CLASSICAL CHINESE

MW01031923

含英咀華集

關福德
劉紹銘 合編

賴恬昌題

Classical Chinese Literature

An Anthology of Translations

Volume I: From Antiquity to the Tang Dynasty

Edited by

John Minford and Joseph S. M. Lau

Columbia University Press
New York

The Chinese University Press
Hong Kong

Copyright © 2000 Columbia University Press and
The Chinese University of Hong Kong

All rights reserved. No part of this publication may be reproduced or
transmitted in any form or by any means, electronic or mechanical, including
photocopying, recording, or any information storage and retrieval system,
without permission in writing from the copyright holders.

Columbia University Press gratefully acknowledges a gift from the China Times
Foundation toward the costs of publishing this work.

ISBN: Columbia University Press   978-0-231-09676-8 (cloth : alk.paper)
                                  978-0-231-09677-5 (pbk : alk.paper)
      The Chinese University Press   962–201–625–1

Published for North America and Europe by:
   Columbia University Press
   Publishers Since 1893
   New York   Chichester, West Sussex
   U.S.A.

Published for the rest of the world by:
   The Chinese University Press
   The Chinese University of Hong Kong
   Sha Tin, N.T., Hong Kong
   Fax: +852 2603 6692
        +852 2603 7355
   E-mail: cup@cuhk.edu.hk
   Web site: www.chineseupress.com

Library of Congress Cataloging-in-Publication Data
Classical Chinese Literature / John Minford and Joseph S. M. Lau,
   editors.
      p. cm.
   Includes bibliographical references.
   Contents: v. 1. From antiquity to the Tang.
   ISBN 978-0-231-09676-8 (Columbia University Press)
   1. Chinese literature — Translations into English.   2. Chinese
literature — History and criticism.   I. Minford, John.   II. Lau,
Joseph S. M., 1934–   .
PL2658.E1C59   1996
895.108—dc20
                                                95–49940

For list of permissions see pages 1157–1164.

For

David Hawkes

with admiration
and affection

Contents

Part 2: The Han Dynasty and the Period of Disunion
(206 B.C.–A.D. 589)

Contents

Part 3: The Sui, Tang and Five Dynasties
(589–960)

Foreword

Cyril Birch

The longer the book, the shorter should be the foreword. This book is not only vast but varied, comprehensive, and a monument to industrious scholarship. It is both innovative and conservative; it explores some of the lesser-known regions of Chinese literature and, at the same time, restores to view translations made decades, even centuries, ago. By this dedication to translations of long ago as well as of recent years and the present day, the editors celebrate the ways in which Chinese works in prose and verse have been enjoyed by many generations of foreign readers.

No doubt the exact nature of this enjoyment would have come, in some cases, as a surprise to the original Chinese author. The translator, inevitably more or less of an outsider to the culture whose values he or she is trying to convey, has his or her own idea of what poetry is, of what beauty or goodness is and of what might be an appropriate response to a given manifestation. Perhaps few readers of Chinese works, not born into the culture, have ever responded in the way their authors might have expected. And the translators represented in this giant anthology are certainly a mixed bunch. They include Britons and Americans, Chinese expatriates and continental European scholars, beat poets and an early Governor of Hong Kong, Christians and Buddhists, men of the cloth and cheerful agnostics, professional philologists and diplomats, mellifluous Victorians and spare modern imagists. But each has had his or her love affair, of shorter or longer duration and of greater or lesser intensity, with Chinese writings, and has helped, as the editors say, to make Chinese literature part of world literature, in Goethe's sense.

Many of the writings these men and women have translated assume forms familiar to the Western reader: lyric verse, prose tales, and so on. Other pieces derive from genres particularly favored by the Chinese tradition, but less likely candidates for literary appreciation in recent times in the West: oracles, chronicles, philosophical writings, hagiographies. Changing styles in the English language and in the translation process are illustrated, for example by the inclusion of twenty different versions of a single poem from the *Book of Songs*. Fortunately, of the two hundred or so English renderings of *The Way and Its Power* the editors offer extracts only from one, the best.

The appeal of a particular poem may be ultimately indefinable. Tao Yuanming has a wonderfully ironic statement of the poet's dilemma when he ends a poem, "Written While Drunk," with lines that William Acker translates:

> The mountain air is fine at evening of the day
> And flying birds return together homewards.
> Within these things there is a hint of Truth,
> But when I start to tell it, I cannot find the words.

If the poet "cannot find the words" (though obviously Tao Yuanming has just done so with his images), how are we to hope that the translator will succeed in expressing the ineffable? Did Acker warm his belly with some good rice wine before tackling these lines "written while drunk," and did it help?

I remember once seeing a publisher's announcement of a new history of painting which promised to "take all the mystery out of Art." Promise, or threat? Acker did all a good translator can do — cherish, retain, preserve the mystery that lies at the heart of the true work of literature. This is the case with many if not all of the translations collected in these volumes, and the editors have accumulated merit in Heaven by ensuring the continued survival of these gallant forays into the literary heritage of China.

"Snow Studio."
Seal carved by He Zhen (fl. 1626)

Music from Two Rooms

Editors' Introduction

"China is the land of countless anthologies. Probably no other country has produced so many, over so long a period." So wrote Arthur Waley in his elegant little preface to *A Harp with a Thousand Strings*, the anthology edited during the Second World War by his gifted Chinese friend, the writer Xiao Qian. Xiao's book is a wonderful attic stuffed full of China-jumble, a fascinating miscellany of writers across the centuries, mostly Western observers, from Marco Polo and Friar Odoric in the thirteenth and fourteenth centuries, to Osbert Sitwell and William Empson in the twentieth. Xiao wanted his readers to put aside the old stereotypes, "the melody of China on one string," and instead to hear "many fingers plucking many strings."[1] This anthology of ours has equally polyphonic ambitions. But unlike Xiao Qian's it is made up not of exquisite pieces of chinoiserie, not of tantalizing legends of Cathay and curious travelers' tales, but entirely of translations from the Chinese.

LETTING CHINA SPEAK FOR HERSELF

"There is no better means of instruction on China than letting China speak for herself."[2]

As early as the sixteenth century, the Jesuits — those accomplished cosmopolitan scholars — had begun to do more than tell stories about China. They had started to translate. The translators of the seventeenth, eighteenth and nineteenth centuries provided the raw material for a new and more substantial legend than that of the old Cathay. Bit by bit, they breached the Great Wall of the Chinese language, which, more than any

---

[1] Xiao Qian (Hsiao Ch'ien), *A Harp with a Thousand Strings* (London: Pilot Press, 1944), Preface and Notes from the Compiler, pp. xii–xiii. Of the 560 pages of the book, less than a hundred are devoted to translations from the Chinese. Xiao Qian himself was a fine writer and translator, and completed (with his wife Wen Jieruo) a translation of James Joyce's *Ulysses* (Nanjing: Yilin, 1994). He died in early 1999.

[2] "Il n'y a pas de meilleur moyen de s'instruire de la Chine, que par la Chine même." Thomas Percy, quoting Du Halde on the title page of *Hau Kiou Choaan or The Pleasing History* (London: Dodsley, 1761).

edifice of stone, had succeeded over the ages in defining, containing and isolating Chinese culture. It was a language that amazed, obsessed, and bewildered. Some saw in it the ante-diluvian, pre-Babelian, universal tongue.[3] A few bold spirits were inspired to struggle with its intractable difficulties, enabling their fellow Europeans to read for themselves for the first time the literature of the Chinese. Slowly, Chinese philosophy, poetry, prose, fiction and drama came out into the world.

One very early attempt at translating from the Chinese into a European language was the "hastily transcribed" Latin version of "un libro molto piccolo," sent back to Rome in manuscript by the Jesuit Michele Ruggieri in 1581.[4] Ten years later Ruggieri finished a Latin translation of the Confucian Four Books, which was never published either. By the end of 1593, Matteo Ricci, Ruggieri's successor in China, did his own Latin version of the Four Books — but this too remained in manuscript. It was only in the third quarter of the seventeenth century that the Jesuit fathers finally published a collaborative Latin version of three of the Four Books, which was quickly translated into other European languages. The 1691 English adaptation of a part of this, *The Morals of Confucius: A Chinese Philosopher*, marks the true starting point of English translation from the Chinese (albeit indirect — a free paraphrase, via the French and Latin).[5] This little book enunciated, in strong seventeenth-century prose, the "infinitely sublime, pure, sensible" qualities of Confucianism, "drawn from the purest fountains of Natural Reason."

A long Experience is requir'd to know the Heart of Man. I imagin'd,

---

[3] See for example John Webb, *An Historical Essay Endeavouring a Probability that the Language of the Empire of China Is the Primitive Language* (London: Nathan Brook, 1669). The Jesuit polymath Athanasius Kircher held that the Chinese written characters had been brought from Egypt by the biblical Ham and his sons when they migrated to China. Lach and Van Kley, *Asia in the Making of Europe* (Chicago: University of Chicago Press, 1965–),Vol. 3, Book 4, p. 1717.

[4] See Paul A. Rule, *K'ung-tzu or Confucius: The Jesuit Interpretation of Confucianism* (Sydney: Allen & Unwin, 1986), pp. 6–7, and Knud Lundbæk, "The First European Translations of Chinese Historical and Philosophical Works," in Thomas H. C. Lee, ed., *China and Europe: Images and Influences in the Sixteenth to Eighteenth Centuries* (Hong Kong: The Chinese University Press, 1991), pp. 36–7. See also David Mungello, *Curious Land: Jesuit Accommodation and the Origins of Sinology* (Honolulu: University of Hawaii Press, 1985).

[5] The translation by Father Prospero Intorcetta and his colleagues, *Confucius Sinarum Philosophus*, had appeared in Paris in 1687, and was itself the culmination of a series of earlier versions stretching back to 1662. Extracts from both Latin and English versions can be found in chapter 4. This was incidentally a great age for English prose, and for translation (Dryden's versions of Juvenal and Virgil appeared in 1693 and 1697).

when I was young, that all Men were Sincere; that they always Practis'd what they said; in a word, that their Mouth always agreed with their Heart: But now that I behold Things with another Eye, I am convinc'd that I was mistaken. At present I hear what Men say, but I never rely thereon. I will examine whether their Words are agreeable to their Actions.

Many other Jesuit translations from the Classics and from Chinese poetry, prose, fiction and drama followed, and some of these found their way into widely read eighteenth-century collections, such as Du Halde's *Description de la Chine* (1735).[6] Several filtered through into the popular imagination. Voltaire's play, *L'Orphelin de la Chine* (1755), was based on a Yuan dynasty drama; Oliver Goldsmith included a free adaptation of a Ming dynasty story, "The Story of a Chinese Matron," in the eighteenth of his Chinese Letters (*The Citizen of the World*, 1760–1762); in 1761, that enterprising editor Bishop Thomas Percy presented a collection of poetic fragments from the Chinese (as an appendix to the fourth volume of the novel *The Pleasing History*), taking his versions mainly from Du Halde. They include what must surely be the first English version of a poem by the great Tang poet Du Fu.

> Ye great Men of this world, do not laugh at that poor peasant,
> Who hath only coarse vessels of common earth to contain his wine,
> And who poureth it out himself that he may drink it:
> While ye quaff it out of vessels of gold and silver,
> While ye are waited on by numbers of slaves:
> When you have drunk freely after your fashion,
> If both of you chance to be intoxicated,
> Ye will sleep together without ceremony under the same tree.[7]

It is all too easy to lose sight of the enormous difficulty of the task these early translators were undertaking. Working with the Chinese language (especially the classical literary language) has never been easy, and in those days most of the basic aids (dictionaries, reference works, things that we take for granted today) were lacking. A few hand-written copies of the Chinese-Latin dictionary of Basil of Glemona circulated in the eighteenth century. But that was about it. An early dilettante-translator, Stephen Weston, spoke for many:

---

[6] Jean-Baptiste Du Halde, *Description géographique, historique, chronologique, politique de l'Empire de la Chine* (Paris: Lemercier, 1735).

[7] Thomas Percy, ed., *Fragments of Chinese Poetry*, appendix to Vol. 4 of *Hau Kiou Choaan or The Pleasing History* (London: Dodsley, 1761), pp. 247–8.

The Chinese tongue ... may be mastered for the purpose of knowing what it contains, if one has courage enough to scale the wall that surrounds it, and to force a way through the hedge of aloes, and prickly pears, with which it is fenced, by learning the mode of using its dictionaries, and by an acquaintance with its roots, or claves ...[8]

A few years after Weston, Robert Morrison, the indefatigable Scot who established the first Protestant mission to China, and translated the Bible into Chinese, published his great Dictionary, and laid solid, practical foundations for future students of the language and literature. Morrison and his friend, Sir George Staunton (who had first learned Chinese as his father's page-boy on Lord Macartney's embassy to the Chinese court in 1793), stand at the head of a long line of British sinologists and translators: among them Sir John Francis Davis (the second of Hong Kong's governors), the missionary James Legge, and Herbert Giles, the most prominent of a whole generation of talented consular sinologists. By the last decade of the nineteenth century, Oscar Wilde was able to read the whole of the Taoist philosopher Zhuangzi in Herbert Giles' 1889 translation.[9] "The most caustic criticism of modern life I have met with for some time," Wilde commented, and quoted from it in his essay "The Soul of Man under Socialism."[10] In the early years of the present century, Lytton Strachey read Chinese poems in Giles' late-Victorian versions:

We hear them, and we are ravished; we hear them not, and we are ravished still. But, as in the most fluctuating sounds of birds and breezes, we can perceive a unity in their enchantment, and, listening to them, we should guess these songs to be the work of a single mind,

---

[8] Stephen Weston, *Fragments of Oriental Literature* (London: 1807), p. xii. The early-nineteenth-century missionary William Milne has left a vivid description of the difficulties of learning the Chinese language: "A work for men with bodies of brass, lungs of steel, heads of oak, hands of spring-steel, eyes of eagles, hearts of apostles, memories of angels, lives of Methuselah." See Stephen Neill, rev. Owen Chadwick, *A History of Christian Missions* (London: Penguin, 1990), p. 238.

[9] H. A. Giles, trans., *Chuang Tzu: Mystic, Moralist and Social Reformer* (Shanghai: Kelly & Walsh, 1889).

[10] Oscar Wilde, *Reviews* (London, 1908), pp. 528–538. See Isobel Murray, "Oscar Wilde's Absorption of Influences: The Case History of Chuang Tzu," *Durham University Journal* 64/1 (Dec. 1971), pp. 1–13. Extracts from the Giles version of *Zhuangzi* can be found in chapter 4, together with others by Burton Watson and A. C. Graham.

pursuing through a hundred subtle modulations the perfection which this earth has never known.[11]

Here is just one example of Giles' facility at versifying Chinese poetry:

The clear dawn creeps into the convent old,
The rising sun tips its tall trees with gold, —
As, darkly, by a winding path I reach
Dhyana's hall, hidden midst fir and beech.
Around these hills sweet birds their pleasure take,
Man's heart as free from shadows as this lake;
Here worldly sounds are hushed, as by a spell,
Save for the booming of the altar bell.[12]

And then in 1915 came *Cathay*, a slim volume containing free versions of Chinese poetry done by the young Ezra Pound, the "inventor of Chinese poetry for our time" (T. S. Eliot's words).[13]

What is the use of talking, and there is no end of
    talking,
There is no end of things of the heart.
I call in the boy,
Have him sit on his knees here
    To seal this,
And send it a thousand miles, thinking.[14]

---

[11] Lytton Strachey, "An Anthology," collected in *Characters and Commentaries* (New York, 1933). Xiao Qian's anthology includes an interesting essay by Arthur Waley, "A Debt to China," in which Waley refers to Strachey's "unprintable parodies of my translations of Chinese poetry." Strachey much preferred Giles. Waley and Giles engaged in a bitter public argument in the early twenties; but Waley, in his own *170 Chinese Poems*, praised Giles' versions as combining "rhyme and literalness with wonderful dexterity."

[12] Chang Jian (eighth century), "Dhyana," Giles, *Chinese Poetry in English Verse* (Shanghai: Kelly & Walsh, 1884), p. 112. Dhyana is the school of Buddhism which the Chinese call Chan, the Japanese Zen. Giles' characteristic note reads: "A state of mental abstraction, by recourse to which the Buddhist gradually shakes off all desire for sublunary existence. In every monastery there is a hall in which priests may be seen sitting for hours together with their eyes closed." For another translation of this poem, see chapter 21.

[13] T. S. Eliot, Introduction to *Ezra Pound: Selected Poems* (London: Faber & Faber, 1928). Pound's very first, pre-*Cathay* ventures into Chinese poetry were re-workings of Giles. See Wai-lim Yip, *Ezra Pound's Cathay* (Princeton: Princeton University Press, 1969) pp. 45(n. 23), 60–1, and 64, and Hugh Kenner, *The Pound Era* (Berkeley: University of California Press, 1971), pp. 194–7.

[14] "Exile's Letter" is Pound's superb version of Li Bo's poem, "Remembering our Excursion in the Past: A Letter sent to Commissary Yan of Chao County."

These are the concluding lines of "Exile's Letter," one of the startling "translucencies," with which Pound in a sense re-invented the realm of Cathay, just as he had re-invented Provençal culture through his versions of the troubadour poets. In fact, in his recently transcribed and published journal of a 1912 walking tour of Southern France, Pound more than once "sees" China in the Languedoc.[15]

> Foix ... We are come again to a place where the waters run swiftly & where we have always this Chinese background. The faint grey of the mountains ... Above Quillan the rd. leads into Chinese unreality ... Dwarfed cedars clutch at the crevices. At bottom the stream is almost as green as they are. There is a Chinese bridge of poles across this current.[16]

Pound's 1919 edited version of Fenollosa's essay "The Chinese Written Character as a Medium for Poetry — An Ars Poetica," propounded the thesis that "the Chinese think and feel in concrete terms, hence are eminently poetic in the working of their mind, and that Chinese characters are pictograms and ideograms and nothing else."[17] Exaggerated though this view was, it was a powerful inspiration for a poet bent on making European poetic language more imagistic.

Pound's contemporary, the great translator and formidable scholar Arthur Waley, in his fifty productive years (he died in 1966), gave Chinese literature another, more restrained voice. His translations captured a way of putting things, a sensibility, that became for many readers the quintessence of the Chinese poet:

> Sent as a present from Annam —
> A red cockatoo.
> Colored like the peach-tree blossom,
> Speaking with the speech of men.
> They did to it what is always done
> To the learned and eloquent.
> They took a cage and stout bars
> And shut it up inside.[18]

---

[15] At the same time, *Cathay*, with its "exiled bowmen, deserted women, levelled dynasties, departures for far places, lonely frontier guardsmen and glories remembered from afar," is, as Hugh Kenner has pointed out, Pound's own powerful response to the first winter of the Great War. *The Pound Era*, p. 202.

[16] Richard Sieburth, ed., *A Walking Tour in Southern France: Ezra Pound among the Troubadours* (New York: New Directions, 1992), pp. 48 and 51–2.

[17] Achilles Fang, "Fenollosa and Pound," *Harvard Journal of Asiatic Studies*, 20 (1957), p. 215.

[18] Bo Juyi, "The Red Cockatoo" (A.D. 820).

Above all Waley succeeded in proving that English translations of Chinese could make for fluent, enjoyable reading. "Despite their imperfections my translations have in the past done something towards inspiring a number of people with the idea that, for lovers of poetry, Chinese is a language worth learning. I hope that this book may serve the same purpose and in particular do something to dispel the common idea that all Chinese poetry belongs to a remote antiquity."[19] In the words of his friend David Hawkes, Waley "belonged not only to the world of oriental studies, but to the world of literature."[20] He never once set foot in China, never held a university chair, and yet with extraordinary empathy he enabled Chinese writers, and especially poets, to speak to the world. "Poets hitherto unknown in English are called back from their distant centuries to take modern form and yet preserve the individuality of their own lives and age."[21]

European culture, which for centuries had renewed itself through a continuous process of translation and transmission, was looking to the East. As Hugh Kenner wrote of Pound:

That Li Po should reach Kensington by way of Tokyo, through the intercession of a Harvard-educated enthusiast of Spanish descent [Fenollosa], was but a global recapitulation of the steps by which the Arabs transmitted Aristotle to 12th-century Paris ... [22]

WE POETS KNOCK ON SILENCE FOR AN ANSWERING MUSIC

This anthology then is a new *Cathay*, pieced together from the work of translators of the past three hundred years. It presents the three-thousand-year-old literary tradition of China, from its very beginnings to the fall of the Manchu dynasty in 1911, seen through a Western tradition of translation and interpretation that itself (as we have seen) stretches back to the last decades of the seventeenth century. For over a dozen years now, the editors of this anthology have been eavesdropping at two

---

[19] *Yuan Mei* (London: Allen & Unwin, 1956), p. 204. Quoted by David Hawkes in *Classical, Modern and Humane: Essays in Chinese Literature* (Hong Kong: The Chinese University Press, 1989), p. 255.

[20] David Hawkes, "From the Chinese" (*Times Literary Supplement*, 3 March 1961) and "Arthur Waley" (*Asia Major*, New Series, XII, 1967). Both essays are reprinted in Hawkes, *Classical, Modern and Humane.*

[21] J. M. Cohen, *English Translators and Translations* (London: Longmans, Green & Co., 1962), p. 37.

[22] *The Pound Era*, p. 222.

doors, transcribing from adjoining rooms sounds which while they exhibit an astonishing variety, share one underlying quality: they can all be
read not as curios or curiosities, but as literature. The Cambridge don
Goldsworthy Lowes Dickinson (1862–1932), the man whom E. M. Forster
called the "Hellenist on the Confucian plane," put in the mouth of his
John Chinaman a powerful evocation of the universal calling of literature:

> A rose in a moonlit garden, the shadow of trees on the turf, almond
> bloom, the scent of pine, the wine-cup and the guitar; these and the
> pathos of life and death, the long embrace, the hand stretched out in
> vain, the moment that glides for ever away, with its freight of music
> and light, into the shadow and hush of the haunted past, all that we
> have, all that eludes us, a bird on the wing, a perfume escaped on the
> gale — to all these things we are trained to respond, and the response
> is what we call literature …[23]

"What is of the greatest importance in literature is the Vital Breath,"
wrote one of China's own earliest critics, Cao Pi (187–226), Emperor
Wen of the Wei dynasty. "The use of the Vital Breath is bound to vary
from singer to singer in rendering the same song." In the language of
traditional Chinese aesthetics, the quality prized above all, whether in
playing or listening to music, in writing or reading literature, or more
generally in the marriage of true minds, in the relationship between true
friends, is the ability to "know the sound."[24] "We poets knock upon
Silence for an answering Music," wrote the third-century poet-general Lu
Ji.[25] The translator too must knock and listen: listen to the sound of the
text and reach through it to the original silence. A "knowing-the-sound"
affinity (the Chinese call it *yinyuan*) needs to exist between translator
and author, an "insinuation of self into otherness." George Steiner calls
it the "final secret of the translator's craft."[26] This is the counterpoint we
have tried to catch.

---

[23] Goldsworthy Lowes Dickinson, *Letters from John Chinaman* (London: Allen & Unwin, 1901), Fifth Letter. E. M. Forster wrote in his notes to the new edition of 1946: "Dickinson's feeling for China was profound and he once amused an English audience by saying: 'I am speaking to you about China, not because I know anything about the subject nor because I once visited the country, but because in a previous existence, I actually was a Chinaman.'"

[24] It is also the ability to hear oneself. As the great pianist Walter Gieseking has written, "Critical self-hearing is by far the most important factor in all of music study!" Foreword to *Piano Technique* (New York: Dover reprint, 1972).

[25] For both of these writers, see chapter 15.

[26] Steiner, *After Babel* (second edition, Oxford: Oxford University Press, 1992), p. 378.

Two of our earliest and most illustrious predecessors — Jean-Baptiste du Halde and Bishop Thomas Percy — wrote in the age before sinology, when "the interest in China was rather humanistic than philological or pragmatic".[27] In the two centuries since then, the increasing "accuracy" of scholarship and intensity of specialization have not always been informed by the same broad sympathy (or "knowing of the sound"). Our aim in this anthology has been to record the humanistic lineage, to pick the moments when translators have been able to draw Chinese literature into the culture of their times. The publication of Ezra Pound's *Cathay* poems was one such moment, a turning-point in the early twentieth-century modernist movement; so were Gary Snyder's Cold Mountain poems, and the Wilhelm/Baynes *Book of Changes*, both of which became popular reading in the 1960s and 1970s. Arthur Waley's translation of Bo Juyi's long poem "The Temple" was included by Yeats in his 1936 *Oxford Book of Modern English Verse*, only a few pages after Pound's "The River-Merchant's Wife: a Letter" (another poem from *Cathay*).

These and other transformations have helped to fulfil the dream of Goethe, himself so deeply interested in things Chinese, who wrote to Eckermann in 1827: "The age of world-literature is at hand, and everyone should endeavor to hasten its coming." Translators are, together with their original authors, partners in the creation of this world-literature. Translation is a celebration of the diversity and the oneness of humanity.

The American poet and translator Witter Bynner and his Chinese collaborator Kiang Kang-hu, in the preface to their fine collection *The Jade Mountain* (1929), quoted from Li Shangyin:

Literature endures, like the universal spirit,
And its breath becomes a part of the vitals of all men.

Twenty years later, from the more sombre surroundings of his Nanjing prison, Kiang wrote to Bynner, this time quoting a Chinese saying:

All human beings are of the same heart,
And all human hearts are for the same reason.[28]

---

[27] Qian Zhongshu (Ch'ien Chung-shu), "China in the English Literature of the Eighteenth Century," *Quarterly Bulletin of Chinese Bibliography* (1941).

[28] Witter Bynner, "Remembering a Gentle Scholar," in *The Chinese Translations* (New York: Farrar, Straus, Giroux, 1978), p. 11. Kiang Kang-hu (Jiang Kanghu) was imprisoned as a Japanese collaborator in 1945. He wrote to Bynner from prison on August 13, 1948. He finally died in prison in December 1954.

DIVERS FLEECES, MANY FLOWERS

It will not come as a surprise to find that our anthology contains as great a variety of ways of translating as it does ways of writing. Since Western men and women of letters first began to deal with the problems of translating Chinese, there have been countless changes in fashion, in the ways of writing and reading literature, of which translation is but a part. Each generation must translate for itself; Pound's versions may seem to a future generation to have been very much a product of their time, good examples of "Windsor translation."[29] By contrast, the neglected late-nineteenth-century translations by "V. W. X" from the *Book of Songs* (see chapter three) seem strikingly modern today.

We have been happy to give our readers this variety, while trying wherever possible to provide an individual Chinese author or text with a recognizable voice or set of voices in English. There is an old Western misconception of a timeless sameness running through the ages of Chinese literature, which is no more accurate than the impression that Chinese people "all look the same." In fact Chinese poetry, prose and fiction cover an astonishingly wide range, across time and often within the same period; both in style — from the austerely classical to the racily colloquial — and in content — from the severely didactic to the un-ashamedly erotic.

Poetry-lovers can find here folksong and ballad, euphuistic rhapsody, regular (i.e. regulated) verse of all kinds (poetry written in lines of equal length, according to strict schemes of rhyme and tone), and poignant lyrics to music from the singsong quarters (written in unequal, lilting lines). Prose-lovers can find a wealth of historical, philosophical, critical, descriptive and epistolary writings. Those whose pleasure it is to read a story, can find tantalizingly fragmentary myths, zany Taoist parables, poignant biographies and hagiographies, carefully chiselled miniatures and epigrammatic anecdotes, crafted classical tales of romance and the supernatural, early examples of vernacular story-telling. For drama and the fully-fledged story and novel, readers will have to wait for the second volume.

The sameness of Chinese literature is an illusion, but the unbroken continuity is a fact. In some ways the reader of this anthology will be able to see this, to spot some of the references and quotations, the intercon-nections, variations on a theme, that bind together this most self-refer-ring and continuous of all literatures. But an anthology like ours

---

[29] T. S. Eliot, op. cit.

(without an extensive critical apparatus) has only a limited chance of preserving and reproducing in any detail this quality which is so important and apparent to literate Chinese readers of their own tradition.[30] The continuum is too bound up with the ubiquitous use of allusion, and with the nature of the language itself, the interplay between classical and vernacular Chinese, between "free" and "regulated" verse, regular and irregular metre, parallel prose and "old style" prose. These connections and distinctions are often masked or lost in translation, especially in a collection such as this, where the translations themselves cover a span of three hundred years.

In fact, our anthology may from time to time give quite the reverse impression. There may be a sense of discontinuity, arising out of the process and history of translation itself. In chapter three, for example, our readers will encounter among the English versions of the ancient *Book of Songs* some that read like twentieth-century modernist verse, some like country ballads from the American South, some like Tennyson or Longfellow, some written in the Scottish style; while among the versions of the later more colloquial Chinese lyrics (see chapter thirty) some will come across as deliberately quaint, almost Swinburnian, others as sharp Audenesque pastiche of Horace. In chapters three and four can be found versions of Confucius in prose styles varying from the pithy Jacobean (*The Morals of Confucius*), to the high-flown Augustan ("As In a Mirror") and the High Victorian (James Legge's *Chinese Classics*). The Taoist Masters sometimes converse in Herbert Giles' late Victorian English (as if they had been reincarnated with Walter Pater and John Ruskin), sometimes in Arthur Waley's exquisite Bloomsbury (*The Way and Its Power*). Sometimes they exchange quips or tell tales in Angus Graham's crisp modern dialectic (his *Zhuangzi* and *Liezi*), sometimes with Burton Watson's dry, transatlantic wit (his *Zhuangzi*). All are indeed possible, for the fact of the matter is that what they actually spoke was ancient Chinese. The affinity between author and translator is no respecter of history. It has led to some wonderful matchings that have a strange temporal logic of their own. The rooms at which we have been eavesdropping adjoin in their own time-and-space continuum.

We have also refrained from imposing an all-knowing editorial voice when introducing and framing the material we have assembled. Instead we have, wherever possible, anthologized again, prefacing each chapter

---

[30] Stephen Owen's *An Anthology of Chinese Literature: Beginnings to 1911* (New York: W. W. Norton, 1996), in nature very different from ours, succeeds in conveying this intertextuality very well.

with a few thought-provoking remarks (from both Chinese and Western sources), then choosing and editing an informative paragraph or two from an acknowledged authority. We have tried our utmost to be scrupulous in our attributions, following the principle of Robert Burton in *The Anatomy of Melancholy* ("Democritus to the Reader"):

> As a good housewife out of divers fleeces weaves one piece of cloth, a bee gathers wax and honey out of many flowers, ... I have laboriously collected this cento out of divers writers, and ... have wronged no authors, but given every man his own ...

ARRANGEMENTS

In many ways this is an old-fashioned, straightforward selection, arranged simply and chronologically in two volumes of thirty chapters, representing, we hope, most of the widely accepted Chinese masters and masterpieces of the principal genres and periods. We have kept in mind the needs of teachers and students (of Chinese literature and of translation), but we hope that these two volumes will also be of value to all lovers of literature.

The very first chapter (Pattern and Sign) is a collection of materials (some verbal, some visual) about the Chinese script itself. The written character, the medium in which the Chinese writer works, is by its nature different from anything available to the Western writer. It therefore seemed essential to provide a brief initiation into the language, before, in the very process of translation, it disappears from sight.

The third chapter (The *Book of Songs*) is a miniature anthology in its own right, a case study in translation history (echoes of this will be found in other chapters). Since the mid-eighteenth century, just about every translator from the Chinese has attempted at least a poem or two from this classic, the fountainhead of Chinese lyricism. The earliest complete version (the Latin of Father Lacharme, which existed in manuscript in about 1750) is the one Ezra Pound praised (and leaned on heavily) in the 1950s, when doing his own complete "reworking," *The Classic Anthology as Defined by Confucius.* We have quoted the Latin sparingly. The occasional Latin version of other works has been included elsewhere (see chapter four), not out of some obscurantist whim, but in order to document the extraordinary achievement of the Jesuits, working in what was then the European scholarly *lingua franca.* Similarly, the few nineteenth-century French versions in chapters nineteen and twenty (by the Marquis d'Hervey de Saint-Denys and Judith Gautier, daughter of the poet Théophile) are there to demonstrate the influential French traditions of creative scholarship on the one hand, and poetic license on the other. The Marquis was not only a student of the great French sinologue Stanislaus Julien, but also an authority on the interpretation of dreams, while Gautier's strangely transmogrified *Le Livre de Jade* was for many years the principal source for European knowledge of Chinese verse.

We have from time to time included lesser-known versions by pioneer translators (such as Milne, Collie, Morrison, Kidd, Medhurst), whose names have been overshadowed by those of their successors (Legge, Giles, Waley), just as Wycliffe, Tyndale and Coverdale have tended to disappear into the Authorized Version of the Bible.

Chapters four (The Source), fourteen (Green Bags and Yellow Covers) and twenty-seven (Return to the Source) are miscellanies of prose writing from the three periods into which this volume falls: the Pre-Han, the Han and Six Dynasties, and the Tang respectively. These letters, memorials and essays were memorized by generations of Chinese schoolboys, and their brevity and elegance have helped to form the style of many an aspiring writer.

Narrative prose written in the classical language can be traced through chapters two (Heavenly Questions), four (especially the wonderful Taoist parables of Zhuangzi and Liezi), seven (Mortals and Immortals), sixteen (Spirits and Humours), and twenty-eight (The World in a Pillow). These superbly crafted miniatures and short tales are an acquired taste, a type of story-telling in which the Chinese have always excelled, exploiting the elliptical qualities of their classical language to perfection. The beginnings of the more informal narratives in the vernacular (which flourished in subsequent dynasties, and which will occupy large parts of the second volume) can be seen in the Buddhist stories from Dunhuang (chapter twenty-nine).

Chapter ten (Bamboo Grove, Golden Valley, and Orchid Pavilion) is built around three literary coteries of the third and fourth centuries. Chinese men of letters and artists have often functioned best in the convivial and congenial context of a group, clique or club (this is still true today). In evoking such a group collectively one can convey something of the spirit of an epoch. In similar fashion a part of chapter twenty-three is built around the intense friendship between two poets — Bo Juyi and Yuan Zhen. Literary friendship could itself constitute the basis for another anthology.

Chapters five (The *Songs of the South*) and six (Red and Purple Threads) trace the development of one particular strand of poetic writing — the rhapsody — that derives from the shamanistic outpourings of the South. Further examples of this genre are to be found in other chapters, notably in chapter ten and chapter fifteen (The Carving of Dragons). Chapters eight (We Fought South of the City Wall) and nine (Tigers Setting the Wind Astir) follow the evolution of popular, folk-style poetry on the one hand and more refined, literary poetry on the other; while chapters eleven (Tao Yuanming) and twelve (The Murmuring Stream and the Weary Road) introduce three outstanding individual poets of the fourth and fifth centuries. Chapter thirteen (New Songs from a Jade Terrace) provides a selection of the fashionable court poetry of the fifth and sixth centuries. Eight whole chapters (seventeen to twenty-four), with substantial parts of three others (twenty-five, twenty-six and thirty), are devoted to the poetry of the Tang dynasty (618–907). Four of these chapters are taken up by individual Tang poets (Wang Wei, Li Bo, Du Fu and Bo Juyi), four by the four "Seasons" or periods of Tang poetry (the Early, High, Mid, and Late Tang). From the Han dynasty onwards, poetry was the Chinese medium of literary self-expression par excellence, and after the Confucian Classics the Chinese literati regarded the corpus of Tang verse as the foundation of their literary culture. Every self-respecting Chinese man of letters wrote verse. As the Abbé Grosier wittily remarked, in 1788:

> The Chinese say of a man of letters, that he has the talent of making verses, almost in the same manner as if one should praise, in Europe, a captain of dragoons, for being an excellent performer on the violin.[31]

It is no accident that all told, of the thirty chapters in this anthology, nineteen (and parts of three others) are devoted to poetry. The very last chapter (Among the Flowers) records the birth of the new style of lyric verse, set to the beguiling music of the singsong quarters. This genre of poetry was to be popular in all the subsequent dynasties, and will be well represented in the second volume, as will the rich tradition of lyric drama.

Chapter twenty-five (Red Leaf) and chapter twenty-six (Cold Mountain) each covers several centuries, the first being dedicated to women poets, the second to a special preoccupation of poets, Zen Buddhism and the Tao. Each of these chapters could have been divided up and allocated to the relevant period. But while chronology is a useful frame, it is also refreshing to step back occasionally and pick out a strand.

Chapter twenty (Du Fu) is the only chapter in which Chinese characters

---

[31] Jean Baptiste Gabriel Alexandre Grosier, *A General Description of China* (London: G.G.J. and J. Robinson, 1788).

have been provided for some of the translated texts (there will, however, be two separate volumes, giving the complete Chinese texts of the anthology).[32] More than any other Chinese writer, this Tang poet defies translation, and demands an initiation into the original language. The seven detailed explications taken from David Hawkes' *Little Primer of Tu Fu* presuppose no knowledge of Chinese, and the reader for whom this word-by-word approach is helpful can go on to read the remaining poems in that excellent book.[33]

In addition to the twenty versions of the first poem of the *Book of Songs* in chapter one, the reader will find in chapters eighteen, nineteen and twenty, several poems in different versions. It is an illuminating experience, to read a Chinese poem through the prism of varying translations.[34] This could in itself be an alternative method of organizing a complete anthology.

When introducing individual writers or works, we have given more or less rudimentary biographical sketches or other relevant information, taken (unless otherwise stated) from the material provided by the translator in question. In some cases we have used Giles' old (1898) *Biographical Dictionary* (which needs to be checked for veracity — but Giles, like his contemporary Lytton Strachey, had a knack for encapsulating a personality in a few memorable phrases). Otherwise we have relied on the more recent and indispensable *Indiana Companion to Traditional Chinese Literature* (1986). Chinese men of letters often have several names, but we have tried to simplify matters by sticking to the most common one wherever possible (e.g. Tao Yuanming, not Tao Qian). We have kept footnotes to a minimum, preserving just as many as seemed necessary to an understanding of the translation. They are the translator's, unless otherwise stated. By contrast, several titles of poems, stories or essays, are our own additions.

Every chapter concludes with a brief list for Further Reading, which doubles as a source-list of translations (and illustrations) used. There are also general lists for Further Reading at the back of the book. If the source of a translation is not given in the individual list, it can be found

---

[32] These companion volumes, edited by Agnes Chan and Joanne Tsui, are available from the Chinese University Press, Hong Kong, either separately or together with the English volumes.

[33] Available as a Renditions Paperback, published by the Research Centre for Translation, The Chinese University of Hong Kong.

[34] See for example the excellent little book by Eliot Weinberger and Octavio Paz, *Nineteen Ways of Looking at Wang Wei: How a Chinese Poem is Translated* (Wakefield, Rhode Island: Moyer Bell, 1987).

in the general one. Occasionally, where it seemed of particular interest, we have appended an informal editorial note about the translations to the very end of the chapter.

The system of romanization of Chinese characters used is the one known as *Hanyu pinyin*, adopted in China since the early 1950s, and now widely used internationally. We have added hyphens in giving reign periods (e.g. the Tian-bao period) and cyclical terms (the day *geng-shen*). For a very few well-known place names and terms we have kept the old spellings throughout (Peking, Yangtze, the Tao), and in a small number of early translations, the old transliterations have been preserved, to convey a sense of period. At the back of the book there is a brief note on how to pronounce certain elements of *Hanyu pinyin*, and conversion tables for the benefit of readers more familiar with the older system known as Wade-Giles. There are two indices, one to authors, and one to translators, and a quick finding list for those readers who only recognize an author's name in the Wade-Giles system.

Illustrations have been carefully selected to complement, not to distract. They are a gesture to the inevitable loss in translation of what can only be called the Chinese "flavor" of the originals. We have included examples of Chinese calligraphy, paintings, traditional woodblock illustrations, seals and rubbings from old tiles or stones. The Chinese characters on the title page, and at the beginning of each chapter, were written by our dear friend T. C. Lai, doyen of Hong Kong calligraphers, translators and gourmets.

ACKNOWLEDGMENTS

This anthology has been well over a dozen years in the making. The editors have worked on it together in Hong Kong, Auckland, Oxford and Taipei; separately in Madison (Wisconsin), Tuchan (France), and Canberra (Australia). It began as the bright idea of our friend T. L. Tsim (a man of many bright ideas), who was then director of The Chinese University Press. Over the years he has been unfailingly generous with his support and enthusiasm. Throughout we have been fortunate in the dedicated team working at the Chinese University Press, especially Patrick Kwong, who as acting director saw the book through an important stage, Paul Wong, Steven Luk, Y. K. Fung, and a number of hardworking editors, including Wong Ching-yu, Tse Wai-keung, Ivy Siu and above all Esther Tsang. Since Columbia University Press entered into the project, Jennifer Crewe, Anne McCoy and Debra Soled have brought a sense of realism that helped the book come to fruition.

Of the many sources of material support, first thanks must go to the Council for Cultural Promotion and Development of Taiwan's Executive Yuan. It was their grant that enabled the editors to spend the summer of 1990 in Oxford, when many of the chapters took on their final form, between periodic sorties into the treasures of the Bodleian Library, and sessions over a long kitchen table in a village beneath the Berkshire Downs. Other opportunities for the editors to work together were created by the generosity of the Institute of Chinese Studies of The Chinese University of Hong Kong (special thanks to its Director, Chen Fong-ching), and the Auckland University Foundation.

Obtaining permissions has been not only a time-consuming business, but an expensive one. Grants towards this expense have been forthcoming from the Pacific Cultural Foundation and the China Times Foundation. Special thanks also to the following generous individuals — Chuang Liang-yu, Kuo Chao-yung, Lam Shan Muk, and W. K. Lau — for their contributions.

We owe a great debt of gratitude to Cyril Birch for his touching Foreword, and to the many translators who have come forward with translations, either new and unpublished, or published but available only in small, inaccessible editions: these include Daniel Bryant, John Cayley, Robert Joe Cutter, Kenneth DeWoskin, Bill Dolby, Elling Eide, C. H. Kwock, Richard Mather, William H. Nienhauser, Stephen Owen, and Benjamin Penny. We have received welcome advice and timely assistance from Geremie Barmé, Anne Birrell, Duncan Campbell, Agnes Chan, Don Cohn, Mark Elvin, Alain Ginesty, Ed Gunn, David Hawkes, Nick Koss, André Lévy, H. C. Li, Liu Ts'un-yan, William McNaughton, Rachel May, Stephen Soong, Joanne Tsui, Wang Ch'iu-kuei, Wang Der-wei and Timothy Wixted. Finally, we would like to record our appreciation for the friendly co-operation of the staff of the various libraries we have consulted, including the Bodleian Library, Oxford; the Menzies Library, Australian National University; the National Library of Australia; the Hong Kong University Library; the Library of the Hong Kong Polytechnic University; and the Library of the Royal Asiatic Society (Hong Kong branch).

"Cottage of the Distant Voice," "Pleasures of Sight and Sound."
Twin seals carved by Qian Song (1807–1860)

About the Editors

JOHN MINFORD has taught Chinese literature and literary translation in China, Hong Kong, and New Zealand. He has translated, with David Hawkes, the Penguin Classics edition of *The Story of the Stone* by Cao Xueqin and is the coeditor, with Geremie Barmé, of *Seeds of Fire: Chinese Voices of Conscience.* He is currently working on the *Strange Tales of Pu Songling, The Art of War* by Sunzi, and the martial arts fiction of the contemporary Hong Kong novelist Louis Cha.

JOSEPH S. M. LAU is Chair Professor of Translation and head of the Department of Chinese at Lingnan University. He is coeditor of *Traditional Chinese Stories: Themes and Variations* (Columbia, 1978); *Modern Chinese Stories and Novellas, 1919–1949* (Columbia, 1981); *The Columbia Anthology of Modern Chinese Literature* (Columbia, 1995), and editor of *Chinese Stories from Taiwan* (Columbia, 1976) and *The Broken Chain: An Anthology of Taiwan Fiction Since 1926* (Indiana, 1983).

Part 1

Before the Han Dynasty (to 206 B.C.)

"Besotted with the words of the ancients, hearing them every day."
Wang Chong, *Animadversions*
Seal carved by Deng Shiru (1743–1805)

Chapter 1

Pattern and Sign

The Chinese Language

We understand further that it is the use of China and the kingdoms of the high Levant to write in Characters Real, which express neither letters nor words in gross, but Things or Notions.

> — Francis Bacon, *The Advancement of Learning*, 1605

Now to give a Language the first or premier rank, as to succinct Sweetness, and graceful Brevity, is a great step towards the granting of it to be the Primitive Language; considering which, together with the exemplary Vitality; remarkable Modesty; admirable Generality; great Simplicity, and high Antiquity; we may from these Arguments almost dare to affirm, that the Language of the Empire of China is the Primitive Language.

> — John Webb, *An Historical Essay Endeavouring a Probability That the Language of the Empire of China Is the Primitive Language*, 1669

The Chinese has no resemblance with any dead or living Language that we are acquainted with.... The *Chinese* have only Figures to express their Thoughts.... In the beginning of their Monarchy, they communicated their Ideas by drawing on Paper the Natural Images of the Things they would express: for instance, a Bird, Mountains, Trees, Wavy Lines, to express Birds, Mountains, a Forest, and Water.

> — Du Halde, *A Description of the Empire of China*, 1738

Boswell: "What do you say to the written character of their language?"
Johnson: "Sir, they have not an alphabet. They have not been able to form what all other nations have formed."
Boswell: "There is more learning in their language than in any other from the immense number of their characters."
Johnson: "It is only more difficult from its rudeness; as there is more labour in hewing down a tree with a stone than with an axe."

> — James Boswell, *Life of Johnson*, 1791

Wen: drawn lines, design; striped; ornaments, ornate; written character; literary document, literature; accomplished; civil (as opposed to military); embellish. The early graph shows a man with tattooing on the breast.

> — Bernhard Karlgren, *Grammata Serica Recensa*, 1957

SCRIPT

ꙮꙮꙮꙮꙮꙮꙮꙮꙮꙮꙮꙮꙮꙮꙮꙮꙮꙮꙮꙮꙮꙮꙮꙮꙮꙮꙮꙮꙮꙮꙮꙮꙮꙮꙮ

LIU XIE (c. 465–c. 520)

The Pattern of the Tao

Translated by Vincent Yu-chung Shih

Wen, or pattern, is a very great virtue indeed. It is born together with heaven and earth. Why do we say this? Because all color-patterns are mixed of black and yellow, and all shape-patterns are differentiated by round and square. The sun and moon like two pieces of jade manifest the pattern of heaven; mountains and rivers in their beauty display the pattern of earth. These are, in fact, the pattern (*wen*) of the Tao itself. And as one sees above the sparkling heavenly bodies, and below the manifold forms of earth, so there is established a difference between high and low estate, giving rise to the two archetypal Forms (Yin and Yang). Man, and man alone, forms with these the Great Trinity, and he does so because he alone is endowed with spirituality. He is the refined essence of the five elements — indeed, the mind of the universe.

Now with the emergence of mind, language is created, and when language is created, writing (*wen*) appears. This is the Tao of nature. If we extend our observations, we find that all animals and plants have patterns of their own. Dragons and phoenixes in their picturesque form embody the auspicious, tigers and leopards with their stripes and spots recall the individuality of virtuous men. The sculptured colors of the clouds surpass the painter's art in their exquisite beauty, the blooming flower depends on no embroiderer's skill for its marvellous grace. Can this beauty be considered external adornment? No, it is natural, it is just so of itself. The sounds of the forest wind blend into a melody like that of reed pipe or lute, the music of spring water striking the rock is as tuneful as the ring of jade chime or bronze bell. In physical bodies there is plastic pattern, in sound there is musical pattern. Now if insentient objects have such adornment, can that which is endowed with mind lack a pattern proper to itself?

Human pattern originated in the Supreme, the Ultimate. "Mysteriously manifesting the divine light," the Images of the *Book of Changes* were the first such pattern. Fu Xi began the *Changes* by drawing the eight trigrams, and Confucius completed it by writing the "Patterned Words.".... Patterned words are indeed the mind of the universe! From the Plan of the Yellow River were born the eight trigrams, and from the

Figure 1. (left) "Cang Jie, soothsayer of the Yellow Emperor, studied the tracks of birds and wild animals, and understood that different patterns could be used to represent different realities. And so he devised writing ..." Xu Shen (30–124), Afterword to *Shuowen jiezi*. (Source: *Sancai tuhui*, Ming dynasty); (right) Fu Xi inventing the eight trigrams (Source: Williams, C. A. S. *Encyclopedia of Chinese Symbolism and Art Motives* [Shanghai: Kelly & Walsh, 1932])

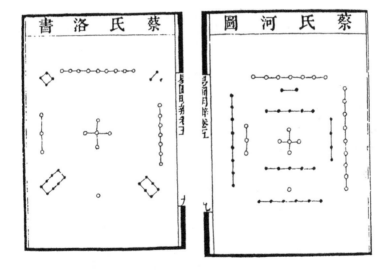

Figure 2. The Scroll of the River Luo (left) and The Plan of the Yellow River (right). According to the legend, which was given its final shape by Kong Anguo (2nd century B.C.), a "dragon-horse" emerged from the waters of the Yellow River and presented on its back an arrangement of symbols, whence the divine ruler Fu Xi elucidated the system of the Eight Trigrams. And while the Great Yu was engaged in draining off the floods, a "divine tortoise" presented to his gaze a scroll of writing on its back, composed of the numbers from one to nine, which the sage interpreted and made the basis of his ninefold exposition of philosophy — W. F. Mayers, 1874. (Source: Hu Wei, *Yitu mingbian*, 1706)

Scroll of the River Luo came the nine categories. For these and for the fruits contained in the jade and gold decorated tablets and the flowers blooming in red words and green strips was anyone responsible? No. They are natural, organic expressions of the Divine.

When bird's markings replaced knotted cords, writing first came into being.... Both the first sage Fu Xi, who invented writing, and Confucius, the "Uncrowned King," who transmitted the teachings, drew their literary embellishment from the mind of the Tao, both of them taught by reference to divine principles. Both took images from the Plan of the Yellow River and the Scroll of the River Luo, and both divined by means of milfoil stems and tortoise shells. Both observed the pattern of the heavens in order to exhaust its changes; both studied the pattern of man in order to achieve transformation. In this way they were able to master the warp and woof of the universe, to encompass permanent principles, to achieve glorious deeds and make their words shine forth. From this we know that the Tao is handed down in writing through the sages, and that the sages make the Tao manifest in their writings.... Words are able to arouse the world because they are the Pattern of the Tao.

> — from "On Tao, the Source," chapter 1 of
> *The Literary Mind and the Carving of Dragons*[1]

The Beginnings of Chinese Writing

Jerry Norman

The Chinese script appears as a fully developed writing system in the late Shang dynasty (fourteenth to eleventh centuries B.C.). From this period we have copious examples of the script inscribed or written on bones and tortoise shells, for the most part in the form of short divinatory texts. From the same period there also exist a number of inscriptions on bronze vessels of various sorts. The former type of graphic record is referred to as the oracle bone script, while the latter is commonly known as the bronze script. The script of this period is already a fully developed writing system, capable of recording the contemporary Chinese language in a complete and unambiguous manner. The maturity of this early script has suggested to many scholars that it must have passed

---

[1] All subsequent quotations from *The Literary Mind* are based on Vincent Shih's translation, with the exception of the lengthy extracts in chapters 6 and 15. The interpretation and wording of this extract have been reworked in the light of James Liu's translation and commentary, to be found in chapter 2 of his *Chinese Theories of Literature. Eds.*

through a fairly long period of development before reaching this stage, but the few examples of writing which precede the fourteenth century are unfortunately too sparse to allow any sort of reconstruction of this development. On the basis of available evidence, however, it would not be unreasonable to assume that Chinese writing began sometime in the early Shang or even somewhat earlier in the late Xia dynasty or approximately in the seventeenth century B.C.

From the very beginning the Chinese writing system has basically been morphemic: that is, almost every graph represents a single morpheme. Since the overwhelming majority of Old Chinese morphemes were monosyllables, this means that, at the phonological level, every graph represents a single syllable. The Chinese script differs from purely syllabic scripts (like Japanese *kana*) in that homophonous syllables are represented by different graphs when they have different meanings. For example, *shou* "head" and *shou* "hand" are represented by different graphs, even though they are homophonous as far back as they can be traced.

The earliest Chinese writing shows that it had a basically pictographic origin. At the earliest stages of its development, it is quite clear that the chief device for creating graphs was to draw a picture of what was to be represented. Examples of this sort of graph are shown in Figure 3. The more truly representational a graph is, the more difficult and time-consuming it is to depict. There is a natural tendency for such graphs to become progressively simplified and stylized as a writing system matures and becomes more widely used. As a result, pictographs gradually tend to lose their obvious pictorial quality. The graph for *quan* "dog" shown in Figure 4 can serve as a good illustration of this sort of development.

Not all the elements of language could be easily represented in pictorial form. Faced with this problem, the early creators of the Chinese script resorted to various other devices. One was to use a more abstract representation; for example, to write *shang* "above" [see Figure 5a] they

Figure 3. Pictographs in early Chinese writing. (Source: Jerry Norman, *Chinese* [Cambridge: Cambridge University Press, 1988])

Figure 4. The graph for *quan* "dog." (Source: Jerry Norman, *Chinese* [Cambridge: Cambridge University Press, 1988])

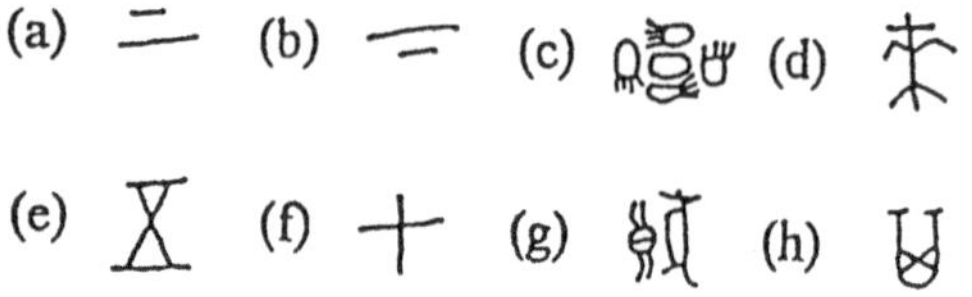

(a) ⸗   (b) ⸗   (c) 🐍   (d) 禾

(e) ✕   (f) 十   (g) 𤰈   (h) ⩁

Figure 5. Other early pictographs. (Source: Bernhard Karlgren, *Grammata Serica Recensa* [Stockholm: Museum of Far Eastern Antiquities, 1964])

drew a horizontal line and placed another shorter horizontal line above it; *xia* "below" [5b] was written similarly, but with a short line below a longer horizontal line. The word *wei* "surround" [5c] was written by depicting four small graphs for "foot" around an empty square, probably representing a walled city. In all these cases the graphic representations are linked directly to their corresponding morphemes without any reference to the sound or pronunciation of the word in question. But these devices also proved inadequate to represent early Chinese in a complete fashion. Ultimately, as in all fully developed writing systems, the pronunciation of elements to be written had to be taken into account. One way to do this was to use the *rebus* principle, that is, to employ a pictograph or other nonphonetic representational graph for its sound value alone; for example, the word *lai* "come" would be difficult to represent relying on the pictographic or other purely representational devices. One solution to this problem was to borrow the graph for a homophone or a near-homophone. In this particular case a pictograph representing *lai* "wheat" [5d] was chosen; in the subsequent history of the language this word for "wheat" became obsolete and the graph in question now survives only in its "borrowed" sense of "come." Grammatical elements were particularly hard to represent in pictorial form; as a result, virtually all the early graphs for such elements are based on this "phonetic borrowing" principle.

In addition to the types of characters described above, a very small number of early graphs were apparently purely arbitrary signs bearing no representational or phonetic relationship to the word depicted. An example of this sort of graph is that for *wu* "five" which is written with an X [5e], or the word for *qi* "seven," written with a simple cross [5f].

In early China another device for character formation was developed, which in subsequent centuries was to become progressively more important: this was the device of phonetic compounding. A character of this type consists of a semantic element combined with a second element used to indicate the pronunciation of the new graph; for example, the word *lang* "wolf" was written with the graph for *quan* "dog" on the left and a graph pronounced *liang* (meaning "good") on the right [5g]. The phonetic element here is generally used for its sound value alone, independent of its meaning. The original impetus for creating characters of this type may have been the need to distinguish graphs that looked alike and could easily be confused. The numerous characters for types of birds, for example, could be distinguished more clearly if such phonetic elements were added to them. Another impetus was probably the increased borrowing of simple graphs for their phonetic values to write words otherwise difficult to depict. As this device was used more and more, the danger of ambiguity and confusion undoubtedly increased. This ambiguity could be resolved by adding semantic indicators. An example of this is the very early use of the pictograph for *ji* "winnowing basket" [5h] for the word *qi*, a modal particle denoting probability or futurity; since the grammatical word *qi* had a much higher textual frequency than *ji*, the graph *zhu* "bamboo" was eventually added to *ji* to distinguish it from *qi*. The Shang script then contained characters of two basic types; one type was semantically representational without any indication of the pronunciation of the words represented, and the other type was in some fashion tied to the pronunciation of the words. In both cases it is essential to keep in mind that the individual graphs or characters of the Shang writing system represented specific words in the Shang language, each of which had its own semantic and phonological characteristics. The notion which is sometimes encountered that Chinese characters in some platonic fashion directly represent ideas rather than specific Chinese words is patently absurd and leads to gross misunderstandings concerning both the Chinese script and the nature of writing in general. For this reason, the term ideograph, which has often been used to refer to Chinese characters, is best avoided. Chinese characters represent Chinese words, and an understanding of the semantic and phonological makeup of these words is essential to an understanding of how the Chinese writing system works.

— from "The Chinese Script," chapter 3 of *Chinese*, 1988

ORACLE BONES

Texts of Divination

Stanley Mickel

Shang dynasty (c. 1600–c. 1028 B.C.) oracle-bone inscriptions are texts incised or sometimes written with a brush on cattle scapula or turtle shells. (These are the so-called dragon-bones, first rediscovered a hundred years ago.) With the exception of some record-keeping texts, oracle-bone inscriptions record divinations seeking either the meaning of past events or the course of future events. Some divinations about the past tried to interpret it: "The King dreamed of white cattle, shall there be a disaster?" Some sought the cause of problems: "Sick tooth, is Father Yi causing harm?" The bulk of the divinations attempted to pin down the future: "Shall it rain?", "Shall the western areas receive a harvest?", "Shall we kill ten Qiang persons in sacrifice to Ancestor Yi?"

A full inscription (a rarity) has four parts: (1) the preface: "On *jia-shen* [the shell] was cracked and Ke divined"; (2) the charge: "The Wife Hao will give birth, shall it be a happy event?"; (3) the prognostication: "The King read the cracks saying, 'If the birthing is on *ding*, it shall be a happy event. If the birthing is on *geng*, it will be hugely auspicious!' " and (4) the verification: "Three weeks and one day, *jia-yin*, the birthing was not a happy event, it was a female." Some texts also include a postface giving the time or place of divination, but most divination inscriptions consist of just the preface and charge. In the first of the five oracle-bone periods, a positive version of the divination is frequently echoed on the other half of the scapula or plastron by a mirror-image negative: "The King shall make a city, shall Di approve?" "The King shall not make a city, shall Di approve?"

The oracle-bone texts are generally less than fifteen characters long. Only a very few exceed fifty characters, and texts of thirty characters are unusual. Although the oracle inscriptions were not composed with a literary intent, they often pulse with examples of Shang sensitivity and awareness of language, both in the manner in which characters were constructed and in the way in which they were used in writing. The character for "toothache" shows teeth with a worm in them, a deer in a pit represents "trap," and "kill in sacrifice" shows a person transfixed at the neck by a halberd. Words were used for more than one level of meaning: the king as well as the sun "goes forth," clouds "send down" rain and ancestors "send down" disasters. Some word usages reveal an awareness of metaphor: the image of a singing bird was used when the king divined about a ringing in his ears, and in contrast to the plain "female" used when a girl's birth was noted, the use of "happy event" to refer to the birth of a boy speaks clearly of the values of the society as well as a basic skill with metaphor.

Phrases of considerable poetic power enliven the oracle texts, especially in the more spontaneous first period. The tip of a rainbow sips from the Yellow River rather than just touching it. A feeling of stretching and experimenting with metaphor apparent in this text is reinforced by the arched, open mouthed serpentine form of the character for "rainbow"; "There is an eating of the moon" is indicative of Shang concern with natural phenomena and of their skilled use of implied simile.

Shang diviners possessed a well-developed ability to narrate a story within the particular constraints of the oracle inscriptions. If plot is understood as a sequence of events which can be followed presented within a definite timeframe, narrative skill is clearly present in the birthing text given above. It is also evident in the following text in which the king's prognostication that the coming week will have some form of disaster is verified as: "On *jia-wei* the King chased rhinoceroses. A minor official drove the chariot. The horses hit a rock, overturning the King's chariot. Prince Yang also fell out." In addition to a sequence of events which the reader can easily follow, evidence of a subtle skill with words is shown in hinting at but avoiding direct reference to the king's human fallibility in falling out of the chariot by stating simply that the prince also fell out.

Further demonstrations of Shang facility with linear, historical time in telling of events are present in many other inscriptions. One of the longest oracle texts (see Figure 6) gives important historical information about interstate conflicts of the time and tells a story at the same time: "On *gui-si* [the bone] was cracked and Ke divined: 'Shall the week be without any disaster?' The King looked at the cracks and said, 'There shall be a disaster, there will be a coming of bad news.' Upon the fifth day, *ding-you*, there indeed was a coming of bad news, from the west. Zhi Xia told us saying, 'The state of Tu surrounded our eastern area destroying two cities. The state of Gong also encroached on the fields of our western area' ." ...

The oracle-bone inscriptions were not written with a literary intent, and the greatest part of them contain no features which could claim kinship with literature. Nevertheless, they contain many examples of skilled use of language, and prototypes of some later Chinese literary techniques are scattered throughout them.

— *Indiana Companion*, 1986

Figure 6. Rubbing of Shang dynasty oracle bone. (Source: Kwang-chih Chang, *Shang Civilization* [New Haven: Yale University Press, 1980])

Divining the Future — Reading the Past

David N. Keightley

The sun's rays glint first on mountains to the west, then, moments later, touch the thatched roofs of the temples and pit dwellings that follow the curve of the Huan. The river, still in shadow at the foot of the earthen cliff, winds to the southeast between clearings of sprouting millet, on its way to merge with the powerful He. The year is the eleventh of Wu Ding's reign, the season spring, the day *xin-wei,* eighth of the week.

Filtering through the portal of the ancestral temple, the sunlight wakens the eyes of the monster mask, bulging with life on the garish bronze tripod. At the center of the temple stands the king, at the center of the four quarters, the center of the Shang world. Ripening millet glimpsed through the doorway shows his harvest rituals have found favor. Bronze cauldrons with their cooked meat offerings invite the presence of his ancestors, their bodies buried deep and safely across the river, but their spirits, some benevolent, some not, still reigning over the royal house and the king's person. One is angry, for the king's jaw ached all the night, is aching now, on the eve of his departure to follow Zhi Guo on campaign against the Ba-fang.

Five turtle shells lie on the rammed-earth altar. The plastrons have been polished like jade, but are scarred on their inner side with rows of oval hollows, some already blackened by fire. Into one of the unburned hollows, on the right side of the shell, the diviner Que is thrusting a brand of flaming thorn. As he does so, he cries aloud, "The sick tooth is not due to Father Jia!" Fanned by an assistant to keep the glowing tip intensely hot, the stick flames against the surface of the shell. Smoke rises. The seconds slowly pass. The stench of scorched bone mingles with the aroma of millet wine scattered in libation. And then, with a sharp, clear, *puk*like sound, the turtle, most silent of creatures, speaks. A *bu*-shaped (⼘) crack has formed in the hollow where the plastron was scorched. Once again the brand is thrust, now into a matching hollow on the left side of the shell: "It is due to Father Jia!" More time passes … another crack forms in response. Moving to the next plastron, Que repeats the charges: "It is not due to Father Jia!" *Puk!* "It is due to Father Jia!" He rams the brand into the hollows and cracks the second turtle shell, then the third, the fourth, and the fifth.

The diviners consult. The congregation of kinsmen strains to catch their words, for the curse of a dead father may, in the king's eyes, be the work of a living son. Que rubs wood ash from the fire into the new set of cracks and scrutinizes them once more. But the shell has given no indication. The charge must be divined again. Two more cracks are made in each of the five plastrons … and there is again no sign.

Another brand is plucked from the fire and the new charge cried: "The sick tooth is not due to Father Geng! … It is due to Father Geng." Father Geng — the king's senior uncle. This time the indications are clear. His sons, the king's older cousins, turn away in dismay at the diviner's reading of the cracks. The spirit, their father, has been blamed. But still the work of spiritual identification continues. "It is not due to Father Xin! … It is due to Father Xin!" Que moves methodically down the row of five plastrons, reciting the negative and positive charges and cracking each shell twice in this way. No judgment can be made. Once again, as for Father Jia, ten more cracks are burned. "Auspicious!" Que points to two cracks on the second and fourth shells. Father Xin is without blame, his descendants relieved….

Now the king speaks. Assistants drag two victims into the temple. There is the barking and bleating of animals in panic, then silence.

Blood stains the earth floor. The king dismembers the victims as Que proposes a new charge: "We sacrifice a dog to Father Geng and butcher a sheep." The brand flames … *puk* … *puk* … *puk* … the plastrons crack in slow and stately sequence. Has the sacrifice mollified the dead uncle? Will the pain in the sick tooth depart? The king, his hands still sticky with blood, scans the cracks.…

In such an atmosphere and in such ways — in a routine that must have consumed tens of thousands of hours during the Shang historical period — the Shang kings and their diviners sought to know and fix the future. As the ceremony ended, the diviner handed the five plastrons to scribes,

Figure 7. The legendary Shun Emperor and his ministers, including the Great Yu, consulting the oracles of the tortoise-shell and the milfoil. Late Qing dynasty illustration. (Source: Sun Jianai et al., eds. *Shujing tushuo*, 1905)

who began the task of carving into the shell's smooth front a record of the charges proposed and results observed.

The Shang kings read the mantic cracks to divine the wishes of their ancestors. We read the mantic inscriptions to divine the wishes of the Shang kings. May the oracle bones, once used to read the future, now be used to read the past!

— Preamble, *Sources of Shang History: The Oracle-Bone Inscriptions of Bronze Age China*, 1978

Eight Oracle Bone Inscriptions

Interpreted by Lionel C. Hopkins

1

On the day *ren-xu*, inquiry was made through the tortoise-shell of the Royal Guest Shi-ren whether the next day would be without objection for sacrificing.

2

On the day *bing-zi*, inquired of the guest through the tortoise-shell, whether the *fang* officer should go out in force in the seventh moon.

3

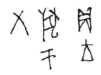

Inquired whether the King should hunt in Ai.

4

On the day *wu-yin*, divined in Gao and inquired if the King hunted in Yi, whether the chase would be without mishap.

5

On the day *gui-wei*, divined as to fishing on the day *ding-hai*.

6

On the day *geng-shen*, divined, inquiring as to our millet harvest. Third moon.

7

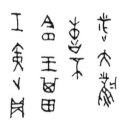

On the day *ren-yin*, divined inquiring if the King hunted today, whether he would not encounter high wind.

8

Inquired whether today, being *bing-wu*, there would be prolonged rain.

— "Working the Oracle," 1919

BRONZE INSCRIPTIONS

Texts of Ritual

Stanley Mickel

Intaglio texts are found on bronze implements cast during the late Shang, Zhou, Qin, and early Western Han periods. Bronze inscriptions range in length from single clan marks on some late Shang pieces to texts nearly five hundred characters in length on pieces from the Zhou period. Texts occur on swords, musical instruments, coins, seals, and other bronze objects. However, the inscriptions of greatest length, content, and literary importance are those on bronze sacrificial vessels cast to immortalize success and status.

The first true bronze texts contain two or three characters which indicate the ancestor in whose memory the vessel was cast: "Ancestor Gui," "Wife Hao," and so on. These texts were soon followed by those which name the ancestor or patron as well as the type of vessel: "Make Father Ji a *ding*," "Make Lü a *ding*," etc. The vast majority are similarly simple, but a few are of much greater complexity. The longest known Shang text has forty-one characters.

The practice of composing commemorative texts for casting in bronze reached its zenith in the Western Zhou. While many bronzes of the period contain no texts, and many others contain inscriptions which simply state that the vessel was made in the honor of a certain ancestor or by a particular person, others display texts hundreds of characters in length. These lengthy texts generally focus on the meritorious deeds of the patrons of the bronzes and the largesse of the Zhou rulers.

Shang and Zhou bronze texts were composed to tell a story from a particular point of view to a particular audience. While characterizations are often neglected, a sophisticated artistic ability is frequently revealed in the narrative techniques employed. By the middle of the Zhou period narrative style had evolved from a completely detached, reportorial stance to the inclusion of unmistakable commentary. When these writing skills are considered in conjunction with the fact that many bronze vessels with lengthy texts were so poorly made as to be little more than a means to present the text to the reader, it becomes clear that bronze texts should be considered as works of literary art.

— *Indiana Companion*, 1986

Early Emblems Related to Professions

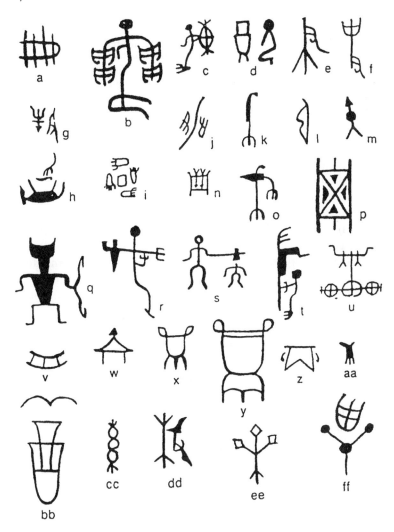

a. animal herder; *b.* trader; *c.* carrier; *d.* food service; *e.* painter; *f.* archivist; *g.* herder; *h.* butcher; *i.* guardsmen; *j.* messenger; *k.* knife-maker; *l.* bow-maker; *m.* arrow-maker; *n.* quiver-maker; *o.* halberd-maker; *p.* shield-maker; *q.* bowman; *r.* halberder; *s.* executioner; *t.* flag-maker; *u.* chariot-maker; *v.* boat-maker; *w.* house-builder; *x. ding*-tripod-maker; *y. yan*-steamer-maker; *z. li*-tripod-maker; *aa. jue*-cup-maker; *bb.* wine-maker; *cc.* silk-maker; *dd.* woodsman; *ee.* orchard grower; *ff.* net-hunter. (Source: Kwang-chih Chang, *Shang Civilization* [New Haven: Yale University Press, 1980])

Five Bronze Inscriptions

Interpreted by Léon Wieger

Whensoever the ancient Chinese noblemen had been favored by their princes, or had experienced some kind of success or luck, they used to cast a bronze vase, in memoriam. Symbols and Characters relating the fact, were molded on the interior side of the vase, which was placed in the ancestral temple of the family, and served henceforth as a ritual vessel, when oblations and libations were offered to the Manes. On the exterior side of the vase, the two eyes of the Ancestor, were figured, looking at his sons and grandsons with benevolence.

1. The most frequent of all symbols is a right hand making an offering, which is neither a flame, nor incense, but the smell of the offered meat, ascending toward the Ancestors.
   Almost every time, beneath this symbol of offering meat, there is a sort of tear, symbol of the poured-down libation of wine.
2. Ordinarily the son offering to his father (and ancestors) is represented in an ethereal shape, which figures his being raptured and transported mentally in the presence of his ancestors, by his filial love and desire to please them. Sometimes arms and legs of the son are figured.
3. Besides the smell of meat and the libation of wine, three things are presented at almost all solemn offerings. These are:
   a. a box containing jade, cowries, and pottery,
   b. an amphora of wine, presented by two hands, with a ladle,
   c. a distaff-load of textile fibers, with two or four hands spinning.
   The idea is very clear. The Ancients offered to their deceased Ancestors, all the things which the living could not do without: viz, valuables, money, vases, stuff for clothes, wine.
4. "In the presence of my Ancestors, I offered raw meat, a libation, wine and flax."
5. On the day *geng-shen*, the new emperor, Wuding, went to the eastern gate of the city, to salute the rising sun. On the evening of the same day, he ordered Minister Hu to deliver five man-loads of cowries, to be presented with the ordinary offerings, as a token of gratitude for the prints of feet and hands of the deceased emperor, Xiaoyi, which had been noticed in the ancestral temple, five times, during the sixteen months of mourning. This vase was cast and placed in the sanctuary, to commemorate the fact. — 1273 B.C.

— *Caractères*, 1900[2]

---

[2] Some of Father Wieger's interpretations (and those of Lionel Hopkins) have been questioned, in the light of more recent archaeological and linguistic research. *Eds.*

1   2   3

4   5

Qiang the Historian
A Bronze Inscription of the Early Zhou Dynasty

Translated by Cho-yün Hsü and Katheryn M. Linduff

In antiquity, King Wen reigned. God bestowed upon him virtues that allowed him to possess a multitude of states between Heaven and Earth. The powerful King Wu campaigned in four directions, took over the Shang people, and quelled the troubles with the (nomadic) Di and the Yi peoples (on the east coast). The wise, sage King Cheng was assisted by strong helpers and consolidated the Zhou. The virtuous King Kang was the one who divided the territory (by enfeoffing feudal lords). The broad-minded King Zhao campaigned southward in the region of Chu-Jing. The brilliant King Mu developed a model to educate the current Son of Heaven in the ways of the old Zhou kings Wen and Wu. A Son of Heaven who enjoyed long life and good health, who served the deities well, who glorified the previous kings and royal ancestors, who brought

Figure 8. Rubbing from the inscription on the Shi Qiang *pan* bronze, reign of King Gong (946–935 B.C.) (Source: Cho-yün Hsü & Katheryn M. Linduff, *Western Chou Civilization* [New Haven: Yale University Press, 1988])

good harvest and made people of all places come to pay their respects, was the model.

Our ancestor resided in Wei at the time when King Wu conquered the Shang. Our great-grandfather was the historian of the Wei state and came to the court of King Wu. King Wu ordered the Duke of Zhou to assign him a residence at Qizhou. Our great-grandfather Zuxin gave birth to many of the descendants of many branches. He brought them blessings and happiness. To him we should offer sacrifices. Our father Yi Gong, wise and virtuous, engaged in farming and managed well, for no one uttered criticism of him. I, Shi Qiang, who love my parents and my brothers, work hard all day and night. Qiang received grace from the king to cast this precious vessel. It is the fortune built by my forefathers that gave the Qiang their land. May good luck and blessings last until my hair turns white and my skin becomes dry. May we serve our king well. May the vessel be treasured ten thousand years.

CALLIGRAPHY

Rhythm and Meaning

François Cheng

It is no accident that calligraphy, which exalts the visual beauty of the ideograms, became a major art. In the practice of this art, the calligrapher seeks to rediscover the rhythm of his deepest being, and to enter into communion with the elements. Through the signifying strokes, he may completely surrender himself. Their thickness and their slenderness, their contrasting and balancing relationships, permit him to express the multiple aspects of his own sensibility: forcefulness and tenderness, abandon and quietude, tension and harmony. In the accomplishment of the unity of each character and in the balance among them, the calligrapher, even in the act of expressing things, achieves his own unity. These immemorial and always restrained gestures provide the cadence, instantaneously achieved with the strokes, which, as in a sword dance, thrusts and crosses, soars and plunges, holding a meaning of its own, and adding another to the codified meaning of the word. It is appropriate, when we speak of calligraphy, to speak of meaning; its gestural and rhythmic nature must not make us forget that it works on signs. In the course of execution, the *signified* of the text is never completely absent from the mind and spirit of the calligrapher, nor is the choice of the text either gratuitous or a matter of indifference.

The calligrapher's preferred texts are poetic texts, poems, and poetic prose. When a calligrapher begins a poem, he does not limit himself to a simple act of copying. Through his calligraphy, he attempts to revive the entire gestural movement and imaginative power of the signs. This is his manner of penetrating the profound reality of each of the signs, of marrying them within the uniquely physical cadence of the poem, and, finally, of recreating the poem itself. Another type of text, the sacred and no less incantatory texts of Taoism (and Buddhism), is equally attractive to the calligrapher. Here calligraphic art is seen as restoring to the signs their original magical and sacred functions. Taoist monks gauge the efficacy of a talisman (or charm) that they draw in terms of the quality of their calligraphy, as it is that quality which assures good communication with the beyond. The Buddhist faithful believe that they may gain merit by copying canonical texts; and here too the efficacy of the result is in direct relation to the quality of the calligraphy.

— from the Introduction to *Chinese Poetic Writing*, 1982

The Historical Development of Four Characters

	1. *xia* below, under, down.	2. *ma* horse.	3. *de* to get, attain.	4. *qing* nobility, court-official.
Pre-historical marks	T			
Oracle Bone Inscription	⌐	𓅂	𓂃	𓊝
Great-seal	T	𓄀	𓇳	𓋹
Small-seal	下	馬	得	卿
Clerical	下	馬	得	卿
Grass	下	马	得	心
Regular	下	馬	得	卿
Running	下	馬	得	卿

(Source: Tseng Yuho, *A History of Chinese Calligraphy* [Hong Kong: The Chinese University Press, 1993])

Five Styles of Calligraphy

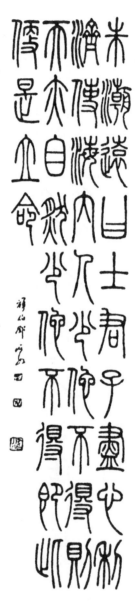

Seal Style: Deng Shiru (1743–1805)

為離此圖美：皆向左番風之夕
浦前呈爛熳晴烟低葉紛婀娜縈
柔初觀駴目若零歊諦視凝神還
衣磬薄裸但覺書紙如書空惟知
變化縱橫無不可他人之式已云
雖不能知蘭之飆杰頗＝載觀品
窳嚴人肌骨寒手必不置行與坐

Clerical Style: Zhu Yizun (1629–1709)

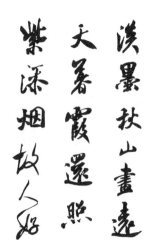

Regular Style: Liu Gongquan
(778–865)

Running Style: Mi Fei (1051–1107)

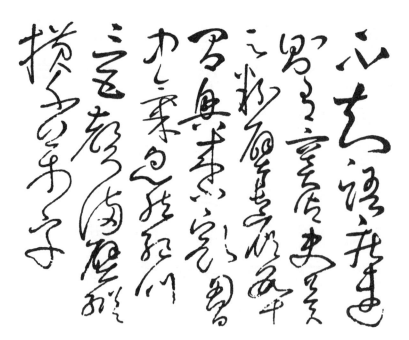

Grass Style: Huai-su (seventh century)
(Source: Chiang Yee, *Chinese Calligraphy: An Introduction to Its Aesthetic and Technique*
[Cambridge, Mass.: Harvard University Press, 1973])

Charms, Talismans, and Stone Books

J. J. M. de Groot

In China, written characters are not merely dead figures, but things essentially endowed with the faculty of producing the reality they represent.

— *The Religious System of China*, 1892

The character for "blessing" repeated a hundred times.

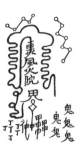

Charm which destroys spectres of illness.

Charm to annul bad dreams.   Charm for protection in the grave.

These characters, in the Seal Style, were engraved on stone slabs measuring thirty centimetres by twenty, which were placed in the grave of Yang Qichuan of Amoy (1801–1859). They read: "Sepulchral Biography with Inscription for Mr. Yang, Intendant Expectant of a Circuit, promoted three degrees, on whom the Imperial Qing dynasty has conferred the title of honour of the second rank."

OUTLINES, CHARACTERS, SIGNS

A Language Ancient and Wonderfully Composed

Sir William Jones

According to a Chinese Writer named Li Yang Ping, "the ancient characters used in his country were the outlines of visible objects earthly and celestial; but, as things merely intellectual could not be expressed by those figures, the grammarians of China contrived to represent the various operations of the mind by metaphors drawn from the productions of nature; thus the idea of roughness and rotundity, of motion and rest, were conveyed to the eye by signs representing a mountain, the sky, a river, and the earth; the figures of the sun, the moon, and the stars, differently combined, stood for smoothness and splendor, for anything artfully wrought, or woven with delicate workmanship; extension, growth, increase, and many other qualities were painted in characters taken from clouds, from the firmament, and from the vegetable part of the creation; the different ways of moving, agility and slowness, idleness and diligence, were expressed by various insects, birds, and quadrupeds: in this manner passions and sentiments were traced by the pencil, and ideas not subject to any sense were exhibited to the sight; until by degrees new combinations were invented, new expressions added; the characters deviated imperceptibly from their primitive shape, and the Chinese language became not only clear and forcible, but rich and elegant in the highest degree."

In this language, so ancient and so wonderfully composed, are a multitude of books, abounding in useful, as well as agreeable, knowledge.

— "On the Second Classical Book of the Chinese,"
Asiatic Researches, 1799

ANON

Precious as Jade: The Written Character (?1870)

Translated by Herbert Giles

They honor their Characters in the most common Books, and if by chance they find any printed Leaves, they gather them up with Respect; they think it would savour of ill-breeding to make a prophane Use of them, to trample them under their Feet, or even to throw them away in a careless manner.

— Du Halde, *A Description of the Empire of China*, 1738

One of the most remarkable national peculiarities of China is their extraordinary addiction to letters, and the very honorable pre-eminence which, from the most remote period, has been universally conceded to that class which is exclusively devoted to literary pursuits. Everything that is subservient to, or connected with, literary objects in China is carried to a degree of refinement, and blended with all their ordinary concerns of pleasure and of business, in a way that may seem extravagant and puerile. Their customary reverence for letters is such that they will not tread upon written or printed paper.

— Sir George Staunton, 1822

From of old down to the present time our sages have devoted themselves to the written character — that fairest jewel in heaven above or earth beneath. Those, therefore, who are stimulated by a thirst for *fame*, strive to attain their end by the excellency of their compositions; others, attracted by desire for wealth, pursue their object with the help of day-books and ledgers. In both cases men would be helpless without a knowledge of the art of writing. How, indeed, could dispatches be composed, agreements drawn up, letters exchanged, and genealogies recorded, but for the assistance of the written character? By what means would a man chronicle the glory of his ancestors, indite the marriage deed, or comfort anxious parents when exiled to a distant land? In what way could he secure property to his sons and grandchildren, borrow or lend money, enter into partnership, or divide a patrimony, but with the testimony of written documents? The very laborer in the fields, tenant of a few acres, must have his rights guaranteed in black and white; and household servants require more than verbal assurance that their wages will not fail to be paid. The prescription of the physician, about to call back some suffering patient from the gates of death, is taken down with pen and ink; and the prognostication of the soothsayer, warning men of evil or predicting good fortune, exemplifies in another direction the use of the written character. In a word, the art of writing enriches and ennobles man, hands him over to life or death, confers upon him honors and distinctions, or covers him with abuse and shame.

Of late, however, our schools have turned out an arrogant and ignorant lot — boys who venture to use old books for wrapping parcels or papering windows, for boiling water, or wiping the table; boys, I say, who scribble over their books, who write characters on wall or door, who chew up the drafts of their poems, or throw them away on the ground. Let all such be severely punished by their masters that they may be saved, while there is yet time, from the wrath of an avenging heaven. Some men use old pawn-tickets for wrapping up things — it may be a cabbage or a pound of beancurd. Others use lottery tickets of various descriptions for wrapping up a pickled vegetable or a slice of pork, with no thought of the crime they are committing as long as there is a cash to be made or saved. So also there are those who exchange their old books for pumeloes or ground-nuts, to be defiled with the filth of the wastepaper basket, and passed from hand to hand like the checks of the barbarian. Alas, too, for women when they go to fairs, for children who are sent to market! They cannot read one single character: they know not the priceless value of written paper. They drop the wrapping of a parcel in the mire for every passer-by to tread under foot. Their crime, however, will be laid at the door of those who erred in the first instance (i.e., those who sold their old books to the shopkeepers). For they hoped to squeeze some profit, infinitesimal indeed, out of tattered or incomplete volumes; forgetting in their greed that they were dishonoring the sages, and laying up for themselves certain calamity. Why then sacrifice so much for such trifling gain? How much better a due observance of time-honored custom, ' ensuring as it would a flow of prosperity continuous and everlasting as the waves of the eastern sea! O ye merchants and shopkeepers, know that in heaven as on earth written words are esteemed precious as the jade, and whatever is marked therewith must not be cast aside like stones and tiles. For happiness, wealth, honors, distinctions, and old age may be one and all secured by a proper respect for written paper.

— *Chinese Sketches*, 1876

The Acts of Signifying

François Cheng

Signs incised upon the shells of tortoises, upon the bones of oxen. Signs borne upon bronze vessels, sacred and mundane. Divinatory or utilitarian, these signs are manifest first of all as tracings, emblems, fixed attitudes, visualized rhythms. Each sign, independent of sound and invariable, forms a unity of itself, maintaining the potential of its own sovereignty and thus the potential to endure. From its beginning the Chinese writing system has refused to be simply a support for the spoken language: its development has been characterized by a constant struggle to assure for itself both autonomy and freedom of combination.... Through these signs, obeying a primordial rhythm, the spoken word may burst forth, and in every area go beyond its act of signifying. To define and delimit the reality of these signs, to demonstrate the specific nature of the Chinese ideograms, and to clarify their connections with other signifying practices is already to reveal essential traits of Chinese poetry.

Man and Nature

François Cheng

What should be emphasized above all is the affirmation of the place of man in the bosom of the universe. Man, heaven, and earth constitute, for the Chinese, the Great Trinity; these participate in a relationship of both correspondence and complementarity. The role of man consists not only of "fitting out" the universe, but of interiorizing all things, in recreating them so as to rediscover his own place within. In this process of "co-creation," the central element, with regard to literature, is the notion of *wen*. This term is found in many later combinations signifying language, style, literature, civilisation, and so forth. Originally it designated the footprints of animals or the veins of wood and stone, the set of harmonious or rhythmic "strokes" by which nature signifies. It is in the image of these natural signs that the linguistic signs were created, and these are similarly called *wen*. The double nature of *wen* constitutes an authority through which man may come to understand the mystery of nature, and thereby his own nature. A masterpiece is that which restores the secret relationship between things, and the breath that animates them as well.

— *Chinese Poetic Writing*, 1982

🙢 *Further Reading* 🙢

Chang, Kwang-chih. *Shang Civilization.* New Haven: Yale University Press, 1980.

Cheng, François. *L'Ecriture poétique chinoise.* Paris: Editions du Seuil, 1977. Trans. Donald A. Riggs & Jerome P. Seaton as *Chinese Poetic Writing: With an Anthology of T'ang Poetry* (Bloomington: Indiana University Press, 1982).

Chiang Yee. *Chinese Calligraphy: An Introduction to Its Aesthetic and Technique.* 3d rev. ed., Cambridge, Mass.: Harvard University Press, 1973.

Giles, Herbert. *Chinese Sketches.* London: Trubner, 1876.

Groot, J. J. M. de. *The Religious System of China.* 5 vols. Leiden: Brill, 1892.

Hopkins, Lionel C. "Working the Oracle." *New China Review* (1919).

Hsü, Cho-yün, & Katheryn M. Linduff. *Western Chou Civilization.* New Haven: Yale University Press, 1988.

Jones, Sir William. "On the Second Classical Book of the Chinese." In *Asiatic Researches*, Vol. 1. London: Bengal Asiatic Society, 1799.

Karlgren, Bernhard. *Sound and Symbol in Chinese.* London: Oxford University Press, 1923.

———. *Grammata Serica Recensa.* Stockholm: Museum of Far Eastern Antiquities, 1957.

Keightley, David N. *Sources of Shang History: The Oracle-Bone Inscriptions of Bronze Age China.* Berkeley: University of California Press, 1978.

Legeza, Laszlo. *Tao Magic: The Secret Language of Diagrams and Calligraphy.* London: Thames & Hudson, 1975.

Liu, James J. Y. *Chinese Theories of Literature*. Chicago: University of Chicago Press, 1975.

Norman, Jerry. *Chinese*. Cambridge: Cambridge University Press, 1988.

Shih, Vincent Yu-chung, trans. *The Literary Mind and the Carving of Dragons: A Study of Thought and Pattern in Chinese Literature*. Rev. ed. Hong Kong: The Chinese University Press, 1983.

Tseng, Yuho. *A History of Chinese Calligraphy*. Hong Kong: The Chinese University Press, 1993.

Wieger, Léon. *Caractères*. Ho-kien fu: Catholic Mission Press, 1900. Trans. L. Davrout as *Chinese Characters*, 2d rev. ed. (Ho-kien fu: Catholic Mission Press, 1927).

🖫 Editors' Note 🖫

Between them, the medieval critic Liu Xie (see chapter 15) and the contemporary Paris-based critic, poet, and translator François Cheng provide an initiation into the nature of the Chinese script and the very special relationship between the literature written in that script, and the Tao — the "Chinese Way," that untranslatable, impalpable, "eternally nameless," all-embracing first principle of the Chinese universe. The Chinese script is the Pattern of the Tao. Samples of epigraphy and calligraphy serve to illustrate the efficacy of this underlying magic.

Four scholar-translators of the turn of the century appear here for the first time in the anthology. Lionel C. Hopkins, younger brother of the poet Gerard Manley Hopkins, served in the Chinese consular service from 1874 to 1908 and wrote many imaginative studies of the newly discovered oracle bones. Léon Wieger, born in Alsace in 1856, was the most prolific of the French Jesuit sinologists and translators of his time. The Dutch scholar de Groot, in his monumental work *The Religious System of China*, translated into pleasant English a huge amount of the Chinese literature concerning the dead and the realm of departed spirits. Herbert Giles, another product of the Chinese consular service, later professor of Chinese at Cambridge, is a translator whose name will recur frequently in subsequent chapters. He was the most accomplished English translator of Chinese literature (as opposed to the philosophical classics) in the late Victorian and Edwardian period. Of his translations of Chinese verse, Lytton Strachey wrote in 1908: "One would be tempted to say that the poetry in it is the best that this generation has known, save that it has been written for the last ten centuries."

Characters based on Zhou Dynasty Bronze Inscriptions.
Seal carved by Wu Zi (1813–1858)

Chapter 2

Heavenly Questions

Early Myths and Legends

For besides that in the *Great Annals* it is read that *Fohi*'s [Fu Xi's] Mother accidentally stepping into a Place where a Giant had passed, she was suddenly encompass'd with a Rainbow, and that 'twas at this very moment that she perceiv'd herself with Child of the Founder of the Chinese Monarchy; where it is also related that this Founder had the Head of a Man, and Body of a Serpent. 'Tis true, that these Fables being very gross, the Generality of the Chinese derides them.

— *The Morals of Confucius: A Chinese Philosopher*, 1691

Please tell me who the Chinese are,
Teach me how to cling to memory.
Please tell me the greatness of this people
Tell me gently, ever so gently.
Please tell me: Who are the Chinese?
Whose hearts embody the hearts of Yao and Shun?
In whose veins flow the blood of Jing Ke and Nie Zheng?
Who are the true children of the Yellow Emperor?

— Wen Yiduo, 1927 (*translated by Hsü Kai-yü*)

China has never had monumental works putting all these myths and legends together, as in the Greek epics. In our literature myths and legends serve merely as allusions and embellishments in poetry or prose. They left their mark, too, on later fiction.

It seems likely that Chinese myths remained separate fragments for the following reasons. First, the early dwellers in the Yellow River Valley were not an imaginative people; and since their life was hard and they devoted most of their energy to practical matters without indulging in flights of fancy, they did not combine all the old legends into one great epic. Secondly, Confucius appeared with his teaching about the way to cultivate morality, regulate the family, rule the state and bring peace to the world. Since he disapproved of talk of the supernatural, the old myths were not quoted by Confucian scholars, and instead of undergoing further development many of them were lost.

— Lu Xun, *A Brief History of Chinese Fiction*, 1931
(*translated by Xianyi and Gladys Yang*)

Heavenly Questions
Selections, from the Songs of the South

Translated and annotated by David Hawkes

The "Heavenly Questions" is a long questionnaire that begins with questions about the sky but soon progresses from cosmological, astronomical, and meteorological subjects to questions about the earth and its marvels and thence to questions about the affairs of men: the legendary heroes of antiquity and the kings and princes of a more recent past....

The commentator Wang Yi (d. A.D. 158) gives an ingenious but highly improbable reconstruction of the circumstances in which the "Heavenly Questions" were written. After his banishment, he says, Qu Yuan (c. 340–278 B.C.)[1] wandered about in great distress of mind through mountains, marshes, and plains, lifting up his eyes and *crying out to heaven* as he went. Sometimes, exhausted by his wanderings, he would sink down to rest under the walls of the ancestral temples of former kings and ministers of the southern Kingdom of Chu. Looking up and observing the pictures with which the walls were covered — pictures representing the mysteries of heaven and earth and the acts of the men of old, both wise and wicked — he would write these questions on the walls "to ease his mind." (Wang Yi is a great believer in the therapeutic value of creative writing.) After his death the people of Chu felt sorry for him, so they copied down and collected together what he had written. That is why the questions often appear to be in the wrong order....

It is clear that in the "Heavenly Questions" we have a remarkably rich sourcebook of Chinese mythology, untainted by the euhemerism, systematizing, and rationalizations that mythology underwent in so many Chinese texts; but our uncertainty as to whether or not an obscure passage is in the right context, added to our realization that the story it refers to may in any case be lost, tantalizingly reduces the use we are able to make of its treasures....

"Heavenly Questions" is written in an archaic language to be found nowhere else in the Chu anthology, the *Songs of the South*, with the exception of one or two short passages of "On Encountering Trouble." It is my belief that its somewhat odd combination of archaic riddles with questions of a speculative or philosophic nature may be due to the fact that it started as an ancient, priestly riddle-text (a sort of catechism to be used for mnemonic purposes), which was rewritten and greatly enlarged by a secular poet; and since Sima Qian unhesitatingly ascribes "Heavenly Questions" to Qu Yuan and "On Encountering Trouble" is undoubtedly related to "Heavenly Questions" in one way or another (the same stories, the same attitudes, even, once or twice, the same phrases, are found in both), I have assumed that Qu Yuan was this adapter. The tradition that Qu Yuan was inspired to write these questions by looking at pictures on temple walls has at least this much substance in it: that it seems to recognize the fact that this was not a wholly original work by the great poet but an ancient one having priestly, i.e. shamanistic, associations, which he took over and improved.

— *The Songs of the South*, 1985

---

[1] For Qu Yuan and the *Songs of the South*, see chapter 5. Eds.

Figure 9. Painted pottery head. Gansu, 2nd millenium B.C. (Source: William Watson, *China Before the Han Dynasty* [London: Thames & Hudson, 1961])

1. Who passed down the story of the far-off, ancient beginning of things? How can we be sure what it was like before the sky above and the earth below had taken shape? Since none could penetrate that murk when darkness and light were yet undivided, how do we know about the chaos of insubstantial forms?

2. What manner of things are the darkness and light? How did Yin and Yang[2] come together, and how could they originate and transform all things that are by their commingling?

---

[2] From the composition of the characters with which they are written, the earliest meaning of these words would seem to have been "shady" and "sunny"; hence the somewhat confusing fact that the south side of mountains and the north side of eastward-flowing rivers are both called "yang," these being, in the northern hemisphere, the sides which face the sun. Later they came to be thought of in an abstract sense as two principles or forces, each equally important in the process of creation, which in the advanced thought of Qu Yuan's day was conceived of as a spontaneous, natural process: viz. the emergence of these two forces from a primordial, undifferentiated One, their polarization of formless matter into a Yang heaven and a Yin earth, and their engendering, by an infinite number of interactions and combinations, of the Ten Thousand Things — the myriad forms of organic life which inhabit the earth.

3. Whose compass measured out the ninefold heavens?[3] Whose work was this, and how did he accomplish it? Where were the circling cords fastened, and where was the sky's pole fixed? Where did the Eight Pillars meet the sky, and why were they too short for it in the southeast?[4]

4. Where do the nine fields of heaven[5] extend to and where do they join each other? The ins and outs of their edges must be very many: who knows their number?

---

[3] In the worldview of the ancient Chinese, the earth was square and comparatively flat, whilst the sky was round and suspended over it like an inverted bowl. The sky was "ninefold" in a double sense. It was divided, like the earth, into nine regions or "fields"; it was also ninefold in the sense that it was made up of nine layers, like a very heavy plywood. It is in the latter sense that "ninefold" is intended here. Chinese philosophers associated "nine" with "heaven" because the sky is Yang and nine is a perfect Yang number.

[4] The Eight Pillars were eight mountains situated at the eight points of the compass around the edges of the earth. They feature in a cosmological myth designed to explain (1) why the Celestial Pole around which the sky appears to revolve is not at the zenith immediately overhead but north of it, and (2) why the earth (i.e., China) inclines downwards towards the southeast, causing the major rivers to flow in an easterly direction: in a word, why the cosmos, instead of being perfect and symmetrical, as you would expect it to be, is askew. The myth, which is invoked here in connection with the northward tilting of the Celestial Pole, is referred to again in connection with the downward tilting of the earth. A version of it is preserved in *Huainanzi* (second century B.C.): "Long, long ago Gong Gong contended with Zhuan Xu for mastery of the world. Enraged by his defeat, he butted against the Buzhou Mountain, breaking the supporting pillar, snapping the cords, and causing the sky to tilt downward toward the northwest. That is why the sun, moon, and stars revolve from east to west and why the earth is lower on its southeast side, so that water and silt drain away from it in a southeasterly direction." Buzhou Mountain was the northwestern of the Eight Pillars. The "perfect" cosmos, as it existed before Gong Gong's assault on it, would have been a motionless firmament, supported at the center by a Celestial Pole, rising vertically from the middle of the earth to the zenith above, and at the edges by the Eight Pillars, to which, as an additional reinforcement, cords from the top of the Celestial Pole were fastened, like guy-ropes sustaining a mast. Apart from breaking the Pillar, the shock of Gong Gong's assault snapped the cords and dislodged the sky from its eight supports, causing the Celestial Pole to heel over toward the north, the sky to start spinning in an eastwest direction (which it has continued to do ever since), and the earth to tilt downward on the southeast side. Qu Yuan's evident unhappiness about the dynamics of this myth must have been shared by many others to judge from the attempts at improving on it made in later versions.

[5] The nine fields of the sky are best thought of in relation to the Nine Lands into which the earth was thought to have been divided by the demiurge Yu. Yu invented drainage and irrigation, which turn the landscape, wherever it is a comparatively flat one, into a grid. The simplest grid having a square as its center is made by the right-angled intersection of two pairs of parallel lines inside a larger square, and this is how Yu is supposed to have divided the earth. The nine fields of the sky represent a somewhat arbitrary attempt to give the earthly pattern a celestial counterpart.

5. How does heaven coordinate its motions? Where are the Twelve Houses divided?[6] How do the sun and the moon hold to their courses and the fixed stars keep their places?

6. Setting out from the Gulf of Brightness and going to rest in the Vale of Murk, from the dawn until the time of darkness, how many miles is that journey?

7. What is the peculiar virtue of the moon, the Brightness of the Night, which causes it to grow once more after its death? Of what advantage is it to keep a toad in its belly?[7]

8. How did the Mother Star get her nine children without a union? Where is Lord Bluster, the Wind Star, and where does the warm wind live?

9. What is it whose closing causes the dark and whose opening causes the light? Where does the Bright God hide before the Horn proclaims the dawning of the day?[8]

---

[6] The Twelve Houses were the twelve stations of the imaginary Counter-Jupiter planet. It was by means of this imaginary planet that the twelve-year (actually 11.86- year) cycle of Jupiter was correlated with the twelve cyclical characters and with the twelve lunations of the year. The solar, lunar, and sidereal years are all different but eventually "come together" (approximately) inside larger cycles, just as, in the ancient Chinese calendar, the cycles of ten and twelve eventually "came together" at the end of each sexagenary cycle. Qu Yuan is asking, in effect, what mysterious, complicated mechanism coordinates the movements of the sun, moon, and planets with those of the fixed stars.

[7] The characters *gutu* appear to mean "backward-looking hare" and have been so understood by most interpreters of this passage. Certainly there was a tradition — though I think it was rather a late one — that the dark shadows on the moon's surface represent a hare perpetually engaged in the pounding of magic herbs; yet most early sources, pictorial ones included, suggest that the moon's sole inhabitant was a toad. The scholar Wen Yiduo (1899–1946), in a lengthy note on this passage, adduced what seem to me convincing reasons for believing that the characters *gutu* are used here as an alternative way of writing one of the words for "toad." Chang E, wife of the fox-hunting Lord Yi, is supposed to have stolen the herb of immortality from her husband and fled with it to the moon, where she turned into a toad. The advantage to the moon, which "dies" every month (many Zhou inscriptions actually refer to the "death" of the moon in recording the date), of harboring a creature which possesses the secret of immortality must be obvious.

[8] The Bright God is the sun. The Horn is the name of a constellation consisting of α Virginis, i.e. Spica, and one much fainter star. It was the first of the twenty-eight *xiu* which divided the Celestial Equator. Its two stars were also called the Gate of Heaven. These questions are thought to refer to the heliacal rising of this constellation in the first month of spring, i.e. the beginning of the year.

10. If Gun was not fit to allay the flood, why was he given this charge?[9] All
said, "Never fear! Try him out and see if he can do it." When the
bird-turtles linked together, how did Gun follow their sign? And if he
accomplished the work according to his will, why did the high lord
punish him? Long he lay cast off on Feather Mountain: why for three
whole years did he not rot? When Lord Gun brought forth Yu from
his belly, how was he transformed?[10] Yu inherited the same tradition
and carried on the work of his father. If he continued the work
already begun, in what way was his plan a different one? How did he
fill the flood waters up where they were most deep? How did he set
bounds to the Nine Lands? What did the winged dragon trace on the
ground? Where did the seas and rivers flow?

---

[9] Gun's failure to control the floodwaters and his consequent punishment by exposure on
the Feather Mountain are cited in "On Encountering Trouble," as an awful example of
the danger of clinging too persistently to a discredited theory. The story of Gun and Yu,
the unsuccessful father and the successful son, appears to have existed in a number of
different versions. It seems to symbolize the transition from one mode of subsistence to
another among peoples inhabiting the flood plains of the Yellow River and its tributaries
in ancient times. Gun represents a more primitive society whose small-scale reclamation
of areas rising somewhat above the level of the surrounding marshes may have been
eked out with floating "gardens" of brushwood and soil like those made by some riverine
peoples in our own day. (One version of the myth maintains that Gun was punished for
stealing magic soil from God with which to "fill up the waters".) Yu represents a society
able to organize itself on the much vaster scale required for constructing networks of
ditches and canals capable of eliminating the marshes altogether. The seemingly
miraculous transformation of the landscape, which drainage brings about, is reflected in
the myth's portrayal of Yu as a demiurge responsible for every feature of China's
geography. In fact the "Nine Lands" into which he is supposed to have divided the
inhabited earth are simply the basic drainage grid on a very large scale. The Chinese
term means literally "nine islands," viz., lands surrounded or intersected by water
channels. (The word for "island" used in this expression has a riverine rather than
maritime connotation.) Qu Yuan's opening question refers to the text of the ancient
Book of History, with which most educated men in his time would be familiar. In the
section of it called "The Canon of Yao" [see pp. 50–54] the high lord sits in council and
asks his assembled chieftains what he should do about the flood: "On every hand the
waters spread havoc; they encircle the hills; they rise up level with their summits; they
threaten the sky; the people below cry out. Is there any one who can control them?" The
assembly unanimously recommend Gun, and the high lord, despite some misgivings,
appoints Gun to control the flood. "For nine years he labored," says the text, "but he did
not succeed." But not all texts make Gun out to have been a failure. The story about his
stealing god's magic soil, for instance, seems to imply that he was punished not for
failure but for succeeding all too well. Qu Yuan probably knew several versions of the
story and was puzzled by their inconsistency.

[10] Three years after his death on Feather Mountain Gun's belly was cut open and his son
Yu came out. His body turned into a yellow dragon — some accounts said a turtle or a
bear — which dived into a nearby lake.

11. What did Gun plan and what did Yu accomplish? Why, when the Wicked One was enraged, did the earth sink down toward the southeast? Why are the lands of the earth dry and the river valleys wet? They flow eastwards without ever getting exhausted: who knows the cause of this? What are the distances from east to west and from south to north? From north to south the earth is longer and narrower. What is the difference between its length and breadth? Where is Kunlun with its Hanging Garden? How many miles high are its ninefold walls? Who goes through the gates in its four sides? When the northeast one opens, what wind is it that passes through? What land does the sun not shine on and how does the Torch Dragon light it? Why are the Ruo flowers bright before Xi He is stirring? What place is warm in winter? What place is cold in summer? Where is the stone forest? What beast can talk? Where are the hornless dragons which carry bears on their backs for sport? Where is the great serpent with nine heads and where is the Shu Hu? Where is it that people do not age? Where do giants live? Where is the nine-branched weed? Where is the flower of the Great Hemp? How does the snake that can swallow an elephant digest its bones? Where is the Black Water that dyes the feet, and where is the Mountain of Three Perils? The folk there put death off for many years: what is the limit of their age? Where does the man-fish live? Where is the Monster Bird?

12. When Lord Yi shot down the suns, why did the ravens shed their feathers?[11]

13. Yu labored with all his might. He came down and looked on the earth below. How did he get that maid of Tushan and lie with her in Taisang? The lady became his mate and her body had issue. How came they to have appetite for the same dish when they sated their hunger with the morning food of love?[12]

---

[11] At one time the ten suns of Fusang came out together and dried up the earth. Lord Yi, the Mighty Archer, was commanded by God to shoot them down. The ravens are the ravens of the suns. (A raven was said to inhabit the sun just as a toad or hare was said to inhabit the moon.) Perhaps their feathers were meteorites.

[12] Yu's labors involved him in perpetual journeying and left little time over for domesticity. The mother of his only son, Qi, is said to have been a mountain nymph, the Lady of Tushan, whom he met on his travels. Visiting her some time later, when she was pregnant, Yu was unwise enough to let her see him when he had changed himself (as he sometimes did, apparently) into a bear. This gave the lady so great a shock that she turned into stone. Yu called out anxiously to the petrified mother to give him his son, whereupon the stone burst open, revealing the infant Qi inside. (The name means "open.")

14. Who built the ten-storeyed tower of jade? Who foresaw it all in the beginning, when the first signs appeared?[13]

15. By what law was Nü Wa raised up to become high lord? By what means did she fashion the different creatures?[14]

16. King Mu was a breeder of horses. For what reason did he roam about? What was he looking for when he made his circuit of the earth?[15]

17. When the witches were tied up together, what was it that was crying in the marketplace? Whom was You of Zhou punishing when he got that Bao Si?[16]

---

[13] The subject of this question is an unbroken mystery.

[14] Readers of the 18th-century novel *The Story of the Stone* will remember Nü Wa as the goddess who repaired the broken sky in the novel's opening chapter. A late arrival in the Chinese pantheon, she was given a place among the sage-kings and early "emperors" somewhat before that of the Yellow Ancestor. (In the pseudo-history of what was called "high antiquity" the latest arrivals were made to antedate their predecessors because there was nowhere else to put them.) Mythology makes her the wife or sister of Fu Xi and the pair of them are represented iconographically as human above and serpentine below, with their lower serpent-halves intertwined. Generally they are shown holding carpenter's tools in their hands, or sometimes the sun and moon. Evidently they were a personification of the male and female principle, the Yin and Yang, by which all other things were created. Sometimes (as in this question) Nü Wa alone was said to be the creator. The second-century lexicographer Xu Shen refers to this alternative tradition.

[15] King Mu was the fifth of the Zhou kings, the son of King Zhao. He was a great traveler. A fictitious account of this journey to the far west called *The Travels of Mu, Son of Heaven* [see pp. 57–65] was discovered in the third century A.D. in the tomb of a fourth-century B.C. king of Liang. The names of his horses and of their driver, Bo Le, who is supposed to have had a preternatural flair for assessing equine capabilities, make frequent appearances in the poems of Qu Yuan and his imitators, who saw in them a parable of the wise king who is able to choose the right statesmen for harnessing to the chariot of state.

[16] Xuan, the eleventh of the Zhou kings (r. 827–781 B.C.), heard a prophecy that a mulberry bow and a bamboo quiver would destroy the kingdom of Zhou. A man and his wife caught selling these objects were tied up and exposed in the marketplace. At this time a waiting-maid at the palace had given miraculous birth to a fatherless child (she was impregnated by a terrifying flood of dragon-sperm which someone had imprudently let out of a chest) which she then abandoned. The couple, escaping from their bonds, heard its cries and fled with it to the land of Bao. The abandoned infant grew up to become King You's queen Bao Si, whose follies hastened the downfall of Western Zhou. The only thing which ever made Queen Bao Si smile, it is said, was the expression of angry surprise on the faces of the King's vassals when they turned out with their armies in response to the kindling of the warning beacons which the King had caused to be lit for her amusement. Unfortunately, like the boy in the fable who cried "wolf," King You found that his joke was an expensive one, for when his barbarian enemies really did come marching down over the hills and he lit the beacon fires to summon his vassals, no one would turn out to protect him. The answer to the second question is the Lord of Bao. It was in order to avert a punitive expedition that the men of Bao sent the beautiful Bao Si to the court of King You.

18. King Millet was his firstborn: why did the high lord treat him so
cruelly? When he was left out on the ice, how did the birds keep him
warm? Drawing his bow to the full and grasping the arrow, how did
he become a war-leader? After giving the high lord so great a shock,
how did he come to have a glorious future?[17]

THE NORTHERN LANDS BEYOND THE SEA
Book 8 of the Book of Hills and Seas

Translated by H. C. Cheng, H. C. Pai Cheng, and K. L. Thern[18]

The *Book of Hills and Seas* is a fantastic geography of ancient China and surrounding

Figure 10. Deities from the Chu Silk Manuscript. (Source: Noel Barnard, *The Ch'u Silk Manuscript: Translation and Commentary* [Canberra: Australian National University Press, 1973])

---

[17] The corn god King Millet was the First Ancestor of the Zhou people. His mother, Jiang Yuan, conceived him by stepping in a giant footprint left by God. As a fatherless child, he was exposed shortly after his birth (his name Qi means "the castaway" or "the abandoned one"), but, as in the case of other heroic infants, all attempts at getting rid of him were frustrated: "They laid him in a narrow lane / But the sheep and oxen stood over him and protected him / They laid him in a wood / But the woodcutters found him and brought him back / They laid him on the cold ice / But the birds came and covered him with their wings." [compare p. 49] In the "modernized" version of the myth which Qu Yuan appears to be referring to here, Di Ku, or Gao Xin, instead of being the name of God, has become Jiang Yuan's earthly husband, the high lord Gao Xin. In this version it was Di Ku, presumably, who exposed King Millet: hence the question "Why did the high lord treat him so cruelly?" The custom of killing the firstborn was noted by the ancient Chinese among certain neighboring tribes. They explained it by saying that the women-folk among these peoples were unchaste, and that it was only in this way that fathers could make sure that the first son they reared would be their own. The point of the last two questions in this passage is obscure.

[18] The translation has been revised by the editors. Much of the text is obscure, and in places the translation is tentative. *Eds.*

lands. Liu Xin (c. 50 B.C.–A.D. 23), the Han editor of this text, ascribed it to the thearch Yu (twenty-third century B.C.), mythological regulator of the great Chinese flood, and his assistant Yi. Supposedly, Yu traveled the world during his heroic labors and learned much about the mountains, seas, inhabitants, and gods of his own and other lands. Yu's travelogue was written down by his assistants in thirty-four sections, which were edited millennia later by Liu Xin into the present eighteen-section classic.

In the traditional Chinese bibliographical literature, *Hills and Seas* is variously categorized as a work of geomancy, geography, or fiction. However the book is classified, its chief value lies in its preservation of much ancient Chinese myth and folklore. Such material is organized according to a geographical scheme that gives the precise spatial location of the various fantasies it describes. David Hawkes perceives in this work some "ritual-religious intent" and several Chinese scholars, Lu Xun the most prominent, have linked it to the early Chinese shamanistic tradition. *Hills and Seas* has been commonly assigned to the southern Chu literary realm and compared to the rather mysterious poetic work "Heavenly Questions" …

Hills and Seas is of considerable literary significance. It is described by Hu Yinglin (1551–1602) as "the ancestor of ancient and modern works that discuss the strange." As such, it has been listed as a forerunner of the traditional Chinese tales of the supernatural. The narrative sections of the work are extremely brief and somewhat disjointed, but they contain valuable fragments of early Chinese mythology.

— William H. Nienhauser, *Indiana Companion*

These are the places beyond the sea, from the northeast corner to the northwest corner.

No Calf Land lies east of Long Leg Land. The people have no calves.

The Spirit of Goblet Mountain is named Torch Dark. When it opens its eyes, that is the daytime, and when its eyes are closed, that is the night. When it blows it makes the winter, and when it inhales it makes the summer. It does not drink, neither does it eat or breathe. If ever it does breathe, then that is the wind. Its body is one thousand *li* long. It is to be found east of No Calf Land. In bodily form it has the face of a man and the body of a snake, and is red in color. It resides below Goblet Mountain.

One Eye Land lies to the east. These people have one eye in the center of the face.

The Land of Soft-and-Easy lies east of One Eye. These people have one hand and one foot and can bend back their knee, so the leg folds up altogether.

The minister of Gong Gong is named Willow. He has nine heads with which to eat on the Nine Mountains. The places where Willow dug holes became ravines and swamps. Yu the Thearch killed Willow, and his blood made such an evil stench that no grain could be planted there. Yu dug the soil out three times in these places and each time the blood soaked it again. Some soil was used to build a Mound Tower to all the emperors. This is north of Kunlun and east of Soft-and-Easy. Willow has nine heads and faces, the body of a snake, and is green in color. He dares not shoot north, for awe of the Mound Tower of Gong Gong. The Mound Tower is to the east, built square; it has a snake on the corner, with tiger markings, facing south.

Deep Eye Land is to the east. Here the people have deep eyes and one hand raised. Some say this is east of the Mound Tower of Gong Gong.

No Bowels Land is to the east of Deep Eye. Here the people are tall and have no bowels.

Pendant Ear Land is east of No Bowels Land. Here they train two striped tigers and hold their ears in their hands. They live in a village surrounded by sea and get many rare things from the water. The two tigers are to the east.

Big Daddy chased the sun. As the sun went down he was thirsty and wanted a drink, so he drank from the Yellow and Wei Rivers. They were not enough, so he started north to drink from the Great Marsh, but on the way he died of thirst. He threw away his staff, and it became the Forest of Deng.

Big Daddy Land is east of Pendant Ear. Here the people are large. In their right hand they hold a green snake, in their left a yellow one. The Forest of Deng lies to the east. Two trees in the Forest are called Big Fellow by some.

The Mountain of Rocks Piled by the Great Yu lies to the east. This is where the Yellow River enters.

The Land of Goiter lies to the east. Here with one hand they support the goiter on their necks.

The *xun* tree is a thousand *li* high and is found south of Goiter, growing above the Yellow River, to the northwest.

Tiptoe Land lies to the east of Goiter. Here the people are large, and so are their feet. Some call the place Big Heel.

Spitting Silk Wilderness lies east of Big Heel. Here a girl kneels against a tree spitting silk.

Three Mulberry Trees with no branches grow east of Spitting Silk, two hundred and fifty meters tall.

The Forest of Fan is three hundred *li* square and lies east of the Three Mulberry Trees. Islands surround it.

Wu Yu Mountain: Emperor Zhuan Xu is buried on the south side, and his nine concubines on the north. Some say bears, striped tigers, and other animals are to be found here.

Level Hill lies east of the Three Mulberry Trees. Here are to be found jet, the green horse, the willow, the sweet haw, the sweet flower, and all the fruits that grow. It lies in a valley between two hills.

In the North Sea lives an animal resembling the horse, called the *taotu*. Also to be found there is an animal called the *jiao*, resembling a white horse, but with saw teeth. It eats tigers and leopards. There is also a white animal that looks like a horse, called the *ang'ang*, and a green animal like the tiger, called the *luo-luo*.

Yu Qiang of the north has a human face and the body of a bird. In its ears it wears two green snakes and it treads on two more.

HOU JI (LORD MILLET), PROGENITOR OF ZHOU
A *Dynastic Legend from the* Book of Songs *(Song 245)*

Translated by William Jennings

The House of Zhou traced their pedigree back to Hou Ji, and when the dynasty was founded, sacrificial honors were paid to him. The Duke of Zhou is said thereupon to have written this Ode.... The strange and easy birth was regarded by his mother as an unlucky omen, and this explains why she is represented as "exposing" him to be trampled on by cattle, then in the forest's solitude, then on the ice. From all these dangers he had wonderful escapes, and she therefore took him back.... His early talent for husbandry grew with the years, and the Emperor Yao at length made him minister of husbandry.

— *The Shi King,* 1891

> Our folk's first origin
> Is dated from Jiang Yuan:
> Now sing we how this origin occurred:
> Once worshipping was she,

Figure 11. Four creatures from the *Book of Hills and Seas*. (Source: Yuan Ke, *Zhongguo shenhua chuanshuo cidian* [Hong Kong: Commercial Press, 1986])

Praying, "Pity childless me,"
Then, treading on God's toe-print, she was stirred;
This brought her blessing, brought her rest,
Conception, privacy;
Then came an infant to her breast;
That infant was Hou Ji.

When all her months had run,
Came forth her first-born son,
Came as a lamb comes, without manglement,
Or injury or throe,
The Prodigy to show!
Thus did not God vouchsafe to her content?
Thus did not her pure offerings please?
That she should have her child with ease.

She exposed him in a narrow lane,
The kine yet showed him care.
She exposed him in the forest-plain,
Wood-cutters found him there.
She exposed him on the ice-bound river, cold;
A bird with outspread wings did him enfold.
At length, forsaken by the bird,
He cried for it to stay,
And long and loud his wails were heard
Along the whole highway.

When he could creep and crawl,
More wit had he than all;
When he grew on to feeding without aid,
He took to sowing beans,
And finely grew his beans,
And smiling rows of rice his toil repaid;
His hemp and wheat abundant grew,
His little gourds prolific too.

He taught the husbandman,
"Aid nature where you can:
First all the rank and grassy herbage clear;
Then sow your golden grain,
Well forced and put in train;
Thus sown 'twill soon above the soil appear,
And shoot aloft, and fructify,
Grow strong and fair to see,

Full awned and eared" — and this was why
The House of Dai won he.

And thus good seed men find,
Of millets every kind —
The black, the double-grained, the brown, the white.
Those first we see all round
Stacked on the reaping-ground;
The white and brown, again a common sight,
On back and shoulders home we bear,
To make our first-fruit offerings there.

These how do we prepare?
Many the duty share:
Some thresh, some hull, some winnow well the grain;
'Tis washed, with swish and swirl!
Distilled, and vapors curl!
We fix the day, keep vigil, and abstain;
Bring southernwood, to offer with the fat,
The rams for the gods of roads;
Flesh roast and boiled; good fortune that
For future years forebodes.

The sacred bowls, the pair
Of wood and earthenware,
We fill; and odors sweet begin to rise;
Pleased God is with the smell,
So fragrant, timed so well.
Hou Ji it was began this sacrifice;
And none can rightfully regret
That it continues with us yet.

THE CANON OF YAO
from the Book of History

Translated by W. H. Medhurst

The first Chinese work of history — taking the word in its broadest sense to mean a record of past events — is the *Book of History*, also known as the *Documents of Antiquity*. According to tradition, the documents which make up the work were assembled and arranged by Confucius, who wrote brief introductions to each one explaining the circumstances of its composition. There may well be a core of truth in this account, since it is known that Confucius and his disciples often cited passages from some of the documents in their teaching. Whatever Confucius' collection of documents may have been, however, it was certainly added to in the centuries after his death....

Figure 12. The six Xi and He brothers receive their commission from the Emperor Yao. Late Qing dynasty illustration. (Source: *Shujing tushuo*, 1905)

The language of the *Book of History* in both its narrative and its speech passages, is extremely difficult. Bernhard Karlgren terms it lapidary, which seems a particularly apt way of conveying the terse, archaic impression which it gives: something stiff, stone-carved, difficult to make out, and blurred in places beyond intelligibility. It stands with the *Book of Songs* and the older portions of the *Book of Changes* at the dawn of Chinese literature, preceded by the bone inscriptions discovered in the last century and paralleled by inscriptions on bronze, but set apart in style and vocabulary from everything that follows. No one, not even a scholar, picks up the *Book of History* and reads it right off; the meaning of many passages remains today the subject of endless dispute among specialists. Nevertheless, in spite of individual words or phrases whose meaning is doubtful or lost, the general sense of the text can still be made out. As in later Chinese style, there is a tendency to use balanced, parallel phrases, and to treat ideas in the forms of numerical categories — the five felicities, the three virtues, and so on. The basic ideas expressed in the *Book of History* have influenced later Chinese thought to an incalculable degree. But the style, because of its difficult and archaic quality, cannot be said to have had a similar influence.

— Burton Watson, *Early Chinese Literature*, 1962

Now on examining into the ancient Emperor Yao, we must say that he was vastly meritorious, reverential, and intelligent; his external accomplishments and internal reflections were easy and unconstrained; he was sincerely respectful, and capable of yielding, while his fame extended to the four distant quarters, reaching to heaven above and earth beneath.

He was able to display his superior virtue, in order to bind closer the nine degrees of kindred; the nine kindreds being rendered harmonious, he equalized and illumined the people of the Imperial domain; his own people having become intelligent, he harmonized the various states of the Empire, and the black-haired people. Oh! how were they reformed by this cordial agreement!

He then commanded Xi and He, in reverent accordance with the motions of the expansive heavens, to arrange by numbers and represent by instruments the revolutions of the sun, moon, and stars, with the lunar mansions, and then respectfully to communicate to the people the seasons adapted for labor.

He then separately directed Xi's younger brother to reside at Yuyi, called the Orient Valley, where he might respectfully hail the rising sun, adjust and arrange the eastern (or vernal) undertakings, notice the equalization of the days, and whether the star culminating at night fall was the middle constellation of the bird, in order to hit the center of mid-spring; he might also observe whether the people began to disperse abroad, and whether birds and beasts were begining to pair and copulate.

He further commanded Xi's third brother to reside at the southern border, to adjust and arrange the southern (or summer) transformations, respectfully to notice the extreme limit of the shadow, when the days attain their utmost length, and the star in the zenith is that denominated "Fire": in order to fix the exact period of mid-summer, when the people disperse themselves more widely, and birds and beasts begin to molt and cast their skins.

He then distinctly commanded He's younger brother to dwell in the west, at a place called the Dark Valley, where he might respectfully attend upon the setting sun, and equalize and adjust the western (or autumnal) completions, notice the equalization of the nights, and see whether the culminating star was emptiness (Aquarius), in order to adjust midautumn, when the people would be more at ease, and the birds and beasts would be sleek and plump.

He further directed He's third brother to dwell at the northern region, called the Dismal City, where he might properly examine the reiterations and alterations, and see whether, when the days were at the shortest, the culminating star was Pleiades, in order to adjust mid-winter, when the people would remain at home, and birds and beasts get their down and hair.

The Emperor said, "Listen! you, Xi and He; an entire year consists of three hundred sixty and six days; do you therefore employ an intercalary month to settle the four seasons and complete the tropical year. Regulate at the same time with exactness the hundred kinds of labor, and your abundant merits will be universally diffused."

The Emperor said, "Who will enquire for one who, complying with these times, may be elevated to employment?" Fang Qi said, "Your son and heir, Zhu, is beginning to display intelligence." The Emperor said, "Tush! he is insincere and litigious; can he do?"

The Emperor said, "Who will enquire for someone, who can accord with my mode of managing business?" Huan Dou said, "Excellent! There is the superintendant of works, who has just consolidated his affairs, and displayed merit." The emperor said, "Tush! when there is nothing to do, he can talk; but employ him, and he belies his profession, while he has only the resemblance of respect."

The Emperor said, "Oh! you, President of the four eminences, the swelling flood occasions hurt; it spreads far and wide, it encompasses the hills, and overtops the mounds; vast and expansive it rises up to heaven; so that the lower people lament and sigh. If there be any persons of ability, I will set them to manage this matter." They all said, "Lo, there is Gun!" The Emperor said, "Tush! nonsense! he disobeys orders and ruins his companions." The President said, "Notwithstanding, just try if he can manage this matter only." The Emperor said, "Go; but take care." For nine years he labored, but did not accomplish anything.

The Emperor said, "Oh! you, President of the four eminences, I have now been on the throne seventy years; and since you are able to follow out my regulations, I will resign my throne to you."

The President said, "With my poor qualities, I should only disgrace the Imperial throne." The Emperor replied, "Bring to light those who are in brilliant stations, and set forth those of low rank." All the courtiers then addressed the Emperor saying, "There is a solitary individual, in a mean station, called Shun of Yu." The emperor said, "Good! I have heard of him; but how are his qualities?" The President said, "He is a blind man's son, his father is stupid, and his mother insincere, while Xiang (his brother) is overbearing; but he has been able to harmonize them by his filial piety, so that they have gradually advanced toward self-government and have not gone to the extreme lengths of wickedness." The emperor said, "Had I not better take him on trial! I will marry my daughters to this man, and thus observe his manner of acting with my two daughters."

Having thus arranged matters, he sent down his two daughters to the north of Gui and married them to Shun; when the Emperor said to them, "Take care!"

THE SAGE KINGS
Selections from the Bamboo Annals

Translated and annotated by James Legge

The *Bamboo Annals*, a book in the form of a chronicle, recording events from the Yellow Emperor until 299 B.C., was found, together with several other texts, in A.D. 281 in a royal tomb of circa 300 B.C. The *Annals* are important as a source for ancient history and legend, though the text itself is unreliable.

— Timoteus Pokora, in Leslie et al., *Essays on the Sources for Chinese History*, 1973

The Yellow Emperor; Dynastic Title Xuanyuan

Note.[19] His mother was called Fubao. She witnessed a great flash of lightning, which surrounded the star Chu of the Great Bear with a brightness that lightened all the country about her, and thereupon became pregnant. After twenty-five months, she gave birth to the emperor in Shouqiu. When born, he could speak. His countenance was dragonlike; his virtue that of a sage. He could oblige the host of spirits to come to his court and receive his orders. He employed Yinglong to attack Chiyou, the fight with whom was maintained by the help of tigers, panthers, bears, and grisly bears. By means of the heavenly lady Ba, he stopped the extraordinary rains caused by the enemy. When the empire was settled, his sage virtue was brightly extended, and all sorts of auspicious indications appeared. The grass *Juyi* grew in the courtyard of the palace. When a glib-tongued person was entering the court, this grass pointed to him so that such men did not dare to present themselves.

In his first year, when he came to the throne, he dwelt in Youxiong. He invented the cap with pendants, and the robes to match. In his twentieth year, brilliant clouds appeared; and he arranged his officers by names taken from the colors of the clouds.

Note. The auspicious omen of brilliant clouds was in this way: The vapors of the red quarter (the south) extended so as to join those of the green (the east). In the red quarter were two stars, and in the green, one; all were of a yellow color, and appeared, when the heavens were clear and bright, in Sheti, and were named the brilliant stars. The emperor in yellow robes fasted in the Middle palace. When he was sitting in a boat on the Xuanhu, above its junction with the Luo, there came together phoenixes, male and female. They would not eat any living insects, nor tread on living grass. Some

---

[19] Legge's "notes" are taken from the commentaries added to the text in later centuries, including those of Shen Yue (441–513) and Hu Yinglin (1551–1602). *Eds.*

of them abode in the emperor's eastern garden; some built their nests about the corniced galleries of the palace; and some sang in the courtyard, the females gambolling to the notes of the males. *Qilins* [the mythical beast, sometimes called the Chinese unicorn] also appeared in the parks; and other spiritlike birds came with their measured movements. Four-horned *lou* were produced as large as a goat, and the yin worms like rainbows. The emperor, considering that the influence of earth was thus predominant, reigned by the virtue of earth.

In his fiftieth year, in the autumn, in the seventh month, on the day *geng-shen* (fifty-seventh of cycle), phœnixes, male and female, arrived. The emperor sacrificed at the river Luo.

Note. Beginning with *geng-shen*, the heavens were wrapt in the mist for three days and three nights. The emperor asked Tianlao, Li Mu, and Rongcheng what they thought of it. Tianlao said, "I have heard this: When a kingdom is tranquil, and its ruler is fond of peace, then phœnixes come and dwell in it; when a kingdom is disordered, and its ruler is fond of war, then the phœnixes leave it. Now the phœnixes fly about in your eastern borders rejoicing, the notes of their singing all exactly harmonious, in mutual accord with Heaven. Looking at the thing in this way, Heaven is giving your majesty grave instructions, which you must not disobey." The emperor then called the recorder to divine about the thing, when the tortoise-shell was only scorched. The recorder said, "I cannot divine it; you must ask your sage men." The emperor replied, "I have asked Tianlao, Li Mu, and Rongcheng." The recorder then did obeisance, twice, with his face to the earth, and said, "The tortoise will not go against their sage wisdom, and therefore its shell is only scorched."

When the mists were removed, he made an excursion on the Luo, and saw a great fish; and sacrificed to it with five victims, whereupon torrents of rain came down for seven days and seven nights, when the fish floated off the sea, and the emperor obtained the map-writings. The dragon-writing came forth from the He [the Yellow River], and the tortoise-writing from the Luo.

In red lines, and the seal character, they were given to Xuanyuan. He entertained the myriad spirits in Mingting, the present valley of Hanmen.

In his fifty-ninth year, the chief of the "Perforated Breasts" came to make his submission. So also did the chief of the "Long Legs." In his seventy-seventh year, Changyi (one of the Yellow Emperor's sons) left the court and dwelt by the Ruo-water; he begat the emperor Qianhuang. In his hundredth year, the earth was rent. The emperor went on high.

Emperor Yao; Dynastic Title Tao and Tang

Note. His mother was called Qingdu. She was born in the wild of Douwei, and was always overshadowed by a yellow cloud. After she was grown up, whenever she looked into any of the three rivers, there was a dragon following her. One morning the dragon came with a picture and writing. The substance of the writing was: "The red one has received the favor of Heaven." The eyebrows of the figure were like the character eight, and of variegated colors. The whiskers were more than a cubit long; and the height was seven cubits two inches. The face was sharp above, and broad below. The feet trode on the constellation Yi. After this came darkness and winds on every side; and the red dragon made Qingdu pregnant. Her time lasted fourteen months, when she brought forth Yao in Danling. His appearance was like that in the picture. When he was grown up, his height was ten cubits. He had the virtue of a sage, and was invested with the principality of Tang. He dreamed that he climbed up to heaven. When Gaoxin was decaying, the empire turned to him.

In his first year, which was *bing-zi* (thirteenth of cycle), when he came to the throne, he dwelt in Ji; and commanded Xi and He to make calendaric calculations and delineations of the heavenly bodies. In his fifth year, he made the first tour of inspection to the four mountains. In his seventh year, there was a *Qilin*. In his twelfth year, he formed the first standing army. In his sixteenth year, the chief of Jusou came to make his submission. In his nineteenth year, he ordered the minister of Works to undertake the regulation of the He. In his twenty-ninth year, the chief of the Pygmies came to court in token of homage and offered as tribute their feathers, which sank in water. In his forty-second year, a brilliant star appeared in Yi. In his fiftieth year, he traveled for pleasure about Mount Shou, in a plain carriage drawn by dark-colored horses. In his fifty-third year, he sacrificed near the Luo. In his fifty-eighth year, he caused his son Zhu to be sent in banishment by prince Ji to Danshui. In his sixty-first year, he ordered the baron Gun of Chong to regulate the He. In his sixty-ninth year, he degraded Gun. In his seventieth year, in the spring, in the first month, he caused the chief of the four mountains to convey to Shun of Yu his charge to succeed to the throne.

Note. When the emperor had been on the throne seventy years, a brilliant star issued from the constellation Yi, and phœnixes appeared in the courtyards of the palace; the pearl grass grew, and the admirable grain flourished; sweet dews moistened the ground, and crystal springs issued from the hills; the sun and moon appeared like a pair of gems, and the five planets looked like threaded pearls. In the imperial kitchen there appeared of itself a piece of flesh, as thin as a fan, which, when shaken, raised such a wind that all eatables were kept cool and did not spoil. It was called the fan flitch. A kind of grass, moreover, grew on each side of the palace stairs. On the first day of the month, it produced one pod, and so on, every day a pod, to the fifteenth; while on the sixteenth one pod fell off, and so on, every day a pod, to the last day of the month; and if the month was a short one (of twenty-nine days), one pod shrivelled up, without falling. It was called the felicitous bean, and the calendar bean. When the flooded waters were assuaged, the emperor, attributing the merit of that to Shun, wished to resign in his favor. He thereon purified himself and fasted, built altars near the He and the Luo, chose a good day, and conducted Shun and others up Mount Shou. Among the islets of the He, there were five old men, walking about, who were the spirits of the five planets. They said to one another, "The river scheme will come and tell the emperor of the time. He who knows us is the double-pupiled yellow Yao." The five old men on this flew away like flowing stars and ascended into the constellation Mao. On the second month, on the *xin-chou* day, between the dark and light, the ceremonies were all prepared; and when the day began to decline, a glorious light came forth from the He, and beautiful vapors filled all the horizon; white clouds rose up, and returning winds blew all about. Then a dragonhorse appeared, bearing in his mouth a scaly cuirass, with red lines on a green ground, ascended the altar, laid down the scheme, and went away. The cuirass was like a tortoise shell, nine cubits broad. The scheme contained a tally of white gem, in a casket of red gem, covered with yellow gold, and bound with a green string. On the tally were the words "With pleased countenance given to the emperor Shun." It said also that Yu and Xia should receive the appointment of Heaven. The emperor wrote these words and deposited them in the Eastern college. Two years afterward, in the second month, he led out all his ministers and dropped a jade *bi* in the Luo. The ceremony over, he retired, and waited for the decline of the day. Then a red light appeared; a tortoise rose from the waters, with a writing in red lines on its back, and rested on the altar. The writing said that he should resign the throne to Shun, which accordingly the emperor did.

In his seventy-first year, he commanded his two daughters to become wives to Shun. In his seventy-third year, in the spring, in the first month, Shun received the resignation of the emperor in the temple of the accomplished ancestor. In his seventy-fourth year, Shun of Yu made his first tour of inspection to the four mountains. In his seventy-fifth year, Yu, the superintendent of Works, regulated the He. In his seventy-sixth year, the superintendent of Works smote the hordes of Cao and Wei and subdued them. In his eighty-sixth year, the superintendent of Works had an audience, using for his article of introduction a dark-colored mace. In his eighty-seventh year, he instituted the division of the empire into twelve provinces. In his eighty-ninth year, he made a pleasure palace in Tao. In his ninetieth year, he took up his residence for relaxation in Tao. In his ninety-seventh year, the superindendent of Works made a tour of survey through the twelve provinces. In his hundredth year, he died in Tao.

THE WHEELS OF HIS CHARIOT, THE HOOFS OF HIS HORSES
Selections from The Travels of Mu, Son of Heaven

Translated by Cheng Te-k'un

The Travels of Mu, Son of Heaven is an anonymous historical romance describing the journeys of the Zhou dynasty Emperor Mu (r. 1032–983 B.C.). The work was probably written during the first years of the fourth century B.C. but was lost until a copy was discovered in a tomb in A.D. 281 along with numerous other ancient works, including the *Bamboo Annals*.

Along with the *Book of Hills and Seas*, *The Travels of Mu* is often noted as an important precursor of Chinese fiction. However, the influence of the two works is very dissimilar. The laconic, enigmatic depictions of various mythical figures in the *Book of Hills and Seas* often served as the source for later, more elaborate fictional depictions — but the work itself contains no extended narratives or "fiction" as such. *The Travels of Mu*, on the other hand, is a relatively unified piece which could be considered historical fiction. Moreover, it is the earliest extant work which treats a human, rather than mythical, protagonist.

— William H. Nienhauser, *Indiana Companion*

Preface

In the second year of the reign of Tai-kang, Buzhun of Jixian rifled an ancient tomb in which he found a number of books. Among these, one is entitled *The Travels of Mu, Son of Heaven.*

The book is made of slips of bamboo, pasted with white silk. Measuring the leaves with the ancient ruler which (Xun) Xu, Your Majesty's servant, has determined before, they are each two feet and four inches long, containing forty characters written in black ink....

The book records the travels of King Mu of the Zhou dynasty. "King Mu," says the *Zuo Commentary* on the *Spring and Autumn Annals,* "wished to satisfy his ambition by touring around the world and by marking the countries under the sky with the wheels of his chariots and the hoofs of his horses." The accounts of his travels have been recorded in this book.

The King, having the fine steeds Daoli and Lu'er, and the excellent driver Zao Fu, traveled around the world. He visited the four remote corners of the world, crossing the desert on the north, ascending the Kunlun Mountain on the west and paying a visit to the Royal Mother of the West.[20] This same story can also be found in the *Records of the Grand Historian.*

But unfortunately, the book was not well preserved in Jixian and most of the leaves have been either destroyed or disarranged.

Although the stories do not conform to classical ideas, yet it is an ancient book and is indeed worth reading.

Therefore, Your Majesty's servant has carefully translated the old text on yellow sheets of paper two feet in size, and begs that when at leisure, Your Majesty will order the court secretary to copy it out together with the original text and store it up in the third hall as one of the Middle Classics.

Your obedient servant writes this preface,

Xun Xu

---

[20] Elsewhere translated as the Western Queen Mother or Goddess of the West. *Eds.*

1

On the day *mou-yin* the emperor made his way to the west, marching on as far as the Yangyu Mountain, where in ancient days Wu Yi,[21] the God of the River, had established his family, the house of Hezong. A member of this house, Bo Yao, welcomed the emperor at the Yanren Mountain, offering as presents a piece of silk fabric and a *bi* jade[22].... The emperor ordered Ji Fu to receive them.

On the day *gui-chou*, the emperor gave an audience on the Yanran Mountain, by the River. He ordered Jing Li and Liang Gu to have the six divisions of soldiers ready at his disposal.

On the auspicious day *mou-wu*, the emperor robed himself appropriately in the ceremonial costume, the cap, the gown, the handkerchief, the girdle and the *hu* tablet[23] with ornamental hangings on both sides. And, holding a *bi* jade in his hands, he took his stand in Hanxia, facing the south. Zeng Zhu was the assistant at the ceremony. When the officials had arranged the sacrificial animals in their proper order, the emperor presented the *bi* to the God of the River. Bo Yao received it from him, turned to the west and submerged the present in the River. After performing this he knelt before the Son of Heaven and touched his head to the earth many times. Zeng Zhu then submerged the sacrificial animals ... the ox, the horse, the pig, and the sheep. Then the God of the River appeared from the water and bearing good tidings from God he addressed the emperor by name, saying: "Mu Man, be Thou forever on the throne and may Thy rule be wise and prosperous!"

To the south the emperor bowed many times.

"Mu Man," continued the God of the River, "let me show Thee the precious articles of Chun Mountain and the beautiful palaces of Kunlun,[24] where there are four plains from which flow seventy springs. Proceed, then, to ... Kunlun Mountain, and behold the precious articles of Chun Mountain."

The voice dropped low and died away. The emperor listened to the heavenly decree with respect; and to the south he bowed again.

---

[21] This god, according to the *Book of Hills and Seas*, has the face of a man and rides on two dragons. He lives in the Stream of Congji, which is 300 feet deep.

[22] Round jade disk symbolizing Heaven.

[23] A tablet nearly three feet long, made of ivory, precious stones, wood or bamboo, held before the breast by courtiers at audience as late as the Ming dynasty.

[24] This mountain was the center of Chinese mythology. It is fully described in the *Book of Hills and Seas*.

On the day *ji-wei* the emperor gave an audience on the Yellow Mountain, where he inspected the map and the inscriptions on the precious vessels which were stored there for the Son of Heaven. It is said that the precious vessels of the emperor were made of beautiful jades, valuable stones, pure silver, and pure gold. A precious vessel of the emperor cost ten thousand pieces of gold ..., a precious vessel of a scholar cost fifty pieces of gold and that of an ordinary person cost ten pieces of gold.

The bows and arrows of the emperor killed people very easily like the sword of Bu[25].... The horses of the emperor ran a thousand *li* in one day, faster than any fast racing horses or any other powerful animals. His hounds ran a hundred *li* and were still strong enough to capture tigers and leopards.

"The hunting birds," Bo Yao informed the emperor, "have powerful wings. The black eagle flies one hundred *li* and the heron flies eight hundred *li*. The common animals have strong legs. The young lion runs one thousand *li*, the wild horse runs five hundred *li*, the *ang'ang-juxu* runs one hundred *li* and the elk runs twenty *li*."

It is said that after performing all the ceremonies due to the family of the God of the River, Bo Yao accompanied the emperor on his travels. Riding on the horse named Quhuang he went forward in the vanguard of the company and led the march to the extreme west of the empire.

On the day *yi-chou* the emperor passed over the River to the west.... There was in this region a valley called Letu,[26] which was warm in the winter and in which there was a traveling resort of the family of Hechong.

On *bing-yin*, the next day, by the decree of the emperor, all the officials were gathered for the inspection of the precious articles obtained. Jiao Fu, the chief minister of state, was ordered to inspect the governments of the border states and see if the commands of the emperor were carried out in full.

The eight steeds of the emperor were then allowed to take their rest and had their drink in the little pool which had its source from the River, south of the Rockpile[27] Mountain. The eight steeds were called Chiji, Daoli, Baiyi, Yulun, Shanzi, Quhuang, Hualiu, and Lu'er.

The hounds of the emperor were named Zhonggong, Cheshan, Guanxia, Zhonghuang, Nandan, and Laibai.

---

[25] A famous weapon used by the King of Yue.

[26] Literally "Happy Land."

[27] When the Great Emperor Yu drained the country of the flood, he reshaped all the rivers' courses and led them to the seas. He piled up the stones of this mountain to check the rushing flow of the mighty flood.

The drivers of the emperor's chariots were Zao Fu, Can Bai, Geng Xiao, and San Ji.

2

On the day *ding-mao*, in the last month of the summer, the emperor ascended Chun Mountain on the north, from where he could see the wilderness stretching in four directions.

It is said that the mountain was the highest mountain on earth. The flowers of the *zimu*,[28] which grew on the peak, were not afraid of snow. The emperor gathered some of the seeds and planted them in his royal garden when he returned from the excursion.

It is also said that on Chun Mountain, there was a pond which was filled by a spring of pure and warm water. There was no violent wind to disturb the peace of the pond, and it was here that birds of the sky and animals of the earth gathered for their drink. This is the place which our ancestors called Xianbu or the Hanging Garden.[29] The emperor kept in this garden the best specimens of the *yuze* and *chisi* jade.

Again it is said that Chun Mountain was the home of all sorts of animals and the resting place for all the birds in the sky. Here was a kind of fierce animal which devoured tiger and leopard. It was like an elk, but thinner, ... it also resembled a small hornless deer with a small head and a big nose. Here were the red leopard, the white tiger, the bear, the jackal, the wild horse, the wild buffalo, the goat, and the wild boar. Here were also the white bird and the black hawk which could capture a big goat and devour a boar and a deer.

And again, it is said that the emperor roamed over Chun Mountain for five days, and on the rock of the Hanging Garden he engraved for future generations a record of this visit.

3

On the day *ren-shen* the emperor rode to the west and on *jia-xu*, two days later, he arrived at Chi Niao, or the domain of the Red Bird. Qi, of the Red Bird tribe, presented to the emperor one thousand measures of wine, nine hundred horses for food, three thousand cattle and one

---

[28] Traditional commentators identify this with the Cinnabar tree in the *Book of Hills and Seas*.

[29] According to the *Book of Hills and Seas*, the Hanging Garden is a hill separated from the Kunlun Mountain and is the garden of the Heavenly God.

hundred carts fully loaded with millet and wheat. Ji Fu accepted the presents by the emperor's order.

It is said that the head of the house of the Red Bird was a descendant of the royal family of Zhou. When Danfu, an early ancestor of the family, first developed the region on the west, he conferred on his eldest son the right to rule over the country of Eastern Wu, with the title of the Great Earl of Wu, giving him as a token a slab of gold and the precious jade of the Zhou house. He also conferred on his favorite minister, Zhang Jichuo, the right to rule over the valley of Chun Mountain, marrying him to his eldest daughter and giving him as a token a slab of jade. There his minister ruled and performed sacrifices to the ancestors of the Zhou house. Therefore, the emperor bestowed upon Qi four black carriages, forty *yi*[30] of gold, fifty girdles made of shell, and three hundred pearls. Qi accepted the gift after prostrating himself.

It is said that Chun Mountain was the richest mountain in the world, a store of precious stones and valuable jades. It was a place where the most flourishing crops grew and the trees were tall and the bushes beautiful. The emperor gathered some species of these excellent crops so that he might cultivate them in the central kingdom when he returned.

It is also said that the emperor rested at the foot of the mountain for five days and amused himself with the *Guang* music. Qi then presented to the emperor many beautiful women. Among them, Lady Ting and Lady Lie soon became his favorite concubines. It is said that the country of the Red Bird was famous for its beautiful women and valuable jade.

4

On the auspicious day *jia-zi*, the emperor, carrying a white *gui* scepter[31] and a black *bi* jade, paid a visit to the Royal Mother of the West. To her he offered as presents one hundred pieces of embroidered silk and three hundred pieces of *wu* fabric. After bowing many times, the Royal Mother accepted the presents.

On *yi-chou*, the next day, the emperor invited the Royal Mother to a banquet on Emerald Pond. During the occasion she sang extempore:

Hills and mountains come into view
As fleecy clouds ascend the sky.

---

[30] A weight of the Zhou dynasty, equal to 20 taels.
[31] Small stone scepter given to nobles as a sign of rank and held in both hands at court levees. The size varied according to the bearer's rank.

Figure 13. The Royal Mother of the West on the magic mountain Kunlun. (Source: Wu Hung, *The Wu Liang Shrine: The Ideology of Early Chinese Pictorial Art* [Stanford: Stanford University Press, 1989])

Far and wide, divided by waters and ranges
Our countries separately lie.
Should long life preserve thee,
Come again.

To this the emperor responded:

When I to east return
To millions bringing order and peace;
When they enjoy prosperity and ease
To thee shall I return;
From this day count three years
To this country again shall I come.

The emperor then rode on Xi Mountain and on the rocks engraved a record of this visit. He planted a memorial tree of sophora and named the place Mountain of the Royal Mother of the West.

From here the emperor took his way back to the east. He was sad and distressed as he thought of his people at home and expressed his sorrow by composing the following poem:

In the distant west she rules,
Happily on the wide, wide plain,
Accompanied by tigers and leopards,
Sleeping with crows and jackdaws.

The Heavenly decree changes not,
A son of Heaven I am made.
But the will of Heaven I follow not,
Leaving my people in distress.

Tears suddenly fill my eyes
When the parting music is sounding,
And my heart is filled with sadness
As I think of my millions, hoping for my return.

On the day *ding-wei*, the emperor took a drink at Hot Mountain and went out fowling the next day, *mou-shen*. The following day, he drank at the bank of the Ru River and gave orders to the six divisions of soldiers to gather together.

In this region there were forests, marshy swamps and ponds full of water, and there were also smooth plains and high plateaux where big birds scattered their feathers. Now the six divisions of soldiers had concentrated in this wide region where it is said the emperor stayed for three months.

5

On the day *mou-xu*, the emperor traveled westward and conducted a chase in the forest. It was a time when the leaves of the trees had fallen and the grass and bushes were scarce. He ordered the people under the land officers to chop down the trees and clear away the bushes, which he gave them for fuel and other purposes. While the people were engaged in their work the emperor went to Bing, where he played at chess with Duke Jing. On the third day of the game the He River overflowed its banks, and the gap was not filled up until the day *xin-chou*.

When the hot summer days had passed away, he returned to his tower and stayed there to attend to the government of the empire. He also examined the population of the border states, looking for clever men who were identified and recorded in books.

... the emperor was very much pleased and ordered a tower to be built, which he named Fantai, and here he came for pleasure.

A tiger was crouching under a bush when the emperor drew near. Gao Benrong, a member of the seven regiments, offered to capture the animal alive. He did it successfully and presented the victim unhurt. The emperor ordered a cage to be made for the wild animal and that it be kept in the Eastern *Yu*, which he called the "Tiger Jail." The emperor rewarded the hero with ten teams of four hunting horses each and a set of sacrificial animals, which consisted of an ox, a sheep, and a pig. Gao

Benrong accepted the prize kneeling before the emperor and touching his head to the ground several times.

On the day *bing-shen*, the emperor spent his time in the northern forest.

In the second month of the autumn, on the day *jia-xu*, the emperor traveled eastward. He arrived at Qiaoliang, where he sunned his books eaten by worms in Yulin.

6

... presented wine to the emperor while he was enjoying the *Guang* music. Sometime before, the magic drum of the emperor had disappeared, transforming itself into a yellow snake and now it sounded from under the ground. Therefore, the emperor planted in this region parasol trees which furnished good material for making powerful drums, weapons and musical instruments.

The emperor rowed on the Yellow Pond to the East and spent a night at the bend of the Luo River. He ordered his followers to play a melody while he sang the following song:

O, Yellow Pond
The horses have disturbed Thy sand.
Glory and Power attend the Royal Family.

O, Yellow Pond
The horses have disturbed Thy jade.
Old Age and Happiness attend the Royal Family!

Figure 14. Jade *bi*. (Source: Berthold Laufer, *Jade: A Study in Chinese Archaeology and Religion* [Chicago: Field Museum of Natural History, 1912])

🔲 *Further Reading* 🔲

Barnard, Noel. *The Ch'u Silk Manuscript: Translation and Commentary.* Canberra: Australian National University Press, 1973.

Birch, Cyril. *Chinese Myths and Fantasies* (a retelling). London: Oxford University Press, 1961.

Birrell, Anne. *Chinese Mythology: An Introduction.* Baltimore: Johns Hopkins University Press, 1993.

Cheng, H. C., H. C. Pai Cheng, & K. L. Thern, trans. *Shan Hai Ching: Legendary Geography and Wonders of Ancient China.* Taipei: National Institute for Compilation and Translation, 1985.

Cheng, Te-k'un, trans. "The Travels of Emperor Mu." *Journal of the North China Branch of the Royal Asiatic Society* (1933–34), 64–65.

Christie, Anthony. *Chinese Mythology.* London: Hamlyn, 1968.

Field, Stephen, trans. *Tian Wen: A Chinese Book of Origins.* New York: New Directions, 1984.

Hawkes, David, trans. *The Songs of the South: An Ancient Chinese Anthology of Poems by Qu Yuan and Other Poets.* Harmondsworth: Penguin Books, 1985.

Jennings, William, trans. *The Shi King: The Old "Poetry Classic" of the Chinese, a Close Metrical Translation with Annotations.* London: Routledge, 1891.

Legge, James, trans. *The Chinese Classics, Vol. 3, The Shoo King* (includes the *Bamboo Annals*). Hong Kong: Legge, 1865.

Loewe, Michael. *Ways to Paradise: The Chinese Quest for Immortality.* London: Allen & Unwin, 1979.

Medhurst, W. H., trans. *Ancient China: The Shoo King; or, The Historical Classic.* Shanghai: Mission Press, 1846.

Watson, Burton. *Early Chinese Literature.* New York: Columbia University Press, 1962.

Watson, William. *China Before the Han Dynasty.* London: Thames & Hudson, 1961.

Werner, E.T.C. *Myths and Legends of China.* London: Harrap, 1922.

Yuan, Ke. *Zhongguo shenhua chuanshuo cidian.* Hong Kong: Commercial Press, 1986.

🔲 *Editors' Note* 🔲

Two of the Victorian translators here represented, Walter Medhurst Sen. (1796–1857), and James Legge (1814–1897), were missionaries, both working for the London Missionary Society, the first for the greater part of his life in Shanghai, the second in Hong Kong until his return to Britain in 1873, after which he was appointed first Professor of Chinese at Oxford. Medhurst was known primarily for his work translating the Bible into Chinese, and his *Book of History* was soon superseded by Legge's, and forgotten. Its presence in this chapter serves as a reminder of the achievement of the early pioneer translators, without whose work subsequent development would have been so much harder. Just as the Authorized Version of the Bible relied heavily on earlier versions, so the "standard" translations of Legge were made possible by the work of earlier translators such as Robert Morrison, David Collie and Medhurst.

James Legge's 5-volume work, *The Chinese Classics*, was published in Hong Kong from 1861 to 1872. Other material from it is included in Chapters 3 and 4. His scholarship was tireless, his native helpers were first rate, and his high-flown High Victorian prose remained for several generations *the* voice of the Confucian sages.

The rhyming verse of William Jennings is particularly well suited to the retelling of the dynastic legend of Lord Millet. Jennings was, in 1891, vicar of Beedon in

Berkshire, having previously been Colonial Chaplain at the Cathedral of St John's, Hong Kong. More of his versions of the *Book of Songs* are included in chapter 3.

David Hawkes was professor of Chinese at Oxford from 1959 to 1971. His erudite and eloquent translations of the "Songs of the South" (see chapter 5) and of the eighteenth-century novel *The Story of the Stone* (see Vol. 2) have set the standard for the present generation of translators.

"I never weary of studying the Ancients."
Seal from the Vernal Radiance Collection

Chapter 3

The Book of Songs

The Earliest Anthology of Chinese Poetry

The third Booke is *Xikim*, and is of ancient poesie, all under metaphors and poeticall figures, concerning the naturall inclinations of mankind, and also of diverse customs.... Poesie hath ever been much esteemed in China.... The Chinese have a great advantage over all others, because they are very modest, in whatsoever they write; and it is very rare to find a loose word in their verses: and (what is more) they have no letters whereby to expresse the privy parts.

— Alvarez Semedo, *The History of China*, 1655

[The *Xikim* is the same book as the *Che-king, Chi-king, Shi-king, Sheeking, Shih-ching*, or *Shijing*. All are romanizations of the same two Chinese words meaning Book, or Classic, of Songs.]

Ars poetica est apud Sinas antiquissima, et varia vario metro carmina complectitur. [The Art of Poetry is very ancient with the Chinese and embraces various types of song in various meters.]

— Martino Martini, *Sinicae Historiae Decas Prima*, 1658

The second Volume ... is intituled *Xi Kim*.... 'Tis a Collection of Odes, and several other little Poems of this Nature: For Musick being greatly esteemed and much used in *China*, and whatever is published in this Volume having respect only to the Purity of Manners, and Practise of Virtue, those that wrote it composed it in Verse, to the end that every one being enabled to sing the things therein contained, they might be in everyone's Mouth.

— *The Morals of Confucius: A Chinese Philosopher*, 1691

The poetry of the *She king* is so beautiful and harmonious, the lovely and sublime tone of antiquity rules in it continually, its pictures of manners are so naive and minute.... In the following ages we find nothing, I will not say equal to these ancient odes, but nothing worthy to be compared with them.... We are not afraid to say that it yields only to the Psalms of David in speaking of the Divinity, of Providence, of virtue, &c., with a magnificence of expressions and an elevation of ideas which make the passions cold with terror, ravish the spirit, and draw the soul from the sphere of the senses.

— *Mémoires concernant les Chinois: Par les Missionaires de Pékin*, Tôme Premier: "Essai sur l'antiquité des Chinois," 1776 (*translated by James Legge*)

The praises of the Chinese can never be exhausted when they speak of the sublimity, softness, simplicity, and ancient taste of these pieces; they confess that all the succeeding ages have not been able to produce anything which can be put in competition with them.... The six virtues, say they, are like the soul of the *Chi-king*; no age has been able to wither the brilliant flowers with which they are crowned, and no age will produce any so beautiful.

— Abbé Grosier, *A General Description of China*, 1788

It will never occur to an educated Chinese that the songs might be of popular origin.

— Marcel Granet, *Fêtes et chansons anciennes de la Chine*, 1919
(*translated by E. D. Edwards*)

And Kung said, "Without character you will
    be unable to play on that instrument
"Or to execute the music fit for the Odes.
"The blossoms of the apricot
    blow from the east to the west,
"And I have tried to keep them from falling."

— Ezra Pound, *Cantos XIII*, 1924

There sprang up from under the tangle of misconceptions and distortions that hid them from me a succession of fresh and lovely tunes. The text sang, just as the lines of Homer somehow manage to sing despite the barbarous ignorance with which we recite them.

— Arthur Waley, *The Book of Songs*, 1937

Is there any other major classic in a great language, of which distinguished scholars could make such widely divergent interpretations? This is partly thanks to the Confucian schoolmen twisting a simple poem to their taste. But should modern readers not look at the original poems more independently? And at the world outside?

— Arthur Cooper, Lecture Notes, c. 1970

There was once a time, in China as well as Europe, when to versify was to sing and to sing spontaneously, when to make a poem was to manipulate a professional stock of formulaic phrases.

— C. H. Wang, *The Bell and the Drum*, 1974

Introduction

C. H. Wang

The *Book of Songs* is one of the six classics of the Confucian school and the fountainhead of Chinese literature. It is an anthology of 305 poems edited by Confucius (551–479 B.C.), as the traditional belief has it, on the basis of about three thousand compositions collected for the education of his disciples. The book remained a classic and required reading for the literati for more than two thousand years; not until the turn of the twentieth century did it cease to be read as scripture and begin to be appreciated as a collection of poetic compositions.

The poems may be dated from the twelfth century to the seventh century B.C. External and internal evidence attests that the earliest pieces of the corpus are the Zhou hymns (nos. 266–296). But many of their stylistic qualities underwent modification until the time of Confucius, when these hymns, together with later poems (including the so-called Shang hymns, which were composed in the state of Song long after the fall of the Shang dynasty), assumed their final shape. The book in its definitive form was officially banned in the third century B.C., along with the other Confucian Classics, but the text survived orally and in hidden manuscripts so that it was possible to restore the collection under imperial sanction during the Han dynasty. Four separate versions were reconstructed. Of the four, the text preserved by a certain master Mao and commented on by some of the most thoughtful scholars in Chinese history, has survived almost intact to the present day, while those of the other three schools exist only in fragments.

The *Book of Songs* is divided into four sections, Folk Songs (Legge: Lessons from the States), Elegantiae (Legge: Minor Odes of the Kingdom), Greater Odes of the Kingdom, and Odes of the Temple and Altar. The first section (nos. 1–160) comprises fifteen groups of songs with salient folk features, from fifteen geographical areas. The second section (nos. 161–234) includes some poems which overlap with the Folk Songs in folk attributes, and others which constitute celebrations composed for banquets and feasts. The third section (nos. 235–265) contains poems of greater scope, more grandiloquent in style and more sublime in theme. Scattered in this section are some important pieces, which together can be seen as an epic of early Zhou history [see chapter 2]. This section also contains hyperbolic odes extolling heroism. Finally, the fourth section (nos. 266–305) is divided into the Zhou hymns, Lu hymns, and Shang hymns. Most of these are formal, ritual hymns that praise the ancestors envisioned in the rites.

The subject matter of the poems in the *Book of Songs* varies greatly from one section to another. Love, war, agriculture, sacrifice, and dynastic legends are among the most prominent themes. While in the presentation of themes the tone may be positive and eulogistic or licentious and censuring, Confucius argued that a single judgment could describe all the poems: "Having no depraved thoughts."

The style is, in general, straightforward and natural, typical of ancient literature in terms of the immediacy of imagery and pervasive musical quality. The modes of expression, however, are by no means simple: the poems are rich in metaphors and similes, both indirect (*xing*) and direct (*bi*), as well as narrative displays (*fu*). An unmistakable formulaic language, furthermore, characterizes the style, and reveals that the majority of the poems were composed spontaneously before specific audiences. It indicates, too, that the poetic tradition before Confucius was primarily oral.

— *Indiana Companion*, 1986

SIXTY SONGS IN VERSIONS SPANNING
TWO AND A HALF CENTURIES

To understand well in what the Excellency of the Chinese Poetry consists, it is
necessary to be skilled in their Language; but as that is no Easy Matter, we cannot give
the Reader a very good notion of it.

> — Jean-Baptiste du Halde, *A Description of the Empire of China*, 1738

La langue poétique des Chinois est véritablement intraduisible; on pourrait peut-être
ajouter qu'elle est souvent inintelligible. [The Chinese poetic language is truly untranslatable. One could perhaps add that it is often unintelligible.]

> — Jean-Pierre Abel Rémusat (1788–1832), quoted by
> Sir John Francis Davis, "On the Poetry of the Chinese," 1829

FOLK SONGS

1: Guan-ju
(twenty versions, arranged historically)

i. Epithalamium

Translated into Latin by Father Alexandre de Lacharme (c. 1750)

Aves Tsu-kiou in aquaticis terris mas et foemina ambae vices agunt suas
cantando. Plenam majestatis, oris splendore et eximia virtute puellam vir
sapiens matrimonio jungere gaudet.

In this chapter, which provides translations of sixty of the three hundred and five *Songs*, the
traditional number and conventional Chinese romanized title for each poem are given
before the translation (thus, "1: *Guan-ju*"). Where more than one version is given, the
versions are numbered separately (using Roman numerals). Within the translations themselves, early romanizations have in many places been retained, to give something of a sense
of period — especially for translations done before the nineteenth century. It is only in the
last decade or so that the Chinese system of romanization, *Hanyu pinyin* (which is used
throughout this anthology), has become internationally accepted. For several centuries
different systems evolved and co-existed — the Portuguese, French, German and the old
English systems (Morrison, Wade-Giles), together with a number of others.

We have also provided commentary of two kinds (although they sometimes overlap).
The first kind, which occurs mainly with the differing versions of *Song* 1, concerns attitudes
towards the process of translation — rhyme versus free verse, close versus loose translation,
etc. The second kind concerns interpretation of the meaning of the *Songs*. The reader will
be able to glimpse from extracts taken from James Legge's commentary the more or less
traditional Chinese commentator's view (Legge synthesized the Han dynasty Mao, the Song
dynasty Zhu Xi and other commentators, while leaning heavily towards the Zhu interpretation). Legge's commentary may sometimes be at variance with the translation which it

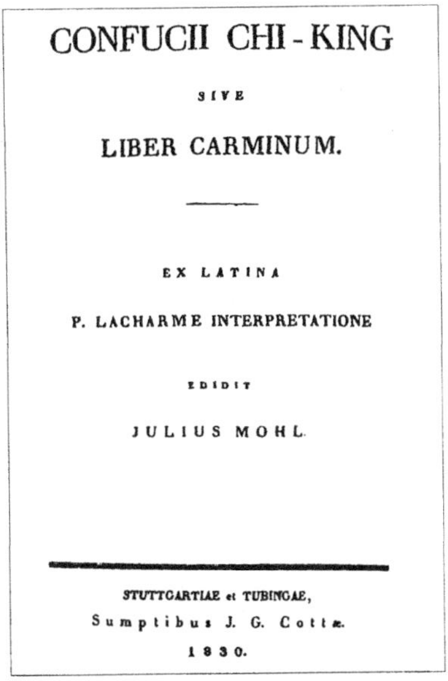

CONFUCII CHI - KING

SIVE

LIBER CARMINUM.

———

EX LATINA

P. LACHARME INTERPRETATIONE

EDIDIT

JULIUS MOHL.

STUTTGARTIAE et TUBINGAE,
Sumptibus J. G. Cottæ.
1 8 3 0.

Figure 15. Title page of first printed edition (1830) of Lacharme's Latin translation of the *Book of Songs* (the manuscript dates from c. 1750)

Inaequali altitudine plantam King-tsai dictam, modo ad dextram, modo ad sinistram usque ferri videmus, quo aqua in qua adcrevit, ipsam impellit. Puellam nostram vigilando, dormiendo exoptant, cumque hanc sibi velint in uxorem, necdum obtinuerint, ipsam vel inter quiescendum, sive vigilent, sive dormiant, usque cogitant; et in lecto versant corpus in omnes partes, modo supini modo in faciem jacentes.

Plantae nostrae hinc, inde fit delectus. Plena majestatis est, oris splendore, et eximia virtute puella. Kin et Che fit concentus musicus.

Planta nostra hinc inde decerpta suscipitur. Plena majestatis est, oris splendore et eximia virtute puella. Campanae et tympani sonis musicis aures recreantur.

About the Translation:
M. Callery [Joseph Gaetan Pierre-Marie Callery, French Lazarist missionary, born in 1810, author of *Systema Phoneticum Scripturae Sinicae*, 1841, was in China 1836–1842, and subsequently until his death in 1862 was Secretary-Interpreter to Napoleon III] has characterized Lacharme's translation as "la production la plus indigeste et la plus ennuyeuse dont la sinologie ait à rougir [the most undigested and tiresome product

---

accompanies. But it provides an interesting insight into the (often distorted) traditional way of reading the poem. From Marcel Granet's brief notes on the Themes of the *Songs*, the reader can glimpse the possibilities inherent in a fresh look beneath the incrustations of the Confucian tradition.

Song 245, "Hou Ji (Lord Millet), Progenitor of Zhou," can be found in chapter 2. *Eds.*

to disgrace sinology]." The translation is, indeed, very defective, and the notes
accompanying it are unsatisfactory and much too brief.

— James Legge, Preface to his *She-King*, 1871

I have concentrated in this memoir my investigations on the *Book of Songs*, the reading
of which is, to say the least, greatly facilitated by the Latin translation of Lacharme.
That translation, made in China by this missionary, has been published by the zeal
of M. Mohl; and if we can discover in it some inaccuracies, in consequence of the
author's having used in great measure the Manchëw version of the original, we owe,
as a compensation, to the learned missionary, a series of notes extracted from the
commentaries, very useful in throwing light upon the historical allusions, as well as
the probable identification of the animals and vegetables mentioned in the text with
those with which we are acquainted.

— Edouard Biot (1843), translated in James Legge,
Prolegomena to his *She-King*, 1871

P. Lacharme ex soc. Jesu. A very learned man most skilled in Chinese and Tartar
languages, of whose life no trace remains save this notable work, begun in 1733 and
not really finished when he left off about 1752. Seventy-one sheets once belonged to
a certain Delisle, later handed on to the Ministry of Marine, then to the society of
Astronomers, Paris. Chinese words written in Portuguese style. Julius Mohl wrote
'em out in French style when preparing his edition in Paris, 1829, printed or published
Stuttgart and Tubingen sumptibus D. G. Cotta, 1830....

The translation lay eighty years in ms. and I suppose Mohl's edition missed the
boat. Latin having by 1830 ceased to be the lingua franca of Western culture.

Now we WANT the ideograms, even where Lacharme is clear reading....

Did Père Lacharme's Latin arouse NO curiosity whatsoever. We must assume
Lacharme's Latin as a basis. Who saw it before Mohl? and after Mohl's edition where
did it lie doggo for one hundred and seven years? ...

What puzzles me is that the Latin has led nobody to dig down into the original
during a hundred years. The English translation before me (pub. 1891) is an infamy.

I admit that I have owned the Lacharme for fifteen or twenty years, but I can
account for at least part of my time during that interval.

The yoke of the universities has been heavy.

— Ezra Pound, *Guide to Kulchur*, 1938

The German Poet Rückert turned Lacharme into German verse, paraphrasing his
imperfect translation and using the utmost poetical license, omitting what was too
prosy and remodelling what was not poetical enough in itself with the help of his
own rich store of poetic imagination. The consequence of course is, that it is difficult,
even for the best Chinese Scholar, to recognize any single Chinese Ode as translated
by Rückert. We can scarcely call them translated at all, unless we use the word in the
sense which Quince gives to it, "Bless thee, Bottom! bless thee! thou art translated."

— Ernst Eitel, *China Review*, 1873

ii. Kwan Ts'eu

Translated by James Legge (1871)

The ode celebrates the virtue of the bride of King Wen.

[King Wen built up the strength of the Zhou state, when it was still a dependency of the Shang rulers. His name in Chinese is literally synonymous with "culture" or "civilization." He is remembered for his piety towards the gods and ancestors, and his concern for the well-being of his people.

King Wen ruled well when earth he trod;
Now moves his spirit near to God.
A strong-willed, earnest king was Wen,
And still his fame rolls widening on. (*Song* 235)

King Wen was succeeded by his son, King Wu "the warlike," who was the true founder of the Zhou dynasty. "Confucius looked back to and carried forward the tradition of the Sage Emperors Yao and Shun, he emulated and illuminated the ways of Kings Wen and Wu." *The Doctrine of the Mean, XXX.*]

We hear the friends of a bridegroom expressing their joy on the occasion of his marriage with the virtuous object of his love, brought home in triumph, after long quest and various disappointments. According to the school of Mao (Han dynasty), the bride's virtue is her freedom from jealousy, and her constant anxiety and diligence to fill the harem of the king with virtuous ladies to share his favours with her and assist her in various duties. And the ode was made by her. According to the school of Zhu Xi (Song dynasty), the virtue is her modest disposition and retiring manners, which so ravished the inmates of the harem, that they sing of her, in the first stanza, as she was in her virgin purity, a flower unseen; in the second, they set forth the king's trouble and anxiety while he had not met with such a mate; and in the third, their joy reaches its height, when she has been got, and is brought home to his palace.

Kwan-kwan go the ospreys,
On the islet in the river.
The modest, retiring, virtuous, young lady: —
For our prince a good mate she.

Here long, there short, is the duckweed,
To the left, to the right, borne about by the current.
The modest, retiring, virtuous, young lady: —
Waking and sleeping, he sought her.
He sought her and found her not,
And waking and sleeping he thought about her.
Long he thought; oh! long and anxiously;
On his side, on his back, he turned, and back again.

Here long, there short, is the duckweed;
On the left, on the right, we gather it.
The modest, retiring, virtuous, young lady: —
With lutes, small and large, let us give her friendly welcome.
Here long, there short, is the duckweed;
On the left, on the right, we cook and present it.
The modest, retiring, virtuous young lady: —
With bells and drums let us show our delight in her.

About the Translation:

My object has been to give a version of the text which should represent the meaning of the original, without addition or paraphrase, as nearly as I could attain to it. The collection as a whole is not worth the trouble of versifying. But with my labors before him, anyone who is willing to undertake the labor may present the pieces in "a faithful metrical version." My own opinion inclines in favor of such a version being as nearly literal as possible. In Bunsen's *God in History*, Book III, chap. V., poetical versions are given of several passages from the *Songs*, which that various writer calls "The Book of Sacred Songs." Versified, first in German, from the Latin translation of Lacharme, and again from the German version in English, if the odes from which they are taken were not pointed out in the footnotes, it would be difficult, even for one so familiar with the Chinese text as myself, to tell what the originals of them were. Such productions are valueless, either as indications of the poetical merit of the odes, or of the sentiments expressed in them....

The traditional interpretation of the *Songs*, which we may suppose is given by Mao, is not to be overlooked; and, where it is supported by historical confirmations, it will often be found helpful. Still it is from the pieces themselves that we must chiefly endeavor to gather their meaning. This was the plan on which Zhu Xi proceeded; and, as he far exceeded his predecessors in the true critical faculty, so China has not since produced another equal to him....

Whatever completeness belongs to my own Work is in great measure owing to the unpublished *Explanations of Mao's Songs*, prepared expressly for my own assistance by my friend Wang Tao [1828–1898, Legge's distinguished collaborator. Wang was a scholar, poet, and essayist from Suzhou, who sought refuge in Hong Kong in 1862, when suspected by the Chinese authorities of collusion with the Taiping rebels. He worked with Legge for eleven years. The manuscript of the work to which Legge refers is now in the New York Public Library.].

— James Legge, Prolegomena to his *She-King*, 1871

iii. The Song of the Ospreys

Translated by "An Accomplished Friend of Ernst Faber" (1874)

Ernst Faber (1839–1899) was a German missionary and scholar who worked in Hong Kong, Shanghai and Qingdao. This anonymous translation, together with a musical setting, was contributed by a friend of his to the pages of the *China Review*.

— Editors

Where, from islands in the river,
        Ospreys clang, there dwells apart,
Sweet and fair, a modest maiden
        Meet to win our Prince's heart.

Where the water-lilies waver
        In the stream — from dark to dawn,
To the dear maid, to win her favor
        Sweet and fair, his thoughts are drawn:

For he sought her, sought her vainly;
        But day and night his fancies go

To find her, and the night is sleepless,
    Full of tossings to and fro.

Pluck the water-lilies gladly!
    Sweet and fair, she comes at last!
Lute and harp lend all your music!
    Sweet and fair, let lilies cast

Sacrificial to her welcome
    Usher in the bride to be!
Join, ye people, all your voices
    With the merry minstrelsie!

iv. The Kuan Chü

Translated (versified) by James Legge (1876)

Mainly allusive. Celebrating the virtue of the bride of King Wen, his quest for her, and welcoming her to his palace.

Hark! from the islet in the stream the voice
Of the fish hawks that o'er their nest rejoice!
From them our thoughts to that young lady go,
Modest and virtuous, loth herself to show.
Where could be found, to share our prince's state
So fair, so virtuous, and so fit a mate?

See how the duckweed's stalks, or short or long,
Sway left and right, as moves the current strong!
So hard it was for him the maid to find!
By day, by night, our prince with constant mind
Sought for her long, but all his search was vain.
Awake, asleep, he ever felt the pain
Of longing thought, as when on restless bed,
Tossing about, one turns his fevered head.

Here long, there short, afloat the duckweed lies;
But caught at last, we seize the longed-for prize.
The maiden modest, virtuous, coy, is found;
Strike every lute, and joyous welcome sound.
Ours now, the duckweed from the stream we bear,
And cook to use with other viands rare.
He has the maiden, modest, virtuous, bright;
Let bells and drums proclaim our great delight.

v. The Ospreys Woo

Translated by "V. W. X." (1878)

As the ospreys woo
On the river ait,
So the graceful lass
Has her manly mate.

As the coy marsh flowers
Here and there do peep,
So the graceful lass
In his wakeful sleep.

But he seeks in vain,
Brooding night and day,
Ah me! ah me!
Tossing rest away!

As the coy marsh-flower
Chosen here and there,
So the graceful lass;
He in tune with her.

As the coy marsh-flower
Gathered here and there,
So the graceful lass,
Bells now ring for her.

About the Translation:
These lines claim to be as nearly as possible literal translations of the ballads of the
Shi-king [*Book of Songs*]. Moreover, each line of the original is represented by one line
only of translation; and each line follows the sense of the corresponding line of
the Chinese. It has been attempted to convey in the translation the exact amount of
humor, exultation, or despair to which the original characters give expression.... The
translator is so convinced of the true poetry contained in the *Shi-king* ballads that he
ventures to submit them in their own simple garb to the aesthetic ear of the foreign
critic.

— "V. W. X.," *China Review,* 1878

vi. King Wen's Epithalamium

Translated by Clement Allen (1891)

They sent me to gather the cresses, which lie
And sway on the stream, as it glances by,

That a fitting welcome we might provide
For our prince's modest and virtuous bride.

I heard, as I gathered the cress, from the ait
The mallard's endearing call to its mate;
And I said, as I heard it, "Oh may this prove
An omen of joy to our master's love!"

Long, long for his bride has the prince been yearning,
With such desire has his heart been burning,
That his thoughts by day and his dreams by night
Have had but her as his sole delight.

But a doubt tormented his anxious brain,
And sleep was banished by aching pain,
As tossing in fear and distress he lay
Till the long night watches had passed away.

And now he has won her, this lady fair,
With her modest mind and her gracious air.
Let our lutes and our music and feasting show
The love we to her and our master owe.

About the Translation:
I must say a word or two in defense of my freedom of translation. Sir John Davis, in his "Poetry of the Chinese," remarks: "A verbal translation from Chinese must of necessity degenerate into a horrible jargon, which few persons will undergo the disgust of perusing." Let the verses of V. W. X. (who has sacrificed everything to accuracy, with appalling consequences) prove the truth of this observation. To avoid a similar fate I have assumed the utmost license, but I plead that license is not necessarily inaccuracy. I go further, and say that in these cases it is unfair to the original author of a poem to reproduce his work in a form that strikes the perception of those who have to take it in, as harsh and barbarous. A poem in stanzas of four lines, each of four words, is to Chinamen composed in a simple form of poetic expression. Such a composition in English is at best a *tour de force* requiring the skill of Mr. Swinburne to infuse anything like music into it. Humbler versifiers must alter the structure and recast it in a more melodious shape. This is what I have tried to do, using my best endeavors to compose verses in honest flowing meter suitable to the subjects of the poems. When a piece consists of one sentence expressed three or four times over with the least possible variation, I have often compressed the whole of it into one stanza. Moreover, I have avoided the use of Chinese names as far as I can, knowing how the general reader dislikes them. I have also allowed myself considerable license in the use of botanical terms. I have relegated the Jujube, the dolichos creeper, the ephemeral hedge tree, the polygonum, and the broussonetia, — to say nothing of *T'ung, I* and *Tzu* trees — to the footnotes; substituting for them better known plants and trees, or using some such generic term as creepers, shoots, shrubs, trees, or flowers in their stead.

— Clement Allen, from the Preface to his *Book of Chinese Poetry*, 1891

vii. *Song of Welcome to the Bride of King Wen*

Translated by William Jennings (1891)

Waterfowl their mates are calling,
　　On the islets in the stream.
Chaste and modest maid! fit partner
　　For our lord (thyself we deem).

Waterlilies, long or short ones,
　　Seek them left and seek them right.
'Twas this chaste and modest maiden
　　He hath sought for, morn and night.
Seeking for her, yet not finding,
　　Night and morning he would yearn
Ah, so long, so long! — and restless
　　On his couch would toss and turn.

Waterlilies, long or short ones,
　　Gather, right and left, their flowers.
Now the chaste and modest maiden
　　Lute and harp shall hail as ours.
Long or short the waterlilies,
　　Pluck them left and pluck them right.
To the chaste and modest maiden
　　Bell and drum shall give delight.

About the Translation:
The following version I have ventured — from the expressed opinion of some eminent sinologists in Hong Kong — to call a *close translation*.... I have availed myself much of the great work of Dr Legge.... His work will doubtless remain always the standard one for students; and the erudition, the evidence of wide reading, and the patience and care displayed in it, make one indeed stand aghast. It seems to be the general opinion, however, that in the metrical version which followed, in which he availed himself of coadjutors (*not* sinologists) in England and elsewhere, he has been far from equaling himself.

— William Jennings, Introduction to *Shi King: The Old
"Poetry Classic" of the Chinese*, 1891

viii. *Les Mouettes*

Translated into French by Marcel Granet (1919)

Thème de la rencontre près des eaux, — du concours de cueillettes, — des appréhensions, — de la séparation et de la retraite de la fille, — de l'insomnie, — de l'accord et de la musique. Noter les reprises de vers et les enchainements qui donnent quasiment à la pièce une allure de pantoum. *Vide* Skeat, *Malay Magic*, p. 483.

A l'unisson crient les mouettes
dans la rivière sur les rocs!
La fille pure fait retraite,
compagne assortie du Seigneur!

Haute ou basse, la canillée:
à gauche, à droite, cherchons-la!
La fille pure fait retraite:
De jour, de nuit, demandons-la!
Demandons-la! Requête vaine!
de jour, de nuit, nous y pensons!
Ah! quelle peine! Ah! quelle peine!
De-ci, de-là, nous nous tournons!

Haute ou basse, la canillée:
à gauche, à droite, prenons-la!
La fille pure fait retraite:
guitares, luths, accueillez-la!
Haute ou basse, la canillée:
à gauche, à droite, cueillons-la!
La fille pure fait retraite:
cloches et tambours, fêtez-la!

ix. The Ospreys

Translated from the French of Marcel Granet by E. D. Edwards (1932)

The themes are the meetings by the rivers; the assembly for the gathering of plants; misgivings; separation and the retirement of the girl; sleeplessness; harmony and music. Observe the repetition of lines and the concatenation, which give the poem almost the air of a mime. See Skeat, *Malay Magic*, p. 483.

In harmony the ospreys cry
In the river, on the rocks.
The maiden goes into retirement,
A fit mate for the Prince.

Long or short the duckweed:
To left and right let us seek it.
The maiden goes into retirement,
Day and night let us ask for her.
Ask for her! Useless quest!
Day and night let us think of her!
Ah! what pain! Ah! what pain!
This way and that we toss and turn!

Long or short the duckweed:
To left and right let us take it.
The maiden goes into retirement,
Guitars and lutes should welcome her.

Long or short the duckweed:
To left and right let us gather it.
the maiden goes into retirement,
Bells and drums should welcome her.

About the Translation:

The language of the *Book of Songs* is both ancient and difficult. Neither the sinologue nor the educated Chinese himself has immediate access to it. This is most true of the odes of the first part of the book. How then can they be understood? One may apply to a literary Chinese or have recourse to the learned editions. In making use of the commentaries there is always the strong probability that one will be influenced by their symbolic interpretation even while declaring from time to time their absurdity. If, on the other hand, help is sought from an educated Chinese, it is probable that he will, if he has cast off the shackles of classical orthodoxy, be conscious of the charm of the text, but he certainly will not seek in it anything more than the satisfaction of his æsthetic taste. He will explain an ode from the *Book of Songs* just as one would explain a pleasing poem, examining the *literary processes of the poet* and pointing out the *art of the writer*. It will never occur to him that the songs might be of popular origin.

I propose to show that it is possible to go beyond the simple literary explanation, and, beyond the symbolic interpretation, to discover the original meaning of the odes.

— Marcel Granet, *Fêtes et chansons anciennes de la Chine*, 1919

x. Fair, Fair, Cry the Ospreys

Translated by Arthur Waley (1937)

"Fair, fair," cry the ospreys
On the island in the river.
Lovely is this noble lady,
Fit bride for our lord.

In patches grows the water mallow;
To left and right one must seek it.
Shy was this noble lady;
Day and night he sought her.

Sought her and could not get her;
Day and night he grieved.
Long thoughts, oh, long unhappy thoughts,
Now on his back, now tossing on to his side.

In patches grows the water mallow;

To left and right one must gather it.
Shy is this noble lady;
With great zithern and little we hearten her.

In patches grows the water mallow;
To left and right one must choose it.
Shy is this noble lady;
With gongs and drums we will gladden her.

About the Translation:
When in 1913 I first began to read them ... it was simply as poetry that I read the *Songs*, and strangely enough, perhaps, even more as music than as poetry. For though I soon distrusted the Confucian interpretation, I had nothing to put in its place, and was often forced to accept the *Songs* as meaningless incantations. And yet as I read there sprang up from under the tangle of misconceptions and distortions that hid them from me a succession of fresh and lovely tunes. The text sang, just as the lines of Homer somehow manage to sing despite the barbarous ignorance with which we recite them.

The *Songs* are no longer unintelligible to me; save for a line here and there I believe that I understand them fairly well, and they have become, through their unique importance as documents of early metric, ritual mythology, an incentive to studies that extend far beyond ancient China. But they have never lost for me their early attraction. The music, perhaps utterly unauthentic, that accompanied my first discovery of them, has followed me through repeated reading and rereading. Above all, in the last three years, when the text has been continually before me, the jumble of problems linguistic, botanic, zoological, historical, geographical which the translator of such a work must face, has never robbed the *Songs* of their freshness; and I trust that some part of my delight in them, despite the deadening lack of rhyme and formal metric, has found its way to the reader of the foregoing translations....

The true nature of the poems was realized by M. Granet, whose *Fêtes et chansons anciennes de la Chine*, published in 1919, deals with about half the courtship and marriage songs. Since that time sinology has made enormous advances. I differ from M. Granet as regards some general questions and many details. But his book was epoch-making, and I can only hope that the next translator of the *Songs* will feel as much respect for my present versions as I do for those of M. Granet.

— Arthur Waley, *The Book of Songs*, 1937

xi. Kuan ts'ü

Translated by Bernhard Karlgren, 1944–1945

1. *Kwan-kwan* cries the *ts'ü-kiu* bird, on the islet of the river; the beautiful and good girl, she is a good mate for the lord. 2. Of varying length is the *hing* waterplant, to the left and the right we catch it; the beautiful and good girl, waking and sleeping he sought her: wished for her; he wished for her but did not get her, waking and sleeping he thought of her; longing, longing, he tossed and fidgeted. 3. Of varying length is the *hing* waterplant, to the left and the right we gather it; the beautiful and

good girl, guitars and lutes befriend her: hail her as a friend. 4. Of varying length is the *hing* waterplant, to the left and the right we cull it as a vegetable; the beautiful and good girl, bells and drums cheer her.

About the Translation:
This translation was not intended to have any literary merits. I endeavored, on the contrary, to make it as literal as possible, intending it to serve such students of sinology who wish to acquaint themselves with this grand collection, which has played such an enormous part in the literary and cultural history of China.

— Bernhard Karlgren, *The Book of Odes*, 1950

xii. The Mallards

Translated by Robert Payne et al. (1947)

> *Kwang-kwang* cry the mallards
> On the island in the river.
> Such a noble young lady
> Were fit bride for her lord.
>
> There grow the tangled marsh mallows,
> Left and right you will see them.
> Such a noble young lady,
> Waking and sleeping he will see her.
>
> He sought her, could not find her;
> Waking and sleeping, he grieved.
> He longed for her with long thoughts,
> And tumbled over on his side.
>
> There grow the tangled marsh mallows,
> Left and right you may gather them.
> For this noble young lady
> We will sing with small and great flutes.
>
> There grow the tangled marsh mallows,
> Left and right you may choose among them.
> Such a noble lady —
> With bells and drums we will gladden her heart.

About the Translation:
The aim throughout was to have translations by skilled Chinese scholars rather than the adaptations that have been made by Western scholars. Chinese scholars were asked to translate the poems they believed they were most fitted to translate on the basis of their experience and scholarship; these were then revised by me and submitted to them, until final agreement was reached.... There are limitations in all translation, and we have made no effort to break through these limitations, but rather

we have attempted to use them for our own advantages, which are delight in poetry and the understanding of a foreign soul.

— "Method of Translation," from *The White Pony*, 1947

xiii. Kuan Kuan

Translated by Wong Man (1950)

"Kuan Kuan" the chü's
On river's isle:
O virtuous maid,
Love he pursues.

Long and short play the weeds,
Left and right miss thee:
O virtuous maid,
Wake and sleep he seeks thee.

Seeks thee in vain,
Wake and sleep sad,
Long hours long hours,
Tossing insane.

Long and short play the weeds,
Left and right catch thee,
O virtuous maid,
May lute and string charm thee?

Long and short play the weeds,
Left and right hold thee,
O virtuous maid,
May bell and drum cheer thee?

About the Translation:
In some of these translations an attempt has been made to reproduce the image of the original in form, meter, rhyme, couplet-symmetry, and order of words, even to the use of monosyllabic words and a narrow vocabulary; while in others more liberties (feeling guilty all the time) had been taken.

— Wong Man, "Introductory Note" to *Poems from China*, 1950

xiv. Hid! Hid!

Translated by Ezra Pound (1954)

"Hid! Hid!" the fish-hawk saith,
by isle in Ho the fish-hawk saith:
      "Dark and clear,

Dark and clear,
So shall be the prince's fere."

Clear as the stream her modesty;
As neath dark boughs her secrecy,
    reed against reed
    tall on slight
as the stream moves left and right,
    dark and clear,
    dark and clear.

To seek and not find
as a dream in his mind,
    think how her robe should be,
    distantly, to toss and turn,
    to toss and turn.

High reed caught in *ts'ai* grass
    so deep her secrecy;
lute sound in lute sound is caught,
    touching, passing, left and right.
Bang the gong of her delight.

About the Translation:
Thus all translators of the Odes must take courage in their hands; after all, translators are interpreters among other things....

As the translator of the *Classic Anthology*, Pound now emerges as a Confucian poet. Instead of taking the present volume merely as another addition to the long list of Sinological translations, we have to "try with thoughts to comprehend the intention," as Hsien-ch'iu Meng was told by Mencius.

— Achilles Fang, Introduction to Pound's *Classic Anthology Defined by Confucius*, 1954

Invariably one has to compare Pound's *Classic Anthology* with the Waley translation of the same poems because, by a coincidence, they are both appearing in the bookshops together. Read as literature, the Waley is delicate, fresh, sensitive. The Pound — hauntingly beautiful, clownishly funny, or just tomfool-silly — is good Pound....

The trouble with Pound's translations is not that he does not know Chinese (he could certainly use a Chinese dictionary in 1919 when he published Fenollosa's essay "The Chinese Written Character as a Medium for Poetry"), but that a sort of willful obscurantism prevents him from making proper use of the cribs. Pound derived, from Fenollosa, the half-baked theory that all the parts of a Chinese character are significant in the same way; when, in fact, a majority of the characters contain one element which is used for the sound alone. It is as though in writing English we were to draw an eye to represent "eye," and eye with a little man beside it to represent "I." To Pound the second symbol would mean, not "I," but "I, the watcher." ...

Translators should, I feel, be fairly self-effacing people, more anxious for the faithful interpretation and good reception of the original than for their own creative development or greater glory. Though wholly unimpressed by Pound the Confucian, I enjoyed reading these poems immensely. But I should hesitate to describe them all as translations; and I should recommend anyone who is looking for a definitive translation to study the Waley too, and, if he is interested in the technical problems of translation, to glance at the writings of Karlgren.

— David Hawkes, "Translating from the Chinese," 1955

He [Ezra Pound] does not translate words. The words have led him into the thing he expresses.

— Hugh Kenner, introduction to *The Translations of Ezra Pound*, 1970

xv. Crying Ospreys

Translated by Xianyi and Gladys Yang (1955)

Merrily the ospreys cry,
On the islet in the stream.
Gentle and graceful is the girl,
A fit wife for the gentleman.

Short and long the floating water plants,
Left and right you may pluck them.
Gentle and graceful is the girl,
Awake he longs for her and in his dreams.

When the courtship has failed,
Awake he thinks of her and in his dreams.
Filled with sorrowful thoughts,
He tosses about unable to sleep.

Short and long the floating water plants,
Left and right you may gather them.
Gentle and graceful is the girl,
He'd like to wed her, the *qin* and *se*[1] playing.

Short and long the floating water plants,
Left and right you may collect them.
Gentle and graceful is the girl,
He'd like to marry her, bells and drums beating.

---

[1] Two traditional Chinese musical instruments, rather like the zither; the former has seven strings and the latter twenty-five strings.

xvi. Epithalamium

Translated by Arthur Cooper (1971)

Waterbirds on
River islands!
Shy the nymph our
Shepherd's chosen.

Waterlilies
Wreathe around her,
Shy the nymph he
Waking, sleeping,
Never reaches;
Waking, sleeping,
Longing, longing,
Turning, tossing.

Waterlilies
To adorn her,
Shy the nymph we
Greet with zither,

Waterlilies
To array her,
To the shy nymph
Bell, drum bring glee!

About the Translation:
The last English word in my translation of *Guan-ju*, namely glee, represents a Chinese word written with the character 樂 which stands for both of the meanings that "glee" had in Old English: that is, "joy" and "music."...

As an exception to the general Chinese rule that a character represents the sound of a word of one syllable together with its meaning, this particular character represents not only both the meanings of "glee" in English ("joy" and "music") but differently pronounced syllables, in modern Chinese *le* and *yue*, for these two meanings respectively. The explanation of this anomaly is interesting, for it has been shown by the great Swedish sinologue Karlgren that each of these modern syllables once began with a sound like the "gl-" of our own word "glee." There is, however, no need at all to suppose a surprising historical relationship between Old Chinese and Old English: the "gl-" may have been felt as a gleeful sound by the speakers of both languages; while the Chinese at the time the character was created were conscious, even though the two words in their language were already not pronounced quite the same, of an etymological identity between them.... The point I wish to make is that the associations represented in these characters, like the nymph, shepherd, and waterlilies as well as the music of the *Guan-ju* song itself, belong to a *universal language* of the human mind.

— Arthur Cooper, Introduction to *Li Po and Tu Fu*, 1973

xvii. "Guan!" Cries the Hawk

Translated by William McNaughton (1971)

"Guan! Guan!" The fish-hawk
Keeps to the river-strait.
Nilling-willing noble daughter,
Royal son's perfect mate.

Ragged, jagged *xing* plants
Leftward, rightward drifting;
Nilling-willing noble daughter —
Waking-sleeping sought her
Sought her yet not got her
And waking-sleeping thought of her.
    You-zai! You-zai!
Turning, churning, still distraughter

Ragged, jagged *xing* plants
Leftward, rightward lifting:
Nilling-willing, noble daughter,
Lute and zither brought her!

Ragged, jagged *xing* plants
Leftward, rightward sifting:
Nilling-willing noble daughter,
Bells and drums, applaud her!

xviii. Courtship Song

Translated by John Turner (1976)

Sea-hawks are calling
By the river-board.
A modest sweet maid
Is to wed a lord.

Sprayey Floating Hearts
Trail we left and right.
A modest sweet maid
He seeks dark and light.

Seeking her in vain,
Dark and light he yearns,
Longing, aye longing,
He tosses and turns.

Sprayey Floating Hearts
Cull we left and right.
A modest sweet maid
Lute and harp invite.

Sprayey Floating Hearts
Left and right we tell.
A modest sweet maid
Welcome drum and bell.

About the Translation:

My intention is to make the translation of a poem to read like a poem itself. Accordingly, I do not comply with the modern fashion of putting Chinese verse into line by line prose, or into unmeasured sprung rhythm, which is the same thing. Besides, I believe that poetry cannot really be translated into prose. The translation of a poem into prose, which is merely verbally accurate, is not itself a poem and remains a crib. It misses the point and soul and reason of a poem, its specific beauty.

The superiority of poetic translations over prose ones is borne out by English literary history. The good translations of poetry which have been made in English were made by poets; by Chaucer, Spenser, Jonson, Dryden, Pope, Shelley, Fitzgerald.

Chinese poetry tends strongly to be epigrammatic, and most short Chinese poems are epigrams. Now if an effective epigram is transformed into prose, it becomes inconsequential. For the point of epigrammatic and antithetical poetry (and Chinese poetry is both) is carried by its rhyme and rhythm. This is very clearly shown by taking any good epigram and de-rhyming it.

Balance and antithesis is of the essence of *all* Chinese art, and Chinese artistic unity is firmer than any other. Chinese poets always have observed the rules of Chinese rhetoric which are just slightly more streamlined than those of Greek rhetoric; and every Chinese poem has a point, firmly and tellingly driven home.

— John Turner, from the introduction to *A Golden Treasury of Chinese Poetry*, 1976

xix. Kuan-kuan, the Ospreys

Translated by Wai-lim Yip (1976)

When the poet finishes his *Guan-ju* in praise of a girl by mentioning the bell and the drum, whose music delights her heart, he does not present her a manuscript, but a song. The last line of *Guan-ju* betrays the mechanism of the poem, and of all other early Chinese poems. The poet sings, in accord with the pitch, tone, and rhythm produced by various musical instruments; the bell and the drum are used mainly in the case of the *Book of Songs*.

— C. H. Wang, Preface to *The Bell and the Drum*, 1974

Kuan-kuan, the ospreys.
On the river's isle.
Delicate, a good girl:
A gentleman's fit mate.

Long and short, duckweeds.
Fetch some — left and right.
Delicate, a good girl.
Waking, sleeping: seek her.
To seek her and possess not —
Waking, sleeping: think of her.
So distant, so deep;
Toss and turn in bed.
Long and short, duckweeds.
Pluck some — left and right.
Delicate, a good girl:
With music to befriend her.
Long and short, duckweeds.
Pick some — left and right.
Delicate, a good girl:
With bells and drums to meet her.

About the Translation:
All these translators, starting with Giles, must have been led by the sparseness of syntax
in the original to believe that the Chinese characters must be telegraphic — in the
sense that they are shorthand signs for a longhand message — and so they took it as
their task to translate the shorthand poetry into prose, adding commentary all along
to aid understanding, not knowing that these are "pointers" toward a finer shade of
suggestive beauty, which the discursive, analytical, longhand unfolding process
destroys completely.

— Wai-lim Yip, Introduction to *Chinese Poetry*, 1976

xx. *Gwan! Gwan! Cry the Fish Hawks*

Translated by Burton Watson (1984)

This is said to be a wedding song for a member of the royal family; the fish hawks are
symbolic of conjugal affection.

Gwan! gwan! cry the fish hawks
on sandbars in the river:
a mild-mannered good girl,
fine match for the gentleman.

A ragged fringe is the floating-heart,
left and right we trail it:
that mild-mannered good girl,
awake, asleep, I search for her.

I search but cannot find her,
awake, asleep, thinking of her,

endlessly, endlessly,
turning, tossing from side to side.

A ragged fringe is the floating-heart,
left and right we pick it:
the mild-mannered good girl,
harp and lute make friends with her.[2]

A ragged fringe is the floating-heart,
left and right we sort it:
the mild-mannered good girl,
bell and drum delight her.

About the Translation:

As pointed out by David Lattimore, among others, classical Chinese poetry was only successfully translated into English when the translators were willing to set aside the rhymes and meters of traditional English verse, as well as Western concepts of what constitutes poetic diction and subject matter, and create a freer form that would permit the power and expressiveness of the originals to shine through. This act of creation, as is well known, was brought about largely through the efforts of Pound, Waley, and other translators of their ilk in the early decades of the present century, and all of us who work in the field today stand immensely in their debt.

— Burton Watson, introduction to *Columbia Book of Chinese Poetry*, 1984

Confucius and the Traditional Interpretation of the Book of Songs

As in a Mirror

The following extract from the works of CONFUCIUS, will be no improper introduction to the succeeding pages, as it bears such honorable testimony to the moral cast of the ancient CHINESE POETRY, and contains an argument in favor of the utility and respectableness of that fine art in general. It is much to the honor of Poesy, that she hath been in all ages, the first conductress to wisdom and virtue.

CONFUCIUS, exciting his disciples to the study of the ancient Poesy, saith, O my children, why do not you study the book of ODES?

For if we grovel on the earth, if we lie useless and inglorious: by the instructions in the Odes, we may as it were be erected again, and rise up to true and perfect honor.

In the Odes, as in a mirror, we may behold what becomes us, as also what is misbecoming: by contemplating which we may be strongly affected with a wholesome indignation.

Under the influence of the Odes we may come forth sociable, and affable, and pleasant: for as Music aptly tempereth sounds, even so doth

---

[2] The bride is welcomed into the groom's house.

Poesy our passions and appetites. We may hate without anger, we may admit any other natural sensation, and gratify it without vice.

The Odes teach us how at home ewe may serve our parent: how abroad (we may serve) our prince. [*Analects* XVII:9]

In another place, CONFUCIUS addressing himself to his son Pe-yu [Bo Yu], says, Dost thou exercise thyself in the first chapters of the Odes, called *Cheu-nan* [*Zhou-nan*] and *Chao-nan* [*Shao-nan*]? He who doth not exercise himself in those chapters is like a man standing with his face to a wall; he is rendered totally insignificant and useless, for he can neither move a step forward, nor contemplate any object. [*Analects* XVII:10]

— from Thomas Percy, Introduction to
Fragments of Chinese Poetry, 1761

No Evil Thoughts

When Confucius spoke of "poetry" he was referring to the *Book of Songs*, which was all the poetry that was available to him, or at least all that he would have accepted as such. We are therefore justified in taking what he said about this anthology as representing his views on poetry in general.

"The *Three Hundred Songs* may be summed up in one phrase: 'No evil thoughts.' " [*Analects* II:2]

"Be inspired by the Songs, confirmed by ritual, and perfected by music." [*Analects* VIII:8]

"Though a man can recite the *Three Hundred Songs*, if he canot carry out his duties when entrusted with affairs of state, and cannot answer questions on his own when sent on a mission abroad, what is the use of having studied the poems, no matter how many?" [*Analects* XIII:5]

"If you do not study the *Songs*, you will not be able to speak (properly)." [*Analects* XVI:13]

"Young men, why do you not study the *Songs*? They can be used to inspire, to observe,. to make you fit for company, to express grievances; near at hand, they will teach you how to serve your father, and, looking further, how to serve your sovereign; they also enable you to learn the names of many birds, beasts, plants and trees." [*Analects* XVII:9]

— from James J. Y. Liu, *Chinese Theories of Literature*, 1975

Some Traditional Interpretations of Song 1: Guan-ju

Translated (unless otherwise stated) by Pauline Yu

Exegesis could extract a relevant message from the most unpromising material. A lyric which likened the dimpling smile and flashing eyes of a princess to "embroidery on a white silk ground" was read by a disciple of Confucius to mean that "morality takes precedence over the rules of etiquette": an interpretation that does not seem strikingly obvious to us, though it met with whole-hearted approval from the Master.

— David Hawkes, "The Age of Exuberance,"
in *Classical, Modern and Humane*, 1989

Confucius (551–479 B.C.), *Analects* III:20:

In the *Guan-ju* there is joy without wantonness and sorrow without self-injury.

Sima Qian (c. 145–c. 85 B.C.), *The Records of the Grand Historian*:

Alas! When the house of Zhou was in decline, the *Guan-ju* was composed. (The traditional commentary expands: "The poem criticizes King Kang and his wife of the eleventh century B.C., by presenting contrastive, positive images of male-female decorum." But in Sima's own *Records* King Kang's reign is described as being so peaceful that no punishments needed to be levied for over forty years.)

The Mao Heng (Han dynasty) interpretation:

The earliest systematic commentary on the *Songs* is that found in the Mao text, consisting of brief introductions to each poem explaining its general meaning and usually assigning it to some period of early Zhou history, as well as glosses on individual words. Presumably these comments represent the views of a scholar named Mao (or, according to another version, two scholars of that name), who served at the court of Liu De, a son of Emperor Jing of the Former Han who was enfeoffed as king of the region of Hejian in 155 B.C. Mao is at best a shadowy figure, but these comments attributed to him, along with a general preface to the *Songs* (now generally believed to have been written by a scholar of the first century A.D. named Wei Hong) have had an enormous influence upon later interpretations of the *Songs*.

These comments in the Mao text are designed, in almost all cases, to give the songs a political significance and, wherever possible, to relate them to some specific historical person or event. If the song expresses joy or contentment or reflects a state of social order, for example, Mao assigns it to the reign or domain of a "good" ruler, since, according to Confucian doctrine, these are the conditions that prevail among the people when a truly wise sovereign is present to lead them in the path of virtue. If the song grumbles or complains of some ill (no matter how private), Mao attributes it to the time of an "evil" ruler and interprets it as political satire or reprimand. In cases where the grievance seems to be too personal in nature to admit such a view, he resolves the difficulty by interpreting the whole poem metaphorically — for example a jilted lover or an abandoned wife becomes a metaphor for an abused and misunderstood official complaining to his lord.

Though some Mao interpretations (see *Song* 41: "Cold is the North Wind", and *Song* 91: "The Student's Blue Collar") appear far-fetched indeed, Mao and the commentators who followed him, such as Zheng Xuan, did not concoct their theory of the political import of the *Songs* out of thin air. By tradition the *Songs* were collected by officials of the king specifically for the purpose of keeping him informed of the sentiments and grievances of the people, and if one accepts this idea one is already obliged to find political significance in at least some of the poems.... Moreover we know that, during the Spring and Autumn period, statesmen and diplomats were in the habit of quoting the Songs as a means of expressing their opinions discreetly and with becoming indirection. The *Zuo Commentary* [see chapter 4] is full of descriptions of meetings and diplomatic conferences at which the exchange of ideas is carried on almost exclusively in this medium (and woe to the statesman who failed to recognize an allusion and interpret it correctly!). In the process, lines were often quoted out of context, or whole poems used to express ideas or sentiments quite foreign to the original meaning of the poem. Thus in time the poems, particularly those of the "Folk Songs" section, acquired a set of allegorical connotations, usually of a political nature, and it was no doubt these which Mao used as the basis of his interpretations.

— Burton Watson, *Early Chinese Literature*, 1962

Guan-guan is the cry of birds responding to each other, and this variety observes the separation of the sexes. In the first two lines, the queen takes joy in the virtue of her lord, and there is nothing on which she does not accord with him, nor is she wanton about her beauty. Her prudence is firm and her seclusion deep, like the ospreys in their separation. Only afterward can her influence transform the world. When husbands and wives observe the separation of the sexes, then fathers and sons will maintain familial relations.... In lines three and four the 'young lady' is King Wen's queen, who possesses the virtue of the ospreys by living in seclusion and thus makes a suitable mate for the ruler.... In the second stanza, she is picking the edible water plants — because she "possesses the virtue of the ospreys" she can begin preparations for the ancestral sacrifices.

The "Lesser" Mao Preface (? first century A.D.):

Guan-ju speaks of the virtues of the queen. It is the beginning of the Airs, by which all under heaven was transformed and relations between husband and wife were ordered.... The *Guan-ju* takes joy in obtaining a pure young lady as a mate for the lord and is anxious to present her worth, without being wanton about her beauty....

Zheng Xuan (127–200):

The "pure young lady" refers not to the queen herself, but rather to palace ladies whom their mistress, in her virtue and jealousy-free seclusion, is seeking as additional mates for the king; thus it is she who tosses and turns until finding them."

Han Ying (Han dynasty):

Whatever we may have lost through the perishing of Han Ying's other works, we have not gained anything towards the understanding of the *Book of Songs* by the preservation of his *Illustrations of the Songs*. The editors of the catalogue of the imperial library under the present dynasty [Manchu], in the conclusion of their notice of it, quote with approval the judgement of Wang Shizhen of the Ming dynasty, that "Han quotes the *Songs* to illustrate his narratives, and does not give his narratives to illustrate the meaning of the *Songs*."

— James Legge, Prolegomena to his *She-King*, 1871

Zixia asked, "Why is the *Guan-ju* made to begin the 'Guo-feng' [Folk Songs] section of the *Songs*?"

Confucius said, "The *Guan-ju* is perfection.[3] Now in its relation to man, the *Guan-ju* above is like Heaven; below it is like Earth. Mysterious and dark is the virtue it hides; abundant and rich the Way it puts into practice. Its transformations are like those of the supernatural dragon. It is complete in its brilliancy and order. Oh great is the Way of the *Guan-ju*! It is that which connects all things and on which the life of human beings is dependent.

"The He and the Luo Rivers gave forth the writing and the diagram; the *lin* [Chinese unicorn] and the phoenix frequented the suburbs: by what means should this be brought about except by following the Way of the *Guan-ju*, and by taking the subject of the *Guan-ju* for a model? Now the writings of the Six Classics all are devoted to exhaustive discussion, but they derive their matter from the *Guan-ju*. The subject of the *Guan-ju* is great! Vast and soaring, 'from the east to the west, from the south to the north, there is not a thought but does it homage.' May you exert yourself to emulate it, and cherish it in thought. Neither human beings between Heaven and Earth nor the origin of the Kingly Way are outside its compass."

Zixia sighed deeply and said, "Great indeed is the *Guan-ju*; it is the very foundation of Heaven and Earth."

---

[3] Confucius is made to express himself more cautiously in the *Analects*: "The *Guan-ju* is expressive of enjoyment without being licentious, and of grief without being hurtfully excessive." [*Analects* III:20. Hightower is here quoting Legge. As Legge himself put it, "Confucius expressed his admiration of the Song, but his words afford no help towards the interpretation of it." Compare Pauline Yu's translation: "joy without wantonness and sorrow without self-injury."]

The Song says,
   With bells and drums let us show our delight in it.

   — from *Han Ying's Illustrations of the Didactic Application of the*
                    Classic of Songs (translated by J. R. Hightower)

Zhu Xi (1130–1200):

King Wen of the Zhou possessed a sage virtue from birth and obtained
the sage young lady of the Si clan to be his mate. The ladies of the palace,
upon her arrival, saw her retiring, chaste, and tranquil virtue, and thereupon wrote this poem. It says that those ospreys join together and cry
guan-guan to each other on the islet in the river; how will this secluded
young lady not make a good mate for their lord? It says that their joining
together in mutual joy and respect is like that of the ospreys, whose
feelings for each other are extremely strong yet who maintain the separation of the sexes.

Yan Can (fl. 1248):

Ospreys by nature mate only once but reside in different places: this is
maintaining the separation of the sexes and not being licentious. Also by
nature they like to stay put; once settled they do not move again: this is
an image of reclusion and proper quietude.

Yao Jiheng (b. 1647):

The poem has nothing to do with King Wen or his queen at all, but is a
simple epithalamium for some nobleman and his bride. But the joyful
marriage is an omen that the house of Zhou's fortunes are rising.... The
water-plants are simply objects chosen from the same scene — the water-
bound islet — from which the ospreys were taken.

2: Ge-tan
Shade o' the Vine

Translated by Ezra Pound

   Shade o' the vine,
   Deep o' the vale,
   Thick of the leaf,

the bright bird flies
singing, the orioles
gather on swamp tree boles.

Shade of the vine,
Deep o' the vale,
Dark o' the leaf
    here 'neath our toil
    to cut and boil
stem into cloth, thick or fine
No man shall wear out mine.

Tell my nurse to say I'll come,
    Here's the wash and here's the rinse,
    Here's the cloth I've worn out since,
Father an' mother, I'm comin' home.

Commentary:

The old interpreters held that this ode was of King Wen's Queen in her virgin prime. We see her in her parents' house, with her mind bent on woman's work; thrifty and economical, wearing her washed clothes, and honoring and reverencing her matron-teacher. Zhu Xi makes it a narrative piece, in which the queen tells first of her diligent labours, and then how, when they were concluded, she was going to pay a visit of duty and affection to her parents. The imperial editors prefer Zhu Xi's view in this instance. "Anciently, the rules to be observed between husband and wife required the greatest circumspection. When the wife wished to visit her parents, she intimated her purpose through the nurse. Inside the door of the harem, no liberty could be taken any more than with a revered guest. Thus was the instruction of the people made to commence from the smallest matters, with a wonderful depth of wisdom!" (Legge)

3: Juan-er
Curl-Grass

Translated by Ezra Pound

She:

    Curl-grass, curl-grass,
    to pick it, to pluck it
    to put in a bucket
    never a basket load
Here on Zhou road, but a man in my mind!
    Put it down here by the road.

He:

    Pass, pass

up over the pass,
a horse on a mountain road!
A winded horse on a high road,
give me a drink to lighten the load.
As the cup is gilt, love is spilt.
          Pain lasteth long.

Black horses, yellow with sweat,
are not come to the ridge-top yet.
          Drink deep of the rhino horn
But leave not love too long forlorn.

Tho' driver stumble and horses drop,
we come not yet to the stony top.
Let the foundered team keep on,
How should I leave my love alone!

Commentary:
Zhu Xi ascribes the ode to King Wen's Queen. Her husband, "the man of her heart"
[Pound's "man in my mind."], is absent on some toilsome expedition; and she sets
forth her anxiety for his return, by representing herself, first as a gatherer of
vegetables, unable to fill her basket through the preoccupation of her mind; and then
as trying to drive to a height from which she might see her husband returning, but
always baffled. [Pound changes the subject in the second stanza.] All this is told in her
own person, so that the piece is narrative. The whole representation is, however,
unnatural; and when the baffled rider proceeds to console herself with a cup of spirits,
I must drop the idea of King Wen's Queen altogether, and can make nothing more of
the piece than that someone is lamenting in it the absence of a cherished friend in
strange fashion. (Legge)

The themes are the chase on the mountains; harvestings; misgivings; drinkings.
Observe the rhinoceros horn. A horse-race may be indicated. (Granet)

4: Jiu-mu
South, Droops a Tree

Translated by "V. W. X."

Refers to the happy household of the queen and her husband's concubines.

South, droops a tree,
Creeper surround her.
Our lady's joy
Fortune hath found her!

South, droops a tree,
Creepers entrance her:

Our lady's joy
Fortune enhance her!

South, droops a tree,
Creepers beset her:
Our lady's joy
Fortune beget her!

Commentary:
The piece is allusive, supposed to be spoken or sung by the ladies of the harem, in praise of King Wen's Queen, who was not jealous of them, and did not try to keep them in the background, but cherished them rather, as the great tree does the creepers that twine round it. (Legge)

6: Tao-yao
Like the Slender Peach

Translated by "V. W. X."

Like the slender peach
With her flowers red-hot,
So speeds the bride
To chaste room and cot.

Like the slender peach
With her fruit in bloom,
So speeds the bride
To chaste cot and room.

Like the slender peach
With exuberant leaves,
So speeds the bride
With her virgin slaves.

Commentary:
Praise of a bride going to be married. The young peach tree is allusive of the bride in the flush of youth, and its brilliant flowers of her beauty. (Legge)

A marriage-song. Theme: the growth of plants. (Granet)

7: Tu-zhi
Hares

Translated by Arthur Cooper

Ware, ware, snares for hares,
　　Peg 'em down, tack, tack:

Fair, fair, the warriors
    My Lord's
Bucklers and Bastions!

Ware, ware, snares for hares,
    Spread 'em in the tracks:
Fair, fair, the warriors
    My Lord's
Dearest companions!

Ware, ware, snares for hares,
    Spread 'em in the woods:
Fair, fair, the warriors
    My Lord's
Soul and opinions!

Commentary:
Praise of a rabbit-catcher, as fit to be a Prince's mate. The influence of King Wen (according to Zhu Xi), or of his Queen (according to Mao), was so powerful and beneficial, that individuals in the lowest rank were made fit by it to occupy the highest positions. (Legge)

10: Ru-fen
Along Yew's Banks

Translated by "V. W. X."

The last stanza contains a covert allusion to the approaching downfall of the tyrant Zhou and the triumph of Prince Wen.

Along Yew's banks
As the brush I clove,
Ah! where my lord?
Sad, hungered love!

Along Yew's banks
As the stumps I cut,
Lo! here my lord!
He forgets me not!

As the bream-tails flush
So Court passions fly,
Let them seethe away!
Our saviour's nigh!

Commentary:
This song belongs to the closing time of the Shang dynasty, under the tyranny of King

Zhou, when King Wen was consolidating his power and influence. The effects of his very different rule were felt in the country about the Yew [Ru] River, and animated the wife of a soldier (or officer), rejoicing in the return of her husband from a toilsome service, to express her feelings and sentiments. (Legge)

The themes are the walk beside the river, the bundles of fuel, separation and the restlessness of love. Observe that the vividness of the picture gives the impression of pain and loss. (Granet)

12: Que-chao

i. The Robber-Bird

Translated by Sir John Francis Davis (1829)

According to the commentary, the ode has a reference to the success of a rich and powerful suitor, who carries off the bride that has already been contracted to a humble rival.

> The nest yon winged artist builds,
> The robber-bird shall tear away;
> So yields her hopes th'affianced maid,
> Some wealthy lord's reluctant prey.
>
> The anxious bird prepares a home,
> In which the spoiler soon shall dwell;
> Forth goes the weeping bride, constrain'd,
> A hundred cars the triumph swell.
>
> Mourn for the tiny architect,
> A stronger bird hath ta'en its nest;
> Mourn for the hapless, stolen bride,
> How vain the pomp to soothe her breast!

About the Translation:
The bulk of these curious vestiges of antiquity in the *Sheeking* do not rise beyond the most primitive simplicity, and their style and language, without the minute commentary that accompanies them, would not be always intelligible at the present day.... In this paraphrase, it has been necessary to embody the full sense of what is only hinted at in the original.

— Sir John Francis Davis, *Poeseos Sinicae Commentarii*, 1829

Sir John Davis has made a little poem, more interesting than the original, but altogether away from the obvious meaning of that original, on a view of it not hinted at in any commentary.

— James Legge, *The She-King*, 1871

ii. The Dove in the Magpie's Nest

Translated by Clement Allen (1891)

> The dove, that weak and timid bird,
> Scant wit hath she her nest to build;
> Unlike the pie, whose house well lined
> Within, and strong with labor skilled,
> Might seem a palace. Yet the dove
> Will to herself appropriate
> The magpie's nest, and snug therein
> Dwell in contentment with her mate.
>
> My sweet, thou art the tender dove!
> Hath fate's decree then nought more fair
> For thee than in these barren fields
> A peasant's hut and life to share?
> My lands are wide, my halls are high,
> And steeds and cars obey my call;
> My dove, within my magpie nest,
> Thou shalt be mistress of them all.

About the Translation:

I have made a very free paraphrase in translating this ballad, but I believe I have hit on its meaning. Most Chinese commentators say that the poet's object was to laud the virtues of the lady, among which was her *stupidity*, which is typified by the clumsiness of the dove, which is unable to build itself a decent nest.... But why need we trouble ourselves with such absurdities? Surely the motive of the piece is the same as that of "King Cophetua and the Beggar Maid," "The Lord of Burleigh," and a dozen other pieces. The prince is the magpie, the strong, handsome, skillful bird. The peasant girl is the dove, who does not forcibly rob the magpie of his nest, but by her softness and gentleness persuades him to allow her to occupy it.

Sir John Davis's translation of this ballad ... is very pretty, but does not, in my opinion, in any way express the meaning of the original.

— Clement Allen, *The Book of Chinese Poetry*, 1891

iii. The Wedding-Journey of a Princess

Translated by William Jennings (1891)

> The magpie has a nest;
> The dove yet takes possession.
> Lo! the young bride departs,
> In many-wheeled procession.
>
> The magpie has a nest;

The dove yet there will quarter.
Lo! the young bride departs;
And countless cars escort her.

The magpie has a nest;
The dove will fit it (quickly).
Lo! the young bride departs,
With chariots mustered thickly.

Commentary:

I do not know that it is a fact that the dove is to be found breeding in a magpie's nest, as is here assumed; but Mao Qiling (1623–1716) vehemently asserts it, and says that any one with eyes may see about the villages a flock of doves contending with as many magpies, and driving the latter from their nests. The virtue of the bride is thought to be emblemed by the quietness and stupidity of the dove, unable to make a nest for itself, or making a very simple, unartistic one. The dove is a favourite emblem with all poets for a lady; but surely never, out of China, because of its "stupidity." But says Duan Changwu (towards the end of the Song dynasty), "The duties of a wife are few and confined; there is no harm in her being stupid." (Legge)

A marriage-song. Themes: birds; the carriage of the bride. (Granet)

13: Cai-fan
Pluck the Quince

Translated by Ezra Pound

Pluck the quince
to serve a prince,
by isle, and pool.

Plucking quinces
in service of princes,
in vale, pluck again
and carry to fane.

In high wimple
bear to the temple
ere dawn light,
then home
for the night, leisurely, leisurely.

Commentary:

The ladies of a harem, in one of the States of the South, admiring and praising the way in which their mistress discharged her duties, her industry and reverence, assisting him in sacrificing. According to Zhu Xi, it refers to her duties in his silk-worm establishment. (Legge)

14: Cao-chong
Hopper-Grass

Translated by Ezra Pound

1

> "Chkk! chkk!" hopper-grass,
> nothing but grasshoppers hopping past;
> tell me how a lady can
> be gay if she sees no gentleman?
>
> But when I've seen a man at rest,
> standing still, met at his post,
> my heart is no more tempest-toss'd.

2

> I climb South Hill to pick the turtle-fern,
> seeing no man
> such climb's heart-burn
>
> but to see a good man at rest,
> standing still, met at his post,
> I no more think this trouble lost.

3

> To climb South Hill picking the jagged fern
> and see no man, who shall not pine and yearn?
>
> But to see good man at rest
> standing still there at his post
> is the heart's design's utmost.

Commentary:

The wife of some great officer bewails his absence on duty, and longs for the joy of his return. According to the view of Zhu, she is moved by the phenomena of the different seasons which she observes, and gives expression to the regrets and hopes which she cherished. (Legge)

The themes are: the excursions on the heights; the mating of animals; harvestings; the restlessness of love; and its satisfaction. (Granet)

15: Cai-bin
I Pluck the Grass

Translated by "V. W. X."

This poem tells of the decent and profitable employment of women under King Wen.

    I pluck the grass
    From the brooklet's bank,
    I pluck the weed
    From the puddle dank.

    In what shall I put it?
    In pail and pottle.
    How shall I cook it?
    In pan and kettle.

    And where shall I set it?
    On the altar sill.
    Who sacrifice it?
    The vestal will.

16: Gan-tang

i. *That Shady Crab*

Translated by "V. W. X."

This poem offers the people's affectionate recollection of Prince Shao's virtues.

    Ah! that shady crab!
    Cut not, nor lop!
    Here Prince Shao did stop.

    Ah! that shady crab!
    Cut not, nor spoil!
    Here he sat awhile.

    Ah! that shady crab!
    Cut not, nor shear!
    For Prince Shao stayed here.

ii. *Don't Chop That Pear Tree*

Translated by Ezra Pound

    Don't chop that pear tree,
    Don't spoil that shade;

Thaar's where ole Marse Shao used to sit,
Lord, how I wish he was judgin' yet.

Commentary:
The love of the people for the memory of the Duke of Shao makes them love the trees beneath which he had rested. The Duke had won the hearts of the people, and his memory was somehow connected with the tree which the poet had before his mind's eye, who makes the people therefore "think of the man and love the tree." (Legge)

18: Gao-yang
In His Lambskin Coat

Translated by "V. W. X."

In his lambskin coat,
With five plain thread seams,
Home to sup from his work,
How smart he seems!

In his lambskin cape,
With five plain thread stitches,
How smart he seems,
As he homeward fetches!

In his lambskin cloak,
With five plain thread coils,
How smart he seems,
Going home from his toils.

20: Piao-you-mei
Like Falling Fruit

Translated by "V. W. X."

This is a song of a marriageable girl who fears her chance will never come.

Like falling fruit
Near a third is gone.
Come, wooers all
Time is getting on!

Like falling fruit
A good half is cast.
Come, wooers all
Time is flying fast!

Like falling fruit
Gathered in the pail.
Come, wooers all
Tell your marriage tale!

Commentary:
The critics contend that it is not the desire merely to get married which is here
expressed, but to be married in accordance with propriety, and before the proper
time was gone by. (Legge)

A harvest song. Theme: invitation. (Granet)

23: Ye-you si-jun
Lies a Dead Deer

Translated by Ezra Pound

Lies a dead deer on yonder plain
whom white grass covers,
A melancholy maid in spring
                    is luck
                    for
                    lovers.

Where the scrub elm skirts the wood,
be it not in white mat bound,
as a jewel flawless found,
                    dead as doe is maidenhood.

Hark!
Unhand my girdle-knot,
                    stay, stay, stay
                    or the dog
                    may
                    bark.

Commentary:
A virtuous young lady resists the attempts of a seducer. (Legge)

Themes: invitation and half-refusal; bundles of fireweood; hunting. (Granet)

26: Bo-zhou
That Boat of Cypress Wood

Translated by James Legge

An officer of worth bewails the neglect and contempt with which he is treated. The
state of the unemployed officer is like that of a boat floating uselessly about with the

current. His mind is firmer than a stone, and more even and level than a mat. In the
State of Wei, the ruler was at this time obscured by the unworthy officers, who abused
his confidence and directed the government: the sun had become small, and the
moon had taken its place.

It floats about, that boat of cypress wood,
    Now here, now there, as by the current borne.
Nor rest nor sleep comes in my troubled mood;
    I suffer as when painful wound has torn
    The shrinking body. Thus I dwell forlorn,
And aimless muse, my thoughts of sorrow full.
    I might with wine refresh my spirit worn;
I might go forth, and, sauntering try to cool
The fever of my heart; but grief holds sullen rule.

My mind resembles not a mirror plate,
    Reflecting all the impressions it receives.
The good I love, the bad regard with hate;
    I only cherish whom my heart believes.
    Colleagues I have, but yet my spirit grieves,
That on their honor I cannot depend.
    I speak, but my complaint no influence leaves
Upon their hearts; with mine no feelings blend;
With me in anger they, and fierce disdain contend.

My mind is fixed, and cannot, like a stone,
    Be turned at will indifferently about;
And what I think, to that, and that alone,
    I utterance give, alike within, without;
    Nor can like mat be rolled and carried out.
With dignity in presence of them all,
    My conduct marked, my goodness who shall scout?
My foes I boldly challenge, great and small,
If there be aught in me they can in question call.

How full of trouble is my anxious heart!
    With hate the blatant herd of creatures mean
Ceaseless pursue. Of their attacks the smart
    Keeps my mind in distress. Their venomed spleen
    Aye vents itself; and with insulting mien
They vex my soul; and no one on my side
    A word will speak. Silent, alone, unseen,
I think of my sad case; then opening wide
My eyes, as if from sleep, I beat my breast, sore-tired.

Thy disc, O sun, should ever be complete,
    While thine, O changing moon, doth wax and wane.
But now our sun hath waned, weak and effete,
    And moons are ever full. My heart with pain
    Is firmly bound, and held in sorrow's chain,
As to the body cleaves an unwashed dress.
    Silent I think of my sad case; in vain
I try to find relief from my distress.
Would I had wings to fly where ills no longer press!

Commentary:

This poem is a protest of woman with a "troubled mood" caused by a host of "mean creatures" who attempt to marry her against her inclinations. She sails the river recounting her troubles, of which the greatest seems to be her brothers' rude refusal to help her out of the predicament. *Song* 45 begins with the same motif of sailing, and the boat is also built of cypress. The word *bo*, in its archaic pronunciation *bak*, is phonologically identical with *po/bak*, meaning "press" or "compel." The English word "cypress" is not in any way etymologically related to "press," but by pure accident it may well illustrate the Chinese effect, the motif word "cypress" punning to evoke the type-scene, the woman "under pressure." The grief of the woman in *Song* 45 is substantially identical with that of the one in this poem, being caught in a situation where she is to marry someone against her wishes, and cannot secure any family support in her resistance to her suitors. The concatenate motifs of the theme are roughly as follows: the cypress boat; unwanted marriage at hand; no help in resistance from the next of kin; amd an unavailing appeal to the heaven-sun-moon statue, which is not yet personalized in the Chinese tradition.

— C. H. Wang, *The Bell and the Drum*, 1974

27: Lü-yi
Green Robe

Translated by Ezra Pound

Green robe, green robe, lined with yellow,
Who shall come to the end of sorrow?

Green silk coat and yellow skirt,
How forget all my heart-hurt?

Green the silk is, you who dyed it;
Antient measure, now divide it?

Nor fine nor coarse cloth keep the wind
from the melancholy mind;
Only antient wisdom is
solace to man's miseries.

Commentary:

The complaint, sad but resigned, of a neglected wife. The ode leads us further into the harem of the State of Wei, and show us the dissatisfactions and unhappiness that prevailed there. (Legge)

30: Zhong-feng
Wild and Windy

Translated by Arthur Waley

> Wild and windy was the day;
> You looked at me and laughed,
> But the jest was cruel, and the laughter
>   mocking.
> My heart within is sore.
>
> There was a great sandstorm that day;
> Kindly you made as though to come,
> Yet neither came nor went away.
> Long, long my thoughts.
>
> A great wind and darkness;
> Day after day it is dark.
> I lie awake, cannot sleep,
> And gasp with longing.
>
> Dreary, dreary the gloom;
> The thunder growls.
> I lie awake, cannot sleep,
> And am destroyed with longing.

34: Pao-you ku-ye
Bitter Blade

Translated by Arthur Cooper

> He: "The Gourd now sprouts its bitter blade:
>   The ford is now too deep to wade!"
>
> She: "Where it is deep, there are stepping stones,
>   Where it is shallow just raise your clothes!"
>
> He: "But see how the raging waters fall,
>   And hark to the pheasant's grating call!"

She: "Carts could still cross with their axles dry!
      That was the pheasant's mating cry.

      Riverbirds mingle their voices now
      As a new sun rises over the brow,

      But he who would bring a bride to his bed
      Should never wait till the frosts have fled!

      Beckons and beckons the boatman aboard:
          Let others cross but no, not I,
          Let others cross but no, not I,
              I shall await my love and lord!"

Commentary:
The themes are: crossing the river, invitation, and the song of birds. Various marriage customs are recalled. (Granet)

35: Gu-feng
The Valley Wind

Translated by Arthur Waley

Zip, zip the valley wind,
Bringing darkness, bringing rain.
"Strive to be of one mind;
Let there be no anger between you."
He who plucks greens, plucks cabbage
Does not judge by the lower parts.
In my reputation there is no flaw,
I am yours till death.

Slowly I take the road,
Reluctant at heart.
Not far, no, near;
See, you escort me only to the gateway.[4]
Who says that sow-thistle is bitter?
It is sweeter than shepherd's-purse.
You feast your new marriage-kin,
As though they were older brothers, were
      younger brothers.

---

[4] He hustles her off the premises without courtesy.

"It is the Wei that makes the Jing look dirty;
Very clear are its shoals.[5]
You feast your new relations,
And think me no fit company.
"Do not break my dam,
Do not open my fish-traps.
Though for my person you have no regard,
At least pity my brood."[6]

Where the water was deep
I rafted it, boated it;
Where the water was shallow
I swam it, floated it.
Whether a thing was to be had or no
I strove always to find it.
When any of your people were in trouble
I went on my knees to help them.

Why do you not cherish me,
But rather treat me as an enemy?
You have spoilt my value;
What is used, no merchant will buy.
Once in times of peril, of extremity
With you I shared all troubles.
But now that you are well-nurtured, well-fed,
You treat me as though I were a poison.

I had laid by a good store,
Enough to provide against the winter;
You feast your new kin,
And that provision is eaten up.
Then you were violent, were enraged,
And it gave me great pain.
You do not think of the past;
It is only anger that is left.

---

[5] It is only in comparison with the new wife that I seem shabby. These lines are no doubt a proverb; the poem comes from Henan and not from Shaanxi. The Jing flows into the Wei to the east of the old Zhou capital in Shaanxi.

[6] These lines, several times repeated in the *Songs*, must be a quotation.

41: Bei-feng
Cold Is the North Wind

Translated by Burton Watson

Cold is the north wind,
the snow falls thick.
If you are kind and love me,
take my hand and we'll go together.
You are modest, you are slow,
but oh, we must hurry!

Fierce is the north wind,
the snow falls fast.
If you are kind and love me,
take my hand and we'll go home together.
You are modest, you are slow,
but oh, we must hurry!

Nothing redder than the fox,
nothing blacker than the crow.
If you are kind and love me,
take my hand and we'll ride together.
You are modest, you are slow,
but oh, we must hurry!

Commentary:

Though the identity of the speaker is not clear, the poem is quite obviously a love song of some kind. Yet Mao gives it an uncompromisingly political interpretation: the peasants, oppressed by a cruel government (the cold wind of the song), urge each other to flee to another state. The private dilemma of two lovers is transformed into a public crisis; what in the original is a timeless expression of urgent pleading is given a specific temporal an factual context.

— Burton Watson, *Early Chinese Literature*, 1962

Themes: the weather; invitation. Indication of the part played by forcible persuasion. (Granet)

45: Bo-zhou
Like a Lonely Bark

Translated by "V. W. X. "

A young widow remonstrates with her mother for urging a second marriage.

Like a lonely bark

In the stream I be,
My curly-haired lad
Was the mate for me!
To the death I will widowed be!
Oh! gentle mother!
Why urge another?

Like a drifting bark,
I helpless move,
My curly-haired lad
Was my only love!
To the death I will faithful prove!
Oh! nature's mother!
Why urge another?

46: Qiang-you-ci
Off the Wall

Translated by "V. W. X."

This poem includes a cautious allusion to the disgraceful doings of a royal Duke, who was rumored to have committed incest with his stepmother.

Off the wall those prickles
So ill be swept,
So the harem secrets
Were better kept.
　　To tell the same,
　　Would bring but shame.

Off the wall those prickles
Can ill be brushed,
So the harem secrets
Were better hushed.
　　To tell the tale,
　　All words would fail.

Off the wall those prickles
Were ill abated,
So the harem secrets
Were best not prated.
　　Such things to tell
　　Would not look well.

Commentary:
The things done in the harem of the Palace of Wei were too shameful to be told. A plant like the *tribulus terrestris* on the wall [V. W. X.'s "prickles"] was unsightly and injurious to it; but the attempt to remove it would be still more injurious, and it is therefore let alone. So with the deeds done in the harem, vile and disgusting, so that it was better not to speak of them openly. (Legge)

48: Sang-zhong
Hunting the Dodder

Translated by "V. W. X."

Love song.

> Hunting the dodder,
> Through the lanes I pass,
> But my thoughts are hunting
> Yon pretty lass!
> In this thicket she should be,
> About this rustic spot, said she,
> And promised to go back with me.
>
> Gleaning the wheat-ears,
> I pass the street,
> But my thoughts are gleaning
> Yon pretty sweet!
> In this thicket she should be,
> About this rustic spot, said she,
> And promised to go back with me.
>
> Hunting the shallots
> I pass the moat,
> But my thoughts are hunting
> A petticoat!
> In this thicket she should be,
> About this rustic spot, said she,
> And promised to go back with me.

Commentary:
Themes: assignations by the rivers; harvestings. (Granet)

55: Qi-yu

i. Behold That Bay

From Thomas Percy (1761)

Verses in Praise of VU-CUNG [Wu-gong] Prince of the Kingdom of GUEY [Wei] from an Ancient Ode.

Behold that bay, which is formed by the winding of the river KI:[7]
Beset with tufts of verdant canes, how beautifully luxuriant!
So is our prince adorned with virtues.
He is like one, that carveth and smootheth ivory.

He is like one that cutteth and polisheth diamonds,[8]
O how sublime, yet profound is he!
O how resolute, yet cautious! How removed and respectable!
We have a prince adorned with virtues:
Whom to the end of time we never can forget.

About the Translation:
The flowers of Poesy are of so delicate a nature that they will seldom bear to be
transplanted into a foreign language.... The beauties of the Chinese Poetry must of
all other be the most incapable of transfusion into other languages, and especially
into those, whose idioms are so remote and unsuitable as are those of Europe.

— Thomas Percy, *Fragments of Chinese Poetry*, 1761

ii. A Chinese Ode

Translated by Sir William Jones (1799)

Behold yon reach of the river KI;
Its green reeds how luxuriant! how luxuriant!
Thus is our Prince adorned with virtues;
As a carver, as a filer, of ivory,
As a cutter, as a polisher, of gems.
O how elate and sagacious! O how dauntless and composed!
How worthy of fame! How worthy of reverence!
We have a Prince adorned with virtues,
Whom to the end of time we can not forget.

---

[7] Ki [Qi] is a river in the province Hu-quang [Hunan and Hubei], that gives name to a city,
which is watered by its streams *Vid Martini Atlas*. [Percy's notes, like his translations, were
based on the work of the Jesuits, especially Du Halde.]

[8] The *Chinese* commentator Tseng-tsu (for the *Chinese* have their commentators and
scholiasts) explains the fourth and fifth verses, as expressing the unwearied care and
attention of this prince to reform and improve himself and his subjects: as a nice artist,
who deals in works of the most elegant kinds, never rests till he hath brought his
manufacture to the most exquisite perfection.

About the Translation:
A native of Canton ... has favoured me with the Three Hundred Odes in the original.
But he seems to think that it would require three or four years to complete a
translation of them; and Mr Cox informs me that none of the Chinese, to whom he
has access, possess leisure and perseverance enough for such a task.

— Sir William Jones, "On the Second Classical Book of the Chinese," 1799

iii. A Chinese Ode

Paraphrased by Sir William Jones (1799)

Behold, where yon blue riv'let glides
    Along the laughing dale;
Light reeds bedeck its verdant sides,
    And frolick in the gale.

So shines our Prince! In bright array
    The Virtues round him wait;
And sweetly smil'd th'auspicious day,
    That rais'd Him o'er our State.

As pliant hands in shapes refin'd
    Rich iv'ry carve and smoothe,
His laws thus mold each ductile mind,
    And every passion soothe.

As gems are taught by patient art
    In sparkling ranks to beam,
With Manners thus he forms the heart,
    And spreads a gen'ral gleam.

What soft, yet awful, dignity!
    What meek, yet manly grace!
What sweetness dances in his eye,
    And blossoms in his face!

So shines our Prince! A sky-born crowd
    Of Virtues round him blaze:
Ne'er shall Oblivion's murky cloud
    Obscure his deathless praise.

Translator's Note:
The prediction of the poet has hitherto been accomplished; but he little imagined,
that his composition would be admired, and his Prince celebrated in a language not
then formed, and by the natives of regions so remote from his own.

iv. Praise of Duke Wu of Wei

Translated by William Jennings (1891)

See in that nook, where bends the K'i,
The green bamboos, how graceful grown!
Ay, and a gifted prince have we,
Polished, — as by the knife and file,
The graving-tool, the smoothing-stone!
What grace, what dignity is there!
What splendor, bruited everywhere!
A gifted prince indeed have we,
And ne'er forgotten shall he be.

See in that nook, where bends the K'i,
The green bamboos, so stout, so fine!
Ay, and a gifted prince have we: —
Rare costly stones his ears adorn,
Gems on his bonnet starlike shine!
What grace, what dignity is there!
What splendor, bruited everywhere!
A gifted prince indeed have we,
And ne'er forgotten shall he be.

See in that nook, where bends the K'i,
The green bamboos, how thick they stand!
Ay, and a gifted prince have we:
Pure as the gold or tin refined,
Sound as the scepter in his hand!
What ease, what freedom in his gait!
Yet see him in his car of state!
In pleasantry and jest expert,
Withal so careful none to hurt!

Commentary:

The praise of Duke Wu of the State of Wei (ruled 811–757 B.C.), his assiduous cultivation of himself; his dignity; his accomplishments. The critics all agree to accept Duke Wu as the subject of this ode. The K'i [Qi] was a famous river in the State of Wei, rising at the hill of Dahao and flowing eastwards from the present district of Lin. It was famous in old times for the luxuriance and quality if its bamboos. The sight of them, so rich and beautiful, suggested to the poet the idea of Duke Wu, with his admirable and attractive qualities. The *Shuowen* says that the Ki fell into the Yellow River, but it now pursues a different course to the sea. (Legge)

58: Meng
To a Man

Translated by Herbert Giles

You seemed a guileless youth enough,
Offering for silk your woven stuff;[9]
But silk was not required by you:
I was the silk you had in view.

With you I crossed the ford, and while
We wandered on for many a mile
I said, "I do not wish delay,
But friends must fix our wedding-day ...
Oh, do not let my words give pain,
But with the autumn come again."

And then I used to watch and wait
To see you passing through the gate;
And sometimes when I watched in vain,
My tears would flow like falling rain;
But when I saw my darling boy,
I laughed and cried aloud for joy.
The fortune-tellers, you declared,
Had all pronounced us duly paired;
"Then bring a carriage," I replied,
"And I'll away to be your bride."

The mulberry-leaf, not yet undone
By autumn chill, shines in the sun.
O tender dove, I would advise,
Beware the fruit that tempts thy eyes![10]
O maiden fair, not yet a spouse,
List lightly not to lovers' vows!
A man may do this wrong, and time
Will fling its shadow o'er his crime;
A woman who has lost her name
Is doomed to everlasting shame.

---

[9] Pieces of stamped linen, used as a circulating medium before the introduction of the
     bank-note.
[10] The dove is very fond of mulberries, and is said to become intoxicated by them.

The mulberry-tree upon the ground
Now sheds its yellow leaves around.
Three years have slipped away from me,
Since first I shared your poverty;
And now again, alas the day!
Back through the ford I take my way.
My heart is still unchanged, but you
Have uttered words now proved untrue;
And you have left me to deplore
A love that can be mine no more.

For three long years I was your wife,
And led in truth a toilsome life;
Early to rise and late to bed,
Each day alike passed o'er my head.
I honestly fulfilled my part;
And you, — well, you have broke my heart.
The truth my brothers will not know,
So all the more their gibes will flow.
I grieve in silence and repine
That such a wretched fate is mine.

Ah, hand in hand to face old age! —
Instead, I turn a bitter page.
Oh for the river-banks of yore;
Oh for the much-loved marshy shore;
The hours of girlhood, with my hair
Ungathered, as we lingered there.
The words we spoke, that seemed so true,
I little thought that I should rue;
I little thought the vows we swore
Would some day bind us two no more.

Commentary:
A woman, who had been seduced into an improper connection, now cast off, relates and bemoans her sad case. Mao refers the piece to the time of Duke Xuan, of dissolute character. He thinks, accordingly, that the piece was directed against the times, and holds up to approval the woman who relates her case in it, as a reformed character. The ode, however, gives no note of the time when it was composed, nor does anything more appear in it beyond what I have expressed in the above summary. The whole piece is addressed to the man who had first led the woman astray and then cast her off. *Meng* [the title and first word of the poem], means "one of the people." The woman intimates by the term that "at first she did not know the man nor anything about him." (Legge)

Themes: markets; meetings; excursions on the heights and beside the rivers; antiphonal lines; the intermediary; hill climbs in autumn; divinatory practices; carriage;

the custom of trousseaux for women; crossing rivers; and the young men's wooing.
(Granet)

59: Zhu-gan
This Rod

Translated by "V. W. X."

A young wife longs for her native village once more.

> As soon could this rod
> Catch my native fish,
> As my homesick heart
> Have its secret wish!
>
> Where the brook meanders,
> Where the river trends,
> When I left these to marry,
> I lost my friends!
>
> The familiar river,
> The well-known brook,
> Where, in laughing girlhood,
> My walks I took!
>
> On that flowing river
> In my little boat,
> Where I, sailing, discovered
> Grief's antidote!

63: You-hu
There's Fox

Translated by Arthur Cooper

> There's fox creeps creeps
> on yon Qi dam:
> heart the grief oh!
> The childe lacks robe.
>
> There's fox creeps creeps
> on yon Qi ford:
> heart the grief oh!
> The childe lacks belt.

There's fox creeps creeps
on yon Qi side:
heart the grief oh!
The childe lacks costume.

66: Jun-zi yu-yi

i. He's to the War

Translated by Ezra Pound

He's to the war
for the duration;
Hens to wall-hole,
beasts to stall,
shall I not remember
him at night-fall?

He's to the war
for the duration,
fowl to their perches,
cattle to byre;
is there food enough;
drink enough
by their camp fire?

ii. Ode (scoticè)

Translated by James Legge

The feelings of a wife on the prolonged absence of her husband on service, and her
longing for his return.

The gudeman's awa, for to fecht wi' the stranger,
   An' when he'll be back, oh! my hert canna tell.
The hens gae to reist, an' the beests to their manger,
   As hameward they wend frae their park on the hill.
      But hoo can I, thus left alane,
      Help thinking o' my man that's gane?

The gudeman's awa, for to fecht wi' the stranger,
   An' lang will it be ere he see his fireside.
The hens gae to reist, an' the beests to their manger,
   As the slantin' sunbeams throu the forest trees glide.
      Heaven kens the lanesome things I think.

Heaven sen' my man his meat an' drink!

67: Jun-zi yang-yang
The Gudeman's Come Hame (*scoticè*)

Translated by James Legge

This poem depicts the husband's satisfaction, and the wife's joy, on his return.

> The gudeman's come hame, an' his face weers a bloom,
>   His organ o' reeds he hads in his left han';
> An' his richt han' ca's me to come till his room: —
>   It's siccan a joy; it's mair nor I can stan'.
>
> The gudeman's come hame, an' he's pleesed I'll engage,
>   His gran' fether screen he hads in his left han';
> An' his richt han' ca's me to come till the stage: —
>   It's siccan a joy; it's mair nor I can stan'.

72: Cai-ge

i. Taedium

Translated by Ezra Pound

> Plucking the vine leaves, hear my song:
> "A day without him is three months long."
>
> Stripping the southernwoods, hear my song:
> "A day without him is three autumns long."
>
> Reaping the tall grass hear my song:
> "A day without him's three years long."

ii. Bean Flower

Translated by Wong Man

> That bean flower O,
> Day out of sight
> As three months O.
>
> That weed flower O,
> Day out of sight
> As three falls O.

That field flower O,
Day out of sight
As three years O.

Commentary:
A lady longs for the society of the object of her affection. So Zhu interprets this little piece; and his view of it is more natural than that of the old interpreters, who held that it indicates the fear of slanderers, entertained by the officers of the royal domain of Zhou. According to Zhu's interpretation a short absence from the loved object seems to be long, and longer the more it is dwelt upon. The lady fancies her lover engaged as the first lines describe, and would fain go and join him in his occupations. (Legge)

A very simple piece on the subjects of harvesting and absence. (Granet)

76: Jiang Zhong-zi
Hep-Cat Chung

Translated by Ezra Pound

Hep-Cat Chung, 'ware my town,
don't break my willows down.
The trees don't matter
but father's tongue, mother's tongue
      Have a heart, Chung,
          it's awful.

Hep-Cat Chung, don't jump my wall
nor strip my mulberry boughs,
The boughs don't matter
But my brothers' clatter!
      Have a heart, Chung,
          it's awful.

Hep-Cat Chung, that is *my* garden wall,
Don't break my sandalwood tree.
The tree don't matter
But the subsequent chatter!
      Have a heart, Chung,
          it's awful.[11]

Commentary:
A lady begs her lover to let her alone, and not excite the suspicions and remarks of her

---

[11] "Banish the songs of Cheng." — K'ung, the Anthologist. K'ung-fu-tsy [Confucius] seems to have regarded the tunes to these verses as a species of crooning or boogie-woogie.

parents and others. Such is the interpretation of this piece given by Zhu Xi; and no one, who draws his conclusions simply from the stanzas themselves, can put any other on it. The Little Preface, however, gives an historical interpretation of it, which is altogether different, and for which something like an argument has been constructed. It must be said, without hesitation, that if this be the correct interpretation, then the piece is a riddle, which only appears the more absurd, when the answer to it is told. (Legge)

81: Zun-da-lu
If Along the Highroad

Translated by Arthur Waley

If along the highroad
I caught hold of your sleeve,
Do not hate me;
Old ways take time to overcome.

If along the highroad
I caught hold of your hand,
Do not be angry with me;
Friendship takes time to overcome.

Commentary:
Old friendship should not be hastily broken off. Zhu hears in it the words of a woman entreating her lover not to cast her off. But the highway is a strange place for a woman to be detaining her lover in, and pleading with him. (Legge)

Themes: quarrels; excursions; forcible persuasion. (Granet)

82: Nü-yue ji-ming
The Cock Is Crawin' (*scoticè*)

Translated by James Legge

This poem presents a pleasant picture of domestic life. A wife sends her husband from her side to his hunting, expresses her affection, and encourages him to cultivate virtuous friendships.

Says oor gudewife, "The cock is crawin'."
Quoth oor gudeman, "The day is dawin'."
"Get up, gudeman, an' take a spy;
See gin the mornin' star be high,
Syne tak a saunter roon' aboot;
There's rowth o' dyukes and geese to shoot.

"Lat flee, and bring them hame to me,
An' sic a dish as ye sall pree.
In comin' times as ower the strings
Your noddin' heed in rapture hings,
Supreme ower care, nor fasht wi' fears,
We'll baith grow auld in worth and years.

"An' when we meet the friends ye like,
I'll gie to each some little fyke: —
The lasses beads, trocks to their brithers,
An' auld-warld fairlies to their mithers.
Some knickknack lovin' hands will fin'
To show the love that dwalls within."

Commentary:
Themes: dawn; separation at dawn (the affianced lovers have passed the night
together); the chase, the communal feast, harmony; presents and love-tokens; conjugal vows. (Granet)

87: Qian-shang
Gird Your Loins

Translated by Arthur Waley

If you tenderly love me,
Gird your loins and wade across the Zhen;
But if you do not love me —
There are plenty of other men,
Of madcaps maddest, oh!

If you tenderly love me,
Gird your loins and wade across the Wei;
But if you do not love me —
There are plenty of other knights,
Of madcaps maddest, oh!

90: Feng-yu
Cold Wind, and the Rain

Translated by Ezra Pound

"As on the Last Day of the Moon"

Cold wind, and the rain,

cock crow, he is come again,
                    my ease.

Shrill wind and the rain
and the cock crows and crows,
I have seen him, shall it suffice
                    as the wind blows?

Wind, rain and the dark
as it were the dark of the moon,
What of the wind, and the cock's never-ending cry;
Together
again
he and I.

91: Zi-jin
The Student's Blue Collar or Lapel

Translated by Ezra Pound

Blue, blue collar, my heart's delight,
I can't come out,
Why shouldn't you write?

Blue, blue sash, heart's misery.
I cannot come out, but you might come to me.

You swish about
between gates of the towered wall,
So far, no wrong.
One day without you
is three months long.

Commentary:
Zheng Xuan (127–200) wrote a sub-commentary on Mao's version of the *Songs*, and his strongly political and moralistic interpretations were accepted with little opposition until the Song dynasty. In the case of this song, granted that students in ancient China may, as Mao asserts, have worn uniforms with blue collars, can one seriously believe that this is a complaint against students who do not go to school but spend their time idly walking the gate towers of the city? This is what Mao says it is, and scholars of later generations who wished to pass the government examinations in the Confucian Classics were no doubt obliged to give sequacious assent, since his was the officially approved interpretation. But privately there must have been many with grave misgivings. It remained for the great Song-dynasty scholar Zhu Xi (1130–1200) to clear away the worst of this nonsense. (Burton Watson, *Early Chinese Literature*, 1962)

A lady mourns the indifference and absence of her lover. I cannot adopt any other interpretation of this piece than the above, which is given by Zhu Xi. The old interpreters find in it a condemnation of the neglect and disorder into which the schools of Zheng had fallen. The attendance at them was become irregular. Some young men pursued their studies, and others played truant; and one of the former class is suposed to be here upbraiding a friend in the second. The imperial editors approve of this view, and say that Zhu Xi himself once held it; but the language of the ode is absurd upon it. (Legge)

93: Chu-qi dong-men
At the Great Gate

Translated by Ezra Pound

At the great gate to the East
Mid crowds
be girls like clouds
who cloud not my thought in the least.

> Gray scarf and a plain silk gown
> I take delight in one alone.

Under the towers toward the East
be fair girls like flowers to test,

> Red bonnet and plain silk gown
> I take delight with one alone.

94: Ye-you man-cao
Mid the Bind-Grass

Translated by Ezra Pound

Mid the bind-grass on the plain
that the dew makes wet as rain
I met by chance my clear-eyed man,
>   then my
>   joy began.

Mid the wild grass dank with dew
lay we the full night thru,
>   that clear-eyed man and I
>   in mutual felicity.

110: Zhi-hu
Young Soldier Thinks of Home

Translated by Rewi Alley (1954)

I climb a barren hill and ponder
over my folk at home, thinking
of my father
          how he will be wondering about me
          saying to everyone he meets,
          "My boy is away at the war
          with little rest by day or night. I hope
          he takes care of himself, and
          is back soon. Can't get him
          out of my mind;"

          then of my mother and of what
          she will be saying —
          "My child is a soldier now —no sleep
          day or night; oh, that he
          would take care and come
          home, not leaving his body
          in such far places;"

then I climb further
and think of my brother

          how he will be explaining
          "My brother is away fighting,
          struggling day and night; he must
          return to us, alive."

Commentary:
A young soldier on service solaces himself with the thought of home. According to the
Preface, the service in which the young man was engaged was service extracted from
the State of Wei by a more powerful State, in which there was no room for patriotism,
no opportunity for getting glory. The sentiment is one of lamentation over the poor
and weak Wei, whose men were torn from it to fight the battles of its oppressors.
(Legge)

113: Shi-shu
Rats

Translated by Ezra Pound

RATS,

stone-head rats lay off our grain,
three years pain,
enough, enough, plus enough again.

More than enough from you, deaf you,
we're about thru and ready to go
where something will grow
untaxed.
Good earth, good sown,
and come into our own.

RATS,
big rats, lay off our wheat,
three years deceit,
and now we're about ready to go
to Lo Kuo, happy, happy land, Lo Kuo, good earth
where we can earn our worth.

RATS,
stone-head rats, spare our new shoots,
three years, no pay.
We're about ready to move away
to some decent border town.
Good earth, good sown,
and make an end to this endless moan.

Commentary:
Against the oppression and extortion of the government of Wei. The piece is purely
metaphorical, the writer, as representative of the people, clearly having the oppressive
officers of the government before him, under the figure of large rats. (Legge)

124: Ge-sheng
The Kudzu Spreads Till It
Darkens the Brier

Translated by Burton Watson

A woman swears to be faithful to her absent lover until the grave.

The kudzu spreads till it darkens the brier,
the bindweed blankets the fields.
My beautiful one — he's not here —
who would I live with, if not alone?

The kudzu spreads till it darkens the thorn tree,
the bindweed blankets the graves.

My beautiful one — he's not here —
who would I sleep with, if not alone?

My pillow of horn gleams brightly,
my brocade coverlet glows,
my beautiful one — he isn't here —
who would I greet the dawn with, if not alone?

Days of summer,
winter nights:
after a hundred years have passed,
I'll join you in your dwelling.

Nights of winter,
summer days:
after a hundred years are over,
I'll join you in your room.

Commentary:
A wife mourns the death of her husband, refusing to be comforted, and will cherish
his memory till her own death. The first two lines of the first stanzas are taken by Mao
and Zhu as allusive: the speaker being led by the sight of the weak plants supported by
the trees, ground, and tombs, to think of her own desolate, unsupported condition.
But we may also take them as narrative, and descriptive of the battle ground, where
her husband had met his death. In the third stanza, the pillow of horn and the
embroidered coverlet had been ornaments of the bridal chamber; and as the widow
thinks of them, her grief becomes more intense. In the last two stanzas, the lady shows
the grand virtue of a Chinese widow, in that she will never marry again. The "dwelling"
and the "room" are to be understood as the grave. (Legge)

143: Yue-chu

i. A Moon Rising

Translated by Arthur Waley (1937)

A moon rising white
Is the beauty of my lovely one.
Ah, the tenderness, the grace!
Heart's pain consumes me.

A moon rising bright
Is the fairness of my lovely one.
Ah, the gentle softness!
Heart's pain wounds me.

A moon rising in splendor

Is the beauty of my lovely one.
Ah, the delicate yielding!
Heart's pain torments me.

ii. Moonrise

Translated by John Cayley (1990)

The moon comes out, both full and bright. Ah
She I'm bound to's-beauty makes me burn, now
It's raveled round the coil of light within, how
It wastes and gnaws my troubled heart. So

The moon comes out, to warn of light. Ah
She I'm bound to's beauty eats my soul, now
It's raveled round the sorrow that we share, how
It cuts and tears my troubled heart. So

The moon comes out, and earth's alight. Ah
She I'm bound to's beauty's made me ash, now
It's raveled in a silken knot of death, how
It fills and stops my troubled heart. So.

Commentary:
A gentleman tells all the excitement of his desire for the possession of a beautiful lady.
There is no difference of opinion as to the character of the piece, only the Preface
moralizes over it, according to its wont, and says that it was directed against the love of
pleasure. (Legge)

145: Ze-bi
By That Swamp's Shore

Translated by Arthur Waley

By that swamp's shore
Grow reeds and lotus.
There is a man so fair —
Oh, how can I cure my wound?
Day and night I can do nothing;
As a flood my tears flow.

By that swamp's shore
Grow reeds and scented herbs.
There is a man so fair —
Well-made, big and strong.

Day and night I can do nothing;
For my heart is full of woe.

By that swamp's shore
Grow reeds and lotus-flowers.
There is a man so fair —
Well-made, big and stern.
Day and night I can do nothing;
Face on pillow I toss and turn.

147: Su-guan

i. The White Cap

Translated by James Legge (1871)

Some one deplores the decay of filial feeling, as seen in the neglect of the mourning
habit. By the "white cap" we are to understand the cap worn by mourners for their
parents at the end of two years from the death. The "white dress (a skirt or lower robe
of plain white silk)" and the "white knee-covers (a sort of leather apron covering the
knee)" were the proper accompaniment of the "white cap." [These, in this interpretation, would have been worn by a "proper" mourner, who would have been "thin and
worn by grief and abstinence."] The second stanza expresses the speaker's love and
admiration of such a mourner.

If I could but see the white cap,
And the earnest mourner worn to leanness! —
My toiled heart is worn with grief!

If I could but see the white dress! —
My heart is wounded with sadness!
I should be inclined to go and live with the wearer!

If I could but see the white knee-covers! —
Sorrow is knotted in my heart!
I should almost feel as of one soul with the wearer!

ii. Plain Cap

Translated by Arthur Waley (1937)

That the mere glimpse of a plain cap
Could harry me with such longing,
Cause pain so dire!

That the mere glimpse of a plain coat
Could stab my heart with grief!

Enough! Take me with you to your home.

That a mere glimpse of plain leggings
Could tie my heart in tangles!
Enough! Let us two be one.

148: Shi-you chang-chu
In the Lowlands

Translated by Arthur Waley

In the lowlands is the goat's-peach;[12]
Very delicate are its boughs.
Oh, soft and tender,
Glad I am that you have no friend.

In the lowlands is the goat's-peach;
Very delicate are its flowers.
Oh, soft and tender,
Glad I am that you have no home.

In the lowlands is the goat's-peach;
Very delicate is its fruit.
Oh, soft and tender,
Glad I am that you have no house.

154: Qi-yue
In the Seventh Month

Translated by Arthur Waley

The piece which follows is not a calendar but a song made out of sayings about "works
and days," about the occupations belonging to different seasons of the year. There is
no attempt to go through these in their actual sequence. "Seventh month," "ninth
month," and so forth, means the seventh and ninth months of the traditional, popular
calendar, which began its year in the spring; whereas "days of the First," "days of the
Second" means, according to the traditional explanation, the days of the first and
second months in the Zhou calendar, which began its year round about Christmas,
that is to say, at the time of the winter solstice. "The Fire ebbs" is explained as meaning
"Scorpio is sinking below the horizon at the moment of its first visibility at dusk." Did

---

[12] The goat's-peach was later identified with the Chinese gooseberry, which now only grows
a long way south of the Yangtze. The same names were applied to the *Actinidia Chinensis*,
which grows in the north and is probably what is meant here.

this happen in northern China round about September during the eighth and
seventh centuries B.C., the probable period of this song? That is a question which I
must leave to astronomers.

> In the seventh month the Fire ebbs;
> In the ninth month I hand out the coats.
> In the days of the First, sharp frosts;
> In the days of the Second, keen winds.
> Without coats, without serge,
> How should they finish the year?
> In the days of the Third they plough;
> In the days of the Fourth out I step
> With my wife and children,
> Bringing hampers to the southern acre
> Where the field-hands come to take good cheer.

> In the seventh month the Fire ebbs;
> In the ninth month I hand out the coats.
> But when the spring days grow warm
> And the oriole sings
> The girls take their deep baskets
> And follow the path under the wall
> To gather the soft mulberry-leaves:
> "The spring days are drawing out;
> They gather the white aster in crowds.
> A girl's heart is sick and sad
> Till with her lord she can go home."

> In the seventh month the Fire ebbs;
> In the eighth month they pluck the rushes,
> In the silk-worm month they gather the
>   mulberry-leaves,
> Take that chopper and bill
> To lop the far boughs and high,
> Pull toward them the tender leaves.
> In the seventh month the shrike cries;
> In the eighth month they twist thread,
> The black thread and the yellow:
> "With my red dye so bright
> I make a robe for my lord."

> In the fourth month the milkwort is in spike,
> In the fifth month the cicada cries.
> In the eighth month the harvest is gathered,

In the tenth month the boughs fall.
In the days of the First we hunt the racoon,
And take those foxes and wild-cats
To make furs for our Lord.
In the days of the Second is the great Meet;
Practice for deeds of war.
The one-year-old[13] we keep;
The three-year-old we offer to our Lord.

In the fifth month the locust moves its leg,
In the sixth month the grasshopper shakes its
        wing,
In the seventh month, out in the wilds;
In the eighth month, in the farm,
In the ninth month, at the door.
In the tenth month the cricket goes under
        my bed.
I stop up every hole to smoke out the rats,
Plugging the windows, burying the doors:
"Come, wife and children,
The change of the year is at hand.
Come and live in this house."

In the sixth month we eat wild plums and
        cherries,
In the seventh month we boil mallows and
        beans.
In the eighth month we dry the dates,
In the tenth month we take the rice
To make with it the spring wine,
So that we may be granted long life.[14]
In the seventh month we eat melons,
In the eighth month we cut the gourds,
In the ninth month we take the seeding hemp,
We gather bitter herbs, we cut the ailanto for firewood,
That our husbandmen may eat.

In the ninth month we make ready the stackyards,
In the tenth month we bring in the harvest,

---

[13] Boar.

[14] Wine increases one's *de* (inner power) and consequently increases the probability of one's prayers being answered. That is why we drink when we wish people good luck.

Millet for wine, millet for cooking, the early
    and the late,
Paddy and hemp, beans and wheat.
Come, my husbandmen,
My harvesting is over,
Go up and begin your work in the house,
In the morning gather thatch-reeds,
In the evening twist rope;
Go quickly on to the roofs.
Soon you will be beginning to sow your
    many grains.

In the days of the Second they cut the ice
    with tingling blows;
In the days of the Third they bring it into
    the cold shed.
In the days of the Fourth very early
They offer lambs and garlic.
In the ninth month are shrewd frosts;
In the tenth month they clear the stackgrounds.
With twin pitchers they hold the village feast,
Killing for it a young lamb.
Up they go into their lord's hall,
Raise the drinking-cup of buffalo-horn:
"Hurray for our lord; may he live for ever and ever!"

ELEGANTIAE

161: Lu-ming
Salt Lick!

Translated by Ezra Pound

"Salt
lick!" deer on waste sing:
grass for the tasting, guests to feasting;
strike lute and blow
pipes to show how
feasts were in Chou,
        drum up that basket-lid now.

"Salt

lick!" deer on waste sing:
sharp grass for tasting, guests to feasting.
In clear sincerity,
here is no snobbery.
This to show how
good wine should flow
            in banquet mid true
            gentlemen.

"Salt
lick!" deer on waste sing,
k'in plants for tasting, guests to feasting;
beat drum and strumm
lute and guitar,
lute and guitar to get
deep joy where wine is set
mid merry din
let the guest in, in, in, let the guest in.

Commentary:
A festal ode, sung at entertainments to the King's ministers, and guests from the
feudal states. The plant in the third stanza [Pound's "k'in plants"], is a marshy plant,
with leaves like the bamboo, a creeper. Cattle generally are fond of it, as well as deer.
Williams [1812–1884, American missionary, diplomat and author, professor of
Chinese at Yale from 1877, author of a *Syllabic Dictionary of the Chinese Language*] says,
"perhaps a kind of salsola." From the deer browsing happily the writer proceeds to the
guests and their entertainment. (Legge)

162: Si-mu
Request for Furlough

Translated by Ezra Pound

Toiling stallions, winding road,
Would I were home, the king's load
is heavy as heart, on Chou Road,

Heavy team ever strains,
They be black with white manes;
would I were home, I am oppresst
by duty that gives a man no rest.

Doves can fly, then rest on oak
but the king's yoke heavy is
and my father in distress.

Weary pigeon can come to tree,
I cannot serve my mother fittingly.
There's no rest in
the king's livery.

By the black manes of my white horse
I yoke these words in remorse with this refrain:
Let me report to my mother again.

167: Cai-wei
We Pick Ferns, We Pick Ferns

Translated by Burton Watson

This poem depicts men on duty guarding the country from the Xianyun tribes of the
north.

We pick ferns, we pick ferns,
for the ferns are sprouting now:
oh to go home, to go home
before the year is over!
No rooms, no houses for us,
all because of the Xianyun,
no time to kneel or sit down,
all because of the Xianyun.

We pick ferns, we pick ferns,
the ferns now are tender:
oh to go home, to go home!
Our hearts are saddened,
our sad hearts smolder and burn.
We are hungry, we are thirsty,
no limit to our border duty,
no way to send home for news.

We pick ferns, we pick ferns,
now the ferns have grown tough.
oh to go home, to go home
in the closing months of the year!
The king's business allows no slacking,
no leisure to kneel or rest.
Our sad hearts are sick to death,
this journey of ours has no return!

What splendor is here?
The splendor of cherry flowers.
What chariot is this?
The chariot of our lord.
The war chariot is yoked,
four stallions sturdy and strong.
How would we dare to stop and rest?
In one month, three engagements!

We yoke those four stallions,
four stallions stalwart and strong,
for our lord to ride behind,
for lesser men to shield.
Four stallions stately,
ivory bow-ends, fish-skin quivers:
could we drop our guard for a day?
The Xianyun are fearfully swift!

Long ago we set out
when willows were rich and green.
Now we come back
through thickly falling snow.
Slow slow our march,
we are thirsty, we are hungry,
our hearts worn with sorrow,
no one knows our woe.

170: Yu-li
Fine Fish to Net

Translated by Ezra Pound

Fine fish to net,
ray, skate;
Milord's wine is
heavy and wet.

Fish to trap,
bream, tench,
Milord has wine
to drink and quench.

Fine fish to trap,
carp and mud-fish,

Milor' has wine
in quantities'h.

Food in plenty
say good food
Plenty of food
all of it good,

This the song each guest agrees on:
Milor's good food all fits the season.

Commentary:

An ode used at district entertainments, celebrating the abundance of everything and
the prosperity of the times. The net in the first stanza was an exceedingly simple
contrivance, made of bent bamboos, by which fish were caught as they passed through
the openings of a dam. That fish of so many kinds should be taken in so inartificial a
contrivance showed how good government produced an abundance of all material
resources. The abundant supply of good spirits was also a proof of the general
prosperity. (Legge)

201: Gu-feng

i. *The Zephyr's Sigh*

Translated by Sir John Francis Davis (1829)

Now scarce is heard the zephyr's sigh
    To breathe along the narrow vale:
Now sudden bursts the storm on high,
    In mingled rush of rain and hail.
— While adverse fortune louring frown'd
    Than our's no tie could closer be;
But lo! when ease and joy were found,
    Spurn'd was I, ingrate — spurn'd by thee.

Now scarce is felt the fanning air
    Along the valley's sloping side;
Now winds arise, and light'nings glare,
    Pours the fell storm its dreadful tide!
— While fears and troubles closely prest,
    By thee my love was gladly sought:
But once again with quiet blest,
    Thou view'st me as a thing of nought!

The faithless calm shall shift again,
    Another gale the bleak hill rend,
And every blade shall wither then,

And every tree before it bend:
— Then shalt thou wail thy lonesome lot,
    Then vainly seek the injur'd man,
Whose virtues thou hadst all forgot,
    And only learn'd his faults to scan.

ii. The Valley Wind

Translated by Arthur Waley (1937)

Zip, zip the valley wind!
Nothing but wind and rain.
In days of peril, in days of dread
It was always "I and you."
Now in time of peace, of happiness,
You have cast me aside.

Zip, zip the valley wind!
Nothing but wind and duststorms.
In days of peril, in days of dread
You put me in your bosom.
Now in time of peace, of happiness
You throw me away like slop-water.

Zip, zip the valley wind
Across the rocky hills.
No grass but is dying,
No tree but is wilting.
You forget my great merits,
Remember only my small faults.

206: Wu-jiang da-ju
Don't Walk Beside the Big Carriage

Translated by Burton Watson

Don't walk beside the big carriage,
you'll only get yourself dusty.
Don't brood on a hundred worries,
you'll only make yourself sick.

Don't walk beside the big carriage,
the dust will blacken and blind you.
Don't brood on a hundred worries,
you'll never reach a brighter land.

Don't walk beside the big carriage,
the dust will swallow you up.
Don't brood on a hundred worries,
you'll only weigh yourself down.

Commentary:
Some officer, overloaded in the King's service, thinks it better to try and dismiss his troubles from his mind. (Legge)

219: Qing-ying
Buzz Buzz, the Blue Flies

Translated by Burton Watson

Buzz buzz, the blue flies,
lighting on the fence:
my joyous and gentle lord,
don't listen to slanderous words!

Buzz buzz, the blue flies,
lighting on the thorn:
slandering men know no limits,
they destroy every state around!

Buzz buzz, the blue flies,
they light on the hazel:
no end to slanderers' doings —
they set the two of us to quarreling!

Commentary:
Against listening to slanderers. From the last line we must infer that the speaker had fallen under the king's suspicion in consequence of being slandered. Two commentators adduce here the *History of Han*, to the effect that the King of Changyi dreamt one night of the Emperor Xiaowu, that he saw a great accumulation of filth left by these blue flies on the stairs of the palace, and consulted one of his officers on the subject, who quoted this ode, and told him that the dream indicated that there were many calumniators about him. (Legge)

GREATER ODES OF THE KINGDOM

237: Mian
The House of Zhou

Translated by James Legge

Legends of the early days. The small beginnings and subsequent growth of the House

of Zhou. Its removal from the principality of Bin under Duke Tanfu, grandfather of
King Wen, and settlement in Zhou, down to the time off King Wen.

In long trains ever increasing grow the gourds.
When our people first sprang,
From the country about the Cu and the Qi rivers,
The ancient duke Tanfu,
Made for them kiln-like huts and caves,
Ere they had yet any houses.

The ancient duke Tanfu
Came in the morning, galloping his horses,
Along the banks of the western rivers,
To the foot of Mount Qi;
And there, he and the lady Jiang
Came, and together looked for a site on which to settle.

The plain of Zhou looked beautiful and rich,
With its violets and sowthistles sweet as dumplings.
There he began with consulting his followers;
There he singed the tortoise-shell, and divined.
The responses were — there to stay, and then;
And they proceeded there to build their houses.

He encouraged the people and settled them;
Here on the left, there on the right.
He divided the ground into larger tracts and small portions;
He dug the ditches; he defined the acres;
From the west to the east,
There was nothing which he did not take in hand.

He called his superintendent of works;
He called his minister of instruction;
And charged them with the building of the houses.
With the line they made everything straight;
They bound the frame-boards tight, so that they should rise regularly.
Uprose the ancestral temple in its solemn grandeur.

Crowds brought the earth in baskets;
They threw it with shouts into the frames;
They beat it with responsive blows;
They pared the walls repeatedly, and they sounded strong.
Five thousand cubits of them arose together,
So that the roll of the great drum did not overpower
The noise of the builders.

They set up the gate of the *enceinte*;
And the gate of the *enceinte* stood high.
They set up the court gate;
And the court gate stood grand.
They reared the great altar to the Spirits of the land,
From which all great movements should proceed.

Thus though he could not prevent the rage of his foes,
He did not let fall his own fame.
The oaks and the *yi* trees were gradually thinned,
And roads for travelling were opened.
The hordes of the Kun disappeared,
Startled and panting.

The chiefs of Yu and Rui were brought to an agreement,
By King Wen's stimulating their natural virtue.
Then, I may say, some came to him, previously not knowing him;
And some, drawn the last by the first;
And some, drawn by his rapid successes;
And some, by his defence of the weak from insult.

Commentary:

The growth of Zhou from its very small beginnings is compared with the spreading of
the tendrils and leaves of the gourd. The poem describes the removal from Bin to the
plain of Zhou, the process of erecting the buildings of the new settlement, especially
the palace of Duke Tanfu and the ancestral altar. It tells of the Duke's trouble with the
wild barbarian hordes (the Kun). Then it tells of King Wen's growing influence over
the surrounding states. (Legge)

242: Ling-tai
He Measured Out His Spirit Tower

Translated by Heng Kuan

King Wen, father of King Wu, the founder of the Zhou dynasty, built near his capital
of Hao (close to modern Xi'an, in Shaanxi province) an observation tower, called the
Spirit Tower, complete wth a park and animals.

He measured out his spirit tower
Measured it and planned it;
All the people rushed to work
And they built it in a day.
Measured it out, saying "No hurry,"
All the people flocked like children.

The King rests in his spirit park
Where doe and stag lie about,
Doe and stag so sleek
And the white birds glisten.
The King stands by his spirit pond
Where fishes leap all around.

On solid cedar H-frames, spiked,
Hang the dented ornaments:
Grand drums and bells all perfectly tuned
To the ceremony of his crescent moat.

Grand drums and bells all perfectly tuned
To the ceremony of his crescent moat:
B'ung, b'ung, lizard-skin drums —
Blind musicians make report of public event.

ODES OF TEMPLE AND ALTAR

276: Chen-gong
King's Serfs

Translated by Wong Man

(Overseer)

Hail you, King's serfs!
Heed you your task,
The King inspects,
Come to reckon.

(King)

Hail you, overseer!
Time of late spring,
Have you more wants?
How the new crops?

(Overseer)

Barley and wheat
Nearing sprouting,
Praise to high God
We reap good years.

(King)

> Tell my people:
> Take spud and hoe —
> Soon shall use scythes.

Commentary:
Instructions given to the officers of husbandry, probably after the sacrifice in spring to God for a good year. (Legge)

277: Yi-xi
Halloa!

Translated by Wong Man

Written in the time of King Cheng, the second King of Zhou (approx. 1115–1079 B.C.), this song shows the kind of mass farming then in existence, employing 10,000 hands, supervised by the King himself.

> Halloa! King Cheng
> Has called you here.
> Prime your farm men
> To sow the grains.
>
> Horse-swift out tools:
> Full thirty *lis*
> Are yours to plough
> Ten thousand paired.

279: Feng-nian
Good Year

Translated by Wong Man

> Good year,
> Much wheat much rice,
> We have high barns,
> Millions suffice.
>
> Make wine, make brew,
> To ancestors
> Honor all rites
> That they bless us.

Commentary:
An ode of thanksgiving for a plentiful year. (Legge)

290: Zai-shan
Weed Grass

Translated by Wong Man

Weed grass weed root,
Spuds clinking true,
Thousands harnessed
Down dale up hill;
King and nobles,
Chiefs and barons,
Weak and strong too.

Eager for food,
Daydream for love,
They dig the earth,
They ply the spades,
Pressing southward
they scatter seeds
Deep into glades.

Quick quick their sprouts,
Comely their shoots,
Green green their seedlings,
Long last their fruits.

Reaping in hosts,
Solid the stores
Piled to great heights.
Make wine make brew,
To ancestors
Honor all rites.

Rice that tastes sweet,
The land's glory;
Wine ambrosian
Ripen old age:
Not thus awhile,
Nor thus a day,
But ever so.

Commentary:
The cultivation of the ground, from the first breaking of it up, till it yields abundant harvests. Available specially for sacrifices and on festive occasions. Whether intended to be used on occasions of thanksgiving, or in spring when praying for a good year,

cannot be determined. It brings before us a series of pleasing pictures of the husbandry of those early times. (Legge)

EIGHT ANCIENT POEMS FROM THE FOUNTAIN OF OLD POEMS

Compiled by the 18th-century anthologist Shen Deqian and translated by James Legge

I have thought it would be interesting to many of my readers to see a good proportion of the ditties, songs and other versified compositions, which have as high an antiquity attributed to them as the poems of the *Book of Songs*. Some of them indeed are referred to a much more remote age — on, to my mind, quite insuffucient evidence.

Song of the Peasants in the Time of Yao

This is the ancient folk song used by Ezra Pound in Canto XLIX, ll. 41–5. *Eds.*

> We rise at sunrise,
> We rest at sunset,
> Dig wells and drink,
> Till our field and eat; —
> What is the strength of the emperor to us?

Prayer at the Winter Thanksgiving

> Clods, return to your place;
> Water, flow back to your ditches;
> Ye insects, appear not;
> Grass and trees, grow only in your marshes.

Yao's Warning

> Be tremblingly fearful;
> Be careful night and day.
> Men trip not on mountains;
> They trip on anthills.

Inscription on a Bathing Vessel

> Than to sink among men,
> It is better to sink in the deep.

He who sinks in the deep
May betake himself to swimming.
For him who sinks among men
There is no salvation.

Inscription on a Staff

Where are you in peril?
In giving way to anger.
Where do you lose the way?
In indulging your lusts.
Where do you forget your friends?
Amid riches and honors.

Inscription on a Robe

Here is the toil of silkworms,
And the labor of women's work.
If, having got the new, you cast away the old,
In the end you will be cold.

A Writing on a Door

Go out with awe;
Come in with fear.

A Writing on an Ink-Stone

Where the stone and the ink meet, there is blackness.
Let not a perverse heart and slanderous words
Stain what is white.

▣▣ Further Reading ▣▣

Allen, Clement F. R., trans. *The Book of Chinese Poetry, Being the Collection of Ballads, Sagas, Hymns, and Other Pieces Known as the Shih Ching or Classic of Poetry*. London: Kegan Paul, Trench, Trubner, 1891.

Alley, Rewi. *Peace Through the Ages: Translations from the Poets of China*. Beijing: Rewi Alley, 1954.

Bynner, Witter. *The Chinese Translations*. New York: Farrar, Straus, & Giroux, 1978.

Cayley, John. "Translations" (unpublished, 1990).

Cooper, Arthur, trans. *Li Po and Tu Fu*. Harmondsworth: Penguin Books, 1973.

Davis, Sir John Francis. *The Poetry of the Chinese: Poeseos Sinicae Commentarii.* London: J. L. Cox, 1829; rev. ed., London: Asher, 1870.

Du Halde, Jean-Baptiste. *Description géographique, historique, chronologique, politique de l'empire de la Chine,* 4 vols. Paris: Lemercier, 1735. Trans. by R. Brookes as *A Description of the Empire of China,* 2 vols. (London: Edward Cave, 1738).

Eitel, Ernst. *China Review* (1873).

Giles, Herbert, trans. *Chinese Poetry in English Verse.* Shanghai: Kelly & Walsh, 1884.

———. *Gems of Chinese Literature: Verse.* London: Quaritch, 1926. (2d rev. ed. of the above.)

Granet, Marcel. *Fêtes et chansons anciennes de la Chine.* Paris: Albin Michel, 1919. Trans. by E. D. Edwards as *Festivals and Songs of Ancient China* (London: Routledge, 1932).

Grosier, Abbé. *Description générale de la Chine.* Paris: Moutard, 1785. Trans. as *A General Description of China* (London: Robinson, 1788).

Hawkes, David. "Translating from the Chinese." *Encounter* (July 1955), 5 (1).

Hightower, J. R., trans. *Han Shih Wai-chuan: Han Ying's Illustrations of the Didactic Application of the Classic of Songs.* Cambridge, Mass.: Harvard University Press, 1952.

Jennings, William, trans. *The Shi King, the Old "Poetry Classic" of the Chinese, a Close Metrical Translation with Annotations.* London: Routledge, 1891.

Jones, Sir William. "On the Second Classical Book of the Chinese." In *Asiatic Researches,* Vol. 1. London: Bengal Asiatic Society, 1799.

Karlgren, Bernhard, trans. *The Book of Odes.* Stockholm: Museum of Far Eastern Antiquities, 1950.

Kenner, Hugh. "Introduction" to *The Translations of Ezra Pound.* Enlarged ed., London: Faber and Faber, 1970.

Lacharme, Alexandre, trans. *Confucii Chi-King Sive Liber Carminum.* Stuttgart & Tübingen: D. G. Cotta, 1830.

Legge, James, trans. *The Chinese Classics, Vol. IV, The She-King, or the Book of Poetry.* Hong Kong: Lane Crawford, 1871.

———. *The She-King: or the Book of Ancient Poetry, Translated in English Verse.* London: Trubner, 1876.

Liu, James J. Y. *Chinese Theories of Literature.* Chicago: University of Chicago Press, 1975.

McNaughton, William. *The Book of Songs.* New York: Twayne, 1971.

Payne, Robert, ed. *The White Pony: An Anthology of Chinese Poetry from the Earliest Times to the Present Day.* New York: John Day, 1947.

Percy, Thomas, ed. *Fragments of Chinese Poetry* (appendix to Vol. 4 of *Hau Kiou Choann or The Pleasing History*). London: Dodsley, 1761.

Pound, Ezra. *Guide to Kulchur.* New York: New Directions, 1938.

———. trans. *The Classic Anthology Defined by Confucius.* Cambridge, Mass.: Harvard University Press, 1954.

Rückert, Friedrich, trans. *Schi-King, Chinesisches Liederbuch, gesammelt von Confucius.* Altona: Hammerich, 1833.

Turner, John, trans. *A Golden Treasury of Chinese Poetry.* Hong Kong: Chinese University Press, 1976.

"V.W.X.," trans. "The Ballads of the Shi-king." *China Review* (1878–80).

Waley, Arthur, trans. *The Book of Songs.* London: Allen & Unwin, 1937.

Wang, C. H. *The Bell and the Drum: Shih Ching as Formulaic Poetry in an Oral Tradition.* Berkeley: University of California Press, 1974.

Watson, Burton, trans. and ed. *The Columbia Book of Chinese Poetry: From Early Times to the Thirteenth Century.* New York: Columbia University Press, 1984.

Wong, Man, trans. *Poems from China.* Hong Kong: Creation Books, 1950.

Xu, Yuanzhong, trans. *Shijing: Book of Poetry.* Changsha: Hunan Press, 1993.

Yang, Gladys, and Yang, Xianyi, trans. *Selections from the "Book of Songs."* (Contains translations first published in *Chinese Literature.*) Beijing: Foreign Languages Press, 1983.

Yip, Wai-lim, trans. and ed. *Chinese Poetry: Major Modes and Genres.* Berkeley: University of California Press, 1976.

Yu, Pauline. *The Reading of Imagery in the Chinese Poetic Tradition.* Princeton: Princeton University Press, 1987.

▣ Editors' Note ▣

In this chapter we trace the path of Western understanding and translation of one of the great Chinese classics over a period of more than three hundred years, from the first inklings of the Portuguese Jesuit Semedo in the mid-seventeenth century, the eighteenth-century Latin of the Jesuit Alexandre de Lacharme (in China 1728–1767; his work was itself based on a Manchu translation), through the painstaking scholarship of the great Victorian Legge (without whose work the later and freer versions would not have been possible), to the multi-disciplinary insights of Marcel Granet and C. H. Wang (himself a distinguished poet, and translator of Yeats, writing in Chinese under the pen-name Yang Mu) and the two complete literary translations of Waley and Pound in this century (both remarkable in their own way). This classic is the "fountainhead" of Chinese poetry and has occupied the attentions of many generations of scholars and translators. The twenty versions of the first Song constitute a miniature anthology. Here we see every possible approach to the problems of translating Chinese poetry.

The mysterious translator "V. W. X." was very much ahead of his time with his bare, striking versions of the *Songs.* These were published in the late 1870s, in the China Coast periodical the *China Review,* and although they attracted a certain amount of (mainly negative) critical attention when they first came out, they have since then been largely forgotten. Exhumed over a hundred years later, they are startlingly modern in their attempt to recreate the folksong quality of the originals.

"Drum."
Seal of the Warring States period

Chapter 4

The Source

Prose of the Ancients:
Early Narrative and Philosophy

The Classics have deep roots and luxuriant branches and foliage. The language is concise, but the content is meaningful; the facts are commonplace, but their metaphorical implications are unlimited. So, although they are ancient, their flavor remains fresh. Later scholars take them up and do not feel that they have become outmoded; scholars in the past long used them and never felt that they were ahead of their time. They may be compared to Mount Tai, which waters all the lands about, or to the Yellow River, which moistens one thousand *li*....

If one's writing is based on the Classics, one's style will be especially distinguished by one of the following six characteristics: deep feeling untainted by artificiality, unmixed purity of form, empirical truth untarnished by falsehood, moral ideas uninvolved in perversity, simple style free from verbosity, and literary beauty unmarred by excess. Master Yang compared the writing of the Classics to the carving of jade into vessels, meaning that literary pattern is innate in the five Classics.

> — Liu Xie (c. 465–c. 520), *The Literary Mind and the Carving of Dragons*, chapter 3, "The Classics"

The deep and ultimate source of literature should be the Classics.... These writers (of later times), after seeing the trembling leaves, fail to discover the roots and, having contemplated the billows of a stream, they do not trace its source. If the wisdom of our forefathers is not proclaimed, there is no way in which the later generations can be helped.

> — Liu Xie, *The Literary Mind and the Carving of Dragons*, chapter 50, "Postscript"

I walk the path of human-heartedness and righteousness and linger at the source — the *Book of Songs* and the *Book of History* — lest I lose the path, lest I be cut off from the source. This I shall have to do until the end of my days.

> — Han Yu(768–824), "Letter to Li Yi" (*translated by Chen Yu-shih*)

The Books which the Ancient Chineses have writ, are exceeding numerous, but the chief are those which are called *Ukim*, that is to say, the five Volumes, and those intituled *Su Xu*, that is to say, the four Books.

> — *The Morals of Confucius: A Chinese Philosopher*, 1691

In this Language (of Books) there are many Degrees of Superiority, before they can arrive to the Majestick and Sublime Beauty of the Books called *King*.... Each thought is generally expressed in four or in six Characters. One finds nothing to shock the nicest Ear, and the Variety of the Accents, artfully managed, affords a sound altogether soft and harmonious.

> — Du Halde, *A Description of the Empire of China*, 1738

NARRATIVE

꧁꧁꧁꧁꧁꧁꧁꧁꧁꧁꧁꧁꧁꧁꧁꧁꧁꧁꧁꧁꧁꧁꧁꧁꧁꧁꧁꧁꧁꧁꧁꧁

THE BOOK OF HISTORY
Two Selections

The first and chiefest of these five Volumes is called *Xu Kin* [the *Book of History*]. It is not necessary very amply to discourse of the Antiquity of this Work; 'tis sufficient to say, that in perusing it we find, that the Author wrote a long time before Moses.... This whole Volume, not to multiply words, is only an Historical Relation, and Collection of Moral Maxims, of Harangues spoken by Princes, of Sentences uttered by the Mouths of Kings and particular Persons, and of Precepts and Councils given to Princes, wherein so much Prudence, Policy, Wisdom and Religion is set forth, that they might be given to all Christian Princes.

— *The Morals of Confucius: A Chinese Philosopher*, 1691[1]

A Dialogue Upon the Maxims of the Ancient Kings, or the Counsels of Kau Yau

Translated from the French of Du Halde (1738)

Du Halde himself identifies the French translation used in his compendium as being by the Jesuit Joseph-Henri de Prémare (1666–1736). The English version published by Edward Cave in two volumes (1738–1741) was done by John Green (alias Bradock Mead, fl. 1730–1753, an Irish cartographer) and William Guthrie (a Scottish historian, 1708–1770). The young Samuel Johnson, who himself was writing and translating for Cave's *Gentleman's Magazine* at this time, may have had a hand in revising the translation. He commented much later (1780) that "Green said of Guthrie, that he knew no English, and Guthrie of Green, that he knew no French." (Boswell's *Life of Johnson*)

Kau Yau (Gao Yao) was minister of crime under the Sage King Shun, and subsequently chief minister under his successor Yu (legendary founder of the Xia dynasty). He was esteemed for the wisdom of his judgements. James Legge summarizes the opening of this dialogue as follows (*Chinese Classics* 3, 68-70): "It enunciates the principle that in government the great thing is for the prince to pursue the course of virtue, which will be seen in his knowledge of men, and giving repose to the people. It illustrates the knowing of men, the virtues by which they may be known, and the importance of the emperor's personal example."

The (no doubt disobedient) official Huantou, the rebellious prince of the Miao people, and Gong Gong, the minister held responsible for the great floods, were three of the "four criminals" of the reign of the Sage King Yao, whom Shun had punished.

— Editors

Make me, replies the Emperor, like the Person you speak of; learn me to

---

[1] For more on the *Book of History*, see chapter 2. *Eds.*

follow your Lessons so well, that my Example may be as an impetuous, yet kindly, Wind, which carries along with it all Hearts; so that real Happiness may be diffused through all the Parts of my Empire.[2]

When a King is solidly virtuous, says *Kau yau* [Gao Yao]; he thus enters into all the good Counsels that are given him, and always acts in Concert with the wise Ministers he has chosen.

Nothing is so true, says the Emperor; but explain yourself a little more circumstantially.

A good King, replies *Kau yau*, has no Passion so predominant as to advance more and more in the Study and Practice of Wisdom, so that he puts no Bounds to so useful an Exercise. By this fine Example, he first instructs all his royal Family; this is afterwards communicated to all his Subjects, and in the End, spreads among the most distant People. Of so great Importance it is for a King to be Virtuous!

Yu applauds, and respectfully receives, these Words, which are so full of Wisdom.

All may be reduced to two Points, says *Kau yau*, To know the Characters of Men, and to render the People happy.

Is that all? (interrupts *Yu*) Our good King, how perfect soever he is, will find a great deal of Difficulty in this. To know the Characters of People thoroughly, is never to err in the Choice of those we employ. To render a People happy is to load them with Favours, and entirely to gain their Love. When a Prince has so great Qualities as these, what Dread needs he have of such a wretch as *When tew* [Huantou]? What difficulty will he find to subdue such a Rebel as *Myau* [Miao]? And what harm can a Sycophant and a Hypocrite like Kong kong [the Minister of Works, Gong Gong] do him?

Nevertheless, says *Kau yau*, you may add, that there are Nine Virtues, which a Prince ought well to know, in order to make them familiar to him. It is not enough that he has a general Notion, that such a Man has such and such a Virtue: He must moreover know what Proofs that Man has given of his really possessing it. You ask what these Nine Virtues are?

I require,[3] continued *Kau yau*, a Greatness of Soul, neither haughty nor insensible; a noble Indifference, but without Inactivity; a charming

---

[2] It is agreed that the *Shu King* [the *Book of History*] has suffered many Alterations; that the half of it is lost: and that what escaped the Flames and the Worms has been patch'd up in the best manner they could.

[3] It is in such passages as these, that we see the sublime Brevity of Style in these antient Books. Eighteen Letters convey a clear Idea of these nine Virtues, with the Quality each Virtue ought to have to prevent its degenerating into Vice; and all this in a Manner so lively and so fine that it must suffer by a Translation into any European language.

Goodness, but without Indolence or Coarseness; a Genius delicate, but industrious and laborious; a Humanity and Politeness attended with Resolution and Courage; an Uprightness of Mind, which knows how to temper Severity with Mercy; an Understanding that comprehends the greatest, yet neglects not the smallest Matters; a Mind firm, but neither stubborn nor fierce. In short, a Magnanimity which yields only to Justice: These are the Nine Virtues upon which a Prince ought to regulate himself, that he may distinguish the different Characters of Men. For this is the greatest good Fortune a King can wish for, that he may reward the Virtuous.

The Metal-Bound Coffer

Translated by James Legge (1865)

King Wu [founder of the Zhou dynasty] is very ill, and his death seems imminent. His brother, the duke of Zhou, apprehensive of the disasters which such an event would occasion to their infant dynasty, conceives the idea of dying in his stead, and prays to "the three kings," their immediate progenitors, that he might be taken and King Wu left. Having done so, and divined that he was heard, he deposits the prayer in the metal-bound coffer, where important archives were kept. The king gets well, and the duke is also spared; but five years after, Wu really dies, and is succeeded by his son, a boy only thirteen years old. Rumors are spread abroad that the duke has designs upon the throne, and he withdraws for a time from the court. At length in the third year of the young king, Heaven interposes. He has occasion to open the metal-bound coffer, and the prayer of the duke is found. His devotion to his brother and the interest of his family is brought to light. The boy monarch weeps because of the unjust suspicions he had harbored, and welcomes the duke back to court, amid unmistakable demonstrations of the approval of Heaven.

The whole narrative is a very pleasing episode in the history of the times, and is more interesting to the foreign reader than most other portions of the *Book of History*. It divides itself naturally into two chapters: the first, ending with the depositing the prayer in the coffer; and the second, detailing how it was brought to light, and the duke cleared by means of it from the suspicions which had been cherished of him.

— James Legge, *The Shoo King or Book of Historical Documents*,
vol. 3 of *The Chinese Classics*, 1865

The date of "The Metal-Bound Coffer" is uncertain; the narrative portions, in particular, may well be of quite late date. The typically primitive and naive belief, expressed in the prayer of the duke of Zhou, that one can hoodwink the spirits, and the miraculous reversal of the wind, however, suggest that the legend, if not the wording of the piece, date from rather early Zhou times. If the piece is in fact earlier in composition than the *Zuo Commentary*, it represents the oldest example we have of the historical narrative style in Chinese literature, with its typical dramatic form and large admixture of direct speech.

— Burton Watson, *Early Chinese Literature*, 1962

Two years after the conquest of Shang, the king fell ill and was quite disconsolate. The two other great dukes said, "Let us reverently consult the tortoise shell about the king."

But the duke of Zhou said, "You must not so distress our former kings."

He then took the business on himself and reared three altars of earth on the same cleared space. Having made another altar on the south of these, and facing the north, he took there his own position. Having put a round symbol of jade, *bi*, on each of the three altars and holding in his hands the long symbol of his own rank, *gui*, he addressed the kings Tai, Ji and Wen.

The Grand Historiographer had written on tablets his prayer, which was to this effect: "Your great descendant is suffering from a severe and violent disease. If you three kings in heaven have the charge of watching over him, Heaven's great son, let me, Dan, be a substitute for his person. I was lovingly obedient to my father; I am possessed of many abilities and arts which fit me to serve spiritual beings. Your great descendant, on the other hand, has not so many abilities and arts as I, and is not so capable of serving spiritual beings. And moreover he was appointed in the hall of God to extend his aid all over the kingdom, so that he might establish your descendants in this lower earth. The people of the four quarters all stand in reverent awe of him. Oh! do not let that precious Heaven-conferred appointment fall to the ground, and all the long line of our former kings will also have one in whom they can ever rest at our sacrifices. I will now seek your decision from the great tortoise shell. If you grant me my request, I will take these symbols and this mace, and return and wait for your orders. If you do not grant it, I will put them by."

The duke then divined with the three tortoise shells and all were favorable. He opened with a key the place where the oracular responses were kept, looked at them, and they also were favorable. He said, "According to the form of the prognostic the king will take no injury. I, the Little Child, have got the renewal of his appointment from the three kings, by whom a long futurity has been consulted for. I have now to wait for the issue. They can provide for our One Man."

When the duke returned, he placed the tablets of the prayer in a metal-bound coffer and next day the king got better.

Afterward, upon the death of King Wu, the duke's elder brother, he of Guan, and his younger brothers, spread a baseless report through the kingdom to the effect that the duke would do no good to the king's young son. On this the duke said to the two other great dukes, "If I do not take the law to these men, I shall not be able to make my report to the former kings."

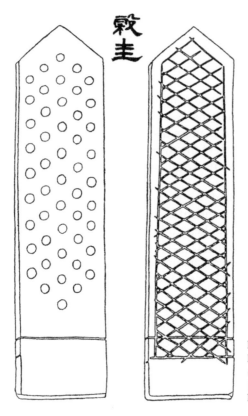

Figure 16. Jade *gui* tablet. (Source: Berthold Laufer, *Jade: A Study in Chinese Archaeology and Religion* [Chicago: Field Museum of Natural History, 1912])

He resided accordingly in the east for two years, when the criminals were taken and brought to justice. Afterward, he made a poem to present to the king and called it "The Owl." The king on his part did not dare to blame the duke.

In the autumn, when the grain was abundant and ripe but before it was reaped, Heaven sent a great storm of thunder and lightning, along with wind, by which the grain was broken down and great trees torn up. The people were greatly terrified. The king and great officers, all in their caps of state, proceeded to open the metal-bound coffer and examine the writings in it, where they found the words of the duke when he took on himself the business of being a substitute for King Wu. The two great dukes and the king asked the historiographer and all the other officers acquainted with the transaction about the thing, and they replied, "It was really thus. But ah! the duke charged us that we should not presume to speak about it."

The king held the writing in his hand and wept, saying, "We need not now go on reverently to divine. Formerly the duke was thus earnest for the royal house, but I, being a child, did not know it. Now Heaven has moved its terrors to display his virtue. That I, the Little Child, now go with my new views and feelings to meet him, is what the rules of propriety of our kingdom require."

The king then went out to the borders to meet the duke, when Heaven sent down rain and, by virtue of a contrary wind, the grain all rose up. The two great dukes gave orders to the people to take up the trees that had fallen and replace them. The year then turned out very fruitful.

THE SPRING AND AUTUMN ANNALS

Book 3, Reign of Duke Zhuang (692–661 B.C.), Years 1–6

Translated and annotated by James Legge (1872)

To the fourth Volume Confucius has given the Title of *Chun Cieu* [*Chunqiu*]; words which signifie the *Spring* and *Autumn*. He composed it in his Old Age. He discourses like an Historian of the Expeditions of Divers Princes; of their Virtues and Vices; of the Fatigues they underwent, with the Recompences they received.... The title is an Emblematic Title, because that States flourish when their Princes are endowed with Virtue and Wisdom; which is represented by the *Spring*; and that on the contrary they fall like the Leaves, and are utterly destroyed, when their Princes are dispirited, or are wicked, which is represented by the *Autumn*.

— *The Morals of Confucius: A Chinese Philosopher*, 1691

The *Spring and Autumn Annals* is a chronological record of the chief events in the State of Lu between the years 722 and 481 B.C. and is generally regarded as the work of Confucius, whose native State was Lu. The entries are of the briefest, and comprise notices of incursions, victories, defeats, deaths, murders, treaties, and natural phenomena....

The *Spring and Autumn* owes its name to the old custom of prefixing to each entry the year, month, day, and season when the event recorded took place; spring, as a commentator explains, including summer, and autumn, winter. It was the work which Confucius singled out as that one by which men would know and commend him, and Mencius considered it quite as important an achievement as the draining of the empire by the Great Yu: "Confucius completed the *Spring and Autumn*, and rebellious ministers and bad sons were struck with terror." Consequently, just as in the case of the *Book of Songs*, native wits set to work to read into the bald text all manner of hidden meanings, each entry being supposed to contain approval or condemnation, their efforts resulting in what is now known as the praise-and-blame theory. The critics of the Han dynasty even went so far as to declare the very title elliptical for "praise life-giving like spring, and blame life-withering like autumn."

— Herbert Giles, *History of Chinese Literature*, 1901

The mass of Chinese scholars and writers, for nearly 2,000 years, have not scrupled to accept the history of the Spring and Autumn period given by Zuo (in his *Commentary on the Spring and Autumn Annals*) as in the main correct, maintaining at the same time their allegiance to Confucius as "the teacher of all ages," the one man at whose feet the whole world should sit, accepting every paragraph from his *stylus* as a divine oracle. The thing is to me inexplicable. There have been many times when I have mused over the subject in writing the pages of this volume, and felt that China was hardly less strange a country to me than Lilliput or Laputa would be.

The scholars of China are ready, even forward, to admit that Confucius in the *Spring and Autumn* often conceals the truth about things. The *Gongyang Commentary* says: "The *Spring and Autumn* conceals the truth on behalf of the high in rank, out of regard for kinship, and on behalf of men of worth." The *Zuo Commentary* says that it was the rule for the historiographers to conceal any wickedness which affected the character of the State. But this "concealing" covers all the ground occupied by our three English words — ignoring, concealing, misrepresenting....

Well, we have examined the model summary of history from the *stylus* of the sage, and it testifies to three characteristics of his mind which it is painful to have thus distinctly to point out. First, he had no reverence for truth in history — I may say no reverence for truth, without any modification.... Second, he shrank from looking the truth fairly in the face.... Third, he had more sympathy with power than with weakness.

> — James Legge, *The Ch'un Ts'ew [Spring and Autumn Annals]*
> *with the Tso Chuen [Zuo Commentary]*, vol. 5 of *The Chinese Classics*, 1872

First Year

1. It was the duke's first year, the spring, the king's first month.

There is here the same incompleteness of the text as in Book I; and no doubt for the same reason, that the usual ceremonies at the commencement of the rule of a new marquis were not observed. The young marquis' father had been basely murdered; he took his place; but with as little observation as possible.

2. In the third month, the late duke's wife retired to Qi.

She probably felt her position in Lu exceedingly unpleasant. Guilty of incest with her brother, and of complicity in the murder of her husband, she could not be looked kindly on by her son or the people of Lu.

3. In summer, the earl of Shan escorted the king's daughter to Lu.
4. In autumn, a reception house was built for the king's daughter outside the city wall.

The case was a hard one, as Zhuang was still in mourning for his father. To be managing the marriage of the king's daughter to the man who had murdered his own father was a greater difficulty still. The case was met, in part at least, by not receiving the lady in the palace or the ancestral temple, but building a sort of hall or reception-house for her outside the city.

5. In winter, in the tenth month, or *yi-hai*, Lin, marquis of Chen, died.

6. The king sent Shu of Yong to Lu to confer on duke Huan certain symbols of his favor.

To confer these symbols, as here, on a dead man, seems very strange; and on a man who had been stained with crime, is stranger still. Whatever the gifts were, they would be treasures in Lu as royal testimonials to the excellence of the late duke Huan.

7. The king's daughter went to her house in Qi.
8. An army of Qi carried away the inhabitants of Ping, Jin, and Wu, cities of Ji.

Qi here takes an important step in carrying out its cherished purpose of extinguishing the State of Ji.

Second Year

1. In the duke's second year, in spring, in the king's second month, there was the burial of duke Zhuang of Zhen.
2. In summer, duke Huan's son Qingfu led a force and invaded Yuyuqiu.

Qingfu was the name of a half-brother of duke Zhuang, older than he, but the son of a concubine.... From the foreign, barbarous, tri-syllabic aspect of the place-name, we may infer that the State was that of some wild tribe, not far from Lu.

3. In autumn, in the seventh month, the king's daughter, married to the marquis of Qi, died.

The *Lieguo zhi* [*History of the States*] says the lady pined away and died broken-hearted, on finding what sort of a husband she was mated to.

4. In winter, in the twelfth month, the late duke's wife, the lady Jiang, had a meeting with the marquis of Qi in Zhuo.

The *Zuo Commentary* says plainly that the object of the meeting was a repetition of the former crime.

5. On *yi-you*, Ping, duke of Song, died.

Third Year

1. In the duke's third year, in spring, in the king's first month, Ni joined an army of Qi in invading Wei.
2. In summer, in the fourth month, there was the burial of duke Zhuang of Song.
3. In the fifth month, there was the burial of King Huan.
4. In autumn, the third brother of the marquis of Ji entered with the city of Hui under the protection of Qi.
5. In winter the duke halted in Huai.

Fourth Year

1. In the duke's fourth year, in spring, in the king's second month, duke Huan's wife, the lady Jiang, feasted the marquis of Qi at Zhuqiu.

It appears from this that the duke's mother had returned to Lu, after her meeting with her brother in the Second Year. Her now getting him to come to Lu, and openly feasting him, shows how they were becoming more and more shameless.

2. In the third month, duke Yin's eldest daughter, who had been married to the marquis of Ji, died.
3. In summer, the marquis of Qi, the marquis of Qin, and the earl of Zheng met at Qi.
4. The marquis of Ji made a grand leaving of his state.

The poor marquis was unable to cope with his relentless enemy, and rather than sacrifice the lives of the people in a vain struggle, he gave the state over to his brother, who had already put himself under the jurisdiction of Qi.... the *Gongyang Commentary*, indeed, argues that the style of the paragraph, concealing the fact that Qi now *extinguished* the state of Ji, was designed to gloss over the wickedness of the marquis of Qi in the act, because he thereby revenged the wrong done in 893 B.C. to one of his ancestors, who was boiled to death at the court of Zhou, having been slandered by the then lord of Ji! The marquis of Ji, therefore, was only discharging a duty of revenge in destroying the House of Ji! Into such vagaries do the critics fall, who will find "praise or censure" in the turn of every sentence in this Classic.

5. In the sixth month, on *yi-zhou*, the marquis of Qi interred duke Yin's eldest daughter, the late wife of the marquis of Ji.

The leaving his wife unburied shows to what straits the prince of Ji had been reduced, when he went away.

6. It was autumn, the seventh month.
7. In winter, the duke and an officer of Qi hunted in Zhuo.

Du Yu (222–281) says that the nature of the whole transaction — the duke's crossing his own borders and hunting in another State with one of inferior rank — is sufficiently apparent.

Fifth Year

1. It was the duke's fifth year, the spring, the king's first month.
2. In summer, duke Huan's wife, the lady Jiang, went to the army of Qi.
3. In autumn, Lilai of Ni paid a visit to our court.
4. In winter, the duke joined an officer of Qi, an officer of Song, an officer of Chen, and an officer of Cai, and invaded Wei.

Sixth Year

1. In the duke's sixth year, in spring, in the king's first month, Zitu, an officer of the king, endeavored to relieve the capital of Wei.

2. In summer, in the sixth month, Su, marquis of Wei, entered the capital of Wei.

3. In autumn, the duke arrived from the invasion of Wei.

4. There were the *ming*-insects.

This is the record of a plague. The *ming* is described as a grub that eats the heart of the growing grain. It develops into the locust.

5. In winter, an officer of Qi came to present to Lu the spoils of Wei.

Figure 17. A *ding* bronze vessel of the Zhou dynasty. (Source: C. A. S. Williams, *Encyclopedia of Chinese Symbolism and Art Motives* [Shanghai: Kelly & Walsh, 1932])

THE ZUO COMMENTARY
Selected Episodes

Translated and annotated by Burton Watson (1989)

The *Zuo Commentary* takes its name from its putative author, Zuo Qiuming or Zuoqiu Ming, who has sometimes been identified with a man of the same name praised by Confucius in the *Analects*. In fact, however, nothing is known of who he was, when he lived, or what connection he had with the work that bears his name.

Most scholars today agree that the *Zuo* is a genuine work of Zhou times, compiled probably in the third century B.C., though it appears to contain additions made toward the end of the Former Han....

We do not know what the original form of the work was. At present its accounts of events in the various feudal states are broken up and arranged chronologically to fit with entries in the bare chronicle of events in the state of Lu, the *Spring and Autumn Annals*. Some entries in the *Annals* have no corresponding passages of explanation in the *Zuo*, however; some passages in the *Zuo* have no corresponding entry in the *Annals*; and sometimes the accounts in the two texts are in conflict. It would seem, therefore, that the two works were originally quite separate, though it may have been an interest in the events mentioned in the *Annals* itself which inspired the compilation of the *Zuo*....

The *Zuo* begins in 722 B.C., the first year of the *Annals*, but carries its narrative down to 468 B.C., thirteen years after the *Annals* stops. Undoubtedly the narrative contains a large admixture of legend and romance. The lengthy, formal speeches of its numerous rulers and statesmen, in particular, are in most cases probably no more than literary fictions. Yet it undoubtedly includes a great deal of sound fact and information of real value on the life and history of the period. If we had only the *Annals* to go by, we could construct no more than the barest outline of the history of the age. With the *Zuo*, however, we have a portrait which, while perhaps somewhat idealized and confined almost wholly to the life of the aristocracy, is remarkably vivid and detailed. Regardless of what light it can be made to shed as a commentary on the *Annals*, therefore, it is a work of primary importance for the study of Zhou history and society. At the same time, because of its vivid, powerful style and wealth of detail, it ranks with the *Zhuangzi* as one of the greatest prose works of ancient China.

— Burton Watson, *Early Chinese Literature*, 1962

A Wife's Dilemma

The rulers and high ministers of the Spring and Autumn period, whose intrigues and predatory strikes kept the society of the time in such perpetual turbulence, may be said to have brought upon themselves the sufferings that ensued. But often their wives and daughters as well, though in most cases innocent of any part in the planning of such exploits, were fearfully embroiled in the consequences. Sometimes, as in the episode below, they were confronted with agonizing conflicts of loyalty.

Zhai Zhong monopolized power, much to the distress of the ruler of Zheng. The latter ordered Zhai Zhong's son-in-law, Yong Jiu, to kill Zhai Zhong, inviting him to a banquet in the suburbs of the capital in order to do so.

Yong Jiu's wife was aware of the plot (against her father) and said to her mother, "Which is dearer, a father or a husband?"

Her mother replied, "All men are potential husbands, but you have only one father. How could there be any comparison?"

In the end she informed her father, saying, "Yong is deliberately foregoing his own house and holding the banquet in the suburbs. I have told you because I am suspicious of the arrangement."

Zhai Zhong killed Yong Jiu and threw his corpse into the Zhou family pond. The ruler of Zheng loaded the corpse on his carriage and fled from the capital, saying, "He told even his wife about the plot — no wonder he died!"

— Duke Huan fifteenth year, 697 B.C.

Chong'er: The Years of Wandering

After the downfall and suicide of Prince Shensheng of Jin, Shensheng's younger half brother Chong'er or Double Ears fled to his fief in Pu and then from his native state altogether. The following narrative focuses on the history of Prince Chong'er during his years of wandering abroad, where he acquires an assortment of wives. Like many heroes in romance, he is accompanied by a small band of faithful attendants and is subjected to various ordeals.

When the troubles accompanying the death of Prince Shensheng occurred, the men of Jin attacked the Jin ducal son Chong'er at his walled city of Pu. The men of Pu wanted to fight, but Chong'er refused permission. "Through the kind command of my father the ruler I have received a stipend to insure my living, and in this way have gathered these men around me. If, having acquired followers, I should use them to resist my father, I could be guilty of no greater crime! I had far better flee!"

He thereupon fled to the territory of the Di barbarians.[4] He was accompanied by Hu Yan, Zhao Cui, Dian Xie, Wei Wuzi, and the minister of works Jizi.

The Di people attacked the Qianggaoru and seized Shu Wei and Ji Wei, the two daughters of their leader.[5] They handed them over to Prince Chong'er. Chong'er took the younger, Ji Wei, for his wife, and she bore him two sons, Bochou and Shuliu. He gave Shu Wei to his follower Zhao Cui to be his wife, and she bore him a son named Zhao Dun.

When Chong'er was about to leave the territory of the Di and journey to the state of Qi, he said to his wife Ji Wei, "Wait for me twenty-five years. If I don't return by that time, then remarry."

Ji Wei replied, "I am twenty-five now. If I am to wait that long before remarrying, I'll be laid in my grave! With your permission, I'll just wait."

Chong'er remained among the Di for twelve years before moving on.

As he was passing through the state of Wei, Duke Wen of Wei failed to treat him with courtesy. When Chong'er was leaving the state by way of Wulu, he begged one of the peasants to give him something to eat. The peasant gave him a clod of earth.

The prince, enraged, was about to whip the man, but his attendant Hu Yan said, "Heaven presents this to you!"[6] The prince thereupon bowed his head, accepted the clod of earth, and placed it in his carriage.

---

[4] Non-Chinese tribes who lived along the northern border of the Chinese states at this time.

[5] According to commentators, the Qianggaoru were a branch of the Di people.

[6] The clod of earth was an omen that the prince in time would become the ruler of a state. During these wanderings, Chong'er is being tested to see if he has the qualities of mind and character needed to make him a worthy ruler. At the same time, the rulers of the various states through which he passes are being tested to see how wisely they respond to his presence.

When he reached the state of Qi, Duke Huan of Qi gave him one of his daughters for a wife, along with twenty carriages and eighty horses to pull them.

The prince was content to stay in Qi, but his followers, convinced it was wrong to do so, gathered under a mulberry tree to plot how they could bring about his departure. A serving woman was up in the tree gathering mulberry leaves, and she reported what she overheard to the prince's wife, the daughter of Duke Huan of Qi. The wife had the woman killed.

His wife said to the prince, "I know your ambition is to roam to the four directions. Someone overheard this, but I have had her killed."

The prince said, "I have no such ambition!"

His wife replied, "Just go! Too much concern for comfort and the ties of affection will undo your fame!"

When the prince declined to leave, his wife plotted with Hu Yan and together they contrived to get him drunk and send him off in a carriage. When he sobered up, he chased after Hu Yan with a halberd.

When the prince visited the state of Cao, Duke Gong of Cao, having heard that the prince's ribs were all grown together, wanted to catch a glimpse of him naked.[7] When the prince took a bath, therefore, he peered in through the curtain.

The wife of Xi Fuji, a minister of Cao, said to her husband, "I have observed the followers of the prince of Jin, and all are worthy to serve as chief minister of a state. If they continue to assist him, he is bound in time to return to his own state. Once he returns to his state, he will be able to do as he pleases with the other feudal lords, and when he can do as he pleases, he will surely punish those who failed to show him the proper courtesy. And Cao will be the first to feel it! Why don't you hurry and do something to show you regard him differently from the others!"

Xi Fuji accordingly sent the prince a supper heaped on a platter, and placed a jade disk in with the food. The prince accepted the supper but returned the jade.

When the prince passed through Song, Duke Xiang of Song sent him off with a gift of eighty horses.

When the reached Zheng, Duke Wen of Zheng, like some of the other rulers, failed to treat him courteously. Shu Zhan remonstrated with the

---

[7] The *Jinyu* chapters of the *Conversations from the States* contain an account of the career of Chong'er that roughly parallels this, though the two often differ considerably. Neither the *Zuo Commentary* nor the *Conversations*, however, gives any details on this physical peculiarity, *pianxie* or "linked ribs," which is said to be a sign of great strength. It is of course one of the marks of a hero that he should have some unusual physical feature.

duke, saying, "I have heard that when heaven is opening up the way for a man, others cannot touch him! There are three proofs that this ducal son of Jin is such a man. Heaven, it would seem, intends to make him a ruler. You would do well to treat him with courtesy!

"Ordinarily, when a man and woman of the same surname marry, their offspring do not prosper. Yet this prince of Jin, though born of a mother of the Ji surname, has been able to come this far.[8] This is the first proof. He has had the misfortune to wander abroad, and yet heaven has not in the meantime brought peace to the state of Jin, no doubt because it intends to open the way for him there. This is the second proof. He has three gentlemen with him capable of ranking above others, yet they consent to be his followers. This is the third proof.

"Jin and Zheng are of equal rank. If even a younger son of the Jin ruling house were passing through, you should surely treat him courteously, to say nothing of one for whom heaven is opening the way!"

The duke ignored this advice.

When the prince visited Chu, the ruler of Chu[9] entertained him at a banquet. "If you return to the state of Jin, Prince, what will you give me as a reward for this?" he asked.

The prince replied, "Men and women, jewels, silks — all these you have, my lord. Feathers, furs, tusks and hides — these your own land produces, and what is more than enough for you overflows and reaches as far as the state of Jin. What could I give you as a reward?"

The ruler of Chu said, "Be that as it may, how will you reward me?"

The prince replied, "If, due to your kind assistance, I am able to return to Jin, and if Jin and Chu should take up arms and meet on the plain of battle, then for your sake I will withdraw my forces for a distance of three days' march. If, having done that, you fail to command your troops to withdraw, however, then I will seize my whip and bow in my left hand, take my arrow case and bow case in my right, and I will go round and round with you!"

Ziyu Dechen of Chu begged to be allowed to kill the prince. But the ruler of Chu said, "This prince of Jin is broad-visioned and disciplined,

---

[8] Chong'er's mother, though a daughter of the Greater Rong people, bore the same surname, Ji, as the ruling family of Jin. Chinese custom was generally very strict in prohibiting marriage between persons of the same surname.

[9] King Cheng (r. 671–626). Though in theory only the Zhou ruler was entitled to employ the title *wang* or king, the rulers of the southern state of Chu, which in some ways considered itself outside the Chinese cultural sphere, had for several centuries been calling themselves kings.

refined and courteous, and his followers are respectful and generous, loyal and of great strength and ability. The present ruler of Jin is without allies; those inside and outside the state alike hate him. I have heard it said that the family of the Ji surname, the descendants of Tangshu, will be the last to wane in power. This must be because of this prince of Jin. When heaven is about to raise a man up, who can put him down? To oppose heaven can only lead to grave consequences!"

So in the end the Chu ruler sent off the prince to the state of Qin.

When the prince arrived in Qin, the ruler of Qin, Duke Mu, assigned five of his daughters to wait on him, among them the wife of Yu.[10] She waited on him with a washbasin while he washed his hands. When he had finished, he flicked the water off his hands and spattered her.

The daughter of the Qin ruler, angered at this, said, "Qin and Jin are equals — why do you treat me so rudely!"

The prince, alarmed, removed his upper garment and bowed in the humble posture of a prisoner.

Another day the duke of Qin invited the prince to a banquet. Hu Yan said to the prince, "When it comes to polite accomplishments, I am no match for Zhao Cui. I beg you to let Zhao Cui accompany you to the banquet."

At the banquet the prince recited the poem "River Water."[11]

The duke responded with the poem "Sixth Month."[12]

Zhao Cui said, "Chong'er gratefully accepts the gift (of this poem)." The prince thereupon bowed his head to the ground.

The duke of Qin descended a step and indicated he was unworthy of such obeisance.

Zhao Cui said, "My lord, you have referred to Chong'er as one capable of 'assisting the Son of Heaven.'[13] How would he dare fail to make obeisance?"

— Duke Xi twenty-third year, 637 B.C.

---

[10] The son of Chong'er's younger brother, Yiwu, the ruler of Jin. He had been a hostage in Qin but in 638 escaped and returned to Jin.

[11] No such poem is found in the present text of the *Book of Songs*. Du Yu says it describes how the waters of the rivers all flow into the sea. The prince was implying that in like manner the feudal lords all pay homage to the ruler of Qin.

[12] *Book of Songs* 177, a poem that praises the military leader Jifu for assisting King Xuan of Zhou to win victory over the barbarian tribes. The duke is comparing Chong'er to the military leader Jifu.

[13] Zhao Cui is quoting from the poem "Sixth Month." One of course needed a thorough understanding of the *Book of Songs* in order to know how to respond to such implied compliments, which is why Hu Yan urged the prince to take Zhao Cui with him to the banquet.

The Death of Duke Jing of Jin

Duke Jing of Jin, a grandson of the illustrious Chong'er or Duke Wen of Jin, headed
the state from 599 until his death in 581. During this time Jin won a noteworthy victory
over the state of Qi. But, as in the reigns of Duke Jing's two predecessors, awesome
power continued to be wielded by members of the Zhao family, relatives of Chong'er's
faithful follower Zhao Cui, and in fact Duke Jing came to power because one of the
family, Zhao Chuan, murdered the previous ruler, Duke Ling, in 600. The most
memorable thing about Duke Jing, an otherwise somewhat colorless figure, is perhaps
his macabre death, which is described in the passage below.

Duke Jing dreamed that he saw a huge ogre with disheveled hair that
hung down to the ground, beating his chest and leaping around, saying,
"You killed my grandsons, an evil deed!¹⁴ God has promised me
revenge!" The ogre broke down the main gate of the palace, and then
the door to the inner apartments, and came in. The duke fled in terror
to his chamber, but the ogre broke down that door as well. At that
moment the duke awoke and sent for the shaman of Mulberry Field. The
shaman described the duke's dream just as it had been.

"What will become of me?" asked the duke.

"You will not live to eat the new grain!" replied the shaman.

The duke fell gravely ill and sent for a doctor from the state of Qin.
The ruler of Qin dispatched a physician named Huan to treat the duke.
Before the physician arrived, the duke dreamed that his illness appeared
to him in the form of two little boys. One boy said, "He is a skilled
physician and I am afraid he will do us injury. Where can we flee?" The
other replied, "If we reside in the region above the diaphragm and below
the heart, what can he do to us?"

When the physician arrived, he told the duke, "I can do nothing for
your illness. It is situated above the diaphragm and below the heart,
where treatment cannot affect it, acupuncture will not penetrate, and
medicine will not reach. There is nothing I can do."

"You are a good doctor," said the duke and, entertaining him with all
courtesy, he sent him back home.

---

¹⁴ In 583 Duke Jing put to death the high officials Zhao Tong and his brother Zhao Kuo on
charges that they were plotting rebellion. The charges, which were probably slanderous,
were brought by a woman who had had an adulterous affair with their youngest brother,
Zhao Yingqi, who had been banished from the state. All three brothers were sons of
Zhao Cui by Duke Wen's daughter. At this point, the Zhao family was very nearly wiped
out. According to the traditional interpretation of this passage, as represented in Du Yu's
commentary, the ogre was the spirit of one of the Zhao family ancestors who was seeking
revenge for the death of the Zhao brothers, though it should be noted that the *Zuo*
narrative itself does not state this.

In the sixth month, the day *bing-wu*, the duke decided he wanted to taste the new grain and ordered the steward of his private domain to present some. When his butler had prepared it, he summoned the shaman of Mulberry Field and, pointing out the error of his prophecy, had him executed. Then he started to eat the grain, but his stomach swelled up and, hurrying to the privy, he fell down the hole and died.

One of the duke's servants had dreamt in the early morning hours that he was carrying the duke on his back up to heaven, and consequently he was delegated that day to bear the duke's body on his back out of the privy, after which he was executed so that he could attend the duke in death.

— Duke Cheng tenth year, 581 B.C.

The Death of Duke Zhuang of Zhu

The following brief death scene centers upon Duke Zhuang, the ruler of a small state called Zhu in the Shandong Peninsula near the state of Lu. Elsewhere in the *Zuo Commentary*, one of the characters observes that "a man will meet his end doing what he enjoys," and indeed in the *Zuo* the particular manner of death is taken as an important key to the individual's personality, and vice versa. Duke Zhuang of Zhu succeeded his father, Duke Dao, as ruler of Zhu in 541, and by the time of his demise was probably well along in years — old enough, that is, to have had better control of his temper.

Second month, the day *xin-mao*. The ruler of Zhu was on the terrace at the top of the palace gate, looking down into his courtyard. The gatekeeper at the time was dousing the courtyard with water from a pitcher. The ruler, spying him from afar, was greatly annoyed. When he questioned the gatekeeper, the latter said, "Yi Yegu pissed in the court there!"

The ruler ordered Yi Yegu arrested. When Yi Yegu could not be found, the ruler, more furious than ever, flung himself down on his bed with such violence that he fell off into the ashes of the brazier and burned to death.

Before dying, he gave instructions that five chariots be buried with him and five men put to death to accompany his spirit. Duke Zhuang was a very excitable and fastidious man, and therefore he came to such an end.

— Duke Ding third year, 507 B.C.

Attitudes Toward the Supernatural

The following collection of brief episodes, culled from different sections of the *Zuo Commentary* and arranged in chronological order, will give some idea of the typical attitude displayed in the *Zuo* toward questions relating to portents, the service of the spirits, and other supernatural concerns. In reading these passages, it is well to keep in mind the pronouncement of Confucius recorded in *Analects* VI, 22: "To treat the spirits and gods with reverence but keep one's distance from them may be called wise."

The Battle of the Snakes

The first excerpt deals with a strange battle of snakes in the capital of the state of Zheng. At the time of the incident, Duke Li (r. 700–697; 680–673), the ruler of Zheng, had been forced to flee the state and was residing abroad. In 680 his efforts to regain control of the state and return to his capital were finally successful. The battle of the snakes that had taken place six years previously was interpreted as an omen of this event.

Earlier, the snakes living within the city and those from outside had engaged in battle in the middle of the southern gate to the capital of Zheng. The snakes living within the city died. Six years later, Duke Li of Zheng returned to the capital.

When Duke Zhuang of Lu heard of this, he questioned his minister Shen Xu about it, saying, "Are there really such things as portents?"

Shen Xu replied, "When people have something they are deeply distressed about, their vital energy flames up and takes such shapes. Portents arise because of people. If people have no dissensions, they will not arise of themselves. When men abandon their constant ways, then portents arise. That is why these particular portents came about."

— Duke Zhuang fourteenth year, 680 B.C.

Human Sacrifice

The next two items concern the practice of human sacrifice. Archeological excavation at Shang dynasty sites has revealed that human sacrifices were carried out by the Shang people on the occasion of royal burials or the consecration of buildings or city walls, and presumably on other occasions as well. In most cases the victims were probably slaves or prisoners of war. References in literary sources dealing with the succeeding Zhou period indicate that the practice was continued in Zhou times, at least sporadically, though it is vehemently condemned by thinkers of the period.

In the summer the duke of Song ordered Duke Wen of Zhu to use the ruler of Zeng as a sacrifice at the shrine of Cisui. He hoped in this way to win over the Yi barbarians of the east.[15]

---

[15] The Song ruler is Duke Xiang (r. 650–637). On the ruler of Zeng, see note 17 below. The shrine was on the Sui River in present day Henan; the deity worshipped there was apparently revered by the Yi people of the east.

The marshal Ziyu of Song said, "In ancient times the six domestic animals were not used interchangeably.[16] For a minor affair one does not use a large sacrifice. And how would one ever dare use a human being? Sacrifices and prayers are carried out for the sake of human beings. The people act as hosts to the gods. If one uses a human being as a sacrifice, what god will ever accept it?

"Duke Huan of Qi ensured the preservation of three states that would otherwise have perished and in that way won over the other feudal lords, but even then men who were concerned about righteousness claimed that he was lacking in virtue. Now the ruler of Song holds one meeting of the feudal lords and treats the rulers of two feudal states with brutality.[17] And in addition he wants to use one of them in sacrifices to some unknown and disreputable spirit being![18] He hopes in this way to become a hegemon among the feudal rulers, but that will be hard, will it not? He will be lucky if he dies a natural death!"

— Duke Xi nineteenth year, 641 B.C.

In the summer there was a great drought. Duke Xi of Lu wanted to burn the shaman Wang alive.[19]

Zang Wenzhong said, "That won't remedy the drought! Repair your inner and outer city walls. Eat simply, reduce expenses, pay heed to agricultural matters, encourage people to share. These are what you should tend to. What can shaman Wang do? If heaven wants him killed, it shouldn't have brought him into existence in the first place. And if he can really cause a drought, then burning him alive will only make it worse!"

The duke followed this advice. The year was one of dearth, but the people suffered no harm.

— Duke Xi twenty-first year, 639 B.C.

---

[16] The six domestic animals, which were used for sacrifices, are the horse, ox, sheep, pig, dog, and fowl.

[17] The ruler of Song held a meeting of the feudal lords in the third month of this year, at which time he seized the ruler of Teng. In the sixth month he seized the ruler of Zeng. Teng and Zeng were tiny states in the area east of Song.

[18] The word translated here as "disreputable," *yin*, also means "excessive" or "obscene," and is often employed in early texts to stigmatize sacrifices or other religious activities of which the Chinese disapproved.

[19] Presumably because the shaman's prayers had failed to produce rain or because he was thought to be in some way responsible for the drought. Some commentators believe that the shaman indicated here was a woman.

Destiny

The following brief narrative concerns the ruler of Zhu, a small state in Shandong adjoining Lu, and the concept of *ming*, fate or destiny, which may refer to either one's mission in life or one's allotted life span. The discussion plays on these two meanings of the word.

Duke Wen of Zhu divined by the tortoise shell to determine if he should move his capital to the city of Yi. The historian who conducted the divination replied, "The move will benefit the people but not their ruler."

The ruler of Zhu said, "If it benefits the people it benefits me. Heaven gave birth to the people and set up a ruler in order to benefit them. If the people enjoy benefit, I am bound to share in it."

Those around the ruler said, "If by taking warning from the divination you can prolong your destiny, why not do so?"

The ruler replied, "My destiny lies in nourishing the people. Whether death comes to me early or late is merely a matter of time. If the people will benefit thereby, then nothing could be more auspicious than to move the capital."

In the end he moved the capital to Yi. In the fifth month, Duke Wen of Zhu died.

The gentleman remarks: he understood the meaning of destiny.

— Duke Wen thirteenth year, 614 B.C.

The Speaking Stone

In the episode that follows, an event of seemingly prodigious nature is reported to Duke Ping of Jin. When the duke questions his wise adviser Shi Kuang or Music Master Kuang, the latter adroitly uses the opportunity to deliver a reprimand. The narrative concludes with remarks by another sage of Jin, Yangshe Shuxiang.

Eighth year, spring. A stone spoke in Weiyu in Jin. Duke Ping of Jin questioned Shi Kuang, saying, "How can a stone speak?"

Shi Kuang replied, "A stone cannot speak. But perhaps something took possession of it. If not, then the people who reported it must have made a mistake. Nevertheless, I have heard it said that if enterprises are not undertaken at the proper time, resentment and grumbling will arise among the people. And then even things that do not speak will do so.

"Now our halls and palaces are lofty and lavish, and the people's strength is impaired and exhausted. Resentment and grumbling continually arise, for the people cannot go on living as human beings. It is hardly surprising that a stone should speak!"

At this time the ruler of Jin was engaged in building the palace at Siqi. Yangshe Shuxiang of Jin remarked, "Shi Kuang's words are those of a gentleman. The words of a gentleman are trustworthy and capable of proof. Therefore resentment never comes near him. The words of a petty man are irresponsible and lacking in proof. Therefore resentment and blame fall on him. This is what the *Songs* means when it says:

> Pitiful is he who cannot speak!
> His words have barely left his tongue
> when his body encounters distress.
> Lucky is he who can speak!
> His skillful words are like a current
> bearing his body to a place of rest.[20]

"When the Siqi palace is completed, the other feudal lords will surely turn against Jin, and our ruler will suffer blame. This gentleman, Shi Kuang, understands this."

— Duke Zhao eighth year, 534 B.C.

Fighting Dragons

There was a great flood in Zheng. Dragons fought with one another in the deeps of the Wei River outside the Shi Gate of the Zheng capital.

The people of the state asked permission to perform sacrifices to them. But Zichan refused, saying, "When we fight, the dragons do not watch us. When the dragons fight, why should we watch them? We might pray for their removal, but the river is after all their home. If we ask nothing of the dragons, the dragons will ask nothing of us."

This ended the matter.

— Duke Zhao nineteenth year, 523 B.C.

Omens

King Zhao of Chu was temporarily driven from his capital by the Wu invaders in 506–505 B.C. He was eventually able to return to his state and resume rule. Some years later, in 489, the Wu forces invaded the small state of Chen on Chu's northern border. Chen had for generations been an ally of Chu and King Zhao was bound by oath to defend it. Though by this time he was in poor health, he chose to be faithful to his oath and died, presumably of illness, as he was launching an attack on the Wu invaders. Immediately after describing his death, the *Zuo* records the following two incidents concerning omens that were thought to pertain to the king's destiny.

This year there was a cloud like a flock of red birds that pressed in on either side of the sun and flew in the sky for three days. King Zhao of Chu

---

[20] *Book of Songs* 194. I have translated the lines in a way that seems to fit the context here.

sent an envoy to consult the grand historian of the Zhou court concerning its meaning. The grand historian replied, "It concerns the king's own person. But if he will perform a propitiatory sacrifice, the ill effects can be shifted to the prime minister or the marshals of the state."

King Zhao said, "If an illness that threatens the heart and bowels of the nation should be shifted to the legs and arms, what good would that do?[21] If I have not committed any grave error, would heaven cut short my life prematurely? And if I have committed a fault, I must accept punishment. How can I shift it off on others?" So in the end he refused to perform a propitiatory sacrifice.

Some years earlier, when King Zhao was ill, divination was made by the tortoise shell and the answer given: "The Yellow River is exercising a malign influence."

The king, however, declined to perform sacrifices to the Yellow River. When his officials begged him to carry out such sacrifices in the suburbs of the capital, he replied, "Under all three dynasties of antiquity, with regard to sacrifices it has been ordained that one shall not sacrifice to mountains or rivers beyond the borders of one's own domain. The rivers that Chu sacrifices to are the Yangtze, the Han, the Ju, and the Zhang. Whatever good or ill fortune comes to us comes from these alone. Though I may be a person of no virtue, I have done nothing to offend the Yellow River!" In the end he declined to perform the sacrifice.

Confucius said: King Zhao of Chu understood the Great Way. No wonder he did not lose his kingdom.

— Duke Ai sixth year, 489 B.C.

INTRIGUES OF THE WARRING STATES
Selected Anecdotes

Translated by J. I. Crump (1979)

The *Spring and Autumn Annals*, and the period to which it lends its name, ended in 481 B.C. It has been estimated that at the beginning of the Spring and Autumn period, China was divided into over a hundred feudal states and principalities. By the end of the period, the number had been reduced to about forty, the smaller and weaker states having been conquered and absorbed by their more powerful neighbors. This process continued until in 403 B.C., when the old state of Jin officially split into three parts, there were only seven important states left. The period from 403 until the

---

[21] In Chinese rhetoric the ruler represents the heart or mind of the state and the chief ministers are the legs and arms.

unification of the empire under Qin Shihuangdi, the first emperor of the Qin dynasty, a process which was completed in 221 B.C., is known as the Warring States period and gives its name to this work.

Actually some of the material in the *Intrigues* deals with events as early as 475 B.C., and it thus covers, though in a sketchy way, the entire period from the end of the *Zuo Commentary* to the unification of the empire. It is, however, by no means a year by year account of the period, but rather a collection of anecdotes arranged in more or less chronological order in sections devoted to twelve states: the Zhou court, the seven "Warring States" — Qin, Qi, Chu, Zhao, Wei, Han, and Yan — and a few smaller ones that perished early.

The *Intrigues* contains a certain amount of valuable historical information, and it was used as early as the Han dynasty as a source for the history of the period, there being no other comparable work on the history of the period extant. For this reason Chinese scholars have often classified it as a work of history. But at other times they have treated it as a philosophical work, and this is the more realistic view.

The *Zuo Commentary*, while dealing with historical or semihistorical persons and events, is, so far as we can judge, less interested in presenting an objective account of the past than in displaying the lessons which the past has to teach. It is a work on ritual and ethics cast in historical form. In the case of the *Intrigues*, the connection with anything that we today could call history becomes even more tenuous. If the *Zuo Commentary* is a handbook on morality illustrated by historical cause and effect, the *Intrigues*, while making use of the same "examples from history" form, is a handbook on rhetoric and persuasive speaking.

We do not know when, where, or by whom the *Intrigues* was written or compiled, though it probably dates from the early part of the second century B.C.

— Burton Watson, *Early Chinese Literature*, 1962

The Handsome Man

Zou Ji was tall and fair of face and figure. He put on his court robes and cap and looked in the mirror.

"Am I more handsome than Mr. Tardy of Northwall?" he asked his wife.

"You are much more so," replied his wife. "How can Mr. Tardy even be compared with you?"

Now, Mr. Tardy was a man known in Qi for his beauty, and Zou Ji was not content, so he asked his concubine:

"Am I more handsome than Mr. Tardy?"

"How can there be any comparison?" she replied.

Next morning when guests, not members of his family, came and he sat with them and talked, he asked them:

"Who is the more handsome, Mr. Tardy or I?"

"Mr. Tardy is not as handsome as you are, sir," they replied.

The day after that Mr. Tardy himself came. Zou Ji examined him closely and decided he was not as handsome as Mr. Tardy. Then he looked in the mirror at himself and decided he was much less well favored than was Mr. Tardy. When he went to bed that night he thought about it:

"My wife thinks me handsome because she is close to me, my concubine because she fears me, and my guests because they want something of me."

He then went to the court, had audience with King Wei and said:

"Your servant knows he is really not as handsome as Mr. Tardy. My wife is close to me, my concubine fears me, and my guests want something of me, so they all say I am more handsome than he. Now in the thousand square *li* of our country and in its one hundred and twenty cities there is no woman of the king nor attendant who is not close to him. In the court there is no minister who does not fear him, and within the borders of the land there is no one who does not seek something of the king. If one looks at it this way, the king has been monstrously hoodwinked!"

"It is so," said the king and he sent down an order:

"To all ministers, officers and citizens who will criticize the king's faults to his face will go the highest reward; those who will remonstrate with the king in writing will be given the next highest reward, and to those who overhear criticism of the king and convey it to his ears will go the least reward."

As soon as the order had been given, ministers came in with remonstrations; the doorway to the chamber looked like a marketplace. In a few months there were occasional petitioners, and after a year none who spoke to the king had petitions to present.

When Yan, Zhao, Han and Wei heard of this they all came to court at Qi. This is what is meant by "winning a battle from the throne room."

— Book of Qi

The Treasury Report

Lord Jingguo said to the king of Qi, "It is absolutely necessary that you listen to your five officials' treasury report each day and frequently inspect the treasure itself."

"It shall be done," said the king, but when he had done it once he was wearied with the task and gave it over to Lord Jingguo.

— Book of Qi

The Tiger and the Fox

"I hear that the North fears Zhao Xixu," said King Xuan to his ministers. "What say you to this?"

None of them replied, except Jiang Yi, who said, "The tiger hunts all the animals of the forest and devours them, but once when he caught a fox, the fox said, 'You dare not eat me. The Lord of Heaven ordained me chief among beasts; if you now kill me you will be disobeying the will of Heaven. If you doubt it, follow behind me through the forest and watch the animals flee when they see me.' The tiger did indeed doubt the fox and therefore followed him. Animals saw them and fled, but the tiger did not know that the animals ran because they feared him. He thought they were afraid of the fox.

"Now your majesty's country is five thousand *li* square and in it are a million first-class troops, all of whom are under Zhao Xixu. Therefore when the North fears Xixu, in reality it fears your majesty's arms, just as the animals of the forest feared the tiger."

— Book of Chu

Yurang's Revenge

The grandson of Bi Yang of Jin, one Bi Yurang, had once been in the service of Fan and Zhonghang, but being discontented had left to join the Hegemon of Jin, Earl Zhi. The latter favored him greatly.

When Earl Zhi was killed and the Three Jin divided his lands, Viscount Xiang, ruler of Zhao, hating the Hegemon more than all the rest, had his skull made into a drinking cup.

Yurang fled to the mountains and there cried out: "Alas, the true warrior requites the lord who knew his worth by dying for him, just as a woman makes herself beautiful for the man who delights in her. Let me, then, avenge the name of the Hegemon!"

He changed his name and mutilated himself to be taken as a convict. Having got entrance to the palace by pretending to be a plasterer, he hid in the privy to murder Viscount Xiang. When Viscount Xiang entered the privy he was suspicious of the plasterer and had him held while he was questioned. It was in truth Yurang, who had sharpened his trowel to a knife-edge and sworn to avenge the Hegemon.

His attendants would have killed him, but Viscount Xiang intervened: "He is a warrior of honor," said Viscount Xiang. "I will henceforth simply be careful to avoid him. The Hegemon is dead and his family extirpated, yet here is his officer doing his utmost to avenge him. Truly a worthy of the realm!" He released Yurang.

After this Yurang rubbed lacquer into his skin until it ulcerated like that of a leper. He destroyed his hair and eyebrows, scarred his face and went forth as a beggar. He went to his wife who did not recognize him but said: "How can this man whose face and form are not those of my husband yet have a voice that is the same as his?" After that he swallowed ashes till his voice became only a croak.

His friends chided him: "Your way is most difficult and will be bootless. We must admit to your honor, but not to your intelligence. If one of your abilities were to serve Viscount Xiang and serve him well, it would not be long before you were advanced and in his favor, and being there you could do what you want to do. This would be most easily done and certain of success."

Yurang laughed at them and replied: "And so I would abuse him who uses me now for him who used me first; betray a new lord for the sake of a former lord. Nothing could more confuse the principle of righteousness between lord and servant! In all I have done I have tried to make clear this principle; I have not tried to do what is easily done. To exchange pledges with a lord and serve him while also planning to assassinate him is fealty with two hearts. What I now do may be most difficult, but it will remain to shame those men in generations to come who would practice fealty with two hearts."

A little later, when Viscount Xiang had need to travel, Yurang hid himself beneath a bridge over which the ruler must pass. Viscount Xiang's horse shied as they reached the bridge and Viscount Xiang knew that Yurang must be there. He sent his retainers to look and it was indeed Yurang.

Then Viscount Xiang held a reckoning face to face with Yurang. "Did you not once serve Fan and Zhonghang?" he asked. "Earl Zhi the Hegemon, destroyed Fan and Zhonghang, but you, far from seeking revenge for them, indeed made pledge to serve Earl Zhi. The Hegemon is now dead. Why do you strive so mightily to avenge him?"

"When I served Fan and Zhonghang they treated me like a common man. When they were killed I treated their revenge as a common man would. When I served the Hegemon he treated me as a hero, and I treat his revenge as a hero should."

Viscount Xiang wept. "Alas, Yurang, what you have already done for the Hegemon was enough to make your name. I pardoned you once, and that too was enough. You must have known, Yurang, that I could not spare you again."

He ordered his men to surround Yurang, who then said: "I have heard that a true ruler does not hide the righteousness of a man, and that a faithful man is not chary of his life if he can gain honor. You, sir, have already graciously granted me my life, and all men speak of your virtue because of it. For this deed I today do willingly submit to punishment. Would your grace but give me his cloak that I may strike it, I should die without regret. I do but ask, not hope, that I may show my kidney!"

Viscount Xiang granted him his honor and sent an attendant to him with the cloak. Yurang drew his sword and leaped, shouting as he struck the cloak, "In this way alone can I avenge Earl Zhi."

Then he fell on his sword and died; and on the day he died the warriors in Zhao all wept.

— Book of Zhao

PHILOSOPHY

೧೧

We have here [in the translation into English of Chinese philosophical concepts]
indeed what may very probably be the most complex type of event yet produced in the
evolution of the cosmos.

— I. A. Richards, "Towards a Theory of Translating,"
in Wright, ed., *Studies in Chinese Thought*, 1953

The translator of a complex text is a juggler with a dozen balls to keep in simultaneous
flight, and some of them are always bouncing on the floor.

— A. C. Graham, *Chuang-tzu: The Inner Chapters*, 1981

THE BOOK OF CHANGES

The Third Volume is called *Ye Kim* [*Book of Changes*]. In this Volume, which is the
Ancientest, if it may be called a Volume, nothing but Obscurity and Darkness is
observed. *Fohi* [Fu Xi] had no sooner founded his Empire, than he gave Instructions
to the Chinese; but the use of Characters and Writing being unknown, this Prince ...
thought at last upon making a Table, composed of some little Lines which it is not
necessary to describe.... Five hundred Years after appeared Confucius, who en-
deavoured to untie this *Gordian* Knot. He explain'd, according to his Understanding,
the little Lines of the Founder, with the Interpretations that had been made before
him, and refers all to the Nature of Beings and Elements; to the Manners and
Discipline of Men.

— *The Morals of Confucius: A Chinese Philosopher*, 1691

Ce n'étoit pas proprement un livre, ni quelque chose d'approchant; c'étoit une
énigme très obscure, et plus difficile cent fois à expliquer que celle du sphinx.

[It was not properly speaking a book, or anything approaching a book; it was a
most obscure enigma, a hundred times more difficult to explain than that of the
sphinx.]

— Claude Visdelou, "Notice du livre Chinois nommé
Y-King [*Book of Changes*]," 1728

The *I King* [*Book of Changes*] is purely Symbolical, being a series of Images of this
Visible World, expressive of the properties of Creatures, and the Matter of which all
Beings are formed.... Fohi [Fu Xi], who was the Inventor of this ... formed to himself
a particular method of Hieroglyphicks, which have no relation to Words, but are
immediate Images of Things and Thoughts, or at least Symbols arbitrary ... In short,
his Design was to point out by sensible Signs, the Principles of all Beings, in the same
Manner as the Lines and Notes of music do the Tone and alteration of the Voice ... To
apply to the Study of other Books and neglect that of the *I King* is to seek after the
Stream and neglect the Fountain.

— Du Halde, *A Description of the Empire of China*, 1738

The *Yeking*, or the book of Changes, believed to have been written by Fo, the Hermes
of the East, and consisting of right lines variously disposed, is hardly intelligible to the

most learned Mandarins; and Cun Fu Tsu [Confucius] himself, who was prevented by
death from accomplishing his design of elucidating it, was dissatisfied with all the
interpretations of the earliest commentators.

— Sir William Jones, *Asiatic Researches*, 1799

The *Book of Changes* preserves an ancient system of divination which is based upon the
sixty-four possible combinations of a broken line (the so-called yin line) and an
unbroken line (yang line) in six places. In the course of transmission, this divination
manual acquired numerous layers of textual explanation and commentary, eventually
becoming a compendium of the Chinese philosophy of transformation. Since the text
is a storehouse of image and symbol from which Chinese literati frequently drew, a
knowledge of its basic terminology is necessary to the understanding of many later
literary references and allusions. Plainly the text as we have it today is not the product
of a single time but consists of materials produced over almost a millenium. According
to the traditional "four-sage" theory of authorship, the hexagrams (the symbols which
form the basic building blocks of the divination system) were fashioned by King Wen
while he was imprisoned by the Shang (c. 1140 B.C.). These hexagrams were constructed by doubling the eight trigrams which had been invented long before by the
mythical Emperor Fu Xi (twenty-fourth century B.C.). The next of the venerable four
sages, the Duke of Zhou (d. 1104 B.C.), supposedly added the earliest textual layer
consisting of the hexagram judgment texts and the line texts. Confucius, who was very
fond of the *Book of Changes*, added a series of commentaries known as the "Ten Wings."
Although all of these attributions of authorship are questionable, the "four-sage"
theory recognizes that the text today is the product of a long period of accretion.

— Stephen Durrant, *Indiana Companion*, 1986

Y-KING: Antiquissimus Sinarum Liber [The Book of Changes: The Most Ancient Book of the Chinese]

The First Hexagram: *Kien [Qian]*

*Latin version by The Jesuit Fathers Jean-Baptiste Régis (1664–1738), Joseph-
Anne-Marie de Moyriac de Mailla (1669–1748), and Pierre Vincent de Tartre
(1669–1724)*

The translation of Régis and his Jesuit coadjutors (first published by Mohl in 1834) is
indeed capable of improvement; but their work as a whole, and especially the
prolegomena, dissertations, and notes, supply a mass of correct and valuable information. They had nearly succeeded in unraveling the confusion and solving the enigma
of the *Changes*.

Régis's coadjutors in the work were the Fathers Joseph de Mailla, who turned the
Chinese into Latin word for word, and compared the result with the Manchu version
of the *Changes*; and Pierre de Tartre, whose principal business was to supply the
historical illustrations. Régis himself revised all their work and enlarged it, adding his
own dissertations and notes. [Régis worked on the translation from 1707. His cor-
rected manuscript is dated 1736.]

— James Legge, Introduction to *The Texts of Confucianism*,
part 2, *The Yi King*, 1882

De Explicatione Textuum, Libri Y-King, Caput Primum

Kien: Coelum

Epigraphe, principis Ouen-Ouang
Magnum, penetrans, conveniens, solidum.

Ephiphonema Primum, principis Tcheou-Kong
In primum nonum.
Draco est absconditus.
Interpretatio: Sit vir tam fortis sagaxque quam Draco; si detinetur fit inutilis.

Ephiphonema Secundum, principis Tcheou-Kong
In secundum nonum.
Draco exivit. Est in campis. Oportet convenire magnum virum.
Interpretatio: Vir tam fortis sagaxque quam Draco esse vulgo dicitur, si tandem aliquando e coeno emergat, liberque in lucem campumque prodeat, tunc vero ita occultas hactenus virtutes exerit, ut dignus sit quem caeteri sequatur (etiam necdum suprema assecutum).

Ephiphonema Tertium, principis Tcheou-Kong
In tertium nonum.
Sapiens quotidie sibi invigilans, singulis serotinis maxime timet — est quod timeat, sed nulla est culpa.

Ephiphonema quartum, principis Tcheou-Kong
In quartum nonum.
Videtur assurgere. Est in profundo. Nulla est culpa.

Epiphonema Quintum, principis Tcheou-Kong
In quintum nonum.
Draco volans est in coelo. Oportet convenire magnum virum.

Epiphonema Sextum, principis Tcheou-Kong
In sextum nonum.
Draco transgressus est, est quod poeniteat.

Epiphonema Ultimum
Si videas Draconum multitudinem sine capite, bonum est, vel bona fortuna est.

The First and Second Hexagrams: Qian and Kun

Translated by James Legge

I wrote out a translation of the *Book of Changes*, embracing both the Text and the Appendixes, in 1854 and 1855; and have to acknowledge that when the manuscript was completed, I knew very little about the scope and method of the book. I laid the volumes containing the result of my labor aside, and hoped, believed indeed, that the light would by and by dawn and that I should one day get hold of a clue that would guide me to a knowledge of the mysterious classic.

Before that day came, the translation was soaked, in 1870, for more than a month in the water of the Red Sea. By dint of careful manipulation it was recovered so as to be still legible; but it was not till 1874 that I began to be able to give the book the prolonged attention necessary to make it reveal its secrets. Then for the first time I got hold, as I believe, of the clue, and found that my toil of twenty years before was of no service at all....

The written characters of the Chinese are not representations of words, but symbols of ideas, and the combination of them in composition is not a representation of what the writer would say, but of what he thinks. It is vain therefore for a translator to attempt a literal version.... There is not so much an interpretation of the characters employed by the writer as a participation of his thoughts; there is the seeing of mind to mind.

— James Legge, preface to *The Texts of Confucianism,*
part 2, The Yi King, 1882

The First Hexagram: Qian

Explanation of the entire figure by King Wen

Qian represents what is great and originating, penetrating, advantageous, correct and firm.

Explanation of the separate lines by the Duke of Zhou

1. In the first (or lowest) line, undivided, we see its subject as the dragon lying hid in the deep. It is not the time for active doing.
2. In the second line, undivided, we see its subject as the dragon appearing in the field. It will be advantageous to meet with the great man.
3. In the third line, undivided, we see its subject as the superior man active and vigilant all the day, and in the evening still careful and apprehensive. The position is dangerous, but there will be no mistake.

4. In the fourth line, undivided, we see its subject as the dragon looking as if he were leaping up, but still in the deep. There will be no mistake.
5. In the fifth line, undivided, we see its subject as the dragon on the wing in the sky. It will be advantageous to meet with the great man.
6. In the sixth (or topmost) line, undivided, we see its subject as the dragon exceeding the proper limits. There will be occasion for repentance.
7. The lines of this hexagram are all strong and undivided, as appears from the use of the number nine. If the host of dragons thus appearing were to divest themselves of their heads, there would be good fortune.

The Second Hexagram: Kun

Explanation of the entire figure by King Wen

Kun represents what is great and originating, penetrating, advantageous, correct and having the firmness of a mare. When the superior man here intended has to make any movement, if he take the initiative, he will go astray; if he follow, he will find his proper lord. The advantageousness will be seen in his getting friends in the southwest, and losing friends in the northeast. If he rest in correctness and firmness, there will be good fortune.

Explanation of the separate lines by the Duke of Zhou

1. In the first line, divided, we see its subject treading on hoarfrost. The strong ice will come by and by.
2. The second line, divided, shows the attribute of being straight, square, and great. Its operation, without repeated efforts, will be in every respect advantageous.
3. The third line, divided, shows its subject keeping his excellence under restraint, but firmly maintaining it. If he should have occasion to engage in the king's service, though he will not claim the success for himself, he will bring affairs to a good issue.
4. The fourth line, divided, shows the symbol of a sack tied up. There will be no ground for blame or for praise.
5. The fifth line, divided, shows the yellow lower garment. There will be great good fortune.

6. The sixth line, divided, shows dragons fighting in the wild. Their blood is purple and yellow.
7. The lines of this hexagram are all weak and divided, as appears from the use of the number six. If those who are thus represented be perpetually correct and firm, advantage will arise.

The Fifty-Second Hexagram: Gen

Translated into German and annotated by Richard Wilhelm
English version by Cary F. Baynes

The *Book of Changes* is unquestionably one of the most important books in the world's literature. Its origin goes back to mythical antiquity, and it has occupied the attention of the most eminent scholars of China down to the present day. Nearly all that is greatest and most significant in the three thousand years of Chinese cultural history has either taken its inspiration from this book, or has exerted an influence on the interpretation of its text. Therefore it may safely be said that the seasoned wisdom of thousands of years has gone into the making of the *Book of Changes*. Small wonder then that both of the two branches of Chinese philosophy, Confucianism and Taoism, have their common roots here. The book sheds new light on many a secret hidden in the often puzzling mode of thought of that mysterious sage, Laozi, and of his pupils, as well as on many ideas that appear in the Confucian tradition as axioms, accepted without further examination.

Indeed, not only the philosophy of China but its science and statecraft as well have never ceased to draw from the spring of wisdom in the *Changes*, and it is not surprising that this alone, among all the Confucian classics, escaped the great burning of the books under Qin Shihuangdi.[22] Even the commonplaces of everyday life in China are saturated with its influence. In going through the streets of a Chinese city, one will find, here and there at a street corner, a fortune-teller sitting behind a neatly covered table, brush and tablet at hand, ready to draw from the ancient book of wisdom pertinent counsel and information on life's minor perplexities. Not only that, but the very signboards adorning the houses — perpendicular wooden panels done in gold on black lacquer — are covered with inscriptions whose flower language again and again recalls thoughts and quotations from the Changes. Even the policymakers of so modern a state as Japan, distinguished for their astuteness, do not scorn to refer to it for counsel in difficult situations.

... A living stream of deep human wisdom was constantly flowing through the channel of this book into everyday life, giving to China's great civilization that ripeness of wisdom, distilled through the ages, which we wistfully admire in the remains of this last truly autochthonous culture.

— Richard Wilhelm, Introduction to *The I Ching, or Book of Changes*, 1924

Looked at from such a historical perspective, I see Wilhelm in the guise of one of those great gnostic intermediaries who brought the cultural heritage of Asia into

---

[22] 213 B.C.

contact wih the Hellenic spirit, and thereby caused a new world to rise out of the ruins of the Roman Empire....

Toward the foreign culture of the East, Wilhelm displayed an extraordinarily large amount of modesty, something unusual in an European. He erected no barrier against it, no prejudices, no assumptions of knowing better, but instead, opened heart and mind to it. He let himself be gripped and shaped by it, so that when he came back to Europe, he brought us not only in his spirit but also in his nature, a true image of the East. This deep transformation was certainly not won by him without great sacrifice, because our historical premises are so entirely different from those of the East....

Wilhelm fulfilled his mission in every sense of the word. Not only did he make accessible to us the dead treasures of the Chinese mind but, as I have pointed out, he brought with him its spiritual root, the root that has lived all these thousands of years, and planted it in the soil of Europe.

— Carl Gustav Jung, "In Memory of Richard Wilhelm," 1931

Legge translated what the text said, while Wilhelm translated what the text meant; that is, Legge was primarily a translator while Wilhelm was more of an interpreter, interested in the overall significance of the text for Chinese intellectual life. Wilhelm was fascinated with the significance of the text for Chinese intellectual tradition, but perhaps even more, he was drawn toward the possible significance of the text as an aspect of world literature. The immense popularity of the Wilhelm translation can only be accounted for by the realization that, for Wilhelm, the *Changes* was not a lifeless artifact of archaic China, but transcended even China. Richard Wilhelm had an insight that separated him from his predecessors: the ultimate significance of the *Changes* is as a guide for one's personal psychic understanding. This is how it was used in old China; that is, the meaning of the book in China was to help one find perspective amid the constant changes of life. Wilhelm saw that it might have that significance also for the West, and therefore in his translation and interpretation he kept the text as faithful to the Chinese understanding as possible. In this way Richard Wilhelm raised the *Changes* to the status of world literature.

— Gerald W. Swanson, Introduction to Shchutskii,
Researches on the I Ching, 1979

Gen/Keeping Still, Mountain

☶ *above* Gen: keeping still, mountain
☶ *below* Gen: keeping still, mountain

The image of this hexagram is the mountain, the youngest son of heaven and earth. The male principle is at the top, because it strives upward by nature; the female principle is below, since the direction of its movement is downward. Thus there is rest because the movement has come to its normal end.

In its application to man, the hexagram turns upon the problem of achieving a quiet heart. It is very difficult to bring quiet to the heart. While Buddhism strives for rest through an ebbing away of all movement in nirvana, the *Book of Changes* holds that rest is merely a state of polarity that always posits movement as its complement. Possibly the words of the text embody directions for the practice of yoga.

The Judgment
Keeping still. Keeping his back still

So that he no longer feels his body.
He goes into his courtyard
and does not see his people.
No blame.

True quiet means keeping still when the time has come to keep still, and going forward when the time has come to go forward. In this way rest and movement are in agreement with the demands of the time, and thus there is light in life.

The hexagram signifies the end and the beginning of all movement. The back is named because in the back are located all the nerve fibers that mediate movement. If the movement of these spinal nerves is brought to a standstill, the ego, with its restlessness, disappears as it were. When a man has thus become calm, he may turn to the outside world. He no longer sees in it the struggle and tumult of individual beings, and therefore he has that true peace of mind which is needed for understanding the great laws of the universe and for acting in harmony with them. Whoever acts from these deep levels makes no mistakes.

The Image
Mountains standing close together:
The image of keeping still.
Thus the superior man
Does not permit his thoughts
To go beyond his situation.

The heart thinks constantly. This cannot be changed, but the movements of the heart — that is, a man's thoughts — should restrict themselves to the immediate situation. All thinking that goes beyond this only makes the heart sore.

The Lines
Six at the beginning means:
Keeping his toes still.
No blame.
Continued perseverance furthers.

Keeping the toes still means halting before one has even begun to move. The beginning is the time of few mistakes. At that time one is still in harmony with primal innocence. Not yet influenced by obscuring interests and desires, one sees things intuitively as they really are. A man who halts at the beginning, so long as he has not yet abandoned truth, finds the right way. But persisting firmness is needed to keep one from drifting irresolutely.

Six in the second place means:
Keeping his calves still.
He cannot rescue him whom he follows.
His heart is not glad.

The leg cannot move independently; it depends on the movement of the body. If a leg is suddenly stopped while the whole body is in vigorous motion, the continuing body movement will make one fall.

The same is true of a man who serves a master stronger than himself. He is swept along, and even though he may himself halt on the path of wrongdoing, he can no longer check the other in his powerful movement. Where the master presses forward, the servant, no matter how good his intentions, cannot save him.

Nine in the third place means:
Keeping his hips still.
Making his sacrum stiff.
Dangerous. The heart suffocates.

This refers to enforced quiet. The restless heart is to be subdued by forcible means. But fire when it is smothered changes into acrid smoke that suffocates as it spreads.

Therefore, in exercises in meditation and concentration, one ought not to try to force results. Rather, calmness must develop naturally out of a state of inner composure. If one tries to induce calmness by means of artificial rigidity, meditation will lead to very unwholesome results.

Six in the fourth place means:
Keeping his trunk still.
No blame.

As has been pointed out above in the comment on the Judgment, keeping the back at rest means forgetting the ego. This is the highest stage of rest. Here this stage has not yet been reached: the individual in this instance, though able to keep the ego, with its thoughts and impulses, in a state of rest, is not yet quite liberated from its dominance. Nonetheless, keeping the heart at rest is an important function, leading in the end to the complete elimination of egotistic drives. Even though at this point one does not yet remain free from all the dangers of doubt and unrest, this frame of mind is not a mistake, as it leads ultimately to that other, higher level.

Six in the fifth place means:
Keeping his jaws still.
The words have order.
Remorse disappears.

A man in a dangerous situation, especially when he is not adequate to it, is inclined to be very free with talk and presumptuous jokes. But injudicious speech easily leads to situations that subsequently give much cause for regret. However, if a man is reserved in speech, his words take ever more definite form, and every occasion for regret vanishes.

Nine at the top means:
Noblehearted keeping still
Good fortune.

This marks the consummation of the effort to attain tranquillity. One is at rest, not merely in a small, circumscribed way in regard to matters of detail, but one has also a general resignation in regard to life as a whole, and this confers peace and good fortune in relation to every individual matter.

THE ANALECTS OF CONFUCIUS (c. 551–c. 479 B.C.)

And certainly this excellent Man (Confucius) was also endow'd with admirable Qualifications. He had an Aspect both grave and modest; he was faithful, just, cheerful, civil, courteous, affable: and a certain serenity, which appear'd in his Countenance, gain'd him the hearts and respect of all those that beheld him. He spake little, and meditated much. He eagerly pursued his Study, without tiring his Spirit. He contemn'd Riches and Honors when they were Obstacles to his Designs. His whole Delight was in teaching and making his Doctrine savoury to many. He was severer to himself than others. He had a continual Circumspection over himself, and was a rigid Censurer of his own Conduct. He blam'd himself for not being assiduous enough in instructing; for not shewing vigilance enough in correcting his own Faults, and for not exercising himself, as he ought, in the practice of Virtue. In fine, he had one Virtue rarely found in great Men, *viz.* Humility: for he not only spake with an extreme Modesty of himself, and what concern'd him, but he with a singular sincerity declar'd to the whole World, that he ceased not to learn, and that the Doctrine he taught was not his own, but the Doctrine of the Ancients. But his Books are his true Pourtraiture.

— *The Morals of Confucius: A Chinese Philosopher,* 1691

On eagle wings the poet of tonight
Soars for fresh virtues to the source of light,
To China's eastern realms: and boldly bears
Confucius' morals to Britannia's ears.

— William Whitehead, Prologue to Arthur Murphy, trans.,
The Orphan of China, 1759

I have read the books of Confucius with attention, I have made extracts from them; I found that they spoke only the purest morality.... He appeals only to virtue, he preaches no miracles, there is nothing in them of religious allegory.

— Voltaire (1694–1778), *Essai sur les Moeurs,* translated by Honour,
Chinoiserie: The Vision of Cathay, 1961

I hope I have not done him injustice; the more I have studied his character and opinions, the more highly have I come to regard him. He was a very great man, and his influence has been on the whole a great benefit to the Chinese, while his teachings suggest important lessons to ourselves who profess to belong to the school of Christ.

— James Legge, Prolegomena to *Confucian Analects,*
vol. 1 of *The Chinese Classics,* 1861

The *Analects* ... are the oddments which Kung's [Confucius] circle found indispensable, and for 2,500 years the most intelligent men of China have tried to add to them or to subtract....
    Points define a periphery. What the reader can find here is a set of measures whereby at the end of the day, to learn whether the day has been worth living.

— Ezra Pound, *The Analects,* 1951

Confucius is believed to have died in 479 B.C. It was probably a hundred years or more before the *Analects,* the earliest work we have on his life and teachings, attained anything like its present form. It consists of twenty chapters, divided into 497 sections, some of them no more than the briefest pronouncements. There is no order to the chapters nor continuity in the sections. What we have in the *Analects* is not a book in the modern sense, but a collection of fragments, of varying dates and degrees of reliability, united only by the fact that they all deal with Confucius and his teachings. Imagine a handful of earnest scholars working through the years to contact the former students of the late Professor So and so, or the students of his students, collecting their reminiscences of the professor and his sayings, and finally pasting together the results in a book. Allow for the special difficulties of such a procedure in the China of twenty-five hundred years ago, and you will have an idea of how the *Analects* was most likely formed.

— Burton Watson, *Early Chinese Literature*, 1962

Confucius Sinarum Philosophus [Confucius, Chinese Philosopher]: Scientiae Sinicae Liber Tertius: Ratiocinantium Sermones Versio Litteralis, Una cum Explanatione: Pars Prima [Wisdom of the Chinese, Third Book: Discourses]

Latin version of the Analects *by the Jesuit Fathers Prospero Intorcetta (1625–1696), Christian Herdtrich (1624–1684), François de Rougemont (1624–1676), and Philippe Couplet (1624–1692), published in Paris, 1687; the opening sentences, together with the English version of James Legge (1861)*

Then his majesty [James II, r. 1685–1689] told Dr. Hyde [the Bodleian librarian] of a book of Confucius translated from the China language by the Jesuits (4 in number) and asked whether it was in the library? To which Dr. Hyde answered that it was, and that "it treated of philosophy, but not so as that of European philosophy."

— Anthony Wood (1632–1695), from Clark ed.,
The Life and Times of Anthony Wood, vol. 3

This magnificently printed folio (dedicated to the "most Christian king" of France, Louis XIV) contains translations of the first three of the Four Books (*The Analects, The Great Learning*, and *The Doctrine of the Mean*) and a life of Confucius with a full-page, icon-like portrait of the sage. The translations are long-winded paraphrases.

— Knud Lundbaek, "The first European translations of Chinese historical and philosophical works," in Lee ed., *China and Europe*, 1991

Confucius Sinarum Philosophus was widely circulated, translated and analysed. (*La Morale de Confucius* [1688] and *The Morals of Confucius* [1691] were essentially popular abridgements.) It was the basis of the popular image of "Confucius, the Philosopher of China," which haunted European thought for a century or more. Its publication marks the beginning of the vogue for *chinoiserie* in art and literature as well as the serious impact of China on the intellectuals of Europe.

— Paul Rule, *K'ung-tzu or Confucius?*, 1986

Fol. 1, pag. 1, §1

Confucius ait: Operam dare imitationi sapientium, & assidue exercitare
sese in hujusmodi studio imitandi, nonne olim delectabile erit? Quasi
dicat: suae principiis fere omnibus difficultates insunt ac spinae; verum-
tamen si devoraveris istas magno animo vicerisque, tu quisquis sectator es
virtutis ac sapientiae, si exemplis simul ac documentis virorum sapien-
tum ob oculos tibi positis constantiam junxeris cum labore, plane fiet ut
recuperata paulatim claritate & integritate primæva naturæ nostræ, insig-
nis etiam facilitas atque peritia sequatur tuam exercitationem, delectatio
vero peritiam & facilitatem.
(Legge: The Master said, "Is it not pleasant to learn with a constant
perseverance and application?")

Fol. 1, pag. 1, §2

Postquam autem te excolueris tam feliciter hujusmodi cum labore &
constantiæ, si dentur tunc sectatores & amici e longinqua regione adven-
tantes, consulturi te, atque in disciplinam tuam tradituri sese, fama scilicet
virtutis ac sapientiæ tuæ excitati, nonne tum multo etiam vehementiùs
laetaberis, & prodes omnino sensum hunc exultantis animi tui.
(Legge: "Is it not delightful to have friends coming from distant
quarters?")

Fourteen Maxims from The Morals of Confucius (1691)

*Translated from the French work, La Morale de Confucius, philosophe de la
Chine (Paris, 1688)*

Confucius's third Book is a Contexture of several Sentences pronounc'd at divers
times, and at several places, by Confucius and his disciples. Therefore it is intituled
Lun Yu, that is to say, *Discourses of several Persons that Reason and Philosophize together....*
He declaims against Pride, Self-Love, Indiscretion, and against the ridiculous Vanity of
those that affect to be Masters everywhere, against those Self-Conceited Men, who
momentarily cite their own Actions, and against great Talkers, and drawing afterward
the Portraiture of the Wise man, he says, that Humility, Modesty, Gravity, and Neigh-
borly Affection, are Virtues which he cannot one moment neglect, without departing
from his character ...

He would have us avoid Idleness; to be serious, and not precipitate in our Answers;
and that setting our selves above everything, we should never be troubled, either that
we are contemn'd, or not known in the World.

He compares Hypocrites to those lewd Villains, who the better to conceal their
Designs from the Eyes of Men, do appear Wise and Modest in the Daytime, and who
by the favor of the Night, do Rob Houses, and commit the most infamous Robberies.

[The Maxims selected here are taken from the eighty which form the last section of *The Morals of Confucius*. The previous section ends with the words: "Confucius relates an infinite number of other Things of this Nature, which concern the Conduct of all sorts of Men; but most of the Things that he says, or which his Disciples do say, are Sentences and Maxims, as we have already declar'd, the most considerable of which are these that follow." These pithy, epigrammatic sayings illustrate well the nature of the 1691 text. The reader should remember that it was translated (into wonderful English prose) from the French, which was itself a free adaptation of the Latin of the Jesuits, which itself had been greatly expanded from the original Chinese.]

1. He that in his Studies wholly applies himself to Labour and Exercise, and neglects Meditation, loses his time; and he that only applies himself to meditation, and neglects Labour and Exercise, does only wander and lose himself. The first can never know anything exactly, his Lights will be always intermixt with Doubts and Obscurities; and the last will only pursue Shadows; his Knowledge will never be certain, it will never be solid. Labour, but slight not meditation; Meditate, but slight not Labour.

2. Do unto another as thou wouldst be dealt with thyself: Thou only needest this Law alone; 'tis the Foundation and principle of all the rest.

3. A long Experience is requir'd to know the Heart of Man. I imagin'd, when I was young, that all Men were Sincere; that they always Practis'd what they said; in a word, that their Mouth always agreed with their Heart: But now that I behold Things with another Eye, I am convinc'd that I was mistaken. At present I hear what Men say, but I never rely thereon. I will examine whether their Words are agreeable to their Actions.

4. 'Tis not enough to know Virtue, it is necessary to love it; but it is not sufficient to love it, it is necessary to possess it.

5. The Way that leads to Virtue is long, but it is thy Duty to finish this long Race. Alledge not for thy excuse, that thou hast not strength enough; that Difficulties discourage thee, and that thou shalt be at last forc'd to stop in the midst of the Course. Thou knowest nothing, begin to run: "'Tis a sign thou hast not as yet begun, thou shouldst not use this Language."

6. Eschew Vanity and Pride. Although thou hadst all the Prudence and Ability of the Ancients, if thou hast not Humility, thou hast nothing, thou art even the Man of the World that deserves to be contemned.

7. Learn what thou know'st already, as if thou hadst never learn'd it: Things are never so well known but that we may forget them.

8. Wouldst thou learn to die well? Learn first to live well.

9. Innocence ceases to be a Virtue, most of the Great Ones are fallen therefrom. But if thou demandest what must be done to recover this Virtue, I answer, That it is necessary to conquer thyself. If all Mortals could, in one Day, gain over themselves this happy Victory, the whole Universe would, from this very Day, reassume a new Form; we should all be perfect, we should all be innocent. 'Tis true, the Victory is difficult, but it is not impossible; for in short, to conquer thyself is only to do what is agreeable to Reason. Turn away thine Eyes, stop thine Ears, put a Bridle upon thy Tongue, and rather remain in an Eternal Inaction, than to imploy thine Eyes in beholding Sights where Reason is stifled; than to give Attention thereunto, or to Discourse thereon. Behold how thou mayst overcome! The Victory depends on thyself alone.

10. 'Tis good to Fast some times, to give the Mind to Meditation, and to the Study of Virtue. The Wise Man is taken up with other Cares, than with the continual Cares of his Nourishment. The best cultivated Earth frustrates the hopes of the Labourer, when the Seasons are irregular: All the Rules of Husbandry could not secure him from Death, in the time of a hard Famine; but Virtue is never fruitless.

11. We have three Friends that are Useful to us, a Sincere Friend, a Faithful Friend, a Friend that Hears every Thing, that Examines what is told him, and that Speaks little. But we have three also whose Friendship is pernicious, a Hypocrite, a Flatterer, and a great Talker.

12. The Natural Light is only a perpetual Conformity of our Soul with the Laws of Heaven. Men can never lose this Light. It is true, that the Heart of Man being inconstant and wavering, it is sometimes covered over with so many Clouds, that it seems wholly extinguish'd. The Wise Man experiences it himself; for he may fall into small Errors, and commit light Offences: Yet the Wise Man cannot be Virtuous, whilst he is in this state, it would be a Contradiction to say it.

13. The Wise Man seeks the cause of his Defects in himself; But the Fool avoiding himself, seeks it in all others besides himself.

14. Contract Friendship with a Man whose Heart is upright and sincere; with a Man that loves to learn, and who can teach thee something, in his turn. Other Men are unworthy of thy Friendship.

Seventeen Fragments from The Analects

Translated by James Legge (1861)

James Legge worked on his version of *The Analects*, the first of his many translations from the Chinese Classics, in Malacca and then in Hong Kong. It appeared in 1861 with a dedication "to the memory of the Hon. Joseph Jardine, Esq., by whose munificent assistance it is now published, and but for which it might never have been published." Jardine, head of the great Hong Kong trading house that built its fortune on the opium trade, had said to Legge in 1856: "If you are prepared for the toil of the publication, I will bear the expense of it. We make our money in China, and we should be glad to assist in whatever promises to be of benefit to it."

— Editors

I:3

The Master said, "Fine words and an insinuating appearance are seldom associated with true virtue."

I:4

The philosopher Zeng said, "I daily examine myself on three points: whether, in transacting business for others, I may have been faithful; whether, in intercourse with friends, I may have been sincere; whether I may have not mastered and practiced the instructions of my teacher."[23]

II:4

The Master said, "At fifteen, I had my mind bent on learning. At thirty, I stood firm. At forty, I had no doubts. At fifty, I knew the decrees of Heaven. At sixty, my ear was an obedient organ for the reception of truth.

---

[23] Compare the corresponding passage in *The Morals of Confucius*:

In the first place there is represented a Disciple of this famous Philosopher, who declares, that he spent not a Day wherein he render'd not an account to himself of these three things.

1. Whether he had not undertaken some Affair for another, and whether he manag'd and follow'd it with the same Eagerness and Fidelity as if it had been his own Concern.

2. If when he has been with his Friends, he has discours'd with them sincerely, if he has not satisfied himself with shewing them some slight appearance of Kindness and Esteem.

3. Whether he has meditated on his Master's Doctrine; and whether after having meditated on it, he has us'd his utmost Endeavors to reduce it to practice. *Eds.*

At seventy, I could follow what my heart desired, without transgressing what was right."

II:10

The Master said, "See what a man does. Mark his motives. Examine in what things he rests. How can a man conceal his character? How can a man conceal his character?"

IV:8

The Master said, "If a man in the morning hear the right way, he may die in the evening without regret."[24]

IV:9

The Master said, "A scholar, whose mind is set on truth, and who is ashamed of bad clothes and bad food, is not fit to be discoursed with."

VI:15

The Master said, "Who can go out but by the door? How is it that men will not walk according to these ways?"[25]

VI:21

The Master said, "The wise find pleasure in water; the virtuous find pleasure in hills. The wise are active; the virtuous are tranquil. The wise are joyful; the virtuous are long-lived."

VII:4

When the Master was unoccupied with business, his manner was easy, and he looked pleased.

---

[24] Compare *The Morals of Confucius*:
He that in the Morning hath heard the Voice of Virtue, may die at Night. This Man will not repent of living, and Death will not be any pain unto him. *Eds.*

[25] Compare Ezra Pound (*Confucius*, 1951):
He said: The way out is via the door, how is it that no one will use this method? *Eds.*

VII:5

The Master said, "Extreme is my decay. For a long time, I have not dreamed, as I was wont to do, that I saw the duke of Zhou."

VII:6

The Master said, "Let the will be set on the path of duty. Let every attainment in what is good be firmly grasped. Let perfect virtue be accorded with. Let relaxation and enjoyment be found in the polite arts."

VII:8

The Master said, "I do not open up the truth to one who is not eager to get knowledge, nor help out anyone who is not anxious to explain himself. When I have presented one corner of a subject to anyone, and he cannot from it learn the other three, I do not repeat my lesson."

VII:15

The Master said, "With coarse rice to eat, with water to drink, and my bended arm for a pillow; I have still joy in the midst of these things. Riches and honors acquired by unrighteousness are to me as a floating cloud."

VII:20

The subjects on which the Master did not talk, were extraordinary things, feats of strength, disorder, and spiritual beings.

IX:16

The Master standing by a stream, said, "It passes on just like this, not ceasing day or night!"

IX:17

The Master said, "I have not seen one who loves virtue as he loves beauty."

IX:21

The Master said, "There are cases in which the blade springs, but the plant does not go on to flower! There are cases where it flowers, but no fruit is subsequently produced!"

Six Fragments

Translated and annotated by Ku Hung-ming (1898)

Ku Hung-ming (Gu Hongming, 1857–1928) was born into a Fujianese family in Penang, educated at Edinburgh and in Germany, and later became the secretary to the statesman Zhang Zhidong (1837–1909). Ku was the ageing Philosopher portrayed so brilliantly by Somerset Maugham in his *On a Chinese Screen* (1922). "Five days in a sampan were needed to reach the Upper Yangtze ... Here lived a philosopher of repute, the greatest authority in China on the Confucian learning. He was said to speak English and German with facility ... On certain days in the week all through the year he opened his doors to such as sought after knowledge, and discoursed on the teaching of Confucius ... He was an old man, tall, with a thin grey queue, and bright large eyes under which were heavy bags. His teeth were broken and discoloured. He was exceedingly thin, and his hands, fine and small, were withered and claw-like. I had been told that he was an opium-smoker. He was very shabbily dressed in a black gown, a little black cap, both much the worse for wear, and dark grey trousers gartered at the ankle ... His study of Western philosophy had only served in the end to satisfy him that wisdom after all was to be found within the limits of the Confucian canon. He accepted its philosophy with conviction. It answered the needs of his spirit with a completeness which made all foreign learning seem vain." At Maugham's departure, Ku wrote out for him a couple of poems in his own calligraphy. When Maugham asked him to give him a translation, Ku's reply was: "*Tradutore — tradittore.* You cannot expect me to betray myself. Ask one of your English friends. Those who know most about China know nothing, but you will at least find one who is competent to give you a rendering of a few rough and simple lines."

— Editors

Anyone now, even without any acquaintance with the Chinese language, who will take the trouble to turn over the pages of Dr. Legge's translation, cannot help feeling how unsatisfactory the translation really is. For Dr. Legge, from his raw literary training when he began his work, and the utter want of critical insight and literary perceptions he showed to the end, was really nothing more than a great sinologue, that is to say, a pundit with a very learned but dead knowledge of Chinese books. But in justice to the memory of the great sinologue who, we regret to hear, has recently died, it must be said that notwithstanding the extremely hard and narrow limits of his mind, which was the result of temperament, he was, as far as his insight allowed him, thoroughly conscientious in his work.... To the generality of the English reading people we cannot but think the intellectual and moral outfit of the Chinaman as presented by Dr. Legge in his translation of the Chinese books, must appear as strange and grotesque as to an ordinary Englishman's eyes, unaccustomed to it, the Chinaman's costume and outward appearance.

— Ku Hung-ming, preface to *The Discourses and
Sayings of Confucius*, 1898

III:23

Confucius remarked to the Grand Kapel Meister of his native State, "I think I know the way in which a piece should be played with a full orchestra. At first, the full volume of sound in the piece should be heard. Then, as you proceed, you must pay attention to and bring out each note of the piece, distinct and clear, but flowing, as it were, without break or interval, thus to the end."

VII:26

Confucius sometimes went out fishing, but always with the rod and angle; he would never use a net. He sometimes went out shooting, but he would never shoot at a bird except on the wing.

VIII:9

Confucius remarked, "The common people should be educated in what they ought to do; not to ask why they should do it."

Goethe, in his latter years, was inclined to believe that Martin Luther put back the civilization of Europe because he appealed to the multitude to judge of things which they could not possibly be in a position to understand. The real and true principle of modern democracy, on the other hand, is contained in that saying of Confucius: "Greatly fear the aspirations (the inarticulate, not the mere articulate aspirations) of the people."

IX:18

Confucius remarked, "Suppose a man wants to raise a mound, and just as it wants only one basket more of earth to complete the work, suppose he were suddenly to stop: the stopping depends entirely upon himself. Suppose again a man wants to level a road, although he has just thrown over it only one basket of earth; to proceed with the work also depends entirely upon himself."

"Life lies before us as a huge quarry lies before the architect.... Men seem to me like people who have taken up a notion that they must and will erect a tower, but who yet expend on the foundation not more stones and labour than would be sufficient for a hut." — Goethe, *Wilhelm Meister*

XI:5

A disciple of Confucius was fond of repeating the verse:

A fleck on the stone may be ground away;
A word misspoken will remain alway.

Confucius married his niece to him.

XIII:3

A disciple, the intrepid Chung Yu, said to Confucius on one occasion when the reigning prince of a certain State was negotiating for Confucius to enter his service: "The prince is waiting, sir, to entrust the government of the country to you. Now what do you consider the first thing to be done?"

"If I must begin," answered Confucius, "I would begin by defining the names of things."

"Oh! really," replied the disciple, "but you are too impractical. What has the definition of names to do here?"

"Sir," replied Confucius, "you have really no manners. A gentleman when he hears anything he does not understand, will always wait for an explanation.

"Now, if names of things are not properly defined, *words* will not correspond to *facts*. When words do not correspond to facts, it is impossible to perfect anything. Where it is impossible to perfect anything, the arts and institutions of civilization cannot flourish, law and justice cannot attain their ends; and when law and justice do not attain their ends, the people will be at a loss to know what to do.

"Therefore a wise and good man can always specify whatever he names; whatever he can specify, he can carry out. A wise and good man makes it a point always to be exact in the word he uses."

Confucius here points out, as a characteristic of his time, what the Revd. Mr. Smith in his *Chinese Characteristics* has lately very cleverly pointed out as a characteristic of the Chinese of the present day, namely "a want of exactness," which, wherever and whenever it exists, makes it impossible for the arts of civilization to flourish. But "the want of exactness" in the use of words, we fancy, is not entirely confined to China now.

THE WAY AND ITS POWER
Six Chapters

Translated by Arthur Waley

He [Laozi] was a philosopher, contemporary of Confucius, who, they assert, was born after a gestation of eighty years, hence his name, which means Old Philosopher. He did not leave a book of his teachings nor did he claim to create a new school, but after his death his followers, who are called *tausu* [*daoshi*], took him as their leader and produced many books different from those of other schools, full of fantastic stories told with a lot of frills.

— Matteo Ricci (1552–1610), *Fonti Ricciane*, vol. 1

His followers say of Lao-tsö [Laozi] himself that he is Buddha who as man became the ever-existent God. We still have his principal writings; they have been taken to Vienna and I have seen them there myself.... Without a name *Tao* is the beginning of Heaven and Earth, and with a name she is the Mother of the Universe. It is only in her imperfect state that she is considered with affection; who desires to know her must be devoid of passions....

Nothing, emptiness, the altogether undetermined, the abstract universal ... this is called *Tao*, or reason.

— G. W. F. Hegel, *Lectures on the History of Philosophy*, 1816

Of the three most famous Taoist texts, *The Way and Its Power*, the *Zhuangzi*, and the *Liezi*, *The Way* has traditionally been accepted as the oldest. It was attributed to a sage and recluse named Lao Dan [Laozi] who was supposed to have been a contemporary of Confucius. Scholars now generally agree that the biographical accounts of Lao Dan are no more than a jumble of confused legends, and that the text called *The Way* is probably no older than the fourth or third century B.C., though it may incorporate older material. It is impossible to say anything about its authorship other than that it may well have been the work of a single writer.

The work as we have it at present is in eighty-one brief paragraphs or stanzas. There is little formal structure to the work or systematic development of ideas. Much of it is made up of what appear to be ancient maxims, often rhymed, interspersed with passages of interpretation in verse or prose. The style is highly formal and parallelistic like that of much late Zhou literature.

What distinguishes *The Way* so sharply from other works of the period is its mystical, rhapsodic tone. Not only is much of it in verse, but it is dominated throughout by a poetic and highly symbolic manner of expression. The ideas are not explained or elaborated, but rather flung in the reader's face. "Truth sounds like its opposite!" proclaims the author, and he proceeds to lay before the world his own perception of truth, couched in as bold and paradoxical language as he can devise. The rhythm and balance of the sentences drum the reader on his way, the trenchant symbolism draws him along, and he may go for pages before he wakes with a start to realize that he has only a hazy idea of what is being said.

This is of course the secret of the work's inexhaustible charm. To render it into another language, the translator must always be more explicit than the original; he must choose one of a number of possible meanings before he can produce any kind of coherent version. Yet the original remains magnificently elusive and suggestive, which is no doubt why it has been translated so many times. Each new translator of the work is fired with a determination to bring out hidden meanings and subtleties which his predecessors have overlooked.

— Burton Watson, *Early Chinese Literature*, 1962

Chapter 1

The Way that can be told of is not an Unvarying Way;

The names that can be named are not unvarying names.
It was from the Nameless that Heaven and Earth sprang;
The named is but the mother that rears the ten thousand
    creatures, each after its kind.
Truly, "Only he that rids himself forever of desire can see
    the Secret Essences";
He that has never rid himself of desire can see only the
    Outcomes.
These two things issued from the same mold, but
    nevertheless are different in name.
This "same mold" we can but call the Mystery,
Or rather the "Darker than any Mystery,"
The Doorway whence issued all Secret Essences.

Chapter 4

The Way is like an empty vessel
That yet may be drawn from
Without ever needing to be filled.
It is bottomless; the very progenitor of all things in the world.
In it all sharpness is blunted,
All tangles untied,
All glare tempered.
All dust smoothed.[26]
It is like a deep pool that never dries.
Was it too the child of something else? We cannot tell.
But as a substanceless image[27] it existed before the Ancestor.[28]

Chapter 5

Heaven and Earth are ruthless;
To them the Ten Thousand Things are but as straw dogs.
The Sage too is ruthless;
To him the people are but as straw dogs.

---

[26] Dust is the Taoist symbol for the noise and fuss of everyday life.
[27] A *xiang*, an image such as the mental images that float before us when we think.
[28] The ancestor in question is almost certainly the Yellow Ancestor, who separated Earth
from Heaven and so destroyed the Primal Unity, for which he is frequently censured in
Zhuangzi.

Yet Heaven and Earth and all that lies between
Is like a bellows
In that it is empty, but gives a supply that never fails.[29]
Work it, and more comes out.
Whereas the force of words[30] is soon spent.
Far better is it to keep what is in the heart.[31]

Chapter 6

The Valley Spirit never dies.
It is named the Mysterious Female.
And the Doorway of the Mysterious Female
Is the base from which Heaven and Earth sprang.
It is there within us all the while;
Draw upon it as you will, it never runs dry.[32]

Chapter 9

Stretch a bow[33] to the very full,
And you will wish you had stopped in time;
Temper a sword-edge to its very sharpest,
And you will find it soon grows dull.
When bronze and jade fill your hall
It can no longer be guarded.
Wealth and place breed insolence
That brings ruin in its train.
When your work is done, then withdraw!
Such is Heaven's[34] Way.

---

[29] Though ruthless (as the Realists never tired of maintaining), nature is perpetually bounteous.

[30] Laws and proclamations.

[31] For *zhong* as 'what is within the heart,' see *The Zuo Commentary*, Duke Yin 3rd year and *Guanzi*, 37, beginning. The comparison of Heaven and Earth to a bellows is also found in *Guanzi* (11, beginning).

[32] *Liezi* quotes these six lines as coming from the Book of the Yellow Ancestor, but it does not follow that the *The Way and Its Power* is actually quoting them from this source. They may belong to the general stock of early Taoist rhymed teaching.

[33] The expression used can also apply to filling a vessel to the brim; but 'stretching a bow' makes a better parallel to 'sharpening a sword.'

[34] As opposed to the Way of man.

Chapter 10

> Can you keep the unquiet physical-soul from straying,
>   hold fast to the Unity, and never quit it?
> Can you, when concentrating your breath, make it soft
>   like that of a little child?
> Can you wipe and cleanse your vision of the Mystery till
>   all is without blur?
> Can you love the people and rule the land, yet remain
>   unknown?
> Can you in opening and shutting the heavenly gates play
>   always the female part?[35]
> Can your mind penetrate every corner of the land, but you
>   yourself never interfere?
> Rear them, then, feed them,
> Rear them, but do not lay claim to them.
> Control them, but never lean upon them;
> Be chief among them, but do not manage them.
> This is called the Mysterious Power.

ZHUANGZI (c. 369–c. 286 B.C.)

Zhuang Zhou attained freedom and spontaneity in his elucidation of the Tao.

— Liu Xie, *The Literary Mind and the Carving of Dragons*, chapter 17

The *Zhuangzi*, a work in thirty-three chapters, was said to have been written by Zhuang Zhou, a philosopher whose dates are tentatively given as 369–286 B.C.... The *Zhuangzi* is unique in early Chinese literature for two reasons. One is that it is the only prose work of the ancient period which does not, at least in part, deal with questions of politics and statecraft. Zhuangzi has little advice for the rulers of his time.... He is concerned only with the life and freedom of the individual. Freedom is the central theme of the work — not political, social, or economic freedom, but spiritual freedom, freedom of the mind....

The second thing which makes the *Zhuangzi* unique is the remarkable wit and imagination with which this philosophy is expounded. Other works of Chinese history and philosophy abound in anecdotes that are obviously based on no more than myth or legend, but are always put forward in a solemn, pseudo-historical manner. The *Zhuangzi*, on the contrary, deals in deliberate and unabashed fantasy.... Nowhere else in early Chinese literature do we encounter such a wealth of satire, allegory, and poetic fancy. No single work of any other school of thought can approach the *Zhuangzi* for sheer literary brilliance.

— Burton Watson, *Early Chinese Literature*, 1962

---

[35] Read *wei*, not *wu*. This is the original Wang Bi reading, as the commentary shows.

Four Passages

Translated and annotated by Herbert Giles (1889)

Oscar Wilde read Giles' version of Zhuangzi with great interest and called it "the most caustic criticism of modern life I have met with for some time." He quoted from it in his 1891 essay "The Soul of Man under Socialism." In his prefatory note to the translation, the Rev. Aubrey Moore wrote: "It is impossible in reading this chapter on The Identity of Contraries not to be reminded of Heraclitus."

— Editors

Big and Useless

Huizi

A celebrated schoolman, contemporary with and antagonistic to Zhuangzi.

said to Zhuangzi, "The prince of Wei gave me a seed of a large-sized kind of gourd. I planted it, and it bore a fruit as big as a five-bushel measure. Now had I used this for holding liquids, it would have been too heavy to lift; and had I cut it in half for ladles, the ladles would have been ill adapted for such purpose. It was uselessly large, so I broke it up."

"Sir," replied Zhuangzi, "it was rather you who did not know how to use large things. There was a man of Song who had a recipe for salve for chapped hands, his family having been silk-washers for generations. Well, a stranger who had heard of it came and offered him 100 oz. of silver for this recipe; whereupon he called together his clansmen and said, 'We have never made much money by silk-washing. Now, we can make 100 oz. in a single day. Let the stranger have the recipe.'

"So the stranger got it, and went and informed the prince of Wu, who was just then at war with the Yue state. Accordingly, the prince used it in a naval battle fought at the beginning of winter with the Yue state, the result being that the latter was totally defeated.

They suffered from chapped hands, while their rivals of the Wu state were protected by their patent salve.

The stranger was rewarded with territory and a title. Thus, while the efficacy of salve to cure chapped hands was in both cases the same, its application was different. Here, it secured a title; there, a capacity for washing silk.

"Now as to your five-bushel gourd, why did you not make a boat of it, and float about over river and lake? You could not then have complained of its not holding anything! But I fear you are rather woolly inside."

Like it. This, of course, is a sneer. Huizi could not see that the greatness of a thing depends upon the greatness of its application.

Huizi said to Zhuangzi, "Sir, I have a large tree, of a worthless kind. Its trunk is so irregular and knotty that it cannot be measured out for planks; while its branches are so twisted as to admit of no geometrical subdivision whatever. It stands by the roadside, but no carpenter will look at it. And your words, sir, are like that tree — big and useless, not wanted by anybody."

"Sir," rejoined Zhuangzi, "have you never seen a wild cat, crouching down in wait for its prey? Right and left it springs from bough to bough, high and low alike, — until perchance it gets caught in a trap or dies in a snare.

> The tiger-cat screams now, that whined before,
> That pried and tried and trod so gingerly,
> Till in its silliness the trap-teeth join. — *Browning*

"On the other hand, there is the yak with its great huge body. It is big enough in all conscience, but it cannot catch mice.

> The adaptability of a thing is oft-times its bane. The inability of the yak to catch mice saves it from the snare which is fatal to the wild cat.

"Now if you have a big tree and are at a loss what to do with it, why not plant it in the domain of non-existence,

> Beyond the limits of our external world. Referring to the conditions of mental abstraction in which alone true happiness is to be found.

whither you might betake yourself to inaction by its side, to blissful repose beneath its shade?

> Why does the horizon hold me fast, with my joy and grief in this centre? — *Emerson*

There it would be safe from the axe and from all other injury; for being of no use to others, itself would be free from harm."

> Illustrating the advantage of being useless. That which is small and useful is thus shown to be inferior to that which is large and useless.

— from chapter 1, "Transcendental Bliss"

Life is a Dream

Ju Qiao addressed Zhangwuzi

> A disciple and tutor of antiquity.

as follows: "I heard Confucius say, 'The true sage pays no heed to mundane affairs. He neither seeks gain nor avoids injury. He asks nothing at the hands of man. He adheres, without questioning, to Tao. Without speaking, he can speak; and he can speak and yet say nothing.

And so he roams beyond the limits of this dusty world. These,' added
Confucius, 'are wild words.'

Hanfeizi tells us that Laozi, whose doctrines Confucius seems to be here deriding,
said exactly the opposite of this; viz.: "The true Sage is beforehand in his attention to
mundane affairs." i.e., "takes time by the forelock."

Now to me they are the skillful embodiment of Tao. What, Sir, is your
opinion?"

"Points upon which the Yellow Emperor doubted," replied
Zhangwuzi, "how should Confucius know?

Laozi and the Yellow Emperor have always been mixed up in the heads of Taoist
writers, albeit separated by a chasm of some two thousand years. Confucius is here
evidently dealing with the actual doctrines of Laozi.

You are going too fast. You see your egg, and expect to hear it crow. You
look at your cross-bow, and expect to have broiled pigeon before you. I
will say a few words to you at random, and do you listen at random.

"How does the Sage seat himself by the sun and moon, and hold the
universe in his grasp? He blends everything into one harmonious whole,
rejecting the confusion of this and that. Rank and precedence, which the
vulgar prize, the Sage stolidly ignores. The revolutions of ten thousand
years leave his Unity unscathed. The universe itself may pass away, but he
will flourish still.

"How do I know that love of life is not a delusion after all? How do I
know but that he who dreads to die is not as a child who has lost the way
and cannot find his home?

"The Lady Li Ji was the daughter of Ai Feng.

A border chieftain.

When the Duke of Jin first got her, she wept until the bosom of her dress
was drenched with tears. But when she came to the royal residence, and
lived with the Duke, and ate rich food, she repented of having wept. How
then do I know but that the dead repent of having previously clung to
life?

"Those who dream of the banquet, wake to lamentation and sorrow.
Those who dream of lamentation and sorrow, wake to join the hunt.
While they dream, they do not know that they dream. Some will even
interpret the very dream they are dreaming; and only when they awake
do they know it was a dream.

Who knows but life may after all be death,
   And death be life.— Plato in *Gorgias*, quoting Euripides
Peace, peace! he is not dead, he doth not sleep —
   He hath awakened from the dream of life.— Shelley in *Adonis*

"By and by comes the Great Awakening, and then we find out that this life is really a great dream. Fools think they are awake now, and flatter themselves they know if they are really princes or peasants. Confucius and you are both dreams; and I who say you are dreams, — I am but a dream myself. This is a paradox. Tomorrow a sage may arise to explain it; but that tomorrow will not be until ten thousand generations have gone by."

— from chapter 2, "The Identity of Contraries"

Prince Hui's Cook

Prince Hui's cook was cutting up a bullock. Every blow of his hand, every heave of his shoulders, every tread of his foot, every thrust of his knee, every *whshh* of rent flesh, every *chhk* of the chopper, was in perfect harmony, — rhythmical like the dance of the Mulberry Grove, simultaneous like the chords of the Jing Shou.

Commentators are divided in their identifications of these ancient *morceaux*.

"Well done!" cried the Prince. "Yours is skill indeed."

"Sire," replied the cook, "I have always devoted myself to Tao. It is better than skill. When I first began to cut up bullocks, I saw before me simply *whole* bullocks. After three years' practice, I saw no more whole animals.

Meaning that he saw them, so to speak, in sections.

And now I work with my mind and not with my eye. When my senses bid me stop, but my mind urges me on, I fall back upon eternal principles. I follow such openings or cavities as there may be, according to the natural constitution of the animal. I do not attempt to cut through joints: still less through large bones.

For a curious parallelism, see Plato's *Phaedrus*.

"A good cook changes his chopper once a year, — because he cuts. An ordinary cook, once a month, — because he hacks. But I have had this chopper nineteen years, and although I have cut up many thousand bullocks its edge is as if fresh from the whetstone. For at the joints there are always interstices, and the edge of a chopper being without thickness, it remains only to insert that which is without thickness into such an interstice. By these means the interstice will be enlarged, and the blade will find plenty of room. It is thus that I have kept my chopper for nineteen years as though fresh from the whetstone.

"Nevertheless, when I come upon a hard part where the blade meets with a difficulty, I am all caution. I fix my eye on it. I stay my hand, and gently apply my blade, until with a *hwah* the part yields like earth crumbling to the ground. Then I take out my chopper, and stand up, and look around, and pause, until with an air of triumph I wipe my chopper and put it carefully away."

"Bravo!" cried the Prince. "From the words of this cook I have learned how to take care of my life."

— from chapter 3, "Nourishment of the Soul"

Autumn Floods

It was the time of autumn floods. Every stream poured into the river, which swelled in its turbid course. The banks receded so far from one another that it was impossible to tell a cow from a horse.

Then the Spirit of the River laughed for joy that all the beauty of the earth was gathered to himself. Down with the stream he journeyed east, until he reached the ocean. There, looking eastward and seeing no limit to its waves, his countenance changed. And as he gazed over the expanse, he sighed and said to the Spirit of the Ocean, "A vulgar proverb says that he who has heard but part of the truth thinks no one equal to himself. And such a one am I.

"When formerly I heard people detracting from the learning of Confucius or underrating the heroism of Bo Yi, I did not believe. But now that I have looked upon your inexhaustibility — alas for me had I not reached your abode, I should have been forever a laughing-stock to those of comprehensive enlightenment!"

The Spirit of a paltry river learns that the ripple of his rustic stream is scarcely the murmur of the world.

To which the Spirit of the Ocean replied, "You cannot speak of ocean to a well-frog, — the creature of a narrower sphere.

I seem to be a frog abiding in a dried-well.— *Upanishad*

"You cannot speak of ice to a summer insect, — the creature of a season. You cannot speak of Tao to a pedagogue: his scope is too restricted. But now that you have emerged from your narrow sphere and have seen the great ocean, you know your own insignificance, and I can speak to you of great principles.

"There is no body of water beneath the canopy of heaven which is greater than ocean. All streams pour into it without cease, yet it does not overflow. It is constantly being drained off, yet it is never empty. Spring and autumn bring no change; floods and droughts are equally unknown.

And thus it is immeasurably superior to mere rivers and brooks, — though I would not venture to boast on this account, for I get my shape from the universe, my vital power from the Yin and Yang. In the universe I am but as a small stone or a small tree on a vast mountain. And conscious thus of my own insignificance, what is there of which I can boast?

"The Four Seas, — are they not to the universe but like puddles in a marsh? The Middle Kingdom, — is it not to the surrounding ocean like a tare-seed in a granary? Of all the myriad created things, man is but one. And of all who inhabit the land, live on the fruit of the earth, and move about in cart and boat, an individual man is but one. Is not he, as compared with all creation, but as the tip of a hair upon a horse's skin?"

— from chapter 17, "Autumn Floods"

Twelve Passages

Translated by Burton Watson (1968)

Zhuangzi, though he writes in prose, uses words in the manner of a poet, particularly in the lyrical descriptions of the Way or the Taoist sage, where meaning often takes second place to sound and emotive force. In the broader sense of the word, his work is in fact one of the greatest poems of ancient China ... No other text of early times, with the possible exception of the *Zuo Commentary*, so fully exploits the beauties of ancient Chinese: its vigor, its economy, its richness and symmetry and it is for this reason that I have chosen to render the wording of the original as closely as possible, even though the English which results may at times sound somewhat strange. Zhuangzi uses words in unconventional ways and he deserves a translation that at least attempts to do justice to his imaginativeness ...

Giles, who produced the first complete English translation, is very free in his rendering, and again and again substitutes what strike me as tiresome Victorian clichés for the complex and beautiful language of the original. In spite of his offensively "literary" tone, however, he generally gets at what appears to me to be the real meaning of the text ...

Every translator who takes up the text will produce his own *Zhuangzi*, and the more that are available for the reader to enjoy and compare, the better.

The Transformation of Things

Once Zhuang Zhou dreamed he was a butterfly, a butterfly flitting and fluttering around, happy with himself and doing as he pleased. He didn't know he was Zhuang Zhou. Suddenly he woke up and there he was, solid and unmistakable Zhuang Zhou. But he didn't know if he was Zhuang Zhou who had dreamt he was a butterfly, or a butterfly dreaming he was

Zhuang Zhou. Between Zhuang Zhou and a butterfly there must be *some* distinction! This is called the Transformation of Things.

— from chapter 2, "Discussion on Making All Things Equal"

The Freeing of the Bound

Master Si, Master Yu, Master Li, and Master Lai were all four talking together. "Who can look upon nonbeing as his head, on life as his back, and on death as his rump?" they said. "Who knows that life and death, existence and annihilation, are all a single body? I will be his friend!"

The four men looked at each other and smiled. There was no disagreement in their hearts and so the four of them became friends.

All at once Master Yu fell ill. Master Si went to ask how he was. "Amazing!" said Master Yu. "The creator is making me all crookedy like this! My back sticks up like a hunchback's and my vital organs are on top of me. My chin is hidden in my navel, my shoulders are up above my head, and my pigtail points at the sky. It must be some dislocation of the yin and yang!"

Yet he seemed calm at heart and unconcerned. Dragging himself haltingly to the well, he looked at his reflection and said, "My, my! So the Creator is making me all crookedy like this!"

"Do you resent it?" asked Master Si.

"Why no, what would I resent? If the process continues, perhaps in time he'll transform my left arm into a rooster. In that case I'll keep watch on the night. Or perhaps in time he'll transform my right arm into a crossbow pellet and I'll shoot down an owl for roasting. Or perhaps in time he'll transform my buttocks into cartwheels. Then, with my spirit for a horse, I'll climb up and go for a ride. What need will I ever have for a carriage again?

"I received life because the time had come; I will lose it because the order of things passes on. Be content with this time and dwell in this order and then neither sorrow nor joy can touch you. In ancient times this was called the 'freeing of the bound.' There are those who cannot free themselves, because they are bound by things. But nothing can ever win against Heaven — that's the way it's always been. What would I have to resent?"

Suddenly Master Lai grew ill. Gasping and wheezing, he lay at the point of death. His wife and children gathered round in a circle and began to cry. Master Li, who had come to ask how he was, said, "Shoo! Get back! Don't disturb the process of change!"

Then he leaned against the doorway and talked to Master Lai. "How marvelous the Creator is! What is he going to make of you next? Where is he going to send you? Will he make you into a rat's liver? Will he make you into a bug's arm?"

Master Lai said, "A child, obeying his father and mother, goes wherever he is told, east or west, south or north. And the yin and yang — how much more are they to a man than father or mother! Now that they have brought me to the verge of death, if I should refuse to obey them, how perverse I would be! What fault is it of theirs? The Great Clod burdens me with form, labors me with life, eases me in old age, and rests me in death. So if I think well of my life, for the same reason I must think well of my death. When a skilled smith is casting metal, if the metal should leap up and say, 'I insist upon being made into a Moye!'[36] he would surely regard it as very inauspicious metal indeed. Now, having had the audacity to take on human form once, if I should say, 'I don't want to be anything but a man! Nothing but a man,' the Creator would surely regard me as a most inauspicious sort of person. So now I think of heaven and earth as a great furnace, and the Creator as a skilled smith. Where could he send me that would not be all right? I will go off to sleep peacefully, and then with a start I will wake up."

— from chapter 6, "The Great and Venerable Teacher"

Brief, Sudden, and Chaos

Do not be an embodier of fame; do not be a storehouse of schemes; do not be an undertaker of projects; do not be a proprietor of wisdom. Embody to the fullest what has no end, and wander where there is no trail. Hold on to all that you have received from Heaven but do not think you have gotten anything. Be empty, that is all. The Perfect Man uses his mind like a mirror — going after nothing, welcoming nothing, responding but not storing. Therefore he can win out over things and not hurt himself.

The emperor of the South Sea was called Shu (Brief), the emperor of the North Sea was called Hu (Sudden), and the emperor of the central region was called Hundun (Chaos). Shu and Hu from time to time came together for a meeting in the territory of Hundun, and Hundun treated them very generously. Shu and Hu discussed how they could repay his kindness. "All men," they said, "have seven openings so they can see, hear, eat, and breathe. But Hundun alone doesn't have any. Let's try boring him some!"

---

[36] A famous sword of King He Lü (r. 514–496 B.C.) of Wu.

Every day they bored another hole, and on the seventh day Hundun died.

— from chapter 7, "Fit for Emperors and Kings"

I'll Drag My Tail in the Mud

Once, when Zhuangzi was fishing in the Pu River, the king of Chu sent two officials to go and announce to him: "I would like to trouble you with the administration of my realm."

Zhuangzi held on to the fishing pole and, without turning his head, said, "I have heard that there is a sacred tortoise in Chu that has been dead for three thousand years. The king keeps it wrapped in cloth and boxed, and stores it in the ancestral temple. Now would this tortoise rather be dead and have its bones left behind and honored? Or would it rather be alive and dragging its tail in the mud?"

"It would rather be alive and dragging its tail in the mud," said the two officials.

Zhuangzi said, "Go away! I'll drag my tail in the mud!"

— from chapter 17, "Autumn Floods"

Are You Trying to Shoo Me?

When Huizi was prime minister of Liang, Zhuangzi set off to visit him. Someone said to Huizi, "Zhuangzi is coming because he wants to replace you as prime minister!" With this Huizi was filled with alarm and searched all over the state for three days and three nights trying to find Zhuangzi. Zhuangzi then came to see him and said, "In the south there is a bird called the Yuanchu — I wonder if you've ever heard of it? The Yuanchu rises up from the South Sea and flies to the North Sea, and it will rest on nothing but the Wutong tree, eat nothing but the fruit of the Lian, and drink only from springs of sweet water. Once there was an owl who had gotten hold of a half-rotten old rat, and as the Yuanchu passed by, it raised its head, looked up at the Yuanchu, and said, 'Shoo!' Now that you have this Liang state of yours, are you trying to shoo me?"

— from chapter 17, "Autumn Floods"

What Fish Really Enjoy

Zhuangzi and Huizi were strolling along the dam of the Hao River when Zhuangzi said, "See how the minnows come out and dart around where they please! That's what fish really enjoy!"

Huizi said, "You're not a fish — how do you know what fish enjoy?"

Zhuangzi said, "You're not I, so how do you know I don't know what fish enjoy?"

Huizi said, "I'm not you, so I certainly don't know what you know. On the other hand, you're certainly not a fish — so that still proves you don't know what fish enjoy!"

Zhuangzi said, "Let's go back to your original question, please. You asked me *how* I know what fish enjoy — so you already knew I knew it when you asked the question. I know it by standing here beside the Hao."

— from chapter 17, "Autumn Floods"

Peace in a Vast Room

Zhuangzi's wife died. When Huizi went to convey his condolences, he found Zhuangzi sitting with his legs sprawled out, pounding on a tub and singing. "You lived with her, she brought up your children and grew old," said Huizi. "It should be enough simply not to weep at her death. But pounding on a tub and singing — this is going too far, isn't it?"

Zhuangzi said, "You're wrong. When she first died, do you think I didn't grieve like anyone else? But I looked back to her beginning and the time before she was born. Not only the time before she was born, but the time before she had a body. Not only the time before she had a body, but the time before she had a spirit. In the midst of the jumble of wonder and mystery a change took place and she had a spirit. Another change and she had a body. Another change and she was born. Now there's been another change and she's dead. It's just like the progression of the four seasons, spring, summer, fall, winter.

"Now she's going to lie down peacefully in a vast room. If I were to follow after her bawling and sobbing, it would show that I don't understand anything about fate. So I stopped."

— from chapter 18, "Perfect Happiness"

Lack-Limb and Lame-Gait

Uncle Lack-Limb and Uncle Lame-Gait were seeing the sights at Dark Lord Hill and the wastes of Kunlun, the place where the Yellow Emperor rested. Suddenly a willow sprouted out of Uncle Lame-Gait's left elbow. He looked very startled and seemed to be annoyed.

"Do you resent it?" said Uncle Lack-Limb.

"No — what is there to resent?" said Uncle Lame-Gait. "To live is to borrow. And if we borrow to live, then life must be a pile of trash. Life and death are day and night. You and I came to watch the process of change, and now change has caught up with me. Why would I have anything to resent?"

— from chapter 18, "Perfect Happiness"

The Skull

When Zhuangzi went to Chu, he saw an old skull, all dry and parched. He poked it with his carriage whip and then asked, "Sir, were you greedy for life and forgetful of reason, and so came to this? Was your state overthrown and did you bow beneath the ax, and so came to this? Did you do some evil deed and were you ashamed to bring disgrace upon your parents and family, and so came to this? Was it through the pangs of cold and hunger that you came to this? Or did your springs and autumns pile up until they brought you to this?"

When he had finished speaking, he dragged the skull over and, using it for a pillow, lay down to sleep.

In the middle of the night, the skull came to him in a dream and said, "You chatter like a rhetorician and all your words betray the entanglements of a living man. The dead know nothing of these! Would you like to hear a lecture on the dead?"

"Indeed," said Zhuangzi.

The skull said, "Among the dead there are no rulers above, no subjects below, and no chores of the four seasons. With nothing to do, our springs and autumns are as endless as heaven and earth. A king facing south on his throne could have no more happiness than this!"

Zhuangzi couldn't believe this and said, "If I got the Arbiter of Fate to give you a body again, make you some bones and flesh, return you to your parents and family and your old home and friends, you would want that, wouldn't you?"

The skull frowned severely, wrinkling up its brow. "Why would I throw away more happiness than that of a king on a throne and take on the troubles of a human being again?" it said.

— from chapter 18, "Perfect Happiness"

Gamecocks

Ji Xingzi was training gamecocks for the king. After ten days the king asked if they were ready.

"Not yet. They're too haughty and rely on their nerve."

Another ten days and the king asked again.

"Not yet. They still respond to noises and movements."

Another ten days and the king asked again.

"Not yet. They still look around fiercely and are full of spirit."

Another ten days and the king asked again.

"They're close enough. Another cock can crow and they show no sign of change. Look at them from a distance and you'd think they were made of wood. Their virtue is complete. Other cocks won't dare face them, but will turn and run."

— from chapter 19, "Mastering Life"

Look for Me in the Dried Fish Store

Zhuang Zhou's family was very poor, and so he went to borrow some grain from the marquis of Jianhe. The marquis said, "Why, of course. I'll soon be getting the tribute money from my fief, and when I do, I'll be glad to lend you three hundred pieces of gold. Will that be all right?"

Zhuang Zhou flushed with anger and said, "As I was coming here yesterday, I heard someone calling me on the road. I turned around and saw that there was a perch in the carriage rut. I said to him, 'Come, perch — what are you doing here?' He replied, 'I am a Wave Official of the Eastern Sea. Couldn't you give me a dipperful of water so I can stay alive?' I said to him, 'Why, of course. I'm just about to start south to visit the kings of Wu and Yue. I'll change the course of the West River and send it in your direction. Will that be all right?' The perch flushed with anger and said, 'I've lost my element! I have nowhere to go! If you can get me a dipper of water, I'll be able to stay alive. But if you give me an answer like that, then you'd best look for me in the dried fish store!' "

— from chapter 26, "Eternal Things"

Confucius

A disciple of Lao Laizi was out gathering firewood when he happened to meet Confucius. He returned and reported, "There's a man over there with a long body and short legs, his back a little humped and his ears set way back, who looks as though he were trying to attend to everything within the four seas. I don't know who it can be."

Lao Laizi said, "That's Kong Qiu. Tell him to come over here!"

When Confucius arrived, Lao Laizi said, "Qiu, get rid of your proud bearing and that knowing look on your face and you can become a gentleman!"

Confucius bowed and stepped back a little, a startled and changed expression on his face, and then asked, "Do you think I can make any progress in my labors?"

Lao Laizi said, "You can't bear to watch the sufferings of one age, and so you go and make trouble for ten thousand ages to come! Are you just naturally a boor? Or don't you have the sense to understand the situation? You take pride in practicing charity and making people happy — the shame of it will follow you all your days! These are the actions, the 'progress' of mediocre men — men who pull each other around with fame, drag each other into secret schemes, join together to praise Yao and condemn Jie, when the best thing would be to forget them both and put a stop to praise! What is contrary cannot fail to be injured, what moves when it shouldn't cannot fail to be wrong. The sage is hesitant and reluctant to begin an affair, and so he always ends in success. But what good are these actions of yours? They end in nothing but a boast!"

— from chapter 26, "Eternal Things"

Two Passages

Translated by A. C. Graham (1981)

Zhuangzi illustrates to perfection the kind of battering which a text may suffer between being written in one language and being transferred to another at the other end of the world some two thousand years later. In the first place ancient Chinese thinkers did not write books, they jotted down sayings, verses, stories, thoughts and by the third century B.C. composed essays, on bamboo strips which were tied together in sheets and rolled up in scrolls ...

They [the previous English translators] treat *Zhuangzi* as though it were what is nowadays understood by a "book" ... If we are to risk something more ambitious [than the "smooth flow of a whimsical, garrulous old wiseacre"], it is our duty to remember that the ideal of integral translation is in this case meaningless ... A Taoist philosopher is a thinker who despises thoughts, yet values, and finds the imagery and rhythm to convey, any spontaneously emerging process of thinking which he senses is orienting him in the direction of the Way. My own private final test of whether translation is really working is whether it catches any of the extraordinary rhythmic energy of Zhuangzi's writing, not merely for the lift of the heart which it gives but because to lose it falsifies the paces and shifts and stresses of his thinking ...

The Pipes of Heaven

Ziqi of Nanguo reclined elbow on armrest, looked up at the sky and exhaled, in a trance as though he had lost the counterpart of himself. Yancheng Ziyou stood in waiting before him.

"What is this?" he said. "Can the frame really be made to be like withered wood, the heart like dead ashes? The reclining man here now is not the reclining man of yesterday."

"You do well to ask that, Ziyou! This time I had lost my own self, did you know it? You hear the pipes of men, don't you, but not yet the pipes of earth, the pipes of earth but not yet the pipes of Heaven?"

"I venture to ask the secret of it."

"That hugest of clumps of soil blows out breath, by name the 'wind.'
Better if it were never to start up, for whenever it does ten thousand
hollow places burst out howling, and don't tell me you have never heard
how the hubbub swells! The recesses in mountain forests, the hollows
that pit great trees a hundred spans round, are like nostrils, like mouths,
like ears, like sockets, like bowls, like mortars, like pools, like puddles.
Hooting, hissing, sniffing, sucking, mumbling, moaning, whistling, wailing, the winds ahead sing out AAAH!, the winds behind answer EEEH!,
breezes strike up a tiny chorus, the whirlwind a mighty chorus. When the
gale has passed, all the hollows empty, and don't tell me you have never
seen how the quivering slows and settles!"

"The pipes of earth, these are the various hollows; the pipes of men,
these are rows of tubes. Let me ask about the pipes of Heaven."

"Who is it that puffs out the myriads which are never the same, who in
their self-ending is sealing them up, in their self-choosing is impelling
the force into them?

— from chapter 2, "The Sorting Which Evens Things Out"

The Axis of the Way

What is It is also Other, what is Other is also It. There they say "That's it,
that's not" from one point of view, here we say "That's it, that's not" from
another point of view. Are there really It and Other? Or really no It and
Other? Where neither It nor Other finds its opposite is called the axis of
the Way. When once the axis is found at the center of the circle there is
no limit to responding with either, on the one hand no limit to what is *it*,
on the other no limit to what is not. Therefore I say: "The best means is
Illumination." Rather than use the meaning to show that the meaning is
not the meaning, use what is *not* the meaning. Rather than use a horse to
show that a horse is not a horse, use what is *not* a horse. Heaven and earth
are the one meaning, the myriad things are the one horse.

— from chapter 2, "The Sorting Which Evens Things Out"

MENCIUS (372–289 B.C.)
Three Passages

Translated by David Collie (1828)

None of the Disciples of Confucius, says Su Ma [Sima Qian], Author of the Annals of
the Empire, has expressed that Philosopher's Sense and Energy so well. And whoever
would be instructed in his Doctrine aright, ought to begin his studies with the Work of
Mencius.

His Book is divided into two Parts; the first containing six Chapters, and the second eight. He treats of good Government, almost throughout this Work: And as at that time, the whole Empire was filled with Commotions and civil Wars, above all things, he recommends Uprightness of Heart and Equity. For this Reason, he proves, that the Re-establishment of Peace and Tranquility in the Empire, was not to be attain'd by the force of Arms, but by the Examples of Virtue.

— Du Halde, *A Description of the Empire of China*, 1738

Some will say that in many instances the rendering is too literal and in others too free, and in many cases the spirit and force of the original have been lost. Others may observe so many Chinesisms and Scotticisms in the style that they will be apt to say it does not deserve the name of an *English* version. To such charges we are ready to plead guilty; but trust that the frequent obscurity and uniform conciseness of the original, will, in some degree, be admitted as our apology. At least if such considerations as those do not tend to soften the severity of criticism, we have no other to offer, for the translation was written with due deliberation and with good native assistance, and with the same assistance every page of it has been carefully compared with the original; nor has the Translator failed to avail himself of the aid to be derived from the English and Latin Versions of the Four Books to which he had access.

— David Collie, from the preface to *The Chinese Classical Work Commonly Called the Four Books*, 1828

The *Mencius*, a work in seven chapters dealing with the teaching of the Confucian philosopher Mencius (372–289 B.C.), resembles the *Analects* in many ways. It too was probably compiled by the philosopher's disciples after his death, though tradition credits Mencius himself with a part in the work of compilation. As in the case of the *Analects*, there is little suggestion of system or order in the arrangement of the material. However, though some of the pronouncements are presented without context, many of them are given a fairly elaborate anecdotal setting, usually in the form of an interview between Mencius and one of the feudal rulers of the time.

— Burton Watson, *Early Chinese Literature*, 1962

The Compassionate Heart

Mencius said, "All men have compassionate hearts (or hearts that cannot bear to do anything cruel). The former kings had compassionate hearts and exhibited them in their compassionate government. He who possesses a compassionate heart and practices compassionate government, in ruling the empire may turn it in the palm of his hand. What is meant by saying that all men have compassionate hearts may be thus illustrated; if one see a child about to fall into a well, the latent compassion of his heart is suddenly aroused. Nor is this because he wishes to gain the favor of the child's parents, or to gain a name in the neighborhood, or because he is afraid of a bad name.

"Look at the subject in this light and you will see that he who has not a latent principle of compassion in his heart is not a man, that he who is void of shame and hatred is not a man, that he who has no humility and modesty is not a man, and that he who knows not right and wrong is not a man. A latent principle of compassion in the heart is the spring of benevolence. Shame and hatred form the rising principle of justice. Humility and modesty constitute the source of a correct and polite behavior. A sense of right and wrong is the germ of wisdom. Man has these four sources in himself, the same as he has four members. To possess these four principles and yet to say that we are not able to act well is to rob ourselves and to say that our Prince is not capable of acting aright is to rob our Prince.

"All who possess these four principles, if they know how to expand and fill them up, they will resemble the breaking out of fire, or the rising of water; carry them to perfection, and you will be able to preserve the four seas. If you do not fill them up, you cannot preserve your own father and mother."

— Book 2, part 1, chapter 6

The Man of Qi

There was a man of Qi who had a wife and concubine living in the same house. When their husband went out he always returned crammed with flesh and wine. When his wife asked with whom he ate and drank, he said, always with the rich and honorable. His wife informed his concubine, saying, "When our husband goes out he is sure to return full of flesh and wine, and when I ask with whom he eats and drinks, he says that they are all rich people.

"But I have never seen them come here. I will spy out where our husband goes." She rose early in the morning and looked after her husband. In the town no one stood to speak with him. At last he went to the east suburbs of the town among those who were offering sacrifices at the tombs, and begged what was left, which, not satisfying him, he looked round for more. This was the way in which he crammed himself. His wife returned and informed his concubine how the man on whom they depended for life was acting and then united with his concubine in reprobating their husband. Both sat down in the hall and wept. The husband, ignorant of all this, entered in a jovial manner and behaved in a pompous way. Mencius said, according to the views of a superior man there are few of the wives and concubines of those who seek riches, honor, and profit who have not occasion to be ashamed and weep.

— Book 4, part 2, chapter 33

Fish and Bear's Paw

Mencius said, "I love fish, so do I bear's paw; but if I cannot get both at once, I give up fish and take bear's paw. I love life, and I love justice; but if I cannot preserve both at once, I would give up life and hold fast justice. Although I love life, there is that which I love more than life; hence I will not act irregularly to obtain life. Although I hate death, yet there is that which I hate more than death; hence there are evils, or danger, which I will not avoid.

"If it were the case that man desired nothing more than life, then why not use every means by which it may be preserved; and were it true that there were nothing which man hated more than death, then why not use every means by which danger may be avoided?

"From this virtuous nature a man will not do what is wrong to save life nor what is unjust to avoid calamity. Hence, there is that which is desired more than life, and that which is hated more than death. Nor is it only men of superior virtue and talents who possess this heart, but all men originally possess it. The virtuous are able to preserve it.

"Suppose one is in such a state that one basket of food, or one dish of soup would save his life, while the want of them would occasion his death; if you call rudely to him and give these to him, even a man on the highway will not receive them; if you strike the ground with your foot and offer them to a common beggar he will deem them unclean.

"Now, if I, without asking whether it is just or not, receive ten thousand Zhong, of what consequence will these be to my person (compared with the basket of rice and dish of soup), but to beautify my mansions, afford me the attendance of wives and concubines, and the praises of the harem?

"Formerly to save you from death, you would not receive, but now you receive in order to beautify your mansions. Formerly you would not receive to save you from death, but now you receive to obtain the services of wives and concubines. Formerly you would not receive to save your body from death, but now you receive to obtain the praises of the poor. Is it not time to stop? This is what we call losing the original heart."

Mencius says, "Benevolence is man's heart, and justice is man's path. To lose the way, and no longer walk therein — to let one's heart go, and not know how to seek it, how lamentable! If a man lose his fowls, or his dogs, he knows how to seek them. There are those who lose their hearts, and know not how to seek them.

"The duty of the student is no other than to seek his lost heart."

— Book 6, part 1, chapters 10 and 11

HAN FEIZI (d. 233 B.C.)
Two Passages

Translated by Burton Watson (1967)

The book *Han Feizi* is a long work, in fifty-five sections, a large part of which is undoubtedly from the hand of Han Feizi himself, a highly educated thinker, writer, and would-be statesman, who attracted the attention of the king of Qin but was immediately forced by a political rival to commit suicide in 233 B.C. Some sections, however, may be by later writers of the Legalist school.

The *Han Feizi* dates from the same period as the *Intrigues of the Warring States*. The two works share many of the same anecdotes and are marked by the same air of urbanity, wit, and pervading cynicism. Both show a keen interest in rhetoric, the *Han Feizi* actually containing an essay devoted to the subject of persuasive speaking.

The *Han Feizi*, however one reacts to the ideas expressed, is almost always a delight to read. Lucidly and cogently argued, it is couched in a clear, balanced, yet seldom monotonous style, and enlivened by anecdotes and parables, which, though they do not match those of the *Zhuangzi* in originality, are often witty and incisive.

— Burton Watson, *Early Chinese Literature*, 1962

Mr. He's Jade

Once a man of Chu named Mr. He, having found a piece of jade matrix in the Chu Mountains, took it to court and presented it to King Li. King Li instructed the jeweler to examine it, and the jeweler reported, "It is only a stone." The king, supposing that He was trying to deceive him, ordered that his left foot be cut off in punishment. In time King Li passed away and King Wu came to the throne, and He once more took his matrix and presented it to King Wu. King Wu ordered his jeweler to examine it, and again the jeweler reported, "It is only a stone." The king, supposing that He was trying to deceive him as well, ordered that his right foot be cut off. He, clasping the matrix to his breast, went to the foot of the Chu Mountains, where he wept for three days and nights, and when all his tears were cried out, he wept blood in their place. The king, hearing of this, sent someone to question him. "Many people in the world have had their feet amputated — why do you weep so piteously over it?" the man asked. He replied, "I do not grieve because my feet have been cut off. I grieve because a precious jewel is dubbed a mere stone, and a man of integrity is called a deceiver. This is why I weep." The king then ordered the jeweler to cut and polish the matrix, and when he had done so a precious jewel emerged. Accordingly it was named "The Jade of Mr. He."

Rulers are always anxious to lay their hands on pearls and precious stones. Though He presented a matrix whose true beauty was not yet apparent, he certainly did no harm to the ruler thereby; and yet he had to have both feet cut off before the real nature of his treasure was finally recognized. This is how hard it is to get a treasure acknowledged. Rulers nowadays are not nearly so anxious to get hold of laws and state policies as they are to get hold of He's jade, and they are concerned about putting a stop to the private evils and deceptions of the officials and common people. Under these circumstances, if a man who truly understands the Way hopes to avoid punishment, his only resort is simply not to present to the ruler any uncut jewels of wisdom and statecraft.

If the ruler follows set policies, then the high ministers will be unable to make arbitrary decisions, and those who are close to him will not dare try to sell their influence. If the magistrates enforce the laws, then vagabonds will have to return to their farm work and wandering knights will be sent to the battlefield where they belong to face the dangers of their profession. In effect, then, laws and policies are actually inimical to the private interests of the officials and common people. Hence, if a ruler does not have the strength of character to defy the counsels of the high ministers, rise above the criticisms of the common people, and heed only that advice which truly accords with the Way, then the planners of law and policy may persist, like Mr. He, until they face the death penalty itself, and yet the true value of their words will never be acknowledged.

— from section 13, "Mr. He"

The Stump-Watcher

In the most ancient times, when men were few and creatures numerous, human beings could not overcome the birds, beasts, insects, and reptiles. Then a sage appeared who fashioned nests of wood to protect men from harm. The people were delighted and made him ruler of the world, calling him the Nest Builder. The people lived on fruits, berries, mussels, and clams — things rank and evil-smelling that hurt their bellies, so that many of them fell ill. Then a sage appeared who drilled with sticks and produced fire with which to transform the rank and putrid foods. The people were delighted and made him ruler of the world, calling him the Drill Man.

In the age of middle antiquity there was a great flood in the world, but Gun and Yu of the Xia dynasty opened up channels for the water. In the age of recent antiquity Jie and Zhou ruled in a violent and perverse way, but Tang of the Yin dynasty and Wu of the Zhou dynasty overthrew them.

Now if anyone had built wooden nests or drilled for fire in the time of the Xia dynasty, Gun and Yu would have laughed at him, and if anyone had tried to open channels for the water during the Yin or Zhou dynasties, Tang and Wu would have laughed at him. This being so, if people in the present age go about exalting the ways of Yao, Shun, Yu, Tang, and Wu, the sages of today are bound to laugh at them. For the sage does not try to practice the ways of antiquity or to abide by a fixed standard, but examines the affairs of the age and takes what precautions are necessary.

There was a farmer of Song who tilled the land, and in his field was a stump. One day a rabbit, racing across the field, bumped into the stump, broke its neck, and died. Thereupon the farmer laid aside his plow and took up watch beside the stump, hoping that he would get another rabbit in the same way. But he got no more rabbits, and instead became the laughing-stock of Song. Those who think they can take the ways of the ancient kings and use them to govern the people of today all belong in the category of stump-watchers!

— from section 49, "The Five Vermin"

LIEZI
Ten Passages

Translated by A. C. Graham (1960)

Taoism is the greatest philosophical tradition of China after Confucianism. From its first maturity in the third century B.C. we find references to a certain Liezi, who traveled by riding the wind. His historicity is doubtful, and it is not even clear when he is supposed to have lived; some indications point to 600, others to 400 B.C. The book which carries his name is a collection of stories, sayings, and brief essays grouped in eight chapters, each loosely organized around a single theme....

Some authorities still maintain that it belongs to the third century B.C. It certainly contains material coming from this period; but the predominant opinion of scholars in China is now that it was written as late as A.D. 300.

Possessing the Way

Shun asked a minister:

"Can one succeed in possessing the Way?"

"Your own body is not your possession. How can you possess the Way?"

"If my own body is not mine, whose is it?"

"It is the shape lent to you by heaven and earth. Your life is not your possession; it is harmony between your forces, granted for a time by heaven and earth. Your nature and destiny are not your possessions; they are the course laid down for you by heaven and earth. Your children and grandchildren are not your possessions; heaven and earth lend them to you to cast off from your body as an insect sheds its skin. Therefore you travel without knowing where you go, stay without knowing what you cling to, are fed without knowing how. You are the breath of heaven and earth which goes to and fro; how can you ever possess it?"

The Way of Stealing

Mr. Guo of Qi was very rich. Mr. Xiang of Song, who was very poor, traveled from Song to Qi to inquire about his methods.

"I am good at stealing," Mr. Guo told him. "After I first became a thief, within a year I could keep myself, within two I was comfortable, within three I was flourishing, and ever since then I have been the benefactor of the whole neighborhood."

Xiang was delighted; he understood from what Guo said that he was a thief, but misunderstood his Way of being a thief. So he climbed over walls and broke into houses, and grabbed anything in reach of his eye and hand. Before long, he was found guilty of possessing stolen goods, and lost his whole inheritance. Thinking that Guo had deceived him, he went to him to complain.

"In what way have you been stealing?" Guo asked him.

Xiang described what had happened.

"Alas!" Guo said. "Have you erred so far from the true Way of stealing? Let me explain. I have heard it said: 'Heaven has its seasons, earth has its benefits.' I rob heaven and earth of their seasonal benefits, the clouds and rain of their irrigating floods, the mountains and marshes of their products, in order to grow my crops, plant my seed, raise my walls, build my house. I steal birds and animals from the land, fish and turtles from the water. All this is stealing; for crops and seed, clay and wood, birds and animals, fish and turtles, are all begotten by heaven, and how can they become my possessions? Yet I suffer no retribution for robbing heaven. On the other hand precious things such as gold and jade, and commodities such as grain and silk, are collected by men, and how can we claim that it is heaven which provides them? When you steal them, why should you resent being found guilty?"

Xiang was highly perplexed, and thought that Guo was trapping him again. Happening to meet Master Dongguo, he questioned him and got this answer:

"Is not your very body stolen? When you must steal the yin and yang energies in harmonious proportions even to achieve your life and sustain your body, how can you take the things outside you without stealing them? In reality the myriad things of heaven and earth are not separate from each other; and to claim anything as one's own is always wrong-headed. Guo's way of stealing is common to all, and so he escapes retribution; your motive for stealing is private, and so you were found guilty. Whether or not you distinguish between common and private, you are still stealing. It is the power of heaven and earth which makes the common common and the private private. For the man who understands the power of heaven and earth, what is stealing and what is not stealing?"

— from chapter 1, "Heaven's Gift"

The Keeper of Monkeys

There was a keeper of monkeys in Song who loved monkeys so much that he reared flocks of them. He could interpret the monkey's thoughts, and the monkeys too caught what was in his mind. He made his own family go short in order to give the monkeys whatever they wanted. Before long he found himself in need, and decided to give them less to eat. Fearing that the monkeys would not submit to it tamely, he played a trick on them beforehand:

"If I give you three chestnuts in the morning and four in the evening, will that be enough?"

The monkeys all got up in a rage.

"Will it be enough if I give you four in the morning and three in the evening?"

The monkeys were all pleased and lay down again.

It is always the same when the cleverer of two things traps the sillier. The sage by his wisdom gets all the fools into his cage, just as the keeper did to the monkeys. Without taking anything away, in name or reality, he can either please them or enrage them!

— from chapter 2, "The Yellow Emperor"

Dreaming and Waking

There was a man of Zheng who went to gather firewood in the moors, and came on a frightened deer. He stood in its way, struck it, and killed it. Fearing that someone would see the deer, he quickly hid it in a ditch and covered it with brushwood. His joy overwhelmed him. But soon afterward he could not find the place where he had hidden it, and decided that he must have been dreaming.

He came down the road humming to himself about the affair. A passer-by heard him, acted on his words and took the deer. When this man got home he told his wife:

"Just now a woodcutter dreamed he had caught a deer, but did not know where it was. Now I have found it. His dream was a true one."

"Isn't it rather that you dreamed you saw the woodcutter catch the deer? Why should there be any woodcutter? Since you have really got the deer, isn't it your dream which was true?"

"All I know is that I have got it. What do I care which of us was dreaming?"

When the woodcutter got home, he was not reconciled to his loss. That night he had a true dream of the place where he hid the deer, and also of the man who found it. Next morning, guided by the dream, he sought out the man, and then went to law to contest his right to the deer.

The case was referred to the Chief Justice, who said:

"If in the first place you really did catch the deer, you are wrong to say you were dreaming. If you really dreamed that you caught it, you are wrong to say it actually happened. The other man really did take your deer, yet contests your right to it. His wife also says that he recognized it in his dream as another man's deer, yet denies the existence of the man who caught it. Now all I know is that here we have the deer. I suggest you divide it between you."

It was reported to the lord of Zheng, who said:

"Alas! Is the Chief Justice going to dream that he has divided someone's deer?"

The Prime Minister was consulted. He said:

"It is beyond me to distinguish dreaming and not dreaming. If you want to distinguish dreaming from waking, you will have to call in the Yellow Emperor or Confucius. Now that we have lost the Yellow Emperor and Confucius, who is to distinguish them? For the present we may as well trust the decision of the Chief Justice."

— from chapter 3, "King Mu of Zhou"

Still in Jin

There was a man who was born in Yan but grew up in Chu, and in old age returned to his native country. While he was passing through the state of Jin his companions played a joke on him. They pointed out a city and told him: "This is the capital of Yan."

He composed himself and looked solemn.

Inside the city they pointed out a shrine: "This is the shrine of your quarter."

He breathed a deep sigh.

They pointed out a hut: "This was your father's cottage."

His tears welled up.

They pointed out a mound: "This is your father's tomb."

He could not help weeping aloud. His companions roared with laughter: "We were teasing you. You are still only in Jin."

The man was very embarrassed. When he reached Yan, and really saw the capital of Yan and the shrine of his quarter, really saw his father's cottage and tomb, he did not feel it so deeply.

— from chapter 3, "King Mu of Zhou"

Mister Simple of North Mountain

The mountains Taixing and Wangwu are seven hundred miles square, and seven hundred thousand feet high. They stood originally between Jizhou on the North and Heyang on the South. When Mister Simple of North Mountain was nearly ninety, he was living opposite them; and it vexed him that, with the North flank of the mountains blocking the road, it was such a long way round to come and go. He called together the family and made a proposal:

"Do you agree that we should make every effort to level the high ground, so that there is a clear road straight through to South of Yu and down to the South bank of the Han river?"

They all agreed. But his wife raised difficulties:

"You are too weak to reduce even the smallest hillock; what can you do with Taixing and Wangwu? Besides, where will you put the earth and stones?"

They all answered:

"Throw them in the tail of the Gulf of Zhili, North of Yintu."

Then, taking his son and grandson as porters, he broke stones and dug up earth, which they transported in hods and baskets to the tail of the Gulf of Zhili. The son of their neighbor Mr. Jingcheng, born to his widow after his death, and now just cutting his second teeth, ran away to help them.

Mister Simple did not come home until the hot season had given way to the cold. Old Wiseacre of River Bend smiled and tried to stop him, saying:

"How can you be so unwise? With the last strength of your declining years, you cannot even damage one blade of grass on the mountains; what can you do to stones and earth?"

Mister Simple of North Mountain breathed a long sigh, and said:

"Certainly your mind is set too firm for me ever to penetrate it. You are not even as clever as the widow's little child. Even when I die, I shall have sons surviving me. My sons will beget me more grandsons, my grandsons in their turn will have sons, and these will have more sons and grandsons. My descendants will go on forever, but the mountains will get no bigger. Why should there be any difficulty about leveling it?"

Old Wiseacre of River Bend was at a loss for an answer.

The mountain spirits which carry snakes in their hands heard about it and were afraid he would not give up. They reported it to God, who was moved by his sincerity, and commanded the two sons of Kua'er to carry the mountains on their backs and put one in Shuodong, the other in Yongnan. Since this time there has been no high ground from Jizhou in the North to the South bank of the Han river.

— from chapter 5, "The Questions of Tang"

The Size of the Sun

When Confucius was traveling in the East, he saw two small children arguing and asked them the reason. One child said he thought that the sun is nearer to us at sunrise, the other that it is nearer at noon. The first child said:

"When the sun first rises it is as big as the cover of a car; by noon it is as small as a plate or a bowl. Don't you think it must be nearer when it is big than when it is small?"

The other child answered:

"When the sun first rises the air is cool. By noon it is like dipping your hand in hot water. Don't you think it must be nearer when it is hot than when it is cool?"

Confucius could not decide the question. The two children laughed: "Who says you are a learned man?"

— from chapter 5, "The Questions of Tang"

A Good Listener

Bo Ya was a good lute-player, and Zhong Ziqi was a good listener. Bo Ya strummed his lute, with his mind on climbing high mountains; and Zhong Ziqi said:

"Good! Lofty, like Mount Tai!"

When his mind was on flowing waters, Zhong Ziqi said:

"Good! Boundless, like the Yellow River and the Yangtze!"

Whatever came into Bo Ya's thoughts, Zhong Ziqi always grasped it.

Bo Ya was roaming on the North side of Mount Tai; he was caught in a sudden storm of rain, and took shelter under a cliff. Feeling sad, he took up his lute and strummed it; first he composed an air about the persistent rain, then he improvised the sound of crashing mountains. Whatever melody he played, Zhong Ziqi never missed the direction of his thought. Then Bo Ya put away his lute and sighed:

"Good! Good! How well you listen! What you imagine is just what is in my mind. Is there nowhere for my notes to flee to?"

— from chapter 5, "The Questions of Tang"

The Artificial Men

When King Mu of Zhou made his royal tour of the west, he passed Kunlun but did not reach Mount Yan. On the road back, before he arrived in the Middle Kingdom, someone introduced to him a craftsman named Yanshi. King Mu received the craftsman and asked:

"What can you do?"

"Your Majesty may command what he pleases. But I have already made something, and I hope that Your Majesty will look at it first."

"Bring it with you next time, and I will take a look at it with you."

Next day Yanshi asked to see the King. The King received him, and asked:

"Who is that man who has come with you?"

"It is something I made which can do tricks."

The King looked at it in amazement; it was striding quickly looking up and down, undoubtedly it was a man. When the craftsman pushed its cheek it sang in tune; when he clasped its hand it danced in time; it did innumerable tricks, whatever it pleased you to ask. The King thought it really was a man, and watched it with his favorite Sengji and his other concubines.

When the entertainment was about to end, the performer winked his eye and beckoned to the concubines in waiting on the King's left and right. The King was very angry, and wanted to execute Yanshi on the spot. Yanshi, terrified, at once cut open the performer and took it to pieces to show the King. It was all made by sticking together leather, wood, glue, and lacquer, colored white, black, red, and blue. The King examined it closely; on the inside the liver, gall, heart, lungs, spleen, kidneys, intestines, and stomach, on the outside the muscles, bones, limbs, joints, skin, teeth, and hair were all artificial, but complete without exception. When they were put together, the thing was again as he had seen it before. The King tried taking out its heart, and the mouth could not speak; tried taking out its liver, and the eyes could not see; tried taking out its kidneys, and the feet could not walk. The King was at last satisfied, and said with a sigh:

"Is it then possible for human skill to achieve as much as the Creator?"

He had it loaded into the second of his cars, and took it back with him.

Gongshu Ban's ladder which reached the clouds, Mozi's flying kite, seemed to them the utmost of which men are capable. When their disciples Dongmen Jia and Qin Guli heard of Yanshi's skill, they told the two philosophers, who never dared to speak again of their accomplishments to the end of their lives, and always carried compass and square.

— from chapter 5, "The Questions of Tang"

Duke Jing's Tears

Duke Jing of Qi went on an excursion to Ox Mountain. He looked Northward down on the walls of his capital, and said with tears streaming:

"How beautiful, this city of mine, teeming and thriving! Why must the drops fall one by one, why must I some day leave this city and die? If from of old there had been no death, should I ever leave it for another?"

Shi Kong and Liangqiu Ju both followed his example and wept, saying:

"Your servants owe it to your bounty that we are lucky enough to have tough meat and coarse rice to eat, jaded hacks and plain carriages to ride. Yet even we do not wish to die, and how much less our master!"

Yanzi alone was smiling to himself. The Duke wiped away his tears, turned to Yanzi and said:

"My excursion today has been a melancholy one. Kong and Ju both wept as I did; why should you alone be smiling?"

"If by merit we could hold on to life," Yanzi answered, "your ancestors Taigong and Duke Huan would have lived forever. If by courage we could hold on to life, Duke Zhuang and Duke Ling would have lived forever. If these princes had held on to life, my lord would now be standing in the ricefields wearing a grass coat and bamboo hat, caring about nothing but his work, with no time to think about death! For how does my lord come to be sitting on this throne? Because your ancestors occupied and left it one after another until it was your turn; and it is ignoble that you should be the only one to shed tears over it. I see an ignoble lord and flattering ministers; and this sight is the reason why I alone ventured to smile."

Duke Jing was ashamed of himself. He lifted his winecup and sconced himself, and sconced his two ministers two cups each.

— from chapter 6, "Endeavor and Destiny"

▣ Further Reading ▣

Chang Chung-yuan, trans. *Tao: A New Way of Thinking.* New York: Harper & Row, 1975.

Clark, Andrew, ed. *The Life and Times of Anthony Wood, Antiquary, of Oxford,* 5 vols. Oxford: Oxford Historical Society, 1891–1900.

Collie, David, trans. *The Chinese Classical Work Commonly Called the Four Books.* Malacca: Mission Press, 1828.

Crump, J. I., trans. *Chan-kuo Ts'e.* Rev. ed., San Francisco: Chinese Materials Center, 1979.

Dawson, Raymond, trans. *Confucius: The Analects.* Oxford: Oxford University Press, 1993.

D'Elia, Pasquale, ed. *Fonti Ricciane.* Rome: Librerio dello Stato, 1942–1949.

Du Halde, Jean-Baptiste. *Description géographique, historique, chronologique, politique de l'empire de la Chine,* 4 vols. Paris: Lemercier, 1735. Trans. as *A Description of the Empire of China,* 2 vols. (London: Edward Cave, 1738–41).

Duyvendak, J. J. L., trans. *Tao Te Ching: The Book of the Way and Its Virtue.* London: John Murray, 1954.

Giles, Herbert, trans. *Chuang Tzu: Mystic, Moralist and Social Reformer.* Shanghai: Kelly & Walsh, 1889. 2nd rev. ed., re-entitled *Chuang-tzu: Taoist Philosopher and Chinese Mystic.* London: Allen & Unwin, 1926.

Graham, A. C., trans. *The Book of Lieh-tzu.* London: John Murray, 1960.

———. *Chuang-tzu: The Seven Inner Chapters and Other Writings.* London: Allen & Unwin, 1981.

Intorcetta, Prospero, *et al.,* trans. *Confucius Sinarum Philosophus, sive Scientia Sinensis, latine exposita.* Paris: Horthemels, 1687.

Jung, Carl Gustav. "In Memory of Richard Wilhelm." Trans. C. F. Baynes. In *The Secret of the Golden Flower: A Chinese Book of Life,* trans. Richard Wilheim. London: Kegan Paul, 1931.

Ku Hung-ming, trans. *The Discourses and Sayings of Confucius: A New Special Translation, Illustrated with Quotations from Goethe and Other Writers.* Shanghai: Kelly & Walsh, 1898.

Lau, D. C., trans. *Lao Tzu: Tao Te Ching.* Harmondsworth: Penguin Books, 1963.

———. *Mencius.* Harmondsworth: Penguin Books, 1970.

———. *The Analects.* Harmondsworth: Penguin Books, 1979.

Laufer, Berthold. *Jade: A Study in Chinese Archaeology and Religion.* Chicago: Field Museum of Natural History, 1912.

Lee, Thomas, ed. *China and Europe: Images and Influences in the Sixteenth to Eighteenth Centuries.* Hong Kong: The Chinese University Press, 1991.

Legge, James, trans. *The Chinese Classics, Vol. 1: Confucian Analects etc.* Hong Kong: Legge, 1861.

———. *The Chinese Classics, Vol. 3: The Shoo King.* Hong Kong: Legge, 1865.

———. *The Chinese Classics, Vol. 5: The Ch'un Ts'ew with the Tso Chuen.* Hong Kong: Legge, 1872.

———. *The Sacred Books of the East: Vol. 16—The Texts of Confucianism, Pt. 2: The Yi King.* Oxford: Clarendon Press, 1882.

———. *The Sacred Books of the East: Vols. 39 and 40—The Texts of Taoism: The Tao Teh King and The Writings of Kwang-Sze.* Oxford: Clarendon Press, 1891.

Leys, Simon (Pierre Ryckmans), trans. *The Analects of Confucius.* New York: W. W. Norton, 1997.

Lin Yutang, ed. and trans. *The Wisdom of Confucius.* New York: Random House, 1938.

———— . *The Wisdom of Laotse.* New York: Random House, 1948.

Lynn, Richard, trans. *The Classic of Changes: A New Translation of the I Ching As Interpreted by Wang Bi.* New York: Columbia University Press, 1994.

The Morals of Confucius: A Chinese Philosopher, Who Flourished about Five Hundred Years Before the Coming of Christ. London: Randal Taylor, 1691.

Pound, Ezra, trans. *Confucius: The Great Digest, The Unwobbling Pivot, The Analects.* New York: New Directions, 1951.

Régis, Jean-Baptiste, trans. *Y-King: Antiquissimus Sinarum Liber.* Stuttgart: J. G. Cotta, 1834.

Rule, Paul. *K'ung-tzu or Confucius: The Jesuit interpretation of Confucianism.* Sydney: Allen & Unwin, 1986.

Shchutskii, Iulian K. *Researches on the I Ching.* Trans. William L. MacDonald, and Tsuyoshi Hasegawa, with Hellmut Wilhelm. London: Routledge & Kegan Paul, 1979.

Waley, Arthur, trans. *The Way and Its Power: A Study of the Tao Te Ching and Its Place in Chinese Thought.* London: Allen & Unwin, 1935.

———— . *The Analects of Confucius.* London: Allen & Unwin, 1938.

———— . *Three Ways of Thought in Ancient China.* London: Allen & Unwin, 1939.

Watson, Burton, ed. and trans. *Early Chinese Literature.* New York: Columbia University Press, 1962.

———— . *Basic Writings of Mo Tzu, Hsün Tzu and Han Fei Tzu.* New York: Columbia University Press, 1967.

———— . *The Complete Works of Chuang Tzu.* New York: Columbia University Press, 1968.

———— . *The Tso Chuan: Selections from China's Oldest Narrative History.* New York: Columbia University Press, 1989.

Wilhelm, Richard, trans. *I Ging: Das Buch der Wandlungen.* Jena: Diederichs, 1924. *The I Ching, or Book of Changes.* English translation by Cary F. Baynes. New York: Pantheon, 1950.

Wright, Arthur F., ed., *Studies in Chinese Thought.* Chicago: Chicago University Press, 1953.

⳾ Editors' Note ⳾

In this chapter, as in the previous one, we encounter a wealth of early versions. When the West first began to inform itself seriously about China, it was the way of thinking, the history, and social organization of this fabulous land that demanded attention, more so than its literature. So the great classics of Confucianism were well served. The original manuscript of the Latin *Book of Changes* by Jean-Baptiste Régis (1664–1738) and his fellow Jesuits dates from the first half of the eighteenth century, though it was not published until 1832. Few readers now possess the Latin to appreciate the beauty of his "*Draco absconditus*" (Legge's "dragon lying hid in the deep"), but it is nonetheless salutary to be reminded of the very high standards attained by these early Jesuits, who combined vast erudition with insights gained from years in China and contacts with learned mandarins. They used Latin not to impress, but because it was still at that time the *lingua franca* of the scholarly world. Richard Wilhelm's version of the same work, coming two centuries later (the preface to his original German text is dated Peking, 1923), is one of the rare examples of a major Chinese classic becoming undeniably part of *weltliteratur*. Wilhelm worked closely with Lao Naixuan, a distinguished scholar of the old school, and entered deeply into the many-layered world of this ancient text. His German version was translated into English in its entirety in 1950 and became one of the key books of twentieth-century literature. As Jung points out, in his moving memorial, Wilhelm was more than just a translator, he was a "gnostic intermediary."

The *Confucian Analects* had been translated, or paraphrased, into Latin in the late seventeenth century (1687), by another team of Jesuits, and it was on the basis of this paraphrase that other books summarizing the "Morals of Confucius" appeared rapidly (1688, 1691) in French and English. Jean-Baptiste du Halde's *Description géographique, historique, chronologique, politique de l'empire de la Chine*, published in 4 volumes in 1735, an epitome of the work of the great Jesuits of the previous century and a half, was put into English twice in quick succession (1736 and 1738). Apart from summarizing large amounts of descriptive information about China, this work was in a sense the first European anthology of translations from the Chinese. Its English version, written in resonant Augustan prose, was part of the well-educated gentleman's reading, in a way that no anthology of Chinese has ever been since.

Apart from the Jesuits, there were the Protestant missionaries of the early nineteenth century such as Robert Morrison, whose *Dictionary of the Chinese Language* appeared in the Portuguese colony of Macao, in six volumes (1815–1823), and David Collie, who translated Mencius while principal of the Anglo-Chinese College in Malacca.

Chinese translators of Chinese literature will be a rarity in this anthology. There have been many of them, but few have had a mastery of the English language to match their undoubted familiarity with the original texts. The *Analects* of Ku Hung-ming (1857–1928) is a rare exception.

Prominent in this chapter (the *Zuo Commentary, Zhuangzi, Han Feizi*) is the work of the contemporary American translator Burton Watson, whose name has already occurred in the previous chapter and will recur regularly throughout this anthology. Since the early 1960s he has delighted and instructed countless readers and students with his limpid prose, his fluent free verse, his lively wit, and his great learning lightly worn. In addition to his translations, we have also included a number of his succinct introductions (taken from such books as his *Early Chinese Literature*).

"He who has contemplated the sea finds it difficult to think of other waters."
Mencius, Book VII, Part I, Chapter 24
Seal carved by Wu Xizai (1799–1870)

Chapter 5

The Songs of the South

Shamanism and Poetry

When we examine both the bone structure of the work and the musculature and integument which that structure sustains, we see that, although the work adopts the basic idea of the Classics, there are yet magnificent literary expressions which are the original work of the authors themselves. Thus "On Encountering Trouble" and the "Nine Pieces," brilliant and beautiful, communicate frustrated desires; the "Nine Songs" and "Nine Changes," delicate and lyrical, express grief; the "Heavenly Questions" and "Far-off Journey," odd and eccentric, exhibit great artfulness; and the "Summons of the Soul" and "Great Summons," gorgeous and dazzling, are imbued with profound beauty. The "Divination" reveals the true manner of one in exile; and "The Fisherman" manifests the unique talent of a recluse. For these reasons, their spirit is in harmony with the spirit of the ancients and their language meets the need of the present day. With their startling grace and unique beauty, they are indeed incomparable.

> Without Qu Yuan
> How could there be "On Encountering Trouble"?
> His startling talent sweeps like wind,
> And his vigorous patterns roll like clouds.
> The mountains and streams he describes have no horizons,
> And the emotions and ideas he expresses are those of one who has suffered much.
> All the phases and forms of the works are of gold and jade,
> And its minutest fragments overflow with beauty.
>
> — Liu Xie, *The Literary Mind and the Carving of Dragons*,
> chapter 5, "On the *Songs of the South*"

With respect to their Poetry, besides their Ancient Books, some of which are in Verse, the poems of *Kiu iwen* [Qu Yuan] are extremely delicate and sweet.

> — Du Halde, *A Description of the Empire of China*, 1738

Introduction

David Hawkes

North and South

The first thing to be lost when Chinese poetry is translated is not some subtle nuance of the meaning but the poetic form. The traditional forms of Chinese poetry are most of them extraordinarily antique. Some of those used by the late Mao Zedong in his occasional verse — some, for that matter, used by the thousands of amateurs who continue to write traditional-style Chinese poetry today — had already been perfected by the time of Charlemagne, and some were developed even earlier, in the second century A.D. Before the second century A.D. Chinese poetry was formally very different — at least as different as Old English alliterative verse from the poetry of Chaucer, Milton, and Pope. Yet if we look beyond the superficialities of form and seek to understand the spirit of Chinese poetry — the Chinese poet's way of looking at the world, his vocabulary of images, and the various assumptions that he makes — it is to the ancient poetry that we must turn. In the ancient poetry of China we may, indeed, find clues to the dual origin of all poetry: the expression of men's feelings as social beings and the expression of their feelings as isolated individual souls.

For Chinese poetry has a dual ancestry, a Northern and a Southern, corresponding in some respects to these two poetic functions. The Southern ancestor is less ancient than the Northern one and can, in a very roundabout sort of way, be derived from it; but the differences between them are so great that it is more convenient to think of them as two separate sources, contributing in equal measure to the new kind of poetry that began to emerge in the second century A.D. The Northern of these two ancestors is the *Book of Songs*; the Southern one is the *Plaints of Chu* or *Songs of the South*. In these two anthologies is contained all that we know of ancient Chinese poetry.

"Northern" and "Southern" are relative terms and therefore apt to be misleading. The people who produced the songs of the *Book of Songs*, many of which date from the ninth and eighth centuries B.C., certainly did not think of themselves as Northerners, though they lived in what we should nowadays call North China: the North China Plain and the loess plateaux to the west of it. On the other hand, they would certainly have regarded the Chu noblemen who wrote the early *Songs of the South* poems in the fourth and third centuries B.C. as Southerners, though the kingdom of Chu occupied what to us is Central China: the lakelands of the central valley of the Yangtze and the lands traversed by its tributaries, the Han and the Xiang.

China's First Poet

Perhaps the biggest of the differences (between the Northern and Southern ancestors of Chinese poetry) was the great gulf separating the oral, anonymous nature of the *Book of Songs* from the personal, essentially literary character of the *Songs of the South*.

Of the three hundred and five songs of the *Book of Songs* there are exactly three in which the singer identifies himself by name.

Ji Fu made this song
Clear and cool as a breeze.
Lord, long worn by care,
May it bring your heart ease

concludes one of them at the end of several stanzas celebrating the achievements of a nobleman called Zhongshan Fu. We know that Zhongshan Fu was a great officer at the court of King Xuan of Zhou at the end of the ninth century B.C., but "Ji Fu" means nothing to us; the name was as common as "Thomas" or "Peter" is today. Was he an amateur or a professional, a squire in Zhongshan Fu's employment or a bard? We have no means of knowing. No hint of his own personality is revealed to us in his poem. We have even less idea of him than of the anonymous footsoldier who sings, elsewhere in the *Songs*, about the hardships of campaigning, or of the disillusioned wife who sings about her betrayal by a faithless husband. But all the songs, with their short stanzas and frequent refrains, are oral poetry, circulating, in some cases perhaps, for centuries before they were committed to writing.

The *Songs of the South* are quite different. Qu Yuan, whose great poem "On Encountering Trouble" stands at the head of the collection, thrusts himself from the very first line on our attention:

Scion of the high lord Gao Yang,
Bo Yong was my father's name.
When She Ti pointed to the first month of the year
On the day *geng-yin* I passed from the womb ...

And throughout the whole of the long poem he remains in the forefront: "I ... I ... I ..." He bares his breast to us, examines his motives, admits his doubts, reveals his aspirations, argues, cites historical precedents in defense of his opinions — in short, he is no mere bard or song-maker like Ji Fu, but a *poet*. China's First Poet we can with some justice call him.

Chuci: *The Songs of the South*

The poetry of Qu Yuan and his immediate successors has reached us as part of an anthology of Chu poetry edited and annotated by Wang Yi, a librarian employed in the Imperial Library at Luoyang by the Later Han emperor Shun in the second century A.D. The anthology consists of seventeen works, of which about half are ascribed by Wang Yi to Qu Yuan whilst the other half are mostly imitative works in the Chu style written by poets of the Han dynasty.

The title that Wang Yi gave his anthology, *Chuci*, means literally "Words of Chu." (The term *ci* was used to denote an oral or written text: the words of a song, an oath, a treaty, a speech, a poem, and so forth.) Long before Wang Yi used it as the title of his anthology it was in use as a vague collective title for the various works associated with Qu Yuan and the early Chu poets, just as *Matière de Bretagne* was used in medieval Europe as a collective title for the vast corpus of prose and verse woven round the legend of King Arthur and his knights, and the quest of the grail. *Chuci* was, as it were, the *Matière de Chu*, the name of a literary tradition.

— General Introduction to *The Songs of the South*, 1985

Qu Yuan (c. 340–278 b.c.)
On Encountering Trouble

Translated by David Hawkes

The key to this extraordinary poem is in its first and last lines. In the opening line of the poem the poet tells us that he is a nobleman, descended from the gods; in the closing lines he cries out despairingly that there is no one "worthy to work with in making good government" and that he intends to abandon the corrupt world which is incapable of understanding him and join the company of the holy dead.

Armed with this knowledge, we are able to understand that the inconstant "Fair One" who rejects him is the weak-minded, vacillating king who rejected his policies, and that his unsuccessful quest for a suitable "mate" among the goddesses and legendary princesses who inhabit the spirit world which he journeys through after his rejection is an allegorical survey of the political alternatives: employment in one or other of the neighboring states. His conclusion is that all are equally bad and that his only real alternative is death.

We can only guess at the nature of the recitals which Chu shamans may be supposed to have given recounting the aerial journeys or "flights" they made into the land of spirits, but by studying "On Encountering Trouble" and the "Nine Songs" we can fairly easily deduce that they must have been dramatic ("Here I am, suddenly, in this House of Spring," "On Encountering Trouble," l. 217) and that they must have employed various formulaic devices for conveying the passage of time. (It has always been held, and by other peoples besides the Chinese, that time in the spirit world passes more quickly than our earthly time.)

The dreamlike changes and shifts of focus in "On Encountering Trouble" are a product not of textual corruption, as has sometimes been suggested, but of this shamanistic convention.

The most remarkable thing about this very remarkable poem is that we can see a genius at work in it actually in the process of inventing a completely new sort of poetry out of an old oral tradition. Qu Yuan's despairing cry signals, paradoxically — or perhaps not so paradoxically — the birth of literature.

> Scion of the high lord Gao Yang,[1]
> Bo Yong was my father's name.
> When She Ti pointed to the first month of the year,[2]
> On the day *geng-yin* I passed from the womb.[3]

---

[1] Gao Yang, also known as Zhuan Xu, was one of a pair of high lords, *di* (the other one being Gao Xin), from whom nearly all the princely houses of Qu Yuan's day believed themselves to be descended. Later genealogists gave them a common ancestor in the person of the Yellow Emperor.

[2] She Ti was the name of a Chinese constellation made up of two groups of three stars to left and right of the bright star Arcturus in Boötes.

[3] This was the twenty-seventh day in the sixty-day cycle. It had some special significance for the people of Chu and was clearly quite the best day in the year either to be born or to die on.

My father, seeing the aspect of my nativity,
Took omens to give me an auspicious name.
The name he gave me was True Exemplar;
The title he gave me was Divine Balance.

Having from birth this inward beauty,
I added to it fair outward adornment:
I dressed in selinea and shady angelica,
And twined autumn orchids to make a garland.
Swiftly I sped as in fearful pursuit,
Afraid Time would race on and leave me behind.
In the morning I gathered the angelica on the mountains;
In the evening I plucked the sedges of the islets.

The days and months hurried on, never delaying;
Springs and autumns sped by in endless alternation:
And I thought how the trees and flowers were fading and falling,
And feared that my Fairest's beauty would fade too.[4]
"Gather the flower of youth and cast out the impure!
Why will you not change the error of your ways?
I have harnessed brave coursers for you to gallop forth with:
Come, let me go before and show you the way!

"The three kings of old were most pure and perfect:
Then indeed fragrant flowers had their proper place.
They brought together pepper and cinnamon;
All the most-prized blossoms were woven in their garlands.
Glorious and great were those two, Yao and Shun,[5]
Because they had kept their feet on the right path.
And how great was the folly of Jie and Zhou,[6]
Who hastened by crooked paths, and so came to grief.

---

[4] In ancient China the word *meiren* (literally "beautiful person") was sexually ambiguous. Is the poet imagining himself as a handsome, flower-decked youth and his king as a beautiful maiden whom he seeks to woo? Or is the poet representing himself as a woman and the king as a man? Or is it a homosexual relationship: flower-decked male poet in pursuit of beautiful male lover? The text is non-committal.

[5] Yao and Shun were the two "sage-kings" constantly referred to by Qu Yuan and his contemporaries as symbols of a Golden Age in high antiquity when rulers ruled by good example alone and won the allegiance of distant tribes not by military conquest but by cultural magnetism.

[6] Jie and Zhou were the last kings of the Xia and Shang dynasties respectively. Both kings were represented as monsters of iniquity.

"The fools enjoy their careless pleasure,
But their way is dark and leads to danger.
I have no fear for the peril of my own person,
But only lest the chariot of my lord should be dashed.
I hurried about your chariot in attendance,
Leading you in the tracks of the kings of old."
But the Fragrant One refused to examine my true feelings:
He lent ear instead to slander, and raged against me.

How well I know that loyalty brings disaster;
Yet I will endure: I cannot give it up.
I called on the ninefold heaven to be my witness,
And all for the sake of the Fair One, and no other.
There once was a time when he spoke with me in frankness;
But then he repented and was of another mind.
I do not care, on my own count, about this divorcement,
But it grieves me to find the Fair One so inconstant.

I had tended many an acre of orchids,
And planted a hundred rods of melilotus;
I had raised sweet lichens and the cart-halting flower,
And asarums mingled with fragrant angelica,
And hoped that when leaf and stem were in their full prime,
When the time had come, I could reap a fine harvest.
Though famine should pinch me, it is small matter;
But I grieve that all my blossoms should waste in rank weeds.

All others press forward in greed and gluttony,
No surfeit satiating their demands:
Forgiving themselves, but harshly judging others;
Each fretting his heart away in envy and malice.
Madly they rush in the covetous chase,
But not after that which *my* heart sets store by.
For old age comes creeping and soon will be upon me,
And I fear I shall not leave behind an enduring name.

In the mornings I drank the dew that fell from the magnolia;
At evening ate the petals that dropped from chrysanthemums.
If only my mind can be truly beautiful,
It matters nothing that I often faint for famine.
I pulled up roots to bind the valerian
And thread the castor plant's fallen cluster with;
I trimmed sprays of cassia for plaiting melilotus,
And knotted the lithe, light trails of ivy.

I take my fashion from the good men of old:
A garb unlike that which the rude world cares for;
Though it may not accord with present-day manners,
I will follow the pattern that Peng Xian has left.[7]
Heaving a long sigh, I brush away my tears,
Sad that man's life should be so beset with hardship.
Though goodness and beauty were my bit and bridle,
I was slandered in the morning and cast off that same evening.

Yet, though cast off, I would wear my orchid girdle;
I would pluck some angelicas to add to its beauty;
For this it is that my heart takes most delight in,
And though I died nine times, I should not regret it.
What I regret is the Fair One's waywardness,
That never once stops to ask what is in men's minds.
All your ladies were jealous of my delicate beauty;
In their spiteful chattering they said I was a wanton.

Truly this generation are cunning artificers,
From square and compass turn their eyes and change the true
    measurement,
Disregard the ruled line to follow their crooked fancies;
To emulate in flattery is their only rule.
But I am sick and sad at heart and stand irresolute:
I alone am at a loss in this generation.
Yet I would rather quickly die and meet dissolution
Before I ever would consent to ape *their* behavior.

Eagles do not flock like birds of lesser species;
So it has ever been since the olden time.
How can the round and square ever fit together?
How can different ways of life ever be reconciled?
Yet humbling one's spirit and curbing one's pride,
Bearing blame humbly and enduring insults,
But keeping pure and spotless and dying in righteousness:
Such conduct was greatly prized by the wise men of old.

Repenting, therefore, that I had not conned the way more closely,
I halted, intending to turn back again —
To turn about my chariot and retrace my road

---

[7] Peng Xian may refer to a shaman who lived at the court of one of the Shang kings and drowned himself in protest when his loyal advice was rejected.

Before I had advanced too far along the path of folly.
I walked my horses through the marsh's orchid-covered margin;
I galloped to the hill of pepper-trees and rested there.
I could not go in to him for fear of meeting trouble,
And so, retired, I would once more fashion my former raiment.

I made a coat of lotus and water-chestnut leaves,
And gathered lotus petals to make myself a skirt.
I will no longer care that no one understands me,
As long as I can keep the sweet fragrance of my mind.
Higher still the hat now that towered on my head,
And longer the girdle that dangled from my waist.
Fragrant and foul mingle in confusion,
But my inner brightness has remained undimmed.

Suddenly I turned back and let my eyes wander.
I resolved to go and visit all the world's quarters.
My garland's crowded blossoms, mixed in fair confusion,
Wafted the sweetness of their fragrance far and wide.
All men have something in their lives that gives them pleasure:
With me the love of beauty is my constant joy.
I could not change this, even if my body were dismembered;
For how could dismemberment ever hurt my mind?

My Nü Xu was fearful and clung to me imploringly,[8]
Lifting her voice up in expostulation:
"Gun in his stubbornness took no thought for his life
And perished, as result, on the moor of Feather Mountain.[9]
Why be so lofty, with your passion for purity?
Why must you alone have such delicate adornment?
Thorns, king-grass, curly-ear hold the place of power:
But you must needs stand apart and not speak them fair.

"You cannot go from door to door convincing everybody;

---

[8] Whether this refers to the poet's wife, concubine, sister or friend it is quite impossible to say.
[9] According to legend, Gun, the son of Gao Yang, was given the task of dealing with the great flood that occurred during the time of the high king Yao. His chosen methods — building dykes and infilling — were unsuccessful and he was put to death as a punishment, his body being exposed on Feather Mountain, where it lay for three years without rotting. At the end of that time it was cut open, releasing his son, Yu the Great. Yu the Great was more successful in dealing with the flood. In fact, the whole Chinese landscape is supposed to have been his creation. See chapter 2, "Heavenly Questions."

No one can say, 'See, look into my mind!'
Others band together and like to have companions:
Why must you be so aloof? Why not heed my counsel?"
But I look to the wise men of old for my guidance.
So sighing, with a full heart, I bore her upbraidings
And crossing the Yuan and Xiang, I journeyed southwards
Till I came to where Chong Hua was and made my plaint to him.[10]

"Singing the Nine Songs and dancing the Nine Changes,
Qi of Xia made revelry and knew no restraint,
Taking no thought for the troubles that would follow:[11]
And so his five sons fell out, brother against brother.
I loved idle roaming and hunting to distraction,
And took delight in shooting at the mighty foxes.
But foolish dissipation has seldom a good end:
And Han Zhuo covetously took his master's wife.

"Zhuo's son, Jiao, put on his strong armor
And wreaked his wild will without any restraint.
The days passed in pleasure; far he forgot himself,
Till his head came tumbling down from his shoulders.[12]
Jie of Xia all his days was a king most unnatural,
And so he came finally to meet with calamity.
Zhou cut up and salted the bodies of his ministers;
And so the days were numbered of the House of Yin.

---

[10] Chong Hua was the name of the high king Shun. He is supposed to have died while campaigning against the Miao tribes in what was then the Deep South, near the source of the River Xiang in South Hunan. His two queens, the daughters of the high king Yao, were supposed to have wandered southwards along the banks of the Xiang looking for him. They turned into river goddesses (two of the "Nine Songs" are addressed to them) and their tears are supposed to have turned into the markings on a certain sort of bamboo which grows in that area.

[11] Qi, the son of Yu the Great, wrested the kingship from the chieftain to whom his father, following the custom of his predecessors, had entrusted it, thereby bringing the Golden Age to an end and instituting the hereditary monarchy (the Xia dynasty). Qi was believed to have visited heaven and been entertained by God and to have brought back the Nine Songs (not the ones in this anthology) and the Nine Shao Dances. After Qi's death, Lord Yi took advantage of the quarrelling among Qi's five sons to seize power for himself in the Central Plain. Then Lord Yi's wife and henchman Han Zhuo plotted against him. They waylaid and killed him on his return from the hunt, cooked his body and served his flesh up to his son. When the son refused to eat it, they killed him too.

[12] Jiao the Strong Man was one of the two sons of Han Zhuo and Lord Yi's treacherous wife. He was slain by the young Xia prince Shao Kang.

"Tang of Shang and Yu of Xia were reverent and respectful;
The House of Zhou chose the true way without error,
Raising up the virtuous and able men to government,
Following the straight line without fear or favor.
High God in Heaven knows no partiality;
He looks for the virtuous and makes them his ministers.
For only the wise and good can ever flourish
If it is given them to possess the earth.

"I have looked back into the past and forward to later ages,
Examining the outcomes of men's different designs.
Where is the unrighteous man who could be trusted?
Where is the wicked man whose service could be used?
Though I stand at the pit's mouth and death yawns before me,
I still feel no regret at the course I have chosen.
Straightening the handle, regardless of the socket's shape:
For that crime the good men of old were hacked in pieces."

Many a heavy sigh I heaved in my despair,
Grieving that I was born in such an unlucky time.
I plucked soft lotus petals to wipe my welling tears
That fell down in rivers and wet my coat front.
I knelt on my outspread skirts and poured my plaint out,
And the righteousness within me was clearly manifest.
I yoked a team of jade dragons to a phoenix-figured car
And waited for the wind to come, to soar up on my journey.

I started out in the morning on my way from Cangwu;
By evening I had arrived at the Hanging Garden.[13]
I wanted to stay a while in those fairy precincts,
But the swift-moving sun was dipping to the west.
I ordered Xi He to stay the sun-steeds' gallop,[14]

---

[13] A terrestrial paradise on the mythical mountain of Kunlun. After his ascent of Kunlun,
Qu Yuan's journey is mainly an aerial one. As the highest mountain in the world, Kunlun
was naturally a suitable place for the ancient space-traveller to take off from.

[14] In Chinese as in Greek mythology, the sun was *driven* across the sky, but the charioteer
was, originally at any rate, not a male god but a woman. According to some ancient
sources, Xi He gave birth to the sun — or rather suns, for there were ten of them, one
for each day of the week. They roosted in the branches of the Fusang tree, a giant tree at
the eastern edge of the world, corresponding to the Ruo tree at the world's western end
whose leaves give off the red glow that we see in the sunset sky. Xi He bathed them in the
Gulf of Brightness before driving one of them on its day-long journey across the sky.

To stand over Yanzi mountain and not go in;[15]
For the road was so far and so distant was my journey,
And I wanted to go up and down, seeking my heart's desire.

I watered my dragon steeds at the Pool of Heaven,[16]
And tied their reins up to the Fusang tree.
I broke a sprig of the Ruo tree to strike the sun with:
First I would roam a little for my enjoyment.
I sent Wang Shu ahead to ride before me;
The Wind God went behind as my outrider;[17]
The Bird of Heaven gave notice of my comings;
The Thunder God warned me when all was not ready.

I caused my phoenixes to mount on their pinions
And fly ever onward by night and by day.
The whirlwinds gathered and came out to meet me,
Leading clouds and rainbows, to give me welcome.
In wild confusion, now joined and now parted,
Upwards and downwards rushed the glittering train.
I asked Heaven's porter to open up for me;
But he leant across Heaven's gate and eyed me churlishly.

The day was getting dark and drawing to its close.
Knotting orchids, I waited in indecision.
The muddy, impure world, so undiscriminating,
Seeks always to hide beauty, out of jealousy.
I decided when morning came to cross the White Water,
And climbed the peak of Langfeng, and there tied up my steeds.[18]
Then I looked about me and suddenly burst out weeping,
Because on that high hill there was no fair lady.

---

[15] Yanzi belongs, like Kunlun, to mythical cosmography rather than to real geography. It was one of the mountains behind which the setting sun was supposed to go down into the Vale of Murk.

[16] The Pool of Heaven is the name of a constellation corresponding very roughly to our Auriga.

[17] Wang Shu was, according to the second-century B.C. *Huainanzi*, the lady driver of the moon (the lunar counterpart of Xi He). The Wind God is usually represented as a winged deer. The aerial journey made like a royal progress across the heavens with gods and spirits in attendance seems at one time to have been a regular feature of Chinese shamanism.

[18] The White Water was one of the different colored rivers flowing out of the magic mountain of Kunlun. Langfeng was one of Kunlun's terraces.

"Here I am, suddenly, in this House of Spring.[19]
I have broken off a jasper branch to add to my girdle.
Before the jasper flowers have shed their bright petals,
I shall look for a maiden below to give it to."
So I made Feng Long ride off on a cloud
To seek out the dwelling-place of the lady Fu Fei.
I took off my girdle as a pledge of my suit to her,
And ordered Lame Beauty to be the go-between.[20]

Many were the hurried meetings and partings:
All wills and caprices, she was hard to woo.
In the evenings she went to lodge in the Qiongshi mountain;
In the mornings she washed her hair in the Weipan stream.
With proud disdain she guarded her beauty,
Passing each day in idle, wanton pleasures.
Though fair she may be, she lacks all seemliness:
Come! I'll have none of her; let us search elsewhere!

I looked all around over the earth's four quarters,
Circling the heavens till at last I alighted.
I gazed on a jade tower's glittering splendor
And spied the lovely daughter of the Lord of Song.[21]
I sent off the magpie to pay my court to her,
But the magpie told me that my suit had gone amiss.
The magpie flew off with noisy chatterings.
I hate him for an idle, knavish fellow.

---

[19] The House of Spring was the home of the Green God of the East; it was also one of the four equatorial palaces of ancient Chinese astronomy.

[20] Feng Long seems to have been Rain God, Cloud God and Thunder God — in other words, different aspects of the same god. Fu Fei was a water goddess, the guardian of the River Luo. According to Wang Yi, Fu Fei was the daughter of Fu Xi, who played an important part in the creation myths of several of the peoples inhabiting China in ancient times. He and his sister Nü Wa, like Deucalion and Pyrrha in the Greek legend, were thought to have peopled the earth after a great flood. They were both serpents from the waist down. According to one source, Nü Wa founded the institution of marriage and was the first go-between. Conceivably she is the matchmaker used here and "Lame Beauty" is a "kenning" for her invented by the poet. With a serpent's tail instead of legs she could certainly be thought of as "lame."

[21] This is Jian Di, the First Ancestress from whom the kings of the Shang dynasty were descended. She was shut up in a tower like Danaë, but became pregnant by swallowing an egg brought to her by a swallow sent by "Heaven."

My mind was irresolute and havering;
I wanted to go, and yet I could not.
Already the phoenix had taken his present,
And I feared that Gao Xin would get there before me.
I wanted to go far away, but had nowhere to go to:
Where could I wander to look for amusement?
Before they were married to Prince Shao Kang,
Lord Yu's two daughters were there for the wooing.[22]

But my pleader was weak and my matchmaker stupid,
And I feared that this suit, too, would not be successful.
For the world is impure and envious of the able,
Eager to hide men's good and make much of their ill.
Deep in the palace, unapproachable,
The wise king slumbers and will not be awakened.
That the thoughts in my breast should all go unuttered —
How can I endure this until I end my days?

I searched for the holy plant and twigs of bamboo,
And ordered Ling Fen to make divination for me.[23]
He said, "Beauty is always bound to find its mate:
Who that was truly fair was ever without lovers?
Think of the vastness of the wide world:
Here is not the only place where you can find your lady.
Go farther afield," he said, "and do not be faint-hearted.
What woman seeking handsome mate could ever refuse you?

"What place on earth does not boast some fragrant flower?
Why need you always cleave to your old home?
The world today is blinded with its own folly:
You cannot make people see the virtue inside you.

---

[22] When the Strong Man Jiao killed Prince Xiang (one of the five quarrelling sons of Qi mentioned above), Xiang's wife, who was pregnant at the time, escaped to her own people and gave birth to Shao Kang. Shao Kang obtained employment as a cook with the Lord of Yu, who subsequently gave him his two daughters in marriage and enfeoffed him with lands.

[23] Perhaps this is the same person as the Shaman Fen, mentioned in the *Book of Hills and Seas* as one of the Ten Shamans who lived on a holy mountain in the West. Chopped-up pieces of bamboo were a recognized substitute for the milfoil stalks normally used in the kind of divination associated with the *Book of Changes*.

Most people's loathings and likings are different,
Only these men here are not as others are;
For they wear mugwort and cram their waistbands with it,
But the lovely valley orchid they deem unfit to wear.

"Since beauty of flower, then, and of shrub escapes them,
What chance has a rarest jewel of gaining recognition?
They gather up muck to stuff their perfume bags with;
The spicy pepper-plant they say has got no scent at all."
I wanted to follow Ling Fen's auspicious oracle,
But I faltered and could not make my mind up.
I heard that Wu Xian was descending in the evening,[24]
So I lay in wait with offerings of peppered rice-balls.

The spirits came like a dense cloud descending,
And the host of Doubting Mountain came crowding to meet him.
His godhead was manifested by a blaze of radiance,
And he addressed me in these auspicious words:
"To and fro in the earth you must everywhere wander,
Seeking one whose thoughts are of your own measure.
Tang and Yu sought sincerely for the right helpers;
So Yi Yin and Gao Yao worked well with their princes.[25]

"As long as your soul within is beautiful,
What need have you of a matchmaker?
Yue labored as a builder, pounding earth at Fuyan,
Yet Wu Ding employed him without a second thought.[26]
Lü Wang wielded the butcher's knife at Zhaoge,
But King Wen met him and raised him up on high.[27]

---

[24] Wu Xian was the greatest of all the Shaman Ancestors (shamans worshipped after their death and taken by living shamans as their "guides").

[25] Yi Yin was the Chief Minister of Tang the Successful, the founder of the Shang dynasty. Gao Yao was first the colleague and then the minister of Yu the Great, the founder of the Xia dynasty.

[26] Wu Ding, the seventeenth Shang king, dreamed of the man best qualified to help him with the government of his empire and afterwards painted a likeness of the man he had seen in his dream so that he could have a search made for him throughout his dominions. He was eventually discovered in a gang of convicts ramming earth at a place called Fuyan.

[27] Lü Wang, chief adviser of King Wen, father of the King Wu who overthrew the last Shang king and established the Zhou dynasty, was, according to one tradition, a butcher when King Wen first "discovered" him.

Ning Qi sang as he fed his ox at evening;
Duke Huan of Qi heard him and took him as his minister.[28]

"Gather the flower of youth before it is too late,
While the good season is still not yet over.
Beware lest the shrike sound his note before the equinox,
Causing all the flowers to lose their fine fragrance."
How splendid the glitter of my jasper girdle!
But the crowd make a dark screen, masking its beauty.
And I fear that my enemies, who never can be trusted,
Will break it out of spiteful jealousy.

The age is disordered in a tumult of changing:
How can I tarry much longer among them?
Orchid and iris have lost all their fragrance;
Flag and melilotus have changed into straw.
Why have all the fragrant flowers of days gone by
Now all transformed themselves into worthless mugwort?
What other reason can there be for this
But that they all have no more care for beauty?

I thought that orchid was one to be trusted,
But he proved a sham, bent only on pleasing his masters.
He overcame his goodness and conformed to evil counsels:
He no more deserves to rank with fragrant flowers.
Pepper is all wagging tongue and lives only for slander;
And even stinking dogwood seeks to fill a perfume bag.
Since they only seek advancement and labor for position,
What fragrance have they deserving our respect?[29]

Since, then, the world's way is to drift the way the tide runs,
Who can stay the same and not change with all the rest?

---

[28] Duke Huan of Qi, the fifteenth Duke, who inherited the duchy of Qi in the eleventh
generation after Lü Wang, was the first of the Great Hegemons who led the confederacy
of Zhou states in the days of the royal house's decline and the most progressive ruler of
his day. Like many other successful autocrats, he preferred men of humble origin as his
chief advisers. One of them, Ning Qi, was a travelling merchant when he first came to the
Duke's attention.

[29] The "orchid" here and the "pepper" four lines below it are, according to a well-established Han tradition, the names of real people: King Huai of Chu's younger son, Prince
Lan, and a nobleman called Lord Jiao, who were Qu Yuan's principal enemies at court.

Seeing the behavior of orchid and pepper-flower,
What can be expected of cart-half and selinea?
They have cast off their beauty and come to this:
Only my garland is left to treasure.
Its penetrating perfume does not easily desert it,
And even to this day its fragrance has not faded.

I will follow my natural bent and please myself;
I will go off wandering to look for a lady.
While my adornment is in its pristine beauty
I will travel around looking both high and low.
Since Ling Fen had given me a favorable oracle,
I picked an auspicious day to start my journey on.
I broke a branch of jasper to take for my meat,
And ground fine jasper meal for my journey's provisions.

"Harness winged dragons to be my coursers;
Let my chariot be of fine work of jade and ivory!
How can I live with men whose hearts are strangers to me?
I am going a far journey to be away from them."
I took the way that led towards the Kunlun mountain:
A long, long road with many a turning in it.
The cloud-embroidered banner flapped its great shade above us;
And the jingling jade yoke-bells tinkled merrily.

I set off at morning from the Ford of Heaven;[30]
At evening I came to the world's western end.
Phoenixes followed me, bearing up my pennants,
Soaring high aloft with majestic wing-beats.
"See, I have come to the Desert of Moving Sands!"
Warily I drove along the banks of the Red Water,[31]
Then, beckoning the water-dragons to make a bridge for me,
I summoned the God of the West to take me over.

So long the road had been and full of difficulties,

---

[30] This is the name of a constellation. The poet appears to be airborne once more. The Chinese thought of the Milky Way as a celestial river. The Ford of Heaven was their name for the stars in Sagittarius which span its narrowest part.

[31] The Red Water, like the White Water, was one of the colored rivers flowing out of Kunlun. The Moving Sands may be based on travellers' tales of the Central Asian deserts, but, like the Red Water, belong to the wonderland of shamanistic cosmography rather than to any real geography.

I sent word to my escort to take another route,
To wheel around leftwards, skirting Buzhou Mountain:[32]
On the shore of the Western Sea we would reassemble.
When we had mustered there, all thousand chariots,
Jade hub to jade hub we galloped on abreast.
My eight dragon steeds flew on with writhing undulations;
My cloud-embroidered banners flapped on the wind.

In vain I tried to curb them, to slacken the swift pace:
The spirits soared high up, far into the distance.
We played the Nine Songs and danced the Shao Dances,[33]
Borrowing the time to make a holiday.
But when I had ascended the splendor of the heavens,
I suddenly caught a glimpse below of my old home.
My groom's heart was heavy and the horses for longing
Arched their heads back and refused to go on.

Luan

Enough! There are no true men in the state: no one understands me.
Why should I cleave to the city of my birth?
Since none is worthy to work with in making good government,
I shall go and join Peng Xian in the place where he abides.

The Nine Songs

Translated by David Hawkes

The first thing to be observed about the "Nine Songs" is that there are eleven of them: nine addressed to various gods and goddesses, a tenth to the spirits of warriors killed in battle, and a short concluding hymnor recessional at the end. The "Nine Songs" can best be described as religious drama; but though it is obvious from the most cursory reading of them that they were written for performance, the absence of stage directions indicating who at any given point was supposed to be singing, or what they were doing while they sang, makes it impossible to be sure how they were performed. In some cases, we cannot even be sure whether what we are reading is monologue or

---

[32] Somewhere west of Kunlun. Buzhou Mountain was the north-western of the eight pillars which once supported the sky.

[33] These were the Nine Songs brought back from heaven by Qi (see note 11). The Shao was the dance, or dances, that went with them. Confucius heard the music for the Shao dances when he was visiting a neighboring state and was so overcome that he scarcely noticed what he was eating for weeks afterwards. "I never realized that music could be so perfect," he told his disciples.

dialogue or dialogue with choric interruptions. Everyone who interprets the songs has to begin by making his own reconstruction; and because the uncertainties are so numerous, there are almost as many reconstructions as there are interpreters.

The words themselves provide us with some clues. It appears that the actors or dancers in these dramas were gorgeously dressed shamans; that musical accompaniment was provided by an orchestra of lithophones, musical bells, drums, and various kinds of wind and string instruments; that — to judge from one or two references to a "hall"— the performance took place indoors. In several of the songs a shaman appears in the first half to be invoking or searching for some god or goddess, and in the second half to be complaining because the god or goddess either failed to turn up or left after too short a visit; in others it is the god or goddess him- or herself who appears to be addressing us.

Wang Yi [second century A.D.] thought that the "Nine Songs" were written by Qu Yuan during his exile…. Sima Qian [c. 145–c. 85 B.C.], who may quite likely have seen the "Nine Songs" performed, appears to have been unaware that they were in any way connected with Qu Yuan. Tai Yi, the "Great Unity," chief of the gods to whom the "Nine Songs" are dedicated, is first mentioned as an object of religious worship in the reign of Sima Qian's employer, the Han emperor Wu [r. 141–87 B.C.]. Emperor Wu was a keen patron of shamans and had a weakness for lavish ritual, particularly for night-time rituals involving massed choirs and troops of dancers in which songs and dances specially composed for him by the poets and musicians of his court were performed by the light of thousands of flickering torches. He was introduced to the worship of Tai Yi by his favorite shamans. Tai Yi was "their" god — the god whom they would undertake to summon into his presence. He was attended, they told him, by various lesser gods, one of them the Master of Fate, to whom Songs V and VI of the

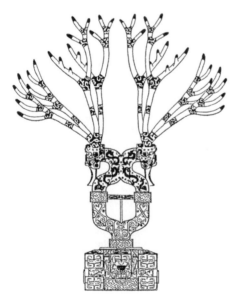

Figure 18. Tomb-guarding animal, Warring States period, Kingdom of Chu. (Source: Li Xueqin, *Eastern Zhou and Qin Civilizations* [New Haven: Yale University Press, 1985])

"Nine Songs" are dedicated. Song V does in fact speak of the Master of Fate "conducting the *di* (presumably Tai Yi) to the height of heaven."

It might be thought that the obvious conclusion to draw from all this is that the "Nine Songs" were written or compiled for Emperor Wu and date from no earlier than his reign. In the 1940s some Chinese scholars did in fact advocate this view. The great objection to it is that all the songs, with the exception of I, X, and XI, show obvious traces of Chu dialect or contain linguistic features similar to ones that we find in "On Encountering Trouble." In content the "Nine Songs" are as eclectic as a Baroque suite including dance-tunes from half a dozen different countries, but from their outward form it is clear that they can only have been written by a Chu poet.

For a number of reasons I believe this to have been a poet (or poets) at the Chu court in Shouchun [241–223 B.C.].... It is my belief that Liu An [d. 122 B.C.], who became Prince of Huainan some sixty years after the extinction of the Warring States kingdom of Chu and who had his provincial capital at the former Chu capital of Shouchun, revived and perhaps re-edited the "Nine Songs" and introduced them to the imperial court, where they were used, perhaps after further editing, in Emperor Wu's Tai Yi spectaculars.

There are still many questions about these songs that remain unanswered ...

Fortunately their beauty remains unaffected by our understanding of how they were performed or when they were written and continues to be an inspiration to Chinese poets and painters as it has been throughout the ages.

I. The Great Unity, God of the Eastern Sky

On a lucky day with an auspicious name
Reverently we come to delight the Lord on High.
We grasp the long sword's haft of jade,
And our girdle pendants clash and chime.
From the god's jeweled mat with treasures laden
Take up the fragrant flower-offerings,
The meats cooked in melilotus, served on orchid mats,
And libations of cinnamon wine and pepper sauces!
Flourish the drumsticks, beat the drums!
The singing begins softly to a slow, solemn measure:
Then, as pipes and zithers join in, the sound grows shriller.
Now the priestesses come, splendid in their gorgeous apparel,
And the hall is filled with a penetrating fragrance.
The five notes mingle in a rich harmony;
And the god is merry and takes his pleasure.

II. The Lord Within the Clouds

We have bathed in orchid water and washed our hair with perfumes,
And dressed ourselves like flowers in embroidered clothing.
The god has halted, swaying, above us,
Shining with a persistent radiance.

He is going to rest in the House of Life.[34]
His brightness is like that of the sun and moon.
In his dragon chariot, dressed in imperial splendor,
Now he flies off to wander round the sky.

The god had just descended in bright majesty,
When off in a whirl he soared again, far into the clouds.
He looks down on Jizhou and the lands beyond it;
There is no place in the world that he does not pass over.
Thinking of that lord makes me sigh
And afflicts my heart with a grievous longing.

III. The Goddess of the Xiang

The goddess comes not, she holds back shyly.
Who keeps her delaying within the island,
Lady of the lovely eyes and the winning smile?
Skimming the water in my cassia boat,
I bid the Yuan and Xiang still their waves

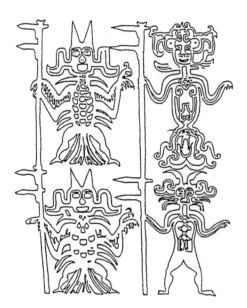

Figure 19. Figures of deities, Warring
States tomb, Kingdom of Chu.
(Source: Li Xueqin, *Eastern Zhou and
Qin Civilizations* [New Haven: Yale
University Press, 1985])

---

[34] Literally, Palace of Longevity — a chapel specially constructed for the reception of spirits
conjured up in shamanistic séances.

And the Great River make its stream flow softly.
I look for the goddess, but she does not come yet.
Of whom does she think as she plays her reed-pipes?

North I go, drawn by my flying dragon,[35]
Steering my course to the Dongting lake:
My sail is of fig-leaves, melilotus my rigging,
And iris my flag-pole, my banner of orchids.
Gazing at the distant Cenyang mooring,
I waft my magic across the Great River.

I waft my magic, but it does not reach her.
The lady is sad, and sighs for me;
And *my* tears run down over cheek and chin:
I am choked with longing for my lady.

My cassia oars and orchid sweep
Chip all in vain at ice and snow.
I am gathering wild figs in the water!
I am looking for lotuses in the tree-tops!
The wooing is useless if hearts are divided;
The love that is not deep is quickly broken.

The stream runs fast through the stony shallows,
And my flying dragon wings swiftly above it.
The pain is more lasting if loving is faithless:
She broke her tryst; she told me she had not time.

In the morning I race by the bank of the river;
At evening I halt at this north island.
The birds are roosting on the roof-top;
The water laps at the foot of the hall.
I throw my thumb-ring into the river.[36]
I leave my girdle-gem in the bay of the Li.
Pollia I've plucked in the scent-laden islet
To give to the lady in the depths below.
Time once gone cannot be recovered:
I wish I could play here a little longer.

---

[35] I take it that a dragon boat, i.e. a boat which, like a Viking ship, had a carved dragon on its prow, is meant here. Boats of this kind survive to the present in places where the Dragon Boat festival is still celebrated.

[36] The thumb-ring, usually made of jade, was worn as a protection by archers. It marks the shaman as a male.

IV. *The Lady of the Xiang*

The Child of God, descending the northern bank,
Turns on me her eyes that are dark with longing.
Gently the wind of autumn whispers;
On the waves of the Dongting lake the leaves are falling.

Over the white sedge I gaze out wildly;
For a tryst is made to meet my love this evening.
But why should the birds gather in the duckweed?
And what are the nets doing in the tree-tops?

The Yuan has its angelicas, the Li has its orchids:
And I think of my lady, but dare not tell it,
As with trembling heart I gaze on the distance
Over the swiftly moving waters.

What are the deer doing in the courtyard?
Or the water-dragons outside the waters?
In the morning I drive my steeds by the river;
In the evening I cross to the western shore.
I can hear my beloved calling to me:
I will ride aloft and race beside her.
I will build her a house within the water
Roofed all over with lotus leaves;

With walls of iris, of purple shells the chamber;
Perfumed pepper shall make the hall.
With beams of cassia, orchid rafters,
Lily-tree lintel, a bower of peonies,
With woven fig-leaves for the hangings
And melilotus to make a screen;
Weights of white jade to hold the mats with,
Stone-orchids strewn to make the floor sweet:
A room of lotus thatched with the white flag
Shall all be bound up with stalks of asarum.
A thousand sweet flowers shall fill the courtyard,
And rarest perfumes shall fill the gates.
In hosts from their home on Doubting Mountain
Like clouds in number the spirits come thronging.[37]

I'll throw my thumb-ring into the river,

---

[37] Doubting Mountain was the burial-place of Shun, the goddess's husband.

Leave my girdle-gem in the bay of the Li.
Sweet pollia I've plucked in the little islet
To send to my far-away Beloved.
Oh, rarely, rarely the time is given!
I wish I could play here a little longer.

V. *The Great Master of Fate*

Open wide the door of heaven!
On a black cloud I ride in splendor,
Bidding the whirlwind drive before me,
Causing the rainstorm to lay the dust.

In sweeping circles my lord is descending:
"Let me follow you over the Kongsang mountain![38]
See, the teeming peoples of the Nine Lands:
The span of their lives is in your hand!"

Flying aloft, he soars serenely,
Riding the pure vapor, guiding yin and yang.
Speedily, lord, I will go with you,
Conducting High God to the height of heaven.
My cloud-coat hangs in billowing folds;
My jade girdle-pendants dangle low:
A yin and a yang, a yin and a yang:
None of the common folk know what I am doing.

I have plucked the glistening flower of the Holy Hemp
To give to one who lives far away.
Old age already has crept upon me:
I am no longer near him, fast growing a stranger.

He drives his dragon chariot with thunder of wheels;
High up he rides, careering heavenwards.
But I stand where I am, twisting a spray of cassia:
The longing for him pains my heart.

It pains my heart, but what can I do?
If we only could stay as we were, unchanging!

---

[38] The *Book of Hills and Seas* has a Kongsang Mountain "on which neither tree nor herb grows and which is covered with snow both winter and summer alike." It appears to have been somewhere in northern Shanxi.

But all man's life is fated;
Its meeting and partings not his to arrange.

VI. *The Lesser Master of Fate*

The autumn orchid and the deer-parsley
Grow in a carpet below the hall;
The leaves of green and the pure white flowers
Assail me with their wafted fragrance.

The autumn orchids bloom luxuriant,
With leaves of green and purple stems.
All the hall is filled with lovely women,
But his eyes swiftly sought me out from the rest.

Without a word he came in to me, without a word he left me:
He rode off on the whirlwind with cloud-banners flying.
No sorrow is greater than the parting of the living;
No happiness is greater than making new friendships.

Wearing a lotus coat with melilotus girdle,
Quickly he came and as quickly departed.
At night he will lodge in the High God's precincts.
"Whom are you waiting for at the cloud's edge?"

I will wash my hair with you in the Pool of Heaven;
You shall dry your hair on the Bank of Sunlight.
I watch for the Fair One, but he does not come.
Wildly I shout my song into the wind.

With peacock canopy and kingfisher banner,
He mounts the ninefold heaven and grasps the Broom Star;
He brandishes his long sword, protecting young and old:
"You only, Fragrant One, are worthy to be judge over men."

VII. *The Lord of the East*

With a faint flush I start to come out of the east,
Shining down on my threshold, Fusang.
As I urge my horses slowly forwards,
The night sky brightens, and day has come.

I ride a dragon car and chariot on the thunder,
With cloud-banners fluttering upon the wind.
I heave a long sigh as I start the ascent,
Reluctant to leave, and looking back longingly;

For the beauty and the music are so enchanting,
The beholder, delighted, forgets that he must go.

Tighten the zither's strings and smite them in unison!
Strike the bells until the bell-stand rocks!
Let the flutes sound! Blow the pan-pipes!
See the priestesses, how skilled and lovely,
Whirling and dipping like birds in flight,
Unfolding the words in time to the dancing,
Pitch and beat all in perfect accord!
The spirits, descending, darken the sun.

In my cloud-coat and my skirt of the rainbow,
Grasping my bow I soar high up in the sky.
I aim my long arrow and shoot the Wolf of Heaven;[39]
I seize the Dipper to ladle cinnamon wine.
Then holding my reins, I plunge down to my setting,
On my gloomy night journey back to the east.

VIII. *The River Earl*

I wander with you by the Nine Mouths of the river
When the storm wind rises and lashes up the waves.
I ride a water chariot with a canopy of lotus;
Two dragons draw it, between two water-serpents.

I climb the Kunlun mountain and look over the four quarters,
And my heart leaps up in me, beating wildly.
Though the day will soon end, I forget to go in my pleasure:
Longingly I look back to that distant shore.
Of fish-scales his palace is, with a dragon-scale hall;
Purple cowrie gate-towers; rooms of pearl.
And what does the god do, down there in the water?

Riding a white turtle, he chases the spotted fishes.
Let me play with you among the river's islets,
While the swollen waters come rushing on their way!
Eastward you journey, with hands stately folded,
Bearing your fair bride to the southern harbor.
The waves come racing up to meet me,
And shoals of fishes are my bridal train.

---

[39] This is the star Sirius, part of Canis Major, the Dog.

IX. The Mountain Spirit

There seems to be someone in the fold of mountain
In a coat of fig-leaves with a rabbit-floss girdle,
With eyes that hold laughter and a smile of pearly brightness:
"Lady, your allurements show that you desire me."

Driving tawny leopards, leading the striped lynxes;
A car of lily-magnolia with banner of woven cassia;
Her cloak of stone-orchids, her belt of asarum:
She gathers sweet scents to give to one she loves.

"I am in the dense bamboo grove, which never sees the sunlight,
So steep and hard the way was, therefore I am late."
Solitary she stands, upon the mountain's summit:
The clouds' dense masses begin below her.

From a place of gloomy shadow, dark even in the daytime,
When the east wind blows up, the goddess sends down her showers.
Dallying with the Fair One, I forget about returning.
What flowers can I deck myself with, so late in the year?

I shall pluck the thrice-flowering herb among the mountains,
Where the arrowroot spreads creeping over the piled-up boulders.
Sorrowing for my lady, I forget that I must go.
My lady thinks of me, but she has no time to come.

The lady of the mountains is fragrant with pollia;
She drinks from the rocky spring and shelters beneath the pine trees.
My lady thinks of me, but she holds back, uncertain.

The thunder rumbles; rain darkens the sky:
The monkeys chatter; apes scream in the night:
The wind soughs sadly and the trees rustle.
I think of my lady and stand alone in sadness.

X. Hymn to the Fallen

Grasping our great shields and wearing our hide armor,
Wheel-hub to wheel-hub locked, we battle hand to hand.

Our banners darken the sky; the enemy teem like clouds:
Through the hail of arrows the warriors press forward.

They dash on our lines; they trample our ranks down.
The left horse has fallen, the right one is wounded.

The wheels are embedded, the foursome entangled:
Seize the jade drumstick and beat the sounding drum!
The time is against us: the gods are angry.
Now all lie dead, left on the field of battle.

They went out never more to return:
Far, far away they lie, on the level plain,
Their long swords at their belts, clasping their Qin bows,
Head from body sundered: but their hearts could not be vanquished.

Both truly brave and also truly noble;
Strong to the last, they could not be dishonored.
Their bodies may have died, but their souls are living:
Heroes among the shades their valiant souls will be.

XI. Honoring the Dead

The rites are accomplished to the beating of the drums;
The flower-wand is passed on to succeeding dancers.
Lovely maidens sing their song, slow and solemnly.
Orchids in spring and chrysanthemums in autumn:
So it shall go on until the end of time.

Figure 20. Silk painting from a Chu
tomb. (Source: Li Xueqin, *Eastern
Zhou and Qin Civilizations* [New
Haven: Yale University Press, 1985])

ᄆᄆ *Further Reading* ᄆᄆ

Hawkes, David, trans. *The Songs of the South: An Ancient Chinese Anthology of Poems by Qu Yuan and Other Poets.* Harmondsworth: Penguin Books, 1985. (A revised version, with greatly expanded, and fascinating, commentary, of *Ch'u Tz'u: The Songs of the South* [Oxford: Oxford University Press, 1959].)

Li, Xueqin. *Eastern Zhou and Qin Civilizations.* New Haven: Yale University Press, 1985.

Lim, Boon Keng. *The Li Sao, an Elegy on Encountering Sorrow, by Ch'ü Yüan.* Shanghai: Commercial Press, 1929.

Waley, Arthur, trans. *The Nine Songs, a Study of Shamanism in Ancient China.* London: Allen & Unwin, 1955.

Waters, Geoffrey R. *Three Elegies of Ch'u: An Introduction to the Traditional Interpretation of the Ch'u Tz'u.* Madison: University of Wisconsin Press, 1985.

Yang, Xianyi, and Gladys Yang, trans. *Li Sao and Other Poems of Chu Yuan.* Beijing: Foreign Languages Press, 1953.

"I fear I shall not leave behind an enduring name."
Seal carved by Chen Yuzhong (1762–1806)

Part 2

The Han Dynasty
and the Period of Disunion
(206 B.C.–A.D. 589)

Han dynasty seal

Chapter 6

Red and Purple Threads

Rhapsodies from the Han and Six Dynasties

Poetry traces emotions daintily;
  Rhapsody embodies objects brightly.

> — Lu Ji (261–303), "Literature: A Rhapsody" (*translated by Achilles Fang*)

Beautiful words and refined ideas will match and complement each other, like the apportioning of red and purple threads in a piece of woven goods, or the application of black and yellow pigment in a painting. The patterns, though novel, will be supported by sound substance; the colors, though varied, will be laid on a firm base. This is the essential point in fashioning a rhapsody....

The rhapsody derives from poetry,
A fork in the road, a different line of development;
It describes objects, pictures their appearance,
With a brilliance akin to sculpture or painting.
What is clogged and confined it invariably opens up;
It depicts the commonplace with unbounded charm;
But the goal of the form is beauty well-ordered,
Words retained for their loveliness when weeds have been cut away.

> — Liu Xie, *The Literary Mind and the Carving of Dragons*, chapter 8,
> "Elucidating the Rhapsody" (*translated by Burton Watson*)

As for rhapsodies

Narrating a single event
Celebrating a single object —
Poems inspired by winds, clouds, plants, and trees,
Pieces on fish, insects, birds, and beasts —

One could extend and broaden the list
And never record them all.

> — Xiao Tong (501–531), preface to the *Literary Anthology*
> (*translated by David Knechtges*)

His [Sima Xiangru's] glittering torrent of words has never since poured from the pen of any writer in the world, and besides him Euphues seems timid and Apuleius cold.

> — Arthur Waley, *The Temple*, 1923

The long, ornate, rhapsodic *fu*, in so far as it had an ancestor, derived from the shaman-chants of the South. Its lexical richness, euphuism and hyperbole suited an expansive, adventurous age in which Chinese armies penetrated deep into Central

Asia and Chinese merchandise regularly found its way into European markets, but were deeply disturbing to right-minded Confucians, and therefore, ultimately, to the writers themselves; so that, amidst all the self-confident exuberance, a note of guilt and unease kept stealing in.

— David Hawkes, "The Age of Exuberance," in
Classical, Modern and Humane, 1989

Introduction

Burton Watson

Sima Xiangru, one of the earliest and greatest writers in the rhapsody or rhyme-prose (*fu*) form, left no statement as to what he thought the characteristics of the form ought to be or how it should be employed. It is probable that, like many artistic creators of genius, he allowed his works to find their own form, without undue worry as to whether in doing so he was abiding by or departing from patterns set by previous writers. There would seem to have been few important works in the rhapsody form before his appearance on the literary scene — only one in this selection, Jia Yi's "Rhapsody on the Owl," is certainly earlier — and in many respects he is its virtual creator. Nearly all the themes of the typical Han rhapsody — the great hunts, palaces, and ceremonies of the capital; rivers and mountains; birds, beasts, flowers, and trees; beautiful women and musical instruments; journeys or meditations on the past — can be traced back to some passage in his works. As the reader will observe when he comes to the rhapsody "The Mighty One," Sima Xiangru adorns his works with an almost endless profusion of scenes and objects, any one of which might be borrowed by a later writer and made the subject of a single poem.

The rhapsody in its early form generally consists of a combination of prose and rhymed verse (hence the other English term "rhyme-prose"), prose serving for the introduction that explains the genesis of the piece, as well as for occasional interludes, verse taking over in the more rhapsodic and emotionally charged passages.... End rhyme is used throughout the verse portions, as well as frequent alliteration, assonance, and other euphonic effects. Rhetorical devices such as parallelism and historical allusion abound, and the diction is rich with onomatopoeias, musical binomes descriptive of moods or actions, and lengthy catalogues of names, often of rare and exotic objects, that are calculated to dazzle the reader and sweep him off his feet. The rhapsody, in fact, though it is a purely secular form, owes much to the shaman songs and chants of the folk religion, incantations empowered to call down deities or summon lost or ailing souls, such as are found in the earlier *Songs of the South*. The works of Sima Xiangru in particular seem capable of bewitching one with the sheer magic of rhythm and language, and it is not surprising that Emperor Wu, when he had finished reading one of them, announced that he felt as though he were soaring effortlessly over the clouds.

It was this very exuberance and wildness of language that in some quarters occasioned reservations about the value of works in the rhapsodic form.

One of the most important critics to express such doubts was the philosopher Yang Xiong. In his youth he wrote ornate works in the rhapsody form, descriptive of imperial hunts and outings in the manner of Sima Xiangru, whom he admired and took as his model, laboring so fervently over one of them, we are told, that he brought on a nervous collapse and was ill for a whole year. But later, he abandoned the writing of rhapsodies. He felt, it seems, that the element of reprimand, which was held up as the justification for such works, was too often lost in the torrent of verbiage, and that the effect was often quite the opposite, actually lending encouragement to the Han rulers in their costly and luxurious ways.

As time went by, there was a growing tendency towards realism, and with increasing realism came a more personal and subjective note, a turning away from the great public themes of palace, hunt, and royal garden to expressions of private moods and concerns. Wang Can's "Climbing the Tower" was written in the region of the upper Yangtze, far from courts and capitals, to voice the sorrows and frustrations of a lonely traveler.

One post-Han work in this selection stands as a later representative of the relatively objective and impersonal type of rhapsody, the "Rhapsody on the Sea," by Mu Hua. This work does not display any substantial advance over the descriptive powers of earlier masterpieces by men such as Sima Xiangru, but it applies these powers to a wholly new subject, the sea. The novelty of the subject raises the poem above the level of imitation and gives it a fascination all its own. In such works we see the rhapsody form being returned to what was probably one of its earliest and most important usages, that of providing a pleasant literary pastime for men of taste, a fitting accompaniment to the pleasures of music, wine, and good fellowship.[1]

— *Chinese Rhyme-Prose*, 1971

SONG YU (c. 290–c. 223 B.C.), attrib.
The Wind

Translated by Burton Watson

The "Rhapsody on the Wind" is attributed to Song Yu, a writer of the third century B.C. who served at the court of the state of Chu and was a disciple of the famous poet-statesman Qu Yuan. The style of the poem, however, and the fact that it is not recorded in earlier works have led many modern scholars to question its authenticity. It represents a type very important in rhapsody literature, the poetic description of a particular object or phenomenon, in this case the wind. The poem may be intended simply to delight the reader with its gusty portrait of the two winds of the land of Chu. But, if commentators are to be believed, a more serious purpose underlies it, the expression of veiled reproaches against a king whose way of life is so far removed from that of his impoverished subjects that the very winds that blow upon them are of a different nature.

King Xiang of Chu was taking his ease in the Palace of the Orchid Terrace, with his courtiers Song Yu and Jing Cha attending him, when a sudden gust of wind came sweeping in. The king, opening wide the collar of his robe and facing into it, said, "How delightful this wind is! And I and the common people may share it together, may we not?"

But Song Yu replied, "This wind is for Your Majesty alone. How could the common people have a share in it?"

"The wind," said the king, "is the breath of heaven and earth. Into every corner it unfolds and reaches; without choosing between high or low, exalted or humble, it touches everywhere. What do you mean when you say that this wind is for me alone?"

---

[1] Other rhapsodies can be found below in chapters 10, 11, 12, and 15. *Eds.*

Song Yu replied, "I have heard my teacher say that the twisted branches of the lemon tree invite the birds to nest, and hollows and cracks summon the wind. But the breath of the wind differs with the place which it seeks out."

"Tell me," said the king. "Where does the wind come from?"

Song Yu answered:

"The wind is born from the land
And springs up in the tips of the green duckweed.
It insinuates itself into the valleys
And rages in the canyon mouth,
Skirts the corners of Mount Tai
And dances beneath the pines and cedars.
Swiftly it flies, whistling and wailing;
Fiercely it splutters its anger.
It crashes with a voice like thunder,
Whirls and tumbles in confusion,
Shaking rocks, striking trees,
Blasting the tangled forest.
Then, when its force is almost spent,
It wavers and disperses,
Thrusting into crevices and rattling door latches.
Clean and clear,
It scatters and rolls away.
Thus it is that this cool, fresh hero wind,
Leaping and bounding up and down,
Climbs over the high wall
And enters deep into palace halls.
With a puff of breath it shakes the leaves and flowers,
Wanders among the cassia and pepper trees,
Or soars over the swift waters.
It buffets the mallow flower,
Sweeps the angelica, touches the spikenard,
Glides over the sweet lichens and lights on willow shoots,
Rambling over the hills
And their scattered host of fragrant flowers.
After this, it wanders into the courtyard,
Ascends the jade hall in the north,
Clambers over gauze curtains,
Passes through the inner apartments,
And so becomes Your Majesty's wind.
When this wind blows on a man,

At once he feels a chill run through him,
And he sighs at its cool freshness.
Clear and gentle,
It cures sickness, dispels drunkenness,
Sharpens the eyes and ears,
Relaxes the body and brings benefit to men.
This is what is called the hero wind of Your Majesty."

"How well you have described it!" exclaimed the king. "But now may I
hear about the wind of the common people?" And Song Yu replied:

"The wind of the common people
Comes whirling from the lanes and alleys,
Poking in the rubbish, stirring up the dust,
Fretting and worrying its way along.
It creeps into holes and knocks on doors,
Scatters sand, blows ashes about,
Muddles in dirt and tosses up bits of filth.
It sidles through hovel windows
And slips into cottage rooms.
When this wind blows on a man,
At once he feels confused and downcast.
Pounded by heat, smothered in dampness,
His heart grows sick and heavy,
And he falls ill and breaks out in a fever.
Where it brushes his lips, sores appear;
It strikes his eyes with blindness.
He stammers and cries out,
Not knowing if he is dead or alive.
This is what is called the lowly wind of the common people."

The Gao Tang Rhapsody

Translated by Arthur Waley

This rhapsody begins with a prose introduction setting the scene. King Xiang of Chu,
accompanied by Song Yu, is visiting the great marsh of Yunmeng (Cloud-Dream
Terrace). After an exchange of dialogue, the king asks the poet to compose for him a
rhapsody on the wonders of Mount Gao Tang in the region. In a long, rhymed
passage, sometimes in lines of six words, sometimes in lines of four or three, the poet
proceeds to describe the appearance of the mountain, its rushing streams and the fish
and reptiles which inhabit them, its flowering trees, its steep and rugged heights and
the strange creatures, flowers, birds, and immortal spirits who dwell there. The king is

then pictured setting out upon a hunt, and is finally admonished to "deal kindly for ever with the thousand lands, sorrow for the wrongs of his people, promote the wise and good, and make whole whatever was amiss." Thus, after enchanting the king (and the reader) with his vivid and exotic descriptions, the poet delivers a little homily on good government.

— Burton Watson, *Early Chinese Literature*, 1962

Once when Xiang, King of Chu, was walking with Song Yu on the Cloud-Dream Terrace, he looked up at the Gao Tang Shrine. Above it was a coil of mist, now pointing steadily skyward like a pinnacle of rock, now suddenly dissolving and in a single moment diffused into a thousand diverse shapes. Then the King questioned Song Yu, saying, "What Cloud-spirit is this?" And Yu answered: "It is called Morning Cloud." The King said: "Why has it this name?" and Yu answered: "Long ago a former king was wandering upon this mountain of Gao Tang. When night came he was tired and slept beyond the dawn. And early in the morning he dreamt that a lady stood before him saying, 'I am a girl from the Witches' Hill. I have come as a stranger to Gao Tang, and hearing that my lord the King was traveling on this same mountain, I desired to offer him the service of pillow and mat.' So the king lay with her, and when they parted, she said to him: 'My home is on the southern side of the Witches' Hill, where from its rounded summit a sudden chasm falls. At dawn I am the Morning Cloud; at dusk, the Driving Rain. So dawn by dawn and dusk by dusk I dwell beneath the southern crest.'

"Next day at sunrise he looked towards the hill, and it was even as she had said. Therefore he built her a shrine in the place where she had come to him and called it the Temple of the Morning Cloud."

Then King Xiang questioned Song Yu, saying, "Tell me of this Morning Cloud, in what guise does she first appear?" And Yu answered: "Still is she and somber as a forest of tall pines, where tree stands close to tree; but soon she kindles with a shimmering light; as when a beautiful lady, looking for her lover, raises lawn sleeves to shade her eyes from the sun. Suddenly her being is transformed; swiftly now she races as a chariot whirled onward by galloping steeds, with feathery flags outspread. From the rain a dankness she borrows, and from the wind an icy breath. But soon the wind has dropped, the rain has cleared, and Morning Cloud has vanished from the sky."

The King said: "May I too visit the mountain whereon she was met?" Song Yu answered: "Your Majesty may do so." The King said: "What manner of place is it?" Yu answered: "It is a high, conspicuous hill, from whose summit immeasurable prospects may be scanned. Broad is it and vast; parent and home of ten thousand creatures. Its summit is in the realms of Heaven; its base is founded in the deep. Its marvels cannot be

told, nor its giant prodigies rehearsed." The King said: "Nevertheless I
beg you to sing of it for me," and Song Yu did not refuse.

> To what shall I liken this high and desolate hill?
> In all the world it has no kin.
> The Witches' Mountain[2]
> Knows no such terraces, such causeways of coiling stone.
> Climb the treeless rocks, look down into the deep,
> Where under their tall banks the gathered waters lie.
> After long rain the sky has cleared afresh.
> A hundred valleys hold concourse! In silent wrath
> Mad waters tussle, the high floods
> Brim abreast and tumble to their home.
> The shallows spread and spread, the restless pools
> Mount their steep shores.
> Ever the wind blows; great waves are piled
> Like barrows on a lonely field;
> Now on a widening bed
> They jostle savagely or beat upon their shores;
> Now cramped, they draw together and are at peace.
> Now in precipitous creeks, with violence renewed,
> High they bound as breakers that an ocean-ship
> Sees on the Stony Foreland flung.
> The pebbles grind their flinty sides, grate and churn
> With a din that shakes the sky.
> The great rocks drown; rise up, and sink again,
> Or suddenly above the waves stand high and bare.
> The turbulent eddies reel and swirl;
> Great waves go floundering;
> They run, they leap into the air, they dance;
> Scrimmage like clouds, could clouds echo
> With cataractine roar.
> Wild beasts dance in terror, fly headlong from the flood.
> Quaking tiger, panther, wolf and buffalo dismayed —
> Panting they skelter; eagle and osprey, falcon and kite
> Take wing and hide themselves away;

---

[2] The Witches' Mountain (Wu Shan) of ancient times was near Jingzhou, in Hubei. The modern Wu Shan is much higher up the Yangtze.

Haunch quaking, breath bated —
No heart to pounce or snatch.

And now the creatures of the water, scaly kind
And serpent, chased by panic from their dens,
Mount to safe sunshine one and all upon an island-
    bank;
Scorpion and alligator, turtle and giant crab
In scrambling shoals criss-crossed,
Fins floundering, scales flourished —
Now slithering, now twining,
They gain the middle bank and stare afar.

They see dark trees whose winter-flowers
Dazzle the eye; white shine those woods
As a full heaven, where star is blent with star.
And over many woods of chestnut-trees
Thick leaf and blossom brood;
Here twin catalpas trail their cups
From branches subtly twined.
Through the dark leafage ripples roam,
Tides run; to east and west
The forest spreads her wings
In delicate wafting of innumerable thrills;
Green leaves, purple fruit-skins,
Red buds, white stems
And slender branches wailing
Reed-music to the wind.

Climb higher, look afar.
Tall cliffs by their dizzy winding
Confound the eye. Yonder in rank are propped
Stupendous spires; here are great boulders split
In hideous escarpment, leaning crags,
And cliffs from whose disrupted crest
Rock slithers after rock
Into a chaos of disastered stone.
Horned pinnacles rear back at the chasm's brink,
Dismayed and staggering.

So in huge conglomeration
Bulk is strewn on bulk, pile heaped on pile;
Till, topping all, the pillared summit soars
Like a great mowers'-stone

Erect beneath the towering of the inland hills.

Above, a rainbow glistens on the hill's grave crest;
Below, a void whose chasms seem
Bottomless, save for the voice
Of pine-trees carried upward on the wind.

Steep tilts the sodden bank, noisy with filtering waters;
Bear-wise clambers the traveler, slinging from tree to tree.
Will the climbing never be ended?
Sweat pours from his limbs;
He stops, he is bewildered, dares not move.
Loneliness besets him, disappointment and weak irresolute grief.
Often in such case
The soul is changed, fears causeless come,
Hearts fabled stout, of Meng Fen or Xia Yu,[3]
Forget their boldness. For suddenly (whence came they?)
Flock bestial legions, hairy multitudes,
Creatures magically spawned, childen of ghost or god,
Some winged, some footed; all terrible, huge and strange,
Beyond the power of tale to tell.

Around the shrine
Flat spreads the mountain-roof and wide,
A mighty flail, on whose broad palm
Thick grow the scented herbs, orchis and river-broom,
Crow's-fan, clustering thyme, gray lavender.
Delicately the grasses dip and myriad bushes blend
The scent of tender boughs, wherein,
Each seeking his lost mate,
Small birds lament; from neighboring twig
Trill answers trill — the royal-coot,
The yellow witwall, herald-of-dusk, warbler of Chu,
Desolate-bride, sister-come-home-again
And trailing pheasant housed in his high nest
In the fresh season carol at their play
Lusty and heedless; or in sudden choir declaim
Skilled music matched to the stream's pause and flow.

Here dwell masters of magic, wizards of the North;

---

[3] Legendary heroes.

On high they roam in happy throngs,[4] to gather in
The sacrificial grain. See, now they dedicate
The stainless victim, hymn the Lord
Of the Revolving Chamber, to the many Gods
Libations pour; with worship venerate
The Unity Supreme.
The prayers are over, the liturgies incanted.
Then shall my lord the King
Ride in a magic chariot of jade
By tawny dragons drawn.
Banners and tall gonfalons shall he trail
Whose pennons intertwine. Harpers shall pluck
Their giant chords, and courtly music flow,
Tinged by the eager winds that pass
With sadness not its own;
Legends of anguish, sorrowful tales shall the singer's voice
Temper to that unhappy tune
Till they that listen throb with answering sighs.

Last come the serried huntsmen, knee to knee,
Many as the stars of heaven. For winged hunt
The word is passed; they set the gags between their teeth
And suddenly are dumb.
Not yet from arbalest or bow
Is arrow shot; no net is spread.
Over wide streams they wade, through tangled thickets stride.
Ere the bird take wing to fly or the beast set foot to roam,
Suddenly, through stroke invisible, blood spurts on haunch or claw.
The huntsman's work is ended; the carts are heavy with prey.
Such is the Mountain of Gao Tang.

But should my lord desire to hunt there he must needs practice long abstinence and fasting, and by augury select the day and hour. He must be dressed in black; he must be carried in an unpainted chair. His banner must be woven with clouds; his streamers must be fashioned like the rainbow, his awning, of halcyon feathers.

Then the wind shall rise, the rain shall cease, and for a thousand leagues the clear sky shall be unfurled. And when the last cloud has vanished, he shall go quietly to the place of meeting.

Thereafter shall my lord the King deal kindly for ever with the

---

[4] The text of this line and the next is corrupt and my translation only conjectural.

thousand lands, sorrow for the wrongs of his people, promote the wise and good, and make whole whatever was amiss. No longer shall the apertures of his intelligence be choked; to his soul's scrutiny all hidden things shall be laid bare. His years shall be prolonged, his strength eternally endure.

JIA YI (200–168 B.C.)
The Owl

Translated by Burton Watson

"The Owl" by Jia Yi is the earliest work in the rhapsody form whose authorship and date of composition are reasonably certain. The text is recorded in the biography of the poet in the *Records of the Grand Historian* by Sima Qian, compiled around 100 B.C. Sima Qian describes the circumstances under which the work was composed: "Three years after Jia Yi became grand tutor to the king of Changsha a hoot-owl one day flew into his lodge and perched on the corner of his mat.... Jia Yi had been disgraced and sent to live in Changsha, a damp, low-lying region, and he believed that he did not have long to live. He was filled with horror and grief at the appearance of the bird and, to console himself, composed a poem in the rhapsody style." The position of tutor to the king of Changsha, in a remote region of the Yangtze, was actually a form of banishment, and this fact, along with the poet's failing health, accounts for the air of gloom that pervades the work. Using the owl as his mouthpiece, Jia Yi preaches himself a fervently Taoist sermon on the equality of life and death, drawing his ideas and images principally from the writings of Zhuangzi.

In the year *dan-e,*
Fourth month, first month of summer,
The day *gui-zi,* when the sun was low in the west,
An owl came to my lodge
And perched on the corner of my mat,
Phlegmatic and fearless.
Secretly wondering the reason
The strange thing had come to roost,
I took out a book to divine it
And the oracle told me its secret:
  "Wild bird enters the hall;
  The master will soon depart."
I asked and importuned the owl,
"Where is it I must go?
Do you bring good luck? Then tell me!
Misfortune? Relate what disaster!
Must I depart so swiftly?
Then speak to me of the hour!"

The owl breathed a sigh,
Raised its head and beat its wings.
Its beak could utter no word,
But let me tell you what it sought to say:
All things alter and change,
Never a moment of ceasing,
Revolving, whirling, and rolling away,
Driven far off and returning again,
Form and breath passing onward,
Like the mutations of a cicada.
Profound, subtle, and illimitable,
Who can finish describing it?
Good luck must be followed by bad,
Bad in turn bow to good.
Sorrow and joy throng the gate,
Weal and woe in the same land.
Wu was powerful and great;
Under Fucha it sank in defeat.
Yue was crushed at Kuaiji,
But Goujian made it an overlord.
Li Si, who went forth to greatness, at last
Suffered the five mutilations.
Fu Yue was sent into bondage,
Yet Wu Ding made him his aide.[5]
Thus fortune and disaster
Entwine like the strands of a rope.
Fate cannot be told of,
For who shall know its ending?
Water, troubled, runs wild;
The arrow, quick-sped, flies far.
All things, whirling and driving,
Compelling and pushing each other, roll on.
The clouds rise up, the rains come down,
In confusion inextricably joined.
The Great Potter fashions all creatures,

---

[5] Wu and Yue were rival states in the southeast during Zhou times and Fucha and Goujian the rulers who led them to defeat and glory respectively. Li Si, prime minister to the First Emperor of the Qin, later fell from favor and was executed. Wu Ding was a king of the Yin dynasty who dreamed of a worthy minister and later discovered the man of his dream in an ex-convict laborer, Fu Yue.

Infinite, boundless, limit unknown.
There is no reckoning Heaven,
Nor divining beforehand the Tao.
The span of life is fated;
Man cannot guess its ending.
Heaven and earth are the furnace,
The workman, the Creator;
His coal is the yin and the yang,
His copper, all things of creation.
Joining, scattering, ebbing and flowing,
Where is there persistence or rule?
A thousand, a myriad mutations,
Lacking an end's beginning.
Suddenly they form a man:
How is this worth taking thought of?
They are transformed again in death:
Should this perplex you?
The witless takes pride in his being,
Scorning others, a lover of self.
The man of wisdom sees vastly
And knows that all things will do.
The covetous run after riches,
The impassioned pursue a fair name;
The proud die struggling for power,
While the people long only to live.
Each drawn and driven onward,
They hurry east and west.
The great man is without bent;
A million changes are as one to him.
The stupid man chained by custom
Suffers like a prisoner bound.
The sage abandons things
And joins himself to the Tao alone,
While the multitudes in delusion
With desire and hate load their hearts.
Limpid and still, the true man
Finds his peace in the Tao alone.
Transcendent, destroying self,
Vast and empty, swift and wild,
He soars on wings of the Tao.
Discarding wisdom, forgetful of form,
Borne on the flood he sails forth;

He rests on the river islets.
Freeing his body to Fate,
Unpartaking of self,
His life is a floating,
His death a rest.
In stillness like the stillness of deep springs,
Like an unmoored boat drifting aimlessly,
Never looking on life as a treasure,
He embraces and drifts with Nothing.
Comprehending Fate and free of sorrow,
The man of virtue heeds no bounds.
Petty matters, weeds and thorns —
What are they to me?

MEI SHENG (d. 141 B.C.)
The Seven Exhortations to Rise

Translated by John Scott

Mei Sheng was a provincial court poet to the royal princes Wu and Xiao. His fame rests
on this rhapsody, known for its great length and its use of the rhetorical technique
known as *feng*, or satirical criticism.

The Crown Prince of Chu was ailing and a courtier of Wu inquired after
his condition: "I have heard that the Prince's jade frame is ill at ease. Has
there been any improvement?" The Prince replied: "How exhausted I
feel! But I thank you kindly for your solicitude." The courtier then said:
"The nation is at peace, the four quarters of the globe enjoy harmony,
and Your Majesty has a rich future to look forward to. I am of the opinion
that you have been long addicted to pleasure, day and night without end.
Evil humors have attacked you, and your internal organs are congealed.
You are pallid and afeared. Your breathing has been affected by a surfeit
of drink. Alarmed and troubled you rest but find no sleep. You are
debilitated to such an extent that you shrink from the sound of voices.
Your energy seeps away. A hundred maladies will arise. Hearing and
eyesight will grow dull, anger and happiness succeed each other for no
reason. If you persist in this course it will be difficult to abandon these
bad habits, and your life will be imperiled. Is it not this way with you, my
Prince?" The Prince replied: "I thank you for your solicitude. It is true
that, relying upon my imperial power, I have from time to time indulged
myself a little, but I would not say it has gone as far as you have suggested." The courtier replied: "You, like the sons of all noblemen, have

lived secure in the Palace apartments. At home you have had a nurse, and journeying out you have been accompanied by a tutor. If you had desired to choose your own friends you could have found no opportunity of doing so. When eating and drinking you have enjoyed rich and delicate flavors, succulent meats, and the finest liquor. Your wardrobe is extensive, fine clothing as warm as a summer's day; so even were your physique as tough as steel or stone it would be hard not to be melted and broken down. How much the more so when you are but a man of bone and muscle. Therefore I say: if you give vent to the desires of your ears and eyes, covet the joys of the flesh, you will interrupt the harmony of your bloodstream. If for every trip you make, you travel by chariot, I can safely say you will end up a cripple. The pleasures of the bedroom and the passion-palace are called The Go-Between of Fever. White teeth and fine moth eyebrows are known as The Axe Which Beheads Life. Rich foods and liquors are known as The Drug Which Rots The Stomach. Now, my Prince, your flesh is too tender, your countenance pale, your limbs have no energy, your marrow has gone soft, your bloodstream curdled, your hands and feet without strength. Ladies from Yue attend you in front, and concubines from Qi follow behind. With them you come and go to banquets, venting your lusts in the twisting corridors and hidden bedrooms. Such enjoyment is like drinking poison. Dalliance of this sort is playing with the claws and teeth of a wild animal. Things have gone far enough, but if you persist much longer, even if you summoned a physician as wise as Bian Qiao to attend to your internal organs or the fabled shaman Wu Xian to attend to your external person, nothing could be done. When dealing with the malady that you are suffering from, my Prince, only the world's great sages are competent, men of profound experience and extensive knowledge, who would seize the opportunity to persuade you to a change of heart. They would be constantly at your side to guide you. And then where would you find the means to protract your pleasures, pamper your lustful notions and indulge your urge for dissipation?" Then said the Prince: "I agree with you, but I am still unwell. When I am feeling better, I will do just as you suggest." But the courtier replied: "It is not by means of cautery and acupuncture that your disease will be cured, but by succinct words and excellent teaching. Do you wish to hear more?" The Prince replied: "I would like to." Then the courtier spoke:

"At Dragon Gate Mountain stands a turpentine tree
    a hundred feet high to the lowest branch,
In it for ever multiply the age-rings,
    its roots spread far and wide,

Behind it towers the eight-thousand-foot peak,
    a hundred feet below it rushes a torrent,
Turbulent waves, conflicting currents wash
    its roots half life half death,
In winter it is stabbed by frost, fierce wind and swirling snow
    in summer assailed by flashes of lightning, peals of thunder,
In the morning the oriole settles there,
    the *hantan* bird cries in its branches,
In the evening the bereaved female bird
    and the lost male
    rest there,
Upon it the solitary snow-goose sings in the dawn,
    the crane mournfully circles and cries below it.
Now the year turns its back on autumn, and winter comes:
    the master lute-maker hews it down for his instrument.
Wild silk cocoons become the lute-strings,
    the orphans' jewelry adorns it,
    its frets are the ear-rings of the widow with nine children.
I will cause Confucius's music-teacher, Master Tang, to play
    upon it the time-honored melodies,
And Bo Ya the fabled lute-player will sing this song to it:
    Among the thick ear-rings of wheat
      the wild cockerel flies at dawn.
    Facing the desolate village, alas,
      the bird turns its back on the withered ashtree.
    The paths and road are blocked, alas,
      I face the everflowing torrent.
The birds will hear it,
    fold their wings and be unable to fly,
The wild beasts will hear it,
    droop their ears and be unable to walk,
The creeping ants and insects will hear it,
    cease their gnawing and be unable to move.
This song is the sum of the world's sadness:
    can the Prince force himself to rise and listen to it?"
The Prince said: "I am ill,
    I am not yet well enough."

The courtier said:
"Cook
    the flesh of a young calf
      garnished with the tenderest shoots,

Brew
    a harmonious broth from plump dogflesh,
       cap it with a layer of mountain truffles,
Prepare the rice of Chu
    and the fine cereals of the South,
       choice dainties,
Rolled into balls,
    dropped in the mouth,
       they will melt at a taste,
Summon the master chef Yi Yin to perform the cuisine,
    the famed cook Yi Ya will blend and spice it,
And then prepare well-cooked bear's paw,
    add a sweet sauce,
Take delicately sliced, braised lean meats,
    slivers of fresh carp,
Adorn the whole with autumn-yellow sapan,
    September mushrooms plucked amidst white dew,
Serve with wine steeped in orchids,
    a sip will freshen the mouth,
Then add the flesh of wild pheasant,
    the fetus of home-reared leopards,
Taste a little rice,
    drink much thin gruel,
And it will be like sun melting snow.
This is the sum of the world's cuisine:
    can the Prince force himself up to savor it?"
The Prince replied "I am ill,
    I am not yet well enough."

The courtier said: "Bring fine horses of the Kingdom of Zhao,
    matched by age and harnessed to chariots,
The front span as swift as flying birds,
    the rear span as frisky as the heavenly gazelle.
Feed them a fine mash of wheat —
    their mettle will be without compare.
Caparisoned with stout harness and bit
    they will gallop the level roads.
Then have the horse-fancier Bo Le
    to choose the order of the team,
Wang Liang and Cao Fu, as master-charioteers,
    brave Qin Que and stout Lou Ji to be outriders.
With men like these to control such fiery horses

or right the toppled chariot,
Then you may lay wagers of a thousand talents,
    compete in races of a thousand miles.
These are the sum of the world's mettle —
    Can the Prince force himself up to mount his chariot?"
The Prince replied: "I am ill,
    I am not yet well enough."

The courtier said: "Ascend the pagoda of Jing Yi,
    to the south you will look out to Mount Jing
    to the north you will see the vast waters of Ru,
To the left the mighty Yangtze,
    to the right Lake Dongting
    the world holds few such joys.
Then you may summon scholars learned in disputation
    who will in verse describe the mountains and rivers,
    exhaustively name each tree and plant,
All these they will marvellously classify —
    to make the Sum of Things.
After this brief excursion
    you will come down to feast and wine in Yu Huai Palace
    whose corridors are belvederes,
With story upon story painted dark green,
    interconnecting carriageways,
    sinuous ornamental ponds.
Amongst birds reared here is the white-striped Hunzhang,
    the Eastern Egret, the Peacock, the Kungu Jungle Fowl,
    the Mandarin Duck, the Green Crested Grebe;
Some birds sport turquoise crests of kingfisher feather,
    others boast purple throat-bands;
The hornless Dragon-Fowl, the Virtuous Shepherd-Bird —
    their song harmonizes.
Endless varieties of fish leap and splash
    their fins strumming the waters.
By the fresh green rivulets grow
    elegant grasses and marsh-reeds,
The convolvulus and opulent water-lily,
    tender mulberry-bushes and river willows
    with white leaves and purple stems;
Mighty pine-trees and camphor laurels
    whose branches brush the heavens,
    the turpentine tree and the coir palm

form forests as far as the eye can see.
Manifold thick fragrant shade blends
    with every sound of rustling
    the treetops are pliant to the wind,
    the foliage shifts from light to shadow.
Orator Jing Chun serves the drinks,
    Lutemaster Du Lian sees to the music.
Dainty foods are laid out,
    dishes of fish and fowl stand ready.
Exquisite colors charm the eye,
    fine sonorities delight the ear.
Then like a whirlwind the tunes of the South strike up:
    the melodies of lubricious Zheng and lascivious Wei
    float upon the air.
Then are summoned Lady Xi Shi, concubine Zheng Shu,
    Lady Sun-Pattern, Mistress Broken Stem,
    South Baby, Lu Zhou, Fu Yu and other lovely women
    trailing dresses of every color,
    hair hanging like swallowtails,
    eyes provocative, bosoms hinting at
    dark permissiveness.
They bring water to bathe in,
    turmeric unguents perfume their naked bodies,
Their hair piled up like dust-clouds
    where floats the scent of orchids,
They slip on flimsy silks to await the lovemakers' couch.
This is the sum of the world's expansive luxury:
    can the Prince force himself up to dally?"
The Prince replied: "I am ill,
    I am not yet well enough."

The courtier said: "Well then for you I would offer
    to break in steeds,
    harness them to paneled light chariots.
Mounted in a car drawn by noble stallions
    in your right hand you will grasp
      Prince Xia's quiver of straight arrows,
    in your left, the bow, crowblack, of the Yellow Emperor.
Then set out to Cloud-Dream Forest,
    drive through the Orchid Lowlands,
    halt by the Great River's flood,
    rest among the marsilea plants,

swallow the transparent wind,
　　get drunk on the sun's air,
　　unshackle your spring heart,
Pursue the crafty beasts of the field,
　　shoot down light-soaring birds,
Try out the talents of hound and horse,
　　tire out the wild beasts' hoof,
　　exhaust the charioteer, his skill,
Tiger and leopard flushed out of hiding will take fright,
　　birds of prey will fly on wings of panic.
As the horse runs full tilt the harness-bells will tinkle;
　　they will leap like fish, butt like stags.
You will tread deer and hare, trample down antelope.
　　The beasts will sweat, cower, fall exhausted,
　　they will die unscathed, of fright.
Your chariots in the rear will be piled with game.
The world knows no mightier hunt:
　　can you force yourself to rise and join the meet?"
The Prince replied: "I am ill,
　　I am not yet well enough."
But in his eyes glinted a livelier light,
　　a happy look began to steal upon his majestic countenance.

Seeing the Prince's look of joy,
　　the courtier developed his theme, and said:
"Night hunting fires will light up the heavens,
　　war chariots roll like thunder,
The standards flutter aloft
　　and feather-pennants crazy in array,
You will set the riders in hot pursuit;
　　scenting the killed game,
　　they will compete for first place.
The undergrowth will be beaten flat
　　clear to the very frontiers.
A beast perfect in hide and pelt will later be sacrificed
　　to your ancestors."
Then came the Prince's interruption: "Excellent.
　　I should like to hear more of this."

The courtier said: "That is not all there is to it.
There, within the hazel forests, the deep marshlands,
　　enveloped in dusk-smoke
　　rhinoceros and tiger appear together,

Stout hunting warriors, fierce and steadfast,
    their sleeves rolled up to do battle,
White blades glinting like white rocks,
    a tangle of lances and spears all stabbing.
The bag's recorded, achievements written down,
    prizes of gold and silk awarded,
They roll out grass mats, spread couches,
    and for the chief sacrificer prepare a feast:
The finest wine, the choicest dishes,
    thin cuts well braised to banquet the retainers.
Such loyalty is a hardness
    firmer than iron or rock.
Loud they sing and tell of deeds,
    long life to the King, unwearying.
This is truly something you, my Prince, could delight in.
    Can you not force yourself up to join this venture?"
The Prince said: "Indeed I would like to take part.
    It's just that I feel my presence a hindrance
    to the other lords."
Yet nonetheless he took on color.

The courtier said: "Soon comes the eighth month,
    the fifteenth day.
Then princes from far regions journey together with their brothers
To look down at Guangling's mighty flood-bore.
Till now they have not seen the power of waves,
    even the looking bowls you over,
Seeing it rushing and rising,
      tearing and pulling,
        rending and hurrying,
      rearing together,
        pouring away.
Had you but the words to describe it,
    its shape would elude you like its curves.
O see it, fear it, be stunned by it, ground by it,
    sudden flusterer, roller and roysterer,
      pouring forth, roaring away, massive in onslaught,
Swallowing up the Southern hills,
    evilly lusting for the Eastern sea,
A rainbow vaulting the blue skies,
    building a cliff in the mind,
It flows and roars without end,

    seeking a path to the Sun-mother's home.
Now up it drives and down it goes,
    No telling where its end,
The waves in confusion flow and tear,
    Clash suddenly and no return.
Look there at the Southern bank,
    rushing to the distance.
You are empty and filled with a violent fear,
    an impression of waves so deeply staining your heart
      it cannot be washed away.
But water refreshes the lungs,
    purges the bowels, cleanses the hands and feet,
      soaks the teeth and hair,
Drives away languid humors,
    cleans off all dust and dirt,
Makes certain uncertainties,
    rinses the ears and eyes.
Suppose now there was some despondency,
Why, even the hunchback would straighten up,
    the cripple walk,
The deaf would hear, the blind would be enlightened
    to gaze upon this scene.
How much more for those with but light afflictions,
    disciples of wine, hangover-sick.
As it is said of old, Truly no words of mine
    could make a sum of this enlightenment."
The Prince said: "Excellent.
    Yet what is the nature of this flood?"

The courtier said: "It is not recorded.
    Yet I have heard my teacher say
      the water possesses three things
    that spirits lack:
Sudden thunder heard from a hundred miles;
    the sea-bore flowing back against itself,
      blanketing mountains in the cloud
    endlessly day and night;
Slowly it starts, gathering speed
    till the ominous swell of waves
      builds up a mighty rhythm
    like the Eastern egret soaring,
Advancing and tipped with small white crests

as bright
as the silken parasols of white chariots
driven by white horses.
Then the chasers become cloud-confused,
rushing forward like a full-geared army
With small waves hurrying lightly —
generals on the wing riding light chariots.
A team of six dragons pulling Great White the water spirit's car
a massing perspective of rainbows together,
pressing ahead,
High and high, low and low,
forward and back hustling and crowding,
Now like a castellated fort,
now like a cavalry and footsoldiers forward advancing,
Its noise is a roaring, it fills the sky with seething,
its strength cannot be withstood.
See the two banks, massive flood-anger around them,
for a moment dark and lowering,
suddenly then it's palpable,
to overwhelm, to undermine,
The waves like brave soldiers
forward rushing without fear,
smashing down walls and stopping breaches,
It roars round curves, leaps over sandbanks,
those it meets die, those who oppose are smashed,
Gathers up speed to thunder past Encircling Ford,
with a fearful rush it fills the valleys,
Its maelstrom whirls round Green Splint
laying a muffled ambush for Sandalwood Forest,
Descending on Mount Wu Zixu
for the assault on Bone-Mother Battlefield,
It cuts Red Crag away, sweeps past Purple Mulberry Grove,
its advance is impetuous thunder.
Truly it robs warriors of spirit
in its enraged vibration,
in its gulping and gurgling,
the strength of galloping horses,
in its swirling and swallowing,
the sound of hungry drum-thunder.
Clear rising, the back waves leap clear over,
follow up to do battle at the mouth of Crashing River.
Fish are stranded, beasts cannot run, birds cannot fly,

they flap their wings, winged waves like clouds.
It violates the Southern Mountain,
    steals up to attack the Northern shore,
Tearing down dykes, flattening the Western Weir,
In dangerous sport it playfully swallows reservoirs,
    victory alone will check it,
But the quick advance of the gurgling flood
    rips out everything with its mighty waves.
This is the sum of cruelty,
    fish and turtle are helpless, tossed and turned,
    floating and bloated, stranded,
Even the spirits would be afeared:
    so many abilities baffling speech
That men fall down in fright,
    faint from fear,
    slowly to regain consciousness.
This is the world's most varied, strange and terrible vista:
    can the Prince not force himself up to look at it?"
The Prince said: "I am ill,
    I am not yet well enough."

The courtier said: "Then let me summon
    men of skill and knowledge,
Schooled in policy and debate:
    Master Zhuangzi the Taoist,
    Yangzi the Individualist,
    Mo Di the Chivalrous Altruist,
    Bian Juan, Zhan He and others,
To expound to you the nature of the world,
    reason out the rights and wrongs of Manifold Existence.
Confucius and Laozi could test and observe,
    Mencius could investigate and assess,
    out of ten thousand wisdoms
    not one would be lacking:
Such is the sum of succinct words and excellent teaching:
    why not listen, my Prince?"
The Prince heaved himself up with both hands,
    saying:
    "Things are clear, it is as if
    I hear the wise disputers' words."
His fever broke
    and in a sweat

Suddenly
    his sickness had ended.

SIMA XIANGRU (179–117 B.C.), attrib.
The Beautiful Person

Translated by John Scott

One of the great romantic figures in Chinese literature, Sima Xiangru led a rather bohemian existence for a number of years, until eventually he came to the notice of the discerning Martial Emperor [Emperor Wu of the Han dynasty], who made him an Attendant of the Imperial Secretariat. Whilst at court he composed rhapsodies for the imperial delectation. Only six of these survive, of which "The Beautiful Person" stands in a class by itself — this has led later critics to doubt its authenticity. Before "making good" at the court, Xiangru had eloped with a millionaire's daughter, called Lady Zhuo Wenjun. For some time the scandalous couple kept alive runnng a humble tavern where she served the drinks behind the counter whilst he, wearing nothing but a loincloth, washed the empties at the public trough in the marketplace. Eventually her father relented and more than amply compensated his daughter and son-in-law with trousseau and gifts. Perhaps this rhapsody is a true reflection of his "younger and more vulnerable years." At all events, it is the first example of erotic writing in Chinese literature to have survived the literary prescriptions of later and less enlightened generations.

Handsome Sima Xiangru was at leisure in the Capital. He had journeyed to see the Prince of Liang, who delighted in his conversation. But Zhou Yang vilified him to the Prince, saying: "True it is that Xiangru is a fine figure of a man. But despite his elegant dress, his noble features, there is deceit and disloyalty in his good looks and he uses his flattering command of rhetoric to achieve pleasure. He has been wandering about the seraglio of Your Highness. I wonder if you have noticed this?" The Prince asked Xiangru: "Are you addicted to lust?" "I am not," he replied. Then the Prince said: "Well, you must be like Confucius and Mo Di." But Xiangru answered: "Those ancients avoided all acquaintance with sensual delights. The like of Confucius and Mo Di had only to hear of a beautiful woman and they made themselves scarce. If they heard a woman of the palace singing in the distance, they would turn their chariots around. It was as if they considered women as dangerous as raging fire and deep water, and hid away from them on secluded mountains. Seeing they found no opportunity for temptation, how can we be sure that they were not libertines?

When I was young
    long years in the West
        I dwelt by myself in a solitary place.

My mansion was vast and rambling,
    yet I found no diversions.
My neighbor to the East had a daughter
    black her hair, comely her figure,
        moth eyebrows and white teeth,
Features full and sensual,
    a luster like flashing light.
She often gazed towards my residence
    as if she would wish me to join her;
As she mounted her steps
    she would pause and look at me.
Though I lived there three years
    I avoided her and never complied,
      for I was mindful of Your Highness's
    strict standards:
      you had commanded me to ride eastwards.
My journey took me through lascivious Zheng
      and lubricious Wei,
        my path took me through Sang Zhong.
In the morning I set off from the region of Zhun Wei,
    in the evening I lodged at a great mansion.
This mansion was an empty but elegant residence
    all by itself among the clouds:
    its doors had been shut to the light.
      It seemed a fairy palace.
I pushed my way in through the shuttered door,
    found my way to the hall;
Exotic perfumes and fine scents hovered in the air,
    rich screens and tapestries furnished it.
And there in this room a lady waited alone:
    curvaciously beautiful, reclining on the bed
In sweetly perfumed and languid charm,
    her skin clear, her features vivid.
Seeing hesitation in my step,
    she smiled and said:
'Sir, what country are you from?
    Have you traveled far to this place?'
She offered me wine,
    brought out a bird-toned lute;
So I touched the strings
    and played White Snow
      and the Dark Orchid.

And then she sang this poem:
    'In solitude here, alas,
      in empty vastness, no one to care for me,
    I long for my handsome prince, alas,
      I am wounded with sorrow.
    Here is my handsome prince, alas,
      but how long he delays,
    Till day becomes evening, alas,
      and my flower complexion fades.
    To you I dare confide my body,
      long may you and I be intimate.'
She was so close that her jade hairpins
    brushed my hat,
      her gauze sleeves whispered against my clothes.
The sun went down in the West,
    mysterious dusk set in,
      the light was swallowed up.
Outside, the wind flowed sad and chill,
    cold silk snow swirling.
In our closed room all was quiet,
    not a sound was heard.
On the bed were laid
    exotic coverlets and sheets.
A golden brazier breathed out scented smoke,
    the curtains round the bed were lowered,
The quilt turned back,
    the ivory pillow set horizontal.
She stepped out of her robe,
    showed off her undergarments,
Revealed her white body,
    full delicate nakedness,
      shapely beauty.
Then she came close to me
    wrapping her soft body
      slipping like paste around me.
My pulse of course was regular,
    my heart was purposeful within my breast:
As the *Songs* say:
    'Clearly we were sworn to good faith':
      I held my resolution upright,
      there could be no faltering.
With such lofty example I made my long goodbye."

The Mighty One

Translated by Burton Watson

Sima Qian, the Grand Historian, who gives this rhapsody in full in his biography of
Sima Xiangru, adds: "When Sima Xiangru presented his ode in praise of the Mighty
One, the emperor was overcome with delight, declaring that it made him feel as
though he were already soaring effortlessly over the clouds and filled him with a
longing to wander about the earth and the heavens."

In this world there lives a Mighty One
Who dwells in the Middle Continent.[6]
Though his mansion stretches ten thousand miles,
He is not content to remain in it a moment
But, saddened by the sordid press of the vulgar world,
Nimbly takes his way aloft and soars far away.
With crimson carriage flags interwoven with crystal rainbows,
He mounts upon the clouds and wanders on high;
He raises his long standard of yellow flame
Tipped with multicolored plumes of shimmering radiance,
Streaming with starry pennants
And banderoles of comets' tails.
Drifting with the wind, he threads his way;
With banners fluttering, he wanders aloft.
He snatches a shooting star for a flag
And sheathes his flagstaff in a broken rainbow.
A blaze of vermilion, dazzling the eyes,
He whirls before the gale and drifts upon the clouds.
His elephant-carved chariot is drawn by winged dragons,
With red serpents and green lizards writhing at their sides.
High and low they gallop,
Lifting their heads in lordly pride;
Lithely bending and rearing their backs,
They slither and curl their winding way.
Now they stretch their necks and peer about,
Raising their heads and pausing in passage;
Now with fearless and lofty assurance
They bolt forward in tumultuous flight.
Onward they bound, twisting and turning,
Left side and right leaping in harmony,
Tumbling forward in dauntless array,

---

[6] In other words China. The Mighty One is of course intended to be Emperor Wu himself.

Prancing in unison.
Straining at the bridle and uttering strange cries,
They swoop down to tread the earth;
Springing upward in breathless flight,
They careen wildly across the sky.
Pressing forward, chasing after,
They swirl like sparks, they stream like lightning,
Plunging boldly into the mists
And fading out of sight among the clouds.[7]
Thus the Mighty One crosses to the eastern limit and ascends to the
    end of the north,
Searching out other immortal spirits.
Together they wheel about and drive far to the right;
Slanting across the Valley of Leaping Springs, they turn again east.
He summons all the fairies of the Magic Garden
And a host of gods to ride behind him on the Star of Pure Light.
He orders the Emperors of the Five Directions to be his guides,
Beckons to his side the Great Single Star and the immortal Ling
    Yang.
On his left rides the deity Black Night, on his right, the Thunder
    Bearer,
While before and behind the gods Luli and Yuhuang attend him.
He has the War Earl Qiao as his footman, the genie Xianmen as
    his page,
And the physician Qibo to prepare his medicine cup.
The god of fire Zhurong goes in front to clear the road
And disperse the foul vapors before his coming.
His cortege boasts ten thousand carriages,
Their canopies woven of cloud, their flowered pennants flying.
He calls the god of the east Jumang to wait upon him,
Saying, "I would journey south to take my pleasure!"
He visits the sage Emperor Yao on Mount Chong
And Emperor Shun on the Mountain of Nine Peaks.
In endless massive ranks his retinue advances;
Pressing upon each other, they gallop on their way,
Veering and jostling
Amidst a tangle of chariots,
Swooping onward in eternal procession

---

[7] In this passage, a mass of obscure onomatopoetic compounds, commentators are able to
give only tentative suggestions as to the exact meaning of the words.

Like a mighty river rolling by;
Spurring forward in serried ranks,
A host of countless numbers advancing,
Fanning out across the heavens,
Their columns scattered and broken.
Straight they ride into the din and clangor of the Thunder Hall
And swoop through the craggy confines of Devil Valley.
They survey the eight directions and the four outer wastes,
Ford the Nine Rivers and pass over the Five Streams,
Traverse the Flaming Mountain and the River of Weak Waters,
Embark among the floating islets and cross the drifting sands;
They rest upon the Congling Ranges and idle by their waters,
While the goddess Nü Wa strikes the lute and the Lord of the River
    dances.
At times, when the sky grows dark and threatening,
They summon Pingyi, the messenger of the gods,
And send him to chastise the Wind Earl and punish the Rain Master.
They gaze west to the hazy contours of the Kunlun Mountains,
Then gallop off to the Mountain of the Three Pinnacles.
They batter at the gates of Heaven, enter the palace of the Celestial
    Emperor,
And invite the goddess Jade Maiden to return in their chariots.
They roam the slopes of Langfeng and sit down to rest,
Like ravens that circle on high and come to roost again.
They wander among the Dark Hills,
Winging their way in crooked flight.
"Behold!" cries the Mighty One, "the Queen Mother of the West,[8]
With her hair of silvery white
And her burden of hairpins, living in a cave!
Fortunately she has her three-legged crow to bring her food.
Yet if she must live in this state forever,
Though it be for ten thousand ages, what joy can she find?"
Then he wheels his carriage about and departs from her abode,
Making his way across Mount Buzhou.
He stops to dine at the Hill of the Somber City;
He sucks up the midnight vapors of the northland

---

[8] An immortal spirit whose cult was very popular in Han times, said to dwell in a cave west of the Kunlun Mountains. The poet makes fun of her constrained way of life, contrasting it with the freedom and luxury of The Mighty One.

And feasts on golden morning mists;
He nibbles the blossoms of the herb of immortality
And savors the flowers of the Ruby Tree.
Then he rises and resumes his journey,
His chariot dancing wildly towards the heavens.
He threads through the streams of lightning that pour from
    Heaven's portals
And traverses the drenching torrents of the Cloud Master.
With his attendant carriages, he gallops the long road downward,
Racing through the mists and off into the distance.
He presses beyond the borders of the narrow universe
And, with slackened pace, emerges beyond the bounds of the north.
He leaves his attendants behind at the Dark Pass
And rides ahead of them out of the Cold Gate of the North.
Beneath him in the vastness, the earth has disappeared;
Above his head the heavens vanish in endless space.
Gazing about, his eyes swim and grow sightless;
His ears are deafened and discern no sound.
Riding upon the Void, he mounts on high,
Above the world of men, companionless, to dwell alone.

YANG XIONG (53 B.C.–A.D. 18)
The Sweet Springs Palace

Translated by David Knechtges

This rhapsody describes an imperial progress to the Sweet Springs Palace, located three hundred *li* northwest of Chang'an. The Palace was the site of sacrifices to the supreme deity, the Grand Unity, at an altar first established in 113 B.C. by Emperor Wu. In 16 B.C. the Emperor Cheng [r. 32–7 B.C.], being without an heir, requested the Empress Dowager to issue an edict restoring the sacrifices.

During the reign of the Filial Emperor Cheng, there was an imperial retainer who recommended my compositions as resembling those of Sima Xiangru. His Highness was about to perform the boundary sacrifices at the Grand Altar in Sweet Springs and to Queen Earth at Fenyin, in order to seek an heir and successor. He summoned me to await appointment in the courtyard of the Hall of Received Brilliance. In the first month, I accompanied His Majesty to Sweet Springs. When I returned, I presented the "Sweet Springs Palace Rhapsody" in order to sway (the emperor's opinion). The piece reads:

1

He is Han's tenth generation, and intending to offer the boundary sacrifices to the Supreme Mystery and establish the Grand Altar, He gathers unto Himself divine blessings, honors the lustrous appellations, matches tally with the Three Emperors, registers merit equal to that of the Five Lords, shows concern for the succession, bestows largesse, broadens His pathway, and inaugurates new ventures. Thereupon, He orders the numerous officers to reckon an auspicious day and correlate an efficacious hour.

As the stars spread out and Heaven begins to move:

2

He summons Twinkling Indicator and Grand Yin,[9]
Commands Angular Array to take charge of the troops,[10]
Assigns Geomancer to the ramparts,[11]
Cudgels Demon Drought and flogs Flying Frenzy.[12]
The Eight Spirits race off, heralding and clearing the road:
Swarming in tumultuous throngs, in battle dress,
Peers of Chiyou[13]
Girding on Ganjiang swords, grasping jade axes,[14]
Fly hurry-scurry, run leaping and lurching;
Jointly massed and mustered, grouped and gathered,
    twined and tangled,
Swift as whirlwinds, fleet as clouds, they rush helter-skelter;
Ranged in ranks, arrayed in columns, melding and merging
    like fishscales,
Higgledy-piggledy, diversely disposed, they leap like fish,
    glide like birds;
Bright and blazing, in a blinding blur, gathering like fog,
    closing in like mist,
Scattering and spreading, radiant and resplendent,
    they form an intricate pattern.

---

[9] Two heavenly bodies, a star in the Northern Dipper and the counter Jupiter respectively.
[10] A group of six stars located within the Purple Palace. It had charge of the military guard.
[11] This is possibly the spirit of geomancy, who attends to the building of the ramparts.
[12] Two malevolent spirits.
[13] A warrior who rebelled against the Yellow Emperor.
[14] A famous swordmaker of Wu made two swords. The male was called Ganjiang; the female, Moye.

3

And then the Emperor thereupon
Mounts the phoenix car, shaded by a floriate mushroom,[15]
With a four-in-hand of azure wiverns, a six-in-hand of ecru dragons:

Coiling and uncoiling, lush and luxuriant,
Streaming out, floridly festooned,
Suddenly they gather in darkness,
Abruptly they open to the light.
They overleap the pure empyrean, pass floating phosphors:
How the falcon and tortoise standards so straight and tall
    flap and flutter!
Spangled oxtail pennants streaming forth, flashing like lightning,
Blend with halcyon-plume canopies and simurgh banners.

Assembling a myriad riders in the central camp,
Mustering a thousand rigs of jade-encrusted chariots,
Their sounds rumbling and roaring, echoing and re-echoing,
Nimbly outpacing rapid thunder, outgalloping the swiftest wind,
He scales the lofty heights of a high plateau,
Crosses the crystalline clarity of winding waters,
Ascends Chuanluan and alights at Heaven's gate,[16]
Gallops through Changhe and enters its trembling terror.[17]

4

At this time, while yet to reach Sweet Springs,
He gazes upon the continuous splendor of the Sky-Piercing Tower.[18]
The base, submerged in shade, is chilly and cold;
The spire, a vast chaos, complexly conjoined,
Straight, tall and towering, reaches to Heaven:
Its height, alas, cannot be fully measured!
A level plain, broad and spaciously sprawling,
Is lined with peony trees in groves and thickets;

---

[15] An elaborate mushroom-shaped canopy.

[16] Chuanlan was a mountain south of Sweet Springs.

[17] Changhe is the name of the main portal of the Purple Palace, the barrier of fifteen stars
the Chinese pictured as encircling the celestial pole. It was known as the palace of the
Celestial Emperor and theoretically the Han emperor's palace was a replica of it.

[18] This exceptionally high structure was built by Emperor Wu in 109 B.C. for the purpose of
attracting immortals to the Sweet Springs Palace.

Clustered windmill palms and field mint
Rampantly spread and scatter without limit.

Lofty the proud hauteur of hills and barrows!
Deep moats, steeply scarped, form ravines.
Hither and thither, detached palaces outspread,
    lighting one another;
Great Peak and Stone Gate wind and weave, endlessly extended.[19]

5

And then
A grand edifice, illusory as clouds, deceptive as waves,
Precipitously piled, forms a tower.
Raising and lifting His head to look on high,
His eyes, blurred and blinded, see nothing.
Straight ahead, the view full and flowing, vast and wide,
Points to a spacious sweep east and west.
All dizzy and giddy,
His soul is dazed and dazzled, confounded and confused.

As he clutches the grilled dash and gazes all around,
Suddenly the vista is broad and boundless, without limit.
Halcyon-colored the virescent luster of jade trees,
Prase-hued the sparkling splendor of horses and rhinos.
Bronze figures, brave and bold, upholding bell-stands,
Cragged and crenate, scaled like dragons,
Brandish lighted torches of lustrous brilliance,
Trail a fervid fulgor of luminous flame.[20]
All this befits the Hanging Garden of the Lord's abode,[21]
And images the majestic spirit of Grand Unity.[22]
The massive terrace thrusts itself upward in solitary prominence,
Reaching the supernal heights of the Northern Pole.

Constellations now stretch across the upper crests,
The sun and moon pass through the middle eaves,
Thunder rumbles and roars in its crags and crannies,

---

[19] Two viewing towers on Stone Gate mountain, northeast of the palace.
[20] The bronzemen were ten-foot statues the Chinese captured from the Xiongnu in 120 B.C.
[21] The name of a peak in the Kunlun mountains.
[22] The Sweet Springs Palace would have been considered a terrestrial replica of the Celestial Lord's palace.

Lightning darts and dashes in its walls and fences.
Even ghosts and demons cannot reach the top;
Halfway up its long course, they tumble down again.
It passes Upturned Phosphors, traverses Flying Bridge,[23]
Drifts through Murky Mist, and brushes Heaven.
Gouging Spear left, Mysterious Darkness right,[24]
Flaming Watchtower front, and the receiving gate rear,[25]
It shades the Western Sea and Dark Capital,[26]
Where bubbling wine spurts forth to form a stream.
A dragon coils and curls along the eastern cliff;
The White Tiger fiercely guards the Kunlun.[27]

6

Gazing, roaming round at Lofty Radiance,[28]
At ease, He lingers and loiters at a western repose.
The front hall stands tall and towering,
With Jade-of-He glittering and glistening,
And flying rafters on floating posts raised aloft,
As if spirits, with mighty heaves, brace their collapse.
It spires upward, gaping and yawning, open and wide,
Like the precipitous profundity of Purple Palace.
Row by row, joined one to another, its buildings spread and sprawl,
Long and narrow, tall and towering, intertwining,
Climbing into cloud-capped turrets, rising and falling,
Tangling in a murky mass, as if from chaos formed.
Trailing a long stream of scarlet color,
Wafting a curling wreath of azure vapor,

---

[23] The Upturned Phosphors are luminous bodies in the highest part of the sky, so called because the light of the sun and moon shone upward to them. The Flying Bridge is identified by one commentator as the elevated passageway used by spirits in ascending to Heaven.

[24] The names of a comet and the guardian deity of the north.

[25] The Flaming Watchtower was a red structure located on the southern side of the palace complex.

[26] This seems to have been considered the portal at the extreme northwestern point of the world.

[27] The Azure Dragon was the guardian animal of the east, the White Tiger the guardian of the west. It is possible that these were statues or mural paintings of figures associated with the Grand Unity.

[28] A hall in the Sweet Springs Palace.

It is heir to the Jade Chamber and the Hundred-Acre Palace,[29]
And as He climbs this height to gaze afar,
He is awe-struck, as if poised on an abyss.[30]

7

A swirling whirlwind vents its pulsing fury,
Scattering cinnamon and pepper, gathering poplar and willow:
Fragrance, pungent and strong, arching upward,
Strikes the brackets, grazes the eaves.

Sounds rapidly reverberate with a clashing and clanging,
Musical echoes, pealing and chiming, pass through the bells;
It pushes jade doors open, joggles bronze knockers,
Whisking off thoroughwort, sweet basil, and hemlock parsley.

Curtains bulge and billow, shake and shudder;
Gradually all becomes dark and dim, deeply silent.
Yin and yang, clear and turbid, solemn and gay echo one another,
As if Kui and Ya were playing their zithers.[31]

Ban and Chui would discard their knives and chisels;
Wang Er would throw down his compass and plumb.[32]
Even to a Zheng Qiao or Wo Quan[33]
It would be a vague vision as if in a dream.

8

And then, events change and things transform, His eyes start and ears
whirr. The Son of Heaven then sedately stands in the midst of precious
terraces, leisure lodges, jade finials, nephrite petals, all crinkled-and-
curled, scrolled-and-scalloped. For this is a means to cleanse His mind,
purify His soul, gather His vitality, and concentrate His thoughts, to
influence Heaven and Earth, and receive blessings from the Three

---

[29] Structures built by the last rulers of the Xia and Shang dynasties. This line is a subtle
warning to Emperor Cheng, whose obsession with lavish and ostentatious living could
bring about the fall of his dynasty.

[30] The emperor should take careful note of the great danger presented by his hedonistic
activities.

[31] Kui was the Great Shun's Master of Music. Bo Ya was a legendary player of the zither or
lute (*qin*).

[32] Lu Ban was a master carpenter of the Zhou period. Chui was master of artisans under
Emperor Yao. Wang Er was another great artisan.

[33] Famous Immortals.

Spirits. Whereupon, He seeks partners, searches for mates, cohorts like Gao and Yi,[34] peerless exemplars, superlative talents, who enfold the kindness of the "Sweet Pear," and embrace the intent of the "Eastward March,"[35] together to purify themselves in the palace of the yang spirit:[36]

He spreads fig leaves for mats,
Snaps carnelian branches for their fragrance,
Sips flowing mists in cerulean clouds,
Drinks from the dewy petals of the Ruo Tree.[37]
They assemble in the enclosure for rites to the gods.
Ascend the hall for lauding the earth-spirits.

He raises the long swallowtail streamers of dazzling brilliance,
Displays the lush luxuriance of the floriate sunshade,
Grasps the Jade Armil and downward looks,[38]
Casts His roving gaze over the Triperil peaks.[39]
Deploying His many chariots over the eastern slope,
He releases the jade wheel-locks and gallops downward;
Drifting on Dragon Pool, circling the Nine Divisions,[40]
He peers under the earth and turns upward.
Winds, blasting and blustering, propel His axles;
Simurghs and phoenixes tangle in His chariot fringe.
Bridging Weak River's shallow shoals,[41]
Treading Buzhou's twisting tracks,[42]

[34] Gao Yao was the Wise Minister of Justice under Yao. Yi Yin was minister to Tang, founder of the Shang dynasty.
[35] Referring to the two virtuous ministers, the Dukes of Shao and Zhou. The "Sweet Pear" is *Song* 16, which, according to the Mao interpretation, praises the virtues of the Duke of Shao. In *Song* 157 is the line "The Duke of Zhou marches east."
[36] The sacred hall in which the emperor sacrificed to Heaven.
[37] The magic tree sometimes described as having ten suns on its top. The light from its blossoms illumines earth below.
[38] The Jade Armil is the name of an ancient astronomical instrument, often identified as the armillary sphere. It also refers to the four stars of the bowl of the Northern Dipper.
[39] An ancient legendary mountain commonly located south of Dunhuang.
[40] The Dragon Pool may refer to a river of the same name over sixty *li* southwest of Shanggui (Gansu Province). The Nine Divisions may be the nine layers of the Dragon Pool.
[41] A legendary stream located in the northwest. Some sources say it is the home of the Queen Mother of the West. It was so named because it was believed that even a goose feather would sink in its waters.
[42] The peak that the rebel Gonggong butted, snapping the pillars of Heaven and the cords of Earth so that Heaven slanted northwest and Earth tilted southeast.

He recalls Queen Mother of the West, and joyfully salutes her
   longevity.[43]
He rejects Jade Maiden, expels Consort Fu.[44]
Jade Maiden has no place to gaze her limpid orbs;
Consort Fu can no longer flaunt her pretty eyebrows.
Now He grasps the essential firmness of the Way and Virtue,
And equal to the gods, consults with them.

9

And then
Reverently He makes a burnt offering, devoutly prays:
The holocaust perfumes the august heavens,
Hoisted by pyre to Grand Unity.

He raises Great Sustenance,
Plants the Sacred Pennant.[45]

Firebrands and burning stalks ascend together,
Scatter into the four directions:
Eastward illumining the Azure Sea,
Westward dazzling the Flowing Sands,[46]
Northward brightening the Dark Capital,
Southward singeing the Cinnabar Shore.[47]
In His Black ladle, curved and contoured,
The millet libation fragrantly froths,
Spreading and scattering, rich and full,
Savory and sapid, sweetly scented.
The flames stir the yellow dragon;
The blaze rouses the giant unicorn.[48]

---

[43] See note 8. *Eds.*

[44] The Jade Maiden is the goddess of Mt Hua, a Taoist deity. According to tradition, she was once a palace lady of the First Qin Emperor. Consort Fu is usually identified as the goddess of the Luo River [Fufei in Cao Zhi's rhapsody]. Clearly Yang Xiong intended these two to stand for concubines who improperly accompanied the Imperial carriage.

[45] The Sacred Pennant was used during ceremonies in honor of the Grand Unity. It was painted with the sun, moon, Northern Dipper, and a soaring dragon to symbolize the Grand Unity.

[46] This may refer to the Gobi.

[47] I suspect that this may be a variant for Vermilion Shore, one of the names for Hainan Island off the south coast of China.

[48] Auspicious omens.

He selects Shaman Xian to hail the Lord's gatekeeper,[49]
To open the celestial court and invite the spirit multitudes.

Visitants, thickly thronging, descend on the pure altar;
Auspicious omens, profusely abundant, heap into mountains.

10

And then
The service ended, and His merit expanded,
He wheels His chariot and returns,
Crossing Tri-Peak Tower, resting at Pear Palace:[50]
Heaven's threshold is agape, Earth's boundary is open,
The Eight Barrens are in harmony, the myriad states are in accord.

He scales Changping and thunder drums rumble;[51]
Their celestial sounds rise forth and brave warriors wax fierce.
Clouds fly and soar, rains swell and surge;[52]
Now all are virtuous, to beautify a myriad ages.

11

The finale:
Tall, so tall, the circular mound,[53]
Arching upward, concealing the sky,
Climbing and plunging, twisting and twining,
Sinuously curls and coils.

Storied palaces, jaggedly jutting,
Stand abreast, peaked and pinnacled,
Deep and steep, towering tier upon tier,
Cavernous, without bound.

The actions of high Heaven,
Are mysteriously swift and sudden.
Our Sage Sovereign, solemn and stately,
Truly is Heaven's compeer.

---

[49] This is the diviner whom Qu Yuan consulted in his "On Encountering Trouble."

[50] Tri-Peak Tower may be the same as the Great Peak Tower, located inside the walls of the Sweet Springs Park. The Pear Palace was located south of the Sweet Springs Park.

[51] Changping was the name of a slope on the bank of the Jing River in modern Shaanxi Province.

[52] The clouds and rains are figures for imperial grace and favor.

[53] The circular mound is the altar used for sacrifices to Heaven. Its shape was intended to symbolize the roundness of Heaven.

Reverently He comes to sacrifice to the bounds;
He is one on whom the gods rely.
Wandering and wavering, rambling and roving,
The divinities now rest and repose.

With a bright brilliance glistering and glittering,
They send down their blessing:
    "Son after son, grandson after grandson,
    Forever, without end."

ZHANG HENG (78–139)
The Bones of Zhuangzi

Translated by Arthur Waley

Zhang Heng was a great astronomer and mathematician.[54] In A.D. 132 he constructed the first seismograph. Eight copper dragons on springs sat round a bowl. Each dragon had a copper ball in his mouth. In the middle of the bowl squatted a toad with wide-open mouth. When there was an earthquake the dragon nearest the direction from which the shock came dropped his ball into the toad's mouth.

On one occasion a dragon released his ball, but no shock was felt and there was no news of an earthquake. The Confucians of the capital, who regarded Zhang Heng as an impious charlatan, were delighted that his contrivance should have proved to be fallible. But in a few days a messenger arrived from the extreme northwest of China announcing that there had been an earthquake in that region.

I, Zhang Pingzi, had traversed the Nine Wilds and seen
    their wonders,
In the eight continents beheld the ways of Man,
The Sun's procession, the orbit of the Stars,
The surging of the dragon, the soaring of the phoenix in his flight.
In the red desert to the south I sweltered,
And northward waded through the wintry burghs of Yu.
Through the Valley of Darkness to the west I wandered,
And eastward traveled to the Sun's extreme abode,
The stooping Mulberry Tree.

So the seasons sped; weak autumn languished,
A small wind woke the cold.
And now with rearing of rein-horse,
Plunging of the tracer, round I fetched

---

[54] For another poem by Zhang Heng see chapter 9. For Zhuangzi, see chapter 4. *Eds.*

My high-roofed chariot to westward.
Along the dykes we loitered, past many meadows,
And far away among the dunes and hills.
Suddenly I looked and by the roadside
I saw a man's bones lying in the squelchy earth,
Black rime-frost over him; and I in sorrow spoke
And asked him, saying, "Dead man, how was it?
Fled you with your friend from famine and for the last grains
Gambled and lost? Was this earth your tomb,
Or did floods carry you from afar? Were you mighty, were you wise,
Were you foolish and poor? A warrior, or a girl?"
Then a wonder came; for out of the silence a voice —
Thin echo only, in no substance was the Spirit seen —
Mysteriously answered, saying, "I was a man of Song,
Of the clan of Zhuang; Zhou was my name.
Beyond the climes of common thought
My reason soared, yet could I not save myself;
For at the last, when the long charter of my years was told,
I, too, for all my magic, by Age was brought
To the Black Hill of Death.
Wherefore, O Master, do you question me?"
Then I answered:
"Let me plead for you upon the Five Hill-tops,
Let me pray for you to the Gods of Heaven and the Gods of Earth,
That your white bones may arise,
And your limbs be joined anew.
The God of the North shall give me back your ears;
I will scour the Southland for your eyes.
From the sunrise I will wrest your feet;
The West shall yield your heart.
I will set each several organ in its throne;
Each subtle sense will I restore.
Would you not have it so?"
The dead man answered me:
"O Friend, how strange and unacceptable your words!
In death I rest and am at peace; in life, I toiled and strove.
Is the hardness of the winter stream
Better than the melting of spring?
All pride that the body knew
Was it not lighter than dust?
What Chao and Xu despised,
What Bocheng fled,

Shall I desire, whom death
Already has hidden in the Eternal Way —
Where Li Zhu cannot see me,
Nor Zi Ye hear me,
Where neither Yao nor Shun can reward me,
Nor the tyrants Jie and Xin condemn me,
Leopard nor tiger harm me,
Lance prick me nor sword wound me?
Of the Primal Spirit is my substance; I am a wave
In the river of Darkness and Light.
The Maker of All Things is my Father and Mother,
Heaven is my bed and earth my cushion,
The thunder and lightning are my drum and fan,
The sun and moon my candle and my torch,
The Milky Way my moat, the stars my jewels.
With Nature my substance is joined;
I have no passion, no desire.
Wash me and I shall be no whiter,
Foul me and I shall yet be clean.
I come not, yet am here;
Hasten not, yet am swift."
The voice stopped, there was silence.
A ghostly light
Faded and expired.
I gazed upon the dead, stared in sorrow and compassion.
Then I called upon my servant that was with me
To tie his silken scarf about those bones
And wrap them in a cloak of sombre dust;
While I, as offering to the soul of this dead man,
Poured my hot tears upon the margin of the road.

WANG YANSHOU (c. 124–c. 148)
The Nightmare

Translated by Arthur Waley

One night, about the time I came of age, I dreamt that demon creatures
fought with me while I slept.... When I woke I told this vision in verse,
that the dreamers of posterity might use my poem as a spell to drive off
evil dreams. And so often has it proved its worth that I dare not any
longer hide it from the world. The words are these:

Once, as in the darkness I lay asleep by night,
Strange things suddenly saw I in my dream;
All my dream was of monsters that came about me while I slept,
Devils and demons, four-horned, serpent-necked,
Fishes with bird-tails, three-legged bogies
From six eyes staring; dragons hideous,
Yet three-part human.
On rushed the foul flocks, grisly legions,
Stood round me, stretched out their arms,
Danced their hands about me, and sought to snatch me from my
    bed.
Then cried I (and in my dream
My voice was thick with anger and my words all awry)
"Ill-spawned elves, how dare you
Beset with your dire shapes Creation's cleanest
Shapeliest creature, Man?" Then straightway I struck out,
Flashed my fists like lightning among them, thumped like thunder,
Here slit Jack-o'-Lantern,
Here smashed fierce Hog-Face,
Battered wights and goblins,
Smote venturous vampires, pounded in the dust
Imps, gnomes and lobs,
Kobolds and kelpies;
Swiped bulge-eyed bogies, oafs and elves;
Clove Tough-head's triple skull, threw down
Clutching Night-hag, flogged the gawky Ear-wig Fiend
That floundered toward me on its tail.

I struck at staring eyes,
Stamped on upturned faces; through close ranks
Of hoofs I cut my way, buried my fingers deep
In half-formed flesh;
Ghouls tore at my touch; I slit sharp noses,
Trod on red tongues, seized shaggy manes,
Shook bald-heads by the beard.
Then was a scuffling. Arms and legs together
Chasing, crashing and sliding; a helter-skelter
Of feet lost and found in the tugging and toppling,
Cuffing, cudgeling, frenzied flogging....

So fought I, till terror and dismay
Shook those foul flocks; panic spread like a flame
Down mutinous ranks; they stand, they falter,

Those ghastly legions; but fleeing, suddenly turn
Glazed eyes upon me, to see how now I fare.
At last, to end their treachery
Again I rushed upon them, braved their slaver and snares,
Stood on a high place, and lashed down among them,
Shrieking and cursing as my blows crashed.
Then three by three and four by four
One after another hop-a-trot they fled,
Bellowing and bawling till the air was full of their breath —
Grumbling and snarling,
Those vanquished ogres, demons discomfited,
Some that would fain have run
Lolling and lurching, some that for cramped limbs
Could not stir from where they stood. Some over belly-wounds
Bent double; some in agony gasping and groaning.
Suddenly the clouds broke and (I knew not why)
A thin light filtered the darkness; then, while again
I sighed in wonder that those disastrous creatures,
Dire monstrosities, should dare assail
A clean and comely man, … there sounded in my ears
A twittering and crowing. And outdoors it was light.
The noisy cock, mindful that dawn was in the sky,
Had crowed his warning, and the startled ghosts,
Because they heard dawn heralded, had fled
In terror and tribulation from the rising day.

Translator's Note:
In an epilogue the poet seeks consolation in the fact that many evil dreams and
occurrences have in the past been omens of good. Duke Huan of Qi, while hunting in
the marshes, saw in a vision an ogre "as broad as a cartwheel and as long as a shaft,
wearing a purple coat and red cap." It was an omen that he would rise to the
Pentarchy. Wu Ding, Emperor of the Shang dynasty, was haunted in a dream by the
face of the man who afterwards became his wise counselor and friend. Wen, Duke of
Jin, dreamt that the Marquis of Chu held him prostrate and sucked out his brains; yet
his kingdom defeated Chu. Laozi made use of demons, and thereby became leader
among the Spirits of Heaven. "So evil turns to good."

WANG CAN (177–217)
Climbing the Tower

Translated by Burton Watson

"Ascending to the high places" is cited by Ban Gu as one of the occasions upon which rhapsodies are customarily composed.[55] By climbing to a height, the poet expands his horizon and acquires a breadth of vision greater than that which he ordinarily enjoys, in itself an aid to inspiration. With this wider view inevitably come thoughts of his own relative insignificance, and as his eyes wander in space, so do his thoughts in time. These motifs of the vastness of nature, the relentless passing of time, and the isolation of man are present in this work by Wang Can, in which the "high place" ascended is a tower, probably situated at the city of Dangyang on the Ju River, near the place where the Zhang River enters it, in present-day Hubei. To these universal concerns Wang Can has added a very personal note of nostalgia and frustration, for the poem was written when he was sojourning in the region known as Jing or Chu, in the upper Yangtze valley, far from his native land. Around A.D. 195, the troubled political and social conditions in the north had forced him to flee Chang'an, the Western Capital of the empire, and wander south in search of greater safety. The poem, written some "twelve years or more" after this event, expresses the desperate loneliness of the traveler, his homesickness for the north, and his fears that the political situation will never right itself to the point where he may hope to exert his talents in the service of the emperor.

> Climb the tower so I can see in four directions —
> An idle day may help to lessen care.
> I scan the ground the building stands on,
> Broad and open, few sites to match it,
> The lower sweep of the clear Zhang angling in on one side,
> The other bound by long shoals of the crooked Ju,
> Backed by humps and flatlands of the wide plateau,
> Looking over marshy borders of the fertile streams,
> Reaching north to the range where Lord Tao lies,
> West touching the barrow of King Zhao.[56]
> Flowers and fruit trees blanket the meadow,
> Two kinds of millet rich in the fields,
> But lovely as it is, it is not my land —
> How have I the heart to stay for long?
> Facing troubled times, I set off to wander;
> Twelve years and more have slipped by since then;
> Thoughts forever taken up with memories of home,
> Who can endure such longing and pain?
> Propped on the railing, I gaze into the distance,
> Fronting the north wind, collar open wide.
> The plain is far-reaching, and though I strain my eyes,
> They are blocked by tall peaks of the mountains of Jing.

---

[55] For another poem by Wang Can, see also chapter 9. *Eds.*

[56] Lord Tao, better known as Fan Li, and King Zhao are figures associated with the history of the state of Chu in the late sixth and early fifth centuries B.C.

The road winds back and forth, endless in its turning;
Rivers are wide and deep where one would ford.
I hate to be so cut off from my native land;
Tears keep coming in streams I am helpless to check.
Confucius long ago in Chen
Cried out in sorrow, "Let me return!"[57]
Zhong Yi, imprisoned, played the music of Chu;
Zhuang Xie, though honored, sang the songs of Yue.[58]
All shared this feeling, the yearning for home —
Neither success nor failure can change the heart.
And I think how the days and months glide by,
Waiting for the River that never runs clear.[59]
Hoping to see the king's way at last made smooth,
So I may take to the highroad and try my strength;
I fear to be a bitter gourd uselessly dangling,[60]
A well whose waters, though purified, remain undrunk.
Aimlessly I wander, hesitating, halting;
Suddenly the bright sun is on the point of setting.
Winds, sad and sighing, rise up all around;
The sky darkens till all color has gone.
Beasts peer anxiously, searching for the herd;
Birds call back and forth and beat their wings.
Country fields are empty and unpeopled;
Only the traveler pushes on without stop.
My heart, wounded, stirs in sorrow;
Thoughts are gloomy, drowned in despair.
Rung by rung, I climb down the ladder,
At each step a greater grief cramped in my breast.
Midnight comes and still I cannot sleep;
Brooding, restless, I toss from side to side.

[57] *Analects* V, 21.

[58] Zhong Yi, a native of Chu, was taken prisoner to Jin; when given a lute, he played the music of his homeland. Zhuang Xie, a commoner of Yue, acquired wealth and high office in Chu, but when he fell ill, he sang the songs of Yue.

[59] It is said that when the waters of the Yellow River run clear, a sage will appear in the world.

[60] *Analects* XVII, 7: "The Master said, ... 'Am I a bitter gourd? How can I bear to be hung up and not eaten?'"

CAO ZHI (192–232)
The Goddess of the Luo

Translated by Burton Watson

Though the introduction to Cao Zhi's rhapsody on "The Goddess of the Luo" gives the third year of the Huang-chu era as the date of the events that inspired the poem, it is likely that this is a mistake for the fourth year of the era, A.D. 223, when the poet had been in the capital, Luoyang, to pay his respects to his elder brother Cao Pi, ruler of the Wei dynasty, and was on his way back to his fief in Yongqiu in the east.[61] After a brief description of his departure from the capital, Cao Zhi introduces the subject of the work, a beautiful woman who miraculously appears to him on the banks of the Luo River. Since his coachman lacks the power to see her, the poet obliges both him and the reader by presenting an elaborate depiction of her charms. Some critics, not content to accept the vision of the goddess on its own terms, have attempted to impose an allegorical interpretation on the poem, seeing it as a declaration of loyalty addressed by the poet to his brother the emperor; others find the goddess so compelling that they believe her to be modeled after an actual love of the poet's youth.

In the third year of the Huang-chu era, I attended court at the capital and then crossed the Luo River to begin my journey home. Men in olden times used to say that the goddess of the river is named Fufei. Inspired by the example of Song Yu, who described a goddess to the king of Chu,[62] I eventually composed a rhapsody which read:

> Leaving the capital
> To return to my fief in the east,
> Yi Barrier at my back,
> Up over Huanyuan,
> Passing through Tong Valley,
> Crossing Mount Jing;
> The sun had already dipped in the west,
> The carriage unsteady, the horses fatigued,
> And so I halted my rig in the spikenard marshes,
> Grazed my team of four at Lichen Fields,
> Idling a while by Willow Wood,
> Letting my eyes wander over the Luo.
> Then my mood seemed to change, my spirit grew restless;
> Suddenly my thoughts had scattered.
> I looked down, hardly noticing what was there,

---

[61] For other poems by Cao Zhi, see also chapter 9. *Eds.*

[62] A reference to the "Goddess Rhapsody" by Song Yu, in which the poet describes to King Xiang of Chu a woman of supernatural beauty who visited him in a dream; the work was apparently one of the principal models for Cao Zhi's poem.

Looked up to see a different sight,
To spy a lovely lady by the slopes of the riverbank.

I took hold of the coachman's arm and asked, "Can you see her? Who could she be — a woman so beautiful!" The coachman replied, "I have heard of the goddess of the River Luo, whose name is Fufei. What you see, my prince — is it not she? But what does she look like? I beg you to tell me!"
And I answered:

Her body soars lightly like a startled swan,
Gracefully, like a dragon in flight,
In splendor brighter than the autumn chrysanthemum,
In bloom more flourishing than the pine in spring;
Dim as the moon mantled in filmy clouds,
Restless as snow whirled by the driving wind.
Gaze far off from a distance:
She sparkles like the sun rising from morning mists;
Press closer to examine:
She flames like the lotus flower topping the green wave.
She strikes a balance between plump and frail;
The tall and short of her are justly proportioned,
With shoulders shaped as if by carving,
Waist narrow as though bound with white cords;
At her slim throat and curving neck
The pale flesh lies open to view,
No scented ointments overlaying it,
No coat of leaden powder applied.
Cloud-bank coiffure rising steeply,
Long eyebrows delicately arched,
Red lips that shed their light abroad,
White teeth gleaming within,
Bright eyes skilled at glances,
A dimple to round off the base of the cheek —
Her rare form wonderfully enchanting,
Her manner quiet, her pose demure.
Gentle-hearted, broad of mind,
She entrances with every word she speaks;
Her robes are of a strangeness seldom seen,
Her face and figure live up to her paintings.
Wrapped in the soft rustle of silken garments,
She decks herself with flowery earrings of jasper and jade,
Gold and kingfisher hairpins adorning her head,

Strings of bright pearls to make her body shine.
She treads in figured slippers fashioned for distant wandering,
Airy trains of mistlike gauze in tow,
Dimmed by the odorous haze of unseen orchids,
Pacing uncertainly beside the corner of the hill.
Then suddenly she puts on a freer air,
Ready for rambling, for pleasant diversion.
To the left planting her colored pennants,
To the right spreading the shade of cassia flags,
She dips pale wrists into the holy river's brink,
Plucks dark iris from the rippling shallows.
My fancy is charmed by her modest beauty,
But my heart, uneasy, stirs with distress:
Without a skilled go-between to join us in bliss,
I must trust these little waves to bear my message.
Desiring that my sincerity first of all be known,
I undo a girdle-jade to offer as pledge.
Ah, the pure trust of that lovely lady,
Trained in ritual, acquainted with the Songs;[63]
She holds up a garnet stone to match my gift,
Pointing down into the depths to show where we should meet.
Clinging to a lover's passionate faith,
Yet I fear that this spirit may deceive me;
Warned by tales of how Jiaofu was abandoned,[64]
I pause, uncertain and despairing;
Then, stilling such thoughts, I turn a gentler face toward her,
Signaling that for my part I abide by the rules of ritual.
The spirit of the Luo, moved by my action,
Paces to and fro uncertainly,
The holy light deserting her, then reappearing,
Now darkening, now shining again;
She lifts her light body in the posture of a crane,
As though about to fly but not yet taking wing.
She walks the heady perfume of pepper-scented roads,
Strides through clumps of spikenard, scattering their fragrance,
Wailing distractedly, a sign of endless longing,

---

[63] The *Book of Songs*, where many exchanges of pledges between lovers are described.
[64] Zheng Jiaofu met two women beside the Yangtze and, unaware that they were goddesses of the river, asked them for their girdle stones. They obliged, but shortly after he had put the stones into the breast of his robe, both the stones and the women vanished.

Her voice, sharp with sorrow, growing more prolonged.
Then a swarm of milling spirits appears,
Calling companions, whistling to their mates,
Some sporting in the clear current,
Some hovering over sacred isles,
Some searching for bright pearls,
Some collecting kingfisher plumes.
The goddess attends the two queens of Xiang in the south,
Joins hands with Wandering Girl from the banks of the Han,
Sighs that the Gourd Star has no spouse,
Laments that the Herdboy must live alone.[65]
Lifting the rare fabric of her thin jacket,
She makes a shield of her long sleeve, pausing in hesitation,
Body nimbler than a winging duck,
Swift, as befits the spirit she is;
Traversing the waves in tiny steps,
Her gauze slippers seem to stir a dust.
Her movements have no constant pattern,
Now unsteady, now sedate;
Hard to predict are her starts and hesitations,
Now advancing, now turning back.
Her roving glance flashes fire;
A radiant warmth shines from her jadelike face.
Her words, held back, remain unvoiced,
Her breath scented as though with hidden orchids;
Her fair face all loveliness —
She makes me forget my hunger!
Then the god Bingyi calls in his winds,
The River Lord stills the waves,
While Pingyi beats a drum,
And Nü Wa offers simple songs.
Speckled fish are sent aloft to clear the way for her carriage,
Jade bells are jangled for accompaniment;
Six dragon-steeds, solemn, pulling neck to neck,
She rides the swift passage of her cloudy chariot.

---

[65] The two queens are E'huang and Nüying, wives of Emperor Shun, who after his death became goddesses of the Xiang River in the south. Wandering Girl is identified as the goddess of the Han River. The legend pertaining to the Gourd Star is unknown. The Herdboy, another star, is separated from his love, the Weaving Lady star, by the Milky Way, and they are permitted to meet only one night a year.

Whales dance at the hubs on either side,
Water birds flying in front to be her guard.
And when she has gone beyond the northern sandbars,
When she has crossed the southern ridges,
She bends her white neck,
Clear eyes cast down,
Moves her red lips,
Speaking slowly;
Discussing the great principles that govern friendship,
She complains that men and gods must follow separate ways,
Voices anger that we cannot fulfill the hopes of youth,
Holding up her gauze sleeve to hide her weeping,
Torrents of teardrops drowning her lapels.
She laments that our happy meeting must end forever,
Grieves that, once separated, we go to different lands.
    "No way to express my unworthy love,
       I give you this bright earring from south of the Yangtze.
       Though I dwell in the Great Shadow down under the waters,
       My heart will forever belong to you, my prince!"
Then suddenly I could not tell where she had gone;
To my sorrow the spirit vanished in darkness, veiling her light.
With this I turned my back on the lowland, climbed the height;
My feet went forward but my soul remained behind.
Thoughts taken up with the memory of her image,
I turned to look back, a heart full of despair.
Hoping that the spirit form might show itself again,
I embarked in a small boat to journey upstream,
Drifting over the long river, forgetting to return,
Wrapped in endless remembrances that made my longing greater.
Night found me fretful, unable to sleep;
Heavy frosts soaked me until the break of day.
I ordered the groom to ready the carriage,
Thinking to return to my eastern road,
But though I seized the reins and lifted up my whip,
I stayed lost in hesitation and could not break away.

Mu Hua (fl. c. 300)
The Sea

Translated by David Knechtges

This is one of many early rhapsodies written about the sea. Because it was preserved in the sixth-century *Literary Anthology* (*Wen Xuan*), Mu Hua's piece is the only complete rhapsody on the subject to survive. The Jin dynasty critic Li Chong gave it a mixed review: "Master Mu's 'Rhapsody on the Sea' is powerful indeed! But its head and tail are disjointed. Although it has the appearance of a polished piece, yet it seems incomplete." What Li Chong perhaps criticizes is the lack of an introduction and epilogue, which most rhapsodies have. Mu's rhapsody begins abruptly with an allusion to the myth of the Great Yu, who tamed a giant deluge by channeling all the waters into the sea. Most of the remainder of the rhapsody describes the sea's waters, particularly its waves (Mu uses at least half a dozen different words for wave), replete with all manner of binomial descriptives. The work is notable for its reference to luminous marine organisms, and possibly icebergs, as well as a long passage on a giant whale.

1

Of old, under Emperor Gui,[66]
In the era of the great Tang,[67]
Heaven's guiderope began to froth and foam,[68]
Causing blight, bringing on disease.
Giant breakers spread and sprawled
A myriad miles, without bound;
Long swells rolled and tossed,
Streaming and stretching into the eight marches.

And then Yu
Pared mounds and hills overlooking the banks,
Breached dikes and ponds allowing the water to drain,
Opened Dragon Gate, jaggedly jutting,
Broke open hills and peaks, chiseling and boring through.
Once the massing mountains had been demarcated,
And the hundred streams were dispersed underground,
Broad and boundless, calm and clear,
The leaping waves sped off with the current.

When the Jiang and the He had been channeled,
Through a myriad crevices all the waters began to flow,

---

[66] The Sage Emperor Shun. After he married the two daughters of Yao, he took up residence at the bend of the Gui River (modern Shanxi).

[67] The Sage Emperor Yao. Before Shun became emperor, he served under Yao.

[68] According to Li Shan's commentary, the water covered such a vast expanse, it served as "Heaven's guiderope." Mu Hua is here alluding to the great deluge that began in the time of Yao and was eventually tamed by the Great Yu, who dredged the Nine Streams and cleared the courses of the rivers to carry the water to the sea.

Leaving the Five Peaks pushing and poking upward,
The Nine Continents drained and dried.

Dribbling droplets, soaking waters,
Dense and dark as clouds and fog;
Burbling streams trickling and trilling,
None failed to come pouring in.
Oh, this vast numinous sea,
Long has it received and transported!
Such breadth,
Such wonderment,
All befit its greatness!

2

And such is its form:
Flooding and flowing, tossing and tumbling,
It floats the sky, shoreless,
Surging and swelling, profoundly plunging,
Remotely ranging, distantly distended;
Waves like serried mountains,
Now joined, now scattered;
Inhaling and exhaling the hundred rivers,
Cleaning and clearing the Huai and Han;
Engulfing broad salt flats,
Mingling and merging far and wide.

Now when
The Grand Luminary turns its reins toward the Metallic Pivot
      grotto,[69]
And Soaring Brightness swiftly speeds from Fusang's ford,[70]
Tossing sand and swashing against rocks
The wind rages and roars on island beaches.
And then roused to fury,
Welling waves heave and foam,
Clashing and colliding with one another,
Scattering spray, lifting breakers.

Their form is like the wheels of Heaven,

---

[69] The Grand Luminary must here refer to the moon.

[70] Soaring Brightness is the sun. Fusang is the name of a "solar tree" located above the
Dawn Valley at the extreme eastern limits of the world.

Revolving and rotating, furiously turning;
Or like the axles of earth,
Thrusting, pushing, vehemently spinning.
Their ridges and crests soar on high, then falter and fall,
Like the Five Peaks swaying and swirling, pounding one upon
    another.
Wildly they surge and sink, piled and packed together;
Swollen, they dash and dart, crest and collapse.
Whirling and twirling, they form raging troughs;
Combing and rolling, they jet into pointed peaks.
Swiftly, riffles and ripples popple on the sides,
While the giants, merging and melding, clash with one another.
Startled waves thunderously race,
Stampeding waters scatter and gather again:
They open and close, dissolve and merge,
Spurting and spouting, shaking and shuddering,
Spreading and sprawling, crowded and cramped,
Frothing and foaming, pitching and plunging.

3

Then when
Dust clouds and dark skies recede and dissolve,
Nothing moves, nothing stirs,
And the lightest dust does not fly,
Nor the tenderest vines quiver.
Still gaping and gulping,
Remnant waves continue their solitary heaving,
Swelling and surging, steep and tall,
Jaggedly jutting like mounts and hills.

Further, branches and forks, spuming and seething,
Turbulent and tempestuous, form tributaries.
They divide us from the Man, separate us from the Yi,
And wind one after another for ten thousand miles.

If then
Border wastes must see swift report,
Or royal command must be quickly proclaimed,
They gallop fleet steeds, ply their sweeps,
To cross the sea or scale mountains.

And then,
They await a strong wind,

Hoist the hundred-foot,[71]
Secure long yards,
Hang sails and sheets.

Watching the waves, they depart for afar,
Glistening brightly, gliding like a soaring bird,
Swift as a startled duck lost from its mate,
Sudden as if drawn by six dragons.
At once they cover three thousand miles,
Before morning's end they reach their destination.

4

But if a man
Approaches the deep laden with sin,
Swearing empty oaths, uttering false prayers,
Then sea elves block his way,
Horse-swallowers impede his path,
Tianwu suddenly appears, dimly descried,[72]
Wangxiang briefly shows himself, a fleeting specter.[73]
A host of demons meets and confronts him,
Glaring and glowering, beguiling and bewitching.

Tearing the sails, splitting the mast,
Fierce winds begin their dreadful destruction.
All is opened wide, as if transformed by spirits,
Then turns dark and dim, like sombrous dusk.
Their breath, like heavenly vapors,
Misty and murky, spreads like clouds.
Fleeting and flashing, like streaking lightning,
A hundred hues weirdly appear,
Spewing and spuming, pale and pallid,
Flickering and fluttering without measure.

Surging billows grind together,
Their turbulent forces colliding.
Like crumbling clouds, spattering rain,
Swashing and splashing,

---

[71] The main mast.

[72] Also known as the Earl of the Waters, Tianwu is described as an eight-headed creature
with human faces. He had eight feet and eight tails, which were green and yellow.

[73] Wangxiang is identified as a man-eating "prodigy of the water."

Wambling and wobbling, advancing and retreating,
Sputtering and spouting, flowing and flooding,
Pitching and plunging, rolling and tossing,
Sweeping the clouds, dousing the sun.

5

And then
Sailors and fishermen
Travel south and to the extreme east.
Some are smashed and drowned in caverns of turtles and alligators,
Some are hung and caught on jagged reefs,
Some are hauled and dragged to the realm of naked men,
Some drift and float to the land of Black Teeth men,[74]
Some glide like duckweed, scudding and whirling along,
Some following the homing winds, return on their own.
They only know how frightful were the wonders they saw,
And are oblivious of whether the places they passed were near or far.

But these are the general limits:
South it soaks the Vermeil Shore,[75]
North waters the Heavenly Barrens,[76]
East extends to Split Wood,[77]
West pushes upon Qing and Xu.[78]
The area it spans, dim and distant,
Stretches ten-ten-thousand leagues and more.
It spouts clouds and rainbows,
Enfolds dragons and fish,
Hides the scaly *kun*,[79]
Conceals spirit dwellings.
How does it only collect

---

[74] The land of the Black Teeth was located above Dawn Valley. Its people had black teeth, and ate rice and snakes.

[75] Vermeil is often symbolic of the south, and this probably designates the southern limit of the world.

[76] A lunar mansion located in the north part of the heavens.

[77] Split Wood is the name of the Jupiter station corresponding to the northeast areas of Yan and You (northern Hebei).

[78] Areas along the Shandong coast.

[79] A legendary fish of the Northern Sea.

Tai Dian's precious cowry,[80]
Or Lord Sui's luminous pearl?[81]
Could it be that one frequently hears of things collected by the
    world,
While those unnamed seem nonexistent?
Moreover, for things rarely heard of in this world,
How can one discern their names?
Thus, one can only vaguely visualize their features.
Dimly depict their forms.

6

Now,
Within their watery respository,
And the courts of their unplumbed depths,
There are lofty islands borne by giant turtles,[82]
Tall and towering, standing alone,
Cleaving the giant waves,
Pointing to Grand Clarity,[83]
Thrusting mighty boulders,
Roosts for a hundred numina.
When the Balmy Breeze rises, southward they travel;
When the Broad Blast arrives, northward they journey.[84]
Within their shores there are:
Natural jewels, aquatic wonders,
Houses of the mermen,
The eery shimmer of scarlet stones,
The strange essence of scale and shell.

And now,
A cloudy brocade spreads a pattern along sandy shores,
A gauzy gossamer casts luster over the seams of mussels and snails.

---

[80] Taidian and other loyal vassals of King Wen of Zhou obtained a large cowry shell from
the water and presented it as ransom for their lord, when he was captured by King Zhou
of Yin.

[81] The Marquis of Sui encountered an injured snake and cured its wounds with medicine.
Later, the snake appeared to him with a large "luminous moon" pearl, which glowed in
the dark.

[82] Mu Hua is probably referring to the fifteen legendary giant turtles that supported the
islands of the Eastern Sea on their backs.

[83] A place in the heavens located forty *li* from the earth.

[84] The southern wind and the northern wind respectively.

Manifold colors brandish their splendor,
A myriad hues conceal their brilliance:
Sunlit ice that does not melt,[85]
Shadowy fires burning underwater;[86]
Glowing coals that rekindle themselves,[87]
Casting their fulgor into the Nine Springs;[88]
Vermilion flames, green smoke,
Dark and dense, curling and swirling upward.

7

Of fish
There is the sea-spanning whale,
Looming lordly, swimming alone,
Leveling cragged peaks,
Toppling tall breakers,
Devouring the scaled and shelled,
Swallowing dragon boats.
He sucks in waves and giant rollers mass and merge;
He blows out billows and the hundred streams backward flow.
If perchance he flounces and flounders in spent waves,
And beached dies on salty flats,
His giant scales shall pierce the clouds,
His dorsal fins shall prick the sky,
The bones of his skull will form peaks,
And his oozing oil will become ponds.

8

Now,
In bights of cragged isles,
Shelves of sand and stone,
The winged and feathered engender their chicks,
Breaking the eggs to bring young birds to life.
Ducklings, fluffy and flossy,
Baby cranes, sleek and silky,

---

[85] This may describe icebergs.

[86] Probably some sort of marine bioluminescence.

[87] This may refer to the self-kindling fire of Xiaoqiu, a mountain located in the Southern Sea.

[88] In the underworld.

Flying in flocks, bathing in pairs,
Play in the openings, float on the deeps.
Like hovering fog they soar aloft,
Gliding gracefully in a steady stream.
Their fluttering motion creates thunder,
Their thrumming wings become a grove.
Back and forth they screech and squawk,
Wondrously hued, unique in voice.

9

And then,
When the three luminaries shine clear,[89]
Heaven and Earth glow and gleam,
Without drifting on Lord Yang's billows,[90]
One may ride his arches and break away,
To view Anqi on Penglai,[91]
See the Lord's image on Mount Qiao.[92]

A host of immortals, distantly descried,
Feast on jade by pristine shores,
Walk in sandals left at Fuxiang,
Dress in plumes and pinions, dangling and drooping.

They soar to the pond of Heaven,
Play in the barren murk.[93]
Though revealing their forms, they have no desires;
Forever and ever, eternally they live.

10

Further, as for the sea's capacities:

---

[89] The sun, moon, and stars.
[90] The Marquis of Yang drowned and became known as the spirit of the waves.
[91] Master Anqi, a native of Fuxiang, sold medicines on the shore of the Eastern Sea. After
he became renowned as the Thousand-Year-Old Man, the First Qin Emperor sought him
out and conversed with him for three days and nights. After the emperor left, Anqi
disappeared, leaving only a pair of sandals behind. In a letter he announced, "Some
years hence seek me on Penglai Mountain." The emperor dispatched two envoys to find
him, but they had to turn back when they encountered a storm at sea.
[92] The Yellow Emperor's tumulus was on Mount Qiao.
[93] The Northern Sea.

It embraces Donator's mysteries,
Enfolds Receptor's realm.[94]
The gods here reside,
Also spirits here dwell.
What wonder does it not have?
What marvel does it not store?
Broad and boundless, this accumulation of streams!
Though receiving their forms, empty within it remains.
Vast indeed the Abysmal's power![95]
In lowness it makes its abode.
Enlarging what goes forth, accepting what comes in,
It is the grand eminence, the metropolis.
Of the assorted things and living species,
What does it have, what does it not?

ꄻ Further Reading ꄻ

Bischoff, Friedrich A. *Interpreting the Fu, a Study in Chinese Literary Rhetoric.* Wiesbaden: Steiner, 1976.

Hughes, E. R. *Two Chinese Poets: Vignettes of Han Life and Thought* (Rhapsodies by Ban Gu and Zhang Heng). Princeton: Princeton University Press, 1960.

Knechtges, David R. *The Han Rhapsody, a Study of the Fu of Yang Hsiung.* Cambridge: Cambridge University Press, 1976.

———. trans. *Wen Xuan or Selections of Refined Literature.* Several vols. Princeton: Princeton University Press, 1980–.

Scott, John (in collaboration with Graham Martin), trans. *Love and Protest: Chinese Poems from the Sixth Century B.C. to the Seventeenth Century A.D.* London: Rapp & Whiting, 1972.

Waley, Arthur. *The Temple and Other Poems.* London: Constable, 1923.

Watson, Burton. *Chinese Rhyme-Prose: Poems in the Fu Form from the Han and Six Dynasties Periods.* New York: Columbia University Press, 1971.

———. ed. and trans. *Early Chinese Literature.* New York: Columbia University Press, 1962.

Wu Hung. *The Wu Liang Shrine: The Ideology of Early Chinese Pictorial Art.* Stanford: Stanford University Press, 1959.

"Snow whirled by the driving wind."
Seal carved by Su Xuan (fl. 1621)

---

[94] The Donator (Qian) and Receptor (Kun) trigrams represent Heaven and Earth respectively.

[95] The Abysmal (Kan) trigram represents water.

Chapter 7

Mortals and Immortals

Historical and Pseudo-Historical Writings from the Han and Six Dynasties

Man lives in his bodily shape between heaven and earth and his life is like the span of the summer fly, like the passing of a white colt glimpsed through a crack in the wall. Yet he is shamed to think that within those years his merit will not be known, and grieved that after his departure his name will not be heard. Thus from emperors and kings down to the poorest commoner, from the gentlemen of the court to the hermits in their far-off hills and forests, there is truly none who is not tireless in pursuing merit and fame and impassioned in his thoughts of them. Why is this? Because all have their heart set on immortality. And what, then, is immortality? No more than to have one's name written in a book.

If the world had no books, if the ages were without their historiographers, then whether men were sage rulers like Yao and Shun or tyrants like Jie and Zhou ... once death had changed their form, the earth on their graves would hardly have dried before the good and the evil would have become indistinguishable from one another, and both beauty and ugliness would have perished forever. But so long as the office of historiographer is carried on, so long as books continue to exist, then though men die and enter into darkness and empty silence, their deeds remain, shining like the stars of the Milky Way. Then when a man hereafter shall study them, he has only to lift the scrolls from their boxes and his spirit may commune with the vast ages of antiquity; he need not go beyond his courtyard door and his vision can encompass a thousand years. He sees the worthy men and thinks to equal them; he sees the unworthy and his thoughts turn to introspection.

— Liu Zhiji (661–721), *Understanding History*, chapter 11
(*translated by Burton Watson*)

As for history, no people have been more careful to write and preserve the annals of their empire.

— *The Chinese Traveller*, vol. 2, 1775

The *Records of the Grand Historian* had a profound impact upon the style and structure of much later Chinese historical writing, one that has extended to the popular Chinese genre of "historical fiction." Indeed, in the Chinese tradition the boundary between "history" and "fiction" is even less clear than it is in the West, and this ambiguity derives, in some measure, from the influence of the stylistic devices of the *Records*.

— Stephen Durrant, *Indiana Companion*, 1986

MORTALS

ꕥꕥꕥꕥꕥꕥꕥꕥꕥꕥꕥꕥꕥꕥꕥꕥꕥꕥꕥꕥꕥꕥꕥꕥꕥꕥꕥꕥꕥꕥꕥꕥꕥꕥ

SIMA QIAN (c. 145–c. 85 B.C.)
RECORDS OF THE GRAND HISTORIAN
Three Biographies

Translated by Burton Watson

Sima Qian was the son of Sima Tan, a scholar who served as grand historian at the court of Emperor Wu of the Han dynasty (r. 141–87 B.C.). Though Sima Tan's official duties were confined to matters pertaining to astronomy and the calendar, he believed, as on his deathbed he told his son, that the ancestors of the Sima family in ancient times had been actual court chroniclers and that it was his duty to them and to his own age to compile a history of the famous men and great deeds of the past.... Sima Qian succeeded his father to the post of grand historian at Emperor Wu's court and, in obedience to his father's wishes, began work on the history. Midway in his labors, he incurred the displeasure of the emperor by speaking out in defense of Li Ling, a general who had failed in a campaign against the Xiongnu barbarians of the north and had been forced to surrender.[1] As a result Sima Qian was condemned to undergo castration, the severest penalty next to death. Rather than commit suicide, as was customary in such circumstances, he underwent the punishment in order to be able to finish his history, sacrificing honor and reputation for the sake of a work which he hoped would redeem his name in ages to come. Fortitude has been rewarded by the acclaim of centuries.

Whatever sort of work his father may have envisioned, Sima Qian stopped short of nothing less than a history of the entire knowable past, not only of China itself but of all the peoples and regions known to the Chinese of his time. Thus in scope the *Records* far surpass anything that had previously been attempted. To present such a wealth of material, Sima Qian abandoned the simple chronological form of earlier works and created five large divisions under which he arranged the one hundred and thirty chapters of his work.... The work ends with seventy chapters called *liezhuan*: biographies of famous statesmen, generals, philosophers, etc., or accounts of foreign lands and peoples, closing with an autobiography of Qian himself....

Like earlier historical works, Sima Qian's narrative is almost always focused upon the life and deeds of the individual. He gives far more attention than his predecessors to the influence of geography, climate, economic factors, customs, and institutions upon the course of history. He is quick to give genealogical information where he feels that lineage may have some significance in explaining the character of an individual. But when all other factors have been noted, it is still primarily the will of the individual which, in his opinion, directs the course of history.

---

[1] See chapter 14, for Li Ling's "Reply to Su Wu" and Sima Qian's "Letter to Ren An." *Eds.*

Lü Buwei: Wealth and Power

He strengthened family ties between Zichu and his royal kin and set the counselors of the feudal lords to vying with one another, seeing who could lend most eloquent support to his bid for power in Qin. Thus I made "The Biography of Lü Buwei."

Lü Buwei was a great merchant of Yangdi who, by traveling here and there, buying cheap and selling dear, had accumulated a fortune amounting to thousands in gold.

In the fortieth year of the reign of King Zhaoxiang of Qin (267 B.C.), the crown prince died, and two years later, in the forty-second year of his reign, the king designated his second son, Lord Anguo, as crown prince. Lord Anguo had over twenty sons. He had a concubine of whom he was extremely fond and whom he had designated as his consort with the title of Lady Huayang, but she had borne him no sons. By another concubine, of the Xia family, who no longer enjoyed his favor, he had a son named Zichu, one of the younger among his twenty or more sons. Zichu had been sent by the state of Qin to be a hostage at the court of Zhao,[2] and since, in spite of this, Qin had several times invaded Zhao, the Zhao court accordingly treated Zichu with scant respect. Being merely a grandson of the king of Qin and the son of a concubine, and having been sent as hostage to one of the other feudal states, Zichu was poorly provided with carriages and other equipment and had to live in straitened circumstances, unable to do as he pleased. Lü Buwei, visiting Handan, the capital of Zhao, on business, saw him and was moved to pity. "Here is a rare piece of goods to put in my warehouse!" he exclaimed.

He then went and called on Zichu, remarking, "I know how to enlarge your gate for you!"

Zichu laughed and said, "You'd better enlarge your own gate before you worry about mine!"

"You don't understand," said Lü Buwei. "The enlarging of my gate *depends* on the enlarging of yours!"

Zichu, guessing what was in his mind, led him to a seat in an inner room and the two were soon deep in conversation. "The king of Qin is old and Lord Anguo has been designated crown prince," Lü Buwei said. "I am told that Lord Anguo is very much in love with Lady Huayang, and

---

[2] Younger sons of rulers were often sent to reside at the courts of allied states, where they acted as hostages to encourage the continuance of peaceful relations between the states.

since she has no son of her own, it will be up to her alone to decide which son shall be appointed as the rightful heir. Now you have twenty or more brothers, and from the point of view of age, you are about halfway down the line. You enjoy no particular favor and have been a hostage at the court of one of the other feudal lords for a long time. If your grandfather, the old king, should pass away and Lord Anguo become king, I'm afraid you would have little chance of competing for the position of crown prince with your elder brothers or with your other brothers who are there in person morning and evening to wait upon your father."

"True," said Zichu. "But what can I do about it?"

Lü Buwei said, "You are poor and living in a foreign land. You have nothing to use as gifts to present to the members of your family or to attract a band of followers about you. I too am poor, but with your permission I would like to take a thousand measures of gold and travel west on your behalf to Qin, where I will wait upon Lord Anguo and Lady Huayang and see to it that you are made the rightful heir."

Zichu bowed his head and said, "If indeed it should turn out as you say, when the day comes I hope you will allow me to divide the state of Qin and share it with you!"

Lü Buwei accordingly took 500 measures of gold and presented it to Zichu to be used as expense money in attracting a band of followers, and with another 500 he purchased various rare objects, trinkets, and toys, which he took with him west on a trip to Qin. There he sought an interview with the elder sister of Lady Huayang and asked that the gifts he had brought be presented to Lady Huayang. He took the opportunity to mention how virtuous and wise Zichu was, how he had friends among the followers of the various feudal lords all over the world, how he was constantly heard to exclaim, "Her Ladyship is as precious as Heaven itself to me!" and how he wept day and night with longing for his father, the crown prince, and Lady Huayang. Lady Huayang was very pleased with this message.

Lü Buwei then persuaded the elder sister to speak to Lady Huayang to this effect: "They say that one who has only beauty to offer a man will find, as beauty fades, that his love grows cold. Now you wait upon the crown prince but, though he loves you dearly, you have no son. Before it is too late, should you not take this opportunity to choose one of his sons whom you deem worthy and befriend him, seeing to it that he is elevated to the position of rightful heir and treating him as your own son? Then, as long as your husband lives, you will enjoy honor; and when his hundred years of life are ended and the one whom you call son becomes king, you need never fear any loss of position. This is what they call 'speaking one word that brings ten thousand years of gain.' But if now in blossom time you do not make certain that your roots are firm, then when beauty has faded and love grown cold, though you might hope for a chance to 'speak one word,' how could you gain a hearing? Now Zichu is a worthy man and, being far down the line, knows that he cannot hope to become heir by the normal order of succession. In addition, his mother enjoys no favor, and so he offers all his devotion to you. If you were truly willingly to use this moment to pluck him from the line of succession and make him the heir, then to the end of your days you would enjoy favor in the state of Qin!"

Lady Huayang, convinced of the truth of this argument, waited until her husband, the crown prince, was at leisure and then casually mentioned that Zichu, who had been sent as hostage to Zhao, was a man of outstanding worth and that everyone coming from abroad praised him highly. Then, with tears in her eyes, she said, "I have been fortunate enough to be assigned to your women's quarters, but not so fortunate as to bear a son. I beg you to give me Zichu for a son and to set him up as the rightful heir so that I may have someone to entrust my fate to!"

Lord Anguo gave his consent and had a jade tally engraved to this effect, which he divided with Lady Huayang, promising that he would make Zichu his rightful heir.[3] Then Lord Anguo and Lady Huayang sent rich gifts to Zichu and asked Lü Buwei to act as his tutor. As a result, Zichu became increasingly renowned among the feudal lords.

Lü Buwei had selected from among the ladies of Handan one of matchless beauty and great skill in dancing and had lived with her, and in time he learned that she was pregnant. Zichu, joining Lü Buwei in a drinking bout, happened to catch sight of her and was pleased. Immediately he stood up, proposed a toast to Lü's long life, and asked if he might have her. Lü Buwei was outraged, but soon recalled that he had by now invested all of his family's wealth in Zichu in hopes of fishing up some wonderful prize, and so in the end he presented the woman to him. She concealed the fact that she was pregnant, and when her time was up, she bore a son who was named Zheng. Zichu eventually made her his consort.

In the fiftieth year of his reign (257 B.C.) King Zhaoxiang of Qin sent Wang Yi to lay siege to Handan and, when the situation grew critical, the men of Zhao wanted to kill Zichu. Zichu and Lü Buwei plotted together, however, and distributed 600 catties of gold to the officers who were in

---

[3] In such cases the tally was broken in two, the pieces to be held by the two parties to the agreement. Since Lord Anguo was himself only crown prince, he could not at this time make public his decision.

charge of guarding them. In this way Zichu managed to escape, make his way to the Qin army, and eventually return home. The men of Zhao then proposed to kill Zichu's wife and child, but because his wife was the daughter of a wealthy family in Zhao, she was able to go into hiding; thus both mother and son escaped alive.

King Zhaoxiang of Qin passed away in the fifty-sixth year of his reign (251 B.C.). The crown prince, Lord Anguo, succeeded him as king, Lady Huayang became queen, and Zichu was made crown prince. The state of Zhao obliged by sending Zichu's wife and son Zheng to their new home in Qin. The king of Qin passed away after one year of rule and was given the posthumous title of King Xiaowen. The crown prince Zichu succeeded him and is known as King Zhuangxiang. Queen Huayang, whom King Zhuangxiang had come to treat as a mother, was given the title of Queen Dowager Huayang, and his real mother, whose family name was Xia, was called Queen Dowager Xia.

In the first year of his reign (250 B.C.), King Zhuangxiang made Lü Buwei his chancelor and enfeoffed him as marquis of Wenxin with the revenue from 100,000 households in Henan and Luoyang.

King Zhuangxiang passed away after three years on the throne and the crown prince Zheng became king. He honored Lü Buwei with the position of prime minister and as a mark of respect addressed him as *Zhongfu* or Uncle. The new king of Qin was still young and his mother, the former concubine of Lü Buwei, who had now become queen dowager, from time to time had sexual relations with Lü Buwei in secret. Lü Buwei had some 10,000 male servants in his household.

This was the period of Lord Xinling of Wei, Lord Chunshen of Chu, Lord Pingyuan of Zhao, and Lord Mengchang of Qi, all men who were willing to humble themselves before others and who delighted in gathering bands of followers about them, seeking in this way to outdo one another. Lü Buwei felt that, since Qin was a powerful state, it was disgraceful for it not to do likewise, and so he too set about attracting gentlemen to his service with offers of generous rewards and treatment, and in time gathered as many as 3,000 men who lived and ate at his expense. This was also the period when there were many skilled debaters in the various feudal states, men such as Xun Qing[4] who wrote books and circulated them throughout the world. Lü Buwei accordingly ordered each of his retainers to write down what he himself had learned, and then collected and edited the results into a work comprising eight *lan* or "surveys," six *lun* or "discussions," and twelve *ji* or "records," totaling over

---

[4] The famous Confucian philosopher Xun Zi (fl. 250 B.C.), author of a work in 32 sections.

20,000 characters. It was intended to embrace all the affairs of heaven, earth, the ten thousand things, yesterday, and today, and was entitled "The Spring and Autumn of Mr Lü."[5] The text was posted on the market gate of Xianyang, the Qin capital, with 1,000 pieces of gold suspended above it. An invitation to the wandering scholars and retainers of the various feudal lords informed them that the 1,000 in gold would be awarded to anyone who could add or subtract a single character from it.

The king of Qin, who was later to bear the title of First Emperor of the Qin, in time grew to manhood, but his mother, the queen dowager, did not cease her wanton behavior. Lü Buwei began to fear that, if her conduct were ever brought to light, he himself would become involved in the scandal. He therefore searched about in secret until he found a man named Lao Ai who had an unusually large penis, and made him a servant in his household. Then, when an occasion arose, he had suggestive music performed and, instructing Lao Ai to stick his penis through the center of a wheel made of paulownia wood, had him walk about with it, making certain that the report of this reached the ears of the queen dowager so as to excite her interest. She received the report and, as had been expected, wanted to have the man smuggled into her quarters. Lü Buwei then presented Lao Ai, at the same time getting someone to pretend to accuse him of a crime for which the punishment was castration. Lü Buwei spoke to the queen dowager in private, pointing out that, if the man were subjected to a mock castration, he could then be taken into service in the queen's private apartments. The queen accordingly sent lavish gifts in secret to the official who was in charge of performing the castration, who then pretended to carry out the sentence, plucking out the man's beard and eyebrows and making him into a "eunuch." In this way he eventually came to wait on the queen, who carried on clandestine relations with him and grew to love him greatly. In time she became pregnant and, fearing discovery, pretended to conduct a divination that indicated that, in order to avoid a period of evil influences, she should move from the palace and take up residence in Yong. Lao Ai was constantly in attendance on her and received lavish gifts and awards. All decisions were made by Lao Ai, who was waited upon by an entourage of several thousand male servants. His followers numbered over 1,000, all men who flocked to him in hopes of attaining government office.

In the seventh year of the king's reign (240 B.C.) Queen Dowager Xia, the mother of King Zhuangxiang, passed away. Earlier Queen Dowager

---

[5] The work is still extant and provides invaluable information on Qin period thought and language.

Huayang, the queen of King Xiaowen, had been buried with her husband, King Xiaowen, at Shouling, and Queen Dowager Xia's son, King Zhuangxiang, had been buried at Zhiyang. Accordingly, Queen Dowager Xia was buried separately at a spot east of Du where, in her words, "I may look eastward to my son and westward to my husband. After 100 years, a city of 10,000 households will surely grow up by my side."

In the ninth year of the king's reign someone reported that Lao Ai was not a real eunuch at all, but had constantly been engaging in secret misconduct with the queen dowager, and that she had borne him two sons, both of whom were being kept in hiding. "He and the queen dowager have agreed," said the report, "that, when the present king passes on, one of these sons shall succeed him."

The king thereupon referred the matter to his officials for investigation and all the facts were brought to light, including those that implicated the prime minister Lü Buwei. In the ninth month Lao Ai and his there sets of relatives were executed, the two sons whom the queen dowager had borne were put to death, and the residence of the queen was officially transferred to Yong. Lao Ai's followers were all deprived of their household goods and sent into exile in Shu.

The king of Qin wanted to put the prime minister Lü Buwei to death as well but, because he had won great distinction in the service of the former king, and because so many followers and men of eloquence came forward to speak on his behalf, the king could not bring himself to apply the death penalty. In the tenth month of the tenth year of his reign the king of Qin removed Lü Buwei from the office of prime minister.

Later Mao Jiao, a man of Qi, spoke to the king of Qin and persuaded him to send to Yong for his mother, the queen dowager, and allow her to return to residence in Xianyang. The king also ordered Lü Buwei, the marquis of Wenxin, to leave the capital and proceed to his fief in Henan. A year or so later he learned that so many of the followers and envoys of the various feudal lords were traveling to Henan to call on Lü Buwei that their carriages were never out of sight of each other on the road. Fearful that there might be some plot afoot, the king sent a letter to Lü Buwei saying, "What did you ever do for the state of Qin that Qin should enfeoff you in Henan with the revenue from a 100,000 households? What relation are you to the ruler of Qin that you should be addressed as 'Uncle'? Be so good as to take your family and retinue and move your residence to Shu!"

Lü Buwei judged that he would only have to suffer increasing insult and, fearing the death penalty,[6] he drank poison and died. With Lü

---

[6] Because it would involve his whole family in the punishment.

Buwei and Lao Ai, the two men who had been the butt of his anger, both dead, the king recalled Lao Ai's retainers who had been exiled to Shu. In the nineteenth year of his reign his mother, the queen dowager, passed away and was given the posthumous title of Empress Dowager. She was buried with her husband, King Zhuangxiang, at Zhiyang.

The Grand Historian remarks: Lü Buwei and Lao Ai were both honored with fiefs, the former receiving the title of marquis of Wenxin. When accusations were first made against Lao Ai, Lao got word of it. The king of Qin questioned those about him as to the truth of the charges but had not yet uncovered any definite evidence when he set off for Yong to perform the suburban sacrifice. Lao Ai, fearful that calamity was about to befall him, plotted with the members of his clique and, using the queen dowager's seal of authority without her permission, called out troops and initiated a revolt in the Qinian Palace. The king dispatched officers to attack Lao Ai's forces and Lao Ai fled in defeat. He was pursued and cut down at Haozhi, and eventually his whole clan was wiped out. This marked the beginning of Lü Buwei's fall from power. What Confucius said about the "man of fame" might well apply to this Master Lü, might it not?[7]

— from chapter 85, "The Biography of Lü Buwei"

Nie Zheng, Man of Valor[8]

Nie Zheng was from the village of Deep Well in Zhi. He killed a man and, in order to escape retaliation, went with his mother and elder sister to the state of Qi, where he made a living as a butcher. Some time later Yan Zhongzi of Puyang, an official in the service of Marquis Ai of Han, had a falling out with Han Xialei, the prime minister of Han. Fearful that he might be put to death, Yan Zhongzi fled from the state and traveled about to other states searching for someone who would be willing to get back at Xialei for him.

---

[7] Confucius, contrasting the true man of distinction with one who merely enjoys a good reputation, said, "The man of fame may be one who puts on the appearance of virtue but in practice acts quite differently." (*Analects* XII, 20)

[8] The biographies of Nie Zheng and Jing Ke are two of five biographies that make up chapter 86 of the *Records of the Grand Historian*, "The Biographies of the Assassin-Retainers." The *cike* or "assassin-retainers" are men who undertake an assassination or threat of assassination in order to avenge some wrong done to their lord or to right a political wrong.

When he arrived in Qi, someone told him that Nie Zheng was a man of valor and daring who, fleeing from his enemies, was hiding out among the butchers. Yan Zhongzi went to his door and requested an interview, but was several times turned away. He then prepared a gift of wine, which he asked to be allowed to offer in the presence of Nie Zheng's mother. When the drinking was well under way, Yan Zhongzi brought forth a hundred taels of yellow gold, which he laid before Nie Zheng's mother with wishes for a long life. Nie Zheng was astounded at such generosity and firmly refused the gift. When Yan Zhongzi just as firmly pressed it on him, Nie Zheng repeated his refusal, saying, "I am fortunate enough to have my old mother with me. Though our family is poor and I am living in a strange land and earning my way as a dog butcher,[9] I am still able, come morning and evening, to find some sweet or tasty morsel with which to nourish her. She has everything she needs for her care and comfort — I could not be so bold as to accept your gift."

Yan Zhongzi asked the others present all to withdraw and spoke to Nie Zheng in private. "I have an enemy," he said, "and I have already traveled about to a great many states. When I reached Qi, however, I was privileged to learn that you, sir, are a man of extremely high principles. Therefore I have presented these hundred taels of gold, hoping that you may use them to purchase some trifling gift of food for your honored parent and that I may have the pleasure of your friendship. How would I dare hope for anything more?"

Nie Zheng replied, "I have been content to humble my will and shame my body, living as a butcher here by the marketplace and well, only because I am fortunate enough to have my old mother to take care of. While she lives, I dare not promise my services to any man!"

Yan Zhongzi continued every effort to persuade him, but to the end Nie Zheng was unwilling to accept the gift. Yan Zhongzi nevertheless did all that etiquette demands of a proper guest before taking his leave.

Some time later Nie Zheng's mother died and, when she had been buried and the mourning period was over, Nie Zheng said to himself, "Ah! I am a man of the marketplace and well, swinging a knife and working as a butcher, while Yan Zhongzi is chief minister to one of the feudal lords. And yet he did not consider it too far to come a thousand miles, driving far out of his way just to make friends with me. I treated him very shabbily indeed! I have accomplished no great deeds for which I might be praised, yet Yan Zhongzi presented a hundred taels of gold to my mother with wishes for her continued good health. Though I did not

---

[9] Dogs were raised to be eaten.

accept it, it is clear that he did so simply because he has a profound appreciation of my worth. Now a worthy gentleman, burning with anger and indignation, has offered friendship and trust to a poor and insignificant man. Can I bear to remain silent and let it end there? Earlier, when he made his request of me, I refused only because my mother was still alive. Now that her years have come to a close, I shall offer my services to one who truly understands me!"

Thereupon he journeyed west to Puyang in Wey[10] and went to see Yan Zhongzi. "The reason I would not agree earlier," he said, "was simply that my mother was still alive. Now, unfortunately, the years Heaven gave her have come to a close. Who is this enemy that you wish to take revenge on? I request permission to undertake the task!"

Yan Zhongzi then related to him the whole story. "My enemy is Han Xialei, the prime minister of Han. He is also the younger uncle of the ruler of Han. His clan is numerous and powerful and there are many armed guards stationed wherever he happens to be. I had hoped to send someone to stab him to death, but so far no one has been able to accomplish it. Now if you are so kind as not to reject my plea for help, I hope you will allow me to give you additional carriages and men to assist you in the job."

But Nie Zheng said, "Han and Wey are near neighbors. Now if one is going to murder the prime minister of another state, and the prime minister also happens to be a close relative of the ruler, then the circumstances make it unwise to send a large party of men. If you try to use a lot of men, then there are bound to be differences of opinion on how best to proceed; if there are differences of opinion, then word of the undertaking will leak out; and if word leaks out, then the whole state of Han will be up in arms against you! What could be more dangerous?"

Nie Zheng therefore declined to accept any carriages or attendants, but instead took leave and set off alone, disguising his sword as a walking stick, until he reached Han. When he arrived, the Han prime minister, Xialei, happened to be seated in his office, guarded and attended by a large body of men bearing lances and other weapons. Nie Zheng walked straight in, ascended the steps, and stabbed Xialei to death. Those about the prime minister were thrown into great confusion, and Nie Zheng, shouting loudly, attacked and killed thirty or forty of them. Then he flayed the skin of his face, gouged out his eyes, and, butchering himself

---

[10] This is the old state in the lower Yellow River valley. I have romanized the name "Wey" in order to distinguish it from the state of Wei that was created in 403 B.C. by the partition of the state of Jin.

as he had once done animals, spilled out his bowels and in this way died.

The ruler of Han had his corpse taken and exposed in the marketplace, offering to reward anyone who could identify him, but no one knew who he was. The ruler then hung up the reward, promising to give a thousand pieces of gold to anyone who could say who it was that had killed Prime Minister Xialei. A long time passed but no one came forward with the answer.

Meanwhile Nie Zheng's elder sister, Rong, heard that someone had stabbed and killed the prime minister of Han, but that the blame could not be fixed since no one knew the culprit's name. His corpse had been exposed in the marketplace with a reward of a thousand pieces of gold hanging above it, she was told. Filled with apprehension, she said, "Could it be my younger brother? Ah — Yan Zhongzi certainly knew what he was capable of!"

Then she set off at once and went to the marketplace of Han, where she found that the dead man was indeed Nie Zheng. Throwing herself down beside the corpse, she wept in profound sorrow, crying, "This man is called Nie Zheng from the village of Deep Well in Zhi!"

The people passing back and forth through the market all said to her, "This man has committed an act of violence and treachery against the prime minister of our state and our king has posted a reward of a thousand gold pieces for anyone who can discover his name — have you not heard? How dare you come here and admit that you were acquainted with him?"

Rong replied, "Yes, I have heard. But Zheng was willing to accept shame and disgrace, throwing away his future and making a living in the marketplace, because our mother was still in good health and I was not yet married. After our mother had ended her years and departed from the world, and I had found a husband, then Yan Zhongzi, recognizing my brother's worth, lifted him up from hardship and disgrace and became his friend, treating him with kindness and generosity. So there was nothing he could do. A gentleman will always be willing to die for someone who recognizes his true worth. And now, because I am still alive, he has inflicted this terrible mutilation upon himself so as to wipe out all trace of his identity. But how could I, out of fear that I might be put to death, allow so worthy a brother's name to be lost forever?"

Having astounded the people of the marketplace with these words, she cried three times in a loud voice to heaven and then died of grief and anguish by the dead man's side. When the inhabitants of Jin, Chu, Qi, and Wey heard of this, they all said, "Zheng was not the only able one — his sister too proved herself a woman of valor!"

If Zheng had in fact known that his sister would be unwilling to stand by in silence but, heedless of the threat of execution and public exposure, would make her way a thousand miles over the steep passes, determined to spread his fame abroad, so that sister and brother would both end as criminals in the marketplace of Han, then he would surely never have agreed to undertake such a mission for Yan Zhongzi. And as for Yan Zhongzi, it can certainly be said that he knew how to recognize a man's ability and win others to his service.

— from chapter 86, "Biographies of the Assassin-Retainers"

Jing Ke, Assassin

Some 220 years later there was the affair of Jing Ke in Qin. Jing Ke was a native of Wey, though his family came originally from Qi. The men of Wey referred to him as Master Qing, the men of Yan, as Master Jing. He loved to read books and practise swordsmanship. He expounded his ideas to Lord Yuan of Wey, but Lord Yuan failed to make use of him. Later, Qin attacked Wey, established Dong Province, and moved the collateral kinsmen of Lord Yuan of Wey to Yewang.

Jing Ke once visited the area of Yuci, where he engaged Gai Nie in a discussion on swordsmanship. In the course of the talk, Gai Nie got angry and glared fiercely at Jing Ke, who immediately withdrew. Someone asked Gai Nie if he did not intend to summon Jing Ke back again. "When I was discussing swordsmanship with him a little while ago," said Gai Nie, "we had a difference of opinion and I glared at him. Go and look for him if you like, but I'm quite certain he has gone. He wouldn't dare stay around!" Gai Nie sent a messenger to the house where Jing Ke had been staying, but Jing Ke had already mounted his carriage and left Yuci. When the messenger returned with this report, Gai Nie said, "I knew he would go. I glared at him and frightened him away."

Again, when Jing Ke was visiting the city of Handan, he and a man named Lu Goujian got into a quarrel over a chess game. Lu Goujian grew angry and began to shout, whereupon Jing Ke fled without a word and never came to see Lu Goujian again.

In the course of his travels Jing Ke reached the state of Yan, where he became close friends with a dog butcher and a man named Gao Jianli who was good at playing the lute. Jing Ke was fond of wine, and every day he would join the dog butcher and Gao Jianli to drink in the marketplace of the Yan capital. After the wine had begun to take effect, Gao Jianli would strike up the lute and Jing Ke would join in with a song. In the middle of the crowded marketplace they would happily amuse themselves, or if their mood changed they would break into tears, exactly as though there were no one else about. But, although Jing Ke spent his time with drunkards, he was a man of depth and learning. Whatever feudal state he traveled to, he always became close friends with the most worthy and influential men. When he went to Yan, Master Tian Guang, a gentleman of Yan who was living in retirement, treated him very kindly, for he realized that he was no ordinary man.

After Jing Ke had been in Yan some time, Prince Dan, the heir apparent of Yan, who had been a hostage in Qin, escaped and returned home. Previously Prince Dan had been a hostage in Zhao. Zheng, the king of Qin, was born in Zhao, and in his youth had been very friendly with Prince Dan; later, when Zheng became king, Prince Dan went as a hostage to the Qin court. But the king of Qin treated him very shabbily until, in anger, he escaped from the state and returned to Yan. After his return, he looked about for someone who would undertake to get back at the king of Qin for him; but because Yan was small and powerless, there was nothing he could do. Meanwhile, Qin day by day dispatched more troops east of the mountains, attacking Qi, Chu, Hann,[11] Wei, and Zhao and gradually eating away at the lands of the other feudal lords, until it became obvious that Yan's turn would be next. The ruler of Yan and his ministers all feared imminent disaster, and Prince Dan, likewise worried over the situation, asked his tutor Ju Wu what could be done.

Ju Wu replied, "Qin's lands fill the world and its might overawes the rulers of Hann, Wei, and Zhao. To the north it occupies the strongholds at Sweet Springs and Valley Mouth, and to the south the fertile fields of the Jing and Wei river valleys; it commands the riches of Ba and Han and the mountain ranges of Long and Shu to the west, and the vital Hangu and Yao passes to the east. Its people are numerous and its soldiers well trained, and it has more weapons and armor than it can use. If it should ever decide to march against us, we could find no safety south of the Great Wall or north of the Yi River.[12] Angry as you are at the insults you have suffered, you surely would not want to brush against its bristling scales!"[13]

"Then what should I do?" said Prince Dan.

"Let me retire and think it over," replied Ju Wu.

Shortly afterward the Qin general Fan Yuqi, having offended the king of Qin, fled to Yan, where Prince Dan received him and assigned him

---

[11] One of the states created in 403 B.C. by the partition of the state of Jin. It is romanized in this way to distinguish it from the later Han dynasty.

[12] The boundaries of the state of Yan.

[13] The deadly scales that protrude from the throat of a dragon.

quarters. Ju Wu admonished the prince, saying, "This will not do! Violent as the king of Qin is, and with the resentment he nurses against Yan because of your escape, it is already enough to make one's heart turn cold. And what will he be like when he hears where General Fan is staying? This is what men call throwing meat in the path of a starving tiger — there will be no help for the misfortune that follows! Even if you had ministers as wise as Guan Zhong and Yan Ying, they could think of no way to save you! I beg you to send General Fan at once to the territory of the Xiongnu barbarians to get him out of the way. Then, after you have negotiated with Hann, Wei, and Zhao to the west, entered into alliance with Qi and Chu on the south, and established friendly relations with the leader of the Xiongnu to the north, we may be able to plan what move to make next."

"The scheme you propose will require a great deal of time," said Prince Dan. "As anxious as I feel at the moment, I am afraid I cannot wait that long! And that is not all. General Fan, having been hounded throughout the world, has come to entrust his fate to me. No matter how much I might be pressed by Qin and its power, I could never bear, when he is in such a pitiful plight, to betray his friendship and abandon him by sending him off to the Xiongnu! This is a matter of life and death to me. I beg you to consider the question once more."

Ju Wu said, "To pursue a dangerous course and hope for safety, to invite disaster while seeking good fortune; with too little planning and too much hatred to disregard a serious threat to the whole nation because of some lately incurred debt of friendship to one man — this is what is known as 'fanning resentment and abetting disaster'! Drop a swan's feather into a burning brazier and puff! — it is all over in an instant. And when Qin, like a ravening hawk, comes to vent its anger, will Yan be able to last any longer? However, there is a certain Master Tian Guang in Yan who is a man of deep wisdom and great daring. He would be a good person to consult."

"I would like you to introduce me to him," said Prince Dan. "Can you arrange it?"

"With pleasure," said Ju Wu, and went to see Master Tian, informing him that the crown prince wished to consult him on matters of state. "I will be happy to comply," said Master Tian. He went to call on the prince, who came out to greet him, politely led him inside, knelt, and dusted off a mat for him to sit on.

When Tian Guang was settled on his seat and those about them had retired, the prince deferentially moved off his mat and addressed his request to his visitor: "Yan and Qin cannot both stand! I beg you to devote your mind to this problem."

"They say," replied Tian Guang, "that when a thoroughbred horse is in its prime, it can gallop 1,000 *li* in one day; but when it is old and decrepit, the sorriest nag will outdistance it. It appears that you have heard reports of how I was when I was in my prime, but do not realize that my strength is by now wasted and gone. Nevertheless, though I myself would not venture to plan for the safety of the state, I have a friend named Master Jing who could be consulted."

"I would like you to introduce me to him," said Prince Dan. "Is it possible?"

"With pleasure," said Tian Guang and, rising from his mat, he hurried from the room. The prince escorted him as far as the gate and there warned him, "What we have been discussing is a matter of vital concern to the nation. Please do not let word of it leak out!"

Tian Guang lowered his gaze to the ground and replied with a laugh, "I understand."

Then, stooped with age, he made his way to the house of Master Jing. "Everyone in Yan knows that we are good friends," he said. "The crown prince, having heard reports of me when I was in my prime and unaware that by now my powers have failed, has told me that Yan and Qin cannot continue to exist side by side and begged me to devote my mind to the problem. Rather than refuse his request, I took the liberty of mentioning your name. May I ask you to go call on him at his palace?"

"I will be glad to comply," said Jing Ke.

"They say," Tian Guang continued, "that a worthy man does not act in such a way as to arouse distrust in others. Now the prince has warned me that the matter we discussed is of vital concern to the nation and begged me not to let word of it leak out. Obviously he distrusts me, and if my actions have aroused his distrust, then I am no gentleman of honor!" Tian Guang had decided to commit suicide in order to spur Jing Ke to action, and he continued: "I want you to go at once and visit the prince. Tell him I am already dead, so he will know that I have not betrayed the secret!" With this he cut his throat and died.

Jing Ke went to see the prince and informed him of Tian Guang's death and last words. The prince bowed twice and then, sinking to his knees, crawled forward, the tears starting from his eyes. After some time he said, "I only cautioned Master Tian not to speak so that we could be sure of bringing our plans to a successful conclusion. Now he has actually killed himself to show me that the secret will never be betrayed — as though I could have intended such a thing!"

After Jing Ke had settled himself, the prince moved off his mat, bowed his head, and said, "Master Tian, unaware of how unworthy a person I am, has made it possible for me to speak my thoughts to you. It is clear from this that Heaven has taken pity upon Yan and has not abandoned me altogether.

"Qin has a heart that is greedy for gain, and its desires are insatiable. It will never be content until it has seized all the land in the world and forced every ruler within the four seas to acknowledge its sovereignty. Now, having already taken captive the king of Hann and annexed all his lands, Qin has mobilized its troops to strike against Chu in the south, while in the north it stands poised for an attack on Zhao. Wang Jian, leading several hundred thousand troops, is holding Zhang and Ye, while Li Xin leads another force against Taiyuan and Yunzhong. Zhao, unable to withstand the might of Qin, will undoubtedly submit and swear allegiance to it. And when Zhao has gone under, Yan will stand next in line for disaster!

"Yan is small and weak, and has often fared badly in war. Even if we were to mobilize the entire nation, we obviously could not stand against Qin; and once the other feudal lords have bowed to its rule, none of them will dare to become our allies. Nevertheless, I have a scheme of my own which, foolish as it may be, I would like to suggest — that is, to find a really brave man who would be willing to go as our envoy to the court of Qin and tempt it with some offer of gain. The king of Qin is greedy, and under the circumstances would surely listen to our offer. If this man could then somehow threaten the king, as Cao Mei threatened Duke Huan of Qi,[14] and force him to return to the feudal lords all the land he has seized, that would be the best we could ask for. And if that proved impossible, he might still be able to stab and kill the king. With the Qin generals free to do as they wished with the troops in the outlying areas, and the Qin court in a state of confusion, dissension would surely arise between ruler and subject. The feudal lords could then take advantage of the situation to band together once more, and in that case the defeat of Qin would be inevitable. This is what I would like to see more than anything else, but I do not know who could be entrusted with such a mission. I can only ask that you give it some thought!"

After some time Jing Ke said, "This is a matter of grave importance to the state. I am a person of little worth and I fear I would be unfit for such a mission."

---

[14] Cao Mei or Cao Mo, a general of the state of Lu, had several times been defeated by the forces of the neighboring state of Qi and forced to concede lands to Qi. When the rulers of Lu and Qi came together for a meeting, Cao Mei, brandishing a dagger, threatened the Qi ruler, Duke Huan (r. 685–643 B.C.), and forced him to return the lands to Lu. Cao Mei's is the first of the five "Biographies of the Assassin-Retainers."

The prince moved forward and, bowing his head, begged and begged Jing Ke to accept the proposal and not to decline any longer, until at last Jing Ke gave his consent. The prince then honored him with the title of Chief Minister and assigned him the finest quarters in the capital. Every day the prince went to call at his mansion, presenting gifts of food, supplying him with all manner of luxuries, and from time to time pressing him to accept carriages, rider attendants, and waiting women, indulging his every wish so as to ensure his cooperation.

Time passed, but Jing Ke showed no inclination to set out on the mission. Meanwhile the Qin general Wang Jian defeated Zhao, took prisoner its king, and annexed its entire territory. Then he advanced north, seizing control of the land as he went, until he reached the southern border of the state of Yan. Crown Prince Dan, filled with terror, begged Jing Ke to set off. "Any moment now the Qin forces may cross the Yi River, and if that happens, though I might wish to continue to wait upon you, how could I do so?"

"I intended to say something, whether you mentioned it or not," said Jing Ke. "The trouble is that, if I set off now, without any means of gaining the confidence of the king of Qin, I will never be able to get close to him. The king of Qin has offered 1,000 catties of gold and a city of 10,000 households in exchange for the life of his former general, Fan Yuqi. If I could get the head of General Fan and a map of the Dukang region of Yan, and offer to present these to the king of Qin, he would certainly be delighted to receive me. Then I would have a chance to carry out our plan."

But the prince replied, "General Fan has come here in trouble and distress and entrusted himself to me. I could never bear to betray the trust of a worthy man for the sake of my own personal desires. I beg you to think of some other plan."

Jing Ke realized that the prince would never bring himself to carry out his suggestion, and so he went in private to see Fan Yuqi. "Qin's treatment of you has been harsh indeed!" he said. "Your father, your mother, and all the members of your family have been done away with; and now I hear that Qin has offered a reward of 1,000 catties of gold and a city of 10,000 households for your head! What do you intend to do?"

Fan Yuqi looked up to Heaven and gave a great sigh, tears streaming down his face. "I think of nothing else, until the ache of it is in my very bones! But I do not know what I can do!"

"Suppose I said that one word from you could dispel the troubles of the state of Yan and avenge the wrong you have suffered?"

Fan Yuqi leaned forward. "What is it?" he asked.

"Give me your head, so that I can present it to the king of Qin! Then he will surely be delighted to receive me. With my left hand I will seize hold of his sleeve, with my right I'll stab him in the breast, and all your wrongs will be avenged and all the shameful insults which Yan has suffered will be wiped out! What do you say?"

Fan Yuqi bared his shoulder and gripped his wrist in a gesture of determination. Moving forward, he said, "Day and night I gnash my teeth and eat out my heart trying to think of some plan. Now you have shown me the way!" Then he cut his throat.

When the crown prince heard what had happened, he rushed to the spot and, throwing himself upon the corpse, wept in deep sorrow. But, since there was nothing that could be done, he took Fan Yuqi's head and sealed it in a box. Earlier he had ordered a search for the sharpest dagger that could be found, and had purchased one from a man of Zhao named Xu Furen for 100 measures of gold. He ordered his artisans to coat the blade with poison and try it out on some men; though the thrust drew hardly enough blood to stain the robe of the victim, every one of the men dropped dead on the spot. The prince then began to make final preparations for sending Master Jing on his mission. There was a brave man of Yan named Qin Wuyang who at age thirteen had murdered someone, and was so fierce that no one dared even to look at him crossly. This man the prince ordered to act as a second to Jing Ke.

There was another man whom Jing Ke wished to have along in his party, but he lived a long way off and had not yet arrived in Yan. Meanwhile preparations for the journey were completed but, though time passed, Jing Ke still did not set off. The prince began to fret at the delay and to suspect that Jing Ke had changed his mind. He therefore went to Jing Ke and pressed his request. "The day for departure has already passed, and I am wondering what you intend to do. Perhaps I should send Qin Wuyang on ahead ..."

"What do you mean, send Qin Wuyang on ahead?" roared Jing Ke angrily. "Send that little wretch alone and you may be sure he'll never return successful — setting off with a single dagger to face the immeasurable might of Qin! The reason I have delayed is that I was waiting for a friend I wanted to go with me. But, if you feel it is growing too late, I beg to take my leave."

Then he set out. The crown prince and all his associates who knew what was happening put on white robes and caps of mourning to see the party off, accompanying them as far as the Yi River. After they had sacrificed to the god of the road and chosen their route, Gao Jianli struck up his lute and Jing Ke joined in with a song in the mournful *bianzhi* mode. Tears streamed from the eyes of the company. Jing Ke came forward and sang this song:

Winds cry *xiao xiao*,
  Yi waters are cold.
Brave men, once gone,
  Never come back again.

Shifting to the *yu* mode with its martial air, Jing Ke sang once more;
this time the eyes of the men flashed with anger and their hair bristled
beneath their caps. Then he mounted his carriage and set off, never
once looking back.

In time he arrived in Qin, where he presented gifts worth 1,000
measures of gold to Meng Jia, an attendant to the sons of the nobility and
one of the king's favorite ministers. Meng Jia in turn spoke on his behalf
to the king of Qin: "The king of Yan, trembling with awe before Your
Majesty's might, has not ventured to call out his troops to oppose our
forces, but requests that he and all his people may become vassals of Qin,
so that he may be ranked among the other feudal lords and present
tribute and perform labor services in the manner of a province or a
district; in this way he hopes to be allowed to continue the sacrifices at
the temple of his ancestors, the former kings of Yan. In his terror he has
not dared to come and speak in person, but has respectfully sent the
severed head of Fan Yuqi sealed in a box, along with a map of the Dukang
region in Yan, to be presented to you. Bowing respectfully in his courtyard, he has sent these gifts, dispatching his envoys to inquire Your
Majesty's pleasure. He awaits your command."

When the king of Qin heard this, he was delighted and, donning his
court robes and ordering a full dress reception, he received the envoys of
Yan in the Xianyang Palace. Jing Ke bore the box with Fan Yuqi's head,
while Qin Wuyang carried the map case; step by step they advanced
through the throne room until they reached the steps of the throne,
where Qin Wuyang suddenly turned pale and began to quake with fear.
The courtiers eyed him suspiciously. Jing Ke turned around, laughed at
Qin Wuyang, and then stepped forward to apologize: "This man is a
simple rustic from the barbarous region of the northern border, and he
has never seen the Son of Heaven. That is why he shakes with fright. I beg
Your Majesty to pardon him for the moment and permit me to complete
my mission before you."

"Bring the map he is carrying!" said the king to Jing Ke, who took the
map container from Qin Wuyang and presented it to the king. The king
opened the container, and when he had removed the map, the dagger
appeared. At that moment Jing Ke seized the king's sleeve with his left
hand, while with his right he snatched up the dagger and held it pointed
at the king's breast, but he did not stab him. The king jerked back in

alarm and leaped from his seat, tearing the sleeve off his robe. He tried to draw his sword, but it was long and clung to the scabbard and, since it hung vertically at his side, he could not, in his haste, manage to get it out.

Jing Ke ran after the king, who dashed around the pillar of the throne room. All the courtiers, utterly dumbfounded by so unexpected an occurrence, milled about in disorder.

According to Qin law, no courtier or attendant who waited upon the king in the upper throne room was permitted to carry a weapon of any kind. The palace attendants who bore arms were ranged in the lower hall, and without a command from the king they were forbidden to ascend to the throne room. In his panic the king had no chance to give a command to the soldiers to appear, and thus Jing Ke was able to pursue him. Having nothing with which to strike at Jing Ke, the king in panic-stricken confusion merely flailed at him with his hands. At the same time the physician Xia Wuju, who was in attendance, battered Jing Ke with the medicine bag he was carrying.

The king continued to circle the pillar, unable in his confusion to think of anything else to do. "Push the scabbard around behind you!" shouted the king's attendants, and, when he did this, he was at last able to draw his sword and strike at Jing Ke, slashing him across the left thigh. Jing Ke, staggering to the ground, raised the dagger and hurled it at the king, but it missed and struck the bronze pillar. The king attacked Jing Ke again.

Jing Ke, wounded now in eight places, realized that his attempt had failed. Leaning against the pillar, his legs sprawled before him, he began to laugh and curse the king. "I failed because I tried to threaten you without actually killing you and exact a promise that I could take back to the crown prince!" As he spoke, the king's attendants rushed forward to finish him off.

It was a long time before the king regained his composure. When at last he came to himself, he discussed with his ministers the question of who deserved a reward for his part in the incident, and who deserved punishment. To the physician Xia Wuju he presented 200 taels of gold, "because Xia Wuju, out of love for me, hit Jing Ke with his medicine bag."

After this the king in a rage dispatched more troops to join his army in Zhao and commanded Wang Jian to attack Yan. Ten months later the Qin army captured the city of Ji. King Xi of Yan, Prince Dan, and the others of the court, leading their best troops, fled east to Liaodong for safety. The Qin general Li Xin pursued and attacked them with ever increasing fury.

King Jia of Dai sent a letter to King Xi of Yan which read: "It is all because of Prince Dan that Qin is harassing you with such vehemence. If you would only do away with the prince and present his corpse to Qin, the king's anger would surely be appeased and he would leave you in peace to carry on the sacrifices to your altars of the soil and grain."

Shortly after this, Li Xin pursued Prince Dan as far as the Yan River, where the prince hid among the islands of the river. Meanwhile the king of Yan sent an envoy to cut off the prince's head, intending to present it to Qin, but Qin dispatched more troops and reopened its attack on Yan. Five years later, Qin finally destroyed the state of Yan and took its ruler, King Xi, prisoner. The following year (221 B.C.), the king of Qin united all the empire under his rule and assumed the title of August Emperor.

The Qin ruler then began a campaign to ferret out the associates of Prince Dan and Jing Ke, and as a result they all went into hiding. Gao Jianli, who was among the group, changed his name, hired himself out as an indentured workman, and went into hiding in a household in the city of Songzi, enduring for a long time the hardships of a laborer's life. Whenever he heard some guest of the family playing the lute in the main hall of the house, he would linger outside, unable to tear himself away, and after each performance he would say, "That man plays well" or "That man is not very good." One of the servants reported this to the master of the house, saying, "That hired man must know something about music, since he ventures to pass judgment on everyone's playing."

The master of the house summoned Gao Jianli to appear and play the lute before his guests, and when he did so, everyone in the company praised his playing and pressed wine on him. Gao Jianli thought of the long time he had been in hiding, and of the seemingly endless years of hardship and want that lay ahead; finally he went back to his room, got his lute and good clothes out of the trunk where he had stored them and, changing his clothes, appeared once more in the hall. The guests were overcome with surprise and, bowing and making room for him as an equal, they led him to the seat of honor and requested him to play the lute and sing. When the performance was over, there was not a guest who left the house dry-eyed.

Gao Jianli was entertained at one home after another in Songzi, and in time his fame reached the ears of the Qin emperor. The emperor summoned him to an audience, but when he appeared, someone who had known him in the past exclaimed, "This is Gao Jianli!" The emperor, unable to bring himself to kill such a skilled musician, ordered his eyes put out and commanded him to play in his presence. The emperor never failed to praise his playing and gradually allowed him to come nearer and nearer. Gao Jianli then got a heavy piece of lead and fastened it inside his lute, and the next time he was summoned to play at the emperor's side, he raised the lute and struck at the emperor. He missed and was summarily executed, and after that the emperor never again permitted any of the former followers of the feudal lords to approach his person.

When Lu Goujian heard of Jing Ke's attempt to assassinate the king of Qin, he sighed to himself and said, "What a pity that he never properly mastered the art of swordsmanship! And as for me — how blind I was to his real worth! That time when I shouted at him in anger, he must have thought I was hardly human!"

The Grand Historian remarks: When people these days tell the story of Jing Ke, they assert that at the command of Prince Dan the heavens rained grain and horses grew horns. This is of course a gross error. They likewise say that Jing Ke actually wounded the king of Qin, which is equally untrue. At one time Gongsun Jigong and Master Dong were friends of the physician Xia Wuju and they learned from him exactly what happened. I have therefore reported everything just as they told it to me.

Of these five men,[15] from Cao Mei to Jing Ke, some succeeded in carrying out their duty and some did not. But it is perfectly clear that they had all determined upon the deed. They were not false to their intentions. Is it not right, then, that their names should be handed down to later ages?

— from chapter 86, "Biographies of the Assassin-Retainers"

Ban Gu (32–92)
History of the Former Han
Two Biographies

Translated by Burton Watson

The *History of the Former Han*, which deals with the period from 206 B.C. to A.D. 23, is one of the most renowned and influential of all Chinese historical works. Admired for the rich detail of its narrative and the purity and economy of its style, it served as a model for the official histories that were compiled in later centuries to cover all the dynasties of Chinese imperial history. From the time of its appearance in the first century A.D. until the present, no one in China or the countries within the sphere of Chinese cultural influence could consider himself truly educated who was not thoroughly familiar with its pages....

Ban Gu, though considerably more fortunate than Sima Qian, suffered a somewhat similar experience. His father Ban Biao (A.D. 3–54), a scholar and possessor of a

---

[15] The five men whose biographies make up Sima Qian's chapter, including Nie Zheng.

superb private library, began work on a continuation of the *Records of the Grand Historian*, though how far he had progressed by the time of his death we do not know. Ban Gu took up his father's labors but decided that, rather than produce a mere continuation of Sima Qian's work, he would undertake a history of the entire Former Han period. He had not devoted himself to this task for long, however, when someone submitted a letter to the ruler, Emperor Ming (r. A.D. 58–77), accusing him of attempting as a private citizen to write a history of the Former Han, which had been ruled by members of the same Liu family to which Emperor Ming belonged. Ban Gu was taken to prison in the capital for questioning and his writings were confiscated....

When the emperor examined Ban Gu's writings, however, he not only released the historian but appointed him to a post in the imperial archives and encouraged him to continue his literary labors. Ban Gu was thus given access to government files and was allowed to complete the writing of his history under highly favorable circumstances. The *History of the Former Han* was probably finished around A.D. 80 and is said to have won immediate acclaim among the scholars of the day.

Dongfang Shuo, Jester Extraordinary

Dongfang Shuo was rich in words, a man of jests and witticisms, an actor and a buffoon. In condemning the Shanglin Park and blocking Dong Yan's entrance into the hall of state, he voiced a just reprimand and exposed error, yet he thrust the meat into the breast of his robe and dirtied the palace. He had his stiff moods and his relaxed ones, his bobbings and his sinkings. So I have transmitted the Biography of Dongfang Shuo.

Dongfang Shuo, whose polite name was Manqian, was a native of Yanci in Pingyuan. When Emperor Wu first came to the throne, he sent out a call to the empire for the promotion of men who were "honest and upright," "worthy and good," or noted for scholarly or literary talents or unusual strength, offering to assign them to posts without requiring them to advance in the ordinary fashion. As a result, many men from all quarters submitted letters to the throne with their suggestions on policy; thousands came forward to peddle and parade their abilities in this way. Those who did not seem worthy of selection were summarily informed that their papers had been examined and were then dismissed.

When Dongfang Shuo first came forward, he submitted a letter to the throne, which said: "When I was young, I lost my father and mother and was brought up by my older brother and his wife. At the age of twelve I began to study writing, and after three winters I knew enough to handle ordinary texts and records. At fifteen I studied fencing; at sixteen, the *Songs* and *History*; and soon I had memorized 220,000 words. At nineteen I studied the works on military science by Masters Sun and Wu, the equipment pertaining to battle and encampment, and the regulations concerning drum and gong.[16] Once more I memorized 220,000 words, so that in all I could recite 440,000 words. In addition I always kept in mind Zilu's words.[17] I am twenty-two years in age, measure nine feet three inches,[18] have eyes like pendant pearls, teeth like ranged shells, and am as brave as Meng Ben, nimble as Qingji, scrupulous as Bao Zhu, and loyal as Wei Sheng. I am fit to become a great minister to the Son of Heaven. Daring death, I bow twice and submit this report."

Dongfang Shuo's words were so lacking in humility and he praised himself so extravagantly that the emperor, concluding that he was no ordinary man, ordered him to await the imperial command in the office of public carriage. His stipend was meager, however, and he had not yet been granted an audience with the emperor.

After some time, Shuo played a trick on the dwarfs who worked in the stable, telling them, "His Majesty has decided that you fellows are of no benefit to the government. In plowing fields and raising crops you are surely no match for ordinary men. Given official posts and put in charge of the multitude, you would never be able to bring order to the people. Assigned to the army and dispatched to attack the barbarians, you would be incapable of handling weapons. You contribute nothing to the business of the state — all you do is use up food and clothing! So now he has decided to have you killed."

The dwarfs, thoroughly terrified, began weeping and moaning, whereupon Shuo instructed them, saying, "When His Majesty passes by, knock your heads on the ground and beg for mercy." After a while, word came that the emperor was on his way. The dwarfs all wailed and bowed their heads, and when the emperor asked them why they were doing that, they replied, "Dongfang Shuo told us Your Majesty was going to have us all executed!"

The emperor, knowing that Shuo was a man of many devices, summoned him and asked him what he meant by terrifying the dwarfs in this fashion. Shuo replied, "I will speak out, whether it means life or death for me! The dwarfs are somewhat over three feet in height, and as a stipend they receive one sack of grain and 240 cash each. I am somewhat over nine feet in height, and as a stipend I too receive one sack of grain and

---

[16] In battle the drum sounded the call to advance, the gong that to retreat.

[17] *Analects* XI, 25: "Zilu briskly replied, 'Give me a country of a thousand war chariots.... and I can make the people do brave deeds, and furthermore understand the right direction to go in!'"

[18] The Han foot was about three-fourths of an English foot.

240 cash. The dwarfs are about to die of overeating, I am about to die of hunger. If my words are of any use, I hope I may be treated differently from them. If my words are of no use, then dismiss me. There's no point in merely keeping me around to eat up the rice of Chang'an!"

The emperor roared with laughter and accordingly assigned him to await command at the Golden Horse Gate. Little by little, Shuo gained the confidence of the emperor.

Once the emperor ordered his various tricksters to play "guess-what's-under-it."[19] He placed a gecko lizard under the cup and asked them to guess, but no one was able to get the answer. Shuo then volunteered his services, saying "I have received instruction in the *Book of Changes* — let me try guessing." He then divided up the milfoil stalks, laid out the hexagrams, and announced, "I would take it for a dragon but it has no horns. I'd say it was a snake except that it has legs. Creeping, crawling, peering here and there, good at moving along the wall — if it's not a gecko, it's bound to be a skink!"

"Splendid!" said the emperor, and presented him with ten rolls of silk. Then he ordered him to guess some other objects. Again and again Shuo guessed correctly, and was immediately presented with more silk.

At this time there was an actor named Courtier Guo who enjoyed great favor with the emperor for his never-ending fund of waggery and was constantly in attendance at the ruler's side. "Shuo just happened to make a few lucky hits!" he asserted. "This is not true art. I would like to have Shuo guess again. If he guesses correctly, I am willing to accept a hundred blows of the cane; but if he fails, I am to be given all the presents of silk!" Then he put a round tree fungus under the cup and ordered Shuo to guess. Shuo replied, "It's a saucer."

"There!" said the actor, "I knew he couldn't guess it!" But Shuo replied, "Fresh meat — you call it a stew; dried meat — you call it jerky. Growing on a tree, you call it a fungus; under a cup, you call it a saucer!" The emperor ordered the official in charge of actors to have Guo beaten. Unable to bear the pain, Guo squealed in anguish, but Shuo only laughed at him and said, "Ugh! Mouth with no hair — voice all ablare — rear end in the air!"

Infuriated, the actor screamed, "Shuo is brazenly trying to hoodwink and humiliate an attendant of the Son of Heaven! His corpse ought to be exposed in the marketplace!"

---

[19] A game in which an object is placed under an overturned cup or bowl and the participants try to guess what it is.

The emperor then asked Shuo why he was trying to humiliate the man, but Shuo replied, "How would I dare humiliate anyone? I was just making up some riddles for him, that's all."

"What riddles?" asked the emperor.

"'Mouth with no hair,'" said Shuo, "that's the dog's private door.[20] 'Voices all ablare' — fledglings at supper, calling for more. 'Rear end in the air' — a crane, bending over, pecking at the floor."

But Guo refused to acknowledge defeat. Instead, he said, "Now I would like to ask Shuo some riddles. If he can't solve them, he too ought to be given the cane!" Then he put together this absurd jingle:

"Law pot snaggle-toothed
age cypress mud-grooved
yi-yu-ya
ngi-ngu-nga

What does that mean?"

Shuo replied, "Law — an ordination. Pot — to store your ration. Snaggle-toothed — nonconformation. Age — what all men hail. Cypress — the spirits' vale. Mud-grooved — a soggy trail. *Yi-yu-ya* — words merely jangling. *Ngi-ngu-nga* — two dogs tangling!" Whatever Guo asked, Shuo would immediately come back with an answer in rhyme, twisting things around, distorting, popping out in any number of weird ways so that no one could pin him down. The company was reduced to utter astonishment.

The emperor appinted Shuo a gentleman in constant attendance and eventually bestowed great affection and favor on him.

Some time later, during the hottest days of summer, the emperor ordered that a gift of meat be given to his attendants. But, although the day grew late, the assistant to the imperial butler did not appear to distribute the gift. Shuo then took it upon himself to draw his sword and cut off a portion of meat, saying to his fellow officials, "In these hot days one ought to go home early. With your permission, therefore, I will take my gift." Then he put the meat into the breast of his robe and went off. The imperial butler reported him to the emperor, and when Shuo appeared at court, the emperor said, "Yesterday when the gift of meat was being given out, you did not wait for the imperial command but cut off a piece of the meat with your sword and made away with it. What do you mean by such behavior!"

---

[20] The small opening in a gate or wall for dogs to go in and out; the word "mouth" may also mean "door."

Shuo doffed his cap and apologized, but the emperor said, "Stand up, sir, and confess your faults!"

Shuo bowed twice and said, "All right now, Shuo! You accepted the gift without waiting for the imperial command — what a breach of etiquette! You drew your sword and cut the meat — what singular daring! When you carved it up, you didn't take much — how abstemious of you! You took it home and gave it to the little lady — how big-hearted!"

The emperor laughed and said, "I told you to confess your faults and here you are praising yourself!" Then he presented him with a further gift of a gallon of wine and a hundred catties of meat and told him to take them home to "the little lady."

— from chapter 65, "The Biography of Dongfang Shuo"

Madam Li, Imperial Concubine

Madam Li, a concubine of Emperor Wu the Filial, originally entered service in the palace as an entertainer. Her elder brother Li Yannian, who had an innate understanding of music, was skilled at singing and dancing and Emperor Wu took a great liking to him. Whenever he presented some new song or musical composition, there were none among his listeners who were not moved to admiration. Once when he was attending the emperor, he rose from his place to dance and sing this song:

> Beautiful lady in a northern land,
> standing alone, none in the world like her,
> a single glance and she upsets a city,
> a second glance, she upsets the state!
> Not that I don't know she upsets states and cities,
> but one so lovely you'll never find again!

The emperor sighed and said, "Splendid! — but I doubt there's anyone that beautiful in the world." The emperor's elder sister Princess Pingyang then informed him that Li Yannian had a little sister, and he forthwith had her summoned and brought before him. She was in fact strikingly beautiful and skilled at dancing as well, and because of this she won his favor.

She bore him a son, known posthumously as King Ai of Changyi, but died shortly afterwards at a very young age. The emperor, filled with grief and longing, had a portrait of her painted at the Palace of Sweet Springs. Later, Empress Wei was removed from the position of empress, and four years afterward, when Emperor Wu passed away, the general in chief He

Guang, following what he knew to have been the emperor's wishes, had sacrifices performed to Madam Li in the emperor's mortuary temple as though she had been his official consort, posthumously honoring her with the title Empress of Emperor Wu the Filial.

Earlier, when Madam Li lay critically ill, the emperor came in person to inquire how she was, but she pulled the covers over her face and, apologizing, said, "I have been sick in bed for a long time and my face is thin and wasted. I cannot let Your Majesty see me, though I hope you will be good enough to look after my son the king and my brothers."

"I know you've been very sick, and the time may come when you never rise again," said the emperor. "Wouldn't you feel better if you saw me once more and asked me face to face to take care of the king and your brothers?"

"A woman should not appear before her lord or her father when her face is not properly made up," she said. "I would not dare let Your Majesty see me in this state of disarray."

"Just let me have one glimpse of you!" said the emperor. "I'll reward you with a thousand pieces of gold and assign your brothers to high office!"

But Madam Li replied, "It is up to Your Majesty to assign offices as you please — it does not depend on one glimpse of me."

When the emperor continued to insist on one last look at her, Madam Li, sobbing, turned her face toward the wall and would not speak again. The emperor rose from his seat in displeasure and left.

Madam Li's sisters berated her, saying, "Why couldn't you let him have one look at you and entreat him face to face to take care of your brothers! Why should you anger him like this!"

"The reason I didn't want the emperor to see me," she said, "was so I could make certain he would look after my brothers! It was because he liked my looks that I was able to rise from a lowly position and enjoy the love and favor of the ruler. But if one has been taken into service because of one's beauty, then when beauty fades, love will wane, and when love wanes, kindness will be forgotten. The emperor thinks fondly and tenderly of me because he remembers the way I used to look. Now if he were to see me thin and wasted, with all the old beauty gone from my face, he would be filled with loathing and disgust and would do his best to put me out of his mind. Then what hope would there be that he would ever think kindly of me again and remember to take pity on my brothers?"

When Madam Li died, the emperor had her buried with the honors appropriate to an empress. After that, he enfeoffed her eldest brother, Li Guangli, the Sutrishna general, as marquis of Haixi, and appointed her brother Li Yannian as a chief commandant with the title Harmonizer of the Tones.

The emperor continued to think longingly of Madam Li and could not forget her. A magician from Qi named Shaoweng, announcing that he had the power to summon spirits, one night lit torches, placed curtains around them, and laid out offerings of wine and meat. He then had the emperor take his place behind another curtain and observe the proceedings from a distance. The emperor could see a beautiful lady who resembled Madam Li circling within the curtains, sitting down and then rising to walk again. But he could not move closer to get a good look and, stirred more than ever to thoughts of sadness, he composed this poem:

> Is it she?
> is it not?
> I stand gazing from afar:
> timid steps, soft and slow,
> how long she is in coming!

He then ordered the experts of the Music Bureau to devise a string accompaniment and make it into a song.

He also composed a work in *fu* or rhapsody form to express his grief at the loss of Madam Li....

Later, Li Yannian and his younger brother Li Ji were tried on charges of immoral behavior with the women of the palace, and Li Guangli, the eldest brother, surrendered to the Xiongnu. As a result, all the members of the Li family were put to death.

— from chapter 97, "Accounts of Families Related
to the Emperors by Marriage"

DOCTORS, DIVINERS, AND MAGICIANS

These biographies focus on a group of men who made their imprint on early Chinese history with technical skills in medicine, divination, and magic combined with talent for storytelling and political persuasion. From our present-day perspective, their personalities and lives were diverse, as were their particular arts and techniques. But in their own times, from the third century B.C. to the fourth or fifth century A.D., they were classified under the common rubric *fangshi*, and it became the practice of dynastic histories from the *History of the Later Han* on to present a selection of *fangshi* lives in a collective biography. [This brought new material into the literary tradition, and helped pave the way for the fictional genre of the Supernatural Tale, which has continued to fascinate the Chinese literary mind well into the twentieth century. *Eds.*]

During the flourishing days of the *fangshi*, the Han and early Six Dynasties (second century B.C. to fourth century A.D.), *fangshi* influence was significant in many areas of culture. Some people identified as *fangshi* were deeply involved in scientific thinking and technological activities, especially in the applied areas of calendrics, metallurgy, meteorology, pharmacology, geography, and biology. During periods of substantial imperial patronage, some *fangshi* achieved personal wealth and eminence in official-dom. Imperial favor was won by means of three promised contributions to the throne: maintenance of the emperor's youth and vitality; correction and maintenance of the standards of time, of space, of weight, and of pitch; and perception and interpretation of omens foretelling the future, illuminating obscurities of the present, and guiding the policies of the government so as to gain the favor of heaven.

FAN YE (398–445)
HISTORY OF THE LATER HAN
Three Biographies

Translated by Kenneth DeWoskin

Areas of Fan Ye's history clearly overlap with the newly popular Tales of the Strange and Supernatural [see chapter 16]. He indulged his personal interest in the occult arts to such an extent that his narratives were criticized for being "irregular," or "out of line."

Guo Yu, Physician

Guo Yu was a native of Luo in Guanghan. No one knew his origins nor where his father came from. Because Yu's father was always fishing in the Pei River, the people gave him the nickname Old Man Pei. Though his father mostly begged for his food, sometimes when he happened across a sick person he would perform acupuncture. When he did, it was always an effective treatment. He wrote two books, the *Classic of Acupuncture* and *Method of Examining Pulse*, both of which still circulate today. A disciple named Cheng Gao sought the old man's instruction for many years and was finally accepted. Gao too chose the life of a recluse.

Yu during his youth took Gao as his master, studying techniques for measuring and examining the six visceral functions and arts of the subtle side of yin and yang pulses.

During the reign of Emperor He (89–105), he served as assistant to the grand physician. His therapies proved to be highly effective. The emperor's curiosity was piqued by Yu, and he wanted to put Yu's skills to the test. So he selected a catamite with very delicate hands and wrists and placed him behind a curtain alongside a girl, so that each put out one arm. He then had Yu examine the pulse of both arms and asked him to identify the ailment of the "patient." Yu said, "The left arm is yang and the right arm is yin. A pulse is distinctly male or female. But this case would seem to be something different and your servant is puzzled as to why." The emperor sighed in admiration and praised his skill.

Yu was compassionate and loving, and he was never arrogant. Even for a patient as poor as the poorest peasant, Yu would exhaust his heart and soul. On the other hand, sometimes when treating a noble he was unable to effect a cure. On one occasion, the emperor ordered an ailing aristocrat to put on shabby clothes and move outside the palace. Guo Yu was able to cure him with a single needle. The emperor summoned Yu and asked him to explain this. Yu replied:

"The word 'medicine' *yi* embodies the idea of 'attention' *yi*. The regions of the skin are very finely divided. Following the flow of energy requires consummate skill. When inserting needles, an error of a hair's breadth will mean failure. A kind of spirit connects the physician's heart with his hand, and that is something I can know but cannot explain.

"Now, when it comes to the nobles, they look down at me from the heights of their distinguished place, and I am filled with anxiety that I might not please them. Curing nobles presents four difficulties. First, they do as they please and not as I advise. Second, they are not at all careful in caring for their own health. Third, their bones are frail, so they cannot bear strong medicine. Fourth, they love a life of ease and hate labor. Though the acupuncture needles demand precise measure, with them I am often in error. I am burdened with a heart full of trepidation compounded by a will reduced in strength. Thus attention is not fully there. Consider what influence this has on treating the disorder! This is the reason I cannot bring about a cure."

The emperor was pleased with this answer. Guo Yu died at an advanced age, still at his post.

Fei Changfang, Magician

Fei Changfang was a native of Runan. At one time, he served as a guard in the marketplace. There was an old man there who sold medicine at a stand with a large gourd hanging in front. When the market closed each day, the old man would promptly leap into the gourd. No one in the marketplace was able to see this, but Changfang, from his second-story vantage point, could. Thinking this very curious, Changfang went to pay a visit to the old man with gifts of wine and dried beef. Now, the old man knew that Changfang had an interest in his spiritual powers, so he told him, "You may come again tomorrow." Early the following morning, Changfang appeared again. This time the old man took Changfang with him into the gourd. Everywhere Changfang looked there were jade halls of awesome beauty and fine wines and rare delicacies overflowing. The two had a drink together and then came out again. The old man extracted a promise from Changfang that he would not discuss this event with anyone else.

Sometime later, the old man climbed up to Changfang's guard post to talk with him. "I am a spirit immortal, in exile as punishment for a transgression I committed. But today my sentence ends, and I must be leaving. Would you like to be able to come with me? In any case, downstairs I have a little wine to give you as a parting gift."

Changfang sent a man down to pick up the wine, but he could not. So Changfang sent ten men down to hoist it up, but they could not budge it either. When the old man heard this he laughed and went down himself. He returned carrying the wine with a single finger. The container appeared to be slightly more than a cup, but the two men drank from it all day and could not exhaust its contents.

Changfang developed a desire to seek the Way with the old man, but he feared his family would worry about him if he simply wandered off. The old man took a fresh bamboo stick and cut it off to the same height as Changfang's body. He had this hung behind the house, and when the family saw it, it appeared to them to be Changfang himself. They thought he had hung himself, and young and old alike wailed in shock and dismay. The body was quickly shrouded and interred. During all of this, Changfang stood to the side watching, but no one was able to see him.

With his funeral over, Changfang followed the old man deep into the mountains. Hiking over thick brambles, they eventually entered into the midst of a pack of tigers. The old man left Changfang alone there, but Changfang was not afraid. The old man then had him lie down in an open chamber with a ten-ton boulder over his heart, suspended by nothing more than a rotten piece of rope. A swarm of snakes crawled over each other for a chance to gnaw the rope in half, but Changfang did not so much as flinch. The old man returned and patted him. "You can indeed be taught."

But he tested him a third time by having him eat a pile of feces, foul with the worms of decay. The stench and filth were particularly loathsome, and deep inside Changfang felt disgust at this. The old man then told him, "You came so close to getting the Way. How regrettable that you should fail at this point. Alas, that's too bad!"

So Changfang said goodbye and was about to leave for home when the old man gave him a staff and said, "Ride this back to your home province so that you will be able to find your way alone. As soon as you arrive, take the staff and toss it into the Gebei Lake." He also made a charm for Changfang. "Take this and you will be master of terrestrial ghosts and spirits." So Changfang rode upon the staff and arrived home in no time at all. By his estimate, he had been away from his family for about ten days, but in reality it had been over ten years. As soon as he had tossed the staff into the lake, he could see it was a dragon. Now, the members of Changfang's family protested that he had been long dead and they refused to believe he was himself. Changfang explained to them, "What you buried so long ago was nothing more than a bamboo stick." Thereupon they dug up the grave, hacked open the coffin, and found the stick still there.

From that time on, Changfang was capable of curing all manner of illnesses. He could exorcise a hundred demons and was master of the deities of the local soil god altars. Once when he was sitting with a group of people, he suddenly showed signs of a great rage. Asked about this, he explained, "I was reprimanding some demons for breaking rules."

Year after year in the commandery of Runan, there appeared a demon dressed in the robes of the grand protector and impersonating him. He would visit the district office and pound on the alarm drums. Everyone in the commandery feared this demon. The time the demon was due just happened to coincide with a visit Fei Changfang himself was making to the grand protector. The demon was so terrified at this encounter he could not even retreat. He came forward, removed his false robes, and kowtowed, begging for his life. Changfang commanded him sternly, "Go to the courtyard and return to your original form!" He immediately transformed himself into an old tortoise, big as a wagon wheel, with a neck stretching some ten feet. Changfang then ordered the demon to approach the grand protector and beg forgiveness. Finally, he gave him a citation of warning to deliver to the Master of Gebei Lake. The tortoise kowtowed and wept bitterly. He carried off the wooden slip, and by the side of the lake stuck it end up in the ground. Then he wrapped his neck around the slip and died.

At a later time, the Master of Donghai paid a visit to the Master of Gebei Lake. During the visit, the Master of Donghai had illicit relations with Gebei's wife; so Changfang punished him with three years of confinement. As a consequence of this, a great drought beset the entire Donghai region. When Changfang visited that coast, he witnessed the people there pleading for rain, and so he explained to them, "Your Master of Donghai committed a crime, and I sentenced him to three years of confinement in Gebei. I will let him go now and have him make rain for you." Rain began to fall immediately.

Once when Changfang was traveling with some others, the group came upon a student riding bareback and wearing a yellow turban. As soon as they met, the student leaped down from the horse and began to kowtow. Changfang said to him, "Return the horse and I will pardon you for this capital crime!" When his friends asked what had transpired, Changfang explained, "This is a raccoon demon who stole the horse from the spirit of the local soil god altar."

And once when sitting with dinner guests, Changfang decided to go all the way to Yuan to buy salted fish. He went and returned in an instant, and the guests all were able to eat the fish. In other instances, Changfang was seen in several places, thousands of *li* apart, within a single day's time.

Later, he lost the charm that gave him his power and was murdered by a swarm of ghosts.

Zuo Ci, Magician

Zuo Ci, styled Yuanfang, was a native of Lujiang.[21] When he was young, it was apparent that he possessed a spiritual Way. There was an occasion on which he was a guest at a banquet given by the imperial grand clerk Cao Cao.[22] Cao casually turned to his guests at one point and remarked, "This is a distinguished assembly, for which fine and rare delicacies have been prepared. All that is missing is river perch from the Song River in the Wu region.[23] Zuo Ci, from his seat among the less honored guests, responded, "That can be gotten!" He called for a brass basin filled to the brim with water. Then he took a bamboo pole, baited a hook, and began fishing in the basin. Before long, he pulled out a perch. Cao smiled and applauded enthusiastically, while the guests all stood astonished. Then Cao said, "But one fish will not make the rounds of these tables. Can you

21 Anhui Province.
22 Subsequently founded the Wei dynasty. [See chapter 9.]
23 Southeast of Soochow.

get more?" Zuo Ci baited his line again, dropped it in, and in a little while he pulled out another fish. Both were over three feet long, and both were absolutely fresh and delicious. Cao had the fish minced before the very eyes of the guests and immediately passed around for everyone to enjoy.

Then Cao said, "Well, now that we have the fish, it is too bad that we do not have any fresh ginger from Shu." Ci replied, "That too can be gotten." Suspecting that there was some place nearby where Ci could get the ginger, Cao added to the test, "Sometime ago I dispatched a man to Shu to buy embroidered cloth. If you should happen to run into him, please tell him to increase the order by two bolts." He had hardly finished his instructions when Ci returned with the ginger in hand. He also reported success in passing on the new instruction to Cao's messenger. Much later, when that man returned from Shu, he was questioned about how he came to know to increase the order. His report coincided with what the guests had seen, down to the very hour of the very day.

On a later occasion, Cao was traveling outside the city in the company of over one hundred officials. For provisions, Ci carried along only a single cup of wine and one slab of dried meat. He personally did the serving and pouring, and not a single person among the hundred failed to get drunk and completely filled. Cao thought this was very strange and sent out people to investigate the matter. Upon visiting all the wine shops in the area, the investigators discovered that their stocks of wine and meat had been totally depleted. Cao was naturally quite unhappy to hear this, so he had Zuo Ci charged and arrested, and he planned to execute him. But Ci simply walked right through the wall and disappeared without a trace.

Then someone spied him in the marketplace and placed him under arrest. That same instant, however, every person in the marketplace changed into an exact image of Ci, and it became impossible to determine who was the real one. After that, someone came across him on Yangcheng Mountain.[24] Cao Cao pursued him there, chasing Ci into a flock of goats. Knowing that he could not simply grab him, Cao ordered his troops to go into the flock and announce, "Cao is no longer trying to kill you. It was originally nothing more than a test of your arts." Suddenly an old ram stood up like a man, his two front legs dangling down, and said, "What a sudden change!" All Cao's soldiers rushed forward to subdue the ram, but then the entire flock of several hundred changed into mirror images of the old ram, standing up like men, with their two

---

[24] Henan Province.

front legs dangling down, and saying, "What a sudden change!" Once again, there was no way to determine which one to capture.

Figure 21. Fei Changfang and the old man in the gourd. (Source: *Sancai tuhui*, Ming dynasty)

Figure 22. Zuo Ci. (Source: *Sancai tuhui*, Ming dynasty)

CHEN SHOU (233–297)
RECORDS OF THE THREE KINGDOMS
Two Biographies

Translated by Kenneth DeWoskin

Zhu Jianping, Physiognomist

Zhu Jianping was a native of Peiguo.[25] He was a skillful practitioner of the physiognomic arts among the common folk, and the effectiveness of his

---

[25] Jiangsu Province.

techniques had been proven many times. When the Grand Ancestor of our dynasty was Duke of Wei,[26] he heard about Jianping and summoned him to court to be a court gentleman. [His son, the future] Emperor Wen was serving as commander in chief, and there were over thirty retainers in his presence. Emperor Wen asked Jianping how long he could hope to live and then had him go about the room and make a physiognomic analysis of all the guests present.

"General," Jianping began, "Your lifespan should be eighty years, but at forty you will have a small crisis. Please take care to protect yourself." He told Xiahou Wei, "You will become a provincial governor. At the age of forty-nine, you will face a crisis, but if you manage to survive it, you will live to be seventy and rise to the post of ducal attendant."

He then told Ying Qu, "Sir, at age sixty-two you will become a high attendant official and will face a crisis. A year before that happens, you will see an apparition of a white dog, but it will be invisible to the people standing around you." Finally, Jianping told Cao Biao, "Sir, you will be occupying a vassal state and, when you reach fifty-seven, will become entangled in a military action. You should take care to prevent it."

Originally, Xun You and Zhong You, both of Yingchuan, were the most intimate of friends. Xun died first, when his son was still in infancy. His friend Zhong was naturally called to be executor of the estate and wanted to take Xun's concubine. He wrote the following to someone: "Xun You and I together once had Zhu Jianping do a divination for us. He told me then, 'Although Xun You is your junior, in fact it is fated that you will be left to manage his affairs.' When I heard that, I joked with him, saying, 'I will get his concubine Aying, and that's all!' What does it mean that now he has indeed died, and what I said only as a joke has come to be realized? Today I want to marry Aying; clearly it would be a good thing to do so. When I think back to the subtle vision of Jianping, I realize that even Tang Ju and Xu Fu could have added nothing to his prophecy."[27]

During the seventh year of the Huang-chu reign (226), Emperor Wen turned forty years old, and he was plagued with a grave illness. He told his attendants of the right and left, "The eighty years of which Jianping spoke must have been half in days and half in nights. I now face the point of crossing." In a very short while, he died.

---

[26] Cao Cao.

[27] Xu Fu was a celebrated diviner of the Former Han; Tang Ju was a celebrated physiognomer of the Warring States period who could perceive the future of anyone simply by glancing at him.

Xiahou Wei indeed became governor of Yan province. Early in the last month of the year, when he was forty-nine years old, he fell ill. Recalling Jianping's words, he reasoned that his lot was in fact to die at this time, so he began issuing his last testament and making preparations for the funeral so that everything would be in order when the time came. But two or three weeks later, his health turned about, and he recovered, almost to his former strength. On the afternoon of the last day of the month, he had his recording clerk pour some wine, and then he said, "The ailment from which I have been suffering has gradually subsided. Tomorrow morning when the cock crows, I will reach age fifty and the danger period in Jianping's prophecy will have passed." But after Wei bade his clerk good night and closed his eyes, the illness began to stir again. In the middle of the night he died.

At the age of sixty-one, Ying Qu became a palace attendant. When crossing through the inner palace he suddenly spied a white dog. He asked all the people around him, but not a single other person could see it. As a result of seeing this apparition, he began giving parties and chasing about on pleasure trips away from the capital. He gave himself over to drinking, and, after another year had passed, at age sixty-two, he died.

Cao Biao was enfeoffed as the king of Chu, but at age fifty-seven he conspired against the emperor with Wang Ling. When his plot was discovered, Cao was ordered to commit suicide.

In explaining the fates of this entire group, Jianping never missed the mark. But I am not too clear on some of the details, so I have just recorded the rough outlines of several events. Only in the prophecies of the minister of works, Wang Chang, the general of the northern expedition, Cheng Xi, and the major general, Wang Su, were there discrepancies. Su was sixty-two years old when he became critically ill. All his doctors felt that nothing could be done to save him, so his wife asked if he had any last words. Su said, "Jianping predicted that I would pass seventy and that I would rise to occupy one of the three ducal posts. Now none of this has come to pass, but I for one will not have to worry about it." Then he finally died.

Jianping was also skilled in divining the fates of horses. Once when Emperor Wen was about to go riding, he had his horse brought into the courtyard. Jianping happened upon the scene and said, "The physiognomy of this horse tells me he will die today." When the emperor was about to mount him, the horse shied at the fragrance of the emperor's robes, turned in fright, and nipped the emperor's knee. Emperor Wen was enraged by this and immediately had the beast put to death.

Jianping died in the middle of the Huang-chu reign (220–226).

Figure 23. Physiognomist's charts analyzing four typical faces. Clockwise from top right: "cold and lonely," "wicked and defiant," "crude and befuddled," and "weak and frail." (Source: *Sancai tuhui*, Ming dynasty)

Zhou Xuan, Diviner of Dreams

Zhou Xuan, styled Konghe, was a native of Le'an[28] and a commandery official. Grand Protector Yang Pei dreamed that someone came to him and said, "On the first day of the eighth month Duke Cao will arrive. He will give you a staff and fete you with medicinal wine." Pei had Xuan divine the meaning of this dream. This occurred right at the time that the Yellow Turban rebels[29] were on the rise, and Xuan said, "A staff assists the weak in standing and medicines cure the infirmities of men. On the

---

[28] Shandong Province.

[29] The Yellow Turbans were a widespread peasant rebel group at the end of the Later Han dynasty. Under the leadership of Zhang Jue, they embraced an ideology based on religious Taoism and wrapped their heads in yellow cloths when they banded together to fight. Their ranks numbered several hundred thousand, and they were a significant factor in the final demise of the Han.

first day of the eighth month, the rebels will be eliminated." When that day arrived, the rebels were indeed defeated.

Sometime later, Liu Zhen of Dongping dreamed of a snake that had four feet and dwelled in a hollow within his gatehouse. He asked Xuan to interpret this and was told, "This dream has relevance for the state. It does not concern your particular household, but foretells the killing of women who are bandits." In fact, before long, two female bandits, one of the Zheng clan and one of the Jiang clan, were wiped out. Xuan understood this because a snake ordinarily is an auspicious sign for women, but a snake should not have feet.

Emperor Wen asked Xuan, "I dreamed that two tiles fell from the palace ceiling and were transformed into a pair of mandarin ducks. What does this portend?"

Xuan explained, "In the rear palace [the women's quarters] someone will suffer a violent death." But the emperor confessed to Xuan, "I was only teasing you!" To this Xuan replied, "The fact is, dreams are nothing more than conceptions of the heart. If they even take form enough to be articulated, the waxing or waning fortunes they indicate can be divined." He had hardly finished speaking when the prefect of the yellow gate reported to the emperor that there had been a murder among the palace ladies.

Not much time had passed when Emperor Wen told Xuan, "Last night, I dreamed of a green vapor that arose from the ground and attached itself to the heavens."

Xuan explained, "A woman of noble birth will die unjustly." At that time the emperor had just dispatched a messenger to serve an imperial sentence on Lady Zhen. When he heard Xuan say this, he regretted having ordered the punishment, and immediately dispatched another man after the messenger to rescind the execution order. But the second man arrived too late.

The emperor also asked, "I dreamed that I was rubbing away at the design on a coin, trying to make it disappear. But the design only became brighter. What does this mean?"

Xuan was distraught, and he hesitated to answer. The emperor pressed him with the question again, and Xuan said, "This derives from a problem in Your Majesty's own household. Although you are wishing for something, the imperial mother does not concur. This is the reason the pattern only brightens, although you would like to rub it away."

At that time, it was true that the emperor wanted to inflict a punishment on his younger brother, Cao Zhi, and he was pressuring his mother to permit it. But the imperial mother was willing only to reduce Zhi in rank. The emperor recognized Xuan's abilities by making him a gentleman of the household attached to the office of the grand clerk.

Once someone asked Xuan, "Last night I dreamed that I saw a straw dog.[30] What does this portend?" Xuan replied, "Sir, you are about to have something very good to eat. That is all." A short while later he was traveling and happened to be invited to a great feast.

He subsequently asked Xuan, "Last night I dreamed again that I saw a straw dog. What about that?" Xuan replied, "Sir, you will fall from a cart and break your leg. Please be cautious!" And soon this too happened, exactly as Xuan had predicted.

And then the man asked again, "Last night I had the same dream of a straw dog. What this time?" Xuan replied, "Your house, sir, is in danger of being destroyed by fire. You should take good care to protect it." Almost immediately, a fire broke out.

After all this, the man said to Xuan, "From the very first to the very last, these dreams I reported to you never really happened. I just thought I would test you; that's all. How is it that the predictions you made from what I reported all came true?"

Xuan replied to him, "It is because you were moved and made to speak of these events by spiritual powers exactly as would have been the case with genuine dreams."

The man continued his questions: "Three times I reported dreams of a straw dog. Yet, all the predictions you made were different. How is that?"

Xuan said, "Straw dogs are things used in sacrifices to the spirits. Thus, when you reported your first dream, it meant that you would go to a great feast. As soon as the sacrifices are completed, the straw dogs are run over by a cart. Thus the second case indicated that you would fall from a cart and break your leg. After the straw dogs are crushed by the cart, they are loaded on it to be carried back and used for fuel. Therefore the final dream indicated concern over a fire."

All Xuan's descriptions of dreams were of this kind. He was right on target in eight or nine cases out of ten, and the people of his time likened his talent to the physiognomic skills of Jianping. The rest of his divinations were similar to the ones I have described above, so I will not continue to list them. Xuan died in the final years of the reign of Emperor Ming (226–239).

---

[30] Sacrificial effigies used especially in prayer for rain. As Zhou Xuan later explains, once the ritual is over, the straw bundles are crushed and burned.

IMMORTALS

𝄢𝄢𝄢𝄢𝄢𝄢𝄢𝄢𝄢𝄢𝄢𝄢𝄢𝄢𝄢𝄢𝄢𝄢𝄢𝄢𝄢𝄢𝄢𝄢𝄢𝄢𝄢𝄢𝄢

LIU XIANG (c. 79–c. 6 B.C.), attrib.
LIVES OF IMMORTALS
Five Biographies

Translated by Lionel Giles

The *Lives of Immortals* is the earliest extant collection of hagiographies of Taoist adepts who supposedly achieved the goal of immortality. Its seventy brief "biographies" typically list the Taoist skills acquired by the adept and describe a single important event from his life, often a dramatic departure from the "dusty" world. As a result of its fantastic content, the collection is sometimes seen as a forerunner of the Tales of the Strange and Supernatural of the Six Dynasties period [see chapter 16].

— Stephen Durrant, *Indiana Companion*, 1986

Ma Shi Huang, Horse Doctor

Ma Shi Huang was a horse doctor in the time of the Yellow Emperor. He knew the vital symptoms in a horse's constitution, and on receiving his treatment the animal would immediately get well. Once a dragon flew down and approached him with drooping ears and open jaws. Huang said to himself: "This dragon is ill and knows that I can effect a cure." Thereupon he performed acupuncture on its mouth just below the upper lip, and gave it a decoction of sweet herbs to swallow, which caused it to recover. Afterwards, whenever the dragon was ailing, it issued from its watery lair and presented itself for treatment. One morning the dragon took Huang on its back and bore him away.

Mao Nü, Hairy Woman

Mao Nü ("Hairy Woman"), whose style is Yujiang, has been seen by hunters on Mount Huayin[31] for many generations. Her body is covered with hair. She professes to be one of the ladies from Qin Shihuang's palace who, during the troubles that attended the downfall of the Qin dynasty, became a wandering fugitive and took refuge on the mountain. There she encountered the Taoist recluse Gu Chun, who taught her to

---

[31] This is Mt. Hua, the Sacred Peak of the West, not far from Chang'an.

eat pine-needles. In consequence of this diet she became immune from cold and hunger, and her body was so etherealized that it seemed to fly along. For over 170 years the mountain grotto in which she makes her abode has resounded to the thrumming of a lute.

Duzi, Master Calf

Duzi ("Master Calf") was a native of Ye. As a young man, he used to gather fir-cones and *fuling*[32] on the Black Mountain to diet himself with. For several hundred years he alternated between robust youth and old age, good looks and ugliness, so that he came to be recognized as an immortal. His usual round took him past the establishment of the vintner Yang Du, whose daughter sold wine in the marketplace. Her eyebrows met in the middle, and her ears were long and delicate. These marks were considered extraordinary, and everybody declared that she was a celestial being.

Now Duzi, while he was leading a yellow calf along the road, happened to meet Yang Du's daughter, and was so delighted with the girl that he arranged to keep her as his handmaid. She, therefore, went out in Duzi's company to gather peaches and plums. They would spend one night away and then return with a number of sacks full of fruit. People in the town tried to follow and keep a watch on them, but although they went out of the gate together, still leading the calf, no runner was able to overtake them, and there was nothing for it but to return.

The couple continued to frequent the marketplace for thirty years or more, and then they departed. They have been seen at the foot of Mt. Pan selling their peaches and plums in winter.

Wen Bin, Vendor of Straw Sandals

Wen Bin was a villager of Taiqiu (the modern Yongchengxian, Henan) who made his living as a vendor of straw sandals. He took a number of wives, turning them away after thirty years or so. At a later period, one of his former wives, who had now passed the age of ninety, saw Wen Bin again. He was still in the full vigor of manhood, and the old lady wept, and pleaded with him to take her back. Wen Bin excused himself, saying: "It wouldn't do; but could you perhaps meet me at the altar west of the

---

[32] Tubers of *Pachyma cocos*, a fungus growth upon the roots of fir-trees.

village pavilion, at daybreak on the first of the first moon?" Accordingly, the old lady, accompanied by her grandson, traveled over ten *li* by night and sat by the altar waiting for Pin. In a short time he arrived and was greatly surprised to see her. — "So you really love Tao, then?" he said. "Had I known that before, I should never have sent you away." He then instructed her to swallow chrysanthemum petals, *difu* (*Kochia scoparia*, Schr.), certain epiphytes of the mulberry, and pine-seeds. Thus increasing her store of vital energy, she too became rejuvenated, and was seen for more than a hundred years afterwards.

Yin Sheng, Beggar Boy

Yin Sheng was a beggar boy who lived under a bridge spanning the river Wei at Chang'an. He used to take up his stand in the marketplace and beg from those who did business there. On one occasion, disgusted by his importunity, they bespattered him with filth. Yet, when he appeared in his place again, his clothes were in their normal condition and showed no trace of dirt. The authorities, getting wind of the affair, had him arrested and thrown into chains; and yet he continued to beg in the marketplace. Being again arrested, and threatened with the death penalty, he left the city. But the houses of all those who had bespattered him collapsed in ruins, killing some dozen people. Hence the jingle which is current in Chang'an:

> If you meet a beggar boy, give him a drink,
> Or your house will fall down before you can wink.

GE HONG (283–343), attrib.
LIVES OF DIVINE IMMORTALS
Two Biographies

Translated by Lionel Giles

Lives of Divine Immortals continues the tradition of Taoist hagiography that began with the Han collection *Lives of Immortals*. But Ge Hong's biographies are longer and more detailed, which allows for a more satisfying portrayal of the immortals' personalities and activities. The collection's lively and entertaining narratives place it squarely within the tradition of the Six Dynasties Tales of the Strange and Supernatural. Interestingly, Gan Bao, author of the famous collection of tales *In Search of Spirits*, was a close associate of Ge Hong.

— Stephen Durrant, *Indiana Companion*, 1986

Liu An, Prince of Huainan

Liu An was Prince of Huainan under the Han dynasty.[33] In those days the young feudal princes made a virtue of extravagance: they spent their lives in music, making love, and hunting with dogs and horses. Liu An, on the contrary, maintained a humble demeanor, paying respectful attention to the learned. Scholarship was his constant and beloved pursuit, and he also acquired proficiency in prophecy and magic.

Taoists from all parts of the country visited Liu An's abode, and among others, eight worthies whose beards and eyebrows were all hoary white. The doorkeeper went first secretly and informed the Prince, who ordered him, as if on his own initiative, to put some puzzling questions to the newcomers. Accordingly he said: "Uppermost in our Prince's mind is a desire to seek the Tao that makes one live long without growing old; next, he wishes to find great scholars with a wide range of learning and intimate knowledge of abstruse subjects; and lastly, he wants lusty devil-may-care fellows whose strength is equal to the lifting of weighty tripods or attacking tigers unarmed. Now you, Sirs, are too old, and it is evident that you lack the magic means of warding off senility. How can you investigate profundities, or exercise control over things at a distance, thoroughly assimilate eternal principles, or perfect your moral nature? As you are wanting in these requirements I dare not announce you to the Prince."

To this the Eight Worthies smilingly replied: "If his Highness dislikes our antiquity, we will become young." Scarcely had they spoken these words than they all turned into youths of fourteen or fifteen. Their coils of hair became black and silky, and their complexions like peach-bloom. The doorkeeper, much amazed, went and told the Prince. Directly the Prince heard the news, he went, without putting on his shoes, barefooted to welcome them, and conducted them up to the Terrace of Meditation on Immortality, where he spread brocaded hangings over an ivory couch, kindled the Hundred Harmonies Incense, and placed before them tables of gold and jade.

The Prince paid them deference as if he were their disciple. Facing north,[34] he made obeisance to them, saying: "I am a man of mediocre ability. Since childhood I have loved Tao and the virtue it manifests. Fettered with ordinary occupations and sunk in the depths of mundane affairs, I cannot escape from my trammels and shoulder my satchel in order to live in the mountains and forests. Yet morning and evening I

---

[33] The following account has been somewhat abbreviated.
[34] Because the Eight occupied the place of honor facing South.

hunger and thirst while meditating on the glories of spiritual life, and long to wash away my muddy sediment of mortality... Earnestly I beg you Princes of Tao to pity and instruct me. Then, though now a crawling insect, I shall borrow the wings of a heron and be enabled to soar up into the sky."

Thereupon the eight youths turned into old men again and, addressing the Prince, said: "Although our knowledge is incomplete, and we possess merely the education of children, yet hearing that the Prince loves scholars, we have come to join him; but we have still to learn the Prince's mind and what it is he desires. One of us is able without effort to call up wind and rain, instantaneously to raise clouds and mists. He can trace lines across the land and they become rivers, and by scooping up the soil he can make mountains. Another of us can cause high hills to collapse, and the sources of deep springs to dry up. He can tame tigers and panthers, summon scaly monsters and dragons to appear, and press the spirits of heaven and earth into his service. Another of us can divide his personality and transform his shape, and is also able to become visible or invisible at will. He can hide whole army corps, and turn midday into night. Another can ride the clouds and tread the empyrean, cross the sea and walk upon the waves. He can go in and out where there is no crevice, or travel in a breath one thousand *li*. Another can enter flames unscathed and plunge into water without a wetting. He is invulnerable by sword or shaft. He feels no cold in winter frosts, nor does he sweat in summer heat. Another is capable of a myriad transformations: bird, beast, plant or tree — as the fancy takes him, he can become each or any of these. He can move mountains and bring rivers to a halt; he can transport a palace or shift a house. Another can boil mud into gold, or freeze lead into silver. He can fuse the eight minerals of the alchemist into a liquid from which pearls fly aloft in lieu of steam. He rides in a chariot of clouds with dragons for his team, and floats above the Great Purity.[35]

"Thou, O Prince, hast but to choose which of these powers thou desirest."

The upshot was that the magic drug was duly prepared, but the Prince did not yet proceed to swallow it. Before ascending to heaven he met some of the Immortal nobility. Having had but little practice in doing honor to others, and having seldom had occasion to perform the ceremonies of self-abasement, he showed some lack of politeness in his

---

[35] Taoists distinguish "Three Purities," each being the abode of Immortals: (1) Jade Purity; (2) Upper Purity; and (3) Great Purity. The latter is 40 *li* above the earth and of crystalline hardness.

demeanor, talked in too loud a voice, and made a blunder in referring to himself as the Solitary One.[36]

Thereupon the chief of the Immortal nobles formally accused him of disrespectful behavior, and said that he ought to be expelled from their company. The Eight Worthies, however, interceded for him, and a milder penalty was substituted: he was condemned to be Keeper of the Latrines at the capital for three years, after which he was to become an Immortal of the rank and file, ineligible for any official post, and merely exempted from mortality.

It is related by men who were living at this time that when Liu An and the Eight Worthies at last took their departure from this earth, the vessel containing the dregs of the elixir was left lying in the courtyard, and that the contents were finished up by the dogs and poultry of the establishment, with the result that they too sailed up to heaven; thus, cocks were heard crowing in the sky, and the barking of dogs resounded amidst the clouds.

Jiao Xian: Fire and Snow

Jiao Xian was a native of Hedong (Shanxi). At the age of one hundred and seventy he was in the habit of eating white stones after boiling them thoroughly like yams and used to distribute them to others. Every day he went into the mountains to cut fuel, which he gave away to the headman and other villagers in turn, after which he began afresh. Carrying the fuel on his back, he would deposit it outside each man's door. Anyone who happened to see him would spread a mat and invite him in to partake of a meal. Jiao Xian would then sit down but say not a word to his host. If he saw no one when he came with his fuel, he would put it down silently at the door and go away. So it went on year after year.

When the House of Wei established their dynasty, he was dwelling on the bank of the Yellow River, having built himself a thatched hut in which he lived quite alone. He had no proper bed, but sat on a straw mattress. His body was dirty, as if he had been soused in liquid mud. Sometimes he would go several days without eating. In walking he did not keep to the path. He shunned the company of women. When his clothes wore out he would sell some firewood in order to buy old garments to replace them. Winter and summer alike, he wore clothing of a single thickness.

The Governor Dong Jing went to pay him a visit, but Xian refused to speak to him. This only heightened Jing's opinion of his worth.

---

[36] A title used only by the reigning emperor.

Eventually his hut was caught in a forest fire, and men who came to look for Xian found him sitting upright and motionless under the roof. When the fire had burned itself out and the hut lay in ashes, Xian got up quite calmly, and then it appeared that his clothes were not even singed.

After he had made himself another hut, there suddenly came a great snowfall, which wrecked a large number of houses. Xian's hut collapsed, and a party of rescuers, seeing no trace of him, feared that he must have frozen to death. But on digging their way into the hut they found him fast asleep under the snow, with a ruddy face and breathing freely, just like a man lying drunk in the height of summer.

People recognized that he was no ordinary being, and many wished to learn from him about Tao; but Xian declared that there was no Tao in him. Thus he continued, now old and now young, for more than two hundred years. At last he parted from his fellow men and went no one knows whither. Those who had questioned him got not a single word to appease their curiosity.

Three Biographies

Translated by Benjamin Penny

Shen Jian: Balls of Medicine

Shen Jian was a native of Danyang. His family had been senior officials for generations but Jian only loved the Tao and refused to take up an official career. He studied gymnastics and the ingestion of drugs as well as the methods for turning back the years and reversing aging. He could also treat disease. Whether the disease was serious or mild — if Jian treated it, it was cured. Several hundred families honored him.

Once when he was about to go on a long journey he gave a ball of medicine to each of his four or five slaves and servants, to his donkey, and to his several tens of goats. He said to the man in charge, "Just tether them up in the house. Don't bother giving them food or drink." Then he left. The man in charge thought this very strange and said, "This gentleman has provided less than a foot-long strip of food for more than fifteen slaves and beasts. What should I do?"

After Jian left, the man in charge gave food and drink to the slaves and servants. When the slaves tasted the food they spat it out and would not look at it. He also gave grass to the donkey and the goats, but they avoided it and would not eat. Then they started to butt people. The man in charge was astounded.

More than a hundred days later the bodies of the slaves and servants were glowing and shining — different from when they had been eating. The donkeys and goats were fat. Shen Jian returned after three years and gave each of the slaves and servants and the donkey and goats another ball of medicine, and they returned to eating and drinking as before.

Jian then gave up grains and stopped eating. He was able to make his body rise up and fly around, sometimes leaving and sometimes coming back. It was like this for more than three hundred years. Then he disappeared without trace. Nobody knows where he went.

Li Babai: Eight Hundred

Li Babai, which means eight hundred, was a native of Shu. No one knew his given name. He had been seen generation after generation, so people of that time reckoned he was already eight hundred years old. That was how he got his name. Sometimes he lived as a recluse in the mountain forests; sometimes he lived in the market.

Eight Hundred knew that Tang Gongfang of Hanzhong had the will but had not met with an enlightened teacher. Wanting to hand the knowledge over to Gongfang, Eight Hundred first went to test him out, working in his household as a servant. Gongfang did not know that he was an Immortal. Eight Hundred ran errands for him, and served him with a devotion exceeding that expected of the other servants; so Gongfang loved him all the more.

Later Eight Hundred feigned an illness that brought him to the verge of death. Gongfang ordered a doctor to come and blend herbs — the cost was several hundred thousand cash but he did not grudge the expense. His thoughts were full of grief; and it showed on his face. Eight Hundred then produced evil boils all over his own body through cyclical transformation. The boils burst, they were rank and foul-smelling, and nobody was able to get close to him. Gongfang wept, "You have become so sick after working hard for my family over the years. I really want you to be healed. There is nothing I would not do for you to get better! What else can I do?" Eight Hundred said, "My boils can be healed. Hurry and get somebody to lick them." Gongfang ordered three female slaves to lick them. Then Eight Hundred said, "The licking of slaves cannot heal me. If you, Sir, will lick them, then healing will result." Gongfang then licked them himself. Eight Hundred said, "Your licking cannot heal me either. If your wife will lick them I will be cured." Gongfang then made his wife lick them. Eight Hundred said, "My boils are gone! Please fetch one hundred and fifty gallons of the finest wine for me to bathe in and I will be completely healed." Gongfang then prepared the wine and poured it into a bath. Eight Hundred washed and was healed. The texture of his skin was as smooth as congealed fat, and there was no scarring. Then he told Gongfang, "I am an Immortal. You had the will, so I came here to test you, and you certainly can be taught. Now I can give you the instructions for transcending the generations." Then he sent Gongfang, his wife, and the three servants who had licked his boils to bathe in the remaining wine themselves. After they had washed they were all young again. Their faces were beautiful and full of joy. Eight Hundred handed the *Elixir Scripture* in one roll over to Gongfang. Gongfang then entered Mount Yuntai and blended the elixir. When it was complete, he swallowed it and went off as an Immortal.

Jie Xiang: Minced Fish and Ginger

Jie Xiang was a native of Kuaiji. He studied the five classics thoroughly, had broadly examined the words of the hundred schools of philosophy, and was able to write literary compositions. Later he studied the Tao and entered Mount Dong. He was expert in the techniques of transcending the generations and inhibiting with *qi*. He was able to light a fire on a thatched roof, cook a chicken in it, and yet not burn the thatch. He could command that all the cooking in the households a mile round would not produce cooked food and that their dogs and chickens would not bark or cluck for three days. He could command that all people in a market sit and be unable to rise. He could disguise himself by transforming himself into plants, trees, birds, or animals.

When he heard of the *Five Elixirs Scripture* he went all over the empire to seek it out but did not find a teacher. Then he entered the mountains and refined his thoughts in the hope of meeting an Immortal. At the height of exhaustion, he lay down on a rock. A tiger approached and licked him on the forehead. He awoke and saw the tiger and spoke to him. "If Heaven sent you to come and protect me, you may desist. If the mountain spirits sent you to test me out, then hurry off!" The tiger then left.

Xiang entered a mountain ravine. At the head of it were some stones that were purple and brilliant, very beautiful and as big as hen's eggs. It was impossible to estimate how many there were. He took two of them. The ravine was so deep he could not go on, so he went back the way he had come.

In the mountains he saw a beautiful girl of about fifteen or sixteen. Her face was extraordinary, and her clothes were of many colors. She was an Immortal. Xiang begged for a recipe for long life. The girl said, "If you, Sir, were to return what you have in your hands it would be possible. You ought not to have taken them, so I must cease attending to you." When Xiang returned the stones he saw the girl in front of him. She said, "You have not completely cleared yourself of the *qi* of flesh. Stop eating grains for three years and then come back. I shall stay here." Xiang went home.

After doing without grains for three years he returned and saw the girl in front of him in the same place as before. She then presented Xiang with the *Reversion Elixir Scripture* in one chapter and she announced to him, "With this you can attain immortality — you will need nothing else."

Xiang normally slept at the residence of his disciple Luo Tingya. On a screen couch below the curtains, there were several students discussing the meaning of the *Zuo Commentary* and they could not agree. Xiang, listening from the side, could not forbear and angrily resolved the issue. The students knew that he was not an ordinary man and secretly recommended him to Sun Quan, the Ruler of the state of Wu. When Xiang knew of this he wanted to leave and said, "I fear that official service will constrain me." But Tingya insisted that he stay.

When Sun Quan heard about Xiang, he summoned him to Wuchang, where he did him great honor and addressed him as Lord Jie. He had a house erected, supplied him with imperial screens, and gave him a great deal of money. From Xiang he learnt the techniques of hiding his form. He tried them out when returning to the Rear Palace, where the women lived, and left through the gate of the hall without being seen.

He also made Xiang perform transformations: Xiang planted melons, vegetables, and all sorts of fruit that all immediately grew and could be eaten.

Sun Quan discussed with Xiang which kind of minced fish was the tastiest. Xiang said, "The *zi* fish is best." Then Sun Quan said, "I was talking about fish that come from local districts. That is a sea fish. Would it be possible to get one?" Xiang said, "It is possible." Then he ordered someone to go into the hall and dig a square hole. He filled it with water, asked for a hook, baited up a line, and dangled it in the hole. After a short time he had caught a *zi* fish. Sun Quan was amazed and delighted. "Is it edible?" he asked. Xiang said, "I caught it so that Your Majesty could have fresh minced fish. Why would I dare catch something inedible?" Then he sent it to the kitchen to be chopped up.

Sun Quan said, "I have heard that an emissary of the state of Shu came. If we had some Shu ginger to use as a garnish, it would be very tasty, but alas, he will have gone by now." Xiang said, "Shu ginger is easy to get. Can you spare a messenger and the money for it?" Sun Quan then indicated one of his attendants and gave him fifty cash. Xiang wrote a talisman and inserted it into a green bamboo staff. He told the traveler to close his eyes and mount the staff. When the staff stopped he was to buy ginger, then close his eyes again. After taking in these instructions, the man mounted the staff and in a short time it came to a halt. He had arrived in Chengdu but did not know where he was, so he asked someone. That person said he was in the Shu market, so he bought ginger. Just at that time, Zhang Wen, the emissary from Wu, who was already resident in Shu, happened to be in the market and recognized him. He was extremely surprised and wrote a report to send home. When the man had bought the ginger, he took the report, put the ginger on his back, mounted the staff and closed his eyes. In a short time he was back in Wu. In the kitchen, the fish had only just been cut up.

Later Xiang announced that he was ill. Sun Quan sent his courtiers and concubines to give Xiang a makeup case full of beautiful pears. Xiang ate them and a short time later was dead. Sun Quan interred him. He died at noon, but by mid-afternoon of the same day Xiang reached Jianye. He handed over seeds from the pears he had been given to the orchard official to plant. Later the official sent in a report about it. Then Sun Quan immediately disinterred the coffin and looked inside. There was nothing but a talisman there. He pondered on this and erected a shrine. From time to time he went there himself and made offerings. White cranes would often come and gather on the shrine, then slowly return whence they came.

Later a disciple saw him in Mount Lanzhu. He looked as if he had become his youthful self again.

▣ Further Reading ▣

DeWoskin, Kenneth J., ed. and trans. *Doctors, Diviners, and Magicians of Ancient China: Biographies of Fang-shih*. New York: Columbia University Press, 1983.

Dubs, Homer H., trans. *The History of the Former Han Dynasty by Pan Ku*. 3 vols. Baltimore: Waverly, 1938–55.

Giles, Lionel, ed. and trans. *A Gallery of Chinese Immortals: Selected Biographies*. London: John Murray, 1948.

Nienhauser, William H., Jr., ed. and trans. *The Grand Scribe's Records: The Basic Annals of Pre-Han China*. 9 vols. Bloomington: Indiana University Press, 1994–.

Watson, Burton, ed. and trans. *Courtier and Commoner in Ancient China: Selections from the History of the Former Han by Pan Ku*. New York: Columbia University Press, 1974.

———. trans. *Records of the Grand Historian of China*. 2 vols. New York: Columbia University Press, 1961. (A revised edition in 3 volumes was published by Columbia University Press/*Renditions* in 1993.)

Yang, Gladys and Xianyi, eds. and trans. *Records of the Historian*. Hong Kong: Commercial Press, 1974.

Chapter 8

We Fought South of the City Wall

Ballads and Folksongs of the Han and Six Dynasties

When men and women had anything they were grieved or angry about, they got together and made a song, the hungry man singing of a meal, the weary man singing of his task.

> — He Xiu (129–182), commentary on the *Gongyang Commentary*,
> Duke Xuan, 15th year (*translated by Burton Watson*)

Ordinary men and women express their feelings in local folk songs; these songs were gathered by official poetry collectors and set to music by music masters. These feelings set silk strings and bamboo reeds vibrating while the living spirit informed the brass instruments and stone bells.

> — Liu Xie, *The Literary Mind and the Carving of Dragons*, chapter 7, "Ballads"

Introduction: Ballads from the Music Bureau

Burton Watson

Emperor Wu of the Han (140–87 B.C.) set up an office called the Yuefu or Music Bureau, one of whose functions was to collect folksongs from the countryside, as had been done in antiquity, and use them to determine the mood of the populace. It is probably due to Emperor Wu's bureau, and the importance which educated men in general attached to works in the folksong form, that we possess a number of songs, known collectively by the term *yuefu*, which date from Han times.... The ailing wife, the orphan, or the gray-haired veteran who returns after years of service to his old village are among the most famous figures in the *yuefu* songs of the Han. Love, as in earlier times, continues to be an important theme, sometimes that of unnamed lovers, sometimes of historical or pseudo-historical personages. By far the longest poem of the period, a ballad entitled "Southeast the Peacock Flies," which tells of a young couple who are forced by the groom's mother to separate and who eventually commit suicide, is said to have been based upon an actual tragedy of that nature that occurred in the Jian-an period (196–220). Many of the songs are meant merely to amuse and entertain, pleasant accompaniments to the banquets and drinking bouts of the well-to-do, but others, such as those which complain of the hardships of military service or the poverty of the oppressed peasantry, are clearly intended as works of social protest in the old tradition of the *Book of Songs*....

   In the period of disunity that followed the Han, love songs like those of the *Book of Songs* appeared again. Perhaps, as traditional scholars would no doubt claim, their appearance indicates a decline of public morality due to the temporary waning of Confucian influence; perhaps it only means that literate men at this time felt daring enough to record what had existed all along but had earlier been passed over in silence. Whatever the reason, the impatient lovers who in the time of the *Songs* had slipped out to a rendezvous by the city gate or climbed over walls and crept into midnight chambers once more make their entrance on the poetic scene.

   The love songs are brief and usually quite direct. Like the Japanese *kouta*, which they closely resemble, they rely for their effect upon simple nature imagery, often indicative of the particular season, puns and word plays, and an engaging air of sauciness and candor.

— *Chinese Lyricism*, 1971

Figure 24. Beating the drum. Han dynasty rubbing. (Source: *Chinese Rubbings* [Beijing: Guoji shudian, n.d.])

HAN DYNASTY

Eleven Poems

Translated by Anne Birrell

Greening Yang

One of a set of seasonal hymns which liturgically articulate the Han cosmological theory of the Five Elements and Yin and Yang.

Greening Yang starts to stir,
Causing root and bulb to obey,
Its rich moisture loving all alike.
Padpaw creatures their own ways come forth,
The sound of thunder brings out flowers' glory.
Lair-dwellers lean to hear.
The barren again give birth,
And so fulfill their destiny.
All the people rejoice, rejoice.
Blessings are on the young and pregnant.
All living things are quickened, quickened.
Such is the good gift of Spring.

A Withered Fish

The moral of the fable is that the imprudent and the unwary will come to a sad end.

A withered fish by a river wept.
Too late for remorse now!
He wrote a letter to carp and bream
Warning them: Mind how you come and go!

The Ballad of the Orphan Boy

One of the most lucid narrative ballads in the Han repertoire.

The life of an orphan boy;
An orphan boy's encounter with life.
Fated to be wretched and alone.
When Father and Mother were alive
We rode in a strong carriage,
Drove a team of four horses.
Now Father and Mother are gone,

My older brother and his wife make me trade;
South to Jiujiang,
East to Qi and Lu.
In the La month I come home,[1]
But daren't speak of my misery.
My hair is full of nits,
My face and eyes full of dust.
My big brother says, "Get the meal ready."
My big sister says, "Look after the horses."
Up I go to the high hall,
Then hurry down to the lower hall.
The orphan boy's tears fall like rain.
They make me go and draw water at dawn,
At dusk I must fetch water again.
My hands have become chapped,
My feet go without straw sandals.
Aching, aching I tread on frost,
Among many prickly root crops I walk.
I pull up and break the thorns,
My calves hurt so I want to scream.
Tears fall spurting, spurting,
Clear tears flooding, flooding.
In winter I have no lined coat,
In summer no unlined robe.
To live unhappily
Is not as good as an early death,
Following on down to Yellow Springs.
Spring air quickens,
Grass shoots sprout.
In the third month silkworm mulberry,
In the sixth month I harvest melons.
Pushing the melon cart
I come back home again.
When my melon cart overturns
A few help me,
But many devour my melons.
I want people to give back the vines —
Brother and his wife are strict.

---

[1] The twelfth lunar month.

Empty-handed, I'd better hurry home
To face their reckoning.

Envoi

"In the village what shouting, shouting!
I want to send a foot-long letter
To the underworld to Father and Mother:
With Brother and his wife I can't live much longer!"

At Fifteen I Joined the Army

This powerful anti-war ballad is possibly the work of a lettered poet, adapting a
popular song.

At fifteen I joined the army,
At eighty I first came home.
On the road I met a villager,
"At my home what kin are there?"
"Look over there — that's your home!"
Pine, cypress, burial mounds piled, piled high,
Hares going in through dog-holes,
Pheasants flying in through rafter tops;
The inner garden grown wild with corn,
Over the well wild mallow growing.
I pound grain to serve for a meal,
I pick mallow to serve for broth.
Once broth and meal are cooked
I'm at a loss to know whom to feed.
I leave by the gates, look east.
Tears fall and soak my clothes.

We Fought South of the City Wall

Despite its difficulties of interpretation, and fraught as it is with textual problems, this
stark song of protest retains its age-old power to inspire admiration and sympathy.

We fought south of the city wall.
We died north of the ramparts.
In the wilderness we dead lie unburied, fodder for crows.
Tell the crows for us:
"We've always been brave men!
In the wilderness we dead clearly lie unburied,

So how can our rotting flesh flee from you?"
Waters deep, rushing, rushing,
Reeds and rushes, darkening, darkening.
Heroic horsemen fought and died fighting,
Flagging horses whinnied in panic.
Raftered houses we built,
And south, alas! and north;
If grain and millet aren't reaped, what will you eat, Lord?
We longed to be loyal vassals, but how can that be?
I remember you, good vassals,
Good vassals I truly remember:
In the dawn you went out to glory,
At nightfall you did not return.

Mulberry on the Bank

In this fine example of Han balladic art, the mulberry-picking girl responds to an attempted seduction with a forthright refusal.

Sunrise at the southeast corner
Shines on our Qin clan house.
The Qin clan has a fair daughter,
She is called Luofu.
Luofu loves silkworm mulberry,
She picks mulberry at the wall's south corner.
Of green silk her basket strap,
Of cassia her basket and pole.
On her head a twisting-fall hairdo,
At her ears bright moon pearls.
Of apricot silk her lower skirt,
Of purple silk her upper blouse.
Passersby see Luofu,
They drop their load, stroke their beard.
Young men see Luofu,
They take off their caps, put on headbands.
The ploughman forgets his plough,
The hoer forgets his hoe.
They come home cross and angry,
All from seeing Luofu.

A prefect comes from the south,
His five horses paw the ground.
The prefect sends his sergeant forward:

"Ask: Whose is the pretty girl?"
"The Qin clan has a fair daughter,
She is called Luofu."
"Luofu, how old is she?"
"Not yet quite twenty,
A bit more than fifteen."
The prefect invites Luofu:
"Would you like to ride with me?"
Luofu comes forward and rejoins:
"The Prefect is so foolish!
The Prefect has his own wife,
Luofu has her own husband.

"In the east more than a thousand horsemen,
My bridegroom is in the lead.
How would you recognize my bridegroom?
His white horse follows jet-black colts,
Green silk plaits his horses' tails,
Yellow gold braids his horses' heads.
At his waist a Lulu dagger[2]
Worth maybe more than ten million cash.
At fifteen he was a county clerk,
At twenty a palace official,
At thirty a gentleman-in-waiting,
At forty lord of his own city.
As a man he has a pure white complexion,
Bushy whiskers on both cheeks.
Majestic he steps to the courthouse,
Solemn he strides to the courtroom,
Where several thousand in audience
All say my bridegroom is unique!"

West Gate Ballad

The singer ends this *carpe diem* song by ruefully admitting to poverty. He is unable to pay for the fun he has been advocating.

Leaving by West Gate
I pace and think of it:
If today I don't make merry,

---

[2] A dagger the hilt of which was decorated with a well-pulley motif.

How long must I wait?
Hasten to make merry!
Hasten to make merry —
While there's time!
Can sad despair overwhelm me?
Must I keep waiting for next year?
Brew fine wine!
Roast the fat ox!
Call for my heart's delight,
May be to dispel dull care.
Man's life does not last a century,
He ever nurses worries of one thousand years.
Morning is short alas! night is long,
Why not hold a candle and have fun?
Let's go and have fun, away! away! as clouds pass on.
But a worn cart, a lean nag, that's my lot!

Dew on the Shallot

An early hearse-puller's song.

On the shallot the dew —
How easily it dries!
The dew dried at bright dawn once more will drop.
Man dies — once he's gone when will he come back?

Artemisia Village

Another graveyard song. According to an old legend, when a person died, his two souls, the *hun* and *po*, went back to live in Artemisia Village.

Artemisia Village — whose is this land?
It's for teeming souls and spirits, none wise, none fool.
The King of Ghosts, how he hurries them along!
Man is fated never to linger long.

Almighty on High!

A love song, sung by a girl to her lover, in the form of a mock-serious oath to the supreme deity.

Almighty on High!
I long to know my lord,

Let our love never fade or die
Till mountains have no peaks,
Or rivers run dry,
Till thunder roars in winter,
Or snow pours down in summer,
Till the skies merge with the ground —
Then may I die with my lord!

The One I Love

More than a simple plaint about a fickle lover, this song depicts the giddy romance of an impulsive, naive young girl of a well-to-do family, who believed that the attentions of a young official were serious.

The one I love
Is south of the great lakes.
What shall I send you?
A tortoiseshell hatpin with twin pearls,
With jade I'll braid and plait it.
I hear that you have another love —
I will break it, smash and burn it,
Smash and burn it,
Face into the wind, scatter its ashes.
From this day on
Nevermore will I love you.
My love for you is severed.
Cocks crow, dogs bark.
My brother and his wife must find out.
Alas! Oh my!
Autumn winds sough, sough. Dawn Wind hastens.[3]
The east at a blink whitening will find out!

Ten Old Poems

Translated by Arthur Waley

The following ten poems are from a series known as the Nineteen Pieces of Old Poetry. Some have been attributed to Mei Sheng [first century B.C. — see chapter 6], and some to Fu Yi [first century A.D.]. They are manifestly not all by the same hand nor

---

[3] The peregrine falcon, a metaphor for the swift passage of time.

of the same date. Internal evidence shows that the third poem below at least was written after the date of Mei Sheng's death. These poems had an enormous influence on all subsequent poetry, and many of the habitual clichés of Chinese verse are taken from them.

Life-Parting

On and on, always on and on
Away from you, parted by a life-parting.[4]
Going from one another ten thousand *li*,
Each in a different corner of the World.
The way between is difficult and long,
Face to face how shall we meet again?
The Tartar horse prefers the North wind,
The bird from Yüe nests on the Southern branch.
Since we parted the time is already long,
Daily my clothes hang looser round my waist.
Floating clouds obscure the white sun,
The wandering one has quite forgotten home.
Thinking of you has made me suddenly old,
The months and years swiftly draw to their close.
That I'm cast away and rejected I must not repine;
Better to hope that you eat your rice and thrive.

The Grass by the River-Bank

Green, green,
The grass by the river-bank.
Thick, thick,
The willow trees in the garden.
Sad, sad,
The lady in the tower.
White, white,
Sitting at the casement window.
Fair, fair,
Her red-powdered face.
Small, small,
She puts out her pale hand.

---

[4] The opposite of a parting by death.

Once she was a dancing-house girl,
Now she is a wandering man's wife.
The wandering man went, but did not return.
It is hard alone to keep an empty bed.

The Cypress on the Mound

Green, green,
The cypress on the mound.
Firm, firm,
The boulder in the stream.
Man's life lived within this world
Is like the sojourning of a hurried traveler.
A cup of wine together will make us glad,
And a little friendship is no little matter.

Yoking my chariot I urge my stubborn horses,
I wander about in the streets of Wan and Luo.[5]
In Luo Town how fine everything is!
The "Caps and Belts"[6] go seeking each other out.
The great boulevards are intersected by lanes,
Wherein are the townhouses of Royal Dukes.
The two palaces stare at each other from afar,
The twin gates rise a hundred feet.
By prolonging the feast let us keep our hearts gay,
And leave no room for sadness to creep in.

Man in the World Lodging

Of this day's glorious feast and revel
The pleasure and delight are difficult to describe.
Plucked from the lute in a swift, tumultuous jangling
The new melodies in beauty reached the divine.
Skillful singers intoned the high words,
Those who knew the tune heard the trueness of their singing.
We sat there each with the same desire
And like thoughts by each unexpressed:

---

[5] Nanyang and Luoyang in Henan.
[6] High officers.

"Man in the world lodging for a single lifetime
Passes suddenly like dust borne on the wind.
Then let us hurry out with high steps
And be the first to reach the highways and fords,
Rather than stay at home wretched and poor,
For long years plunged in sordid grief."

Man's Life a Sojourning

I drive my chariot up to the Eastern Gate;
From afar I see the graveyard north of the Wall.
The white aspens how they murmur, murmur;
Pines and cypresses flank the broad paths.
Beneath lie men who died long ago;
Black, black is the long night that holds them.
Deep down beneath the Yellow Springs,
Thousands of years they lie without waking.

In infinite succession light and darkness shift,
And years vanish like the morning dew.
Man's life is like a sojourning,
His longevity lacks the firmness of stone and metal.
For ever it has been that mourners in their turn were mourned,
Saint and Sage — all alike are trapped.
Seeking by food to obtain immortality
Many have been the dupe of strange drugs.
Better far to drink good wine
And clothe our bodies in robes of satin and silk.

No Road Back

The dead are gone and with them we cannot converse;
The living are here and ought to have our love.
Leaving the city gate I look ahead
And see before me only mounds and tombs.
The old graves are ploughed up into fields,
The pine and cypresses are hewn for timber.
In the white aspens sad winds sing;
Their long murmuring kills my heart with grief.
I want to go home, to ride to my village gate;
I want to go back, but there's no road back.

Take a Lamp and Wander Forth

The years of a lifetime do not reach a hundred,
Yet they contain a thousand years' sorrow.
When days are short and the dull nights long,
Why not take a lamp and wander forth?
If you want to be happy you must do it now,
There is no waiting till an after-time.
The fool who's loath to spend the wealth he's got
Becomes the laughing-stock of after ages.
It is true that Master Wang[7] became immortal,
But how can we hope to share his lot?

The Year Draws to Its End

Cold, cold the year draws to its end,
The mole-cricket makes a doleful chirping.
The chill wind increases its violence.
My wandering love has no coat to cover him.
He gave his embroidered furs to the Lady of Luo,
But from me his bedfellow he is quite estranged.
Sleeping alone in the depth of the long night
In a dream I thought I saw the light of his face.
My dear one thought of our old joys together,
He came in his chariot and gave me the front reins.
I wanted so to prolong our play and laughter,
To hold his hand and go back with him in his coach.
But when he had come he would not stay long
Nor stop to go with me to the Inner Chamber.
Truly without the falcon's wings to carry me
How can I rival the flying wind's swiftness?
I go and lean at the gate and think of my grief,
My falling tears wet the double gates.

At the Beginning of Winter

At the beginning of winter a cold spirit comes,
The North Wind blows — chill, chill.

---

[7] Wang Ziqiao, who ascended to Heaven on a white crane. [See chapter 14.]

My sorrows being many, I know the length of the nights,
Raising my head I look at the stars in their places.
On the fifteenth day the bright moon is full,
On the twentieth day the "toad and hare" wane.[8]
A stranger came to me from a distant land
And brought me a single scroll with writing on it;
At the top of the scroll was written "Do not forget,"
At the bottom was written "Good-bye for ever."
I put the letter away in the folds of my dress,
For three years the writing did not fade.
How with an undivided heart I loved you
I fear that you will never know or guess.

The Bright Moon

The bright moon, oh how white it shines,
Shines down on the gauze curtains of my bed!
Racked by sorrow I toss and cannot sleep;
Picking up my clothes, I wander up and down.
My absent love says that he is happy,
But I would rather he said he was coming back.
Out in the courtyard I stand hesitating, alone;
To whom can I tell the sad thoughts I think?
Staring before me I enter my room again;
Falling tears wet my mantle and robe.

Southeast the Peacock Flies

Translated by Burton Watson

A brief preface of unknown date states that the following poem, which concerns a
government clerk of Lujiang in Anhui named Jiao Zhongqing and his young wife, Liu
Lanzhi, is based on an actual event that took place in the Jian-an era (196–220).

Southeast the peacock flies,
and every five *li* it hesitates in flight.

"At thirteen I knew how to weave plain silk,
at fourteen I learned to cut clothes;

---

[8] The "toad and hare" correspond to our "man in the moon." The waning of the moon
symbolizes the waning of the lover's affection.

at fifteen I played the many-stringed lute,
at sixteen recited from the *Songs* and *History*.
At seventeen I became your wife,
but in my heart there was always sorrow and pain.
You were a clerk in the government office,
I guarded my virtue and was never untrue.
At cockcrow I began my work at the loom,
night after night never resting.
In three days I turned out five measures of cloth,
but the Great One[9] grumbled at my slowness.
It's not that I'm so slow at weaving,
but it's hard to be a bride in your home.
The work is more than I can cope with —
what use in my staying any longer?
So I beg of your honored mother,
let her send me away at once!"

When the clerk heard this,
he ascended the hall, addressed his mother:
"Your son is blessed with little fortune,
but luckily I've found this wife.
From the time we bound our hair,[10] we've shared pillow and mat,
and we'll go together to the Yellow Springs.[11]
But it's scarcely been two or three years,
no time at all since we married.
There's nothing wrong in the woman's conduct —
why do you treat her so harshly?"

His mother said to the clerk,
"How can you be so foolish and doting!
This wife knows nothing of propriety,
her actions are selfish and willful.
For a long time I've found her infuriating —
how dare you try to have your own way!
The family east of us have a virtuous daughter —
Qin Luofu is her name,
beautiful in form, no one to rival her —
your mother will arrange it for you.

---

[9] The groom's mother.
[10] Men bound up their hair at twenty, women at fifteen, as a sign they had reached maturity.
[11] The land of the dead.

This other must be sent away at once.
Send her off and don't dare detain her!"

The clerk, humbly kneeling, replied,
"I beg to say this to my mother,
if this wife of mine is sent away,
till death I will never have another!"
His mother, hearing this,
pounded on her chair in a fit of rage.
"Little one, have you no caution?
How dare you speak up for your wife!
I've wasted kindness enough on her already —
you'll never have my permission for this!"
The clerk was silent, unspeaking;
he bowed once more, then returned to his room,
started to tell his wife what had happened
but sobs choked him till he couldn't speak.
"I'm not the one who's sending you away —
my mother forces me to it.
Just go home for a little while.
I must report to my office,
but before long I will return
and then I will surely come and fetch you.
Let these words of mine calm your fears,
take care and do not disobey them!"

The young wife said to the clerk,
"No more of this muddling talk!
Once in the past, in early spring,
I left my family, came to your noble gate,
did all I could to serve your honored mother —
when was I ever willful in my ways?
Day and night I kept at my duties,
though ache and exhaustion wrapped me around.
I know of no fault or error of mine —
I strove only to repay the great debt I owe her.
And now I'm being driven away —
how can you speak of my coming again?
I have an embroidered vest
so lovely it shines with a light of its own.
I have double bed curtains of scarlet gauze
with scent bags hanging from each of the four corners.
I have boxes and hampers, sixty or seventy,

tied with cords of green and turquoise and blue.
Each is a little different from the rest,
and in them are articles of all kinds.
But if a person is lowly, her things too must be worthless —
they would never do for the one who comes after.
But I leave them so they may be used for gifts.
From now on we won't be meeting again —
look at them sometimes if it should please you,
and over the long years, do not forget me!"

Cocks crowed, outside the dawn was breaking;
the wife rose, dressing herself with care,
put on her lined embroidered skirt,
going through each motion four or five times.
On her feet she wore silken shoes,
on her head shone a tortoiseshell comb;
round her waist she wrapped some flowing white gauze,
in her ears fastened moon-bright pearls.
Her fingers were slim as scallion roots,
her mouth as though lined with vermillion or cinnabar.
Lithely she walked, with delicate steps,
in loveliness unequaled in all the world.
She ascended the hall, knelt before the mother;
the mother agreed to let her go, did nothing to stop her.
"In the past when I was a child,
being born and bred in the countryside,
I had no proper training or instruction,
and added to my disgrace by entering your noble family.
I've received from you numerous coins and bolts of cloth,
yet have never succeeded in serving you well.
Today I go back to my old home,
though I fear my departure may leave your household short-
    handed."
Then she went to take leave of her little sister-in-law,
tears falling like strands of pearls.
"When I first came here as a bride,
you could barely stand up by holding to the bed,
yet today, when I'm being sent away,
you're fully as tall as me!
Be diligent, take good care of your mother,
and look out for yourself as well.
When the seventh and the twenty-ninth come round,

remember the games and good times we had together."[12]
Then she went out the gate, mounted the carriage and left,
her tears falling in a hundred streams or more.

The clerk had ridden off on horseback,
the wife set out later by carriage;
bump-bump, rumble-rumble went the wheels,
when the two chanced to meet at the entrance to the highway.
The clerk dismounted, climbed into the carriage,
lowered his head and spoke into her ear,
"I swear I will never leave you —
only go home for a little while.
I must be off to the government office
but before long I will be back.
I swear to Heaven I won't be untrue!"

The young wife said to the clerk,
"I am grateful for your kind concern.
If indeed you think so much of me,
I may hope you will come before long.
You must be like the solid boulder,
I like a rush or a reed.
Rushes and reeds can be strong as well as pliant,
just so the boulder does not move.
But I have a father and older brother
with tempers as violent as thunder.
I doubt they will let me have my way —
just thinking of it makes my heart blanch!"
They lifted their hands in endless endearments,
two souls bound by a single longing.

Through the gate, into her house went the young wife,
not knowing how to face her family.
Her mother slapped her palms together:
"I never expected *this* child to return!
At thirteen I taught you to weave,
at fourteen you knew how to cut clothes;
at fifteen you played the many-stringed lute,

---

[12] On the seventh and twenty-ninth days of the month, women were allowed to rest from
their work. Some commentators take the seventh to refer to the festival of the Herdboy
and the Weaving Maiden held on the night of the seventh day of the seventh month,
when girls prayed for skill in weaving and needlework.

at sixteen understood the rules of decorum.
At seventeen I sent you to be a bride,
thinking you would never betray your vows.
But now, if you haven't committed some fault,
why have you come home unsummoned?"
Lanzhi was ashamed before her mother,
"Truly, I've done nothing wrong!"
and her mother felt great pity for her.

When she had been home ten days or so,
the magistrate sent his matchmaker:
"It concerns the magistrate's third son,
a handsomer young man nowhere in the world,
just turned eighteen or nineteen,
clever in speech, a boy of many talents —"
The mother said to her daughter,
"Here is a proposal worth answering!"
But her daughter, tear-choked, replied,
"When I came home this time,
the clerk pleaded with me again and again,
and we made a vow that we'd never part.
Today if I went against those feelings,
I fear nothing lucky could come of it!
Let us break off these negotiations,
or say we need time to think it over slowly."
The mother informed the matchmaker,
"This child of our poor and humble home
has just been sent back from her first marriage.
If she wasn't fit to be the wife of a clerk,
how could she be suitable for a magistrate's son?
I beg you to make inquiries elsewhere —
we could never give our consent."

A few days after the matchmaker left,
an aide came from the governor with a like request,
saying that Lanzhi's family
for generations had served as officials,
that the governor's fifth son,
a favorite child, was as yet unmarried,
that the aide had been sent as go-between,
had come with a secretary to open discussions.
"In the governor's family," he reported,
"there's this fine young gentleman —

they wish to conclude a marriage alliance
and hence have sent me to your honored house."
The mother apologized to the matchmaker:
"My daughter has given her word elsewhere —
what can an old woman like me say?"

When Lanzhi's older brother heard of this,
he was troubled and angry in heart.
He went and said to his little sister,
"How thoughtless a way to plan things!
Formerly you were married to a clerk,
now you could marry this gentleman.
Your lot would be as different as heaven from earth —
you could assure yourself of a brilliant future!
If you do not marry this fine gentleman,
how do you intend to get along?"
Lanzhi lifted her head and answered,
"What you say is quite reasonable, brother.
I left my family, went to serve a husband,
but midway came back to my brother's house.
Your wishes should rule in this matter —
how could I hope to have my way?
Though the clerk and I made our promises,
I seem fated never to see him again.
Let us give our consent at once
and get on with the marriage arrangements."

The matchmaker got down from his seat,
with "Yes, yes," and then "Fine, fine!"
He returned and reported to the governor,
"Your servant has carried out his task —
the talks have ended in splendid agreement."
When the governor heard this,
his heart was filled with delight.
He looked at the calendar, consulted his books,
decided that this month was just right.
"The six accords are right now in agreement,[13]
the thirtieth is an auspicious day.

[13] The "six accords" may refer to the positions of the sun, moon, and four stars in the Big
Dipper, though the meaning is uncertain.

Today is already the twenty-seventh —
go again and arrange the wedding!"

Talks were held, preparations rushed,
unceasing bustle like streams of floating clouds.
Green sparrow and white goose boats,
dragon pennants at their four corners
fluttering gracefully in the wind,
golden carriages with jade-trimmed wheels,
dapple-gray horses stepping slowly,
gold-threaded saddles with colored pompons,
a wedding gift of three million cash,
all the coins strung on green cords,
three hundred bolts of cloth in assorted hues,
rare seafoods purchased in Jiao and Guang,[14]
attendants, four or five hundred,
all setting out in droves from the governor's gate.
The mother said to her daughter,
"You have received the governor's letter.
Tomorrow they will come to fetch you —
why aren't you making the clothes you'll need?
Don't go and spoil things now!"
The daughter was silent, unspeaking,
her handkerchief muffling her sobs,
her tears coming down in cascades.
She moved her crystal-studded couch,
placed it in front of the window,
in her left hand took her knife and ruler,
in her right hand held her satins and gauzes.
By morning she had finished her lined embroidered skirt,
by evening she had finished her unlined gauze jacket,
and as the day wore away and darkness fell,
with somber thoughts she went out the gate weeping.

When the clerk heard of this change in matters,
he asked leave to go home for a while,
and when he was still two or three *li* away,
his weary horse began to neigh sadly.
The young wife recognized the horse's neigh,
stepped into her shoes, went out in greeting,

---

[14] The provinces of Jiaozhou and Guangzhou on the far southern seacoast.

peering into the distance anxiously,
and then she knew that her husband had come.
Raising her hand, she beat on the saddle,
with sobs that tore at her heart.
"Since I took leave of you,
unimaginable things have happened!
I can no longer be true to my former promise,
though I doubt you will understand why.
I have my parents to think of,
and my brother has pressed me as well,
making me promise myself to another man —
how could I be sure you would return?"
The clerk said to his wife,
"I compliment you on your rise in the world!
The boulder is square and solid —
it can last for a thousand years.
But the rush or the reed — its moment of strength
lasts no longer than dawn to dusk!
You will grow mightier, more exalted daily —
I will go alone to the Yellow Springs."[15]
The young wife said to the clerk,
"What do you mean by such words!
Both of us were forced against our will,
you were, and so was I!
In the Yellow Springs we will meet again —
no betraying the words I speak today!"
They clasped hands, then went their separate ways,
each returning to his own family.
Still alive, they were parted as though by death,
with grief and regret beyond describing,
thinking now to take their leave of the world,
knowing that their lives could last no longer.

The clerk returned to his home,
ascended the hall, bowed to his mother:
"Today the winds blow fierce and cold,
the cold winds break the tree limbs,
and harsh frost collects on the orchids in the garden.[16]

---

[15] The Nether World.
[16] His wife's name, Lanzhi, means Orchid Plant.

Your son today goes into darkness,
leaving you behind all alone.
I do this bad thing of my own will —
do not rail at the gods or spirits.
May your years be like the rock on the southern mountain,
your four limbs sturdy and straight."
When his mother heard this,
her tears fell in time to her words:
"You are the son of a great family
who have served in high government office.
Don't be foolish and die for this woman,
when she is so far beneath you!
The family to the east have a virtuous daughter,
her beauty the boast of the whole city.
Your mother will arrange for you to have her,
it will be done in the space of a day!"
The clerk bowed once more and withdrew,
in his empty bedroom sighed unendingly,
then made his plan, determined to see it through,
turned his head, looked toward the door,
grief pressing in on him more cruelly than ever.

That day the cattle lowed, the horses neighed,
when the bride entered the green enclosure.[17]
And after the darkness of evening had come,
when all was still and people had settled down,
she said, "My life will end today,
my soul take leave, my body remaining."
She lifted her skirt, stepped out of her silken shoes,
and threw herself into the clear pond.
When the clerk heard of this,
he knew in his heart they must part forever.
He circled the tree in the garden,
then hanged himself from the southeast limb.

The two families agreed to bury them together,
to bury them by the side of Flower Mountain.
To east and west they planted pine and cypress,
left and right set out parasol trees.
The branches came together to make a canopy,

---

[17] A curtained enclosure that the bride enters as part of the wedding ceremony.

leaf entwined about leaf.
And in their midst a pair of flying birds,
the kind called mandarin ducks,
raised their heads and cried to each other
night after night till the hour of dawn.
Travelers halted their steps to listen,
widows got up and paced the room.
And this I say to you of later ages:
take warning and never forget this tale!

A Sad Song

Translated by Burton Watson

Can a sad song take the place of crying?
Can peering in the distance take the place of going home?
I think with longing of the old village,
my spirits downcast, fretful and forlorn.
I want to go home but there's no one there,
I want to cross the river but there is no boat —
thoughts in my heart I can find no words for,
like cartwheels going round in my belly!

THE SIX DYNASTIES

SOUTHERN DYNASTIES
Seven Ziye Songs

Translated by John Frodsham

The Six Dynasties period witnessed the rapid development of two types of *yuefu* ballad, the Northern and the Southern. The Southern *yuefu* is generally languid and erotic. The Northern reflects the simpler martial spirit of nomad peoples but lately settled in China. Both types produced poems which must be ranked high in the achievements of Chinese literature.

The forty-two *Ziye* songs are probably the best known of the Southern folksongs during this period. Legend has it that they were composed during the Jin dynasty by a girl called Ziye (Midnight).

At Sunset I Strolled

At sunset I strolled out of the front gate.
Not far from me, I spied you passing by.
Such clouds of hair around your lovely face,
Its fragrance filled the very road you trod.

Was I Not Made for Love?

Last night no comb held back my hair,
My silken tresses covered both my shoulders.
As I stretched myself upon your knees
Was I not made for love?

The First Time I Set Eyes on You

The first time I set eyes on you,
I thought our hearts would be as one.
I fed my thread into a broken loom
It would not make a bolt of cloth.[18]

---

[18] A pun on *pi*, which means both "mate" and "a roll of cloth." Hence our line also means, "You would not marry me."

So Long and Still No Mate

Today I parted from my love.
When will we meet again?
The bright lamp shines on the empty chess-board —
So long and still no mate.[19]

Spring

The spring wind stirs my romantic heart,
I let my eyes roam over mountain and forest.
Strange yet lovely, the colors of mountain and forest,
Birds in the sun let fall their limpid songs.

Summer

She has done with silkworms and the fieldwork,
This pensive wife, who yet laments her lot.
In summer heat she is packing fine linen clothes,
To send away to her husband on his journeys.

Autumn

The autumn wind sweeps in through the windows,
The thin silk curtains flutter in the breeze.
I lift my head and look at the bright moon,
And send my love on its beams a thousand leagues.

Four Ziye Songs

Translated by Burton Watson

The Fragrance Comes from the Scent I Wear

(In Reply to "At Sunset I Strolled")

(She)
The fragrance comes from the scent I wear,
a lovely face I wouldn't dare claim.

---

[19] Another pun, this time on *qi*, "a game of chess," and *qi*, "a meeting."

Heaven's not deaf to a body's pleas —
that's why it has brought you to me!

Summer

In the hottest time, when all is still and windless
and summer clouds rise up at dusk,
under the dense leaves, take my hand
and we'll float melons on the water, dunk crimson plums.

Autumn

Cool breezes — I sleep by the open window
where the light of the setting moon shines in.
At midnight there are no voices,
but within my gauze curtains, a pair of smiles.

Winter

When ice on the pond is three feet thick
and white snow stretches a thousand miles,
my heart will still be like the pine and cypress,
but your heart — what will it be?

NORTHERN DYNASTIES
Three Northern Yuefu Ballads

Translated by John Frodsham

The Ballad of Mulan

Our earliest account of this legend states that Mulan, whose surname is unknown, lived during the Northern Wei dynasty (386–534), when the north of China was ruled by the Toba.

Heaving a sigh and then another sigh,
Mulan was sitting weaving at her door.
You could not hear the noise of loom and shuttle,
But only the sound of the girl lamenting.
"O lady, are you thinking of your love?
O lady, are you brooding on your love?"
"Indeed, I have no love at all to think of,

Indeed I have no love at all to brood on.
But then last night I heard the battle-roll,
The Khan is calling up a mighty levy.
The battle-roll was written in twelve scrolls,
And every scroll carried my father's name.
My father has no grown-up son at all,
And I myself have got no elder brother.
I want to buy a saddle and a horse,
To take my father's place in the expedition."
In the eastern market she bought a noble horse,
In the western market bought a blanket and saddle.
In the southern market bought a bridle and reins,
In the northern market bought a long whip.
At break of day she took leave of her father and mother,
At evening camped on the banks of the Yellow River.
She did not hear her father and mother calling for their daughter,
She only heard the Yellow River's flowing waters murmuring.
At break of day she left the Yellow River,
At dusk she came to the edge of the Black Hills.
She did not hear her father and mother calling for their daughter,
She only heard the nomad horses whinnying on the hills of Yan.
Ten thousand leagues she rode on missions of war,
Passes and mountains she crossed like a bird on the wing.
On the northern wind came the sound of the sentry's drum.
The wintry light glinted upon her armor.
After a hundred battles the general was killed,
Ten years passed by and the warriors could go home.
When she came back she was summoned by the Son of Heaven,
The Son of Heaven was seated in the Hall of Light.
For her brave deeds she was raised up full twelve ranks,
And given a reward of one hundred cash.
The Khan asked her to state just what she wanted.
"Oh, I do not want to be a court official.
But lend me a camel will go a thousand leagues a day,
To take me back to my old home."
When her father and mother heard their daughter was back,
Leaning on each other, they went out of the suburb gates.
When the elder sister heard her little sister had come,
She went to the door and put rouge on her face.
When her little brother heard his elder sister had come,
He whetted his knife and darted like lightning
Towards the pigs and goats.

"I opened the gates that led to the eastern apartments,
I sat down on my bed in the western apartments.
Then I took off my soldier's robes
And put on the dress that I was wont to wear.
I stood at the window to dress my cloudy hair.
I went to the mirror and put on my yellow makeup.
I went out of the gates and saw my mess-mates,
And what a shock they got on seeing me!"
"Oh we were living with you for full twelve years,
Yet never knew that Mulan was a girl!"
For the male hare tucks its feet in when it sits,
And the female hare is known by her bleary eye.
But when two hares are bounding side by side,
How can you then tell female from the male?

Breaking a Willow-Branch

This song may originally have been translated into Chinese from one of the nomad languages. A willow-branch was customarily given to the traveler setting off on a journey.

Mounting your horse, you did not take your whip,
Instead you broke a branch from the willow-tree.
Walking and sitting I played on my flute,
Its sadness would break any traveler's heart.

Deep down within me I was miserable,
Oh! how I wished that I could be your whip!
Coming and going, I'd be worn at your wrist,
Journeying and halting to rest upon your knee.

Far off you can descry the Mengjin ford,[20]
And all its clumps of dancing willow-trees.
But I am only a girl of a nomad tribe,
And cannot understand your Chinese songs.

A hero needs a horse that's swift of foot,
And a horse that's swift of foot needs have a hero.
As hooves go thundering through the yellow dust,
I shall soon know who was the victor.

---

[20] A ford across the Yellow River.

Driving Goats Into a Valley

Driving goats into a valley,
A white goat in the lead,
This girl grown old, unmarried still,
Stamps the earth and cries to heaven.

"Alack, alas and woe the day!
My thoughts are ever on you.
Pillowed on your left arm,
I rolled onto my side.

I used to stroke your beard
And gaze up at your face.
But since then you've forgotten me,
You could not be forced to love."

Qiyuge

Translated by Burton Watson

Man — pitiful insect,
out the gate with fears of death in his breast,
a corpse fallen in narrow valleys,
white bones that no one gathers up.

▣▣ Further Reading ▣▣

Allen, Joseph R., trans. *In the Voice of Others: Chinese Music Bureau Poetry.* Ann Arbor: University of Michigan Press, 1992.

Birrell, Anne, trans. *New Songs from a Jade Terrace: An Anthology of Early Chinese Love Poetry.* London: Allen & Unwin, 1982.

——— . *Popular Songs and Ballads of Han China.* London: Unwin Hyman, 1988.

Frankel, Hans H. *The Flowering Plum and the Palace Lady: Interpretations of Chinese Poetry.* New Haven: Yale University Press, 1976.

Frodsham, John D., ed. and trans., with the collaboration of Ch'eng Hsi. *An Anthology of Chinese Verse: Han, Wei, Chin and the Northern and Southern Dynasties.* Oxford: Oxford University Press, 1967.

Mayhew, Lenore, and William McNaughton, trans. *A Gold Orchid: The Love Poems of Tzu Yeh.* Rutland, Vt.: Tuttle, 1972.

Waley, Arthur, trans. *Chinese Poems.* London: Allen & Unwin, 1946.

Watson, Burton. *Chinese Lyricism: Shih Poetry from the Second to the Twelfth Century.* New York: Columbia University Press, 1971.

——— . ed. and trans. *The Columbia Book of Chinese Poetry: From Early Times to the Thirteenth Century.* New York: Columbia University Press, 1984.

Chapter 9

Tigers Setting the Wind Astir

**Poets of the Han,
Wei and Jin Dynasties**

Cao Zhi and Liu Zhen sit and whistle, tigers setting the wind astir —
In the four seas none could compare
  with these two heroes.

— Yuan Haowen (1190–1257), "Thirty Poems on Poetry," 2
(translated by J. Timothy Wixted)

Introduction

Burton Watson

The middle years of the Han dynasty saw a highly significant development in the history of Chinese poetry, the appearance of a new kind of *shi* poetry that employs a five-character or five syllable line rather than the four-character line typical of the *Book of Songs*. The new form seems to have been of popular origin and was perhaps influenced by changes in the music of the time. By the first century A.D. it had been taken up by the literati, and soon became the favorite vehicle for lyric expression. A variant of the form employing a seven-character line appeared about the same time but did not gain wide acceptance until several centuries later.

A tone of brooding melancholy informs most of the *shi* poems by known writers of the late Han, and of its brief successor, the Wei dynasty (220–264). These writers include Cao Cao, the powerful military leader who opened the way for his son Cao Pi to ascend the throne as the first emperor of the Wei, and his younger son Cao Zhi, one of the finest poets of the period. Flourishing under the patronage of the Cao family were the so-called Seven Masters of the Jian-an Era (196–220), represented in this selection by Kong Rong, Ruan Yu, Xu Gan, Wang Can, Chen Lin, and Liu Zhen. The last three, it may be noted, died in an outbreak of plague in 217.

The works of these men for the most part mirror the harsh realities of the period, depicting in realistic detail the civil strife, unrest, and political intrigue that accompanied the downfall of the Han dynasty. In some, such as Chen Lin's poem on the Great Wall, the poet borrows a persona from the *yuefu* ballad tradition; in others he speaks in his own voice.

The decay and collapse of the Han served in some degree to discredit the Confucian doctrines that had formed the official foundation of the state and to clear the way for a revival of interest in the transcendental thought of the Taoist philosophers Laozi and Zhuangzi. This new intellectual trend is represented in the Taoist-flavored, spiritedly anti-Confucian work by Zhongchang Tong in this selection.

At the same time, as disease, warfare, peasant uprisings, and the sudden shifts in political power made life increasingly perilous for members of the ruling class, there was growing speculation concerning the possibilities of employing drugs or dietary regimen to prolong life or even perhaps achieve the state of a *xian* or immortal spirit, a figure often depicted in Taoist writings. In the centuries that followed, the themes of reclusion and the dream of flight to some freer, happier realm constitute one of the major concerns of Chinese poetry.

— *Columbia Book of Chinese Poetry*, 1984

XIANG YU (232–202 B.C.)
The Hegemon's Lament

Translated by Burton Watson

In 202 B.C., when Xiang Yu, the military leader who had challenged the founder of the Han dynasty, Liu Bang, for control of the empire, was surrounded by his enemies and faced certain defeat, he is said to have composed this song in farewell to his horse, Dapple, and his beautiful companion, Lady Yu.

My strength plucked up the hills,
    my might shadowed the world.
But the times were against me
    and Dapple runs no more.
When Dapple runs no more,
    what then can I do?
Ah Yu, my Yu,
    what will your fate be?

LIU BANG, EMPEROR GAO OF HAN (256–195 B.C.)
Song of the Great Wind

Translated by Burton Watson

Liu Bang, founder and first emperor of the Han dynasty, composed this poem in 196 B.C., when he visited his native village in his old age and reflected upon his accomplishments.

A great wind came forth,
    the clouds rose on high.
Now that my might rules all within the seas,
    I have returned to my old village.
Where will I find brave men
    to guard the four corners of my land?

LIU CHE, EMPEROR WU OF HAN (157–87 B.C.)
Two Poems

Translated by Arthur Waley

The Autumn Wind

Emperor Wu came to the throne when he was only sixteen. In this poem he regrets that he is obliged to go on an official journey, leaving his mistress behind in the capital. He is seated in his state barge surrounded by his ministers.

Autumn wind rises; white clouds fly.
Grass and trees wither; geese go south.
Orchids, all in bloom; chrysanthemums smell sweet.
I think of my lovely lady; I never can forget.
Floating-pagoda boat crosses Fen River;
Across the mid-stream white waves rise.
Flute and drum keep time to sound of rowers' song;

Amidst revel and feasting sad thoughts come;
Youth's years how few, age how sure!

Li Furen

This poem is supposed to have been written by Emperor Wu when his mistress, Li
Furen, died [see the biography of Madam Li, chapter 7].

The sound of her silk skirt has stopped.
On the marble pavement dust grows.
Her empty room is cold and still.
Fallen leaves are piled against the doors.
    Longing for that lovely lady
How can I bring my aching heart to rest?

LIU FULING, EMPEROR ZHAO OF HAN (?95–74 B.C.)
Written in Early Autumn at the Pool of Sprinkling Water

Translated by Amy Lowell and Florence Ayscough

Liu Fuling was the youngest son of Liu Che, Emperor Wu, whom he succeeded in 86
B.C. as seventh emperor of the Han.

In Autumn, when the landscape is clear, to float over the wide,
    water ripples,
To pick the water-chestnut and the lotus-flower with a quick,
    light hand!
The fresh wind is cool, we start singing to the movement of
    the oars.
The clouds are bright; they part before the light of dawn; the
    moon has sunk below the Silver River.
Enjoying such pleasure for ten thousand years —
Could one consider it too much?

ZHANG HENG (78–139)
Epithalamium

Translated by John Frodsham

Zhang Heng is best known for his rhapsodies, including the "Rhapsody of the Two
Capitals," a masterpiece ten years in the making [see chapter 6 for "The Bones of
Zhuangzi"]. Besides being a poet, he was also a skilled astronomer and mathemati-
cian. His contemporary, Cui Yuan, said of him on his burial stele: "His mathematical

computations plumbed the heavens and the earth. His inventions were like those of the Transforming Power. The brilliance of his talents, the excellence of his art, put him on a level with the spirits." Little of Zhang Heng's poetry has survived, but the following poem is one of the very few pieces of frankly erotic love poetry to escape the scissors of the neo-Confucian moralists.

> By good luck I was granted a meeting with you,
> And now have entered your women's apartments.
> Although I long for my first union with you,
> I feel as though my hands touch boiling water.[1]
> Untalented, I shall struggle to do my best,
> Your worthless consort knows her duties well.
> United with you, I shall supervise your kitchen,
> Perform the rites and help at the sacrifices.
> I long to become a mat of sedge and arum,
> To act as a covering for your square couch.
> I want to be your coverlet and canopy,
> To lie over you and protect you from wind and frost.
> I have sprinkled and swept clean the pillow and mat,
> My sandals are fragrant with exotic perfumes.
> The double doors are locked with golden bars,
> Above and below, ornamental lanterns burn.
> I take off my clothes, wait on you with towel and powder,
> Unroll the picture-scroll beside the pillow.[2]
> The Plain Girl will now be my instructress,
> I shall learn ten thousand postures to adopt.
> Very few men have ever seen these arts,
> Which the Old Man of Heaven taught to the Yellow Emperor.
> No joy will be like the joy of this first night,
> We shall never forget it, however old we may grow.

---

[1] *Analects* XVI. 11.

[2] This was a handbook of sex mentioned in the bibliography of the *History of the Former Han* — the *Sex Handbook of the Old Man of Heaven and Others*. Written in the form of a dialogue between the Old Man of Heaven and the Yellow Emperor, it was illustrated with pictures showing various sexual postures and was used for the instruction of brides. The Plain Girl is one of the three female guardians of the arcana of sexual lore.

KONG RONG (153–208)
A First-Born

Translated by Herbert Giles

One of the Seven Masters of the Jian-an period, Kong Rong was a descendant of Confucius in the twentieth generation, and an antiprohibitionist. "If my halls are full of guests," he said, "and my jars are full of wine, I am happy." He was put to death by Cao Cao.

The wanderer reaches home with joy
    From absence of a year and more;
His eye seeks a beloved boy —
    His wife lies weeping on the floor.

They whisper he is gone. The glooms
    Of evening fall; beyond the gate
A lonely grave in outline looms
    To greet the sire who came too late.

Forth to the little mound he flings,
    Where wild-flowers bloom on every side ...
His bones are in the Yellow Springs,
    His flesh like dust is scattered wide.

"O child who never knew thy sire,
    For ever now to be unknown,
Ere long thy wandering ghost shall tire
    Of flitting friendless and alone.

"O son, man's greatest earthly boon,
    With thee I bury hopes and fears."
He bowed his head in grief and soon
    His breast was wet with rolling tears.

Life's dread uncertainty he knows,
    But oh for this untimely close!

LIU HONG, EMPEROR LING OF THE LATER HAN (156–189)
Proclaiming the Joy of Certain Hours

Translated by Amy Lowell and Florence Ayscough

Liu Hong succeeded to the throne in 168 as eleventh emperor of the Later Han.

Cool wind rising. Sun sparkling on the wide canal.
Pink lotuses, bent down by day, spread open at night.

There is too much pleasure; a day cannot contain it.
Clear sounds of strings, smooth flowing notes of flageolets —
    we sing the "Jade Love-Bird" song.
A thousand years? Ten thousand! Nothing could exceed
    such delight.

Cao Cao (155–220)
Graveyard Song

Translated by John Frodsham

Cao Cao fought his way up from obscurity during the wars that marked the breakup of the Han empire, eventually gaining control of the north, which he ruled as the kingdom of Wei. Most of his surviving verse is in the *yuefu* ballad form.

After the two great Taoist rebellions of 184 the Han dynasty was so weakened that its generals became warlords in their own domains. In 189 Dong Zhuo (d. 192) rose in revolt, sacking the capital the following year. He was opposed by a coalition under the leadership of Yuan Shao. But the allied armies refused to move against Dong Zhuo, who was by then firmly entrenched in Luoyang. Yuan Shao and Yuan Shu then split away from Cao Cao, only to turn against each other. Each sponsored his own claimant to the throne.

East of the Passes there were loyal knights,
Who rose in arms to crush all wickedness.[3]
They were meant to meet together in Mengjin,[4]
To set their hearts on getting to Xianyang.[5]
Yet the allied armies would not pull together,
But marched about like lines of aimless geese.
A lust for power led them at last to wrangle,
In a little while they were at each other's throats.
A young man was styled emperor in Huainan.[6]
An imperial seal was carved out in the north.[7]
Their armor was alive with breeding lice,
Ten thousand families were all wiped out.
Their white bones lay and bleached in the wilderness,

---

[3] To attack Dong Zhuo.
[4] An historical analogy. When King Wu of Zhou attacked the tyrant Zhou, he assembled all the feudal lords together in Mengjin, Henan.
[5] The attack on Luoyang is likened to Xiangyu's attack on Xianyang, capital of the detested Qin dynasty, in 207 B.C.
[6] In 197 Yuan Shu had himself proclaimed emperor.
[7] In 191 Yuan Shao had tried to set up Liu Yu as emperor.

For a thousand leagues not a cock was heard to crow.
Of the people, barely one in a hundred survived,
Remembering this is enough to break your heart.

Song on Enduring the Cold

Translated by Burton Watson

This poem was probably written in 206 when Cao Cao, the most powerful military
leader of the time, was crossing the Taihang Mountains in northern Shanxi to attack
a rival.

North we climb the Taihang Mountains;
the going's hard on these steep heights!
Sheep Gut Slope dips and doubles,
enough to make the cartwheels crack.

Stark and stiff the forest trees,
the voice of the north wind sad;
crouching bears, black and brown, watch us pass;
tigers and leopards howl beside the trail.

Few men live in these valleys and ravines
where snow falls thick and blinding.
With a long sigh I stretch my neck;
a distant campaign gives you much to think of.

Why is my heart so downcast and sad?
All I want is to go back east,
but waters are deep and bridges broken;
halfway up, I stumble to a halt.

Dazed and uncertain, I've lost the old road,
night bearing down but nowhere to shelter;
on and on, each day farther,
men and horses starving as one.

Shouldering packs, we snatch firewood as we go,
chop ice to use in boiling our gruel —
That song of the Eastern Hills is sad,
a troubled tale that fills me with grief.[8]

---

[8] Eastern Hills, *Book of Songs* 156, describes the hardships of a military campaign similar to
the one Cao Cao was engaged in.

Ruan Yu (d. 212)
Driving My Chariot Through the Northern Suburbs Gate

Translated by John Frodsham

Ruan Yu was one of the Seven Masters of the Jian-an period. He had once been secretary to the great scholar Cai Yong (133–192); later he became secretary to Cao Cao. He was renowned for his skill in drafting memorials and addresses to the throne. He was the father of Ruan Ji [see chapter 10].

I drove my chariot through the Northern Suburbs Gate,
When my horses balked and refused to gallop on.
I got down from my chariot, not knowing what to do,
Looked up and broke a branch from a dead willow-tree.
Turning my head, I heard from a funeral-grove,
The sorrowful sound of someone weeping there.
I called to the mourner, begged him to come out,
And asked him what had brought him to this place.
"My mother died and left me all alone,
My stepmother hates me, orphan that I am.
Hungry and cold, I have no clothes or food,
At every move I am beaten with a whip.
My bones dissolve, my flesh is cut away,
My body is like the bark of a withered tree.
They hide me away within an empty room,
When my father comes home, he does not know where I am.
I came to this graveyard to look for our old tomb,
But the living and dead are thrust apart for ever.
How can I ever see my mother again?
My tears fall down, my voice is hoarse with sobbing.
They have cast me away and left me in this place,
What have I done to merit such poverty and danger?"
I have set down this story for later generations,
That through this they may understand such things.

Xu Gan (171–217)
The Wife's Thoughts

Translated by Burton Watson

Xu Gan, one of the Seven Masters of the Jian-an period, spent his last years in the service of Cao Cao.

Clouds that drift so far and free
I'd ask to bear my message,
but their whirling shapes accept no charge;
wandering, halting, I long in vain.
Those who part all meet once more;
you alone send no word of return.
Since you went away,
my shining mirror darkens with neglect.
Thoughts of you are like the flowing river —
when will they ever end?

WANG CAN (177–217)
Poem of Seven Sorrows

Translated by John Frodsham

Wang Can was one of the Seven Masters of the Jian'an period. He came from a noted family, which had served the Later Han with distinction. In spite of this, he joined the forces of Cao Cao. [See also chapter 6 for his rhapsody "Climbing the Tower."]

The "Seven Sorrows" was the name of a *yuefu* ballad that appeared during the period of anarchy and civil war at the end of the Later Han dynasty. The Tang commentator, Lü Xiang, says that this ballad got its name from the fact that all the seven senses — smell, speech, sight and hearing, feeling, pain, resentment, and the sense of justice — were afflicted by the breakup of Han society.

Wang Can wrote this poem on the occasion of his flight from Chang'an (the Western Capital), to Jingzhou in 192. The "wolves and tigers" are the rebel generals of Dong Zhuo. [See the "Graveyard Song" of Cao Cao and Cai Yan's "Poem of Sorrow."]

When wild disorder gripped the Western Capital,
Tigers and wolves added to our despair.
So I turned about and fled the Middle Kingdom,[9]
To far-off Jing, among the Man tribes there.[10]
My relatives stood facing me in sorrow,
My friends came with me, tried to hold me back.
Beyond the city-gates there was nothing to see
But white bones strewn across the level plain.
Upon the road I met a starving woman,

---

[9]   North China, generally known as the Central Plain.

[10] Jingzhou was the territory of the ancient state of Chu. The Man were an aboriginal tribe inhabiting this region of South China. Wang Can fled south to put himself under the protection of Liu Biao, governor of Jingzhou, an old friend of his paternal grandfather.

Who had left her suckling child to die in the grass.
She turned her head to listen to its crying,
But brushed away her tears and would not return.
"Since I do not know the place where death will take me,
How can I manage to care for my child as well?"
I spurred my horse and left her far behind,
For I could not bear to hear the words she spoke.
As I journeyed south, I climbed up Baling tomb,[11]
Then I turned my head and gazed toward Chang'an.
Now I understand the Song of the Falling Spring![12]
The sighs I heave are enough to break my heart.

CHEN LIN (d. 217)
Song: I Watered My Horse at the Long Wall Caves

Translated by Burton Watson

Chen Lin was an official whose checkered career reflected the uncertainty of the closing years of the Later Han. His literary reputation rests on the letters, proclamations and official documents he wrote on behalf of his powerful patrons, who included Yuan Shao and Cao Cao. It is said that Cao Cao, laid up one day with a high fever, felt suddenly restored to health after reading the works of Chen Lin. He is numbered among the Seven Masters of the Jian-an period, and is chiefly remembered for this ballad, about a conscript engaged in the construction of the Great Wall.

— Jean-Pierre Diény, *Indiana Companion*, 1986

I watered my horse at the Long Wall caves,
water so cold it hurt his bones;
I went and spoke to the Long Wall boss:
"We're soldiers from Taiyuan — will you keep us here forever?"
"Public works go according to schedule —
swing your hammer, pitch your voice in with the rest!"
A man'd be better off to die in battle

---

[11] Baling, in Shaanxi, was the place where Emperor Wen of Han (r. 179–156 B.C.) was buried. The poet is contrasting the time of peace and prosperity under Emperor Wen with the chaos of his own time.

[12] *Book of Songs* 153:

Cool is that falling spring
Soaking the henbane all around.
Groaning, I wake from my sleep.
Thinking of the capital of Zhou.

than eat his heart out building the Long Wall!
The Long Wall — how it winds and winds,
winds and winds three thousand *li*;
here on the border, so many strong boys;
in the houses back home, so many widows and wives.
I sent a letter to my wife:
"Better remarry than wait any longer —
serve your new mother-in-law with care
and sometimes remember the husband you once had."
In answer her letter came to the border:
"What nonsense do you write me now?
Now when you're in the thick of danger,
how could I rest by another man's side?"
(HE)   If you bear a son, don't bring him up!
        But a daughter — feed her good dried meat.
        Only *you* can't see, here by the Long Wall,
        the bones of the dead men heaped about!
(SHE) I bound up my hair and went to serve you;
        constant constant was the care of my heart.
        Too well I know your borderland troubles;
        and I — can I go on like this much longer?

LIU ZHEN (d. 217)
Poem Without a Category

Translated by Burton Watson

Liu Zhen is ranked second to Cao Zhi in the coterie of Jian-an poets. *Eds.*

Office work: a wearisome jumble;
ink drafts: a crosshatch of deletions and smears.
Racing the writing brush, no time to eat,
sun slanting down but never a break;
swamped and muddled in records and reports,
head spinning till it's senseless and numb —
I leave off and go west of the wall,
climb the height and let my eyes roam:
square embankments hold back the clear water,
wild ducks and geese at rest in the middle —
Where can I get a pair of whirring wings
so I can join you to bob on the waves?

ZHONGCHANG TONG (179–220)
Speaking My Mind

Translated by Burton Watson

A nonconformist thinker known by his contemporaries as "the madman," Zhong-chang Tong joined the staff of Cao Cao. [See also chapter 14 for his "On Happiness."]

> The Great Way — simple as it is,
> few spy out its secrets.
> Follow the will and you do no wrong;
> go along with things — none are in error.
> From times past, ties and entanglements,
> cricks and coils, this petty lot,
> these hundred worries — what are they?
> All that's most important rests in you!
> Hand your woes to the sky above,
> bury your troubles in the ground,
> flout and discard the *Five Classics*,
> put an end to the *Songs*.
> And those muddled scraps that are the hundred philosophers —
> consign them please to the flames!
> Lift your ambitions to the hills and westward,
> let your mind wander east of the sea.
> With the Primal Breath as your boat,
> the little winds for a rudder,
> sail and soar in the Great Purity,
> do what you want to, handsome and blithe!

CAO PI (187–226)
A Song of Yan

Translated by John Frodsham

Cao Pi, eldest son of Cao Cao, came to the throne in A.D. 220 as Emperor Wen. Though his verse cannot compare with that of his younger brother, Cao Zhi, it still ranks high in achievement. [See also chapter 15 for his treatise "On Literature."]

Yan was an ancient state in the northeast of China, in the area of modern Peking and southern Manchuria. It had been extinguished by Qin in the third century B.C. Originally, "Yan Songs" had been songs set to the music of Yan. Later, after the music was lost, a "Yan Song" came to be a song about parting, where the lover or husband was away on a long journey or at a frontier war. During Emperor Wen's time the old territory of Yan was occupied by the Murong tribe of the Xianbi, a fact that would lend the song an added poignancy.

The autumn wind blows drearily,
The breath of heaven is cold.
Flower and leaf fall fluttering down,[13]
Dew turns to frost.[14]
All the swallows cry farewell,
The snow-geese wing off south.
I think of you journeying far from home,
And brooding breaks my heart.
Dissatisfied, you think of coming back,
Longing for your old home.
So why then do you tarry there,
Lingering in that strange land?
You have left me here in solitude,
Keeping these empty rooms.
I am plunged in grief when I think of you,
Yet never dare forget.
I do not feel the tears fall,
The tears that soak my dress.
I pick up my lute and its singing strings
Emit a clear *shang*.[15]
The song is short, the notes are faint,
But more I cannot do.
The brilliant moon, so dazzling bright,
Is shining on my bed.
The starry river's flowing west,[16]
The night is halfway done.
The Herdboy and the Weaving-lady[17]
Gaze far-off, each to each.
Why ever are you sundered by
The bridge across that river?[18]

---

[13] These opening lines are strongly reminiscent of lines from "The Nine Changes" in the *Songs of the South*:
   Sad is the breath of autumn,
   Drearily flower and leaf fall fluttering to decay.
[14] *Book of Songs* 129:
   The white dew turns to frost.
[15] The note of the pentatonic scale associated with autumn.
[16] The starry river is the Milky Way.
[17] See Cao Zhi, "Miscellaneous Poem no. 3." *Eds.*
[18] This refers to the bridge formed by magpies across the Milky Way. Over this the Herdboy and the Weaving-lady may cross to meet each other on the seventh day of the seventh month.

CAO ZHI (192–232)
Seven Poems

Translated by John Frodsham

Cao Zhi, third son of Cao Cao, is undoubtedly one of the greatest of all Chinese poets. His outstanding literary talents were evident from the time he was quite young. He excelled not only in poetry but also in the rhapsody [see chapter 6, "The Goddess of the Luo"] and almost every other literary genre. His father was so impressed with his capabilities that he once thought of making him Crown Prince over the head of his elder brother, Pi. The feud between the two was exacerbated by Cao Zhi's love for the Lady Zhen, the woman who later became Pi's consort. Pi took his revenge when he came to the throne by systematically persecuting his brother. There is a well-known story, almost certainly apocryphal, that Pi, jealous as ever of his brother's talents, once commanded him to compose a poem in the time it took to walk seven paces. Zhi promptly produced the following:

> Once, boiling beans while beanstalks fed the flame,
> The beans within the pot began to cry.
> We sprang together from the self-same root,
> So why are you so bent on cooking us?

Four of Six Miscellaneous Poems

These poems were written after Cao Zhi had been sent out to Ying, in Hubei, before his enfeoffment in A.D. 223.

1

The commentators put an elaborate, allegorical interpretation on this poem. The tall towers represent the capital, the mournful winds imperial edicts, the morning sun the wisdom of the Emperor, and the northern woods evil men. But this would be tedious, even if it were true. It is better to understand it as a poem of exile.

> Round the tall towers blow many mournful winds,
> The morning sun shines on the northern woods.
> This man has gone ten thousand leagues away,
> Rivers and lakes distant and deep between.
> In a double boat how shall I travel there?[19]
> The thought of parting is very hard to endure.
> A lonely goose goes wandering, southward winging.
> As it passes the house it gives a long, sad cry.

---

[19] "A double boat" — high officials traveled in a boat which was joined side by side with another one. This made the journey safer and more comfortable.

I think with yearning of my far-off love,
Would I could send some news to him this way.
But body and shadow suddenly vanish from sight;[20]
Those beating wings have racked my heart with pain.

2

The poem is not just a literary pose. There is evidence that Cao Zhi suffered bitter hardships in the campaigns of his early years.

The tumbleweed that leaves its root and stock,
Drifts with the big wind, hither and thither blown.
Why did I think to ride on the whirlwind's back?
It blew me up into the very clouds.
Higher and higher, up through the infinite,
What ending is there to the roads of Heaven?
This is the life the wanderer must lead,
Who pledges himself to fight in far-off wars.
The coarse hair-cloth not enough to cover his body,
His belly never full, not even with bracken or beans.
Away, away, never speak of this again.
It is our bitter sorrows have made us old.

3

The Weaving-lady corresponds to the star Vega in the Constellation Lyra. Though she weaves for ever, she never finishes a single piece of cloth. Traditionally, she pines away for the Herdboy, the star Altair.

In the northwest there is a Weaving-lady,
How dazzling are her silks, both flowered and plain!
From the bright dawn she plies her loom and shuttle,
When the sun goes down, not a piece of cloth is made!
All through the long night she sighs heavily,
Her mournful cries pierce the clouds in the blue.
"Your handmaid now must keep her empty chamber,
Her husband has gone marching off to war.
Although he swore to return in three years' time,

---

[20] The goose flies out of sight, just as we ourselves must one day vanish away. Life is as brief as the flight of a bird.

Nine months of spring have now already passed.
A solitary bird goes winging round the trees,
Its plaintive cry tells it has lost the flock.
I wish I were the sun that shines in the south,
To send my beams hastening to see my lord."

4

In the south country there lives a lovely lady,
Her face as delicate as peach or plum.[21]
In the morning she wanders on the north shore of the River,
In the evening she wanders on an islet in the Xiang.[22]
But these days rosy cheeks are out of fashion,
No one is there to see her dazzling smile.
In the blink of an eye, the year's night is on us,
Such fleeting beauty cannot last for long.

Far-Off Journey

On my far-off journey all round the Four Seas,
I looked up and down and gazed on the mighty waves.
There was a vast, great fish like a mountain cove,
That breasted the waves, let them go sliding past.
A magic turtle carried Fangzhang on its back,[23]
There were spirit mountains, majestic, precipitous.
Immortals flew about the coigns of the hills,
While the Jade Girl was playing on their peaks.[24]
Petals of jade were enough to dull my hunger,
I rinsed my mouth, head back, with mountain mist.
Kunlun mountain is my original home,
The central provinces are not my dwelling place.
I shall return and visit Dongwangfu,[25]

---

[21] *Book of Songs* 24: How rich it is, the bloom of peach and plum.
[22] The river Xiang, which is over 2,000 *li* long, rises in Guangxi province and runs north-east, passing through Changsha in Hunan, into the Dongting lake.
[23] Fangzhang is one of the three islands of the Immortals.
[24] An Immortal.
[25] A Taoist divinity, the "Father King of the East," most important of the ten thousand gods and the counterpart of the Goddess of the West. He reigns over Mount Penglai, another of the three islands of the Immortals.

With a single bound, I shall cross the Moving Sands.[26]
Beating my wings, I shall dance on the seasonal wind,
With a long whistle, I shall sing like the pure breeze.
Metal and stone easily crumble away,
But I shall be radiant as the sun and moon.
Enduring as long as Heaven and Earth together,
What do I care for a realm of ten thousand chariots?

Emotion

A trace of shadow veils the light of the sun,
A pure breeze is ruffling at my robe.
Swimming fishes dive through the limpid water,
Wheeling birds fly up to touch the sky.
Far, far away the traveler has journeyed,
From such a voyage he can never return.
When he first set out, a cruel frost prevailed,
Now he journeys on as the white dew dries in the sun.
The traveler sighed at the song of the Drooping Millet,[27]
Those who stayed home sang "Oh, how few, how few!"[28]
Now quite cast down I face my honored guests,
Stricken with grief, my heart is full of sorrow.

White Horses

White horses, all adorned with golden bridles,
On flying hooves go galloping northwest.
Who are the men who are riding these white horses?

---

[26] A region frequently mentioned in ancient texts and probably located in the extreme
northwest of China. Laozi, for example, is supposed "to have roamed through the region
of the Moving Sands" with the Warden of the Passes, after he had left China.

[27] *Book of Songs* 65:
  The wine-millet is drooping,
  The cooking millet sprouts.
  Slowly I journey on, bowed down
  By the cares that trouble my heart.

[28] *Book of Songs* 36: Strictly speaking this line of the Song means "It's no use at all!" But Cao
Zhi would have followed the orthodox commentary.

They are wandering knights, who come from You and Bing.[29]
They left their native towns when they were young,
To make their names on the desert's sandy borders.
For many years they have gripped their trusty bows,
And held their redthorn arrows, both short and long,
Drawing their bows, they shatter the lefthand targets,
Shooting from the right, they wipe out the Yuezhi.[30]
They raise their hands to shoot those flying monkeys,
Then bend in the saddle to scatter the horses' hooves.[31]
More cunning and wily they are than monkeys or apes,
Fierce and fleet of foot, like leopards or dragons.
Many a time they have startled the border-towns,
And again and again defeated the slavish Huns.
When the feathered summons from the north comes flying.[32]
They spur their horses over the tall dikes.
On the right they go galloping over the Xiongnu,[33]
On the left turn back to trample the Xianbi.[34]
They give their bodies to the mercy of point and blade,
Never for a moment do they think of their own lives.
They cannot spare a thought for father and mother,
Still less pay heed to their children or their wives.
Their fame is written in the annals of the bold,
For selfish interests have no weight with them.
They die to save their country from its dangers,
And look on death as a sudden journey home.

---

[29] You and Bing are two of the Nine Provinces of ancient China. You corresponded roughly to present-day Liaoning and Hebei; Bing to North Shanxi and Shaanxi.

[30] The Yuezhi were an Indo-European people who had been driven out of Western Gansu by the Xiongnu early in the second century B.C. They moved west into North India, where they set up the Kushan dynasty. Here the term seems to have been a name for a kind of target used in archery practice.

[31] "Monkeys": literally, "nao monkeys." The nao is a golden-haired monkey with a long, hairy tail (hapale jacchus). Horses' hooves were used as targets for archery.

[32] The feathered summons was a call to arms, so styled because a cock's feather was attached to it as a sign of urgency.

[33] A Turkish-speaking people who were a constant menace to the Chinese for many centuries. They were gradually growing in power throughout the third century of our era.

[34] A proto-Mongolian people. Towards the end of the third century A.D. they made periodic raids on the Wei empire.

Figure 25. Tiger. Han dynasty rubbing. (Source: *Chinese Rubbings* [Beijing: Guoji shudian, n.d.])

Fu Xuan (217–278)
Pity Me!

Translated by Anne Birrell

Fu Xuan rose from poverty and obscurity to wealth and fame through his literary talent. He served as censor and lord chamberlain under the Jin Emperor Wu.

Pity me! my body is female,
My lowly state is hard to describe.
A boy faces door and gate,
Comes down on earth with a natural birthright,
His manly heart burns for the four seas,
Ten thousand leagues he yearns for windy dust.

A girl is born, there is no celebration,
She is not her family's prized jewel.
Grown up she is hidden in private rooms,
Veils her head, too shy to look on others.

Shedding tears she marries in another village,
Sudden like a cloudburst of rain.
With bowed head she calms her features,
White teeth clenched beneath red lips.
She kneels down countless times
To maids and concubines like grim guests.
Happy love is like Cloudy Han,
Like mallow or bean that lean toward spring sun.

Loving hearts in conflict are worse than water on fire,
One hundred wrongs are heaped upon the girl.

Her jade face with the years alters,
Her husband takes many new loves.
Once they were form and shadow,
Now they are Hun and Chinese.
Hun and Chinese sometimes see each other.
Love once severed is remote as Antares and Orion.

ZHANG HUA (232–300)
Emotion

Translated by John Frodsham

Zhang Hua was said to have begun life as a poor orphan employed as a goatherd. But his literary talents, especially his skill in writing rhapsodies, brought him to high office under the Western Jin dynasty. This is the third of a series of five poems under the title "Poems of Emotion," all of which have as their theme a wife's sorrow at her husband's absence.

A pure breeze billows bed-curtains and blinds,
The moon of dawning lights the secluded room.
My husband is away on a distant journey,
The light of his face has gone from the orchid chamber.
I clutch the vacant shadows to my breast,
Only a light quilt covers the empty bed.[35]
At the height of our joy, we grieved the nights were so short,
Now in my despair I resent the length of the dark.
I stroke my pillow, sigh in my loneliness,
Whelmed in sorrow, my heart is torn within me.

PAN YUE (247–300)
Homeward

Translated by Anne Birrell

Pan Yue was famous for his poetry and his good looks. It was said that when he drove through Luoyang women used to mob him, offering him peaches (the emblem of

---

[35] The bed is empty because she is unable to sleep while her husband is away.

immortality, or eternal youth). Charged with treasonous involvement in the revolt of
the Prince of Qi, he was executed.

Alone I pine. Where is the one I desire?
Man's life is like the morning dew.
Through boundless space I cleave to my severed land,
With tender passion I remember the way we were.
Your love pursues me even here,
And my heart looks homeward to you.
Our bodies parted cannot touch,
Our souls embrace midway.

Don't you see the hilltop pine?
In dead of winter it never changes from old.
Don't you see the cypress in the glen?
In yearend chill it keeps the same appearance.
Don't say I sought this separation,
From far away the bonds of love grow firmer.

In Mourning for His Dead Wife

Translated by Kenneth Rexroth

Winter and Spring have come and gone.
Once more Autumn overtakes
Summer. She has returned to
The Hidden Springs. And all the
World separates us forever.
Who will listen to my secrets
Now? Who will I live for now?
I try to do my job at Court,
And reluctantly go through
The motions of duty, and
Take up the tasks I had dropped.
When I come home I can think
Only of her. When I come
Into our room I expect to see her.
I catch her shadow on the
Screens and curtains. Her letters
Are the most precious examples
Of calligraphy. Her perfume
Still haunts the bedroom. Her clothes
Still hang there in the closet.

She is always alive in
My dreams. I wake with a start.
She vanishes. And I
Am overwhelmed with sorrow.
Two birds made a nest and then
There was only one. A pair
Of fishes were separated
And lost in the current.
The Autumn wind blows. The morning
Is misty, with dripping eaves.
All through the troubled night I was
Not able to forget in sleep.
I hope the time will come when
I am calm enough to beat
On a pot like Zhuangzi did
In mourning for his dead wife.

Lu Ji (261–303)
Summoning the Recluse

Translated by John Frodsham

Lu Ji was the grandson of the great Lu Xun, who had helped to establish the kingdom of Wu in A.D. 229. When Wu fell before the forces of Jin, Ji and his younger brother Yun escaped to their family estate at Huating, in the Yangtze delta, where they lay low for some ten years. In 290 the two of them went to Luoyang to take service with the Jin dynasty, under the patronage of the poet Zhang Hua. In 301 Ji got himself involved in Huan Xiu's plot to overthrow the Emperor and narrowly escaped execution. The following year he was persuaded to join the forces of a rebel prince in an attack on the capital. In the battle that ensued the troops under his command sustained a heavy defeat. Convinced that Ji had turned traitor, the prince ordered him to be executed along with his two sons and his brother. Ji is known as a writer of rhapsodies rather than as a lyric poet. [See chapter 15 for his "Literature: A Rhapsody."]

At break of day my heart is still unquiet,
I dress myself, then stand there hesitating.
I hesitate, not knowing where I should go —
A recluse may dwell in a secluded valley.
In the morning he culls cress in the southern gorge,
At night he rests at the foot of the western hill.
Light branches lace above him like the clouds,
Thick foliage forms a tent of kingfisher-green.
Eddying winds linger in the grove of magnolias,

Their fragrance swirls to meet the graceful trees.
The pleasant plashing of the mountain burn,
A waterfall rinsing the singing jade!
Mournful music wells from these magic waters,
Their falling notes echo in coigns of the crags.
Such perfect joy can simply not be feigned,
Why harm the Primal Unity with meddling?
If wealth and renown are difficult to obtain,
Better halt my carriage and do what I want to do.

ZUO SI (d. 306)
Summoning the Recluse

Translated by John Frodsham

Zuo Si is renowned above all as a writer of rhapsodies. His trilogy, the "Rhapsodies of the Three Capitals," is a masterpiece that was so widely copied out when it appeared that the price of paper in Luoyang was said to have risen as a result.

Leaning on my staff, I summon the recluse,
Since ancient times this wild road has lain here.
The cave in the crags is bare of criss-cross beams,
But among these hills is the sound of a singing lute.
White snow still lies on the mountain's shadowy side,
Red petals flare on the sunny side of the woods.
A stony spring washes over precious jade,
Delicate fishes are swimming in its depths.
No need of strings, or bamboo instruments,
When mountains and waters give forth their pure notes.
Why bother now to whistle or to sing,
When bushy trees are humming mournfully?
Autumn chrysanthemums are food enough for me,
The lonely orchid I wear as a buttonhole.
My feet are tired from all this pacing about,
I would like to throw my hat-pins clean away.[36]

---

[36] His official hat-pins, sign of his rank.

Guo Pu (226–324)
First Poem of Wandering Immortals

Translated by John Frodsham

Guo Pu was a scholar with a wide range of interests who wrote commentaries to ancient dictionaries, to the fabulous travellers' tales of the *Book of Hills and Seas* and *The Travels of Mu, Son of Heaven* [see chapter 2], and to the *Songs of the South* [see chapter 5]. But he is best known for his introduction of the terminology of neo-Taoist Dark Learning into verse. His "Fourteen Poems of Wandering Immortals" are his chief claim to fame. As the sixth century critic Zhong Rong astutely pointed out, these verses are not really about Immortals at all, but are simply an expression of his own unhappiness. Ironically enough, for all his yearnings for immortality, he was executed at the age of forty-eight by the rebel minister Wang Dun.

> The capital is a cave for wandering knights,
> Mountains and forests are hiding-places for hermits.
> What lustre lies in those vermilion gates?
> They cannot compare with a dwelling on Mount Penglai.
> The hermit drinks from the clear waves of the spring,
> Then climbs the hills to gather cinnabar buds.[37]
> Hidden from the world, he can stroll by Magic Stream,[38]
> So why should he care to climb the Ladder to the Clouds?
> A haughty official once lived in Lacquer Garden,[39]
> Master Lai's wife was fond of the hermit's life.[40]
> Advancement will surely let you see the dragon,[41]
> But try to retire, you're a goat with horns in the hedge.[42]
> Let me flee to the mountains, out of the wind and dust,
> And bowing low, take farewell of Yi and Qi.[43]

---

[37] Young cinnabar mushrooms, believe to confer immortality on those who ate them.

[38] The name of a stream west of Dacheng in Jingzhou. The hermit can enjoy himself on earth and need not ascend to the Taoist heaven.

[39] Zhuangzi was once official in Qiyuan (Lacquer Garden), according to his pseudo-biography in the *Records of the Grand Historian*.

[40] The *Biographies of Famous Women* records that the wife of Lao Laizi, a hermit on Mount Meng, dissuaded him from taking office with the king of Chu by threatening to leave him.

[41] To "see the dragon" is to take office and appear before the emperor. See *Book of Changes*, Hexagram 1.

[42] *Book of Changes*, Hexagram 42: "A goat butts against a hedge. It cannot retreat, it cannot advance."

[43] The hermits Bo Yi and Shu Qi.

Vision: Second Poem of Wandering Immortals

Translated by Graeme Wilson

To guard my body from the blight of age
I scoured those heights where magic simples thrive.
By breath-control, by drafts of powdered jade,
Within my breast a new Me came alive.

I grew immortal, coaxed a team of dragons
To wear my harness so that I might ride
The roll of thunder while, through whirling clouds,
White lightnings flickered from their scaly hide.

I dropped the reins of the charioteer of the sun
And stamped my foot to open heaven's gate.
Like some small horse's hoofprint filled with water
The ocean gleamed below me, and the great
Hunch of the world's most sky-assaulting mountain
Lay like an anthill in a shaven park.

Enormous sadness filled me as I watched
Earth's aimless turning in an empty dark.

YANG FANG (fourth century)
The Joy of Union

Translated by Burton Watson

Yang Fang served the Western Jin dynasty (265–317), before retiring to the countryside.

The loadstone beckons to the long needle,
the burning glass calls down fire and smoke;
gong and *shang* blend their voices;[44]
hearts alike draw closer still.
My love binds me to you,
shadow in pursuit of form;
we sleep side by side beneath close-woven quilts,
stuffed with wadding from a concord of cocoons.
In heat our waving fans are two wings that touch,

---

[44] *Gong* and *shang* are the first two notes of the musical scale.

in cold the felt mat seats us shoulder to shoulder.
You laugh and suddenly I am laughing too;
you grieve and all my joy has vanished.
Coming, I match my steps with yours;
going, we share the very same dust;
equals of the *qiongqiong* beasts,[45]
in no act forsaking one another.
My only wish is that we never part,
that we unite our bodies in a single form,
in life partners of a common chamber,
in death two people in one coffin.
Lady Xu proclaimed her love the truest;
our love surpasses words.[46]

Yu Chan (fl. 317)
Looking at Stone Drum Mountain

Translated by John Frodsham

Yu Chan is a little-known poet, only eighteen of whose poems are extant. His chief claim to fame is that he would appear to have been China's first nature poet, writing the type of verse known as "mountains-and-waters" poetry, nearly a century before this genre really came to maturity under Xie Lingyun [see chapter 12].

I called for my carriage and went to look at strange rarities,
Hastening on my way I went to the Magic Mountain.
In the morning I crossed the shores of a pure stream,
In the evening I rested by the Five Dragon Spring.
The Singing Stone holds a hidden music,
Thunderous and startling, it shakes the Nine Heavens.
It is not that there are no such things as Mysterious Transformations,
But that no one knows of the Spontaneity of the Spirits.
Flying mist brushes the blue peaks,
A green torrent washes between the crags.
I rinse my hands in the vernal purity of the spring,
While my eyes enjoy the fresh beauty of flowers in the sun.

---

[45] The *qiongqiong*, a fabulous beast, is an inseparable companion of the equally fabulous *juxu* beast, hence a symbol of fidelity.

[46] Xu Shu was the wife of an official of the Eastern Han named Qin Jia; several love poems are attributed to the devoted couple.

Zhan Fangsheng (fl. 386)
Poem About My Study at the Back of the House

Translated by John Frodsham

Zhan Fang-sheng must remain very much an enigma to us, since nothing is known about his career beyond the fact that he was at one time Administrative Counselor to the Army of Defense under the Eastern Jin (317–420). Only nine of his poems are extant. Some fit into the landscape genre; others are closer to the type of poem known as "garden poetry," at which Tao Yuanming [see chapter 11] excelled.

> I loosened my cap strings and put on serge clothes again,
> I said farewell to the Court and went back to my marshes.
> No carriages can get through my gates,
> My homestead is not even a full acre.
> Thick grasses fence in my courtyard,
> Orchids in profusion brush against my windows.
> I fondle my sons and nephews,
> I clasp the hands of my friends.
> We eat vegetables from the garden,
> And drink this spring wine.
> I open the lattice window and gaze out for a long time,
> I sit and look at the river and hills.
> Who can tell what I am feeling?
> There is no one I can tell my feelings to.
> Unpainted beams are easy to look after,
> The "dark root" does not easily rot.
> If you go towards it it will not be far away,
> The dark root can endure for ever.

꘎ Further Reading ꘎

Birrell, Anne, trans. *New Songs from a Jade Terrace: An Anthology of Early Chinese Love Poetry.* London: Allen & Unwin, 1982.

Frodsham, John D. *The Murmuring Stream: The Life and Works of the Chinese Nature Poet Hsieh Ling-yün.* Kuala Lumpur: University of Malaya Press, 1967.

——— . ed. and trans., with the collaboration of Ch'eng Hsi. *An Anthology of Chinese Verse: Han, Wei, Chin and the Northern and Southern Dynasties.* Oxford: Oxford University Press, 1967.

Kent, George W., trans. *Worlds of Dust and Jade: 47 Poems and Ballads of the Third Century Chinese Poet Ts'ao Chih.* New York: Philosophical Library, 1969.

Lowell, Amy (with Florence Ayscough), trans. *Fir-Flower Tablets: Poems Translated from the Chinese.* Boston: Houghton Mifflin, 1922.

Miao, R. C. *Early Medieval Chinese Poetry, the Life and Verse of Wang Ts'an.* Wiesbaden: Steiner, 1982.

Rexroth, Kenneth, trans. *One Hundred More Poems from the Chinese: Love and the Turning Year.* New York: New Directions, 1970.

Watson, Burton, ed. and trans. *The Columbia Book of Chinese Poetry: From Early Times to the Thirteenth Century.* New York: Columbia University Press, 1984.

"Pen-Song, Ink-Dance."
Seal carved by Deng Shiru (1743–1805)

Chapter 10

Bamboo Grove, Golden Valley, Orchid Pavilion

Coteries of the Third and Fourth Centuries

Ruan Ji, at the end of the Wei dynasty, was a man given to wine and reckless of all his actions. He would bare his head, let loose his hair and sit naked with his legs spread out. Later idle young aristocrats took him as their spiritual ancestor and said they had obtained the Root of the Great Way. They threw away their bonnets, took off their clothes and showed forth their ugliness like any animal. The more extreme were called Universal, and the less, Enlightened.

> — Wang Yin, *Jin Shu* (340) (*translated by Donald Holzman*)

While Liu Shi was visiting Shi Chong, he went to the privy, and saw there red silk curtains, a large bed, cushions, and rush mats, all very beautiful. Two female slaves were holding brocaded aromatic sachets. Liu turned around and retreated in haste, saying to his host, "Just now by mistake I entered your bedroom." Shi Chong replied, "It's just the privy."

> — Pei Qi, *Forest of Conversations* (362) (*translated by Richard Mather*)

Beaming flowers in the thicket,
Sporting fishes in the clear stream.
At the bank, cast a line —
Fully content — fish or no fish.

> — Wang Binzhi (fl. 350), "Orchid Pavilion Poem" (*translated by Wai-lim Yip*)

Introduction

Jacques Gernet

The period of four centuries from the decline of the Han dynasty to the formation of the aristocratic Sui and Tang empires was one of the richest and most complex in the intellectual history of the Chinese world. It was astonishingly fertile and abounded in innovations. It witnessed the development of a metaphysics completely free of the scholasticism of the Han age and enriched from the beginning of the fourth century by the Buddhist contribution of the Great Vehicle, the doctrine of the universal void. It also witnessed the affirmation of a sort of artistic and literary dilettantism, a pursuit of aesthetic pleasure for its own sake which was in complete contradiction with the classical tradition; it witnessed the first, remarkable attempts at literary and artistic criticism; the promotion of painting from the rank of craft to that of a skilled art, rich in intellectual content; the first appearance in world history of landscape as a subject for painting and as an artistic creation; and an unprecedented efflorescence of poetry....

The metaphysical movement (the revival of Taoist speculation) expressed itself, in the world of the literati, in nonconformist attitudes — contempt for rites, free and easy behavior, indifference to political life, a taste for spontaneity, love of nature. Independence and freedom of mind, a horror of conventions, a passion for art for art's sake are characteristic of the whole troubled age from the third to the sixth century. It would be legitimate to say that a sort of "aestheticism" was dominant throughout the Chinese Middle Ages. The first figures to show signs of these tendencies, which were so clearly opposed to the classical tradition, were the ones who were to be christened the Seven Sages of the Bamboo Grove, a little group of Bohemian literati, the best known of whom is the poet and musician Xi Kang. The same attitudes of mind, the same taste for nature and freedom persisted in aristocratic circles after the exodus to the valley of the Yangtze. We find them in the group headed by the famous poet and calligrapher Wang Xizhi, with whose name is connected one of the most famous episodes in the history of Chinese literature and calligraphy, the Gathering at the Orchid Pavilion at Kuaiji (in the neighborhood of present-day Shaoxing in Zhejiang), where, after many a libation, forty-one poets competed at improvising poems.

— *A History of Chinese Civilization*, 1982

SEVEN SAGES OF THE BAMBOO GROVE

Portraits from a late fourth-century tomb, with commentary by Ellen Johnston Laing, and anecdotes from *A New Account of Tales of the World* by Liu Yiqing (403–444)

Translated by Richard B. Mather

Ruan Ji of Chenliu (Henan), Xi Kang of Jiao Principality (Anhui), and Shan Tao of Henei (Henan) were all three of comparable age, Xi Kang being the youngest. Joining this company later were Liu Ling of Pei Principality (Jiangsu), Ruan Xian of Chenliu, Xiang Xiu of Henei, and Wang Rong of Langye (Shandong). The seven used to gather beneath a bamboo grove, letting their fancy free in merry revelry. For this reason the world called them the Seven Sages of the Bamboo Grove.

— from *A New Account of Tales of The World*, chapter 23[1]

Translator's Note: The problem of the real or fancied existence of a group known as the Seven Sages of the Bamboo Grove, flourishing at the end of the Wei kingdom in a place identified as Bamboo Grove, has been treated by many scholars. There is no doubt that the seven were contemporaries and that at least some were close friends. But it seems quite clear that the nostalgic refugees of Eastern Jin (317–420) reconstructed the supposed association in their effort to idealize the spirit of freedom and transcendence the Seven came to symbolize. The recent discovery in 1960 of a stamped brick representation of them from a tomb at Xishanqiao near Nanjing, dating from the fourth century, is further evidence of their popularity in the southern capital.

WANG RONG (234–305)

Commentary: Wang Rong, the first figure on the north panel, was a shrewd man of noble family, noted for his tremendous wealth and avarice. He is depicted as seated on a mat placed between a gingko and a willow. Although not known as a contortionist, he sits in an extremely peculiar posture with both legs bent vertically in opposite directions so that the foot of one leg is near the knee of the other. Beside him are a handled bowl, presumably of wine, in which floats a miniature duck. He reclines casually against a square, boxlike arm rest and dallies with a *ruyi*[2] in an off-hand fashion.[3]

---

[1] This work by Liu Yiqing (403–444) is hereafter referred to in this chapter as *Tales*. All translations are by Richard Mather. For an introduction to the work, and further extracts, see chapter 16. *Eds.*

[2] A scepterlike object. See the note to "Coral Trees," chapter 16. *Eds.*

[3] This and subsequent commentaries are by Ellen Johnston Laing. *Eds.*

Figure 26. Wang Rong. Impressed clay brick from a tomb in Nanjing. (Source: Ellen Johnston Laing, "Neo-Taoism and the 'Seven Sages of the Bamboo Grove' in Chinese Painting," *Artibus Asiae* [1974], 36 [1/2])

Spoiling the Mood

Xi Kang, Ruan Ji, Shan Tao, and Liu Ling were in the Bamboo Grove drinking and were well in their cups when Wang Rong arrived. Ruan Ji said, "Here comes this vulgar fellow again to spoil our mood."

Laughing, Wang replied, "Do you mean to say your mood is something that can be spoiled?"

— from *Tales*, chapter 25

Master Huang's Wineshop

Once while Wang Rong was serving as president of the Imperial Secretariat (301–302), wearing his ceremonial robes and riding in a light one-horse carriage, he passed beneath Master Huang's Wineshop.

Looking back, he remarked to the guests in the carriage behind him, "Long ago I used to drink and make merry in this wineshop with Xi Kang and Ruan Ji, and in the outings in the Bamboo Grove I also took a humble part. But ever since Xi Kang's premature death (in 262) and Ruan Ji's passing (263) I've been hemmed in by the times. Today as I look on this place, even though it's so near, it seems as far away as the hills and rivers."

— from *Tales*, chapter 17

SHAN TAO (205–283)

Commentary: Facing Wang Rong, but separated from him by the willow tree, is Shan Tao. He sits erect; in his left hand he holds a wine cup, his right arm clasps the knee

Figure 27. Shan Tao. Impressed clay brick from a tomb in Nanjing. (Source: Ellen Johnston Laing, "Neo-Taoism and the 'Seven Sages of the Bamboo Grove' in Chinese Painting," *Artibus Asiae* [1974], 36 [1/2])

of his raised right leg and his right hand holds back the left sleeve of his garment as he raises the wine cup. His left leg is bent in front of his body. Next to him is a wine bowl. His more modest pose and erect posture contrast with the contorted posture of Wang Rong. Like Wang, Shan devoted his life to civil service, but unlike Wang, was appreciated for his straightforward upright integrity. [See chapter 14 for Xi Kang's famous letter to Shan Tao.]

Unpolished Jade

Wang Rong characterized Shan Tao as follows: "He's like unpolished jade or unrefined gold. Everyone delights in his great value, but no one knows how to name what kind of vessel he is."

— from *Tales*, chapter 8

RUAN JI (210–263)

Figure 28. Ruan Ji. (Source: Ellen Johnston Laing, "Neo-Taoism and the 'Seven Sages of the Bamboo Grove' in Chinese Painting," *Artibus Asiae* [1974], 36 [1/2])

Commentary: To Shan Tao's left is a locust tree and then the figure of Ruan Ji, who sits facing the last figure in the panel, Xi Kang. These two figures are separated by a pine tree; a gingko is placed beyond Xi Kang at the end of the panel. Ruan Ji's official biography stresses his anti-Confucian behavior, tells us that he loved wine, knew how to whistle and was an expert on the *qin*, or Chinese lute. He was also famous for his beautiful and imaginative poetry. He is shown here as seated on a mat with one knee up, the other leg extended; his body is braced by his bare left arm, while the thumb of his right hand is held in front of his mouth and the fingers are extended. This gesture has been interpreted as one of whistling, and indeed, Ruan's lips seem puckered and his cheeks distended.... Ruan was also wont to engage in occult Taoist practices (his whistling may be related to breath control exercises) and he is known to have sought the advice of the mysterious Taoist adept Sun Deng. A great toper, Ruan once remained stone drunk for sixty days to avoid marrying into the usurping Sima clan.

Whistling

When Ruan Ji whistled,[4] he could be heard several hundred paces away. In the Sumen Mountains there appeared from nowhere a Realized Man about whom the woodcutters were all relaying tales. Ruan Ji went to see for himself and spied the man squatting with clasped knees by the edge of a cliff. Ji climbed the ridge to approach him and then squatted opposite him. Ji rehearsed for him briefly matters from antiquity to the present, beginning with an exposition of the Way of Mystical Quiescence of the Yellow Emperor and Shen Nong, and ending with an investigation of the excellence of the Supreme Virtue of the Three Ages. But when Ji asked his opinion about it he remained aloof and made no reply. Ji then went on to expound that which lies beyond Activism, and the techniques of Resting the Spirit and Conducting the Vital Force. But when Ji looked toward him for a reply, he was still exactly as before, fixedly staring without turning. Ji therefore turned toward him and made a long whistling sound. After a long while the man finally laughed and said, "Do it again." Ji whistled a second time, but as his interest was now exhausted, he withdrew. He had returned about halfway down the ridge when he heard above him a shrillness like an orchestra of many instruments,

---

[4] Donald Holzman, in his study of Ruan Ji, gives Sun Guang's (765) definition of "whistling" — "a sound produced by breath striking against the tip of the tongue ..., a method of communicating with the spirits and achieving immortality" — and comments: "Whatever whistling did signify, the important thing to note is that it was an unintellectual art, probably a fairly strange kind of sound divorced from speech and reason.... Like the Zen masters of the Tang dynasty who, with their eructations and physical blows, resemble him so much, the Realized Man knows that the Truth is beyond words.... His whistling is the very breath of Nature." *Eds.*

while forests and valleys re-echoed with the sound. Turning back to look, he discovered it was the whistling of the man he had just visited.

— from Tales, *chapter 18*

Commandant of Infantry

There was a vacancy in the office of the commandant of infantry, in the commissary of which were stored several hundred *hu*[5] of wine. It was for this reason that Ruan Ji requested to become commandant of infantry.

— from Tales, *chapter 23*

Nothing Amiss

The wife of Ruan Ji's neighbor was very pretty. She worked as a barmaid tending the vats and selling wine. Ruan and Wang Rong frequently drank at her place, and after Ruan became drunk he would sleep by this woman's side. Her husband at first was extraordinarily suspicious of him, but after careful investigation he eventually ceased to think anything amiss.

— from Tales, *chapter 23*

A Rough and Rugged Terrain

Wang Gong once asked Wang Chen, "How would Ruan Ji compare with Sima Xiangru?"

Wang replied, "Ruan Ji's breast was a rough and rugged terrain; that's why he needed wine to irrigate it."

— from Tales, *chapter 23*

The Whites of His Eyes

When Ruan Ji was in mourning Xi Xi (brother of Xi Kang) went to pay him a visit of condolence. Now Ji was able to look with the whites of his eyes, and he used the whites of his eyes when greeting worldly gentlemen. When Xi arrived, Ji did not perform the customary weeping. Observing his white eyes, Xi withdrew in dismay.

Later, when Xi's brother, Kang, learned of it, he took a gift of wine, and, tucking his lute under his arm, went to visit Ji, after which they became good friends.

— from commentary to Tales, *chapter 24*

---

[5] A traditional measure equivalent to several gallons. *Eds.*

Eight Poems of My Heart

Translated by Jerome Ch'en and Michael Bullock

Ruan Ji's real importance in the Chinese poetic tradition rests on his eighty-two pentameter poems entitled "Poems of My Heart," which describe his anguish and fear and his desire to find constancy and purity in an inconstant and impure world. His poetry abounds in obscure satire and allegory, and some poems are almost impenetrable. Unable to find fulfilment in politics (the normal realm of action for a man of his class and times), he turned towards philosophy and religion, debating with himself on philosophical and religious problems, and exploring, in a subjective, introverted way, themes unknown in earlier poetry.

— Donald Holzman, *Indiana Companion*, 1986

Sleepless at Midnight

Being sleepless at midnight,
I rise to play the lute.
The moon is visible through the curtains
And a gentle breeze sways the cord of my robe.
A lonely wild-goose cries in the wilderness
And is echoed by a bird in the woods.
As it circles, it gazes
At me, alone, imbued with sadness.

In My Youth

In my youth,
I too was fond of singing and dancing.
I went west to the Capital
And frequented the Li's and the Zhao's.
Before the fun came to an end,
I realized time had been wasted.
On my return journey,
I looked back at the riverside district
Where I had squandered a great deal,
So that not a coin was left.
Coming to the Taihang mountain path,
I was afraid of again losing my way.

Last Rays of the Sun

The last rays of the setting sun,
Which once shone upon me warmly, have now gone.
The wind keeps returning to strike the walls

While cold birds seek warmth in one another's breast.
Clinging to their feathers,
They fear hunger in silence.
O, men of influence
Remember to withdraw in time!
You look sad and frail.
Is it because of power and fame?
I prefer to fly with jays and tits,
Not with hoary herons.
For they travel high and far,
Making the return too hard.

Weird Dances

Weird dances are performed in the north street
And near the river decadent songs are heard.
These flighty, leisured youths,
Enslaved by fads and fashions,
Always take a short cut
To sensual pleasure.
I see no one racing against the sun
Or turning his staff into a forest.
The recipe for a long life
Alone calms my heart.

Inscribe on Your Heart

Inscribe on your heart
Every inch of the time at sunset.
Adjust your sleeves, unsheathe a slender sword,
And look up at the passing clouds.
Among them a dark stork
Raises its head and rattles its beak.
Darting aloft, it vanishes into the sky.
Never again will it be heard.
It is no company for the cuckoos and the crows
That circle round the Court.

Day and Night

Day and night
Revolve,
While my face wrinkles.

And my spirit wanes,
But the sight of injustice still pains me.
One change induces another
That cannot be dealt with by tact or wit.
The cycle goes on for ever.
I only fear that in a moment
Life will disperse in the wind.
I have always trodden on thin ice.
Yet no one knows!

As Dew-Drops Freeze

As dew-drops freeze
Green grass wilts.
Gentlemen do not understand this,
Yet are said to be wise.
Let me ride on a cloud
To visit the immortals.

In the Shadow of Death

I am growing old
In the shadow of death.
My admiration goes to the waves
That come from the same source
        to flow in different ways.
Life is not worthy of mention
Yet hate and enmity have been my tribulation.
Do I really have adversaries?
Or are my sensitive ears deceiving my eyes?
Vision and hearing are both waning.
But malice against me is still waxing.
I shall call on my Taoist friends;
Together we shall go on a journey.

Learning

Translated by Graeme Wilson

Long years ago, at fifteen, maybe less,
How earnestly I loved the Classics then:
Poor as I was, my heart possessed true wealth,
That ache to learn such truths as make good men.

I threw all windows wide upon the world
And climbed high hills to find those truths I sought.
The heights were knobbed with gravemounds.
Hundreds and hundreds
Of hundreds and hundreds all brought down to nought.

Thousands of thousands of thousands of years from now
What will a good name count for? Nothing at all.
At last I understand earth's oldest wisdom
And laught out loud at that lad who was learning's thrall.

In Answer to Fu Yi's Letter

Translated by Donald Holzman

Fu Yi's letter argued that Ruan Ji (whom he did not know intimately) was exactly the kind of man needed by the flourishing Wei dynasty, and that he should use his intelligence and engage in worldly action. "I hear that you roar with indignation and anguish, sobbing pathetically, pouring out tears. Or that at times you strike your belly and laugh loudly, rolling up your eyes, gazing on high. You are by nature domineering and go against the world; you've set your target against the wind and ignore all others as if there were no one else alive." He ended his letter by asking Ruan Ji to explain himself so that he, Fu Yi, could explain him to the rest of the world. Ruan Ji's answer is couched in purely Taoist terms.

The reception of your letter and the perusal of its contents have put me in a mind to send you an answer.

Now, not even the fastest wings can visit the heights of the nine-fold blue skies, nor can the darkest fins fathom the depths of the Four Seas. How much less can the unfeathered and unfinned species talk about them? A dark cloud, too, has no fixed form; the winged dragon has no constant manner. The former will sometimes pass over in the morning and be rolled up at night, its transformations taking place with great rapidity; the latter will sometimes hide in the mud or fly in the sky, descending in the morning and rising in the evening. When they spread themselves out, the Eight Directions do not suffice to contain them; when they squeeze themselves together, they can move with ease in no place at all. But this cannot be seen by a blind man or understood by a tiny insect; great and distant things cannot be examined by men of limited powers; divine changes and spiritual transformations cannot be investigated by men with small capacities. How can you, Sir, in your petty way, endeavor to seek my conception of the Truth?

Men's powers cannot be considered equal and their tastes differ: the phoenix *luan* leaps into the Milky Way to dance and to move its wings, but the dove and the quail are happy to swoop above the brushwood forest; the hornless dragon floats to the Eight Shores to wash his scales, but the gregarious turtle enjoys himself in puddles along the road. Thus we each follow our own preferences in our affections to procure our joy; if you stick to your own taste and criticize another's you will never be able to see all tastes as quite relative and equal, as a truly great man does.

Now, when a man sets up his aims in life, he should spread his net wide to catch the world; how could he complacently march into the net himself? It is he who should set himself up as an example for the vulgar crowd: how could he idly cut down his own natural gifts in order to conform to a label of their giving? And if by chance the moment is not propitious to his designs, if the secret springs of destiny do not conform, then he must let his spirit leap up, he must raise high his will and leave far behind the world as he transcends it. Then he can let his spiritual energy run wild on the outer rim of the Realm of Mystery; he can lift up his marvellous ambitions beyond the limits of heaven and earth, soaring upon rays of light, swooping up and down, mounting chaotically into the heights. Relaxed, he moves together with the sun and the moon. When he encounters fame or renown, he equates them with any other transformation in the world's vicissitudes. He goes above that which has nothing above it and below that which has nothing below it. He dwells in no room and leaves through no gate, equating all the movements of the ten thousand things, following the contractions and swellings of the Six Breaths of the universe. He holds together at the Great Pole all the strings of the Somber Net and caresses the star Celestial One in the chaotic wastes of space. The swirling grime of our world cannot follow in his wake, nor can its flying dust besmirch his purity. He has only left his corporeal body here with us: how could you hope to examine his spirit?

In spite of the fact that, as you say, there are no professions that cannot be heard of, no plans that cannot be told, surely it is not strange to say that intelligence has limits? Just look, Sir, where your desires lead you: you would boast of having money to keep a city-toppling beauty, and then you seek after piddling business affairs; you establish heaven-reaching rituals, and then compare men using superficial social labels. You fatigue your precious body to enslave others, and then harbor the fetid filth such labor produces in your system to hasten your death. You are like a man sunk in a puddle formed in an ox's hoofprint who is indignant because heaven's river, the Milky Way, has no end! To hold these base attitudes is shameful; to engage in these acts is pathetic!

I believe in a transcendent plan of action and have faith in a great Way that is vast and secret. To plod with slow and cramped step along the common road, with no way to cast my thoughts afar, simply makes me melancholy.

A chronic illness has weakened my spirits these last days and I have not been able to put forth many forceful teachings.

XI KANG (223–262)

Figure 29. Xi Kang. (Source: Ellen Johnston Laing, "Neo-Taoism and the 'Seven Sages of the Bamboo Grove' in Chinese Painting," *Artibus Asiae* [1974], 36 [1/2])

Commentary: Xi Kang, depicted playing his lute, or *qin*, with elegant finesse and concentration, is seen in a neatly frontal view with his head turned toward Ruan Ji. The lute rests on Xi's bare left leg which is bent horizontally in front of him; his right knee is raised. Xi, noted as a musician and as a poet, frequently worked at a forge, apparently "to imitate the activity of the Tao, the Great Smith"; and he, too, was acquainted with the mountain recluse, Sun Deng. Despite Xi's efforts to remain aloof from the intrigues of the times, he was unwittingly snared in an unfortunate political trap and executed.

I Came, I'm Leaving

Zhong Hui was thoroughly equipped with ability and reasoning powers, but he had not previously been acquainted with Xi Kang. Zhong wanted to go to visit Kang in company with other worthy and outstanding gentlemen of the time. Kang was at that moment engaged in forging metal beneath a tree, with Xiang Xiu assisting him at the bellows. Kang continued to pound with the hammer without interruption, as if no one else were present. Some time passed without his exchanging a single word, until Zhong finally rose to go. Kang said, "What had you heard that made you come, and what have you seen that now makes you leave?"

Zhong replied, "I came after hearing what I heard, and I'm leaving after seeing what I've seen."

— from *Tales*, chapter 24

Solitary Pine

Xi Kang's body was seven feet eight inches tall, and his manner and appearance conspicuously outstanding. Some who saw him sighed, saying, "Serene and sedate, fresh and transparent, pure and exalted!" Others would say, "Soughing like the wind beneath the pines, high and gently blowing."

Shan Tao said, "As a person Xi Kang is majestically towering, like a solitary pine tree standing alone. But when he's drunk he leans crazily like a jade mountain about to collapse."

— from *Tales*, chapter 14

The Melody Is No More

On the eve of Xi Kang's execution in the Eastern Marketplace of Luoyang (in 262), his spirit and manner showed no change. Taking out his seven-stringed zither (*qin*), he plucked the strings and played the "Melody of Guangling." When the song was ended, he said, "Yuan Jun once asked to learn this melody, but I remained firm in my stubbornness, and never gave it to him. From now on the 'Melody of Guangling' is no more!"

Three thousand scholars of the Grand Academy sent up a petition requesting Xi's release to become their teacher, but it was not granted. Sima Zhao (who had ordered the execution) himself later repented of it.

— from *Tales*, chapter 6

The Lute: A Rhapsody
Extracts

Translated by Robert Van Gulik

During the Jin and Wei periods, when Buddhism spread over China, and neo-Taoism flourished, the magical virtues of the Lute, or *Qin*, were much praised, as being conducive to meditation, and prolonging life. Xi Kang's celebrated rhapsody describes in exquisite language the mysterious virtues of the Lute, and the materials suitable for building it.

1

From the days of my youth I loved music, and I have practiced it ever since.

For it appears to me that while things have their rise and decay, only music never changes;

And while in the end one is satiated by all flavors, one is never tired of music.

It is a means for guiding and nurturing the spirit, and for elevating and harmonizing the emotions.

Nothing equals music in its power to bring solace to those who dwell in poverty and loneliness.

Therefore, if instrumental music proves to be insufficient, one hums a melody to set forth one's intention;

If this is not sufficient, one composes words for the tune, in order fully to express one's thoughts.[6]

2

Brilliant men of former ages have in poetical compositions and odes of praise written about the eight kinds of musical instruments[7] and the various figures of song and dance....

Of all musical instruments the lute has the greatest virtue.

Therefore I have now made a poetical essay, or rhapsody, setting forth my thoughts regarding the lute.

This essay says:

---

[6] This sentence is an elaboration of the second paragraph of the "Greater Preface" to the *Book of Songs*. [See chapter 15.]

[7] Made of stone, metal, silk, bamboo, wood, skin, gourd, and clay.

3

The trees of that species from which lutes are built[8] grow on the lofty ridges of steep mountains.

Rich soil ensures them great age, their tapering stems rise high into the sky.

They are saturated with the pure harmony of Heaven and Earth, they inhale the beneficent splendor of sun and moon.

Their solitary luxuriant growth overtops the surrounding vegetation, their verdure leaps high to the azure vault of heaven.

At twilight they borrow the red glow of the evening sky, in the morning the sun dries the dew on their stems.

For a thousand years they wait for him who shall recognize their value, quietly they repose, forever robust.

4

The scenery there is rugged and irregular, with many a hidden depth.

There are rock-covered heights and lonely mountain peaks, dark rocks and craggy ascents, steep cliffs and precipitous ridges.

Red rocks rise steeply upward, and there are green walls ten thousand fathoms high.

Mountain crest rises above mountain crest, they seem to be pressed down by the clouds.

Lofty and verdurous summits far off show their massive shapes; here and there a solitary peak rising in impressive splendor draws the eye.

5

The spiritual haze that hovers over these mountains mingles with the clouds, and from their mysterious founts stream burst forth.

Tumbling waves gush one after the other; running onwards they vie in crazy torrents, they hurtle themselves against rocks and beat in recesses in a boiling rage.

The wild waters churn, the billows spurt foam, with a roaring noise they turn round and round, like a mass of intertwined, coiling dragons.

Then they spread out and form the great streams that gush forth to water the land.

Farther on, their current slows down, to broaden out into a floating vastness.

---

[8] Trees of the *catalpa* species.

Placidly the waters spread out wider and wider, till they embrace mountains and hills.

6

Now observing more closely what is found growing in this region, the precious products of this mysterious domain, one sees on the slopes of these mountains rare and strangely shaped jadestone, and deep red jasper, massed about in luxuriant abundance.

Vernal orchids cover their eastern sides, their western slopes produce the yellow crab-apple tree.

On their southern sides the immortal Juanzi[9] dwells, in front an ambrosia fountain bubbles up.

Their summits are covered with dark clouds, phoenixes with fluttering wings gather on their peaks.

Pure dew moistens their flanks, a gentle breeze blows over them.

They are quiet in majestic passiveness, they are subtle in serene repose.

Being surrounded by such scenery, these trees naturally are spiritual and beautiful, and suitable for inspiring the love of music.

7

Here it is that wise men fleeing the world, worthy companions of a Yongqi[10] or Qili,[11] together ascend high mountain arches and cross deep-cut vales.

Clinging to branches of fairy trees they climb steep ridges, in order that they may roam under these trees.

Wandering about they remain gazing into the distance for ever; their horizon is as wide as that of a bird in its flight.

Looking upward they see the Kunlun ranges, looking down they discern the marshes that border the ocean.

They point to the Cangwu mountains[12] afar off, they approach the imposing calm of meandering rivers.

---

[9] Said to have been a recluse from the state of Qi, who could command wind and rain and reputedly wrote a treatise entitled *The Mind of the Lute.*

[10] A recluse famous as a lute player, said to have lived on Mount Tai.

[11] A recluse of the beginning of the Han dynasty.

[12] According to the *Book of Hills and Seas*, a mountain range containing Mount Jiuyi, where the mythical Emperor Shun (traditionally the inventor of the lute) was buried.

Then they realize the constraining shackles of worldly life, and longingly they look up to the splendor that lingers over Mount Ji.[13]

Enamoured with the generous broadness of these heights, their hearts are filled with noble emotions, and they forget to return.

8

Their emotions become broad and even, their eyes have a faraway look.

They long to continue the music left by the Yellow Emperor,[14] they cherish the mountain spirit Laodong of the Gui rock,[15] and admire the inspired songs of Tai Yong.[16]

Beholding these trees they grow thoughtful, they long to express the feelings of their hearts in a tangible way.

Then they lop off the young branches, and weigh and measure a block of wood meet to be employed.

Thus, in order to expand their feelings, Superior Men made the Elegant Lute....

9

One should play the lute in a high building or on a towering terrace, in a spacious hall or in a secluded room;

On a wintry night when the air is limpid and a bright moon is shining; clad in rustling new garments whose perfume pervades the air: then the instrument is cool to the touch, and the strings are correctly tuned.

If the heart is tranquil and the hands are able, the touch of the fingers will respond to the thoughts, and the player will be able to express himself in his music....

10

In the first part of the third month, clad in the elegant garb proper to that season, together with some good friends one sets out for a pleasant excursion.

---

[13] The mountain where it is said that Xu You, the famous recluse of antiquity, retired in disgust when the mythical Emperor Yao offered him the empire.

[14] That is, the music of the lute, the Yellow Emperor being also credited with having invented this instrument.

[15] According to the *Book of Hills and Seas*, on Mount Gui lives a spirit whose voice is clear like bronze bells or stone chimes. This spirit is said to have been a son of the Yellow Emperor.

[16] The music master of the Yellow Emperor.

They wander through fragrant gardens, climb hills, rest under old trees or sit under gaily decorated sunshades.

They walk along clear streams, composing new poems. They admire the leisurely movements of water creatures, and enjoy the verdure.

Then is the right time for playing on the lute the songs left by the Emperor Shun, which elevate the spirit and fill one with longing sadness.

Or, when one holds an informal feast in a daily decorated hall, together with one's bosom friends and some intimate guests, enjoying dishes of rare flavor sprinkled with excellent wine of subtle bouquet, then is the right time to play tunes like Nanjing and Xiqin, or to intone the melodies Lingyang and Baren.

All sorts of other melodies may also be played; they will cheer up those who hear them and exalt their spirits....

11

In truth, those people who are not of a free and detached disposition cannot find enjoyment in lute music.

Those who are not profound and serene cannot dwell with it. Those who are not broad-minded cannot ungrudgingly give themselves to it.

Those who are not of the utmost refinement cannot understand its deep significance....

12

In admiration of the rich excellence of this musical instrument, for my own satisfaction I composed this essay.

I shall always cherish the lute, without ever tiring of it. I believe it is a treasure of present and bygone days.

In conclusion, I sing:
Solemn indeed is the virtue of the lute,
It cannot be fathomed.
Purity of body and aloofness of heart,
Difficult indeed it is to attain these heights.
Good instruments and excellent players.
Where are those to be found in the present age?
The silk strings resounding in harmony,
This music surpasses all other arts.
As those who understand music are few.
Who can truly treasure this instrument?
Only to the Superior Man is it given
Completely to understand the elegant lute.

A Song of Disillusionment

Translated by John Turner

Wisdom and learning I abhor:
Wander, my soul, in Quietude!
Wisdom and learning I detest:
In Quietude I set my rest:
Repenting what may be amiss,
All my ambition, all my bliss,
To trail my hook by some ravine,
Lord of a kingdom quite unseen.
And so, bare-headed as I go,
Though all around are scenes of woe,
This be my song for evermore:
Wander, my soul, in Quietude!

Letter to Shan Tao

Translated by J. R. Hightower

In this letter, written shortly before his death, Xi Kang broke off relations with his former friend Shan Tao, who had not kept to his vow of uncompromising integrity, and who, after accepting a high post, had even dared to suggest that Xi Kang should become his assistant. Xi Kang, full of violent indignation, threw the offer back in his face, saying abruptly that his aspirations were not of this world, and explaining with such eloquence what Flaubert somewhere in his letters has expressed in the lapidary formula: *Les honneurs déshonorent, le titre dégrade, la fonction abrutit.*

— Etienne Balazs, 1964

Some time ago you spoke of me to your uncle, the Prefect of Yingchuan, and I must say I found your estimate of me just. But I wondered how you could have come to so accurate an understanding without really knowing what my principles are. Last year when I came back from Hedong, Gongsun Chong and Lü An said you had proposed me as your successor in office. Nothing came of it, but your proposal made it obvious you really did not understand me at all.

You are versatile: you accept most things and are surprised at little. I, on the other hand, am by nature straightforward and narrow-minded: there are lots of things that I cannot put up with. It was only chance that made us friends. When recently I heard of your promotion in office, I was upset and unhappy, fearing that the cook would be shy of doing the carving by himself and would call in the Impersonator of the Dead to help, handing over a kitchen knife soiled with rancid fat. Hence I am writing to make clear what may and may not be done.

It used to be that when in my reading I came across people resolutely above the world, I rather doubted their existence, but now I am convinced that they really do exist after all. One can be so constituted that there are things one cannot endure; honest endorsement cannot be forced. So it is perhaps idle to talk about the familiar "man of understanding" who can put up with anything, who takes no exception to vulgarity around him but who still preserves his integrity within; who goes along with the vacillations of the times without ever feeling a twinge of regret. Laozi and Zhuang Zhou are my masters: they held mean positions. I would hardly criticize *them*. And Confucius, out of his love for all, was ready to hold a coachman's whip; and Ziwen, with no desire for the job, was thrice prime minister: these were gentlemen whose minds were bent on saving the world. This is what is meant by "in success, he shares the benefits with all and does not vacillate; in obscurity, he is content and not depressed."

From this point of view, Yao and Shun's ruling the world, Xu You's retirement to the hills, Zifang's helping Han and Jieyu's singing as he walked all add up to the same thing. When you consider all these gentlemen, they can be said to have succeeded in doing what they wanted. Hence all the various modes of conduct of the gentleman take him to the same goal by different paths. He acts in accordance with his nature and rests where he finds his ease. Thus there are those who stick to the court and never emerge, and those who enter the wilderness and never come back.

Moreover, I am filled with admiration when I read the biographies of the recluses Shang Ziping and Tai Xiaowei and can imagine what sort of men they were. Add to that the fact that I lost my father when young, was spoiled by my mother and elder brother and never took up the study of the Classics. I was already wayward and lazy by nature, so that my muscles became weak and my flesh flabby. I would commonly go half a month without washing my face, and until the itching became a considerable annoyance, I would not wash my hair. When I had to urinate, if I could stand it I would wait until my bladder cramped inside before I got up.

Further, I was long left to my own devices, and my disposition became arrogant and careless, my bluntness diametrically opposed to etiquette; laziness and rudeness reinforcing one another. But my friends were indulgent, and did not attack me for my faults.

Besides, my taste for independence was aggravated by my reading of Zhuangzi and Laozi; as a result any desire for fame or success grew daily weaker, and my commitment to freedom increasingly firmer. In this I am like the wild deer, which captured young and reared in captivity will be docile and obedient. But if it be caught when full-grown, it will stare wildly and butt against its bonds, dashing into boiling water or fire to escape. You may dress it up with a golden bridle and feed it delicacies, and it will but long the more for its native woods and yearn for rich pasture.

Ruan Ji is not one to talk about people's faults, and I have tried to model myself after him, but in vain. He is a man of finer character than most, one who never injured another. Only in drinking does he go to excess. But even so the proper and correct gentlemen with their restrictions hate him as a mortal enemy, and it is only thanks to the protection of Generalissimo Sima Zhao that he survives. But I, without Ruan Ji's superiority, have the faults of being rude and unrestrained, ignorant of people's characters and blind to opportunity, not careful like Shi Fen, but driven to carry things to their end. The longer I were involved in affairs the more clearly would these defects show. I might want to stay out of trouble, but would it be possible?

Furthermore, in society there are prescribed courtesies, and the court has its rules. When I consider the matter carefully, there are seven things I could never stand and two things which would never be condoned. I am fond of lying late abed, and the herald at my door would not leave me in peace: this is the first thing I could not stand. I like to walk, singing, with my lute in my arms, or go fowling or fishing in the woods. But surrounded by subordinates, I would be unable to move freely — this is the second thing I could not stand. When I kneel for a while I become as though paralyzed and unable to move. Being infested with lice, I am always scratching. To have to bow and kowtow to my superiors while dressed up in formal clothes — this is the third thing I could not stand. I have never been a facile calligrapher and do not like to write letters. Business matters would pile up on my table and fill my desk. To fail to answer would be bad manners and a violation of duty, but I would not long be able to force myself to do it. This is the fourth thing I could not stand. I do not like funerals and mourning, but these are things people consider important. Far from forgiving my offense, their resentment would reach the point where they would like to see me injured. Although in alarm I might make the effort, I still could not change my nature. If I were to bend my mind to the expectations of the crowd, it would be dissembling and dishonest, and even so I would not be sure to go unblamed — this is the fifth thing I could not stand. I do not care for the crowd and yet I would have to serve together with such people. Or on occasions when guests fill the table and their clamor deafens the ears, their noise and dirt contaminating the place, before my very eyes they would indulge in their double-dealings. This is the sixth thing I could not stand. My heart cannot bear trouble, and official life is full of it. One's mind is bound with a thousand cares, one's thoughts are involved with worldly affairs. This is the seventh thing I could not stand.

Further, I am always finding fault with Tang and Wu Wang, or running down the Duke of Zhou and Confucius. If I did not stop this in society, it is clear that the religion of the times would not put up with me. This is the first thing which would never be condoned. I am quite ruthless in my hatred of evil, and speak out without hesitation, whenever I have the occasion. This is the second thing which would never be condoned.

To try to control these nine weaknesses with a disposition as narrow and niggling as mine could only result in my falling ill, if indeed I were able to avoid trouble with the authorities. Would I be long in the world of men? Besides, I have studied in the esoteric lore of the Taoist masters, where a man's life can be indefinitely prolonged through eating herbs, and I firmly believe this to be so. To wander among the hills and streams, observing fish and birds, is what gives my heart great pleasure. Once I embarked on an official career, this is something I would have to give up forthwith. Why should I relinquish what gives me pleasure for something that fills me with dread?

What is esteemed in human relationships is the just estimate of another's inborn nature, and helping him to realize it. When you see a straight piece of wood, you do not want to make it into a wheel, nor do you try to make a rafter of a crooked piece, and this is because you would not want to pervert its heaven-given quality, but rather see that it finds its proper place. Now all the four classes of people have each their own occupation, in which each takes pleasure in fulfilling his own ambition. It is only the man of understanding who can comprehend all of them. In this you have only to seek within yourself to know that one may not, out of one's own preference for formal clothes, force the people of Yue to wear figured caps, or, because one has a taste for putrid meat, try to feed a phoenix a dead rat.

Of late I have been studying the techniques of prolonging one's life, casting out all ideas of fame and glory, eliminating tastes, and letting my mind wander in stillness: what is most worthwhile to me is Inaction. Even if there were not these nine concerns, I could still pay no attention to your wishes. But beyond this, my mind tends toward melancholy, increasingly so of late, and I am personally convinced that I would not be able to stand any occupation in which I took no pleasure. I really know myself in this respect. If worse comes to worst and there is no way out, then I shall simply die. But you have no grudge against me that you should cause me to lie lifeless in the gutter.

I am continually unhappy over the recent loss of the company of my mother and elder brother. My daughter is thirteen, my son eight years old — neither grown to maturity, and I am in ill health. This is another fact that pains me so much I cannot bear to speak further of it.

Today I only wish to stay on in this out-of-the-way lane and bring up my children and grandchildren, on occasion relaxing and reminiscing with old friends — a cup of unstrained wine, a song to the lute: this is the sun of my desires and ambitions.

If you keep on relentlessly nagging me, it can only be because you are anxious to get someone for the post who will be of use to the world. But you have always known what an irresponsible, bungling sort of person I am, not at all up on current affairs. I know myself that I am in all respects inferior to our modern men of ability. If you think me unlike ordinary men in that I alone do not find pleasure in fame and distinction, this is closest to my true feelings and deserves to be considered. If a man of great ability and endowments, able to turn his hand to anything, were able to be without ambition, he would be worth your respect. But one like me, frequently ill, who wants to stay out of office so as to take care of himself for the remaining years of his life — in me it is rather a deficiency. There is not much point in praising a eunuch for his chastity. If you insist on my joining you in the king's service, expecting that we will rise together and will be a joy and help to one another, one fine day you will find that the pressure has driven me quite mad. Only my bitterest enemy would go so far. The rustic who took such pleasure in the warm sun on his back, or the one who so esteemed the flavor of celery that they wanted to bring these things to the attention of the Most High: this showed them to be well-meaning, but it also showed their complete ignorance. I hope you will not do as they did. This being the way I feel about it, I have written to explain it to you and at the same time to say farewell.

XIANG XIU (c. 221–300)

Commentary: None of the four figures in the second panel are related to each other by pose or action. The most penetrating portrait of all the eight is that of Xiang Xiu. He is presented in frontal view seated before a gingko tree, his bare right leg bent horizontally in front of him, his left knee raised. His right hand appears to be resting on his right knee. (The placement of his left arm cannot be determined because of damage to the brick.) He slumps to one side and perhaps slightly forward. His eyes are closed and his brow contracted; he appears unaware that his robe has slipped off one shoulder. Xiang is not in a drunken stupor (there is no wine bowl or cup near him as there is for Wang Rong, Shan Tao, Ruan Ji, and Liu Ling), but in a state of profound concentration. This is a fitting and compelling characterization of the man who wrote

Figure 30. Xiang Xiu. (Source: Ellen Johnston Laing, "Neo-Taoism and the 'Seven Sages of the Bamboo Grove' in Chinese Painting," *Artibus Asiae* [1974], 36 [1/2])

the widely acclaimed commentaries elucidating difficult points in the Taoist classics. Xiang was not only a metaphysician, but also assisted Xi Kang at his forge and engaged in the pursuits of alchemy.

Recalling Old Times: A Rhapsody

Translated by Burton Watson

I used to be a near neighbor of Xi Kang and Lü An. Both were men of irrepressible talent. But Xi Kang was high-minded and out of touch with the world, and Lü An, though generous in heart, was somewhat wild. Eventually both of them got into trouble with the law. Xi Kang had a wide mastery of the various arts, and was particularly skilled at string and wind instruments. When he was facing execution, he turned and looked at the shadows cast by the sun, and then called for a lute and played on it.

My travels took me to the west, but later I passed by the old houses
where we used to live. It was the hour when the sun was about to sink into
the Gulf of Yu, and the cold was harsh and biting. Someone nearby
was playing a flute, the sound of it drifting abroad, tenuous and thin. I
thought back to the good times we'd had, the banquets and outings of
long ago, and, stirred to sadness by the notes of the flute, I decided to
write this rhapsody.

> Obeying orders, I journeyed to the distant capital,
> Turned around at last and came back north,
> Setting out by boat to cross the Yellow River,
> Going by way of my old home at Shanyang.
> I scanned the lonely reaches of the spreading plain,
> Halted my horses to rest by a corner of the city wall,
> Walked the roads my two friends had once frequented,
> Passed their empty houses on the humble lane.
> I intoned the "Drooping Millet" with its tears for Zhou,
> Sorrowed with the "Ear of Wheat" over ruins of Yin,[17]
> Thought of the past and those I longed for,
> My heart restless, my steps unsure.
> Roof and ridgepole still there, unbending,
> But those bodies and spirits — where have they gone?
> Long ago, when Li Si went to his death,
> He sighed for his yellow dog with endless longing.[18]
> I grieve that Master Xi had to leave forever,
> Looking at the sun and shadows, playing on a lute,[19]
> Entrusting his destiny to a deeper understanding,
> Giving his life's remainder to that moment of time.
> When I heard the wailing flute with its troubling sound,
> Wonderful notes that break and begin again,

---

[17] "Drooping Millet" and "Ears of Wheat" are two songs attributed to ancient times; according to traditional interpretation, they express sorrow over the vanished glories of the Zhou and Yin dynasties respectively. The first is no. 65 in the *Book of Songs*.

[18] Li Si (d. 208 B.C.) rose to become prime minister to the First Emperor of the Qin dynasty, but was later ousted by a rival and condemned to death. As he was being led to his execution, he said to his son, "I wish you and I were once again tagging after the yellow dog, out the eastern gate of Shang Cai to chase the wily rabbits — but that's all over now!" (*Records of The Grand Historian*).

[19] One may take the "sun and shadows" as symbolic merely of the approaching twilight of Xi Kang's life. But Donald Holzman believes that Xi Kang looked at his own shadow, which stood as proof of his mortality. According to Taoist belief, those who have attained the status of immortal are so pure in substance that they cast no shadow.

I halted my carriage before going farther,
To take a brush and write what is in my heart.

LIU LING (c. 225–280)

Figure 31. Liu Ling. (Source: Ellen Johnston Laing, "Neo-Taoism and the 'Seven Sages of the Bamboo Grove' in Chinese Painting," *Artibus Asiae* [1974], 36 [1/2])

Commentary: A willow separates the figure of Xiang from that of the waggish drunkard, Liu Ling. Liu sits on the diagonal; he holds a rather capacious wine cup in one hand and seems to be gesturing with the other. His head is bent forward as if he is forlornly peering into an already empty cup. His loosened garments cascade around him, but have been pulled back to expose his raised knee. We know nothing factual of Liu Ling other than his mighty passion for wine, a reputation which is confirmed in this portrait of an inebriate.

So Much Earth or Wood

Liu Ling's body was but six feet tall, and his appearance extremely homely and dissipated, yet detached and carefree. He treated his bodily frame like so much earth or wood.

— from *Tales*, chapter 14

The Virtue of Wine

When Liu Ling composed his Hymn to the Virtue of Wine, it was the document to which he committed his whole heart and soul.[20]

— from *Tales*, chapter 4

Hymn to the Virtue of Wine

Translated by Richard Mather

There was a certain Mr. Great Man, for whom
    Heaven and earth were but a morning's span,
    A myriad ages but a flash of time;
    The sun and moon, a door and window's eye,
    The eight directions like a country lane.
    He traveled without leaving track or trace,
    And domiciled in neither room nor hut;
    For curtain — sky, and for a mat — the earth;
    He let his fancy wander where it would.
    At rest he grasped a goblet or a cup,
    And moving, always carried jug or pot.
    For wine, and wine alone, was all his lot.
    How should he know about the rest?
Now there was
    A certain noble duke, Lord High-and-Great,
    And a retired scholar, Sir Silk Sash,
    Who, hearing rumors of our hero's ways,
    Came to discuss with him the hows and whys.
    Waving their sleeves and baring wide their breasts,
    With wildly glaring eyes and gnashing teeth,
    They lectured loud and long on rites and laws,
    While rights and wrongs rose up like spears.

---

[20] For other anecdotes from *Tales* concerning Liu Ling, see chapter 16. *Eds.*

At this the Great Man
  Took the jar and filled it at the vat,
  Put cup to mouth and quaffed the lees;
  Shook out his beard and sat, legs sprawled apart,
  Pillowed on barm and cushioned on the dregs.
  Without a thought, without anxiety,
  His happiness lighthearted and carefree.
  Now utterly bemused with wine,
  Now absently awake,
  He calmly listened, deaf to thunder's crashing roar,
  Or fixed his gaze, unseeing of Mt. Tai's great hulk.
  Of cold or heat he felt no fleshly pangs,
  Of profit or desire no sensual stir;
  He looked down on the myriad things, with all their fuss,
  As on the Jiang or Han with floating weeds.
  And those two stalwarts, waiting by his side —
  How like to blacktail flies their busy buzz!

RUAN XIAN (234–305)

Commentary: The last of the Seven Sages, Ruan Xian (Ruan Ji's cousin) is seated playing the *yuan*, the musical instrument he is said to have invented. He sits erect and cross-legged between a gingko and a broad-leafed tree, possibly a *wutong* (Chinese plane-tree). One sleeve is rolled up to the shoulder, its long drape flares out behind him; the lower edge of his robe spreads out on the mat. He wears a turbanlike hat held in place by cords which pass in front of his ears. Completely oblivious of his sottish neighbor, Ruan devotes earnest attention to his music-making. For Ruan Ji, Xi Kang and Ruan Xian, music (like liquor for Liu Ling) helped produce an ecstatic state of mind in which they could "forget themselves" and be absorbed in the Great Tao.

Underpants

Ruan Xian and Ruan Ji lived on the south side of the street, and all the other Ruans lived on the north (sunny) side. The northern Ruans were all wealthy, while the southern Ruans were poor. On the seventh day of the seventh month the northern Ruans put on a grand sunning of their wardrobes, which all consisted of silk gauzes and colored and plain brocades, while Ruan Xian, using a bamboo pole, hung out a large pair of plain cloth calf-nose underpants in his central courtyard. When someone remarked about this, he replied, "I'm not yet able to be completely free of worldly matters, so I just do this, that's all!"

— from *Tales*, chapter 23

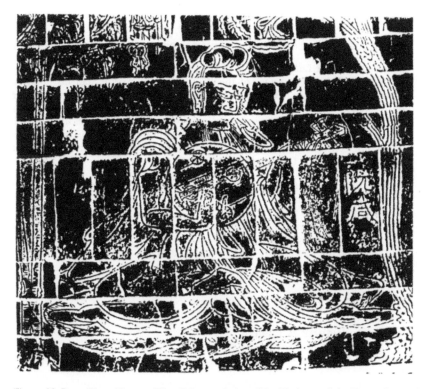

Figure 32. Ruan Xian. (Source: Ellen Johnston Laing, "Neo-Taoism and the 'Seven Sages of the Bamboo Grove' in Chinese Painting," *Artibus Asiae* [1974], 36 [1/2])

Pigs and Men

The Ruans were all great drinkers. When Ruan Xian arrived at the home of any of the clan for a gathering, they no longer used ordinary wine cups for drinking toasts. Instead they would use a large earthenware vat filled with wine, and sitting facing each other all around it, would take large drafts. One time a herd of pigs came to drink and went directly up to the vat, whereupon pigs and men all proceeded to drink together.

— from *Tales*, chapter 23

GOLDEN VALLEY

Golden Valley, near Luoyang, was where the extravagantly wealthy official and poet Shi Chong, near contemporary of the Bamboo Grove coterie, had his luxurious summer villa. Here it was that he gathered his friends and celebrated its "clear springs and verdant woods ... moved by the impermanence of our lives, and dreading the unappointed hour of falling leaves"; here it was, when political disaster finally caught up with him, that his favorite concubine Green Pearl threw herself to her death from a tower. Five centuries later the poet of the late Tang, Du Mu [see chapter 24], wrote a quatrain entitled "Shi Chong's Golden Valley Garden":

> Scattered pomp has fallen to the scented dust.
> The streaming waters know no care, the weeds
>   claim spring for their own.
> In the East wind at sunset the plaintive birds cry:
> Petals on the ground are her likeness still
>   beneath the tower where she fell. (*translated by A. C. Graham*)

SHI CHONG (249–300)

Longing to Return: A Lament

Translated by Helmut Wilhelm

Shi Chong was probably the wealthiest man of his period, brilliantly successful in almost every field of cultural and political endeavor. The calamitous fate, however, that overtook him, his family, and the persons and families of his adherents, demonstrates the price that had to be paid for such eminence, a price from which not even a combination of bureaucratic, military, and economic power could save him. This rhapsodic lament expresses in somewhat conventional form his aspirations for a life of secluded and transcendent leisure, typical of the gentry of that time. His closing wish, that "bad fortune should not come my way," was not to be granted.

> Ascending the corner of the city wall — oh!
>   I gaze down the long stream,
> The supreme sight of boundlessness — oh!
>   Fills my breast with longing.
> The splash of fish — oh!
>   The purposeless flutter of birds,
> Marsh pheasants and migrating ducks — oh!
>   Frolicking in the park,
> The autumn wind's sharp edge — oh!
>   Flights of wild swans and geese,
> The cricket's chirping — oh!
>   Sounding throughout the night,

Falling leaves floating — oh!
　　Barren branches jutting,
Withered grass and herbs — oh!
　　Covering plots and mounds.
Time passes away — oh!
　　The season draws to a close.
Moved by such a year's end — oh!
　　I grieve and mourn for myself,
A lonesome wayfarer — oh!
　　I stagnated in the country and in the city.
I wish I could ride the north wind — oh!
　　And swiftly return to times past.
There metal and stone — oh!
　　Are somber and clear,
Woods are luxuriant — oh!
　　And fragrant herbs abound,
Mysterious springs flow — oh!
　　Coiling around hills and mounds,
Halls and pavilions stand in solitude — oh!
　　Shaded by groves of willows.
There I would play the long flute — oh!
　　And strum the five-stringed lute,
My cheerful song would reach the clouds — oh!
　　And I would enjoy my remaining years.
I would unroll old scrolls — oh!
　　And converse with the sages.
I would discard my bonnet and throw away my sash — oh!
　　Hoping to attain the age of Pengzi and Lao Dan.
Transcending blissful leisure — oh!
　　I would shake off the dust of the world.
Good fortune would not arrive — oh!
　　Nor would bad fortune come my way.

Preface to the Golden Valley Poems

Translated by Richard Mather

This poetical gathering, and its literary celebration, were the direct model for the more famous Orchid Pavilion gathering and for the Preface of Wang Xizhi [see below]. In *Tales*, chapter 16, we read: "Whenever Wang Xizhi heard someone compare his own Orchid Pavilion Preface to Shi Chong's Golden Valley Preface, or again, whenever someone matched him against Shi Chong, he would look extremely pleased."

In the sixth year of the Yuan-kang era (296), in company with the grand master of chariots, I set out from Luoyang as commissioner of military affairs in Qing and Xu provinces (Shandong and northern Anhui and Jiangsu). I own a villa on the outskirts of Henan Prefecture, by Golden Valley Creek (near Luoyang), with some high and some low ground. There are clear springs and verdant woods, fruit trees, bamboos, cypresses, and various kinds of medicinal herbs, all in great abundance. In addition, there are water mills, fish ponds, caves in the earth, and all things to please the eye and delight the heart.

The libationer and General Chastising the West, Wang Xu, was due to return to Chang'an, so I and the other worthies escorted him as far as the creek. Day and night we roamed about and feasted, each time moving to a different place, sometimes climbing to a height and looking down, sometimes sitting by the water's edge. At times seven- or twenty-five-stringed zithers, mouth organs, and bamboo zithers accompanied us in the carriages, and were played in concert along the road. When we stopped, I had each person perform in turn with the orchestra. Then each one composed a poem to express the sentiments in his heart. Whenever anyone could not do so, he had to pay a forfeit by drinking three dipperfuls of wine. Moved by the impermanence of our lives, and dreading the unappointed hour of falling leaves, I have duly recorded below the offices, names, and ages of those who were present. In addition, I have copied their poems and appended them after the names, in hopes some curiosity-seeker of later times may read them.

Biography of Shi Chong
Extract, from the History of the Jin Dynasty (ed. 644–646)

Translated by Helmut Wilhelm

This biography, which makes free use of episodic material in Liu Yiqing's *New Tales of the World* [compare the anecdote in chapter 16], tells the story of Shi Chong's rise and fall with great gusto and an uncanny sense of the dramatic.

After several transfers of office, Shi became Chief of the Cavaliers at Disposal. Emperor Wu, on account of his being the son of a meritorious official and on account of his own great talents, had profound respect for his capacities....

... While Shi Chong was in the South, he obtained a Serpent-eagle and gave it as a present to the General of the Rear Wang Kai. At that time it was against the rules to transport these birds across the river, and he was impeached by the Colonel Fu Di; but he was exculpated by Imperial mandate. The bird, however, was burned in the Public Market.

Shi Chong was a versatile man and had the spirit of a genius; he was bold and never exercised restraint. When he was at Jingzhou he captured envoys and merchants, and thus he became extremely rich. His resources were boundless.... He had a summer resort in Golden Valley north of the river; it was also called Catalpa Pond. Those who accompanied him on his farewell, practically the whole capital, were given a drinking party under specially raised canopies at this place.

When he arrived at his headquarters, he had a drinking bout with the prefect of Xuzhou, Gao Yan, and insulted him. The officer in charge memorialized about it, and Shi was cashiered. Later he was appointed Commander of the Imperial Guard. Together with Pan Yue, he cultivated the acquaintance of the powerful Jia Mi. He became very intimate with Jia, and was known as one of his circle of Twenty-four Friends. Every time the Lord of Guangzheng (Jia Mi) went out, Shi Chong would descend from his carriage and stand at the left of the road, stare into the dust and do obeisance. This was the extent to which he would humble himself in his flattery.

His personal property was extensive. His mansion was vast and elegant and contained over a hundred women's apartments. All his women were richly clad in silk and embroidery, laden with ear ornaments of gold and jade. His musicians were the finest of their time, and his kitchen served every imaginable delicacy of water and land. With the members of the consort clan, such as Wang Kai and Yang Xiu, he competed in the display of luxury. Wang Kai had his pots cleansed with syrup, Shi Chong had his stove fired with wax. Wang Kai produced a canopy made of scarlet silk measuring forty *li*; Shi Chong produced a canopy of brocade measuring fifty *li*, in order to outdo him. Shi Chong polished his rooms with spices, Wang Kai used clay ointment. This was the way they tried to outdo each other in luxury. Emperor Wu always sided with Wang Kai.

Once the Emperor presented Wang Kai with a coral tree over three feet high, luxuriantly branching, such as could hardly be matched in the world. Wang Kai showed it to Shi Chong, who struck it with an iron scepter and broke it with one stroke. Wang Kai was deeply distressed, believing Shi Chong had done it because he envied him his treasure. When Wang Kai raised his voice and showed anger in his face, Shi Chong said: "This is no cause for resentment. I shall presently make amends." Thereupon he ordered his servants to produce all his own coral trees. Among them there were six or seven which were three or four feet high, the span of whose branches surpassed the ordinary and whose luster competed with the sun. There were many to equal the one of Wang Kai. At this Wang Kai was dejected and had to concede defeat....

When it came to the execution of Jia Mi, Shi Chong was dismissed for being of his clique.

At that time the Prince of Zhao, Sima Lun, had usurped the power. Shi Chong's nephew, Ouyang Jian, had a rift with Sima Lun. Shi Chong owned a concubine named Green Pearl, who was of dazzling beauty and knew how to play the flute well. Sun Xiu sent somebody to fetch her away from him. Shi Chong was at that time at his resort in Golden Valley. He had just ascended the terrace to enjoy the landscape, and his women were at his side. When the messenger had stated his request, Shi Chong had every one of his slave girls and concubines, several tens of them, led out, and showed them to the messenger. They were all of them scented with orchid and musk, and dressed in the finest silk gauze. Shi Chong said to the messenger: "Pick any one of these!" But the messenger replied: "This certainly is a great display of beauty. I have, however, received express orders to bring Green Pearl. I would not know which one of these is her." Whereupon Shi Chong changed his countenance and said: "It happens that I love Green Pearl. She is not available." The messenger replied: "Your Excellency, you are conversant with the affairs of past and present, you are equally discerning about affairs remote and close at hand. I beg you to think this over." "No," insisted Shi Chong. The messenger departed and returned again; but Shi Chong was adamant.

Sun Xiu, in his anger, induced Sima Lun to have both Shi Chong and Ouyang Jian executed. But Shi and his nephew learned about their secret plans. Together with the Imperial Secretary Pan Yue they secretly induced Sima Yun, Prince of Huainan, to enter into a conspiracy against Sima Lun and Sun Xiu. Sun Xiu, however, got wind of this and he forged an Imperial mandate to arrest the three of them. Shi Chong was just having his evening meal in the upper story, when the armed guards arrived at the gate. He said to Green Pearl: "Now I shall suffer punishment for you." She burst into tears and said: "It is fitting that I should incur death in front of the officials." Thereupon she threw herself down from the upper story and died. Shi Chong said: "I shall probably just be banished to Jiaozhou or Guangzhou." But when the carriage reached the execution ground of the Eastern Market, Shi Chong said with a sigh: "The scoundrels merely covet my family fortune." The guard answered: "You knew that your wealth would bring you ruin; why did you not disperse it long ago?" Shi Chong had no reply.

Together with Shi Chong, his mother and older brother, his wife and children irrespective of their ages, were all put to death. Altogether fifteen people died. Shi Chong was at that time in his fifty-second year.

ORCHID PAVILION

WANG XIZHI (309–c. 365)

Preface to the Orchid Pavilion Poems

Translated by H. C. Chang

The year 316 saw the collapse of the Jin dynasty in the north, when the capital Chang'an fell to the invading Xiongnu tribesmen. An exodus to the south began, and Nanjing became the capital of the restored dynasty, the Eastern Jin. Shattered by the fateful turn of events, the exiles from the north would forgather in some pavilion overlooking the Yangtze, seemingly their only bulwark against the invaders, to brood on the past and be pleasantly surprised by the beauty of the scenery. For northern eyes, accustomed to plains and plateaus and mountain ranges, the entire region that is now southern Jiangsu and the whole of Zhejiang, abounding in lakes and hills, rivers and watercourses, was nothing short of a revelation. Zhejiang, in particular, nursed the esthetic sense for the apprehension of landscape. In the final years of the fourth century, the painter Gu Kaizhi returned to his post in Hubei after a visit to Kuaiji (i.e., Shaoxing in Zhejiang) and gave his colleagues this account of that famous district:

> The landscape of Kuaiji consists of a thousand rival precipices overhanging ten thousand ravines and gushing torrents, crowned by trees and luxuriant vegetation that appear like variously coloured clouds.

The lofty sentiments, at once jubilant and mournful, expressed in the thirty-seven poems written at the Orchid Pavilion (Lanting, in Kuaiji prefecture) gathering in 353 reflect the state of mind, at once troubled and serene, of a select and influential group. Among those present were the brothers Xie An and Xie Wan, both Ministers at court; the brothers Sun Tong and Sun Chuo, inveterate ramblers; Wang Xizhi, a leading member of the powerful Wang clan, known to posterity as the supreme calligrapher, and a large number of his family. The occasion was the customary ceremony of purification performed on the third day of the third month.

To the poems Wang Xizhi contributed a famous preface. His own calligraphy of that preface is perhaps the single best-known work of Chinese calligraphy (controversy has always surrounded the authenticity of the various surviving copies). It is a magnificent document in the history of Chinese sensibility. For it is the first considered statement on the application of Zhuangzi's doctrine of consonance with the cosmic principle to the contemplation of hills and streams and, summarizing as it does the outlook of several centuries, is a lasting part of the Chinese heritage. In the poems and in the preface itself, man's gaze is directed with childlike wonder to the world he inhabits. The eye does not rest on flower or tree or hill or brook as in earlier verse and in the *Book of Songs*, but roves over them all in a sweeping survey. Not content with the delight this affords, the mind reaches out to the empyrean and beyond. What is more, man's cherished feelings not only find release but positively seek fulfillment in the natural world. The mountain heights, the sheer cliffs, the cascading waterfall, the echoing valley, the ever-widening horizon — these mirror the inner world; aspiration is assuaged by height; magnanimity comes into its own with spaciousness; solitude finds a ready harbor in the woods.

Thus the Orchid Pavilion poets will say:

I release my pent-up feelings
Among these hills and streams;
Serenely I abandon all restraints. (Wang Huizhi)

In these spacious surroundings
My feelings find free scope. (Wang Yunzhi)

Solitary aloofness
Seeks a home on this woody hill. (Xie An)

In former days, when at leisure,
In my mind I roamed these woody hills.
Today I have indeed wandered hither;
My spirit is gladdened, my mind at rest. (Wang Suzhi)

All my hopes and longings
Have as their limit
These mountains and streams. (Sun Tong)

I stretch my gaze as far as the lofty hills.
Then rest my eye
On the woods near the summit. (Xie Wan)

My spirit glides
Between heaven and earth. (Yu Yue)

In the ninth year (353) of the Yong-he reign, which was a *gui-chou* year, early in the final month of spring, we gathered at the Orchid Pavilion in Shanyin in Kuaiji for the ceremony of purification. Young and old congregated, and there was a throng of men of distinction. Surrounding the pavilion were high hills with lofty peaks, luxuriant woods and tall bamboos. There was, moreover, a swirling, splashing stream, wonderfully clear, which curved round it like a ribbon, and we seated ourselves along it in a drinking game, in which cups of wine were set afloat and drifted to those who sat downstream. The occasion was not heightened by the presence of musicians. Nevertheless, what with drinking and the composing of verses, we conversed in whole-hearted freedom, entering fully into one another's feelings. The day was fine, the air clear, and a gentle breeze regaled us, so that on looking up we responded to the vastness of the universe, and on bending down were struck by the manifold riches of the earth. And as our eyes wandered from object to object, so our hearts, too, rambled with them. Indeed, for the eye as well as the ear, it was pure delight! What perfect bliss!

For in men's association with one another in their journey through life, some draw upon their inner resources and find satisfaction in a closeted conversation with a friend, while others follow their inclinations and abandon themselves without constraint to diverse interests and pursuits, oblivious of their physical existence. Their choice may be infinitely varied, even as their temperament will range from the serene to the irascible. When absorbed by what they are engaged in, they are for the moment content, and in their content they forget that old age is at hand. But when eventually they tire of what had so engrossed them, their feelings will have altered with their circumstances, and, of a sudden, complacency gives way to regret. What previously had gratified them is now a thing of the past, which itself is cause for lament. Besides, although the span of men's lives may be longer or shorter, all must end in death. And, as has been said by the ancients, birth and death are momentous events. What an agonizing thought!

In reading the compositions of earlier men, I have tried to trace the causes of their melancholy, which too often are the same as those that

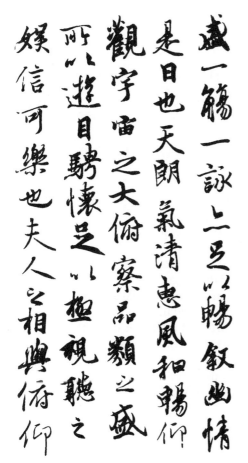

Figure 33. Rubbing of a copy of the Orchid Pavilion Preface. (Source: Chinese University Art Gallery, Hong Kong)

affect myself. And I have then confronted the book with a deep sigh, without, however, being able to reconcile myself to it all. But this much I do know: it is idle to pretend that life and death are equal states and foolish to claim that a youth cut off in his prime has led the protracted life of a centenarian. For men of a later age will look upon our time as we look upon earlier ages — a chastening reflection. And so I have listed those present on this occasion and transcribed their verses. Even when circumstances have changed and men inhabit a different world, it will still be the same causes that induce a mood of melancholy attendant on poetical composition. Perhaps some reader of the future will be moved by the sentiments expressed in this preface.

ZHIDUN (314–366)

Song of My Mountain Dwelling

Translated by John Frodsham

Probably the most admired and the most influential of the Buddhist clergy living in the Jiangsu-Zhejiang area during the Eastern Jin, Zhidun divided his time between monasteries in the capital and Kuaiji, lecturing and participating in "pure conversation" sessions with the great figures of the day. Among his lay-disciples were Wang Xizhi and Sun Chuo.

> The Five Holy Mountains are great works raised by spirits,
> The four rivers have vast and surging floods.
> I went there to seek of myself a true wisdom,
> In its silence I guarded there the heights of tranquil love.
> If I do not feel happy out of my seclusion,
> It is because I have found a constant pleasure there.
> Those who seek heaven will live for ever,
> From my cave I look on those who have left the world of men.
> There is pure jade at the foot of the crags,
> A sound as of metal as the stream washes the nearby banks.
> I went gathering flowers and was hidden in deep mist,
> I shook my coarse clothes and brushed them free of dust.
> What I have done has been like the measuring worm
>   when it draws itself up,
> The Tao stretches like a leaping dragon.
> On this peak is no successor to Shan Bao,[21]

---

[21] "Shan Bao dwelt among the crags and drank from the rivers.... At seventy he still had the complexion of a babe." *Zhuangzi.*

It is not my lot to know the truth revealed on Shouyang.[22]
With a long whistle I go back to my wooded peak,
In that solitary place I shall devote myself to my potter's wheel.

SUN CHUO (314–371)

An Autumn Day

Translated by John Frodsham

In his day considered the "crown of literary men," Sun Chuo was much in demand as a composer of obituaries and eulogies. A devout Buddhist layman and disciple of Zhidun, he attempted to harmonize Buddhism and the contemplative life with Confucianism and an active political career.

A melancholy day in the second month of autumn,
A whirling wind moans, the storm-tossed clouds are high.
Living in the mountains you feel the seasons changing,
Far from home the traveler sings a long ballad.
The empty peaks are thick with frozen ether,
The leafless forest hung with icy winds.
Soaking dew wets garden and forest.
Thick leaves take farewell of wind-blown boughs.
I touch these mushrooms, sorry they will fall so soon.
I pull down a pine-branch, glad that it endures so long.
I cast my line in woods and wilds,
I have my friendships far from market and court.
Gone now is the troubled heart I used to bear,
Surely I am not far from the banks of the river Hao.

Wandering on Mount Tiantai: A Rhapsody

Translated by Burton Watson

Mount Tiantai, situated some fifty miles southwest of Ningbo and north of Yongjia, in Zhejiang, was the earliest seat of Buddhism in East China. Its earliest monasteries were founded in the fourth century. Sun Chuo, when he served as governor of Yongjia, conceived a strong desire to resign from office and retire to Mount Tiantai. He is said to have had maps or diagrams of the mountain drawn for him; and in this rhapsody he realizes his desire by performing the ascent of the mountain in imagination. As he proceeds up the mountain, the scenery becomes increasingly fantastic and idealized, until at the end he reaches a plane of pure philosophy, in which Taoist and Buddhist allusions are carefully balanced one against the other.

---

[22] The mountain on which the legendary hermits Bo Yi and Shu Qi starved to death.

Mount Tiantai is the sacred flower of all mountain ranges. Cross the sea and you will find Fangzhang and Penglai; turn inland and you will come to Siming and Tiantai, all of them places where the sages of the occult wander and perform their transformations, where the holy immortals have their caves and dwellings.[23] The endlessly soaring shapes of these ranges, their miraculous beauty exhaust the wealth and wonder of mountain and sea, embrace all that is brave and admirable among gods and men. The reason that Mount Tiantai is not ranked among the Five Sacred Peaks, that records of it are lacking in the classical texts — is it not that it stands in such a remote and out-of-the-way place, that the road there is so long and hard to trace? Now casting its shadow into the many-fathomed depths, now hiding its summit among a thousand ranges — to reach it one must first travel the paths of goblins and trolls, and finally enter the realm where no human being lives. Few men in all the world have ever succeeded in climbing it; no kings have come to offer sacrifices. Therefore mention of it is not to be found in ordinary writings; its name is celebrated only in the accounts of wonders.

And yet the diagram of the mountain that has been drawn for me — how could it be a deception? Surely if one is not the kind who will abandon the world to amuse himself with the Way, who will give up grain to subsist on a diet of mushrooms, then how can he clamber nimbly up its slopes and make his home there? If one is not the sort who can embark on a far-off journey in order to delve into mysteries, who is fervent in his faith and can make his spirit go where he wishes, then how would he dare attempt to visit it in his distant imagination?

And so it is that I have caused my spirit to gallop and my thoughts to turn round and round, chanting by day and watching by night, until, in less time than it takes to wag one's head, it seems as though I have already twice ascended the mountain! Now I am about to cast off all bonds and shackles and reside forever on these peaks. But because I cannot bear to go on forever with these mumbled imaginings, I have called upon literature to aid me in expressing what is in my heart.

> The Great Void, vast and wide, that knows no boundary,
> Sets in cycle the mysterious Being, So-of-itself;[24]
> Melting, it forms the rivers and waterways;
> Thickening, it turns into mountains and hills.
> Ah, the awesome eminence of Tiantai peak —

---

[23] Fangzhang and Penglai are mythical mountains in the eastern sea, the home of immortal spirits: Siming is just north of the Tiantai range.

[24] The So-of-itself is another name for the Way.

Truly it must be held up by the gods!
Under the Herdboy's protection, it flaunts its bright crests;
Sheltering in the holy land of Yüe, it makes certain of a
    four-square base,[25]
Spreading a net of roots vaster than Mounts Hua and Tai,
Pointing straight upward, taller than the Nine Doubts,
Equal of the "counterpart of Heaven" in the "Canon of Yao,"
A match for the "craggy heights" of the Odes of Zhou.
Yet so far away are those peerless regions,
So remote and mysterious,
That the petty-wise merely gaze but fail to journey there,
And those who go, because the trail runs out, never find the way.
I laugh at such summer insects who doubt that ice exists,[26]
Prepare my light-winged mount, longing to depart.
No inner law stays forever hidden and undisclosed:
See how these two wonders parade their form!
Red Wall, like sunset mists ascending, planted for a guidepost,[27]
The Cataract, leaping and plunging, to blazon the way.
When I glimpse these sacred signs, then I will be off;
Suddenly now I am on my way,
Asking the feathered men on their cinnabar hills[28]
How to find that happy domain where no one ever dies.
If the heights of Tiantai can really be scaled,
Why long for the Storied City?[29]
I'll cast off the constant attachments of this world,
Giving vent to nobler, more exalted feelings;
Clad in shaggy folds of fur and felt,
With the clang-clang of the metal staff I wield,
I'll push through the murk of tangled forests,
Climb the sharp acclivity of precipice and slope,
Across You Creek and straight ahead,
Moving quickly past the point where five counties join.
Then straddling the arc of the soaring stone bridge,
I'll peer down ten thousand feet to untold depths;

---

[25] The Herdboy star is thought to protect the region of Yüe, where Mount Tiantai is situated.

[26] *Zhuangzi* 17: "You can't discuss ice with a summer insect — he's bound to a single season."

[27] The road up Tiantai, we are told, led off from a rise called Red Wall.

[28] The immortal spirits.

[29] The city of God in the fabulous Kunlun Mountains of the far west.

I'll tread the slippery moss-covered stone,
Reach for the cliff that rises like a kingfisher-colored screen,
Snatch the strands of dodder that trail from tall trees,
Cling to the flying stems of creeper and vine.
But though I face a moment's danger, on the brink of a fall,
In the end I gain forever the gift of long life.
So long as I keep faith with the dark and hidden Way,
I may trudge the steepest slopes and they are level plains to me;
And when I have traversed all their nine turnings,
The road will stretch before me unending and clear,
Where my heart will wander unconcerned, my eyes roam free,
And I will let my slow steps take me where they will.
I'll spread a mat of slender grasses, rich and tender,
Sheltering beneath these lanky giants, the tall pines;
Watch the flight of winging *luan* birds,
Listen to the chorus of phoenixes warbling.
And when I've crossed Spirit Gorge and bathed myself there,
All the nagging worries will be cleansed from my chest;
In the swirling flow I'll wash away the last fleck of "dust,"
Free myself from the pursuing darkness of the "five becloudings";[30]
Then I'll set out to follow the matchless ways of Fu Xi
        and Shen Nong.
To tread in the dark footsteps of the two named Lao.[31]
Clambering up and down, camping a night or two,
I'll come at last to the city of immortals,
Its double gates like banks of cloud flanking the road,
Its garnet terrace thrust halfway to the sky, suspended there;
Vermilion portals glowing and resplendent among the trees,
Jade halls now hidden, now bright on the tall turn of the hill,
With rosy clouds arrayed like wings at lattice casements,
The radiant sun streaming through window grilles.
Eight huge cassia trees stand high and unscarred by frost,
Five-hued mushrooms unfold their caps in the morning light.
Gentle breezes pile up fragrance in the sunny woods;

---

[30] According to Buddhist doctrine there are six "dusts" that defile the mind: form, sound, smell, taste, touch, and perception of characteristics; the "five becloudings" that darken the mind are desire, anger, drowsiness, excitability, and doubt.

[31] Fu Xi and Shen Nong are mythical cultural heroes of antiquity; the "two named Lao" are Laozi and Lao Laizi, Taoist sages.

Spring water, sweet to the taste, bubbles through shady channels.
The *jian* tree rises a thousand yards without casting a shadow;
The *qi*-gem tree, sparkling and shining, droops with jewels.
Wang Qiao, a crane for his mount, hurries up to heaven;
The "responders-to-Truth," waving their staffs, pace the void,[32]
Performing the hocus-pocus of their uncanny transformations,
Suddenly emerging from Being to enter Non-being.
    And then,
When I have come full circle in my wandering inspection,
Body stilled, mind at rest,
When whatever "hurts the horses" has been done away with,[33]
And chores of the world all have been renounced,
Then, wherever I move my knife, it will always find the hollow;
I'll eye the ox but never see it whole.[34]
Composing my thoughts beside the somber cliffs,
I'll chant in a clear voice by the endless river.
    And so,
When Xihe, charioteer of the sun, arrives at the point of noon,
And trailing vapors have lifted and dispersed,
The dharma-drums, booming, will wake the echoes,
And countless blends of incense send up pungent smoke,
In preparation for audience with the Heavenly Ancestor,[35]
For the gathering here of the enrolled immortals.
We will dip up the rich oil of black jade,
Freshen our mouths in the springs of Flower Lake,
Spreading doctrines of what is "beyond symbol,"
Expounding texts on what is "without origination";[36]
Till we realize that Being can never wholly be rejected,

---

[32] Wang Qiao is a Taoist Immortal; the "responders-to-Truth" are Buddhist saints.

[33] A reference to *Zhuangzi* 24, the anecdote in which the Yellow Emperor asks a young herder of horses how to govern the empire. The boy replies, "Governing the empire I suppose is not much different from herding horses. Get rid of whatever is harmful to the horses — that's all."

[34] A reference to *Zhuangzi* 3, which describes the remarkable butcher who moved his carving knife through the natural hollows of the ox's body, and no longer "saw the whole ox." [See chapter 4, "Prince Hui's Cook."]

[35] Some identify the Heavenly Ancestor as Laozi, though the term may refer to the sun, moon, and other heavenly bodies, or to deities in general.

[36] The lines refer to Taoism and Buddhism respectively.

That to walk with Non-being still leaves gaps.[37]
We'll destroy both Form and Emptiness, making our path one,
Turn at once to Being, and thereby gain the Way,
Abandoning the two "names" that spring from a single source,
Wiping out the one nothingness of the "three banners."[38]
Then we may chatter as merrily as we like all day long —
It will be the same as utter silence, as though we'd never spoken.
We will merge with the ten thousand images through deepest contemplation;
Unwitting, we'll join our bodies with the So-of-itself.

Further Reading

Balazs, Etienne. *Chinese Civilization and Bureaucracy: Variations on a Theme.* Trans. H. M. Wright, ed. Arthur F. Wright. New Haven: Yale University Press, 1964. (Contains several masterful essays and translations relating to this period.)

Bischoff, Friedrich Alexander. *The Songs of Orchis Tower.* Wiesbaden: Otto Harrassowitz, 1985.

Chang, H. C., ed. and trans. *Chinese Literature, Vol. 2: Nature Poetry.* Edinburgh: University of Edinburgh Press, 1977.

Ch'en, Jerome, and Michael Bullock, trans. *Poems of Solitude.* London: Abelard-Schuman, 1960.

Frodsham, John D., ed. and trans., with the collaboration of Ch'eng Hsi. *An Anthology of Chinese Verse: Han, Wei, Chin and the Northern and Southern Dynasties.* Oxford: Oxford University Press, 1967.

Gernet, Jacques. *Le Monde Chinois.* Paris: Armand Colin, 1972. Trans. J. R. Foster as *A History of Chinese Civilization* (Cambridge: Cambridge University Press, 1982).

Hartill, Graham, and Fu-sheng Wu, trans. *Ruan Ji: Songs of My Heart.* London: Wellsweep, 1988.

Henricks, Robert G. *Philosophy and Argumentation in Third-Century China: The Essays of Hsi K'ang.* Princeton: Princeton University Press, 1983.

Hightower, J. R., trans. "Hsi K'ang's Letter to Shan T'ao." In *Anthology of Chinese Literature,* ed. Cyril Birch (New York: Grove Press, 1965).

Holzman, Donald. *Poetry and Politics: The Life and Works of Juan Chi.* Cambridge: Cambridge University Press, 1976.

Laing, Ellen Johnston. "Neo-Taoism and the 'Seven Sages of the Bamboo Grove' in Chinese Painting." *Artibus Asiae* (1974), 36 (1/2).

[37] Both Taoism and Buddhism teach the student, as a step in his training, to give up concepts of being and purposive action and embrace those of nothingness and non-action; but true enlightenment comes when he can transcend such dualistic thinking and accept things as they exist. The remainder of the poem plays in paradoxical terms on these ideas of transcendence and acceptance.

[38] The two "names" are the named and the nameless (Taoist doctrine); the "three banners" are identified as form, the voidness of form, and meditation (Buddhist doctrine), though the exact meaning of the term is very uncertain.

Mather, Richard B., trans. *A New Account of Tales of the World by Liu I-ch'ing.* Minneapolis: University of Minnesota Press, 1976.

Van Gulik, Robert. *Hsi K'ang and His Poetical Essay on the Lute.* Tokyo: Monumenta Nipponica Monograph, 1941.

Wilhelm, Helmut. "Shih Ch'ung and His Chin-ku-yüan." *Monumenta Serica* (1959), no. 18.

Wilson, Graeme, trans. "Tao: Buddha: Zen." *Denver Quarterly* (1977), 12(2): 45–63.

ᴇᴘ *Editors' Note* ᴇᴘ

This chapter, unlike most others in this anthology, is not built around a work, an author, or a genre, but is rather assembled in collage fashion around three well-known coteries of the third and fourth centuries. It allows the reader to sample something of the mood of this rich and fascinating period, which in recent years has attracted the attention of several Western scholars and translators. Extracts are included here from the Dutch diplomat, sinologue, and bon vivant Robert Van Gulik's translation of Xi Kang's "The Lute: A Rhapsody". Van Gulik, through his prolific translations and monographs (often based on his personal insight as living practitioner of some art or other), illuminated many aspects of traditional Chinese culture — inkstones, sexual customs, the mounting of scrolls, art connoisseurship, the "Way" of music, the gibbon — and even wrote Chinese-style detective stories of his own. The American sinologist Richard Mather has devoted a great part of his life to a scholarly elucidation and witty translation of the wonderful compendium of anecdotes about this period *A New Account of Tales of the World,* extracts from which are included both here and in chapter 16. From this more than any other single work we capture the mood of this era, we hear the voices and see the profiles and postures of the period.

"The orchid is my friend."
Seal carved by Deng Shiru (1743–1805)

Chapter 11

Tao Yuanming (365–427)

The Gentleman of the Five Willow Trees

He did not take his family with him to his official post at Pengce. He sent a servant for his sons and wrote to them: "It is hard for you to provide for your daily needs yourselves. I am sending you this servant to aid you in the labor of gathering wood and drawing water. He too is a man's son and should be well treated." In the public fields he ordered his subordinates to plant only glutinous rice. He said: "It will be enough for me always to get drunk with wine." When his wife and sons earnestly begged him to plant ordinary rice, then he had two hundred and fifty acres planted with glutinous rice and fifty with plain. At the end of the year it happened that an Inspector was sent by the commandery to Tao's district. Tao's subordinates told him that he ought to tie his girdle and call on the Inspector. Tao said with a sigh: "I cannot for five pecks of rice bow before a country bumpkin." The same day he untied his seal-ribbon and gave up the post ... Tao did not understand music, but he kept a plain lute without strings. Whenever there was a drinking party, he fingered it to express his thoughts.

> — "Biography of Tao Yuanming," from the *Song Dynastic History* (488)
> and other sources, *translated by A. R. Davis*

His literary style is spare and limpid, with scarcely a surperfluous word. His sincerity is true and traditional, his verbalized inspirations supple and relaxed. When one reads his works, the fine character of the poet himself comes to mind. Ordinary men admire his unadorned directness. But such lines of his as "With happy face I pour the spring-brewed wine," and "The sun sets, no clouds are in the sky," are pure and refined in the beauty of their air. These are far from being merely the words of a farmer. He is the father of recluse poetry past and present.

> — Zhong Rong (469–518), *The Poets Graded*,
> *translated by J. Timothy Wixted*

The only poet I am particularly fond of is Tao Yuanming. Although the poems he wrote are not many in number, they are unadorned and yet beautiful, spare and yet ample ... Neither Cao Zhi, Liu Zhen, Bao Zhao, Xie Lingyun, Li Bo, nor Du Fu achieves his stature ... This is not to say that I only like Tao for his poetry. I am deeply impressed by what he was as a man.

> — Su Dongpo (1037–1101), quoted by his brother Su Ziyou (1039–1112),
> *translated by J. Timothy Wixted*

I love Tao Yuanming;
With wine, he achieved his true self ...

Just look among Tao's works
At his poems on drinking wine and returning to the fields.
That old man did not write poetry —
He wrote truly what was in his heart.

> — Yuan Haowen (1190–1257), lines from two poems, "After Drinking Wine:
> In Imitation of Tao Yuanming", and "For Zhao Yilu"
> *translated by J. Timothy Wixted*

There is a realm-with-the-self and there is a realm-without-the-self ... Tao Yuanming's lines "I pluck chrysanthemums under the eastern hedge, And gaze afar towards the southern mountains," are examples of the realm-without-the-self ... In this realm the poet perceives things as things, and there is no longer any distinction between thing and perceiver.

> — Wang Guowei (1877–1927), *Poetic Thoughts in the Material World,*
> *translated by John Minford*

The highest realm in art is not passion, but serenity. Perhaps a poet's human experience of joy and sorrow is more passionate than that of other men; but when, as a poet, he comes to express that passion, it matures like a vintage wine, it loses its sharpness, and acquires a mellow bouquet. This is serenity. It is a lofty ideal, and is not to be found in ordinary poetry. Ancient Greece, and especially ancient Greek sculpture, often conveys this sense of serenity. It is a realm of utter enlightenment and peace, rather like that of the contemplative Buddhist Goddess of Mercy, Guanyin. Serenity is above human joy and sorrow. Indeed it washes away joy and sorrow. A realm such as this is seldom found in Chinese poetry. Qu Yuan, Ruan Ji, Li Bo and Du Fu lapse too often into passion and righteousness indignation. But Tao Yuanming is all serenity. Hence his greatness.

> — Zhu Guangqian (1897–1986), "On a poem by Qian Qi,"
> *translated by John Minford*

Extracts and anthologies can be highly misleading. Suppose you take Tao Yuanming's lines "I pluck chrysanthemums under the eastern hedge, And gaze afar towards the southern mountains," and you ignore other poems of his; by lifting lines out of context in this fashion, you can make him into the most wonderfully unworldly figure ... Serious readers should never rely on extracts. They should read more extensively for themselves, and then they will see that none of the great writers of the past was "all serenity." Tao Yuanming was great precisely because he was *not* "all serenity."

> — Lu Xun (1881–1936), "Notes without titles:7,"
> *translated by John Minford*

Tao Yuanming represents the most perfectly harmonious and well-rounded character in the entire Chinese literary tradition. There is a simplicity in his life, as well as in his style, which is awe-inspiring and a constant reproach to more brilliant and more sophisticated natures. And he stands, today, as a perfect example of the true lover of life, because in him the rebellion against worldly desires did not lead him to attempt a total escape, but reached a harmony with the life of the senses.

> — Lin Yutang (1897–1976), *The Importance of Living*

Introduction

Burton Watson

Tao Yuanming, or Tao Qian, is one of the most widely admired of the early Chinese poets. He lived in the period of disunity known as the Six Dynasties, when northern China was in the hands of non-Chinese leaders, and the south, where Tao lived, was ruled by a succession of weak and short-lived dynasties that had their capital at the present-day city of Nanjiing. Tao's poetry fully reflects the unease and anxiety that beset Chinese society at this time. At the same time, however, it strikes a rare and hardwon note of peace and contentment that, though only sporadic, seems to hold out some hope for escape from sorrow and suffering, a hope that is given poignant symbolic expression in his famous fable of the Peach Blossom Spring.

Tao Yuanming was born near modern Jiujiang in Jiangxi province, within sight of the famous Mount Lu, the "southern mountain" that he mentions in his poetry. His father and grandfather had pursued official careers, and though it was against his inclination, he too in time took up a post as adviser to one of the military leaders of the time. He did not fare well in this and subsequent posts, however, and he longed for the quiet rural life of his birthplace. His last post, that of magistrate of Pengze, he quit after only eighty days, retiring to the countryside to become a farmer for the remainder of his years.

His extant poems seem to have been written mainly in his later years, when he was living in a small house on the outskirts of a village with his family (he had five sons). Many poems describe the quiet joys of country life, though others speak of famine, drought, and similar hardships. The Taoist side of the poet's nature no doubt told him he should be content with such a life of seclusion, but his dedication to Confucian ideals kept him longing for the less troubled times of the past, when virtue prevailed and a scholar could in good conscience take an active part in affairs of state. There is an overall ambiguity in his poetry — exclamations upon the beauties of nature and the freedom and peace of rustic life, set uneasily alongside confessions of loneliness, frustration, and fear, particularly fear of death. He sought solace in his lute, his books, and above all in wine, about half of his poems mentioning his fondness for "the thing in the cup," though in one of the poems he wrote depicting his own funeral ["Dirge"], he declares that he was never able to get enough of it.

At a time when Chinese poetry on the whole was marked by ornate diction and elaborate rhetorical devices, Tao Yuanming chose to write in a relatively plain and simple style — in translation he may even sound rather flat on first reading. Probably because of this plainness of style, and the homey and personal nature of most of his poems, he was not highly esteemed by his contemporaries. It was some centuries before the true worth of his works was recognized, though few today would question that he is one of the finest of the pre-Tang poets.

— *Columbia Book of Chinese Poetry: From Early Times*, 1984

The Gentleman of the Five Willow Trees

Translated by J. R. Hightower

A short and fanciful autobiographical sketch, written when the poet was a young man.

Figure 34. Tao Yuanming. Ming dynasty painting. (Source: National Palace Museum, Taiwan)

I don't know where this gentleman was born and I am not sure of his name, but beside his house were five willow trees, from which he took his nickname. He was of a placid disposition and rarely spoke. He had no envy of fame or fortune. He was fond of reading, without puzzling greatly over difficult passages. When he came across something to his liking he would be so delighted he would forget his meals. By nature he liked wine, but being poor could not always come by it. Knowing the circumstances, his friends and relatives would invite him over when they had wine. He could not drink without emptying his cup, and always ended up drunk, after which he would retire, unconcerned about what might come. He lived alone in a bare hut, which gave no adequate shelter against rain and sun. His short coat was torn and patched, his cooking pots were frequently empty, but he was unperturbed. He used to write poems for his own amusement, and in them can be seen something of what he thought. He had no concern for worldly success, and so he ended his days.

Nineteen Poems

Translated by William Acker

Substance, Shadow, and Spirit

Whether nobly born or humble, whether wise or simple, there is none who does not diligently seek to spare his own life, but in so doing men are greatly deluded. Therefore I have done my best to set forth the reasons for this in the form of an argument between Substance and Shadow which is finally resolved by Spirit, who expounds Nature. May gentlemen of an inquiring turn of mind take it to heart.

Substance Speaks to Shadow

Heaven and Earth
    endure and do not perish;
Mountains and rivers
    do not change with time.
Grasses and trees partake
    in this constant principle,
Although the frost and dew
    cause them to wilt or flourish.
Of all things Man, they say,
    is most intelligent and wise,
And yet he alone
    is not like them in this.
Appearing by chance
    he comes into this world,
And suddenly is gone
    never to return.
How is one to feel
    the lack of such a one
When even friends and kinfolk
    scarcely think of him?
Only that the things
    he used in life are left —

Coming across them
    may make us shed a tear.
I have no art
    to soar and be transfigured;[1]
That it must be so
    I cannot ever question.
I only beg that you
    will agree with what I say
And when we can get wine
    never perversely refuse it!

Shadow Replies to Substance

I cannot tell you
    how to preserve life,
And have always been inept
    in the art of guarding it.[2]
Yet truly I desire
    to roam on Kun and Hua[3]
But they are far away
    and the road to them is lost.
Ever since I met you
    and have been with you
I have known no other
    sorrows and joys but yours.
Though I seemed to leave you
    when you rested in the shade,

---

[1] According to popular taoism, which was gradually becoming institutionalized into a church in Tao's time, the adept could achieve these things by the practice of taoist yoga (a system of breath control), an elaborate and strict sexual regimen and, above all, a strict diet with avoidance of grain and meat and reliance on vegetables, herbs, and drugs of various kinds. Tao here shows himself to be rather skeptical of such claims.

[2] This refers specifically to taoist yoga, sexual regimen, and diet, which at the very least were supposed to confer longevity.

[3] After long and successful practice of "the art of preserving life," culminating perhaps in the discovery of some elixir of immortality, the taoist adept was supposed to become transfigured. His very body was transformed into some finer substance, and he soared away to certain realms of the Immortals, where he lived in houses of gold and subsisted on air and dew. The Kunlun mountains far in the west, Mount Hua at the great bend of the Yellow River, and Mount Penglai floating in the midst of the Eastern Ocean were believed to be such abodes.

I never really left you
    until the day was done.[4]
But this association
    cannot last forever;
Mysteriously at last
    we shall vanish in the darkness.
After our death —
    that our name should also perish
At the mere thought of this
    the Five Passions seethe within me.
Should we not labor
    and strive with all our might
To do good in such a way
    that men will love us for it?
Wine, as they say,
    may dissipate our grief,
But how could it ever
    be compared to fame?

Spirit Resolves the Argument

The Great Balance[5]
    has no personal power,
And its myriad veins
    interlace of themselves.[6]

---

[4] The material soul (*po*), which unlike the spirit (*shen* or *hun*) remains with the body after death like a sort of lingering eddy of animal magnetism, was identified with the visible shadow. But it remained with the body, whether visible or not.

[5] The Tao (Way) is the sum totality of all things, spirit, and matter and the laws by which they operate, conceived of as one great monad. But though ultimately all is one, this monad expresses itself, operates, and ceaselessly creates through two apparently opposing forces, *yin* (shade) and *yang* (light). These terms are applied very widely to account for all sorts of dualities such as positive and negative, male and female, active and passive, etc. Neither one of these forces ever destroys or diminishes the other; the quantity and strength of each in the universe as a whole remain constant. The term *Da Jun* ("great scales," "great balance") expresses this truth, and so may almost be taken as an equivalent to Tao itself.

[6] Within the Tao, yin and yang, spirit and matter, the passive and the active, are all inexhaustible, indestructible, and equal. All phenomena and effects, visible or invisible, are produced by their ceaseless motion and constant interplay. Although this view of the universe leaves no room for a personal God, or *deus ex machina*, it cannot be called atheistic or materialistic, but is closer to what we know as pantheism or monism.

That Man has his place
    among the Three Forces,[7]
This is certainly
    due to my presence with you.
And although I am
    different from you both,
At birth I am added
    and joined together with you.
Bound and committed
    to sharing good and evil
How can we avoid
    mutual exchange?
The Three Emperors
    were the Primal Sages.
Now, after all,
    whither are they gone?
And though Grandfather Peng[8]
    achieved longevity
Yet he too had to go
    when he still wished to stay.
Old and young
    all suffer the same death,
The wise and the foolish —
    uncounted multitudes.
Getting drunk daily
    one may perhaps forget
But is not wine a thing
    that shortens one's life?
And in doing good
    you may always find pleasure
But no one is obliged
    to give you praise for it.
Dwelling on such things
    wounds my very life.

---

[7] The Three Cosmic Forces (*San Cai*) are Heaven, Earth, and Man. Chinese thought is by
no means so unanthropocentric as is commonly said.

[8] The Chinese Methuselah, a very shadowy figure who had no special cult, but was merely
proverbial for longevity.

The right thing to do
    is to leave things to Fate,
Let go and float along
    on the great flux of things,
Not overjoyed
    but also not afraid.
When it is time to go
    then we should simply go.
There is nothing, after all,
    that we can do about it.

Five Poems on Returning to Dwell in the Country

1

In youth I had nothing
    that matched the vulgar tone,
For my nature always
    loved the hills and mountains.
Inadvertently I fell
    into the Dusty Net,
Once having gone
    it was more than thirteen years.
The tame bird
    longs for his old forest —
The fish in the house-pond
    thinks of his ancient pool.
I too will break the soil
    at the edge of the Southern moor,
I will guard simplicity
    and return to my fields and garden.
My land and house —
    a little more than ten acres,
In the thatched cottage —
    only eight or nine rooms.
Elms and willows
    shade the back verandah,
Peach and plum trees
    in rows before the hall.
Hazy and dimly seen
    a village in the distance,

Close in the foreground
    the smoke of neighbors' houses.
A dog barks
    amidst the deep lanes,
A cock is crowing
    atop a mulberry tree.
No dust and confusion
    within my doors and courtyard;
In the empty rooms,
    more than sufficient leisure.
Too long I was held
    within the barred cage.
Now I am able
    to return again to Nature.

2

Here in the Country
    I have little to do with people,
In my poor lane
    no noise of wheel and harness.
White sunlight
    bathes the rustic gate,
The empty rooms
    cut off dusty thoughts.
At times I find myself
    again among my neighbors,
Parting the high grass
    we walk about together.
Meeting each other
    we do not talk at random,
But only speak of how
    the hemp and mulberry grow.
Hemp and mulberry
    keep growing day by day
And every day I clear
    the land a little more.
My constant fear
    is of the frost and hail
Which could reduce my crops
    to a mass of tangled grasses.

3

I planted beans beneath the southern hill,
While the grass is thick the bean shoots still are sparse.
Rising at dawn I pull up weeds and tares,
Shouldering my hoe I carry home the moon.[9]
The path is narrow, the grass and bushes high —
The evening dew has thoroughly drenched my clothes.
That my clothes are wet I do not mind at all:
It only makes me wish not to avoid what comes.[10]

4

Long I have loved to stroll among the hills and marshes,
And take my pleasure roaming the woods and fields.
Now I hold hands with a train of nieces and nephews,
Parting the hazel growth we tread the untilled wastes —
Wandering to and fro amid the hills and mounds
Everywhere around us are dwellings of ancient men.
Here are vestiges of their wells and hearthstones,
There the rotted stumps of bamboo and mulberry groves.
I stop and ask a faggot-gatherer.[11]
"These men — what has become of them?"
The faggot-gatherer turns to me and says:
"Once they were dead that was the end of them."
In the same world men lead different lives;
Some at the court, some in the marketplace.
Indeed I know these are no empty words:
The life of man is like a shadow-play
Which must in the end return to nothingness.

---

[9] A figurative expression which appears to mean that, looking back over his shoulder, the poet sees the moon as though it were a bundle suspended from the handle of his hoe. This line is much admired by Chinese critics.

[10] Literally: "to practice non-avoidance" or "non-contrariety," that is to say, to act in conformity with the Tao. Every kind of work brings with it its own discomforts and frustrations, and he must learn to accept the bad with the good.

[11] In Chinese poetry the faggot-gatherer and the fisherman are types of the rustic philosopher. Perhaps the man might have been some sort of hermit. There are endless stories telling how this or that emperor goes out hunting and meets such a man and is so struck with his wisdom that he takes him back to court and gives him high office, or in other cases the man refuses to go.

5

In grief and disappointment I return with my staff alone,[12]
Over the rugged path I thread its hazeled windings.
A mountain stream runs clear and shallow,
Coming upon it I wade and wash my feet.[13]
Arriving home I filter my newly heated wine
And killing chickens invite in all my neighbors.
The sun goes down — it is dark within the hall,
And thornwood faggots take the place of candles.
When such joys come the bitter night is short
And so it goes until the day dawns in the east.

Four Poems Written While Drunk

Living in retirement I had few pleasures, and moreover the autumn
nights were already growing longer. I happened to have some wine from
a famous place, and this I drank every evening. I would finish it alone
sitting self-contentedly, and suddenly would find myself drunk again.
After I was drunk, I would quickly dash off a few verses to amuse myself.
After a while the paper and ink made quite a pile, though the pieces had
no logical sequence, so I merely asked a friend to write them out for me
for a happy laugh.

1

Fortune and misfortune
    have no fixed abode;
This one and the other
    are given us in turn.
Shao Ping working
    in his field of melons
Was much as he had been
    when Lord of Dongling.[14]

---

[12] Reflecting with pain on the words of the faggot-gatherer he feels suddenly old, and as he goes the path seems steep and difficult.

[13] This, presumably, makes him feel better, and he conceives the idea of inviting his neighbors in for feasting and talking.

[14] Shao Ping was Marquis of Dongling when the Han overthrew the Qin dynasty in 206 B.C. Losing all his rank, he was reduced to growing melons on land east of the Chang'an city wall. They were of exceptionally fine quality and became famous as "Dongling melons."

Cold and hot seasons
    follow one another,
And the way of man
    will always be like this.
The intelligent man
    sees that it must be so.
Having gone so far
    he will not doubt again,
But from that moment
    every day and evening
He will be happy
    holding a cup of wine.

2

The Tao has been lost
    nigh on a thousand years
And people everywhere
    are misers of their feelings.
Though they have wine
    they do not dare to drink it,
And think of nothing save
    keeping their reputation.
All the things that make us
    care about our lives —
They are surely compassed
    within a single lifetime.
And how much can that life
    amount to after all —
Swift as the surprise
    of pouring lightning,
Fixed and circumscribed
    within a hundred years —
Hemmed and bound to this
    what can we hope to do?

3

I built my house near where others dwell,
And yet there is no clamor of carriages and horses.
You ask of me "How can this be so?"
"When the heart is far the place of itself is distant."
I pluck chrysanthemums under the eastern hedge,

And gaze afar towards the southern mountains.
The mountain air is fine at evening of the day
And flying birds return together homewards.
Within these things there is a hint of Truth,
But when I start to tell it, I cannot find the words.

4

In the clear dawn
    I hear a knocking at my gate
And skirt on wrong way round
    go to open it myself.
I ask the visitor
    "Pray, sir, who may you be?"
It is an old peasant
    who had a kindly thought,
And has come from far away
    bearing a jug of wine,
Because he thinks I am
    at variance with the times.
"Sitting in patched clothes
    under a thatched roof —
This will never help you
    to get on in the world!
All the world together
    praises that alone,
So I wish, sir, that you too
    would float with the muddy stream."
"Old man, I am deeply
    grateful for your words,
But your advice does not accord
    with my inborn nature.
Even if I could learn
    to follow the curb and reins,
To go against one's nature
    is always a mistake.
Let us just be happy
    and drink this wine together —
I fear my chariot
    can never be turned back."

Two Miscellaneous Poems

1

The bright sun sinks
    beyond the western ridge,
The white moon rises
    behind the eastern range.
Afar, afar
    a myriad miles it flashes,
Immeasurably vast
    its light amidst the sky.
A wind comes
    and enters the bedroom door,
So in the night
    pillow and mat are cold.
The air seems different —
    I awake to the season's change.
I cannot go to sleep
    and know the night's eternity,
I wish to speak
    but there is no friend to talk to.
Raising my cup
    I challenge my lonely shadow.
The days and months
    fling us aside and pass;
We have high purposes
    but cannot realize them.
Thinking of this
    I have grief and pain at heart,
And all night long
    can find no quietness.

2

The days and months do not wish to tarry,
The four seasons urge each other on.
A cold wind sweeps the withered branches,
And fallen leaves cover the long road.
My youthful vigor fails as the years revolve
And my black locks are already turning white.
When once the white signpost is raised above man's head

The road before him begins to seem narrow.
My home is only a hostel by the wayside,
And I a traveler who must soon depart.
On and on I travel — whither am I going?
On the Southern Mountain there is my ancient home.[15]

A Picnic by the Xie River

On the fifth day of the first month of the year *xin-chou* (A.D. 401),[16] the weather being clear and mild and the scene tranquilly beautiful, I went on an excursion to Xie River with a few of my neighbors. Looking down over a long stretch of the river we could see the site of the walled city of Ceng[17] in the distance. As the evening came on we caught the flashing scales of bream and trout leaping from the water, and seagulls circled back and forth on the mild air.

The fame of the sites on the southern foothills of Mount Lu is indeed ancient — it were a pity indeed not to celebrate them anew. There is the site of Ceng with nothing round about it, standing isolated on the riverbank. The sight of it awakened far-off memories of the fame of Mount Ling.[18]

I felt that it was not enough simply to gaze at it enraptured, so on a sudden impulse I composed a poem in which I sorrowed over the way in which our days and months slip by, and grieved over how our years will not tarry. Each of us then noted his age and birthplace to form a record of the occasion.

The fifth day of the New Year
    was here before we knew it,
And we suddenly felt
    our lives were fading fast.
Thinking of this
    our hearts were moved within us,

---

[15] Presumably his family's burial ground.
[16] Thus, in Tao's thirty-seventh year. [Compare this preface with the "Orchid Pavilion" preface in chapter 10.]
[17] In Tao's time a Buddhist temple called the Temple of the Falling Star stood upon this site.
[18] The reference must be to the Vulture Peak in India, where Sakyamuni preached the Law.

So while we yet have time
    we have come to view this spot.
The air is mild
    and the heavens cloudless,
We spread our mats in order
    overlooking the far stream.
Speckled bream
    leapt in the slow eddies —
And crying gulls
    soared in the lonely vale.
We let our eyes wander
    at will over distant lowlands
And gazed with heart-felt longing
    at the far-off hill of Ceng.
True, it is not as high
    as the Nine-Storyed Mountain,[19]
But no other hill commands
    such loving admiration.
Raising the ewer
    I call to my companions,
Draining our cups
    we pledge and pledge again.
After all who knows
    in the time to come
We may not ever
    meet like this again.
Midway in our cups
    we give rein to far-off feelings
And utterly forget
    the "thousand years of sorrow."[20]
Let us just enjoy
    this day to the utmost
And let our tomorrows
    take care of themselves.

---

[19] A fabulous place in the Kunlun Mountains.

[20] "The years of a lifetime do not reach a hundred,
Yet they contain a thousand years' sorrow."
From one of the Nineteen Old Poems. [See chapter 8.]

Written on the First Day of the Fifth Month

Harmonizing with a Poem by the Registrar Dai

> The empty boat[21]
>   drifts on and on at will
> Till it returns at last
>   into infinity.
> After Spring came
>   I had hardly looked around
> When suddenly it was
>   the middle of the year.
> By the southern windows
>   no trace of tiresome things,
> And the northern woods
>   are dense and flowering.
> The deep abyss of Heaven
>   sends the season's rain.
> And the morning's color
>   heralds the south wind.
> Once come into this world
>   there is none but must depart,
> But that is not the end
>   of the meaning of our lives.
> To dwell in what is constant
>   and so await the end,
> Though one's only pillow
>   should be his bended arm[22]
> That will not destroy
>   his inner quietness.
> Becoming an Immortal
>   is a steep and dangerous road
> But to set one's own ideals
>   is a broad and level highway.
> If we are lofty
>   in our everyday pursuits

---

[21] Human life is compared to a boat drifting on the stream of time.

[22] "The Master said, He who seeks only coarse food to eat, water to drink and a bent arm for pillow, will without looking for it find happiness to boot." (*Analects*, VII, 15)

What would be the use
    of climbing Hua or Song.[23]

Putting the Blame on His Sons

White hair covers my temples —
My flesh is no longer firm,
And though I have five sons
Not one cares for brush and paper.
A-shu is sixteen years of age;
For laziness he surely has no equal.
A-xuan tries his best to learn
But does not really love the arts.
Yong and Duan at thirteen years
Can hardly distinguish six from seven;
Tongzi with nine years behind him
Does nothing but hunt for pears and chestnuts.
If such was Heaven's decree
In spite of all that I could do,
Bring on, bring on
The Thing Within the Cup.

In Reply to a Poem by Liu Chaisang

Dwelling in poverty
    I have few human contacts
And at times forget
    the turning of the seasons.
In the empty court
    are many fallen leaves —
With pain at my heart
    I know that Fall has come.
New sunflowers
    shade the north window,
Fine ripe grain
    enriches the southern acres.
If I do not take
    this chance to be happy

---

[23] Mount Hua and Mount Song are two of the Five Sacred Mountains of ancient China, both also fabled abodes of Taoist Immortals and adepts.

How do I know that I
    shall see another harvest?
Calling the children to me
    I take them by the hand
On this fine day
    let us climb and roam afar.

Harmonizing with a Poem by the Registrar Guo

Shady, shady, the woods before the hall,
In the midst of summer treasuring pure shadow.
A gentle wind comes from time to time
And eddying about blows open my lapels.
Parting from company I go and rest at leisure,
Or getting up again I play with books and lute.
Vegetables from my garden provide nourishment to spare,
Of grain from last year's harvest there is still enough in store.
Really I have managed as well as I could do,
To have more than I needed was never my desire.
Husking my millet I brew exquisite wine,
When the wine is ready I dip it out myself.
The young children play beside my seat,
Learning to talk they do not yet form words.
With all these things I have regained happiness
And with their help forget the flowered hairpin.[24]
Afar, afar, I gaze at the white clouds,
And think of olden days with Oh, how deep a longing.

Seeing Off a Guest at Captain Wang's Headquarters

The autumn days
    are terrible and keen,
And the hundred herbs
    will soon all be withered.
Now in the season
    when we tread the frost
I climb on high
    to see you off again.

---

[24] An ornate hairpin used to fasten an official's cap of office in place.

Cold air
   obscures the hills and lowlands
So that the floating clouds
   have no place to rest.
Unthinkably far
   the islets of the ocean,
And the wind and waves
   are often contrary.
As evening comes on
   we enjoy the farewell banquet
Though our parting words
   must at last be sad,
When the birds of dawn
   return to roost at evening
And the setting sun
   gathers his last rays in.
Going and staying —
   to each a different road,
And I grieve how long before
   your chariot returns.
My eyes will follow
   your boat into the distance,
And my emotions fade
   with the Ten-thousand Changes.[25]

Written on the Ninth Day of the Ninth Month of the Year *Yi-you* (A.D. 409)

Slowly, slowly,
   the autumn draws to its close.
Cruelly cold
   the wind congeals the dew.
Vines and grasses
   will not be green again —
The trees in my garden
   are withering forlorn.
The pure air
   is cleansed of lingering lees

---

[25] That constitute Nature.

And mysteriously,
    the Heaven's realms are high.
Nothing is left
    of the spent cicada's song,
A flock of geese
    goes crying down the sky.
The myriad transformations
    unravel one another
And human life
    how should it not be hard?
From ancient times
    there was none but had to die,
Remembering this
    scorches my very heart.
What is there I can do
    to assuage this mood?
Only enjoy myself
    drinking my unstrained wine.
I do not know
    about a thousand years,
Rather let me make
    this morning last forever.

Six Poems

Translated by Gladys Yang and Yang Xianyi

Miscellaneous Poem

I would not work elsewhere but on a farm;
For toil my farm and mulberry leaves suffice.
I do it without other laborers,
And cold and hungry feed on husks of rice.
I only want enough to eat my fill,
Only expect sufficient grain to eat;
For winter satisfied with country cloth,
Rough linen serves me for the days of heat,
Yet even these desires I cannot meet;
This pitiful reflection gives me pain.
All other men can satisfy their needs,
But my attempts prove clumsy and in vain.

If such a fate is destined to be mine,
Let us drink to it with a cup of wine.

Two Poems Written While Drunk

1

My friends appreciate my way of life,
And bearing wine pots all together come;
We clear the weeds to sit beneath the pine,
With several cups of wine we drunk become.
When all the elders midst confusion speak,
And drinking is from all conventions freed;
We do not know if we ourselves exist,
And pay to the material world no heed.
In carefree drinking thus ourselves forget,
For in the wine a deeper truth is set.

2

There lived a scholar who was fond of wine,
But since he had no money could not buy;
Sometimes he was provided by his friends
With wine, if he their problems would untie.
And when the cup was filled he drained it straight,
And when advice was asked would not refuse.
But sometimes he would not his counsel give,
For unjust cause his gift would not abuse.
For when a wise man is desired to teach,
He will not err by silence or by speech.

Three Dirges

Written in Imitation of an Ancient Funeral Song

Tao Yuanming probably wrote these three poems in 427, when he was 63 years old. He died towards the end of the same year, and they are often read as poems written for his own funeral.

— Editors

1

That which has life inevitably dies,
Nor may the early dead their fate's haste blame.
Numbered last night amongst the living men,

Today enrolled amongst the ghosts my name.
Where does the spirit once departed fly
When dry form rests within the hollow wood?
My loving children for their father cry,
Mourning above my corpse my kinsmen good.
No more can I distinguish loss or gain,
No more twixt right and wrong can I decide.
For ages hence when centuries roll by
To know my fame or shame who will abide?
But I regret that in the world above
I longed for wine and never had enough.

2

In former days I wanted wine to drink;
The wine this morning fills the cup in vain.
I see the spring mead with its floating foam,
And wonder when to taste of it again.
The feast before me lavishly is spread,
My relatives and friends beside me cry.
I wish to speak but lips can shape no voice,
I wish to see but light has left my eye.
I slept of old within the lofty hall,
Amidst wild weeds to rest I now descend.
When once I pass beyond the city gate
I shall return to darkness without end.

3

How desolate the weeds appear;
Rustling the leaves of aspen trees forlorn.
In bitter frost, upon an Autumn day,
Far out beyond the city am I borne.
No human habitance on any side,
Only the towering tombs that scattered lie.
Stretching their necks the horses skyward neigh,
While cold winds wailing make the forest sigh.
The gloomy chamber once in darkness sealed,
A thousand years the light of day will fail.
A thousand years the light of day will fail,
While wise and learned nothing can avail.
Those who went forth my coffin to escort
Now homeward to their families repair.

My relatives may feel some sorrow still,
The rest already hum another air.
My body in the mountain side they lay;
No dead and gone, what more is there to say?

The Peach Blossom Spring

Translated by J. R. Hightower

This happy land, where men live in harmony with their neighbors, and are secure against the envy and malice of outsiders; where every man tills his own fields and pays no taxes; where the old and the young do not toil and where all have a sufficiency — it differs in nearly every detail from the world of Tao Yuanming's own experience. That it may have been inspired by the report of a contemporary discovery of such an enclave is interesting but not really relevant, for this is after all an imagined utopia, no less remote and impossible for the modesty of its conception.

During the Tai-yuan period of the Jin dynasty a fisherman of Wuling once rowed upstream, unmindful of the distance he had gone, when he suddenly came to a grove of peach trees in bloom. For several hundred paces on both banks of the stream there was no other kind of tree. The wild flowers growing under them were fresh and lovely, and fallen petals covered the ground — it made a great impression on the fisherman. He went on for a way with the idea of finding out how far the grove extended. It came to an end at the foot of a mountain whence issued the spring that supplied the stream. There was a small opening in the mountain, and it seemed as though light was coming through it. The fisherman left his boat and entered the cave, which at first was extremely narrow, barely admitting his body; after a few dozen steps it suddenly opened out onto a broad and level plain where well-built houses were surrounded by rich fields and pretty ponds. Mulberry, bamboos and other trees and plants grew there, and criss-cross paths skirted the fields. The sounds of cocks crowing and dogs barking could be heard from one courtyard to the next. Men and women were coming and going about their work in the fields. The clothes they wore were like those of ordinary people. Old men and boys were carefree and happy.

When they caught sight of the fisherman, they asked in surprise how he had got there. The fisherman told the whole story, and was invited to go to their house, where he was served wine while they killed a chicken for a feast. When the other villagers heard about the fisherman's arrival they all came to pay him a visit. They told him that their ancestors had fled the disorders of Qin times and, having taken refuge here with wives and children and neighbors, had never ventured out again; consequently they had lost all contact with the outside world. They asked what the present ruling dynasty was, for they had never heard of the Han, let alone the Wei and the Jin. They sighed unhappily as the fisherman enumerated the dynasties one by one and recounted the vicissitudes of each. The visitors all asked him to come to their houses in turn, and at every house he had wine and food. He stayed several days. As he was about to go away, the people said, "There's no need to mention our existence to outsiders."

After the fisherman had gone out and recovered his boat, he carefully marked the route. On reaching the city, he reported what he had found to the magistrate, who at once sent a man to follow him back to the place. They proceeded according to the marks he had made, but went astray and were unable to find the cave again.

A high-minded gentleman of Nanyang named Liu Ziji heard the story and happily made preparations to go there, but before he could leave he fell sick and died. Since then there has been no one interested in trying to find such a place.

> The Ying clan disrupted Heaven's ordinance
> And good men withdrew from such a world.[26]
> Huang and Qi went off to Shang Mountain
> And these people too fled into hiding.[27]
> Little by little their tracks were obliterated
> The paths they followed overgrown at last.
> By agreement they set about farming the land
> When the sun went down each rested from his toil.
> Bamboo and mulberry provided shade enough,
> They planted beans and millet, each in season.
> From spring silkworms came the long silk thread
> On the fall harvest no king's tax was paid.
> No sign of traffic on overgrown roads,
> Cockcrow and dogsbark within each other's earshot.
> Their ritual vessels were of old design,
> And no new fashions in the clothes they wore.
> Children wandered about singing songs,
> Graybeards went paying one another calls.
> When grass grew thick they saw the time was mild,
> As trees went bare they knew the wind was sharp.
> Although they had no calendar to tell,

---

[26] The First Emperor of Qin is here referred to by his clan name Ying.
[27] Huang and Qi were two of the hermits known as the Four White-heads.

The four seasons still filled out a year.
Joyous in their ample happiness
They had no need of clever contrivance.
Five hundred years this rare deed stayed hid,
Then one fine day the fay retreat was found.
The pure and the shallow belong to separate worlds:
In a little while they were hidden again.
Let me ask you who are convention-bound,
Can you fathom those outside the dirt and noise?
I want to tread upon the thin thin air
And rise up high to find my own kind.

The Return: A Rhapsody

Translated by J. R. Hightower

This rhapsody was inspired by the poet's final retirement from official life in the winter of 405, as were the "Five Poems on Returning to Dwell in the Country" of the following year.

I was poor, and what I got from farming was not enough to support my family. The house was full of children, the rice-jar was empty, and I could not see any way to supply the necessities of life. Friends and relatives kept urging me to become a magistrate, and I had at last come to think I should do it, but there was no way for me to get such a position. At the time I happened to have business abroad and made a good impression on the grandees as a conciliatory and humane sort of person. Because of my poverty an uncle offered me a job in a small town, but the region was still unquiet and I trembled at the thought of going away from home. However, Pengze was only thirty miles from my native place, and the yield of the fields assigned the magistrate was sufficient to keep me in wine, so I applied for the office. Before many days had passed, I longed to give it up and go back home. Why, you may ask. Because my instinct is all for freedom, and will not brook discipline or restraint. Hunger and cold may be sharp, but this going against myself really sickens me. Whenever I have been involved in official life I was mortgaging myself to my mouth and belly, and the realization of this greatly upset me. I was deeply ashamed that I had so compromised my principles, but I was still going to wait out the year, after which I might pack up my clothes and slip away at night. Then my sister who had married into the Cheng family died in Wuchang, and my only desire was to go there as quickly as possible. I gave up my office and left of my own accord. From mid-autumn to winter I was

altogether some eighty days in office, when events made it possible for
me to do what I wished. I have entitled my piece "The Return"; my
preface is dated the eleventh moon of the year yi-si (405).

> To get out of this and go back home!
> My fields and garden will be overgrown with weeds —
>   I must go back.
> It was my own doing that made my mind my body's slave
> Why should I go on in melancholy and lonely grief?
> I realize that there's no remedying the past
> But I know that there's hope in the future.
> After all I have not gone far on the wrong road
> And I am aware that what I do today is right, yesterday wrong.
> My boat rocks in the gentle breeze
> Flap, flap, the wind blows my gown;
> I ask a passerby about the road ahead,
> Grudging the dimness of the light at dawn.
> Then I catch sight of my cottage —
>   Filled with joy I run.
> The servant boy comes to welcome me
>   My little son waits at the door.
> The three paths are almost obliterated
>   But pines and chrysanthemums are still here.
> Leading the children by the hand I enter my house
>   Where there is a bottle filled with wine.
> I draw the bottle to me and pour myself a cup;
> Seeing the trees in the courtyard brings joy to my face.
> I lean on the south window and let my pride expand,
> I consider how easy it is to be content with a little space.
> Every day I stroll in the garden for pleasure,
> There is a gate there, but it is always shut.
> Cane in hand I walk and rest
> Occasionally raising my head to gaze into the distance.
> The clouds aimlessly rise from the peaks,
> The birds, weary of flying, know it is time to come home.
> As the sun's rays grow dim and disappear from view
> I walk around a lonely pine tree, stroking it.
>
> Back home again!
> May my friendships be broken off and my wanderings come to
>   an end.
> The world and I shall have nothing more to do with one
>   another.

If I were again to go abroad, what should I seek?
Here I enjoy honest conversation with my family
And take pleasure in books and zither to dispel my worries.
The farmers tell me that now spring is here
There will be work to do in the west fields.
Sometimes I call for a covered cart
Sometimes I row a lonely boat
Following a deep gully through the still water
Or crossing the hill on a rugged path.
The trees put forth luxuriant foliage,
The spring begins to flow in a trickle.
I admire the seasonableness of nature
And am moved to think that my life will come to its close.
        It is all over —
So little time are we granted human form in the world!
Let us then follow the inclinations of the heart:
Where would we go that we are so agitated?
I have no desire for riches
And no expectation of Heaven.
Rather on some fine morning to walk alone
Now planting my staff to take up a hoe,
Or climbing the east hill and whistling long
Or composing verses beside the clear stream:
So I manage to accept my lot until the ultimate homecoming.
Rejoicing in Heaven's command, what is there to doubt?

Elegy

Translated by J. R. Hightower

This autobiographical sketch was written by Tao in the last year of his life, perhaps on his deathbed.

The year is *ding-mao* of the cycle, the season that of the tone *wu-yi*, when days are cold and the nights long, when the wind blows mournfully as the wild fowl migrate, and leaves turn yellow and fall. Master Tao is about to depart from this lodging house to return for all time to his own home. Old friends are grieved and mourn for him: this evening they give him a farewell banquet, offering a sacrificial food, pouring libations of clear wine. They look, and his face is dim; listening, they no longer hear the sound of his voice.

Alas, alas, this vast clod, earth, that illimitable high firmament, together produce all things, even me who am a man. But from the time I attained human estate, my lot has been poverty. Rice-bin and wine-gourd have often been empty, and I have faced winters in thin clothes. Still I have gone happily to draw water from the brook and have sung as I walked under a load of firewood, going about my daily affairs in the obscurity of my cottage. As springs gave way to autumn, I have busied myself in my garden hoeing, cultivating, planting or tending. I have rejoiced in my books and have been soothed by my zither. Winters I have warmed myself in the sun, summers I have bathed in the brook. There was little enough reward for my labor, but my mind enjoyed a constant leisure. Content with heaven and accepting my lot, I have lived out the years of my life.

Men fear to waste their lives, concerned that they may fail to succeed. They cling to the days and lament passing time. During their life they are honored by the world, and after their death they still are mourned. But I have gone my own way, which is not their way. I take no glory in their esteem, nor do I feel defamed by their slander. I have lived alone in my poor house, drinking wine and writing poetry.

Aware of my destined end, of which one cannot be ignorant, I find no cause for regret in this present transformation. I have lived out my lifespan, and all my life I have desired quiet retirement. Now that I am dying, an old man, what have I left to wish for?

Hot and cold hasten on, one after the other. The dead have nothing in common with the survivors. Relatives come in the morning, friends arrive in the evening, to bury me in the meadow and give comfort to my soul. Dark is my journey, desolate the grave. It is shameful to be buried extravagantly as was Huan Tui (whose stone coffin was three years a-making), and ridiculous to be parsimonious like Yang Wangsun (who was buried naked), for after death there is nothing. Raise me no mound, plant me no grove; time will pass with the revolving sun and moon. I never cared for praise in my lifetime, and it matters not at all what eulogies are sung after my death. Man's life is hard enough in truth; and death is not to be avoided.

▧ *Further Reading* ▧

Acker, William, trans. *T'ao the Hermit: Sixty Poems by T'ao Ch'ien.* London: Thames & Hudson, 1952.

Chang, H. C., ed. and trans. *Chinese Literature, Vol. 2: Nature Poetry.* Edinburgh: University of Edinburgh Press, 1977.

Davis, A. R. *T'ao Yüan-ming.* 2 vols. Cambridge: Cambridge University Press, 1984.

Hightower, J. R. *The Poetry of T'ao Ch'ien.* Oxford: Oxford University Press, 1970.

Waley, Arthur, trans. *One Hundred and Seventy Chinese Poems*. London: Constable, 1918. (Contains twelve poems by T'ao, all included in the later [1946] anthology *Chinese Poems*.)

Yang, Gladys and Yang Xianyi, trans. *Tao Yuanming: Selected Poems*. Peking: Chinese Literature Press, 1993.

⌨ *Editors' Note* ⌨

William Acker's 1952 translations convey very well the quality of "unadorned direct-ness" and reclusive tranquillity that characterize so much of Tao Yuanming's poetry. The rhyming versions done by Gladys and Xianyi Yang, although first published in book form in 1993, are in fact the product of their youthful days as students at Oxford fifty years earlier. They capture another facet of Tao's work, perhaps the one Lu Xun had in mind when he said that Tao Yuanming was great precisely because he was *not* "all serenity."

"I pluck chrysanthemums under the eastern hedge, and gaze afar towards the southern mountains."
Seal carved by Ding Jing (1695–1765)

Chapter 12

The Murmuring Stream and the Weary Road

Xie Lingyun (385–433) and Bao Zhao (414–466)

The murmuring stream is the huge tongue of Buddha,
The color of the hills is surely His pure body.

> — Su Dongpo(1037–1101), "Poem for the Abbot of Donglin Monastery"
> (*translated by John Frodsham*)

Men have always spoken and will always speak of the beauty of mountains and streams. High peaks that go soaring into the clouds; translucent torrents, clear to their very bottoms, flanked on either side by cliffs of stone, whose fivefold colors glitter in the sun; green forests and bamboos of kingfisher-blue, verdant through every season of the year. As the mists of dawn roll aside, the birds and monkeys cry discordantly. As the evening sun sinks to rest, the fishes vie at leaping from their deep pools. Here is the true Paradise of the Region of Earthly Desires. Yet, since the time of Xie Lingyun, no one has been able to feel at one with these wonders, as he did.

> — Tao Hongjing (452–536), "Letter in Reply to Secretary Xie"
> (*translated by John Frodsham*)

If my lord would banish sorrow and brood no more,
Let him listen to my songs of the weary road,
Sung to the beat of the drum …

Pour out wine and let us take our ease!
Raise our goblets, sing no more
Of the weary road …

Man runs a rough road through life —
But what is there to say?

> — Bao Zhao, "Songs of the Weary Road" (*translated by John Frodsham*)

When joy comes, I dip the wine alone;
When care arrives, I forthwith write a poem.

> — Bao Zhao, "Answering a Visitor" (*translated by Burton Watson*)

XIE LINGYUN (385–433)
Ten Poems

Translated by John Frodsham

Xie Lingyun, Duke of Kangle, was born into one of the most illustrious families of the Six Dynasties. His great-grand-uncle Xie An (320–385) had been Prime Minister; his grandfather, Xie Xuan (343–388), had thrown back Fu Jian's invading army at the battle of the Fei River in 383, and so prevented the northern "barbarians" from seizing the south. Given such advantages, Lingyun would have seemed assured of a brilliant career at court; yet this persistently eluded him. When the Jin collapsed in 419, he joined forces with the Liu Song dynasty. But in 422 his enemies, jealous of his friendship with the heir to the throne, the Prince of Luling, exiled him to Yongjia (Wenzhou in Zhejiang province) and murdered the prince. It is from this period that his finest verse must be dated: suffering had made a poet out of a competent versifier. For the next ten years he alternated between intervals of seclusion on his estate and spells of discontented service as an official. Finally, he ran foul of a powerful clique at court, was exiled to Guangzhou, and executed there on a trumped-up charge.

Brought up as a Taoist in the esoteric sect of the Way of the Heavenly Master, Lingyun soon became a fervent convert to Buddhism. He joined the community on Mount Lu, under the famous Huiyuan (334–416), and distinguished himself by his essays on Buddhist philosophy and his translation of several sutras. But his real contribution to Chinese literature lies in his nature poetry, which grew out of his love for the picturesque mountains of Zhejiang and Jiangxi. He liked wandering among the hills, and even devised a special pair of mountaineering boots, with removable studs, to enable him to scale the most difficult peaks. As a nature-poet he is unsurpassed; his verse resounds with the roar of mountain torrents, is redolent with the scent of wind-tossed pines. His faults spring from an excess of cleverness: he can never resist the temptation to dazzle his readers with his virtuosity, to strain after an allusion, a recondite and bookish phrase, whenever he can. Yet in spite of this, he is undoubtedly one of the finest poets of the whole period, the inspiration of many later writers, Li Bo and Du Fu among them. Brilliant, sensitive, and eccentric, his verse gives us the measure of the man.

On Spending Some Time at the Bai'an Pavilion

The pavilion lay Southwest of the river Nan, eighty-seven *li* from Yongjia.

On these sandy dikes I shake the world's dust from my clothes,
And leisurely stroll into my tumbleweed house.
Through the rock-strewn gorge a nearby stream goes trickling,
While distant mountains glint through the sparse trees.
So hard to find words for their airy kingfisher blue,
So easy for a fisherman to live.[1]

---

[1] If one bends to one's fate, submits to the inevitable as does a fisherman — symbol of the Taoist sage — then one will preserve one's life.

On these green shores I listen, grasping the creepers,
Spring and my heart have now become as one.
The call of yellow birds among the oaks,
The cry of deer browsing on the duckweed.[2]
Sadly I recall those men of a hundred sorrows,
But delight in your joy at the baskets you received.[3]
Joy and sorrow come and go in turn,
Now failure daunts us, now success makes us glad.
Rather than this, I prefer to be free for ever.
From all the world I choose Simplicity.

On Climbing Stone Drum Mountain, Near Shangshu

The mountain lay some forty *li* west of Yongjia, and derived its name from a stone on its summit which gave off a distinctive note when struck.

The traveler is a prey to endless sorrows,
As one grief goes another comes behind.
Such a long road leading back to my old home,
With rivers and hills between that cannot be crossed.
Time rushes by, yet no one shares my pleasures,
So when spring comes I have to start climbing alone.
Perhaps, I thought, since no one shares my joys,
I shall find a scene to suit my melancholy.
Now I stare out to the plains that lie to the left,
Then turn my gaze to the gorges on my right.
As the sun goes down, the mountain stream swells higher,
As the clouds are born, the peaks are plunged in mist.
White flag is vying with the young tree-creeper,
Green duckweed is just venturing into leaf.
The fragrant plants I pluck brook no forgetting,
All these delights I must enjoy alone.
Not a trace of a friend to come and meet me here,
The distance only mocks my loneliness.

---

[2] These allusions to the *Book of Songs* probably hint at the fate of his friends who had been "sacrificed" after the death of Emperor Wu.

[3] Another allusion to the *Book of Songs*. Here the poet seems to address those of his friends who have still managed to remain in office under the regime which has exiled him. He bears them no grudge for this but rather rejoices in their good fortune.

On Climbing Mount Green Crag in Yongjia

A hill in the Yongning range twenty *li* northwest of Yongjia.

I packed some provisions and took up my light staff,
Climbing the long, winding way to my hidden abode.
As I walked up-stream, the path led me further away,
When I reached the mountain-top, my heart was still rejoicing.
The calm shallows were congealed in frozen beauty,
Glossy bamboos seemed heedless of the frost.
In the windings of the gorge, the water went straying away,
Far-off stretched the forest, with crags crowding it in.
I peered westward, looking for the sickle-moon,
I gazed back to the east, wondering if the sun had set.
I walked on till twilight, then rested until the dawn,
Enshrouding shadows whelming me in their deep.
"Decay" in high places: best to serve no one at all:
"Take second place"; it always pays to push on.[4]
A recluse will always walk the level Way,
Yet his goal lies higher than anything we know.
What difference is there between plain "yes" and a nod?
I shall live in peace, hold fast to Unity.
Once tranquillity and wisdom fuse together,
From that day on, your nature begins to heal.

All Around My New House at Stone Gate Are High Mountains, Winding Streams, Rocky Torrents, Thick Forests, and Tall Bamboos

The poet's second house, built at the top of Stone Gate Crags, was secluded and difficult of access.

I climbed these crags to build a secluded cabin,
Brushing aside the clouds I rested at Stone Gate.
Who can walk on these slippery mosses here,
Or clutch the dolichos plants to keep from falling?
On autumn days the wind goes howling past,
But in the spring the place is full of flowers.
My friend has gone and has not yet returned,
Small hope I have of seeing him again.
Our jewelled mats are thick with scented dust,

[1] These two allusions to the *Book of Changes* are amplified in the two following lines.

While golden beakers brim with crystal wine.
What good to me are the waves on Dongting Lake?
In vain I climb up by the cassia boughs.
I long for someone far off as the Milky Way,
My lonely shadow is left with its memories.
I swim in the lake down at the foot of the rocks,
And looking up, see the apes swing through the trees.
Mornings, I wait for the rush of the evening breeze,
Evenings, I watch for the morning sun to rise.
Light cannot linger under these beetling crags,
In the forest depths the slightest sound carries far.
When sadness has gone then thought can return again,
Once wisdom has come, passion no longer exists.
Would that I were the charioteer of the sun!
Only this would bring some solace to my soul.
Not for the common herd do I say these things,
I should like to talk them over with the wise.

Written on the Lake on My Way Back to the Retreat at Stone Cliff

Xie had founded a small meditation hall on his estate.

Between dusk and dawn the weather is constantly changing,
Bathing mountain and lake alike in radiant sunlight.
This radiant sunlight filled me with such joy,
That lost in delight I quite forgot to go home.
When I left my valley the day had scarcely broken,
When I stepped into my boat the light was growing dim.
Forest and gorge were veiled in somber colors,
The sunset clouds mingled with evening haze.
Gay panoply of water-chestnut, lotus,
Rushes and cattails growing side by side,
I swept them aside with my hands as I hastened southward.
How glad I was to reach my house in the east!
Once the mind stops striving the world loses importance,
Once the heart is content it does not swerve from truth.
I send these words to those who would nurture their lives:
Try using this Method if you want the Truth.[5]

---

[5] The Method of having a tranquil mind and a contented heart, which is the best means of nurturing life.

On Climbing the Highest Peak of Stone Gate

At dawn with staff in hand I climbed the crags,
At dusk I made my camp among the mountains.
Only a few peaks rise as high as this house,
Facing the crags, it overlooks winding streams.
In front of its gates a vast forest stretches,
While boulders are heaped round its very steps.
Hemmed in by mountains, there seems no way out,
The track gets lost among the thick bamboos.
My visitors can never find their way,
And when they leave, forget the path they took.
The raging torrents rush on through the dusk,
The monkeys clamour shrilly through the night.
Deep in meditation, how can I part from Truth?
I cherish the Way and never will swerve from it.
My heart is one with the trees of late autumn,
My eyes delight in the buds of early spring.
I dwell with my constant companions and wait for my end,
Content to find peace through accepting the flux of things.
I only regret that there is no kindred soul,
To climb with me this ladder to the clouds in the blue.

What I Saw When I Had Crossed the Lake on My Way from South Mountain to North Mountain

The poet, on his way across the lakes, stops at the mountainous island separating them, and enjoys the view.

In the morning I set out from the sun-lit shore,
When the sun was setting I rested by the shadowy peaks.
Leaving my boat I gazed at the far-off banks,
Halting my staff, I leant against a flourishing pine.
The narrow path is dark and secluded,
Yet the ring-like island is bright as jade.
Below I see the tops of towering trees,
Above I hear the meeting of wild torrents.
Over the rocks in its path the water divides and flows on,
In the depth of the forest the paths are free from footprints.
What is the result of "Delivering" and "Forming"?[6]

---

[6] Allusions to the *Book of Changes*.

Everywhere is thick with things pushing upward and growing.
The first bamboos enfold their emerald shoots,
The newborn rushes hold their purple flowers.
Seagulls play on the vernal shores,
The heaven-cock flies up on the gentle wind.[7]
My heart never tires of meeting these Transformations,
The more I look on Nature, the more I love her.
I do not regret the departed are so remote,
I am only sorry I have no one as a companion.
I wander alone, sighing, but not from mere feeling;
Unsavored nature yields to none her meaning.[8]

I Follow the Jinzhu Torrent, Cross the Peak, and Go Along by the River

When the monkeys howl, I know that dawn has broken,
Though yet no sun has touched this shadowed valley.
Around the peaks the clouds begin to gather,
While dew still glistens brightly on the flowers.
My path winds round beside a curving river,
Then climbs far up among the rock-bound crags.
With gown held high, I wade the mountain torrent,
Then toil up wooden bridges, ever higher.
Below, the river islets wind around,
But I enjoy following the sinuous stream.
Duckweed floats upon its turbid deeps,
Reeds and cattails cover its clear shallows.
I stand on a rock to fill my cup from a cataract,
I pull down branches and pluck their leafy scrolls.
In my mind's eye I see someone in the fold of the hill,
In a fig-leaf coat and girdle of rabbit-floss.
With a handful of orchids I grieve for my lost friendship,
I pluck the hemp, yet can tell no one how I feel.[9]
The sensitive heart will find beauty everywhere —
But with whom can I discuss such subtleties now?

---

[7] The golden pheasant.

[8] The poet's feeling for nature is no mere sensuous enjoyment, but a religious ecstasy which unites him with the Tao itself.

[9] These four lines contain allusions to the "Nine Songs" [See chapter 5].

When I look at all this, the world of men disappears,
In a flash of enlightenment everything falls from me.

A Poem on Stone House Mountain

In the cool of dawn I sought a strange seclusion,
Cast loose my boat and passed through the suburbs and the Wilds.
Past banks of massed orchids the river went flowing rapidly.
How remote is this high and mossy peak!
Stone House Mountain rises from a corner of the forest,
A waterfall comes hurtling from its summit.
Its vacant flow has gone on for thousands of years;
These sheer heights were not just the work of a day.
Nor sight nor sound here of the world of men,
Wind and mist drive away gatherers of wood and herbs.
Though I never could wander off to distant parts,
Since I was a youth I have admired the ascent of Qiao.[10]
In this magic region he has long been hidden,
If only I could meet with my heart's delight![11]
Of the Tree of Joy I cannot bear to speak,
I pluck a scented frond and play with its cool branches.

Last Poem

The allusions in the first four lines of this poem provide analogies with Xie's own case. Gong Sheng (68 B.C.–A.D. 11) starved himself to death rather than serve the usurper Wang Mang; Li Ye (first century A.D.) also preferred death to serving the usurper Gongsun Shu, who, incensed at his refusal, had him poisoned; Xi Kang (see chapter 10) had been unjustly put to death on the flimsiest of evidence; and Huo Yuan was executed by the would-be usurper Wang Jun (252–314).

Lingyun wrote this last poem on the eve of his execution. On his way to the execution, so the story goes, he cut off his splendid goatee and presented it to the Jetavana monastery in Nanhai to serve as a beard for an image of Vimalakirti. He died as he had lived — philosophical, eccentric, courageous — a poet and an aristocrat to the last. His body was brought back to Kuaiji and laid to rest there among the mountains he loved so well.

---

[10] The Immortal Wang Ziqiao.

[11] This may refer to the bark of the albizzia, supposed to dissipate anger and bring freedom from care; or it may refer figuratively to the joy and harmony between the poet and the mountains.

Gong Sheng had no life left to him,
Li Ye came to an end.
Xi Kang was harassed for his truth,
Master Huo too lost his life.
Thick and green the cypress, heedless of the frost,
Soaked with dew the mushroom, suffering in the wind.
What does a happy life amount to after all?
I am not troubled by its brevity.
I only regret that my resolution as a gentleman
Could not have brought me to my end among the mountains.
To deliver up my heart before I achieved Enlightenment
This pain has been with me for long.
I only pray I may be born again
Where friend and foe alike might share
The same desires.

Replying to a Poem from My Cousin Huilian

Translated by Burton Watson

Written in 430 when the poet was living in retirement at Kuaiji and had received news,
in the form of a poem, that his cousin was on his way to visit.

Brought to bed by sickness, cut off from men,
I hid myself among cloudy peaks.
Cliffs and valleys filled the eye and ear;
the ones I loved — their faces, their voices far away;
gone the hopes of finding a heart's companion,
long regretting I must always be alone,
near the end of the road, I met my honored cousin:
frowns faded, hearts were opened up.

After we had opened our hearts,
my sole contentment was in you.
Across the valleys you searched out my room;
I opened my books, told you all I knew.
At evening I thought how the dawn moon would pale;
mornings I fretted that the sun would set too soon.
We walked together, never tiring;
we met — and now we're parted again.

Parted, taking leave at the western river;
I turned my shadow back to the hills of the east.

When we parted it was sorrowful enough;
since then the pain never seems to end.
One thought — to wait for joyful news;
then came your poem about a "river-crossing,"
about your trials with wind and wave,
of every aspect of the beaches and shoals.

Beaches and shoals where you linger so long,
wind and wave delaying your journey.
Wrapped in your memories of the bright capital far away,
how could I expect you to recall these empty valleys?
And though you favor me with this message,
it serves only to trouble my thoughts.
If — if you would come back as you said,
together we could enjoy the late spring.

Late spring — there would still be time!
more time for pleasure if you came the month before,
when the mountain peach unfurls its crimson petals
and meadow ferns are sheathed in purple.
Already the chatter of birds delights me,
but still there's gloom in my out-of-the-way home.
In dreams I wait your boat returning,
coming to free me from meanness and care.

BAO ZHAO (414–466)
Six Songs of the Weary Road

Translated by John Frodsham

Bao Zhao was born into a gentry family, just sufficiently well-to-do to afford him an education, but not influential enough to enable him to break through the rigid stratification of Six Dynasties society. As a young man he won himself a position at the court of the Prince of Linchuan [Liu Yiqing, author of *A New Account of Tales of the World*, for which see chapter 10 and chapter 16], who had been impressed by his literary talents. But advancement was slow in coming. Bao had to suffer the indignity of seeing well-born idiots rise where he could not.

How long does life drag on?
How long must I limp round
With folded wings?

His life, spent in the occupancy of a series of petty offices, was eventually brought to an end by a group of marauding soldiers, who killed him during the course of a revolt staged by his master, the Prince of Linhai.

His favorite genre was the *yuefu* ballad, and his eighteen Songs of the Weary Road take the genre to heights it had never attained before and has seldom reached since.

A Goblet of Wine

To you, my lord, a gold goblet of vintage wine,
And a carved lute of tortoiseshell in a jade casket.
Feather-edged curtains of seven-colored hibiscus,
And a silken quilt embroidered with nine-flowered vines.
Rosy cheeks will fade as the years roll on,
The chill moon circles round as the seasons pass.
If my lord would banish sorrow and brood no more,
Let him listen to my songs of the weary road,
Sung to the beat of the drum.
You have seen the Cypress Beam and the Brazen Bird?[12]
Where now is the pure music of those ancient flutes?

This Bronze Censer

This bronze censer, from a famous master of Luoyang,
Is fashioned like Mount Bo.[13]
It is carved in a thousand ways,
Engraved in ten thousand.
On its top is the girl of Qin
Leading the Immortal by the hand.[14]
To aid my lord in his pleasures tonight,
I have placed it inside the bed-hangings,
Before the candle's gleam.
Without, it shines with a dragon's scarlet scales,
From within it exhales a purple, musky fragrance.
If my lord's heart should suddenly turn against me,
I should gaze at this and sigh for a thousand years.

---

[12] The Cypress Beam Tower was built by Emperor Wu of Han in 108 B.C. The Brazen Bird Tower was erected by Emperor Wu of Wei (Cao Cao) in A.D. 210. [For poems by both emperors, see chapter 9.]

[13] A mountain in Shandong. Mount Bo censers are still to be seen in collections of Chinese bronzes.

[14] Nongyu was the daughter of Duke Mu of Qin. She married Xiao Shi, who taught her to summon the phoenix on her flute. One day they both climbed on the back of the bird and flew away into the blue.

Water Spilt

Water spilt on level ground,
Runs north, south, east and west.
So man's life is ruled by Fate,
Why be sighing as we journey,
Grieving as we rest?
Pour out wine and let us take our ease!
Raise our goblets, sing no more
Of the weary road.
My heart is not unfeeling wood or stone —
Yet I hesitate, swallow my plaint,
Not daring to speak.

The Grass by the River

Have you not seen the grass by the river?
In winter, withered and dead,
In spring it covers the roads.
Have you not seen the sun above the walls?
Now it is sinking, seems gone for good,
Yet next day it is back with us again.
But no such resurrection comes for us
Who once descended to the Yellow Springs[15]
Have fled this world for ever.
Life is all suffering, very little joy.
Only the young have boundless confidence.
If we should ever realize our aims
Let's try and meet as often as we can,
Keep cash for wine forever by our beds.
Renown in silk or annals of bamboo?
Such things are not for me.
Honor or obscurity, life or death,
High heaven deals out the lot.

---

[15] The tomb [or the nether world].

Folded Wings

At table I could not eat,
I drew my sword and hacked at a pillar[16]
Heaving long sighs.
"How long does life drag on?
How long must I limp round
With folded wings?"[17]
So I gave up my post,
Left office, went away,
Back to my family to rest.
In the morning I bade farewell to my parents,
In the evening I was back with my family again.
I play with the baby romping in front of the cot,
I watch my wife as she sits and weaves at her loom.
Since ancient times, wise men have been poor and unknown,
How much more so the lonely and honest men of today.

A Rough Road

Have you not seen the young men
Going off to the wars?
They have turned into white-haired exiles
Because they can never return.
Their homes are hidden in the distance,
Cut off by night and day.
Rivers and mountain passes
Bar them off from their world.
The desert wind moans sadly,
Scudding white clouds.
Poignant the flutes of the nomads
In the bitter, frontier air.

---

[16] When Han Gaozu came to the throne (202 B.C.) his followers, unaccustomed to court etiquette, behaved as they would in camp and hacked at the pillars of the palace with their swords. Bao is implying that he was too rough and uncultured for the polished society in which he found himself.

[17] As a member of a poor family Bao had no chance of real advancement.

The music fills them with sadness,
But what are they to do?
Climbing a hill and gazing south,
For a while they are young again.
Trampled under nomad horses,
They will see their families no more.
Man runs a rough road through life —
But what is there to say?
Ravaged by endless sorrows,
They get to their feet with a sigh.

Imitating the Old Poems

Translated by Burton Watson

Many strange mountains in Shu and Han;
looking up, I see them level with the clouds,
shaded scarps piled with summer snow,
sunny ravines where autumn flowers fall.
Morning after morning I watch the clouds go home,
evening on evening, hear the monkeys wail,
a melancholy man, sorrow always with me,
a lonely traveler, easily cast down.
From my room I look out, wine jar by my side,
plying the dipper, thinking back on life —
It is the nature of stone to be firm:
do not forsake the friendship we once had!

Ballad in Imitation of "The Prince of Huainan"

Translated by Burton Watson

Liu An, the Prince of Huainan, was a member of the Han imperial family whose name
is associated in popular lore with the cult of the immortals [see chapter 7].

The Prince of Huainan,
craving long life,
tried elixirs and breath control, studied the Classic of the Immortals;
of lapis lazuli his bowls, of ivory his plates;
in golden cauldrons with spoons of jade mixing magic cinnabar,
mixing magic cinnabar,
sporting in purple rooms,
purple rooms where bright-robed ladies toyed with earrings of pearl,

sang like the *luan* bird, danced like phoenixes —
    how they broke my lord's heart!
Nine gates to the vermilion city, each with nine small portals;
I want to chase the bright moon, to enter my lord's bosom,
enter my lord's bosom,
twine myself at his sash.
I hate my lord, I curse my lord, I wait for my lord's love.
May it be firm as a builded city, may it be keen as swords;
may I flourish with him, wane with him, and never be cut off!

Ballad: A Song in the Night

Translated by Joseph R. Allen

The deep winter night; deep in the night you sit singing
I already know your desires before you speak
The frost enters the curtain
The wind blows through the grove
The rosy lamp is put out
And your rosy face is sought
Following your song
Pursuing its sound
Not valuing the voice
But rather its deep intent.

Ballad: The Boatman's Song

Translated by Joseph R. Allen

Ever since childhood this constant traveler
Has floated and drifted without a place to stay
Last fall stationed at the edges of the Yangtze
This spring traveling along the banks of the Yellow
I was sent off up with the corvée laborers
Wanting always to talk of my memories of Chu
In the pool chilly and cold the minnows are few
Along the islands sadly honking the geese call
Heavy and hard the steady wind hammers the boat
Heaving and hauling the sails are raised high
The violent waves offer no way of lingering
The sailors on the boat will not dally there.

The Desolate City: A Rhapsody

Translated by Burton Watson

The poem deals with the city of Guangling, situated north of the Yangtze, not far from its mouth, in present-day Jiangsu. A canal, linking the Yangtze to the Huai River in the north, ran by its side. It saw its first great period of glory in Former Han times as capital of the state of Wu when Liu Pi, the king of Wu, grew rich by boiling sea water to extract salt and by minting cash from the copper ore in its mountains. In 154 B.C. Liu Pi led six other feudal states in an abortive revolt against the supreme ruler, Emperor Jing, which quickly ended in disaster. Much later, in A.D. 459, another feudal lord with his base in Guangling raised a rebellion against the Song dynasty but was soon crushed, his city destroyed, and over three thousand of its inhabitants massacred. Bao Zhao, visiting the area shortly after, recalls the former wealth and grandeur of the city and laments its present sad state.

Broad and far-reaching, the level plain,
Hurrying south to Cangwu and the Sea of Zhang,
Racing north to Purple Barriers, the Wild Goose Gate,
Its barge canal like a tow rope to haul it about,
Its Kunlun of hills to serve as an axle,
A fastness of double rivers, of many-fold passes,
A corridor where four roads meet, where five pass through.
Long ago, at the time of its greatest prospering,
Carriages clashed axle heads,
Men jostled shoulders,
House rows and alley gates crowded the earth,
Songs and piping shrilled to the sky.
There was wealth to be wrung from fields of salt,
Profit to be pared from copper mountains;
Its talented and strong ones grew rich and mighty,
Its horses and riders were handsome and well trained.
So it could flout the laws of Qin,
Overstep the regulations of Zhou,
Troweling smooth its lofty battlements,
Channeling out the deepest moats,
Hoping to prolong its generations with the help of fair fortune.
    Thus
Pounded earth was raised to form a forest of parapets,
An awesome file of turrets and beacon towers,
Taller in measure than the Five Mountains,
Broader across than the Three Dikes,
Precipitous as a sheer escarpment,
Rising straight up like a bank of long clouds.

They were fitted with magnets to guard against assault,[18]
Daubed with russet clay to lend the fancy of design.
Gazing on the firmness of those gates and bastions,
You'd think one lord could hold them for ten thousand years;
Yet now, when three dynasties have come and gone,[19]
Five hundred years and more have passed,
They lie split like melons, like bean pods broken open.

Damp mosses cling to the well,
Tangles of kudzu vine snare the path;
Halls are laced with vipers and crawling things,
Musk deer and flying squirrel quarrel by the stairs.
Tree goblin and mountain sprite,
Field rat, fox in the wall
Howl at the wind, whimper in the rain,
At dusk appearing, scampering off at dawn.
Hungry falcons whet their beaks,
Cold hawks hiss at those who menace their chicks;
Lurking tigers, crouching cats
Suck blood and dine on flesh.
Thickets of fallen trees clog the road,
The old thoroughfare, deep and overgrown;
White poplars shed their leaves early,
Bleak grasses withered long ago;
Breath of frost, keen and biting;
Soo, soo, the bullying of the wind:
A lone tumbleweed trembles by itself,
Puffs of sand for no reason suddenly start up.
Dense copses murky and unending,
A jungle of weeds and brush leaning on each other;
The circling moat caved in long ago,
Towering battlements — they too have tumbled:
One looks straight out a thousand *li* or more,
Seeing only the whirls of yellow dust.
        Dwell on it, listen in silence —
        It wounds the heart, breaking it in two.
        And so
The painted doors, the gaily stitched hangings,

---

[18] The gates of ancient cities were said to have been fitted with loadstones to detect weapons concealed on those who entered.
[19] The Han, Wei, and Jin.

Sites where once were halls of song, pavilions of the dance,
Jasper pools, trees of jadeite,
Lodges for those who hunt in woods, who fish the shores,
Music of Wu, Cai, Qi, Qin,
Vessels in shapes of fish and dragon, sparrow and horse —
All have lost their incense, gone to ash,
Their radiance engulfed, their echoes cut off.
Mysterious princess from the Eastern Capital,
Beautiful lady from a southern land,
With heart of orchis, limbs of white lawn,
Marble features, carmine lip —
None whose soul is not entombed in somber stone,
Whose bones do not lie dwindling in the dust.
Do you recall now what joy it was to share your lord's carriage?
The pain of being banished to a palace apart?
Is it Heaven's way
To make so many taste sorrow?
Bring the lute — I will sing,
Fashioning a song of the Desolate City.
    The song says:

    Border winds hurrying
    Above the castle cold.
    Well and pathway gone from sight,
    Hill and grave mound crumbling.
    A thousand years,
        Ten thousand ages,
    All end thus —
        What is there to say?

🙐 *Further Reading* 🙐

Allen, Joseph R., trans. *In the Voice of Others: Chinese Music Bureau Poetry*. Ann Arbor: University of Michigan, Center for Chinese Studies, 1992.

Chang, H. C., ed. and trans. *Chinese Literature, Vol. 2: Nature Poetry*. Edinburgh: University of Edinburgh Press, 1977.

Chang, Kang-i Sun. *Six Dynasties Poetry*. Princeton: Princeton University Press, 1986.

Ch'en, Jerome, and Michael Bullock, trans. *Poems of Solitude*. London: Abelard-Schuman, 1960.

Frodsham, J. D. *The Murmuring Stream: The Life and Works of the Chinese Nature Poet Hsieh Ling-yün*. 2 vols. Kuala Lumpur: University of Malaya Press, 1967.

———. ed. and trans., with the collaboration of Ch'eng Hsi. *An Anthology of Chinese Verse: Han, Wei, Chin and the Northern and Southern Dynasties*. Oxford: Oxford University Press, 1967.

Chapter 13

New Songs from a Jade Terrace

Court Poetry of the Southern Dynasties

The palace lady takes no delight in idle hours,
But devotes her mind to the latest verse.
For poetry can
Be a substitute for the flower of oblivion,
And can banish the disease of ennui....

Therefore
I have written, burning the midnight oil,
Wielding my pen over times at dawn.
I have selected love-songs,
Ten books in all.

— Xu Ling (507–583), from the preface to *New Songs from a
Jade Terrace (translated by Anne Birrell)*

The Way of Literature has been in decline for five hundred years. The spirit and
substance of the Han and Wei were not transmitted through the Jin and Song.... In
my leisure time I used to peruse the poetry of the Qi and Liang: colorfully gorgeous
and ornate it is, but completely devoid of deeper significance. I would often let out a
long sigh, thinking back to the Ancients, fearing lest matters should continue to
degenerate and the spirit of the *Songs* become dead.

— Chen Zi'ang (661–702), "Letter to Dongfang Qiu"
(*translated by J. Timothy Wixted*)

The state of poetry among the Chinese, as appears from the best accounts of that
people, is very imperfect. Their essays in this way are, for the most part, little slight
pieces, not unlike the sonnets, madrigals, and songs of our European poets.

— Thomas Percy, *Miscellaneous Pieces Relating to the Chinese*, 1762

The Chinese say of a man of letters that he has the talent of making good verses,
almost in the same manner as if one should praise, in Europe, a captain of dragoons,
for being an excellent performer on the violin.

— Abbé Grosier, *A General Description of China*, 1788

Introduction

New Songs from a Jade Terrace [from which the majority of the poems in this chapter are taken] is an anthology of love poems compiled c. 545 A.D. by the court poet Xu Ling. It comprises 656 poems dating from the late third century B.C. to the mid-sixth century A.D. It is traditionally held that Xiao Gang (503–551), crown prince of the Liang dynasty, commissioned this work in order to elevate and preserve the modern sub-genre of love poetry which had become fashionable at his court.

The *Jade Terrace* is a monument to contemporary literature and a repository of palace-style poetry.... This sub-genre is governed by numerous conventions. The setting is a palace boudoir, luxurious and erotic; the persona is a palace lady deserted by her lover; the emotional tenor is melancholy pathos; the expression of love is decorous, graceful, and courtly, avoiding explicit sexuality. The style derives its name from this palatial, courtly ambience.

The title of the anthology is a complex pun: "Jade Terrace" may refer to the erotic mountain haunt of a goddess, to the prison of a legendary princess in antiquity, or to a mirrorstand in the contemporary noblewoman's boudoir. "New" indicates the modern emphasis of the anthology, while "Songs" is a general term for emotional lyricism.

Viewed against the background of Southern Dynasties literary theory and practice, this anthology marks a new departure. Previously the concept of literature was didactic; it was considered a means of ameliorating human nature and of advancing the progress of civilization. In his preface to the *Jade Terrace*, Xu Ling avoids this functional approach, preferring the belletristic view, believing that his selection will entertain his readers, that they will "for long hours be diverted."

— Anne Birrell, *Indiana Companion*, 1986

The Liang dynasty which ruled in Nanjing during the first half of the sixth century is an extreme example of the combination of political darkness and cultural splendor which characterizes this age. The history of its founder Xiao Yan and his numerous progeny reads like a Jacobean tragedy. Xiao Yan, betrayed by his own nephew to a foreign adventurer, died of hunger at the age of eighty-six, imprisoned after a siege of unprecedented awfulness in the course of which most of the inhabitants of Nanjing lost their lives. His brilliant elder son Xiao Tong having died many years previously as a result of a boating accident, the next eldest Xiao Gang was made puppet emperor by the conqueror, but deposed less than two years later in favor of Xiao Tong's eldest son and shortly after pressed to death under sacks of earth. Xiao Gang's ten sons were also put to death. His young nephew, the new puppet-emperor, and the young nephew's two brothers were drowned by the deputy of another uncle when the latter recovered what remained of Nanjing from the conqueror. And so on. It would be tedious to narrate the various violent ends which overtook the wicked uncle and the numerous other Liang princes. Murder and treachery so monotonously reiterated seem to belong to the annals of Roi Ubu rather than to serious human history.

Yet if we turn from the political to the cultural history of the time we find that Xiao Yan was both a devout Buddhist and one of the greatest ever patrons of Chinese Buddhism. He and Xiao Gang were accomplished poets and left quantities of verse which, if somewhat slight, is of very considerable charm. Xiao Gang's protégé, the diplomat Xu Ling, compiled, at his suggestion, *New Songs from a Jade Terrace*, an anthology of lyric verse dating from the first century up to his own day.

— David Hawkes, "The Age of Exuberance," 1983

Yan Yanzhi (384–456)

A Pure Wife

Translated by Anne Birrell

Orphaned and impoverished in his youth, Yan Yanzhi was given to drink. He became a page to the heir apparent and was promoted, serving the first four Liu Song (420–479) emperors, but was subsequently demoted to governor of a district in Zhejiang. His poetry was often ranked with that of Bao Zhao and Xie Lingyun, but the critic Zhong Rong (469–518) compared Yan and Xie in the following terms:

> Xie's poetry is like lotus flowers emerging from water;
> Yan's is like a mix of colors with inlays of gold.

Bao Zhao himself made a similar comparison, in reply to Yan's own question:

> Xie's five-word verse is like a freshly opened hibiscus: its naturalness is simply adorable. Your poetry is like a well laid-out tapestry or embroidery: the details of the stitching fill the eye.

Catalpa leans toward lofty phoenix,
Cold Valley waits for singing pipes.[1]
Shadow and echo, don't they fall in love?
All mates love, distant thought they are.
Lovely the girl in her hidden room
When she became wife in her lord's home.
Strict her virtue, taut with autumn frost,
Radiant her beauty, like the morning sun.
"Good fortune is with us now,
We dearly hope it lasts to the end of our days."

They lived in bliss, but before each knew the other well
Her beloved had to go on a journey long.
He removed his headband to go beyond ten thousand leagues,
Tied on official ribbons to go up to the royal domain.
He ordered his servants to come at break of dawn,
His followers all came to his side.
Driven in his coach he left the suburbs,
His path slow and winding.
If he lived, they would be parted long,
If he died, he would nevermore return.

---

[1] The catalpa was a tree invested with grand and noble qualities, especially in the context of music. It was favoured by the phoenix. It was in Cold Valley, in the ancient state of Yan, that the statesman Zou Yan blew on his pipes, so that millet then grew and flourished.

Oh I hate official travel!
Three hills I suffer from dawn to dark.
Hitching coaches tight we trek through winds chill,
Unsaddling we brave frosty dew.
High plains, wet lowlands redouble our misery,
Whirlwinds roll tall trees.
Scattered beasts appear in wild trails,
Frightened birds flee in panic.
Wretched the man on official circuit,
As he struggles along paths of crag and creek.

Far away the traveler grows distant,
Smoothly roll the years away.
Happy hours turned to such a parting,
Days and months are drawing close to summer.
Who knows how many seasons hot and cold?
In a glance I see nature bloom and wither.
The year ends, I go toward my empty room,
Cold winds stir from the corners.
In bed or rising I feel the days grow colder,
White frost spreads over the garden weeds.

I worked hard, but gave in to homeward thoughts,
The road back skirts hills and rivers.
Long ago I said goodbye before autumn whitened,
Now is the season of flowers.
In silkworm months I see a time of rest,
In mulberry fields all is busy movement.
A lovely girl is doing her work,
Gracefully she draws high branches down.
Who would not look back at her city-razing beauty?
I slow my pace, pause halfway up the ridge.

Years have passed. Such pining they had suffered!
His work was distant, word and image remote.
Though it was a five-year separation,
Each was a stranger to the other's normal life.
He leaves his coach, treads his old path,
A duck among waterplants he gives a quick wink.
Southern gold he by no means undervalues,
But at such a time he counts it as little!
Married love brings many sorrows.
He whispers words of gold and jade.

Her high principles forbid him to dally.
At long last he leaves her, nothing won.
Slow, slow he covers the old path,
Eager, eager he reaches his gate-post.
Going up the hall he offers respectful greetings,
Entering his room he asks, "Where's my wife?"
"At sunset she comes home from picking,
At nature's Mulberry-Elm time."[2]
A beautiful woman arrives toward dusk.
He gasps with shock — he'd been with her before!

Who can stop love once love happens?
Let's tell of this wife's own hardship.
We lived apart year in, year out.
Once parted, river and pass blocked our way.
Spring comes, perhaps he no longer enjoys it?
Autumn falls, he must feel cold sooner?
Till daybreak I fret my sad heart away,
In my room I rise with long sighs.
The year is dark in my bitter anguish,
The sun has set upon my wanderer's face.

Playing high notes causes broken strings,
Intense music comes from high-pitched chords.
Long ago when I enjoyed your bright dust[3]
We vowed to be true from first to last.
Aren't you who made our parting so long
To blame for all that's gone wrong?
Since you betrayed our pure marriage,
With whom will I end my days?
Disgraced like the "Dewdrops"[4] woman
I'd better drown myself in the long river.

---

[2] Twilight.

[3] This image signifies a man's exciting life in the world of politics.

[4] *Book of Songs* 17, in which a woman declares that she will not submit to marriage, no matter how influential her suitor's family is.

SHEN YUE (441–512)
Five Poems

Translated by Anne Birrell

Shen Yue served three successive dynasties, the Liu Song, the Qi, and the Liang, achieving the rank of head of the imperial secretariat. Because his grandfather and father before him had been executed, he pursued a career in politics with utmost caution. He was one of the Eight Comrades, Xiao Yan's literary group. He is credited with classifying, together with Liu Yun, the four tones of literary Chinese and with evolving a system of tonal harmony, which was fully developed into basic prosodic rules in the Tang. He was a great scholar, owning a reputed library of 20,000 books.

I Climb High to Look at Spring

I climb high to look at Luoyang city,
Streets and lanes criss-cross far and wide.
I turn my head to view Chang'an,
City turrets bristle zigzag.
Sunrise glints on jewel pins and kohl,
Passing winds ruffle sheer silks.
Qi boys stamp their red boots.
Zhao girls smooth of kingfisher plume brow.

The spring breeze sways dappled trees,
Rich blooms emerald and cinnabar.
Jewelled lutes, ruby stops,
Gold harness, tortoiseshell saddles.
Youth loiters, sleeps at Xiacai,
Pours wine on the way through Shanglan.[5]
Relaxed eyebrows pucker again
Showing it's hard to keep a dazzling smile.
Lovers linger and dawdle,
Tearful from bliss unfulfilled.
"My honored guest is now out of sight,
Through you I send him long sighs."

Night After Night

The River Han is the Milky Way, which in Chinese folklore separates the lovers, the Weaver and Herdboy stars.

---

[5] Xiacai was a place in Chu famous for its alluring beauties. Shanglan was a Han dynasty palace in the Royal Forest.

River Han long and wide,
Northern Dipper wide and straight,
Starry Han void like this
How can you know of love?

The lone lamp dims, bright no more,
The cold loom at dawn still weaves.
I shed tears. To whom will I speak?
At cockcrow I just heave a sigh.

Spring

Willows tangle like silk threads,
Sheer silk I cannot bear.
Spring grass green and emerald,
The wanderer's heart aches at such an hour.
Kingfisher lichen binds Wei river now,
Jade water brims in the Qi once more.
Sunny florescence brightens Zhao lutes,
Breezy flickers ruffle Yan skirts.
On my collar ten thousand trickling tears
Are because I long only for him.

Peach

Winds come blowing leaves astir,
Winds go, and I fear for flowers wounded.
Red blooms shining now in splendor
Shine richer in sunlight caress.

Singing boys at dusk rehearse their tunes,
Roving girls by night sew their coats.
How will I lessen the tears of spring
That could break a lover's heart?

Green, Green Riverside Grass

Dense, dense dust on the bed,
My inner heart remembers past love.
Past love I cannot bear to remember,
Midnight's endless sighing.
Sighing I imagine his face

Who did not want this long parting.
Separation slowly grown prolonged.
My empty bed. I give in to cups of wine.

KONG ZHIGUI (447–501)

Wandering Round Mount Taiping

Translated by John Frodsham

Kong Zhigui was fortunate enough to have enjoyed a comfortable if undistinguished career at court, without ever involving himself in political intrigue. Very much of a recluse by nature, he liked to drink alone in his overgrown garden, listening to the croaking of the frogs, which he preferred, so he claimed, to the sound of drums and flutes. Only four poems of his are extant; but this one is a minor masterpiece. [See chapter 14 for his "Proclamation on North Mountain."]

Towering rocks rending the sky asunder,
A trelliswork of trees barring the sun.
Into the shadowy gorge spring blossom is falling,
On the cold crags lingers the summer snow.

XIE TIAO (464–499)
Five Poems

Translated by John Frodsham

Xie Tiao came from the same brilliant family that had produced Xie Lingyun [see chapter 12], and many other fine poets. In the middle of an uneventful official career he was unlucky enough to incur the enmity of a powerful prince, then plotting to seize the throne, who had him executed when he refused to join forces with him. Tiao's verse was much admired by his elder contemporary Shen Yue, who once exclaimed: "There has been no verse of this quality for the last two hundred years." The great Tang poet Li Bo [see chapter 19] "regretted that he could not produce poems as startling as those of Xie Tiao."

Complaint of the Jade Staircase

A palace lady is lamenting the absence of the Emperor.

In the palace at dusk the blinds of pearl are unfurled,
Fireflies flit around, then come to rest.
Throughout the long night I sew thin silken garments.
When will my thoughts of you ever come to an end?

A Prince Went Wandering

The title refers the poem to the poem "Summons for a Recluse" in the *Songs of the South*. By the time her lover returns, the girl's beauty will have faded.

The green grass spreads about like silk,
The trees are putting forth their scarlet blossoms.
Why bother saying you will not return?
By the time you do, their scent will have faded forever.

An Autumn Night

On autumn nights the rapid weaver sings[6]
To the hurried beat of batons in the southern suburbs.[7]
My thoughts turn to you, behind those ninefold gates,[8]
Night after night I am standing here in vain.
A flimsy curtain covers the northern window,
Moonbeams are shining through the western door.
How do I know that the glistening dew is falling?
I sit and stare at the droplets on the steps.
How can I live so long apart from you?
Autumn is ending and winter is coming once more.

Looking at the Morning Rain

Weary of the dangers and uncertainties of an official career, he is contemplating becoming a hermit.

The North wind blows the flying rain,
It settles bleakly down upon the River.
Sprinkling the Tower of Hundred Constancies,
It drenches the Terrace of Nine Completions.
The cloudy drizzle hangs in the air like mist,
A wave of water scattered like wind-borne dust.
At dawn I dress myself and then sit down,
While the serried gates seem bolted up for ever.

---

[6] A name for the cricket. Some critics read it as "Hurry-your-weaving," for its cry is supposed to spur on the housewife to weave cloth for the winter.
[7] These were wash-batons, used for pounding clothes.
[8] *Songs of the South*, "The Nine Changes":
I could not help being downcast and longing for my lord.
But his gates were ninefold.

My eyes and ears are undisturbed for a time,
I think of the ancients and how remote they seem.
I have drawn in my wings but am still ambitious,
I swim with the stream, but fear I may not leap the falls.[9]
I find I cannot stir and stay at once,
As though I stood and havered at a cross-roads.
Let me emulate the man who conquered his desires,[10]
And go to gather goosefoot on Mount North.[11]

I Sit in My Lofty Study, High up in My Commandery, Relaxing at Leisure, and Reply to Lü Sengzhen, the Officer of Justice

My house with criss-cross beams is remote from the world,
Into the distance I gaze, out over heights and abysses.
Far-away mountain peaks are framed by my windows,
All round my courtyard, tall trees bow their heads.
As the sun comes out, flocks of birds all scatter,
As the mountains darken, lonely apes start howling.
When I have drunk some wine by the side of the pool,
I play my lute again as the breeze starts blowing.
For no one else but you, of measureless virtue,[12]
Would I drive on my heart to weariness.[13]
You have shown such fond affection for me,[14]
Sent me a poem, lovely as the sparse-hemp's flower.[15]

---

[9] In northwest Shanxi the Yellow River rushes over a series of waterfalls known as Dragon Gates. It is said that if fish manage to leap up these falls they will become transformed into dragons; if not, they will die.

[10] *Hanfeizi* [see chapter 4] includes the story of Zixia, a disciple of Confucius, who overcame his desire for riches and fame after a long struggle with himself.

[11] *Book of Songs* 172: "Goosefoot grows on the northern mountains."

[12] Literally "of measureless beauty," but this would give quite the wrong impression in English. A reference to *Songs* 108, "That gentleman there, of measureless beauty," which was originally a love song sung by a girl.

[13] Alluding to both *Songs* 102 and *Songs* 146. He has wearied his heart with longing for his absent friend.

[14] Almost a direct quotation from *Songs* 41.

[15] *Songs of the South*, "Nine Songs: The Great Master of Fate" [see chapter 5]:
I have plucked the sparse-hemp's lovely flower.
To give to someone who lives far away.

If ever you should walk out of the Golden Gates,[16]
Please visit me on my peak of the Jade Mountain.[17]

In a Provincial Capital Sick in Bed: Presented to the Shangshu Shen

Translated by Burton Watson

Written in 495 when the poet was serving in Xuancheng in present-day Anhui as governor of the province, this poem is addressed to his friend, the poet-official Shen Yue.

The governor of Huaiyang, arm and leg to the ruler,
served his term from a bed of ease.[18]
And this post of mine, far in the southern hills?
Hardly different from a hermit's life!
Incessant rains — busy season for farmers:
straw hats gather in fallow fields to the east.
Daytime my state chambers are always closed,
few law suits to hear on the grass-grown terrace.
Soft mats refresh me in the summer rooms,
light fans stir a cooling breeze.
Tasty bream I am urged to try,
helping myself to the best strained wine.
Summer plums — crimson fruit chilled in water;
autumn lotus root — tender threads to pluck;
but our happy days, when will they come?
Nightly I meet you in my dreams.
I sit whistling while time piles up,
a year already since I came here to govern;
I could never do it with strings and song —
patting the armrest, I chuckle to myself in scorn.[19]

---

[16] Actually the Golden Horse Gates, which were used by high officials.

[17] The Western Queen Mother, an Immortal with teeth like a tiger, was supposed to dwell on the Jade Peak.

[18] Ji An (d. 112 B.C.), an official of the Han who was highly regarded by the emperor, tried to decline the post of governor of Huaiyang on grounds of illness, but the emperor assured him that he could carry out his duties while resting in bed.

[19] Reference to *Analects* XVII, 4, the story of how Confucius's disciple Ziyou governed a city by teaching the people to sing and play stringed instruments.

XIAO YAN (464–549)
Four Poems

Translated by Anne Birrell

Xiao Yan founded the Liang dynasty, reigning as Emperor Wu from 502 until 549, the longest reign in the Southern Dynasties era. Though a distant relative of the Qi royal family, he took up arms against the last Qi emperor because he had executed Xiao Yan's eldest brother. Shen Yue advised Xiao Yan to found his own dynasty. A devout Buddhist, he became a monk twice, retiring to a monastery three times in his lifetime. He was a man of great learning and considerable poetic ability, as were two of his sons, Xiao Tong, compiler of the *Literary Anthology*, and Xiao Gang, poet and patron of *New Songs from a Jade Terrace*. Xiao Yan formed a literary group called the Eight Comrades of Jingling, consisting of himself, Shen Yue, Xie Tiao, and five others.

A Border Guard

The autumn moon risen mid-sky,
Near or far, has no favorites.
It radiates one equal brilliant light
Upon all pining separated lovers.

The Candle

In halls fine silken women
On mats singers and girl dancers
Wait for my waves of splashing light
To shine glancingly for you.

The Flute

At Aspen Pavilion there are marvellous bamboos,
They throb with passion in high and low key,
Sublime sounds pour from jade fingers,
Dragon music echoes with phoenix song.

Morning Sun

Morning sun shines on silk coin windows,
A flickering breeze sways gossamer silk.
Flirting smiles dimple with two melons,
Lovely eyes beam beneath twin moths.

HE XUN (died c. 517)
Three Poems

Translated by John Frodsham

He Xun was highly acclaimed by Shen Yue, who once confessed that he would read his poems three times in a single day, unable to put them down once he had started.

Spring Wind

As the women leaves her lute and takes up her mirror, the spring wind swirls her face-powder about. Alternatively, "powder" may mean "blossoms."

> You can hear it but never see it,
> It can storm or gently touch.
> In front of the mirror falling powder eddies,
> As the lute's last cadence dies away.

Singing-Girls in the Brazen Bird

Cao Cao [see chapter 9] had left instructions that after his death all his concubines and dancing girls should live in the Brazen Bird Tower. Here they were to go on behaving just as though he were still alive. Every morning and evening they had to bring food up to his curtained bed; on the fifteenth day of every month they had to give a dancing display in the presence of guests. His sons were ordered to ascend the tower and gaze out towards the tomb where he was buried.

> The wind of autumn sends leaves fluttering down,
> Its lonely crying clear as strings and flutes.
> We gaze at the tomb and sing his Drinking Song.
> Facing his canopy, we dance The Empty City.[20]
> Broad roofs and eaves stretch peacefully out below,
> The curtains flutter lightly in the breeze.
> When the songs have ended, rising we stare to hear
> Murmur of pines and cypress through the dusk.[21]

---

[20] [Cao Cao's famous poem began with the lines:
Come drink with me and sing,
For life's a fleeting thing.
Full many a day has fled
Like the morning dew ...] "The Empty City" was the name of a dance. Its title enhances the feeling of desolation.

[21] Graveyard trees growing by the royal tombs near the tower.

Watching the New Moon, I Compose These Verses to Show to My Fellow-travelers, Stranded with Me

Our first night on the long Huai river,
And a broken mirror shining out of the clouds.
This evening for a thousand leagues or more,
A second moth is dazzling, water-born.[22]
So crystal-clear, peaceful as the sand,
So shining bright, as gentle as the waves.
We gaze out homewards, everyone is weeping,
I am not the only one with a broken heart.

XIAO ZIHUI (fl. 519)

Winter Dawn

Translated by John Frodsham

Xiao Zihui was a minor member of the royal house of Liang. Only three poems of his are extant, all of them in the "palace" style.

This subtle poem achieves its effects by suggestion. The lady wakes before dawn, lights her candles, snuffs them as dawn breaks, then gets out of bed, and breathes on her frozen mirror as she begins her toilet.

Between verandah railings light is creeping,
At daybreak birds start flying east and west.
Smell of the snuffed-out candles lingers still,
The bed-curtains' fragrance wafts on the dawn wind.
No end to the ice-flowers blossoming everywhere,
Until they fade from the cold looking-glass.

ZHANG SHUAI (475–527)
Two Poems

Translated by Anne Birrell

Zhang Shuai served the Liang as deputy of the imperial chancellory and later became a prefect of Xin'an. Transferred for irresponsibility, he became an official for Xiao Gang in 509 for a decade. His poetry won the admiration of Xiao Yan, Emperor Wu.

---

[22] Moth stands for "moth-eyebrow," the new moon. Chinese ladies painted eyebrows that looked like the new moon. Here the reflection of the new moon forms a second "moth-eyebrow" in the water.

Staring

I'll always love you
However long we're parted.
My beloved's distance is like a drought.
Alone, standing still,
My heart taut inside me,
I stare at clouds gone, gone far away,
Stare at birds flown, flown into nothingness.
Useless staring always ends like this:
Pearl tears that won't be wiped dry.

Pining

Sky River is the Milky Way.

I'll always love you
However long we're parted.
Where is my love? Under distant skies pining.
My heavy heart does not know where to look for you.
On jade steps the moon's twilight glimmer.
Through filmy drapes the wind's nighttime blowing.
Constantly longing for you I cannot sleep,
I sit and stare at Sky River's motion.

YU JIANWU (487–550)

On the Third Day I Wait on the Emperor at a Banquet and Describe the Reflection of the Candles in the Serpentine

Translated by John Frodsham

Yu Jianwu was one of the most renowned poets of his period. Once, when captured by Song Zixian, a general of the rebel Hou Jing, he is said to have saved his life by his ability to compose poems at a moment's notice.

On the third day of the third month it was the custom to float goblets of wine in serpentines during banquets. "Candle-flowers" is a term used to describe the wick of a candle bending over and flaring up.

Candle-flowers two-fold flames like fragrant trees.
Wind blows, the river ripples, transient both in air and water.
Spring branches brushing the bank surge out of mirrored lights,
Goblets circling round the guests go drifting through the dazzle.

Xiao Gang (503–551)
Four Poems

Translated by Anne Birrell

Xiao Gang became heir apparent in 531, when his brother Xiao Tong died. He was the third son of Xiao Yan, and succeeded his father in 540 as Emperor Jianwen of the Liang. He was assassinated two years later by the Tartar general Hou Jing. A statesman of great erudition and literary talent, he was interested in philosophy, religion, literary theory and composition, and surrounded himself with the outstanding literary personalities of the day. He was a believer in Buddhism.

Spiders' Spun Threads

Spiders' spun threads spread through curtains.
Sweet grasses' knotted blades choke the pathways.
Pink cheeks in mute desire weep her life away.
Golden orioles fitful flit, flit past.
Old love, though old, once was new.
New love, though new, also must grow old.

I Play My Zither

I play my zither by the northern window,
Echoes of night full of clear tones sad.
The key raised, a string soon snaps
And my heart mourns the melody lost.

I Can Sigh

I can sigh but cannot think,
Or can think but cannot see.
A string left broken on my guitar bridge,
A trace of lipstick stains my concert fan.

Soft Echoes

Soft, soft echoes of twilight eaves,
Dark, dark colors of drawn curtains.
There's only moss upon the floor tiles,
And I seem to see a spider spinning.

XU LING (507–583)
Three Poems

Translated by Anne Birrell

Xu Ling's father, Xu Chi, was tutor to Xiao Gang while he was a young prince, and he introduced Xu Ling to the prince's court. He showed a penchant for scholarship and literature from an early age. A minister of state under Xiao Yan, he enjoyed Xiao Gang's patronage and was included in his circle with many literary lights of the day. It was he who compiled the anthology *New Songs from a Jade Terrace*.

Bagatelle

> Today, your being so considerate
> Offends, but less than had it been spring.
> Candle-trickling tears I shed this night
> Are not because you bring her home at dark.
> Her dance mat come autumn will fold away,
> Her concert fan will gather sheets of dust.
> Since time began new love supplants the old,
> So why does old love hate to greet the new?
> A sliver of moon peeps into her flowery bed,
> Slight chill creeps under her shawl and scarf.
> Autumn will come when all things wither,
> And touch her body with nature's stealth.

The Dance

The magnificent Jianzhang Palace was built in 104 B.C. by the Emperor Wen of Han.

> At fifteen she belonged to the Princess of Pingyang
> And so came to enter Jianzhang Palace.
> The Princess's house taught well the art of dance,
> The city perfected the craft of dawn make-up.
> With lowered coiffure she nears the silk mat,
> With raised sleeves brushes on floral yellow.
> Candles cast shadows near the window,
> Her dress spreads perfume in her wardrobe.
> The reason she attracts guests so well must be
> That she makes her dance gown deliberately long.

A Maid's Thanks for a Mirror

One legend tells of a king of ancient Kashmir who found a paradise bird. It refused to sing, so his wife told him to do something to stop it pining for its mate. They set a mirror in front of the bird, hoping it would sing to its reflection. The bird did sing, but its song was so sad that it died of a broken heart.

Your messenger came to bring me a jewelled mirror,
Grand, grand as the round moon.
When a mirror ages it shines the brighter,
When a person ages so passions decline.
I accept your mirror, hang it on the empty stand,
To this day never reopened.
Don't you see that lone paradise bird?
From where will lost love's soul appear?

YU XIN (513–581)
Five Poems

Translated by John Frodsham

Yu Xin came from a rich and noble family in present-day Henan. His father was the poet Yu Jianwu. He grew up in the South, then under the rule of the Liang dynasty, and speedily achieved the reputation of being the most accomplished poet of his time. When in 552, Hou Jing rebelled and seized the capital Jiankang (Nanjing), Yu fled with the court to Jiangling, in Hubei. He was then sent as an emissary to the capital of the Western Wei, in Chang'an. But while he was there the Wei invaded the South, sacked Jiangling, and brought thousands of prisoners back with them to Chang'an, among them many of Yu's acquaintances. Shortly after this, in 557, the enfeebled Liang dynasty was replaced by the Chen, while the Western Wei itself gave way to the Northern Zhou. From then on Yu was left stranded at an alien court, with no hope of ever returning home again.

The great Tang poet Du Fu [see chapter 20] wrote of him:

The writings of Yu Xin
    grew more perfect as he grew older,
A mighty brush, overtopping the clouds,
    a mind roaming as it pleased.

The Season of Shadow

In this bitter weather the poet's thoughts turn to the sufferings of the poor Confucian scholar — not, as with Bo Juyi [see chapter 23], to the sufferings of the poor in general.

The season of Shadow draws to an end in silence,
Monotonous, endless clouds cover the sky.
The swarming snow swirls down like crane-feathers falling,
The flying thistledown spins past like whirling wheels.
The homing geese know well where the warm sun is shining,

While birds in their nests contrive to keep out of the cold.
On the river's twin shores, the icy sands gleam white,
And hunters' fires have turned all the mountains red.
Men with clothes like feathers on a hanging quail —
I sigh for their lives in backstreet empty rooms.

Offered in Thanks for a Present of Wine and a Goose

The light from the clouds is dazzling my eyes,
The cry of the wind has stilled my heart to silence.
The shivering apes howl in the shrouding snow,
Down sink the frozen fishes, wrapped in ice.
Today a single pitcherful of wine
Is surely worth a thousand gold pieces and more.
Ungrateful that I am, I cannot thank you,
For I know only the way to the Bamboo Grove.[23]

Harmonizing with Great Officer Yan's Poem "The Start of the Fine Weather"

Great Officer Yan was Yan Zhiyi, a brother of the famous Yan Zhitui (531–591), author of the *Family Instructions for the Yan Clan* [see chapter 14].

Evening sunlight aswim with the river mist,
The setting sun is shining on the dike.
The rain-soaked blossoms cannot flutter far,
Dark storm-clouds mass and lower threateningly.
Feeling the heat the swallows have changed to stone,[24]
The dragons have vanished, turned to mud once more.[25]
I pour out fragrant water from a snow-cold gorge,
And fish from a little skiff on a lotus creek.
Just make the heart look on all things as equal,
And you will not grieve at inequality.[26]

---

[23] For the Seven Sages of the Bamboo Grove, see chapter 10. *Eds.*

[24] Certain stones found in Lingling were known as "stone swallows." They were believed to fly about when it rained, only to turn into stone again when the sun came out. These "swallows" were actually fossil brachiopods, of the family *Spiriferacea*, the shells of which look rather like the wings of a bird.

[25] Clay dragons were set up to bring on rain during periods of drought. When rain finally fell, they naturally turned to mud.

[26] A reference to *Zhuangzi*, chapter 2, "Discussion on Making All Things Equal" [see chapter 4].

Harmonizing with the Monk Heling's Poem "An Outing to the Kunming Pool"

Autumn sunlight gilds the evening sky,
In a fish-hawk boat we drift along the river.[27]
Thick water-chestnut hides the bathing birds,
Tall lotus screens the fisherman's boats from us.
Small pearls lie strewn round snapped chrysanthemums,
Torn silk hangs from the broken lotus-buds.
Falling blossoms urge us to drink our wine,
While we sing "The Roosting Birds" to a one-stringed lute.

Running Into Snow While Journeying Through the Suburbs

The wind and clouds are storming angrily,
While plain and wilds stretch endlessly away.
Flowers of the snow are opening their six petals,
While ice-pearls glisten with a nine-fold fire.
As I push home, I am driving horses of jade,
For a time it seems I am hunting a silver deer.
The serried ranks of clouds move not at all,
On the frozen mountains the fragrant plants are dead.
The Lord of Xue owned a single white fox-fur,[28]
The Marquis of Tang had two horses, Su and Shuang.[29]
As the sun is setting over the ice-hung pass,
Mantled with snow I cross the river bridge.

Knights Errant

Translated by John Minford

An early poetic evocation of the *xia*, or knight errant, that recurring figure of chivalry and honor in the Chinese tradition, whose exploits have so often inspired historians, poets and writers of fiction.

---

[27] A boat with a fish-hawk carved or painted on the prow.

[28] The *Records of the Grand Historian* [see chapter 7] tell how Lord Mengchang, a leading magnate of Chu, was imprisoned by King Zhao of Qin. He managed to escape only by bribing the king's favorite concubine with a unique white fox-fur he possessed. Yu's snow-covered jacket reminds him of this fur.

[29] The *Zuo Commentary* [see chapter 4] carries the story of two magnificent white horses owned by Duke Cheng of Tang, which were coveted by the rapacious Prime Minister of Chu, Zichang, who imprisoned the Duke for three years for not presenting him with the horses. Both this allusion and the one above hint at the way Yu's poetic gifts have led him into captivity.

Knights!
Posse on the move, bit to bridle, bridle to bit,
Gold saddles strewn with sprays of cassia.
Fine dust rising screens the road;
Startled flowers floating dazzle the eye.
The riders, wine-steeped, halfway drunk;
The horses, sweat-drenched, utterly proud:
Homeward bound, fearing nightfall,
Jostling to the river, the bridge.

JIANG ZONG (518–590)

Melancholy in the Women's Apartments

Translated by John Frodsham

Jiang Zong held office under the Liang and Chen dynasties. He formed one of a coterie who were accused of being unduly intimate with Chen Shubao, last Emperor of the Chen dynasty [see below], aiding and abetting him in his carousing, instead of counseling him against the evils of such conduct. This is simply pious Confucian propaganda.

A silent, blue pavilion by the highway,
With white snow fluttering past its silken windows.
The love-birds on the lake are not alone,
Behind the curtains Suhe incense smokes.[30]
The screen seems bent on shutting out the moonlight,
The unfeeling lantern-flame glares on her, sleeping alone.
"In Liaoxi with its frozen rivers, spring is very short,
From Jibei the geese are coming, several thousand leagues.[31]
May you cross quickly over the mountain passes,
Knowing my beauty, like peach or plum, will last but a moment."

CHEN SHUBAO (553–604)

A Jade Tree Blossoms in the Back Garden

Translated by John Frodsham

Chen Shubao, last Emperor of the Chen dynasty (r. 582–589), was notorious for his love of wine, women, and song. When omens of disaster threatened the dynasty, he

---

[30] An expensive incense.
[31] Two commanderies in present-day Hebei Province.

sold himself to a Buddhist monastery as a slave in an effort to avoid the coming storm. Ransomed from his predicament, he went on with his merry-making until the arrival of the Sui forced him to abdicate. His is "palace-style" poetry of the most languid type.

Fine buildings in the fragrant forest face the tall pavilions,
The beauty of her newly made-up face could bring down a city wall.[32]
In the light from the door she composes herself, hesitates a moment,
Comes out from the curtains, controls her feelings, welcomes me
    with a smile.
The bewitching beauty of her face is like a dew-filled flower,
The moving light from the jade tree shines on the back-garden.[33]

⌖ Further Reading ⌖

Allen, Joseph R., trans. *In the Voice of Others: Chinese Music Bureau Poetry.* Ann Arbor: University of Michigan, Center for Chinese Studies, 1992.
Birrell, Anne, trans. *New Songs from a Jade Terrace: An Anthology of Early Chinese Love Poetry.* London: Allen & Unwin, 1982.
Frodsham, John D., ed. and trans. (with the collaboration of Ch'eng Hsi). *An Anthology of Chinese Verse: Han, Wei, Chin and the Northern and Southern Dynasties.* Oxford: Oxford University Press, 1967.
Hawkes, David. "The Age of Exuberance." In *Classical, Modern & Humane: Essays in Chinese Literature.* Hong Kong: Chinese University Press, 1989.
Liu, James J. Y., trans. "Song of Knights Errant." In *The Chinese Knight-Errant.* Chicago: University of Chicago Press, 1967.
Marney, John. *Liang Chien-wen Ti.* Boston: Twayne, 1976.
———. *Chiang Yen.* Boston: Twayne, 1981.
Mather, Richard. *Shen Yüeh: The Reticent Marquis.* Princeton: Princeton University Press, 1988.

"Heirloom."
Yu Xin, "Rhapsody of the Little Garden"
Seal carved by Chen Yuzhong (1762–1806)

---

[32] *Songs* 264:
A clever man can build a city wall,
A clever woman brings it down again.
[33] The jade tree is the lovely woman. "Back-garden" means the women's apartments at the rear of a Chinese house.

Chapter 14

Green Bag and Yellow Covers

A Miscellany of Prose
from the Han and Six Dynasties

A general survey of the nature of letter-writing reveals that its purpose is to state one's feelings in words without reserve, and its function is to unburden the mind of its melancholy thought in the form of elegant colors. Therefore its style should be orderly and smooth, capable of expressing the spirit of the writer, easy and soft and pleasant to the reader. With its language clear and natural, it is indeed the presentation of the sound of the heart.

> — Liu Xie (c. 465–c. 520), *The Literary Mind and the Carving of Dragons*,
> chapter 25, "Epistolary Writing"

The memorial as a form of writing demands as its foundation the qualities of lucidity, truthfulness, simplicity, and sincerity; and it opens with an approach which is analytical and systematic. The ideas expounded should be cogent enough to fire enthusiasm for carrying the task to completion, and the experience of the author broad enough to enable him to follow out all the ramifications of the reasoning. He should consider the principles prevailing in ancient times in his management of the present, and keep the mass of details under control and reduce them to the essential.

> — Liu Xie, *The Literary Mind and the Carving of Dragons*, chapter 23, "On Memorials, II"

When not busy with my duties as Heir Apparent, I have spent many idle days looking through the garden of letters or widely surveying the forest of literature, and always I have found my mind so diverted, my eye so stimulated, that hours have passed without fatigue. Since the Zhou and Han, far off in the distant past, dynasties have changed seven times and some thousands of years have elapsed. The names of famous writers and men of genius overflow the green bag, the scrolls of winged words and flowing brushes fill the yellow covers. If one does not leave aside the weeds and select the flowers, it is impossible, even with the best intentions, to get through the half....

> — Xiao Tong (501–531), preface to the *Literary Anthology*
> *(translated by J. R. Hightower)*

But the most remarkable feature of Chinese composition is the antithesis. Most of the principal words are classed in pairs, such as heaven and earth, beginning and end, day and night, hot and cold, etc. From antithetical words, they proceed to contrast phrases and sentences, and draw up whole paragraphs upon the same principle. In these antithetical sentences, the number of words, the class of expressions, the meaning and intonation, together with the whole sentiment, are nicely and exactly balanced, so that the one contributes to the perspicuity and effect of the other. Such a counting of words, and such a mechanical arrangement of sentences, would be intolerable in European composition, but are quite elegant and almost essential in Chinese.

> — Walter Medhurst, *China: Its State and Prospects* (1838)

LI SI (d. 208 B.C.)

On the Employment of Foreigners

Translated by Herbert Giles

Li Si was for a long period prime minister and trusted adviser of the prince who finally annihilated the feudal system which had prevailed under the Zhou dynasty and seated himself upon the throne as the First Emperor of China. It was then that Li Si suggested the entire destruction of existing literature, with a few trifling exceptions, in order to break off absolutely all connection with the past; a design which was rapidly carried into practical effect, though not to the extent which has been generally supposed, and from the operation of which the sacred books of Confucianism were saved only by the devotion of a few. Li Si was himself an accomplished scholar, and invented a form of writing which remained in vogue for several centuries.

The high officers of State had combined to persuade the Prince of Qin to dismiss all foreign nobles and other strangers from the Court, urging that such persons were there only in the interests of their masters. This proscription would have included me. I therefore sent up the following Memorial:

May it please your Majesty,

The present scheme for proscribing strangers is in every way a fatal step. Have we not innumerable examples in the past of the employment of foreigners, to the greater glory of the State and to the infinite advantage of the people?

From the mountains of Tibet your Majesty receives jade; from elsewhere, jewels. Bright pearls, good blades, fine horses, kingfisher banners, triton-skin drums — of such rarities not one is produced at home, yet your Majesty delights in all. But if nothing is to be used in future save local produce, then will rich pearls shine no more at Court, then will the elephant and the rhinoceros contribute their ivory no more, nor the ladies of Zhao throng the Imperial hareem, nor sleek palfreys stand in the Imperial stables, nor gold, nor pewter-ware, nor brilliant hues glow within the Imperial walls.

And if all, too, which adorns the seraglio, and ministers to the pleasure of eye and ear, must for the future be of local growth; then adieu to pearl-set pins, to jewelled eardrops, to silken skirts and embroidered hems — welcome the humble and the plain, there where beauty no longer reigns supreme.

Take for instance our local music — shrill songs shrieked to earthen and wooden accompaniments — as compared with the magnificent harmonies of other States. Those we have rejected in favor of these, simply because the latter contributed most to the pleasure of sense.

In the choice of men, however, this principle is not to prevail. There is to be no question of capacity or of incapacity, of honesty or of dishonesty. If he be not a native, he must go: all foreigners are to be dismissed. Surely this is to measure men by a lower standard than music and gems! No method this for stretching the rod of empire over all within the boundary of the sea.

As broad acres yield large crops, so for a nation to be great there should be a great population; and for soliders to be daring their generals should be brave. Not a single clod was added to Mount Tai in vain: hence the huge mountain we now behold. The merest streamlet is received into the bosom of Ocean: hence the Ocean's unfathomable expanse. And wise and virtuous is the ruler who scorns not the masses below. For him, no boundaries of realm, no distinctions of nationality exist. The four seasons enrich him; the Gods bless him; and, like our rulers of old, no man's hand is against him.

But now it is proposed to deliver over the black-haired people into the power of the foe. For if strangers are expelled, they will rally round the feudal princes. The leaders of the age will retire, and none will step forth to fill the vacant place. It is as though one should furnish arms to a rebel, or set a premium upon theft.

Many things that are not produced here are nevertheless highly prized. Countless men who were not born here are nevertheless loyal of heart. Therefore to dismiss all foreigners will be to make our enemies strong; for those who suffer expulsion will go to swell the hostile ranks. There will be but hollowness within and bitterness without; and danger will never cease to menace the State.

On reading the above, the Prince of Qin cancelled the edict respecting the proscription of foreigners, and I was restored to office.

CHAO CUO (d. 154 B.C.)

On War

Translated by Herbert Giles

An Imperial counselor, Chao Cuo was chiefly known by his strenuous opposition to the system of vassal princes, which had been in part reestablished under the Han dynasty after the total abolition of feudatory government by their predecessors, the Qin. Ultimately, when a coalition of seven vassal princes threatened the very existence of the dynasty, Chao Cuo was shamefully sacrificed by the Emperor, with a view to appease the rebels and avert the impending disaster.

May it please your Majesty,

Ever since the accession of the House of Han there have been constant irruptions of Tartar hordes, with more or less profit to the invaders.
During one reign they twice fell upon Longxi, besieging the city,
slaughtering the people, and driving off cattle. On another occasion,
they made a further raid, murdered the officials and garrison, and
carried away everything upon which they could lay their hands.

Now, victory inspires men with additional courage: with defeat their
morale disappears. And these three defeats at Longxi have left the inhabitants utterly demoralized, with never a ray of hope for the future.
The officials, acting under the protection of the Gods and armed with
authority from the Throne, may strive to renew the *morale* and discipline
of their soldiers, and to raise the courage of a beaten people to face the
onset of Huns flushed with victory. They may struggle to oppose many
with few, or to compass the rout of a host by the slaughter of its leader.
The question, however, is not one of the bravery or cowardice of our
people, but rather of the strategy of our generals. Thus it is said in the *Art
of War*, "A good general is more indispensable to success than a good
army." Therefore we should begin by careful selection of competent
generals. Further, there are three points upon which the fate of a battle
depends. These are (1) Position, (2) Discipline, and (3) Arms.[1]

We read in the *Art of War*, "(1) A country intersected by ditches and
watercourses, or marshy, or woody, or rocky, or overgrown with vegetation, is favorable to the operations of infantry. Two horsemen are there
not equal to one foot-soldier.

"Gentle slopes of soft earth, and level plains, are adapted to the
manœuvers of cavalry. Ten foot-soldiers are there not a match for one
horseman.

"Where the route lies between high hills some distance apart, or
through defiles with steep precipices on each side, the conditions are
favorable to bowmen. A hundred soldiers with side-arms are there no
match for a single archer.

"Where two armies meet at close quarters on a plain, covered with
short grass and giving plenty of room to manœuver, the conditions are
favorable to lancers. Three men with sword and buckler are not equal to
one of these.

---

[1] These words were penned about two thousand years ago; and yet Mr. Demetrius Boulger
(*horresco referens*), in the June number of the *Fortnightly* for 1883 treats us to the following:
"China has yet to learn that arms alone will not make an efficient army."

"But in jungle and amid thick undergrowth, there is nothing like the short spear. Two lancers are there not equal to one spearman.

"On the other hand, where the path is tortuous and difficult, and the enemy is concealed from view, then swordsmen carry everything before them, one man thus equipped being more than a match for three archers.

"(2) If soldiers are not carefully chosen and well drilled to obey, their movements will be irregular. They will not act in concert. They will miss success for want of unanimity. Their retreat will be disorderly, one half fighting while the other is running away. They will not respond to the call of the gong and drum. One hundred such as these will not hold their own against ten well-drilled men.

"(3) If their arms are not good, the soldiers might as well have none. If the cuirass is not stout and close set, the breast might as well be bare. Bows that will not carry, are no more use at long distances than swords and spears. Bad marksmen might as well have no arrows. Even good marksmen, unless able to make their arrows pierce, might as well shoot with headless shafts. These are the oversights of incompetent generals. Five such soldiers are no match for one."

Therefore, the *Art of War* says, "Bad weapons betray soldiers. Raw soldiers betray their general. Incompetent generals betray their sovereign. Injudicious sovereigns betray their country." The above four points are of vital importance in military matters.

May it please your Majesty. There is a difference in outline between great things and small ones. There is a difference in power between the strong and the weak. There is a difference in preparation between dangerous enterprises and easy ones. To truckle and cringe to the power-ful — this is the behavior of a petty State. To mass small forces against one great force — this is the attitude of a hostile State. To use barbarians as a weapon against barbarians — this is what we do in the Central State.

The configuration of the Hun territory, and the particular skill there available, are not what we are accustomed to at home. In scaling moun-tains and fording rivers our horses do not excel; nor our horsemen in galloping wildly along precipitous mountain paths, shooting as they go; nor our soldiers in endurance of cold, hunger, and thirst. In all these respects the Huns are our superiors. On level ground we beat them out of the field. Our bows, our spears, are incomparably better than theirs. Our armor, our blades, and the manœuvers of our troops, are un-matched by anything the Huns can show. When our good archers dis-charge their arrows, the arrows strike the target all together, against which their cuirasses and wooden bucklers are of no avail. And when it comes to dismounting and hand-to-hand fighting with sword and spear in the supreme struggle, the victory is easily ours. In these respects we excel them. Thus, the Huns may be compared with us in strength as three to five. Besides which, to slaughter their myriads we can bring tens of myriads, and crush them by mere force of numbers. But arms are a curse, and war is a dread thing. For in the twinkling of an eye the mighty may be humbled, and the strong may be brought low. The stake is great, and men's lives of no account. For him who falls to rise no more, the hour of repentance is past.

Now the maxim of our ancient kings was this: "The greatest safety of the greatest number." And as we have among us several thousand barbarians who, in point of food and skill, are closely allied to the Huns, let us clothe them in stout armor and warm raiment, arm them with trusty bows and sharp blades, mount them on good horses, and set them to guard the frontier. Let them be under the command of a competent general, familiar with their customs, and able to develop their *morale* according to the military traditions of this empire. Then, in the event of arduous military operations, let these men go to the front, while we keep back our light war-chariots and horse-archers for work upon level ground. We shall thus have, as it were, an outside and a lining; each division will be employed in the manner for which best adapted; our army will be increased, and the greatest safety of the greatest number will be achieved.

It is written, "The rash minister speaks, and the wise ruler decides." I am that rash minister, and with my life in my hand I dare to utter these words, humbly awaiting the decision of your Majesty.

On the Value of Agriculture

Translated by Herbert Giles

When the people are prosperous under the sway of a wise ruler, familiar with the true principle of national wealth, it is not only the tiller of the soil who fills his belly, nor the weaver alone who has a suit of clothes to his back.

In the days of Yao there was a nine years' flood: in the days of Tang, a seven years' drought. Yet the State suffered not, because of the preparations which had been made to meet such emergencies. Now, all within the boundary of the sea is under one scepter; and our country is wider and its inhabitants more numerous. For many years Heaven has sent upon us no visitation of flood or drought. Why then is our provision against emergency less? The fertility of the soil is not exhausted; and more labor is to be had. All cultivable land is not under tillage; neither have the hills and marshes reached their limit of production; neither has every available idler put his hand to the plough.

Crime begins in poverty; poverty in insufficiency of food; insufficiency of food in neglect of agriculture. Without agriculture, man has no tie to bind him to the soil. Without such tie, he readily leaves his birth-place and his home. He is like unto the birds of the air or the beasts of the field. Neither battlemented cities, nor deep moats, nor harsh laws, nor cruel punishments, can subdue this roving spirit that is strong within him.

He who is cold examines not the quality of cloth: he who is hungry tarries not for choice meats. When cold and hunger come upon men, honesty and shame depart. As man is constituted, he must eat twice daily, or hunger; he must wear clothes, or be cold. And if the stomach cannot get food and the body clothes, the love of the fondest mother cannot keep her children at her side. How then should a sovereign keep his subjects gathered round him?

The wise ruler knows this. Therefore he concentrates the energies of his people upon agriculture. He levies light taxes. He extends the system of grain storage, to provide for his subjects at times when their resources fail.

Man makes for grain, just as water flows of necessity in the direction of a lower level. Gold, silver, and jewels are powerless to allay the pangs of hunger or to ward off the bitterness of cold; yet the masses esteem these things because of the demand for them among their betters. Light and of limited bulk, a handful of such valuables will carry one through the world without fear either of cold or hunger. It is for these things that a minister plays false to his prince. It is for these things that a man lightly leaves his home: a stimulus to theft, the godsend of fugitives!

Grain and cotton cloths come to us from the earth. They are produced in due season by the labor of man, and time is needed for their growth. A few hundred-weight of such stuffs is more than an ordinary man can carry. They offer no inducement to crime; yet to be without them for a single day is to suffer both hunger and cold. Therefore the wise ruler holds grain in high honor, but degrades gold and jewels.

Now in every family of five there is an average of at least two capable husbandmen, who have probably not more than a few roods of land, the yield of which would perhaps be not more than a hundred piculs. In spring they have to plough; in summer, to weed; in autumn, to reap; in winter, to store; besides cutting fuel, repairing official residences, and other public services. Exposed, in spring, to wind and dust; in summer, to scorching heat; in autumn, to fog and rain; in winter, to cold and frost — from year's end to year's end they know not what leisure means. They have besides their own social obligations, visits of sympathy and condolence, the nourishment of orphans, of the aged, and of the young. Then, when flood and drought come upon them, already compassed round with toil and hardship, the government pressing harshly, collecting taxes at unsettled times, issuing orders in the morning to revoke them at night — those who have grain sell at half value, while those who have not borrow at exorbitant usury. Then paternal acres change hands; sons and grandsons are sold to pay debts; merchants make vast profits, and even petty tradesmen realize unheard-of gains. These take advantage of the necessities of the hour. Their men do not till: their women do not spin. Yet they all wear fine clothes and live on the fat of the land. They share not the hardships of the husbandman. Their wealth pours in from the four quarters of the earth. Vying in riches with kings and princes, in power they outdo the authorities themselves. Their watchword is gain. When they go abroad they are followed by long retinues of carriages and servants. They ride in fine coaches and drive sleek horses. They are shod in silk and robed in satin. Thus do they strip the husbandman bare of his goods; and thus it is that the husbandman is an outcast on the face of the earth.

At present, the merchant is *de jure* an ignoble fellow; *de facto*, he is rich and great. The husbandman is, on the other hand, *de jure* an honorable man; *de facto*, a beggar. Theory and practice are at variance; and in the confusion which results, national prosperity is out of the question. Now there would be nothing more presently advantageous than to concentrate the energies of our people upon agriculture; and the way to do this is to enhance the value of grain by making it an instrument of reward and punishment. Let rank be bestowed in return for so much grain. Let penalties be commuted for so much. By these means, rich men will enjoy honors, husbandmen will make money, and grain be distributed over the face of the empire. Those who purchase rank in this way will purchase out of their surplus; and by handing this over to the Imperial exchequer, the burden of taxes may be lightened, one man's superfluity making up for the deficiency of another, to the infinite advantage of the people. The benefits of this plan may in fact be enumerated under the following heads: (1) Sufficiency for Imperial purposes; (2) Light taxation; (3) Impetus given to agriculture.

Then again, at present a horse and cart are taken in lieu of three men under conscription for military service, on the ground that these are part of the equipment of war. But it was said of old, "An you have a stone rampart a hundred feet high, a moat a hundred feet broad, and a million of soldiers to guard the city, without food it shall be of no avail."

From the above it is clear that grain is the basis of all government. Rather then bid men gain rank and escape conscription by payments of grain: this would be better far than payment in horses and carts. Rank can be given at will by the mere fiat of the Emperor, and the supply is inexhaustible; grain can be produced from the earth by man in endless measure; and rank and exemption from penalty are what men above all things desire.

Therefore, I pray your Majesty, bestow rank and commute penalties for grain payments; and within three years the empire will be amply supplied.

LIU AN, PRINCE OF HUAINAN (d. 122 B.C.)

On the Nature of Tao

Translated by Herbert Giles

Liu An [see chapter 7] was the grandson of the founder of the Han dynasty. A student of Taoism, he directed his attention to alchemistic research and to the discovery of an elixir of immortality. The book bearing his name is an eclectic collection compiled by scholars at his court.

Tao roofs over the sky and is the foundation of the earth; it extends north, south, east, and west, stretching to the eight extreme points in those directions. Its height is beyond reach and its depth is unfathomable; it enfolds both the sky and the earth, and produces things which had been formless. It is like the flow of a spring, which starts bubbling up from nothing but gradually forms a volume of rushing muddy water which again gradually becomes clear. Therefore, if set vertically, it will block all the space between the sky and the earth; if set laterally, it will touch the shores of the Four Seas; inexhaustible by use, it knows neither the fullness of morning nor the decay of night; dispersed, it fills space; compressed, it is scarce a handful; scant, it can be ample; dark, it can be light; weak, it can be strong; soft, it can be hard. Though open on all sides, it contains the two cosmogonical Principles; it binds up the universe, while making manifest the sun, moon, and stars; it is thick as clay, and yet is watery; it is infinitesimally fine, and yet it can be subdivided; it makes mountains rise high and valleys sink low; it makes beasts to walk, birds to fly, the sun and moon to shine, the stars to move, the unicorn to come forth, and the phoenix to hover above us.

The first two Emperors of old obtained control of Tao, and established themselves in the center of all things, and by their divine influence brought about civilization and gave peace to the world. Thus, the sky duly turned round, while the earth stood still, and the wheel of human life revolved without ceasing.

SIMA XIANGRU (179–117 B.C.)

Against Hunting

Translated by Herbert Giles

Sima was the famous writer of rhapsodies [see chapter 6].

I had accompanied the Imperial hunt to Changyang. At that time His Majesty (Emperor Wu, second century B.C.) was an ardent follower of the chase, and loved to slaughter bears and wild boars with his own hands. Therefore I handed in the following Memorial:

May it please your Majesty,

I have heard that although the human race is comprised under one class, the capabilities of each individual are widely different. Thus we praise the strength of this man, the swiftness of that, and the courage of a third. And I venture to believe that what is true of us in this respect is equally true of the brute creation.

Now your Majesty enjoys laying low the fierce quarry in some close mountain pass. But one day there will come a beast, more terrible than the rest, driven from its lair; and then disaster will overtake the Imperial equipage. There will be no means of escape, no time to do anything, no scope for the utmost skill or strength, over the rotten branches and decaying trunks which help to complete the disorder. The Huns rising up under your Majesty's chariot-wheels, the barbarians of the west clinging on behind, would hardly be worse than this. And even if, in every case, actual injury is avoided, still this is not a fitting scene for the presence of the Son of Heaven. Besides, even on smooth ground and on a beaten track there is always risk of accident, — a broken rein or a loose pin; how much more so in the jungle or on the rough mountain-side, where, with the pleasure of the chase ahead and no thought of danger within, misfortune easily comes?

To neglect the affairs of a mighty empire and to find no peaceful occupation therein, but to seek for pleasure in the chase, never wholly without peril, — this is what in my opinion your Majesty should not do. The clear of vision discern coming events before they actually loom in sight: the wise in counsel avoid dangers before they definitely assume a shape. Misfortunes often lie concealed in trifles, and burst forth when least expected. Hence the vulgar saying, *He who has piled up a thousand ounces of gold, should not sit with chair overhanging the dais;* which proverb, though trivial in itself, may be used in illustration of great matters. I trust that your Majesty will deign to reflect hereon.

THE PRINCE OF ZHONGSHAN (fl. 110 B.C.)

Music

Translated by Herbert Giles

An Emperor of the Han dynasty was feasting several of his vassal princes who had come to pay their respects at court, when it was observed that one of them shed tears at the sound of the music. His Majesty inquired the cause of his distress, and the following was the prince's reply. He had been a terrified witness of the unexpected fall of a number of his colleagues, apparently without other reason than the caprice of their Imperial master excited by the voice of secret slander, and was evidently afraid that his own turn might be at hand.

May it please your Majesty!

There are moments when those who sorrow must weep, when those who are pensive cannot restrain their sights. And so, when Gao Jianli struck his lute, Jing Ke bowed his head and forgot to eat; when Yong Menzi vented his sorrow in song, Meng Changjun uttered a responsive cry. Now, mine has been a grief pent up for many a day; and whenever music's plaintive strains reach my ear, I know not how it is, my tears begin to flow.

Enough spittle will float a mountain; enough mosquitoes will cause a roar like thunder; a band of confederates will catch a tiger; ten men will break an iron bar. Combination has ever prevailed even against the greatest of the great.

And I, — I live afar off. I have but few friends, and none to intercede on my behalf. Against enough calumny, the purest purity and the ties of kindred cannot prevail. Light things may be piled on a cart until the axle snaps: it is by abundance of feathers that birds can raise their bodies in the air. And when I see so many of my colleagues tangled in the meshes of treason, my tears are beyond control.

When the sun is glowing brightly in the sky, the darkest corners are illumined by its light. Beneath the beams of the clear moon, the eye discerns the insect on the wing. But when dark clouds hide the sky behind their murky veil; when storms of dust thicken the surrounding air; then even mighty mountains are lost to sight behind the screen of intervening things.

Thus I am beyond the pale, while the lying tongues of courtiers chatter behind my back. The way is long, and none will speak on my behalf. Therefore I weep.

Rats are not flooded out of shrines: mice are not smoked out of a house, lest the buildings suffer withal. Now, I am but distantly related to your Majesty: still we are as the calyx and the fruit of the persimmon. My rank may be low: still I address your Majesty as my elder brother. But the courtiers round the Throne: their claims to relationship are thin as the pellicle of the rush, light as the down of the wild goose. Yet they combine, and each supports the other. They bring about separations in the imperial family, until the ties of blood vanish like melting ice. It was this that drove Bo Qi into exile: it was this that hurried Bi Gan to his grave.

It is said in the *Songs*, "Sorrow stabs my heart, and I am overwhelmed with sad thoughts. Vainly trying to sleep, I do naught but sigh. My grief is aging me. My heart throbs with it, like a throbbing head." And such, may it please your Majesty, is my case now.

LIU CHE, EMPEROR WU OF HAN (157–87 B.C.)

Heroes Wanted! A Proclamation

Translated by Herbert Giles

This emperor [see chapter 9] is famous for his long and magnificent reign, for his energetic patronage of scholars engaged in the resuscitation of Confucian literature, for the brilliant exploits of his generals in Central Asia against the Huns, and for the establishment of universities and literary degrees.

Exceptional work demands exceptional men. A bolting or a kicking horse may eventually become a most valuable animal. A man who is the object of the world's detestation may live to accomplish great things. As with the untractable horse, so with the infatuated man; — it is simply a question of training.

We therefore command the various district officials to search for men of brilliant and exceptional talents, to be Our generals, Our ministers, and Our envoys to distant states.

DONGFANG SHUO (154–93 B.C.)

Self-Recommendation

Translated by Herbert Giles

Dongfang Shuo [see chapter 7 for his biography] was popularly known as "The Wag." The following memorial was forwarded by him in response to the Proclamation of Emperor Wu calling for heroes to assist in the government. Dongfang Shuo became at once an intimate friend and adviser of the young Emperor, continuing in favor until his death. On one occasion he drank off some elixir of immortality, which belonged to the Emperor, and the latter in a rage ordered him to be put to death. But

Dongfang Shuo smiled and said, "If the elixir was genuine, your Majesty can do me no harm; if it was not, what harm have I done?"

I lost my parents while still a child, and grew up in my elder brother's home. At twelve I learned to write, and within the year I was well advanced in history and composition. At fifteen, I learned sword exercise; at sixteen, to repeat the *Songs* and the *Book of History* — 220,000 words in all. At nineteen, I studied the tactics of Sun Wu,[2] the accoutrements of battle array, and the use of the gong and drum, also 220,000 words in all, making a grand total of 440,000 words. I also carefully laid to heart the sayings of the bold Zilu.[3]

I am now twenty-two years of age. I am nine feet three inches in height.[4] My eyes are like swinging pearls, my teeth are like a row of shells. I am as brave as Meng Fen, as prompt as Qing Ji, as pure as Bao Shu, and as devoted as Wei Sheng.[5] I consider myself fit to be a high officer of State; and with my life in my hand, I await your Majesty's reply.

SIMA QIAN (c. 145–c. 85 B.C.)

Letter to Ren An

Translated by J. R. Hightower

Li Ling, a military man who was known and admired by the Grand Historian Sima Qian [see chapter 7], had led a force of five thousand men deep into nomadic Xiongnu territory. Poorly supplied and badly outnumbered, Li Ling was defeated and captured. With the exception of Sima Qian, who continued to speak out in support of the general, all Emperor Wu's high officials turned against Li Ling. The emperor, enraged that Li Ling had allowed himself to be captured alive, cast the general's defender, Sima Qian, into prison. Shortly thereafter, Sima was found guilty of "defaming the emperor," a crime carrying the sentence of death. Such a sentence could be commuted upon payment of a large sum of money, but Sima's family was poor and no friends came to his aid. It was fully expected that a man of noble character caught in such an unfortunate situation would commit suicide, but Sima agreed to undergo the humiliation of castration in place of either suicide or execution. Several years later, he wrote to Ren An concerning this episode in a deeply moving text that may be described as a "confession."

— Stephen Durrant, *Indiana Companion*, 1986

---

[2] Author of a famous treatise on the art of war.

[3] One of Confucius' favorite disciples.

[4] We must understand a shorter foot-rule than that now in use.

[5] Wei Sheng was a young man who had an assignation with a young lady beneath a bridge. At the appointed time she did not come, but the tide did; and Wei Sheng, rather than quit his post, clung to a pillar and was drowned.

The Grand Historian Sima Qian, bowing repeatedly, addresses his worthy friend Ren An:

Some time ago you deigned to send me a letter in which you advised me to be concerned for my social contacts and devote myself to the recommendation and advancement of qualified persons. You expressed yourself with considerable vigor, as though you expected I would not follow your advice but would be influenced by the words of the vulgar: I would hardly behave in such a way. I may be a broken hack, but I have still been exposed to the teachings handed down by my elders. However, I see myself as mutilated and disgraced: I am criticized if I act, and where I hope to be helpful I do harm instead. This causes me secret distress, but to whom can I unburden myself? As the proverb says, "For whom do you do it? Who are you going to get to listen to you?" Why was it that Boya never again played his lute after Zhong Ziqi died? A gentleman acts on behalf of an understanding friend, as a woman makes herself beautiful for her lover. Someone like me whose virility is lacking could never be a hero, even if he had the endowments of the pearl of Sui and the jade of Bianhe or conducted himself like Xu You and Bo Yi; he would only succeed in being laughed at and put to shame.

I should have answered your letter sooner, but when I got back from the East in the emperor's suite I was very busy. We were seldom together, and then I was so pressed that there was never a moment's time when I could speak my mind. Now you, Shaoqing, are under an accusation whose outcome is uncertain. Weeks and months have passed until we have now reached the end of winter, and I am going to have to accompany the emperor to Yong. I am afraid that that may come to pass which cannot be avoided, and as a result I will never have the chance to give expression to my grievance and explain myself to you. It would mean that the souls of the departed would carry a never-ending burden of secret resentment. Let me say what is on my mind; I hope you will not hold it against me that I have been negligent in leaving your letter so long unanswered.

I have been taught that self-cultivation is the mark of wisdom, that charity is the sign of humanity, that taking and giving is the measure of decency, that a sense of shame is the index of bravery, that making a name for oneself is the end of conduct. A gentleman who practices these five things can entrust his reputation to the world and win a place among outstanding men. On the other hand there is no misfortune so hurtful as cupidity, no grief so painful as disappointment, no conduct so despicable as disgracing one's forebears, no defilement so great as castration. One who has undergone that punishment nowhere counts as a man. This is not just a modern attitude; it has always been so. Formerly when Duke Ling of Wei rode in the same chariot with the eunuch Yongqu, Confucius left Wei to go to Chen; when Tongzi shared the emperor's chariot, Yuan Si blushed. It has always been occasion for shame. Even an ordinary fellow never fails to be offended when he has business with a eunuch — how much the more a gentleman of spirit. Though the court today may want men, you surely do not expect one who has submitted to the knife to recommend the worthies of the empire for places?

It has been twenty years since I inherited my father's office and entered the service of the emperor. It occurs to me that during that time I have not been able to demonstrate my loyalty and sincerity or win praise for good advice and outstanding abilities in the service of a wise ruler; nor have I been able to make good defects and omissions, or advance the worthy and talented, or induce wise hermits to serve; nor have I been able to serve in the ranks of the army, attacking walled cities and fighting in the field to win merit by taking an enemy general's head or capturing his banners; nor have I been able to win merit through long and faithful service to rise to high office and handsome salary, to the glory of my family and the benefit of my friends. From my failure in all four of these endeavors it follows that I am prepared to compromise with the times and avoid giving offense, wholly ineffectual for good or ill. Formerly as Great Officer of the third grade I once had the chance to participate in deliberations in a minor capacity. Since I then offered no great plans nor expressed myself freely, would it not be an insult to the court and an affront to my colleagues if now, mutilated, a menial who sweeps floors, a miserable wretch, I should raise my head and stretch my eyebrows to argue right and wrong? Alas, for one like me what is there left to say? What is there left to say?

It is not easy to explain just what happened. When I was young I had no outstanding abilities and I grew up unpraised by my fellow townsmen. Fortunately, however, thanks to my father's service, the emperor made it possible for me to put my inconsiderable abilities at his disposal, and I had access to the court. It seemed to me that one cannot get a good view of the sky carrying a platter on one's head, so I broke off relations with my friends and neglected my family affairs that I might day and night devote all my small abilities wholeheartedly to my official duties and so gain the liking and approval of the ruler. But then came the event when I made my big mistake and everything was changed.

Li Ling and I were both stationed in the palace, but we never had a chance to become friends. Our duties kept us apart; we never shared so much as a cup of wine, let alone enjoyed a closer friendship. But I observed that he conducted himself as no ordinary gentleman. He was filial toward his parents, honest with his colleagues, scrupulous about money, decent in his behavior, yielding in matters of precedence,

respectful, moderate and polite to others. Carried away by his enthusiasm he never thought of himself but was ever there where his
country needed him: such was his constant concern. To me he seemed to
have the bearing of a national hero. A subject who exposes himself to a
thousand deaths without regard for his own single life, and rushes to the
defense of his country — that is a great man. That men who had been
solely concerned with keeping themselves and their wives and children
safe and sound should go out of their way to stir up trouble for him when
he had made a single mistake was something that really pained my
inmost feelings.

Moreover Li Ling's troops numbered fewer than five thousand when
he led them deep into the territory of the nomads. They marched to the
khan's court and dangled the bait in the tiger's mouth. They boldly
challenged the fierce barbarians, in the face of an army of a million. For
ten days running they fought the khan, killing more than their own
number, so that the enemy were unable to retrieve their dead or rescue
their wounded. The princes of felts and furs were all terror-stricken; they
called on the neighboring lords to draft bowmen, and the whole nation
joined to attack and surround Li Ling's troops. For a thousand miles they
retreated, fighting as they went, until their arrows were exhausted and
the road cut off. The relieving force had not arrived. Dead and wounded
lay in heaps. But when Li Ling rallied his men with a cry, his soldiers rose
to fight, with streaming tears and bloody faces. They swallowed their
tears and, brandishing their empty bows, braved naked swords. Facing
north they fought to the death with the enemy.

Before Li Ling had reached this extremity a messenger brought news
to the court and all the lords and princes raised their cups to drink to his
success. Some days later the message arrived announcing that he had
been defeated. The news so affected the emperor that he found his food
tasteless and took no pleasure in holding court. The great ministers were
depressed and fearful, now knowing what course to take. When I saw
the emperor in great distress of mind, I took no count of my own humble
position, but wished to express my honest opinion: that Li Ling had
always shared with his men, renouncing the sweet and dividing his short
rations, so that he was able to get them to die for him — no famous
general of antiquity surpassed him in this. And though he was now
involved in defeat, it could be assumed that he intended to do what was
right and make good his obligation to China. The situation was past
remedying, but the losses he had already inflicted on the Xiongnu were
such that his renown filled the empire.

I wished to express these ideas but had no way to do so until by chance
I was ordered to give an opinion. In these terms I extolled Li Ling's

merits, hoping to get the emperor to take a wider view of things and at the same time undo the charges of his enemies. I did not succeed in making myself clear, and the emperor, in his wisdom, did not understand, suspecting that I was criticizing the Second General Li Guangli, who headed the relief column, and that I was indulging in special pleading in behalf of Li Ling. As a result I was turned over to the judges, and despite all my heartfelt sincerity I was unable to justify myself. In the end it was decided that I was guilty of attempting to mislead the emperor.

Being poor, I had insufficient funds to pay a fine in lieu of punishment. None of my friends came to my aid. My colleagues and associates spoke not a word on my behalf. My body is not of wood or stone: and I was alone with my jailors. When one is shut up in the depths of prison is there anyone he can appeal to? You have experienced this yourself, do you think it was otherwise with me?

In giving himself up alive to the Xiongnu, Li Ling disgraced his family; in going to the silkworm chamber after his act I became doubly the laughingstock of the empire. Alas, alas! This is not a thing one can easily talk about to the vulgar. My father never earned tally and patent of nobility; as annalist and astrologer I was not far removed from the diviners and invokers, truly the plaything of the emperor, kept like any singing girl or jester, and despised by the world. Had I chosen to submit to the law and let myself be put to death, it would have been no more important than the loss of a single hair from nine oxen, no different from the crushing of an ant. No one would have credited me with dying for a principle; rather they would have thought that I had simply died because I was at my wit's end and my offense allowed no other way out. And why? They would think so because of the occupation in which I established myself.

A man can die only once, and whether death to him is as weighty as Mount Tai or as light as a feather depends on the reason for which he dies. The most important thing is not to disgrace one's ancestors, the next is not to disgrace one's self, the next not to disgrace one's principles, the next not to disgrace one's manners. Next worse is the disgrace of being put in fetters, the next is to wear a prisoner's garb, the next is to be beaten in the stocks, the next is to have the head shaved and a metal chain fastened around the neck, the next is mutilation, and the very worst disgrace of all is castration. It is said that corporal punishments are not applied to the great officers, implying that an officer cannot but be careful of his integrity. When the fierce tiger is in the depths of the mountain, all animals hold him in fear, but when he falls into a trap he waves his tail and begs for food: this is the end result of curtailing his dignity. Hence if you draw the plan of a jail on the ground, a gentleman will not step inside the figure, nor will he address even the wooden image of a jailor. In this way he shows his determination never to find himself in such a position. But let him cross his hands and feet to receive the bonds, expose his back to receive the whip, and be incarcerated in the barred cell — by then when he sees the jailor he bows his head to the ground and at the sight of his underlings he pants in terror. And why? It is the result of the gradual curtailment of his dignity. If now he claims there has been no disgrace, he is devoid of a sense of shame and wholly unworthy of respect.

Wen Wang was an earl, and yet he was held prisoner in Youli; Li Si was prime minister and yet was visited with all five punishments; Han Xin was a prince and yet he was put in the stocks in Chen; Peng Yue and Zhang Ao each sat on a throne and called himself king, and yet the one was fettered in prison, the other put to death. These were all men of high rank and office and widespread reputation, but when they got into trouble with the law they were unable resolutely to put an end to themselves. It has always been the same: when one lies in the dirt there is no question of his not being disgraced. In the light of these examples, bravery and cowardice are a matter of circumstance, strength and weakness depend on conditions. Once this is understood, there is nothing to be surprised at in their behavior. If by failing to do away with himself before he is in the clutches of the law a man is degraded to the point of being flogged and then wishes to rescue his honor, has he not missed his chance? This is no doubt why the ancients were chary of applying corporal punishment to a great officer.

Now there is no man who does not naturally cling to life and avoid death, love his parents and cherish his wife and children. But the man who is devoted to the right sometimes has no choice but to behave otherwise. I early had the misfortune to lose my father and mother; I had no brothers and was quite alone. You have seen how little my affection for my wife and children deterred me from speaking out. But a brave man will not always die for his honor, and what efforts will not even a coward make in a cause to which he is devoted? I may be a coward and wish to live at the expense of my honor, but I surely know how to act appropriately. Would I have abandoned myself to the ignominy of being tied and bound? Even a miserable slavegirl is capable of putting an end to herself; could you expect less of me, when I had so little choice? If I concealed my feelings and clung to life, burying myself in filth without protest, it was because I could not bear to leave unfinished my deeply cherished project, because I rejected the idea of dying without leaving to posterity my literary work.

In the past there have been innumerable men of wealth and rank whose names died with them; only the outstanding and unusual are known today. It was when King Wen was in prison that he expanded the *Book of Changes*; when Confucius was in straits he wrote the *Spring and Autumn Annals*; when Qu Yuan was banished he composed "On Encountering Trouble"; Zuo Qiu lost his sight and so we have the *Conversations from the States*; Sunzi had his feet chopped off, and *The Art of War* was put together. The general purport of the three hundred poems of the *Book of Songs* is the indignation expressed by the sages. All of these men were oppressed in their minds, and, unable to put into action their principles, wrote of the past with their eyes on the future. For example, Zuo Qiu without sight and Sunzi with amputated feet were permanently disabled. They retired to write books in which they expressed their pent-up feelings, hoping to realize themselves in literature, since action was denied them.

I have ventured not to look for more recent models, but with what little literary ability I possess I have brought together the scattered fragments of ancient lore. I studied the events of history and set them down in significant order; I have written 130 chapters in which appears the record of the past — its periods of greatness and decline, of achievement and failure. Further it was my hope, by a thorough comprehension of the workings of affairs divine and human, and a knowledge of the historical process, to create a philosophy of my own. Before my draft was complete this disaster overtook me. It was my concern over my unfinished work that made me submit to the worst of all punishments without showing the rage I felt. When at last I shall have finished my book, I shall store it away in the archives to await the man who will understand it. When it finally becomes known in the world, I shall have paid the debt of my shame; nor will I regret a thousand deaths.

However, this is something I can confide only to a person of intelligence; it would not do to speak of it to the vulgar crowd. When one is in a compromising situation, it is not easy to justify onself; the world is always ready to misrepresent one's motives. It was in consequence of my speaking out that I met disaster in the first place; were I to make myself doubly a laughingstock in my native place, to the disgrace of my forebears, how could I ever have the face again to visit the grave of my father and my mother? Even after a hundred generations my shame will but be the more. This is what makes my bowels burn within me nine times a day, so that at home I sit in a daze and lost, abroad I know not where I am going. Whenever I think of this shame the sweat drenches the clothes on my back. I am fit only to be a slave guarding the women's apartments: better that I should hide away in the farthest depths of the mountains. Instead I go on as best I can, putting up with whatever treatment is meted out to me, and so complete my degradation.

And now you want me to recommend worthy men for advancement! Is this not rather the last thing in the world I would want to do? Even if I should want to deck myself out with fine words and elegant phrases, it would not help me any against the world's incredulity; it would only bring more shame on me. In short, I can hope for justification only after my death.

In a letter I cannot say everything. What I have written is a crude and general statement of my feelings. Respectfully I bow to you.

LI LING (d. 74 B.C.)

A Reply to Su Wu

Translated by Herbert Giles

Su Wu, the friend to whom this letter was addressed, had been sent in 100 B.C. on a special mission to the court of the Huns [Xiongnu], where, because he would not renounce his allegiance, he was thrown into prison and remained in captivity for nineteen years. He subsequently effected an escape, and returned to China, whence he wrote to Li Ling (who had meanwhile surrendered to the Huns) in a sense that will be gathered from a perusal of the latter's reply.

O Ziqing,[6] O my friend, happy in the enjoyment of a glorious reputation, happy in the prospect of an imperishable name — there is no misery like exile in a far-off foreign land, the heart brimful of longing thoughts of home! I have thy kindly letter, bidding me be of good cheer, kinder than a brother's words; for which my soul thanks thee.

Ever since the hour of my surrender until now, destitute of all resource, I have sat alone with the bitterness of my grief. All day long I see none but barbarians around me. Skins and felt protect me from wind and rain. With mutton and whey I satisfy my hunger and slake my thirst. Companions with whom to while time away, I have none. The whole country is stiff with black ice. I hear nought but the moaning of the bitter autumn blast, beneath which all vegetation has disappeared. I cannot sleep at night. I turn and listen to the distant sound of Tartar pipes, to the whinnying of Tartar steeds. In the morning I sit up and listen still, while

---

[6] Su Wu's literary name or style.

tears course down my cheeks. O Ziqing, of what stuff am I, that should do aught but grieve? The day of thy departure left me disconsolate indeed. I thought of my aged mother butchered upon the threshold of the grave. I thought of my innocent wife and child, condemned to the same cruel fate. Deserving as I might have been of Imperial censure, I am now an object of pity to all. Thy return was to honor and renown, while I remained behind with infamy and disgrace. Such is the divergence of man's destiny.

Born within the domain of refinement and justice, I passed into an environment of vulgar ignorance. I left behind me obligations to sovereign and family for life amid barbarian hordes; and now barbarian children will carry on the line of my forefathers.[7] And yet my merit was great, my guilt of small account. I had no fair hearing; and when I pause to think of these things, I ask to what end I have lived. With a thrust I could have cleared myself of all blame: my severed throat would have borne witness to my resolution; and between me and my country all would have been over for aye. But to kill myself would have been of no avail: I should only have added to my shame. I therefore steeled myself to obloquy and to life. There were not wanting those who mistook my attitude for compliance, and urged me to a nobler course; ignorant that the joys of a foreign land are sources only of a keener grief.

O Ziqing, O my friend, I will complete the half-told record of my former tale. His late Majesty commissioned me, with five thousand infantry under my command, to carry on operations in a distant country. Five brother generals missed their way: I alone reached the theater of war. With rations for a long march, leading on my men, I passed beyond the limits of the Celestial Land, and entered the territory of the fierce Huns. With five thousand men I stood opposed to a hundred thousand: mine jaded foot soldiers, theirs horsemen fresh from the stable. Yet we slew their leaders, and captured their standards, and drove them back in confusion toward the north. We obliterated their very traces: we swept them away like dust: we beheaded their general. A martial spirit spread abroad among my men. With them, to die in battle was to return to their homes; while I — I venture to think that I had already accomplished something.

This victory was speedily followed by a general rising of the Huns. New levies were trained to the use of arms, and at length another hundred

---

[7] He had taken a Tartar wife.

thousand barbarians were arrayed against me. The Hun chieftain himself appeared, and with his army surrounded my little band, so unequal in strength — foot-soldiers opposed to horse. Still my tired veterans fought, each man worth a thousand of the foe, as, covered with wounds, one and all struggled bravely to the fore. The plain was strewed with the dying and the dead: barely a hundred men were left, and these too weak to hold a spear and shield. Yet, when I waved my hand and shouted to them, the sick and wounded arose. Brandishing their blades, and pointing toward the foe, they dismissed the Tartar cavalry like a rabble rout. And even when their arms were gone, their arrows spent, without a foot of steel in their hands, they still rushed, yelling, onward, each eager to lead the way. The very heavens and the earth seemed to gather round me, while my warriors drank tears of blood. Then the Hunnish chieftain, thinking that we should not yield, would have drawn off his forces. But a false traitor told him all: the battle was renewed, and we were lost.

The Emperor Gao, with 300,000 men at his back, was shut up in Pingcheng. Generals he had, like clouds; counselors, like drops of rain. Yet he remained seven days without food, and then barely escaped with life. How much more then I, now blamed on all sides that I did not die? This was my crime. But, O Ziqing, canst thou say that I would live from craven fear of death? Am I one to turn my back on my country and all those dear to me, allured by sordid thoughts of gain? It was not indeed without cause that I did not elect to die. I longed, as explained in my former letter, to prove my loyalty to my prince. Rather than die to no purpose, I chose to live and to establish my good name. It was better to achieve something than to perish. Of old, Fan Li did not slay himself after the battle of Huiji; neither did Cao Mo die after the ignominy of three defeats. Revenge came at last; and thus I too had hoped to prevail. Why then was I overtaken with punishment before the plan was matured? Why were my own flesh and blood condemned before the design could be carried out? It is for this that I raise my face to Heaven, and beating my breast, shed tears of blood.

O my friend, thou sayest that the house of Han never fails to reward a deserving servant. But thou art thyself a servant of the house, and it would ill beseem thee to say other words than these. Yet Xiao and Fan were bound in chains; Han and Peng were sliced to death. Chao Cuo was beheaded, Zhou Bo was disgraced, and Dou Ying paid the penalty with his life. Others too, great in their generation, have also succumbed to the intrigues of base men, and have been overwhelmed beneath a weight of shame from which they were unable to emerge. And now, the misfortunes of Fan Li and Cao Mo command the sympathies of all.

My grandfather filled heaven and earth with the fame of his exploits — the bravest of the brave. Yet, fearing the animosity of an Imperial favorite, he slew himself in a distant land, his death being followed by the secession, in disgust, of many a brother-hero. Can this be the reward of which thou speakest?

Thou too, O my friend, an envoy with a slender equipage, sent on that mission to the robber race, when fortune failed thee even to the last resource of the dagger. Then years of miserable captivity, all but ended by death among the wilds of the far north. Thou left us full of young life, to return a gray-beard; thy old mother dead, thy wife gone from thee to another. Seldom has the like of this been known. Even the savage barbarian respected thy loyal spirit: how much more the lord of all under the canopy of the sky? A many-acred barony should have been thine, the ruler of a thousand-charioted fief! Nevertheless, they tell me 'twas but two paltry millions, and the chancelorship of the Tributary States. Not a foot of soil repaid thee for the past, while some cringing courtier gets the marquisate of ten thousand families, and each greedy parasite of the Imperial house is gratified by the choicest offices of the State. If then thou farest thus, what could I expect? I have been heavily repaid for that I did not die. Thou hast been meanly rewarded for thy unswerving devotion to thy prince. This is barely that which should attract the absent servant back to his fatherland.

And so it is that I do not now regret the past. Wanting though I may have been in my duty to the State, the State was wanting also in gratitude towards me. It was said of old, "A loyal subject, though not a hero, will rejoice to die for his country." I would die joyfully even now; but the stain of my prince's ingratitude can never be wiped away. Indeed, if the brave man is not to be allowed to achieve a name, but to die like a dog in a barbarian land, who will be found to crook the back and bow the knee before an Imperial throne, where the bitter pens of courtiers tell their lying tales?

O my friend, look for me no more. O Ziqing, what shall I say? A thousand leagues lie between us, and separate us for ever. I shall live out my life as it were in another sphere: my spirit will find its home among a strange people. Accept my last adieu. Speak for me to my old acquaintances, and bid them serve their sovereign well. O my friend, be happy in the bosom of thy family, and think of me no more. Strive to take all care of thyself; and when time and opportunity are thine, write me once again in reply.

Li Ling salutes thee!

Lu Wenshu (first century B.C.)

On Punishments

Translated by Herbert Giles

He taught himself to read and write while working as a shepherd and soon attracted attention. Graduating with what was in his day the equivalent of B.A. degree, he rose to some distinction in official life. This memorial was presented in 67 B.C.

May it please your Majesty,

Of the ten great follies of our predecessors, one still survives in the maladministration of justice which prevails.[8]

Under the Qins, learning was at a discount: brute force carried everything before it. Those who cultivated a spirit of charity and duty toward their neighbor were despised. Judicial appointments were the prizes coveted by all. He who spoke out the truth was stigmatized as a slanderer, and he who strove to expose abuses was set down as a pestilent fellow. Consequently, all who acted up to the precepts of our ancient code found themselves out of place in their generation; and loyal words of good advice to the sovereign remained locked up within their bosoms, while hollow notes of obsequious flattery soothed the monarch's ear and lulled his heart with false images, to the exclusion of disagreeable realities. And so the rod of empire fell from their grasp for ever.

At the present moment, the State rests upon the immeasurable bounty and goodness of your Majesty. We are free from the horrors of war, from the calamities of hunger and cold. Father and son, husband and wife, are united in their happy homes. Nothing is wanting to make this a golden age, save only reform in the administration of justice.

Of all trusts, this is the greatest and most sacred. The dead man can never come back to life: that which is once cut off cannot be joined again. "Rather than slay an innocent man, it were better that the guilty escape." Such, however, is not the view of our judicial authorities of today. With them, oppression and severity are reckoned to be signs of magisterial acumen, and lead on to fortune; whereas leniency entails

---

[8] The "ten great follies" which helped to bring about the overthrow of the Qin dynasty were — (1) abolition of the feudal system; (2) melting down all weapons and casting twelve huge figures from the metal; (3) building the Great Wall to keep out the Tartars; (4) building a huge pleasaunce, the central hall of which was over sixty feet in height, and capable of accommodating ten thousand guests; (5) the burning of the books; (6) the massacre of the literati; (7) building a vast mausoleum; (8) searching for the elixir of life; (9) appointing the Heir-Apparent to be Commander-in-Chief; and (10) maladministration of justice.

naught but trouble. Therefore, their chief aim is to compass the death of their victims; not that they entertain any grudge against humanity in general, but simply that this is the shortest cut to their own personal advantage. Thus, our marketplaces run with blood, our criminals throng the jails, and many thousands annually suffer death. These things are injurious to public morals, and hinder the advent of a truly golden age.

Man enjoys life only when his mind is at peace; when he is in distress, his thoughts turn towards death. Beneath the scourge, what is there that cannot be wrung from the lips of the sufferer? His agony is overwhelming, and he seeks to escape by speaking falsely. The officials profit by the opportunity and cause him to say what will best confirm his guilt. And then, fearing lest the conviction be quashed by higher courts, they dress the victim's deposition so to suit the circumstances of the case, so that, when the record is complete, even were Gao Yao[9] himself to rise from the dead, he would declare that death still left a margin of unexpiated crime. This, because of the refining process adopted to ensure the establishment of guilt.

Our magistrates indeed think of nothing else. They are the bane of the people. They keep in view their own ends, and care not for the welfare of the State. Truly they are the worst criminals of the age. Hence the saying now runs, "Chalk out a prison on the ground, and no one would remain within. Set up a jailer of wood, and he will be found standing there alone."[10] Imprisonment has become the greatest of all misfortunes; while among those who break the law, who violate family ties, who choke the truth, there are none to be compared in iniquity with the officers of justice themselves.

Where you let the kite rear its young undisturbed, there will the phoenix come and build its nest. Do not punish for misguided advice, and by-and-by valuable suggestions will flow in. The men of old said, "Hills and jungles shelter many noxious things: rivers and marshes receive much filth: even the finest gems are not wholly without flaw. Surely then the ruler of an empire should put up with a little abuse." But I would have your majesty exempt from vituperation, and open to the advice of all who have aught to say. I would have freedom of speech in the advisers of the Throne. I would sweep away the errors which brought about the downfall of our predecessors. I would have reverence for the virtues of our ancient kings, and reform in the administration of justice, to the utter confusion of those who now pervert its course. Then, indeed,

---

[9]   A famous Minister of Crime in the third millennium B.C. [see chapter 4].

[10]   Contrary to what is believed to have been the case during the Golden Age.

would the golden age be renewed over the face of the glad earth, and the people would move ever onwards in peace and happiness boundless as the sky itself.

WANG CHONG (27–91)

On Spirits

Translated by Herbert Giles[11]

Born in poverty, he managed to pick up a good education and entered official life. After a short spell he retired dissatisfied to his home, and there composed his great work, the *Animadversions* (*Lun Heng*), in which he criticizes freely the teachings of Confucius and Mencius, and tilts generally against the errors and superstitions of his day.

The dead do not become disembodied spirits; neither have they consciousness, nor do they injure anybody. Animals do not become spirits after death; why should man alone undergo this change? That which informs man at his birth is a vital fluid, or soul, and at death this vitality is extinguished, the body decays and becomes dust. How can it become a spirit? Vitality becomes humanity, just as water becomes ice. The ice melts and is water again; man dies and reverts to the condition of the vital fluid. Death is like the extinction of fire. When a fire is extinguished, its light does not shine any more; and when a man dies, his intellect does not perceive any more. The nature of both is the same. If people, nevertheless, pretend that the dead have knowledge, they are mistaken. The spirits which people see are invariably in the form of human beings, and that very fact is enough of itself to prove that these apparitions cannot be the souls of dead men. If a sack is filled with grain, it will stand up, and is obviously a sack of grain; but if the sack is burst and the grain falls out, then it collapses and disappears from view. Now, man's soul is enfolded in his body as grain in a sack. When the man dies, his body decays and his vitality is dissipated. When the grain is taken away, the sack loses its form; why then, when vitality is gone, should the body obtain a new shape in which to appear again in the world?

The number of persons who have died since the world began, old, middle-aged, and young, must run into thousands of millions, far

---

[11] The translator has selected and re-arranged several short extracts. *Eds.*

exceeding the number of persons alive at the present day. If every one of these has become a disembodied spirit, there must be at least one to every yard as we walk along the road; and those who die now must suddenly find themselves face to face with vast crowds of spirits, filling every house and street. If these spirits are the souls of dead men, they should always appear naked; for surely it is not contended that clothes have souls as well as men. It can further be shown not only that dead men never become spirits, but also that they are without consciousness, by the simple fact that before birth they are without consciousness. Before birth man rests in God; when he dies he goes back to God. God is vague and without form, and man's soul is there in a state of unconsciousness. The universe is, indeed, full of disembodied spirits, but these are not the souls of dead men. They are beings only of the mind, conjured up for the most part in sickness, when the patient is especially subject to fear. For sickness induces fear of spirits; fear of spirits causes the mind to dwell upon them; and thus apparitions are produced. Even if disembodied spirits did exist, they could not be either pleased or angry with a sacrifice, for the following reason. We must admit that spirits do not require man for their maintenance; for if they did, they would hardly be spirits. If we believe that spirits only smell the sacrifices, which sacrifices are supposed to bring either happiness or misfortune, how do we picture to ourselves the habitations of these spirits? Have they their own provisions stored up, or must they use the food of man to appease their hunger? Should they possess stores of their own, these would assuredly be other than human, and they would not have to eat human food. If they have no provisions of their own, then we should have to make offerings to them every morning and evening; and according as we sacrificed to them or did not sacrifice, they would be satiated or hungry, pleased or angry, respectively.

CAI YONG (133–192)

Stele for Wang Ziqiao

Translated by Donald Holzman

Cai Yong was a pre-eminent figure in the literary and court life of the final days of the Later Han, a calligrapher of genius, a ritualist, and musician. His importance in literary history lies in his status as one of China's greatest masters of parallel prose, and he is especially famous for his inscriptions such as this one. Liu Xie, in his *Literary Mind and the Carving of Dragons*, commented: "From the Later Han, when stele inscriptions appeared in great number, no one has written inscriptions with more trenchancy than Cai Yong." Wang Ziqiao was a well-known Taoist immortal, whose "biography" is included in the *Lives of Immortals* [see chapter 7].

Wang Ziqiao would seem to be the name of an antique Perfect Man. It is not known during which dynasty he first appeared as an Immortal. Among the numerous Taoists I consulted some say he was from Yingchuan, some say he was born in Meng.[12] This tumulus has been here since the founding of the city, and it has been called "the Wang family tomb" by word of mouth since early times. But the family line was not continued; the tomb has been abandoned without an inheritor for years beyond counting.

In the twelfth month of the first year of the Yong-he era, during the night of the All Saints Festival (17 January 137), very plaintive crying was heard on the tomb. Wang Bo, who lived nearby, thought it strange, and when it became light he ascended the tomb and investigated. There had been a heavy snowfall and no path had yet formed, but there were tracks of a large bird where sacrifices had been held, and the onlookers all took them to be supernatural.[13] Later a man wearing an official's hat and a scarlet unlined robe stood before the sepulture leaning upon a bamboo staff. He called to the young wood-gatherer, Yi Yongchang, and said: "I am Wang Ziqiao. You must not take the trees on our grave mound!"[14] In an inkling he disappeared.

The local magistrate, Wan Xi of Taishan, looked into what the elders had to say about this and felt that there had been an extremely favorable supernatural occurrence. He held an inquest and believed there was sufficient evidence proving that miracles had truly taken place. He then had an ancestral temple built to rejoice the god. Thereupon those who took delight in the Tao came from distant places to assemble there. Some strummed zithers and sang of the Great One;[15] others practiced meditation to visit their Cinnabar Fields.[16] Those who were sick or crippled and who silently bowed and prayed for good fortune were granted it straightaway, but those who were lacking in respect were struck down immediately. Thus it was known that this was a tomb of great virtue, in truth the tomb of the ancestors of the Perfect Man.

In the eighth month, in autumn, of the eighth year of the Yan-xi era (165) the emperor sent an envoy to offer a sacrificial victim and perform a ritual. The purification was accomplished with utmost reverence and dignity. The Counselor-Delegate Wang Zhang of Donglai felt that the

---

[12] Both in Henan.
[13] Wang Ziqiao is said to have risen to heaven on a white crane.
[14] As will soon become clear, this is not Wang Ziqiao's own tomb, but that of his ancestors.
[15] An important divinity since early Han times.
[16] Points in the body upon which the Taoist adept concentrates during his meditations.

place of origin of a divine saint required the erection of an inscription that would make it known to succeeding generations. It is thus that in Laixiang they venerate the vestiges of Laozi and that the people living near the Pass admire the remaining aura of Yin Xi.[17] Wang Zhang then, with his aide Bian Qian, had this stele set up to commemorate and glorify the great acts of the past and for the inspection of those who have set their hearts on the Tao.

Lord Wang,
So virtuous he could commune with the spirits,
Shone with internal brightness,
Keeping himself perfectly pure.
In tune with the great Tao,
He longed for eternal youth.
Rejecting the world and its customs,
He flew away, his body made divine.
Soaring in the highest clouds,
Floating in the Great Purity,
He would ride on a hornless dragon,
Or drive in a car pulled by a crane,
Wearing a multicolored bamboo hat,
Making his metallic bells ring out,
Waving a flag of plumes,
Brandishing a rainbow banner.
His joys know no limits
As he lives for ever and ever, without end.
To manifest his fervent filial piety,
He thought of those who had given him life.
As the year drew to its close
He showed his sincere feelings.
In attendance near the tomb
He sent forth his doleful chant.
By leaving bird tracks
He alerted the old town,
And wearing a scarlet robe,
With purple hat-strings dangling,
He called to the child
And announced his name.

---

[17] Laixiang in eastern Henan (about 60 kilometers south of the Wang Ziqiao stele) is said in the *Records of the Grand Historian* to be the native place of Laozi; Yin Xi is said to have been the Guardian of the Pass when Laozi left China for the West.

At this men understood
And reacted with fear and surprise.
They rebuilt the shrine
And returned the altars and bamboo mats.
They presented sacrificial foods
That spread forth sweet-smelling odors.
As all looked on,
A far-wafting fragrance arose from the pure sacrifice,
Adding to the stream of good fortune
And to the glory of the imperial court.
Heaven will protect our land,
Aid our common people,
Make our great blessings glow,
Shining to the ends of the earth.

ZHONGCHANG TONG (179–220)

On Happiness

Translated from the French of Etienne Balazs by H. M. Wright

We read in his biography in the *History of the Later Han*: "Every time he was called upon to fill a post in a district or a commandery, he immediately excused himself on account of illness and never accepted. He always pronounced the opinion that all those who wander in search of office and visit kings and emperors, have no other aim but to acquire celebrity by making a career. But renown does not last forever, and it is easy to lose one's life. One can, however, amuse oneself by happy wanderings here and there. One can choose a pure and spacious dwelling and thus fulfill one's aspirations." [For one of his poems, see chapter 9.]

Let the place where one lives have good fields and a large house set upon a hillside and looking over a river, surrounded by canals and bamboo-bordered pools. In front are laid out the threshing floor and the vegetable garden, and behind is planted an orchard of fruit trees. There are enough carriages and boats to ensure that one shall not have the trouble of walking or wading; there are enough servants to ensure that one shall not exhaust oneself with menial tasks. For nourishing one's family, the finest viands are at hand; wife and children do not have to bear the burden of doing any hard work.

When good friends pay a visit, they are served with wine and refreshments for their entertainment. When times are prosperous, on feast days a lamb or a suckling pig is roasted and served to them. There is enjoyment to be had between the fields and the garden, and sport to be had in the woods. There is bathing in clear water, or breathing in of fresh winds. One can fish for the darting carp, or shoot at wild geese on the wing. One can chant softly at the foot of the rain altar, or carouse up in the great hall.

One's spirits can be calmed in the interior apartments, or one can meditate on the mysterious void of Laozi, or make one's vital essence harmonious by practicing breathing exercises, in an attempt to become like the supreme men. With one or two initiates,[18] the Way can be discussed and books explained. Upward and downward the Two Powers (Heaven and Earth) can be examined; men and things can be analyzed and explored. The strings of the lute can vibrate with the sublime song "The Southern Wind," or a wondrous melody in the pure *re* mode can be sung. In one's transports all worldly affairs can be transcended, and from on high what lies between Heaven and Earth can be contemplated. The demands of one's times are left unheeded, and life can be prolonged for ever. In this way one can reach the firmament and emerge into a region beyond space and time.

Why then should one be eager to be received by kings and emperors?

ZHUGE LIANG (181–234)

On Deploying the Army

Translated by Robert Joe Cutter

After the abdication of the last Han emperor in A.D. 220, China split into the states of Wei (220–265), Wu (222–280), and Shu Han (221–263). Liu Bei was the ruler of Shu Han and claimed to be the legitimate successor of the Han emperors by virtue of having the surname Liu. Although he proclaimed himself emperor and is naturally referred to as "the late emperor" in this memorial, neither he nor his son Liu Chan are given that distinction in the official history of the period or by later historians in general. Zhuge Liang, the author of the memorial, had been Liu Bei's chief counselor and strategist, and it was largely thanks to his sagacity and military skill that Liu Bei was successful in establishing himself upon the throne.

Your servant Liang states:

The late emperor (Liu Bei) died before his work of restoring the Han was half done. Now the land is divided into three parts, and our people here in Yizhou are worn and tired. This, indeed, is a critical time on which hangs our survival. Yet the officials of the imperial guard persevere

---

[18] *Da* (initiates) combines the meanings of intelligent, penetrating, and free, untrammeled.

at court, and loyal and noble-minded soldiers are selfless in the field. This presumably is because they recall the late emperor's remarkable solicitude and wish to repay it through Your Majesty. To be sure, you should lend a sage ear to a broad range of opinions so as to bring further glory to the virtue of the late emperor and enhance the morale of those patriots in the field. You should not be excessively modest or go wrong in following advice lest you block the channels of loyal criticism.

Those in the palace and the bureaucracy are all one body. They should not be treated differently with regard to promotions, punishments, praise, or censure. People who do evil and break the law and people who are loyal and good should all be turned over to the proper authorities to determine their respective punishments and rewards, thereby demonstrating the fairness and wisdom of Your Majesty's administration. You should not be biased and allow different standards to be applied within and without the palace.

Palace Attendants Guo Youzhi and Fei Hui and Attendant Gentleman Dong Yun are all able and honest. Their aims and ideas are loyal and true, so the late emperor picked them to serve Your Majesty after his death. In my opinion, if you always consult them before taking action on palace matters, no matter how important or trivial, they will surely be able to help remedy errors and omissions and be of vast benefit. General Xiang Chong's character and behavior are exemplary and just, and he is a master of military matters. The late emperor employed him in the past and praised him as capable, so one and all discussed making Chong commander-in-chief. In my opinion, if you always consult him on military strategy, he will surely be able to harmonize the armed forces and properly position the stronger and weaker units.

The Former Han flourished because it favored worthy subjects and kept disreputable people at a distance. The Later Han fell because it favored disreputable people and kept worthy subjects at a distance. Whenever the late emperor and I discussed these concerns, he always sighed with bitter regret over the reigns of Emperors Huan and Ling. Palace Attendants Guo Youzhi and Fei Hui, Imperial Secretary Chen Zhen, Administrator Zhang Yi, and Adjutant Jiang Wan are all staunch and trustworthy subjects willing to die for their integrity. I hope that Your Majesty will be on close terms with them and trust in them, for then the ascendancy of Shu Han will be just around the corner.

I was originally a commoner and farmed in Nanyang. I did whatever it took to save my skin in a turbulent world and did not seek celebrity among the nobles. The late emperor did not consider me contemptible, but rather was kind enough to call on me three times in my thatched hut and consult me about current events. I was moved by this and gave my assent to him, serving at his beck and call. Later, we met a serious defeat, and for twenty-one years I accepted assignments midst a beaten army and was entrusted with missions at a crucial and difficult time. The late emperor knew that I am cautious and prudent, so on his deathbed he charged me with the great affairs of state. Ever since I received his command, I have sighed in distress day and night, fearing that I would fail in my commission and thereby impugn his wisdom. Therefore, in the fifth month we crossed the Lu River and penetrated deep into the desert. Now, while the South is already pacified and our weapons and armor are in good supply, we should encourage the troops and lead them north to pacify the Central Plain. I yearn to use every bit of my limited ability to expel our arch-enemy, restore the house of Han, and return us to the old

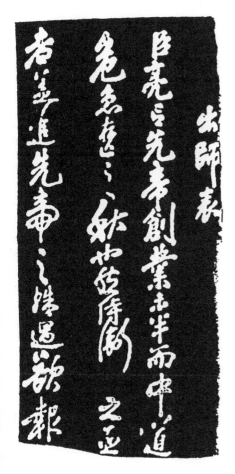

Figure 35. Part of Zhuge Liang's memorial "On Deploying the Army," in the calligraphy of Yue Fei (1103–1141). (Source: *Calligraphy*, September 1979)

capital. In this way, I might repay the late emperor and demonstrate my loyalty to Your Majesty.

It is the duty of Guo, Fei, and Dong to offer honest advice in assessing government policies. But I pray that Your Majesty will entrust the job of suppressing the enemy and restoring the dynasty to me. If I fail, then punish me for my transgression in order to mollify the soul of the late emperor. If Guo, Fei, and Dong have no advice for enhancing your virtue, then rebuke them for their mistakes and expose their dereliction. Your Majesty should also seek solutions on your own, taking counsel and selecting wise policies, weighing and adopting appropriate advice, and bearing very much in mind the last wishes of the late emperor. I am deeply grateful for having received so much favor. Now I must go far away. I weep over this memorial, unaware of what I have said.

WANG SU (195–256)

Jade

Translated by Herbert Giles

Wang Su was a very distinguished scholar who wrote and published many volumes of classical commentaries. He is said to have found, in the house of a descendant of the Sage, the text of *The Family Sayings of Confucius* (from which this piece is taken), and to have published it in 240. But the generally received opinion is that he wrote the work himself, based no doubt upon tradition.

A disciple asked Confucius, saying, "Why, sir, does the superior man value jade much more highly than serpentine? Is it because jade is scarce and serpentine is abundant?" "It is not," replied Confucius; "but it is because the superior men of olden days regarded it as a symbol of the virtues. Its gentle, smooth, glossy appearance suggests charity of heart; its fine close texture and hardness suggest wisdom; it is firm and yet does not wound, suggesting duty to one's neighbor; it hangs down as though sinking, suggesting ceremony; struck it gives a clear note, long drawn out, dying gradually away and suggesting music; its flaws do not hide its excellences, nor do its excellences hide its flaws, suggesting loyalty; it gains our confidence, suggesting truth; its spirituality is like the bright rainbow, suggesting the heavens above; its energy is manifested in hill and stream, suggesting the earth below; as articles of regalia it suggests the exemplification of that than which there is nothing in the world of equal value, and thereby is — Tao itself.

We read in the *Songs* —

When I think of my husband,
As gentle as jade,
In his hutment of planking,
My heart is afraid ...

Li Mi (c. 225–c. 290)

Memorial Expressing My Feelings

Translated by David Knechtges

Li Mi was a native of Wuyang (east of modern Pengshan County, Sichuan) in Qianwei commandery. His father died when Li was an infant. When Li Mi was four, his mother was forced to remarry. Li Mi was sent to live with his maternal grandmother, Lady Liu, who raised him. Li Mi in turn served his grandmother with filial devotion. Whenever Lady Liu was ill, he wept and sobbed, and never took off his clothes. He insisted on tasting all of her drinks, foods, and medicines before giving them to her. Li Mi served as gentleman of the secretariat in his native Shu. When Shu was defeated by the Jin in 264, the Jin emperor Sima Yan wished to appoint him as an aide to the crown prince. On the grounds that he had to care for his aged grandmother, Li Mi refused the appointment. To explain himself, he composed this famous and much anthologized memorial.

Your servant Mi states: Because of a parlous fate, I early encountered grief and misfortune. When I was an infant of only six months my loving father passed away. When I was four my mother's brother forced my mother to remarry against her will. Grandmother Liu took pity on this weak orphan and personally cared for me. When young, I was so often sick that even at the age of nine I could not walk. Solitary and alone I suffered until I reached adulthood. I had neither uncles nor brothers, and my family was so destitute and devoid of good fortune that only late in life did I have offspring. Outside the household, I have no close relatives whom I can mourn; inside, I have not even a boy servant to watch the gate. I am so miserable and alone, my body and shadow console each other. Grandmother Liu long has been ill and is constantly bedridden. I serve her medicinal brews, and I have never abandoned her or left her side.

When I came into the service of this Sage Dynasty, I bathed in Your pure transforming influence. First Governor Kui sponsored me as Filial and Pure. Later Inspector Rong recommended me as a Flourishing Talent. But because there was no one to care for grandmother, I declined and did not take up the appointment. An edict was especially issued appointing me Palace Gentleman. Not long thereafter I received imperial favor and was newly appointed Aide to the Crown Prince. I humbly believe that for a man as lowly and insignificant as I to be deemed worthy of serving in the Eastern Palace is an honor I could never requite you for even by giving my life. I informed you of all the circumstances in a memorial, and I again declined and did not go to my post. Your edict was insistent and stern, accusing me of being dilatory and disrespectful. The commandery and prefectural authorities tried to pressure me and urged me to take the road up to the capital. The local officials approached my door swifter than shooting stars. I wanted to comply with your edict and dash off to my post, but Grandmother Liu's illness daily became more grave. I wished temporarily to follow my personal desires, but my plea was not granted. Whether to serve or retire truly was a great dilemma!

I humbly believe that this Sage Dynasty governs the empire by means of filial piety, and that all among the aged and elderly still receive compassion and care. How much more needful am I whose solitary suffering has been especially severe! Moreover, when young I served the false dynasty,[19] and I have moved through the various gentleman posts.[20] I originally planned to become illustrious as an official, but I never cared about my reputation and character. Now I am a humble captive of a fallen state. I am utterly insignificant and unimportant, but I have received more promotions than I deserve, and your gracious charge is both liberal and generous. How would I dare demur, with the hope of receiving something better? However, I believe that Grandmother Liu is nearing the sunset of her years, and with faint and weakened breath, her life has reached a precarious, delicate stage. One cannot predict in the morning what will happen in the evening. Without grandmother I would not be alive today. Without me grandmother would not have been able to live out her remaining years. Grandmother and grandson have depended upon one another for life. Thus, simply because of my own small, selfish desires I cannot abandon or leave her. I am now in my forty-fourth year, and Grandmother Liu is now ninety-six. Thus, I have a long time in which to fulfill my duty to Your Majesty, and only a short time in which to repay Grandmother Liu for raising me. I am like the crow that feeds its mother, and I beg to be allowed to care for her to her final days. My suffering and misery are not only clearly known by the men of Shu and the governors of the two provinces (of Liang and Yi), they have been perceived by August Heaven and Sovereign Earth. I hope your majesty will take pity on my naïve sincerity and will grant my humble

---

[19] Li Mi is referring to his service with the state of Shu, which was defeated by the Jin.

[20] Under the Shu, Li Mi first served as palace gentleman and then was promoted to gentleman of the secretariat.

wish, so that Grandmother Liu will have the good fortune to preserve the remaining years of her life. While I am alive, I shall offer my life in your service. When dead, I shall "knot a clump of grass" for you.[21]

With unbearable apprehension, like a loyal dog or horse, I respectfully present this memorial to inform you of my feelings.

FAXIAN (c. 337–422)

from *Record of the Buddhistic Kingdoms*
A Chinese Pilgrim in Ceylon

Translated by Herbert Giles

A native of Wuyang in Shanxi, Faxian became a novice in the Buddhist priesthood at the age of three, exchanging his family name of Gong for the religious designation Faxian. On reaching manhood he was ordained and proceeded to Chang'an to make a thorough study of the Buddhist religion. Finding that there was a lack of material for this purpose, and full of zeal and faith, he set out in 399 in company with several others on an overland pilgrimage to India, his object being to obtain a complete set of the Buddhist Canon in the original tongue. Alone of the party he reached the goal and spent some time in India, traveling to various important Buddhist centers and generally fulfilling the purposes of his mission. In 414 he was back in China, having returned by sea, via Ceylon and the Straits of Malacca; and then he spent several years at Nanjing, being prevented by the disturbed state of the empire from carrying his books and sacred relics on to Chang'an. He occupied the time in translating a work on monastic discipline. He also related to his friend and fellow-laborer, Buddha Bhadra, a great Indian Buddhist, then in China, the incidents of his long journey. These Buddha Bhadra committed to writing, thus forming the work now known as the *Record of the Buddhistic Kingdoms*.

At the end of this time he took passage on a large merchant vessel, and setting sail proceeded toward the south-west with the first of the favorable winter monsoon. After fourteen days and nights he reached the Land of the Lion (Ceylon), said by the inhabitants to lie at a distance

---

[21] Viscount Wu of Wei, Wei Zhou, had a favorite concubine who had not given birth to a son. Wei Zhou became ill, and he ordered his eldest son Wei Ke to allow her to remarry after his death. When his illness became grave, Wei Zhou then changed his mind and ordered Wei Ke to have her buried with him. When Wei Zhou died, Wei Ke allowed the concubine to remarry. Later, the Qin general Du Hui attacked Wei Ke. On the battlefield Wei Ke saw an old man knotting a clump of grass that tripped Du Hui, allowing Wei Ke to defeat Du Hui. That night the spirit of the old man appeared to Wei Ke in a dream and told him that he was the father of the concubine. He had tied the clump of grass as a way of repaying Wei Ke for saving his daughter's life. Thus, "knotting grass" is an expression for repaying favor after death. See *Zuo Commentary*.

of seven hundred yōjanas[22] from India. This country is on a great island, measuring fifty yōjanas from east to west and thirty from north to south. The small islands round about are nearly one hundred in number, and are distant from one another ten, twenty, or even two hundred *li.* They are all subject to the mother island, and produce chiefly pearls and precious stones. There is one island where the Mani beads (fine pearls used for Buddhist rosaries) are found; it is about ten *li* square. The king sends men to guard it; and if any pearls are obtained, he takes three-tenths.

This country was not originally inhabited by human beings, but only by devils and dragons, with whom the merchants of the neighboring countries traded by barter. At the time of the barter the devils did not appear, but set out their valuables with the prices attached. The merchants then gave goods according to the prices marked and took away the goods they wanted. And from the merchants going backwards and forwards and some stopping there, the attractions of the place became widely known, and people went thither in great numbers, so that it became a great nation.

The temperature of this country is very agreeable; there is no distinction between winter and summer. Plants and trees flourish all the year round, and cultivation of the soil is carried on as men please, without regard to the season.

When Buddha came to this country, he wished to convert the wicked dragons; and by his divine power he placed one foot to the north of the royal city and the other on the top of Adam's Peak, the two points being fifteen yōjanas apart. Over the footprint to the north of the city a great pagoda has been built, four hundred feet in height and decorated with gold and silver and with all kinds of precious substances combined. By the side of the pagoda a monastery has also been built, called No-Fear Mountain, where there are now five thousand priests. There is a Hall of Buddha of gold and silver carved work with all kinds of precious substances, in which stands his image in green jade, over twenty feet in height, the whole of which glitters with the seven preciosities, the countenance being grave and dignified beyond expression in words. On the palm of the right hand lies a priceless pearl.

Faxian had now been many years away from his own land of Han; the people he had had to deal with were all inhabitants of strange countries; the mountains, the streams, plants, and trees on which his eyes had

---

[22] An ancient measurement described variously as a day's march for the royal army, or eight times the distance at which a bull's bellow can be heard. *Eds.*

lighted were not those of old days; moreover, those who had traveled with him were separated from him — some having remained behind in these countries, others having died. Now, beholding only his own shadow, he was constantly sad at heart; and when suddenly, by the side of this jade image, he saw a merchant make offering of a white silk fan from China, his feelings overcame him and his eyes filled with tears.

A former king of this country had sent an envoy to Central India to get seeds of the Bō tree, which he planted alongside of the Hall of Buddha, and from which a tree grew up to a height of two hundred feet. As this tree bent over towards the south-east, the king feared it would fall, and therefore placed a prop of eight or nine spans in circumference to support it. Where the tree and prop met, the tree shot out; and the shoot, piercing the prop, went right through it to the ground and took root, growing to about four spans in circumference. Although the prop was split through, it still encircles the shoot and has not been taken away. At the foot of the tree a shrine has been built, with the image of Buddha seated inside, an object of ceaseless worship to ecclesiastics and laymen.

In the city, too, a shrine has been built to receive a tooth of Buddha's, both the above being made from the seven preciosities....

Buddha's Tooth is regularly brought out in the middle of the third moon. Ten days previously the king causes a large elephant to be splendidly caparisoned, and a man who speaks well to be dressed up in royal robes and mounted on the elephant. This man will beat a drum and proclaim in a loud voice, "The Bodhisattva during three immeasurable aeons practiced self-mortification and did not spare his person or his life; he gave up his country, his wife, and his child; he gouged out his eyes to give to a fellow-creature; he cut off his flesh to ransom a dove, and his head to give as alms; he flung his body to a hungry tigress, stinting neither his marrow nor his brains. Thus in various ways he suffered for the benefit of living creatures, and so he became a Buddha, tarrying on earth forty-nine years, preaching the Faith and converting sinners, giving rest to the weary and salvation to those who had not been saved. When his relations with living creatures had been fulfilled, he passed away. Since his entry into Nirvāna, fourteen hundred and ninety-seven years ago, the Eye of the world has been put out, and all living creatures have sorely grieved. Now, ten days hence Buddha's Tooth will be brought forth and be taken to the shrine of the No-Fear Mountain. Let all those ecclesiastics and laymen of this country who wish to lay up happiness for themselves, help to level the roads, decorate the streets, and prepare flowers, incense, and implements of worship."

When these words have been recited, the king then proceeds to make on both sides of the road representations of the five hundred different forms in which the Bodhisattva successively appeared; for instance as prince Sudāna, or as a flash of lightning, as the king of elephants, as a stag, or as a horse. These representations are all beautifully painted and have a lifelike appearance. The Tooth is then brought out and passes along the central street, receiving homage of offerings as it goes by. Arriving at the Hall of Buddha in the shrine of the No-Fear Mountain, ecclesiastics and laymen flock together in crowds, burn incense, light lamps, and perform the various ceremonies of the Faith, day and night without ceasing. After ninety days have elapsed, the Tooth is returned to the shrine in the city. On fast-days this shrine is opened for worship according to the Faith.

Forty *li* to the east of the No-Fear shrine, there is the sacred mountain, Mihintale, with a shrine on it called Bhadrika, in which there are about two thousand priests. Among them is a Shaman, the Reverend Dharmagupta, whom all the people of this country respect and look up to. He has dwelt in a stone cell for more than forty years; and by constant exercise of kindness of heart he has succeeded in so influencing snakes and rats that they will live together in the same cell without hurting one another.

Seven *li* to the south of the city there is a shrine called the Great Shrine, with three thousand resident priests. Among them was one reverend Shaman, so pure in his conduct as regards the Disciplines that all suspected him of being a Lohan.[23] When he was at the point of death, the king came to look into the matter; and when, in accordance with the rules of the Faith, he had assembled the priests, he asked, "Has this religious mendicant become a Lohan?" The priests at once told the truth and replied, "He is a Lohan." When he was dead the king accordingly buried him with the ceremonial due to a Lohan, as laid down in the Canon.

Four or five *li* to the east of the shrine a great pile of wood was collected, over thirty feet square and of about the same height. Sandal-wood, garoo wood (lign-aloes), and all kinds of scented woods were placed at the top, and at the four sides steps were made. Over it was spread clean white cashmere which surrounded and quite covered the pyre; and again on the top of this was placed a car, in form like the hearses of China, but without the dragon. At the time of the cremation the king and his subjects collected together from all quarters, and with offerings of flowers and incense followed the car to the burial-ground, the king himself making personal offerings of flowers and incense. When

---

[23] The Lohan, or Arhat, is the enlightened, saintly man in Hīnayāna Buddhism. *Eds.*

these ceremonies were finished, the car was placed on the top of the pyre, oil of sweet basil was poured all over it, and a light was applied. While the fire was blazing, everyone was moved with a feeling of reverence, and each took off his upper garment, and together with feather-fan and umbrella, threw it from a distance into the midst of the flames, so as to help on the cremation. When it was all over, the bones were collected and a pagoda raised over them. Faxian did not arrive while the deceased was yet alive, but only in time to see his funeral....

Faxian remained in this country for two years; and after repeated search he obtained a copy of the Disciplines according to the school of "The Faith Prevailing"; also copies of the long Agamas[24] on cosmogony, and of the miscellaneous Agamas on ecstatic contemplation, and subsequently of a collection of extracts from the Canon, all of which China was without. When he had obtained these in Sanskrit, he took passage on board a large merchant-vessel, on which there were over two hundred souls, and astern of which there was a smaller vessel in tow, in case of accident at sea and destruction of the big vessel. Catching a fair wind, they sailed eastward for two days; then they encountered a heavy gale, and the vessel sprang a leak. The merchants wished to get aboard the smaller vessel; but the men on the latter, fearing that they would be swamped by numbers quickly cut the tow-rope in two. The merchants were terrified, for death was close at hand; and fearing that the vessel would fill, they promptly took what bulky goods there were and threw them into the sea. Faxian also took his pitcher and ewer, with whatever else he could spare, and threw them into the sea; but he was afraid that the merchants would throw over his books and his images, and accordingly fixed his whole thoughts upon Guan Yin, the Hearer of Prayers, and put his life into the hands of the Catholic Church in China, saying, "I have journeyed far on behalf of the Faith. Oh that by your awful power you would grant me a safe return from my wanderings."

The gale blew on for thirteen days and nights, when they arrived alongside of an island, and then, at ebb-tide, they saw the place where the vessel leaked and forthwith stopped it up, after which they again proceeded on their way.

This sea is infested with pirates, to meet whom is death. The expanse of ocean is boundless, east and west are not distinguishable; only by observation of the sun, moon, and constellations is progress to be made. In cloudy and rainy weather, our vessel drifted at the mercy of the wind,

---

[24] General name for the Hīnayāna scriptures. *Eds.*

without keeping any definite course. In the darkness of night nothing was to be seen but the great waves beating upon one another and flashing forth light like fire, huge turtles, sea-lizards, and such-like monsters of the deep. Then the merchants lost heart, not knowing whither they were going, and the sea being deep, without bottom, they had no place where they could cast their stone-anchor and stop. When the sky had cleared, they were able to tell east from west and again to proceed on their proper course; but had they struck a hidden rock, there would have been no way of escape.

And so they went on for more than ninety days until they reached a country named Java, where heresies and Brahmanism were flourishing, while the Faith of Buddha was in a very unsatisfactory condition.

After having remained in this country for five months or so, Faxian again shipped on board another large merchant-vessel which also carried over two hundred persons. They took with them provisions for fifty days and set sail on the 16th of the 4th moon, and Faxian went into retreat on board the vessel.

A northeast course was set in order to reach Canton; and over a month had elapsed when one night in the second watch (9–11 P.M.) they encountered a violent gale with tempestuous rain, at which the traveling merchants and traders who were going to their homes were much frightened. However, Faxian once more invoked the Hearer of Prayers and the Catholic Church in China, and was accorded the protection of their awful power until day broke. As soon as it was light, the Brahmans took counsel together and said, "Having this Shaman on board has been our undoing, causing us to get into this trouble. We ought to land the religious mendicant on some island; it is not right to endanger all our lives for one man." A "religious protector" of Faxian's replied, saying, "If you put this religious mendicant ashore, you shall also land me with him; if not, you had better kill me, for supposing that you land him, when I reach China I will report you to the king who is a reverent believer in the Buddhist Faith and honors religious mendicants." At this the merchants wavered and did not dare to land him just then.

Meanwhile, the sky was constantly darkened and the captain lost his reckoning. So they went on for seventy days until the provisions and water were nearly exhausted, and they had to use seawater for cooking, dividing the fresh water so that each man got about two pints. When all was nearly consumed, the merchants consulted together and said, "The ordinary time for the voyage to Canton is exactly fifty days. We have now exceeded that limit by many days; must we not have gone out of our course?"

Thereupon they proceeded in a northwesterly direction, seeking for land; and after twelve days and nights arrived south of the Lao mountain (on the Shandong promontory) at the boundary of the Prefecture of Chang'guang (the modern Jiaozhou), where they obtained fresh water and vegetables.

And now, after having passed through much danger, difficulty, sorrow, and fear, suddenly reaching this shore and seeing the old familiar vegetables, they knew it was their fatherland; but not seeing any inhabitants or traces of such, they did not know what part it was. Some said that they had not got as far as Canton; others declared that they had passed it. Being in a state of uncertainty, some of them got into a small boat and went up a creek in search of anyone whom they might ask about the place. These fell in with two hunters and brought them back to the vessel, telling Faxian to act as interpreter and interrogate them. Faxian began by reassuring them, and then quietly asked them, "What men are you?" They replied, "We are followers of Buddha." "And what is it you go among the mountains to seek?" continued Faxian. Then they began to lie, saying, "Tomorrow is the 15th day of the 7th moon; we wished to get something for a sacrifice (the lie!) to Buddha." Faxian then said, "What country is this?" They answered, "This is the boundary of the Chang'guang prefecture in Qingzhou; all these parts belong to the Liu family." When they heard this the merchants were very glad, and at once requested that their effects might be landed, sending men off with them to Chang'guang.

KUMĀRAJĪVA (344–413)

Faith Is the Substance

Translated by Herbert Giles

Kumārajīva was an Indian missionary monk who, with learned Chinese assistants, translated various sutras into Chinese, from one of which, the *Diamond Sutra*, the following passage has been taken.

O Subhūti, if a good man, or a good woman, were to give up in the morning as many of his or her lives (in rebirths) as there are sands in the river Ganges, and to do the same at noonday, and again in the evening, and to continue to do this every day for an innumerable number of *kalpas*, each of an innumerable number of years; and if, on the other hand, there should be one who, having heard this *sutra*, should yield up his heart to implicit belief — then the happiness of this last would exceed the happiness of that other. And much more would this be so if he were to write out this *sutra*, hold fast to it himself, and recite and explain it to others. O Subhūti, let me state its importance. This *sutra* has a merit which cannot be conceived of by thought and cannot be estimated by weight or measurement.

If anyone looks for me through the medium of form,
Or seeks me through the medium of sound,
Such a man is walking on a heterodox path,
And will not be able to see the Lord Buddha.

ZONG BING (375–443)

On Landscape Painting

Translated by Wing-tsit Chan

Chinese art is the exclusive province neither of Taoism nor of any other particular philosophy or religion. Nevertheless it cannot be denied that Taoism has supplied much of the inspiration in the formulation of the artistic ideal. Zong Bing was a distinguished painter, none of whose works have survived. He lived for some time in a hut on Mount Heng; but when he began to grow old he returned to civilization, saying: "I can no longer see the hills; I must visit them in imagination from my couch."

The sage embraces the Tao and responds harmoniously to things. The worthy man purifies his mind and enjoys forms. As to landscapes, they exist in material substance and soar into the realm of the spirit. Therefore men like the Yellow Emperor, Yao, Confucius, Guangcheng, Dawei, Xu You, Boyi, and Shuqi insisted on traveling among the mountains of Kongtong, Juci, Miaogu, Jishou, and Dameng. These are also called the delights of the man of humanity and the man of wisdom.[25] Now the sage, by the exercise of his spirit, follows the Tao as his standard, while the worthy man understands this. Mountains and rivers in their form pay homage to the Tao, and the man of humanity delights in them. Do not the sage and mountains and rivers have much in common?

I was strongly attached to the Lu and Heng Mountains and had missed for a long time Mounts Jing and Wu. Like Confucius, I did not realize that old age was coming on. I am ashamed that I can no longer concentrate my vital power or nourish my body, and I am distressed to follow the steps of people like the keeper of the Stone Gate.[26] Therefore I draw

---

[25] *Analects,* VI, 21: "The wise find pleasure in water; the virtuous find pleasure in hills."
[26] Who ridiculed Confucius for attempting the impossible.

forms and spread colors and create these mountain peaks capped with clouds.

Now, the Principle that was lost in ancient times may, through imagination, be found in the thousand years yet to come. Meanings that are subtle and beyond the expression of words and symbols may be grasped by the mind through books and writings. How much more so in my case, when I have personally lingered among the mountains, and with my own eyes observed them all around me, so that I render forms as I find forms to be and apply colors as I see them!

... And so I live in leisure and nourish my vital power. I drain clean the wine-cup, play the lute, lay down the representation of the landscape, face it in silence, and, while still seated, travel beyond the four borders of the land, never leaving the realm where nature exerts her influence, and alone responding to the call of the wilderness. Cliffs and peaks seem to rise to soaring heights, and dense groves in the midst of clouds extend to the vanishing point. Sages and virtuous men of far antiquity come back to live in my imagination and all interesting things come together in my spirit and in my thoughts. What else need I do? I gratify my spirit, that is all. What is there that is more important than gratifying the spirit?

BAO ZHAO (414–466)

Dalei Riverbank: From a Letter to My Sister

Translated by Kang-i Sun Chang

Bao Zhao [see chapter 12] was only twenty-five years old when he wrote this famous letter, on his way from Nanjing to Jiangxi Province, where he was to assume a position as assistant to Liu Yiqing, the Prince of Linchuan. When he stopped by Dalei Riverbank in Anhui Province, he was suddenly overcome with loneliness.

Since I set out there has been cold rain, and few of the days have been spent entirely in travel. Moreover, the autumn rains fall in torrents, and the mountain streams overflow. I cross the boundless waters against the current and travel along dangerous paths. On the cliffside roads I eat my meals under the stars; I spend my nights on lotus beds by the water. As a traveler, I am distressed and toil-worn. The rivers and roads are broad and immense. Thus, by mealtime today, I had only reached Dalei. I have traveled on this road for a thousand *li*; my journey has taken more than ten days. There is severe frost in this merciless season; the grievous wind bites my flesh. To be parted from one's loved ones and to become a wanderer — what, oh what, can be done?

Looking far away to the clear and bright sandbars, I let my eyes wander at dusk. To the east I see the Five Islands' straits; to the west I gaze at the Nine Streams' parting. I spy the extraordinary scenery of the earth's gateway; I view the lone clouds at the sky's edge.

To the southwest I look at Mount Lu,
Again I am struck by how extraordinary it is.
Its base presses down on the river's tide,
Its peaks touch the stars and the Milky Way.
Above it, rosy clouds often gather,
Wrought into an ornamental tapestry.
Evening radiant as the flowers of the *ruo* tree,
Mists pass between cliffs and marshes.
The emerging light scatters varicolored silk,
So red, it seems to redden the sky.
To the left and right, blue vapors
Form a complement to the Purple Sky Peak.
From the ridges up,
Mists are full of golden brilliance.
At the bottom half of the mountain,
It is completely sea blue ...
In it soaring billows leap up to touch the sky,
High waves pour onto the sun.
They swallow and disgorge a hundred rivers,
Rushing and churning up ten thousand ravines.
Light mists lingering,
Water boiling in the splendid cauldron ...
Swirling foam caps the mountains,
Rushing billows empty the valleys.
Hard rocks are smashed by them,
Curving banks are crushed and collapse.
I look at the Big Fire Star above,
And listen to the sound of the waves below.
Shivering I hold my breath,
My heart is startled.

The wind blows in the thundering gale, and I shall be very careful on the road at night. Around the time of the half-moon, I hope I will have arrived at the appointed place. It is difficult to adjust to changes of climate; you must take special care of yourself. Guard yourself well morning and night, and do not worry about me.

KONG ZHIGUI (447–501)

Proclamation on North Mountain

Translated by J. R. Hightower

That seclusion served sometimes as a cloak for the poseur is evident from this satirical Proclamation by Kong Zhigui [for notes on his life see chapter 13]. In this essay the devices of the euphuistic Parallel Prose style so popular during this period are used to great effect to pillory the pretensions of a would-be recluse, Zhou Yong, dignified by the writer as Master Zhou. This man built a retreat he called Grass Hut, on the Bell Mountain named in the opening sentence of Kong's essay. He suffers at the writer's hands by comparison with various genuine immortals and sages whose names dot the piece.

The Spirit of Bell Mountain, the Divinity of Grass Hut Cloister,
hasten through the mist on the post road
to engrave this proclamation on the hillside:
    A man who
Incorruptible, holds himself aloof from the vulgar,
Untrammeled, avoids earthly concerns,
Vies in purity with the white snow,
Ascends straightway to the blue clouds —
    We but know of such.
    Those who
Take their stand outside things,
Shine bright beyond the mist,
Regard a treasure of gold as dust and do not covet it,
Look on the offer of a throne as a slipper to be cast off,
Who are heard blowing a phoenix flute by the bank of the Luo,
Who are met singing a faggot song beside the Yanlai —
    These really do exist.
    But who would expect to find those
Whose end belies their beginning,
Vacillating between black and yellow,
Making Mo Di weep,
Moving Yang Zhu to tears,[27]
Retiring on impulse with hearts still contaminated
Starting out pure and later becoming sullied —
    What imposters they are!
    Alas!

---

[27] "Yang Zhu wept on seeing a cross-road, because it could lead north or south; Mo Di cried on seeing them dye plain silk, because it could become yellow or black." See *Huainanzi*.

Master Shang lives no more[28]
Mister Zhong is already gone[29]
The mountain slope is deserted,
A thousand years unappreciated.
At the present time there is Master Zhou[30]
An outstanding man among the vulgar
Cultured and a scholar
Philosopher and scribe.
    But he needs must
Imitate Yan He's retirement[31]
Copy Nanguo's meditation,[32]
Occupy the Grass Hut by imposture
Usurp a hermit's cap on North Mountain,
Seduce our pines and cassia trees
Cheat our clouds and valleys.
Although he assume the manner by the river side
His feelings are bound by love of rank.
    When first he came, he was going to
Outdo Chaofu
Surpass Xuyou[33]
Despise the philosophers
Ignore the nobility.
His flaming ardor stretched to the sun
His frosty resolve surpassed the autumn.
He would sigh that the hermits were gone forever
Or deplore that recluses wandered no more.
He discoursed on the empty emptiness of the Buddhist sutras
He studied the murky mystery of Taoist texts.
A Wu Guang[34] could not compare with him
A Juanzi[35] was not fit to associate with him.
    But when
The belled messengers entered the valley

---

[28] A first-century recluse.
[29] Zhongchang Tong (179–219). [See above and chapter 9.]
[30] Zhou Yong (d. 485) whose apostasy is being rebuked in the Proclamation. He is better known as an early writer on phonology.
[31] A recluse (native of Lu) who refused a gift from the ruler. See *Zhuangzi*.
[32] Reached a state of trance through meditation. See *Zhuangzi*.
[33] Both refused the empire when Yao offered it to them.
[34] Threw himself into the river when Tang wanted to give him the throne.
[35] Taoist Immortal.

And the crane-summons reached his hill,
His body leapt and his souls scattered
His resolve faltered and his spirit wavered.
    Then
Beside the mat his eyebrows jumped
On the floor his sleeves danced.
He burned his castalia garments and tore his lotus clothes[36]
He raised a worldly face and carried on in a vulgar manner.
Wind-driven clouds grieved as they carried their anger
Rock-rimed springs sobbed as they trickled their disappointment.
Forests and crags appeared to lack something
Grass and trees seemed to have suffered loss.
    When he came to
Tie on his brass insignia
Fasten the black ribbon,
He was foremost of the leaders of provincial towns
He was first among the heads of a hundred villages.
He stretched his brave renown over the coastal precincts
He spread his fine repute through Zhejiang,
His Taoist books discarded for good
His dharma mat long since buried.
The cries and groans from beatings invade his thoughts
A succession of warrants and accusations pack his mind.
The Lute Song is interrupted
The Wine Poem is unfinished.
He is constantly involved in examinations
And is continually swamped by litigation.
He tries to cage Zhang Chang and Zhao Guanghan[37] of past fame
And seeks to shelve Zhuo Mao and Lu Gong[38] of the former records.
He hopes to succeed the worthies of the three Capital Districts
He wants to spread his fame beyond the Governors of the Nine
    Provinces.
    He has left our
High haze to reflect the light unwatched
Bright moon to rise in solitude
Dark pines to waste their shade

---

[36] Worn in imitation of Qu Yuan.

[37] Two successful minor officials of the first century B.C.

[38] Zhuo Mao (53–28 B.C.) was a prefect who treated the people as his children; Lu Gong (A.D. 32–112) was a model administrator whose district was spared by locusts.

White clouds with no companion.
The gate by the brook is broken, no one comes back
The stone pathway is overgrown, vain to wait for him.
    And now
The ambient breeze invades his bedcurtains
The seeping mist exhales from the rafters.
The orchid curtains are empty, at night his crane is grieved[39]
The mountain hermit is gone, mornings the apes are startled.
In the past we heard of one who cast away his cap-pin
    and retired to the seashore
Today we see one loosen his orchids
    and tie on a dirty cap instead.
    Whereupon
The Southern Peak presents us with its scorn
the Northern Range raises its laughter
All valleys strive in mockery
Every peak contends in contempt.
We regret that this vagrant has cheated us
We grieve that no one comes to condole.
    As a result
Our woods are ashamed without end
Our brooks humiliated with no reprieve.
Autumn cassia sends away the wind.
Spring wistaria refuses the moon.
We spread the word of the retirement to West Mountain
We broadcast the report of the resolve of East Marsh.
    Now today
He is hurrying to pack in his lowly town
With drumming oars to go up to the capital.
Though he is wholly committed to the court
He may still invade our mountain fastness.
    How can we permit our
Azaleas to be insulted again
Bili to be shameless
Green cliffs again humiliated
Red slopes further sullied?
He would dirty with his vagrant steps our lotus paths

---

[39] Taoist adepts used cranes for steeds in their flights through the air.

And soil the cleansing purity of the clear ponds.[40]
    We must
Bar our mountain windows
Close our cloud passes
Call back the light mist
Silence the noisy torrent
Cut off his approaching carriage at the valley mouth
Stop his impudent reins at the outskirts.
    Then
Massed twigs shall be filled with anger
Ranked buds shall have their souls enraged
Flying branches shall break his wheels
Drooping boughs shall sweep away his tracks.
Let us turn back the carriage of a worldly fellow
And decline on behalf of our lord a forsworn guest.

WU JUN (469–520)

Pleasure in Mountains and Streams

Translated by H. C. Chang

Several of Wu Jun's poems are included in the anthology *New Songs from a Jade Terrace*
[see chapter 13]. In the first of these two letters, he gives an account of a journey on
the Fuchun river, southwest of Hangzhou; in the second, of the scenery in his native
district near Anji in Zhejiang Province.

1: *From a Letter to Song Yuansi*

There was not a whiff of smoke or mist, and the color of the sky matched
the hills. We drifted with the current, which bore us now in one direction, now in another. Thus we traversed the hundred odd *li* from Fuyang
to Tonglu, through some of the best scenery in the world. The water was
throughout a clear green, and over the deepest pools we fancied we saw
to a depth of hundreds of feet; for we could see the fish swimming and
the pebbles on the riverbed. At times the current was swift as an arrow
and angry waves lashed our boat.

    The hills on either bank were planted with coniferous trees and rose
to a great height, seeming to vie with one another in steepness or

---

[40] The same as the waters of the Ying, where Chaofu washed his ears to remove the taint of
hearing Yao's offer.

eminence. There were hundreds of jutting peaks. The torrents dashed against the rocks as they came rushing down the hillsides, humming and gurgling. The birds sang melodiously in chorus. The chirping of cicadas was interrupted now and then by the apes' shrill cries. Even as the eagle desists from its soaring flight when confronted with a massive mountain, so those engaged in governmental affairs would forgo their worldly ambitions if they set eyes on one of the mysterious ravines, shrouded in perpetual twilight by thick overhanging trees forming a screen through which the sun but seldom penetrates.

2: From a Letter to Gu Zhang

Analects, VI, 21: "The wise find pleasure in water; the virtuous find pleasure in hills." Compare Zhuangzi, XXII: "Woody hills and marshy lakes make me joyful and glad; but before the joy is ended, sadness comes and succeeds to it.... Man's life between heaven and earth is like a white colt's passing a crevice, and suddenly disappearing."

Last month I obtained sick leave and returned to the life of a recluse. To the west of Plum Stream is Stone Gate Hill, whose precipices reflect the afterglow of early evening and whose peak challenges the noonday sun. Clouds glide in and out of its hidden caves, and the gorge below it is verdant with luxuriant vegetation. The cicadas chirp and the cranes squawk; the torrents scream and the monkeys chatter. What a strange chorus of discordant voices, though with a tunefulness all its own!

Having always preferred a life of solitude, I made my home there. It is my good fortune that the place abounds in chrysanthemums. There is also no lack of bamboo seeds, the staple diet and sole produce of those who dwell in this valley. There are no other riches, but it was not said in vain that the good and the wise find pleasure in mountains and streams.

ZU HONGXUN (died c. 550)

Eagle Hill (From a Letter to Yang Xiuzhi)

Translated by H. C. Chang

Zu Hongxun lived in the north and served under the Xianbei dynasty of Eastern Wei and the semi-Chinese dynasty of Northern Qi. This extract, like the two previous ones, demonstrates how the eyes and ears of the literary men of the fifth and sixth centuries were schooled to appreciate the sights and sounds of the natural world.

Being from a poor family with many aging relatives, I have more than once had to leave my official post in order to be with them in our native district. To the west of the county town is Eagle Hill, a secluded spot with a clear stream and rugged rocks, surrounded on all sides by high precipices. There we have several hundred *mou* of cultivated fields. We had a villa, too; but the wars left it in ruins, and now I have had it rebuilt. The rocks provided us with a foundation, and the neighboring woods supplied pillars and beams. A creeping vine adorns the exterior, and a stream winds round our front-door steps. The moonlight on the pinetrees and the winds rustling in the grass mark the boundary of our house. By the pond, like galaxies of stars, the yellow flowers of the leguminous Cloud Fruit glisten under the dancing rays of the sun. The curling smoke rising from our hearth blends with the mists. Against the pines and firs in our garden, the peach and plum trees show up their green foliage.

Setting out from the house, sometimes I would lift my robe and wade through a torrent or with the aid of a stick walk up the peak. As I made my lone ascent, my mind would become increasingly detached; my body would seem afloat and my very being ready to dissolve into nothingness. At such moments, I would no longer seem to be aware that I existed on earth, and I would remain thus a long while before returning home. At other times, I would sit by myself on a rock overhanging the stream and play on my guitar to the sound of rushing water; or recite verses in some concealed nook; or raise my goblet and drink to the moon. The shrill whistling of the wind would inspire my thoughts, and the piercing cry of the crane touch my heart. Then I would long for the state of untrammeled ease advocated by Zhuangzi and approve Shangzi's choice of the simple life.

At still other times, I would put on a coolie hat and a rush-and-grass raincloak to attend to the sowing of the millet and the planting of the rice, from which I would return to wait upon my aged parents. My feet are now my chariot, and I prize inactivity above all the useless bustle. And I shall be content to live thus, forgoing even the pleasure of good conversation.

YANG XUANZHI (fl. c. 550)

The Monasteries of Luoyang
Extracts

Translated by W. J. F. Jenner

Record of the Monasteries of Luoyang is a description of Luoyang, the Northern Wei capital that was founded in 493 and compulsorily evacuated in 534. This memoir, probably written within three years of the author's passing through the deserted ruins of the great capital he had known in both prosperity and decline as a court official, brings Luoyang to life with vivid descriptions of places, events, and people. It is the earliest substantial prose account of the Chinese city to survive. Its language is clear and expressive, avoiding the gratuitous ornateness and obscurity of some other writing of this period. The book's interest today lies in its wealth of factual information on a great and short-lived city — from ruins to a population of over half a million and back to ruins again in forty-one years — presented in a readable and rather informal style. Yang had access to official and private archives and may also have witnessed some of the events he describes. He ranges from palace coups and wars and rebellions to market gossip and ghost stories. The book has in it elements of private history, of the informal jottings of the *biji* (notebook) genre, of urban history, and of an anthology of the city's best writing.

Preface

The sayings of the Three Emperors and Five Kings of high antiquity and the words of the Nine Traditions and Hundred Schools of thought[41] coexist in the domain of men; their principles unify everything beyond the heavens. Of the fundamental teachings of the One Vehicle and Two Kinds of Truth, like the doctrines of the Three Insights and Six Faculties,[42] the West has full details, while the East has no record. After Emperor Xiaoming of the Han (A.D. 58–76) dreamed of a man crowned with the sun and shining like the full moon, figures with long eyebrows adorned the palace gates, and a Buddha with jet-black hair was painted in the Emperor's tomb.[43]

More recently there has been a rush to spread the influence of Buddhism. In the Yong-jia years (307–313) of the Jin dynasty there were only forty-two temples, but after the August Wei came to power and established its capital by Mount Song and the River Luo, Buddhist faith and teaching both flourished. Aristocrats and high officials parted with their horses and elephants as if they were kicking off their sandals; commoners and great families gave their wealth with the ease of leaving footprints. As a result monasteries and pagodas were packed closely together. Men competed in drawing the heavenly beauty of the Buddha, and in copying the image he left in the mountains. Monastery spires were as high as the Spirit Mound,[44] and the preaching halls were as grand as the Epang Palace.[45] It was, indeed, more than just

---

[41] Chinese traditions.

[42] Buddhist doctrines.

[43] The legend that China's conversion to Buddhism began with Emperor Xiaoming's dream was established long before the sixth century.

[44] Symbol of Chinese kingship.

[45] The great palace complex begun west of Xi'an by the First Emperor of Qin in 212 B.C. It was a byword for magnificence. Popularly pronounced "Afang."

Woods clothed in silk and embroidery,
Plaster covered with red and purple.[46]

When the many troubles of the years Yong-xi (532–34) caused the transfer of the imperial capital to Ye the monks and nuns of the temples moved there as well.

In *ding-mao*, the fifth year of Wu-ding (547), my official duties brought me back to Luoyang. The city walls had collapsed, palaces and houses were in ruins; Buddhist and Taoist temples were in ashes; and shrines and pagodas were mere heaps of rubble. Walls were covered with artemisia, and streets were full of thorns. The beasts of the field had made their holes in the overgrown palaces steps, and the mountain birds had nested in the courtyard trees. Wandering herdsmen loitered in the highways, and farmers had planted millet between the ceremonial towers before the palace. At last I knew that the ruins of the Yin capital were not the only ones to evoke sorrow when covered with ears of wheat,[47] and I felt the grief that the Song "Heavy hangs the millet" conveys about the decline of the Zhou.[48]

There had been over a thousand temples inside and outside the city wall, but now all were empty and the sound of their bells was never heard; so I compiled this record in case all this might be lost to posterity. There were so many temples that I could not describe them all. This account in five chapters is confined to the big monasteries, except where strange and miraculous events or popular stories justify the inclusion of the medium-sized and smaller ones. I begin with those inside the city wall and go on to those outside, listing them by city gates to give an idea of the distances. As I have no talent for writing there are many omissions; may gentlemen of later generations fill in my gaps.

Inside the City Wall

The Comptroller Monastery

The Comptroller Monastery was founded by Liu Teng. It was so called because Liu Teng had once been Comptroller of the Empress's Household. It was one *li* north of the imperial highway inside the Xiyang Gate.

---

[46] From *Zhang Heng*'s "Rhapsody on the Western Capital," describing the splendid aristocratic mansions of Han Chang'an.

[47] The former Yin minister Wei Zi is said to have written a poem called "Ears of Wheat" on passing the ruins of the Yin capital after the fall of the dynasty.

[48] *Book of Songs* 65, said to express the grief of a Zhou nobleman at seeing the ruins of Zhou palaces and temples.

This monastery was where the Gold Market of the Jin capital Zhongchao had been. North of the monastery was the Mengsi Pool that was full of water in summer but dry in winter.

Inside the monastery was a three-storyed pagoda the gleam of whose golden urn and sacred pole could be seen throughout the city. There was also a statue of a six-tusked elephant bearing Sākyamuni Buddha on its back through the void.[49] The ornaments and Buddha statues were made entirely of gold and jewels, and its unique workmanship would beggar description. On the fourth of the fourth month it used to be taken out in procession,[50] with lions and gryphons leading the way before it. Sword-swallowers and fire-belchers pranced on one side of the procession; there were men who climbed flagpoles, rope-walkers and every kind of amazing trick. Their skill was greater and their clothes stranger than anywhere else in the capital, and wherever the statue rested spectators would pack round in a solid crowd in which people were often trampled to death.[51]

The Precious Light Convent

The Precious Light Convent, founded by Shizong, the Emperor Xuanwu, was inside the Changhe Gate of the city wall to the north of the imperial highway. Two *li* to the east of it was the Qianqiu (Thousand Autumns) Gate of the palace.

Inside the Qianqiu Gate of the palace and north of the highway was the Xiyou Park (Park of the Westward Journey). Inside the park was the Lingyun (Cloud-Touching) Tower, which had been built by the Emperor Wen of the Cao Wei. Beside the Tower was the Octagonal Well, and to the north of this Emperor Gaozu built the Liangfeng (Cool Breeze) Pavilion. If one climbed this one could see right up the Luo River. Below the Lingyun Tower was the Quchi (Curving Pond) of the Bihai (Jade-green Lake). East of the tower was the Xuanci (Mercy Proclaimed) Pavilion, which was 100 feet high. East of the pavilion was the Lingzhi (Magic Fungus) Fishing Tower, built on wooden piles which raised it over 200 feet above the water. Breezes were born from its doors and windows while clouds rose from its beams and rafters; its red columns and carved beams had immortals painted on them. The Fishing Tower was borne on the back of a carved stone whale that seemed to be leaping up from the

---

[49] To his earthly mother's womb.

[50] Processions of statues in honor of the Buddha's birthday came to China from Central Asia and were an annual event in Pingcheng before the move.

[51] Many of the acts had Central Asian connections. An acrobatic troupe had been established by the dynasty's founder in 403.

ground or flying down from the sky. To the south of the Fishing Tower was the Xuanguang Hall (Hall of Glory Proclaimed); to the north was the Jiafu Hall (Hall of the Great Blessing); to its west was the Jiulong (Nine Dragon) Hall in front of which was a pool filled by water coming from the mouths of nine dragons. All four of these halls were connected by "flying passageways" to the Lingzhi Fishing Tower where the Emperor stayed in the dog days of summer to avoid the heat.

The Precious Light Convent had a five-storyed pagoda five hundred feet high on top of which "immortal hands" touched the void and bells hung down above the clouds. The excellence of the workmanship matched that of the Yongning Monastery. There were over five hundred preaching rooms and nuns' cells. Carved patterns spread from one wall to the next, and the rooms were connected by doors and windows. One could not describe the wealth of rare trees and fragrant plants: "ox-sinew" and "dog-bone" trees, "chicken-heads" (water lilies), and "ducks-feet" (mallows) were all there. This was where the Junior Consorts and Imperial Concubines from the Scented Apartments studied the Way, with the Beauties of the Side Court among them.[52] There were also maidens of famous families who in their love for this place of enlightenment cut off their hair and left their parents to worship in this nunnery. Abandoning their jewelled finery they put on religious habits, placed their faith in the Eightfold Path, and came back to belief in the One Vehicle.

When in the third year of Yong-an (530) Erzhu Zhao entered Luoyang and allowed his troops to loot, some dozens of Hu horsemen from Xiurong entered the nunnery and committed rape. This gave rise to some jeering and the saying went round the capital, "When the women of the capital were desperately braiding their hair,[53] the nuns of precious Light Convent were grabbing husbands."

North of the Precious Light Convent was the Chengming Gate and the Jinyong Castle that had been built by the Cao Wei. During the Yong-kang years (330–331) of the Jin dynasty the Emperor Hui was imprisoned inside this wall. East was the small Luoyang Wall built during Yong-jia (307–313). In the northeast corner of the Jinyong Castle was the Hundred-Foot Tower of the Emperor Wen of the Cao Wei. It still looked as it had when new despite its age. Inside the castle Gaozu built the Guangji Hall (Hall of the Brilliant Ultimate), after which he named the gate in the Jinyong Castle the Guangji Gate. He also built multi-storyed

---

[52] These designations are bureaucratic ranks in descending order.
[53] Presumably to disguise their sex as men they wore a pair of braided topknots.

buildings and flying passageways that soared all around the wall and
looked like clouds when seen from the ground.

The Great Happiness Convent

The Great Happiness Convent was founded by the Grand Instructor
Yuan Yi, Prince Wenxian of Qinghe.

Yuan Yi was a son of the Emperor Xiaowen (Gaozu) and younger
brother of the Emperor Xuanwu (Shizong). The convent was south of
the Changhe (Palace) Gate and east of the imperial highway. The Yongning Monastery was directly opposite to the west of the highway. To the
west of the convent was the High Premier's Office, east of it was the
mansion of the Senior General Gao Zhao, and to the north it bounded
the Yijing (Well of Justice) ward. Outside the north gate of this ward was
a copse of trees under whose foliage was a sweetwater well with a stone
tank and an iron pitcher. This provided water and shade for passersby,
and many people rested here.

In the nunnery there was a Buddha-hall in which was kept a carriage
for a Buddha-statue. The carving in this hall was the finest of the age.
Lodges and porticoes surrounded it on all sides and rooms led from one
to another. Delicate branches brushed against the doors, and blossom
covered the courtyards. At the six maigre-feasts there were always women
musicians.

YAN ZHITUI (531–c. 590)

Last Will

from *Family Instructions for the Yan Clan*

Translated by Teng Ssu-yü

Yan Zhitui lived in troubled times. He served under the Liang dynasty, under the
Northern Qi dynasty (following the fall of the Liang), and finally under the Sui
dynasty (established in 581). Although he wrote poetry and historical and lexi-
cographical works, he is best known for his *Family Instructions*. Some critics identify
him as one of the earliest proponents of the simpler *guwen* (or "ancient") style of
prose, later championed by Han Yu [see chapter 27].

Death is every man's lot; it cannot be avoided. At the age of nineteen, I
experienced the disorder of the destruction of the Liang dynasty. Under
those conditions there were several occasions when I faced a bright
sword, but fortunately, by the merits inherited from my ancestors, I have
survived until now. The ancients said, "Fifty years are not to be regarded
as a short life." I am already over sixty, my heart is quite calm, and I have

no worries for my declining years. I have already suffered from apoplexy and constantly expect a sudden end, so I am jotting down my long-cherished wishes as a warning to you.

Neither my father nor my mother was brought back to our old burial hill at Jianye,[54] but they were buried in the eastern suburb of Jiangling where we were sojourning.[55] At the end of the Cheng-sheng period (555), I reported on this and petitioned the authorities at Yangdu,[56] expressing my desire for removal of the coffins there. Receiving the gracious contribution of a hundred ounces of silver, I had bricks baked north of a small field outside of Yangzhou. The overthrow of our dynasty (556) stopped the work. My wanderings for several decades since that time destroyed any hope for arranging the removal. Though the nation is now (559) reunited, our family means are exhausted. How could we raise funds for the proper interment? Moreover, Yangdu has been entirely destroyed, and nothing remains. It is not a good plan to remove the coffins to a low and damp place. My self-reproach pierces my heart and bones.

My brothers and I should not have entered government service, but because of the decline of our clan fortune, the weakness of our family members, the lack of superior persons within five generations ... I have brazenly taken a public post, hoping to preserve the family status from a fall. Moreover the government regulations in the North are so strict that no one is permitted to retire.

Now, old and sick as I am, if I should suddenly expire, how could I ask for full funeral rites? Just bathe the body on the first day after the arms have stiffened and dress it in ordinary clothes; do not trouble about "recalling the soul." At our late mother's death, which was during a time of famine, our family resources were exhausted and we brothers were young and weak, so the coffin was thin and roughly made; no bricks were used in the grave. I deserve only a pine coffin, two inches thick, and nothing to accompany me into the tomb besides my clothes and hat. On top of the coffin, place only a seven-star board.[57] Other objects such as a waxed crossbow, an ivory or jade pig, and pewter men should all be omitted. Jars of provisions and mortuary figures must not be prepared; a biographical stele and elegiac scrolls cannot be considered. Carry the

---

[54] Near Nanjing.
[55] In Hubei.
[56] Nanjing.
[57] On the so-called seven-star board seven figures as large as pieces of money were cut and linked together by lines to represent the constellation of the seven stars of the Big Dipper on the inner coffin.

coffin on a clamshell hearse, and bury it underground with no grave mound. If you fear that you will not know where to find the grave for future sacrifices, you may build a low wall at the left, right, front and back of the tomb to serve as a private sign. In the soul shrine, do not prepare any pillow or couch. In sacrifices on the first and fifteenth of the month, there must be no wine, meat, cakes or fruit; offer only white congee, clean water, and dry jujubes. Stop all relatives and friends who come to offer libations of wine. If you, my children, disobey my wishes and treat me better than I did my mother, you will make your father seem unfilial. Could you then feel happy?

... I am now wandering like a floating cloud. I know not what district will be my burial place. Wherever I expire, just bury me there. You children should make it your task to hand on what I have done and make known your good name; do not lavish loving attention on what is perishable under the soil and thereby bring destruction upon yourselves.

ZHOU XINGSI (fl. 550)

The Thousand Character Classic
Extracts

Translated by E. C. Bridgman (1835)

This work is unique among all the books in the Chinese language, and its like could not be produced in any other, in that it consists of just a thousand characters, no two of which are alike in form or meaning. There are several more or less apocryphal accounts of how it came to be written. It is China's oldest primer, and has been used for hundreds of years to teach reading to Chinese children and as a text for calligraphers to copy. The text (much of which is doggerel) was so familiar that the characters in it were sometimes used as an alternative way of counting or numbering from one to a thousand.

The heavens are somber; the earth is yellow;
The whole universe at the creation was one wide waste ...
Now this our human body is endowed
With four great powers and five cardinal virtues:
Preserve with reverence what your parents nourished —
How dare you destroy or injure it?
Let females guard their chastity and purity,
And let men imitate the talented and virtuous.
When you know your own errors then reform;
And when you have made acquisitions do not lose them.
Forbear to complain of the defects of other people,

And cease to brag of your own superiority ...
Observe and imitate the conduct of the virtuous,
And command your thoughts that you may be wise.
Your virtue once fixed, your reputation will be established;
Your habits once rectified, your example will be correct.
Sounds reverberate in the deep valleys,
And the vacant hall re-echoes all it hears;
So misery is the penalty of accumulated vice,
And happiness the reward of illustrious virtue ...
Years fly away like arrows, one pushing on the other;
The sun shines brightly through his whole course.
The planetarium revolves where it hangs;
And the moon turns from darkness to light.
To feed the fire, add fuel; so cultivate the root of happiness,
And you will obtain eternal peace and endless felicity....

🔁 *Further Reading* 🔁

Balazs, Etienne (trans. H. M. Wright, ed. Arthur F. Wright). *Chinese Civilization and Bureaucracy: Variations on a Theme.* New Haven: Yale University Press, 1964.
Bridgman, E. C., trans. *"Tseën Tsze Wan, or the Thousand Character Classic." Chinese Repository* (September 1835).
Chang, H. C., ed. and trans. *Chinese Literature, Vol. 2: Nature Poetry.* Edinburgh: University of Edinburgh Press, 1977.
Chang, Kang-i Sun. *Six Dynasties Poetry.* Princeton: Princeton University Press, 1986.
de Bary, William Theodore, Chan Wing-tsit, & Burton Watson, eds. *Sources of Chinese Tradition.* New York: Columbia University Press, 1960. (Contains Zong Bing's essay "On Landscape Painting.")
Giles, Herbert, trans. *The Travels of Fa-hsien.* Cambridge: Cambridge University Press, 1923.
————. *Gems of Chinese Literature: Prose.* 2d rev. ed. London: Quaritch, 1926.
Hightower, J. R. "Some Characteristics of Parallel Prose." In Sören Egerod & Else Glahn, eds. *Studia Serica Bernhard Karlgren Dedicata.* Copenhagen: Ejnar Munskgaard, 1959.
Holzman, Donald. "The Wang Ziqiao Stele." *Rocznik Orientalistyczny,* 47 (2) (1991).
Jenner, W.J.F., trans. *Memories of Loyang: Yang Hsüan-chih and the Lost Capital.* Oxford: Oxford University Press, 1981.
Knechtges, David, trans. *Wen Xuan or Selections of Refined Literature.* Several vols. Princeton: Princeton University Press, 1982–.
Medhurst, Walter. *China: Its State and Prospects.* London: Snow, 1838.
Renditions 33–34, "Special Issue: Classical Prose." Hong Kong: Research Centre for Translation, Chinese University, 1990.
Teng Ssu-yü, trans. *Family Instructions for the Yen Clan.* Leiden: E. J. Brill, 1968.

Chapter 15

The Carving of Dragons

Early Literary Criticism

雕文
龍心

Poetry expresses in words the intent of the heart.
— "The Canon of Shun," from the *Book of History*

What is of the greatest importance in literature is the Vital Breath.
— Cao Pi (187–226), "On Literature"

> We poets struggle with Non-being
> to force it to yield Being;
> we knock upon Silence
> for an answering Music.

— Lu Ji (261–303), "Literature: A Rhapsody"

In my title "literary mind" refers to the application of the mind to literature; as in the titles of Juanzi's *The Lute Mind* [a lost Taoist work] and Wangsunzi's *The Inventive Mind* [a Confucian text, fragments of which survive] ... Literature has since olden times attained form through carving and richness of detail; in my title, "the carving of dragons" [refers to this craft of letters, it] does not refer to [the ornamental skill of] old "Dragon-Carver" Zou Shi [a pre-Qin literary figure].

— Liu Xie (c. 465–520), *The Literary Mind and the Carving of Dragons*, chapter 50, "Afterword"

The Style of the Chinese in their Compositions is abstruse, concise, allegorical, and sometimes obscure to those who are not well versed in the Characters. It requires skill to make no Mistakes in reading an Author; they say many Things in a few Words; their Expressions are lively, animated, and intermix'd with bold Comparisons, and noble Metaphors.

— Du Halde, *A Description of the Empire of China*, 1738

In China letters are respected not merely to a degree but in a sense which must seem, I think, to you unintelligible and overstrained. But there is a reason for it. Our poets and literary men have taught their successors, for long generations, to look for good not in wealth, not in power, not in miscellaneous activity, but in a trained, a choice, an exquisite appreciation of the most simple and universal relations of life. To feel, and in order to feel to express, or at least to understand the expression of all that is lovely in Nature, of all that is poignant and sensitive to man, is to us in itself a sufficient end. A rose in a moonlit garden, the shadow of trees on the turf, almond blossom, the scent of pine, the wine-cup and the guitar; these and the pathos of life and death, the long embrace, the hand stretched out in vain, the moment that glides for ever away, with its freight of music and light, into the shadow and hush of the haunted past, all that we have, all that eludes us, a bird on the wing, a perfume escaped on the gale — to all these things we are trained to respond, and the response is what we call literature.

— G. Lowes Dickinson, *Letters from John Chinaman*, 1901

Introduction

Craig Fisk

The first work of Chinese literature devoted to literary criticism is generally considered to be Cao Pi's essay "On Literature." This work provides a short criticism of each of the Jian-an Masters, who were the leading contemporary writers, as well as of Qu Yuan, Jia Yi, and other earlier poets. It also includes remarks on the characteristics of four genres: memorials, personal letters and essays, the epigraph, and poetic writing in the lyric or ode forms. In the latter section Cao Pi puts forward his theory of the Vital Breath in literature. The quality of a work is a reflection of the Vital Breath of its author, a concept that remains important in later poetry criticism.

After this there gradually came to be more and more writings concerned exclusively with literary criticism during the Six Dynasties. Two factors are important here. One is the making of literary anthologies, to which critical essays largely historical in form were often appended. The other is the influence of abstract modes of thought from early Chinese Buddhism.

Lu Ji's "Literature: A Rhapsody," an elaborate, poetic essay on literature, might best be described as a rhapsody on the metaphysics, craft, and psychology of literary composition.

With Liu Xie's *The Literary Mind and the Carving of Dragons* in the early sixth century, literary criticism becomes a substantial and completely independent enterprise. The fifty chapters of *The Literary Mind* are equally divided between discussions of all the major literary genres and discussions of what might best be called the dynamics of literary works, i.e. their form, style, use of material, and rhetorical structure. Liu Xie seems to be simultaneously motivated by both Confucian and Buddhist ideas, because he argues for the use of the Confucian Classics as models for contemporary writing, yet takes a strongly Buddhist-influenced approach to the abstract analysis that goes into his technical chapters. Secondly, even though he wants writers to take the Confucian Classics as models and to be diverse in their generic capabilities, Liu Xie's technical chapters clearly show that his conception of literature is dominated by the lyric poetry and odes of the early third to the early fifth centuries. Perhaps it is best to say that *The Literary Mind* is a moderately conservative book of criticism written in a period when the distinction between literary and non-literary writing was not yet sharp, and that it redefined the classics *as* literature.

— *Indiana Companion*, 1986

The "Great Preface" to The *Book of Songs*
Extract

Translated by Samuel Kidd (1841)

It is uncertain exactly when the "Great Preface" reached its present form, but we can be reasonably sure that it was no later than the first century A.D. Many readers accepted it as the work of Confucius's disciple Zixia and thus saw in it an unbroken tradition of teaching about the *Book of Songs* that could be traced back to Confucius himself. A more learned and skeptical tradition took the "Great Preface" as the work of one Wei Hong, a scholar of the first century A.D. It is probably anachronistic to apply the concept of "composition" (except in its root sense of "putting together") to the "Great Preface"; rather it is a loose synthesis of shared "truths" about the *Book of Songs*, truths which were the common possession of traditionalists in the Warring States and Former Han periods.

— Stephen Owen, *Readings in Chinese Literary Thought*, 1992

Poetry is the natural tendency of the human will which resides in the heart. Its essence consists in internal excitement; its external form in suitable expressions, which, aided by sighs and groans, broke out into eternal songs, which were still found insufficient to express the emotions of the soul even before posture-making and dancing were discovered as its ultimate requirements. The inward workings of the animal nature, in other words the seven passions — joy, anger, grief, fear, love, hatred, desire — displayed in sounds, which by cultivation became musical, were the true sources of the influence poetry obtained in ruling over the world. If these sounds were peaceful and joyful, they indicated the prosperity of the government; if resentful and acrimonious, its perversity; but if marked by grief and commiseration, then they proclaimed the lost state of the nation. As the passions differ in their nature, so also must the notes of music, which are clear and thick, high and low, swift and slow, mutually responding in harmony; wherefore, in adjusting your affairs of profit and loss, influencing demons and gods, and moving heaven and earth, there is nothing equal to poetry. For the recitation of odes in a musical tone impels the prosperous to the utmost point of harmony and peace, rouses the unfortunate to the highest pitch of anger and resentment, is sufficiently powerful to penetrate the elements of the first two principles (Yin and Yang), to promote felicity and call down calamities. Since poetry proceeds from nature, and is not dependant on human strength, it pierces the deepest recesses of man and penetrates his swiftest movements, to which no other medium of instruction can reach. By poetry, former Kings regulated matrimony, perfected filial piety, honored the human relations, adorned the renovating influences of education, and changed the national customs.

The same extract

Translated by Stephen Owen

The poem is that to which what is intently on the mind goes. In the mind it is "being intent"; coming out in language, it is a poem.

   The affections are stirred within and take on form in words. If words alone are inadequate, we speak them out in sighs. If sighing is inadequate, we sing them. If singing them is inadequate, unconsciously our hands dance them and our feet tap them. The affections emerge in sounds; when those sounds have patterning, they are called "tones." The tones of a well-managed age are at rest and happy; its government is balanced. The tones of an age of turmoil are bitter and full of anger; its government is perverse. The tones of a ruined state are filled with lament and brooding; its people are in difficulty.

Thus to correct achievements and failures, to move Heaven and Earth, to stir the gods and spirits, there is nothing more apposite than poetry. By it the former kings managed the relations between husbands and wives, perfected the respect due to parents and superiors, gave depth to human relations, beautifully taught and transformed the people, and changed local customs.

CAO PI (187–226)

On Literature

Translated by Siu-kit Wong

This essay, by the Emperor Wen of Wei (son of Cao Cao and brother of Cao Zhi), is perhaps the earliest attempt in China to put literature on a pedestal. It is also the earliest evidence of an awareness of literary genres, and genres have subsequently preoccupied the minds of many Chinese critics. The Vital Breath discussed in the essay is also a recurrent theme in all Chinese literary criticism.

It has been the case from the ancient past that men of letters hold one another in scorn. In literary abilities Fu Yi (d. 89 B.C.) was hardly inferior to Ban Gu,[1] and yet was belittled by the latter, who said in a letter to Ban Zhao, his younger brother: "And what of Fu Yi's being made a Librarian of the Palace Library because 'he could write'? As soon as he puts pen to paper he is lost and never knows where to stop." The truth is that it is easy for us to see the particular merits in ourselves; it is also true that, while literature encompasses a variety of styles, few writers are equally accomplished in all of them; as a result, one's own forte often becomes the ground on which to level attacks on fellow-writers gifted in other ways. A common saying has it that the baldest broom in one's own household is worth a thousand pieces of gold. The disparagement of others proceeds from an imperfect knowledge of oneself.

---

[1] See chapter 7. *Eds.*

But there are seven masters in our own generation — Kong Rong, Chen Lin, Wang Can, Xu Gan, Ruan Yu, Ying Yang, and Liu Zhen[2] — who, as men of letters, are impeccable in their scholarship and original each in his own style, and who, in spite of my opening remarks, ride, as it were, the finest steeds, and gallop shoulder to shoulder for thousands of miles on the pastures of literary art, in full appreciation of one another's genius. Is this not a phenomenon rare to behold? It takes men of the finest qualities to judge themselves before they judge others, and to escape the above-mentioned dangers inherent in the discussion of literature.

Wang Can is particularly good at rhapsodies. Xu Gan, though occasionally sluggish in his Vital Breath, is nonetheless a match for Wang. Neither Zhang Heng nor Cai Yong could outshine certain pieces of theirs ... But it would be difficult for Wang and Xu to meet with approbation in other genres of writing. The memorials, petitions, and official records of Chen Lin and Ruan Yu are amongst the most elegant written in our time. Ying Yang has harmony but lacks force. Liu Zhen has force but suffers from looseness. Kong Rong is by nature noble and sublime, and in that he surpasses his contemporaries; but he is incapable of sustained argument, his logic being weaker than his rhetoric; as for his writings in which there is an admixture of elements of mockery and jest, surely, in them he is on a par with Yang Xiong and Ban Gu.[3]

Men of average intelligence are given to treasuring what comes from afar and regarding what comes from nearby with contempt; turning their back on facts, they bow to reputations. They are also prone to overrate themselves out of benighted self-ignorance. Literature is all one thing in essence, but a range of things in its accidental manifestations. Official memorials and discourses on state matters should be formally elegant; letters and essays should be orderly; elegiac and other inscriptions should be reliably factual; poetry and rhapsodies should be ornate. These four types of writing are each distinctive in its own way and a writer is usually capable of handling one of them competently: it takes a genius of many-faceted abilities to do equally well in all four types.

What is of the greatest importance in literature is the Vital Breath, which is either pure or impure in character, and the purity or impurity cannot be attained by force. This may be compared with what obtains in music. Given the same song, in which melody and rhythm may well be harmonious, the tempo and changes in tempo equally well-controlled,

---

[2] For works of six of the Seven Masters of the Jian-an Period, see chapter 9. *Eds.*
[3] For Zhang Heng and Yang Xiong, see chapters 6 and 9. *Eds.*

the use of the Vital Breath is bound to vary from singer to singer in rendering the song, and the degree of skill in the singer is as if predetermined, it is something which even a father cannot change in his son, or an elder brother in his younger brother.

Literature is no less noble an activity than the governing of a state; it is also a way to immortality. The years pass and one's life runs out its natural course. Honors and pleasures cease to be with one's mortal frame. Against these inexorable facts, literature lives on to eternity. Ancient authors who chose the brush and ink as an abode for their being, and expressed themselves on tablets for writing, had their names and reputations perpetuated, and they would have done so even without the help that their positions in their life-time might have lent them. King Wen was a man in dark distress when he wrote his Commentary on the *Book of Changes.* The Duke of Zhou was an eminent person when he devised his code of rites. Misfortune did not deter the one from writing, nor prosperity the other. We can thus see how our fathers, fearing the passage of time, valued a brief moment more than a piece of jade a foot long. Nowadays, how men refuse to apply themselves! In poverty, they tremble with cold and hunger. In wealth, they drift in easy pleasures. The affairs of the day are seen to, but the task that matters more down the ages is altogether ignored. Above, the sun and the moon vanish in turn; below, mortal flesh comes to decay and, sooner than one realizes, suffers disintegration with things in nature. How this must grieve anyone who has a sense of purpose. Kong Rong and his friends are now dead. Perhaps Xu Gan alone succeeded as an original author in his *Discourses.*

LU JI (261–303)

Literature: A Rhapsody

Translated by Achilles Fang

Lu Ji's "Literature: A Rhapsody" [for Lu Ji, see chapter 9] is concerned with the process of writing, from the search that precedes inspiration to the transforming effect on the reader that follows putting down the pen. In between, the writer's task is to harmonize his inner world of thoughts and feelings with the outer world of things, and to find words to match his perception of meaning or truth.... The protagonist of the Rhapsody, like the shaman-hero of the "Far-off Journey" in the *Songs of the South* [see chapter 5], undertakes a cosmic journey or hunt for the right expressions. His flight of fancy — the act of writing — comprises three stages. First he gathers fuel. Next he compresses his far-flung material in his mind, achieving a concentrated view of the world and his work. Finally, the completed work flows from his pen with the force of a rushing wind to carry out literature's task of mortal transformation. This is the first systematic treatment of literary criticism in Chinese and one of only a few to be cast in literary form. It pays attention to the definition of genres in more detail than Cao Pi's "On Literature," and is concerned with the description and solution of faults. Unlike many of its successors, it is unconcerned with questions of literary history, the relative ranking of poets, or the appreciation of famous lines.

— Richard Bodman, *Indiana Companion*, 1986

This compact essay is considered one of the most articulate treatises on Chinese poetics.... Accepting Mr Bernard Berenson's challenge, "Then dare to translate the ancient Chinese and Indian thinkers" (*Sketch for a Self-Portrait*), I felt that I had to make my translation independently [of earlier versions] on the basis of "my little psychosinology." I am grateful to Mr Archibald MacLeish for the interest he has taken in my translation. If it is at all readable, it is due in great measure to him.

— Achilles Fang, 1951

Preface

Each time I study the works of great writers,
    I flatter myself I know how their minds worked.
Certainly expression in language
    and the charging of words with meaning
    can be done in various ways.
Nevertheless we may speak of beauty and ugliness,
    of good and bad in each literary work.
Whenever I write myself,
    I obtain greater and greater insight.
Our constant worry is that our ideas may not equal their objects
    and our style may fall short of our ideas.[4]
The difficulty, then, lies not so much in knowing as in doing.[5]
I have written this rhapsody on literature
    to expatiate on the consummate artistry of writers of the past
    and to set forth the whence and why of good and bad writings as
    well.
May it be considered, someday, an exhaustive treatment.
Now, it is true, I am hewing an ax handle with an ax handle in my
hand:
    the pattern is not far to seek.[6]

---

[4] Essentially a restatement of the Confucian saying in the *Book of Changes*: "The written characters are not the full exponent of speech, and speech is not the full expression of ideas." (Legge's translation)

[5] The incommensurability supposed to exist between knowledge and action had already found expression in the *Zuo Commentary*: "It is not the knowing a thing that is difficult, it is the acting accordingly." (Legge's translation)

[6] Allusion to *Song* 158.

However, the conjuring hand of the artist being what it is,
    I cannot possibly make my words do the trick.
Nevertheless, what I am able to say
    I have put down here.

Preparation

Taking his position at the hub of things,
    the writer contemplates the mystery of the universe;
    he feeds his emotions and his mind
    on the great works of the past.
Moving along with the four seasons,
    he sighs at the passing of time;
    gazing at the myriad objects,
    he thinks of the complexity of the world.
He sorrows over the falling leaves in virile autumn;
    he takes joy in the delicate bud of fragrant spring.
With awe at heart, he experiences chill;
    his spirit solemn, he turns his gaze to the clouds.
He declaims the superb works of his predecessors;
    he croons the clean fragrance of past worthies.
He roams in the Forests of Literature,
    and praises the symmetry of great art.
Moved, he pushes his books away and takes the writing-brush,
    that he may express himself in letters.

Process

At first he withholds his sight,
    and turns his hearing inward;
    he is lost in thought,
    questioning everywhere.
His spirit gallops to the eight ends of the universe;
    his mind wanders along vast distances.
In the end, as his mood dawns clearer and clearer,
    objects, clean-cut now in outline,
    shove one another forward.
He sips the essence of letters;
    he rinses his mouth with the extract of the Six Arts.[7]

---

[7] The Six Arts of the *Zhou Ritual*: ceremonies, music, archery, horsemanship, calligraphy, and mathematics. Or, the Six Confucian "Arts": the Books of *Song, History, Changes, Ceremonies, Music* and the *Spring and Autumn Annals*.

Floating on the heavenly lake, he swims along;
    plunging into the nether spring, he immerses himself.
Thereupon, submerged words wriggle up,
    as when a darting fish with the hook in its gills,
    leaps from a deep lake;
    floating beauties flutter down,
    as when a high-flying bird,
    with the harpoon-string around its wings,
    drops from a crest of cloud.
He gathers words never used in a hundred generations;
    he picks rhythms never sung in a thousand years.
He spurns the morning blossom, now full blown;
    he plucks the evening bud, which has yet to open.
He sees past and present in a moment;
    he touches the four seas in the twinkling of an eye.

Words, Words, Words

Now he selects ideas and fixes them in their order;
    he examines words and puts them in their places.
He taps at the door of all that is colorful;
    he chooses from among everything that rings.
Now he shakes the foliage by tugging the twig;
    now he follows back along the waves
    to the fountainhead of the stream.
Sometimes he brings out what was hidden;
    sometimes, looking for an easy prey,
    he bags a hard one.[8]
Now, the tiger puts on new stripes,
    to the consternation of other beasts;
    now, the dragon emerges,
    and terrifies all the birds.
Sometimes things fit together,
    are easy to manage;
    sometimes they jar each other,
    are awkward to manipulate.
He empties his mind completely,
    to concentrate his thoughts;

---

[8] Like Saul, who sought his father's asses and found a kingdom.

he collects his wits
before he puts words together.
He traps heaven and earth
in the cage of form;
he crushes the myriad objects
against the tip of his brush,
At first they hesitate upon his parched lips;
finally they flow
through the well-moistened brush.
Reason, supporting the matter of the poem,
stiffens the trunk;
style, depending from it,
spreads luxuriance around.
Emotion and expression never disagree:
all changes in his mood
are betrayed on his face.
If the thought touches on joy,
a smile is inevitable;
no sooner is sorrow spoken of
than a sigh escapes.
Sometimes words flow easily
as soon as he grasps the brush;
sometimes he sits vacantly,
nibbling at it.

Virtue

There is joy in this vocation;
all sages esteem it.
We poets struggle with Non-being
to force it to yield Being;
we knock upon Silence
for an answering Music.
We enclose boundless space
in a square foot of paper;
we pour out a deluge
from the inch-space of the heart.
Language spreads wider and wider;
thought probes deeper and deeper.
The fragrance of delicious flowers is diffused;
exuberant profusion of green twigs is budding.

A laughing wind will fly and whirl upward;
    dense clouds will arise
    from the Forest of Writing Brushes.

Diversity

(i) The Poet's Aim

Forms vary in a thousand ways;
    objects are not of one measure.
Topsy-turvy and fleeting,
    shapes are hard to delineate.
Words vie with words for display,
    but it is mind that controls them.[9]
Confronted with bringing something into being
    or leaving it unsaid,
    he groans;
    between the shallow and the deep
    he makes his choice resolutely.
He may depart from the square
    and deviate from the compasses;
    for he is bent on exploring the shape
    and exhausting the reality.
Hence, he who would dazzle the eyes
    makes much of the gorgeous;
    he who intends to convince the mind
    values cogency.
If persuasion is your aim,
    do not be a stickler for details;
    when your discourse is lofty,
    you may be free and easy in your language.

(ii) Genres

Shi (lyric poetry) traces emotions daintily;[10]
    Fu (rhapsody) embodies objects brightly.

---

[9] "For he who has the 'power' of Tao is the Grand Almoner." Arthur Waley, trans., *The Way and Its Power*, p. 239.
[10] The ten literary genres discussed in this and the four following couplets do not, of course, exhaust the literature of Lu Ji's days, and yet they seem to be the most important ones.

Bei (epitaph) balances substance with style;
    Lei (dirge) is tense and mournful.
Ming (inscription) is comprehensive and concise,
    gentle and generous;
    Zhen (admonition), which praises and blames,
    is clear-cut and vigorous.
Song (eulogy) is free and easy,
    rich and lush;
    Lun (disquisition) is rarified and subtle,
    bright and smooth.
Zou (memorial to the throne) is quiet and penetrating,
    genteel and decorous;
    Shuo (discourse) is dazzling bright
    and extravagantly bizarre.

Different as these forms are,
    they all forbid deviation from the straight,
    and interdict unbridled license.[11]
Essentially, words must communicate,[12]
    and reason must dominate;
    prolixity and long-windedness
    are not commendable.

Multiple Aspects

As an object,
    literature puts on numerous shapes;
    as a form,
    it undergoes diverse changes.
Ideas should be cleverly brought together;
    language should be beautifully commissioned.
And the mutation of sounds and tones
    should be like the five colors of embroidery
    sustaining each other.

---

[11] This line alludes to the Confucian dictum on the design of the three hundred *Songs*: "Having no depraved thoughts."

[12] Another Confucian dictum, which can be interpreted in a dozen different ways. At any rate, as Wallace Stevens writes ("Chocorua to Its Neighbor"): "To say more than human things with human voice,/That cannot be; to say human things with more/Than human voice, that, also, cannot be;/To speak humanly from the height or from the depth/Of human things, that is acutest speech." Which is as good an interpretation as any.

It is true that your moods,
    which come and go without notice,
    embarrass you by their fickleness,
But if you can rise to all emergencies
    and know the correct order,
    it will be like opening a channel
    from a spring of water.
If, however, you have missed the chance
    and reach sense belatedly,
    you will be putting the tail at the head —
The sequence of dark and yellow being deranged,
    the whole broidery will be smudged and blurred.

Revision

Now you glance back
    and are constrained by an earlier passage;
    now you look forward and are coerced
    by some anticipated line.
Sometimes your words jar
    though your reasoning is sound;
    sometimes your language is smooth
    while your ideas make trouble;
Such collisions avoided, neither suffers;
    forced together, both suffer.
Weigh merit or demerit by the milligram;
    decide rejection or retention by a hairbreadth.
If your idea or word has not the correct weight,
    it has to go,
    however comely it may look.

Key Passages

Maybe your language is already ample,
    and your reasoning rich,
    yet your ideas do not round out.
If what must go on cannot be ended,
    what has been said in full cannot be added to.
Put down terse phrases here and there at key positions;
    they will invigorate the entire piece.
Your words will acquire their proper values
    in the light of these phrases.

This clever trick will spare you
    the pain of deleting and excising.

Plagiarism

It may be that language and thought
    blend into damascened gauze —
    fresh, gay, and exuberantly lush;
Glowing like many-colored broidery,
    mournful as multiple chords;[13]
But assuredly there is nothing novel in my writing,
    if it coincides with earlier masterpieces.
True, the arrow struck my heart;
    what a pity, then,
    that others were struck before me.
As plagiarism will impair my integrity
    and damage my probity,
    I must renounce the piece,
    however fond I am of it.

Purple Patches

It may be that one ear of the stalk buds,
    its tip standing prominent,
    solitary and exquisite.
But shadows cannot be caught;
    echoes are hard to bind.
Standing forlorn,
    your purple passage juts out conspicuously;
    it can't be woven into ordinary music.
Your mind, out of step,
    finds no mate for it;
    your ideas, wandering hither and thither,
    refuse to throw away that solitary passage.

---

[13] It may here be remembered that a tragic note seems to have prevailed in Chinese poetics since the last days of the Han dynasty; in fact it seems to have become a frame of reference with which to judge poetry. As gaiety was a quality not excluded in Confucian poetics, it would be worth investigating how and exactly since what time sadness has become the key tune in Chinese poetry. Is this tearfulness perhaps merely geographical? The *Songs of the South* are not joyous jingles; could it be, then, that the South was responsible for the whining note in Chinese poetry?

When the rock embeds jade,
the mountain glows;
when the stream is impregnated with pearls,
the river becomes alluring.[14]
When the hazel or arrow-thorn bush
is spared from the sickle,
it will glory in its foliage.
We will weave the market ditty
into the classical melody;[15]
perhaps we may thus rescue what is beautiful.

Five Imperfections

(i) In Vacuo

Maybe you have entrusted your diction
to an anemic rhythm;
living in a desert,
you have only yourself to talk to.[16]
When you look down into Silence,
you see no friend;
when you lift your gaze to Space,
you hear no echo.
It is like striking a single chord —
it rings out,
but there is no music.

(ii) Discord

Maybe you fit your words
to a frazzled music;
merely gaudy,
your language lacks charm.
As beauty and ugliness are commingled,
your good stuff suffers.

---

[14] Compare *Xunzi*: "If there is jade in the mountains, the trees on it will flourish; if there are pearls in the pool, the banks will not be parched." (Dubs' translation)

[15] The commentators agree that these were two ancient melodies, the former being a sort of jazz tune and the latter an Orphean melody.

[16] I like to take the situation described in this and the subsequent couplets as applying to the *haiku*, ancestor of Imagist poetry. Is it possible (I repeat a hackneyed question) to write a long Imagist poem? Can an Imagist draw his breath deep and long?

It is like the harsh note
  of a wind instrument below in the courtyard;
    there is music,
    but no harmony.

(iii) Novelty for Novelty's Sake

Maybe you forsake reason
  and strive for the bizarre;
    you are merely searching for inanity
    and pursuing the trivial.
Your language lacks sincerity
  and is poor in love;
    your words wash back and forth
    and never come to the point.
They are like a thin chord
  violently twanging —
    there is harmony,
    but it is not sad.

(iv) License

Maybe by galloping unbridled,
  you make your writing sound well;
    by using luscious tunes,
    you make it alluring.
Merely pleasing to the eye,
  it mates with vulgarity —
    a fine voice,
    but a nondescript song.
It reminds one of Fanglu and Sangjian[17] —
  it is sad,
  but not decorous.

(v) Insipidity

Or perhaps your writing is simple and terse,
  all superfluities removed —
So much so that it lacks even
  the lingering flavor of a sacrificial broth;

---

[17] Titles of two popular songs, "Keeping Off the Dew" and "Among the Mulberries." *Eds.*

it rather resembles the limpid tune
of the "vermilion chord."[18]
"One man sings, and three men do the refrain";
it is decorous,
but it lacks beauty.

Variability

As to whether your work should be loose or constricted,
whether you should mold it by gazing down or looking up,
You will accommodate necessary variation,
if you would bring out all the overtones.
Maybe your language is simple,
whereas your conceits are clever;
maybe your reasoning is plain,
but your words fall too lightly.
Maybe you follow the beaten track
to attain greater novelty;
maybe you immerse yourself in the muddy water —
to reach true limpidity.
Well, perspicacity may come
after closer inspection;
subtlety may ensue
from more polishing.
It is like dancers flinging their sleeves
in harmony with the beat
or singers throwing their voices
in tune with the chord.
All this is what the wheelwright Bian
despaired of ever explaining;[19]
it certainly is not
what mere language can describe.

---

[18] Sacrificial broth was neither salted nor spiced; "vermilion chord" refers to the zithers played in ancestral temples

[19] *Zhuangzi,* "The Way of Heaven." [See title-page of chapter 26. As Stephen Owen writes in *Readings in Chinese Literary Thought,* p. 36, "Perhaps language doesn't work, gives no access to what is really important in the person. The challenge of Wheelwright Bian haunts the literary tradition and makes writers evermore ingenious in inscribing the essential self in literature. Zhuangzi's dark mockery drives the tradition of Chinese literary thought ... "]

Masterpieces

I have been paying tribute
  to laws of words and rules of style.
I know well what the world blames,
  and I am familiar with what
  the worthies of the past praised.
Originality is a thing
  often looked at askance by the fixed eye.
The *fu*-gems and the jade beads, they say,
  are as numerous as the
  "pulse in the middle of the field,"[20]
As inexhaustible as the space between heaven and earth,
  and growing co-eternally
  with heaven and earth themselves.[21]
The world abounds with masterpieces;
  and yet they do not fill my two hands.[22]

The Poet's Despair

How I grieve
  that the bottle is often empty;
  how I sorrow
  that Elevating Discourse
  is hard to continue.
No wonder I limp along
  with trivial rhythms
  and make indifferent music
  to complete the song.
I always conclude a piece
  with a lingering regret;
  can I be smug and self-satisfied?
I fear to be a drummer
  on an earthen jug;[23]

---

[20] *Song* 196.

[21] Laozi, *The Way and Its Power:* "Yet Heaven and Earth and all that lies between/Is like a bellows/In that it is empty, but gives a supply that never fails." (Waley's translation)

[22] *Song* 226: "All the morning I gather the king-grass,/And do not collect enough to fill my hands." (Legge's translation)

[23] Li Si (d. 208 B.C.), in his letter to the First Emperor of Qin, describes how the Qin made merry: "Beating water-jars and drumming earthen jugs, plucking zithers and slapping their shanks, they sing lugubriously to please their ears — this is genuine Qin music."

the jinglers of jade pendants
will laugh at me.

Inspiration

(i)

As for the interaction of stimulus and response,
  and the principle of the flowing and ebbing of inspiration,
You cannot hinder its coming
  or stop its going.
It vanishes like a shadow,
  and it comes like echoes.
When the Heavenly Arrow
  is at its fleetest and sharpest,
  what confusion is there
  that cannot be brought to order?
The wind of thought bursts from the heart;
  the stream of words rushes through the lips and teeth.
Luxuriance and magnificence
  wait the command of the brush and the paper.
Shining and glittering,
  language fills your eyes;
abundant and overflowing,
  music drowns your ears.

(ii)

When, on the other hand, the Six Emotions[24]
  become sluggish and foul,
  the mood gone but the psyche remaining,
You will be as forlorn as a dead stump,
  as empty as the bed of a dry river.
You probe into the hidden depth of your soul;
  you rouse your spirit to search for yourself.
But your reason, darkened,
  is crouching lower and lower;
  your thought must be dragged out by force,
  wriggling and struggling.

---

[24] According to Li Shan's commentary (c. 630–689), these are like, dislike, pleasure, anger, sorrow, and joy.

So it is that when your emotions are exhausted
   you produce many faults;
   when your ideas run freely
   you commit fewer mistakes.
True, the thing lies in me,
   but it is not in my power to force it out.
And so, time and again,
   I beat my empty breast and groan;
   I really do not know the causes
   of the flowing and the not flowing.

Coda: Encomium

The function of style is, to be sure,
   to serve as a prop for your ideas.
(*Yet allow me to expatiate
   on the art of letters:*)[25]
It travels over endless miles,
   removing all obstructions on the way;
   it spans innumerable years,
   taking the place, really, of a bridge.
Looking down, it bequeaths
   patterns to the future;
   gazing up, it contemplates
   the examples of the ancients.[26]
It preserves the way of Wen and Wu,[27]
   about to fall to the ground;
   and it propagates good ethos,
   never to perish.
No path is too far for it to tread;
   no thought is too subtle
   for it to comprehend.[28]

---

[25] This line has been interpolated by the translator. *Eds.*
[26] "I wish to see the emblematic figures of the ancients — the sun, the moon, the stars, the mountains, the dragon, and the flowery fowl ..." *Book of History* (Legge's translation)
[27] "The doctrines of Wen and Wu have not yet fallen to the ground." *Confucian Analects* (Legge's translation)
[28] "The *Book of Changes* was made on a principle of accordance with heaven and earth, and shows us, therefore, without rent or confusion, the course (of things) in heaven and earth." *Book of Changes* (Legge's translation)

It is a match for clouds and rain
   in yielding sweet moisture;
it is like spirits and ghosts
   in bringing about metamorphoses.[29]
It inscribes bronze and marble,
   to make virtue known;
it breathes through flutes and springs,
and is new always.[30]

LIU XIE (c. 465–c. 520)

On Imagination
Chapter 26 of *The Literary Mind and the Carving of Dragons*

Translated by Siu-kit Wong

When he wrote *The Literary Mind and the Carving of Dragons*, Liu Xie was a lay-scholar in a Buddhist temple. His work attracted the attention of the prominent man of letters Shen Yue, and Liu went on to receive various minor appointments in the courts of the Liang princes. Towards the end of his life he took orders as a Buddhist monk. This work of his is the first book-length study in the Chinese language to address itself to some of the main problems that arise in the study of literature. Literary opinions had been expressed since Confucius in the sixth century B.C., and before, and some of those opinions are as sound as anything we find in *The Literary Mind*. But none of the earlier work had been presented in a single treatise devoted exclusively to literary considerations. This is the first *book* of literary criticism in the Chinese language....

   In the first five chapters, the author presents the theoretical — or, more precisely, doctrinal — foundations of his work. All literature, he states, must have its basis in the Confucian Classics and the wisdom therein. Liu Xie argues that as literature exists with heaven and earth, the writer ought to seek to understand heaven and earth, and its Tao, and that Tao could best be comprehended through the Classics. Chapters 6–25 constitute the second section. They treat the genres of writing known in Liu's time. Liu traces the origin and development of each genre, comments on its name, enumerates some examples, and discusses its general characteristics.

   The third section consists of chapters 26–49. Here Liu is no longer concerned with literature as artifact, but with its making, with what in the West would be called the

---

[29] The couplet refers to the *Book of Changes*. The first half compares style with the omnipotent Qian principle [the first of the Eight trigrams, consisting of three Yang lines], by virtue of which "the clouds move and the rain is distributed"; the second half may allude to a Confucian saying, "He who knows the method of change and transformation may be said to know what is done by that spiritual (power)." (Legge's translation)

[30] "The daily renovation which it produces is what is meant by 'the abundance of its virtue'." Cf. also the inscription on the bathtub of Tang: "If you can one day renovate yourself, do so from day to day." (Legge's translation)

"creative process" but should *not* be here since "creative process" implies an analogy which does not apply in the Chinese case. Liu goes through what he believes is at work in the *writing* process, in the *planning* process that occurs earlier, and in the *preparing* process, which lasts the duration of a writer's life. The writer should be well-educated; for Liu this means familiarity with book-knowledge, together with an awareness of nature....

The fourth, and final section, is a single chapter, the fiftieth. As in several other early Chinese works, this chapter serves most of the purposes of the modern introduction.

"To have your self physically sailing on the open seas; to have your mind tethered to the portals of the palace!" This remark, made so long ago, is what I would use as a definition for imagination.[31] The mysteries of the thinking process involved in the act of writing go far indeed.

You sit in quiet, concentrated contemplation, and your thoughts enter into conjunction with events of thousands of years ago. The muscles of your face flex ever so gently, and you see things far, far away. In softly chanting the lines being composed, in giving utterance to the jade-like, pearl-like tinkling of the music of your verse, you find winds and clouds, mild or violent, presenting themselves before your eyes. That is what happens when you are engaged in thinking in the composition of verse. And when your thinking rises to a sublime height, your spirit has intercourse with all that is outside itself.

Your spirit dwells in your breast and is regulated in a pivotal fashion by your Will and by your Vital Breath. Physical objects traverse your ears and eyes and are controlled through some mechanism by language. When that mechanism functions freely, nothing can remain hidden from you. But when the pivotal regulation of your Great Breath is stopped, your spirit retires into obscurity somewhere in your mind.

As the potter's wheel revolves in the process of writing, what is valuable is to attain a state of calm, receptive quietude: the five internal organs of your body should be cleared of their grime, your mind should be bathed to snowlike purity.

You should at all times accumulate learning as if you were hoarding up treasures. You should practice in reasoning to sharpen your wit. Then, when the moment to write comes you should follow the ordered grains of your thought and select the most suitable words. Direct your mind in search of the right sound and rhythm before you decide on the final form. You will then have your unique insight and be able to apply your abilities according to your vision. These then are the chief techniques in mastering the art of writing, the main rules that govern the organization of a literary piece.

---

[31] Literally "superhuman thinking, thinking that defies analysis or comprehension."

When your imagination is at its most active, millions of avenues are open to you. Rules are no longer intractable, and conscious craft leaves no marks behind. Climb the mountains, and the mountains become filled with your feelings; view the oceans, and the oceans overflow with your emotions. Whether your genius is great or small, it gallops along, shoulder against shoulder, with the wind and the clouds.

But what are you to do if, brush in hand, you find that your execution does not live up to your intention; or if, upon completion, you have said little more than half of what you set out to say? You must take comfort in the thought that ideas, being abstract, are free and volatile, whereas words, being fixed tallies, cannot easily be manipulated with skill. Ideas take form from your thoughts; words fall into formation after your ideas. The gap between your thoughts and your finalized ideas, as that between your ideas and your formulated words, can be nonexistent or several thousand miles wide. Sometimes a sense to be conveyed is really near at hand, but you have to hunt for it beyond the boundaries of your country; in other words, what you wish to say may be a commonplace, but can still take the traversing of rivers and hills before you find it.

If, in ordinary times, you are well trained in the techniques of writing, then, when you finally come to write, there is no need for you to punish yourself with deep thought, or put your emotions to hard labor.

Natural endowments vary from writer to writer: some are gifted with speed, while others are usually tardy. And each literary form demands a different amount of effort. Sima Xiangru[32] gripped his brush with his teeth till the hairs of the brush gradually wore away. Yang Xiong wrote so fast that once, when he had finished a piece, he fell into a nightmarish trance. Huan Tan got himself into such excruciating pain through creative thinking that he became ill as a result. Wang Chong exhausted his energy in deep contemplation. On the other hand, Zhang Heng spent ten years working on his "Rhapsody on the Capitals." Zuo Si, too, gave up a decade to produce his piece on a similar subject. The last two are examples of composition on a grand scale, but there can be no denying that Zhang and Zuo were slow writers. By way of contrast, the Prince of Huainan completed a work in the *sao*[33] style in a single morning. Mei Gao completed a rhapsody immediately upon imperial command, Cao Zhi wrote at the speed of speech, Wang Can lifted his brush and words flowed

---

[32] Most of the authors discussed here by Liu Xie can be found in the earlier chapters of this anthology. *Eds.*

[33] In the style of the "Li Sao" ("On Encountering Trouble") of Qu Yuan, for which see chapter 5. *Eds.*

as if they had been carefully put together the night before, Ruan Yu composed a dispatch on horseback, Mi Heng drafted a memorial whilst feasting. Admittedly these are works of brevity, but the speed of these writers is not to be gainsaid.

Fast and inspired writers have the art of writing ready in their minds; they are sprightly, they write without any need for conscientious planning: the occasion arises and the finished work is immediately there. Writers who are cautious in their thinking allow their mental activities to explore even obscure bypaths, make judgments after much wondering and settle on a verbal construct only after careful search and scrutiny. The accomplishment of an alert thinker is there before you in the twinkling of an eye. The product of a cautious one takes time to emerge.

If some of us find writing an easy task, while others find it difficult, we are all alike in that frequent practice is a help. Writers who are slow for want of learning and writers who are fast without being brilliant are equally failures. In mulling over what is about to be written one should always be aware of two dangers: the thinness of thought that results from crooked reasoning; the chaos that comes from indulgent language. But there are safeguards against these dangers. Wide learning is the food that provides against thinness of thought; a sense of unity is the medicine that cures chaos. What mental application is not strengthened by breadth of learning and a unifying intelligence?

In some works of literature, the feelings are obviously complex and subtle, the chosen form employed with great freedom. In other words, ingenious arguments give birth to a clumsy style, original thoughts burgeon forth in vulgar literary echoes. They are like flax before being woven into cloth; one might judge them worthless, but if the weaving machine is set to work, a product of gorgeous splendor might yet be made. As for works in which both substance and form are wrought with the finest skill, in which there is more than meets the eye — works which one knows are precisely what they should be, works whose excellence goes beyond what critical language can describe, why, these are the products of genius that can be explained to us only by the best critics — critics who understand the way these writings "work" in their variation on a given form. Yi Yin[34] alluded to the flavor of the contents of the ceremonial cauldron as indescribable; the master wheelwright Bian was reduced to silence when asked about his craft: such are the elusive mysteries of the literary art.

---

[34] Yi Yin, who became the minister of King Tang of the Shang dynasty, was originally a cook and, by legend, is said to have been unable to explain the mysteries of his art.

Thus:
The workings of the imaginative power
Penetrate all phenomena;
The workings of the imaginative power
Take place as one's emotion
Is moved to action.
The observed world is captured
As it is seen;
The heart returns an echo
In its ordered way.
Tone and rhyme
Are results of carving and chiseling;
Metaphors and similes, however,
Blossom forth of their own accord.
As you set your mind
To writing,
Draw the curtain, lower the blind,
And triumph is there,
For you to find.

ꙮ *Further Reading* ꙮ

Barnstone, Tony and Chou Ping, ed. and trans. *The Art of Writing: Teachings of the Chinese Masters.* Boston: Shambhala, 1996.

Ch'en, Shih-hsiang, trans. *Essay on Literature Written by the Third-Century Chinese Poet Lu Chi.* Portland, Me.: Anthoensen Press, 1953.

Dickinson, Goldsworthy Lowes. *Letters from John Chinaman.* London: Allen & Unwin, 1901.

Fang, Achilles, trans. "Rhymeprose on Literature: The *Wen-fu* of Lu Chi." *Harvard Journal of Asiatic Studies* (1951), 14.

Hamill, Sam. *Wen Fu: The Art of Writing.* Portland: Breitenbush Books, 1987.

Hughes, E. R., trans. *The Art of Letters: Lu Chi's "Wen Fu."* New York: Pantheon, 1951.

Kidd, Samuel. *China, or Illustrations of the Symbols, Philosophy, Antiquities ... and Literature of the Chinese.* London: Taylor & Walton, 1841.

Knechtges, David. "Rhapsody on Literature," in *Wen Xuan or Selections of Refined Literature,* Vol. 3. Princeton: Princeton University Press, 1996.

Liu, James J. Y. *Chinese Theories of Literature.* Chicago: University of Chicago Press, 1975.

Owen, Stephen. *Readings in Chinese Literary Thought.* Cambridge, Mass.: Harvard University Press, 1992.

Rickett, Adele, ed. *Chinese Approaches to Literature from Confucius to Liang Ch'i-ch'ao.* Princeton: Princeton University Press, 1978.

Shih, Vincent Yu-chung, trans. *The Literary Mind and the Carving of Dragons: A Study of Thought and Pattern in Chinese Literature.* Rev. ed. Hong Kong: Chinese University Press, 1983.

Wong, Siu-kit, ed. and trans. *Early Chinese Literary Criticism.* Hong Kong: Joint Publishing, 1983.

———, Allan Chung-hang Lo, & Kwong-tai Lam, trans. *The Book of Literary Design.* Hong Kong: Hong Kong University Press, 1999.

🔳 *Editors' Note* 🔳

Samuel Kidd (1799–1843) received his first lesson in Chinese from Robert Morrison in London, in 1824. He proceeded as a missionary to Malacca, where he studied with David Collie, whom he later succeeded as principal of the Anglo-Chinese College. He returned to England in 1832, because of poor health, and in 1837 was appointed the first Professor of Chinese at University College, London. He died of an epileptic fit in 1843.

"She bears her fine spirit among the lofty clouds."
Tao Yuanming, "Rhapsody on Quieting the Affections"
Seal carved by Gui Changshi (1574–1645)

Chapter 16

Spirits and Humors

Strange Tales from the Six Dynasties

Coming now to what these records contain, it is enough to make clear that the spirit world is not a lie. On this subject, the countless words and hundred differing schools are too much even to scan. And what one perceives with one's eyes and ears is too much to write down.... I will be fortunate if in the future there come some curious men who enjoy these things, take to heart their basic import, and find something in them with which to enlighten their hearts and fill their eyes; and fortunate too if I am not reproached for this book.

> — Gan Bao (fl. 315), Preface to *In Search of Spirits*
> *(translated by Kenneth DeWoskin)*

As early as the beginning of the third century the classification of personalities became one of the Chinese intelligentsia's favorite subjects of discussion in the free, disinterested talks known as "pure conversations" (*qingtan*). These conversations, in which the interlocutors vied with each other in producing witty remarks, amusing repartee, and polished epigrams, were gradually to extend their range from the study of character to literary, artistic, moral, and philosophical problems. The "pure conversations" became characteristic of the aristocratic coteries of the southern dynasties after the exodus of the early fourth century. Ancient examples have been preserved in a work of the first half of the fifth century, *A New Account of Tales of the World*, by Liu Yiqing.

> — Jacques Gernet, *A History of Chinese Civilization*, 1982

GAN BAO (fl. 315)

In Search of Spirits
Twelve Tales

Translated by Kenneth DeWoskin

During the Six Dynasties a new prose genre, the *zhiguai* tale [or "tale of the strange and supernatural"], emerged clearly from the mass of occasional writings of China's literati. Stimulated by the intellectual ferment of the times, chronic political instability, and a great tide of foreign influences, the growth in the writing of these tales was explosive. With an apparently insatiable appetite for the bizarre and curious, compilers sought everywhere for their materials. In the literary tradition, the classics, histories, informal biographies, geographies, and records of all sorts were combed for notices of strange people and events. Ears were turned to the tales and legends of various local cultures which surrounded many of the Six Dynasties courts, particularly those courts dislocated to the south. Further additions were made of contemporary stories and rumors: to be included, an item needed only to be "strange." In formal terms, the tales mimicked historical writing, and were first regarded as a degenerate branch of history. But they never lost their popularity among readers, and are now regarded as an important development in the early stages of Chinese fiction, and as a repository of invaluable observations on local cultures. Readers familiar with the great monuments of fiction and drama of traditional China will recognize the prototypes of many characters and plots in the *zhiguai* tales.

The work *In Search of Spirits* by Gan Bao, historian in the court of the Eastern Jin Emperor Yuan, stands out as a collection of exceptional diversity and quality and of exceptional importance to the literary tradition. It is fortunately a reasonably well preserved work, though Gan Bao's authorship of a number of the stories has been questioned recently, and the exact history of the text is uncertain. According to his biography in the *Jin History*, Gan Bao was converted to a belief in spirits when he witnessed the miraculous rebirth of his brother and the miraculous preservation of his father's favorite maid, ten years after she was interred alive at the father's funeral. In his own preface, Gan Bao indeed asserts that he undertook the writing of the book to document the existence of spirits and ghosts. However we take these stories and comments, the book as it stands now attests to a remarkable breadth of interest, informative contacts, and a sophisticated skill in the exploitation of the literary possibilities of narrative writing.

The early *zhiguai* tales had a significant influence not only on their own direct descendants (the Tang *chuanqi* tales [see chapter 28], and the Supernatural Tales of the Song, Ming and Qing dynasties [see volume 2]), but also on later drama and fiction of every type. Early collections such as *In Search of Spirits* served as repositories of popular characters and plots, and provided a legacy of character stereotypes, plot devices (e.g. demon impersonators, celestial intervention) and favorite props (e.g. magical mirrors, stones, gems and swords). It can be argued that the *zhiguai* tales established the degrees and kinds of supernaturalism and coincidence — in general, the canons of plausibility — that were tolerable in later literary fiction.

Tongue Splicing and Other Arts

During the Yong-jia reign of the Jin dynasty (307–313), a foreigner from India crossed the Yangtze into the Jiangnan regions [central Hubei]. He was a man of many arts. He could cut off his tongue and reattach it, and he could spit fire.

Wherever he went, a crowd gathered to watch him. In preparing to cut off his tongue, he would first stick it out for all to see. Then he would take a knife and cut it, blood gushing all over the ground. Next he took his tongue, put it in a container, and passed it around for all to see. He would stick out his tongue, which now was only half a tongue. Then he took his tongue back, replaced it, and sat for a moment. The onlookers would then see that his tongue was restored to its original condition, and one could not be sure if his tongue had really been cut off or not.

He did other splicing tricks with cloth. He would take a length of silk and have two men hold opposite ends. With a pair of scissors, the foreigner cut the cloth in the middle, then took the two halves and held them up together for all to see. The cloth would be rejoined, indistinguishable from its original condition.

People of the time suspected that this was some kind of conjuring, so they tried this out themselves in secret, but in fact they just cut their cloth in half. He performed his fire spitting by putting some chemical in a bowl, lighting it, and then mixing millet sugar in. He would breathe this in and out repeatedly, then open his mouth wide to show it filled with flame. Cooking fuel was brought and he could ignite it. Books, paper, and hempen rope could all be set on fire by his mouth. The onlookers could see that these items were completely consumed by the flames. Then the foreigner would rummage around in the ashes and pull things out, things that were in fact the original articles.

The Seance

During the Han dynasty in Yingling on the Gulf of Zhili, there was a Taoist who was able to arrange meetings between the living and the dead. A man from the province had lost his wife many years before, and when he heard about this Taoist he went to see him. "I want you to let me see my wife just one time. I would be willing to die for the chance!"

"Sir, you can go to see her, but when you hear the sound of the drum, come back immediately. Don't tarry."

So he described the technique for making the visit, and in no time the man was able to see his wife. He was able to talk with her, share lovingly moments of joy and moments of sorrow just as if she were alive. After a good while, he heard the sound of the drum, but he just hated to tear himself away. As he rushed out, his pant leg got trapped in the door, and he tore it loose and hastened off.

More than a year later, the man himself passed away. As the family performed the funeral rites for him, they opened the grave for his interment. They could see under the lid of his wife's coffin the torn piece from his trousers.

The Tomb of the Three Kings

Ganjiang Moye of Chu made swords for the king of Chu. The swords took three years to complete, which made the king very angry, so angry he wanted to kill Moye. Now the swords were a pair, one male and one female. Moye's wife was pregnant, about to give birth. Moye told her, "I made swords for the king of Chu, and they took three years to complete. The king is angry, so when I go there he will surely kill me. If when you bear our child, it turns out to be a boy, when it grows up, please pass on these instructions: 'Go out the door. Look to the southern mountains. Find a pine growing over a boulder. The sword is behind it.' "

Then he immediately took the female sword of the pair and went to see the king of Chu. The king was already angry, and when he had the sword examined, he discovered that only the female had been brought, though there were two, one male and one female. In a rage he killed Moye forthright.

Moye's son was named Chi. When he reached adolescence, he asked his mother, "Where is my father?" Chi's mother replied, "Your father made swords for the king of Chu. They took three years to complete, so the king was angry and killed him. When he left us, he passed on this instruction: 'Tell your son to go out the door. Look to the southern mountains. Find a pine growing over a boulder. The sword is behind it.' "

The son indeed went out the door and looked south but did not see mountains. He did, however, see a pine post standing on a stone footing. He took an ax, chopped open the back, and found the sword. Day and night he thought about taking his revenge on the king.

Now the king dreamed that there was a lad, with a footwide bridge between his eye brows, and that lad was talking of taking revenge. The king immediately announced a bounty of a thousand measures of gold. When the lad heard about this, he escaped into the mountains. He wandered about, singing of his plight, when another traveler ran into him and asked, "How can a person so young be so bitterly aggrieved?"

"I am the son of Ganjiang Moye. The king of Chu killed my father, and I want revenge." The traveler replied, "I have heard that the king offers a bounty of a thousand measures of gold for your head. I will take your head and the sword to him, then get vengeance for you."

The lad said, "This is my great fortune," and proceeded to slice through his own neck. With two hands he presented his own head and the sword to the traveler, then stood there stiffly. The traveler announced, "I will not disappoint you," and only then did the body fall over.

The traveler took the head to see the king of Chu. The king was delighted. The traveler told him, "This is the head of a determined warrior. You had best put it in a cauldron and boil it." The king followed this suggestion. He boiled the head for three days and three nights, but it did not disintegrate. Instead it bobbed up high in the boiling water, and its glaring eyes showed great rage. The traveler said further, "This lad's head will not disintegrate. Your majesty should personally go to see it; then it will finally cook."

The king rushed to see the head, and the traveler took the sword and struck the king. The king's head tumbled into the cauldron, and the traveler lopped off his own, which rolled in as well. All three were cooked so thoroughly that you could not tell one from the other. The remains were divided into three equal parts and buried. Thus this was commonly called the Tomb of the Three Kings. It is now in the northern part of Ru'nan [Guangxi Province], on the border of Yichun prefecture.

Han Ping and His Wife

King Kang of Song had a retainer named Han Ping who married a woman of the He family. She was very beautiful, and the king took her. Ping was angry, so the king had him arrested and sent off to labor at building garrison walls.

Ping's wife clandestinely sent him a letter in which she carefully encrypted her thoughts. "The rain falls steadily; the river is broad; the water deep. The sun rises, shining on my heart."

The king got hold of the letter and showed it to his advisers, but none could figure out what it meant. One minister, named Su He, offered an explanation, "'The rain falls steadily' means her thoughts are filled with sorrow. 'The river is broad; the water deep' means they are unable to see one another. 'The sun rises shining on my heart' means that in her heart she has made a vow unto death."

Ping committed suicide right away. His wife secretly let her clothing rot and weaken. Then when she climbed a tower with the king, she threw herself off. Attendants grabbed her, but they could not get hold of her clothing, and she plunged to her death. A last testament was tucked in her belt: "Your majesty favored him in life. I will favor him in death. I beg that my remains be buried together with Ping's."

This enraged the king, who ignored her plea. He instructed the villagers to bury them apart, facing each other. The king then pledged, "The two of you loved each other without end. If you are able to bring your graves together, I will not stand in the way."

Within a day, a catalpa tree sprung up at the head of each grave. Within a fortnight, both trees had filled out completely. The trunks of the trees bent toward each other. Beneath the ground their roots tangled, and above the ground their branches intertwined. Then there came a pair of mandarin ducks to perch in the trees, one male and one female. They were always there, morning and night. With their necks wrapped together, they sang a most piteous song, very moving to all around. The people of Song felt deeply about this and nicknamed it the "tree of mutual love." That name originated with this incident.

In the south people are accustomed to saying that mandarin ducks represent the spirits of Han Ping and his wife. In Suiyang [Henan Province] today there is the wall built by Han Ping, and there are still ballads sung recounting this tale.

Li E Returns from the Dead

In the second month of the fourth year of the Jian-an period in the Han dynasty (A.D. 199), in Wuling commandery [Hunan Province], Chong prefecture, an old woman by the name of Li E died of illness at the age of sixty. She had been buried outside the city some fourteen days when a man named Cai Zhong from her neighborhood heard that she had been wealthy and that great treasures were buried with her. So he stole into the grave in search of her wealth. Zhong took an ax to hack open the coffin. After a few swipes, E called from inside the coffin, "Cai Zhong! You watch out for my head!" Cai was terrified, dashed out of the grave, and ran off.

It just happened that some prefectural officials saw him and had him arrested. According to the law, he was banished from the city. E's son heard that his mother was alive, so he went to bring her out. He took her back home. The grand protector of the province heard that E had died and come back to life, so he summoned her to an audience to ask her what transpired. E told the following tale.

I heard that I had been summoned by the Office of Fate in error, so when I arrived I had to be sent right back. As I was passing outside the West Gate, I happened upon my cousin Liu Bowen. Surprised by this meeting, we fell to questioning each other intensely, weeping and wailing, tears flowing in torrents. I told him, "Bowen, one day I was summoned by mistake, so they had to send me back. But since I do not know the way, I cannot go by myself. Could you arrange an escort for me? Also, since I was called more than ten days have gone by. My family has buried me. When I get back, how can I get out of the tomb?"

Bowen replied, "We should make inquiries about this." So he went over to ask the gate keeper and keeper of corpses: "The Office of Fate one day called in error a woman of Wuling, one Li E. Now she is being sent back. But she has been here several days, and her corpse has been prepared and is likely buried. What should she do to get out? Also, she is frail, and rather than walk alone, shouldn't she have an escort? I am her cousin, and I would be grateful if you would arrange this for her."

They replied, "On the western edge of Wuling there is a man named Li Hei. He is also being sent back and can serve as her escort. At the same time, we will order Li Hei to pass by Li E's neighbor Cai Zhong and have Zhong get her out."

This is how I got out. When I took my leave from Bowen, he entrusted to me a letter for his son Tuo. So Hei and I came back together. This is how the affair happened.

The grand protector heard this and gasped with astonishment, "Indeed, the ways of the world are beyond our knowing!" Then he prepared a memorial:

Although Cai Zhong broke into the grave, he was moved to do so by spirits. Although he was without desire to open the grave, the situation was such that he could not help but do it. So it is appropriate to show leniency.

This was approved when submitted to the higher authorities.

The grand protector wanted to determine how accurate this story was, so he dispatched a mounted official to the western border to interrogate Li Hei. When they got Hei's story, it corroborated the old lady's. And then they delivered the letter to Tuo. Tuo recognized the paper. It was in fact an inscription that had been buried with his father. But the contents of the letter were incomprehensible. Fei Changfang was asked to read it, and he did so as follows:

To Tuo: I will be going out on an inspection tour for the Minister of the Dead (the Lord of Mount Tai). I will be stopping to rest at exactly noon on the eighth day of the eighth month at the river that runs south of Wuling. You must come at that time.

At the appointed time, the whole family set out south of the city to await him. All arrived before long, but they could hear nothing but the murmuring of the horses and the people, as they faced the river. Then they heard a voice call out, "Tuo, you have come. Did you get the letter I sent via Li E?" He answered, "I did get it, and so we have come to this spot."

Bowen then called in turn to each and every member of the family, but after a while, he sadly took his leave. "The living and the dead walk different paths. I am not able to get news of you very often. Since I died, the children and grandchildren certainly have gotten big!"

After a long pause, he told Tuo, "This spring there will be a major epidemic. I am giving you this vial of medicine. Spread it on the doorways, and you can avoid the ravages of this coming plague." When he finished speaking, he was gone in an instant, and for the entire time no one got a glimpse of his form.

When spring came, Wuling indeed had a major epidemic. Even in broad daylight, people saw ghosts everywhere. It was only the house of Bowen that the ghosts dared not approach. Fei Changfang examined the medicine and said, "This is the brains from a *fangxiang* demon!"

Song Dingbo Sells a Ghost

When Song Dingbo of Nanyang [Henan Province] was a young man he was once walking at night, when he ran into a ghost. He asked, "Who are you?" The ghost replied, "I am a ghost."

Then the ghost asked, "Who are you?" Dingbo lied and said, "I am also a ghost." The ghost asked him, "Where are you off to?" Dingbo replied, "I am going to the town of Yuan." "I am also going to Yuan," said the ghost, and he walked along with Dingbo.

After several miles, the ghost complained, "Walking by foot is just too slow. What do you say we run along and take turns carrying each other?" "Great," replied Dingbo. The ghost was first to carry Dingbo, but after several more miles he noted, "You are very heavy! You aren't a ghost."

Dingbo replied, "I'm a new ghost, so my body is still heavy." Dingbo then picked up the ghost and found him to be almost weightless. They went back and forth like this several times, when Dingbo asked, "Being a new ghost, I am not clear what I should fear and avoid." The ghost told him, "The only thing we don't like is human spittle."

So they walked along together some more. Coming to a water crossing, Dingbo asked the ghost to go first. He listened, and lo and behold, there was not a sound. When Dingbo himself crossed, there were all sorts of gurgling noises. The ghost questioned him again, "How is it that you make noises?" "I just died, and I am not practiced in crossing waters. Don't distrust me!"

When they were about to reach Yuan city, Dingbo again picked up the ghost. Once he had him on his shoulders, Dingbo held on tightly. The ghost yelped and yelped to be let down, but Dingbo paid no attention. When they reached the middle of the city he finally put the ghost down, and it transformed into a goat. So Dingbo sold it, but fearing further transformations, he spat on it. He got fifteen hundred cash and left. At that time, a local magnate named Shi Chong was wont to say, "Dingbo sold a ghost and earned fifteen hundred cash!"

Scholar Tan

The Han dynasty scholar Tan was forty years old and unmarried. He would often chant from the *Book of Songs* with great feeling. Once in the middle of the night, a young girl came to see him. She could not have been more than fifteen or sixteen. Her beauty, her clothing, and her jewels were unparalleled in this world.

The girl proposed to Tan that they be man and wife. "I am not like mortals. You must not look at me under torch light. But after three years, you can then do so." So the two became husband and wife, and she bore him a child.

Two years had already gone by when Tan could bear it no longer. One night he waited until she had fallen asleep and then sneaked in with a torch to look at her. From the waist up she was fleshy, just like a person, but from the waist down, she was just dried bones. "You betrayed me! I was on the verge of returning to life, but you could not wait one more year and just had to get a light and look." Tan begged her forgiveness and wept and wept, but the situation could not be saved.

She then spoke to him again. "Although righteousness dictates that we must part forever, I am deeply concerned for the son I bore. If you are poor, you cannot provide for his support, so I want you to come with me for a moment, just so I can give you something."

He followed her into a magnificent chamber. The structure and everything in it was out of this world. She took a pearl coat and handed it to him, "This will support you." Then she tore off the lapel of Tan's robe and vanished with it.

Tan subsequently went to sell off the coat, which was bought by the household of the king of Juyang for ten million cash. The king scrutinized the coat and declared, "This is my daughter's coat! Where did you buy it? It must have been taken from her grave." Tan was apprehended and interrogated under torture.

Tan told the entire story, but the king could not believe him. He set off to look at the girl's grave. The grave was untouched, so they proceeded to open it up. When the lid of the coffin was removed, the torn pieces of Tan's lapel were found inside. The king then called for the son to be brought, and he could see the son closely resembled his daughter. After all of this, the king was convinced. So he immediately summoned Tan and rewarded him all the more lavishly, accepting him as a son-in-law, and the boy was made a Gentleman of the Interior.

The Grave Wedding of Lu Chong

Lu Chong was a man of Fanyang [Hebei Province]. Some ten miles west of his house was the grave of provincial commander Cui. When Chong was twenty years old, one day prior to the winter solstice, he left his house and traveled west to enjoy some hunting. He spotted a roe buck, lifted his bow, and shot it. He hit the buck, and it fell over. But it got up again, so Chong ran after it.

Unaware of how far he had gone, he suddenly noticed several hundred yards north of the road an impressive structure, with towering gates and tile roofs, surrounded on all four sides by houses of attendants and servants. The buck was nowhere to be seen. A watchman at the front gate called Chong to come forward. Chong asked, "Whose mansion is this?" The reply, "It is the mansion of the provincial commander."

Chong said, "My clothes are dirty. How can I pay a visit to the provincial commander?" And immediately someone brought a suit of new clothes for him. "The master presents this to you." As soon as Chong had put on the new clothing, he went in to see the commander and introduced himself. After a few rounds of eating and drinking, the commander said to him, "I recently received a letter from your honorable father, who, excusing the poor circumstances of our house, expressed the wish that you marry my daughter. For this reason, our meeting today was arranged."

He showed the letter to Chong. Chong was quite young when his father died, but he recognized his father's handwriting nonetheless. Startled to the brink of tears, Chong had no way to refuse. The commander instructed his wife, "Groom Lu has already arrived. Have the bride begin her preparations!" Then he told Lu, "Please feel free to proceed to the East Hall, where we will await the dusk."

The wife replied, "The bride's preparations are complete." By the time Lu reached the East Hall, the bride had already dismounted from her carriage and was standing at the head of the mat, where they made their vows. The celebration went on for three days, and as soon as the three days were completed, the commander said to Chong, "You may go back now. My daughter appears to be pregnant. If she bears a son, we will send him to you. Have no doubt of that. If it is a daughter, we will keep her and raise her ourselves."

The commander ordered a carriage be prepared to send the guest back. Chong said his parting words, and Commander Cui escorted him formally to the middle gate, grabbed his hands, and bid him a tearful farewell. Outside the gate Chong saw an oxcart driven by a green-clothed officer. He also saw the clothes he had originally worn and his bow and arrow resting outside the gate, just where he had left them. Another messenger was sent out with a gift of clothing for Chong and presented a message, "Our marriage ceremony is just barely over, and parting brings me the deepest sorrow. Here I present you a suit of clothes and the quilt from our bed."

Chong climbed into the cart and like a flash of lightning was home; it took no time at all. Seeing him again, his family pressed him with questions through tears of sorrow and tears of joy. And even though Chong knew that provincial commander Cui was a dead man and he had entered his grave, he still thought back to his abandoned wife with great sadness and longing.

Some four years later, on the third day of the third month, when Chong was undertaking a ritual bath at the water's edge, he suddenly saw two ox-drawn carriages near the side of the river. When the carriages got closer, Chong could see the people sitting together in them. He approached one and opened the door in the back. There he saw Cui's daughter riding with a three-year-old boy. Chong's heart leaped; and he reached to press her hand. But she raised her hand and pointed to the carriage behind, "My father wishes to see you."

Then he caught sight of the provincial commander. Chong walked back to inquire of him, and his wife came back over to him carrying the child, returning it to Chong. She also gave him a golden bowl and a poem. The poem read as follows:

Immortal substance scintillating bright,
a beauty, a softness, all radiant light.
Flowering lushness, quite clear to all,
with genius and charm that all praises did call.

But to my petals awaiting their bloom,
came a midsummer's frost, a blanket of doom.
Extinguished forever that glistening light,
Never to walk this world's paths was my plight.

Uncomprehending the turning of fate,
Wise husband you came to take me as mate.
Our meeting was brief, our parting so fast,
by spirits and gods are these matters all cast.

What do I have to give you dear one,
Just a golden bowl to feed our small son.

Our love and affection from here do part,
And leave me sore wounded with a shattered heart.

Chong took the child, the bowl, and the poem, and suddenly the two carriages vanished from sight. When Chong took the child back to his house, everyone said it was a dangerous ghost. They cautiously stood back some distance and spat on the child, but it did not change forms. When they asked the child, "Who is your father," he would run into Chong's arms. At first everyone was alarmed and disgusted by this turn of events, but after the poem had been circulated and read, people lamented the sad outcome of this mysterious contact between the living and the dead.

Sometime later, Chong rode into the marketplace to sell the golden bowl. He set the price very high, because he did not want to sell it quickly, in the hope that someone would recognize it. There was but one old woman who did recognize the bowl, and she returned home to tell her mistress, "In the market I saw a man on a cart trying to sell a bowl from the tomb of the daughter of provincial commander Cui." Her mistress was none other than the aunt of Cui's daughter. She in turn sent her son to investigate and he confirmed the old woman's account. So the son climbed on to Chong's cart and explained who he was. He asked Chong:

"Long ago my aunt bore a daughter by provincial commander Cui. She died before she was married. The family grieved bitterly for her and presented her with this golden bowl, placing it in her coffin. Can you explain to me what course of events brought it here?"

Chong explained the entire series of events, and the son was also moved to tears by them. He returned home with the bowl and told it all to his mother, the girl's aunt. She immediately sent a messenger to Chong's house to have him bring the boy to her for inspection. All of the relatives assembled for the meeting. The son indeed had the features of the Cui family and yet his face resembled Chong's. After inspecting both the bowl and the boy, the aunt announced, "My grand nephew was born at the end of the third month, and his father says 'spring is a time of warmth (wen) and he wishes the child to grow to be beautiful (xiu) and strong.' We should name him Wenxiu." If you think about it, Wenxiu can mean "mysterious nuptials," and the first sign of her niece's marriage was the swelling with this child.

The boy grew up to be a fine and prominent young man, who served successively several governors of the commandery with high remuneration. His progeny achieved high official posts generation after generation, and still today the name of one descendant, Lu Zhi, styled Zigan, is known throughout the land.

Li Ji, the Serpent Slayer

In the Eastern Yue regions, the commandery of Minzhong [Fujian Province], there is a Mount Yongling that soars to a height of a dozen miles. In a crevice on its northwest side there is a giant serpent, seventy or eighty feet long and over ten feet around. It was a constant terror to the local people. The garrison commander of Dongzhi and local officials reporting to him had lost many people to it. Sacrifices of sheep and ox produced no improvement in fortune. Perhaps through someone's dream, perhaps through a message communicated to a medium, it became known that the serpent desired to feast on nubile girls in their early teens.

The commander and local officials agonized over this, but the baneful influences continued unabated. So they had no choice but to seek out slave girls born to local families and put them in the care of daughters from criminal families. On a morning of the eighth month, a ritual was performed to dispatch the victim to the mouth of the serpent's cave. The serpent would come out and devour the girl. This went on for many a year, until nine girls had been sacrificed.

On this particular year the officials were preparing for the sacrifice and began to search for a victim. In Jiangle prefecture the family of one Li Tan had six daughters and no sons. His youngest daughter, a girl named Ji, responded to the call for a sacrificial victim and wanted to go. Her parents would not hear of it, but Ji argued, "My dear parents, you are luckless! You have begotten six girls and not a single son. You have children but it is as if you did not. I haven't the merit of a Diying[1] to help you out, so I will never be able to contribute to your support and sustenance. Feeding and clothing me is a total waste. How much better it would be if I died early. By selling me, you could get a bit of cash to provide for yourself. Wouldn't this be for the best?"

But her mother and father loved her too much to let her go. So she slipped off clandestinely, and they could not stop her.

Ji appealed for a sharp sword and a serpent-hunting hound. On the morning of the eighth month off she went to sit at the shrine to the serpent, clutching her sword and leading the dog. She had prepared in advance a fair quantity of steamed rice balls, which she coated with a mixture of honey and roasted barley flour. She placed these in front of the serpent's cave, and the serpent immediately came out. Its head was as

---

[1] Diying was a model filial daughter, born to Former Han official Chunyu Yi. Yi was convicted of a serious crime and sentenced to be executed by laceration. Diying appealed to the emperor, offering herself in exchange for her father's life. The emperor was moved by her filial merit and revoked the sentence.

large as a grain bin, with eyes like mirrors two feet across. First it was drawn to the fragrant scent of the rice balls and went over to eat them. Ji immediately released the dog, and the dog sunk his teeth in. Ji attacked from the back, slashing the serpent again and again. In a fit of pain the serpent slithered all the way out, over to the shrine, and died.

Ji went into the cave and retrieved the bones of the preceding nine girls. She gathered them up, walked out of the cave, and proclaimed, "You were timid and afraid, and so you were devoured by the serpent. It is pathetic." She then walked home at a leisurely pace.

When the King of Yue heard this story, he summoned Ji to be his queen. The king appointed Ji's father to the post of prefect of Jiangle, and he bestowed gifts of great value on her mother and sisters. From this time on, Dongzhi was never again bothered by such demonic banes. Even today a ballad is sung in praise of Ji's exploits.

The Cave of the Sick Dragon

During the Jin dynasty in Weijun [Henan Province], there was a drought. The local farmers prayed before a dragon cave, and when rain came, they prepared to sacrifice to the dragon to show their gratitude. Sun Deng, the renowned recluse, told them, "This is a sick dragon. As for his rain, how can it bring life to your grain crops? If you do not believe me, simply smell the rainwater."

When they did, sure enough it was rank. Just at that time, the dragon had a great lesion on its back. It heard Sun Deng's words and transformed itself into an old man. Presenting himself to Sun Deng, the old man begged for a cure. "If you cure this lesion, you will be rewarded."

Following the cure, it was a matter of just a few days when a great rain fell. Then a boulder split open revealing the mouth of a well, and water came gushing forth. Apparently the dragon had drilled this well as the reward.

People Growing Horns

During the Han dynasty, in the ninth month of the first year of Emperor Jing's reign (156 B.C.), a man from Xiami in the state of Miaodong [Shandong Province], who was over seventy years old, grew horns. The horns had hair on them. The commentary by Jing Fang on the *Book of Changes* says, "When a minister of state monopolizes power, then we have the strange phenomenon of people growing horns." The *Treatise on the Five Phases* takes the position that people should not grow horns, and similarly the feudal lords should not raise troops to send against the imperial armies. Indeed, soon afterwards there was the calamity of the

seven states. Coming up to the time of Jin Emperor Wu, his fifth year
(A.D. 269), a seventy year old man in Yuancheng [Hebei Province] grew
horns. This was probably in response to the attempt by Lun, King of
Zhao, to usurp power (A.D. 301).

Sex Changes

In the thirteenth year of King Xiang of Wei a woman turned into a man,
took a wife, and bore a child. The commentary by Jing Fang on the *Book
of Changes* says, "When a woman turns into a man, it means that the yin
female forces have flourished and a base man will become king. When a
man turns into a woman, it means that the yin forces have defeated the
yang, a sign that the state is about to be lost." Another source says, "When
a man turns into a woman, it means the punishment of castration is
being used too often. When a woman turns into a man, it means the
government is controlled by a woman."

LIU YIQING (403–444)

A New Account of Tales of the World
Twelve Tales

Translated by Richard B. Mather

A New Account of Tales of the World is a collection of anecdotes, *bons mots* and characterizations, mainly garnered from earlier written sources of the second through the
fourth centuries and put together in the year 430 under the sponsorship of Liu Yiqing,
Prince of Linchuan [for other extracts see chapter 10]. The incidents described in it
involve more than six hundred historical individuals who lived between the final years
of Later Han and Liu's own lifetime, but by far the largest number fall within the
immediately preceding dynasty of Eastern Jin (317–420).

Taken as a whole, *Tales of the World* has been loved by all educated Chinese ever
since its first appearance in the fifth century. What appeals most to modern readers is
the laconic but elegant prose style, a style that marks an early stage of greater
expression in the history of Chinese literature. It goes beyond the extreme economy
of classical and Han prose. Even though it is based on earlier documents, the style of
Tales of the World is quite consistent and rather distinctive, using many more disyllabic
expressions and expanding the number and subtlety of the function words. Since
many of the episodes are conversations, including some so-called "pure conversation"
debates, it seems reasonable to infer that the written style owes something to contemporary fourth- and fifth-century colloquial modes of expression. Another appealing
feature is the delightful brand of humor, which even Westerners can appreciate.

Still another aspect of the work that makes it unique is the glimpse it gives of
emerging values of the times — a sense of liberation from the oppressive constraints
of the old Han Confucian orthodoxy. Values such as "cultivated tolerance" — the

ability to maintain complete self-composure in the midst of danger and uncertainty, or total immunity from worldly cares and greed — are illustrated in the case of Ruan Fu and his love of wooden clogs, released from the wracking anxiety that continually plagued the miser, Zu Yue. The new stress on "freedom and nonrestraint," which produced a sort of cult of individuality and eccentricity, is dramatically illustrated by the bibulous exploits of Liu Ling, a member of the reclusive coterie, the Seven Sages of the Bamboo Grove. Following the lead of this group a generation later were the Eight Free Spirits, who carried their liberated life-style to even greater extremes. Still later, Wang Xianzhi, the talented son of the calligrapher Wang Xizhi, acting on a completely spontaneous impulse, traveled all night in a small boat to see a friend. But when he reached the friend's gate he turned back without seeing him, because, as he explained, "the impulse was spent."

On the cautionary side, we are also introduced to the shocking lengths to which members of the aristocracy like Shi Chong and Wang Kai would go in their heedless competition to do one better than each other, and to daredevil exploits like that of the young Don Juan, Han Shou, who used to visit his lady love by leaping over her garden wall.

Other values that surface in this work include a greater sensitivity toward the plight of women and the infiltration of Buddhist ideas into the intellectual and religious climate of the times. The somewhat rarefied, and at least partially fictionalized "world" that these "tales of the world" portray — confined as it is to emperors, princes, courtiers, generals, genteel hermits, and urbane monks — is nonetheless the real world of the exiled aristocrats who had fled the barbarian conquest of their homeland in the north at the beginning of the fourth century and were now losing ground to rising families of the south. In these tales we get a momentary glimpse of their daily lives, a tiny glimmer of what they must have felt and thought in the face of the ever-present threat of extinction.

Figure 36. Detail of a Painted Tomb-tile. Han dynasty. (Source: Boston Museum of Fine Arts)

Riches and Clogs

Stories in chapter 6 illustrate the quality of unperturbability under stress, which was much admired during the third and fourth centuries.

Zu Yue loved riches, while Ruan Fu loved wooden clogs. Both of them constantly devoted themselves to their obsessions, and both were constantly burdened by their labors, so that it was never settled who was superior and who inferior.

Someone once paid a visit to Zu and found him counting and checking over his money and possessions. When the guest arrived the process of putting them away had not yet been completed, and two remaining round baskets had been hastily placed behind Zu's back, while he himself bent his body to screen them, his mind all the while unable to rest at ease.

Someone also went to visit Ruan and found him blowing the fire himself to wax his clogs. While doing so he sighed and remarked, "I never knew how many clogs I would wear in a single lifetime!" Meanwhile his spirit and facial expression remained perfectly relaxed and cheerful. It was only then that it became apparent who was superior and who inferior.

— from chapter 6, "Cultivated Tolerance"

Lady Guo

Incidents in chapter 10 all involve censure or warnings offered by younger or lower-ranking persons to their elders or superiors.

When Wang Cheng was in his fourteenth or fifteenth year he observed that Lady Guo, the wife of his older brother, Chancellor Wang Yan, was avaricious and miserly. Once she ordered a female slave to carry in manure gathered from the street, to be used as fuel. Cheng reprimanded her and told her, moreover, that such a thing was not to be done.

Lady Guo flew into a violent rage and said to Cheng, "Some time ago, when your mother, Lady Ren, was on her deathbed, she put you, little boy, under the care of me, the new bride. She did not put the new bride under the care of the little boy!" Seizing him by the lapel of his coat, she was about to administer a flogging.

Cheng, exerting all his strength, struggled to get free, and, leaping through a window, ran away.

— from chapter 10, "Admonitions and Warnings"

Hearing the Way in the Morning

These are stories of once anti-social characters who reformed themselves and became contributing members of society.

When Zhou Chu was young his cruel and violent knight-errantry was a source of distress to his fellow villagers. Furthermore, in the stream which flowed through his native Yixing (in modern Jiangsu) there was a scaly dragon, and in the hills a roving tiger, both of which were terrorizing the local population. The people of Yixing called the three of them the "Three Scourges," but Zhou Chu was the most dreaded of them all. Someone suggested to Chu that he kill the tiger and behead the dragon, in reality hoping that of the "Three Scourges" only one would be left.

Chu promptly stabbed the tiger to death and proceeded to enter the stream to attack the dragon. But the dragon, now afloat, now submerged, swam on for several tens of *li*, with Chu swimming beside it all the way. After a full three days and three nights, the villagers all assumed he was dead and were congratulating each other more than ever.

Finally, however, Chu killed the dragon and emerged from the water. It was only after he had heard that the villagers were congratulating each other that he realized what a source of distress he had been to the feelings of the others, and he made up his mind to reform himself.

Accordingly, from Wu Commandery (modern Suzhou) he sought out the two Lu brothers, Lu Ji and Lu Yun. Since Lu Ji was not at home at the time, he saw only Lu Yun. After reporting the situation to him in detail, Chu added, "I've wanted to reform my ways, but the years have already slipped by and until now I haven't accomplished it."

Yun said, "The man of antiquity honored the principle of 'Hearing the Way in the morning and dying content in the evening.'[2] How much more promising is your own future course! What's more, even though people are distressed that your ambition has not yet been established, why, indeed, should you worry that your good name will not someday become well known?"

Chu thereupon exerted all his energies in a new direction, and in the end he became a loyal minister and filial son.

— from chapter 15, "Self-Renewal"

Drunk Again

The heroes of chapter 23 embody still another quality highly admired in the third and fourth centuries, namely, the spontaneity of following one's own nature, rather than the artificial restraints of society.

Liu Ling was once suffering from a hangover,[3] and, being extremely

---

[2] *Analects*, V, 8.

[3] *Bingjiu* (literally, "sick from wine") is usually interpreted to mean "dead drunk." Here, however, "sick on awaking from drunkenness" seems closer.

thirsty, begged his wife for some wine. His wife, who had poured out all the wine and smashed the vessels, pleaded with tears in her eyes, "You're drinking far too much. It's no way to preserve your life. You'll have to stop it."

Ling replied, "A very good idea. But I'm unable to stop by myself. It can only be done if I pray to the ghosts and spirits and swear an oath to stop it. So you may now get ready the wine and meat for the ceremony."

His wife said, "As you wish," and, setting out wine and meat before the spirits, requested Ling to start praying and swearing his oath.

Kneeling upright, Ling prayed,

When Heaven produced the man, Liu Ling,
It took wine for his name and fate,[4]
In one draft he will down one gallon;
With five dipperfuls relieve the stupor.
As for what his wife has said,
Be careful that you do not listen.

Whereupon he drained the wine and ate up all the meat, and before he knew it, was already drunk again.

— from chapter 23, "The Free and Unrestrained"

In My Pants

On many occasions, under the influence of wine, Liu Ling would be completely free and unrestrained, sometimes even removing his clothes and sitting stark naked in the middle of his room. Some people once saw him in this state and chided him for it.

Ling retorted, "I take heaven and earth for my pillars and roof, and my house with its rooms as my pants and jacket. What are you gentlemen doing in my pants?"

— from chapter 23, "The Free and Unrestrained"

Liu Bao

When Liu Bao was young he used to go fishing in a grassy marsh. He was a skilled whistler and singer, and everybody who heard him would stop to listen. There was an old woman who recognized him for an unusual man, and who so thoroughly enjoyed his singing and whistling that she slaughtered a suckling pig and served it up to him. Bao consumed the pig down to the last morsel without saying a word of thanks. The old

---

[4.] *Ming*, "name," is used here also as a pun with *ming*, "fate."

woman, seeing that he had not yet eaten to satiety, served him another suckling pig. He ate half of it and left half, which he returned to her.

Later, he became a secretary in the Board of Civil Office, where the old woman's son was serving as a petty clerk, and Bao singled him out above the others for special employment. Not understanding the reason, the young man asked his mother, who told him about the pigs. Thereupon he prepared beef and wine and went to visit Bao.

Bao told him, "Go away! Go away! I have nothing more to repay you."

— from chapter 23, "The Free and Unrestrained"

The Strength of an Impulse

While Wang Huizhi was living in Shanyin (in modern Zhejiang), one night there was a heavy fall of snow. Waking from sleep, he opened the panels of his room and ordered wine. All about him was gleaming white, whereupon he got up and paced back and forth, humming Zuo Si's poem "Summoning the Recluse." All at once he remembered Dai Kui, who was living at the time in Shan (thirty-five kilometers to the south). On the spur of the moment he set out by night in a small boat to visit him. The whole night had passed before he finally arrived. When he reached Dai's gate, he turned back without going in.

When someone asked his reason, Wang replied, "I originally went on the strength of an impulse, and when the impulse was spent I turned back. Why was it necessary to see Dai?"

— from chapter 23, "The Free and Unrestrained"

Shallots

Most of the examples in chapter 29 are of stinginess, the exact opposite of the "extravagance" illustrated in the next. Our selection, however, could perhaps be more kindly described as "frugality."

During Su Jun's rebellion Yu Liang fled southward (from Jiankang) for refuge with Tao Kan, who had always held him in high esteem. Tao himself was by nature economical and frugal. When mealtime came, they were eating uncooked shallots, and on this occasion Yu left the white bulbs uneaten. Tao asked him, "What are you going to do with those?"

Yu replied, "Of course, they can be planted." For this Tao admired him greatly, not only for being a cultivated gentleman but also for possessing a genuine capacity for administration.

— from chapter 29, "Stinginess and Meanness"

An Unusual Flavor

The incidents in chapter 30 illustrate some of the negative aspects of Wei-Jin aristocratic society.

Emperor Wu (Sima Yan) once favored Wang Ji's[5] house with a visit. Wang tendered him a banquet for which he used all colored glass utensils. Over one hundred female slaves wearing silk-gauze trousers and blouses hand-served the food and drinks. The steamed suckling pig was succulent and delicious, with an unusual flavor. The emperor marveled at it and inquired about the recipe. He was told, "They used human milk to feed the suckling pigs."

Deeply offended, even though the meal was not yet over, the emperor left abruptly. It was something even Wang Kai and Shi Chong would never have thought of doing.

— from chapter 30, "Extravagance and Ostentation"

Coral Trees

Compare the biography of Shi Chong in chapter 10. — Editors

In their competition for display, Shi Chong and Wang Kai exhausted every refinement and elegance in ornamenting their carriages and clothing. Since Emperor Wu was Wang Kai's nephew, he frequently helped Kai out, and on one occasion presented him with a coral tree two feet or so in height. Its branches and twigs spread luxuriantly, and in all the world it would have been very hard to find its equal. Kai proudly showed it to Chong, who, after he had finished looking at it, struck it with his iron *ruyi* baton,[6] completely shattering it in one blow.

Kai was not only shocked and indignant, but also suspected that Chong had done it out of jealousy of his own treasure, and both his tone and expression were extremely severe.

Chong responded, "Think nothing of it; I'll repay you today." Whereupon he ordered his attendants to bring out all his own coral trees. There were six or seven of them three to four feet or so in height, with branches and trunks surpassing anything in the world and with luster and color that overwhelmed the eyes. Still other trees, all roughly

---

[5] Wang Ji's wife was the emperor's daughter, the Princess of Changshan.

[6] The *ruyi* baton (literally, "as you like it"), originally a crude backscratcher made of bamboo, was in very high fashion in the third and fourth centuries and was sometimes made of jade or even metal.

comparable to Wang Kai's, abounded in great numbers. Kai stood there speechless and unstrung.

— from chapter 30, "Extravagance and Ostentation"

Temper

The incidents of chapter 31 represent the exact opposite of the "cultivated tolerance" of chapter 6 of *Tales*.

Wang Shu was by nature extremely short-tempered. Once while he was attempting to eat a hard-boiled egg, he speared it with his chopstick, but failed to get hold of it. Immediately flying into a great rage, he picked it up and hurled it to the ground. The egg rolled around on the ground and had not yet come to rest when he got down on the ground and stamped on it with the cleats of his clogs, but again failed to get hold of it. Thoroughly infuriated, he once more picked it up from the ground and put it in his mouth. After biting it to pieces, he immediately spewed it out.

When (Shu's lifelong enemy, the calligrapher) Wang Xizhi heard about it, he laughed aloud and said, "Even if his father, Wang Cheng,[7] had had a temper like this, there still wouldn't be a single redeeming feature about him worth discussing. How much less so in the case of Wang Shu!"

— from chapter 31, "Anger and Irascibility"

Over the Wall

The stories in chapter 35 deal mostly with what we might call "romantic love." Even in the relatively free atmosphere of medieval Chinese society it was not necessarily considered an appropriate relationship between a man and a woman.

Han Shou was handsome in appearance and features, and Jia Chong summoned him for his aide. Every time Chong held a meeting with his staff, his daughter, Jia Wu, would peep in through the blue decorated window. When she saw Shou she immediately took a liking to him and constantly cherished thoughts of him in her heart, which she expressed in chanted poems.

Later, one of her slave girls went to Shou's house, where she related all this and in addition spoke of the girl's radiant beauty. As Shou listened to her he was moved in his heart and accordingly requested the slave girl to carry back a secret message of assignation.

---

[7] Wang Shu's father's reputation was partly based on his unflappable disposition.

On the appointed day he went to spend the night. Shou surpassed all his peers in nimbleness and gained entrance by leaping over the wall, so that no one in the household knew of his visit. Some time after this Chong became aware that his daughter was being rather lavish in applying makeup, and her cheerful elation was different from usual. Later, when he called together his aides he noticed that Shou had about him the aura of an exotic perfume, one that had been sent as tribute from a foreign country. Once it was applied to a person's body it lasted for months without fading.[8] Chong calculated that Emperor Wu had only bestowed this perfume on himself and on his favorite, Chen Jian; no other family possessed any. He suspected that Shou had been intimate with his daughter, yet the walls surrounding his house were double and solid, and the main gate and side entrances were tightly guarded and impenetrable. How could he have gotten in? In the end he attributed it to there having been a burglary and ordered the walls inspected for breaches. The inspectors returned and reported, "Everything is the same as usual, except only that by the northeast corner there seem to be human footprints. Yet the walls are high; they couldn't have been leaped over by any man."

Chong thereupon gathered his daughter's attendants and slave girls and interrogated them closely, and they responded with the facts in the case. Chong kept the matter secret and gave his daughter in marriage to Shou.

— from chapter 35, "Blind Infatuations"

எ **Further Reading** எ

Campany, Robert Ford. *Strange Writing: Anomaly Accounts in Early Medieval China.* Albany: State University of New York Press, 1996.

DeWoskin, Kenneth, trans. "In Search of the Supernatural—Selections from the *Sou-shen chi.*" *Renditions* (1977), 7.

————, & J. I. Crump Jr., trans. *In Search of the Supernatural: The Written Record.* Stanford: Stanford University Press, 1996.

Kao, Karl S. Y., ed. *Classical Chinese Tales of the Supernatural and the Fantastic: Selections from the Third to the Tenth Century.* Bloomington: Indiana University Press, 1985.

Lu, Xun (trans. Yang Xianyi & Gladys Yang). *A Brief History of Chinese Fiction.* Beijing: Foreign Languages Press, 1959.

---

[8] In his commentary Liu Jun speculates that this was probably the same dark, mulberry-based scent that was brought as tribute from Kushana in Central Asia in the first century B.C. If so, it would seem to have been the resin, storax (*Suhe*), which was likewise purple in color and long-lasting in fragrance, and which at that time would have been imported from the Sassanian Kingdom in Iran.

Ma, Y. W., & Joseph S. M. Lau, eds. *Traditional Chinese Stories: Themes and Variations.* New York: Columbia University Press, 1978.

Mather, Richard B., trans. *A New Account of Tales of the World by Liu I-ch'ing, with Commentary by Liu Chün.* Minneapolis: University of Minnesota Press, 1976.

Yang, Gladys and Xianyi, trans. *The Man Who Sold a Ghost: Chinese Tales of the 3rd–6th Centuries.* Hong Kong: Commercial Press, 1958.

——— . *Poetry and Prose of the Han, Wei and Six Dynasties.* Beijing: Foreign Languages Press, 1986.

"I am a crazy person."
Seal from the Vernal Radiance Collection

Part 3

The Sui, Tang and Five Dynasties (589–960)

"Heaven of Poesy, Sea of Wine."
Seal carved by Zhao Zhichen (1780–1860) and Xu Mao (fl. 1825)

Chapter 17

The Great River

Poets of the Early Tang

Your denigrators will have faded into nothingness,
But the Great River will flow on for ever.

> — Du Fu (712–770), writing of the Early Tang masters

They drew the stream of the Six Dynasties into the Early Tang.

> — Huang Jie (1874–1935), writing of the
> Four Talents and Four Heroes of the Early Tang

It was in the first year of the Long-shuo Reign (661) that there was a change in the world of letters. Then they were competing to construct the delicate and subtle, vying to make the ornamented and the crafted, confounding the gold and the jade, the dragon and the phoenix, confusing vermilion and purple, yellow and green, copying each other in their greed for great merit, artificing parallelisms to proclaim the loveliness of their craft. Informing point and spirit were utterly gone; strength and subtleness unheard of.

Yet yearning to excise these faults that they might bring glory to the deeds of their ambition were Xue Yuanzhao of the Secretariat, the elder man of letters in court, who formed friendships with his juniors and urged this total change, and Lu Zhaolin, a genius in the ordinary world, who observed the true pattern and brought a halt to those activities man should strive against.

Those who understood literature joined them; those who understood the men themselves followed them.... In but a single morning the filagree preciousness of many years was swept clear and open, spacious was the garden of brushes, and the forest of fine phrases grew ever more imposing.

> — Yang Jiong (b. 650), Preface to *The Collected Works of Wang Bo*
> *(translated by Stephen Owen)*

Introduction

Stephen Owen

The period in the history of Chinese poetry known as the Early Tang extends from the foundation of the dynasty in 618 until roughly 713, when Xuanzong took the throne. The Early Tang does not represent a unified style in its own right: rather it saw the close of a long era of court poetry and the slow transition to the new style of the High Tang. The tradition of court poetry stands at the center of the changes that were taking place in the seventh century. "Court poetry" here refers specifically to the poetry of the later Southern Dynasties, Sui and Early Tang courts. Although poetry was written in the Chinese courts both before and after this period, it was during the late fifth, sixth, and seventh centuries that the court was the real center of poetic acitivity in China. Not only was a substantial proportion of the surviving corpus written for court occasions, the distinctive "courtly style" also dominated poetry written outside the court.

During the first half of the seventh century the courtly style became increasingly mannered and rigid; strong counter-trends developed which sought either to modify the courtly style or to develop an alternative to it. The thematic scope of poetry began to broaden as poets went beyond the strictly limited range of topics and occasions found in court poetry. Furthermore, the rigid techniques of rhetorical amplification in court poetry came to exert a less mechanical control over the process of composition. In these and other ways, poets of the later seventh and early eighth centuries moved towards a new freedom, while retaining much that was good in the older style.

— from the introduction to *Early Tang Poetry*, 1977

WANG JI (585–644)
Four Poems

Translated by Stephen Owen

Wang Ji was a poet who eschewed the embellished and oblique style of his time, and instead opted for simplicity and directness in the fashion of Tao Yuanming [see chapter 11] and Ruan Ji [see chapter 10], both of whom he admired greatly.

Farmers

The poet chooses the lazy, physical life of this world instead of the quest for immortality.

All his life Ruan Ji was lazy,
And Xi Kang was a carefree spirit.
When they met, they drank their fill,
Sat alone, wrote a few lines,
Tried raising cranes by a tiny pool,
Pastured piglets in tranquil fields.

Grass grew over Tao Yuanming's path,
Flowering trees hid Yang Xiong's cottage.
Lie on your bed, watch your wife weave,
Up a hill and urge your son to hoe —
Then turn your head and the quests for the immortals
Become all one great emptiness.

View of the Wilds

The poet climbs a high place and faces a world of autumn, of old age and decline. The close of the poem powerfully expresses the poet's alienation from the tranquil, pastoral scene, the isolation of someone who is out of place in human society, who has no place to which to "return."

Figure 37. View of the Wilds. Early twentieth-century illustration. (Source: *Zixi huapu daquan* [Complete Painter's Manual] [Beijing: Rongbaozhai, 1982])

Toward evening on East Hill gazing,
Hesitant, uncertain, nothing to depend on,
On tree after tree, the colors of autumn,
On mountain after mountain, radiance of the setting sun.
The herdsman turns back, driving his calves,
The hunter's horse returns, bearing a bird.
I look at them; I do not know them.
A long song and a yearning to "pluck the bracken."[1]

Written on the Tavern Wall

Wang Ji does seem to have been something of an alcoholic, and his obsession with
wine surpasses even that of Tao Yuanming. Chinese poets were usually less interested
in the wine itself than in their vision of themselves drunk.

Last night a jar was emptied,
This morning a new jug opened.
In dream I foresaw that the dream would end,
And I would come back to the tavern.

Drinking Alone

How long can this floating life last?
A formless creature chasing empty glory.
Better to brew a lot of wine,
To tip your cup often in a bamboo grove.

To a Kill-Joy

Translated by Herbert Giles

Indulgence in the flowing bowl
Impedes the culture of the soul;
And yet, when all around me swill,
Shall I alone be sober still?

---

[1] This refers to the story of the hermits Boyi and Shuqi, who refused to serve the newly
founded Zhou dynasty, and instead retired to the hills, eating bracken until they starved
to death.

Record of Drunk-Land

Translated by Herbert Giles

Drunk-Land lies at I cannot say how many thousand *li* from the Middle Kingdom. Its soil is uncultivated and has no boundary. It has no hills nor dangerous cliffs. The climate is equable. Nowhere is there either darkness or light, cold or heat. Customs are everywhere the same. There are no towns; the inhabitants live scattered about. They are very refined; they neither love, nor hate, nor rejoice, nor give way to anger. They inhale the breeze, and drink the dew; they do not eat of the five cereals. Happy in their rest, dignified in their movements, they mingle freely with birds, beasts, fishes, and crustaceans. They have no chariots, nor boats, nor weapons of any kind.

Of old, the Yellow Emperor visited the capital of this country; and when he came back, in his confused state he lost his hold on the empire,[2] all through trying to govern by a system of knotted cords.[3] When the throne was handed on to Yao and Shun, there were sacrifices with a thousand goblets and a hundred flagons, the result being that a divine man had to be shot, in order to secure a passage into this territory, on the frontiers of which will be found perfect peace for life. Under the Great Yu, laws were instituted, rites were numerous, and music of varied kinds, so that for many generations there was no communication with Drunk-Land. Then Xi and He threw up their appointments as astronomers royal and fled,[4] in the hope of reaching this country; but they missed their way and died young, after which there was much unrest in the empire. The last Emperors of the House of Xia and of the House of Yin toiled violently up the steps of the eight-thousand-feet mountain of Grains;[5] but though long gazing southward, they never could see Drunk-Land. The Martial King satisfied his ambition in his generation. He ordered his Grand Astrologer to establish a Department of Wine, with its

---

[2] This statement is based upon imagination only.

[3] Originally used for rudimentary arithmetic and popularly exaggerated into a method of government.

[4] "Now here are Xi and He. They have entirely subverted their virtue and are sunk and lost in wine. They have violated the duties of their office, and left their posts. They have been the first to allow the regulations of heaven to get into disorder, putting far from them their proper business. On the first day of the last month, the sun and moon did not meet harmoniously. The blind musicians beat their drums; the inferior officers and common people bustled and ran about." *Book of History*, book 4, chapter 2, verse 4, translated by James Legge.

[5] From which whisky had been distilled.

proper officials; and he extended his territory for 7,000 *li*, until it reached Drunk-Land. The result was that for forty years punishments were unknown, down to the reigns of King Cruel and King Grim. By the time of the Qins and the Hans, the Middle Kingdom was in a state of confusion and collapse, and communications with Drunk-Land were cut off. However, certain enlightened friends of mine often slipped across on the sly. The poets Ruan Ji, Tao Yuanming, and others, to the number of ten or a dozen, went off to Drunk-Land, disappeared there and never came back; they died there and were buried in its earth. They are known in the Middle Kingdom as the Wine Immortals. Ah me! How different are the customs of the people of Drunk-Land from those of the country of the mother of Fu Xi of old! How pure and peaceful they are! Well, I have been there myself, and therefore I have written this record.

LU ZHAOLIN (634–c. 684)

Lu Zhaolin is traditionally regarded as one of the Four Talents of the Early Tang. These writers, however, did not constitute a real coterie; the social contacts between the four were rare and fleeting, and indeed Lu Zhaolin and Luo Binwang were nearly a generation older than Wang Bo and Yang Jiong.... Lu was early given a position in the private archive of the prince of Deng, seventh son of the founding emperor of the Tang dynasty. A fine scholar, Lu was said to have exhausted the resources of the prince's extensive library; this erudition is evident in the many uncommon allusions employed in his poems. He appears to have been at court until at least 666, when he was a member of the party accompanying the third Tang emperor on his pilgrimage to Mount Tai. Shortly thereafter Lu was posted to Shu (modern Sichuan). During the last years he spent in Shu, he suffered from what seems to have been a debilitating disease that eventually left him lame of foot and palsied in one hand. When his chronic physical agony became unbearable, he drowned himself in the River Ying.

— Paul Kroll, *Indiana Companion*, 1986

Chang'an

Translated by Stephen Owen

During the second half of the seventh century, there were several poems written about the Tang imperial capital. Lu's poem recalls the city when it was the capital of the Han dynasty. Ezra Pound translated the first sixteen lines in *Cathay*, under the title "Old Idea of Choan."

Chang'an's broad avenues
    link up with narrow lanes,[6]

---

[6] The "narrow lanes" are associated with the brothels and entertainment quarters.

There black oxen and white horses,
    coaches of fragrant woods,
Jade-fit palanquins go left and right
    past the mansions of lords,
Gold riding whips in a long train move
    toward barons' homes.
Dragons bite jeweled canopies,
    catching the morning sun,
The phoenix disgorges dangling fringe,
    draped with evening's red clouds.
A hundred yards of gossamer strands
    strain to enwrap the trees,
While a single graceful flock of birds
    join their cries among flowers.
Cries among flowers, playful butterflies,
    by the palace's thousand gates,
The emerald trees, the silver terraces,
    thousands of different colors.
Double-decked passageways, intertwined
    windows make the union of lovers.
Paired tower gates, rising layers of tiles
    which sweep as phoenix wings.
The Liang clan's muraled tower
    rises into the skies,[7]
The Emperor of Han's golden columns
    jut straight beyond the clouds.[8]
But those you gaze on before great
    buildings are those you do not know,
And those you meet upon the paths,
    no acquaintances of yours.
Tell me of her who plays the pipes
    off into purple mists —
She has spent her years of beauty
    in the study of the dance.[9]

---

[7] Liang Yi's famous tower was painted with pictures of the Immortals.
[8] The "golden columns" were erected by Emperor Wu of Han; they supported pans to collect the dew, from which an elixir of immortality was to be made.
[9] The first story referred to here is that of Xiaoshi, the master of the panpipes, who was engaged by Duke Mu of Qin to entertain his daughter. The pair fell in love; Xiaoshi taught her to play the pipes, and they flew off together on a phoenix. The second story refers to Zhao Feiyan, a favorite of Emperor Cheng of Han, who studied the dance in her youth and thus attracted the attention of the emperor.

If we could become the *bimu* fish,
    why should we flee from death?[10]
Could we but be the mandarin ducks,
    no yearnings to be immortals.[11]
The *bimu*, the mandarin ducks,
    are truly worth our yearning —
They go in pairs, they come in pairs —
    can't you see them now?
Most I hate that single phoenix
    woven in the top of the drape,
Most I love the swallow pair
    fixed on the curtained door.[12]
Pairs of swallows fly in their pairs
    around the painted beams,
There, gauze hangings, the kingfisher
    quilt, scent of turmeric.
Then one by one, hairdos like clouds,
    cicada-wing curls hanging,
Eyebrows slender like new moons
    above the tawny oils.[13]
Tawny with oil, white with powder,
    they step from coaches,
Charms within, loveliness within,
    hearts not fixed on one.
Bewitching boys on jeweled horses
    with ironblack spots,
And courtesans, pins of coiling dragons,
    golden legs bent under.
In the office of the Censorate
    the crows cry by night,[14]

---

[10] The *bimu*, conventionally used as a metaphor for lovers, was a legendary fish with two
bodies and one eye shared between them.

[11] Mandarin ducks were traditional symbols of confugal fidelity and happiness.

[12] Swallows were traditionally associated with marital and sexual love.

[13] Cloudlike coiffures, "cicada-wing" curls, and "new moon" eyebrows are the Tang
equivalents of "lips like cherries," "teeth like pearls," and "eyes like stars" — the
metaphorical itemization of feminine beauty.

[14] Crows crying by night in the Censorate, evolving from an incident in Han omenology to
a popular song to a *yuefu* title, may suggest that the Censorate, charged with ferreting out
official corruption, is idle.

By the Constabulary gate
    the sparrows go to roost.[15]
Mightily rising Vermilion Walls
    look down on roads like jade,
In the distance azure carriages
    sink behind gold-fast bastions.
Slings are clasped, falcons flown
    north of Duling,
Lots drawn for killing by sworn companions
    west of the Wei.
Greeting each other the bravos
    with lotus-hilted swords,
Spend nights together on paths to peach
    and plum, the houses of singing girls.[16]
At sunset in singing girls' houses
    are skirts of purple gauze,
And a verse of clear singing
    comes swelling from their mouths.
In the northern halls night after night,
    people move as the moon,[17]
On southern paths at every dawn,
    riders move as the clouds.
Southward paths and northern halls
    link through the Northern Quarter,
Then great crossroads and wide highways
    rein in the Markets.
Pliant willows and green ash
    hang brushing the earth,
Sweet air and red dust
    rise darkening the skies.
Royal heralds of the House of Han come,
    a thousand outriders,

---

[15] Sparrows roosting in the Constabulary suggests corruption and idleness similar to that of the crows crying in the Censorate.

[16] Peach and plum, here used in reference to the singing girls, comes from a much-repeated Han proverb that though peach and plum do not speak, a path forms to them; that is, people come to admire their beauty.

[17] "Northern hall" refers to the women's quarters which were ritually located on the north side of a house. The young gallants are "like the moon" in that they come out by night and retire in the morning.

Then kingfisher-colored liquors
    in parrot-shaped goblets.
Blouses of gauze and jeweled sashes
    are taken off for you,
The songs of Yan, the dances of Wu
    for you performed.
But there are others bold and splendid,
    called "minister," "general,"
The day turns, the heavens roll,
    and neither will yield to the other.
Haughty spirits ever willing
    to push aside a Guanfu,[18]
A hold on power which cannot give
    in the least to a Minister Xiao.[19]
Haughty spirits, hold on power,
    the stuff of ruthless heroes,
Blue Dragon and Purple Swallow,
    great steeds in the spring wind.
They said themselves their songs and
    dances would last a thousand years,
And claimed a pride and extravagance
    beyond the Great Lords.
But the glory of each thing in its
    season was not to wait on them,
Mulberry fields and green oceans
    interchange in an instant.
Where once were the golden stairs,
    the halls of white marble,
We now see only
    the green pines remaining.
Silent there in the emptiness,
    the dwelling of Yang Xiong,[20]
Year after year, every year,
    his whole bed covered with books.
Alone are the cassia flowers,
    blooming on South Mountain,

---

[18] Guanfu was a Han general known both for his moral uprightness and arrogance.
[19] A reference to Xiao Wangzhi, a powerful minister at the time of Emperor Yuan of Han.
[20] Yang Xiong, one of the most outstanding Han writers and intellectuals, appears after the Han as an archetypal scholar-hermit.

They fly back and forth,
fly into his sleeves.

Translator's commentary:
The poems opens with the reader's eyes somewhere on the great roads of Chang'an,
watching the traffic. The aspect which Lu emphasizes about this noble society is that
of socializing, traveling and meeting, visiting patrons and lovers. To this is opposed the
dwelling of Yang Xiong at the end of the poem. But in the capital everything is
movement and mobility, a flux that mirrors the larger theme of impermanence: the
poet focuses on descriptions of coaches, palanquins, passageways, all the means by
which people can move and get together.

The seasonal motif is spring, associated with sexuality and physical prowess in the
young bravos. Spring is a prodigal season and its lushness finds an echo in the
ostentatious extravagance of the wealthy and noble. With this aristocratic society of
the court is associated the yearning for immortality — dragons, phoenixes, buildings
(which symbolically "rise into the sky") painted with murals of the immortals, and the
golden columns with their dewpans from which was to be made the elixir of eternal
life.

But this is a "big city," and like all "big cities," it is full of strangers. With this in
mind, all the traveling and visiting takes on a new aspect, a quest for companions in a
world of strangers. As estrangement undercuts the theme of companionship, the
treatment of this splendid world in terms of spring growth undercuts the quest for
immortality. The sensual life in the capital is identified with the vegetative life of
spring, a fragile and impermanent beauty. By the end of the poem we are left only with
the pines of the tombs and the cassia flowers which endure the cold.

Early in the poem, however, the poet takes a less extreme stand than he does in the
end. He counters the false hope of immortality with an affirmation of the constant but
mortal love of the *bimu*, the mandarin ducks, and the swallows. He sees through the
frantic search for companions in the aristocratic world to its essential solitude and
fickleness; this he hates. This hated solitude is unlike the noble solitude of Yang Xiong
at the end of the poem.

The idleness of the Censorate and Constabulary is seen in the behavior of the
birds. We see the young bravos choosing lots to assassinate their enemies. The mood
of violence and aggression, hidden beneath the beauty of spring, increases as the poet
moves into the political sphere, to the struggles for power of the ministers and
generals. In them the heroic spirit turns to hubris. Here appears the fixed topos which
procedes the description of the city in ruins in Bao Zhao's rhapsody "The Desolate
City" [see chapter 12], and in other poems in that tradition: "They said themselves
their songs and dances would last a thousand years."

Next the poet brings in the explicit theme of impermanence: men and their
empires are cyclical and seasonal, passing from flowering to ripeness to ruin. But Lu
offers the enigmatic alternative of Yang Xiong, appearing as the hermit. His silence
contrasts with the city's bustle; his solitude contrasts with their gregariousness; his bed
of books contrasts with their concerns. And though he is not granted more than a
mortal span, the phrase "year after year, every year" gives a sense of stability and
continuity, set against the impermanence of the struggle for glory and futility of the
quest for immortality in the capital. The cassia, traditional symbol for purity and
virtue, grows on South Mountain, traditional symbol of eternity. The haunting last line
brings back the world of change in the image of the falling blossoms, but beside the

hermit these seem almost inconsequential as they are blown back and forth by the
wind and into his sleeve.

LUO BINWANG (before 640–684)
Two Poems

Translated by Stephen Owen

Like Lu Zhaolin and Wang Bo, Luo Binwang was moving away from the decorum of
court poetry, not toward a new simplicity and directness, but rather toward the
complexity of rhetorical exposition. More than any poet before Han Yu, Luo was an
intellectual poet. He began his career by entering the service of the Prince of Dao. In
678 he was imprisoned for criticizing Empress Wu; in 680 he was exiled to a minor
post in Zhejiang Province. Later he joined the rebellion of Xu Jingye and is presumed
to have been one of thousands who perished in the crushing of that rebellion.

On the Cicada: In Prison

The Western Course: a cicada's voice singing.
A southern cap: longing for home intrudes.
How can I bear those shadows of black locks
That come here to face my Song of White Hair?
Dew heavy on it, can fly no farther toward me,
The wind strong, its echoes easily lost.
No one believes in nobility and purity —
On my behalf who will explain what's in my heart?

Translator's paraphrase:
When the sun moves through the Western Course of the heavens, the cicada sings. Its
singing causes homesickness in me, like that once felt by Zhong Yi of Chu, wearing his
southern cap as a memento of his homeland when a prisoner in the state of Qin. Like
him I am a southerner imprisoned in the North. How can I bear that those wings of
the cicada, so often used to describe the curls of beautiful ladies, come to listen to my
"Song of White Hair,"[21] like that which Zhuo Wenjun sang when Sima Xiangru
abandoned her? Those black cicada wings like curls remind me of youth and attractive beauty, unbearable to one who is growing old and feels rejected by his ruler.
Furthermore, since the singing of the cicada is a reminder of autumn, the season
associated with the coming of old age, how can I bear that it come any closer to me,
reminding me of my own ageing? But perhaps I have misunderstood the cicada:
associated with purity and old age, it may be a kindred spirit. If my ruler hears it, it may
remind him of my purity and old age, and thus obtain my release. In this respect its
singing is like pleading my case to the throne. But it, like me, is caught up in the
autumn situation which it represents: the dew is so heavy on it it can fly no further and

---

[21] See chapter 27 for the "Song of White Hair," attributed to Zhuo Wenjun. *Eds.*

thus will not be able to get into the palace and reach the ruler's ears; furthermore, though I might hope that its singing, or my own in this poem, were to reach near the throne, it would do no good, because no one believes any more in nobility or purity — neither mine, my innocence of crime, nor that of the cicada. Thus there is no one to state my case for me.

Mooring by Jiangzhen in the Evening

The fourfold cycle shifts to the Yin pitchpipes,[22]
The Three Wings float on Baron Yang.[23]
The scent of lotus melts away late summer,
As breath from chrysanthemums enters new autumn.
Night crows chatter on whitewashed battlements.
Geese descend for the night on isles of reeds.
Ocean fogs veil the frontiers,
A wind from the river encircles the fortress tower.
The whirling tumbleweed startles at signs of parting,
The shifted orange grieves for departure's sorrow.
My soul flies to the slopes of the Ba Mounds,
My tears are used up in Lake Dongting's currents.
I'll stir my shadow, my thoughts on the "swan over the plain,"
And flee renown, withdrawing from Anthill.
But then I sigh at how far the capital is —
In vain I gaze on the white clouds drifting.

Translator's paraphrase of the last eight lines:
I, a wanderer like the whirling tumbleweed, am shaken when I see something that reminds me of parting and being away from home; in the same way I am like the orange, which grows only in the South and changes to a different tree if transplanted in the North, thus a symbol of steadfastness and purity. Since my body cannot go there, my soul flies off to the Ba Mounds, near Chang'an where I long to be; since I cannot go there I use up all my tears weeping here in the South. In the *Book of Changes* we read, "The wild swan slowly crosses the plain, but the wanderer does not return." The best visual evidence of my motion will be in my shadow, so I'll set it moving to emulate that wild swan and return home. In avoiding political success and fame I'll be like that tavern keeper at "Anthill" in Chu who left his tavern to avoid meeting Confucius. But even though I would like to return home and renounce worldly glory on one level, I cannot help but yearn for the distant capital and worldly success on another. Thus as I gaze toward the capital, my vision is blocked by white clouds,

---

[22] The cycle of the seasons moves into autumn.

[23] The Three Wings were the three classes of war galleys. Luo had moored one evening in early autumn at the Yangtze port of Jiangzhen, where he saw the ships of the imperial fleet. Baron Yang, as the god of the waves, represents the river.

suggesting to me both those who "block" me from Her Majesty's/His Majesty's favor
and the cloudlike vanity of my desires.

WANG BO (649–676)
Two Poems

Translated by Stephen Owen

Famous for his parallel prose, Wang Bo was another of the Four Talents of the Early
Tang. He was a precocious scholar and wrote a critique of the *History of the Han* at the
age of ten or eleven.

Parting by Moonlight in a River Pavilion

Wang Bo was one of the first poets to use a grand understatement, often a single
image or descriptive line, to close the quatrain. The elegant, courtly opening couplet
of this poem is transformed by the simplicity of the last line.

Wild mists veil the emerald stairs,
The moon in flight heads toward the southern horizon.
Silence, the pavilion where we part is closed —
Mountains and rivers cold this night.

Departing from Yiyang in the Early Morning

I packed my bags in dawn moonlight,
Wait on the fading stars to speed up my riding whip.
From the sheer tower make my way over cinnabar cliffs,
Off twisting bridges reach to azure screens.
Among clouds I'm lost in the shadows of trees,
Then in fog can't make out the forms of the cliffs.
And now again a chill gust comes,
Sets flying night's fireflies in deserted mountains.

CHEN ZI'ANG (661–702)
Seven Poems

Translated by Stephen Owen

Chen Zi'ang, a native of Sichuan, was among the first poets in the Tang dynasty to
express open discontent over the affectedness of contemporary poetry and to advocate a return to the seriousness of the Han-Wei style. His views are contained in the
introduction to his poem "The Tall Bamboos," in which he criticizes the poetry of

the Southern Dynasties for its obsession with formal beauty at the expense of profound feelings and advocates a return to more serious themes. He was recognized for the remainder of the dynasty as an innovative poet who set an example for those poets of later ages concerned with social issues. Du Fu wrote of him:

> Born to the line of Sima Xiangru and Yang Xiong
> Your fame hangs in the heavens with the sun and moon.

Chen was more than once unjustly imprisoned on various charges, and he eventually died in prison.

Meditation on the Past at White Emperor City

White Emperor City is the historic city of Kuizhou, on the Yangtze. This poem, and the next, probably date from his first trip down the Yangtze, to take the examination in Luoyang. He is constantly looking back to Ba (Sichuan) and is careful to note "the domain of Zhou" (which excluded Sichuan), the Chinese heartland encompassed by the "deeds" of Yu (the legendary emperor). He repeats these broad geographical designations as though they held some magic in themselves.

The sun sinks — evening on the blue river;
I rest my oars to ask of local customs.
These walls look out on the land of Ba,
While into the terraces sink the palaces of the King of Han.
A wild region — still in Zhou's domain.
Deep in its mountains remain the deeds of Yu.
Peaks hang, their green cliffs broken off,
Terrain perilous, the emerald stream goes through.
Ancient trees rise at the edge of the clouds,
Homeward sails emerge in the fog.
My river road goes off without end —
This wanderer's longing now seems endless too.

Staying in Luoxiang County for the Evening

My homeland is infinitely far —
Here, setting sun and a solitary journey.
Streams and plains hide my former country,
A road moves out toward frontier walls.
A fortress in the wilds, moor mists break it off,
Deep in the mountains, ancient trees level.
What is it like, the grief of this moment? —
Screeching shrilly, gibbons cry by night.

Entering Qiao Gorge and Anju Creek: The Source of Wood-Chopping Creek was Hidden Far Away, Forests and Peaks Brightened One Another — A Wondrous Experience

This poem was written in the 680s in Luoyang, during Chen's term as Corrector of Characters.

I whistled to companions, sang "Chopping Wood,"[24]
Oars raced the skiff bouncing the ripples.
On a long, winding course I followed the waters,
Splashing through current, upstream in the shallows.
Misty sands split two shores,
Dew-drenched isles flanked by pairs of shoals,
Dense forests of ancient trees reaching the clouds,
And floating peaks, criss-crossed, fallen upon the waters.
Cliff and pool cast lovely light upon each other,
Stream-filled valleys circle round and round.
The road is far, light presses urgently on me,
The mountains deep, my mood still more withdrawn.
Evening — chill brooding of deer and squirrels;
Autumn — sunset sounds of gibbons and birds.
I vow to give up my plans in the Royal Library,
Go traveling in the hermit land of cassia.
Thus I write to take leave of friends and loved ones,
For a thousand years I'll search for Fairy Hill.

Song on Youzhou Terrace

This is probably Chen's most famous poem, a straightforward and moving description of the isolation of the individual in space and time, cut off from past and future, dwarfed by the immensity of the universe.

I look back — I do not see the ancients;
I look ahead — can't see the generations to come.
I brood on the endlessness of Heaven and Earth,
And tears stream down — I stand alone.

---

[24] *Book of Songs* 165. In the traditional Mao interpretation, this song is associated with seeking companions.

Stirred By My Experiences
Three of a Series of Thirty-Eight Poems

1

This much acclaimed series of poems is often seen as descended from Ruan Ji's series, "Poems of My Heart" [see chapter 10]. This, the fifth poem in the series, is divided into two parts, the first representing the crass, rejected world, the second representing the ideal world to which the poet aspires, that of the immortal. Chen's immortals, cold, bemused, and aloof, represent more a point of view than actual transcendent beings.

Men of the marketplace boast their cunning,
Yet in the Way they show child's foolishness.
Crawling over each other in boasting and show,
Unaware of the end they shall meet.
How could they see the Master of Mystery,
Observing the world in his flagon of jade,
Fading away, leaving Heaven and Earth,
Riding Change into the Never-Ending?

2

This, the thirty-second poem of the series, places the longing for old friends in the context of a meditation on impermanence.

How many days now, living in seclusion, in solitude? —
Blazing summer is suddenly in decline.
Bright colors in sunlight all shaded and covered,
Friends and relations — strayed, gone different ways.
Climb a mountain, gaze, cannot see them,
Tears trickle down in an endless stream.
All my life stirred by their faces' beauty,
As though fixing a time to meet the white clouds.
Proud young men on horseback,
Galloping after each other in dumb confusion.
In the mountains of Shu, by the rivers of Chu —
When again shall we join hands?

3

The old theme of the spirit journey through the heavens reappears here in a new guise. The madman of Chu comes in the *Analects*, XVIII:5: "Jieyu, the madman of Chu, passed by Confucius singing: 'Phoenix, O Phoenix! How low has virtue fallen!... It is finished! Those now in government are in danger!' Confucius dismounted desiring to speak with him, but Jieyu fled." The unbalanced sage is closely allied to the figure of

the crazy old Taoist, beneath whose foolishness and seeming incoherence is supposed
to lie deep wisdom.

Just now in wild, free mood I yearn,
But for what? — for Mount Emei in my own Shu;
I long to be with the madman of Chu,
To meet him in white clouds, endlessly far away.
The times must be wrong! I grieve that I've missed mine,
And tears trickle down in an endless stream.
I dreamed I climbed to the caves of Mount Sui,
Then to the south gathered herbs on Mount Wu,
Investigated the Basis, observed all things in Change,
Left the world, chasing a dragon in the clouds.
But when its undulations would seem to last forever,
I awoke. I could not see it.

DU SHENYAN (died c. 705)
Two Poems

Translated by Stephen Owen

The grandfather of Du Fu, he was exiled to Fengzhou (up the Red River from Hanoi)
in 705, accused of complicity in a political conspiracy. The verses written at that time
show the beginning of a new awareness of the deep south.

Written at Jumble-Rock Mountain by the South Sea

This landscape poem was written by Du during his exile of 705.

The Sea of Zhang swells to the very sky,
And a host of mountains rear up high from the earth.
They tell me this place is called Jumble-rock,
The charts and classics tell nothing of it.
Its sheer overhangs are all frightening,
Great or small, none of the ordinary kind.
At once it will reach out to cloudy isles,
Then back up to link with the river of stars.
Suddenly jutting up as though in flight,
Then hanging over sharply on the point of falling.
Dawn's glow makes it blush purple and crimson,
And in moonlight it gleams blue and turquoise.
On the towering summits fog and rain gather;
Sequestered there, fairies and spirits hide.

Ten thousand yards up a crane's nest hangs,
A gibbon's arm dangles over a thousand-foot drop.
When I left home before, seasonal winds moved forth;
By the time I've reached here, the third month has come.
Observing this place, I sing my song,
For long I'll imagine the strangeness of its spirits.

Lodging in Annam

In Jiaozhi the weather is strange,
The cold comes slowly, the warmth hurries back again.
In mid-winter mountain fruits are ripe,
In the first month wildflowers blossom.
Dusky fogs arise from the monsoons,
Light frosts bring down peals of thunder.
My homeland, over ten thousand miles away —
Thoughts of it twice what they once were.

SONG ZHIWEN (d. 712)

On Old Zhang's Pine Tree

Translated by Stephen Owen

Song Zhiwen and Shen Quanqi were two poets whose names are usually paired and whose works are traditionally taken as the epitome of the poetry that marked the transition from the Early Tang to the High Tang. Both men passed the *jinshi* examinations in 675 and were associated with the government of Empress Wu. They were both exiled to the provinces when this government fell in 705. A general amnesty returned them to the capital soon afterward, but Song Zhiwen apparently could not refrain from involvement in the politics of imperial succession and after the accession of the Emperor Xuanzong was ordered to commit suicide.

The pine tree had long been a symbol of solitary rectitude, but in this poem Song handles the theme with exceptional power.

The year grows late beneath the eastern cliff,
I peer all around — how desolate it seems!
The sun sinks in the shadows of western mountains,
And from all plants rises the visage of the cold.
In their midst there is a tall pine,
Which brings me to heave a long sigh.
A hundred feet up without a single branch,
By nature a lifetime straight and alone.

SHEN QUANQI (c. 650–713)

First Reaching Huanzhou

Translated by Stephen Owen

By the time Shen reached Huanzhou [present-day Vietnam], he was in complete despair, certain that his place of exile had been chosen with singular malice.

Banished travelers — eighteen of us —
But the decree for me was unlike the others.
I was exiled the furthest — to the world's very end —
And took longest to arrive, the last of them all.
By water I went through the Dan'er's lands,
Then overland through jungles of tattooed savages.
My soul wandered to the very gate of the ghosts,
And my skeleton will be left in Leviathan's mouth.
Bearing with my hunger I lie down by night,
At dawn move on swiftly, carrying sickness.
I scratch out my hair in this southern wilderness,
Brush away tears gazing at the northern Dipper.
Oh, what year will reprieve arrive,
That I may once again drink the wine of Luoyang?

ZHANG YUE (667–731)
Two Poems

Translated by Stephen Owen

A transitional figure between Early and High Tang, Zhang Yue was an influential statesman.

Hearing Bells at Night in the Mountains

The sounds of a Buddhist temple bell were reminders of the vacuity of existence.

Lying down by night I hear night's bells,
A night so still the mountains resound with them.
A frosty wind blows the cold moon,
Far and deep away it rises in the emptiness.
The first notes have been struck,
Then the later notes sweep flashing over.
I listen for them as though I could see them.
Try to pinpoint them — no fixed form.

Now truly I understand that ultimately we stand
    at the edge of Nothingness,
But futile fantasies of life and death linger in my mind.

Composition in Drunkenness

I'm drunk — my joy is boundless —
In every way better than not being drunk:
Each time I move it's a dance,
Each time I speak it's a poem.

ᴇᴘ *Further Reading* ᴇᴘ

Owen, Stephen. *The Poetry of the Early T'ang.* New Haven: Yale University Press, 1977.

"Snow Peak."
Seal carved by Jiang Ren (1743–1795)

Chapter 18

Wang Wei (701–761)

Poet and Painter

In a former life, I erred in becoming a poet.
In some previous incarnation, I must have been a painter.

— Wang Wei, from No. 6 of "Six Occasional Poems"

Savor his poetry, and there is a painting in each poem; look carefully at his paintings, and each one contains a poem.

— Su Dongpo (1037–1101), *Recollections*

The line

Long river, the falling sun rolls around ("Mission to the Frontier")

is written without any predetermined visual conception; the line

Across the stream, call to the woodcutter ("Mount Zhongnan")

is written without any prior notion.

These are examples of the "this-ness" of the Zen Buddhists.

— Wang Fuzhi (1619–1692),
Notes on Poetry from the Ginger Studio

In the Wheel River quatrains of Wang Wei and Pei Di, each word enters Zen ... These poems are wonderful truths and subtle words. They are just like

Sakyamuni picked a flower
And Kasyapa gently smiled.

— Wang Shizhen (1634–1711),
Remarks on Poetry from the Hall of the Classics
(translations by John Minford)

Wang Wei's commitment to Buddhism is evident not so much in explicit doctrinal argument or vocabulary — of which there is little — as in the attitude implicit in his poetry. His contemplative, dispassionate observations of the sensory world affirm its beauty at the same time as they call its ultimate reality into question, by emphasizing its vagueness, relativity, and "emptiness" ... The simple, natural diction and syntax of much of his poetry suggests an effortlessness analogous to that moment of enlightenment which masks the care taken to achieve it.

— Pauline Yu, *Indiana Companion*, 1986

In Wang Wei, the scenery *speaks* and *acts* ... The objects spontaneously emerge before the reader-viewer's eyes ...

Can landscape in its naive, innocent, original form, without involving the world of concepts, occupy us directly? If the poet's answer to this question is positive, he will attempt to release the objects in Phenomenon from their seeming irrelevance and bring forth their original freshness and thingness — return them to their first innocence, so to speak ... The poet merges with and, in some sense, becomes the objects before the act of composition, and focuses attention upon them in such a way as to allow them to leap out directly and spontaneously to us, unhindered ...

The state of stillness, emptiness, silence, or quiescence is ubiquitous in the landscape poems of Wang Wei and his contemporaries. The "voices" one hears are those one hears in absolute silence ...

— Yip Wai-lim, *Diffusions of Distance*, 1993

Introduction

H. C. Chang

Wang Wei was one of the most gifted of men: a consummate musician at a time when music flourished in China, one of the great masters of Chinese painting, a poet among the first rank in the golden age of Chinese poetry. The combination was not uncommon, but the degree of attainment unusual....Wang Wei was precocious, and even his juvenilia have withstood the test of time. From the age of fourteen we find him more or less continuously in the capital Chang'an, which we might regard as his home. Though he did not always occupy an official position, from the age of nineteen he was a social celebrity.... As musician, as painter and as calligrapher, he was much sought after.

Like other scholars of his time, Wang cherished political ambitions. He was eager to serve under the upright and outspoken Zhang Jiuling, who became Prime Minister in 734. At the age of thirty-three, Wang was made a Reminder, a post within the central administration with duties similar to those of the censors, and he doubtless acquitted his responsibilities with conscientious zeal....

But there was an otherworldly strain in Wang, which came increasingly to the fore with the years. He had been brought up as a Buddhist by his mother, to whom he was utterly devoted, and the piety instilled in him in early childhood never abandoned him. While still in his twenties, he retreated for a time to Mount Song (near Dengfeng in Henan Province), one of the Holy Mountains. It was no more than a trial, at the end of which he again took part in mundane affairs.

Soon after his return from a tour of the northwest frontier, in 738–39, Wang made another retreat, to the Zhongnan Mountains, about thirty-five kilometers south of Chang'an. He was out of office and, following a pattern set by the lives of Tao Yuanming [see chapter 11] and Xie Lingyun [see chapter 12], considered the possibility of retirement.... He explored the Zhongnan and the neighboring Lantian mountains with the joy of discovery. This phase of withdrawal probably lasted only about a year, but it gave him a foretaste of the secluded life which he was to lead five or six years later. It was at this time that Wang found in Pei Di, who was a dozen or so years his junior, a congenial companion, possessing literary gifts and a temperament akin to his own. Pei, too, sought solitude in the Zhongnan Mountains, to whose memory he remained faithful in after years. For both friends, those mountains were ever enduring in a world of change and vicissitudes, and the main Zhongnan peak was almost the embodiment of eternity.

From 742 Wang was continuously in the capital.... But he was now more than ever inclined to a life of detachment and contemplation away from the press and bustle of governmental affairs. As an artist, he had received substantial rewards over a score or more years, so that he could afford to purchase a large estate to provide a permanent retreat for himself and a shrine for his mother's devotions. The estate was ten kilometers southwest of Lantian, a town about forty kilometres to the southeast of the capital. He was thus able to repair to it at regular intervals. And when his mother died, his three-year period of mourning was also spent there.

The acquisition, planning and laying out of the estate — known as "Wang River" or "Wheel River," because at the mouth of the gorge by which it was situated, the swift current of the stream met another stream, as a result of which it whirled round in eddies like so many spoked chariot wheels — probably took place in the years 744–7. The estate had previously belonged to the poet Song Zhiwen [see chapter 17], but there had been a lapse of over thirty years between the two owners. Gardens and Chinese houses decay rapidly, so that we might presume all the twenty views of "Wheel River" to have been planned by Wang. The twenty poems by Wang and the companion poems by Pei Di — together known as the "Wheel River Poems" — would date from the second and third year of the acquisition, when every prospect and vista, every nook and recess, was in accordance with Wang's fastidious taste.

Wang Wei's relatively easy personal circumstances, the stability and prosperity of the times in which he passed most of his days, the unstudied poise of the social celebrity, his placid temperament, Buddhist piety and resignation have all contributed to the perfect calm and transparency of his poems…. In his lightness of touch may be detected the hand of the artist who softened the harsh lines of solid landscapes in the earlier tradition into the graceful curves of his ink washes. For our poet seems to subsume his identity under the conventions of rural and landscape poetry set up by Tao and Xie, namely, the lowly cottage, the cheerful farming neighbors, the fields, banks and furrows, the sowing, the self-imposed seclusion, on the one hand; the lake and hills, the bamboo grove and woods, mountain streams and precipices lit up by the setting sun or rising moon, the sense of adventure, on the other. And yet the man's personality emerges distinctly. One might almost say that the transparency of his personality is the poetic achievement of Wang Wei. Who else has succeeded in transmitting such moods of calmness, tranquillity and ease?

— from *Chinese Literature, vol. 2: Nature Poetry*, 1977

Poems from Wheel River
Ten from a Sequence of Twenty, with Accompanying Poems by Pei Di (b. 716)

Translated by Jerome Ch'en and Michael Bullock

The Cove of the Wall of Meng

WANG: My new house
    is at the beginning of the wall of Meng,
Among old trees
    and remains of decaying willows.
The other, after me,
    who will he be?
Vain his grief
    for this which was mine.

PEI: My new hut
    is under the old wall:
Occasionally I go up
    to the ancient enclosure.
There is nothing of the past now
    about the old wall;

Men of today, uncaring,
   come and go.

The Hill of Huazi

WANG: The birds fly away
   into infinite space:
Over the whole mountain
   returns the splendor of autumn.
Ascending and descending
   Huazi hill,
I feel
   unbounded bewilderment and
      lamentation.

PEI: The sun sets,
   the wind rises among the pines.
Returning home,
   there is a little dew upon the grass.
The reflection of the clouds
   falls into the tracks of my shoes.
The blue of the mountains
   touches my clothes.

Figure 38. "The blue of the mountains touches my clothes." Late Ming (1368–1644) illustration of Pei Di's poem, "The Hill of Huazi." (Source: *Tangshi huapu* [Tang Poems Illustrated] [Shanghai: Guji, 1982])

The Hill of the Hatchet-Leaved Bamboos

WANG: The tall bamboos
    soar to the sky
    and their tops bend.
The deep blue
    in the slight movement of the waves
    trembles.
I walk along
    the unfamiliar Shang hill-roads
Which even the woodman
    does not know.

PEI: In the white moonlight the stream
    winds its way
    and disappears from sight.
The green of the bamboos
    grows denser,
    and then spills over.
Without pause
    I push on along the mountain road;
I walk and sing,
    my eyes on the familiar summits.

The Deer Enclosure

WANG: On the lonely mountain
    I meet no one,
I hear only the echo
    of human voices.
At an angle the sun's rays
    enter the depths of the wood,
And shine
    upon the green moss.

PEI: At the end of the day
    the mountain looks cold.
But a belated wanderer
    still passes on his way.
He knows nothing
    of the life of the wood:
Nothing remains
    but the tracks of the buck.

The Magnolia Enclosure

WANG: The mountain receives
    the last rays of autumn:
Flocks of birds follow
    the first flights.
A flash of emerald
    flares out from time to time.
The darkness of evening
    has nowhere to rest.

PEI: From the vault of light
    at the going down of the sun,
The voices of the birds
    mingle with the voice of the torrent.
The path beside the stream
    winds into the distance;
Joy of solitude,
    will you ever come to an end?

The Path of the Ashtrees

WANG: On the narrow path,
    sheltered by the ashtrees
In the secrecy of their shade
    flourishes the green moss,
Only swept
    when someone answers the gate,
Fearing that the monk from the mountain
    has come to call.

PEI: To the south of the gate,
    along by the ashtrees,
Is the path over the hillcrest,
    that leads to Lake Yi.
When the autumn comes
    it rains much on the mountain;
No one picks up
    the falling leaves.

Lake Yi

WANG: The voice of the flute
    reaches the farthest bank.

It is sunset, and I am coming with you,
    my master.
From the high shore of the lake
    I turn back again to look;
On the green of the mountains
    white clouds are gathering.

PEI: Wide in the emptiness
    spreads the water of the lake:
Its pellucid splendor
    reflects the hue of the sky.
I moor the boat to the bank,
    and whistle contentedly.
The freshness of the breeze
    reaches me from every side.

The Stream at the House of the Luans

WANG: Gusts of wind
    in the autumn rain;
The water falls headlong,
    it spills from the rocks in torrents.
The waves leap capriciously
    one on the other in flight;
The startled white heron
    comes down to earth again.

PEI: The voice of the stream
    resounds to the farthest bay.
I walk along the shore
    toward the southern ford.
Here and there on the water
    ducks and egrets glide,
Always they return, impelled
    to the proximity of men.

The Hermitage of the Bamboos

WANG: In solitude
    sitting in the hidden forest
    of the bamboos,
To the sound of the lute
    I whistle suspended notes.
In the secrecy of the wood
    I see no one:

The bright moon reaches me
with its light.

PEI: I come and go
in the hut
isolated among the bamboos,
Every day
more familiar with the Tao.
I go and come back:
there are none here
but the birds of the mountain.
Where solitude is deepest,
the people of the world
cease.

 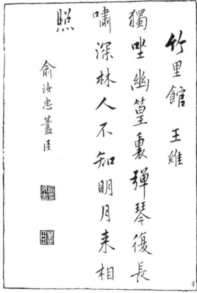

Figure 39. "In the hidden forest of the bamboos." Late Ming (1368–1644) illustration of
Wang Wei's poem, "The Hermitage of the Bamboos." (Source: *Tangshi huapu* [Tang Poems
Illustrated] [Shanghai: Guji, 1982])

The Bank of the Magnolias

WANG: The tops of the hibiscus trees
are in flower,

On the mountains
    the vermilion petals blaze.
Silent is the hut beside the torrent:
    there is no one at home.
By thousands and thousands the flowers
    open and fall.

PEI: On the green bank in springtime,
    when the grass is thick,
The princely descendants
    are already glad to stay.
How much the more, if all around
    the bright-colored flowering
    magnolias mingle
    with the hibiscus.

Letter to Pei Di Written in the Mountains

Translated by H. C. Chang

This letter dates from the winter (probably of 746) preceding the spring in which Pei left Chang'an. From it we learn how the Wheel River Poems — by now completed — were written. Many, at least, of the lines came to Wang and Pei on their walks, whether along the slopes or by some stream.

It being the last month of the year and the weather fine and unexpectedly mild, these our old haunts were well worth visiting. Since I knew that you were engaged in a systematic re-reading of the classics, not wishing to disturb you, I set off by myself for the mountains. After a short rest at Ganpei Temple, where I supped with the monk, I proceeded northwards and was ferried across the black stream of the Ba under a silvery moon that illumined the outskirts of the city [Chang'an]. I ascended Huazi Hill by night. Below, the rippling waves of Wheel River danced with the moonbeams. In the distance, the hills looked cold and bare, although a fire here and there defined the shapes of trees and woods. In a winding lane a dog was barking furiously, the reverberation resembling a leopard's growl. And the noise of the villagers' threshing alternated with the sound of the temple bell.

    At this moment I am seated by myself, with the servants hushed and out of sight. And my thoughts hark back to former days, when hand in hand we would walk along some mountain path to stop before a clear stream, composing verses as we went. It cannot now be long before spring. The plants and trees will put forth leaves and the hills will be

seasonably clad in green for all to admire. Shoals of small, leaflike white
fish will leap out of the water, and the white gulls spread their wings. The
grass on the river bank will be moist with dew, and the wheat fields
echoing of a morning with the crowing of pheasants. Perhaps you will
then be free to roam the hills with me? If I did not know your pure and
unworldly cast of mind, I should not have presumed to ask you to join in
this idle and useless activity, from which, however, one may derive deep
interest and lasting satisfaction. Pray give the matter more than a passing
thought. The dyewood gatherers who will carry this are leaving, and I
must close.

From the mountain-dweller Wang Wei

Nine Poems

Translated by Jerome P. Seaton

To Magistrate Zhang

Late, I love but quietness:
Things of this world are no more my concern.
Looking back, I've known no better plan
Than this: returning to the grove.
Pine breezes: loosen my robe.
Mountain moon beams: play my lute.
What, you ask, is Final Truth?
The fisherman's song, strikes deep into the bank.

Mount Zhongnan

Zhongnan, The Great One, so near the Celestial City,
Linked mount on mount to the sea.
White clouds, where I look back, close in.
Green mists, when I approach, are gone.
Its peak, the pivot of the constellations' change;
Its valleys deep, define both light and shade.
I try to find a place to spend the night,
Across the stream, call to the woodcutter.

Commentary by François Cheng:
In line 1, The Great One is both a notion of Chinese spirituality and an alternate
name for Mount Zhongnan. Celestial City is the name of a star, but also designates
the Tang capital, Zhongnan. Mount Zhongnan is, indeed, located near the capital. In
line 6, "light and shade" alludes to Yin and Yang as well as to the sunny (southern) and
shady (northern) sides of the mountain.

A more "explicit" translation of lines 3 and 4 might be: "The white clouds, when one turns back to contemplate them, melt together into a unity; the green mists, to the extent to which one penetrates them, become invisible." The poem mixes together two orders of being, the celestial and the terrestrial. It relates not so much a simple mountain walk taken by the poet, as the visit to the terrestrial world of a divine spirit who descends little by little from the peak into the valley, finally embodying himself to speak with the woodcutter.

Another Version and Commentary by Yip Wai-lim:
    The poet looks both at and from objects in nature, hence the changing perspectives and nontemporal sequence in Chinese landscape poetry. Like the Chinese landscape painter who uses multiple or revolving perspectives to represent his or her total experience of the mountains (as they are viewed from different vantage points and in their various appearances and moods), the Chinese landscape poet attempts to lay out all moments of experiencing a mountain reality spatially ...

1. The Zhongnan ranges verge on the Capital,
   (viewer on level ground looking from afar — moment 1)
2. Mountain upon mountain to sea's brim.
3. White clouds — looking back — close up.
   (viewer coming out from mountain — moment 2)
4. Green mists — entering — to see nothing.
   (viewer entering — moment 3)
5. Terrestrial division change at the middle peak.
   (viewer atop peak looking down — moment 4)
6. Shade and light differ with every valley.
   (viewer on both sides of mountain — moment 5)
7. To stay over in some stranger's house —
   (viewer down on level ground — moment 6)
8. Across the water, call to ask a woodcutter.

In lines 3 and 4, there are changing perspectives in each line: "White clouds" (shot one), from a distance; "looking back" (shot two), viewer coming out from the mountain from the opposite direction, turning his head back; "close up" (shot three), viewer returning to the same position as for shot one. The visual events are accentuated the way a mime, in order to suggest an event that is not visible, highlights gestures and movements to suggest the energy flow that originally supports that event.

Passing Hidden Fragrance Temple

Who knows the Hidden Fragrance Temple,
How many *li* away, on cloudy peak?
Ancient trees, no trace of path.
Deep mountain, whence the bell?
Sound of the spring, the standing stones, sobbing.
Color of the sun, the green pines, freezing.
Toward dusk, on the curve of the lake,
Quiet Zen, to tame the poison dragon.

Commentary by François Cheng:
Lines 5 and 6 are, by their syntactic structure, ambiguous. Is it the spring that sobs, or the rocks? Is it the sunlight that freezes, or the pines? The poison dragon represents inappropriate passions.

On the Mountain

Jing gorge: white rocks jut.
Cold sky: a few red leaves.
No rain upon this mountain path,
Just azure emptiness, to wet the cloak.

Birdsong Torrent

Man in repose: the cassia flowers falling.
Night calm: spring mountains empty.
Moon surges: startles mountain birds.
Sometimes their cries, within spring's torrent.

In Retirement at Zhongnan

To middle age I loved the Way.
Late now, I lodge upon South Mountain.
If feelings rise, I go alone:
Such scenes as I have seen ...
Walk to where the waters narrow,
Sit, and wait, for the clouds to rise.
Let me meet by chance with any old man:
We laugh and chat, no thought of the return.

Commentary by François Cheng:
Lines 5 and 6 (a parallel couplet) provide an excellent illustration of the profound spirit of parallelism. By referring to the word-for-word translation below, the reader may be able to perceive how the coupling of the parallel elements engenders a deeper significance:

walk	*attain*	*water*	*narrow*	*place*
sit	*see*	*cloud*	*rise*	*moment*

The pair "walk-sit" signifies movement and rest; "attain-see" signifies action and contemplation. "Water-cloud" signifies universal transformation, "narrow-rise" signifies death and rebirth. Finally "place-moment" signifies space and time. Once this series of significations is taken into account, the two lines may be seen to embody the two fundamental dimensions of all life. And the true Way is to choose neither one exclusively, but rather to embrace the Void between the two; to separate neither action and contemplation, nor time and space, but to participate in the universal transformation.

Figure 40. Early twentieth-
century illustration of Wang
Wei's poem, "In Retirement
at Zhongnan." (Source: *Zixi
huapu daquan* [Complete
Painting Manual] [Beijing:
Rongbaozhai, 1982])

Autumn Mountain Evening

Empty mountain, after new rain,
The air of nightfall, autumn.
A bright moon glows among the pines.
The clear stream flows, upon the rocks.
Bamboo rustles, washing maids come home.
Lotus stirs, as fishing boats return.
Fragrance of spring rests here and there.
You too, my gentle friend, may stay.

Mission to the Frontier

A single cart to the frontier
Beyond Quyan, past conquered states,

Wandering grass, beyond our borders.
Wild geese, in alien skies.
Vast desert, lone spire of smoke, stands straight.
Long river, the falling sun rolls round.
At Desolation Pass, met a patrol.
Headquarters camp, on Swallow Mountain.

Commentary by François Cheng:
In lines 5 and 6, Wang Wei, always the poet-painter, suggests a complete picture by contrasting different elements of the landscape. The contrast is carried into the interior of each line; it exists between the two lines of the couplet as well. Literally:

| *immense* | *desert* | *lone* | *smoke* | *straight* |
| *long* | *river* | *setting* | *sun* | *round* |

The desert that extends infinitely; the single straight plume of smoke; the river that flows afar; the sun, fixed for a single instant: these contrasts exist within the lines. And between the lines, the static desert and the dynamic river; the smoke that rises and the sun that descends; the vertical line and the roundness; the black and the red.

Commentary by Yip Wai-lim:
As signs, words function best when they capture the life mechanism of the moment of experience ... Wang Wei suggests the articulation of visual curves and movements:

Vast — desert — lone — smoke — straight

[In the fifth line] "vast desert," a panoramic view; "lone smoke" from possibly one single household, a single object in the midst of an immense expanse of emptiness; "straight," a windless condition true to the actuality of a desert. The line has the appeal of a painting; with the word "straight," it is almost sculptural.

Dike of the Cormorants

Now down among red lotus plunged,
Now out above the bright strand soaring:
Stands alone: the spread of plumage,
Fish in his beak, on a floating log.

A Poem of Farewell

Eight Versions

Der Abschied des Freundes

Translated by Hans Bethge (1907)

The German version of this poem by Hans Bethge, "Der Abschied des Freundes," together with his version of Meng Haoran's "At the Mountain-Lodge" (see chapter 21), "In Erwartung des Freundes," (both included in his 1907 collection *Die Chinesische*

Flöte [*The Chinese Flute*]), formed the basis of Gustav Mahler's "Der Abschied," the final movement of his haunting symphonic song-cycle *Das Lied von der Erde* (*The Song of the Earth*, 1907–8). Consider the various English translations of Wang Wei's bald third line ("*Jun yan bu de yi*" — literally "You say you-are-not satisfied"): Giles' "sick of life's ills," Fletcher's "your hopes unprospered," Bynner's " I am discontent," Watson's "nothing goes right," Yip's "at odds with the world," Owen's "something troubling you," Yu's "you did not achieve your wishes." How strangely flat they all seem against Mahler's poignant rhapsodic setting of his own rewording of Bethge: "Mir war auf dieser Welt das Glück nicht hold!" ("Fortune was not kind to me in this world!"). As Mahler himself wrote in his Draft Orchestral Score, the next line but one, "Ich suche Ruhe" ("I seek rest"), should be "unendlich zart" ("infinitely tender"). And Wang Wei's last line ("*Bai yun wu jin shi*" — literally "White clouds without completion time") contrasts strangely with the mood of ecstatic submission to nature with which Mahler's song ends: "Allüberall und ewig blauen licht die Fernen! Ewig ... Ewig ..." ("Everywhere and forever the distance shines bright and blue! Forever ... forever ...").

As the composer Alban Berg (quoted by Donald Mitchell, *Gustav Mahler: Songs and Symphonies of Life and Death*, 1985) wrote in a letter shortly after Mahler's death (1911), "I have just been passing through the glorious country which sent Gustav Mahler into similar raptures so shortly before his death. The mountains completely under snow show right down to the foothills, then green meadows, brown fields, and that sky: almost unbearably beautiful, I wish you could have seen it, you'd have forgotten all the trials of the journey. But now I must watch all this magnificence sad and alone, and — as I wrote this morning — the sadness won't leave me till tomorrow. The right mood, really, for *The Song of the Earth* ... "

The Parting of Friends: from the eighth-century Wang Wei, consummate musician and painter, lover of nature and poet, social celebrity and Buddhist recluse, through the intermediaries of translation and interpretation in various languages, to the aching weltschmerz of Mahler and Berg in the first years of the twentieth century. Is this, as Donald Mitchell puts the question, a Chinese poem "Europeanized out of all oriental recognition?" Or is there a "residual core of authenticity," deriving from the "ancient originals"? Has the Far East, the visionary China (the words are those of Theodor Adorno) become a mode of "disillusioned romanticism"? Or has something of the ambivalence of Wang Wei, man of the world and Buddhist, survived? Each reader must decide.

— Editors

Ich stieg vom Pferd und reichte ihm den Trunk
Des Abschieds dar. Ich fragte ihn, wohin
Und auch warum er reisen wolle. Er
Sprach mit umflorter Stimme: Du mein Freund,
Mir war das Glück in dieser Welt nicht hold.

Wohin ich geh? Ich wandre in die Berge,
Ich suche Ruhe für mein einsam Herz.
Ich werde nie mehr in die Ferne schweifen,
Müd ist mein Fuss, und müd ist meine Seele,
Die Erde ist die gleiche überall,

Und ewig, ewig sind die weissen Wolken ...

Goodbye to Meng Haoran

Translated by Herbert Giles (1884)

Dismounted, o'er wine we had said our last say;
Then I whisper, "Dear friend, tell me whither away."
"Alas!" he replied, "I am sick of life's ills
"And I long for repose on the slumbering hills.
"But oh seek not to pierce where my footsteps may stray:
"The white clouds will soothe me for ever and ay."

"So Farewell. And If For Ever, Still For Ever Fare Ye Well."

Translated by W. J. B. Fletcher (1919)

Quitting my horse, a cup with you I drank.
And drinking, asked you whither you were bound.
Your hopes unprospered, said you, turned you round
To sleep amid the Range's outer ground.
    You went. I asked no more. The White Clouds pass,
And never yet have any limit found.

At Parting

Translated by Witter Bynner (1929)

I dismount from my horse and I offer you wine.
And I ask you where you are going and why.
And you answer: "I am discontent.
And would rest at the foot of the southern mountain.
So give me leave and ask me no questions.
White clouds pass there without end."

Seeing Someone Off

Translated by Burton Watson (1971)

We dismount; I give you wine
and ask, where are you off to?
You answer, nothing goes right! —
back home to lie down by Southern Mountain.
Go then — I'll ask no more —
there's no end to white clouds there.

To See a Friend Off

Translated by Wai-lim Yip (1972)

Dismount and drink this wine.
Where to? I ask.
At odds with the world:
Return to rest by the South Hill.
Go. Go. Do not ask again.
Endless, the white clouds.

Parting

Translated by Stephen Owen (1977)

Stephen Owen has published three slightly varying versions of this poem, in *Poetry of the Early T'ang* (1977), *The Great Age of Chinese Poetry* (1981), and in his *Anthology of Chinese Literature* (1996). This is the earliest of the three.

— Editors

I get off my horse, offer you wine,
Ask you where you are going.
You say there is something troubling you
And go home to rest at the edge of southern hills.
Be off then — I'll ask no more —
White clouds for eternity.

Farewell

Translated by Pauline Yu (1980)

Dismounting I give you wine to drink,
And inquire where you are going.
You say you did not achieve your wishes
And return to rest at the foot of Southern Mountain.
But go — do not ask again:
White clouds have no ending time.

Six poems translated by various hands

Farewell to Spring

Translated by Sir J. F. Davis (1829)

Sir John Francis Davis (Governor of Hong Kong from 1844 to 1848) was one of the earliest English translators of Chinese poetry and fiction (see chapter 3). His *The*

Poetry of the Chinese, while it contains many errors and distortions, is a brave attempt to come to terms with an alien poetic idiom.

— Editors

Old age hastens on, as each fleet hour passes,
   Though spring ev'ry year re-illumines the glade:
So boys let's be jolly, and fill up our glasses,
   Ah, why should we sigh for the flowers that fade!

Playfully Inscribed on a Large Boulder

Translated by David Lattimore

One can care for   boulders
   that overhang a brook

then too   weeping willows
   brush the cup

if you say   the winds
   of spring are witless

why   do they blow us
   fallen flowers

Melody of Wei City

Translated by William Dolby

This is the poem Pound translates as an epitaph by "Rihaku [Li Bo] or Omakitsu [Wang Wei]" to his "Four Poems of Departure," in *Cathay.*

Light rain is on the light dust
The willows of the inn-yard
Will be going greener and greener,
But you, Sir, had better take wine ere your departure,
For you will have no friends about you
When you come to the gates of Go.

As Hugh Kenner writes in *The Pound Era,* "On its page in *Cathay* the whole poem is scarcely larger than a postage stamp. Its sonoric intricacies would have delighted Pope."

In a letter to Iris Barry written in 1916, Pound describes Wang Wei as an "eighth century Jules Laforgue Chinois." (One wonders on what basis? In the same letter he writes that he has "this day written my first two sentences in Chinese." But also in the same letter he observes, "Really one DON'T need to know a language. One NEEDS, damn well needs, to know the few hundred words in the few really good poems that any language has in it.") The idea of Wang Wei seems to have stuck. Writing in 1917 to

Kate Buss, he describes Wang Wei as "the real modern — even Parisian — of 8th-century China."

— Editors

Morning rain of Wei city
Damps the dust clean.
Fresh by the travelers' inn
Willow's verdant green.

Come, I bid you, sir:
Empty one more cup of wine,
For once you're West, beyond Yang Pass,
All your old friends are gone.

You Come from My Village

Translated by C. H. Kwock and Vincent McHugh

You
    come from my village
You ought to know
        what goes on
            in our part of the world
The day you left
    — outside
    my silk-paned window
that winter plum
    — was it blooming yet?

Weeping for Ying Yao

Translated by Burton Watson

Ying Yao, poet and official, was a close friend of Wang Wei and a fellow student of
Buddhism.

We send you home to a grave on Stone Tower Mountain;
Through the green green of pine and cypress,
        mourners' carriages return.
Among white clouds we've laid your bones — it is ended forever;
Only the mindless waters remain, flowing down to the world of men.

Climbing to the Monastery of Perception

Translated by Pauline Yu

A bamboo path leads up from the lowland —
On lotus peaks emerges the Conjured City.
From within a window all three Chu states;
Above the forests the nine level rivers.
On soft grass monks sit cross-legged;
Tall pines echo their chanting sounds.
Emptily dwelling beyond the Dharma cloud,
They contemplate the world, attaining non-rebirth.

Translator's commentary:
This monastery was located on Mt. Lu in Hubei Province. The poem was probably written during Wang Wei's official mission south in 740. Conjured City (line 2) alludes to a parable in the Lotus Sutra, in which a guide leads a multitude of people on an arduous journey toward a cache of jewels. When they become weary and frightened and wish to turn back, he conjures up a city in which they can rest temporarily, then dissolves it so that they will move on to their ultimate goal … The "nine rivers" (line 4) are the affluents of the Yangtze. Non-rebirth (line 8) denotes the liberation from the cycle of eternal rebirth or attainment of nirvana.

Running parallel to the account of an ascent to a mountain monastery here are allusions to the ten stages of the bodhisattva's progression toward enlightenment. While the "lowland" where the bamboo path begins refers literally to the foot of the mountain, for the Buddhist it simultaneously means the initial stage of entering on the road to Buddhahood…. The tenth stage is dharmamegha, where the bodhisattva gains the fertilizing powers of the "Dharma cloud," which drops its sweet dew everywhere.

🕮 Further Reading 🕮

Bynner, Witter, trans. (from the texts of Kiang Kang-hu). *The Jade Mountain, a Chinese Anthology: Being Three Hundred Poems of the T'ang Dynasty.* New York: Knopf, 1929.

Chang, H. C., ed. and trans. *Chinese Literature, Vol. 2: Nature Poetry.* Edinburgh: University of Edinburgh Press, 1977.

Chang, Yin-nan, and Lewis C. Walmsley, trans. *Poems by Wang Wei.* Rutland, Vt.: Tuttle, 1958.

Ch'en, Jerome, and Michael Bullock, trans. *Poems of Solitude.* London: Abelard-Schuman, 1960.

Cheng, François. *L'Ecriture poétique chinoise.* Paris: Editions du Seuil, 1977. Trans. by Donald A. Riggs and Jerome P. Seaton as *Chinese Poetic Writing: With an Anthology of T'ang Poetry* (Bloomington: Indiana University Press, 1982).

Fletcher, W. J. B., trans. *Gems of Chinese Verse, Translated into English Verse.* Shanghai: Commercial Press, 1919.

Giles, Herbert, ed. and trans. *Chinese Poetry in English Verse.* Shanghai: Kelly & Walsh, 1884.

Kenner, Hugh. *The Pound Era.* Berkeley: University of California Press, 1971.

Mitchell, Donald. *Gustav Mahler: Songs and Symphonies of Life and Death.* London: Faber and Faber, 1985.

Robinson, G. W., trans. *Poems of Wang Wei.* Harmondsworth: Penguin Books, 1973.

Wagner, Marsha. *Wang Wei.* Boston: Twayne, 1982.

Watson, Burton. *Chinese Lyricism: Shih Poetry from the Second to the Twelfth Century.* New York: Columbia University Press, 1971.

Weinberger, Eliot, and Octavio Paz. *Nineteen Ways of Looking at Wang Wei: How a Chinese Poem Is Translated.* Wakefield, R.I.: Moyer Bell, 1987.

Yip, Wai-lim, trans. *Hiding the Universe: Poems by Wang Wei.* New York: Munshin-sha/Grossman, 1972.

———. *Diffusion of Distances: Dialogues between Chinese and Western Poetics.* Berkeley: University of California Press, 1993.

Yu, Pauline. *The Poetry of Wang Wei: New Translations and Commentary.* Bloomington: Indiana University Press, 1980.

"Deep amid the Bamboos."
Seal carved by Yang Xie (1781–1850)

Chapter 19

Li Bo (701–762)

The Banished Immortal

A hundred poems per gallon of wine —
    that's Li Bo,
Who slept in the taverns
    of the market of Chang'an.
The Son of Heaven summoned him, and he
    couldn't stagger on the boat,
Said, "Your servant is indeed
    an immortal in his wine."

— Du Fu, "Eight Drinking Immortals" *(translated by Stephen Owen)*

When the poet Li Bo went from Sichuan to the capital, he lived in a small inn. Secretary-General He Zhizhang, aware of Li's renown, was the first to pay his respects. He marvelled at Li's appearance and asked many times to see specimens of his writings. Li showed him the poem "The Road to Shu is Hard." He waxed lyrical in praise of the poem, before he had even finished reading it, and dubbed Li the Banished Immortal. He then removed his golden tortoise waist-ornament and bartered it for wine. The two men drank until they wobbled, and became inseparable companions, widely known throughout the capital.

— Meng Qi (fl. 841–886), "The Free Spirit of Li Bo," from
The Original Incidents of Poems (translated by Howard Levy)

When He Zhizhang read Li Bo's "Song of the Roosting Crows," he said: "This poem could make gods and ghosts weep."

— Fan Chuanzheng, "Tomb Inscription for Li Bo" (*translated by Stephen Owen*)

Under the Dynasty of the Tang, *Li tsau pe and Tu te mwey* [Li Bo and Du Fu] did not yield to Anacreon and Horace.

— Du Halde, *A Description of the Empire of China*, 1738

Li Tae-pih [Li Bo], the greatest poet of his time, tuned his lyre to notes on the pleasures of wine and of beauty, which would have done honour to Anacreon. Evening feasts amid the parterres of gardens rich with the bloom of a thousand flowers furnished themes upon which he and his imitators were never tired of dilating.

R. K. Douglas, *The Language and Literature of China*, 1875

And Li Po [Li Bo] also died drunk.
He tried to embrace a moon
In the Yellow River.

— Ezra Pound, *Lustra*, 1916

Introduction

Burton Watson

Li Bo would probably be close to the top on almost anyone's list of the greatest Chinese poets of premodern times. It is generally agreed that he and Du Fu raised poetry in the *shi* form to the highest level of power and expressiveness; later poets at times approached but never surpassed them. It was some centuries before the true worth of Du Fu's work was acknowledged, but Li Bo's poetry seems to have gained almost immediate recognition. This may be due to the fact that, unlike Du Fu, Li Bo was no innovator. For the most part he was content to employ the poetic forms inherited from his predecessors and to devote himself to the conventional themes of the past. Of the 1,000 poems attributed to him, about one sixth are in *yuefu* ballad style, which means that they are reworkings of themes drawn from the old folk song tradition, while another group of his poems is entitled *gufeng* or "in the old manner." Li Bo's distinction lies in the fact that he brought an unparalleled grace and eloquence to his treatment of the traditional themes, a flow and grandeur that lift his work far above the level of mere imitations of the past.

Another characteristic of Li Bo's poetry is the air of playfulness, hyperbole, and outright fantasy that infuses much of it. The poem "My Trip in a Dream to the Lady of Heaven Mountain" is a good example, a work in irregular form that in rhapsodic language describes a dream journey to Tianmu, a mountain on the Zhejiang coast associated with Taoist lore. After the poet awakes, he resolves to leave the world of fawning and hypocrisy and retire to the mountains, the carefree life of the recluse being another important theme in his poetry. Other works stress the poet's unique rapport with nature, or his love of wine, the last a trait for which he is proverbial.

Though a wealth of legend has accrued about Li Bo's name, little is known of the facts of his life. (His birthplace is uncertain, perhaps in Central Asia — a minor branch of Li Bo studies centers on the irresolvable question of whether he was of Turkic origin.) He grew up in Sichuan in western China and later traveled extensively in the eastern and central regions. Just what kept him so constantly on the move is difficult to say, since his poetry, unlike that of Du Fu and many other major Chinese poets, tends to be impersonal in tone and to reveal relatively little about the poet's own activities. Around 742 he gained recognition from Emperor Xuanzong and was appointed to a post in the Hanlin Academy, in the government office charged with literary activities, but a few years later he was exiled from the capital as a result of slanders. He fled south at the time of the An Lushan rebellion in 755 and in time entered the service of Prince Yong, a member of the imperial family who was later accused of treason. The prince's downfall involved Li Bo in a second exile, though he was eventually pardoned and resumed his life of wandering.

In spite of such vicissitudes of fortune, Li Bo is little given to expressions of unmitigated despair or bitterness, his poetry on the whole being unusually calm, even at times sunny in outlook. It appears to grow not so much out of actual scenes and experiences of his lifetime as it does out of certain convictions that he held regarding life and art, out of a tireless search for spiritual freedom and communion with nature, a lively imagination and a deep sensitivity to the beauties of language.

— from *The Columbia Book of Chinese Poetry*, 1984

A Preface and Twenty Poems

Translated by Elling Eide

Preface for the Poetry from a Spring Evening Party for My Cousins in a Peach Blossom Garden

This Heaven and Earth are the hostel for Creation's ten thousand forms, where light and darkness have passed as guests for a hundred ages. But our floating lives are like a dream; how many moments do we have for joy? When the ancients took out candles for nighttime revels, they had the right idea. And we the more, when warm spring summons us with misted scenes and the Great Lump of Earth lends us patterned decoration.

Assembled in this garden perfumed by flowering peaches, we shared the happiness of those whom Heaven has related. My young brothers were all talented as the poet Xie Huilian, though my own songs could only shame me before Lingyun, his elder cousin. Yet our quiet enjoyment had not reached an end when the wit of our conversation grew more refined. We spread carnelian mats to sit beneath the flowers, let fly our winged cups and got drunk with the moon.

But if there were no handsome verse, how could you express exquisite feelings? When the poems did not succeed, we exacted forfeits in jars of wine as they did in the Garden of Golden Valley.

Quiet Night Thought

Before my bed the moonlight glitters
Like frost upon the ground.
I look up to the mountain moon,
Look down and think of home.

The Road to Shu Is Hard

This poem is an excellent example of Li Bo *yuefu* in the most extravagant manner. Using wildly irregular line lengths, Sichuanese exclamations (Shu is the old name for Sichuan), and long subordinate clauses normally excluded from both poetry and literary prose, Li hyperbolically describes the difficulties of the mountain journey from Chang'an to Chengdu [the Brocade City]. In reference to poems such as this, Li's contemporary Yin Fan described the poet's work as "Strangeness on top of strangeness."

— Stephen Owen, *Indiana Companion*, 1986

A-eee! Shee-yew! Sheeeeee! So dangerous! So high!
The road to Shu is hard, harder than climbing the sky.
Silkworm Thicket and Fishing Duck[1]
Founded their kingdom in the depths of time,
But then for forty-eight thousand years,
No settlers' smoke reached the Qin frontier.[2]
Yet west on Taibo Mountain, take a bird road there,[3]
You could cross directly to the peaks of Emei's brow.
When earth collapsed and the mountain crashed,
the muscled warriors died.[4]
It was after that when the ladders to heaven
were linked together with timber and stone.
Up above is
the towering pillar where six dragons turn the sun.
Down below on
the twisting river colliding waves dash into the turns.
The flight of a yellow crane cannot cross it;
Gibbons and monkeys climb in despair.

Green Mud Ridge — coiling, winding —
Nine turns in a hundred steps, round pinnacle and snag.
Touch the Triad, pass the Well Stars,
look up to gasp and groan.
Press a hand to calm your chest,
sit down for a lingering sigh.

I wonder as you travel west, when will you return?
I fear that a road so cragged and high is impossible to climb.
All I see is a mournful bird that cries in an ancient tree,
And cocks that fly in pursuit of hens,
circling through the forest.

---

[1] Mythical rulers of the Kingdom of Shu, gods of silkworm-breeding and of fishing. *Eds.*
[2] Qin is now the neighboring province of Shaanxi. The king of Qin was in the third century B.C. to conquer all China and establish the first central government of the Chinese Empire. *Eds.*
[3] Taibo Mountain is on the borders of Qin and Shu. *Eds.*
[4] The "muscled warriors" were five heroes of Shu sent in legend to the King of Qin to bring back his five beautiful daughters for the harem of the King of Shu. On the way back, they saw the tail of a great serpent protruding from a cave and all seized it and pulled, until after a long struggle they at last dragged the creature out; whereupon the great mountain split open with terrible earthquakes, leaving the wild rugged country of present-day Sichuan. *Eds.*

Yet again I hear the cuckoo call in the moonlit night —
sorrow upon the desolate mountain.
The road to Shu is hard, harder than climbing the sky.
Whenever one shall hear this, it wilts his youth away.

Peak after peak missing the sky by not so much as a foot.
Withered pines hang upside-down clinging to vertical walls.

Flying chutes and raging current,
how they snarl and storm!
Pelted cliffs and spinning stones,
ten thousand chasms thunderous roar!
The perils — this is the way they are.
And woe to that man on a road so far —
Oh why, and for what, would he travel here?
Sword Gallery looms above with soaring crags and spines;[5]
One man at the pass,
Ten thousand men are barred.
And if the guards are not our people,
They can change into jackals and wolves.

In the morning avoid fierce tigers.
In the evening avoid long snakes.
They sharpen teeth for sucking blood;
The dead are strewn like hemp.
Let them talk of pleasure in Brocade City,
The better thing is hurrying home.
The road to Shu is hard, harder than climbing the sky.
Edging back, I gaze to the west, long and deep my sighs.

My Trip in a Dream to the Lady of Heaven Mountain
A Farewell to Several Gentlemen of Eastern Lu

This poem, with its flight through space theme, belongs to one of the most venerable traditions in Chinese literature. Many of the images correspond with shamanistic techniques and symbols. Li Bo weaves the supernatural, natural, philosophical, and literary elements into a net that involves the reader in the act of creativity. He becomes a participant in the performance of the poem.

The poem is a technicolor dream and a rhapsody about a real mountain in the Tiantai range [compare Sun Chuo's "Wandering on Mount Tiantai: A Rhapsody" in chapter 10]; a frolic with allusions and word magic and an exercise in rejuvenating an

---

[5] Sword Gallery is a pass in the mountains between Qin and Shu. *Eds.*

ancient theme; a discourse on timeless eternity and the carefully clocked narration of a single day. It is also an essay in Taoist metaphysics, a statement of personal belief, and a magnificent description of a mountain thunderstorm. Probably no one will miss the progression from night to day that parallels Li Bo's progress up the mountain. But note also the progression of the storm: sunlight, gathering clouds, wind, rain, thunder and lightning, and finally clearing with rainbows and the reemergence of the animals and birds. The darkening of trees before the storm is nicely observed, and earlier usage gives gum trees special association with rain; just as dragons and tigers have associations with gathering clouds and rising wind. In all, this description of a thunderstorm seems to compare very well with the highly praised storm in the *mu'allaqa* of Imr al-Qays (fl. c. 530), who was apparently also a wanderer addicted to wine, women, and poetry in the Li Bo manner.

Seafarers tell of a magic island
Hard to find in the vague expanse
of mist and towering waves.

In Yue men talk of the Lady of Heaven[6]
Glimpsed by chance, dissolving and glowing,
amid the rainbows and clouds.

The Lady of Heaven, joining the heavens,
faces the Heavenly Span,[7]
Her majesty conquers the Five Summits
and shadows Vermilion Wall.
Heavenly Terrace rises up forty-eight thousand staves,
Yet tips southeast before her as if it wanted to fall.

Wanting to probe the mystery in a dream of Wu and Yue,
Through a night I flew across the moon on Mirror Lake.

The moon on the lake projected my shadow,
Escorting me to the River Shan.
The place where Duke Xie once retired[8]
stands to the present day;
The lucent waters swiftly purl and
shrill-voiced gibbons cry.
Feet in Duke Xie's cleated clogs
I climbed the ladder of clouds in the blue.
From the slope I could see the sun in the ocean;

---

[6] Yue refers to the present-day province of Zhejiang. *Eds.*

[7] The constellation Auriga, the Waggoner. *Eds.*

[8] Xie Lingyun, the poet and mountaineer (see chapter 12). He invented a detachable and reversible sole with studs or cleats to put on his boots: the short studs in front and the long ones behind for going uphill, the other way round for coming down. *Eds.*

From space I could hear the Rooster of Heaven.

A thousand cliffs, ten thousand turns,
    a road I cannot define;
Dazzled by flowers, I rest on a stone
    and darkness suddenly falls.

Bears grumbling, dragons humming,
    fountains rumbling on the mountainside.
Quaking before a deep forest.
Frightened by impending spires.
Green, green the gum trees. On the verge of rain.
Rough, rough the river. Breaking in spray.

Flashing, cracking, roaring, clapping,
    Hills and ridges crumble and fall.
The stone gates of the Grotto Heavens
    Boom and crash as they open wide.
The Blue Dark is a rolling surge,
    where bottom cannot be seen,
Where sun and moon throw glittering light
    on platforms of silver and gold.

The rainbows are his clothing. His horses are the wind.
The Lord Within the Clouds appears.
All things swirl as he descends.

Tigers strumming zithers. Coaches phoenix drawn.
The immortals now assemble. Arrayed like hemp in rows.
With the suden excitement of my soul,
    my vital force is roused;
I rise distraught and startled, long and drawn my sighs.
There is only the pillow and mat on waking;
Gone are the mists of a moment ago.

The pleasures found within man's world
    are also just this way;
All life's affairs since ancient times
    are an easterly flowing stream.

Parting now I leave you. When shall I return?
Let us set the white deer free[9]

---

[9] The white deer is a Taoist symbol often seen in paintings. It is the animal ridden by the Immortals. *Eds.*

within the blue-green shores;
When I must go, I shall ride away to visit peaks of renown.
How could I ever furrow my brow and bend my back
    in service of rank and power?
To hurry the pleasures of love and wine
    wilts man's youth away.

Xiangyang Song

As west behind Xian Mountain the setting sun would fall,
Put your hat on backwards, get lost beneath the flowers.
And Xiangyang's little urchins will clap their hands in time,
Block the street and jostle and sing "White Copper Greaves."[10]
If passersby should query what makes them laugh this way,
They're jeering Mister Mountain, drunk as a blob of clay.[11]

O cormorant ladle. O parrot shell cup.
In a hundred years six thousand and three
    ten-thousands of days,
and in a day you must be sure three hundred cups to pour.
See the Han's waters far away, green as a mallard's head,
    just like the grape
when the must is set to ferment for a second time.
If that river will transform to make us springtime wine,
Then the risings of yeast could terraces build
    upon that hill of lees.
A steed that's worth a thousand in gold
    I'd swap for a serving girl,
To drunken sit on a saddle carved and sing "Plum Petals Fall."
At the side of a cart I'd hang at a slant
    a single bottle of wine,
With phoenix *sheng* and dragon pipes[12]

---

[10] A popular local song. *Eds.*

[11] At the pool on the southern slopes of Xian Mountain near Xiangyang (birth place of the poet Meng Haoran, in the present-day province of Hubei), the famous governor Shan Jian ("Mister Mountain") liked to picnic, and would return roaring drunk. He became the subject of children's songs. *Eds.*

[12] The *sheng* is a musical instrument, consisting of a number of pipes of different lengths; it has a spout through which the player blows out or sucks in the air, while fingering the keyholes. *Eds.*

to urge each other along.
In the market place at Xianyang, sigh for a yellow dog?[13]
Better by far, beneath the moon, to pour from a golden jar.
Oh, don't you see,
for His Lordship Yang from the days of the Jin,[14]
that chunk of old memorial stone?
His tortoise head erodes away, the moss and lichens grow.
My tears cannot fall for him.
My heart cannot mourn for him.
Who can worry what happens after the body is gone?
Gold ducks and silver mallards bury ashes dead and cold.
The fresh wind and shining moon, no need for a coin to buy;
The jade mountain will fall on its own,
nobody pushes it down.[15]

O Shuzhou ladle. O Ironman pot.
Li Bo to share life and death with you.
King Xiang, the clouds and rain, where are they today?[16]
The river waters eastward flow, at night the gibbons cry.

Take Wine

Grape Wine. Golden Bowls.
And a girl from Wu, just fifteen, bundled on a blooded horse.
Indigo blue she paints her brows, red brocade are her shoes,
Speaking her words a little askew
she temptingly sings her songs.
At the feast on tortoise-shell mats
she gets drunk in your arms.
In bed behind the lotus curtains what will she do to you?

---

[13] When taken out to execution in 208 B.C., Li Si, prime minister of the First Emperor of the Qin dynasty, turned around and told his son how much he missed hunting with his yellow dogs. *Eds.*
[14] Visitors to Xiangyang were supposed to weep at the sight of the stele in memory of the virtuous magistrate Yang Hu. *Eds.*
[15] The poet Xi Kang (223–262) was described as "majestically towering, like a solitary pine tree standing alone. But when he's drunk he leans crazily like a jade mountain about to collapse." See chapter 10. *Eds.*
[16] References to King Xiang, or the "clouds and rain," are usually the unmistakable suggestions of sexual intimacy. *Eds.*

Bring On the Wine

We may note — perhaps with a twinge of envy — that for Li Bo and many others, losing oneself in drink provided a means of blurring the distinctions imposed by the human mind, so that the loneliness of individuality might give way to a comforting sense of identity with the eternal order. Li Bo's *yuefu* poems are studded with golden goblets sloshing with wine, with singing, dancing, and eating. This is the most famous of them. The Chinese poetic tradition had no lack of *carpe diem* poems and drinking poems, but never had there been one before that spoke to its audience with such violent energy.

— Stephen Owen, *The Great Age of Chinese Poetry*, 1981

O don't you see the waters of the Yellow River pouring
from the sky,
Rushing downward to the sea never to return?

O don't you see the mirrors in the mansions where they
grieve for graying hair,
Black silk floss at dawning that by dusk has turned to snow?
When you have some little triumph, you must fully taste the joy,
And never let a golden cup go to waste beneath the moon.

Heaven gave me talent, it will surely be employed.
If I spend a thousand coins, they will come back to me.
Stew the lamb, butcher the ox, and let the fun begin.
We must have three hundred cups once we start our binge.

Master Cen. Young Danqiu.[17]
Don't you stop when the wine is here.
I will sing a song for you.
Please favor me and lend an ear.
Bells and drums and dishes of jade are nothing to be prized:
Just vow to be forever drunk, be done with being sober.
The wise and worthy of ancient times all are silent now;
It's only the good drinkers who have left behind a name.

When the Prince of Chen in former times partied at Pingle Hall,[18]
With dippers of wine, ten times a thousand, they gave themselves to
joking and joy.

---

[17] The identity of Master Cen is uncertain. Danqiu is Yuan Danqiu, a friend referred to several times in Li Bo's works. *Eds.*
[18] The Prince of Chen is Cao Zhi (see chapter 9). *Eds.*

How could the host be saying that the money is running low?
I must quickly buy more wine and pour some more for you.

A horse with five florets. A thousand coin robe.
I'll call the boy to take them out to swap for wonderful wine.
And together we'll dissolve the sorrows of ten thousand things
gone by.

Song of the Heavenly Horse

It is important to note how well elements of this poem, with its elaborate blending of horse imagery, astronomy, anatomy, and references to Li Bo himself and the West, correspond with what we know of Li Bo's career. His exotic origin; early evidence of his great talent; his pride, self-confidence, and ambition; his overnight fame and success at the capital and his association with the emperor and high officials; his rather inexplicable rejection; his desperate efforts to return to service; his disgrace, jail, and exile; and an old age spent far removed from the splendors he had once known.

From the Scythian cave came the heavenly horse,
With tiger-stripe back and dragon-wing bones.
Neighing to clouds in the blue. Shaking a mane of green.
Orchid strong jaw sinew, speed tokened cheeks,
he vanished when he ran.
Over the Kunlun. To the West Edge of Earth.
His four feet never stumbled.
At cockcrow groomed in Yan, at dusk he was foddered in Yue,
The path of a spirit, a lightning flash, galloping past as a blur.

A heavenly horse command. A flying dragon response.
Eyes bright as the Evening Star, his breast a brace of ducks,
His tail was like a comet, his neck like a thirsty crow;
Red light spewed from his mouth,
in his sweat canals were pearls.
He once accompanied the Timely Dragon
to leap in the heavenly streets,
Haltered gold and bridled moon that shone in the City of Stars.
A spirit apart, proud and assured,
he vaulted the Nine Domains;
But even with white jades like a mountain,
who could venture to buy?
He turned and laughed at the Purple Swallows,
Thought to himself, "How dumb your kind."

The heavenly horse dashed forward.
He longed for the sovereign's coach.
The reins let out he could leap and rear
    to tumble the passing clouds.
But his feet moved in check for ten thousand miles,
And he gazed from afar at the gates to the throne.
If you meet no horseman like Master Cold Wind,
    Who will notice a scion of vanishing light?

White clouds in a blue sky,
    The hills are far away.
When the salt wagon piled high climbs the precipitous grade,
One violates custom and runs against reason,
    fearing the close of day.

Bo Le's art to curry and clip was lost along the way;[19]
In my youth they used my strength, they cast me off in age.
I would like to meet a Tian Zifang
    That he, in pity, might care for me,
But though he had Jade Mountain grain,
    My flesh could not be healed.
A hard frost in the Fifth Month
withered the buds on the cinnamon tree;
    In the stall I furrow my brow,
    the bit of injustice in my teeth.
I beg that you will redeem me, send me off to Emperor Mu,
    That I may yet play with my shadow
    and dance by the Jasper Pool.

Early Departure from White Emperor Fortress

This is the walled city on a Gibraltar-like rock at the western entrance to the Yangtze gorges. See Chen Zi'ang's poem in chapter 17.

— Editors

At dawn I took leave of the White Emperor
    in the midst of luminous clouds,
The thousand miles to Jiangling,

---

[19] Bo Le was the driver of the horses of Emperor Mu (or King Mu — see chapter 2). He and his horses occur frequently in the poems of Qu Yuan (see chapter 5), where they are seen as a parable of the wise king who is able to choose the right statesmen for harnessing to the chariot of state. *Eds.*

I have returned in a single day.
With the voices of gibbons on both banks crying incessantly
My frail boat had already passed
ten thousand towering mountains.

A Lu Mountain Song
For the Palace Censor Empty-Boat Lu

This is one of the most complex and skillfully crafted of all Chinese poems. The "threefold zithering of your heart" has a threefold relationship to its context. (1) It denotes making your heart pure as zither music through the Taoist practice of breath control concentrated on the three "cinnabar fields" of the body; (2) it implies the expression of secret feelings by allusion to the poet Sima Xiangru, who "zithered his heart" when he played a "Phoenix Song" to seduce the widow Zhuo Wenjun; and (3) it calls attention to Li Bo's zithering of his own heart with the three refrains of his own "Phoenix Song." When Li Bo refers to the semi-legendary Lu Drifting (Lu Ao), we know that he means his friend Empty-Boat Lu, because in the *Zhuangzi* the ideal man is likened to an untied boat that is both "empty" and "drifting along."

One pictures Li Bo at the mountain top discovering that his elevation so minimizes ground distance that the birds, seen as far-off specks, seem to fly endlessly without getting anywhere. And it is, of course, a "mountain of renown" — one where elixirs can be brewed most satisfactorily. Thus, green shadows and red clouds, the food of would-be immortals who would themselves learn to fly, seem all the more nicely to anticipate the more elaborate elixir, sublimated cinnabar.

Li Bo's friend, Empty-Boat, was appointed to the post of palace censor sometime shortly after 756, at the height of the An Lushan Rebellion.

There is no doubt that Li Bo is having fun, that the dual interpretations and innuendoes are really there, and that this is, indeed, his "Phoenix Song." In fact, two Phoenix Songs.

I am, in fact, the Madman of Chu,
Making fun of Confucius with a Phoenix Song.[20]
In my hand I carry a green jade cane,
And set forth at dawn from Yellow Crane Hall.
On the Five Summits I search for Immortals
and never complain how far,
For all my life I have liked to roam
in the mountains of renown.

---

[20] The Madman of Chu sang a Phoenix Song to Confucius to warn him of political dangers. *Eds.*

Lu Mountain stands in splendor at the side of Southern Dipper,[21]
The nine panels of Folding Screen are covered in cloud brocade,
And shadows fall on the shining lake
giving an eyebrow indigo light.
Golden Gates reveal before me a curtain between two spires,
The Silver River falling down
to drape three bridges of stone.
Incense Burner and waterfall face each other from far away,
The twisted cliffs and serried peaks rise in cerulean blue.
Green shadow and red cloud intensity with the sun at dawn,
And birds fly on, but never arrive,
where the skies of Wu are long.

Atop the heights a majestic view of all the Heaven and Earth,
The Great River rolls forever and going will never return.
Yellow clouds for ten thousand miles color the driving wind,
White waves on the Nine Circuits
are flowing mountains of snow.[22]

I like to sing about Lu Mountain.
Lu Mountain is my source of song.
At rest I gaze in the Mirrors of Stone to purify my heart;[23]
The places Duke Xie traveled, in green moss sink away.

Sublimed cinnabar, taken soon, banishes worldly care,
A threefold zithering of your heart,
and The Way can be attained.
Above I see the immortals in the midst of luminous clouds,
Proceeding to court in the Palace of Jade
with lotuses in their hands.
I have already promised Boundless
to meet on the Ninth Frontier;

---

[21] Lu Mountain is in Jiangxi Province about six miles south of Jiujiang. It is an especially sacred place to the Taoists. *Eds.*

[22] Surveying the world from his lofty perch, Li Bo can contemplate the "yellow wind" from the West, stirred up by the Sogdian An Lushan. That same height would make it hard to see the waves on the "nine rivers" of Jiujiang at the foot of Lu Mountain even if one could conceive of them as "flowing mountains of snow," but the impossibility is the magic of the line, for it forces us to see instead the social order of the Tang flowing away like water to the sea. The Nine Circuits recall the nine divisions into which China was divided by the Great Yu after he had dug the nine rivers to control the flood. *Eds.*

[23] The Mirrors of Stone were a rock formation on the east side of Lu Mountain, perhaps composed of mica which abounds in the area. *Eds.*

Figure 41. Calligraphy attributed to Li Bo. (Source: The Palace Museum, Beijing)

> I wish I could take Lu Drifting along
> to roam the Supremely Pure.

Climbing Xie Tiao's North Tower at Xuan in Autumn

The fifth-century poet Xie Tiao (see chapter 13) was greatly admired by Li Bo.

— Editors

> The river city is as in a picture,
> This mountain evening I gaze through clear skies.
> The two streams are inserted mirrors;
> The paired bridges are fallen rainbows.
> Chimney smoke is chilling the oranges,
> Autumn light ages the phoenix trees.
> Who would suppose that on the North Tower
> Leaning into the wind I'd be filled with Duke Xie?

A Farewell Dinner for My Uncle Li Yun, the Collator, at Xie Tiao's Tower in Xuan Prefecture

> That which has forsaken me,
> the days that were yesterday and could not be detained.

That which has confounded me,
the day that is today full of trouble and woe.
A long wind sends the autumn goose
across ten thousand miles,
Faced with this it is only right to get tipsy upon a tower.

Patterns out of Penglai, the style of Jian-an times,
Along the way, with Little Xie,
they came forth fresh and clear.
Full of soaring inspiration, man's heroic thoughts will fly;
He wants to climb the heavens to inspect the shining moon.

Draw a knife to cut the water, the water still flows on;
Raise a cup to banish grief, grief is grief the more.
When a man's life within this world does not satisfy,
Let him at dawn leave down his hair
and push his boat from shore.

Inscribed at Summit Temple

The night we stayed at Summit Temple
I could reach up and touch the stars.
We did not dare to talk aloud
For fear of disturbing the men in Heaven.

In Praise of a Gold and Silver Painted Scene of the Buddha Manifestation in the Pure Land of the West With a Preface

I hear that west of the golden sky, in the place where the sun sinks away, separated from China by ten trillion Buddhist lands, there is a World of Ultimate Joy. The Buddha of that country has a height of sixty trillion yojanas, as uncountable as the Ganges' sand. The white hairs between His eyebrows curl and turn to the right like five Sumeru mountains, and the light from His eyes is clear and bright like the waters of the four oceans. He sits erect preaching The Law, abiding forever in tranquility.

The lakes there gleam with golden sand; the banks are lined with jewelled trees. Railings and balconies enclose it all, and netting is stretched on every side. Colored glazes and mother-of-pearl from the giant clam decorate the storied halls. From crystal and cornelian comes the splendor of the glittering stains. All this the sundry Buddhas have affirmed; these are not mere empty words.

This gold and silver painted scene of the manifestation in the Pure Land of the West was erected for her late husband, His Lordship Wei, Governor of Hu Prefecture, by the Lady Qin of Pingyi Commandery. Her Ladyship embodies the purity of ice and jade and exemplifies the teaching of the mother's sagelike goodness. In the love and loyalty of the marriage bond, she hopes for him to be lifted up from the dark paths of purgatory, and for the depth of their children's filial devotion to see him perfected in luminous blessing. Thus has she pledged her precious things and sought out famous artisans.

Applying gold they have created the foundation; painting with silver they have supplied the figures. Through the power of the Eight Dharmas, the waves move on the Blue Lotus pools, and fragrant flowers from the seven jewels shine in relief against the golden ground. Whatever is caressed by the refreshing breeze is as if it were producing the five musical notes, so that a hundred and a thousand kinds of sublime music all seem to be set in play.

Be it one who has already expressed the prayer, or one who has not yet expressed the prayer, be it one who has already been born, or one who has not yet been born, devout contemplation for seven days will give him rebirth into that land. Infinite is the power from the merit of this. We may ponder it, but it is hard to explain. In praise I say:

> Looking toward the west where the sun sinks away,
> Behold afar that Face of Great Compassion.
> Eyes pure as the waters of the four oceans,
> His body shines like a mountain of purple gold.

> By diligent contemplation we can surely be reborn,
> Thus the acclaim of Ultimate Joy.
> Mid pearl netting and trees of precious jewels,
> The flowers of Heaven are scattered in fragrant halls.

> In this painting it is all before our eyes,
> And in prayer we entrust ourselves to that spiritual realm.
> On the ocean of power from the merit of this,
> Let divine intercession be our boat and bridge,
> That eight billion kalpas of human sin
> Maybe as frost swept away by the wind.
> Let all think on the Buddha of Eternal Life,
> Even praying for the light of His jadelike hair.

Up Into the Clouds Music

This poem describes a Wenkang performance, a kind of mummery with music, dance, and song that served as the grand finale for certain rather elaborate musical entertainments. The Wenkang musicale that Li Bo describes was probably sponsored by a local official or a nobleman living in the provinces to celebrate either the recovery of Chang'an from An Lushan's rebels in 757 or a subsequent birthday of the new emperor, Su Zong, who had replaced his fleeing father, Xuan Zong, on 12 August 756. The poem was probably commissioned by the sponsor of the celebration and may have been recited during the perfomance. The religious symbolism is a mixture of Buddhism, Taoism, a little Confucianism, and several independent traditions of mythology; in short it is Chinese popular religion.

West of the golden sky,
Where the white sun sinks away,
Old Kang, the Barbarian Birdie,[24]
Was born in that Scythian cave of the moon.[25]
Awesome and craggy the features of his face;
Measured and precise his manner of bearing.
Green jade glowing, glowing, the pupils of his eyes;
Yellow gold curling, curling, the hair upon his temples.

Flowery canopies hang down to his lower lashes,
A lofty mountain looms over his upper lip.[26]
Not seeing his strange, uncanny form,
How could you know the Lord of Creation?
The Great Way was this mummer's stern father,
Primal Ether this mummer's elderly kin.
He played with Pangu, patting his head,[27]
And pushing the carriage turned Heaven's wheels.
He says he saw when the sun and the moon were born,
Cast from water-silver and the essence of fire.[28]

---

[24] People surnamed Kang were often foreigners from the Kangju kingdom located in the vicinity of modern Tashkent and Samarkand. There are several Tang references to performers — usually flute players and presumably foreign — who were called "Barbarian Birdie." *Eds.*

[25] Literally "moon cave," but this means the cave of the "moon people," who may have been the Uti mentioned by Pliny. They were possibly Indo-European Tocharians, but it is conventional to call them "Scythians" since we do not really know who the Scythians were either. *Eds.*

[26] His bushy eyebrows and his foreign nose. *Eds.*

[27] The demiurge who brought order out of chaos to create the world. Old Kang patted him on the head, so Old Kang must be "older than creation." *Eds.*

[28] Water-silver is the element mercury. *Eds.*

While the solar crows had not yet come out of the valley
And the lunar rabbit was still a half-hidden form,[29]
Nü Wa toyed with the yellow earth[30]
And lumped it into ignorant humans,
Scattering them to the Six Directions,
Thick, thick, like dust and sand.
When birth and death go on endlessly,
Who could guess that this barbarian is a realized immortal?

Since the Ruo Tree was planted by the Western Ocean
And the Fu Mulberry was set in the Eastern Sea,[31]
To the present day, how great the time?
The twigs and leaves are ten-thousand miles long.
The Middle Kingdom had Seven Sages,[32]
Then along the way collapsed into chaos.[33]
His Majesty answered the upturn of fortune,
And a dragon flew into the city of Xianyang.[34]
As when the Red Eyebrows set up their Tub,[35]
And White Water restored the Glory of Han,[36]
So, angrily seething, the Four Seas moved,
And for Him great spreading waves arose.
When He stepped to tread the Purple Tenuity,[37]

---

[29] In Chinese mythology, a rabbit lives on the moon, and there were once ten suns, each inhabited by a crow. *Eds.*

[30] Nü Wa was the sister and wife of the legendary Fu Xi. The two are usually depicted with snake-like bodies. In some accounts they were the parents or creators of the human race. *Eds.*

[31] Two of the three or four "world trees" in Chinese mythology. In some accounts the sun rises from the Fu Mulberry and sets in the Ruo Tree. *Eds.*

[32] The Tang emperors prior to Su Zong. *Eds.*

[33] A reference to the An Lushan rebellion that almost toppled the Tang dynasty. *Eds.*

[34] The Qin dynasty capital. Here it represents the Tang capital, Chang'an. The dragon flying in represents the recovery of the capital by the imperial troops in 757. *Eds.*

[35] Peasant rebels of the first century A.D. In 23 they sacked the capital and killed the usurper Wang Mang, setting up as emperor Liu Penzi ("Little Tub" Liu). "Setting up the ritual tripod vessels" means "establishing a new dynasty," and so "setting up a tub" seems perfect for an unsuccessful attempt to found or restore a dynasty. *Eds.*

[36] In 25 A.D. Liu Xiu, who had lived near White Water in what is now Hubei Province, restored the Han by founding the dynasty we know as the Later Han. *Eds.*

[37] When Su Zong became the eighth Tang emperor and returned to Chang'an. The "Purple Tenuity" is a constellation, and so the realm of God, the Emperor of Heaven. Here it represents Chang'an. *Eds.*

Heaven's Gates opened of their own accord,[38]
And the old barbarian responding to Utmost Virtue[39]
Came east to present his immortal actors:
Lions in the five colors,
Phoenixes with the nine perfections.[40]
These are the old barbarian's poultry and hounds;
Singing and dancing they have flown to God's Town;
Proudly prancy, swirly whirly,
Advancing, retreating, and dressing on line.

He is good at barbarian songs. He offers up Chinese wine.
He kneels upon two knees. He presses both elbows together.
Scattering flowers, pointing to Heaven,
raising his pallid arms.
He worships the Dragon Countenance.
He offers long life to The Sage.

Northern Dipper may wobble. South Mountain may fall.
But, O Son of Heaven, as nine nines are eighty-one[41]
and so many times ten thousand years,
long may You drain the ten thousand years cup.

Drinking Alone in the Moonlight

1

Beneath the blossoms with a pot of wine,
No friends at hand, so I poured alone;
I raised my cup to invite the moon,
Turned to my shadow, and we became three.
Now the moon had never learned about drinking,
And my shadow had merely followed my form,
But I quickly made friends with the moon and my shadow;
To find pleasure in life, make the most of the spring.

Whenever I sang, the moon swayed with me;
Whenever I danced, my shadow went wild.

---

[38] Heaven's Gates are a star in the Norther Dipper. The sense of the line is, "The country is at peace, the borders are safe, travel is possible." *Eds.*
[39] The first reign title proclaimed by Emperor Su Zong. *Eds.*
[40] Probably mummers so dressed. *Eds.*
[41] Nine is an especially auspicious number because it is a homonym of the word meaning "eternal." *Eds.*

Drinking, we shared our enjoyment together;
Drunk, then each went off on his own.
But forever agreed on dispassionate revels,
We promised to meet in the far Milky Way.

2

Now, if Heaven didn't love wine,
There wouldn't be a Wine Star in Heaven.
And if Earth didn't love wine,
Earth shouldn't have the town of Wine Spring.
But since Heaven and Earth love wine,
Loving wine is no crime with Heaven.
The light, I hear, is like a sage;
The heavy, they say, is called the worthy.
If I have drunk with the sage and worthy,
What need have I to search for immortals?
Three cups and I've mastered The Way;
A jarful and I am at one with Nature.
A man can get hold of the spirit of drinking,
But no point explaining to those who abstain.

3

Third Month in the city of Xianyang,
And a thousand flowers make the day a brocade.
Who would sorrow alone in the springtime?
Faced with this you must drink straightaway.
Failure, success, and long span or short
Are fates that Creation decreed from the start,
But a cup makes life and death the same
And the ten thousand things are distinguished no more.
I get drunk and lose track of Heaven and Earth;
Sinking, I go to my pillow alone.
Then not to know the existence of me,
This is the pleasure highest of all.

4

I have ten million sources of sorrow,
But only three hundred cups of wine.
My sorrows are many and the cups are few,
But pouring a cup keeps sorrow away.

And I know that I have the sage in my cup,
For in my cups my heart always smiles.
Go hide on Mount Shouyang, refuse the Zhou grain;
Be frequently empty and starve like Yan Hui.
And after a lifetime with no joy in drinking,
What will you do with your hollow fame?
A crab claw is the Golden Elixir;
A hill of dregs is Paradise Mountain.
The thing to do is drink good wine;
Go out with the moon and get drunk on a tower.

Inscription on an Old Tomb at Guangling

The sun it is an arrow. The moon it is a bow.
The four seasons bend man down. Oh, it has no end.
But only if it happens that the moon and heavens die,
Will no one know the Nothing of man flowing with the stream.
Mountains and rivers in splendor. Blue the vault of sky.
And in the very middle, oh, the exalted lady lies.
The gibbons cry, the birds all sigh, the mist is growing dark,
For a thousand and ten thousand years,
wind in the cypress and pines.

Old Dai's Wine Shop

When Old Dai goes down below,
He may still make Young Springtime brew;
But there's no Li Bo on the Terrace of Night,
So who in hell will he sell it to?

Six Poems

Translated by Ezra Pound

from the Chinese of Rihaku,
from the notes of the late Ernest Fenollosa,
and the decipherings of the Professors Mori and Ariga

Pound's erratic romanization (based on the Japanese he found in the notebooks of
Ernest Fenollosa) has been left unchanged. Thus: Rihaku = Li Bo; Chokan = Chang-
gan; Ku-to-yen = Qutang; Chofu-sa = Changfeng sha; Sei-go-yo = Xi Shangyang;
Riokushu = Lü Zhu (Green Pearl, Shi Chong's favorite concubine — see chapter 10);
Han-rei = Fan Li (minister of the king of Yue); So-Kin = Dong Zaojiu; Rakuyo =

Luoyang; Gen = Yuan; Ten-Shin = Tianjin; Raku-hoku = Luo; Sen-Go = Xian-cheng
(City of Immortals); Kan = Han; Shi-yo = Ziyang; San-Ko = Cangxia; Sennin = xianren;
Kan Chu = Hanzhong; So = Chu; Hei-Shu = Bingzhou; Layu = Yang Xiong; Choyo =
Changyang; San = Can; Kojin = guren; Ko-kaku-ro = Huanghelou (Yellow Crane Tower).

— Editors

The River Merchant's Wife: A Letter

Kenneth Rexroth called this version by Ezra Pound "one of the dozen or so major
poems to be written in American in the twentieth century."

— Editors

While my hair was still cut straight across my forehead
I played about the front gate, pulling flowers.
You came by on bamboo stilts, playing horse,
You walked about my seat, playing with blue plums.
And we went on living in the village of Chokan:
Two small people, without dislike or suspicion.

At fourteen I married My Lord you.
I never laughed, being bashful.
Lowering my head, I looked at the wall.
Called to, a thousand times, I never looked back.

At fifteen I stopped scowling,
I desired my dust to be mingled with yours
Forever and forever and forever.
Why should I climb the look out?

At sixteen you departed,
You went into far *Ku-to-yen*, by the river of swirling eddies,
And you have been gone five months.
The monkeys make sorrowful noise overhead.

You dragged your feet when you went out.
By the gate now, the moss is grown, the different mosses,
Too deep to clear them away!
The leaves fall early this autumn, in wind.
The paired butterflies are already yellow with August
Over the grass in the West garden;
They hurt me. I grow older.
If you are coming down through the narrows of the river *Kiang*,
Please let me know beforehand,
And I will come out to meet you
                    As far as *Cho-fu-Sa*.

Poem by the Bridge at Ten-shin

March has come to the bridge head,
Peach boughs and apricot boughs hang over a thousand gates,
At morning there are flowers to cut the heart,
And evening drives them on the eastward-flowing waters.
Petals are on the gone waters and on the going,
        And on the back-swirling eddies,
But today's men are not the men of the old days,
Though they hang in the same way over the bridge-rail.
The sea's color moves at the dawn
And the princes still stand in rows, about the throne,
And the moon falls over the portals of *Sei-go-yo*,
And clings to the walls and the gate-top.
With head gear glittering against the cloud and sun,
The lords go forth from the court, and into far borders.
They ride upon dragonlike horses,
Upon horses with head-trappings of yellow metal,
And the streets make way for their passage.
        Haughty their passing,
Haughty their steps as they go in to great banquets,
To high halls and curious food,
To the perfumed air and girls dancing,
To clear flutes and clear singing;
To the dance of the seventy couples;
To the mad chase through the gardens.
Night and day are given over to pleasure
And they think it will last a thousand autumns,
        Unwearying autumns.
For them the yellow dogs howl portents in vain,
And what are they compared to the lady *Riokushu*,
        That was cause of hate!
Who among them is a man like *Han-rei*
        Who departed alone with his mistress,
With her hair unbound, and he his own skiffsman!

The Jewel Stairs' Grievance

The jewelled steps are already quite white with dew,
It is so late that the dew soaks my gauze stockings,
And I let down the crystal curtain
And watch the moon through the clear autumn.

Pound's Note:
Jewel stairs, therefore a palace. Grievance, therefore there is something to complain
of. Gauze stockings, therefore a court lady, not a servant who complains. Clear
autumn, therefore he has no excuse on account of weather. Also she has come early,
for the dew has not merely whitened the stairs, but has soaked her stockings. The
poem is especially prized because she utters no direct reproach.

Exile's Letter

To *So-Kin* of *Rakuyo*, ancient friend, Chancelor of *Gen*.
Now I remember that you built me a special tavern
By the south side of the bridge at *Ten-Shin*.
With yellow gold and white jewels, we paid for songs and laughter
And we were drunk for month on month, forgetting the kings
  and princes.
Intelligent men came drifting in from the sea and from the west border,
And with them, and with you especially
There was nothing at cross purpose,
And they made nothing of sea-crossing or of mountain-crossing,
If only they could be of that fellowship,
And we all spoke out our hearts and minds, and without regret.
And then I was sent off to South Wei,
  smothered in laurel groves,
And you to the north of *Raku-hoku*,
Till we had nothing but thoughts and memories in common.
And then, when separation had come to its worst,
We met, and traveled into *Sen-Go*,
Through all the thirty-six folds of the turning and twisting waters,
Into a valley of the thousand bright flowers,
That was the first valley;
And into ten thousand valleys full of voices and pine-winds.
And with silver harness and reins of gold,
Out came the East of *Kan* foreman and his company.
And there came also the "True man" of *Shi-yo* to meet me,
Playing on a jewelled mouth-organ.
In the storied houses of *San-Ko* they gave us more *Sennin* music,
Many instruments, like the sound of young phoenix broods.
The foreman of *Kan Chu*, drunk, danced
  because his long sleeves wouldn't keep still
With that music playing,
And I, wrapped in brocade, went to sleep with my head on his lap,
And my spirit so high it was all over the heavens,
And before the end of the day we were scattered like stars, or rain.

I had to be off to *So*, far away over the waters,
You back to your river-bridge.
And your father, who was brave as a leopard,
Was governor in *Hei-Shu*, and put down the barbarian rabble,
And one May he had you send for me,
            despite the long distance.
And what with broken wheels and so on, I won't say it wasn't
      hard going,
Over roads twisted like sheep's guts.
And I was still going, late in the year,
            in the cutting wind from the North,
And thinking how little you cared for the cost,
            and you caring enough to pay it.
And what a reception:
Red jade cups, food well set on a blue jewelled table,
And I was drunk, and had no thought of returning.
And you would walk out with me to the western corner of the castle,
To the dynastic temple, with water about it clear as blue jade,
With boats floating, and the sound of mouth-organs and drums,
With ripples like dragon-scales, going glass green on the water,
Pleasure lasting, with courtesans, going and coming without
      hindrance,
With the willow flakes falling like snow,
And the vermilioned girls getting drunk about sunset,
And the water, a hundred feet deep, reflecting green eyebrows
— Eyebrows painted green are a fine sight in young moonlight,
Gracefully painted —
And the girls singing back at each other,
Dancing in transparent brocade,
And the wind lifting the song, and interrupting it,
Tossing it up under the clouds.
            And all this comes to an end.
            And is not again to be met with.
I went up to the court for examination,
Tried *Layu's* luck, offered the *Choyo* song.
And got no promotion,
            and went back to the East Mountains
            White-headed.
And once again, later, we met at the South bridgehead.
And then the crowd broke up, you went north to *San* palace,
And if you ask how I regret that parting:
It is like the flowers falling at Spring's end

Confused, whirled in a tangle.
What is the use of talking, and there is no end of
   talking,
There is no end of things in the heart.
I call in the boy,
Have him sit on his knees here
      To seal this,
And send it a thousand miles, thinking.

Separation on the River Kiang

Ko-jin goes west from *Ko-kaku-ro*,
The smoke-flowers are blurred over the river.

Figure 42. "Separation on
the River Kiang." Qing
dynasty (1644–1911)
illustration. (Source: *Tangshi
daguan* [Compendium of
Tang Poetry] [Shanghai:
Commercial Press, 1984])

His lone sail blots the far sky.
And now I see only the river,
    The long *Kiang*, reaching heaven.

Taking Leave of a Friend

Blue mountains to the north of the walls,
White river winding about them;
Here we must make separation
And go out through a thousand miles of dead grass.
Mind like a floating wide cloud,
Sunset like the parting of old acquaintances
Who bow over their clasped hands at a distance.
Our horses neigh to each other
        as we are departing.

Four Poems

Translated by Arthur Cooper

On Visiting a Taoist Master in the Daitian Mountains and Not Finding Him

"Visiting a Hermit and Not Finding Him" is a very common theme in Chinese poetry [compare Jia Dao's famous poem in chapter 22]. In such poems the wise hermit gives his "teaching without words" by letting the poet wait and not even meet him. His lesson may be compared with that of Ludwig Wittgenstein in *Philosophical Investigations*: "Don't think: look!"

    Where the dogs bark
    by roaring waters,
        Whose spray darkens
    the petals' colors,
        Deep in the woods
    deer at times are seen;

    The valley noon:
    one can hear no bell,
        But wild bamboos
    cut across bright clouds,
        Flying cascades
    hang from jasper peaks;

No one here knows
which way you have gone:
Two, now three pines
I have leant against!

Abandon

This is perhaps Li Bo's most drunken poem, and yet, in the original, it is also a miraculous work of art. It seems to be a sort of reply (though in no way a retort or a parody) to a poem, famous for its spring freshness, by Li Bo's friend, Meng Haoran:

In Spring one sleeps
absent to morning
Then everywhere
hears the birds singing:

After all night
the voice of the storm
And petals fell —
who knows how many?

[Compare Witter Bynner's translation in chapter 20.]

With wine I sit
absent to Night, till
(Fallen petals
in folds of my gown)

I stagger up
to stalk the brook's moon:
The birds are gone
and people are few!

Longing

The title of this poem is literally something like "long" or "far-away thoughts of one another." A man commonly wrote a love-poem as from the woman; here a professional courtesan and musician.

Sunlight beings to fade,
   mist fills the flowers,
The moon as white as silk
   weeps and cannot sleep,

Zhao zither's Phoenix frets
   no more shall I touch,

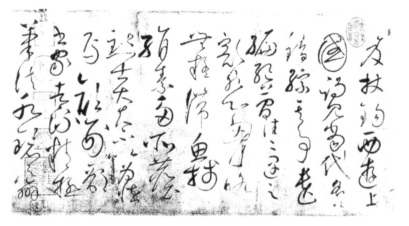

Figure 43. Calligraphy of the Tang dynasty monk Huaisu, much admired by Li Bo. (Source: National Palace Museum, Taipei)

Shu lute's Mandarin Duck strings
    I'll sound instead:

This song has a meaning
    that no one can tell,
It follows the Spring wind
    as far as Yanran

To you far, far away
    beyond the blue sky —

    Whom once I gave
    A sideways glance
    With eyes that now
    Are wells of tears —

If you do not believe
    that my heart breaks,
Come back and look with me
    into this glass!

Hard Is the Journey

The Journey in the title and in the fourth verse is the Journey of Life. The title, some of the detail and much of the spirit of the poem are all derived from ancient songs, but especially from the poetry of Bao Zhao [see chapter 12].

Gold vessels of fine wines,
   thousands a gallon,
Jade dishes of rare meats,
   costing more thousands,

I lay my chopsticks down,
   no more can banquet,
And draw my sword and stare
   wildly about me:

Ice bars my way to cross
   the Yellow River,
Snows from dark skies to climb
   the Taihang Mountains!

At peace I drop a hook
   into a brooklet,
At once I'm in a boat
   but sailing sunward ...

   (Hard is the Journey,
   Hard is the Journey,
   So many turnings,
   And now where am I?)

So when a breeze breaks waves,
   bringing fair weather,
I set a cloud for sails,
   cross the blue oceans!

Four Poems

Translated by David Young

For Du Fu

On Boiled Rice Mountain
I met Du Fu

wearing a big round
bamboo hat
in the hot noon sun

Du Fu
how come

you've grown
so thin?

you must be suffering
too much
from poetry!

To Wang Lun

I was just
shoving off
in my boat

when I heard
someone stomping
and singing on the shore!

Peach Blossom Lake
is a thousand feet deep

but it can't compare
with Wang Lun's love
or the way he said
goodbye

Conversation among the Mountains

You ask why I live
in these green mountains

I smile
can't answer

I am completely at peace

a peach blossom
sails past
on the current

there are worlds
beyond this one

Autumn Lines

Clean fall wind
clear fall moon

leaves heaped by the wind
leaves scattered

a cold raven
flaps slowly
from his roost

thoughts of you
fill my head

will I ever
see you again?

the ache
around my heart
gets bigger

Four Versions

A Statement of Resolutions
After Being Drunk on a Spring Day

Translated by Amy Lowell and Florence Ayscough (1922)

The collaboration between Ezra Pound's arch-rival, the formidable American Imagist "hippo-poet" Amy Lowell (1874–1925), and her Shanghai-born friend Florence Ayscough resulted in the remarkable versions printed in Boston in 1922 as *Fir-Flower Tablets*. In a letter dated 28 June, 1918, Amy wrote ebulliently to Florence: "I tell you we are a great team, Florence, and ought to do wonderful things." On 12 June 1919: "I am absolutely in love with this 'Li T'ai Po,' but Lawks-a massy, my dear, 'taint easy nohow. However, you shall have it somehow. God knows how."

Here we give two poems from *Fir-Flower Tablets*, and some alternative versions by other hands, for comparison.

— Editors

This time of ours
Is like a great, confused dream.
Why should one spend one's life in toil?
Thinking this, I have been drunk all day.
I fell down and lay prone by the pillars in front of the house;
When I woke up, I gazed for a long time
At the courtyard before me.
A bird sings among the flowers.
May I ask what season this is?
Spring wind,
The bright oriole of the water-flowing flight calls.

My feelings make me want to sigh.
The wine is still here, I will throw back my head and drink.

I sing splendidly,
I wait for the bright moon.
Already, by the end of the song, I have forgotten
    my feelings.

Un Jour de Printemps
Le Poète Exprime Ses Sentiments au Sortir de l'Ivresse

French version of the same poem
Translated by the Marquis d'Hervey de Saint-Denys (1862)

The Marquis de Saint-Denys (1823–1892) studied under the great French scholar
Stanislaus Julien (1797–1873). His interests were wide (he wrote a pioneering work on
the interpretation of dreams). His translations combined genuine Chinese scholarship (see, for instance, his notes) with great literary elegance.

— Editors

Si la vie est comme un grand songe,
A quoi bon tourmenter son existence!
Pour moi je m'enivre tout le jour,
Et quand je viens à chanceler, je m'endors
    au pieds des premières colonnes.

A mon réveil je jette les yeux devant moi;
Un oiseau chante au milieu des fleurs;
Je lui demande à quelle époque de l'année nous sommes,
Il me répond à l'époque où le souffle du printemps
    fait chanter l'oiseau.

Je me sens ému et prêt à soupirer,
Mais je me verse encore à boire;
Je chante haute voix jusqu'à ce que la lune brille,
Et à l'heure où finissent mes chants, j'ai de nouveau perdu
    le sentiment de ce qui m'entoure.

Der Trinker im Frühling

German version of the same poem

Translated from the French by Hans Bethge (1907)

Hans Bethge's 1907 German version is freely based on Saint-Denys, with reference to
the earlier German version of Hans Heilmann (1905), and was itself the basis for the

fifth movement of Mahler's *Das Lied von der Erde,* "Der Trunkene im Frühling" (for other poems used by Mahler, see the "Poem of Farewell" by Wang Wei in chapter 18 and "At the Mountain-Lodge of the Buddhist Priest Ye" by Meng Haoran in chapter 21).

— Editors

Wenn nur ein Traum das Dasein ist,
Warum dann Müh und Plag?
Ich trinke, bis ich nicht mehr kann,
Den ganzen lieben Tag.

Und wenn ich nicht mehr trinken kann,
Weil Leib und Kehle voll,
So tauml' ich hin vor meiner Tür
Und schlafe wundervoll!

Was hör ich beim Erwachen? Horch,
Ein Vogel singt im Baum.
Ich frag ihn, ob schon Frühling sei, —
Mir ist als wie im Traum.

Der Vogel zwitschert: ja, der Lenz
Sei kommen über Nacht, —
Ich seufze tief ergriffen auf,
Der Vogel singt und lacht.

Ich fülle mir den Becher neu
Und leer ihn bis zum Grund
Und singe, bis der Mond erglänzt
Am schwarzen Himmelsrund.

Und wenn ich nicht mehr singen kann,
So schlaf ich wieder ein.
Was geht denn mich der Frühling an!
Lasst mich betrunken sein!

"The Best of Life Is But ..."

The same poem
Translated from the original by Herbert Giles (1884)

What is life after all but a dream?
    And why should such bother be made?
Better far to be tipsy, I deem,
    And doze all day long in the shade.

When I wake and look out on the lawn,
    I hear midst the flowers a bird sing;

I ask, "Is it evening or dawn?"
The mango-bird whistles, "'Tis spring."

Overpower'd with the beautiful sight,
    Another full goblet I pour,
And would sing till the moon rises bright —
    But soon I'm as drunk as before.

Two Versions

River Chant

Translated by Amy Lowell and Florence Ayscough (1922)

This is the poem Ezra Pound translated in *Cathay* as "The River Song." Wai-lim Yip, in
his study *Ezra Pound's Cathay*, describes the original as a strong statement against
superficial glory made by the poet "drifting on the river," a "poem about permanence
and impermanence, setting up poetry as the only sign of immortality."

— Editors

Fig-wood oars,
A boat of the wood of the sand-pear.
At either end,
Jade flageolets and pipes of gold.

Amidships,
Jars of delectable wine,
And ten thousand pints
Put by.

A boat-load of singing-girls
Following the water ripples
Going,
Stopping,
Veering —

The Immortal waited,
Then mounted and rode the yellow crane.
But he who is the guest of the sea has no such desire,
Rather would he be followed by the white gulls.

The *ci* and *fu* of Qu Ping[42] hang suspended like the sun and moon.

---

[42] Qu Yuan, Chu poet, author of "On Encountering Trouble" and other poems in the
ancient anthology *The Songs of the South* (see chapter 5). *Eds.*

The terraces and the pleasure-houses
Of the Kings of Chu
Are empty heaps of earth.

I am drunk with wine,
With the sweet taste of it;
When I take up my writing-brush,
I could move the Five Peaks.

When I have finished my poem,
I laugh aloud in my arrogance.
I rise to the country of the Immortals which lies
        in the middle of the sea.
If fame followed the ways of the good official,
If wealth and rank were long constant,
Then indeed might the water of the Han River
        flow Northwest.

En Bateau

French version of the same poem
Translated by the Marquis d'Hervey de Saint-Denys (1862)

Un bateau de *shatang*[43] avec des rames de *mulan;*[44]
De jeunes musiciennes sur les bancs, avec des flûtes d'or
        et de jade;[45]
Du vin exquis dans des coupes mille fois remplies;
Emmener avec soi le plaisir, et se laisser porter
        par les flots.

Les Immortels m'attendent, montés sur leurs cigognes jaunes,[46]
Tandis qu'insouciant et tranquille, je vogue au milieu des mouettes
        blanches.
Les sublimes inspirations de Qu Ping[47] nous restent
        comme un monument qui s'élève à la hauteur des astres;

---

[43] Bois très léger.
[44] Bois très dur.
[45] Expression qui ne doit se prendre qu'au figuré, et pour indiquer le talent de celles qui jouent de cet instrument, comme on dirait en français, pour parler d'un écrivain de talent, *une plume d'or.*
[46] Les personnages de la mythologie *daoshi* qui ont obtenu l'immortalité voyagent dans les airs, montés sur des cigognes jaunes.
[47] Un des surnoms du poète Qu Yuan, auteur du *Lisao,* poème très célèbre en Chine.

Que sont devenus les tours et les pavillons du roi de Chu, jadis
accumulés sur ces collines désertes!

Quand l'ivresse m'exalte, j'abaisse mon pinceau, j'ébranle
de mes chants les cinq montagnes sacrées,[48]
Je suis joyeux et je suis fier, je me ris de toutes les grandeurs,
Puissance, richesse, honneurs, quand vous serez d'assez
longue durée pour que je vous estime,
On verra donc le fleuve jaune partir de l'occident
pour couler vers le nord.

Four Versions

Ivresse d'Amour

Translated by Judith Gautier (1867)

Judith Gautier (1846–1917), the precocious daughter of the poet Théophile Gautier
(1811–1872), completed her wonderful anthology of Chinese poems, *Le Livre de Jade*,
in 1867. She did the versions in collaboration with a Chinese "mandarin refugié," Ting
Tun-ling. Of "Li-Tai-Pé" she wrote in the Prelude: "Like the Persian poet Omar
Khayyam, Li Bo becomes passionately drunk, sings of wine, his sole consolation, and
casts a veil of intoxication, like a gold-spangled shroud, over the bitterness of this life
and apprehensions of the next." The French versions were originally printed as
prose-poems. As can be seen from these two examples, her work was widely translated
and imitated. More recent English translations are given for comparison.

— Editors

Le vent agite doucement, à l'entour du Palais des Eaux, les fleurs
embaumées des nénuphars.

Sur la plus haute terrasse de Kou-sou[49] on peut apercevoir le roi de
Lou, étendu nonchalamment.

Devant lui, Sy-Ché, la beauté même, danse, avec une grâce incomparable, des gestes délicats et sans force.

Puis, elle rit d'être aussi voluptueusement lasse, et, languissante,
vient s'appuyer du côté de l'Orient, au rebord de jade blanc du lit
royal.

---

[48] Les cinq montagnes sacrées sont les cinq grandes montagnes sur lesquelles, dès la plus
haute antiquité, le souverain de la Chine offrait des sacrifices.... L'expression signifie
donc, comme on le voit, faire grand bruit dans le monde entier.

[49] Original romanization has been retained in these three versions. *Eds.*

Sy-che and the King

Translated from the French of Judith Gautier by E. Powys Mathers (1911)

Round the Palace of Waters gently the wind moves the flowers
   of the water-lilies.
On the highest terrace of Kou-Sou one sees the King of Lou
   lazily lying.
And before him Sy-Che, after whom beauty was named, dances
   with lovely grace of delicate weak gestures.
Then she laughs that she is so voluptuously weary,
   and languidly leans to the East
   on the white jade of the royal bed.

Intoxication of Love

Translated from the French of Judith Gautier by James Whittal (1918)

The petals of the water-lilies tremble
as the wind murmurs
through the Palace of the Waters.

The King of Lou
lounges idly on the terrace of Kou-Sou;
before him is Sy-ché;
she is dancing,
and her movements are rhythmical
and full of delicate grace.

Then she laughs,
sensuous in her weariness;
she leans against the royal white jade bed,
and gazes towards the east.

For the Dancer of the King of Wu, When She Is Half Drunk

The same poem
Translated from the original by Robert Payne et al. (1947)

The wind waves the lotuses in the scented palace by the water.
In the Gusu Tower, the King of Wu is carousing.[50]

---

[50] Xi Shi, the most beautiful of all Chinese consorts, was discovered washing her clothes by
   the side of a stream by Gou Jian the King of Yue, who presented her to the King of Wu.

Xi Shi, flushed with wine, dances coy and unresisting.
By the east window, laughing, she leans on a couch of white jade.

Three Versions

La Flûte Mystérieuse

Translated by Judith Gautier (1867)

Un jour, par-dessus le feuillage et les fleurs embaumées, le vent
m'apporta le son d'une flûte lointaine.
Alors, j'ai coupé une branche de saule, et j'ai répondu une chanson.
Depuis, la nuit, lorsque tout dort, les oiseaux entendent une
conversation dans leur language.

The Mysterious Flute

Translated from the French of Judith Gautier by Stuart Merrill (1890)

One day, from beyond the foliage and the perfumed flowers,
    the wind brought me the sound of a distant flute.
I carved a willow branch and I answered with a song.
Since then, at night, when everything is asleep, the birds
    enjoy a conversation in their own language.

A Flute of Marvel

Translated from the French of Judith Gautier by E. Powys Mathers (1911)

Under the leaves and cool flowers
The wind brought to me the sound of a flute
From far away.

I cut a branch of willow
And answered with a lazy song.

Even at night, when all slept,
The birds were listening to a conversation
In their own language.

Spring Night in Luoyang — Hearing a Flute

Translated by Burton Watson (1971)

It has been suggested that this was the poem "behind" Judith Gautier's "mysterious
flute." If that is the case, little has survived except the flute, the wind, and the broken
willow.

— Editors

In what house, the jade flute that sends these dark notes drifting,
scattering on the spring wind that fills Luoyang?
Tonight if we should hear the willow-breaking song,
who could help but long for the gardens of home?

Six Poems

Translated by Various Hands

A Solitary Carouse on a Day in Spring

Translated by R. K. Douglas

The east wind fans a gentle breeze,
The streams and trees glory in the brightness of the Spring,
The bright sun illuminates the green shrubs,
And the falling flowers are scattered and fly away.
The solitary cloud retreats to the hollow hill,
The birds return to their leafy haunts.
Every being has a refuge whither he may turn,
I alone have nothing to which to cling.
So seated opposite the moon shining o'er the cliff,
I drink and sing to the fragrant blossoms.

A Snapshot

Translated by Herbert Giles

A tortoise I see on a lotus-flower resting;
A bird 'mid the reeds and the rushes is nesting;
A light skiff propelled by some boatman's fair daughter,
Whose song dies away o'er the fast-flowing water.

Drinking with a Friend, Among the Mountains

Translated by Jerome P. Seaton

Together, we drink; the mountain flowers open.
A cup, a cup, and one more cup.
Drunk, I'd sleep; you go.
Tomorrow, come again: Do bring your lute.

Night Mooring at Cow's Creek: I Think of the Old Man

Translated by C. H. Kwock and Vincent McHugh

During the Jin dynasty, at this spot on the Yangtze, the general Xie Shang heard the young poet Yuan Hong chanting poems in a nearby boat.

At Cow's Creek
    on Western River
        the night
Sky still blue
    not a rag of cloud
I go on deck
    to look at the bright moon
thinking of
    the great General Xie of old

I also
    can make poetry
but that man's like
    will not be found again
In the morning
    we make sail and go
The maple leaves
    fall as they will.

A Night with a Friend

Translated by Burton Watson

Dousing clean a thousand old cares,
sticking it out through a hundred pots of wine,
a good night needing the best of conversation,
a brilliant moon that will not let us sleep —
drunk we lie down in empty hills,
heaven and earth our quilt and pillow.

Her Presence Was a Roomful of Flowers

Translated by John Scott

Her presence was a roomful of flowers
Her absence is an empty bed
The brocade coverlet rolled up, unslept in

But the perfume left three years ago still lingers.
Though the scent remains
She'll not come again.
A love that is yellow leaves falling
Or white dew wet on the green moss.

🔹 *Further Reading* 🔹

Ayscough, Florence, and Amy Lowell, trans. *Fir-Flower Tablets.* Boston: Houghton Mifflin, 1922.
Bethge, Hans. *Die Chinesische Flöte: Nachdichtungen Chinesischer Lyrik.* Leipzig: Insel Verlag, 1907.
Cheng, François. *L'Ecriture poétique chinoise.* Paris: Editions du Seuil, 1977. Trans. by Donald A. Riggs & Jerome P. Seaton as *Chinese Poetic Writing: With an Anthology of T'ang Poetry* (Bloomington: Indiana University Press, 1982).
Cooper, Arthur, trans. *Li Po and Tu Fu.* Harmondsworth: Penguin Books, 1973.
Demiéville, Paul, ed. *Anthologie de la poésie chinoise classique.* Paris: Gallimard, 1962.
Douglas, R. K. *The Language and Literature of China.* London: Trubner, 1875.
Eide, Elling. "On Li Po," in Wright and Twitchett, eds., *Perspectives on the T'ang.* New Heaven: Yale University Press, 1973.
———. trans. *Poems by Li Po.* Lexington, Ky.: Anvil Press, 1984.
Gautier, Judith, trans. *Le Livre de jade.* Paris: Alphonse Lemerre, 1867.
Heilmann, Hans. *Chinesische Lyrik.* Munich: Piper, 1905.
Hervey de Saint-Denys, trans. *Poésies de l'époque des Thang.* Paris: Amyot, 1862.
Hinton, David, trans. *Selected Poems of Li Po.* New York: New Directions, 1996.
Kwock, C. H., & Vincent McHugh, trans. *Why I Live on the Mountain.* San Francisco: Golden Mountain Press, 1958.
Obata, Shigeyoshi, trans. *The Works of Li Po, the Chinese Poet.* New York: Dutton, 1922.
Owen, Stephen. *The Great Age of Chinese Poetry: The High T'ang.* New Haven: Yale University Press, 1981.
Mathers, E. Powys. *Coloured Stars.* Oxford: Blackwell, 1911.
Merrill, Stuart. *Pastels in Prose.* New York: Harper, 1890.
Payne, Robert, ed. *The White Pony: An Anthology of Chinese Poetry from the Earliest Times to the Present Day.* New York: John Day, 1947.
Pound, Ezra, trans. (from the notes of the late Ernest Fenollosa, and the decipherings of the Professors Mori and Ariga). *Cathay* (for the most part from the Chinese of "Rihaku"). London: Elkin Mathews, 1915.
Scott, John (with Graham Martin), ed. and trans. *Love and Protest: Chinese Poems from the Sixth Century B.C. to the Seventeenth Century A.D.* London: Rapp & Whiting, 1972.
Sun, Yü, trans. *Li Po—A New Translation.* Hong Kong: Commercial Press, 1982.
Waley, Arthur. *The Poet Li Po.* London: East & West, 1919.
———. *The Poetry and Career of Li Po.* London: Allen & Unwin, 1950.
Whittal, James, trans. *Chinese Lyrics from the Book of Jade.* New York: Huebsch, 1918.
Wong, Siu-kit. *The Genius of Li Po.* Hong Kong: University of Hong Kong, 1974.
Yip, Wai-lim. *Ezra Pound's Cathay.* Princeton: Princeton University Press, 1969.
Young, David, trans. *Wang Wei, Li Po, Tu Fu, Li Ho: Four T'ang Poets.* Ohio: Field Translation Series, 1980.

Chapter 20

Du Fu (712–770)

The Sage of Poetry

What do I resemble, blown by wind blown by wind?
A gull on the sand between Heaven and Earth.

— Du Fu, "A Traveller At Night Writes His Thoughts"
(*translated by Florence Ayscough*)

I have said that Du Fu's superb quality is what the Buddhists call "scholarship arriving at non-scholarship." We see how his poetry is like primal energy overflowing, taking shape according to the object. It is comparable to the three rivers and five lakes joining together to form the sea — broad and expansive, without bounds. It is like portentous rays of light or auspicious clouds in countless, description-defying transformations. This is why those who study it find their hearts moved and their eyes startled.

When one becomes thoroughly acquainted with his poetry, seeking out its profundity and chewing it over at length, that which gave enriching moisture to his brush tip, the quintessence of the nine classics and the hundred philosophers of antiquity, seems to find remnant resonance therein.

Now as for gold slivers and cinnabar granules, or mushrooms, fungi, ginseng, and cinnamon, a knowledgeable person can point out and name these. But when it comes to their being joined together and made into a compound, the mysterious functions of lord and minister, subordinate and ambassador, as well as the sweet and bitter, sour and salty, enter into each other, and they can no longer be identified as gold slivers and cinnabar granules, or mushrooms, fungi, ginseng, and cinnamon. Thus, while it can be said that not a single character in Du Fu's poetry is without its literary source, it can also be said that none of his verse comes from the ancients.

— Yuan Haowen (1190–1257), Preface to *A Study of Du Fu's Poetry*
(*translated by J. Timothy Wixted*)

Take any one of Du Fu's poems, or even one line, and everywhere you will see his concern for his country and his love for his sovereign, his compassion for the times and his sadness over disorder, his refusal to compromise in adversity, his integrity in poverty, his way of expressing his indignation and refining his nature by means of enjoying the landscape and drinking with friends, even though he had travelled through rugged, war-torn, bandit-infested terrain: this is Du Fu's visage. Whenever I read him, it leaps before my eyes.

— Ye Xie (1627–1703), *On the Origins of Poetry*
(*translated by James J. Y. Liu*)

Introduction

Burton Watson

If the poetry of Li Bo conveys a feeling of spontaneity and effortless flow, that of his illustrious contemporary Du Fu gives a quite different impression. Though Du Fu wrote in a variety of styles, his most characteristic work is innovative in language and subject matter and densely packed with meaning. He seems to have labored over his compositions, employing parallelisms and other rhetorical and prosodic devices in novel and surprising ways, striving to open up new areas of expression, his professed aim being to startle with the creativeness of his work. This is undoubtedly one reason why his importance was not widely recognized by the readers of his time. As in the case of so many artists whose work is experimental and forward-looking, it remained for posterity to recognize the full extent of his genius.

Du Fu was born in Henan in the region of Luoyang. Though he came from a distinguished literary family and had influential contacts, his early efforts to secure a government position through the examination system or special appointment met with repeated failure. He was forty-three when, in 755, he finally succeeded in obtaining an official post. It was anything but an auspicious time to enter the service of the dynasty.

Emperor Xuanzong, a distinguished and able ruler in his earlier years, had in his sixties become infatuated with the beautiful Yang Guifei, making her his concubine and showering favors on her relations, a move that Du Fu obliquely censures in his "Song of the Beautiful Ladies." With the emperor thus distracted from affairs of state, the court soon became plagued by factionalism and the military leaders in the outlying areas grew dangerously powerful. In 755, the year Du Fu took office, one such leader with his base in the northeast, An Lushan, raised a revolt and began marching toward the Tang capital area. In time Emperor Xuanzong was forced to flee to the west and abdicate in favor of his son, who set up a new regime. Meanwhile, Du Fu and his wife and children fled north to escape the rebel armies. He left his family there while he himself attempted to make his way to the headquarters of the new emperor, but was captured by the rebels and held prisoner in Chang'an.

After a semblance of order had been restored, Du Fu was once more given a post in the capital, but incurred the emperor's displeasure and was removed to a minor provincial position. In 759 he left this post and spent the remainder of his life in restless wanderings, broken by an interval of relative tranquility when he lived on the outskirts of Chengdu in Sichuan. In his last years, much troubled by illness, he journeyed by stages down the Yangtze, attempting to reach his old home in the east, but died along the way.

Since much of Du Fu's poetry is intensely personal, we can follow in it the tortured course of his life as it was molded by the tumultuous events of the time. He was imbued with a strong Confucian sense of duty that kept him striving to serve the dynasty to which he professed such deep loyalty, hoping thereby to help assuage the ills of the nation. As a government official, he proved in his sporadic terms in office to be well-meaning but ineffectual. In a larger sense, however, he fulfilled his moral purpose through his art, in his poems describing in moving terms the griefs that famine, misrule, and civil unrest were inflicting upon his countrymen and himself. His greatest works are at once a lament upon the appalling sorrows that he saw around him, and a reproach to those who, through folly or ignorance, were to some degree responsible for the creation of so much misery. It is no doubt this deeply sincere and compassionate tone in his work that led later ages to bestow on him the epithet the Sage of Poetry, acknowledging him the artistic counterpart of Confucius himself.

Unlike Li Bo, who preferred the relative freedom of the old style verse forms, Du Fu welcomed the technical demands made by the "modern style" or tonally regulated forms, particularly the eight-line regulated verse. Of his approximately 1,450 extant poems, over 1,000 are in such forms. This fact, along with the great compression of language and thought that marks many of his works, makes his poetry particularly difficult to translate. One should keep in mind that many of the beauties of language that Chinese readers admire so greatly in his work inevitably are lost in translation.

— from *The Columbia Book of Chinese Poetry*, 1984

Seven Poems

Chinese texts, with commentary, exegesis, and prose translations by David Hawkes

In this chapter we break with our normal practice, and provide the Chinese characters and romanization for a number of the poems. Aided by David Hawkes' word-for-word exegesis, the reader can observe the Chinese poet at work with his own language.

— Editors

On a Prospect of Mount Tai (*Wang Yue* 望嶽)

1. *Daizong fu ruhe?*
   岱宗夫如何?

2. *Qi Lu qing wei liao.*
   齊魯青未了。

3. *Zaohua zhong shen xiu,*
   造化鍾神秀,

4. *Yin yang ge hun xiao.*
   陰陽割昏曉。

5. *Dang xiong sheng ceng yun,*
   盪胸生曾雲,

6. *Jue zi ru gui niao.*
   決眥入歸鳥。

7. *Huidang ling jue ding,*
   會當凌絕頂,

8. *Yilan zhongshan xiao!*
   一覽眾山小。

Title and Subject

Wang means "gaze at," "look towards," and is commonly used in connection with scenery or distant objects.

Yue is a special word for "mountain" used only of the Five Great Peaks of China: Mount Song in the middle of China (Henan), Mount Tai in the east (Shandong), Mount Hua in the west (Shaanxi), Mount Heng in the south (Hunan), and another Mount Heng in the north (on the borders of Hebei and Shanxi). The "*yue*" of this title is Mount Tai, which was from earliest times regarded by the Chinese with special veneration. The god of Mount Tai was a judge over the dead, and formerly stones representing him stood opposite the openings of side-streets to scare away demons.

This poem was written in 736 when Du Fu was a young unmarried man of twenty-four. His father was at the time assistant prefect of a city only a few miles from the foot of Mount Tai. Du Fu had recently returned there after failing the Civil Service examinations in Chang'an.

"Gazing at Mount Tai" is a typically Chinese title for a poem. Our titles are substantival: "Lycidas," "Home Thoughts from Abroad," "The Rape of the Lock." The Chinese are partial to verbal constructions: "Mourning Lycidas," "Thinking of My Homeland While in a Foreign Country," "Raping the Lock," etc. I should feel no compunction in translating this title "On a Distant Prospect of Mount Tai," or something of the sort.

Note that although this poem is about a view and not an ascent of Mount Tai, Du Fu does, in lines 5 and 6, imagine himself up on the mountainside. He may of course have climbed it a bit already. The poem merely tells us that he had never been to the top.

Form

Although this poem is eight lines long and observes strict verbal parallelism in the two middle couplets (lines 3–4 and 5–6), it is usually classed as a poem "in the Old Style." The reason why it is not thought of as being "in the Modern Style" (or "Regulated Verse" as it is more usual to call it) is that it does not follow the elaborate rules of euphony which have to be observed in Regulated Verse.

The metre is pentasyllabic (five syllables to the line). The rhyme is the same throughout, and is found in alternate lines. Chinese call this type of verse "Five-word Old Style" or "Five Old" for short.

Exegesis

In the literal English translation which follows it will be found that if every word or hyphenated compound or word-group is regarded as a single unit, there are as many units in each line of Chinese as in the corresponding English line; and since the English line follows the Chinese word order, the reader should experience no difficulty in correctly relating the English units to the Chinese units which correspond.

1. Daizong then like-what?
2. Qi Lu green never ends

"Daizong" is one of Mount Tai's names as a god.

Qi and Lu were anciently the names of two states or principalities lying respectively north and south of Mount Tai. Their combined area corresponded roughly to the modern province of Shandong. The names continued to be used as territorial designations long after these states had ceased to exist, rather as "Wessex" and "Provence" continue to be used although they long ago ceased to exist as political entities.

3. Creator concentrated divine beauty
4. Northside southside cleave dark dawn

Yin ang *yang* are familiar enough not to need much explaining. They do not, of course, always mean "northside" and "southside." Their basic sense is "dark" and "sunny." If you use them of river banks, *yin* rather confusingly becomes "southside" and *yang* "northside," since it is the north bank of a river which catches most of the sun.

5. Heaving breast are-born layered clouds
6. Bursting eye-sockets enter returning birds

Inversion is extremely rare in Chinese verse, for the obvious reason that the language contains no grammatical inflections and therefore depends on word-order as a means of expressing grammatical relationships. Any derangement of the usual order is liable to result in impossible ambiguities. These two lines look as if they *ought* to mean

> The heaving breast produces layered clouds,
> The bursting eyes enter the returning birds;

but it has long been recognized that this is a case of poetical inversion. Du Fu's poems contain several such instances. They are considered extremely daring and bizarre by Chinese critics.

7. Really-must surmount extreme summit
8. Single-glance many-mountains little

Zhongshan: literally "the many mountains," "the multitude of mountains"; i.e., "all the other mountains."

Prose Translation

How is one to describe this king of mountains? Throughout the whole of Qi and Lu one never loses sight of its greenness. In it the Creator has concentrated all that is numinous and beautiful. Its northern and southern slopes divide the dawn from the dark. The layered clouds begin at the climber's heaving chest, and homing birds fly suddenly within range of his straining eyes. One day I must stand on top of its highest peak and at a single glance see all the other mountains grown tiny beneath me.

Moonlit Night (*Yue Ye* 月夜)

1. *Jinye Fuzhou yue,*
   今夜鄜州月，

2. *Guizhong zhi du kan.*
   閨中只獨看。

3. *Yao lian xiao ernü,*
   遙憐小兒女，

4. *Wei jie yi Chang'an.*
   未解憶長安。

5. *Xiang wu yunhuan shi,*
   香霧雲鬟濕，

6. *Qing hui yubi han.*
   清輝玉臂寒。

7. *Heshi yi xu huang,*
   何時倚虛幌，

8. *Shuang zhao leihen gan?*
   雙照淚痕乾。

Title and Subject

Yue means "moon"; *ye* means "night."
   Yue ye, therefore, is "Night of Moon" or "Moonlit Night."
   In order to understand the circumstances in which this poem came to be written, it is necessary to know quite a lot about the history of this period and the part that Du Fu played during it.

   On 17 December 755, nineteen years after the date of the last poem, An Lushan, the illiterate barbarian soldier who in 751, as trusted favorite of the Emperor and protégé of the dictator Li Linfu, had become Military Governor over the whole eastern half of the northern frontier of China, raised the standard of revolt in Fanyang (near present-day Peking), ostensibly to "punish" his rival, the Chief Minister, Yang Guozhong. When Tong'guan, the pass controlling the approaches to the capital, was captured by a rebel army in July 756, the Emperor and his immediate entourage slipped out of the city during the night, and Chang'an shortly afterwards fell into enemy hands. At Mawei, about forty miles west of the capital, the Emperor's military escort mutinied, killing Yang Guozhong and demanding the death of Yang Guifei, who was strangled in order to placate them.

   On continuing his journey to his destination in Sichuan — refuge, it will be remembered, of the Chinese Government throughout most of the Second World War — the Emperor, in response to popular representations, left the Crown Prince behind him to organize resistance in the North. In early August, while his father was still making his way down to Chengdu, the Crown Prince set up court at Lingwu beyond the Great Wall, more than four hundred miles north-west of Chang'an. Shortly afterwards he was proclaimed Emperor, the Imperial Seal was sent to him from Sichuan, and historians record the beginning of a new reign, that of the Emperor Suzong.

   About the time when the Tong'guan pass fell, Du Fu, who at forty-four, after long years of unemployment, had just received a small appointment in the capital, appears to have been visiting his wife and children at a place near Fengxian, eighty miles north of Chang'an, where they were living in great poverty. Military operations made it impossible for him to return to the capital, and after its fall and the setting up of a new Imperial government at Lingwu, he seems to have decided to move his family to a place of greater safety and from there make his own way north and offer his services to the Crown Prince. After a nightmarish journey made mostly on foot, leading and carrying their hungry children through country infested with marauding bands of rebels, Du Fu and his wife finally reached Fuzhou, some 130 miles north of Fengxian.

When he had deposited his family in Fuzhou, Du Fu, disguised as a peasant, began the long journey northwest to Lingwu, but on the way was captured by a band of rebel soldiers. Probably used by them as a porter to carry the forage or loot which had no doubt been the object of their expedition, he would appear to have been released when the party reached its destination in Chang'an; for although, like other residents of the occupied city, he was not at liberty to leave it, he does not seem to have been harmed or imprisoned, which he certainly would have been if he had been identified as an official and a partisan of the Imperial government. It is not known where or how he lived in the occupied city during the several months which elapsed before he succeeded in making his escape from it, but one would assume that he found some relation or friend with whom to stay.

This poem was probably written in September 756, a month or two after Du Fu's forcible reentry into Chang'an. The Mid-Autumn Festival fell in mid-September that year. This is a festival traditionally celebrated by eating "moon-cakes" and crabs and drinking wine and, of course, looking at the moon, and tends to be a family affair. The sight of the full moon on this occasion would therefore lend an added poignancy to Du Fu's feelings of anxiety and nostalgia, and he could be almost certain that his wife would be looking at it too and experiencing the same feelings. There is nothing to indicate that the poem was in fact written on the night of the festival, or even that it was written at the full moon; but the assumption he makes in it that his wife would be watching too does make it seem rather probable.

Form

This is a pentasyllabic poem in Regulated Verse. I propose not to explain the complicated rules of euphony which govern the pattern of tones which have to be used in writing this kind of verse, for the simple reason that the tones of Modern Chinese are often not the same as the ones used in Du Fu's day. One of the rules is that the rhyme — which must be the same throughout the poem — must always come on a syllable with a level tone. The rhymes of this poem are still recognizable as rhymes in Modern Chinese, but they are no longer all level-tone syllables: *an* and *gan* in lines 4 and 8 are level-tone syllables, but *kan* and *han* in lines 2 and 6 are not.

The rules that we do need to remember when reading poems in Regulated Verse are (1) that the poem must be one of eight lines in four couplets; and (2) that the two middle couplets (lines 3–4 and lines 5–6) must each be antithetically arranged: i.e., line 4 must parallel line 3 in both grammar and meaning, and line 6 must parallel line 5 in the same way.

Having said that, one has at once to observe that great poets do not always bother about the rules quite as much as their admirers and imitators; and this poem is in fact a rare exception to the general Rule of Parallelism in not having any antithesis in the second couplet (lines 3–4).

Exegesis

1. To-night Fuzhou moon
2. My-wife can-only alone watch

Guizhong, literally "in the women's apartments," is a synonym for "wife." According to the traditional Chinese way of thinking, a wife is the "person inside."

3. Distant sorry-for little sons-daughters
4. Not-yet understand remember Chang'an

Chang'an: used by metonymy for Du Fu himself: "me in Chang'an."

5. Fragrant mists cloud-hair wet
6. Clear light jade-arms cold

Xiang wu: "fragrant mist" is, of course, a poetic conceit. It is the woman's hair which is fragrant and which imparts some of its fragrance to the mist.

Yun "cloudlike" and *yu* "jadelike" are stock epithets for women's hair and arms.

Notice the parallelism in this couplet: "fragrant mist" parallels "clear light," "cloud hair" parallels "jade arms," and "wet" parallels "cold."

7. What-time lean empty curtain
8. Double-shine tear-marks dry

Yi xu huang, literally "lean at the empty curtain," presumably means lean on the open casement from which the curtains have been drawn back.

The *shuang zhao* of line 8 contrasts with the *du kan* of line 2.

The picture which this last couplet is meant to convey is of Du Fu and his wife leaning side by side at the open window and gazing up at the moon while the tears of happiness slowly dry on their checks.

Prose Translation

Tonight in Fuzhou my wife will be watching this moon alone. I think with tenderness of my far-away little ones, too young to understand about their father in Chang'an. My wife's soft hair must be wet from the scented night-mist, and her white arms chilled by the cold moonlight. When shall we lean on the open casement together and gaze at the moon until the tears on our cheeks are dry?

Spring Scene (*Chun Wang* 春望)

1. *Guo po shanhe zai,*
   國破山河在，

2. *Cheng chun caomu shen.*
   城春草木深。

3. *Gan shi hua jian lei,*
   感時花濺淚，

4. *Hen bie niao jing xin.*
   恨別鳥驚心。

5. *Feng huo lian san yue,*
烽火連三月，

6. *Jia shu di wan jin.*
家書抵萬金。

7. *Bai tou sao geng duan,*
白頭搔更短，

8. *Hun yu busheng zan.*
渾欲不勝簪。

Title and Subject

Chun means "spring."

Wang, as in the first poem in this selection, means "gaze at."

Chun wang is "Spring Gazing": i.e., "View in Spring" or "Spring Scene."

This poem was written in occupied Chang'an in the spring of 757. Its occasion may well have been a walk in the deserted Serpentine Park, which is the subject of the next poem. From contemplation of public disasters — so much in contrast with the joyful exuberance of the season — Du Fu turns to contemplation of his personal griefs and worries.

Note the skilful way in which this poem exploits the ambivalence of its images. It is stated

(1) that nature, continuing unchangingly in its annual cycle, is indifferent to human sorrows and disasters;

(2) that, on the contrary, nature is grieving in sympathy with the beholder at the ills which beset him.

The propositions stating this thesis and antithesis are themselves couplets containing antithetical lines. It is partly this involutedness which gives Chinese poetry the extraordinary richness of texture we sometimes find in it.

Notice also the sudden shifting of mood which takes place in the poem. The sombre anguish of the first part ends, as the tragic figure of the opening lines turns into a comic old man going bald on top, on a note of playful self-mockery which is nevertheless infinitely pathetic.

Form

This is a formally perfect example of a pentasyllabic poem in Regulated Verse. Not only the middle couplets, but the first couplet, too, contain verbal parallelism. It is amazing that Du Fu is able to use so immensely stylized a form in so natural a manner. The tremendous spring-like compression which is achieved by using very simple language with very complicated forms manipulated in so skilful a manner that they don't show is characteristic of Regulated Verse at its best. Its perfection of form lends it a classical grace which unfortunately cannot be communicated in translation. That is the reason why Du, one of the great masters of this form, makes so comparatively poor a showing in foreign languages.

Exegesis

1. State ruined mountains-rivers survive.
2. City spring grass-trees thick.
3. Moved-by times flowers sprinkle tears.
4. Hating separation birds startle heart.

Since this is a poem in Regulated Verse, every word and every phrase in this and the following couplet must be arranged antithetically. Notice the skill with which monotony is avoided by a change of grammatical construction. In this couplet the subjects ("flowers," "birds") come in the third place in the line, whilst in the following couplet the compound subjects ("beacon-fires," "letter from home") come at the beginning of the line.

5. Beacon-fires have-continued-for three months.
6. Home-letter worth ten-thousand taels.

In our own history beacons were generally used in order to give warning of invasion. The Chinese used them a good deal in time of emergency, however, as a routine means of maintaining contact between garrisons. For example, two garrisons established at a distance of ten miles apart would light a beacon every evening, and each would know that the other was all right if it saw the fire burning at the appointed hour. To say that the beacons have been burning for three months running is therefore only another way of saying that a state of military emergency has existed throughout that time.

7. White hair scratch even shorter.
8. Quite will-be unequal-to hatpin.

Until their conquest by the Manchus in the seventeenth century, the Chinese, like the Japanese and Koreans and other Far Eastern peoples, dressed their hair in a top-knot on the crown of the head. Their hats, like those of our grandmothers, were anchored to their heads by large hatpins which passed through the knot of hair.

Prose Translation

The state may fall, but the hills and streams remain. It is spring in the city: grass and leaves grow thick. The flowers shed tears of grief for the troubled times, and the birds seen startled, as if with the anguish of separation. For three months continuously the beacon-fires have been burning. A letter from home would be worth a fortune. My white hair is getting so scanty from worried scratching that soon there won't be enough to stick my hatpin in!

Thinking of My Brothers on a Moonlit Night
(*Yueye yi shedi*　月夜憶舍弟)

1. *Shu gu duan ren xing,*
　戍鼓斷人行，

2. *Bian qiu yi yan sheng.*
邊秋一雁聲。

3. *Lu cong jin ye bai,*
露從今夜白，

4. *Yue shi guxiang ming.*
月是故鄉明。

5. *You di jie fen san,*
有弟皆分散，

6. *Wu jia wen sisheng.*
無家問死生。

7. *Ji shu chang bu da,*
寄書長不達，

8. *Kuang nai wei xiu bing.*
況乃未休兵。

Title and Subject

Yueye: "moonlit night," which is the title of the second poem in this selection.

Yi: "think of," "remember," "call to mind."

Shedi. Chinese kinship terms are extremely complicated. For example, there are five words for "aunt" depending on whether you mean mother's sister, father's sister, mother's brother's wife, wife of father's elder brother, or wife of father's younger brother. Matters used to be further complicated by the exigencies of polite language. Thus "your father" was *yanfu* (literally "strict father"), whilst "my father" was *jiafu* (literally "family father"). "My elder brother" was *jiaxiong* with the same *jia*; but "my younger brother" was *shedi* (literally "house younger brother"), *she* being the term used in conjunction with younger relatives: nephews and so forth.

Du Fu's mother died when he was an infant, but he had three half-brothers and a half-sister who were children of his father's second marriage. He was deeply attached to all four of them, and expressed affectionate concern for them in many of his poems.

In this title *yueye* modifies the verb *yi* which follows it: "think of *on* a moonlit night." The whole title therefore means, "Thinking of My Brothers on a Moonlit Night."

The fighting whose overtones darken this poem is that same bloody and protracted civil war which began with the rebellion of An Lushan in December 755. In spite of the murder of An Lushan by his own son and the recovery of Chang'an in 757, it dragged on for a further six years, depopulating and impoverishing Northern China and inflicting such grievous damage on the economic and political fabric of the Tang state that it never afterwards properly recovered.

Some commentators think this poem was written at the end of October 759 after the fall of Luoyang to Shi Siming, a former general of An Lushan who had surrendered to the Tang court in February 758, but rebelled again a few months later and subsequently murdered An Lushan's parricidal son and set himself up as Emperor of Yan in the East. I think it must have been written a little before that, however, because it refers to White Dew, the Chinese name for the chilly part of autumn which follows the Mid-Autumn Festival, which in 759 fell in early September. I strongly suspect that this poem, like "Moonlit Night," may have been written on the occasion of that festival.

Du Fu, for reasons which are still in dispute, threw up his job in Huazhou at the beginning of autumn, 759, and journeyed with his wife and children to the frontier town of Qinzhou, three hundred miles west of Chang'an, near the western end of the Great Wall. He was in Qinzhou no more than six or seven weeks before setting off once more on his travels; but it was a highly productive period. More than sixty of his poems are attributed to it.

Form

This is a formally perfect pentasyllabic poem in Regulated Verse.

Exegesis

1. Garrison drums cut-off people's travel
2. Frontier autumn one goose sound

One distinguished scholar thinks Du Fu wrote this poem while still on his way to Qinzhou; but I think he must be there already, complaining that he feels cut off: no postal services and no visitors. Otherwise I find the first line hard to understand.

Yi yan sheng is an ambivalent image. The migratory wild goose is a symbol of autumn; but a well-known literary convention also associates it with an exile's letter from home. The sound of the wild goose sets in motion the train of thought which begins with a feeling of beleaguerment and a melancholy awareness of winter's approach and ends with anxiety about his absent brothers.

3. Dew from this-night white.
4. Moon is old-home bright

Guxiang: perhaps "homeland" or "homestead" would be a more accurate rendering. We tend to say "home" both for the place (*guxiang*) and the people (*jia* "family"). Unfortunately Du Fu talks about his *guxiang* in this line and then goes on to complain that he hasn't got a *jia* in line 6. But this is quite deliberate. The goose reminds him that this is the mid-autumn moon, and the mid-autumn moon makes him think of his old homestead; but the family who should occupy the homestead is all scattered and has no headquarters to which he can apply for information about its separate members. Everyone has a *guxiang*, since everyone must have been born and brought up somewhere or other, but a person in Du Fu's position could reasonably say that he had no *jia* since the *jia* had been broken up.

5. Have brothers all are-scattered
6. Haven't family ask dead-alive
7. Sent letters always not arrive
8. Especially as not-yet end fighting

Ji shu: it isn't clear whether these are the letters which Du Fu writes to his brothers or those which they write to him. If the former, it could be objected that Du Fu couldn't know whether his letters had reached them or not; if the latter, it could equally well be objected that he had no means of knowing that they had written any. Common sense suggests that this should be understood as a general statement about the breakdown of mails due to the deplorable situation.

Prose Translation

Travel is interrupted by the war-drums of the garrisons. The sound of a solitary wild goose announces the coming of autumn to the frontier. From tonight onwards the dew will be white. The moon is that same moon which shines down on my birthplace. My brothers are scattered in different places. I have no home to tell me whether they are alive or dead. The letters we write never seem to reach their destination; and it will be worse now that we are at war once more.

Dreaming of Li Bo (Meng Li Bo 夢李白)

1. *Sibie yi tunsheng,*
   死別已吞聲，

2. *Shengbie chang cece.*
   生別常惻惻。

3. *Jiangnan zhangli di,*
   江南瘴癘地，

4. *Zhuke wu xiaoxi.*
   逐客無消息。

5. *Guren ru wo meng,*
   故人入我夢，

6. *Ming wo chang xiangyi.*
   明我長相憶。

7. *Kong fei pingsheng hun,*
   恐非平生魂，

8. *Lu yuan bu ke ce.*
   路遠不可測。

9. *Hun lai fenglin qing,*
   魂來楓林青，

10. *Hun fan guansai he.*
    魂返關塞黑。

11. *Jun jin zai luowang,*
    君今在羅網，

12. *Heyi you yuyi?*
    何以有羽翼。

13. *Luo yue man wuliang,*
落月滿屋梁，

14. *You yi zhao yanse!*
猶疑照顏色！

15. *Shui shen bolang kuo,*
水深波浪闊，

16. *Wu shi jiaolong de!*
無使蛟龍得！

Title and Subject

Meng: "dream," here a verb, "dreaming of."

Li Bo: Li Bo and Du Fu are often looked upon as the greatest of all the Tang poets and their very different personalities and styles are frequently contrasted.

Li Bo (701–762) was considerably senior to Du Fu, and when Du Fu first made his acquaintance in Henan in 744 or 745, he was already a famous poet whilst Du Fu was a comparatively unknown young man. Du Fu was completely captivated by the older poet's magnetic personality and treasured the memory of their brief association for the rest of his life, addressing a number of poems to him at different times and from different places.

The An Lushan rebellion which devastated Northern China and wrought so great an upheaval in Du Fu's life almost passed Li Bo by. During its first year he was leading a fairly carefree existence in the Yangtze Valley near Jiujiang. Early in 757, however, he became involved in the fortunes of Prince Lin, a member of the Imperial family who had been given command of a fleet on the Yangtze for the purpose of conducting operations against the rebels, but who, in anticipation of the imminent break-up of the régime, seems to have decided to set up an independent administration of his own centred on Nanjing. At the beginning of 757, when his fleet was anchored at Jiujiang, Prince Lin invited Li Bo on board as a sort of civilian adviser or cultural mascot. After a very enjoyable and convivial cruise down the river, Li Bo apparently realized what was afoot when the fleet reached Yangzhou and deserted, along with many of Prince Lin's officers. Following the defeat and execution of Prince Lin in March 757, Li Bo was arrested near Jiujiang and held in prison for several months. He was released on the initiative of a visiting Government Inspector, but rearrested a year later when the Chief Minister who had been the ultimate authority for his release fell from power. He was sentenced to banishment in Yelang, a malarial district in Guizhou from which an ageing hedonist like Li Bo would have little prospect of returning alive. Fortunately — whether from ineptitude or humanity or a combination of the two — the bureaucratic machine seems not to have hustled him unduly, for when news of an amnesty in which he was included reached him in the early summer of 759, he was little more than half-way to his place of exile.

The exact date of this poem is uncertain. A commonly held view is that it was written while Du Fu was at Qinzhou. Another view is that it must have been written earlier because it seems to imply (in lines 4 and 11) that Li Bo is still in trouble, and must therefore belong to a period earlier than the amnesty. The date will probably always remain uncertain; but I do not in any case find the argument for the second view a very compelling one. It overlooks the fact that Du Fu's news about Li Bo may have been, and, indeed, probably was, months out of date. Scholars accustomed to handling dated sources easily forget that information they can obtain in three-quarters of a minute by taking a book off a shelf may have taken weeks or months to reach a contemporary — particularly one living in a remote frontier city in time of war. Whatever the date of the poem, it is clear that when Du Fu wrote it he thought of Li Bo as a condemned man whose banishment would probably cost him his life.

Form

This is an Old Style pentasyllabic poem.

Exegesis

1. Death-partings have-end-of sobbing
2. Life-partings unremitting anguish
3. Jiangnan pestilential country
4. Banished-man not-any news

In Du Fu's time the name "Jiangnan" was used to designate a vast area in which both Jiujiang and Yelang would be included. It does not therefore give us much indication of where Du Fu imagined Li Bo to be at the time he was writing the poem.

5. Old-friend entered my dream
6. Makes-clear I always think-of-him
7. Afraid is-not living soul
8. Road far cannot-be measured

It is by no means easy to see the connection between these two lines. I think Du Fu means that the distance from Jiangnan to Qinzhou is so immense that Li Bo's soul would be unable to make the journey there and back while he slept. He has a fearful suspicion that Li Bo has died in prison or in exile, and that what he is being visited by is a soul permanently detached from its body. Line 8 is meant to explain line 7. We should perhaps feel the connection more easily if the lines were the other way round.

9. Soul come maple-woods green
10. Soul return passes dark

Fenglin: the maple-woods are on the banks of the River Yangtze. They are also referred to in the third-century B.C. *Summons of the Soul.* It was still light when Li Bo's soul left Jiangnan, but so great is the distance that the journey back through the passes was made at night.

11. You now are-in net
12. How have-got feather-wings

Luowang: i.e., the net of the law. This is dream-logic. "How did you get here? I thought you were supposed to be in prison."

13. Sinking moon fills roof-beams
14. Still doubtful shine-on your-face

These two lines describe Du Fu's feelings on waking. The dream had been so vivid, that when he opened his eyes and saw the whole room bathed in moonlight, he looked around half expecting the moonlight to reveal Li Bo still standing in one of its corners.

15. Water deep waves broad
16. Don't let water-dragons get

Prose Translation

After the separation of death one can eventually swallow back one's grief, but the separation of the living is an endless, unappeasable anxiety. From pestilent Jiangnan no news arrives of the poor exile. That my old friend should come into my dream shows how constantly he is in my thoughts. I fear that this is not the soul of the living man: the journey is so immeasurably far. When your soul left, the maple woods were green: on its return the passes were black with night. Lying now enmeshed in the net of the law, how did you find wings with which to fly here? The light of the sinking moon illumines every beam and rafter of my chamber, and I half expect it to light up your face. The water is deep, the waves are wide: don't let the water-dragons get you!

From a Height (Deng gao 登高)

1. *Feng ji tian gao yuan xiao ai,*
   風急天高猿嘯哀,

2. *Zhuo qing sha bai niao fei hui.*
   渚清沙白鳥飛迴。

3. *Wu bian luo mu xiaoxiao xia,*
   無邊落木蕭蕭下,

4. *Bu jin Changjiang gungun lai.*
   不盡長江袞袞來。

5. *Wan li bei qiu chang zuo ke,*
   萬里悲秋常作客,

6. *Bai nian duo bing du deng tai.*
   百年多病獨登臺。

7. *Jian'nan kuhen fan shuangbin,*
   艱難苦恨繁霜鬢,

8. *Liaodao xin ting zhuo jiu bei!*
   潦倒新停濁酒盃。

Title and Subject

Deng: "climb."
  Gao: "high."
The magnificent sorrow of this threnody for dying nature ends with Du Fu's remark that he has had to give up drinking. Whether the tone intended is fretful or, as I suspect, humorous (cf. the gentle self-mockery at the end of "Spring Scene," which also begins on a note of tragic sorrow), it is hard not to find this ending uncomfortable. Yet Du Fu does this sort of thinking so often that one must look for something other than mere neurotic self-pity if one is to reach any sort of understanding with him at all.

My own view is that Du Fu's famous compassion in fact includes himself, viewed quite objectively and almost as an afterthought. We can perhaps understand this poem if we think of a typical Chinese landscape with a tiny figure in one corner of it looking at the view. In this poem the little figure is Du Fu himself, who, far from solipsistically shrinking the landscape to his own dimensions, lends grandeur to it by contrasting it with his own slightly comical triviality.

Figure 44. "The wind is keen, the sky is high." Early twentieth-century illustration. (Source: *Zixi huapu daquan* [Complete Painting Manual] [Beijing: Rongbaozhai, 1982])

Form

Heptasyllable Regulated Verse.

Exegesis

1. Wind keen sky high apes scream mourning
2. Islet pure sand white birds fly revolving
3. Without limit falling trees bleakly-bleakly shed
4. Not exhaustible long river rolling-rolling come
5. Myriad-*li* melancholy autumn constantly be traveler
6. Hundred-years much sickness alone ascend terrace
7. Difficulties bitter-regrets proliferate frosty temples
8. Despondent newly stop muddy wine cups

Prose Translation

The wind is keen, the sky is high; apes wail mournfully. The island looks fresh; the white sand gleams; birds fly circling. An infinity of trees bleakly divest themselves, their leaves falling, falling. Along the endless expanse of river the billows come rolling, rolling. Through a thousand miles of autumn's melancholy, a constant traveler racked with a century's diseases, alone I have dragged myself up to this high terrace. Hardship and bitter chagrin have thickened the frost upon my brow. And to crown my despondency I have lately had to renounce my cup of muddy wine!

On Yueyang Tower (Deng Yueyang lou 登岳陽樓)

1. *Xi wen Dongting shui,*
   昔聞洞庭水，

2. *Jin shang Yueyang lou.*
   今上岳陽樓。

3. *Wu Chu dong nan che,*
   吳楚東南坼，

4. *Qiankun riye fu.*
   乾坤日夜浮。

5. *Qinpeng wu yi zi,*
   親朋無一字，

6. *Laobing you gu zhou.*
   老病有孤舟。

7. *Rongma guanshan bei,*
   戎馬關山北，

8. *Ping xuan disi liu.*
憑軒涕泗流。

Title and Subject

Deng: "climb"
   Yueyang: a town at the northeastern corner of Lake Dongting, sometimes referred to as Yuezhou.
   Lou: "tower." Here the gatetower in the walls of Yueyang looking westward across the lake.
   Du Fu left Kuizhou in the spring of 768 and sailed 250 miles downstream to Jiangling, where he and his family stayed for a number of months. In the autumn he set off for Yueyang, intending to proceed onwards from there to the junction of the Yangtze and the River Han. He planned to return to the North, to which he had been so long a stranger, by sailing up-river along the Han. News of a Tibetan invasion made

Figure 45. "Today I have climbed up Yueyang tower." Early twentieth-century illustration. (Source: *Zixi huapu daquan* [Complete Painting Manual] [Beijing: Rongbaozhai, 1982])

him alter his plans. Although he reached Yueyang that autumn, he was to spend all the rest of his life in the South.

This poem begins with the poet on top of a high building looking at a view which he has been longing to see for years and ends with him collapsed on the parapet in sobs. Some critics have found it difficult to establish a connection between the first and second halves of the poem, particularly between the magnificent fourth line, in which the whole universe appears to be floating in the ever-moving waters of the vast lake, and the comparatively more trivial fifth line in which the poet complains of the lack of news from his family and friends in the North. The difficulty is due to the rapidity with which one mood succeeds another in the course of the poem. Elation at achieving the long-expected view is followed by awe at its immensity, then by a feeling of isolation and loneliness, then by patriotic worry about the Tibetan invasion and its threat to the metropolitan area, and finally by the tearful breakdown of the last line.

The result of compressing so many mental happenings into so exiguous a form is that the actual wording of the poem becomes a kind of shorthand from which the poet's full meaning has to be reconstructed. Poetry like this, in short, invites us to share some of the process of composition with the poet. That is why much of Du Fu, particularly "late Du Fu," *reads* rather badly but *recollects* wonderfully well.

Form

Pentasyllabics in Regulated Verse. Notice that in this poem, as in "Spring Scene," not only the two central couplets, but also the opening couplet are in parallel arrangement (*xi* balancing *jin*, *wen* balancing *shang*, and *Dongting shui* balancing *Yueyang lou*). This gratuitous bit of extra formalism in a poem which is so heavily loaded with meaning suggests that the creative writer in China cannot have found his elaborately formal medium quite so cramping and inhibiting as is sometimes suggested by iconoclastic modern critics.

Exegesis

1. In-past hear-of Dongting's water
2. Now ascend Yueyang tower
3. Wu Chu east south split
4. Heaven-and-earth day-night float

Qian and *kun* are the names of the first two hexagrams in the *Book of Changes*, the divination scripture of the Confucian canon: they are the symbols of sky and earth; used together here as a compound they form a poetic synonym of *tiandi* "the world," "the universe."

5. Relatives-friends not one word
6. Old-ill have solitary boat

Lao-bing: it should not be thought, from the rather frequent references to ill health which occur in his poems, that Du Fu was a hypochondriac. During the occupation of Chang'an he contracted malaria and some chronic respiratory disease, suffered from rheumatism a great deal during his stay in Chengdu (the "river city"), and after his move to Kuizhou was, at any rate for a time, paralyzed in his right arm. Also while in Kuizhou he became deaf in one ear and lost all his teeth.

7. War-horses passes mountains north
8. Lean-on railing snivel-tears flow
Rongma: reference to the Tibetan invasion. In October 768 the Tibetans invested first Lingwu and then Binzhou, and a state of emergency was declared in the capital. The Tibetan invasion had been successfully stemmed by the time Du Fu wrote this poem, but it is unlikely that news of government successes had yet reached him in Yueyang.

Prose Translation

Long ago I heard about the waters of Dongting, and now today I have climbed up Yueyang tower. The lake cleaves the lands of Wu and Chu to east and south. Day and night the world floats in its changing waters. Of friends and family I have no word. Old and ill I have only my solitary boat. The warhorse stamps north of the passes. I lean on the railing and my tears flow.

Sixteen Poems

Translated by Burton Watson

Song of the Beautiful Ladies

(753) This poem is a veiled attack on the Yang family, relatives of Emperor Xuanzong's favorite, Yang Guifei. The gathering centers on the two elder sisters of Yang Guifei, enfeoffed as the ladies of Guo and Qin respectively; the gentleman who arrives later is Yang Guifei's cousin, Yang Guozhong, a high minister. The scene is the spring outing held on the third day of the third lunar month at Qujiang (the Winding River, or Serpentine), a park in Chang'an.

Third month, third day, in the air a breath of newness;
by Chang'an riverbanks the beautiful ladies crowd,
warm-bodied, modest-minded, mild and pure,
with clear sleek complexions, bone and flesh well matched,
in figured gauze robes that shine in the late spring,
worked with golden peacocks, silver unicorns.
On their heads what do they wear?
Kingfisher glinting from hairpins that dangle by sidelock borders.
On their back what do I see?
Pearls that weight the waistband and subtly set off the form.
Among them, kin of the lady of cloud screen and pepper-scented
    halls,
granted titles to the great fiefs of Guo and Qin.
Humps of purple camel proffered from blue caldrons,
platters of crystal spread with slivers of raw fish;
but ivory chopsticks, sated, dip down no more,

and phoenix knives in vain hasten to cut and serve.
Yellow Gate horses ride swiftly, leaving the dust unstirred,
bearing from royal kitchens unending rare delights.
Plaintive notes of flute and drum, enough to move the gods;
throngs of guests and lackeys, all the highest rank;
and last, another rider, with slow and measured stride,
dismounts at the tent door, ascends the brocade carpet.
The snow of willow catkins blankets the white-flowered reeds;
a bluebird flies away, in its bill a crimson kerchief —[1]
Where power is all-surpassing, fingers may be burned;
take care and draw no closer to His Excellency's glare!

Song of Pengya

(756) This poem recounts the journey made by Du Fu and his family when they fled
north from Chang'an to avoid the rebel armies led by An Lushan.

I remember when we first fled the rebels,
hurrying north over dangerous trails;
night deepened on Pengya Road,
the moon shone over White-water Hills.
A whole family endlessly trudging,
begging without shame from the people we met:
valley birds sang, a jangle of soft voices;
we didn't see a single traveler returning.
The baby girl in her hunger bit me;
fearful that tigers or wolves would hear her cries,
I hugged her to my chest, muffling her mouth,
but she squirmed and wailed louder than before.
The little boy pretended he knew what was happening;
importantly he searched for sour plums to eat.
Ten days, half in rain and thunder,
through mud and slime we pulled each other on.
There was no escaping from the rain,
trails slick, clothes wet and clammy;
getting past the hardest places,
a whole day advanced us no more than three or four *li*.

---

[1] There were rumors that Yang Guozhong was carrying on an intrigue with the Lady of
Guo, and this probably explains the reference to the bluebird, the traditional bearer of
love notes.

Mountain fruits served for rations,
low-hung branches were our rafter and roof.
Mornings we traveled by rock-bedded streams,
evenings camped in mists that closed in the sky.
We stopped a little while at the marsh of Tongjia,
thinking to go out by Luzi Pass;
an old friend there, Sun Zai,
ideals higher than the piled-up clouds;
he came out to meet us as dusk turned to darkness,
called for torches, opening gate after gate,
heated water to wash our feet,
cut strips of paper to call back our souls.
Then his wife and children came;
seeing us, their tears fell in streams.
My little chicks had gone sound to sleep;
he called them to wake up and eat from his plate,
said he would make a vow with me,
the two of us to be brothers forever.
At last he cleared the room where we sat,
wished us goodnight, all he had at our command.
Who is willing, in the hard, bleak times,
to break open, lay bare his innermost heart?
Parting from you, a year of months has rounded,
Tartar tribes still plotting evil,
and I think how it would be to have strong wings
that would carry me away, set me down before you.

Lovely Lady

This poem discribes a woman whose family had been wiped out in the rebellion and whose husband had deserted her.

Lovely lady, fairest of the time,
hiding away in an empty valley;
daughter of a good house, she said,
fallen now among grasses of the wood.
"There was tumult and death within the passes then;
my brothers, old and young, were killed.
Office, position — what help were they?
I couldn't even gather up my brothers' bones!
The world despises you when your luck is down;
all I had went with the turn of the flame.

My husband was a fickle fellow,
his new girl as fair as jade.
Blossoms that close at dusk keep faith with the hour,
mandarin ducks will not rest apart;
but he could only see the new one laughing,
never hear the former one's tears —"
Within the mountain the stream runs clear;
out of the mountain it turns to mud.
Her maid returns from selling a pearl,
braids vines to mend their roof of thatch.
The lady picks a flower but does not put it in her hair,
gathers juniper berries, sometimes a handful.
When the sky is cold, in thin azure sleeves,
at dusk she stands leaning by the tall bamboo.

Presented to Wei Ba, Gentleman in Retirement

Life is not made for meetings;
like stars at opposite ends of the sky we move.
What night is it, then, tonight,
when we can share the light of this lamp?
Youth — how long did it last?
The two of us grayheaded now,
we ask about old friends — half are ghosts;
cries of unbelief stab the heart.
Who would have thought? — twenty years
and once again I enter your house.
You weren't married when I left you;
now suddenly a whole row of boys and girls!
merrily greeting their father's friend,
asking me what places I've been.
Before I finish answering,
you send the boys to set out wine and a meal,
spring scallions cut in night rain,
new cooked rice mixed with yellow millet.
Meetings are rare enough, you say;
pour the wine till we've downed ten cups!
But ten cups do not make me drunk;
your steadfast love is what moves me now.
Tomorrow hills and ranges will part us,
the wide world coming between us again.

The Man with No Family to Take Leave Of

(759) Tian-bao in the first line refers to the outbreak of the An Lushan rebellion in
the fourteenth year of the Tian-bao era, 755.

Ever since Tian-bao, this silence and desolation,
fields and sheds mere masses of pigweed and bramble;
my village of a hundred households or more,
in these troubled times scattered, some east, some west;
not a word from those still living,
the dead ones all gone to dust and mire.
I was on the side that lost the battle,[2]
so I came home, looking for the old paths,
so long on the road, to find empty lanes,
the sun grown feeble, pain and sorrow in the air.
All I meet are foxes and raccoon dogs,
their fur on end, snarling at me in anger.
And for neighbors on four sides, who do I have?
One or two aging widows.
But the roosting bird loves his old branch;
how could he reject it, narrow perch though it is?
Now that spring's here I shoulder the hoe alone,
in the evening sun once more pour water on the fields.
The local officials know I'm back;
they call me in, order me to practice the big drum.[3]
Maybe they'll assign me to duty in my own province —
but still I've no wife, no one to take by hand.
Traveling to a post nearby, I'm one man all alone;
sent to a far-off assignment, I'll be more lost than ever.
But, since my house and village are a wilderness now,
near or far, it's all the same to me.
And always I grieve for my mother, sick so long;
five years I've left her buried in a mere ditch of a grave.
She bore me, but I hadn't the strength to help her;
to the end, both of us breathed bitter sighs.
A living man, but with no family to take leave of —
how can I be called a proper human being?

---

[2] The defeat of the Tang forces at Xiangzhou in 759.
[3] The drum used in battle to signal troop movements.

Five of Seven Songs
Written During the Qian-yuan Era While Staying at Tong'guxian

(759) These are poems recording Du Fu's experiences when, fleeing from famine, he led his family west to Tong'gu in Gansu. Zimei is Du Fu's courtesy name.

1

A traveler, a traveler, Zimei his name,
white hair tousled, dangling below the ears,
through the years gathering acorns in the wake of the monkey pack:
cold skies at dusk within a mountain valley.
No word from the middle plain, no hope of going home;
hands and feet chilled and chapped, skin and flesh grown numb,
Ah-ah, song the first, a song already sad;
mournful winds for my sake come down from the sky.

2

Long hoe, long hoe, handle of white wood,
I trust my life to you — you must save me now!
No shoots of wild taro where mountain snows drift high;
robe so short, pull as I may it will not hide my shins.
And so with you I go empty-handed home;
the boy grumbles, the girls whine, my four walls are still.
Ah-ah, song the second, the song at last breaks free;
village lanes for my sake put on the face of pity.

3

Du Fu had four brothers, the youngest with him in Tong'gu; the others were living in the east.

I have brothers, younger brothers in a place far away,
three of them sickly, not one of them strong;
parted in life, to veer and turn, never to meet;
barbarian dust blackens the sky, the road is long.
Wild geese flying east, behind them the cranes —
if they could only carry me to your side!
Ah-ah, song the third, the singer's third refrain;
if I should die here, how would you find my bones?

4

Zhongli is in Anhui south of the Huai River.

I have a sister, little sister, living in Zhongli,
husband dead these many years, her orphan ones still young.
On the long Huai the waves leap up, dragons and serpents rage;
we haven't met for ten years — when will you come?
I want to go in a little boat but arrows fill my eyes;
far away in that southern land, banners of war abound.
Ah-ah, song the fourth, four times I've sung;
forest monkeys for my sake wail even at noon.

6

Clearly a political allegory, though commentators do not agree on exactly what the dragon and the vipers stand for.

To the south there is a dragon living in a mountain pool,
where old trees, dark and lush, touch limb to bending limb.
When tree leaves yellow and fall, he goes to his winter sleep,
and from the east come vipers to play on the waters there.
Passing by, I marveled that they would dare come forth;
I drew a sword to slash them, but put it up again.
Ah-ah, song the sixth, its purpose long denied;
stream-cut valley, for my sake put on spring clothes again!

On the Spur of the Moment

River slopes, already into the midmonth of spring;
under the blossoms, bright mornings again:
I look up, eager to watch the birds;
turn my head, answering what I took for a call.
Reading books, I skip the difficult parts;
faced with wine, I keep my cup filled.
These days I've gotten to know the old man of Emei;[4]
he understands this idleness that is my true nature.

A Guest Arrives

(760) This was written when Du Fu was living on the outskirts of Chengdu.

North of my lodge, south of my lodge, spring rivers all;
day by day I see only flocks of gulls convening.

---

[4] Emei is a famous mountain southwest of Chengdu.

Flower paths till now have never been swept for a guest;
my thatch gate opening for you, opens for the first time.
For food — the market's far — no wealth of flavors;
for wine — my house is poor — only old muddy brew.
If you don't mind drinking with the old man next door.
I'll call across the hedge and we can finish off what's left.

Restless Night

(762)

The cool of bamboo invades my room;
moonlight from the fields fills the corners of the court;
dew gathers till it falls in drops;
a scattering of stars, now there, now gone.
A firefly threading the darkness makes its own light;
birds at rest on the water call to each other;
all these lie within the shadow of the sword —
Powerless I grieve as the clear night passes.

Quatrain: In Late Sun

(764)

In late sun, the beauty of river and hill;
on spring wind, fragrance of grass and flower;
where mud is soft the swallows fly;
where sands are warm the mandarin ducks doze.

They Say You're Staying in a Mountain Temple

(766) This poem [one of a pair] was written when Du Fu was in Kuizhou on the upper
Yangtze, the Jianghan region mentioned in the poem; his brother was in the seacoast
area south of the Yangtze delta.

My younger brother Feng is alone in the region east of the Yangtze and
for three or four years I have had no word from him; I am looking for
someone to take him these two poems.

They say you're staying in a mountain temple,
In Hangzhou — or is it Yuezhou?
In the wind and grime of war, how long since we parted!
At Jianghan, bright autumns waste away.
While my shadow rests by monkey-loud trees,

my soul whirls off to where shell-born towers rise.
Next year on floods of spring I'll go downriver,
to the white clouds at the end of the east I'll look for you!

On the River

(c. 766) This poem was written while the author was on the upper Yangtze; Jingchu is
the old name for the region.

On the river, every day these heavy rains —
bleak, bleak, autumn in Jingchu!
High winds strip the leaves from the trees;
through the long night I hug my fur robe.
I recall my official record, keep looking in the mirror,
recall my comings and goings, leaning alone in an upper room.
In these perilous times I long to serve my sovereign —
old and feeble as I am, I can't stop thinking of it!

Nine Poems

Translated by Florence Ayscough

Miss Lowell and I had intended to publish a book devoted to the poems of Du Fu, that
grave poet whom the Chinese consider their greatest genius in the realm of poetry,
and a paragraph in a letter which she wrote to me during December, 1923, reads now
in the light of a prophecy: "How is Du Fu coming along? I hope not too rapidly, for
when I finish the Keats book I shall be so exhausted that I shall want quite a long
vacation before I attempt anything else." The "Keats book" of which she spoke was
published in the early spring, 1925, and a few weeks later, Amy Lowell died.

Now all the plans must be revised: the book must be my own.... I realized too that
to render Chinese poems in unrhymed cadence, as Amy Lowell had done, was not
possible for me. After trying many experiments, always bearing in mind that the most
important points to be considered were: What does the poet say? How does he say it?
and, How can I make the text comprehensible? I found that I could give the answers
to these questions best by abandoning all thought of writing conventional English and
by concentrating on the attempt to bring over each ideograph and all that it implies
in the context.

Wasteland — Gazing Far Away

(759)

Limpid Autumn; I gaze, no limit;
Remote, far-off, rise layers of darkness.

Distant waters bind with cold sky;
Lone city blurs in deep mist.

Sparse leaves through wind, still further drop;
Divided peaks through lack of sun, dulled.

Single crane returns home at which sinking of the sun?
Hour of yellow dusk; trees brimful of rooks.

A Traveler at Night Writes His Thoughts

(765)

Fine grass; slight breeze from bank;
High mast; alone at night in boat.

Over level widening waste stars droop — flowers;
Moon flows as water on vast surging stream.

Fame! Is it manifest by essays, poems?
An official, old, sick, should rest.

What do I resemble, blown by wind blown by wind?
A gull on the sand between Heaven and Earth.

Six Cut-Shorts (Quatrains)

Sun Lengthens

(764)

Sun lengthens; streams, hills glorious;
Spring-wind breathes; flowers, grass fragrant.[5]

Vapour rises from wet mud, young swallows fly;
Warmth radiates from soft sand, duck, drake sleep.

River Jade-Gray

(764)

River jade-gray; birds gleam white;
Hills green; flowers burn red.

Now in Spring; I see it pass;
What day will open return-home year?

---

[5] Ayscough ends the line with "frequent," surely a misreading of her handwriting by the typesetter. *Eds.*

Sun Rises from Water
(765)

Sun rises from water East of plaited fence,
Mist exhales mud North of cottage.

Bamboos high; green kingfishers call,
Sands quiet; black water-birds dance.

Shady, Shady
(765)

Shady, shady, flower stamens a tangle;
Flitting, flitting, bees, butterflies a cloud.

Perch in solitude; body reluctant to move;
Should guest come, what shall I do?

West of Hut
(765)

West of hut grow bamboo-shoots; I open another door;
North of ditch stretch pepper-trees; they back on village.

Plums ripe; promised to eat them with old Zhu;
Pines high; proposed a discussion with Sir Yuan.

Yellow Orioles
(765)

Yellow orioles, two, call from willows, kingfisher-green;
White egrets, a line, rise to sky, bright-blue.

Window holds in its lips Western Range; snow of a thousand
        Autumns;
Anchored to gate-post Eastern Wu boats; they travel ten thousand *li*.

Flying from Trouble
(770)

At fifty a white-headed old man,
South, North, I fly from troubles of the State.

Coarse cloth wound round dried bones.
Walk back, forth; alas am still not warm.

Already failing, illness has entered in;
All people within the Four Seas are as mud, charcoal.

Below Heaven, on Earth, throughout ten thousand *li*,
Is no place where a body can be left.

Wife children still follow me;
I turn head, we sigh in grief.

In old home weeds, a mound of ruins;
Our neighbors all divided, scattered.

From this time returning road obscure;
Tears are wept dry on banks of River Xiang.

Eight Poems

Translated by Kenneth Rexroth

All through his life Du Fu wrote fulldress poems of advice to the throne.... I have not translated any of these poems. Others have done them well. They would require too much explanation.... I have chosen only those poems whose appeal is simple and direct with a minimum of allusion to past literature or contemporary politics, in other words, poems that speak to me of situations in life like my own. I have thought of my translations as, finally, expressions of myself.

Written on the Wall at Zhang's Hermitage

An early poem (c. 735).

It is Spring in the mountains.
I come alone seeking you.
The sound of chopping wood echos
Between the silent peaks.
The streams are still icy.
There is snow on the trail.
At sunset I reach your grove
In the stony mountain pass.
You want nothing, although at night
You can see the aura of gold
And silver ore all around you.
You have learned to be gentle
As the mountain deer you have tamed.
The way back forgotten, hidden
Away, I become like you,
An empty boat, floating, adrift.

Visiting Zan, Abbot of Dayun

(756–57) This poem was written while Du Fu was in captivity in Chang'an.

I am sleepless in the glow and shadow of the lamplight.
The heart at peace breathes the incense of dedication.
Between the temple walls the night is bottomless.
The gold wind bells quiver in the breeze.
The courtyard shuts in the deep
Darkness of the Spring night.
In the blackness the crystalline pool
Exhales the perfume of flowers.
The Northern Crown crosses the sky
Cut by the temple roof,
Where an iron phoenix soars and twists in the air.
The chanting of prayers floats from the hall.
Fading bell notes eddy by my bed.
Tomorrow in the sunlight
I shall walk in the manured fields,
And weep for the yellow dust of the dead.

Jade Flower Palace

The stream swirls. The wind moans in
The pines. Gray rats scurry over
Broken tiles. What prince, long ago,
Built this palace, standing in
Ruins beside the cliffs? There are
Green ghost fires in the black rooms.
The shattered pavements are all
Washed away. Ten thousand organ
Pipes whistle and roar. The storm
Scatters the red autumn leaves.
His dancing girls are yellow dust.
Their painted cheeks have crumbled
Away. His gold chariots
And courtiers are gone. Only
A stone horse is left of his
Glory. I sit on the grass and
Start a poem, but the pathos of
It overcomes me. The future
Slips imperceptibly away.
Who can say what the years will bring?

Traveling Northward

(757) This is a fragment from a long poem. — Editors

Screech owls moan in the yellowing
Mulberry trees. Field mice scurry,
Preparing their holes for winter.
Midnight, we cross an old battlefield.
The moonlight shines cold on white bones.

By the Winding River

(758)

Every day on the way home from
My office I pawn another
Of my Spring clothes. Every day
I come home from the river bank
Drunk. Everywhere I go, I owe
Money for wine. History
Records few men who lived to be
Seventy. I watch the yellow
Butterflies drink deep of the
Flowers, and the dragonflies
Dipping the surface of the
Water again and again.
I cry out to the Spring wind,
And the light and the passing hours.
We enjoy life such a little
While, why should men cross each other?

Loneliness

(759)

A hawk hovers in air.
Two white gulls float on the stream.
Soaring with the wind, it is easy
To drop and seize
Birds who foolishly drift with the current.
Where the dew sparkles in the grass,
The spider's web waits for its prey.
The processes of nature resemble the business of men.
I stand alone with ten thousand sorrows.

Clear After Rain

(759)

Autumn, cloud blades on the horizon.
The west wind blows from ten thousand miles.
Dawn, in the clear morning air,
Farmers busy after long rain.
The desert trees shed their few green leaves.
The mountain pears are tiny but ripe.
A Tartar flute plays by the city gate.
A single wild goose climbs into the void.

Brimming Water

(765)

Under my feet the moon
Glides along the river.
Near midnight, a gusty lantern
Shines in the heart of night.
Along the sandbars flocks
Of white egrets roost,
Each one clenched like a fist.
In the wake of my barge
The fish leap, cut the water,
And dive and splash.

Four Poems

Translated by Stephen Owen

Facing the Snow

(756–757)

Weeping over battle, many new ghosts,
In sorrow reciting poems, an old man all alone.
A tumult of clouds sinks downward in sunset,
Hard-pressed, the snow dances in whirlwinds.
Ladle cast down, no green lees in the cup,
The brazier lingers on, fire seems crimson.
From several provinces now news has ceased —
I sit here in sorrow tracing words in air.

800 The Sui, Tang, and Five Dynasties

Translator's commentary:

The political conditions described here have led the traditional commentators to date this poem to Du Fu's period behind rebel lines in Chang'an, after the defeats of the imperial armies at Qingfan and Chentao.

In the symbolic cycle of the seasons, winter was the nadir that followed the destruction of autumn; it was the season of Yin and Darkness, but it was also the season that promised rebirth. The correspondences between the political world, the cosmic cycles manifest in the seasons, and the scene before his eyes all come together in Du Fu's vision of the snow scene.

The title, "Facing the Snow," involves a primary opposition between the poet and the winter world outside.... The first couplet repeats the primary opposition in nominal terms: out there, on the battlefields beyond the horizon, many "new" ghosts, the young dead slain unnaturally before their time; within is the solitary "survivor," the old man for whom death would be appropriate. The city disappears in the poem: there is only the poet who "faces" and the snow world that is "faced," the world of death and winter. This is one of the earliest examples of a characteristic scene in Du Fu's poetry, the self alone in an uninhabited or haunted world.

In the second couplet the world faced grows closer, first in clouds on the horizon, then in the snow whirling before the window. These are nature's correlatives of disorder and rebellion: *luan* clouds, "clouds of rebellion," a "tumult of clouds"; *ji* snow, the "snow of war's alarums," "hard-pressed snow." Double meanings mark the secret correspondences between the human world and the inhabited scene. The poet faces a world of disorder, white in the growing darkness of night, and the predominance of black and white, darkness and light, echoes (as elsewhere in Du Fu's poetry) the interplay of cosmic forces.

As the second couplet treats "what is faced," the third couplet treats the balancing "one who faces" — the poet and the world inside. Each couplet treats one term of the primary opposition, amplifying one line of the first couplet. The antithesis of the winter world is warmth, light, and color — the wine that is gone and the fire that is dying, growing redder as it burns down to the embers.

The poem has been focusing inward, from beyond the horizon ever closer and into the room, to the spot of warmth and color that is the brazier. The "response" of closure demands a corresponding outward movement, but before that can occur, a new term must be introduced into the "facing" relationship: this is blockage, news blocked coming in and messages blocked going out. The poet makes his futile gesture of response upon the interface of two worlds, words written in air, hopeless signs of communication that cannot cross the barrier into the world of winter and disorder. In form, style and concerns, "Facing the Snow" is an early example of the "classic" Du Fu Regulated Poem in which the poet confronts a world of hermetic correspondences. Here the hermetic world can be deciphered; in his later poetry the world can be a configuration of fragments, insistently symbolic, but never falling into such an easily intelligible pattern.

Walking Alone by the Riverbank Seeking Flowers

(760–761) This poem, the second of a series of seven quatrains, may be read with humor or with terror, but the characteristic multiplicity appears in the poet's "in-between" state, young enough to be "driven" by the oppressive lushness of spring, but already too old for it.

Dense flowers, a riot of stamens,
    make the riverbank terrible,
But I walk on, precariously tottering,
    truly afraid of spring,
And bear still the drivings of wine and song,
    I endure,
Not yet finished off — this white-haired old man.

My Thatched Roof Is Ruined by the Autumn Wind

(760–761) Nowhere is the half-humorous, half-pathetic vision of the self more apparent than in this famous poem. Du Fu moves with ease between the naturalistic world of vignette and the world of symbolic vision. The worlds are united by the figure of the poet, at once ridiculous and grandly heroic, pathetic and funny.

In the high autumn skies of September
    the wind cried out in rage,
Tearing off in whirls from my rooftop
    three plies of thatch.
The thatch flew across the river,
    was strewn on the floodplain,
The high stalks tangled in tips
    of tall forest trees,
The low ones swirled in gusts across ground
    and sank into mud puddles.
The children from the village to the south
    made a fool of me, impotent with age,
Without compunction plundered what was mine
    before my very eyes,
Brazenly took armfuls of thatch,
    ran off into the bamboo,
And I screamed lips dry and throat raw,
    but no use.
Then I made my way home, leaning on staff,
    sighing to myself.
A moment later the wind calmed down,
    clouds turned dark as ink,
The autumn sky rolling and overcast,
    blacker towards sunset,
And our cotton quilts were years old
    and cold as iron,
My little boy slept poorly,
    kicked rips in them.

Above the bed the roof leaked,
    no place was dry,
And the raindrops ran down like strings,
    without a break.
I have lived through upheavals and ruin
    and have seldom slept very well,
But have no idea how I shall pass
    this night of soaking.
Oh, to own a mighty mansion
    of a hundred thousand rooms,
A great roof for the poorest gentlemen
    of all this world,
    a place to make them smile.
A building unshaken by wind or rain,
    as solid as a mountain,
Oh, when shall I see before my eyes
    a towering roof such as this?
Then I'd accept the ruin of my own little hut
    and death by freezing.

Autumn Meditation: 7

(766) In the series of poems from which this is taken, Du Fu weaves together scenes of
Kuizhou with his memories of court and, in doing so, produces an extended meditation on the relationship of time and memory to the poetic art.

The waters of Kunming Pool,
    deeds of the days of Han,
The banners and pennons of Emperor Wu
    here before my eyes.
Silk of the loom of the Weaving Girl
    empty in moon of night,
Scales and fins of the whale of stone
    stir in autumn wind.
The waves toss a kumi seed,
    black in sinking cloud,
And dew chills the lotus pod,
    red of falling powder.
Barrier passes stretch to the heavens,
    a road for only the birds;
Lakes and rivers fill the earth,
    one aging fisherman.

Translator's commentary:
The Kunming Pool was an artificial lake in Han Chang'an. The Weaving Girl was a constellation and denizen of the heavens; her statue, like the statue of the stone whale, belonged to the palaces of Han.

The world of the immortals and the Han past (the standard metaphor for the Tang court and empire) merge with the past of Xuanzong's court: all are equally lost in their pastness or their remoteness.... Yet strangely they become equally accessible through the poetic imagination and memory: the "days of Han" are "here before the eyes." This past of the imagination is ghostly and uninhabited, filled with "deeds" and monuments but not with people. And the abandoned statues seem portentous in their isolation, weaving empty fabric in/of moonlight or swimming with mechanical fins through the autumn wind of destruction. The eyes of the imagination focus on the minutest detail, a tiny seed being tossed about by the waves, and the red powder falling from the autumn lotus....

Even the infinitesimal world of the wave-tossed seed and the red powder is filled with omens — of helplessness, dissolution, endings, and autumn. The seventh line brings the poet back to the present in Kuizhou, facing the barriers that block him from Chang'an and the past. Finally... the form of the seed in the "huge" pool reappears in the vast water world that is inhabited only by the single fisherman, the contemplative poet dreaming and writing of the brightly colored past, of the red that has fallen.

Two Ballads

Translated by Arthur Cooper

The Ballad of the Army Wagons

(750) This is one of several famous poems written by Du Fu against war and particularly against the scandals of press-ganging methods of recruitment, some of which were illegal, like making men do more than one period of national service (such as is implied in this poem). Du Fu has followed the convention of setting his poem in the Han dynasty. "Highland" translates the high plateau of Qin. The Black Lake is Kokonor, the great salt lake in Northern Tibet.

The din of wagons! Whinnying horses!
Each marcher at his waist has bow and quiver;
Old people, children, wives, running alongside,
Who cannot see, for dust, bridge over river:

They clutch clothes, stamp their feet, bar the way weeping,
Weeping their voices rise to darkening Heaven;
And when the passers-by question the marchers,
The marchers but reply, "Levies come often:

"They take us at fifteen for up the river,
To garrison the West, they'll take at forty,
Your Headman has at first to tie your turban,

Gray-headed you come home, then back to duty —

"The blood that's flowed out there would make a sea, Sir!
Our Lord, his lust for land knows no degree, Sir!
        But have you not heard
Of House of Han, its East two hundred regions
Where villages and farms are growing brambles?

"That though a sturdy wife may take the plough, Sir,
You can't see where the fields begin and end, Sir?
That Highlanders fare worst, they're hardy fighters
And so they're driven first, like dogs and chickens?

"Although you, Sir, ask such kind questions,
        Dare the conscripts tell their wretchedness?
How, for instance, only last winter
The Highland troops were still in the line
When their Prefect sent urgent demands,
Demands for tax, I ask you, from where?
So now we know, no good having sons,
        Always better to have a daughter:
For daughters will be wed to our good neighbors
When sons are lying dead on Steppes unburied!

        "But have you not seen
        On the Black Lake's shore
The white bones there of old no one has gathered,
Where new ghosts cry aloud, old ghosts are bitter,
Rain drenching from dark clouds their ghostly chatter?"

Ballad on Seeing
A Pupil of the Lady Gongsun Dance the Sword Mime

(767) Du Fu celebrates the work of a fine though aging ballerina, seen at White King
city in the Yangtze Gorges when he was on one of his river tours. Golden Granary was
a hill outside the capital, where the treasuries of grain and gold were, and where the
Glorious Monarch was buried. Qutang is the Yangtze Gorge, near White King city.
"Playing to tortoiseshell" is abbreviated in the translation from "playing to tortoiseshell-bordered mats." The Chinese in Tang times sat on mats on the floor during
banquets, where such ballets were staged. Tortoiseshell-bordered mats were very
grand. "Joy brings the greatest sorrow" is a proverb, evoking, together with the last
verse, a well-known "after-theater" feeling everyone has experienced after witnessing

something especially moving. One has been to the ballet with Du Fu in the eighth century.

On the 19th day of the Tenth Month of Year Two of Da-li (15 November 767), I saw the Lady Li, Twelfth, of Linying, dance the Mime of the Sword at the Residence of Lieutenant-Governor Yan Qi of Kuizhou Prefecture; and both the subtlety of her interpretation and her virtuosity on points so impressed me that I asked of her, who had been her Teacher? She replied: "I was a Pupil of the great Lady Gongsun."

In Year Five of Kai-yuan (A.D. 717), when I was no more than a tiny boy, I remember being taken in Yuyan City to see Gongsun dance both this Mime and "The Astrakhan Hat."

For her combination of flowing rhythms with vigorous attack, Gongsun had stood alone even in an outstanding epoch. No member at all of the *corps de ballet*, of any rank whatever, either of the Sweet Springtime Garden or of the Pear Garden Schools, could interpret such dances as she could; throughout the reign of His Late Majesty, Saintly in Peace and Godlike in War! But where now is that jadelike face, where are those brocade costumes? And I whiteheaded! And her Pupil here, too, no longer young!

Having learned of this Lady's background, I came to realize that she had, in fact, been reproducing faithfully all the movements, all the little gestures, of her Teacher; and I was so stirred by that memory, that I decided to make a Ballad of the Mime of the Sword.

There was a time when the great calligrapher, Zhang Xu of Wu, famous for his wild running hand, had several opportunities of watching the Lady Gongsun dance this Sword Mime (as it was danced in Turkestan); and he discovered, to his immense delight, that doing so had resulted in marked improvement in his own calligraphic art! From *that*, know the Lady Gongsun!

A Great Dancer there was,
    the Lady Gongsun,
And her "Mime of the Sword"
    made the World marvel!

Those, many as the hills,
    who had watched breathless
Thought sky and earth themselves
    moved to her rhythms:

As she flashed, the Nine Suns

fell to the Archer;
She flew, was a Sky God
    on saddled dragon;

She came on, the pent storm
    before it thunders;
And she ceased, the cold light
    off frozen rivers.

Her red lips and pearl sleeves
    are long since resting,
But a dancer revives
    of late their fragrance:

The Lady of Linying
    in White King city
Did the piece with such grace
    and lively spirit

That I asked! Her reply
    gave the good reason
And we thought of those times
    with deepening sadness:

There had waited at Court
    eight thousand Ladies
(With Gongsun, from the first,
    chief at the Sword Dance);

And fifty years had passed
    (a palm turned downward)
While the winds, bringing dust,
    darkened the Palace

And they scattered like mist
    those in Pear Garden,
On whose visages still
    its sun shines bleakly!

                    *

But now trees had clasped hands
    at Golden Granary
And grass played its sad tunes

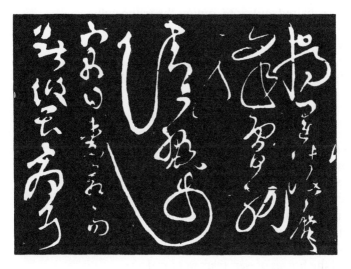

Figure 46. Calligraphy of Zhang Xu (8th century). (Source: *Xi'an beishi shufa huicui* [Xi'an Rubbings] [Xi'an: Shaanxi renmin, 1985])

on Qutang's Ramparts,

For the swift pipes had ceased
playing to tortoiseshell;
The moon rose in the East,
joy brought great sorrow:

An old man knows no more
where he is going;
On these wild hills, footsore,
he will not hurry!

Two Poems

Translated by Jerome P. Seaton

Village by the River

(760–761)

Clear stream, meanders by the village, flowing.
Long summer days, at River Village, everything at ease.
Coming, going, as they please, a pair of soaring swallows.

There, paired and close, out on the water, gulls.
My old wife draws a board for chess.
My son bends pins for fishhooks.
I'm often sick, but I can find good herbs.
What, beyond this, could a simple man ask?

Second Letter to My Nephew Wulang

In front of the hut, she scavenges for dates: let her be.
Hungry, childless, the lone woman,
Only the deepest poverty could bring her to this.
Her fear, her shame, call the more for kindness.
True, she has no reason to distrust her new neighbor.
Yet even a sparse hedge would seem a wall to her.
To think of the taxes: poor to the bone.
And the horses of war: tears wet my sleeve.

Two Poems

Translated by David Lattimore

Night Feast, Zuo Family Village

(c. 735) One of the earliest of the preserved poems of Du Fu. "Thin moon" is a
technical term for the new moon, the second or third night of the lunar cycle. The
"flowered path" is probably covered with fruit-tree blossoms that have fallen at the end
of spring. The poem thus relates to the tradition of the third day of the third lunar
month, when scholars young and old gather by a stream for the rite of lustration,
chanting poems which they have improvised. At its conclusion the poem becomes one
of departure. Presumably Du Fu himself is leaving the south in order to take his
state examinations at Chang'an. He hears his poem chanted in the dialect of Wu (the
Suzhou region), then thinks of Fan Li (fifth century B.C.), who after conquering Wu,
"followed his impulse" and got into a "small skiff," disappearing among the southern
lakes and streams.

Windy   woods thin moon going down
clothes bedewed   clean zither taut
dark streams   race the flowered path
spring stars   wreathe a thatched hall
we con a book   the candles burning short
admire a sword   long do the cups go round
the poem done   is droned in speech of Wu
the small skiff   an impulse not forgotten

Thinking of My Little Boy

(757)

Pony Boy   though it's spring we're still apart
oriole songs in the warmth are at their fullest
separation   seasonal change upsets me
quick and clever   who chatters with you now
a canyon stream   a road in the empty mountains
a rough gate   a village among old trees
I think of you   I grieve and almost sleep
toasting my back   I lean on the sunny rail

Four Late Poems

Translated by A. C. Graham

Midnight

By the West Pavilion, on a thousand feet of cliff,
Walking at midnight under my latticed window.
Flying stars pass white along the water,
Transparent beams of moonset flicker on the sand.
At home in its tree, notice the secret bird;
Safe beneath the waves, imagine the great fishes.
From kinsmen and friends at the bounds of heaven and earth,
Between weapon and buffcoat seldom a letter comes.

The Autumn Wastes: 1 and 2

(767) This poem was written at Kuizhou, in ancient times part of the half-barbarous kingdom of Chu. Du Fu often compares himself with the Chu poet Qu Yuan, who was slandered at court, went into exile, and died by throwing himself into the Miluo river [see chapter 5]. Astrologically the region centered on Mount Min, the destiny of which depended on the Well Rope Star.

1

The autumn wastes are each day wilder:
Cold in the river the blue sky stirs.
I have tied my boat to the Well Rope Star of the barbarians,
Sited my house in a village of Chu.
Though the dates are ripe let others cut them down,
I'll hoe for myself where the mallows run to seed.

From the old man's dinner on my plate
I'll scatter my alms to the fish in the brook.

2

Easy to sense the trend in the drift of life,
Hard to compel one creature out of its course.
In the deepest water is the fish's utmost joy,
In the leafiest wood the bird will find its home.
Age and decline are content to be poor and sick,
Praise and blame belong to youth and glory.
Though the autumn wind blows on my staff and pillow
I shall not weary of the North Mountain's ferns.

Deep in Winter

(768) Du Fu is traveling by boat, evidently up some sidestream after leaving the Yangtze. The "flower in the leaves" is the red sun against blue and violet clouds. "Heaven" is both the power which will bring back the flowers in the spring (and perhaps good fortune to Du Fu) and the sky in which the illusory flower appears. There is a sharp contrast between the images of lines 1 and 3, on the one hand, and 2 and 4, on the other, between the insubstantial promise of spring in the sky and the wintry, stony, precisely visualized present with its scars of the past — the bases of stones showing through the water, the water rising to the marks stained at high level....
  The mysterious first four lines can be read on the assumption that the roseate clouds are conceived as emerging from the red rocks, in accordance with the Chinese belief that clouds are breathed out by mountains and stones.

Flower in the leaves, only as heaven pleases:
From Yangtze to brook, the same roots of stone.
Red cloud of morning's shadow likenesses:
The cold water on each touches its scar.
Easy, Yang Zhu, to shed your tears:
Exile of Chu, hard to call back your ghost.
The waves in the wind are restless in the evening.
I put down my oar to lodge in what man's house?

Six versions

An Evening Shower in Spring

Translated by Sir J. F. Davis (1829)

See how the gently falling rain
  Its vernal influence sweetly showers,

As through the calm and tepid eve
  It silently bedews the flowers.

Cloudy and dark th'horizon spreads,
  Save where some boat its light is burning:
But soon the landscape's tints shall glow
  All radiant, with the morn returning.

La Pluie de Printemps

Translated by the Marquis d'Hervey de Saint-Denys (1862)

Oh! la bonne petite pluie qui sait si bien
  quand on a besoin d'elle!
Qui vient justement au printemps aider
  la vie nouvelle à se développer!
Elle a choisi la nuit, pour arriver doucement avec un vent propice;
Elle a mouillé toutes choses, très finement et sans bruit.

Des nuages sombres planaient hier soir
  au-dessus du sentier qui mène à ma demeure;
Les feux des barques du fleuve se montraient seuls dans l'obscurité
  comme des points lumineux.
Ce matin de fraîches couleurs éclatent au loin
  dans la campagne,
Et je vois, toutes chargées d'une humidité charmante,
  les belles fleurs dont les jardins impériaux sont brodés.

The Kindly Rain

Translated by W. J. B. Fletcher (1918)

The kindly rain its proper season knows.
  With gentle Spring aye born in fitting hour.
Along the Wind with cloaking Night it goes.
  Enmoistening, fine, inaudible it flows.

The clouds the mountain paths in darkness hide.
  And lonely bright the vessels' lanterns glower.
Dawn shows how damp the blushing buds divide.
  And flowers droop head-heavy in each bower.

Spring Night, Happy Rain

Translated by Florence Ayscough (1934)

Happy rain knows time and season;
Should come in Spring, cause life to rise.

Borne on wind, secretly it enters night;
Soaks all growing things, is fine, without sound.

On path in outskirts, clouds all black;
On boat in river, light shines lone.

At dawn, see places where vermilion blooms are wet
Flowers hang heavy in Embroidered Official City.

Spring Rain

Translated by Kenneth Rexroth (1956)

A good rain knows its season.
It comes at the edge of Spring.
It steals through the night on the breeze
Noiselessly wetting everything.
Dark night, the clouds black as the roads,
Only a light on a boat gleaming.
In the morning, thoroughly soaked with water,
the flowers hang their heavy heads.

Good Rain: A Night in Spring

Translated by Jerome P. Seaton (1982)

This poem was composed at Chengdu [during the years 760–761], when, aboard a boat on the river near the town, he witnessed the arrival of a timely spring rain. The following day he contemplated, enraptured, the scene after the rain: the city covered with red flowers gorged with rain. In the last line the poet cleverly chooses an alternate appellation for Chengdu, styling it the Brocade Mandarin City, to suggest that he also, exiled literatus, shares the joy of participating in the festivities of spring.

The good rain knows its season.
Come spring, it comes to life again;
With the wind, so stealthily in the night,
Moistens all things, so delicate, so silent.
On the wild paths, clouds all black.

From river skiff, a lamp, the single light.
In morning's glow, the red wet spots;
Flowers weigh down upon the Brocade Mandarin.

Three versions
The Pressgang

Translated by Herbert Giles (1884)

There, where at eve I sought a bed,
    A pressgang came, recruits to hunt;
Over the wall the goodman sped,
    And left his wife to bear the brunt.

Ah me! the cruel serjeant's rage!
    Ah me! how sadly she anon
Told all her story's mournful page —
    How three sons to the war had gone;

How one had sent a line to say
    That two had been in battle slain:
He, from the fight had run away,
    But they could ne'er come back again.

She swore 'twas all the family —
    Except a grandson at the breast;
His mother too was there, but she
    Was all in rags and tatters drest.

The crone with age was troubled sore,
    But for herself she'd not think twice
To journey to the seat of war
    And help to cook the soldiers' rice.

The night wore on and stopped her talk;
    Then sobs upon my hearing fell....
At dawn when I set forth to walk,
    Only the goodman cried Farewell!

The Conscription

Translated by E. H. Parker (1887)

I was making for the village inn,
    When the press-gang man came stalking in;

Old Darby barely clears the wall,
As Joan advances in the hall.

How now, you hag! The sergeant roars.
What is it, Sir? Poor Joan implores.
I listen while the press-man learns
The dismal story of her bairns.

Look, Sir, one son has writ to tell
How t'other two in battle fell,
He runs for life, my eldest son,
The others (sob) are dead (sob), gone!

We have no man, Sir, here I swear,
But my young grandson over there;
But he must stop to feed his mother,
Let me go carrying, Sir, like another!

Though I'm a poor old shriveled wight,
Yet I will march away this night,
And pay the customary scot,[6]
By serving the men's rations hot.

Done! Said the Sergeant. In my sleep
I heard a sob and footstep creep,
The old pair parting! One *must* go.
Darby or Joan; Joan think you? No!

The Pressgang at Shihao Village

Translated by Jerome P. Seaton

Evening, I found lodging at Shihao.
That night a pressgang came for men.
An old man jumped the wall,
While his wife went through the gate to meet them.
The officer cursed, so full of anger.
The old woman cried, so bitter.
Then I heard her approach him and speak:
"Our three sons went off in defense of Yecheng.
Now one has sent a letter home,

---

[6] An old expression for a contribution or levy. *Eds.*

To tell us that the other two are slain.
He who remains yet clings to life.
They who have gone are dead forever.
At home here there is no one else ...
But a grandson at the breast,
And his mother, not yet able to leave him.
And anyway, she's not a whole skirt to put on ...
This old one, though her strength is ebbing,
Begs you, sir, to let her come tonight,
To answer the draft for Heyang.
I might still help to cook the morning meal."
Night lengthened, the voices died away,
Dwindling to a sound like stifled sobs.
The sky brightened, I climbed back toward the path,
Alone, the old man made farewells.

🙰 *Further Reading* 🙰

Alley, Rewi, trans. *Tu Fu: Selected Poems.* Beijing: Foreign Languages Press, 1962.
Ayscough, Florence. *Tu Fu: The Autobiography of a Chinese Poet.* Vol. 1: A.D. 712–759.
    Boston: Houghton Mifflin, 1929.
———. *Travels of a Chinese Poet: Tu Fu, Guest of Rivers and Lakes.* Vol. 2: A.D. 759–770.
    Boston: Houghton Mifflin, 1934.
Cheng, François. *L'Ecriture poétique chinoise.* Paris: Editions du Seuil, 1977. Trans. by
    Donald A. Riggs & Jerome P. Seaton as *Chinese Poetic Writing: With an Anthology of
    T'ang Poetry* (Bloomington: Indiana University Press, 1982).
Cooper, Arthur, trans.. *Li Po and Tu Fu.* Harmondsworth: Penguin Books, 1973.
Davis, A. R. *Du Fu.* New York: Twayne, 1971.
Davis, Sir John Francis. *The Poetry of the Chinese: Poeseos Sinicae Commentarii.* London: J.
    L. Cox, 1829; rev. ed., London: Asher, 1870.
Fletcher, W.J.B., trans. *Gems of Chinese Verse, Translated into English Verse.* Shanghai:
    Commercial Press, 1918.
Graham, A. C., trans. *Poems of the Late T'ang.* Harmondsworth: Penguin Books, 1965.
Hawkes, David. *A Little Primer of Du Fu.* Oxford: Oxford University Press, 1967.
    (Reprinted as a Renditions Paperback, Hong Kong, Chinese University Press,
    1987.)
Hervey de Saint-Denys, trans. *Poésies de l'époque des Thang.* Paris: Amyot, 1862.
Hinton, David, trans. *Selected Poems of Tu Fu.* New York: New Directions, 1989.
Hung, William. *Tu Fu: China's Greatest Poet.* 2 vols. Cambridge, Mass.: Harvard Univer-
    sity Press, 1952.
Lattimore, David, trans. *Harmony of the World.* Providence, R.I.: Copper Beech Press,
    1980.
Owen, Stephen. *The Great Age of Chinese Poetry: The High T'ang.* New Haven: Yale
    University Press, 1981.
Parker, E. H., trans. "The Conscription." *China Review* (1887).
Rexroth, Kenneth, trans. *One Hundred Poems from the Chinese.* New York: New Direc-
    tions, 1956.

▣ *Editors' Note* ▣

If Du Fu somehow "combines the masteries of every other writer," as Yuan Zhen
claimed, if he is the greatest Chinese poet, by general consensus, as Stephen Owen
states in *The Great Age of Chinese Poetry*, then here more than anywhere else (except
possibly the *Book of Songs*) we need several translators. It has been remarked that none
of the great translators, including Waley, ever tried to represent Du Fu. But many of
them had a shot at some of him. We have Kenneth Rexroth, for whom Du Fu was the
"greatest non-epic, non-dramatic poet to have survived in any language," giving us the
lyrical Du Fu; we have Florence Ayscough giving us the imagistic Du Fu — and
revealing to the English reader much of the underlying bone-structure of the originals
(the versions of Jerome Seaton and David Lattimore are in this tradition); we have
Arthur Cooper giving us the eloquent balladeer; Stephen Owen and A. C. Graham
representing the intellectual subtlety, the verbal dexterity and density (together with
humor and pathos), while Burton Watson gives an idea of his overall range and
versatility. In David Hawkes's *explications de texte*, through careful rendering of allusion
and biographical and historical detail, and through sensitive analysis of the form and
of the Chinese words themselves, we get as close perhaps as we can ever hope to get to
the poet as an individual and a craftsman.

"A gull on the sand between Heaven and Earth."
Seal from the Vernal Radiance Collection

Chapter 21

Spring, River, Flowers, Moon, Night

Poets of the High Tang

In the study of poetry the most important thing is to recognize how things are. You must get on the right course from the very beginning, and your goals must be set high. Take the poets of the Han, Wei, Jin, and High Tang as your teachers; avoid anyone after the Kai-yuan (713–741) and Tian-bao (742–755) eras.

The poets of the High Tang relied only on inspired feelings, like the antelope that hangs by its horns, leaving no traces to be found. Therefore, the miracle of their poetry lies in its transparent luminosity, which cannot be pieced together; it is like sound in the air, color in appearances, the moon in water, or an image in the mirror; it has limited words, but unlimited meaning.

— Yan Yu (fl. 1200), *Canglang's Remarks on Poetry* (*translated by James J. Y. Liu*)

Prose must follow the Jin and Han, poetry the High Tang; all else is not the Way.

— Li Mengyang (1475–1529), quoted by Qian Qianyi (1582–1664), *Poetry Collection of Successive Reigns* (*translated by J. Timothy Wixted*)

Introduction

Stephen Owen

Chinese critics usually designated the periods of literary history by reigns, by dynasties, or by dynastic subdivisions such as "Early," "Middle," and "Late." When they
looked back on the Tang, however, a new term, originally from the vegetative cycle,
intruded between the "Early Tang" and the "Mid Tang." This term reveals the extent
to which wonder overcame the literary historian's usual sobriety: as in the poetry of no
other dynasty, there is a "High Tang," a "Tang in Full Flower." To later readers, this era,
centered in the reign of Xuanzong (712–756), possessed a unique aura of splendor
and greatness, was a moment when cultural efflorescence and literary genius happily
coincided. Their awe was justified: the work of at least three major poets and of a
dozen nearly great shed a light that no reader could ignore. But that very radiance
also obscured the literary-historical realities of the period: a complex process of
continuous change was perceived as a single sunburst of genius and variety that
vanished almost as soon as it appeared, leaving later ages to struggle for its afterglow.

Appearing in the ninth century, growing through the Song dynasty, and firmly
rooted in the minds of all born later was the conviction that the High Tang had been
the apogee of all Chinese poetry. Later poets lamented their own dimness in face of
its luminosity; they imitated it slavishly, revolted against it violently, declared they
would ignore it and write spontaneously according to the dictates of their inner
natures; but in the history of Chinese poetry it remained the fixed center that defined
the positions of all later poets.

Any serious understanding of the period and its poetry demands that we put aside
the myth of radiance. Wang Wei's poems contain an allegory of a mountain temple
whose natural beauty existed to lead the pilgrim to a truth behind the seductive
surface; in a similar way, the myth of the golden age of poetry is not the goal itself, but
an enticement to enter the age and comprehend its true nature.

— from the introduction to *The Great Age of Chinese Poetry: The High Tang*, 1981

Three Poets in a Tavern: An Anecdote

From an Early-Ninth-Century Collection

Translated by Stephen Owen

During the Kai-yuan era (713–741) the poets Wang Changling, Gao Shi,
and Wang Zhihuan were equally famous. In those days before the rebellion the three often traveled around together. One cold day it was about
to snow, and the three poets went into a tavern, ordered wine, and had
been drinking a while, when all of a sudden a group of ten or so
musicians from the Imperial Ensemble came up the stairs for a party. The
three poets left their seats and concealed themselves, huddling behind a
brazier to watch what would happen. A moment later four lovely singing
girls followed the musicians into the room. These girls were a delight to
the eye, voluptuously beautiful, the very height of charm. Soon they

began to play the most famous songs of the age, whereupon Wang
Changling and the others made this agreement: "Each of us has gained
renown for his poetry, and yet we still have not established which is
foremost among us. Let's now listen in secret to what these musicians
sing, and whichever of us has the most poems set to music will be the
master." Soon one of the musicians set the tempo and sang:

Cold rains stretch to the river, by night entering Wu,
At daybreak bid traveler farewell, loneliness in Chu's mountains.
If friends and kin in Luoyang should ask you how I am —
In a vase of whitest jade a heart like a sheet of ice.

Wang Changling made a mark on the wall: "One quatrain for me."
Then another musician sang:

I open the trunk, tears soak my breast,
I see letters you sent me long ago.
The terrace of night lies in utter silence —
Yang Xiong the recluse lives here still.

Gao Shi made a mark on the wall: "One quatrain for me." Then
another musician sang:

Broom in her hand at break of day, golden halls open wide,
She struggles to hold her moon-disk fan, both waver to and fro.
Her face white as jade no rival to the color of winter's crows
That come now, still lit by the beams from the Palace of Shining
    Favor.[1]

Wang Changling made another mark on the wall: "Two quatrains for
me." Wang Zhihuan had been a famous poet for many years, so he said
to his companions: "These fellows are a poor excuse for musicians, and
the songs they are singing are your common village verses — they have
no place beside the truly great songs that a connoisseur of music would
recognize." Then he pointed to the most beautiful of the singing girls
and said: "Let's wait and see what *she* sings — if it's not one of my poems,
I'll never dare enter into competition with you again; but if it *is* my poem,
then you have to pay your respects to me as true master." So saying he
laughed and waited her turn. In a few moments this lady with the lovely
coiffure raised her voice in song:

---

[1] This is a poem about the Imperial Consort Ban Jieyu, who lost the Han emperor's favor
to the Zhao sisters. [See chapter 25 for Ban Jieyu's "Song of Regret."]

Yellow sands rise far away on high among white clouds,
Silhouette of a lonely fortress on a thousand-foot mountain.
Why should this nomad flute be playing wrath at the "leaves" of
willow,
Since the wind of spring will never cross Jade Gate Barrier?

Wang Zhihuan danced with glee and roared with laughter: "Peasants!
Wasn't I right?" Of course, the musicians had had no idea what was
happening, and they went over to the poets: "And what do you
gentlemen find so amusing?" Wang Changling and his companions told
their tale, and the musicians hurried to pay their respects to the poets.
"Our mortal eyes did not recognize the gods. Please grace us with your
presence at our party." The poets joined them and drank the whole day
through.

ZHANG RUOXU (c. 660–c. 720)

Spring, River, Flowers, Moon, Night

Translated by David Lattimore

Little is known about Zhang Ruoxu. He was a native of Yangzhou and once occupied
a minor military post in Yanzhou (Shandong Province). His literary reputation was
established in the capital during the first years of the eighth century in conjunction
with a group of poets, all from the Lower Yangtze Basin, which included He Zhizhang.
This evocation of the languid ambience of a Yangtze riverscape by night is his most
famous poem.

1

Spring river   tidal water
   running level with the sea

on the sea   the bright moon
   rising with the tide

rolling   tossing
   down its waves a million miles

where   spring river
   do you lack for moonlight

2

The river flows   twists   turns
   around the scented park lands

moonlight   sleeting everywhere
   on blooming groves

through the void   flowing frost
   flies unseen

white sand   of the islets
   indistinguishable

3

River   sky   one color
   without a spot of dust

glittering   amid the void
   the bright moon's wheel

on these banks   what people
   first saw the moon

river moon   in what year
   did you first shine on men

4

Life of man   age on age
   unexhausted

river   moon   year by year
   looking at each other

who knows   what person
   the moon in the river waits for

all you see   the long stream
   ushering its waters

5

White cloud   a single swath
   bound far away

maples green   upon the bank
   unquenched sorrow

tonight   where is the household
   of the man in the little boat

what place   does she think of

in the moonlit lodge

6

Piteously   above the lodge
    the moon wavers   wanders

shining back   on the lonely one
    the make-up mirror-stand

blinds   of the jade door
    she twists   but does not go

wash-pounding   on the stone
    though brushed away   returns

7

This is the hour   to gaze afar
    hearing nothing

wishing to follow   the moon-glow
    to flow — to shine on you

wild geese   far flying
    cannot go beyond the light

fish   dragons   churning
    the depths   ripple the surface

8

Last night   by the idle pool
    she dreamt of falling flowers

she grieves   for him at mid-spring
    who does not come home

river waters   wash away
    what's left of spring

river   pool   the falling moon
    slanting westward

9

Slant moon   deep   deep
    in sea-mist hidden

from Jieshi   to Xiaoxiang
  a boundless road

who knows   what people
  come home by moonlight

the moonset   shakes our feelings
  as it fills the river trees.

WANG HAN (fl. 713)

A Reason Fair (Liangzhou Song)

Translated by Herbert Giles

Wang Han was a protégé of Zhang Yue [see chapter 17] and followed the elder
statesman through his shifting political fortunes. He was a notorious drinker,
huntsman, horseman and womanizer. His "Liangzhou Songs" have become minor
classics of frontier poetry. Liangzhou was an important military prefecture northwest
of Chang'an, in modern Gansu Province.

Tis night: the grape-juice mantles high
   in cups of gold galore;
We set to drink — but now the bugle
   sounds to horse once more.
Oh marvel not if drunken we
   lie strewed about the plain;
How few of all who see the fight
   shall e'er come back again!

HE ZHIZHANG (659–745)

The Return

Translated by Herbert Giles

He Zhizhang flourished as a statesman and a poet under the reign of the Emperor
Xuanzong, to whom he introduced the youthful poet Li Bo. He was one of the
so-called Eight Immortals of the Wine-cup, and a lover of dissipation and joviality. On
one occasion he mounted a horse, although a bad rider and drunk at the time: the
result was that he fell into a dry well and was found snoring at the bottom.

Bowed down with age I seek my native place,
Unchanged my speech, my hair is silvered now;
My very children do not know my face,
But smiling ask, "O stranger, whence art thou?"

ZHANG JIULING (678–740)

Climbing a Tall Building on an Autumn Evening:
I Gaze to Where the South River Touches the Shixing Road

Translated by Stephen Owen

Zhang Jiuling also flourished as a statesman and poet under the Emperor Xuanzong. He graduated high on the list of *jinshi* [Advanced Scholars], and his profound learning gained for him the sobriquet Commander-in-chief of the Literary Arena. He soon attracted the notice of Zhang Yue, who introduced him into public life. He later became the patron of several younger writers, including Wang Wei and Meng Haoran.

In this poem, as the poet in "exile" stares at the landscape before him, each element signifies some aspect of his present situation or seems to offer a hidden resolution of his troubles. Paths and fords lead his thoughts if not his body toward the capital; the rolling river in spate reminds him of the world's turmoil and the futile toiling of his life. Clouds and mists exist only to block his vision to the far places he longs to be in. The fluttering of his white hair in the wind reminds him of his age and the absence of the "ribbons of office."

Streaming rivulets draw back, sandflats emerge.
Frost comes down, the sky's vault, crystalline.
Hunched at the railing, I gaze long and far,
Path and ford draw many emotions of distant places.
Longing comes from beyond the rivers and mountains;
Where my gaze breaks off, clouds and mists arise.
A rolling flood where nothing is distinct —
Oh, what is accomplished from all this constant toil?
I came here, wind shaking my frail white locks,
No one could say it shook ribbons of high office.
A stabled horse suffering cramped restraints,
A caged bird longing for faraway journeys.
The year grows ever darker toward its close.
At the end of the day, a pointless restlessness.
All living creatures value fulfilling their natures,
The bonds upon my body grow from recent fame.
I look back, find I'm truly right now —
But when will ease come for sorrow at what is past?

WANG ZHIHUAN (688–742)

Hooded Crane Tower

Translated by Stephen Owen

Wang Zhihuan was well known as a poet during the Kai-yuan period (713–741). Only six of his poems survive, all quatrains, of which this is the most famous. It represents a distinct type in which the persona makes or proposes some mysteriously significant gesture in the closure. Here the reader is invited to consider the relationship between the sunset, the poet's range of vision, and climbing higher in the building. Not only does one increase the range of vision; the sunlight is also briefly regained.

> The bright sun rests on the mountain, is gone,
> The Yellow River flows into the sea.
> If you want to see a full thousand miles,
> Climb one more story of this tower.

MENG HAORAN (689–740)
Seven Poems

Translated by Witter Bynner

Meng was a decade or more older than most of the other famous poets — Li Bo, Wang Wei, Du Fu — who were active during this period. He may thus be regarded, along with Zhang Jiuling, as a senior representative of the so-called High Tang poets. His tie to his native place, Xiangyang (in modern north-central Hubei Province), was exceptionally strong, and he seems to have spent all but eight or ten years of his life there. In contrast to most writers of his day, Meng did not enjoy a career in government service. But a year-long stay in Chang'an, and visits to Luoyang, put him on familiar terms with several of his more successful contemporaries. Li Bo wrote of him:

> I love the Master, Meng Haoran,
> A free spirit known the whole world through.

A Night Mooring on the Jiande River

> While my little boat moves on its mooring of mist,
> And daylight wanes, old memories begin ...
> How wide the world was, how close the trees to heaven,
> And how clear in the water the nearness of the moon!

A Spring Morning

> I awake light-hearted this morning of spring,
> Everywhere round me the singing of birds —
> But now I remember the night, the storm,
> And I wonder how many blossoms were broken.

From a Mooring on the Tonglu to a Friend in Yangzhou

> With monkeys whimpering on the shadowy mountain,
> And the river rushing through the night,
> And a wind in the leaves along both banks,

And the moon athwart my solitary sail,
I, a stranger in this inland district,
Homesick for my Yangzhou friends,
Send eastward two long streams of tears
To find the nearest touch of the sea.

Taking Leave of Wang Wei

Slow and reluctant, I have waited
Day after day, till now I must go.
How sweet the roadside flowers might be
If they did not mean goodbye, old friend.
The Lords of the Realm are harsh to us
And men of affairs are not our kind.
I will turn back home, I will say no more,
I will close the gate of my old garden.

In Summer at the South Pavilion Thinking of Xing

The mountain-light suddenly fails in the west,
In the east from the lake the slow moon rises.
I loosen my hair to enjoy the evening coolness
And open my window and lie down in peace.
The wind brings me odors of lotuses,
And bamboo-leaves drip with a music of dew.
I would take up my lute and I would play,
But, alas, who here would understand?
And so I think of you, old friend,
O troubler of my midnight dreams!

At the Mountain-Lodge of the Buddhist Priest Ye Waiting in Vain for My Friend Ding

A German version of this poem, together with Wang Wei's "Poem of Parting" (see chapter 18), formed the basis of "Der Abschied," in Gustav Mahler's *Das Lied von der Erde* (*The Song of the Earth*).

— Editors

Now that the sun has set beyond the western range,
Valley after valley is shadowy and dim ...
And now through pinetrees come the moon and the chill of evening,
And my ears feel pure with the sound of wind and water ...

Nearly all the woodsmen have reached home,
Birds have settled on their perches in the quiet mist ...
And still — because you promised — I am waiting for you, waiting,
Playing my lonely lute under a wayside vine.

Returning at Night to Lumen Mountain

A bell in the mountain-temple sounds the coming of night.
I hear people at the fishing-town stumble aboard the ferry,
While others follow the sand-bank to their homes along the river.
... I also take a boat and am bound for Lumen Mountain —
And soon the Lumen moonlight is piercing misty trees.
I have come, before I know it, upon an ancient hermitage,
The thatch door, the piney path, the solitude, the quiet,
Where a hermit lives and moves, never needing a companion.

In Passing an Old Friend's Farm

Translated by Soame Jenyns

An old friend has prepared chicken and millet dumpling
And invited me to his home in the fields.
Green trees surround his village on every side,
Blue hills slope away outside the wall.
At the open window the kitchen garden faces me.
We drink wine and talk of mulberry and flax;
Wait till the ninth day of the ninth moon,
I will come again and sample your chrysanthemum wine.

CUI HAO (d. 754)

Yellow Crane Tower

Translated by Stephen Owen

Cui Hao was a friend of Wang Wei and admired by Li Bo. This is one of the most
famous of all poems of the Tang dynasty. It is based on an anecdote about a tavern
keeper whose establishment was frequented by an old man who never paid his bill.
The tavern keeper never importuned the old man for his debts, and after half a year,
the old man came in, took an orange peel, and painted a crane on the tavern wall.
Whenever the guests of the tavern sang, the crane would begin to dance, and the
tavern keeper grew rich from the curious customers attracted by the prodigy. After ten
years the old man returned, summoned his crane from the wall, and flew off into the

sky on its back. In commemoration of the event the tavern keeper built Yellow Crane Tower.

The appeal of this poem can be best explained in terms of certain aspects of Chinese esthetics, and interest in the poem's "energy" and mood. Impermanence and change were compelling themes in their own right: the irrevocable loss of past magic and wonder, nature's luminous indifference and continuity, and the utter isolation of the individual. Yet the poem refrains from any direct expression of emotion until the brilliantly understated last line. High Tang poets learned concealment, learned the energy generated by "seeing through" the text to something deeper, more complex, and often opposite to the surface text.

Hanyang is near where the Han River empties into the Yangtze. Parrot Isle lies in the Yangtze near this spot.

> That man of old has already ridden
>   white clouds away,
> And here in this land there remains only
>   Yellow Crane Tower.
> The yellow crane, once it has gone,
>   will never come again,
> But white clouds of a thousand years
>   go aimlessly on and on.
> Clear and bright in the sunlit stream
>   the trees of Hanyang,
> Springtime's grasses, lush and green,
>   all over Parrot Isle.
> Sun's setting, the passes to home —
>   where can they be?
> Beside this river of misty waves
>   it makes a man sad.

LI QI (fl. 725)

To Zhang Xu

Translated by Stephen Owen

Li Qi was a member of the social network that included High Tang capital poets such as Wang Wei and Wang Changling. His eccentric approach suggests the influence of Li Bo. In this poem the great calligrapher Zhang Xu [see chapter 20, figure 46] does not simply inhabit a landscape poem — he acts. His actions may now seem more comic than eccentric, but they were the kinds of actions associated with eccentricity, just as there were fixed gestures that signified elegance, sensitivity, or resignation.

The "Master Anqi" of the last line was an immortal who met the first Qin Emperor (r. 221–207 B.C.).

> Master Zhang has an inborn craving for wine,

Free and easy, no care for the world's business.
Snow-white hair, total master of cursive and script,
Named by the age "Genius of Great Lake."
Bare-headed he rests on his folding chair,
Gives forth three or four long bellows,
And as his mood comes, daubs ink on the white walls,
Waving his brush like a shooting star.
Round his low cottage the winds moan,
Winter grasses fill his yard.
Do you wonder about his possessions?
To him things of this life are floating weeds.
In his left hand he nibbles a crab claw,
In his right holds alchemical tracts,
And he stares wide-eyed at the river of stars,
Then none can tell if he's drunk or sober.
His guests all come, take their proper seats
As the dawn sun looks down on eastern walls:
He serves Yangtze fish wrapped in lotus leaves,
In white bowls heaps the sweet-scented rice.
Petty salary is beneath his concern,
His spirit roams free to the world's confines.
For those of the age who don't recognize him —
This is the immortal — Master Anqi.

WANG CHANGLING (c. 690–c. 756)
Three Poems

Translated by Stephen Owen

Wang Changling was an eminent poet and critic whose friends included the best-known poets of the day as well as many Buddhist and Taoist priests. He was killed during the An Lushan rebellion.

For him poetry "concentrates the sea of heaven in the inch-space of the heart." He preferred the short poem which crystallized a mood through the observation of nature and which acted as a catalyst for the reader's continuing pleasure; a poem was a living creature, with a "head," a "belly," and a "tail."

Autumn Evening on the Great Lake

This poem is a meteorological prodigy: mist, rain, frost, bright moonlight, and a pervasive darkness that hides the flying geese, dwell together comfortably only in the melancholy mood evoked.

Spend the night on water, mist and rain chill.
Over Lake Dongting the frost comes down faintly.
The moon is bright, the boat shifts on and away,
As in night's stillness the soul returns from dream.
I sense the wind pass over the lake in darkness.
And through its moaning hear wild geese in their flight.

Song by the Walls

Many of Wang's poems celebrate stock characters or express stock situations. In this
one, the feat of transfixing two tigers with one arrow and the brave insouciance of the
last line incarnate the heroism of the stock Handan knight — half soldier, half bravo.

Autumn winds cry through mulberry branches.
The grasses are white, fox and hare exult.
He returns from his dinner at Handan,
    the wine not gone from his blood.
North of the wall in Levelplain County.
    the great hawk held on his arm.
In the empty fortress he shoots and kills
    a pair of leaping tigers
And turns around to the halfmoon,
    the bow tip strung at his waist.

At the Stream's Source in Spring: A Party

Wang Changling is generally acknowledged as the High Tang master of the quatrain.

The spring's source faced the springtime city
    in layers and layers of flowers.
And the river shone with deep azure,
    drawing in the surrounding peaks.
We were drunk together, we lost the road
    that went along Pine Creek.
When, in the immense stillness,
    from a mountain lodge
    came the sound of a bell in the darkness.

Under a Border-Fortress (Written to Music)

Translated by Witter Bynner

Wang Changling was a master of frontier poetry, and this has led many scholars to
assume that he actually spent time in military service on the frontier. The most
reliable evidence, however, suggests that Wang's Central Asia was a combination of the
poetic tradition and his own imagination.

Drink, my horse, while we cross the autumn water! —
The stream is cold and the wind like a sword,
As we watch against the sunset on the sandy plain,
Far, far away, shadowy Lintao.
Old battles, waged by those long walls,
Once were proud on all men's tongues.
But antiquity now is a yellow dust,
Confusing in the grasses its ruins and white bones.

Liu Zhangqing (c. 710–c. 787)
Four Poems

Translated by Witter Bynner

Liu appears to have had an undistinguished career in the capital until shortly before
the outbreak of the An Lushan rebellion in 755. A low-ranking provincial official
when the rebellion began, it is possible he fled his post to avoid capture or death. In
any event, he spent the rest of his long life in central China, holding positions in the
newly organized Salt Administration.

On Parting with the Buddhist Pilgrim Lingche[2]

From the temple, deep in its tender bamboos,
Comes the low sound of an evening bell,
While the hat of a pilgrim carries the sunset
Farther and farther down the green mountain.

While Visiting on the South Stream the Taoist Priest Chang

Walking along a little path,
I find a footprint on the moss,
A white cloud low on the quiet lake,
Grasses that sweeten an idle door,
A pine grown greener with the rain,
A brook that comes from a mountain source —
And, mingling with Truth among the flowers,
I have forgotten what to say.

---

[2] Lingche also wrote poetry (see chapter 26). *Eds.*

Figure 47. "Climbing in
Autumn for a View from the
Temple." Early 20th-century
illustration. (Source: *Zixi
huapu daquan* [Complete
Painting Manual] [Beijing:
Rongbaozhai, 1982])

Climbing in Autumn for a View from the Temple on the Terrace of General Wu

As the seasons have dealt with this ancient terrace,
So autumn breaks my homesick heart ...
Few pilgrims venture climbing to a temple so wild.
Up from the lake, in the mountain clouds.
... Sunset clings in the old defenses.
A stone gong shivers through the empty woods.
... Of the Southern Dynasty, what remains?
Nothing but the great River.

On Seeing Wang Leave for the South

Toward a mist upon the water

Still I wave my hand and sob.
For the flying bird is lost in space
Beyond a desolate green mountain ...
But now the long river, the far lone sail,
The five lakes, gleam like spring in the sunset;
And down an island white with duckweed
Comes the quiet of communion.

Snow on Lotus Mountain

Translated by Kenneth Rexroth

Sunset. Blue peaks vanish in dusk.
Under the Winter stars
My lonely cabin is covered with snow.

Figure 48. "Through snow and wind, someone is coming home." Late Ming illustration. (Source: *Tangshi huapu* [Tang Poems Illustrated] [Shanghai: Guji, 1982])

I can hear the dogs barking
At the rustic gate.
Through snow and wind
Someone is coming home.

CEN SHEN (715–770)
Two Poems

Translated by Stephen Owen

Cen spent some ten years serving in the northwest frontier areas (modern Xinjiang, Gansu, Shaanxi Provinces). This gave much of his poetry a subject matter not commonly seen in Tang poetry.

Song for General Zhao

The frontier quatrain was an established genre. The Heaven Mountain range was far inside Central Asia, running north of Kucha and Bugur. In this poem, both the army and the horse are in winter quarters, idle and waiting. Chess is the substitute for battle, and the general's victory and his "booty" are good omens in the mood of resolute expectation.

November on Heaven Mountain, the wind like a knife,
South of the walls a hunting horse,
    pelt matted short by the cold.
Our general gambles at chess, wins victory in every game,
And has won in the stake the sable-fur greatcoat of the Khan.

On the West Tower in Guozhou

In 758 Cen was demoted and sent to a post in Guozhou, between Chang'an and Luoyang. The western tower is the tower that faces toward Chang'an.

Miscarried, mishandled — a lifetime's affairs,
Slipping and stumbling and now, white hair.
My plans and stratagems all fell through:
I feel my shame even before wife and children.
Though my wise prince has cast me from him,
Loyalty still ceases not in my heart,
But grief comes, and I've nowhere to go —
I can only climb this, the western tower.

GAO SHI (716–765)
Four Poems

Translated by Stephen Owen

Gao had considerable military experience in Central Asia and Tibet. He is often
paired with Cen Shen as a "frontier" poet.

The Ruined Terrace

This poem is the first in a series of poems written in Songzhou, in modern Henan
Province, an area where Gao spent much of his childhood, and which was devastated
during the An Lushan rebellion. It had once been the center of the Han dynasty
princedom of Liang, and Prince Xiao had been the patron of such eminent poets as
Sima Xiangru and Mei Sheng [see chapter 6]. That era of past splendor is contrasted
with the city's present desolation.

When long ago Liang's prince was in his glory,
Among his guests were many men of talent.
And now remote, across a thousand years,
There are only the ruins of his high terrace.
In utter silence I face the autumn grasses,
And a sad wind comes from a thousand miles.

Ji Gate

Ji Gate was very close to modern Peking, though in the Tang dynasty the area was a
frontier. The Han here refers to the Tang armies, willing to give their lives in defence
of the empire.

Dark and brooding beyond the Great Wall,
The sun sinks and again dust, again smoke.
Though nomad horsemen press us hard,
The troops of Han worry not for their lives.
Ancient trees fill the deserted passes,
And brown clouds destroy men with sorrow.

The North Tower of Golden Fort

Golden Fort was about 500 kilometres west-northwest of Chang'an, in modern Gansu
Province. It was on the edge of the frontier region, but not deep in Central Asia. The
bitterness of the last line is presumably that of the troops who must serve in the
garrison at Golden Fort.

Pan Creek's elder was Tai Gong, who was fishing in the creek when King Wen of
Zhou met him and raised him to his councillor. Gao himself has given up all hope of

recognition. But he takes consolation from the story referred to in the following line, which is taken from the *Huainanzi*:

> There was an old man whose horse wandered into nomad territory. His neighbors all offered their sympathy, but the man simply said: "How do you know this isn't a piece of good luck?" Later the horse returned leading an entire herd of nomad horses. His neighbors then congratulated the old man, who replied: "How do you know *this* isn't a misfortune?" Afterwards, the old man's son, who was out riding one of the nomad horses, was thrown and broke his thigh. Again the neighbors commiserated, and again the old man questioned the nature of his fortune. Finally, during a nomad incursion, all the young men of the region were drafted into the militia and most died on the campaign. Only the old man's son, with his broken thigh, was left at home.

From the North Tower my westward gaze
    is filled with clear sky,
Massed waters and linked mountains
    lovelier than a painting.
A swift current over the rapids,
    its sounds like an arrow's,
The waning moon over the fort —
    form of bent bow.
I've bid farewell to Pan Creek's elder,
    his fishing line still dangling,
But my mind is still on the old frontiersman
    who lived within the Way.
Should you ask me of these borderlands,
    what else there is out here —
Ever and now the nomad flutes
    sing bitterness without end.

The Song of the Fisherman

This poem represents the sophistication of the High Tang vignette and its dramatic concealment. The fisherman's complete freedom is here embodied in the poem itself rather than in the physical scene observed in the poem. The fisherman's state of mind cannot be exposed in the limited language of the world. But it can at least be indicated — by silence and a mask of opaque actions that seem to conceal a truth.

By twisting shoreline and deep pool
    an old man of the mountains,
Eyes' movement halted watching the hook,
    the hand does not move.
Here, a worldly man who seeks to know
    the fisherman's name,
Asks him, waits long — the old man

won't open his lips.
A rainhat of young bamboo skins,
    a coat of lotus leaves,
Nothing busying his mind,
    he keeps to the fishing jetty.
I suppose that single boat of his
    has no fixed resting place —
Where will he go this evening,
    his fishing pole in hand?

CHU GUANGXI (fl. 742)
Three Poems

Translated by Kenneth Rexroth

A poet from Jiangsu Province who spent his early life as a prominent figure in
Chang'an society, Chu knew, and exchanged poems with, Wang Wei, Cui Hao, and
others.

A Mountain Spring

There is a brook in the mountains,
Nobody I ask knows its name.
It shines on the earth like a piece
Of the sky. It falls away
In waterfalls, with a sound
Like rain. It twists between rocks
And makes deep pools. It divides
Into islands. It flows through
Calm reaches. It goes its way
With no one to mind it. The years
Go by, its clear depths never change.

Tea

By noon the heat became unbearable.
The birds stopped flying
And went to roost exhausted.
Sit here in the shade of the big tree.
Take off your hot woolen jacket.
The few small clouds floating overhead

Do nothing to cool the heat of the sun.
I'll put some tea on to boil
And cook some vegetables.
It's a good thing you don't live far.
You can stroll home after sunset.

Evening in the Garden, Clear After Rain

Fifth month, golden plums are ripe;
The horizon is hazy; the evening dewfall heavy;
The grass along the lane is bright green.
The sun sets in burning clouds.
The old gardener is glad the rains are over.
He puts the damp mats out to dry
And sets to work repairing the collapsed mud walls.
Twilight, the sky is crystal clear.
The children dance with joy.
They shout and splash in the puddles.
All the world has been made new.
I walk in the garden without a coat.
The hedges are still wet and glittering.
The pond shimmers with a thousand rippling images.
They no sooner appear than
They are erased and appear again.
The beautiful trees are like my heart,
Swelling with boundless happiness.

YUAN JIE (719–772)

Yuan Jie was among the most innovative writers of the mid-eighth century. He condemned literary practice for failing to fulfil its responsibility to explicitly promote moral standards. This, one of his most famous poems, was written when he was prefect of Daozhou (in modern Hunan Province), where the local Chinese population had suffered badly from incursions by the non-Chinese tribes to the south and were further oppressed by rapacious tax collectors sent by the central government.

— David McMullen, *Indiana Companion*, 1986

After the Raiders Have Gone: To Clerks and Officials

Translated by Stephen Owen

In 763 raiders from the western plateaus attacked Daozhou, burning, looting, and murdering. They left only when everything was virtually gone. The following year the raiders struck again, this time at Yongzhou, smashing Shao, but they turned back before they crossed the boundaries of this prefecture. We do not seem to be able to control the enemy by force, and can do no more than endure the wounds we suffer. But how, after all this, can the government envoys increase our hardships with more demands and exactions of taxes? For this purpose I wrote this poem to be shown to the clerks:

> In past years I lived in an age of peace,
> Twenty years amid mountains and forests.
> Springs lay by the door of my yard,
> Caves and ravines, right before my gate.
> Field taxes were taken at regular times;
> At sundown a man could still sleep in peace.
> All at once we came into times of trouble,
> And I served several years under battle flags.
> Now, as I govern this commandery,
> The mountain tribes are running wild.
> The city, so small the raiders didn't sack it,
> But its people are poor, their wounds to be pitied.
> Thus, when the neighboring regions were plundered,
> This prefecture alone remained intact.
> Then come commissioners with royal commands —
> Surely they must be better than the raiders!
> But with their exactions and their collections
> They harry us like a simmering fire —
> What kind of person would end men's lives
> To be a great worthy of the age?
> How I long to cast down my symbols of office,
> Take fishing pole, punt my own boat away,
> Go with my family where there's fish and grain,
> To live out my life by the Yangtze and sea!

QIAN QI (722–c. 780)

After the An Lushan rebellion, Qian Qi made the acquaintance of Wang Wei and gradually became the darling of capital poetry. He was generally considered the poetic successor to Wang Wei.

Kingfisher with Fish in Beak

Translated by Stephen Owen

> Its mind is on something among lotus leaves —
> In the blink of an eye, down from the tall tree.

Splitting the waves it takes the sunken fish,
Then a single dot of azure light departing.

From My Study at the Mouth of the Valley: A Message to Censor Yang

Translated by Witter Bynner

At a little grass-hut in the valley of the river,
Where a cloud seems born from a viney wall,
You will love the bamboos new with rain,
And mountains tender in the sunset.
Cranes drift early here to rest
And autumn flowers are slow to fade ...
I have bidden my pupil to sweep the grassy path
For the coming of my friend.

Figure 49. "From My Study at
the Mouth of the Valley." Early
20th-century illustration.
(Source: *Zixi huapu daquan*
[Complete Painting Manual]
[Beijing: Rongbaozhai, 1982])

Dedicated to the Hermit Cui

Translated by Jerome P. Seaton

Path to the simples, deep in red moss.
Window on the mountain, full of verdure.
I envy you your wine among the flowers;
The butterflies flying, there, in your dream.

CHANG JIAN (fl. 749)

A Buddhist Retreat Behind Broken-Mountain Temple

Translated by Witter Bynner

In the pure morning, near the old temple,
Where early sunlight points the treetops,
My path has wound, through a sheltered hollow
Of boughs and flowers, to a Buddhist retreat.
Here birds are alive with mountain-light,
And the mind of man touches peace in a pool,
And a thousand sounds are quieted
By the breathing of a temple-bell.

QIU WEI (eighth century)

Seeking a Hermit on West Mountain and Not Finding Him

Translated by John Minford

To the thatched hut on the topmost peak
A ten mile climb;
No boy answers the knock,
Nothing but a table or two visible within.
He's gathering firewood in his cart,
Gone fishing in some autumn pool.
All that rough trek, and no encounter:
I pause, head high in this void.
The glint of grass in the fresh rain,
The sound of pines at the evening window;
The perfect stillness of this place

Figure 50. "Seeking a Hermit on West Mountain and Not Finding Him." Early 20th-century illustration. (Source: *Zixi huapu daquan* [Complete Painting Manual] [Beijing: Rongbaozhai, 1982])

Of itself eases the mind.
No meeting, but the spirit of
Peace and purity speaks.
The mood passes; time to descend.
Why wait for the man?

GU KUANG (c. 725–c. 814)

Hard Traveling

Translated by Stephen Owen

Gu Kuang was from Suzhou and passed the *jinshi* [Advanced Scholar] examination in 757. He lived to a ripe old age, and seems to have had no association at all with most of the capital poets.

This *yuefu* ballad [compare Bao Zhao's "The Weary Road" in chapter 12, and Li Bo's "Hard Is the Journey" in chapter 19] often produced poems in which the mood was one of near hysteria. Gu's distress at some unnamed malaise reaches the point of raving. It points forward to the Mid Tang.

Have you not seen them
Bearing snow to block up a well,
    spending their strength in vain,
Or steaming pebbles to be their rice —
    how shall they ever eat it?
For a lifetime a faithful heart
    has been exhausted for others,
And those who recognized it were worse
    than those who recognized it not.
From the winter green of trees there hangs
    the transempyrean vine,
At the year's close its flowers wither,
    but the tree does not.
Each of every living thing
    has its own root, its nature;
The planted grain will never grow
    the sprouts of beans.
Hard traveling, traveling hard,
Where are there level roads?
Whoever's heart is untroubled
    must be noble and rich,
As now I look on you,
    the well-being in your face.

GENG WEI (late eighth century)

Autumn Day

Translated by Stephen Owen

Geng was a member of a group known as the Ten Talents of the Da-li era (766–779), which also included Qian Qi and Li Yi. The image of the stalks of grain echoes *Song* 85, and the rice and millet growing over the Zhou capital. But here it is used for simple purposes of mood, the desolation of autumn and longing to return home.

Sunlight cast back enters the village lanes,
Grief comes — to whom can I tell it.
An ancient road, no one walking there:
The autumn wind stirs the stalks of grain.

DAI SHULUN (732–789)

Su Creek Pavilion

Translated by Stephen Owen

Dai is best known for a statement of his about poetry. "The scene a poet creates is as when the sun is warm on Indigo Fields and the fine jade gives off mist: you can gaze on it, but you cannot fix it in your eyes." [See chapter 24, and Li Shangyin's poem "The Patterned Lute."] His own poetry is full of picturesque and melancholy images, scenes that touch the sentiments but "cannot be fixed in the eyes."

By Su Creek Pavilion
    the grasses spread everywhere —
Who is it leans to the east wind
    on the twelve railings there?
The swallows do not return,
    the last events of spring:
A whole sandbar of misty rain
    and the pear blossoms cold.

WEI YINGWU (737–c. 792)
Five Poems

Translated by Witter Bynner

His landscape poetry is often compared with that of Wang Wei, Meng Haoran and Liu Zongyuan.

Autumn Night Message: To Qiu

As I walk in the cool of the autumn night,
Thinking of you, singing my poem,
I hear a mountain pine-cone fall …
You also seem to be awake.

At Chuzhou on the Western Stream

Where tender grasses rim the stream
And deep boughs trill with mango-birds,
On the spring flood of last night's rain
The ferry-boat moves as though someone were poling.

A Poem to a Taoist Hermit on Quanjiao Mountain

My office has grown cold today;
And I suddenly think of my mountain friend
Gathering firewood down in the valley
Or boiling white stones for potatoes in his hut ...
I wish I might take him a cup of wine
To cheer him through the evening storm;
But in fallen leaves that have heaped the bare slopes,
How should I ever find his footprints!

Mooring at Twilight in Yuyi District

Furling my sail near the town of Huai,
I find for harbor a little cove
Where a sudden breeze whips up the waves.
... The sun is growing dim now and sinks in the dusk.
People are coming home. The bright mountain-peak darkens.
Wildgeese fly down to an island of white weeds.
... At midnight I think of a northern city-gate,
And I hear a bell tolling between me and sleep.

East of the Town

From office confinement all year long,
I have come out of town to be free this morning.
Where willows harmonize the wind
And green hills lighten the cares of the world.
I lean by a tree and rest myself
Or wander up and down a stream.
... Mists have wet the fragrant meadows;
A spring dove calls from some hidden place.
... With quiet surroundings, the mind is at peace,
But beset with affairs, it grows restless again ...
Here I shall finally build me a cabin,
As Tao Qian built one long ago.[3]

---

[3] The famous poet Tao Yuanming (see chapter 11). *Eds.*

Lu Lun (737?–798?)

Two Frontier Songs
Matching Rhymes with General Zhang

Translated by Wong Man

The first poem refers to a story about the great Han general Li Guang: one night the general shot an arrow at what he thought was a tiger, and in the morning the arrow was found to be embedded in a stone.

1

Grass rustle through dim woods,
Warrior shoots into night,
Dawn finds arrow-plume
Lost in rocky heights.

2

Black moon geese fly high,
Tartars flee the dark;
Light horses pursue,
Sword and bow snow-marked.

🕮 *Further Reading* 🕮

Bynner, Witter, trans. (from the texts of Kiang Kang-hu). *The Jade Mountain, a Chinese Anthology: Being Three Hundred Poems of the T'ang Dynasty.* New York: Knopf, 1929.
Cheng, François. *L'Ecriture poétique chinoise.* Paris: Editions du Seuil, 1977. Trans. by Donald A. Riggs & Jerome P. Seaton as *Chinese Poetic Writing: With an Anthology of T'ang Poetry* (Bloomington: Indiana University Press, 1982).
Herdan, Innes, trans. *The Three Hundred T'ang Poems.* Taipei: Far East Book Company, 1973.
Jenyns, Soames, trans. *Selections from the 300 Poems of the T'ang Dynasty.* London: John Murray, 1940.
Jenyns, Soame, trans. *Further Selections from the 300 Poems of the T'ang Dynasty.* London: John Murray, 1944.
Kroll, Paul. *Meng Hao-jan.* New York: Twayne, 1981.
Lattimore, David, trans. *Harmony of the World.* Providence, R.I.: Copper Beech Press, 1980.
Owen, Stephen. *The Great Age of Chinese Poetry: The High T'ang.* New Haven: Yale University Press, 1981.
Rexroth, Kenneth, trans. *One Hundred More Poems from the Chinese: Love and the Turning Year.* New York: New Directions, 1970.
Wong, Man, trans. *Poems from China.* Hong Kong: Creation Books, 1950.

Chapter 22

Stones Where the Haft Rotted

Poets of the Mid Tang

The bones of poetry jut in Meng Jiao,
The waves of poetry surge in Han Yu.

— Meng Jiao (751–814)

I can't bear having the poetry of the Mid Tang even reach my ears.

— Li Panlong (1514–1570)

If I take up any poem or line by Han Yu, I can see his craggy physiognomy throughout.

-— Ye Xie (1627–1703)

Introduction

Stephen Owen

It is difficult to be too close a neighbor to a Golden Age. The major poets of that Golden Age, the High Tang, had always received their due admiration; and no admirers were so fervent as their immediate successors in the Mid Tang. But greatness, if it seems too far out of reach, can become oppressive; and as the magic of High Tang poetry became increasingly unattainable with the passing centuries, it became the object of impotent emulation. An anger was born, directed not at the High Tang itself, but at the poetry of that long interval which separated the Golden Age from the present. Love for the poetry of one period seemed to demand contempt for the poetry of other periods; and the Mid Tang, as the first falling away from High Tang excellence, was open to particular condemnation.

Warnings were issued: a person's taste was in danger of corruption if he read works written after some invisible boundary in the second half of the eighth century. In practice such warnings were ineffective: Mid Tang poetry was still read, as was the even more pernicious poetry of the Late Tang. But there was a consensus that some serious change had occurred in Chinese poetry between the An Lushan Rebellion of the 750s and the 790s, when the major Mid Tang poets began their most characteristic work. This change was as elusive as it was all-encompassing; and it seemed to initiate a process of decline, from which classical poetry never entirely recovered. Later critics like Yan Yu and Li Panlong hoped to leap over that invisible boundary and recapture High Tang innocence. Of course they failed.

For later readers the intuition of some serious change in the transition between High Tang and Mid Tang was inescapable. Mid Tang poems all too often recalled, wilfully or unwittingly, High Tang antecedents; and more often than not, the Mid Tang poem, attractive enough when considered in isolation, became the victim of the comparison....

Sometimes a curse, and sometimes a gift, the one clear mark of the Mid Tang is a lack of restraint: the implicit becomes explicit; the moving becomes sentimental; the plain becomes plainer and the bold, bolder. Consider first Li Bo's "Observing the Past in Yue," an exemplary High Tang quatrain on an ancient site:

When Goujian, then King of Yue,
      came back after smashing Wu,
The royal troops returned to their homes
      dressed all in robes of brocade;
His court ladies, just like the flowers,
      filled the springtime halls,
Where now only
      the partridges are flying.

Contrast Wang Jian's Mid Tang treatment of a similar theme in "Passing by the Palace on Qi Peak":

Its marble mansions have fallen,
      the whitewashed walls lie bare,
Where green hills in fold upon fold
      circle these ancient halls.

The Emperor Wu has come and gone,
    times of gossamer sleeves are done,
Now wildflowers and yellow butterflies
    take command of the wind of spring.

Wang Jian's last line is striking, but there the Mid Tang poet exposes his presence in the word *ling*, "take command." This metaphor of mastery rests uneasily on the indifferent self-absorption of the seasonal phenomena, here where humans once built monuments of their mastery. The Mid Tang poet cannot resist the word that makes the contrast between past and present explicit; he cannot resist the daring word. It is easy to admire Wang Jian's final line; but it too is a "taking command," an assertion of the presence of the poet's interpreting mind, a mind which cannot let nature's changes just "be."

— from "Some Mid-Tang Quatrains," 1984

MENG JIAO (751–814)
Five Poems

Translated by Stephen Owen

Meng Jiao was the eldest and most difficult of the writers who gathered around Han Yu at the turn of the ninth century. Meng was from Huzhou (modern Wuxing in Zhejiang). It was not until 791, when he went to the capital to take the examination and met the young Han Yu, that he began to write poetry in the harsh, idiosyncratic style for which he was later famous. Meng twice failed the examination for the *jinshi*, in 792 and 793, and those failures occasioned angry, disillusioned lyrics that were to win him the shocked contempt of many later readers. As Meng himself so proudly claimed, his style was out of harmony with the gracious occasional poetry of his contemporaries. He conceived of his work as being in the "ancient style," and ethical messages, associated with the mid-Tang revival of Confucian values, occur throughout his poetry. Yet even in his ethics there is discord, and such poems often possess a shrill stridency that undermines and complicates the magisterial calm of the would-be didactic poet.

Laments of the Gorges

1

The edges of the gorges hack up sun and moon,
Sun and moon always ruined in their shining.
All things grow warp and slants,
Bird's wings fly warped and slanting.
Teeth on sunken stones locked;
Spirits of the drowned summoned but don't return.
A blur — armor-shells in a clear spring,
Splotched, the emerald robes on stone.

Hungrily lapping up the howl of rushing waters;
Slavering, seems like whirling, swirling oils.
Don't go strolling through the gorges in springtime —
Stinking grasses grow tiny, tiny.

2

Owls mimic human speech,
Dragons suck in mountainous waves.
They can, during broad daylight,
Coax you with pleasant clear breezes,
Shake judgment, make all living things stumble,
Gather reeking smells to spread from deep vines.
Toothed streams, bleak and bottomless,
Hacksaw froth, found everywhere.
Slanted trees where birds won't nest,
Dangling gibbons swing past them.
You can't listen to the laments of the gorges,
For nothing can be done about the bitterness there.

Apricots Die Young

Apricots die young: their flowers are nipples which the frost cuts and they
fall. They lead me to grieve over my late child and to write these poems.

1

Don't let freezing hands play with these pearls —
If they play with these pearls, the pearls will surely fly loose.
Don't let the sudden frost cut off springtime —
If it cuts off spring, no bright flowering.
Scattering, falling, small nipple buds
In colorful patterns like my dead baby's robes.
I gather them — not a full hand's grasp,
At sunset I return home in hopeless sorrow.

2

In vain I gather up these stars from the ground,
Yet on the branches I see no flowers.
Sad — a solitary old man,
Desolate — a home without children.
Better the duck that sinks in the water,

Better the crow that gathers twigs for nesting.
Duckling in the waves, breaks through them, still flies,
Fledglings in the wind, ruffled, boasting to one another.
But blossoms and baby will live no more,
I sigh in vain, facing these creatures.

Lament for Lu Yin

Poets are usually pure, rugged,
Die from hunger, cling to desolate mountains.
Since this white cloud had no master,
When it flew off, its mind was free from care.
After long sickness, a corpse on a bed,
The servant boy too weak to manage the funeral.
Your old books, all gnawed by famished rats,
Lie strewn and scattered in your single room.
As you go off to the land of new ghosts,
I look on your features white as old jade.
I am ashamed that, when you enter the earth,
No one calls after you, to hold you back.
All the springs lament for you in vain,
As the day lengthens, murmuring waters mourn.

The Stones Where the Haft Rotted

Translated by A. C. Graham

Wang Zhi of the Jin dynasty (265–419) went into the mountains (Stone Bridge Mountain) to gather firewood and saw two boys playing chess. The boys gave him a thing like a date stone, which he ate, and satisfied his hunger. At the end of the game, the boys pointed and said: "Look! Your axe-handle is rotten." When Zhi returned to his village, he was a hundred years old.

Less than a day in paradise,
And a thousand years have passed among men.
While the pieces are still being laid on the board
All things have changed to emptiness.
The woodman takes the road home,
The haft of his axe has rotted in the wind:
Nothing is what it was but the stone bridge
Still spanning a rainbow cinnabar-red.

Risks

Translated by Graeme Wilson

Avoid sharp swords and lovely women.

Swords that are brought too near
Will slice the hand. Too close a beauty
Can cost the heart too dear.
The road's worst threat is not its length,
Ten years can break a wheel,
And the risk of love is not in loving
Too many times. The real
Peril is that a single night
May pierce more deep than steel.

LI YI (748–827)

On Hearing a Flute at Night from the Wall of Shouxiang

Translated by Witter Bynner

The sand below the border-mountain lies like snow,
And the moon like frost beyond the city-wall.
And someone somewhere, playing a flute,
Has made the soldiers homesick all night long.

ZHANG JI (mid-eighth century)
A Night-Mooring near Maple Bridge

Translated by Witter Bynner

While I watch the moon go down, a crow caws through the frost;
Under the shadows of maple-trees a fisherman moves with his torch;
And I hear, from beyond Suzhou, from the temple on Cold
    Mountain,
Ringing for me, here in my boat, the midnight bell.

HAN YU (768–824)

Autumn Thoughts

Translated by Burton Watson

Many of the Mid Tang poets began deliberately working back toward a freer, looser, more colloquial diction and syntax (after the extreme refinement and density of the late Du Fu). One of the most important leaders in this new poetic movement was Han Yu, also famous as a Confucian thinker and creator of the *guwen*, or old prose style [see chapter 27]. His efforts to introduce reforms both in prose and in poetic style were in many ways motivated by the same ideals. In prose he sought to break away from the parallel prose style, with its extreme attention to formal regularity and rhetorical flourish, and to substitute a style embodying the simplicity, naturalness, and respect for speech rhythms that, it was claimed, had characterized the writings of the ancients. In poetry he made a similar effort to do away with stale or contrived diction, to restore freshness to the language of the poem and to encourage greater freedom of form and expression. At the same time he attempted to broaden the subject matter of poetry and to introduce a more openly philosophical note.

2

When white dew descends on the hundred grasses,
mugwort and orchid alike wither and die;
then, green green by my four walls,
they come alive again, spreading over the ground.
The summer cicada has hardly gone silent
when autumn crickets sound their willful cries.
The rounding cycle never ends,
yet each thing differs in the nature it bears.
Each has its season, its own proper time;
why should pine and cypress alone be prized?

6

This morning I can't seem to get out of bed,
instead sit bolt upright through the daylight hours.
Insects chirp, the room grows darker;
a moon pops up, shining in the window.
My mind dazed, as though I'd lost my bearings,
idle thoughts welling up to prick me like thorns —
I'm sick of paying court to the dusty world;
writing — my concerns race solely in that direction.
Yet I must try to curb this perversity —
I have duties in the service of the king.

8

Leaves fall turning turning to the ground,
by the front eaves racing, following the wind;
murmuring voices seem to speak to me
as they whirl and toss in headlong flight.
An empty hall in the yellow dusk of evening:

I sit here silent, unspeaking.
The young boy comes in from outdoors,
trims the lamp, sets it before me,
asks me questions I do not answer,
brings me a supper I do not eat.
He goes and sits down by the west wall,
reading me poetry — three or four poems;
the poet is not a man of today —
already a thousand years divide us —
but something in his words strikes my heart,
fills it again with an acid grief.
I turn and call to the boy:
Put down the book and go to bed now —
a man has times when he must think,
and work to do that never ends.

A Withered Tree

Translated by A. C. Graham

Not a twig or a leaf on the old tree,
Wind and frost harm it no more.
A man could pass through the hole in its belly,
Ants crawl searching under its peeling bark.
Its only lodger, the toadstool which dies in a morning,
The birds no longer visit in the twilight.
But its wood can still spark tinder.
It does not care yet to be only the void at its heart.[1]

Two Poems

Translated by Stephen Owen

To Hou Xi

A Mr. Hou of my circle, Hou Shuqi,[2]
Called to me, "Get your pole and we'll fish in the Wen River."
At daybreak we whipped our horses out the capital gates,

---

[1] The "void at its heart" is both the hollow inside of the tree and the Buddhist ideal of the
mind freed from the illusion of a material body.
[2] Hou Shuqi is Hou Xi.

Then on and on all day long among thorns and brambles.
The Wen is a rather hazy affair — it stops, then flows again,
As deep as a cart track, wide enough for a carriage pole,
Frogs leap over it, there baby wrens can bathe,
But even if there were fish, they wouldn't be worth the trouble.
For Mr. Hou's sake I could not give up,
So we bent needles for hooks,
    broke grains for bait,
      cast them into the slime.
Ramrod stiff we sat from noontime on to yellow dusk,
Hands tired, eyes sore, then finally we got up —
It moved a moment!
    then stopped,
      we couldn't hope —
Shrimps moved, leeches crossed over as though all were in doubt,
I raised the pole and pulled in the line —
    suddenly I had something!
An inch's worth — just old enough to tell the fins from scales.
At this moment Mr. Hou and myself
Gazed mournfully at one another, sighing a good while.
Everything I do these days turns out just like this,
So this experience may well serve as an example for me:
Half of my life spent in a fluster to get chosen for a post,
When I first get that single title, my once young face is old.
Why didn't I see the way things are in this human world?
Bringing pointless suffering on myself, and ultimately for what?
I just ought to take my wife and children by the hand,
Go south into Ying and Ji, never to return.
Hou Xi, your spirit is at its keenest now —
What I say is really important — don't laugh at me! —
If you want to go fishing, you have to go really far,
Do you think a big fish would live in this backwash?

Losing a Tooth

Last year a molar fell out,
This year an incisor fell.
All of a sudden six or seven more fall,
And this tooth-falling condition is hardly over.
Those left are all shaky,
And I suppose this won't stop till they've all fallen.

I remember when the first one fell,
I felt only that the gap was embarrassing.
When two or three had fallen,
I began to worry that this decline meant death.
Now every time one's going to fall,
I feel a constant trembling within.
A shaky tooth prevents me from eating,
I'm so upset I fear rinsing my mouth with water.
Finally it will desert me and fall,
My mood likens it to an avalanche.
Recently I've grown used to the falling,
When one falls, there is similarity in emptiness,
The remaining ones, twenty-odd,
I know they'll fall in succession and that's it.
Now supposing one falls each year,
I've got enough to last me two decades,
On the other hand, if they fall together, emptying me,
It's still the same result as gradually.
People say when the incisors fall,
You can't hope for long life,
But I say life has its limits,
Long or short, all die anyway.
People say when you've got a gap in the incisors,
Those around are startled when they look closely,
But I say what Zhuangzi said,
Trees and geese each have something to be happy about.[3]
Silence is certainly better than telling lies,
Chewing doesn't work, but soft things still taste good.
Thus I sang and finished a poem on it,
With which I inform my wife and children.

---

[3] This refers to the first story in the "Tree on the Mountain" chapter of the *Zhuangzi*.
Zhuangzi's disciples saw that a tree was spared the woodcutter's axe because it lacked
quality; then they observed that in a choice between a goose that could cackle and one
that couldn't, the goose that couldn't cackle — the one that lacked quality — was selected
to be killed. Perplexed at this contradiction, they asked Zhuangzi about it. Zhuangzi
replied that he would take a position between quality and lack of it, but that even that
position was incorrect because it allowed consideration of the distinction between quality
and its lack. Han Yu is saying that such things as whether one has teeth (quality, like the
goose that could cackle and survived) or has not teeth (lacks quality, like the tree that
survived), do not determine survival because they are meaningless distinctions. The tree
was happy to lack quality; the goose that survived was happy to possess it.

Song of the Stone Drums

Translated by Innes Herdan

The Stone Drums were a group of ten dolmens from the Zhou dynasty on which had been carved a number of poems similar in form and style to those of the *Book of Songs.* It was often claimed that they were made in commemoration of one of the hunting expeditions of a Zhou king. They were discovered in the early part of the seventh century lying half-buried in the ground in the province of Shaanxi. They were many times moved, from capital to capital, were (1307) placed in the Confucian Temple in Peking, and are now in the Historical Museum. They are the most hallowed of all the documents in Chinese epigraphy and have been venerated by Chinese scholars from their discovery until the present. Han Yu believed them to have been composed during the reign of King Xuan of Zhou (828–782 B.C.), a period of the restoration of Zhou power, although modern research has shown them to have been written somewhat later. Since the Yuan-he period (806–820), during which this poem was written, was considered to be a "restoration" of Tang power, the stone drums had a special meaning for Han Yu.

Mr. Zhang handed me this rubbing from the Stone Drums
And urged me to compose a Stone Drum Song.
Shaoling has lost its Du Fu, Li Bo "the immortal" is dead —
What can my poor talent do for the Stone Drums?

When the Zhou laws decayed and the Four Seas heaved in turmoil,
King Xuan rose in anger and brandished his sacred sword,
And wide swung the doors of Bright Hall to receive the congratulations
Of feudal princes with their swords and jangling pendants.
To the hunt at Qiyang galloped the brave and handsome,
Birds and game lay strewn over countless miles:
All was wonderfully chiseled in stone, to inform ten thousand
	generations.
Rock was broken from rough hillsides, shaped into drums;
Attendant ministers skilled in the arts, each of the first rank,
Were chosen to carve and inscribe them, and set them on the
	mountain.
Rain drenched, sun baked, wild fire burned them,
Spirits guarded, and drove away what would harm them.
Where could you have found this sheet of tracing?
Absolutely complete down to the finest stroke, with no error.
But severe in expression, obscure in meaning, hard to understand,
The style of calligraphy neither "official" nor "tadpole" —
Of such antiquity, how could it escape disfigurement?
The strokes like living dragons, hewn with a keen sword,

Like phoenix flying and argus wheeling, a crowd of immortals
     descending,
Sea corals and jade trees with branches firmly entwined,
Or golden cords and iron wires strongly twisted and locked,
Like ancient tripods skipping into water or shuttles soaring like
     dragons.
Ignorant scholars collecting poems forgot to include these;
The two books of Solemn Songs were too narrow, lacked scope.
Confucius traveling westward did not reach Qin State —
He gathered a constellation of stars but missed the sun and moon!
How sad that I who love the old culture was born too late!
I look at the drums, and tears stream from my eyes.

I remember, long ago, being summoned to receive my doctorate, —
The year when the reign title changed to Yuan-he:
An old friend with the army at You Fufeng
Advised me where these old drums were buried.
I brushed my cap, washed myself, and spoke with the overseer of
     sacrifices —
Objects so precious, how many could there be in existence?
They should be wrapped in rugs and mats and transported forthwith:
All ten drums could be loaded on just a few camels,
And presented to the Imperial Temple, like a tripod of Gao;
Their splendor and value would increase a hundredfold.
Or if the royal bounty would present them to the University,
Many students could study and diligently decipher them.
In Han days, people came to the Capital over the great Passes,
     to look at the classical texts;
If these drums were set up in public, the whole country
     would scramble to see them.
We would scratch out the moss, scrape away lichen,
     expose the joints and corners,
Set them in a definite place, level and not aslant.
A great building with wide eaves should house them,
Where nothing could happen to them, as it did in the past years.
But the Court officials have grown old in service,
Will not comply with this obligation but keep procrastinating.
So herdboys use them for striking sparks, cows to rub their horns on;
Who would handle them now or stroke them with affection?
Days fade and months melt away, the drums returning to dust:
Six years I looked to the west, chanting my songs in vain.
Wang Xizhi's ordinary script with its bewitching style of brushwork

Could be had, several pages of it, for a few white geese!
Eight dynasties have passed since the Zhou, and wars have ceased:
Why does nobody look after these drums?
We are at peace now, days with no disturbance,
The authorities employ scholars and respect Confucius and Mencius,
How can I bring this subject up for discussion?
I want to borrow an orator's mouth — words tumbling like a
 cataract!

Here I end my song of the Stone Drums —
Alas, alas! my thoughts have gone wandering!

Figure 51. Rubbing from the
Stone Drum inscriptions. (Source:
Li Xueqin, *Eastern Zhou and Qin
Civilizations* [New Haven: Yale
University Press, 1985])

Three Poems

Translated by Herbert Giles

The Wounded Falcon

Within a ditch beyond my wall
I saw a falcon headlong fall.
Bedaubed with mud and racked with pain,
It beat its wings to rise, in vain;

While little boys threw tiles and stones,
Eager to break the wretch's bones.
　　O bird, methinks thy life of late
Hath amply justified this fate!
Thy sole delight to kill and steal,
And then exultingly to wheel,
Now sailing in the clear blue sky,
Now on the wild gale sweeping by,
Scorning thy kind of less degree
As all unfit to mate with thee.
　　　　But mark how fortune's wheel goes round;
A pellet lays thee on the ground,
Sore stricken at some vital part —
And where is then thy pride of heart?
　　　　What's this to me? — I could not bear
To see the fallen one lying there.
I begged its life, and from the brook
Water to wash its wounds I took.
Fed it with bits of fish by day,
At night from foxes kept away.
My care I knew would naught avail
For gratitude, that empty tale.
And so this bird would crouch and hide
Till want its stimulus applied;
And I, with no reward to hope,
Allowed its callousness full scope.
　　　　Last eve the bird showed signs of rage,
With health renewed, and beat its cage.
Today it forced a passage through,
And took its leave, without adieu.
　　　　Good luck hath saved thee, not desert;
Beware, O bird, of further hurt;
Beware the archer's deadly tools! —
'Tis hard to escape the shafts of fools —
Nor e'er forget the chastening ditch
That found thee poor, and left thee rich.[4]

---

[4] In experience of the vicissitudes of life.

Humanity

Oh spare the busy morning fly!
Spare the mosquitos of the night!
And if their wicked trade they ply
Let a partition stop their flight.

Their span is brief from birth to death;
Like you they bite their little day;
And then, with autumn's earliest breath,
Like you too they are swept away.

Discontent

To stand upon the river-bank
and snare the purple fish,
My net well cast across the stream,
was all that I could wish.
Or lie concealed and shoot the geese
that scream and pass apace,
And pay my rent and taxes with
the profits of the chase.
Then home to peace and happiness,
with wife and children gay,
Though clothes be coarse and fare be hard,
and earned from day to day.
But now I read and read, scarce knowing
what 'tis all about,
And eager to improve my mind
I wear my body out.
I draw a snake and give it legs,
to find I've wasted skill,
And my hair grows daily whiter
as I hurry towards the hill.[5]
I sit amid the sorrows
I have brought on my own head,
And find myself estranged from all,
among the living dead.

---

[5] The Chinese prefer hillsides for their burying-grounds.

I seek to drown my consciousness
    in wine, alas! in vain:
Oblivion passes quickly
    and my griefs begin again.
Old age comes on and yet withholds
    the summons to depart ...
So I'll take another bumper
    just to ease my aching heart.

LIU YUXI (772–842)
Two Poems

Translated by Stephen Owen

Liu Yuxi was a close friend of Liu Zongyuan and Bo Juyi, important both as poet and essayist. See chapter 27 for his short prose essay "My Humble Home" and chapter 30 for two of his poems in lyric form.

— Editors

Raven Robe Lane

The lane was in Jinling, the now decayed capital of the Southern Dynasties: this was the aristocratic quarter of great clans such as the Wangs and the Xies.

Beside Red Sparrow Bridge
    wild plants are in flower,
At the entrance to Raven Robe Lane
    evening sunlight sinks down:
The swallows that once were before the halls
    of the former Wangs and Xies
Now fly into the homes
    of the common peasantry.

Gazing on Lake Dongting

The light of the lake and the autumn moon
    are a pair perfectly matched,
No winds ruffle the face of the waters,
    a mirror unpolished.
If you gaze far off into Lake Dongting
    and the azure color of mountain —
In a platter of shining silver
    a single green conch.

朱雀橋邊野草花烏衣巷口
夕陽斜舊時王謝堂前燕
恐一旦尋常百姓家
信大石江寫劉禹錫句

Figure 52. "Beside Red Spar-
row Bridge." Early 20th-
century illustration. (Source:
Zixi huapu daquan [Complete
Painting Manual] [Beijing:
Rongbaozhai, 1982])

Looking at My Knife-Hilt: A Song

Translated by Daniel Bryant

I have always regretted the shallowness of words
Compared with the depth of human hearts.
Today the two of us look at one another
Silently, but with feelings a hundredfold.

The City of Stones

Translated by Amy Lowell and Florence Ayscough

Hills surround the ancient kingdom, they
never change.

The tide beats against the empty city, and
silently, silently returns.
To the East, over the Huai River —
the ancient moon.
Through the long, quiet night it moves
crossing the battlemented wall.

LIU ZONGYUAN (773–819)
Five Poems

Translated by Witter Bynner

For Liu Zongyuan, see chapters 27, 28 and 30. — Editors

Figure 53. "River-Snow." Early
20th-century illustration.
(Source: *Zixi huapu daquan*
[Complete Painting Manual]
[Beijing: Rongbaozhai, 1982])

River-Snow

A hundred mountains and no bird,
A thousand paths without a footprint;
A little boat, a bamboo cloak,
An old man fishing in the cold river-snow.

Reading Buddhist Classics with Chao at His Temple
in the Early Morning

I clean my teeth in water drawn from a cold well;
And while I brush my clothes, I purify my mind;
Then, slowly turning pages in the Tree-Leaf Book,
I recite, along the path to the eastern shelter.
... The world has forgotten the true fountain of this teaching
And people enslave themselves to miracles and fables.
Under the given words I want the essential meaning,
I look for the simplest way to sow and reap my nature.
Here in the quiet of the priest's temple-courtyard,
Mosses add their climbing color to the thick bamboo;
And now comes the sun, out of mist and fog,
And pines that seem to be new-bathed;
And everything is gone from me, speech goes, and reading,
Leaving the single unison.

Dwelling by a Stream

I had so long been troubled by official hat and robe
That I am glad to be an exile here in this wild southland.
I am a neighbor now of planters and reapers.
I am a guest of the mountains and woods.
I plough in the morning, turning dewy grasses,
And at evening tie my fisher-boat, breaking the quiet stream.
Back and forth I go, scarcely meeting anyone,
And sing a long poem and gaze at the blue sky.

From the City-Tower of Liuzhou
To My Four Fellow-Officials at Zhang, Ding, Feng, and Lian Districts

At this lofty tower where the town ends, wilderness begins;
And our longing has as far to go as the ocean or the sky ...
Hibiscus-flowers by the moat heave in a sudden wind,

And vines along the wall are whipped with slanting rain.
Nothing to see for three hundred miles but a blur of woods and
    mountain —
And the river's nine loops, twisting in our bowels …
This is where they have sent us, this land of tattooed people —
And not even letters, to keep us in touch with home.

An Old Fisherman

An old fisherman spent the night here, under the western cliff;
He dipped up water from the pure Xiang and made a bamboo fire;

Figure 54. "From the City-
Tower of Liuzhou." Early 20th-
century illustration. (Source:
Zixi huapu daquan [Complete
Painting Manual] [Beijing:
Rongbaozhai, 1982])

And then, at sunrise, he went his way through the cloven mist,
With only the creak of his paddle left, in the greenness of mountain
    and river.
… I turn and see the waves moving as from heaven,
And clouds above the cliffs coming idly, one by one.

JIA DAO (779–843)
Four Poems

Translated by Stephen Owen

Jia was one of the group of poets who gathered around Han Yu in the early ninth
century, attracted by Han's advocacy of a literary "restoration of antiquity." Early
in life he had entered a Buddhist order, which he left around 810, when he met Han
Yu. Their encounter is part of the lore of Chinese poetry. Jia Dao was riding his
donkey in the streets of Chang'an, gesticulating as he contemplated two lines of
poetry:

> The birds nest in the lake-side trees;
> A monk knocks on a moon-lit door.

He was wondering whether to change "knocks" to "pushes," when he ran into Han Yu,
Governor of the Metropolitan District, who strongly urged him to retain "knocks."
That was the beginning of their friendship.

Weeping for the Zen Master Boyan

Moss covers his stone bed fresh —
How many springs did the master occupy it?
They sketched to preserve his form practising the Way,
But burned away the body that sat in meditation.
The pagoda garden closes in snow on the pines,
While the library locks dust in the chinks.
I hate myself for these lines of tears falling —
I am not a man who understands the Void.

Evening View as the Snow Clears

I lean on my staff, gaze at the sunlit snow,
Clouds and gullies in countless layers.
The woodcutter returns to his plain hut,
As the winter sun falls behind sheer peaks.
A wildfire burns over the grass of the hills;

Figure 55. "Looking for the
Recluse and Not Finding
Him." Early twentieth-century
illustration. (Source: *Zixi
huapu daquan* [Complete Painting Manual] [Beijing:
Rongbaozhai, 1982])

Broken patches of mist rise from among the rocks and pines.
Then, turning back on the mountain temple road,
I hear the bells ring in the evening sky.

Looking for the Recluse and Not Finding Him

Beneath the pines I asked his servant boy,
Said, "The master's gone off picking herbs;
He's somewhere on this mountain,
But the clouds are so thick I can't tell where."

Spending the Night at a Mountain Temple

A host of peaks rear up into the color of cold,
At this point the road splits to the meditation hall.

Shooting stars pierce through the bare trees,
And a rushing moon retreats from moving clouds.
Visitors come but rarely to the very summit;
Cranes do not flock together in the tall pines.
There is a monk, eighty years old,
Who has never heard of what happens in the world.

🀫 *Further Reading* 🀫

Bryant, Daniel. "Chinese Translations." Unpublished.
Bynner, Witter, trans. (from the texts of Kiang Kang-hu) *The Jade Mountain, a Chinese Anthology: Being Three Hundred Poems of the T'ang Dynasty.* New York: Knopf, 1929.
Giles, Herbert A., ed. and trans. *Chinese Poetry in English Verse.* Shanghai: Kelly & Walsh, 1884.
Graham, A. C., trans. *Poems of the Late T'ang.* Harmondsworth: Penguin Books, 1965.
Hartmann, Charles. *Han Yü and the T'ang Search for Unity.* Princeton: Princeton University Press, 1986.
Herdan, Innes, trans. *The Three Hundred T'ang Poems.* Taipei: Far East Book Company, 1973.
Hinton, David, trans. *The Late Poems of Meng Chiao.* Princeton: Princeton University Press, 1997.
Lowell, Amy, trans. (with Florence Ayscough) *Fir-Flower Tablets: Poems Translated from the Chinese.* Boston: Houghton Mifflin, 1922.
Owen, Stephen. "Some Mid T'ang Quatrains." *Renditions* (1984), 21–22.
———— . *The Poetry of Meng Chiao and Han Yü.* New Haven: Yale University Press, 1975.
Watson, Burton, ed. and trans. *The Columbia Book of Chinese Poetry; From Early Times to the Thirteenth Century.* New York: Yale University Press, 1984.
Wilson, Graeme, trans. "Seven Poems." *Renditions* (1974), 2.
Yang, Xianyi, & Gladys Yang, trans. *Poetry and Prose of the Tang and Song.* Beijing: Foreign Languages Press, 1984.

"The Studio of a Hundred Stones."
Seal carved by Qian Song (1807–1860)

Chapter 23
Bo Juyi (772–846)

Madly Singing in the Mountains

And often, when I have finished a new poem,
Alone I climb the road to the Eastern Rock.
I lean my body on the banks of white Stone;
I pull down with my hands a green cassia branch.
My mad singing startles the valleys and hills;
The apes and birds all come to peep.

— Bo Juyi, from the poem "Madly Singing in the Mountains"

All the singing-girls when they saw me coming pointed at me, saying to one another, "That's the one who wrote 'The Everlasting Wrong'!" All the way from Chang'an to Jiangxi — three or four thousand leagues — in village schools, in Buddhist monasteries, at inns and on ships I constantly found poems of mine inscribed, and I heard them chanted by officials, monks, old widow-women and young girls wherever I went. These indeed were mere literary trifles, not the serious works by which I myself set store; but they happen to be just the sort of poetry that it is now the fashion to admire. Nor did old masters such as Tao Yuanming and Xie Lingyun always resist the temptation to produce this kind of work ...

I am accused at the same time of being too obvious and too subtle. No wonder the satires and meditative poems are not liked! In fact the only person of my own generation who does like them is yourself. A hundred, a thousand years hence perhaps someone will come who will understand them as you have done.

— Bo Juyi, letter to his friend Yuan Zhen, 815 (*translated by Arthur Waley*)

Introduction

Arthur Waley

Bo Juyi's childhood was spent in Henan. He tells us that his family was poor and often in difficulties. Soon after settling in Chang'an, he met Yuan Zhen, then aged twenty-two, who was destined to play so important a part in his life. In 804 on the death of his father, and again in 811 on the death of his mother, he spent periods of retirement on the Wei river near Chang'an. Soon after his return to Chang'an, which took place in the winter of 814, he fell into official disfavor. He had criticized the handling of a campaign against an unimportant tribe of Tartars, which he considered had been unduly prolonged. In a series of poems he had satirized the rapacity of minor officials and called attention to the intolerable sufferings of the masses. His enemies soon found an opportunity of silencing him.... He was banished to Jiujiang (then called Xunyang) with the rank of Sub-Prefect. After three years he was given the Governorship of Zhongzhou, a remote place in Sichuan. On the way up the Yangtze he met Yuan Zhen again after three years of separation. In the winter of 819 he was recalled to the capital and became a second-class Assistant Secretary.

In 821 the Emperor Muzong came to the throne. His arbitrary mis-government soon caused a fresh rising in the northwest. Juyi remonstrated in a series of memorials and was again removed from the capital — this time to be Governor of the important town of Hangzhou. Yuan Zhen now held a judicial post at Ningbo, and the two were occasionally able to meet. In 824 his Governorship expired and he went to live in Luoyang.... In 825 he became Governor of Suzhou. Here at the age of fifty-three he enjoyed a kind of second youth, much more sociable than that of thirty years before; we find him endlessly picnicking and feasting. But after two years illness obliged him to retire. He next held various posts at the capital, but again fell ill, and in 829 settled at Luoyang as Governor of the Province of Henan. Here his first son, Acui, was born, but died in the following year. In 831 Yuan Zhen died.

Henceforth, though for thirteen years he continued to hold nominal posts, he lived a life of retirement. In 832 he repaired an unoccupied part of the Xiangshan Monastery at Longmen, a few miles south of Luoyang, and lived there, calling himself the Hermit of Xiangshan [Fragrant Mountain]. In the winter of 839 he was attacked by paralysis and lost the use of his left leg. After many months in bed he was again able to visit his garden carried by Ruman, a favourite monk. He died in 846, leaving instructions that his funeral should be without pomp and that he should be buried not in the family tomb, but by Ruman's side in the Xiangshan Monastery.

The most striking characteristic of Bo Juyi's poetry is its verbal simplicity. There is a story that he was in the habit of reading his poems to an old peasant woman and altering any expression which she could not understand. The poems of his contemporaries were mere elegant diversions which enabled the scholar to display his erudition, or the literary juggler his dexterity. Bo expounded his theory of poetry in a letter to Yuan Zhen. Like Confucius, he regarded art solely as a method of conveying instruction.... But it is obvious that much of his best poetry conveys no moral whatsoever. He admits, indeed, that among his "miscellaneous stanzas" many were inspired by some momentary sensation or passing event. "A single laugh or a single sigh were rapidly translated into verse."

— from *One Hundred and Seventy Chinese Poems*, 1918

Twenty-three Poems

Translated by Arthur Waley

Planting Bamboos

(806?)

Disappointed, my will to serve the State;
At my closed door autumn grasses grow.
What could I do to ease a rustic heart?
I planted bamboos, more than a hundred shoots.
When I see their beauty, as they grow by the stream-side,
I feel again as though I lived in the hills,
And many a time when I have not much work
Round their railing I walk till night comes.
Do not say that their roots are still weak,
Do not say that their shade is still small;
Already I feel that both in courtyard and house
Day by day a fresher air moves.
But most I love, lying near the window-side,
To hear in their branches the sound of the autumn wind.

Passing Tianmen Street in Chang'an and Seeing a Distant View of Zhongnan Mountains

The snow has gone from Zhongnan; spring is almost come.
Lovely in the distance its blue colors, against the brown of the streets.
A thousand coaches, ten thousand horsemen pass down the Nine
    Roads;
Turns his head and looks at the mountains — not one man!

The Flower Market

In the Royal City spring is almost over;
Tinkle, tinkle — the coaches and horsemen pass.
We tell each other "This is the peony season";
And follow with the crowd that goes to the Flower Market.
"Cheap and dear — no uniform price;
The cost of the plant depends on the number of blossoms.
The flaming reds, a hundred on one stalk;
The humble white with only five flowers.
Above is spread an awning to protect them;

Around is woven a wattle-fence to screen them.
If you sprinkle water and cover the roots with mud,
When they are transplanted, they will not lose their beauty."
Each household thoughtlessly follows the custom,
Man by man, no one realizing.
There happened to be an old farm labourer
        Who came by chance that way.
He bowed his head and sighed a deep sigh;
But this sigh nobody understood.
He was thinking, "A cluster of deep-red flowers
Would pay the taxes of ten poor houses."

The Chancelor's Gravel Drive

A Satire on the Maltreatment of Subordinates.

A Government-bull yoked to a Government-cart!
Moored by the bank of Chan River, a barge loaded with gravel.
A single load of gravel,
How many pounds it weighs!
Carrying at dawn, carrying at dusk, what is it all for?
They are carrying it towards the Five Gates,
To the West of the Main Road.
Under the shadow of green laurels they are making a gravel-drive.
For yesterday arrived, newly appointed,
The Assistant Chancelor of the Realm,
And was terribly afraid that the wet and mud
Would dirty his horse's hoofs.
The Chancelor's horse's hoofs
Stepped on the gravel and remained perfectly clean;
But the bull employed in dragging the cart
Was almost sweating blood.
The Assistant Chancelor's business
Is to "save men, govern the country
And harmonize Yin and Yang."
Whether the bull's neck is sore
Need not trouble him at all.

The Charcoal-Seller

A Satire Against "Kommandatur."

An old charcoal-seller

Cutting wood and burning charcoal in the forests of the Southern
  Mountain.
His face, stained with dust and ashes, has turned to the color of
  smoke.
The hair on his temples is streaked with gray: his ten fingers are
  black.
The money he gets by selling charcoal, how far does it go?
It is just enough to clothe his limbs and put food in his mouth.
Although, alas, the coat on his back is a coat without lining,
He hopes for the coming of cold weather, to send up the price of
  coal!
Last night, outside the city — a whole foot of snow;
At dawn he drives the charcoal wagon along the frozen ruts.
Oxen, — weary; man, — hungry; the sun, already high;
Outside the Gate, to the south of the Market, at last they stop in the
  mud.
Suddenly, a pair of prancing horsemen. Who can it be coming?
A public official in a yellow coat and a boy in a white shirt.
In their hands they hold a written warrant: on their tongues — the
  word of an order;
They turn back the wagon and curse the oxen, leading them off to
  the north.
A whole wagon of charcoal,
More than a thousand catties!
If officials choose to take it away, the woodman may not complain.
Half a piece of red silk and a single yard of damask,
The Courtiers have tied to the oxen's collar, as the price of a wagon
  of coal!

Golden Bells

                When I was almost forty
I had a daughter whose name was Golden Bells.
Now it is just a year since she was born;
She is learning to sit and cannot yet talk.
Ashamed — to find that I have not a sage's heart;
I cannot resist vulgar thoughts and feelings.
Henceforward I am tied to things outside myself;
My only reward — the pleasure I am getting now.
If I am spared the grief of her dying young,
Then I shall have the trouble of getting her married.

My plan for retiring and going back to the hills
Must now be postponed for fifteen years!

Lazy Man's Song

(811)

I could have a job, but am too lazy to choose it;
I have got land, but am too lazy to farm it.
My house leaks; I am too lazy to mend it.
My clothes are torn; I am too lazy to darn them.
I have got wine, but I am too lazy to drink;
So it's just the same as if my cup were empty.
I have got a lute, but am too lazy to play;
So it's just the same as if it had no strings.
My family tells me there is no more steamed rice;
I want to cook, but am too lazy to grind.
My friends and relatives write me long letters;
I should like to read them, but they're such a bother to open.
I have always been told that Xi Shuye[1]
Passed his whole life in absolute idleness.
But he played his lute and sometimes worked at his forge;
So even he was not as lazy as I.

Winter Night

This poem was written in 812 during his retirement.

My house is poor; those that I love have left me.
My body is sick; I cannot join the feast.
There is not a living soul before my eyes
As I lie alone locked in my cottage room.
My broken lamp burns with a feeble flame;
My tattered curtains are crooked and do not meet.
"Tsek, tsek" on the door-step and window-sill
Again I hear the new snow fall.
As I grow older, gradually I sleep less;
I wake at midnight and sit up straight in bed.

---

[1] Xi Kang, one of the Seven Sages of the Bamboo Grove. [See chapter 10.]

If I had not learned the "art of sitting and forgetting,"[2]
How could I bear this utter loneliness?
Stiff and stark my body cleaves to the earth;
Unimpeded my soul yields to Change.[3]
So has it been for four tedious years,
Through one thousand and three hundred nights!

The Chrysanthemums in the Eastern Garden

(812)

The days of my youth left me long ago;
And now in their turn dwindle my years of prime.
With what thoughts of sadness and loneliness
I walk again in this cold, deserted place!
In the midst of the garden long I stand alone;
The sunshine, faint; the wind and dew chill.
The autumn lettuce is tangled and turned to seed;
The fair trees are blighted and withered away.
All that is left are a few chrysanthemum-flowers
That have newly opened beneath the wattled fence.
I had brought wine and meant to fill my cup,
When the sight of these made me stay my hand.
       I remember, when I was young,
How quickly my mood changed from sad to gay.
If I saw wine, no matter at what season,
Before I drank it, my heart was already glad.
       But now that age comes
A moment of joy is harder and harder to get.
And always I fear that when I am quite old
The strongest liquor will leave me comfortless.
Therefore I ask you, late chrysanthemum-flower,
At this sad season why do you bloom alone?

---

[2] Yan Hui told Confucius that he had acquired the "art of sitting and forgetting." Asked what that meant, Yan Hui replied: "I have learned to discard my body and obliterate my intelligence; to abandon matter and be impervious to sense-perception. By this method I become one with the all-pervading." *Zhuangzi*, chapter 6.

[3] "Change" is the principle of endless mutation that governs the universe.

Though well I know that it was not for my sake,
Taught by you, for a while I will smooth my frown.

Remembering Golden Bells

Ruined and ill — a man of two score;
Pretty and guileless — a girl of three.
Not a boy — but still better than nothing:
To soothe one's feeling — from time to time a kiss!
There came a day — they suddenly took her from me;
Her soul's shadow wandered I know not where.
And when I remember how just at the time she died
She lisped strange sounds, beginning to learn to talk,
Then I know that the ties of flesh and blood
Only bind us to a load of grief and sorrow.
At last, by thinking of the time before she was born,
By thought and reason I drove the pain away.
Since my heart forgot her, many days have passed
And three times winter has changed to spring.
This morning, for a little, the old grief came back,
Because, in the road, I met her foster-nurse.

Madly Singing in the Mountains

There is no one among men that has not a special failing;
And my failing consists in writing verses.
I have broken away from the thousand ties of life;
But this infirmity still remains behind.
Each time that I look at a fine landscape,
Each time that I meet a loved friend,
I raise my voice and recite a stanza of poetry
And marvel as though a God had crossed my path.
Ever since the day I was banished to Xunyang
Half of my time I have lived among the hills.
And often, when I have finished a new poem,
Alone I climb the road to the Eastern Rock.
I lean my body on the banks of white Stone;
I pull down with my hands a green cassia branch.
My mad singing startles the valleys and hills;
The apes and birds all come to peep.

Fearing to become a laughing-stock to the world,
I choose a place that is unfrequented by men.

Eating Bamboo-Shoots

My new Province is a land of bamboo-groves:
Their shoots in spring fill the valleys and hills.
The mountain woodman cuts an armful of them
And brings them down to sell at the early market.
Things are cheap in proportion as they are common;
For two farthings I buy a whole bundle.
I put the shoots in a great earthen pot
And heat them up along with boiling rice.
The purple skins broken — like an old brocade;
The white skin opened — like new pearls.
Now every day I eat them recklessly;
For a long time I have not touched meat.
All the time I was living at Luoyang
They could not give me enough to suit my taste.
Now I can have as many shoots as I please;
For each breath of the south-wind makes a new bamboo!

The Red Cockatoo

(820)

Sent as a present from Annam —
A red cockatoo.
Colored like the peachtree blossom,
Speaking with the speech of men.
And they did to it what is always done
To the learned and the eloquent.
They took a cage with stout bars
And shut it up inside.

Climbing the Lingying Terrace and Looking North

Mounting on high I begin to realize the smallness of Man's Domain;
Gazing into distance I begin to know the vanity of the Carnal World.
I turn my head and hurry home — back to the Court and Market,
A single grain of rice falling — into the Great Barn.

Realizing the Futility of Life

This poem was written on the wall of a priest's cell, c. 828.

Ever since the time when I was a lusty boy
Down till now when I am ill and old,
The things I have cared for have been different at different times,
But my being busy, that has never changed.
Then on the shore — building sand-pagodas;
Now, at Court, covered with tinkling jade.
This and that — equally childish games,
Things whose substance passes in a moment of time!
While the hands are busy, the heart cannot understand;
When there is no Attachment, Doctrine is sound.
Even should one zealously strive to learn the Way,
That very striving will make one's error more.

The Cranes

(830)

The western wind has blown but a few days;
Yet the first leaf already flies from the bough.
On the drying paths I walk in my thin shoes;
In the first cold I have donned my quilted coat.
Through shallow ditches the floods are clearing away;
Through sparse bamboos trickles a slanting light.
In the early dusk, down an alley of green moss,
The garden-boy is leading the cranes home.

On His Baldness

(832)

At dawn I sighed to see my hairs fall;
At dusk I sighed to see my hairs fall.
For I dreaded the time when the last lock should go ...
They are all gone and I do not mind at all!
I have done with that cumbrous washing and getting dry;
My tiresome comb for ever is laid aside.
Best of all, when the weather is hot and wet,
To have no top-knot weighing down on one's head!
I put aside my messy cloth wrap;
I have got rid of my dusty tasseled fringe.

In a silver jar I have stored a cold stream,
On my bald pate I trickle a ladle full.
Like one baptized with the Water of Buddha's Law,
I sit and receive this cool, cleansing joy.
Now I know why the priest who seeks Repose
Frees his heart by first shaving his head.

To a Talkative Guest

(836)

The town visitor's easy talk flows in an endless stream;
The country host's quiet thoughts ramble timidly on.
"I beg you, Sir, do not tell me about things at Chang'an;
For you entered just when my lute was tuned and lying balanced on
    my knees."

Inscription Written by Me in My Small Garden

I have never battled to buy a fine house,
I have never fought to own great lands.
What I had to fight for, having got a place of my own,
Was to sit tight for more than ten years.
I turn and look at the houses of the Top Clans
Lined up in the heart of this great town —
White walls flanking red gates,
Splendidly staring across the wide streets.
Where are the owners? All have gone away;
They were called to high posts and never came back.
The lakes they dug only the fish enjoy;
The woods they planted belong only to the birds.
Happier far the owner of a small garden;
Propped on his stick he idles here all day,
Now and again collecting a few friends,
And every night enjoying lute and wine.
Why should he pine for great terraces and lakes
When a little garden gives him all that he needs?

Sitting Quietly: Written During My Illness

I have got wine, but am not well enough to drink;
I have got poems, but am too weak to chant them.

My head is giddy, I have had to give up fishing;
My hand is stiff, I have stopped playing my lute.
All day the silence is never broken;
No worries reach me in my place of quiet retreat.
My body is reconciled to its crippled state;
My heart finds refuge in its own mysteries ...
I sit quietly beside the small pond
Waiting for the wind to stir the lapels of my dress.

A Dream of Mountaineering

This poem was written when he was seventy.

At night, in my dream, I stoutly climbed a mountain,
Going out alone with my staff of holly-wood.
A thousand crags, a hundred hundred valleys —
In my dream journey none were unexplored
And all the while my feet never grew tired
And my step was as strong as in my young days.
Can it be that when the mind travels backward
The body also returns to its old state?
And can it be, as between body and soul,
That the body may languish, while the soul is still strong?
Soul and body — both are vanities;
Dreaming and waking — both alike unreal.
In the day my feet are palsied and tottering;
In the night my steps go striding over the hills.
As day and night are divided in equal parts —
Between the two, I get as much as I lose.

Laozi

"Those who speak know nothing;
Those who know are silent."
Those words, I am told,
Were spoken by Laozi.
If we are to believe that Laozi
    Was himself one who knew,
How comes it that he wrote a book
    Of five thousand words?

Last Poem

They have put my bed beside the unpainted screen;
They have shifted my stove in front of the blue curtain.
I listen to my grandchildren reading me a book;
I watch the servants heating up my soup.
With rapid pencil I answer the poems of friends,
I feel in my pockets and pull out medicine-money.
When this superintendence of trifling affairs is done,
I lie back on my pillows and sleep with my face to the South.

Two Ballads

The Everlasting Wrong

Translated by Herbert Giles

(806)
Perhaps the best known of all the works of Bo Juyi is this long narrative poem. It refers
to the ignominious downfall of the Emperor Xuanzong, who had surrounded himself
by a brilliant Court, welcoming such men as Li Bo, at first for their talents alone, but
afterwards for their readiness to participate in scenes of revelry and dissipation,
provided for the amusement of the Imperial Concubine, the ever-famous Yang Guifei.
Gradually the Emperor left off concerning himself with affairs of state; a serious
rebellion broke out, and his Majesty sought safety in Sichuan, returning only after
having abdicated in favor of his son. The poem describes the rise of Yang Guifei,
her tragic fate at the hands of the soldiery, and her subsequent communication
with her heartbroken lover from the world of shadows beyond the grave. The poem
became immensely popular. Bo himself tells us that when a certain general wanted to
hire a singing-girl, she said: "You must not think I am just an ordinary girl. I can sing
'The Everlasting Wrong,'" and put up her price accordingly.

Ennui [4]

His Imperial Majesty, a slave to beauty,
    longed for a subverter of empires;[5]
For years he had sought in vain
    to secure such a treasure for his palace …

---

[4] These headings have been added by the translator. *Eds.*
[5] Referring to a famous beauty of the Han dynasty, one glance from whom would overthrow
a city, two glances an empire.

Beauty

From the Yang family came a maiden,
    just grown up to womanhood,
Reared in the inner apartments,
    altogether unkown to fame.
But nature had amply endowed her
    with a beauty hard to conceal,
And one day she was summoned
    to a place at the monarch's side.
Her sparkling eye and merry laughter
    fascinated every beholder,
And among the powder and paint of the harem
    her loveliness reigned supreme.
In the chills of spring, by Imperial mandate,
    she bathed in the Huaqing Pool,
Laving her body in the glassy wavelets
    of the fountain perennially warm.
Then, when she came forth, helped by attendants,
    her delicate and graceful movements
Finally gained for her gracious favor,
    captivating his Majesty's heart.

Revelry

Hair like a cloud, face like a flower,
    head-dress which quivered as she walked,
Amid the delights of the Hibiscus Pavilion
    she passed the soft spring nights.
Spring nights, too short alas! for them,
    albeit prolonged till dawn —
From this time forth no more audiences
    in the hours of early morn.
Revels and feasts in quick succession,
    ever without a break,
She chosen always for the spring excursion,
    chosen for the nightly carouse.
Three thousand peerless beauties adorned
    the apartments of the monarch's harem,
Yet always his Majesty reserved
    his attentions for her alone.

Passing her life in a "golden house,"[6]
    with fair girls to wait on her,
She was daily wafted to ecstasy
    on the wine fumes of the banquet-hall.
Her sisters and her brothers, one and all,
    were raised to the rank of nobles.
Alas! for the ill-omened glories
    which she conferred on her family.
For thus it came about that fathers and mothers
    through the length and breadth of the empire
Rejoiced no longer over the birth of sons,
    but over the birth of daughters.
In the gorgeous palace
    piercing the gray clouds above,
Divine music, borne on the breeze,
    is spread around on all sides;
Of song and the dance
    to the guitar and flute,
All through the live long day,
    his Majesty never tires.
But suddenly comes the roll
    of the fish-skin war-drums,
Breaking rudely upon the air
    of the "Rainbow Skirt and Feather Jacket."

Flight

Clouds of dust envelop
    the lofty gates of the capital.
A thousand war-chariots and ten thousand horses
    move towards the southwest.
Feathers and jewels among the throng,
    onwards and then a halt.
A hundred *li* beyond the western gate,
    leaving behind them the city walls,
The soldiers refuse to advance;
    nothing remains to be done

---

[6] Referring to Ajiao, one of the consorts of an Emperor of the Han dynasty. "Ah," said the latter when a boy, "if I could only get Ajiao, I would have a golden house to keep her in."

Until she of the moth-eyebrows
    perishes in sight of all.
On the ground lie gold ornaments
    with no one to pick them up,
Kingfisher wings, golden birds,
    and hairpins of costly jade.
The monarch covers his face,
    powerless to save;
And as he turns to look back,
    tears and blood flow mingled together.

Exile

Across vast stretches of yellow sand
    with whistling winds,
Across cloud-capped mountaintops
    they make their way.
Few indeed are the travelers
    who reach the heights of Mount Emei;
The bright gleam of the standards
    grows fainter day by day.
Dark the Sichuan waters,
    dark the Sichuan hills;
Daily and nightly his Majesty
    is consumed by bitter grief.
Traveling along, the very brightness
    of the moon saddens his heart,
And the sound of a bell through the evening rain
    severs his viscera in twain.

Return

Time passes, days go by, and once again
    he is there at the well-known spot,
And there he lingers on, unable
    to tear himself wholly away.
But from the clods of earth
    at the foot of the Mawei hill,
No sign of her lovely face appears,
    only the place of death.
The eyes of sovereign and minister meet,
    and robes are wet with tears.

Eastward they depart and hurry on
   to the capital at full speed.

Home

There is the pool, and there are the flowers,
   as of old.
There is the hibiscus of the pavilion,
   there are the willows of the palace.
In the hibiscus he sees her face,
   in the willow he sees her eyebrows:
How in the presence of these
   should tears not flow —
In spring amid the flowers
   of the peach and plum,
In autumn rains when the leaves
   of the *wutong* fall?
To the south of the western palace
   are many trees,
And when their leaves cover the steps,
   no one now sweeps them away.
The hair of the Pear-Garden musicians
   is white as though with age;
The guardians of the Pepper Chamber[7]
   seem to him no longer young.
Where fireflies flit through the hall,
   he sits in silent grief;
Alone, the lamp-wick burnt out,
   he is still unable to sleep.
Slowly pass the watches,
   for the nights are now too long,
And brightly shine the constellations,
   as though dawn would never come.
Cold settles upon the duck-and-drake tiles,[8]
   and thick hoar-frost,
The kingfisher coverlet is chill,
   with none to share its warmth.

---

[7] A fancy name for the women's apartments in the palace.
[8] The mandarin duck and drake are emblems of conjugal fidelity. The allusion is to ornaments on the roof.

Parted by life and death,
    time still goes on,
But never once does her spirit come back
    to visit him in dreams.

Spirit-Land

A Taoist priest of Linchong,
    of the Hongdu school,
Was able, by his perfect art, to summon
    the spirits of the dead.
Anxious to relieve the fretting mind
    of his sovereign,
This magician receives orders
    to urge a diligent quest.
Borne on the clouds, charioted upon the ether,
    he rushes with the speed of lightning
High up to heaven, low down to earth,
    seeking everywhere.
Above, he searches the empyrean;
    below, the Yellow Springs,
But nowhere in these vast areas
    can her place be found.
At length he hears of an Isle of the Blest
    away in mid-ocean,
Lying in realms of vacuity,
    dimly to be descried.
There gaily decorated buildings
    rise up like rainbow clouds,
And there many gentle and beautiful Immortals
    pass their days in peace.
Among them is one whose name
    sounds upon lips as Eternal,
And by her snow-white skin and flowerlike face
    he knows that this is she.
Knocking at the jade door
    at the western gate of the golden palace,
He bids a fair waiting-maid announce him
    to her mistress, fairer still.
She, hearing of this embassy
    sent by the Son of Heaven,

Starts up from her dreams
    among the tapestry curtains.
Grasping her clothes and pushing away the pillow,
    she arises in haste,
And begins to adorn herself
    with pearls and jewels.
Her cloudlike coiffure, disheveled,
    shows that she has just risen from sleep,
And with her flowery headdress awry,
    she passes into the hall.
The sleeves of her immortal robes
    are filled out by the breeze,
As once more she seems to dance
    to the "Rainbow Skirt and Feather Jacket."
Her features are fixed and calm,
    though myriad tears fall,
Wetting a spray of pear-bloom,
    as it were with the raindrops of spring.
Subduing her emotions, restraining her grief,
    she tenders thanks to his Majesty,
Saying how since they parted
    she has missed his form and voice;
And how, although their love on earth
    has so soon come to an end,
The days and months among the Blest
    are still of long duration.
And now she turns and gazes
    towards the abode of mortals,
But cannot discern the Imperial city
    lost in the dust and haze.
Then she takes out the old keepsakes,
    tokens of undying love,
A gold hairpin, an enamel brooch,
    and bids the magician carry these back.
One half of the hairpin she keeps,
    and one half of the enamel brooch,
Breaking with her hands the yellow gold,
    and dividing the enamel in two.
"Tell him," she said, "to be firm of heart,
    as this gold and enamel,
And then in heaven or on earth below
    we two may meet once more."

At parting, she confided to the magician
    many earnest messages of love,
Among the rest recalling a pledge
    mutually understood;
How on the seventh day of the seventh moon,
    in the Hall of Immortality,
At midnight, when none were near,
    he had whispered in her ear,
"I swear that we will ever fly
    like the one-winged birds,[9]
Or grow united like the tree
    with branches which twine together."[10]
Heaven and Earth, long-lasting as they are,
    will some day pass away;
But this great wrong shall stretch out for ever,
    endless, for ever and ay.

Song of the Lute: Preface and Poem

Translated by Burton Watson

(816)

In the tenth year of the Yuan-he era (815), I was exiled to the district of
Jiujiang (Jiangzhou) with the post of marshal. In the autumn of the
following year, I was seeing a visitor off at the Pen River landing when I
heard someone on one of the boats playing a *pipa* lute in the night.
Listening to its tone, I could detect a note of the capital in its clear
twanging. When I inquired who the player was, I found it was a former
singing girl of Chang'an who had once studied the lute under two
masters named Mu and Cao. Later, when she grew older and her beauty
faded, she had entrusted herself to a traveling merchant and became his
wife.

I proceeded to order wine and lost no time in requesting her to play a
few selections. After the selections were over, she fell into a moody
silence and then told us of the happy times of her youth and of her
present life of drifting and deprivation, moving about here and there in
the region of the Yangtze and the lakes.

---

[9] Each bird having only one wing must always fly with a mate.
[10] Such a tree was believed to exist and has often been figured by the Chinese.

Two years had passed since I was assigned to this post, and I had been
feeling rather contented and at ease. But this evening, moved by her
words, I realized for the first time just what it means to be an exile.
Therefore I have written this long song to present to her. It contains a
total of 612 characters and is entitled "Song of the Lute."

Xunyang on the Yangtze, seeing off a guest at night;
maple leaves, reed flowers, autumn somber and sad:
the host had dismounted, the guest already aboard the boat,
we raised our wine, prepared to drink, though we lacked flutes and
  strings.
But drunkenness brought no pleasure, we grieved at the imminent
  parting;
at parting time, vague and vast, the river lay drenched in moonlight.
Suddenly we heard the sound of a lute out on the water;
the host forgot about going home, the guest failed to start on his
  way.
We traced the sound, discreetly inquired who the player might be.
The lute sounds ceased, but words were slow in coming.
We edged our boat closer, inviting the player to join us,
poured more wine, turned the lamps around, began our revels again.
A thousand pleas, ten thousand calls, and at last she appeared,
but even then she held the lute so it half hid her face.

She turned the pegs, brushed the strings, sounding two or three
  notes —
before they had formed a melody, already the feeling came through.
Each string seemed tense with it, each sound to hold a thought,
as though she were protesting a lifetime of wishes unfulfilled.
Eyebrows lowered, hand moving freely, she played on and on,
speaking of all the numberless things that were in her heart.
Lightly she pressed the strings, slowly plucked, pulled and snapped
  them,
first performing "Rainbow Skirts," then "Waists of Green."
The big strings plang-planged like swift-falling rain;
the little strings went buzz-buzz like secret conversations;
plang-plang, buzz-buzz mixed and mingled in her playing
like big pearls and little pearls falling on a plate of jade,
or the soft call of warbler voices resonant under the blossoms,
the hidden sobbing of springs and rills barely moving beneath the
  ice.
Then the icy springs congealed with cold, the strings seemed to
  freeze,

freeze till the notes no longer could pass, the sound for a while cut
    off;
now something different, hidden anguish, dark reproaches taking
    form —
at such times the silence was finer than any sound.
Then a silver vase would abruptly break, water come splashing forth,
iron-clad horsemen would suddenly charge, swords and halberds
    clanging.
As the piece ended, she swept the plectrum in an arc before her
    breast,
and all four strings made a single sound, like the sound of rending
    silk.
In the boat to the east, the boat to the west, stillness, not a word;
all we could see was the autumn moon white in the heart of the
    river.

Lost in thought, she put down the plectrum, tucked it among the
    strings,
straightened her robes, rose, put on a grave expression,
told us she had once been a daughter of the capital,
living in a house at the foot of Toad Barrow.
By the age of thirteen she had mastered the lute,
was famed as a member of the finest troupe of players.
Whenever a piece was over, her teachers were enthralled;
each time she donned full makeup, the other girls were filled with
    envy.
Young men from the five tomb towns vied to give her presents;[11]
one selection won her she knew not how many red silks.
Silver hairpins set with inlay — she beat time with them till they
    broke;
blood-colored gauze skirts — she stained them with overturned wine.
This year brought joy and laughter, next year would be the same;
autumn moons, spring breezes — how casually she let them pass!
"Then my younger brother ran off to the army, the woman I called
    'mother' died;
and as evenings went and mornings came, my looks began to fade.

---

[11] The tomb towns, sites of imperial graves, were suburbs of the capital where wealthy
families lived.

My gate became still and lonely, few horses or riders there;
getting on in years, I gave myself as wife to a traveling merchant.
But merchants think much of profit and little of separation;
last month he went off to Fouliang to buy tea.
Since coming here to the river mouth, I've guarded my boat alone;
in the bright moonlight that encircles the boat, the river waters are
    cold.
And when night deepens, suddenly I dream of those days of youth,
and my dream-wept tears, mixed with rouge, come down in streams
    of crimson."

Earlier, when I heard her lute, already I felt sad;
listening to her story, I doubled my sighs of pity.
Both of us hapless outcasts at the farther end of the sky;
meeting like this, why must we be old friends to understand one
    another?
Since last year when I left the capital,
I've lived in exile, sick in bed, in Xunyang town.
Xunyang is a far-off region — there's no music here;
all year long I never hear the sound of strings or woodwinds.
I live near the Pen River, an area low and damp,
with yellow reeds and bitter bamboo growing all around my house.
And there, morning and evening, what do I hear?
The cuckoo singing his heart out, the mournful cry of monkeys.
Blossom-filled mornings by the spring river, nights with an autumn
    moon,
sometimes I fetch wine and tip the cup alone.
To be sure, there's no lack of mountain songs and village pipes,
but their wails and bawls, squeaks and squawks are a trial to
    listen to.
Tonight, though, I've heard the words of your lute,
like hearing immortal music — for a moment my ears are clear.
Do not refuse me, sit and play one more piece,
and I'll fashion these things into a lute song for you.

Moved by these words of mine, she stood a long while,
then returned to her seat, tightened the strings, strings sounding
    swifter than ever,
crying, crying in pain, not like the earlier sound;
the whole company, listening again, forced back their tears.
And who among the company cried the most?
This marshal of Jiujiang, wetting his blue coat.

BO JUYI AND YUAN ZHEN: RECORD OF A POETIC FRIENDSHIP

Translated by Arthur Waley

Poem for Yuan Zhen

(805)

>   Since I left home to seek official state
>   Seven years I have lived in Chang'an.
>   What have I gained? Only you, Yuan;
>   So hard it is to bind friendships fast.
>   We have roamed on horseback under the flowering trees;
>   We have walked in the snow and warmed our hearts with wine.
>   We have met and parted at the Western Gate
>   And neither of us bothered to put on Cap or Belt.
>   We did not go up together for Examination;
>   We were not serving in the same Department of State.
>   The bond that joined us lay deeper than outward things;
>   The rivers of our souls spring from the same well!

At the End of Spring
To Yuan Zhen

(810)

>   The flower of the pear tree gathers and turns to fruit;
>   The swallows' eggs have hatched into young birds.
>   When the Seasons' changes thus confront the mind
>   What comfort can the doctrine to Tao give?
>   It will teach me to watch the days and months fly
>   Without grieving that Youth slips away;
>   If the Fleeting World is but a long dream,
>   It does not matter whether one is young or old.
>   But ever since the day that my friend left my side
>   And has lived an exile in the City of Jiangling,
>   There is one wish I cannot quite destroy:
>   That from time to time we may chance to meet again.

The Letter

(810)

Preface. After I parted with Yuan Zhen, I suddenly dreamt one night that I saw him. When I awoke, I found that a letter from him had just arrived, and, enclosed in it, a poem on the *paulovnia* flower.

We talked together in the Yongshou Temple;
We parted to the north of the Xinchang ward.
Going home — I shed a few tears,
Grieving about things — not sorry for you.
Long, long the Lantian road;
You said yourself you would not be able to write.
Reckoning up your halts for eating and sleeping —
By this time you've crossed the Shang mountains.
Last night the clouds scattered away;
A thousand leagues, the same moonlight scene.
When dawn came, I dreamt I saw your face;
It must have been that you were thinking of me.
In my dream, I thought I held your hand
And asked you to tell me what your thoughts were.
And *you* said: "I miss you bitterly,
But there's no one here to send to you with a letter."
When I awoke, before I had time to speak,
A knocking on the door sounded "Doong, doong!"
They came and told me a messenger from Shangzhou
Had brought a letter — a single scroll from you!
Up from my pillow I suddenly sprang out of bed,
and threw on my clothes, all topsy-turvy.
I undid the knot and saw the letter within;
A single sheet with thirteen lines of writing.
At the top it told the sorrows of an exile's heart,
At the bottom it described the pains of separation.
The sorrows and pains took up so much space
There was no room left to talk about the weather!
But you said that when you wrote
You were staying for the night to the east of Shangzhou;
Sitting alone, lighted by a solitary candle
Lodging in the mountain hostel of Yangcheng.
Night was late when you finished writing,
The mountain moon was slanting toward the west.
What is it lies aslant across the moon?
A single tree of purple paulovnia flowers —
Paulovnia flowers just on the point of falling
Are a symbol to express "thinking of an absent friend."
Lovingly — you wrote on the back side,
To send in the letter, your "Poem of the Paulovnia Flower."
The Poem of the Paulovnia Flower has eight rhymes;
Yet these eight couplets have cast a spell on my heart.

They have taken hold of this morning's thoughts
And carried them to yours, the night you wrote your letter.
The whole poem I read three times;
Each verse ten times I recite.
So precious to me are the fourscore words
That each letter changes into a bar of gold!

Yuan Zhen to Bo Juyi

(816)

Other people too have friends that they love;
But ours was a love such as few friends have known.
You were all my sustenance; it mattered more
To see you daily than to get my morning food.
And if there was a single day when we did not meet
I would sit listless, my mind in a tangle of gloom.
To think we are now thousands of miles apart,
Lost like clouds, each drifting on his far way!
Those clouds on high, where many winds blow,
What is their chance of ever meeting again?
And if in open heaven the beings of the air
Are driven and thwarted, what of Man below?

Bo Juyi to Yuan Zhen: A Letter

(817)

Letian speaks. Weizhi, Weizhi, it is three years since I saw you and almost
two years since I had a letter from you.[12] Is life so long that we can afford
such estrangements as this? ... Soon after I came here Xiong Rudeng
arrived, bringing with him a note written the year before last, when you
were so very unwell. In it you told me something about the nature of your
illness and its effect on your spirits and referred to our successive meetings and partings, but said that at the moment you had not the strength
to write more, but that you had put together several packets of your
writings and written on the outside: "To be sent some time or another to
Bo Juyi." For the moment, you hoped I would accept this brief note in
lieu of a proper letter. I was feeling rather sad that you should treat me
like this when I came across another enclosure — the poem you wrote on
hearing that I had been exiled:

---

[12] Letian was Bo Juyi's "literary name" (*zi*), and Weizhi was Yuan Zhen's. *Eds.*

In the last flicker of a dying lamp the shadows beat like wings;
Then it was that I heard this news: you are banished to Jiujiang!
I who was lying sick to death rose startled to my feet;
Through the cold window a dark blast blew the rain on my face.

These are lines that even a stranger might well find almost unen-
durable in their pathos, and you may imagine their effect upon me! I still
find them profoundly moving each time I repeat them. I will not dwell
upon this, but will tell you something of my recent preoccupations. I
have now been three years at Jiujiang. I am in good health and my mind
is completely at rest. All the members of my household are also well, and
my elder brother arrived here last summer from Xuzhou bringing with
him six or seven little orphan cousins belonging to various branches of
the family. Thus for the moment I have under my eye all those about
whose welfare I am particularly concerned.... That is the first reason for
my peace of mind. Here on the River it is rather cooler than is general in
the South and there is not much malaria. Poisonous snakes and
troublesome insects do of course exist; but there are not very many of
them. The fish of the Pen river are particularly fat and the River wine is
excellent. Most of the other things one gets to eat and drink are pretty
much the same as in the North. I have now rather a large number of
mouths to provide for and my marshal's salary is not large; but by
keeping a careful watch on expenditure I can manage to clothe and feed
them without calling for any contributions from outside. This is the
second reason for my peace of mind. In the autumn of last year, I began
making excursions into the Lu Shan and found a spot between the two
Forest Monasteries, just under the Incense Burner Peak, where the
clouds and waters, fountains and rocks were more lovely than at any
other place on the mountain. The situation delighted me so much that I
built myself a cottage there. There is a group of high pine trees in front
of it and a fine cluster of tall bamboos. I have covered the walls with green
creepers and made paved paths of white rock. A stream almost encircles
it and I have a waterfall at my very eaves. There is white lotus in my pool
and red pomegranate on its banks....

Every time that I go to be alone here for a few hours the visit tends to
prolong itself to one of many days, for everything that has always given
me most pleasure is to be found in this place. I forget all about going
home and would be content to stay here till the end of my days. I have
begun by telling you of these causes for my present happiness, thinking
that as you have had no news of me for so long, you must be feeling
anxious. Other items of news are as follows....

Weizhi, Weizhi, the night I wrote this letter I was sitting in my cottage
under a window that looks out on to the mountains. I let my brush run
on as it would, setting down my thoughts at random, just as they occurred
to me. And now as I make ready to seal the letter up I suddenly find that
dawn has almost come. Looking out I see one or two monks, some sitting,
some asleep. From above comes the sad cry of the mountain monkeys,
and from below the twittering of the valley birds. Friend of all my life, ten
thousand leagues away, thoughts of our days together in the world's dusty
arena rise before me and for a moment quite blot out this lovely scene.
Yielding to the habit of old times again I address you in verse:

Long ago I sealed up a letter that I had written to you at night
Behind the Hall of Golden Bells, as day was coming in the sky.
Tonight again I seal a letter — in a hut on the Lu Shan,
Sitting at the first tinge of dawn, by a lamp that still burns.
The bird in its coop, the monkey in its cage are still not dead;
Though the years pass, they yet may meet somewhere in the world
  of men.

Weizhi, Weizhi! I wonder if you know all that is in my heart as I write
this tonight? Letian bows his head.

Dreaming That I Went with Li and Yu to Visit Yuan Zhen

This poem was written in exile.

At night I dreamt I was back in Chang'an;
I saw again the faces of old friends.
And in my dreams, under an April sky,
They led me by the hand to wander in the spring winds.
Together we came to the ward of Peace and Quiet;
We stopped our horses at the gate of Yuan Zhen.
Yuan Zhen was sitting all alone;
When he saw me coming, a smile came to his face.
He pointed back at the flowers in the western court;
Then opened wine in the northern summer-house.
He seemed to be saying that neither of us had changed;
He seemed to be regretting that joy will not stay;
That our souls had met only for a little while,
To part again with hardly time for greeting.
I woke up and thought him still at my side;
I put out my hand; there was nothing there at all.

The Death of Yuan Zhen

On the twenty-second of the seventh month [of 831] Yuan Zhen died at Wuchang after only one day's illness. Some three months later Bo sacrificed to his spirit and in the address that accompanied the offering he speaks of "laying his hand upon the coffin." It would seem, then, that the body was brought to Chang'an by way of Luoyang. At the end of the address Bo says that according to the Buddhist scriptures such a relationship as theirs could only have come about through friendship in many previous incarnations. "In this life we are parted; but who knows whether in some future incarnation we shall not meet again?"

— Arthur Waley

Dreaming of Yuan Zhen

(839)

At night you came and took my hand and we wandered together in
    my dream;
When I woke in the morning there was no one to stop the tears
    that fell on my handkerchief.
At the Zhang Inlet[13] your aged body three times passed through
    sickness;
At Xianyang[14] to the grasses on your grave eight autumns have come.
You — buried beneath the Springs, your bones mingled with clay;
I — lodging in the world of men, my hair white as snow.
Awei and Hanlang[15] both followed in their turn;
Among the shadows of the Terrace of Night did you know them or
    not?

On Hearing Someone Sing a Poem by Yuan Zhen

This was written long after Yuan Zhen's death, c. 840.

No new poems his brush will trace;
    Even his fame is dead.
His old poems are deep in dust
    At the bottom of boxes and cupboards.
Once lately, when someone was singing,
    Suddenly I heard a verse —

---

[13] Near Dangyang, central Hubei.
[14] Near Chang'an.
[15] Familiar names of Yuan Zhen's son and son-in-law.

Before I had time to catch the words
A pain had stabbed my heart.

YUAN ZHEN (779–831)

The Pitcher

Translated by Arthur Waley

I dreamt I climbed to a high, high plain;
And on the plain I found a deep well.
My throat was dry with climbing and I longed to drink,
And my eyes were eager to look into the cool shaft.
I walked round it, I looked right down;
I saw my image mirrored on the face of the pool.
An earthen pitcher was sinking into the black depths;
There was no rope to pull it to the well-head.
I was strangely troubled lest the pitcher should be lost,
And started wildly running to look for help.
From village to village I scoured that high plain;
The men were gone; fierce dogs snarled.
I came back and walked weeping round the well;
Faster and faster the blinding tears flowed —
Till my own sobbing suddenly woke me up;
My room was silent, no one in the house stirred.
The flame of my candle flickered with a green smoke;
The tears I had shed glittered in the candle-light.
A bell sounded; I knew it was the midnight-chime;
I sat up in bed and tried to arrange my thoughts:
The plain in my dream was the graveyard at Chang'an,
Those hundred acres of untilled land.
The soil heavy and the mounds heaped high;
And the dead below them laid in deep troughs.
Deep are the troughs, yet sometimes dead men
Find their way to the world above the grave.
And tonight my love who died long ago
Came into my dream as the pitcher sunk in the well.
That was why the tears suddenly streamed from my eyes,
Streamed from my eyes and fell on the collar of my dress.

Three Poems

Translated by John Scott

You're No Exception

Birds cannot walk, beasts cannot fly
Not understanding each other's understanding, they feel no
    mutual scorn
Dogs do not drink dew, cicadas do not gnaw flesh
Change the cicada with the dog, the cicada'll die, the dog'll
    starve
The swallow sits on the beam, the mouse hides below-stairs
To each his bolt-hole, don't try changing places
Women like needlework, men read the classics
The boy's the ancient, the girl's the wife — each one's knowledge
    is a separation
Fearing your deafness I cup my ear,
Copying your pain I wrinkle my forehead
I am not unless you are, you are without if I am unless

The Song of the Pearl-Fishers

Waves of the sea, fathomless, pearls submerged in the sea.
The pearl-divers pit their lives against death to collect them.
Ten thousand risks to the snatching of one pearl.
Rich men buy concubines by the pearl-load,
Where are the divers?
As year goes by and year comes in, the pearls avoid them.
For the Sea Spirit himself has lately taken up collecting
And when he collects, the pearls die out.
With the bright pearls dead, the sea is empty water.
For the pearls are the sea's, and the sea is the Spirit's.
If the Spirit collects, what chance do mortals have?

Nearly a Sky Half Clear, Not Yet Half Light

Nearly a sky half clear, not yet half light,
Drunk I smell the scent of flowers,
    sleeping I hear the oriole.
My Little One trembled to hear the sacred bell.

That was twenty years ago,
   love knowingly dawn-stolen in an old temple.

▣ *Further Reading* ▣

Levy, Howard. *Translations from Po Chü-i's Collected Works.* 4 vols., New York: Paragon; &
   San Francisco: Chinese Materials Center, 1971–78.
Palandri, Angela Jung. *Yüan Chen.* Boston: Twayne, 1977.
Scott, John (with Graham Martin), ed. and trans. *Love and Protest: Chinese Poems from the
   Sixth Century* B.C. to the Seventeenth Century A.D. London: Rapp & Whiting, 1972.
Waley, Arthur. *The Life and Times of Po Chü-i.* London: Allen & Unwin, 1949.
———, trans. *One Hundred and Seventy Chinese Poems.* London: Constable, 1918.
———. *More Translations from the Chinese.* London: Allen & Unwin, 1919.
———. *The Temple and Other Poems.* London: Allen & Unwin, 1923.
———. *Chinese Poems.* London: Allen & Unwin, 1945.

▣ *Editors' Note* ▣

In Arthur Waley, Bo Juyi found the perfect translator. There can be no better or more
enjoyable introduction to the world of the Chinese poet than Waley's *Life and Times.*
He was in total sympathy with Bo's work and personality (which was very far from the
case with Li Bo, whom Waley disliked), and he brought to his translations of Bo's verse
a sensitivity, an impeccable craft, and a wonderful sense of humor and lightness of
touch. As David Hawkes wrote after Waley's death, "Greatness in men is a rare but
unmistakable quality. In our small profession it is unlikely we shall see a man of such
magnitude again."

"Traces of old Hangzhou wine on my gown."
Bo Juyi, "An Old Shirt"
Seal carved by Zhao Yi (fl. 1813)

Chapter 24

The Patterned Lute

Poets of the Late Tang

The scene created by a poet is like the sun warm on Indigo Fields, like fine jade giving off mist: you can gaze on it but you cannot fix upon it in your eyes.

— Dai Shulun (732–789), from Sikong Tu's "Letter to Ji Pu"
(*translated by Stephen Owen*)

Prose is difficult, but poetry is even more difficult. There have been many metaphors for this from ancient to modern times, but I think one must be discerning in "flavor" before one can discuss poetry.

— Sikong Tu (837–908), from "Letter to Mr. Li Discussing Poetry"
(*translated by J. Timothy Wixted*)

A mist-cloud hanging on the river bank,
Pink almond-flowers along the bough,
A flower-girt cottage beneath the moon,
A painted bridge half seen in shadow,
A golden goblet brimming with wine,
A friend with his hand on the lute ...
Take these and be content;
They will swell thy heart beneath thy robe.

— Sikong Tu, "Embroideries," from "The Twenty-Four Modes of Poetry"
(*translated by Herbert Giles*)

Tang poetry burns with intensity. The moment in which the poem is born is one of the most vital instants in a man's life, in his headlong plunge towards death. He must fix his eyes upon the instant and pour his feelings into it. The emotion must cohere, it must jet forth, it must explode.

— Yoshikawa Kojiro (1904–1980), "T'ang Poetry and Sung Poetry: A Contrast," in
An Introduction to Sung Poetry (*translated by Burton Watson*)

Some of Li Shangyin's poems, such as "The Patterned Lute," actually deal with more than love, using several levels of reality and fusing the past with the present, the real with the imaginary, and the historical with the mythical.

— James J. Y. Liu, *Indiana Companion*, 1986

Introduction

James J. Y. Liu

In cultural history, the ninth century in China is comparable to the seventeenth in Europe. Chinese literary historians customarily divide Tang poetry into four periods, dubbed Early, High, Mid and Late. This division, based mainly on the rise and fall of dynastic power, is somewhat artificial and not entirely satisfactory. It would be better to describe the development of Tang poetry in terms of three successive phases: a formative phase (c. 618–710) marked by experimentation and relative naïvety; a phase of full maturity (c. 710–770) characterized by great creative vitality and technical perfection; and a phase of sophistication (c. 770–900) typified by tendencies toward the exuberant or the grotesque. It is not too fanciful to see a parallel between these three phases of Tang poetry and three successive periods of English poetry: the Tang poets of the formative phase are comparable to English poets of the early sixteenth century like Wyatt and Surrey, those of the mature phase to the great Elizabethans, and those of the sophisticated phase to the seventeenth-century poets traditionally called "metaphysical" and more recently labeled "baroque," such as Donne, Marvell and Crashaw.

In brief, the ninth century in China came after an age of expansion and creativity and preceded one (the Song period, 960–1279) that might be called neo-classical in its conservatism, its emphasis on reason rather than emotion in poetry and art, and its advocacy of imitation of earlier poets rather than spontaneous expression. To compare the ninth century in China to the baroque period in Europe is therefore not as far-fetched as it may seem.

— from *The Poetry of Li Shang-yin: Ninth-Century Baroque Chinese Poet*, 1969

LI HE (791–817)
Eight Poems

Translated by John Frodsham

The Li He of legend is the demon-talented poet, tall and cadaverous, his hair white as snow round his haggard face, who on his deathbed is summoned to heaven by a spirit-messenger riding a red dragon. Such legends have their uses, for they direct us to an important truth about the poet: namely, that his verse and his personality alike were considered odd both by his contemporaries and by later critics. He is, in fact, close to the Western idea of the *poète maudit* — and this is not a stock type of literary man at all in China. Chinese poets were almost invariably members of the bureaucracy, cultivated officials who yet secreted poetry as naturally as oysters produce pearls.

It was Li He's great misfortune never to have attained high office. His failure to do so was all the more humiliating since he was not only renowned for his literary talents but had for his patron one of the most eminent literary men of the time, the great Confucian scholar Han Yu.

In his sensuality and the despairing intensity with which he strives to hold the passing moment burning eternally in his art, like a frozen flame, he is akin to Keats: and like Keats — or Trakl, whom he also resembles — he is half in love at times with easeful death. He wrote in the shadow of the grave: and no philosophy, no religion, no consoling belief could quite keep out its ineluctable cold. Only at the white radiance of his own poetic visions could he warm himself for a while before making his final journey to those cypress-shadowed tombs where he had wandered so often during his brief lifetime like some pallid and melancholy ghost.

Chang'gu
A Poem Written on the Twenty-Seventh Day of the Fifth Month

In this poem, Li He is describing the country around his house (in modern Henan), where the Chang'gu river flows past the foot of Mount Nüji (Maiden's Table).

Paddy fields at Chang'gu, in the fifth month,
A shimmer of green covers the level water.
Distant hills rise towering, crag on crag,
Precarious greenery, fearful of falling.
Dazzling and pure, no thoughts of autumn yet,
A cool wind from afar ruffles this beauty.
The bamboos' fragrance fills this lonely place,
Each powdered node is streaked with emerald.
The long-haired grass lets fall its mournful tresses,
A bright dew weeps, shedding its secret tears.
Tall trees form a bright and winding tunnel,
A scented track where fading reds sway drunkenly.
Swarms of insects etch the ancient willows,
Cicadas cry from high sequestered spots.
Long sashes of yellow arrowroot trail the ground.
Purple rushes criss-cross narrow shores.
Stones coined with moss lie strewn about in heaps,
Plump leaves are growing in glossy clusters.
Level and white are the wave-washed sands,
Where horses stand, printing dark characters.[1]
At evening, fishes dart around joyfully,
A lone, lean crane stands stock-still in the dusk.
Down in their damp, mole-crickets chirp away.
A muted spring wells up with startled splash.
Crooked and winding, Jade Purity Road,
Where the Divine Maiden dwells among orchid blossoms.[2]

---

[1] The shadows of the horses on the waters resemble the ancient Chinese character for "horse."

[2] The road to the Temple of the Divine Maiden of Orchid Fragrance, tutelary deity of Mount Nüji.

Cotton-moss winds around the stones in the stream,
Crimson and purple, mountain fruits hang down.
Small cypresses with leaves like layers of fans,
Plump pines oozing essence of cinnabar.
A singing stream runs on melodiously,
Ripe wheat on the dike trails its glowing head.
Orioles trill songs of a girl from Min,[3]
A waterfall unfurls satin robes from Chu.
Windblown dew fills laughing eyes
That blossom or wither in crannies and clefts.
Tangled branches jut from stony heights,
Tiny throats chatter by an island spring,
The sun's rays sweep aside the shadow of dusk,
New-risen clouds open their ornate deeps.
Pure and still, these oppressive summer days,
Yet a west wind whispers of a cooling air.
Luminous, on high her jade-white face
As I burn cinnamon on the Heavenly Altar.
Her robes of mist are fluttering in the night,
She drowses by Her altar, pure of dreams.
The simurghs have aged, awaiting the Emperor's carriage,
The pepper-walls of the ancient palace are ruined.[4]
Yet several of the bells still tinkle faintly,
Arousing this wandering courtier to desolate thoughts.
Dark creepers twine about the scarlet bolts,
In dragon-curtains lurk the mountain trolls.
Flowering tamarisk clings to emerald brocades,
These scented quilts served nobles long since dead.
No songs now stir the dust on worm-eaten beams,
Where dancers' colored robes hang like long clouds.
This precious land is cut from fissured silk,
Our villagers prize truth and righteousness.
No sound of pestles is heard when a neighbor mourns,
No evil rites are used to drive off plagues.
The fish-skinned oldsters, virtuous and kind,

---

[3] Min is the old name for Fujian Province, where the speech of the aborigines was thought
to sound like the song of birds.
[4] A description of the Fuchang palace, originally built by the Sui (589–618) and rebuilt in
657, the ruins of which lay to the east of the valley. As was customary, its inner rooms had
once been painted with a paint containing oil of pepper.

The horn-haired children, modest, quick to shame.[5]
The county justices have nothing to do,
No dunning tax collectors call on us.
In bamboo groves we repair our tattered books,[6]
From stony jetties drop in the hook and bait.
Winding rivers girdle us with water,
Banana leaves are slanting paper from Shu.
Light on the peaks, a dazzling silk collar,
The setting sun brushes away my cares.
Our springs are beakers of Governor Tao's wine,[7]
Our moon, the brow of Xie's singing-girl.[8]
Clang of a hidden bell far away
On high, a solitary bird wings home.
Rose-mist pinnacles, red and black peaks,
High cataracts roaring as they contend.
Pale moths floating in calm emerald,[9]
A veiled moon, distant, faint and sad.
Its cold light penetrates the river gorge,
Infinite my thoughts among these mountains.
The fisherman's boy lowers his midnight nets,
Frost-white birds soar up on misty wings.
On the pool's mirror, slippery spume of dragons,
And floating pearls exhaled by fishes at play.
Windy *tong* trees, lutes in jasper cases,
Fire-flies' stars, envoys to Brocade City.[10]
Willows join their long green sashes,
Bamboos quiver, short flutes playing.
The base of the crag emerges from green moss,
Reed-shoots are peering from the cinnabar pond.
Ripples and eddies sport with sky's reflection,

---

[5] The hair of young children was braided into horns.
[6] Bamboo-strips were an ancient writing material.
[7] The poet Tao Yuanming, a renowned toper.
[8] The favorite concubine of the great statesman Xie An (320–385).
[9] "Pale moths": the reflections of the peaks. Some commentators gloss as "the moon."
[10] During the reign of Emperor He of the Later Han (r 88–106) two imperial envoys, traveling in disguise to Sichuan, stopped for the night at the house of a certain Li He (not to be confused with our poet) and were astonished to discover that he knew who they were. He explained that two "envoy-stars" (shooting-stars) had just appeared over Sichuan, hence he was expecting them. Chengdu, in Sichuan, is called "City of Brocade" because of the beauty of its surroundings. Our line means simply: "The fire-flies are like the envoys in the story and Chang'gu is as beautiful as Chengdu."

The hands of ancient junipers grasp the clouds.
The mournful moon is curtained with red roses,
Thorns of fragrant creeper catch the clouds.
The bearded wheat lies level for hundreds of leagues,
On the untilled acres stand a thousand shops.
This man from Chengji, restless and fretful,[11]
Would like to emulate Master Wine-sack's ways.[12]

Figure 56. "Bamboos at
Chang'gu." Late Ming
illustration. (Source:
Tangshi huapu [Tang
Poems Illustrated]
[Shang-hai: Guji,
1982])

---

[11] The Li family came from Chengji county, Gansu.

[12] "Master Wine-sack skin" was the name taken by the great statesman Fan Li (fl. fifth century B.C.) when he retired to Qi after helping Yue defeat Wu. Li He means he should like to retire to Chang'gu but only after achieving high office.

Under the Walls of Ping City

Ping City was a northern border outpost in present Datong county, close to the Great Wall. The Han settlement of this name lay east of the Tang fort. In 200 B.C. Emperor Gaozu of the Former Han was besieged in Ping City, which became the scene of the great battle.

Hungry and cold, under Ping City's walls,
Night after night we guard the shining moon.
Our farewell swords have lost their sheen,[13]
The Gobi wind cuts through our temple-hair.[14]

Endless desert merges with white void,
But see — far off — the red of Chinese banners,
In their black tents they're blowing short flutes,
Mist and haze soaking their painted dragons.

At twilight, up there on the city walls,
We stare into the shadows of those walls,
The wind is blowing, stirring dead tumbleweed,
Our starving horses whinny within the walls.

"Just ask the builders of these walls
How many thousand leagues from the Pass we are?[15]
Rather than go home as bundled corpses
We'll turn our lances on ourselves and die."[16]

Song of the Magic Strings

A female shaman exorcises evil spirits. A ballad of this title existed as early as the third century A.D. It originated in the south, long the home of shamanistic culture.

As the sun sets in the western hills
The eastern hills grow dark,
A whirlwind blows the horses along,
Steeds trampling the clouds.[17]
Painted zithers and plain flutes
Play soft, weird tunes,

---

[13] "Farewell swords" — swords presented as parting mementoes.
[14] Literally "Sea-wind"; but "Sea" here stands for the Gobi, a desert being a sea of sand.
[15] The Hangu Pass was regarded as the gateway to China.
[16] The bodies of men who had died on active service were sent back home for burial, wrapped in horsehides.
[17] The god arrives, riding the whirlwind.

To the rustle of embroidered skirts
She treads the autumn dust.[18]

Cassia leaves stripped by the wind,[19]
Cassia seeds fall,
Blue racoons are weeping blood
As shivering foxes die.[20]
On the ancient wall, a painted dragon,[21]
Tail inlaid with gold,
The Rain God is riding it away
To an autumn tarn.
Owls that have lived a hundred years,
Turned forest demons,[22]
Laugh wildly as an emerald fire
Leaps from their nests.

Magic Strings

The witch pours out a libation of wine,
And clouds cover the sky,
In a jade brazier charcoal burns —
The incense booms.[23]
Gods of the sea and mountain demons
Flock to her seat,
Crackle of burning paper money[24]
As a whirlwind moans.

She plays a love-wood lute[25] adorned
With golden, dancing simurghs,
Knitting her brows, she plucks a note
For each word uttered.
She calls down stars and summons demons

---

[18] The shaman dances.
[19] The spirit brings the wind.
[20] Both animals were greatly feared by the Chinese.
[21] "Horned dragon": painted on the wall of the shrine.
[22] Owls were considered unlucky. Forest demons were four-legged beasts with human faces.
[23] This is synaesthesia, sound and scent blending into one.
[24] Paper money is burned at Chinese funerals. Here it is used as an offering to the spirit.
[25] Wood of a tree mentioned in the *Intrigues of the Warring States*. Planted on the grave of a wife who had died while her husband was away on a campaign, its branches would turn toward the quarter where he happened to be.

To savor meat and drink,
When mountain-goblins come to eat,
Men are breathless and hushed.
Colors of sunset low in a coign
Of Zhongnan range,[26]
Long lingers the Spirit. Something or Nothing?
We cannot tell.
The Spirit's anger, the Spirit's delight
Shows in her face,
Ten thousand riders escort him back
To the emerald hills.

Farewell Song of Magic Strings

This is the shaman's farewell song to the departing goddess.

The Maiden of Witch Mountain now departs
Behind a screen of clouds,[27]
In spring a breeze blows flowers of pine
Down from the mountainside.
Alone beneath her emerald canopy she returns
Through fragrant paths,[28]
White horses and flower-decked poles
Dazzle before her.

On the River of Shu blows a limpid wind,
Water like gauze,[29]
Who will float on a fallen orchid
To come to see her?[30]
A cassia tree on a southern hill
Is dying for her,[31]

---

[26] A mountain range which stretches for over 800 *li* across Central China.

[27] It was on Witch Mountain (Mount Wu, a famous twelve-peaked range, rising on the northern banks of the Yangtze and stretching from Sichuan to Hubei) that Jade Beauty, daughter of the legendary Scarlet Emperor, was buried. King Huai of Chu (fl. third century B.C.) once spent the night with her, not knowing who she was. When she left him she told him that in the morning she took the form of clouds on Mount Wu, in the evening she marshalled the rain. Huai's son, King Xiang, had the same experience. [See chapter 6, Song Yu's "Gao Tang Rhapsody."]

[28] This must refer to the goddess and not to the shaman.

[29] The Yangtze flows at the foot of Mount Wu.

[30] "Fallen orchid": a boat.

[31] Mount Zhongnan, near Luoyang, perhaps.

Her robes of cloud are slightly stained
By its rouged petals.[32]

Song of an Arrowhead from Changping

Changping, seven miles west of Kaoping county, was the site of an ancient battlefield.
Here, in 260 B.C., the forces of Qin were said to have captured and then buried alive
400,000 men of Zhao. Farmers were still turning up relics of the massacre in He's day,
over a thousand years later. He may have written this poem in 814, when he was on his
way to Luzhou, which is not far from Changping.

Flakes of lacquer, dust of bones,
Red cinnabar,
The ancient blood once spurted forth
And bore bronze flowers.
White feathers and its metal stem
Have rotted in the rain.
Only the three spines still remain,[33]
Broken teeth of a wolf.

I searched this plain of battle
With a pair of nags,
In stony fields east of the post-station,
On a weed-grown hill.
An endless wind, the day short,
Desolate stars,
Black banners of damp clouds
Hung in void-night.
Souls to the left, spirits to the right,
Gaunt with hunger, wailing.[34]

I poured curds from my tilted flask,
Offered roast mutton.[35]
Insects silent, the wild geese sick,
Reed shoots reddening,
A whirlwind came to see me off,
Blowing the ghost-fires.[36]

---

[32] The cassia flowers in spring and autumn. The last line hints that this may also be a love
poem. Perhaps Li He himself is the cassia-tree of the penultimate line.
[33] "Three spines": the triangular arrow-head.
[34] The dead were crying out with hunger, since they had not been buried with proper rites
nor offered libations.
[35] Curds and mutton are the food of the northern nomads, not of the Chinese.
[36] "Ghost-fires": will-o'-the-wisps.

In tears I sought this ancient field,
Picked up a broken arrow,
Its shattered point, scarlet and cracked,
Once drove through flesh.
In South Street, by the eastern wall,
A lad on horseback
Urged me to exchange the metal
For a votive-basket.[37]

Song: A Lovely Girl Combing Her Hair

Xi Shi dreaming at dawn,
In the cool of silken curtains,[38]
Scented coils of her falling chignon,
Half aloes and sandalwood.[39]

The turning windlass of the well,
Creaking like singing jade,
Wakes with a start this lotus-blossom,
That has newly slept its fill.

Twin simurghs open her mirror,
An autumn pool of light.[40]
She loosens her tresses before the mirror,
Stands by her ivory bed.

A single skein of perfumed silk,
Clouds cast on the floor,
Noiseless, the jade comb lights upon
Her lustrous hair.

Delicate fingers push up the coils —
Color of an old rook's plumes,
Blue-black, so sleek the jeweled pins

---

[37] The money from the sale of the relic was to be used for buying a basket in which to offer sacrifices to appease the spirits of the fallen.

[38] Xi Shi who came from Yue (Zhejiang) during the Warring States period was the most renowned of all Chinese beauties. Her name stands for any beautiful woman.

[39] The girl is wearing her hair in a "falling-from-your-horse chignon," a chignon set on one side of the forehead, like a rider slipping from the saddle. This style, which originated during Han times, persisted well into the nineteenth century. Half the perfume of her hair is aloes and sandalwood, the rest, her natural fragrance.

[40] The back of the mirror was decorated with simurghs (huge, legendary birds).

Cannot hold it up.
Light-heartedly the spring breeze vexes
Her youthful languor,
Just eighteen, with hair so rich,
Her strength has fled.

Her coiffure over, the well-dressed chignon
Sits firm and does not slip.
In cloudy skirts, she takes a few steps,
A wild goose treading sand,
She turns away in silence —
Where is she off to now?
Just down the steps to pick herself
A spray of cherry blossom.

Song: Dragons at Midnight

A curly-haired nomad boy
With eyes of green,
By a tall mansion, in the still of the night
Is playing his flute.
Every note seems to have come
Down from heaven.
Under the moon a lovely girl weeping,
Sick for home.

Deftly he fingers the seven holes,
Hiding their stars,
Gong and Zhi secretly harmonize
With the pure breeze.[41]
Deep autumn on the roads of Shu,
A cloud-filled forest.
From the Xiang river at midnight
Startled dragons rise.[42]

A lovely girl in her jade room
Broods on the frontier.
Bright moonshine on her sapphire window —
Sadly she hears the flute.

---

[41] Gong and zhi are the first and fourth notes of the pentatonic scale.
[42] Images evoked by the music.

A hundred feet of glossed silk beaten
On the cold fulling-block;[43]
Tears congeal as pearls in her powder,
Soak her red gown.

Play no more the Longtou tune,
Nomad boy!
No one knows a girl's heart is breaking
Beyond that casement.

DU MU (803–852)
Four Poems

Translated by A. C. Graham

Du Mu is most admired as a master of the New Style quatrain with an AABA rhyme
scheme like that of Omar Khayyam. With his acutely sensual delight in wine, women,
spring landscapes, and the brilliant colors of birds and flowers, he is a refreshing
exception among the generally somber poets of this period. The times when he
wandered putting up in the monasteries in Jiangnan south of the Yangtze, favorite
region of the Song landscape painters, or rioting in the pleasure quarter of Yangzhou
at the river's mouth, cost him some regrets; but there is more joy in him than in any
Tang poet later than Li Bo.

Easing My Heart

By river and lakes at odds with life I journeyed, wine my freight:
Slim waists of Chu broke my heart, light bodies danced into my
    palm.
Ten years late I wake at last out of my Yangzhou dream
With nothing but the name of a drifter in the blue houses.[44]

To Judge Han Chuo at Yangzhou

Over misted blue hills and distant water
In Jiangnan at autumn's end the grass has not yet wilted.
By night on the Four-and-Twenty Bridges, under the full moon,
Where are you teaching a jade girl to blow tunes on your flute?[45]

---

[43] The sound of silk being beaten on the fulling-blocks in autumn, to make winter clothes,
is a familiar symbol of parting and sorrow.

[44] "Blue houses": brothels.

[45] "Jade girl": singsong girl. *Eds.*

Recalling Former Travels

1

Whirled ten years beyond all bounds,
Treating myself in the taverns, drinking my own health.
In autumn hills and spring rain in the places where I idly sang
I lolled against the pillar of every monastery in Jiangnan.

2

Li Bo put it in a poem, this West-of-the-Waters Abbey.
Old trees and crooked cliffs, wind in the upper rooms.
Between drunk and sober I drifted three days
While blossoms white and crimson opened in the misty rain.

Six Poems

Translated by R. F. Burton

Egrets

With snowy coats, snowy crests, and sapphire bills,
    They flock to fish, reflected in the brook.
In startled flight, they shine on emerald hills
— petals from a pear tree in an evening breeze.

A Mountain Walk

Far up Cold Mountain slants a rocky path.
There, where clouds are born, are people's dwellings.
Halt the carriage. Sit. Enjoy the maple woods at dusk.
The frosted leaves are redder far
    than flowers that bloom in March.

Spring South of the River

Orioles sang in a thousand hamlets,
    red glowing on green.
Waterside villages, mountain ramparts,
    wineshop pennants blowing.
Of four hundred and eighty temples,
    those of the Southern Dynasties,

how many towers are there now
   in misty rain?

A Tower by the Yangtze River

Alone, I pour out spring wine,
   Then climb the tower half tipsy.
Who startled the line of geese
that broke through the Yangtze clouds?

Basin Pond

Picks broke the green-mossed clod.
It stole a slip of sky.

Figure 57. "A Mountain Walk."
Early 20th-century illustration.
(Source: *Zixi huapu daquan* [Com-
plete Painting Manual] [Beijing:
Rongbao-zhai, 1982])

White clouds spawn in the depths of the mirror.
The bright moon dips at the step.

Plantains

For the way that plantains move in the rain
I grew some facing the window.
I'm at one with the ditch, for the sound of the dripping
    Carries me back in a dream to my homeland.
A vain dream: I'll never go home again.
I wake from sleep, turn over again.

Three Poems

Translated by Herbert Giles

Too Late

When ordered to a distant post, he said to his fiancée, "Within ten years I shall be Governor. If I do not return by then, marry whomsoever you please." He came back after fourteen years to find her married and the mother of three children.

Too late, alas! ... I came to find
    the lovely spring had fled.
Yet must I not regret the days
    of youth that now are dead;
For though the rosy buds of spring
    the cruel winds have laid,
Behold the clustering fruit that hangs
    beneath the leafy shade.

A Wilderness

A wilderness alone remains,
    all garden glories gone;
the river runs unheeded by,
    weeds grow unheeded on.
Dusk comes, the east wind blows, and birds
    pipe forth a mournful sound;

Petals, like nymphs from balconies,
    come tumbling to the ground.

Old Love

Old love would seem as though not love today:
Spell-bound by thee, my laughter dies away.
The very wax sheds sympathetic tears
And gutters sadly down till dawn appears.

Take the Bottle, and Ascend

Translated by Robert Morrison (1815)

The original title of this poem, "Climbing the Heights of Mount Qi on the Ninth Day,"
refers to the Double Yang Festival (the ninth day of the ninth lunar month), and to
Mount Qi in present-day Anhui Province, where Du Mu was posted at the time.

— Editors

When the autumnal rivers receive the shadow
    of the first flying swallow;
Let us, companions, take the bottle
    and ascend the lofty mountain.
In this impure world, it is difficult to meet
    with a mouth open laughing;
Let us today with the *ju* flower[46]
    decorate our heads and return.
We'll get merrily drunk, and keep up
    this happy season.
'Tis in vain to ascend the hill, and sigh
    about the sun setting:
Old times have passed away, the present come,
    and still it is thus;
What's the use of staining our garments with tears,
    like the man of Cow Hill?[47]

---

[46] The chrysanthemum. *Eds.*

[47] Cow Hill was a hill to the south of Linzi, capital of the ancient state of Qi (present-day
Shandong Province). The man of Cow Hill was Duke Jing of Qi, who climbed the hill
with his courtiers and, gazing down upon his capital, wept as he reflected on the
transience of human existence. *Eds.*

LI SHANGYIN (c. 813–858)
Three Poems

Translated by James J. Y. Liu

Of Li Shangyin's 598 extant poems one group consists of ambiguous poems, either labeled "Without Title" or bearing titles that are simply the opening words. Apparently concerned with clandestine love, these poems are subjects of controversy. Some scholars interpret them as autobiographical poems about secret love affairs with court ladies and Taoist priestesses. It seems fruitless to read them as *poèmes à clef* and try to identify the supposed prototypes of the *dramatis personae*; instead, it is more rewarding to reconstruct, from the text of each poem, a dramatic context which allows a consistent reading, without identifying the speaker with the author. Seen in this light, these poems are effective explorations of various facets of love: desire, hope, joy, frustration, jealousy, tenderness, and despair. They are unusual among Chinese poems for their intensity and complexity of emotion and their density and richness of language. Some of them, such as "The Patterned Lute," his most famous poem, actually deal with more than love, using several levels of reality and fusing the past with the present, the real with the imaginary, and the historical with the mythical.

Li Shangyin's poetry embodies passion, commitment, and conflict. It contains elements of Confucianism, Buddhism, and Taoism without reaching a complete synthesis of the three. There are signs of a conflict between Confucian puritanism and Buddhist asceticism, on the one hand, and sybaritic hedonism associated with the popular Taoist quest for the elixir of life, on the other. There is also a conflict between the Confucian ideal of public service and the wish to withdraw from society, prompted by both Buddhism and Taoism. These conflicts remain unresolved in Li's poetry, although toward the end of his life he embraced Buddhism and wrote a *gatha* on his deathbed.

In general, Li Shangyin extended the scope of Chinese poetry by exploring spheres of experience previously untouched by poets, or by exploring familiar worlds with a new intensity and a self-awareness that often led to irony. It is perhaps this last quality, together with his striking use of language, that makes him particularly appealing to sophisticated modern readers. At the same time, his exploitation of the potentials of the Chinese language has exerted a profound influence on later poetry.

Without Title

At eight, she stole a look at herself in the mirror,
Already able to paint her eyebrows long.
At ten, she went out to tread on the green,[48]
Her skirt made of lotus flowers.[49]

---

[48] "Treading on the green" — a custom in Tang times of going out into the country or to the Meandering Stream in Chang'an on the third day of the third month.

[49] This line alludes to the *Songs of the South*, but also literally describes the lotus flowers embroidered on her skirt.

At twelve, she learnt to play the small zither:
The silver plectrums she never took off.
At fourteen, she was hid among her relatives,
And, one imagined, not married yet.
At fifteen, she weeps in the spring wind,
Turning her face away from the swing.

Translator's commentary:
This seemingly simple poem has been interpreted in various ways. Feng Hao takes it to be an allegorical expression of the poet's disappointment at his lack of success despite his precocious talents and cites a passage from one of Li's letters which contains verbal similarities:

"I began to study the Classics in my fifth year, toyed with the writing brush and the ink-slab in my seventh, and wrote essays in my sixteenth."

This interpretation is plausible but not strictly necessary, for the poem is poignant enough taken at its face value as a lament for an ill-fated precocious beauty, who, at the early age of fifteen (Chinese reckoning), is either unhappily married or unhappy because she is not yet married, so that she has no further use for the swing, a symbol of youthful gaiety. Moreover, the phraseology of the poem can be considered a conscious imitation or an unconscious echo of some lines from the anonymous ancient ballad known as "Southeast the Peacock Flies" [see chapter 8], which tells how a young man was forced by his mother to divorce his wife and how the young couple both committed suicide.... The resemblance of Li's poem to certain lines of the ballad makes it possible to take it as a description of an unhappy girl, without any allegorical significance. Another interpretation is offered by Miss Su Xuelin, who thinks that the poem alludes to the two Court entertainers Feiluan and Qingfeng, with both of whom the poet was allegedly in love. Thus, the poem can be taken on three different levels: as a description of an ill-fated beauty, as an allegorical self-lament, and as an oblique reference to a clandestine love. But its total significance transcends all three. Whatever the poet may have had in mind, the effect of the poem is to make us feel sadness at the loss of youth, beauty, and talent, no matter where and how such loss was incurred. We may compare this poem with Keats's "La Belle Dame Sans Merci," which may be taken at its face value as a fairy tale, or as an expression of the poet's unhappy infatuation for Fanny Brawne, or as an allegory of his intoxication with Beauty, or as all three at once, for the total meaning of the poem transcends them all, though none of them needs be excluded.

High Noon

The doorknockers with tags of old brocade can be lightly pulled;[50]
The jade key does not turn, the side door is locked.
Who is it that lies asleep inside the crystal curtain,
Her hair piled up like red peonies at high noon?

---

[50] Doors in the palace had tags made of old brocade tied to the knockers to make it easier to pull them.

The floating fragrance ascends the clouds
  to complain to heaven in spring,
But oh, the twelve cloud-stairs and the ninefold gates![51]
What hope is there for one who takes life lightly?
The white moth dies stiff upon the folding screen.

Translator's commentary:
Feng Hao takes this poem to be a veiled reference to the Emperor, who is as hard to
approach as heaven, and the moth to represent a loyal official risking death in his
attempt to admonish the sovereign. This seems too farfetched and does not fit all the
details of the poem. Zhang Zaitian takes it as an allegory about the poet's longing for
the favor of the influential Linghu Tao and the latter's inaccessibility. This too seems
forced. A more likely interpretation is that the poem describes a hopeless passion for
some palace lady, whether this passion is felt by the poet himself or imaginary. The
door looks inviting enough; it could be pulled open easily, yet the key does not turn,
and the door remains locked. The beauty lies tantalizingly within the transparent
curtain: one can see her but cannot come near. One would like to complain to heaven
(or perhaps she would like to complain to heaven), but heaven is inaccessible with its
manifold stairs and gates. Even if one takes life lightly and does not mind risking
death, what hope is there? One can only despair and die like the moth that courts its
own destruction by throwing itself against the screen. This image of the moth reminds
one of Shelley's well-known lines:

> The worship the heart lifts above
>   And the Heavens reject not;
> The desire of the moth for the star,
>   Of the night for the morrow;
> The devotion to something afar
>   From the sphere of our sorrow.

Thus, the whole poem may be regarded as a symbol of a kind of romantic *désir de
l'impossible*, of universal human aspirations for the unattainable, not merely as the
expression of a personal longing for a particular woman or for the favor of a particular
patron.

Chamber Music

There was a kind of ancient Court music called "Chamber Music," but the poet is
borrowing the name to suggest the intimacy of the bedchamber, since the poem is a
lament for his wife.

The roses shed tears on their delicate white petals;
The emerald belts carry small flower-coins.
The spoiled boy is silly like a cloud

---

[51] There are supposed to be twelve jade towers (which presumably have stairs of clouds) in
the palace of the goddess Queen Mother of the West. The palace of Heaven is said to
have ninefold gates.

Hugging the sun by the west curtain in the morning.
The pillow is made of a stone from the dragon palace:
It has reaped the color of your eyes, clear as autumn waves.
The jade mattress has lost your tender flesh;
Only the green silk coverlet remains.
I remember the spring of the year before last —
You said nothing but were full of sadness.
Now I have returned but you are gone!
The ornamented zither[52] has lasted longer than you.
Today, a pine at the bottom of the valley;
Tomorrow, a *bo* tree on top of the hill![53]
I shall grieve till heaven and earth turn round,
Till we no longer recognize each other face to face!

Translator's commentary:
Written, probably, soon after the death of the poet's wife in 851, the poem expresses his deep grief. The first line, by comparing the dewdrops on the rose to tears, at once sets the mood of the poem. (The fact that this image is derived from an earlier writer does not make it less effective.) In the next line, the "emerald belts" probably stand for the twigs, and the "flower-coins" for the seeds. (The seeds of the elm tree are commonly called "elm coins," an analogous usage.) The significance of the whole line, as one commentator suggested, seems to be that the poet's wife has left behind young children like the seeds of the flowers. Lines 3–4 are somewhat ambiguous. The "spoiled boy" has been taken to refer to the poet himself, which is absurd. This must surely refer to his son, who is called "silly" because he is too young to understand that his mother is dead. But some ambiguity still remains, for it is not clear whether the two lines mean that the boy hugs his father like a cloud hugging the sun, or that he is hugging the sunshine in his sleep. On the whole, I think the first interpretation is better, but I have left the ambiguity of the two lines by not using a comma either after the word "silly" or after the word "cloud." (In the original there is, of course, no punctuation.) In lines 5–8, the poet describes how the deserted pillow and the empty bed remind him of his wife: the color of the pillow reminds him of her eyes, and the hard mattress, which used to be a foil to her tender flesh, now bears nothing but a coverlet. The comparison of a beautiful woman's eyes to "autumn waves" is a hackneyed image in Chinese poetry, but it is enriched here by associations aroused by the imagery of the preceding line: the dragon palace evokes the splendors of a rich mansion under the water, and the water image then blends with the picture of the beautiful eyes. Moreover, the mention of the dragon palace may suggest that she is a dragon king's daughter and no common mortal. (There is a story about a dragon king's daughter who married a man called Liu Yi [see chapter 28].) Lines 9–10 allude to the poet's departure for Xuzhou in 849 and lines 11–12 refer to his wife's death. In the next two lines the poet laments his sad lot. The pine at the bottom of the valley

---

[52] This is the "Patterned Lute" of A. C. Graham's translation; see next selection. *Eds.*

[53] Also called "yellow *bo*," a tree whose bark and fruit have a bitter taste and are used for medicinal purposes.

seems to represent his humble position, and the *bo* tree, which has a bitter taste, suggests the bitterness in his heart. As the commentator Qu Fu pointed out, there is an anonymous ancient song containing the lines,

> The yellow *bo* has been growing since spring,
> Its bitter heart growing day by day,

where "bitter heart" is an obvious pun. Further, the sudden change of position from the valley to the hill may indicate that the poet will soon have to leave home again. The last two lines dramatically declare the poet's refusal to cease mourning as long as heaven and earth remain and as long as he himself retains his consciousness. One commentator explained these lines as meaning "Even if my grief could turn heaven and earth around, how could we ever see each other again?" This does not quite fit the last line, which literally says, "Look at each other but not recognize each other." I prefer to paraphrase the last two lines thus: "I will go on mourning your death, until heaven and earth have turned around and you and I would no longer recognize each other even if we met again."

Nine Poems

Translated by A. C. Graham

Untitled Poems

1

Coming was an empty promise, you have gone, and left no footprint:
The moonlight slants above the roof, already the fifth watch sounds.
Dreams of remote partings, cries which cannot summon,
Hurrying to finish the letter, ink which will not thicken.
The light of the candle half encloses kingfishers threaded with gold,
The smell of musk comes faintly through embroidered water-lilies.
Young Liu complained that Fairy Hill[54] is far.
Past Fairy Mountain, range above range, ten thousand mountains
    rise.

Commentary by James Liu:
Let us imagine that the lover has waited all night for his beloved, who has failed to come ... He sees the fading moonlight on the roof and hears the bells striking the fifth watch, announcing the arrival of dawn. He writes a letter in haste (the traditional way of preparing ink in China is to rub an ink-stick with water on an ink-slab, so that it takes some time for the ink to reach the desired degree of thickness). After the messenger has gone with the letter, he looks wistfully at the light of the candle, which

---

[54] Fairy Hill, or Penglai, is one of the mountains of the immortals in the Eastern Sea. Young Liu is a slightly contemptuous reference to the Emperor Wu of Han's search for immortality.

half encompasses the kingfisher feathers mixed with gold on the quilt, and smells the perfume, which has gradually penetrated the embroidered bed-curtain: all these elaborate preparations have been in vain!

2

The East wind sighs, the fine rains come:
Beyond the pool of water-lilies, the noises of faint thunder.
A gold toad gnaws the lock. Open it, burn the incense.
A tiger of jade pulls the rope. Draw from the well and escape.
Jia's daughter peeped through the screen
      when Han the clerk was young,
The goddess of the river left her pillow for the great Prince of Wei.
Never let your heart open with the spring flowers:
One inch of love is an inch of ashes.[55]

Commentary by James Liu:

The opening couplet recalls the scene of a secret rendezvous. The scene would seem to be set in the palace and the woman involved would appear to be a Court lady risking grave dangers in coming to meet her lover. The thunder adds to the already menacing atmosphere created by the wind and the rain, and emphasizes the desperate passion of the lovers. The next two lines are puzzling. Perhaps the burnt incense that enters through the lock (fashioned in the shape of a golden toad) represents messages that have managed to get through to her. The jade tiger pulley may represent a messenger commuting between the lovers. The following couplet contains two allusions. Jia's daughter was the daughter of Jia Chong (217–282), prime minister of the Jin dynasty. She peeped through the curtain at her father's handsome young secretary Han Shou, and subsequently had a love affair with him. The affair was discovered by Jia Chong when he smelt on Han's clothes a rare imported perfume which he himself had given to his daughter. Thereupon the young lovers were allowed to be married. The goddess of the river refers to the famous rhapsody "The Goddess of the River Luo" [see chapter 6] by Cao Zhi, Prince of Wei. Cao Zhi was in love with the Princess Fu, but was unable to marry her. Instead she became the wife of his elder brother Cao Pi, first Emperor of the Wei dynasty. After her death the Emperor gave her pillow to Cao Zhi. Legend has it that when Cao Zhi left the capital and reached the River Luo, she appeared to him in a vision, in which their love was fulfilled. Li Shangyin is either drawing an analogy or pointing a contrast. Either he is saying, "You have shown your favor to me, as Jia's daughter did to Han Shou and the Princess Fu did to to Cao Zhi," or he is saying, "I am not as handsome as Han, nor am I as gifted as Cao: how can I hope to win your love?" In the last couplet, the lover apparently warns himself not to let his heart blossom forth with love, for he knows only too well what suffering this will bring. And yet we sense that he cannot really help it. Such is the intensity of his passion that he cannot stop his longing, but can only watch his heart being consumed by his unfulfilled desire until it turns to the ashes of despair.

---

[55] Thoughts are in a hollow space in the heart, one inch square. The last line also suggests two of Li Shangyin's favorite images of love, a continuing thread and a candle flame.

3

Bite back passion. Spring now sets.
Watch little by little the night turn round.
Echoes in the house; want to go up, dare not.
A glow behind the screen; wish to go through, cannot.
It would hurt too much, the swallow on the hairpin;
Truly shame me, the phoenix on a mirror.
On the road back, sunrise over Hengtang.[56]
The blossoming of the morning-star
    shines farewell on the jewelled saddle.

4

For ever hard to meet, and as hard to part.
Each flower spoils in the failing East wind.
Spring's silkworms wind till death their heart's threads:
The wick of the candle turns to ash before its tears dry.
Morning mirror's only care, a change at her cloudy temples:
Saying over a poem in the night, does she sense
    the chill in the moonbeams?
Not far, from here to Fairy Hill.
Bluebird, be quick now, spy me out the road.

Commentary by James Liu:
I take this poem to be an expression of love for a woman who lives within easy reach
but with whom the poet cannot openly communicate. In the first of the central
couplets, just as the silkworm imprisons itself in the cocoon formed by its own endless
silk, so does the poet enwrap himself in the endless sorrow of his own making, and just
as the candle is consumed by its own heat, so is the poet by his own passions. These
justly famous images are universal symbols of heart-rending sorrow and of hoping
against hope. In the next couplet, the poet imagines how his beloved sits alone before
the mirror in the morning, grieving that her beauty may fade away, or recites poetry
at night, feeling lonely in the chilly moonlight.

5

Where is it, the sad lyre which follows the quick flute?
Down endless lanes where the cherries flower,
    on a bank where the willows droop.
The lady of the East house grows old without a husband.
The white sun at high noon, the last spring month half over.

---

[56] Hengtang was a pleasure quarter.

Princess Liyang is fourteen,
In the cool of the day, after the Rain Feast,
   with him behind the fence, look.
... Come home, toss and turn till the fifth watch.
Two swallows in the rafters hear the long sigh.

The Walls of Emerald

1

Twelve turns of the rail on walls of emerald:
A sea-beast's horn repels the dust, a jade repels the cold.
Letters from Mount Langyuan have cranes for
   messengers,
On Lady's couch a hen-phoenix perches in every tree.
The stars which sank to the bottom of the sea show up
   at the window:
The rain has passed where the River rises, far off you
   sit watching.
If the pearl of dawn should shine and never leave its
   place,
All life long we shall gaze in the crystal dish.

2

To glimpse her shadow, to hear her voice, is to love her.
On the pool of jade the lotus leaves spread out across
   the water.
Unless you meet Xiao Shi with his flute, do not turn
   your head:
Do not look on Hong Ya, nor ever touch his shoulder.
The purple phoenix strikes a pose with the pendant of
   Chu in its beak:
The crimson scales dance wildly to the plucked strings
   on the river.
Prince O despairs of his night on the boat,
And sleeps alone by the lighted censer beneath the
   embroidered quilts.

3

On the Seventh Night she came at the time appointed.
The bamboo screens of the inner chamber have never
   since lifted.

On the jade wheel where the hare watches the dark
    begins to grow,
The coral in the iron net has still to put forth branches.
I have studied magic, can halt the retreat of day:
I have fetched phoenix papers and written down my love.
The Tale of the Emperor Wu is a plain witness:
Never doubt that the world of men can share this
    knowledge.

Translator's commentary:
"The Walls of Emerald" is as obscure in Chinese as in English; it may well be that Li
Shangyin did not even wish to be understood except by the woman to whom he
addressed it (his Taoist nun?). *The Tale of the Emperor Wu* records how the Western
Queen Mother descended from the sky on the Seventh Night of the Seventh Month to
teach the Emperor the science of immortality; it is hardly worthwhile to explain the
other recognizable allusions. In Chinese the poem is an extraordinary example of a
constellation of images which holds its irrational spell a thousand years after its
meaning has been lost; readers may judge for themselves whether or not it survives the
further transplantation to another language and culture.

The Patterned Lute

The Background of the Poem
    Fu Xi ordered the White Lady to strum the fifty-string lute. Because it was too sad,
he forbade her to play, but she would not stop; so he broke her lute and left twenty-five
strings.
    Once Zhuangzi dreamed that he was a butterfly.... He does not know whether he
is Zhuangzi who dreamed that he was a butterfly or a butterfly dreaming that he is
Zhuangzi.
    Wangdi, legendary ruler of Shu, sent Bie Ling to deal with the floods and
debauched his wife. He was ashamed and, considering Bie Ling a better man than
himself, abdicated the state to him. At the time when Wangdi left, the nightjar began
to call. That is why the nightjar's call is sad to the people of Shu and reminds them of
Wangdi.
    When Wangdi died his soul turned into a bird called the "nightjar."
    Bo Ya strummed his lute, with his mind on climbing high mountains; and Zhong
Ziqi said: "Good! Lofty, like Mount Tai!" When his mind was on flowing waters, Zhong
Ziqi said: "Good! Boundless like the Yellow River and the Yangtze!"
    When the moon is full the oyster has pearls, when the moon is dark the oyster is
empty.
    Beyond the South Sea there are mermaids ("shark people") who live in the water
like fish, but spin like women on land: their weeping eyes can exude pearls.
    When the King was dressing and combing himself, suddenly he saw Purple Jade.
"How can it be that you are alive?" he asked in his amazement, sad and happy at
once. Purple Jade kneeled and said: "Once young Han Zhong came to seek me in
marriage, and Your Majesty would not allow it; I lost my good name and atoned for it
by my death...." Her mother heard them and came out to embrace her, but Purple
Jade dissolved like smoke.

Dai Shulun (732–789) said that the scene presented by a poet is like the smoke which issues from fine jade when the sun is warm on Blue Mountain ("Indigo Field"); it can be seen from a distance but not from close to.

Mere chance that the patterned lute has fifty strings.
String and fret, one by one, recall the blossoming years.
Zhuangzi dreams at sunrise that a butterfly lost its way,
Wangdi bequeathing his spring passion to the nightjar.
The moon is full on the vast sea, a tear on the pearl.
On Blue Mountain the sun warms, a smoke issues from the jade.
Did it wait, this mood, to mature with hindsight?
In a trance from the beginning, then as now.

Translator's commentary:
"The Patterned Lute" has long been famous as the most haunting and the most puzzling of Li Shangyin's poems. The commentators Zhu Heling (1606–1683) and Feng Hao (1719–1801) dismissed older stories that it recalls a nobleman's concubine or a maidservant of the poet's first political patron Linghu Chu (766–837), and insisted that it is a lament for his wife. A "patterned lute that lasted longer than you" is in fact mentioned in a lament for his wife, entitled "Chamber Music" [see James Liu's translation]. But although this is still the most popular explanation, the reference to the adulterous love of Wangdi points strongly to the dangerous intrigue of the "Untitled Poems." These notes are offered with the warning that this dense poem has as many readings as readers.

Lines 1, 2. The fifty strings suggest a woman playing sadly like Fu Xi's White Lady; playing them, the poet recalls an experience of his youth; the number also suggests a private chronological reference which has never been convincingly explained.

Lines 3, 4. The memory is of an adulterous love like Wangdi's; like Zhuangzi's dream it sometimes seems unreal, sometimes more real than the rest of life; like the nightjar which was once Wangdi, the poet, changed for the worse by time, sings of a love which he remembers as though it happened to a different person.

"Zhuangzi dreams at sunrise that a butterfly lost its way" raises the possibility that it was in waking from sleep that Zhuangzi began to dream; it also allows one to take, not the dreamer, but the woman of whom he dreams, as the lost butterfly.

Lines 5, 6. As he plays, the music evokes the picture of a moonlit sea; the moon suggests a pearl in a sea of tears, pearls growing in the oyster with the waxing of the moon, mermaids who weep pearls, the girl who is moon, mermaid, and pearl. Then it conjures up Mount Lantian (Blue or Indigo Mountain) in the mist which is the smoke of its jade warmed by the sun, Purple Jade who died when she lost her lover and who dissolved like smoke when her mother tried to embrace her ghost, finally the girl who dissolves when the poet tries to fix her in his memory, whom he sees like a pearl behind a moist film or a precious stone through mist.

The striking parallel with Dai Shulun's aphorism about poetry is often dismissed as a coincidence. If we accept its relevance, the couplet has another dimension. Maturing through time, like pearls forming as the moon waxes, painful experience becomes poetry, which crystallizes out of grief like a pearl from a tear, and depends for its beauty on distance, like the mountain mist.

Lines 7, 8. Is it only in memory that the experience has turned into a dream? Even at the time, it was lived as though in a trance.

WEN TINGYUN (c. 813–870)
Four Poems

Translated by Witter Bynner

Wen's failure to distinguish himself in the examinations or later in public service may have resulted from his personal habits and mannerisms, for the historical sources describe him as an arrogant nonconformist, a decadent ne'er-do-well, and a habitué of the gay quarters.... His familiarity with the world of popular entertainment had other important consequences, for it was in that environment that the new musical and lyric patterns were then much in vogue [see chapter 30]. Inspiration gained in that milieu, along with his own talents as a musician, explain why he was the first literati poet to seriously explore the potentials of the *ci* lyric form as a medium of polite verse. His regular verse reveals a greater range of diction than is the case with his lyric verse.

— William Schultz, *Indiana Companion*, 1986

She Sighs on Her Jade Lute

A cool-matted silvery bed; but no dreams ...
An evening sky as green as water, shadowed with tender clouds;
But far off over the southern rivers the calling of a wildgoose,
And here a twelve-story building, lonely under the moon.

To a Friend Bound East

The old fort brims with yellow leaves ...
You insist upon forsaking this place where you have lived.
A high wind blows at Hanyang Ferry
And sunrise lights the summit of Yingmen ...[57]
Who will be left for me along the upper Yangtze
After your solitary skiff has entered the end of the sky?
I ask you over and over when we shall meet again,
While we soften with winecups this ache of farewell.

Near the Lizhou Ferry

The sun has set in the water's clear void,
And little blue islands are one with the sky.

---

[57] Hanyang Ferry was a crossing over the Yangtze River near present-day Wuhan in Hubei Province. Mount Yingmen is south of the Yangtze, northeast of Yidu County, also in Hubei. *Eds.*

Figure 58. "The sun has set in
the water's clear void." Early
20th-century illustration.
(Source: *Zixi huapu daquan*
[Complete Painting Manual]
[Beijing: Rongbaozhai, 1982])

On the bank a horse neighs. A boat goes by.
People gather at a willow-clump and wait for the ferry.
Down by the sand-bushes sea-gulls are circling,
Over the wide river-lands flies an egret.
… Can you guess why I sail, like an ancient wise lover,
Through the misty Five Lakes, forgetting words?

The Temple of Su Wu

For Su Wu, the Han dynasty envoy sent by Emperor Wu and thrown into prison by the
Xiongnu, see chapter 14.

— Editors

Though our envoy, Su Wu, is gone, body and soul,
This temple survives, these trees endure …

Wildgeese through the clouds are still calling to the moon there,
And hill-sheep unshepherded graze along the border.
... Returning, he found his country changed
Since with youthful cap and sword he had left it.
His bitter adventures had won him no title ...
Autumn-waves endlessly sob in the river.

Two Poems

Translated by Kenneth Rexroth

In the Mountains as Autumn Begins

Cold air drains down from the peaks.
Frost lies all around my cabin.
The trees are bare. Weak sunlight
Shines in my window. The pond
Is full and still. The water
Is motionless. I watch the
Gibbons gather fallen fruit.
All night I hear the deer stamping
In the dry leaves. My old harp
Soothes all my trouble away.
The clear voice of the waterfall
In the night accompanies my playing.

Passing a Ruined Palace

Heavy dew. Thick mist. Dense grass.
Trees grow on the broken balconies.
Willows choke the empty moat.
Fallen flowers litter the courts.
The drunken parties are long gone.
At the fifth watch, under the waning moon,
A nightingale is singing.
I dream of those perfumed lives
That died in inconsolable grief.
The ancient palace is a heap of ruins.
The road has vanished.
The landscape is the same.
The works of men are being obliterated.

Figure 59. "In the Mountains as Autumn Begins." Early 20th-century illustration. (Source: *Zixi huapu daquan* [Complete Painting Manual] [Beijing: Rongbaozhai, 1982])

When I pass by the broken gate
My horse whinnies again and again.

WEI ZHUANG (c. 836–910)

The Lament of the Lady of Qin

Translated by Lionel Giles

Qin was the feudal state that coincided with the modern province of Shaanxi. This long poem (which, though famous in its time, has survived only in handwritten copies found this century in the Dunhuang caves) describes in harrowing detail the brutal sack of Chang'an by the brigand forces of Huang Chao — whose rebellion (879–885) was one of the most disastrous episodes undergone by the Chinese in the course of

their long history, and heralded the end of the Tang dynasty. Wei Zhuang was an
official in his forties when he witnessed the rape of Chang'an. He later moved to
Sichuan, where he became Chief Minister of the state of Shu. He was a leading writer
of lyric verse (see chapter 30).

Section headings have been added by the translator.

— Editors

Introductory: The Poet Meets with the Lady

In the *gui-mao* year of Zhong-he, in the third month of spring,[58]
Outside the city walls of Luoyang, the blossom was like snow.
East and west, north and south, wayfarers were at rest;
The green willows were still, their fragrant scent was departed.
Suddenly, by the wayside I saw a flowerlike lady
Reclining in solitude beneath the shade of the green willows.
Her phoenix head-dress was awry, and a lock of hair
    lay athwart her temples.
Her face showed traces of care, and there was a pucker
    between her eyebrows.
I made bold to question her, saying: "O Lady, whence do you come?"
Looking distressed, she was about to speak, when a sob
    choked her utterance.
Then, turning her head and gathering up her sleeves,
    she apologized to the traveler:
"Tossed and engulfed in the waves of revolution,
    how can I find words to speak?
Three years back I fell into the hands of the rebels
    and was detained in the land of Qin,
And the things that happened in Qin seem engraved in my memory.
If you, Sir, can loosen your golden saddle to hear my story,
I for my part will stay my jade footsteps in your company …

The Lady's Story: The Coming of the Rebels

The year before last, on the fifth day of the sacrificial moon in
    geng-zi,[59]
I had just shut the golden birdcage after giving a lesson to my parrot,
And was looking sidelong in my phoenix mirror as I lazily
    combed my hair,

---

[58] April–May 883.
[59] 8 January 881.

Idly leaning the while on the carved balustrade in silent thought,
When suddenly I beheld a cloud of red dust rising outside the gates,
And men appeared in the streets beating metal drums.
The citizens rush out of doors half-dazed with terror,
And the courtiers come flocking in, still suspecting a false rumor.
Meanwhile, Government troops are entering the city from the west,
And propose to meet the emergency by marching to the Tong Pass.
The general cry is that the Boye troops are holding the enemy in
      check,
And all agree that the rebel army, though on the way,
      has not yet arrived.
Yet a little while, and my husband gallops up on horseback;
Dismounting, he enters the gate; stupefied he stands, like a drunken
      man.
Even now he had met the Emperor's Purple Canopy
      departing into exile,
And had seen the white banners of the rebels advancing
      from all parts of the country ...

The Sack of Chang'an

Supporting the infirm and leading children by the hand,
      fugitives are calling to one another in the turmoil;
Some clamber on to roofs, others scale walls, and all is in disorder.
Neighbors in the south run into hiding with neighbors in the north,
And those in the east make for shelter with those in the west.
Our northern neighbor's womenfolk, trooping all together,
Dash wildly about in the open like stampeding cattle.
Boom, boom! — Heaven and earth shake with the rumbling
      of chariot wheels,
And the thunder of ten thousand horses' hoofs
      re-echoes from the ground.
Fires burst out, sending golden sparks high up into the firmament,
And the twelve official thoroughfares are soon seething
      with smoke and flame.
The sun's orb sinks in the west, giving place to the cold pale
      light of the moon.
God utters never a word, but His heart is surely bursting within him.
A dark halo of misty cloud seems to encircle the moon with many
      rings,
And the Eunuch Stars, gliding in their courses,
      assume the color of blood;

The Purple Exhalation secretly follows the Emperor's Throne
    as it shifts from place to place,
And baleful rays are stealthily shooting at the Tai Stars
    for their destruction.
Every home now runs with bubbling fountains of blood,
Every place rings with a victim's shrieks — shrieks that cause
    the very earth to quake.
Dancers and singing-girls must all undergo secret outrage;
Infants and tender maidens are torn living from their parents' arms.

The Fate of the Four Girls

Our eastern neighbor had a daughter, whose eyebrows
    were but newly painted:
A beauty above all price, to overthrow a city or a state;
Between tall spears she is escorted into a warrior's chariot,
Turning to gaze back at her fragrant boudoir, while her
    handkerchief is soaked with tears.
So now she is pulling out golden thread and learning to sew banners,
Or she is raised upon a carved saddle and made to sit a galloping
    steed.
Now and again, from her horse, she catches sight of her goodman,
But dares not turn her eyes upon him, and has to shed tears in vain.

Our western neighbor had a daughter — verily, a fairy maiden!
Sidelong glances flashed from her large limpid eyes,
And when her toilet was done, she reflected the spring in her mirror;
Young in years, she knew naught of the world outside her door.
A ruffian comes leaping up the steps of her abode;
Pulling her robe from one bare shoulder, he attempts
    to do her violence,
But, though dragged by her clothes, she refuses to pass
    out of the vermilion portal,
And thus with her rouge and fragrant unguents she meets her death
    under the knife.

Our southern neighbor had a daughter — I cannot recall her name;
'Twas but the other day that a worthy go-between
    had brought her betrothal presents.
She had heard no footfalls on her steps of glazed tiles,
And saw but the shadows of men on her blind of kingfisher blue.
Suddenly the clash of sword-blades is heard in the courtyard below,

And in a moment's space heads and trunks are lying severed
 on the ground.
Raising their eyes to heaven, then covering their faces,
 and uttering one wail of horror,
She and her sister threw themselves together into a well.

At our northern neighbor's, the youthful matron was being urged
 to depart;
So she was shaking out her cloudlike tresses, and wiping the paint
 from her eyebrows,
When she heard the noise of men battering down the lofty gates,
And instinctively she climbed the stairs into the upper story.
But soon on every side there appeared the blaze of fire,
And when she would have descended again, the staircase itself
 was destroyed.
Then came loud screams from amidst the smoke, still imploring
 for rescue,
But ere long her corpse, hanging over the cross-beams,
 was reduced to ashes.

The Lady in the Rebels' Camp

By good hap, I was able to preserve myself intact
 from murderous weapons;
But daring not stand irresolute nor look back at the home I was
 leaving,
I combed the hair over my brows to follow the army on their march,
And, forcing a cheerful expression, issued forth
 from the door of my dwelling.
No means, after this, of returning to my old village;
No place, henceforth, where I could seek my kith and kin;
For since I fell into the rebels' hands three years have run their
 course,
And always I have been prey to anxious care, my heart
 quaking with fear.
At night I lie encircled by a thousandfold ring of swords and spears,
In the morning I have to make a meal off minced human livers.
Albeit I am taken to a nuptial couch, how can it give me joy?
Though I have jewels and riches in plenty, they are not
 my heart's desire.
Their hair is unkempt, their faces begrimed, their eyebrows
 shaggy and red:
Often when I turn my eyes upon them, I cannot endure the sight.

Their clothes are put upon all awry, the language they speak is
    strange;
Overweening pride in their prowess is writ large in their faces.
Their officers of the Cypress Terrace are a lot of cunning foxes,
Their members of the Orchid Office are so many slinking rats.[60]
In their close-cropped hair they would fain stick ornamental
    hairpins.
Without removing their Court robes they roll themselves
    in embroidered coverlets.
Clutching their ivory tablets upside down, they masquerade
    as Ministers of State;
With the golden fish at their girdles wrong way up, they play
    the part of Court officials.
In the morning I hear them entering the Audience Chamber
    to present their memorials,
But in the evening one sees them brawling as they make their way
    to the wine tavern.

A Forlorn Hope

One morning, in the fifth watch, everybody gets up in alarm,
With much shouting and excited clamour, as though discussing
    some secret news.
During the night, it seems, a mounted scout had ridden
    into the Imperial City
To say that the previous day the Government troops
    had occupied Chishui.
Now, Chishui is but a hundred *li* from the city,
And if they set out at dawn they ought to be here by nightfall.
The ruffianly crew sit in gloomy silence on their horses,
But the female attendants in my chamber give secret vent to their
    joy.
All say that our grievous wrongs will now be avenged,
And we confidently expect that the villainous horde will this day
    meet their doom.
Horsemen galloping hither and thither fill the air
    with exciting rumours:
'Tis said that our army is on the march to enter the capital
    in full strength!

---

[60] Both of these were names for the Censorate.

Big Peng and little Peng look at each other in distress,
While What's-his-name and What-d'ye-call-him cling to their saddles
   and weep.
Thus things drift on for several days, and still there is no news,
So we must suppose that these advancing troops already
   have jade tablets in their mouths,[61]
And that they came waving flags and brandishing swords
   only in order to submit;
Further it is reported that all the Government armies
   have been routed and put to flight.

Desolation of the City After the Storm

After this, great misery and distress prevail on every side;
A bushel of gold is the price of a single peck of grain;
In Shang Rang's kitchen the bark of trees is used as food,[62]
On Huang Chao's table human flesh is carved.[63]
Communication is cut off from the southeast, and there is no road
   for supplies.
Gradually the ditches and streams are choked up, while
   the population dwindles.
Stiffening corpses lie in heaps outside the Liujun Gate,
And the Qijia Camp is strewn with those who have starved to death.
Chang'an lies in mournful stillness: what does it now contain?
— Ruined markets and desolate streets, in which ears of wheat
   are sprouting.
Fuel-gatherers have hacked down every flowering plant
   in the Apricot Gardens,
Builders of barricades have destroyed the willows
   along the Imperial Canal.
All the gaily-colored chariots with their ornamented wheels
   are scattered and gone,

---

[61] In token of submission.

[62] Shang Rang was one of Huang Chao's lieutenants.

[63] These gruesome facts are corroborated in the histories. "The rebels used their prisoners as food, thousands of men daily. They prepared a number of huge pestles, with which they pounded their bones and skin to a pulp in mortars, and then devoured them." (*New Tang History*) "In Chang'an a bushel of rice would fetch 30,000 cash. The rebels sold human beings to the Government troops as food,... the price of a man running to several hundred thousand cash, and varying according to his degree of plumpness." (*Comprehensive Mirror of History*)

Of the stately mansions with their vermilion gates less than half
    remain.
The Hanyuan Hall of Audience is the haunt of foxes and hares,
The approach to the Flower-calyx Belvedere is a mass of brambles
    and thorns.
All the pomp and magnificence of the olden days
    are buried and passed away;
Only a dreary waste meets the eye: the old familiar objects are no
    more.
The Inner Treasury is burnt down, its tapestries and embroideries
    a heap of ashes;
All along the Street of Heaven one treads on the bones of State
    officials.

The Journey Through the Ruined Countryside

Day was breaking when we arrived at the highway east of the city,
And outside the walls wind-borne smoke tinged the landscape
    with the dismal hue of the frontier regions.
Along the road we sometimes saw roving bands of soldiers;
At the foot of the Slope[64] was heavy silence — no speeding
    nor welcoming of guests.
Looking eastwards from Baling, we see no trace of human life
    or habitation;
From Mount Li, bosomed in trees, the wealth of blue and gold
    has utterly departed.
All the great roads are now become thickets of brambles,
And benighted travelers sleep in ruined shells, under the light
    of the moon.
Next morning, at dawn, we arrive at Sanfenglu,
Where of countless inhabitants not a single household remains;
The deserted fields and gardens show nothing but weeds;
The trees and bamboos are destroyed, and everything is ownerless ...

Episode of the Golden God

I turn to interrogate a Golden God in his wayside shrine,
But the Golden God is silent: he is more melancholy than ourselves.

---

[64] It appears to have been customary for inhabitants of the capital to escort departing
guests to this range of low hills outside the city.

Of the aged cypresses before the temple only mangled stumps
    remain;
The bronze incense-burners in the sanctuary secrete nothing but
    dust.
"Ever since the frenzied Robber brought the Middle Kingdom
    under his yoke,
Heaven and earth have been shrouded in gloom and darkened
    with storms;
The holy water before the altar has failed in its magic power,
The warriors of the underworld, painted on the wall, have been
    unable to repel the invaders.
In days of ease (says the God) I was merely content to enjoy
    the food offerings bounteously provided,
But in time of stress I can bring no aid, nor manifest
    my supernatural power.
Now I am ashamed of being such a helpless God:
Let me flee far into the mountains and there hide me as best I can.
Within these precincts I hear no sound of flutes and pipes,
In the place of offering I look in vain for a sacrificial victim.
Therefore let some hideous demon be installed in my place
    near the village,
Who shall torture and slay the unhappy people from morning to
    night."
— When I heard these words, my melancholy grew deeper still.
Heaven sends down calamities in their season which are not
    in our power to control.
If a God can flee thus from trouble into the mountains,
Why should we look with censure on the noblemen in the East?[65]

On the Road to Luoyang

The year before last, I was also taken over the Yangzhen Pass,
And, raising my head, saw Mount Jing towering into the clouds.
It was like passing out of hell into the company of living men
To be suddenly ware of a world untroubled and at peace.
The Governor of Shanzhou is loyal and upright:
He excites no clash of arms, but contents himself with guarding his
    city.

---

[65] The princes and satraps in other provinces who have been false to their trust and yielded
to the rebels.

The Governor of Pujing is able to repress the spirit of war,
And all is tranquil for a thousand *li*: no sound of weapons is heard.
By day you may carry your valuables abroad, and no man
    will interfere with you;
By night you may travel all alone, with gold hairpins sticking
    in your coiffure.

The Old Man Reduced to Beggary

Next morning, as we passed eastwards of Xin'an,
We fell in with an old man begging for rice-gruel by the wayside,
His hair sprinkled with white, his face of a livid hue,
Who was crouching for concealment amidst the undergrowth of
    weeds.
I asked him, saying: "To what village do you belong?
And why are you lying under the cold sky, exposed to frost and dew?"
The old man stood up for a moment and was about to tell his story,
But sank back with his head in his hands and wailed aloud to heaven.
— "My native homestead was on the register of Dongji County,[66]
And every year I had land covered with crops and mulberry trees,
    seven thousand acres;
The fertile lands which I sowed each year were over two thousand
    acres in extent;
The household tax I paid annually came to thirty million cash.
My daughters were practised in weaving cloaks of serge and sarcenet,
My daughters-in-law were able to cook meals of red millet.
A thousand granaries were mine! Ten thousand wagons too!
And after Huang Chao's passage, a moiety was still left.
But ever since the armed hosts have been encamped in Luoxia,
Day and night, patrolling bands have entered the village ramparts;
The glittering blade, like unto the Green Serpent, is plucked
    from its scabbard;
The wind above our heads blows out the flags and reveals
    the White Tiger.
Entering the gates, they dismount and swoop down like a whirlwind,
Ransack the buildings, empty the money-bags: everything is swept
    bare.
And when all my patrimony is gone, even my flesh and blood
    are torn from me.

---

[66] Part of the city of Luoyang.

So that now, in my declining years, I am left alone in my
    wretchedness.
Alone in my wretchedness, ah me! yet what call have I to lament? —
In the hills there are thousands on thousands like myself,
Who spend their days searching for wild berries to still their hunger,
And sleep by night under the frosty sky, couching
    upon the rank weeds."

Reports from Other Provinces

On hearing this old fellow's heart-rending tale of woe,
Tears coursed down my cheeks all day like rain.
Stirring abroad, I heard but the hooting of the owl, that bird
    of revolution.
We intended to hasten still further east, to find some place of abode,
But now we hear that all traffic by boat or cart is stopped
    on the road to Bian.[67]
They also say that there has been mutual slaughter at Pengmen,
Where the aspect of the countryside would cause even a warrior
    to swoon,
And where the rivers and streams are half composed of the blood
    of murdered men ...

A Visitor from Jiangnan

Now I happen to hear that a visitor has arrived from Jinling,[68]
Who reports that in Jiangnan things are quite otherwise than here;
For ever since the Great Brigand invaded the Central Plain,
No warhorses have been bred on the frontiers of that land.
The Governor there regards the extirpation of thieves and robbers
    as a work of heavenly merit,
While he treats his people as tenderly as though they were
    newborn babes.
His walls and moats offer secure protection, as if made of metal
    and filled with boiling water,
And with the levies and taxes that pour in like rain he provides
    troops and ramparts.
While the whole Empire, alas! is in a state of ferment,
This one district remains smoothly tranquil and undisturbed;

---

[67] The modern Kaifeng.
[68] The modern Nanjing.

It is only the denizens of the capital that must flee to escape calamity,
So that in our yearning for peace we must envy even
   the ghosts of Jiangnan.

Envoi

— I pray, Sir, that when you have plied the oar once more
   and journeyed back to the East,
You will present His Excellency this lengthy ballad that I have sung."

SIKONG TU (837–908)

The Twenty-Four Modes of Poetry

Translated by Herbert Giles

Sikong Tu owes his place in literary history to his "Twenty-four Modes," commonly
considered to be one of the most important works of Tang literary criticism. This
series of twenty-four poems does not give a classification or evaluation of poets, it does
not give names; more than any other work of Chinese literary criticism, it tries to
penetrate into the realm of poetry itself. The twenty-four pieces describe literary
"qualities," "modes," and "moods" in highly artistic language. A certain vagueness
results from the lack of concrete examples and from this intuitive method. The
language is highly suggestive, betraying strong Buddhist and Taoist influences.

— Volker Klöpsch, *Indiana Companion,* 1986

For another annotated version of this extraordinary series of poems, see Stephen
Owen, *Readings in Chinese Literary Thought.* Owen comments: "It is a measure of the
strangeness and the problems of 'The Twenty-Four Categories of Poetry' that if the
title did not contain the word 'poetry,' there would be no way even to guess to what
these elusive verses referred. They could just as easily be 'characters' in traditional
psychology or more transient 'moods,' or they could refer to categories of painting,
calligraphy, or music, or any other activity in which categories of manners played an
important role."

— Editors

Energy — Absolute

Expenditure of force leads to outward decay,
Spiritual existence means inward fulness.
Let us revert to Nothing and enter the Absolute,
Hoarding up strength for Energy.
Freighted with eternal principles,
Athwart the mighty void,
Where cloud-masses darken,

And the wind blows ceaseless around,
Beyond the range of conceptions,
Let us gain the Centre,
And there hold fast without violence,
Fed from an inexhaustible supply.

Tranquil Repose

It dwells in quietude, speechless,
Imperceptible in the cosmos,
Watered by the eternal harmonies,
Soaring with the lonely crane.
It is like a gentle breeze in spring,
Softly bellying the flowing robe;
It is like the note of the bamboo flute,
Whose sweetness we would fain make our own.
Meeting by chance, it seems easy of access,
Seeking, we find it hard to secure.
Ever shifting in semblance,
It shifts from the grasp and is gone.

Slim — Stout [69]

Gathering the water-plants
From the wild luxuriance of spring,
Away in the depth of a wild valley
Anon I see a lovely girl.
With the green leaves the peach-trees are loaded,
The breeze blows gently along the stream,
Willows shade the winding path,
Darting orioles collect in groups.
Eagerly I press forward
As the reality grows upon me ...
'Tis the eternal theme
Which, though old, is ever new.

Concentration

Green pines and a rustic hut,
The sun sinking through pure air,

---

[69] Owen: *"Delicate-Fresh and Rich-Lush."* Eds.

I take off my cap and stroll alone,
Listening to the song of birds.
No wild geese fly hither,
And she is far away;
But my thoughts make her present
As in the days gone by.
Across the water dark clouds are whirled,
Beneath the moonbeams the eyots stand revealed,
And sweet words are exchanged
Though the great River rolls between.[70]

Height — Antiquity

Lo the Immortal, borne by spirituality,
His hand grasping a lotus flower,
Away to Time everlasting,
Trackless through the regions of Space!
With the moon he issues from the Ladle,[71]
Speeding upon a favorable gale;
Below, Mount Hua looms dark,
And from it sounds a clear-toned bell.
Vacantly I gaze after his vanished image,
Now passed beyond the bounds of mortality ...
Ah, the Yellow Emperor and Yao,
They, peerless, are his models.

Refinement

A jade kettle with a purchase of spring,[72]
A shower on the thatched hut
Wherein sits a gentle scholar,
With tall bamboos growing right and left,
And white clouds in the newly-clear sky,
And birds flitting in the depths of trees.
Then pillowed on his lute in the green shade,
A waterfall tumbling overhead,

---

[70] Owen comments: "There is great disagreement about these lines, and the various explanations are only suppositions. Most commentators see in the river an image of security, ubiquitousness, or openness of either the condition of being 'Firm and Self-Possessed' [Giles' 'Concentration'] or of words uttered in such a condition." *Eds.*

[71] The Great Bear.

[72] Wine, which makes man see spring at all seasons.

Leaves dropping, not a word spoken,
The man placid, like a chrysanthemum,
Noting down the flower-glory of the season —
A book well worthy to be read.

Wash — Smelt

As iron from the mines,
As silver from lead,
So purify thy heart,
Loving the limpid and clean.
Like a clear pool in spring,
With its wondrous mirrored shapes,
So make for the spotless and true,
And, riding the moonbeam, revert to the Spiritual.
Let your gaze be upon the stars of heaven,[73]
Let your song be of the hiding hermit;
Like flowing water is our today,
Our yesterday, the bright moon.[74]

Strength

The mind as though in the void,
The vitality as though of the rainbow,
Among the thousand-ell peaks of Wu,
Flying with the clouds, racing with the wind,
Drink of the spiritual, feed on force,
Store them for daily use, guard them in your heart,
Be like Him in His might,
For this is to preserve your energy;[75]
Be a peer of Heaven and Earth,
A co-worker in Divine Transformation ...

---

[73] Emblems of purity.

[74] Our previous state of existence at the eternal Centre to which the moon belongs. [Owen comments: "The reference here is clearly to the figure of moonlight in the water, whose strong Buddhist associations are reinforced by the terminology of reincarnation in the last line.... The reflected poetic image is compared to the process of reincarnation, in which the soul may be perfected towards Buddhahood in realizing the 'emptiness' of the world (emptiness being also associated with the reflected light and the flowing water)."]

[75] The Power who, without loss of force, causes things to be what they are — God. [Owen: "Heaven's motions."]

Seek to be full of these,
And hold fast to them alway.

Embroideries

If the mind has wealth and rank,
One may make light of yellow gold.
Rich pleasures pall ere long,
Simple joys deepen ever.
A mist-cloud hanging on the river bank,
Pink almond-flowers along the bough,
A flower-girt cottage beneath the moon,
A painted bridge half seen in shadow,
A golden goblet brimming with wine,
A friend with his hand on the lute ...
Take these and be content;
They will swell thy heart beneath thy robe.

The Natural

Stoop, and there it is;
Seek it not right and left.
All roads lead thither —
One touch and you have spring![76]
As though coming upon opening flowers,
As though gazing upon the new year,
Verily I will not snatch it.
Forced, it will dwindle away.
I will be like the hermit on the hill,
Like duckweed gathered on the stream,[77]
And when emotions crowd upon me,
I will leave them to the harmonies of heaven.[78]

Conservation

Without a word writ down,
All wit may be attained.
If words do not affect the speaker,

---

[76] Alluding to the art of the painter.
[77] A creature of chance, following the doctrine of Inaction.
[78] Owen: "As it may, his heart will be enlightened — / The Potter's Wheel of Heaven goes on and on forever." *Eds.*

They seem inadequate to sorrow.
Herein is the First Cause,
With which we sink or rise,
As wine in the strainer mounts high,
As cold turns back the season of flowers.
The wide-spreading dust-motes in the air,
The sudden spray-bubbles of ocean,
Shallow, deep, collected, scattered —
You grasp ten thousand, and secure one.

Set Free

Joying in flowers without let,
Breathing in the empyrean,
Through Tao reverting to ether,
And there to be wildly free,
Wide-spreading as the wind of heaven,
Lofty as the peaks of ocean,
Filled with a spiritual strength,
All creation by my side,
Before me the sun, moon, and stars,
The phoenix following behind.
In the morning I whip up my leviathans[79]
And wash my feet in Fusang.[80]

Animal Spirits

That they might come back unceasingly,
That they might be ever with us! —
The bright river, unfathomable,
The rare flower just opening,
The parrot of the verdant spring,
The willow-trees, the terrace,
The stranger from the dark hills,
The cup overflowing with clear wine …
Oh, for life to be extended,

---

[79] Owen: "The immense turtles of myth that dwell in the ocean." *Eds.*

[80] Variously identified with Saghalien, Mexico, and Japan. [Owen: "The *fu-sang* tree is where the sun rises. The last four lines are a common type of description of the 'great man,' one mode of Taoist adept whose mastery of universal process is symbolized by his movement through the cosmos with an entourage of mythical creatures doing his bidding."]

With no dead ashes of writing,
Amid the charms of the Natural —
Ah, who can compass it?

Close Woven

In all things there are veritable atoms,
Though the senses cannot perceive them,
Struggling to emerge into shape
From the wondrous workmanship of God.[81]
Water flowing, flowers budding,
The limpid dew evaporating,
An important road, stretching far,
A dark path where progress is slow ...
So words should not shock,
Nor thought be inept.
But be like the green of spring,
Like the snow beneath the moon.[82]

Seclusion

Following our own bent,
Enjoying the Natural, free from curb,
Rich with what comes to hand,
Hoping some day to be with God.
To build a hut beneath the pines,
With uncovered head to pore over poetry,
Knowing only morning and eve,
But not what season it may be ...
Then, if happiness is ours,
Why must there be action?
If of our selves we can reach this point,
Can we not be said to have attained?

Fascination

Lovely is the pine-grove,
With the stream eddying below,
A clear sky and a snow-clad bank,

---

[81] Owen: "The process of creation is already wondrous." *Eds.*
[82] Each invisible atom of which combines to produce a perfect whole.

Fishing-boats in the reach beyond.
And she, like unto jade,
Slowly sauntering, as I follow through the dark wood,
Now moving on, now stopping short,
Far away in the deep valley ...
My mind quits its tenement, and is in the past,
Vague, and not to be recalled,
As though before the glow of the rising moon,
As though before the glory of the autumn.

In Tortuous Ways

I climbed the Taihang mountain
By the green winding path,
Vegetation like a sea of jade,
Flower-scent borne far and wide.
Struggling with effort to advance,
A sound escaped my lips,
Which seemed to be back ere 'twas gone,
As though hidden but not concealed.
The eddying waters rush to and fro,
Overhead the great rukh soars and sails;
Tao does not limit itself to a shape,
But is round and square by turns.

Actualities

Choosing plain words
To express simple thoughts,
Suddenly I happened upon a recluse,
And seemed to see the heart of Tao.
Beside the winding brook,
Beneath dark pine-trees' shade,
There was one stranger bearing a faggot,
Another listening to the lute.
And so, where my fancy led me,
Better than if I had sought it,
I heard the music of heaven,
Astounded by its rare strains.

Despondent

A gale ruffles the stream
And trees in the forest crack;

My thoughts are bitter as death,
For she whom I asked will not come.
A hundred years slip by like water,
Riches and rank are but cold ashes,
Tao is daily passing away,
To whom shall we turn for salvation?
The brave soldier draws his sword,
And tears flow with endless lamentation;
The wind whistles, leaves fall,
And rain trickles through the old thatch.

Form and Feature

After gazing fixedly upon expression and substance
The mind returns with a spiritual image,
As when seeking the outlines of waves,
As when painting the glory of spring.
The changing shapes of wind-swept clouds,
The energies of flowers and plants,
The rolling breakers of ocean,
The crags and cliffs of mountains,
All these are like mighty Tao,
Skilfully woven into earthly surroundings ...
To obtain likeness without form,
Is not that to possess the man?

The Transcendental

Not of the spirituality of the mind,
Nor yet of the atoms of cosmos,
But as though reached upon white clouds,
Borne thither by pellucid breezes.
Afar, it seems at hand,
Approach, 'tis no longer there;
Sharing the nature of Tao,
It shuns the limits of mortality.
It is in the piled-up hills, in tall trees,
In dark mosses, in sunlight rays ...
Croon over it, think upon it;
Its faint sound eludes the ear.

Abstraction

Without friends, longing to be there,
Alone, away from the common herd,
Like the crane on Mount Hou,[83]
Like the cloud at the peak of Mount Hua.
In the portrait of the hero
The old fire still lingers;
The leaf carried by the wind
Floats on the boundless sea.
It would seem as though not to be grasped,
But always on the point of being disclosed.
Those who recognize this have already attained;
Those who hope, drift daily farther away.

Illumined

Life stretches to one hundred years,
And yet how brief a span;
Its joys so fleeting,
Its griefs so many!
What has it like a goblet of wine,
And daily visits to the wistaria arbor,
Where flowers cluster around the eaves,
And light showers pass overhead?
Then when the wine-cup is drained,
To stroll about with staff of thorn;
For who of us but will some day be an ancient?
Ah, there is the South Mountain in its grandeur![84]

Motion

Like a whirling water-wheel,
Like rolling pearls —
Yet how are these worthy to be named?
They are but illustrations for fools.
There is the mighty axis of Earth,
The never-resting pole of Heaven;
Let us grasp their clue,

---

[83] Owen comments: "The bird on which the immortal Wang Ziqiao was said to have ascended to Heaven." *Eds.*

[84] This remains, while all other things pass away.

And with them be blended into One,
Beyond the bounds of thought,
Circling for ever in the great Void,
An orbit of a thousand years —
Yes, this is the key to my theme.

▣ *Further Reading* ▣

Burton, R. F., trans. *Du Mu: Plantains in the Rain*. London: Wellsweep, 1990.
Bynner, Witter, trans. (from the texts of Kiang Kang-hu). *The Jade Mountain, a Chinese Anthology: Being Three Hundred Poems of the T'ang Dynasty*. New York: Knopf, 1929.
Frodsham, John D., trans. *Goddesses, Ghosts and Demons: The Collected Poems of Li He*. London: Anvil Press, 1983. (Originally published as *The Poems of Li Ho* [Oxford: Oxford University Press, 1970].)
Giles, Herbert, trans. "The Twenty-Four Modes of Poetry," (original title "Taoism"). *A History of Chinese Literature* (London: Heinemann, 1901).
Giles, Lionel, trans. "The Lament of the Lady of Ch'in." *T'oung Pao* (1926), 24.
Graham, A. C., trans. *Poems of the Late T'ang*. Harmondsworth: Penguin Books, 1965.
Liu, James J. Y. *The Poetry of Li Shang-yin: Ninth-Century Baroque Chinese Poet*. Chicago: University of Chicago Press, 1969.
Morrison, Robert. *Translation from the Original Chinese*. Canton: East India Company, 1815.
Owen, Stephen, trans. "The Twenty-Four Categories of Poetry." *Readings in Chinese Literary Thought* (Cambridge, Mass.: Harvard University Press, 1992), 299–357.
Rexroth, Kenneth, trans. *One Hundred Poems from the Chinese*. New York: New Directions, 1956.
———. *One Hundred More Poems from the Chinese: Love and the Turning Year*. New York: New Directions, 1970.
Tu, Kuo-ch'ing. *Li Ho*. Boston: Twayne, 1979.
Yates, Robin. *Washing Silk: The Life and Selected Poetry of Wei Chuang*. Cambridge, Mass.: Harvard University Press, 1988.

▣ *Editors' Note* ▣

James Liu's application in the 1960s of post-Empsonian critical techniques (his recognition of several "kinds of ambiguity" in Chinese verse) to the interpretation and translation of Chinese poetry, especially of Late Tang poetry, marked the beginning of an important new stage in the introduction of Chinese poetry to the West (the previous stage having been associated with the Imagists some fifty years earlier). His work paved the way for the fine translations of Angus Graham and John Frodsham.

"Our yesterday, the bright moon."
Sikong Tu, "The Twenty-four Modes of Poetry"
Seal carved by Qian Song (1807–1860)

Chapter 25

Red Leaf

Women Poets from the First Century B.C. to the Tenth Century A.D.

A Poem Written on a Floating Leaf

> How fast this water flows away!
> Buried in the women's quarters,
> The days pass in idleness.
> Red leaf, I order you —
> Go find someone
> In the world of men.

— Han Cuipin, a palace lady of the Tang (9th century)
(*translated by Kenneth Rexroth and Ling Chung*)

Introduction

Ling Chung

In the popular anthology *Three Hundred Poems of the Tang Dynasty* (1763), there is only one poem written by a woman. In the standard work *Complete Poems of the Tang Dynasty* (1707), among the 2,200 authors, there are only around 190 women poets. In the Tang dynasty women were not encouraged to write poetry and very few received any literary training.

Young girls in the families of the wealthier officials were sometimes allowed to study with boys in the school of their clan, or under private tutors. Daughters of great scholars or historians often became renowned scholars themselves — for instance, the poet Cai Yan; but usually they were only educated enough to study books on women's conduct, which taught women to be passive and yielding toward their husbands and parents-in-law, and modest, moderate and plain in thought, speech, and appearance.

Empresses and imperial concubines from noble families were often well-educated. Lower ranking women of the Imperial Palace usually numbered in the thousands, came from families of commoners, or were forfeited female relatives of officials convicted of crimes. These women sometimes became learned and were appointed by the emperor as court scholars to staff the imperial library, or as tutors to other palace women, or as monitors of the harem. The poetry of the Palace, such as that of Lady Hua Rui, generally had two subjects — praise of the emperor and of palace life, and loneliness.

According to the *Zhou Li* (The Rites of the Kingdom of Zhou), an emperor should have one empress and 126 concubines. In reality the number of his formal consorts varied from several to more than one hundred, and the remaining palace attendants, musicians, and dancers were also at his disposal. As long as they lived in the palace, many for their lifetimes, the only male they were allowed to see, except eunuchs and little boys, was the emperor. Since one man cannot satisfy several thousand women, these women expressed their sexual deprivation in poems of forlorn hope. According to legend, the "Poem Written on a Floating Red Leaf," attributed to a palace lady, Han Cuipin, reached the external world by floating out on a conduit into the waters of the Palace moat.

A class of cultivated courtesans, of girls sold for reasons of poverty, or who came from disgraced official households, or were kidnapped, had flourished at least since the Six Dynasties. They were owned by a brothel or whoremaster, and were freer than housewives and concubines. They could write love lyrics without being condemned for spoiling the family reputation. The more talented they were as poets, the more successful they were with their customers. In the Six Dynasties, China came to have something resembling a Western aristocracy, and the wealthier members kept in their palaces bands of literate women musicians and dancers called "house courtesans," who entertained at banquets.

In the Tang dynasty another class of cultivated courtesans flourished, called "official courtesans," because they entertained at official festivities and came from the most expensive brothels in the capital. Prosperous courtesans' houses were built across from the hall for the imperial examinations, and when the winners were announced, the courtesans traditionally held a celebration. Leading courtiers and officials, and even the emperor, frequented these houses. When the court held great banquets these women would all be summoned. Familiar with the entire art of poetry, the most talented, such as Zhao Luanluan, would be treated as equals and join in the discussions of poetry and poetry contests that were the highlights of the banquet. Many were ransomed by wealthy, powerful men and became their concubines, among them the poet Guan Panpan. Many men wrote of the beauty and talent of the courtesan poets Guan Panpan, Su Xiaoxiao, and Xue Tao.

In the Tang dynasty, Taoist priestesses also became a special social class and enjoyed even more freedom than courtesans, for the priestess was no one's property. She could move, travel, and associate freely. Unlike a Buddhist nun, she was not prohibited from having intimate relations with males. Indeed, Taoist priestesses were in great demand as sexual teachers and initiators. During this period many princesses and wealthy women became priestesses and their temples became the centers of social gatherings for the scholar gentry, and they took lovers at will. The poets Yu Xuanji and Li Ye were among the most influential priestesses of their times.

— From *Women Poets of China*, 1972

ZHUO WENJUN (fl. 150–115 B.C.), attrib.

A Song of White Hair

Translated by Kenneth Rexroth and Ling Chung

Daughter of a wealthy family in Sichuan, Zhuo Wenjun was widowed at seventeen, whereupon Sima Xiangru, the famous writer of rhapsodies, then a poor young man, fell in love with her. She eloped with him. Disowned and poverty-stricken, they opened a wineshop together. This so humiliated her father that he gave them a large sum of money. Sima Xiangru became the leading court poet of the Emperor Wu of Han and took a concubine. Broken-hearted, Zhuo Wenjun wrote this poem, which so moved her husband that he gave up the concubine and returned to her. This attribution is probably pure legend. In many collections the poem is anonymous.

My love, like my hair, is pure,
Frosty white like the snow on the mountain
Bright and white like the moon amid the clouds.
But I have discovered
You are of a double mind.
We have come to the breaking point.
Today we pledged each other
In a goblet of wine.
Tomorrow I will walk alone
Beside the moat,
And watch the cold water
Flow East and West,
Lonely, mournful
In the bitter weather.
Why should marriage bring only tears?
All I wanted was a man
With a single heart,
And we would stay together

As our hair turned white,
Not somebody always after wriggling fish
With his big bamboo rod.
The integrity of a loyal man
Is beyond the value of money.

BAN JIEYU (first century B.C.), attrib.

Song of Regret

Translated by Burton Watson

Lady Ban, a favorite concubine of Emperor Cheng (r. 32–37 B.C.), is known by her
court title Jieyu or Beautiful Companion, her personal name being unknown. She
bore the emperor two sons but both died in infancy. Later, when she lost favor and was
slandered by rivals, she asked permission to take up residence in the eastern palace,

Figure 60. Lady Ban. Early 20th-
century illustration. (Source:
Zixi huapu daquan [Complete
Painting Manual] [Beijing:
Rongbaozhai, 1982])

the Palace of Lasting Trust, where she waited on the empress dowager. The poem is of uncertain date, though it has traditionally been attributed to Lady Ban.

To begin I cut fine silk of Qi,
white and pure as frost or snow,
shape it to make a paired-joy fan,
round, round as the luminous moon,
to go in and out of my lord's breast;
when lifted, to stir him a gentle breeze.
But always I dread the coming of autumn,
cold winds that scatter the burning heat,
when it will be laid away in the hamper,
love and favor cut off midway.

CAI YAN (born c. 178), attrib.

Poem of Sorrow

Translated by John Frodsham

Cai Yan was the grand-daughter of the famous man of letters Cai Yong [see chapter 14]. After the death of her first husband she returned, childless, to her home. During the period of civil war toward the end of the Later Han she was kidnapped by the Xiongnu tribesmen, who married her off to the king of the Southern Xiongnu. On his death, in accordance with tribal custom, she was married to his son. After twelve years' sojourn with the Xiongnu she was ransomed by Cao Cao and brought back to China, where she married for the fourth time.

When Han declining lost its grasp of power,
Dong Zhuo upset the constant Way of Heaven.[1]
He planned to depose and kill his emperor,
But first he murdered the wise and able men.[2]
He made everybody move to the ancient capital,
And set up an emperor by force to strengthen himself.[3]
Within this land there rose up a righteous army,
Who banded together to repress that wicked man.
Zhuo's company came down upon the east,[4]

---

[1] See the notes to Cao Cao's "Graveyard Song" in chapter 9. *Eds.*
[2] In 189 Dong Zhuo deposed the Emperor, Liu Bian, after a reign of only four months and had him killed in the third month of the following year.
[3] The Eastern Han capital was Luoyang. In 190 Dong Zhuo forced Emperor Xian (r. 189–220) to move westward to Chang'an, along with several hundred thousand of his subjects.
[4] Dong Zhuo, Li Cui, Guo Si, Zhang Ji, and others were the chief rebels. In 195 Li, Guo, and the rest brought the Emperor back to Luoyang. By this time Dong Zhuo himself was dead. Nomad troops had been called in as mercenaries to fight against the imperial forces.

Figure 61. Cai Yan. Early 20th-
century illustration. (Source:
Zixi huapu daquan [Complete
Painting Manual] [Beijing:
Rongbaozhai, 1982])

Their metal armor glinting in the sun.
The men of the plains were weak and cowardly,
The invading soldiers were all Hu and Qiang.[5]
Trampling across the fields, they invested the cities,
In the towns they attacked, everything was destroyed.
Heads were lopped off till no one was left to kill,
Just bones and corpses propping each other up.
On their horses' flanks they hung the heads of men,
On their horses' backs they carried off women and girls.
We galloped for days westwards into the passes,
The endless road was dangerous and steep.

---

[5] Nomad tribes.

When I looked back, into the mist-hung distance,
I felt as though my very heart was breaking.
In all they captured over ten thousand women,
Our captors would not let us keep together.
Sometimes when sisters found themselves side by side,
Longing to speak, they dared not utter a word.
If by some trivial fault we angered the soldiers,
At once they'd bawl out: "Kill these prisoners!
We'd better take our knives and finish them,
Why waste our time in keeping them alive?"
I had no desire to go on living longer,
I could not bear their cursing and reviling.
Sometimes they flogged us with rods as well,
And the pain we felt was mingled with our hatred.
During the day we trudged on weeping and crying,
At night we sat there, groaning to ourselves.
We longed to die, but could not get the chance.
We longed to live, with nothing left to live for.
How could the Blue Above be so unjust
To pour on us such anguish and misfortune?
The border wilds are different from China,
And men know little of Righteousness and Truth.
It is a place where frost and snow abound,
And the northern wind blows spring and summer long.
It sent my clothes flapping about as it blew,
And whistled shrilly all around my ears.
Moved by the seasons, I thought of my father and mother,
My grief and sighing never came to an end.
When a stranger arrived from the world outside,
I was always overjoyed to hear of it,
I would welcome him, ask him what news he had,
Only to find his district was not mine.
By luck my constant wish was gratified,
My relatives sent someone to rescue me.[6]
But now when I was able to escape,
I found I had to leave my children there.[7]
Natural bonds tie children to a woman's heart,
I thought of our parting, never to meet again,

---

[6] Cao Cao sent an envoy to rescue her.
[7] The Xiongnu would allow none of their children to be brought up in China.

In life and death eternally separated —
I could not bring myself to say goodbye.
My children came and clung around my neck,
Asking their mother where she was going to.
"They say that you have got to go away,
How can you ever come back to us again?
Mother, you were always so loving and so kind,
Why have you now become so harsh to us?
We have not yet even grown into men,
How can you not look back and think of us?"
The sight of them destroyed me utterly,
I grew confused, behaved like one run mad.
Weeping and wailing, I fondled and caressed them;
When I had to set out, I turned back time and again.
The women who were taken captive with me
Came to bid me farewell and see me off.
They were glad that I could go back, though alone;
The sound of their crying hurt me grievously.
Because of this the horses stood hesitating,
Because of this the carriage did not move.
All the lookers-on were crying and wailing,
Even the passers-by were crying too.
But I had to go! I had to harden my heart;
Daily our caravan hurried me further away.
On and on we went, three thousand leagues;
When would I ever see those I had left behind?
I brooded on the children of my womb,
The heart in my breast was broken evermore.
I got home to find my family was wiped out,
Nor had I any kin at all alive.[8]
My home town had become a mountain-forest,
In its ruined courts the thorns and mugworts grew,
And all around, white bones of unknown men,
Lay scattered with no one to bury them.
Outside the gates I heard no human voices,
Only wolves were howling, barking all around.

---

[8] Literally, "Even my mother's brothers' children and my father's sisters' children." Her family was completely wiped out. This explains Cao Cao's concern for Cai Yong, whose spirit would have remained unconsoled by any ancestral sacrifices if Cai Yan had not been brought back.

I stood alone, facing my lonely shadow,
My cry of anguish battered at my heart.
I climbed a hill and gazed into the distance,
And soul and spirit suddenly fled from me.
A bystander encouraged me to patience,
Kept urging me to try and go on living.
Though I went on living, what had life left for me?
I entrusted my fate to yet another man,
Exhausted my heart to summon strength to go on.[9]
My wanderings have made all men despise me,
I live in fear of being cast aside once more.
How long can a woman's life go dragging on?
I shall know sorrow till the very end of my days.

SU XIAOXIAO (late fifth century)

A Song of Xiling Lake

Translated by Kenneth Rexroth and Ling Chung

Su was a legendary courtesan of Hangzhou, reputed to have been one of the two most beautiful women who ever lived. (The other was Yang Guifei [see chapter 23] who by current standards would probably be considered obese.)

I ride in a red painted carriage.
You pass me on a blue dappled horse.
Where shall we bind our hearts
In a love knot?
Along Xiling Lake under the cypress trees.

BAO LINGHUI (fl. 464)
Two Poems

Translated by Anne Birrell

Linghui was the younger sister of the poet Bao Zhao [see chapter 12].

---

[9] She is speaking of her marriage to Dong Si. For a widow to remarry at all was considered shameful in China. But Cai Yan had been married three times before her marriage to Dong Si. It was for this reason that she was despised. It may well have been known that she had been the wife not only of the Xiongnu prince but also of his son, a proceeding that would have seemed incestuous to the Chinese. We may suppose that Dong Si was persuaded to marry her only after being suitably bribed with high office by Cao Cao.

In the Key of Farewell

A traveler came from far away,
He brought me a lacquer singing lute.
On its wood a loving you design,
Its strings were set in the key of farewell.
All my life I will keep this chord,
The year grown cold will not change my heart.
I long to compose a *Sunny spring* tune
With *do* and *re* for ever in pursuit.

Poem Sent to a Traveler

Ever since you went away
My tense face near the porch won't soften,
Pounder and block no longer sound at night,
Tall gates at noon stay locked.
Into my bedcurtains drift fireflies,
In front of the garden purple orchids bloom.
Nature withers, sensing the change of season,
Swans arrive telling of travelers cold.
Your journey may end at winter's close,
I'll wait till late spring for your return.

SHEN MANYUAN (fl. 540)
Two Poems

Translated by Anne Birrell

Manyuan was the grand-daughter of the poet Shen Yue [see chapter 13].

Her Tiara Flowers

Pearl blooms ring kingfisher plumes,
Jewel leaves inset with gold jade.
Artificial lotus seemingly uncontrived
Are flowers of apparent natural life.
Lower stems stroke her broidered collar,
Tiny footsteps set the jewels aquiver.
Just let me fix it on her cloudy coiffure,
Then moth eyebrows will be soon painted.

Parody of the Other Woman

Bright pearl, kingfisher plume bed drapes,
Gold leaf, sheer green silk door tapestries
Lifting now and then with the wind.
I imagine I see your charming face
At dawn when you put on your tiara,
At dark when you slip off your silk dress.
Well, give yourself to Mr. Libertine!
Does love have to be selfish?

LI YE (eighth century)

A Greeting to Lu Yu

Translated by Kenneth Rexroth and Ling Chung

Li Ye was a Taoist priestess renowned for her beauty, wit, poetry, calligraphy, and skill on the lute. The poets Liu Zhangqing [see chapter 21], Jiaoran [see chapter 26] and Lu Yu (author of the *Tea Classic*) were her close friends. In her old age she was summoned to court by the Emperor Xuanzong.

Last time you left
The moon shone on heavy frosts.
Now today you have come through bitter fog
To visit me, still lying here ill.
When I try to speak, tears start.
You urge me to drink Tao Yuanming's wine,
And I chant Xie Lingyun's poems of welcome.
It is good to get drunk once in a while.
What else is there to do?

ZHAO LUANLUAN (? eighth century)
Five Poems

Translated by Kenneth Rexroth and Ling Chung

Zhao was an elegant prostitute in the pleasure quarters of Chang'an. Her poems were a common type, a sort of advertising copy in praise of the parts of a woman's body, written for courtesans and prostitutes.

Slender Fingers

Slender, delicate, soft jade,
Fresh peeled spring onions —

They are always hidden in emerald
Sleeves of perfumed silk.
Yesterday on the lute strings
All their nails were painted scarlet.

Red Sandalwood Mouth

Small cherries sip delicately
At the edge of the wine cup.
Beautiful speech floats on jasmine perfume.
Like the mouth of the singer Fan Su,
The concubine of Bo Juyi,
The teeth are like white melon seeds,
And the lips like pomegranate blossoms.

Willow Eyebrows

Sorrows play at the edge of these willow leaf curves.
They are often reflected, deep, deep,
In my water blossom inlaid mirror.
I am too pretty to bother with an eyebrow pencil.
Spring hills paint themselves
With their own personality.

Cloud Hairdress

My disordered perfumed clouds are still damp,
Iridescent as a blackbird's throat feathers,
Glossy as a cicada's wing.
I pin a gold phoenix by my ear.
After I have adorned myself,
My man smiles at me.

Creamy Breasts

Fragrant with powder, moist with perspiration,
They are the pegs of a jade inlaid harp.
Aroused by spring, they are soft as cream
Under the fertilizing mist.
After my bath my perfumed lover
Holds them and plays with them
And they are cool as peonies and purple grapes.

XUE TAO (768–831)
Five Poems

Translated by Jeanne Larsen

In her childhood she moved from Chang'an to Sichuan, where her father had a government appointment. After her father's death, to support herself and her widowed mother, she became a courtesan. She became well known as a poet at an early age and was honored at banquets and poetry contests given by the Governor of Sichuan. She was befriended and admired by the leading poets of her day, Bo Juyi and Yuan Zhen [see chapter 23] and Liu Yuxi [see chapter 22].

Cicadas

Dew-rinsed:
their pure notes
carry far.

Windblown:
as dry, fasting leaves
are blown.

Chirr after chirr,
as if in unison.

But each perches
on its own branch,
alone.

Wind

Seeking marsh
orchids, a light
zephyr ranges.

It wafts over strings;
they dry out,
one chord.

Twigs in the woods
sing in whistles and rustles.

Along paths through the pine trees:
night-bracing,
fresh.

Dog Parted from Her Master

Yes, she's a good dog,
lived four or five years
within his crimson gates,

fur sweet-smelling,
feet quite clean,
master affectionate.

Then by chance she
took a nip
and bit a well-loved guest.

Now she no longer sleeps
upon his red silk rugs.

Parrot Parted from Her Cage

A single figure
alone in the desert wastes:

she flew, departing,
and, flying, came
to ascend the brocade seat.

Then all because she blurted
something indiscreet,

she no longer calls out
for him
from her deserted cage.

Crabapple Brook

Spring sets the scene among
celestial dawn-pink clouds.

On the face of the water:
the shapes of fish,
each one trailing flowers.

Our world forgets the
otherness
of numinous green things.

While these trees compete
to dye light sands
with their rosy, dappled silk.

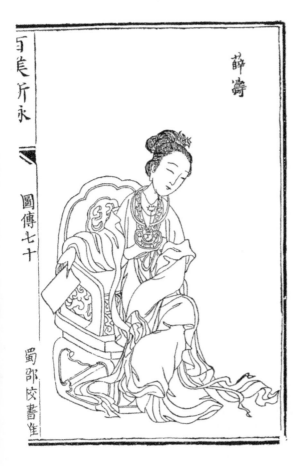

Figure 62. Xue Tao. Qing
dynasty illustration.
(Source: *Baimei xinyong*)

GUAN PANPAN (eighth to ninth century)

Mourning

Translated by Kenneth Rexroth and Ling Chung

Guan was a celebrated courtesan of Xuzhou. She was a favorite of the Governor of the
district, Zhang Yin, and entertained such leading poets as Bo Juyi, who wrote: "When
we had all had a good deal to drink he sent for Panpan to make us merry. And merry
we certainly were. I gave her a poem in which I compared her lovely but helpless

movements (for she had drunk heavily) to the swaying of a peony in the wind." When Zhang died in 806, she lived alone in a house that had belonged to him, in a building known as Swallow Mansion.

In the cemetery on North Hill
Heavy mist envelops the pines and cypresses.
In Swallow Mansion
I sit quietly thinking of you.
Since you were buried
Your singers are scattered like dust.
And the red perfume in their red sleeves
Has faded away for ten years now.

YU XUANJI (c. 844–868)
Five Poems

Translated by Genevieve Wimsatt

Born in Chang'an, she became the concubine of an official, Li Zi'an. His wife, who was jealous, tortured her and drove her from the house. She became a Taoist priestess and entered a Taoist Monastery in the capital, where she held open house for young scholars and officials. She traveled widely and had many lovers, including the poet Wen Tingyun [see chapter 24].

Divided by the Han River

Sent to Li Zi'an

South of the River, north of the River, wandering comfortless,
Remembering you, longing for you, sighing in loneliness;
Mandarin Ducks alight on the warm sand mound,
Cranes flock lazily toward forests yellowed and browned;
Faint ... faint ... in the dusk a song whispers its plea,
Moonlight lies on the wharf, somber profound ...
In love a disunion of ten feet is wide as a myriad *li* —
Listen! In home upon home the washing paddles resound!

Spring Passion

Sent to Li Zi'an

Not of steep mountain trails or perilous ascents
Will I complain, but of the hard, hard ways of love!
Ice melting in far streams beats a refrain,

Snow on cold, distant peaks recalls your lineaments;
Loathing light songs, sick of spring wine,
I bid no guests to evening chess ...
Our vows were of the greenness of the pine,
of the rock's steadfastness;
Sometimes even the One-winged Birds remain too long as twain.
Hating to walk alone when winter sunsets fade,
Eager for meeting when the moon is full above,
What can I give you, O Departed Love of mine?
Only a song of tears falling in the spring sunshine.

Voicing Deepest Thoughts

Idle ... nothing to do ...
Abandoned in the wilds, with time to spare ...
Rivers and clouds ... the moon breaks through ...
Unmoored the boat drifts here and there ...
In Xiaoliang Temple raising the lute strain,
On Youliang Tower humming an air ...
The bamboo cluster is a friend of mine,
The rock a comrade true;
Swallows and sparrows I disdain,
Silver and gold unvalued shine,
But my cup is full of green spring wine!
Facing the moon I touch the lute again;
The pool wells clear and clean about the stair;
I draw my pin and slash ripples in twain,
Then, the book finished, on the couch I drowsily recline.
Rising, half drunk, to comb my hair.

Selling Wilted Peonies

Sigh, for the petals whirl before the gust!
The fragrant essence melts — and spring is over!
Too costly, it has found no master-lover,
Too sweet, it daunts the hovering butterfly;
Red blooms, where is your rightful high resort?
Green leaves, how can you bear the dew and dust?
Yet set this shoot in the imperial court,
And lords will covet what they may not buy.

Vanishing Spring Moves to Regret

Sent to a Friend

Oriole chattering shattering cruel dreams ...
Face worn with tears ... Toilet in disarray ...
Bamboo shadows show thin in the faint moonbeams,
Heavy the evening smoke, muted the streams;
Swallows with wet beaks carry clay,
Bees with perfumed antennae flutter petals along ...
Lonely, despondent, with yearnings ever astray,
I finish singing the Pine Branch Song.

HUANGFU MEI (fl. 910)

The Story of Yu Xuanji

Translated by Jeanne Kelly

This story represents the popular tradition of Yu Xuanji's life. It has been suggested that she was unjustly charged of her maid's death.

At the Universal Temple in the Western Capital there lived a nun by the name of Yu Xuanji. She was a courtesan, famed both for her beauty and for her literary accomplishments. She was especially given to the art of poetry. At the age of sixteen, she decided to dedicate herself to the Taoist teachings.

She became a nun at the beginning of the Xian-tong reign period (860–875). Her verses describing the delights of love were widely known among the literati. She herself was by nature as frail as the orchid, and of a free disposition. She had numerous amorous attachments with the young gallants of the capital, who would compete with one another to win her favor. Some would visit her bringing wine, and she would often sing verses to the accompaniment of the lute....

She had a maidservant named Lüqiao, who was as clever as she was attractive. One day Xuanji was unexpectedly invited to a neighboring temple. As she was about to go, she instructed her maid not to go out. "If a friend of mine calls, just tell him where I am."

Xuanji was detained by her companion and did not return to the temple until the evening. Her maid met her at the door and said: "A little while ago a guest came. When he learned that you were not in, he went on without dismounting."

It happened that the guest in question was an old patron of Xuanji's, and she suspected that her maid had betrayed her. That night she hung out the lanterns and bolted the doors. Then she ordered Lüqiao to her bedroom, where she questioned her. The maid replied: "I have waited on you for many years now and have always conducted myself properly. I would never allow such a thing to happen and thus incur your displeasure. When the patron came and knocked at the door, I told him through the door that you were not in. Without a word, he rode away. As for romantic sentiments, it has been years since I had such feelings. I pray that you will not suspect me." Xuanji became even more incensed. She stripped Lüqiao naked and gave her a hundred lashes. But the maid still denied everything. Finally, when she was on the point of collapse, Lüqiao asked if she could have a cup of water. She poured it on the ground in libation and said: "You seek the way of the Tao and of immortality, yet you cannot forget the pleasures of the flesh. Instead you become suspicious and falsely accuse the chaste and the righteous. I will certainly die by your evil hands. If there is no Heaven, then I will have no recourse. If there is, who can suppress my fervent soul? I vow never to sink dully into the darkness and allow your lascivious ways to go on." Having thus spoken her mind, she expired on the floor. Frightened, Xuanji dug a pit in the back yard and buried her, assuring herself that no one would know of it.

The time was the first month of spring of the *wu-zi* year of the Xian-tong reign (868). Whenever anyone asked about Lüqiao, Xuanji would reply: "She ran away after the spring rains."

A guest was once dining in Xuanji's room and happened to go out to urinate in the back yard, on the very spot where the maid had been buried. There he saw a cloud of black flies swarming over the earth. He chased them off, but they came back. Taking a closer look, he saw what seemed to be traces of blood, and smelt a foul stench. The guest left presently and confided this to his servant, who went home and told his brother. This brother, a watchman, had once asked Xuanji for money. She had rejected him, and he had harbored a grudge against her ever since. He hurried to the temple gate to spy. He noticed people about conversing casually, but there was no sign of Lüqiao. He called the other watchmen and, carrying shovels, they forced their way into Xuanji's yard and uncovered the body. The maid looked just as she had done when alive. The watchmen reported Xuanji to the city authorities, and she was questioned and wrote a confession.

In court circles there were many who spoke in her behalf. The city authorities reported the case to the emperor. In the autumn, nonetheless, she was executed. While in prison she still wrote poetry:

It is easier to obtain a priceless treasure
Than it is to find a lover who is true.

And:

The bright moon shines into the dim corner;
The crisp breeze opens the collar of my gown.

These were among her beautiful lines.

🕮 *Further Reading* 🕮

Ayscough, Florence. *Chinese Women Yesterday and Today.* London: Jonathan Cape, 1938.

Birrell, Anne, trans. *New Songs from a Jade Terrace: An Anthology of Early Chinese Love Poetry.* London: Allen & Unwin, 1982.

Frodsham, John D., ed. and trans. (with the collaboration of Ch'eng Hsi). *An Anthology of Chinese Verse: Han, Wei, Chin and the Northern and Southern Dynasties.* Oxford: Oxford University Press, 1967.

Kelly, Jeanne, trans. "The Story of Yü Hsüan-chi." In Y. W. Ma & Joseph S. M. Lau, eds. *Traditional Chinese Stories: Themes and Variations.* New York: Columbia University Press, 1978.

Larsen, Jeanne, trans. *Brocade River Poems: Selected Works of the Tang Dynasty Courtesan Xue Tao.* Princeton: Princeton University Press, 1987.

Rexroth, Kenneth, & Ling Chung, trans. & eds. *Women Poets of China.* New York: New Directions, 1982. (Originally published as *The Orchid Boat: Women Poets of China* [New York: Seabury Press, 1972].)

Wimsatt, Genevieve. *Selling Wilted Peonies: Biography and Songs of Yü Hsüan-chi, T'ang Poetess.* New York: Columbia University Press, 1936.

———. *A Well of Fragrant Waters, a Sketch of the Life and Writings of Hung Tu (Hsüeh T'ao).* Boston: J. W. Luce, 1945.

"Beautiful Person, Fragrant Grass."
Qing dynasty seal, in imitation of He Zhen (fl. 1626)

Chapter 26

Cold Mountain

Poetry of Zen and the Tao

Duke Huan was one day reading in his hall, when a wheelwright named Bian who was working below flung down his hammer and chisel, and mounting the steps said, "What words may your Highness be studying?"

"I am studying the words of the Sages," replied the Duke.

"Are the Sages alive?" asked the wheelwright.

"No," answered the Duke; "they are dead."

"Then the words your Highness is studying," rejoined the wheelwright, "are only the dregs of the ancients."

"What do you mean, sirrah!" cried the Duke, "by interfering with what I read? Explain yourself, or you shall die."

"Let me take an illustration," said the wheelwright, "from my own trade. In making a wheel, if you work too slowly, you can't make it firm; if you work too fast, the spokes won't fit in. You must go neither too slowly nor too fast. There must be coordination of mind and hand. Words cannot explain what it is, but there is some mysterious art herein. I cannot teach it to my son; nor can he learn it from me. Consequently, though seventy years of age, I am still making wheels in my old age. If the ancients, together with what they could not impart, are dead and gone, then what your Highness is studying must be the dregs."

— *Zhuangzi*, chapter 13, "The Way of Heaven" (*translated by Herbert Giles*)

The fish trap exists because of the fish; once you've gotten the fish, you can forget the trap. The rabbit snare exists because of the rabbit; once you've gotten the rabbit, you can forget the snare. Words exist because of meaning; once you've gotten the meaning, you can forget the words. Where can I find a man who has forgotten words so I can have a word with him?

— *Zhuangzi*, chapter 26, "External Things" (*translated by Burton Watson*)

Before I had studied Zen for thirty years, I saw mountains as mountains, and waters as waters. When I arrived at a more intimate knowledge, I came to the point where I saw that mountains are not mountains, and waters are not waters. But now that I have got its very substance I am at rest. I see mountains once again as mountains, and waters once again as waters.

— *Qingyuan* (d. 740), in *Transmission of the Lamp* (*translated by Alan Watts*)

SENG CAN, THE THIRD ZEN PATRIARCH (d. 606)

The Believing Mind

Translated by Graeme Wilson

What is, is not; and what is not, yet is.

Till you have grasped this truth, you might as well
Waste no more time on fool philosophies:
But once you've grasped what these my teachings tell,
That anything is all things, that the one
Is every and the same, then where's the call
To fret for deeper knowledge? There is none
More deep than all-is-one and one-is-all.

The believing mind knows no duality
And what is dual denies the believing mind
Which, though I word you, inexpressibly
Extends beyond all language to allow
One truth in contradictions. You will find
It has no past, no future and no now.

XUANJUE (665–713), attrib.

Four Quatrains from the Canticle of the Way

Translated by Jerome P. Seaton

Xuanjue was a Zen Buddhist monk, disciple of the Sixth Zen Patriarch.

Roar of the Lion

Roar of the Lion   Voice beyond fear
When the beasts hear they shiver.
Even the elephant flees in awe.
Only the Heavenly Dragon knows to delight.

Heart's Mirror Clear

Heart's mirror clear   Reflects beyond fetter.
The void stripped clean, innumerable worlds.
All things in their majesty, shadowed and seen there.
The single gleaming jewel; not within, not without.

The One Moon Seen

The one moon seen, in all the waters.
All waters' moon, that one moon holds.
Dharmakaya of the Buddhas in my being.[1]
My being with the Thus Come one.[2]

Let Them Mock!

Let them mock! Let them laugh!
Light heaven with a torch? They toil in vain.
Their cries to me: taste of sweet dew.
Melted away, suddenly enter, the realm of No-thought.

WANG THE ZEALOT (Tang dynasty)
Four Poems

Translated by C. H. Kwock and Vincent McHugh

"Wang the Zealot" is the name associated with a sizable corpus of Tang vernacular
poetry, the vast majority of which exists only in manuscript copies found at Dunhuang
in the early part of this century [see chapters 29 and 30]. "The Zealot" is not a given
name, but a title, a Chinese equivalent of the Sanskrit *brahmacarin*, which designates a
lay Buddhist zealot.

Bumping on an Ass

Other people ride
        great big horses
I'm the only one
        bumping on an ass
But look!
back there
        — I feel a little better
A pack of dry sticks
        riding on a man

---

[1] Dharmakaya: Body of the law, the sacred body.
[2] Thus Come: the Tathagata, the Buddha.

Get Blind Drunk

All of us receive
    an empty body
All of us
    take
    the universe's breath
We die
    and still
    must live again
come back to earth
    all recollection lost
Ai! no more than this?
    Think hard about it
All things turn
    stale and flat on the tongue
It comforts people? No
    Better
    now and again
to get blind drunk on the floor
    alone

A Piece of the Loot

    tract houses
Building
    country houses
    No end in sight
What! already
    wailing voices in the hall
    — he's dead
The mourners
relatives
    Every man jack
    gets a piece of the loot
They weep, yes
    but if the truth were known
    a happy-hearted crew

The Ghosts Clap Hands

Hundred-year men?
    None in the world

But we slave to make
    thousand-year songs
beating out iron
    to bar out death
Seeing,
    the ghosts
        clap hands
        and laugh

"COLD MOUNTAIN" (Hanshan, Tang dynasty)
Fourteen Poems

Translated by Gary Snyder

Hanshan, "Cold Mountain," takes his name from where he lived. He is a mountain madman in an old Chinese line of ragged hermits. When he talks about Cold Mountain he means himself, his home, his state of mind. He lived in the Tang dynasty, traditionally 627–650, although Hu Shi dates him 700–780. This makes him roughly contemporary with Du Fu, Li Bo, Wang Wei, and Bo Juyi. His poems, of which three hundred survive, are written in Tang colloquial: rough and fresh. The ideas are Taoist, Buddhist, Zen. He and his sidekick Shide [pronounced "Shir-Dir"] became great favorites with Zen painters of later days — the scroll, the broom, the wild hair and laughter. They became Immortals, and you sometimes run into them today in the skidrows, orchards, hobo jungles, and logging camps of America.

Body Asking Shadow

The path to Hanshan's place is laughable,
A path, but no sign of cart or horse.
Converging gorges — hard to trace their twists
Jumbled cliffs — unbelievably rugged.
A thousand grasses bend with dew,
A hill of pines hums in the wind.
And now I've lost the shortcut home,
Body asking shadow, how do you keep up?

In a Tangle of Cliffs

In a tangle of cliffs I chose a place —
Bird-paths, but no trails for men.
What's beyond the yard?
White clouds clinging to vague rocks.

Now I've lived here — how many years —
Again and again, spring and winter pass.
Go tell families with silverware and cars
"What's the use of all that noise and money?"

In the Mountains

In the mountains it's cold.
Always been cold, not just this year.
Jagged scarps forever snowed in
Woods in the dark ravines spitting mist.
Grass is still sprouting at the end of June,
Leaves begin to fall in early August.
And here am I, high on mountains,
Peering and peering, but I can't even see the sky.

The Wrecked Town

I spur my horse through the wrecked town,
The wrecked town sinks my spirit.
High, low, old parapet-walls
Big, small, the aging tombs.
I waggle my shadow, all alone;
Not even the crack of a shrinking coffin is heard.
I pity all these ordinary bones,
In the books of the Immortals they are nameless.

Cold Mountain

I wanted a good place to settle:
Cold Mountain would be safe.
Light wind in a hidden pine —
Listen close — the sound gets better.
Under it a gray-haired man
Mumbles along reading Huang and Lao.
For ten years I haven't gone back home
I've even forgotten the way by which I came.

The Way to Cold Mountain

Men ask the way to Cold Mountain
Cold Mountain: there's no through trail.

In summer, ice doesn't melt
The rising sun blurs in swirling fog.
How did I make it?
My heart's not the same as yours.
If your heart was like mine
You'd get it and be right here.

Settled at Cold Mountain

I settled at Cold Mountain long ago,
Already it seems like years and years.
Freely drifting, I prowl the woods and streams
And linger watching things themselves.
Men don't get this far into the mountains,
White clouds gather and billow.
Thin grass does for a mattress,
The blue sky makes a good quilt.
Happy with a stone underhead
Let heaven and earth go about their changes.

The Cold Mountain Path

Clambering up the Cold Mountain path,
The Cold Mountain trail goes on and on:
The long gorge choked with scree and boulders,
The wide creek, the mist-blurred grass.
The moss is slippery, though there's been no rain
The pine sings, but there's no wind.
Who can leap the world's ties
And sit with me among the white clouds?

Rough and Dark

Rough and dark — the Cold Mountain trail,
Sharp cobbles — the icy creek bank.
Yammering, chirping — always birds
Bleak, alone, not even a lone hiker.
Whip, whip — the wind slaps my face
Whirled and tumbled — snow piles on my back.
Morning after morning I don't see the sun
Year after year, not a sign of spring.

Back at Cold Mountain

In my first thirty years of life
I roamed hundreds and thousands of miles.
Walked by rivers through deep green grass
Entered cities of boiling red dust.
Tried drugs, but couldn't make Immortal;
Read books and wrote poems on history.
Today I'm back at Cold Mountain:
I'll sleep by the creek and purify my ears.

House Without Walls

Cold Mountain is a house
Without beams or walls.
The six doors left and right are open
The hall is blue sky.
The rooms all vacant and vague
The east wall beats on the west wall
At the center nothing.

Borrowers don't bother me
In the cold I build a little fire
When I'm hungry I boil up some greens.
I've got no use for the kulak
With his big barn and pasture —
He just sets up a prison for himself.
Once in he can't get out.
Think it over —
You know it might happen to you.

Happy Among These Cliffs

If I hide out at Cold Mountain
Living off mountain plants and berries —
All my lifetime, why worry?
One follows his karma through.
Days and months slip by like water,
Time is like sparks knocked off flint.
Go ahead and let the world change —
I'm happy to sit among these cliffs.

Like a Drifting Boat

Once at Cold Mountain, troubles cease —
No more tangled, hung-up mind.
I idly scribble poems on the rock cliff,
Taking whatever comes, like a drifting boat.

Try and Make It

When men see Hanshan
They all say he's crazy
And not much to look at —
Dressed in rags and hides.
They don't get what I say
& I don't talk their language.
All I can say to those I meet:
"Try and make it to Cold Mountain."

JIAORAN (730–799)
Four Poems

Translated by Stephen Owen

Jiaoran dominated the literary scene on the lower Yangtze in the late eighth century with his versatility as a poet and his adeptness as a conversationalist equally well-read in Buddhist, Confucian and Taoist thought. Born and raised in Changcheng (modern Zhejiang), he took orders at Lingyin Temple before the An Lushan Rebellion, was indoctrinated in *vinaya* teachings, traveled widely to study at monasteries throughout the country, and remained a Buddhist all his life.

Cold Mountain

Encroaching on the emptiness, riot of color,
I love this uniquely, my own middle peak.
No cares at all, I lean on light staff,
I walk on calmly, following hidden tracks.
On all the mountains falling of leaves is over.
And cold, azure mists form, layer upon layer.

Playful Poem

Yammering, squabbling — all of it
    in a world bound by "true" and "false";

Who understands the peace of mind
    I feel the whole day long?
A chance visitor sings wildly —
    and why does he do what he does?
He wants only to force himself
    to care about human affairs.

Spontaneous Poems

1

I hide my heart and not my deeds,
And I even desire to dwell in men's world.
If I lack trees, I transplant one in spring;
If I miss the mountains, I look at a painting.
I reside in noise, and I haven't gone wrong —
Truth is here.

2

I don't like foreign languages; I won't study them;
And I've never translated barbarian words.
Tell you of Zen? It's what's topsy-turvy,
What makes the Prince of the West die of laughter.

LINGCHE (746–816)
Two Poems

Translated by Stephen Owen

Lingche's long life spanned the later eighth century and the Mid Tang, but so many
of his poems are from late in his life that he should probably be considered a Mid
Tang poet.

In Reply to Wei Dan

Now old, my heart is at peace
    and nothing external bothers me.
The robes of hemp and seat of grass —
    enough for my body.
Everyone I meet tells me
    how grand it would be to quit office
Yet never once here in the woods
    have I seen a single one.

Spending the Night at East Forest Temple

The skies are cold; fierce tigers
    roar through the snow of peaks;
Here in the forest, no one —
    and moonlight shines unseen.
A thousand years of effigy worship
    is heard no more today,
And the burning of incense is pleasing
    only to the ghosts.

XUANJIAN (782–865)

Zen Sermon

Translated by Graeme Wilson

Drink when thirsty, eat when hungry,
Piss and shit when nature calls.
Sleep when sleepy. Any other
Rules for living are pure balls.

There are neither buddhas nor patriarchs.
Bodhidharma was nothing more
Than some old wog with a growth of beard.
That nig-nog Prince and his quarter-score
Of dark disciples with unpronounceable
Fancy monikers, what were they
But some daft gang of dunghill-coolies
Jabbering bad joss away?

And all those doctrines? Rotten tree-stumps
Which conveniently provide
Snags to which whole droves of donkeys,
You my brothers can be tied.
The roll of saints? A list of ghosts.
The sacred scriptures? Use them thus,
Their only use, to wipe your boil-heads
Of their overload of pus.

Drink when thirsty, eat when hungry,
Piss and shit when nature calls.
Sleep when sleepy. All the other
Rules for living are pure balls.

GUANXIU (832–912)
Four Paradise Poems

Translated by Edward H. Schafer

This talented poet-painter monk (famous for his pictures of sixteen arhats) left the northland during the disasters of the end of the ninth century, stayed in Hangzhou until he lost the favor of the lords of Wuyue, got the patronage of Cheng Rui, warlord of Jingnan in the central Yangtze region, and finally moved to Shu (Sichuan), where he was loaded with honors by Wang Jian, the master of that realm, in 907. There he died. He was a dreamer and visionary, many of whose poems are suffused with a luminous atmosphere, intimating the white light of eternity.

1

I came in a dream to a mountain in the sea,
Entered a certain house of white silver,
Chanced to see a Gentleman of the Way,
Who said he was Li, Eighth Sire.

2

Three or four young sylph women,
Bodies garbed in ultramarine dress,
Held in their hands luminous moon beads,
To knock down golden-hued pears.

3

The nacreous land had no dust —
I went on, and came to the shore of a gemmy pool:
Under the thickset cedrela trees
A white dragon came to smell a man.

4

Palace halls loomed high, encaged in purple vapor,
In golden canals, sanded with jade, was five-colored water,
The guardian doorkeepers, sylphine maids, lay asleep, one on the
    other;
Stealthily I plucked from the coiled peachtree, and almost
    fell to the ground.

HAN WO (844-923)

Letter to a Zen Master

Translated by Graeme Wilson

Han is remembered as a statesman and poet who remained loyal to the Tang in its final decade and subsequently fled to the southeast coast, where he spent the remainder of his life in poverty, studying Taoist alchemy.

> From Nothingness into a massive Being
> Huge Mountains build their bulk into the sky.
> From Being back into mere Nothingness
> Blue lightning flashes in a lightning-flash.
> Both are illusions: mountains, however huge,

Figure 63. The Ink-splash Immortal, by Liang Kai (thirteenth century). (Source: National Palace Museum, Taipei)

Are never born and lightnings never die.
All is illusion: nothing at all is real.
But the world prefers its babble of balderdash.

🙰 *Further Reading* 🙰

Kwock, C. H., & Vincent McHugh, trans. *The Lady and the Hermit.* San Francisco: Golden Mountain Press, 1962.

Nielson, Thomas P. *The T'ang Poet-Monk Chiao-jan.* Tempe, Ariz.: Center for Asian Studies, 1972.

Owen, Stephen. *The Great Age of Chinese Poetry: The High T'ang.* New Haven: Yale University Press, 1981.

Schafer, Edward H. "Mineral Imagery in the Paradise Poems of Kuan-hsiu." *Asia Major* (1963), 10.

———. *Mirages on the Sea of Time: The Taoist Poetry of Ts'ao T'ang.* Berkeley: University of California Press, 1985.

Seaton, Jerome P., and Dennis Maloney, eds. *A Drifting Boat: An Anthology of Chinese Zen Poetry.* Fredonia: White Pine Press, 1994.

Snyder, Gary, trans. "Cold Mountain Poems." *Evergreen Review* (autumn 1958), 2 (6); also in *Riprap & Cold Mountain Poems,* San Francisco: Four Seasons Foundation, 1965.

Waley, Arthur, trans. "Twenty-seven Poems by Han-shan." *Encounter* (1954), 3 (3).

Watson, Burton, trans. *Cold Mountain: 100 Poems by the T'ang Poet Han-shan.* New York: Columbia University Press, 1962.

Watts, Alan W. *The Way of Zen.* New York: Pantheon, 1957.

Wilson, Graeme, trans. "Tao: Buddha Zen." *Denver Quarterly* (1977), 12 (2).

Wu, John C. H. *The Golden Age of Zen.* Rev. ed., Taipei: United Publishing Center, 1975.

"Plain as water."
Seal carved by He Zhen (fl. 1626)

Chapter 27

Return to the Source

Essays of the Tang Dynasty

The Principles of Tao and Virtue (i.e., the Confucian ethos) have long been in decline, and how much more has literature, which is the external expression of that ethos.

If you wish to attain the height of achievement of the ancient masters, then you must not expect quick results, nor should you be lured away by what is advantageous and profitable. Nurture the root and await the fruit; add oil to the lamp and expect it to burn bright. Where the roots thrive, the fruit will be good; where oil abounds, light will be radiant. When a man lives by human-heartedness and righteousness, his words will be gentle and graceful.

... I walk the path of human-heartedness and righteousness and linger at the source — the *Book of Songs* and the *Book of History* — lest I lose the path, lest I be cut off from the source. This I shall have to do until the end of my days.

The vital force (*qi*) is like water, and language is like something floating on it. When a body of water is large, anything floats, will float, regardless of its size. So it is with the vital force and language; if the vital force is abundant, then, whether speech be short or long, its tone proud or humble, it will be appropriate.

— Han Yu, "Letter to Li Yi" (801) (*translated by Chen Yu-shih*)

Introduction

J. R. Hightower

The elaborate Parallel Prose style [for an example of which see Kong Zhigui's "Proclamation on North Mountain" in chapter 14], which had developed during the Six Dynasties, continued to be almost universally practised during the first two centuries of the Tang dynasty. Its most salient features were a preponderance of couplets, in which metrical identity (most often four or six words) and syntactic parallelism occurred between corresponding lines. However, its inadequacy as a vehicle for effective communication had been recognized by the first Emperor of the Sui dynasty, who made an unsuccessful attempt to prevent its use in chancery documents. Occasionally Tang dynasty writers raised objections to the style on aesthetic or ethical grounds and advocated a return to pre-Han models of free prose. The practical difficulty of using Parallel Prose for extended narrative led the early Tang historians to abandon it in their work. Some of them expressed dissatisfaction with the style as decadent and unsuited to the properly didactic function of literature. The reaction developed into a full-fledged literary movement with political and philosophical overtones under the leadership of Han Yu, whose writings are at once the prototype and the model for the reformed prose known as *guwen* (Ancient Style, in contrast to the current Parallel Style).

Ancient Style Prose as written by Han Yu and his followers drew its inspiration from pre-Han models of expository prose and certain Han writers of history and narrative. However, it was not confined to a slavish imitation of these models, either in vocabulary or syntax. Like its models, Ancient Style Prose obeys no arbitrary rules of prosody; it is a true prose, with prose rhythms and only occasional adventitious ornaments of the sort that characterized Parallel Prose. At the same time it is an artificial style in the sense that even in Tang times it was not derived from a living colloquial language; still, it was probably influenced by the spoken language to some extent. Giving considerable scope for individual expression, it revived the moribund essay and provided a medium for fiction, a genre that had developed little since Han times.

That Ancient Style Prose was accepted for a time as a serious competitor of Parallel Prose was only in part because of a recognition of its merits. It found in Han Yu an advocate who was also an effective propagandist. Known as a Confucian, a moralist, and a staunch conservative, he was in a position to damn with authority the "new style" prose along with the other heresies, native or imported, of Taoism and Buddhism. For Han Yu Ancient Style Prose was only a part of a program, if an essential part, concerned with reforming the times by a return to antiquity, a revival of the way of Confucius as transmitted through Mencius. He set himself up as a teacher in the Confucian tradition, attracted disciples, and founded a school....

Han Yu's attitude toward literature was essentially a restatement of the traditional theory, with its insistence on the primarily didactic function of all writing. Suspicious of art as artificiality, he insisted that prose should be straightforward and unadorned. Since he valued content above manner, there should be no place in his aesthetic canon for frivolity. But Ancient Style Prose was a suitable vehicle for narration as well as for exposition, and the writers of tales and anecdotes turned it to their own uses, which were not always edifying to a Confucian moralist [see chapter 28]. After Han Yu's death the chief practitioners of the style he had tried to popularize were the authors of such tales, especially toward the end of the dynasty, when a revival of Parallel Prose displaced the Ancient Style for official and serious use.

— from *Topics in Chinese Literature*, 1953

LI HUA (died c. 769)

On an Old Battlefield

Translated by Herbert Giles

Li Hua was an influential prose stylist of the mid-eighth century. He became widely known without ever rising to high position in government. When Xuanzong fled to Sichuan, he hurried to Chang'an to rescue his mother, but was captured by the rebels and given unwanted office. After the restoration, he was exiled to an administrative post in Hangzhou. In 760, when he was again offered a post in the central government, he refused. Late in life he turned to Buddhism. In his old age he was one of the most respected men of letters in the empire.

Like most men of letters of his time, Li composed in both Parallel Prose and Ancient Style prose. This well-known dirge is a highly rhetorical composition, using imagery from the period of Han frontier expansion and evoking the combination of romantic fascination and pity that literary men felt for those who died in battle on the northern and western borders.

Vast, vast, — a limitless extent of flat sand, without a human being in sight; girdled by a stream and dotted with hills; where in the dismal twilight the wind moans at the setting sun. Shrubs gone: grass withered: all chill as the hoar-frost of early morn. The birds of the air fly past: the beasts of the field shun the spot; for it is, as I was informed by the keeper, the site of an old battlefield. "Many a time and oft," said he, "has an army been overthrown on this spot; and the voices of the dead may frequently be heard weeping and wailing in the darkness of the night."

Oh, sorrow! Oh, ye Qins, ye Hans, ye dynasties now passed away! I have heard that when the men of Qi and the men of Wei gathered at the frontier, and when the men of Jing and the men of Han collected their levies, many were the weary leagues they trod, many were the years of privation and exposure they endured. Grazing their horses by day, fording the river by night, the endless earth beneath, the boundless sky above, they knew not the day of their return; their bodies all the time exposed to the pitiless steel, with many other unspeakable woes.

Again, since the Qin and the Han dynasties, countless troubles have occurred within the boundaries of the empire, desolating the Middle Kingdom. No age has been free from these. In the olden days, barbarians and Chinese alike meekly followed their Imperial guide. But the place of right was usurped by might; the rude soldier cast aside the obligations of morality, and the rule of reason lost its sway.

Alas! methinks I see them now, the bitter wind enveloping them in dust, the Tartar warriors in ambuscade. Our general makes light of the foe. He would give battle upon the very threshold of his camp. Banners wave over the plain; the river closes-in the battle array. All is order, though hearts may beat. Discipline is everything: life is of no account.

And now the cruel spear does its work, the startled sand blinds the combatants locked fast in the death-struggle; while hill and vale and stream groan beneath the flash and crash of arms. By-and-by, the chill cold shades of night fall upon them, knee-deep in snow, beards stiff with ice. The hardy vulture seeks its nest: the strength of the warhorse is broken. Clothes are of no avail; hands frost-bitten, flesh cracked. Even nature lends her aid to the Tartars, contributing a deadly blast, the better to complete the work of slaughter begun. Ambulance wagons block the way: our men succumb to flank attacks. Their officers have surrendered: their general is dead. The river is choked with corpses to its topmost banks: the fosses of the Great Wall are swimming over with blood. All distinctions are obliterated in that heap of rotting bones …

Faintly and more faintly beats the drum. Strength exhausted, arrows spent, bow-strings snapped, swords shattered, the two armies fall upon one another in the supreme struggle for life or death. To yield is to become the barbarian's slave: to fight is to mingle our bones with the desert sand …

No sound of bird now breaks from the hushed hillside. All is still, save the wind whistling through the long night. Ghosts of the dead wander hither and thither in the gloom: spirits from the nether world collect under the dark clouds. The sun rises and shines coldly over the trampled grass, while the fading moon still twinkles upon the frost-flakes scattered around. What sight more horrible than this!

I have heard that Li Mu led the soldiers of Zhao to victory over their Tartar foes, clearing the country for miles, and utterly routing the Huns. The men of Han, on the other hand, exhausted in vain the resources of the empire. They had not the man, and their numbers availed them naught.

The men of Zhou, too, drove back the barbarous hordes of the north; and having garrisoned the country, returned safely home. Then they offered thanks to the Gods, and gave themselves up to the universal enjoyment which peace alone can bring.

The men of Qin built the Great Wall, stretching far away to the sea. Yet the poison-breath of war decimated the people, and mile upon mile ran with their red blood.

The men of Han beat down the Huns, and seized Yinshan. But their corpses lay pillowed over the plain, and the gain was not equal to the loss.

O high Heaven! which of these but has father and mother, who bore them about in childhood, fearing only lest maturity should never come? Which of these but has brothers, dear to them as themselves? Which of these but has a wife, bound by the closest ties? They owe no thanks for life, for what have they done to deserve death? They may be alive or dead — the family knows it not. And if one brings the news, they listen, half doubting, half believing, while the heart overflows with grief. Sleeping and waking, they seem to see the lost one's form. Sacrifices are made ready and libations poured, with tearful eyes strained towards the far horizon; heaven and earth, nay, the very trees and plants, all seeming to sympathize with their sorrow. And when, in response to prayers and libations, these wanderers return not, where shall their spirits find repose? Verily there shall be a famine over the land,[1] and the people be scattered abroad. Alas! such is life, and such it has ever been. What resource then is left but to keep within our frontier lines?[2]

HAN YU (768–824)
Five Essays

Translated by Herbert Giles

From Mr Watters' invaluable *Guide to the Tablets in a Confucian Temple*, we learn that we should wash our hands in rosewater before taking up the works of Han Yu. Known as the "Prince of Literature," and generally regarded as the most striking figure in the Chinese world of letters, he certainly ranks high as a poet [see chapter 22], essayist, and philosopher. In official life, he got himself into trouble by his outspoken attacks upon Buddhism, at that time very fashionable at court, and was banished to the then barbarous south, where he gained great kudos by his wise and incorrupt administration.

The Source: On the True Faith of a Confucianist

Universal love is called *Charity*: right conduct is called *Duty*. The product of these two factors is called the *Method*; and its practice, without external stimulus, is called *Exemplification*.[3]

---

[1] In allusion to some words attributed to Laozi.
[2] I doubt if the Peace Society, to whom this essay might well be dedicated, has ever published a more graphic description of the horrors of war. [Giles wrote this note in 1884.]
[3] This last term cannot be satisfactorily rendered. It is usually translated by "virtue": but that, to go no farther, would make nonsense of the next clause. The meaning, however, may be sufficiently gathered from the context. I need hardly add that "method" must be here understood in its philosophical sense.

Charity and Duty are constant terms. Method and Exemplification are variable. Thus, there is the Method of the perfect man, and the Method of the mean man; while Exemplification may be either good or evil.

Laozi merely narrowed the scope of charity and duty; he did not attempt to do without them altogether. His view of them was the narrow view of a man sitting at the bottom of a well and inferring the size of the heavens from the small portion visible to himself. He understood Charity and Duty in a limited, individual sense; and narrowness followed as a matter of course. What he called the Method was a Method he had determined was the Method. It was not what I call the Method. What he called Exemplification was different from what I call Exemplification. What I call Method and Exemplification are based upon a combination of Charity and Duty; and this is the opinion of the world at large. What Laozi called Method and Exemplification were based upon a negation of Charity and Duty; but that was the opinion of one man.

Under the Zhou, the true Method began to decay; the influence of Confucius to wane. Under the Qin, came the burning of the books. Under the Han, the doctrines of Laozi prevailed, followed by the Buddhism of succeeding dynasties. Those who then occupied themselves with morals sided either with Yang Zhu or with Mozi,[4] or embraced the tenets either of Laozi or of Buddha. Such a one was necessarily led to denounce the teachings of Confucius. His adopted faith became all in all to him; his former faith, an outcast. He glorified the new; he vilified the old. And now those who would cultivate morality, hesitate between a choice of guides!

The followers of Laozi say, "Confucius was a disciple of our Master." The followers of Buddha say, "Confucius was a disciple of our Master."[5] And the followers of Confucius, by dint of repetition, have at length fallen so low as themselves to indulge in such random talk, saying, "Our Master also respected Laozi and Buddha." Not only have they uttered this with their tongues, but they have written it down in books; and now, if a man would cultivate morality, from whom should he seek instruction?

Great is the straining of mankind after the supernatural! Great is their neglect of fundamentals in this yearning for the supernatural alone!

---

[4] Founders of the egoistic and altruistic schools, respectively.
[5] Confucius is reported to have said "There is a prophet in the West," and the Buddhists have explained this to mean Buddha. A few centuries later and the Jesuits would inevitably have appropriated it as a palpable allusion to Christ.

Of old, the people were divided into four classes. They are now divided into six.[6] Of old, there was but one faith. Now, there are three. The husbandman tills his field, and six classes eat of its fruits. The artisan plies his craft, and six classes profit by his skill. The trader barters his goods, and six classes are enriched by the exchange. Is it then surprising that beggary and crime are rampant?

In ancient times, man stood face to face with many dangers. Sages arose and taught him the secret of society. They gave him rulers for the people and teachers for the young. They drove away the beasts of the field and the birds of the air, and established him at the center of the earth.[7] He was cold, and they gave him clothes. He was hungry, and they gave him food. He entrusted his life to the hazard of a branch, or slept himself into sickness on the bare ground; and they built him palaces and houses to live in. They taught him handicrafts that he might furnish himself with useful things; they taught him trade that the deficiency of one region might be supplied from the abundance of another. They taught him medicine that he might battle against premature death; they taught him burial and sacrifice that the memory of the dead might be perpetuated for ever. They taught him ceremonial in order to secure a rule of precedence; they taught him music as a means of dissipating the melancholy of his heart. They taught him punishment in order to weed out the vicious. As a safeguard against fraud, they made for him seals and measures and scales. As a safeguard against robbery, they built walls and organised militia. Thus did they take precautions against whatsoever evils might come upon him.

But now forsooth we are told that "unless our sages are put to death, deeds of violence will not cease"; and that "if we destroy our measures and break our scales, the people will have no further cause for dissension." What thoughtless talk is this![8]

Had there been no sages of old, the race of man would have long since become extinct. Men have not fur and feathers and scales to adjust the temperature of their bodies; neither have they claws and fangs to aid them in the struggle for food. Hence their organization, as follows: — The sovereign issues commands. The minister carries out

---

[6] Alluding to the priests of Laozi and Buddha.

[7] Which the Chinese then believed to be square and flat.

[8] The doctrine elaborated by Zhuangzi, namely, that if good was not defined, evil could not exist.

these commands and makes them known to the people. The people produce grain and flax and silk, fashion articles of everyday use, and interchange commodities, in order to fulfill their obligations to their rulers. The sovereign who fails to issue his commands loses his *raison d'être* : the minister who fails to carry out his sovereign's commands and to make them known to the people, loses his *raison d'être*: the people who fail to produce grain and flax and silk, fashion articles of everyday use, and interchange commodities, in order to fulfill their obligations to their rulers, — should lose their heads.

But now the rule runs thus: — "Discard the relationships of sovereign and subject, of father and son." These social obligations are put out of sight in order to secure, as they say, "perfect purity in abstraction from a world of sense." Happily, indeed, these doctrines were not promulgated until after the Three Dynasties, when they were unable to interfere with the already established landmarks of our great Sages. Unhappily, it might be said, because they have thus escaped demolition at the hands of those mighty teachers of men.

Now the title of emperor is different from that of king; yet the wisdom of each is the same. To slake thirst by drinking and to appease hunger with food; to wear grass-cloth in summer and fur in winter, — these acts cannot be regarded as identical; yet the rationale of each is the same. Those who urge us to revert to the inaction of extreme antiquity, might as well advise us to wear grass-cloth in winter, or to drink when we are hungry. It is written, "He who would manifest his good instincts to all mankind, must first duly order the State. But previous to this he must duly order his Family. And previous to that his own Self. And previous to that his Heart. And previous to that his Thoughts." It will be seen therefore that there was an ulterior motive in thus ordering the heart and the thoughts. What, on the other hand, is the object of the followers of Laozi and Buddha? To withdraw themselves from the world, from the State, and from the family! To deny the eternal obligations of society so that sons need no longer submit themselves to their fathers, so that subjects need no longer own allegiance to their sovereigns, so that the people need no longer occupy themselves with their natural duties!

When Confucius wrote his *Spring and Autumn*,[9] he treated as barbarians those of the feudal princes who used a barbarian ceremonial, while those who adopted the ceremonial of the Central State were treated by him as men of the Central State. It is written in the *Book of*

---

[9] The name given to the *Annals*, said, but not universally admitted to be, from his pen.

Changes, "A barbarian prince is not the equal of a Chinese peasant."[10] It is written in the *Book of Songs*, "Oppose the hordes of the west and north: punish the tribes of Jing and Shu." But now when they would take the rule of life of barbarians and graft it upon the wisdom of our ancient kings, — is not this the first step on the road to barbarism itself? For what was the wisdom of our ancient kings? It was this: — "Universal love is called charity: right conduct is called duty. The resultant of these two factors is called the Method; and their exemplification, without external stimulus, is called instinct." Their canon comprised the *Book of Songs*, the *Book of History*, the *Book of Changes*, and the *Spring and Autumn*. Their code embraced Ceremonial, Music, Punishment, and Administration in general. They divided the people into four classes; — Literati, Husbandmen, Artisans, and Traders. Their relationships were those between sovereign and subject, between father and son, with teacher and with friend, between host and guest, between elder and younger brother, and between husband and wife. Their clothes were of cloth or of silk. They dwelt in palaces or in ordinary houses. They ate grain and vegetables and fruit and fish and flesh. Their Method was easy of comprehension: their doctrines were easily carried into practice. Hence their lives passed pleasantly away, a source of satisfaction to themselves, a source of benefit

---

[10] As I was leaving China in 1883, I was presented by a literary friend with a complimentary poem, in which the following lines occurred:

"We may easily meet once more: still it is hard to part.
The chrysanthemums will have faded ere I shall see you again.
Deep have been your researches in our Sacred Books;
Shallow, alas! my wit to expound those books to you.
From of old, literature has illumined the nation of nations:
And now its influence has gone forth to regenerate a barbarian official."

The word used for "barbarian" was the character tabooed by Treaty; and yet the writer was undoubtedly conscious only of an effort to please. Just now, there is a feeling in certain quarters that the term "Chinaman" is offensive to the Chinese people, and recently a young "Chinese" wrote to *The Times* on the subject. Incidentally, he spoke of us as "Britishers," which though harmless is scarcely a term of respect. Britishers, however, are not so foolish as to resent this: nor I think should the Chinese show themselves too sensitive in regard to "Chinaman," which may be too playful but is certainly not meant offensively, considering that they have but lately dropped the less endearing term "foreign devils," and even now may be occasionally detected in the use of *fan* "barbarian." Meanwhile, our American rivals have advised the use of "Chinese" by "Americans who are desirous of improving the relations between the United States and China" (*see* "Commercial Handbook of China," published by the United States Department of Commerce). [This original footnote, which says so much about Giles and his times, has been kept in its entirety. The "literary friend" was probably Gu Hongming (Ku Hung-ming), who was one of Giles' friends at the time. *Eds.*]

to mankind. At peace within their own hearts, they readily adapted themselves to the necessities of the family and of the State. Happy in life, they were remembered after death. Their sacrifices were grateful to the God of Heaven, and the spirits of the departed rejoiced in the honors of ancestral worship.

And if I am asked what Method is this, I reply that it is what I call *the* Method, and not merely a method like those of Laozi and Buddha. The Emperor Yao handed it down to the Emperor Shun; the Emperor Shun handed it down to the Great Yu; and so on until it reached Confucius, and lastly Mencius, who died without transmitting it to any one else. Then followed the heterodox schools of Xun and Yang, wherein much that was essential was passed over, while the criterion was vaguely formulated. In the days before Zhou Gong, the Sages were themselves rulers; hence they were able to secure the reception of their Method. In the days after Zhou Gong, the sages were all high officers of State; hence its duration through a long period of time.

And now, it will be asked, what is the remedy? I answer that unless these false doctrines are rooted out, the true faith will not prevail. Let us insist that the followers of Laozi and Buddha behave themselves like ordinary mortals. Let us burn their books. Let us turn their temples into dwelling-houses. Let us make manifest the Method of our ancient kings in order that men may be led to embrace its teachings. Thus, and thus only, will there be wherewithal to feed the widow and the orphan, to nourish the cripple and the sick; — and the scheme is feasible enough.

On a Bone from Buddha's Body: A Memorial to the Throne

Your Majesty's servant would submit that Buddhism is but a cult of the barbarians, and that its spread in China dates only from the later Han dynasty, and that the ancients knew nothing of it.

Of old, Huangdi [the Yellow Emperor] sat on the throne one hundred years, dying at the age of one hundred and ten. Shao Hao sat on the throne eighty years and died at the age of a hundred. Zhuan Xu sat on the throne seventy-nine years and died at the age of ninety-eight. Di Gu sat on the throne seventy years and died at the age of a hundred and fifty. The Emperor Yao sat on the throne ninety-eight years and died at the age of a hundred and eighteen; and the Emperors Shun and Yu both attained the age of one hundred years. At that epoch the Empire was tranquil, and the people happy in the attainment of old age; and yet no Buddha had yet reached China. Subsequently, the Emperor Tang of the Yin dynasty reached the age of a hundred years; his grandson Tai Mou reigned for seventy-five years; and Wu Ding reigned for fifty-nine years. Their exact ages are not given in the annals, but at the lowest computation these can hardly have been less than a hundred years. King Wen of the Zhou dynasty reached the age of ninety-seven, King Wu reached the age of ninety-three; and King Mu reigned for one hundred years; and as at that date likewise the Buddhist religion had not reached China, these examples of longevity cannot be attributed to the worship of the Lord Buddha.

The Buddhist religion was in fact introduced during the reign of Emperor Ming of the Han dynasty; and that Emperor sat on the throne but eighteen years. After him came rebellion upon rebellion, with short-lived monarchs.

During the Song, Qi, Liang, Chen, and Wei dynasties, and so on downward, the Buddhistic religion gradually spread. The duration of those dynasties was comparatively short, only the Emperor Wu of the Liang dynasty reigning for so long as forty-eight years. Thrice he devoted himself to the service of Buddha; at the sacrifices in his ancestral shrines no living victims were used; he daily took but one single meal, and that composed of fruits and vegetables; yet he was harassed by the rebel He Jing and died of hunger at Taicheng, soon after which his dynasty came to an end. He sought happiness in the worship but found misfortune instead; from which it must be clear to all that Buddha himself is after all but an incompetent God.

When Gaozu [founding emperor of the Tang dynasty] obtained the Empire he contemplated the extermination of this religion; but the officials of that day were men of limited capabilities; they did not understand the way of our rulers of old; they did not understand the exigencies of the past and present; they did not understand how to avail themselves of His Majesty's wisdom, and root out this evil. Therefore, the execution of this design was delayed, to your servant's infinite sorrow.

Now your present Majesty, endowed with wisdom and courage such as are without parallel in the annals of the past thousand years, prohibited on your accession to the throne the practice of receiving candidates, whether male or female, for priestly orders, prohibiting likewise the erection of temples and monasteries; which caused your servant to believe that the mantle of Gaozu had descended on Your Majesty's shoulders. And even should prohibition be impossible, patronage would still be out of the question. Yet your servant has now heard that instructions have been issued to the priestly community to proceed to Fengxiang and receive a bone of Buddha, and that from a high tower in the palace Your Majesty will view its introduction into the Imperial Palace; also that orders have been sent to the various temples, commanding that the relic be received with the proper ceremonies. Now, foolish though your servant may be, he is well aware that Your Majesty does not do this in the vain hope of deriving advantages therefrom; but that in the fullness of our present plenty, and in the joy which reigns in the hearts of all, there is a desire to fall in with the wishes of the people in the celebration at the capital of this delusive mummery. For how could the wisdom of Your Majesty stoop to participation in such ridiculous beliefs? Still the people are slow of perception and easily beguiled; and should they behold Your Majesty thus earnestly worshipping at the feet of Buddha they would cry out, "See! the Son of Heaven, the All-Wise, is a fervent believer; who are we, his people, that we should spare our bodies?" Then would ensue a scorching of heads and burning of fingers; crowds would collect together, and tearing off their clothes and scattering their money, would spend their time from morn to eve in imitation of Your Majesty's example. The result would be that by and by young and old, seized with the same enthusiasm, would totally neglect the business of their lives; and should Your Majesty not prohibit it, they would be found flocking to the temples, ready to cut off an arm or slice their bodies as an offering to the God. Thus would our traditions and customs be seriously injured, and ourselves become a laughing-stock on the face of the earth; — truly, no small matter! For Buddha was a barbarian. His language was not the language of China; his clothes were of an alien cut. He did not utter the maxims of our ancient rulers, nor conform to the customs which they have handed down. He did not appreciate the bond between prince and minister, the tie between father and son. Supposing, indeed, this Buddha had come to our capital in the flesh, under an appointment from his own State, then your Majesty might have received him with a few words of admonition, bestowing on him a banquet and a suit of clothes, previous to sending him out of the country with an escort of soldiers, and thereby have avoided any dangerous influence on the minds of the people. But what are the facts? The bone of a man long since dead and decomposed, is to be admitted, forsooth, within the precincts of the Imperial Palace! Confucius said, "Pay all respect to spiritual beings, but keep them at a distance." And so, when the princes of old paid visits of condolence to one another, it was customary for them to send on a magician in advance, with a peach wand in his hand, whereby to expel all noxious influences previous to the arrival of his master. Yet now Your Majesty is about to causelessly introduce a disgusting object, personally taking part in the proceedings without the intervention either of the magician or of his peach wand. Of the officials, not one has raised his voice against it; of the censors, not one has pointed out the enormity of such an act. Therefore your servant, overwhelmed with shame, implores Your Majesty that this bone may be handed over for destruction by fire or water, whereby the root of this great evil may be exterminated for all time, and the people know how much the wisdom of Your Majesty surpasses that of ordinary men. The glory of such a deed will be beyond all praise. And should the Lord Buddha have power to avenge this insult by the infliction of some misfortune, then let the vials of his wrath be poured out upon the person of your servant who now calls Heaven to witness that he will not repent him of his oath.

   In all gratitude and sincerity Your Majesty's servant now humbly presents, with fear and trembling, this Memorial for Your Majesty's benign consideration.

A Bone of Fo

Another version of the same essay, translated by R. Brookes from the French of Jean-Baptiste Du Halde (1738)

The same Emperor *Hyen tsong* [Xianzong], having received a certain kind of a Bone, which was said to be a Bone of Fo,[11] caused it to be introduced, with Ceremony, into the innermost Parts of his Palace, where he kept it guarded with great Respect for three Days, in order to cause it to be transported solemnly into the Temple of that Sect. The People, the Literati, the *Kong,* and great Numbers of the *Vang*[12] approved of this Festival. *Han yu,* who was only *She lang* in the Tribunal of Crimes, presented the Emperor with the following *Remonstrance.*

   Sir; let me be permitted respectfully to represent to you, that the Doctrine of *Fo* is, at the Bottom, a vile Sect of some Barbarians. It began to insinuate itself into our Empire, under the last Emperors of the *Han;* at least, it is certain, that anciently it was not known. *Whang ti,* it is said, reigned a hundred Years, and lived a hundred and ten. *Shau hau* reigned ninety Years, and lived a hundred. *Chwen hyo* reigned seventy-nine Years, and lived only ninety-eight. *Ti ko* reigned seventy Years, and lived one hundred and five. *Yau* reigned ninety Years, and lived one hundred and eighteen. *Shun* and *Yu,* each lived one hundred Years. Under these great Princes, the Empire enjoyed a profound Peace: Their Subjects being happy and contented, lived to a good old Age. Yet *Fo* and his Sect were not yet known in *China: Ching tang,* the first Emperor of the *Shang,* likewise lived his hundred Years. *Ven vang* and *Vû ti* alone reigned for a

---

[11] The Name of a Sect and Sectary, which came from *India.* [Original romanization has been retained. *Eds.*]

[12] A Title of Honor next to the *Heu;* They are Kings, but Feudatory. At present, this Dignity is a mere Title without any Possessions.

long time. This Prince, from his Bigotry to the Sect of *Fo* would not kill Animals, even for the *Tsi*[13] of his Ancestors. He reduced himself to one Meal a Day, and that consisted of Pulse and Fruits. In short, three times during his Reign, did he debase himself to honor *Fo* by Meannesses unworthy of his Rank. Where did all this end? He was besieged in *Tay ching*, and press'd so close by *Hew king*, that he died of Famine, and his Empire passed into other Hands. These Princes, who have founded their Empires upon the Honors they paid to *Fo*, have been still more unhappy. Let us then conclude, that the Service of *Fo* is, at least, an useless Thing.

The illustrious Founder of our Dynasty, *Tang*, when he became Master of the Empire, entertained a Thought of extirpating this Sect. He put the Affair under Deliberation: But unhappily they who were in Post, were Men of a narrow Way of thinking. They were not conversant in Antiquity, and, for the most part, they were ignorant of the Doctrine of our ancient Kings, which is so agreeable to all Times: So that, instead of profiting by the good Dispositions of *Kau tsû*, to extirpate that Error out of *China*, they let the Proposal drop. How heartily do I curse them, whenever I think of this!

Your Majesty, whom so much Wisdom, and so much Valor, exalt above the most of the Princes who have reigned these many Years; your Majesty, I say, in the Beginning of your Reign, prohibited this Sect from building new Temples, and any of your Subjects from becoming a *Bonze* in time to come. This makes me believe, and say with Joy, that at least, under your Reign, the Designs of *Kau tsû* will be executed. Yet, your Orders have as yet been without Effect: This is too much Condescension already. But besides, how can you yourself annul them by running into an Extreme directly opposite? It is said to be by your Majesty's Orders, that all the *Bonzes* assemble solemnly to conduct in Procession one of the Bones of *Fo*, into the inner Part of your Palace, where you design to place it with Honor in an exalted Hall. Notwithstanding the Poorness of my Judgment, I know well that your Majesty, tho' you have given Orders about this Pomp of Worship, Processions and Prayers, is no way devoted at the Bottom to the Sect of *Fo*. I know well, your real Motive is; that you may render the Joy which fills all Hearts, more solemn, for this plentiful Year. Indulging this Disposition, you have a mind to give some Spectacle, or new Diversion; and for that Reason, you have permitted this Pomp of extraordinary Ceremonies.

---

[13] It is said, that in their Stead, he made the Animals appointed for these Ceremonies, of Paste.

For in short, is it probable, that a Prince, so understanding as you are, should have any Belief in that Sect? No! I am persuaded you have not; but the ignorant stupid Vulgar, are easy to be seduced, but hard to be reclaimed. When they perceive that your Majesty pays these outward Honors to *Fo*, they are convinced that you really honor him: And they don't fail to say; Our great and wise Emperor, giving himself so much ado about honoring *Fo*; why should we poor People spare our Persons and Lives? There needs no more to persuade them, by Dozens and Hundreds, to burn their Heads and Fingers. The only Contest then among them will be, who shall soonest squander what he has, in order to take the Habit of a *Bonze*. At least, from Evening to Morning, the Roads leading to the Bonzaries will be filled with Pilgrims. Old and Young will be seen running thither in Crowds; and for fear of what may happen, divest themselves of what they have. They will go still farther, and if this should be prevented by rigorous Prohibitions affixt to the Bonzaries, there will be simple People enough found, who will slash their Arms and other Parts of their Bodies in honor of *Fo*.[14]

This Abuse, you must be sensible, will be greatly prejudicial to good Morals, hurt our Policy, and render us ridiculous to all the World. But what was this same *Fo*? A barbarous Foreigner, whose Tongue and Cloaths were different from ours. He never was capable to speak that Language, which our ancient Princes have transmitted to us: Nor did he ever wear any Cloaths made in the Fashion regulated by these great Men. He either was ignorant of, or neglected, the most essential Duties of Prince to Subject, and of Son to Father.

In short, let us suppose that this *Fo* were still alive, and that his Prince had deputed him in his Name, to repair to your Court to pay you Homage; how would your Majesty receive it? At most, after a short Audience, you either would treat him hospitably according to the Rites; and make him a Present of a compleat Habit, or else you would order him a Guard which should have an Eye to his Conduct, and which should convey him to your Frontiers, without allowing him an Opportunity of endeavouring to seduce your People. In this manner would you treat *Fo*. If he were yet alive, and sent hither by his Prince, why then should he be so much revered so many Years after his Death? Where then is the Decorum of introducing in Pomp into your Palace, and to its innermost Parts, whose Access is so severely prohibited, a rotten Bone, the sorry stinking Remains of his Carcass? Respect the *Quey shin* [spirits], said

---

[14] The best of Religions when its Professors lose Reason in *Enthusiasm* or *Priestcraft*, degenerates into the like Absurdities.

Confucius, but don't go near them. It has been seen in Antiquity, that *Chu hew* being obliged to perform a funeral Ceremony without the Bounds of his own State, was afraid of troublesome Consequences: And that in order to guard against the Badness of the Omen, he sent one of these U [magicians], who, by using the Herb *Lye* and other Formalities, averted the Misfortunes.

At present, your Majesty, without taking any Precaution, and without the least Necessity, draws near a rotten stinking Bone, and stops to look at it. Notwithstanding this, your Officers keep Silence, and suffer you to do it, the *Yu tsï* [censors] themselves, who by their Employment are more oblig'd to speak, have not made the least Remonstrance. Indeed I blush with Shame. Give up, I conjure you, give up that Bone to your Officers of Justice: Let them cast it into the Water or the Fire, and thus root up the Evil. Thereby you will prevent the Progress of those Suspicions and Doubts, which you have given Rise to in your Empire, prepossess Posterity against these Errors, and verify by your Example, that Sages of the first Rate, in concerting and executing their Designs, far exceed the Generality of Mankind. Oh! How glorious and how graceful would that be in you? Oh! What a Joy would that give to me, and to every truly zealous Subject! Dread no troublesome Consequences: I take these all upon my self. If *Fo* really can do any thing, let him discharge all his Wrath upon me. *Shang tyen* [Heaven], who sees us inwardly, knows that my Sentiments answer to my Words, and that I am incapable to prevaricate. Happy should I be, if your Majesty would indulge my earnest Prayer. I should not then know how to express my loyal Gratitude.

Hyen tsong, having read this Writing, was in so great an Anger, that he designed to put *Han yu* to Death. But he was appeased at last by *Tswi kyun, Fey tû*, and some others. He was satisfied with banishing *Han yu* to the Provinces, where he gave him a Post much inferior to that he had at Court.

The *Emperor Kang hi's* Remark [Emperor Kangxi (1662–1723) of the Qing dynasty]. The Expressions here are close and full of Honesty; and at the Bottom, reasonable and sensible. It ought to have been sufficient to have reclaim'd the first Man of the Literati of that Dynasty from the vulgar Errors, and to have given a Value for its Author.

I leave the Reader to judge, both of the Discourse of *Han yu*, and what the Emperor and he says of it, by which he will know in what manner the *Chinese* reason, when they refute strange Religions.

Proclamation to the Crocodile

This diatribe has reference to the alleged expulsion of a crocodile which had been devastating the water-courses round Chaozhou, whither Han Yu had been sent in disgrace.

On a certain date, I, Han Yü, Governor of Chaozhou, gave orders that
a goat and a pig should be thrown into the river as prey for the crocodile,
together with the following proclamation: —

"In days of yore, when our ancient rulers first undertook the administration of the empire, they cleared away the jungle by fire, and
drove forth with net and spear such denizens of the marsh as were
obnoxious to the prosperity of the human race, away beyond the boundaries of the Four Seas. But as years went on, the light of Imperial
virtue began to pale; the circle of the empire was narrowed; and lands
once subject to the divine sway passed under barbarian rule. Hence,
the region of Chaozhou, distant many hundred miles from the capital,
was then a fitting spot for thee, O crocodile, in which to bask, and
breed, and rear thy young. But now again the times are changed. We
live under the auspices of an enlightened prince, who seeks to bring
within the Imperial fold all, even to the uttermost limits of sea and sky.
Moreover, this is soil once trodden by the feet of the Great Yü himself;
soil for which I, an officer of the State, am bound to make due return,
in order to support the established worship of Heaven and Earth, in
order to maintain the Imperial shrines and temples of the Gods of our
land.

"O crocodile! thou and I cannot rest together here. The Son of
Heaven has confided this district and this people to my charge; and thou,
O goggle-eyed, by disturbing the peace of this river and devouring the
people and their domestic animals, the bears, the boars, and deer of the
neighborhood, in order to fatten thyself and reproduce thy kind, —
thou art challenging me to a struggle of life and death. And I, though of
weakly frame, am I to bow the knee and yield before a crocodile? No! I
am the lawful guardian of this place, and I would scorn to decline thy
challenge, even were it to cost me my life.

"Still, in virtue of my commission from the Son of Heaven, I am bound
to give fair warning; and thou, O crocodile, if thou art wise, will pay due
heed to my words. There before thee lies the broad ocean, the domain
alike of the whale and the shrimp. Go thither, and live in peace. It is but
the journey of a day.

"And now I bid thee be gone, thou and thy foul brood, within the
space of three days, from the presence of the servant of the Son of
Heaven. If not within three days, then within five; if not within five, then
within seven. But if not within seven, then it is that thou wilt not go, but
art ready for the fight. Or, may be, that thou hast not wit to seize the
purport of my words; though whether it be wilful disobedience or stupid
misapprehension, the punishment in each case is death. I will arm some
cunning archer with trusty bow and poisoned arrow, and try the issue

with thee, until thou and all thy likes have perished. Repent not then, for it will be too late."[15]

In Memoriam — 1

This exquisite morceau, written in memory of the author's cousin, tells its own tale, coupled with several interesting details of the writer's own life.

Seven days had elapsed after the news of thy death ere I could control my grief and collect my thoughts. I then bade one go and prepare, dear boy, some choice votive offering to thy departed spirit.

Ah, me! betimes an orphan; growing up without a father's care; dependent solely upon an elder brother, thy father, and his wife. And when, in mid-career, that brother died far away in the south, thou and I, mere boys, followed the widow home with the funeral *cortège.* Then our life together, orphans each, never separated for a day.

My three brothers all early died, leaving only us, a grandson and a son, to carry on the ancestral line. We were two generations, with but one body, one form, one shadow. And often when thy mother bore thee in her arms, she would point at me and say, "Of two generations of the house of Han, these are all that remain." Thou wert too young to remember that now; and I, though I remember the words now, did not understand the sorrow that they expressed.

At sixteen, I went to the capital, returning home after the lapse of four years. Then four years more, after which I repaired to the family burying-ground, and met thee there, standing by thy mother's grave. Another two years of official life: a short reunion during thy visit of a year: leave of absence to bring my family to my home. The next year my chief died, and I quitted my post; but thou didst not come. In the same year another appointment elsewhere, whence the messenger sent to fetch thee had barely started ere I again had left. Once more thou camest not. Yet I knew that had we gone eastwards together it would have been but for a short time, and that I should do better to make for the west, where we might all gather round the old home.

Alas! why leave me thus and die? To me it seemed that both were young in years, and that although separated for a time, we might still hope to pass our lives together. Therefore we parted, and I went to the

---

[15] The crocodile went.

capital in search of place; but could I have foreseen what was to happen, the many-charioted territory of a duke should not have tempted me one moment from thy side.

Last year I wrote thee, saying, "Not forty yet: sight dim, hair gray, strength sapped. Father and brothers, lusty men all, died in their prime; — can then this decaying frame last long? I may not go: thou wilt not come. Alas! I fear lest at any moment I may be cut off and leave thee to unutterable grief." Yet who would have thought that the young man was to perish and the old man to live? the strong youth to sink into a premature grave, the sick man to be made whole? Is it reality or a dream? Was it truth they told me? Reality — that the line of my noble-hearted brother should be thus ended in premature death? Reality — that thy pure intelligence shall not survive to continue the traditions of his house? Reality — that the young and strong thus early fade and die, while the old and decaying live on and thrive? Reality indeed it is; and no dream, and no lie. Else why this letter, this notice of death, now lying before me? It is so. The line of my noble-hearted brother has indeed been prematurely cut off. Thy pure intelligence, hope of the family, survives not to continue the traditions of his house. Unfathomable are the appointments of what men call Heaven: inscrutable are the workings of the unseen: unknowable are the mysteries of eternal truth: unrecognizable those who are destined to attain to old age!

Henceforth, my gray hairs will grow white, my strength fail. Physically and mentally hurrying on to decay, how long before I shall follow thee? If there is knowledge after death, this separation will be but for a little while. If there is no knowledge after death, so will this sorrow be but for a little while, and then no more sorrow for ever.

Thy boy is just ten; mine five. But if the young and the strong are to be thus cut off, who shall dare hope that these babes in arms may not share the same unhappy fate?

Thy last year's letters told me of the tender foot and its increasing pains; but I said to myself, "The disease is common in Jiangnan, and need cause no alarm." Was it then this that extinguished thy life, or some other disease that brought thee to the grave?

Thy last letter is dated 17th of the 6th moon. Yet I hear from one that death came on the 2nd, while another sends a letter without date. The messenger never thought to ask; and the family, relying on the letter's date, never thought to tell. I enquired of the messenger, but he replied at random, so that I am still in doubt. I have now sent to sacrifice to thy departed spirit, and to condole with thy orphan and foster-mother, bidding them wait, if possible, until the final rites are paid, but if not, then to come to me, leaving the servants to watch over thy corpse. And when perchance I am able, I will some day see that thy bones are duly laid in our ancestral burying-place.

Alas! of thy sickness I knew not the time; of thy death I knew not the hour. Unable to tend thee in life, I was debarred from weeping over thee in death. I could not touch thy bier: I could not stand by thy grave. I have sinned against Heaven: I have caused thee to be cut off in thy prime. Wretch that I am, separated from thee alike in life and death — thou at one end of the earth, I at the other — thy shadow did not accompany my form, neither shall thy spirit now blend with my dreams. The fault, the blame are mine alone.

O ye blue heavens, when shall my sorrow have end? Henceforth, the world has no charms. I will get me a few acres on the banks of the Ying, and there await the end, teaching my son and thy son, if haply they may grow up, — my daughter and thy daughter, until their day of marriage comes. Alas! though words fail, love endureth. Dost thou hear, or dost thou not hear? Woe is me: Heaven bless thee!

In Memoriam — 2

This was written in memory of his dear friend Liu Zongyuan.

Alas! Zihou, and hast thou come to this pass? — fool that I am! is it not the pass to which mortals have ever come? Man is born into the world like a dream: what need has he to take note of gain or loss? While the dream lasts, he may sorrow or may joy; but when the awakening is at hand, why cling regretfully to the past?

'Twere well for all things an they had no worth. The excellence of its wood is the bane of the tree. And thou, whom God released in mid-career from earthly bonds, weaver of the jeweled words, thou wilt be remembered when the imbeciles of fortune and place are forgot.

The unskillful bungler hacks his hands and streams with sweat, while the expert craftsman looks on with folded arms. O my friend, thy work was not for this age; though I, a bungler, have found employment in the service of the State. Thou didst know thyself above the common herd; but when in shame thou didst depart, never to return, the philistines usurped thy place.

Alas! Zihou, now thou art no more. But thy last wish, that I should care for thy little son, is still ringing sadly in my ears. The friendships of the day are those of self-interest alone. How can I feel sure that I shall live to carry out thy behest? I did not arrogate to myself this duty. Thou thyself hast bidden me to the task; and, by the Gods above, I will not betray thy trust.

Thou hast gone to thy eternal home, and wilt not return. With these sacrifices by thy coffin's side, I utter an affectionate farewell.

LIU YUXI (772–842)

My Humble Home

Translated by Herbert Giles

For Liu Yuxi, see chapter 22. — Editors

Hills are not famous for height alone: 'tis the Genius Loci that invests them with their charm. Lakes are not famous for mere depth: 'tis the residing Dragon that imparts to them a spell not their own. And so, too, my hut may be mean; but the fragrance of Virtue is diffused around.

The green lichen creeps up the steps: emerald leaflets peep beneath the bamboo blind. Within, the laugh of cultured wit, the words of the Diamond Sutra, marred by no scraping fiddle, no scrannel pipe, no hateful archives of official life.

Kongming[16] had his cottage in the south; Yang Xiong[17] his cabin in the west. And the Master[18] said, "What foulness can there be where virtue is?"

LIU ZONGYUAN (773–819)

Four Essays

Translated by Herbert Giles

Liu was one of the most celebrated poets and essayists of the Tang dynasty, and also famous as a calligraphist. After rising to be secretary in the Board of Rites, he became involved in the conspiracy of Wang Shuwen and in 805 was sent as a minor official to Yongzhou in Hunan. In 815 he was banished to Liuzhou in Guangxi, with the appointment of Prefect, in which post he died. Some of his poems are deeply tinged with Buddhist doctrines, and he also wrote a remarkable essay in defense of his partiality. He was on very intimate terms with Han Yu from whom he received more than one severe rebuke for his leaning towards the "strange doctrine."

---

[16] Zhuge Liang [see chapter 14, for his memorial "On Deploying the Army"], the "Sleeping Dragon," great general of the Three Kingdoms, to whose cottage Liu Bei came three times in quest of his transcendent talent.

[17] Eminent man of letters of the Han dynasty [see chapter 6 for his rhapsody "The Sweet Spring Palace"].

[18] Confucius.

Catching Snakes

In the wilds of Huguang [Hubei and Hunan] there is an extraordinary kind of snake, having a black body with white rings. Deadly fatal, even to the grass and trees it may chance to touch; in man, its bite is absolutely incurable. Yet if caught and prepared, when dry, in the form of cakes, the flesh of this snake will soothe excitement, heal leprous sores, remove sloughing flesh, and expel evil spirits. And so it came about that the Court physician, acting under Imperial orders, exacted from each family a return of two of these snakes every year; but as few persons were able to comply with the demand, it was subsequently made known that the return of snakes was to be considered in lieu of the usual taxes. There-upon there ensued a general stampede among the people of those parts.

However, there was one man whose family had lived there for three generations; and from him I obtained the following information: — "My grandfather lost his life in snake-catching. So did my father. And during the twelve years that I have been engaged in the same way, death has several times come very near to me." He was deeply moved during this recital; but when I asked if I should state his sad case to the authorities and apply for him to be allowed to pay taxes in the regular manner, he burst into tears and said, "Alas! sir, you would take away my means of livelihood altogether. The misery of this state is as nothing when compared with the misery of that. Formerly, under the ordinary conditions of life, we suffered greatly; but for the past three generations we have been settled in this district, now some sixty years since. During that period, my fellow-villagers have become more and more im-poverished. Their substance has been devoured, and in beggary they have gone weeping and wailing away. Exposed to the inclemency of wind and rain, enduring heat and cold, they have fled from the cruel scourge, in most cases, to die. Of those families which were here in my grandfather's time, there remains not more than one in ten; of those here in my father's time, not more than two or three; and of those still here in my own time, not more than four or five. They are all either dead or gone elsewhere; while we, the snake-catchers, alone survive. Harsh tyrants sweep down upon us, and throw everybody and everything, even to the brute beasts, into paroxysms of terror and disorder. But I — I get up in the morning and look into the jar where my snakes are kept; and if they are still there. I lie down at night in peace. At the appointed time, I take care that they are fit to be handed in; and when that is done, I retire to enjoy the produce of my farm and complete the allotted span of my existence. Only twice a year have I to risk my life: the rest is peaceful enough and not to be compared with the daily round of annoyance which falls to the share of my fellow-villagers. And even though I were to die now in this employ, I should still have outlived almost all my contemporaries. Can I then complain?"

This story gave me food for much sad reflection. I had always doubted the saying of Confucius that "bad government is worse than a tiger," but now I felt its truth. Alas! who would think that the tax-collector could be more venomous than a snake? I therefore record this for the information of those whom it may concern.

Congratulations on a Fire

I have received the letter informing me that your house has been attacked by fire, and that you have lost everything. At first, I felt shocked: then doubtful: but now I congratulate you from the bottom of my heart. My sorrow is turned into joy. Still, we are far apart, and you give no particulars. If you mean that you are utterly and irretrievably beggared, then I have further reason to offer you my congratulations.

In the first place, it was only because I knew your happiness to be bound up with the happiness of your parents, and feared that this calamity would disturb the even tenor of their lives, that I felt shocked.

Secondly, the world is never weary of citing the fickleness of fortune and the uncertainty of her favors. And it is an old tradition that the man who is to rise to great things must first be chastened by misfortune and sorrow: and that the evils of flood and fire, and the slanders of scoundrels, are sent upon him solely that he may shine thereafter with a brighter light. But this doctrine is absurdly far-fetched, and could never command the confidence even of diviner intellects than ours. Therefore I doubted.

My friend, you are widely read in ancient lore. You are an accomplished scholar: a man, in fact, of many gifts. Yet you have failed to rise above the common rank and file. And why? Because you were known to be rich; and men jealous of their reputation refrained from speaking your praises. They kept their knowledge of your virtues to themselves, fearing the calumnious imputations of the world. To speak on your behalf would be to raise a titter, coupled with queries as to the amount transferred.

As for me, it is now some years since I became aware of your literary power; but all that time I selfishly said nothing, disloyal not only to you but to the cause of truth. And even when I became a Censor and a high functionary of State, and rejoiced in my proximity to the Throne and in the liberty of speech which enabled me to bring forth your merits into the blaze of day, — I was only laughed at as one recommending his friends. I have long hated myself for this want of straightforwardness and fear of the world's censure, and with our friend Meng Ji have often bewailed the impracticability of the position. But now that Heaven has sent this ruin upon you, the suspicions of men vanish with the smoke of the fire and are refuted by the blackened walls which proclaim your poverty to all. Your talents have now free play, without fear of reproach. Verily the God of Fire is on your side. In one night he has done more to set your praises before men than your own bosom friends have accomplished during the space of ten years. Have patience awhile, and those who have always believed in your genius will be able to open their mouths; and those with whom your advancement lies, will advance you without fear. You must remain in obscurity no longer. I can help you now, and therefore I congratulate you from my heart.

In the olden days, when the capitals of four States were burnt to the ground,[19] the other States, with one exception, sent to condole with the sufferers. The omission on the part of that one State incurred the disapprobation of the superior man. But I have gone even farther. I congratulate where the world condoles; and as for the care of your parents, with the examples of antiquity before you, there need be no cause for fear.

The Beauties of Buddhism

My learned and estimable friend Han Yu has often reproached my *penchant* for Buddhism and the intercourse that I hold with its priests. And now a letter from him has just reached me, in which he blames me severely for not having denounced the religion in a recent address forwarded to another friend.

In point of fact, there is much in Buddhism which could not well be denounced; *scilicet*, all those tenets which are based on principles common to our own sacred books. And it is precisely to these essentials, at once in perfect harmony with human nature and the teachings of Confucius, that I give in my adhesion.

Han Yu himself could not be a warmer advocate of moral culture (as excluding the supernatural) than was Yang Xiong; and the works of the

---

[19] Owing, as it was said, to the appearance of a great comet.

latter, as well as those of other heterodox writers, contain a great deal that is valuable. Why then should this be impossible in the case of Buddhism? Han Yu replies, "Buddha was a barbarian." But if this argument is good for anything, we might find ourselves embracing a criminal who happened to be a fellow-countryman, while neglecting a saint whose misfortune it was to be a foreigner! Surely this would be a hollow mockery indeed.

The lines I admire in Buddhism are those which are coincident with the principles enunciated in our own sacred books. And I do not think that, even were the holy sages of old to revisit the earth, they would fairly be able to denounce these. Now, Han Yu objects to the Buddhist commandments. He objects to the bald pates of the priests, their dark robes, their renunciation of domestic ties, their idleness, and life generally at the expense of others. So do I. But Han Yu misses the kernel while railing at the husk. He sees the lode, but not the ore. I see both; hence my partiality for the faith.

Again, intercourse with men of this religion does not necessarily imply conversion. Even if it did, Buddhism admits no envious rivalry for place or power. The majority of its adherents love only to lead a simple life of contemplation amid the charms of hill and stream. And when I turn my gaze towards the hurry-scurry of the age, in its daily race for the seals and tassels of office, I ask myself if I am to reject those in order to take my place among the ranks of these.

The Buddhist priest, Haochu, is a man of placid temperament and of passions subdued. He is a fine scholar. His only joy is to muse o'er flood and fell, with occasional indulgence in the delights of composition. His family — for he has one — follow in the same path. He is independent of all men; and no more to be compared with those heterodox sages of whom we make so much, than with the vulgar herd of the greedy, grasping world around us.

Pas Trop Gouverner: Camel-back the Gardener

I do not know what Camel-back's real name was. Disease had hunched him up behind, and he walked with his head down, like a camel. Hence, people came to give him the nickname of Camel. "Capital!" cried he, when he first heard of his sobriquet; "the very name for me." And thereafter he entirely left off using his proper name, calling himself "Camel-back."

He lived in the village of Peace-and-Plenty, near the capital, and followed the occupation of a nursery-gardener. All the grand people of the city used to go and see his show; while market-gardeners vied with each other in securing his services, since every tree he either planted or transplanted was sure to thrive and bear fruit, not only early in the season but in abundance. Others in the same line of business, although they closely watched his method, were quite unable to achieve the same success.

One day a customer asked him how this was so; to which he replied, "Old Camel-back cannot make trees live or thrive. He can only let them follow their natural tendencies. Now in planting trees, be careful to set the root straight, to smooth the earth around them, to use good mold, and to ram it down well. Then, don't touch them; don't think about them; don't go and look at them; but leave them alone to take care of themselves, and nature will do the rest. I only avoid trying to make my trees grow. I have no special method of cultivation, no special means for securing luxuriance of growth. I only don't spoil the fruit. I have no way of getting it either early or in abundance. Other gardeners set with bent root, and neglect the mold. They heap up either too much earth or too little. Or if not this, then they become too fond of and too anxious about their trees, and are for ever running backwards and forwards to see how they are growing; sometimes scratching them to make sure they are still alive, or shaking them about to see if they are sufficiently firm in the ground: thus constantly interfering with the natural bias of the tree, and turning their affection and care into an absolute bane and a curse. I only don't do these things. That's all."

"Can these principles you have just now set forth be applied to government?" asked his listener. "Ah!" replied Camel-back, "I only understand nursery-gardening: government is not my trade. Still, in the village where I live, the officials are for ever issuing all kinds of orders, as if greatly compassionating the people, though really to their utter injury. Morning and night the underlings come round and say, "His Honor bids us urge on your plowing, hasten your planting, and superintend your harvest. Do not delay with your spinning and weaving. Take care of your children. Rear poultry and pigs. Come together when the drum beats. Be ready at the sound of the rattle." Thus are we poor people badgered from morn till eve. We have not a moment to ourselves. How could any one flourish and develop naturally under such conditions? It was this that brought about my illness. And so it is with those who carry on the gardening business."

"Thank you," said the listener. "I simply asked about the management of trees, and I have learnt about the management of men. I will make this known, as a warning to government officials."

Two Records of Yongzhou

Translated by A. R. Davis

Liu Zongyuan's "Eight Records of Yongzhou" (809–812) established the landscape essay as a genre, and gained him a position as a major stylist in Chinese literary history.

— Indiana Companion, 1986

Yongzhou is in the extreme south of Chu; in appearance it is similar to Yue. When I am depressed, I go out for an excursion. But when I go, I again have many fears. For when I go over the rough ground, there are poisonous snakes and great wasps. Looking up in the air and down at the ground, inching my way, I grow weary. When I approach the water, I am afraid of "water-archers" and sand-leeches that, full of malice, stealthily come out and strike at men's bodies and shadows, bringing them out in sores and contusions. Sometimes I come to shady trees and fine rocks, and for a while I laugh. Yet once more I am not happy. Why? I am like a prisoner confined in a prison. As soon as I meet with a fine day, I rub my back against the wall and stretch my limbs. At such a time I am indeed at ease, but when I look at the earth and peer at the sky, it is but eight or ten feet. In the end I cannot get out. How can I be cheerful for long? In an enlightened age the common people all find gladness, yet I, a scholar, who know the ways of government in ancient and modern times, alone am so distressed. Truly I am not fit to be a petty official in an orderly age. Even with foolish men and women I cannot compare, and I secretly pity myself.

— from "A letter to Li Jian" (809)

On First Making an Excursion to the Western Hill

Since I was disgraced, I have lived in this prefecture in constant unease. In my idleness I slowly strolled and aimlessly wandered. Daily with my companions I went up high hills and into deep woods, and traced out winding streams: there was no secluded spring or strange rock, however far, I did not go to. When we arrived, we would sit down upon the grass and pour wine until we were drunk. When we were drunk, we slept, pillowed upon one another. As we slept, we dreamed, and whatever the range of our thoughts, our dreams would have the same tendency. When we awoke, we would get up, and, getting up, return home. I thought that I had seen all the remarkable forms of hill and stream in this prefecture, but I had not learned of the singular wonder of the Western Hill.

On the twenty-eighth day of the ninth month of this year (9th November), as I was sitting in the Western Pavilion of the Fahua Monastery, I gazed at the Western Hill and for the first time pointed to it with wonder. Then I ordered my servants to take me across the Xiang River, go along the Ran Stream, cut down the brushwood and burn the rushes right to the crest of the hill. I clambered up and, squatting down, gazed around. The lands of several prefectures lay before my mat. The undulating aspect had deep folds and hollows, appearing but mounds and holes; in feet and inches were a thousand *li*; contracted and piled up, nothing could be hidden. Surrounded by blue and bound by white, the outer limit of the scene merged into the sky; whichever way one looked was as one. Then I knew that this hill stood alone; it was not of a kind with mounds of earth, but ranged away into unity with the Great Force, where none could achieve its limit; overflowed into companionship with the Creator and its end could not be known.

Taking up the winecup, I filled it full. Falling into drunkeness, I did not know the sun had set. Deep blue, the evening hues came from far until nothing could be seen. Yet still I did not wish to return. My mind was fixed, my body dissolved, darkly merged in Creation. Then I knew that hitherto I had made no excursion; this was my first excursion. Therefore I wrote this piece as a record. This year was the fourth year of Yuan-he (809).

The Small Hill West of the Flat-Iron Lake

Eight days after I had discovered the Western Hill, tracing out the northwestern track through the pass for two hundred paces I also discovered the Flat-Iron Lake. Twenty-five paces to the west, where the water is swift and deep, there is a fishtrap and above it a small hill, where bamboos and trees grow. Its rocks which are sheer and towering, rising out of the earth and rivaling each other in strange forms, are almost innumerable. As they stand erect together and sweep downward, they are like oxen or horses drinking from a stream; as they thrust upward and ascend, they are like bears clambering up a slope. The small extent of the hill is less than a sixth of an acre: it can be enclosed as one man's land.

I enquired its owner and was told: it is the abandoned land of a certain Tang; he had been unable to sell it. I enquired the price and was told: Only four hundred cash. So out of pity I bought it. Li Shenyuan and Yuan Keji sometimes made an expedition with me there and both greatly delighted in it beyond their expectation. Then we took implements to cut down the rank plants and to cut out the poor trees, and burnt them on bonfires. Thus the fine trees stood out, excellent bamboos were revealed and unusual rocks disclosed. As one gazed out from the middle of the hill, the loftiness of the mountains, the drifting of the clouds, the flowing of the streams and the passage of birds and beasts, presented a delightful, changing show, so that as one reclined on a mat beneath this hill, pure forms would meet the eye, murmuring waters greet the ear, a remote dispassionateness enter the spirit and a deep calm enter the heart. In less than ten days I had discovered two remarkable places. Even the connoisseurs of the past may not have been able to achieve this.

Ah! if one brought the scenery of this hill to Feng, Hao, Hu, or Du, then noble and idle gentlemen, striving with one another to buy it, would daily add a thousand cash to the offer, and still be unable to obtain it. Now it was abandoned in this place where peasants and fishermen despised it as they passed by. At a price of four hundred cash, year after year it could not be sold, and only I, with Shenyuan and Keji, delighted to find it. This was indeed a chance encounter. So I have made an inscription on a rock to celebrate coming upon this hill.

ᘓᘏ Further Reading ᘓᘏ

Ch'en, Yu-shih. *Images and Ideas in Chinese Classical Prose.* Stanford: Stanford University Press, 1988.

Davis, A. R. "The Fortunate Banishment: Liu Tsung-yüan in Yung-chou." *Journal of the Oriental Society of Australia* (December 1966), 4 (2).

Du Halde, Jean-Baptiste. *Description géographique, historique, chronologique, politique de l'empire de la Chine.* 4 vols. Paris: Lemercier, 1735. Translated by R. Brookes as *A Description of the Empire of China,* 2 vols. (London: Edward Cave, 1738).

Edwards, E. D., ed. and trans. *Chinese Prose Literature of the T'ang Period.* 2 vols. London: Arthur Probsthain, 1937–38.

Giles, Herbert A., ed. and trans. *Gems of Chinese Literature.* Shanghai: Kelly & Walsh, 1884.

Hartmann, Charles. *Han Yü and the T'ang Search for Unity.* Princeton: Princeton University Press, 1986.

Liu, Shih Shun. *Chinese Clasical Prose: The Eight Masters of the T'ang-Sung Period.* Hong Kong: Chinese University Press, 1979.

Nienhauser, William H., et al. *Liu Tsung-yüan.* New York: Twayne, 1973.

Renditions (1990), 33–34. "Special Issue: Classical Prose."

Strassberg, Richard, ed. and trans. *Inscribed Landscapes: Travel Writings from Imperial China.* Berkeley: University of California Press, 1994.

"My mind is with the ancients."
Seal carved by Deng Shiru (1743–1805)

Chapter 28

The World in a Pillow

Classical Tales of the Tang Dynasty

We must study the Tang stories. Even small incidents are exquisitely moving, and often — without realizing it themselves — the authors are inspired. These stories and Tang poetry are the wonder of their age.

> — Hong Mai (1123–1202), *Notes from Tolerance Studio*
> (*translated by Xianyi and Gladys Yang*)

Tales of miracles and the other worlds were popular during the Six Dynasties, but these were not entirely imaginary: most of them were based on hearsay and false reports. The Tang dynasty scholars, on the other hand, deliberately invented strange adventures and wrote as fiction.

> — Hu Yinglin (1551–1602), *Jottings from a Mountain Retreat*
> (*translated by Xianyi and Gladys Yang*)

Fiction, like poetry, underwent radical changes in the Tang dynasty. Though tales were still written about marvels and strange phenomena, the plots became more elaborate and the language more polished. By this time writers were consciously writing fiction, they were consciously romancing.

> — Lu Xun (1881–1936), *A Brief History of Chinese Fiction*
> (*translated by Xianyi and Gladys Yang*)

Introduction

J. R. Hightower

In Tang times the tale written in the classical language reached its maturity as a literary form. The various earlier types provided themes and contributed to the narrative technique of the Tang Classical Tale (*chuanqi*), but the stimulus for the production of this more sophisticated narrative came from factors new to Chinese society. One factor was the new prose medium — the Ancient Prose style — promoted by Han Yu and his followers [see chapter 27].

The practice of having candidates for the civil service examinations submit to their examiners a "practice composition" in which they were to demonstrate their ability at narration, exposition, and versification has been linked with the contemporary development of the Classical Tale, as these tales frequently contain the three elements. Such a demand would certainly lead to the widespread practice of this type of composition as preparation for acceptance in the examinations, and successful candidates as well as those who failed might have continued to write stories for amusement even after the practical demand had ceased to apply....

The bulk of Tang fiction in the literary language can be conveniently described as belonging in five categories. Of these, the fictional biographies of historical persons were a direct continuation of the Han tradition, and like their prototype were cast in a form imitating the biographies in the Standard Histories [see chapter 7]. They deal with contemporary Tang figures, chiefly poets or the more notorious of the imperial concubines. These sketches show no technical advance over their predecessors, and probably should not be considered as Classical Tales proper.

The few Tang hero stories also have Han prototypes, but reflect a very different attitude toward their subject. The adventures of the hero are no longer bound to follow a prescribed ritual pattern. His motivation may be chivalrous or capricious; there is not the undercurrent of predetermined fate that characterizes the earlier hero story. The intrusion of the supernatural or marvelous appears as a fortuitous ornament rather than as a token of divine concern with the hero's fate.

The religious Classical Tales are more elaborate than the Six Dynasties apologues and through better characterization have greater interest as stories. The moral is less obtrusive, even in the tales retold from earlier versions. Both Taoism and Buddhism provide the materials for Classical Tales; in addition there are many stories containing attacks on the clergy and on the beliefs of the two religions. Among the stories that depend on Buddhist or Taoist cosmology for their setting are those which use the other world as a vehicle for social criticism. Since the world of the dead is a faithful replica of this world in its social organization, abuses and inequalities could be safely attacked by describing the corrupt and bungling administration of the spirit world.

The most remarkable group of Classical Tales is that of love stories. There was no precedent in Tang times for love as a subject for fiction. Mildly erotic accounts of the relationship between emperors and favorite concubines were known, but no tales of romantic attachment. The Tang love stories are the most realistic of the Classical Tales and depend less on supernatural agencies for the working out of their plots. The love affairs described sometimes involve girls of good family, but more often the girl is either a courtesan or a fox-fairy. The connections are nearly all illicit; only exceptionally is the love of a married couple the subject for a story. It is probable that the sudden appearance of this new topic in fiction reflects a changed status of women in Chinese society, possibly as a result of the reign of the Tang Empress Wu. The brothels which flourished in the capitals and commercial centers, providing an opportunity for men to meet educated and attractive young women, were also a factor in popularizing romantic attachments that could provide material for stories. At least one of these tales (*The Story of Yingying*) is known to be autobiographical, and it is likely that others had a basis in fact or current gossip.

Besides the preceding categories of tales there are a large number which can be classified only as tales of the marvelous, a description which applies in a broader sense to all of the Tang Classical Tales. The unusual phenomena or events which are recorded may belong to the supernatural — feats of magic, the behavior of witches, and the fulfillment of omens; or we find brief paragraphs instructing the reader in dragon lore; these all are subjects which had appeared in the Standard Histories since Han times, and which were undoubtedly accepted as factual even out of such a context. Other, more elaborate tales deal with unusual situations of everyday life: exemplary behavior, devoted friends, eccentric people. For these too precedents existed in Han and Six Dynasties stories [see chapter 16].

— from *Topics in Chinese Literature*, 1953

Shen Jiji (c. 741–c. 805)
Two Tales

Translated by Chi-chen Wang

Shen Jiji was an official from Wuxing in modern Zhejiang, who enjoyed a chequered career. He is now chiefly remembered for these two stories.

The World in a Pillow

This story takes its basic plot from an earlier work of the Six Dynasties (compare the stories from *In Search of Spirits* in chapter 16). It tells of a man who dreams of the passage of an entire lifetime while dozing with his head on a hollow pillow made of green porcelain. He wakes to find that this "lifetime" of his has "lasted" less than the time needed to cook a bowl of millet gruel. The story can be understood in the light of contemporary Buddhist and Taoist ideas concerning the illusory nature of life and the vanity of striving after worldly gain.

— Editors

In the seventh year of Kai-yuan (719) a Taoist priest by the name of Lü Weng, who had acquired the magic of the immortals, was traveling on the road to Handan, in the province of Shandong. He stopped at an inn and was sitting and resting with his back against his bag when he was joined in a very genial conversation by a young man named Lu Sheng, who wore a plain, short coat and rode a black colt and who had stopped at the inn on his way to the fields. After a while Lu Sheng suddenly sighed and said, looking at his shabby clothes, "It is because fate is against me that I have been such a failure in life!" "Why do you say that in the midst of such a pleasant conversation?" Lü Weng said. "As far as I can see you suffer from nothing and appear to enjoy the best of health." "This is mere existence," Lu Sheng said. "I do not call this life." "What then do you call life?" asked the priest, whereupon the young man answered, "A man ought to achieve great things and make a name for himself; he should be a general at the head of an expedition or a great minister at court, preside over sumptuous banquets and order the orchestra to play what he likes, and cause his clan to prosper and his own family to wax rich — these things make what I call life. I have devoted myself to study and have enriched myself with travel; I used to think that rank and title were mine for the picking, but now at the prime of life I still have to labor in the fields. What do you call this if not failure?"

After he finished speaking he felt a sudden drowsiness. The innkeeper was steaming some millet at the time. Lü Weng reached into his bag and took out a pillow and gave it to Lu Sheng, saying, "Rest your head on this pillow; it will enable you to fulfill your wishes." The pillow was made of green porcelain and had an opening at each end. Lu Sheng bent his head toward it and as he did so the opening grew large and bright, so that he was able to crawl into it. He found himself back home. A few months later he married the daughter of the Cui family of Qinghe, who was very beautiful and made him exceedingly happy. His wealth increased and the number of luxuries with which he surrounded himself multiplied day by day. The following year he passed the examinations and thus "discarded his hempen coat" and joined the ranks at court. He was made a member of the imperial secretariat and had the honor of composing occasional poems at the Emperor's command. After serving a term as inspector of Weinan, he was promoted to the Censorate, and made secretary in attendance. In the latter capacity he took part in the drafting of important decrees.

Then followed a succession of provincial posts, in one of which, as the governor of Shanzhou, he built a canal eighty *li* in length, which brought so many benefits to the people of the region that they commemorated his achievement upon stone. Next he was made governor of the metropolitan district. In the same year the Emperor's campaigns against the encroaching barbarians reached a critical stage, and when the Turfan and Zhulong hordes invested Guazhou and Shazhou and menaced the region of the Yellow River and the Huang River, the Emperor, in his search for new talent, made Lu Sheng associate director of the Censorate and governor-general of the Hexi Circuit. Lu Sheng routed the barbarians, killing seven thousand men. He conquered nine hundred *li* of territory and built three cities to guard the frontier. The people of the frontier region built a monument on Zhuyan Mountain to commemorate his exploits, and when he returned to court he was received with triumphal honors and was made vice-president of the Board of Civil Service and then president of the Board of Revenue. No name carried so much prestige as his and he had the universal acclaim of popular sentiment. But this incurred the jealousy of the other ministers at court, and as a result of their slanderous attacks he was banished to a provincial post. Three years later, however, he was recalled to court and for more than ten years, with Xiao Song and Pei Guangting, he held the reins of government. Sometimes he received as many as three confidential messages from the Emperor in one day and was ever ready to assist His Majesty with his wise counsel.

Then again he fell victim to the jealousy of his colleagues. They charged him with conspiring with frontier generals to overthrow the dynasty and caused him to be thrown into prison. When the guards came to arrest him, he was stricken with terror and perplexity and said to his wife and sons: "Back in Shandong we have five hundred acres of good land, quite sufficient to keep us from cold and hunger. Why should I have sought rank and title, which in the end have only brought calamity? It is now too late to wish that I could again ride back and forth on the Handan road as I once did, wearing my plain hempen coat!" Thereupon he drew his sword and attempted to kill himself, but was prevented from doing so by his wife. All those implicated in the plot were executed, but Lu Sheng escaped death through the intercession of one of the eunuchs in the confidence of the Emperor. His sentence was commuted to exile to Huanzhou. In a few years the Emperor, having ascertained his innocence, recalled him, made him president of the Imperial Council, and gave him the title of Duke of Yanguo.

He had five sons, all of whom were gifted and were admitted into official ranks. They all married daughters of influential families of the time and presented him with more than ten grandchildren. And so he lived for over fifty years, during which he was twice banished to the frontier wilds only to be recalled to court, vindicated, and rewarded with greater honors than before. He was given to extravagance and was addicted to pleasures. His inner apartments were filled with dancers and beautiful women, and innumerable were the gifts of fertile lands, mansions, fleet horses, and such treasures that the Emperor bestowed upon him.

When advanced age made him wish to retire from court life, his petitions were repeatedly refused. When at last he fell ill, emissaries sent by the Emperor to inquire after his condition followed upon one another's heels and there was nothing left undone that eminent physicians could do. But all was in vain and one night he died. Whereupon he woke up with a start and found himself lying as before in the roadside inn, with Lü Weng sitting by his side and the millet that his host was cooking still not yet done. Everything was as it had been before he dozed off. "Could it be that I have been dreaming all this while?" he said, rising to his feet. "Life as you would have it is but like that," said Lü Weng. For a long while the young man reflected in silence. Then he said, "I now know at last the way of honor and disgrace and the meaning of poverty and fortune, the reciprocity of gain and loss and the mystery of life and death, and I owe all this knowledge to you. Since you have thus deigned to instruct me in the vanity of ambition, dare I refuse to profit thereby?" With this he bowed profoundly to Lü Weng and went away.

Miss Ren, or The Fox Lady

This story too is based on an earlier tale. The author has elaborated a simple plot into a story of considerable length, providing his characters with well-rounded personalities, enlivening his narration with scenes of excitement, vigorous action, and suspense. He has endowed his fox lady, Miss Ren, not only with dazzling beauty, but also with admirable qualities, more admirable than those seen in her human acquaintances. This is one of the first full treatments of the theme of the fox lady, a theme which has continued to haunt the Chinese imagination until the present day. These were-vixen (*hulijing*) were shape-shifting succubae, beautiful, sensual, irresistible creatures, who could be destructive and heartless, ruthless and vindictive (sucking out the essence of their lovers, as Miss Ren puts it), but could also be tender and vulnerable, and capable of deep love and loyalty. They were an expression of the deeply ambivalent attitude of the Chinese literati towards women. The power of feminine beauty and sexuality, as personified by the fox lady, inspired them, and simultaneously incapacitated them, with a mixture of infatuation, fascination, and terror. This fear lay at the root of the sexual vampirism conducted under the guise of the so-called Taoist techniques of the bedchamber, and later (in the Song dynasty) led to the openly sadistic practice of female mutilation known euphemistically as "footbinding."

— Editors

Miss Ren was a fox lady.

Wei Yin, a retired provincial governor, was the ninth in seniority of his family and a grandson of the Prince of Xin'an on his mother's side. As a young man he had been unconventional and fond of drinking. He had a boon companion called Zheng Liu (I do not recall his personal name) who married one of Yin's cousins. In his youth Zheng had trained in the martial arts and was as fond of wine and women as Yin himself. Being poor, he attached himself to his wife's family. He and Yin were on intimate terms and the one was seldom seen without the other.

In the sixth month of the ninth year of Tian-bao (A.D. 750) the two friends were one day riding through the streets of Chang'an on their way to the Xinchang quarter to attend a party. As they reached a point south of Xuanping, Zheng suddenly recalled some matter that he had to attend to and so he begged his friend to excuse him and promised that he would join him at the party later on. Yin went toward the east on his white horse while Zheng rode to the south on his donkey. Inside the northern gate of the Shengping quarter he encountered three women walking on the street, among whom there was one dressed in white whose beauty arrested his attention. He followed them on his donkey, sometimes riding a little distance ahead and sometimes just behind them, and was several times on the point of accosting them but did not do so for lack of courage. Finally the encouraging glances of the one in white emboldened him and he said to them, "Why are you ladies, beautiful as you are, going about the streets of Chang'an on foot?" "What else can we do," said the one in white, "since no one has offered us his mount?" Zheng answered, "My shabby beast is hardly worthy of the honor of bearing such a beautiful lady as you, but I gladly offer it to you and will walk behind you myself." They looked at each other and laughed. The other women, too, encouraged him and soon succeeded in putting him at his ease. Zheng followed them east and it was dark when they finally reached the Leyou Gardens. They stopped before a house with a mud wall around it and a carriage gate through the wall; inside, the buildings were neat. The woman in white went in, and asked Zheng to wait outside a while before he entered, leaving one of the women, who was evidently her maid, to keep him company. The maid asked him his name and where he lived, which he told her, and then he in turn asked her who the woman in white was and was told that her name was Miss Ren and that she was the twentieth of her family.

In a little while Zheng was invited to go in, which he did after securing his donkey to the gate post and putting his hat on the saddle. A woman in her thirties came out to meet him; she was, he found, the elder sister of Miss Ren. Inside candles had been lit and a feast spread out. After a few cups of wine, Miss Ren came out herself, having changed her dress. They drank heartily and became very merry. When the night grew late, Zheng retired with Miss Ren and thus had an opportunity to marvel at the beauty of her form and the exquisite texture of her skin. He was intoxicated with her singing and her laughing and the grace of her carriage, all of a loveliness hardly possible in the mortal world. Before dawn, Miss Ren said to him, "It is time for you to go, for my sisters and myself are attached to the *jiaofang*[1] and must be at our posts early in the morning." Zheng went away, after having agreed on another meeting.

---

[1] A government bureau founded in the early part of the seventh century. It had charge of musicians and dancers. Often used in the sense of the courtesans' quarter.

The gate to the quarter was not yet open when he reached it, but the Tartar baker who kept a shop nearby was already up and building the fire in his oven by the light of a lamp. He went inside and engaged the baker in conversation while waiting for the gate to open. Pointing in the direction whence he had just come, he asked, "Who lives in the house around the bend to the east?" The baker answered, "It is only a deserted yard; there is no one living there." "But I have just come from there and saw signs that it is occupied," Zheng insisted, whereupon the baker seemed to be struck with a thought and said, "Ah, I know now. There is a fox in there that has been bewitching men. She has been seen three times recently. Did you run into her?" Zheng blushed and answered with an evasive "no." He went back to look at the place and found the mud wall and carriage gate as before, but when he peeped in he saw nothing but wild bramble and grass and occasional patches that still showed signs of former cultivation.

When he returned home, his friend Yin took him to task for not having kept his engagement. Zheng made up an excuse but said nothing to him of his extraordinary encounter. He could not, however, forget Miss Ren. He was enamored of her beauty and longed to see her again in spite of what he now knew.

Then some ten days later Zheng suddenly came upon her in a dress shop in the West Market district that he happened to go into. She was accompanied by the same maid whom he had met. Zheng called to her, but she avoided him by stepping into a nearby crowd. Zheng kept on calling to her and following her. Only then did she stand still, with her face averted and concealed behind a fan. "Since you know me for what I am," she said, "why do you seek me still?" Zheng answered, "What harm is there, even though I know?" "I am ashamed," she said, "and find it hard to look you in the face." "But how could you bear to abandon me?" said Zheng. "I long so much for you!" "Abandon you?" she replied. "It is only that I feared that I would revolt you." Zheng swore his love and became all the more insistent. Thereupon Miss Ren turned to face him with her fan drawn aside and showed herself to be as dazzlingly beautiful as ever. "There are many women just as desirable as myself," she said to Zheng. "You have not met them, that's all. Do not embarrass me by behaving as if I were the only one." When Zheng begged her for another meeting, she said, "The reason why our kind incur the revulsion of mankind is that we draw upon men's essence and thus harm them. In this, however, I am different from my kind. If you do not detest me, I shall be willing to serve as your handmaid the rest of my life."

Zheng was more than glad at the proposal and they fell to discussing plans for setting up house. "East of here," Miss Ren said, "there is a house

on a quiet street for rent; you can recognize it by a big tree that rises
above the wall. It will suit us well. Just before you met me the last time you
were with a man on a white horse who left you and rode east. Is he not a
cousin of your wife? You'll find that he has furniture stored away that you
can borrow."

Zheng found the house she had described and then went to Wei Yin
to borrow furnishings, for it happened that one of the latter's uncles was
away on an extended mission and had stored away all his household
things. Yin was incredulous when Zheng told him the purpose of his
request and described the beauty of Miss Ren. "For," said he, "your face
being what it is, how could you capture the heart of a woman as beautiful
as you say?"

He sent, therefore, one of his confidential servants with the curtains
and beds and other articles of furnishing that he readily lent Zheng, so
that he could verify the latter's claim. Soon the servant returned, panting
and covered with perspiration. "Is there a woman?" asked Yin, "and how
does she look?" "It is indeed a strange thing!" the servant answered, "for
I have never seen anyone so beautiful." Now Yin had numerous relatives
and had, moreover, met many beautiful women in his time. So he
mentioned four or five of the most beautiful among them and asked his
servant how Miss Ren compared with them, but to each name the servant
invariably answered that she could not compare to Miss Ren. Finally he
named the most beautiful woman he knew, the sixth daughter of the
Prince of Wu, one of his wife's cousins, but again the servant answered
that she was no match for the lady he had just seen. "How could there be
such a beauty in the world!" Yin exclaimed.

He ordered water to be brought and bathed himself, put on his best
clothes and set out for Zheng's new house. There he found that his
friend had just gone out. When he went inside he saw only a boy servant
engaged in sweeping the yard and a maid at the door. He enquired of the
boy, but the boy denied that there was anyone else in the house. Not
satisfied, Yin went into the room and looking about him he caught a
glimpse of a red skirt under the door to the inner chamber. He pressed
forward and found Miss Ren hiding behind a screen. When he brought
her out into the light and looked at her, she was even more beautiful
than the reports had described her. He was so enamored of her that
he behaved like a madman and tried to force himself upon her. She
would resist him as long as she could and then would say that she
would let him have his will, but the instant he relaxed his hold on her
she would struggle against him as before. After this had happened a few
times Yin exerted all his might against her and she, exhausted and
perspiring profusely, knew that she could no longer resist him, and

ceased to struggle. However, there had suddenly come into her face such a look of misery that Yin was prompted to ask, "Why do you appear so unhappy?" "Because," she said with a long sigh, "I pity Zheng Liu!" "Why do you say that?" Yin asked, and she answered, "Zheng Liu has a stature of six feet like the rest but he cannot protect a woman! He is hardly worthy of the name of man! You, sir, are rich and have known many women just as beautiful as I, while Zheng Liu is poor and has only myself to gladden his heart. Could you, sir, who have more than enough to fill your heart, bear to rob him who has so little? I pity him because he is poor and dependent upon you for the clothes he wears and the food he eats. It must be because of this that you take such liberties. If Zheng Liu had but some chaff that he could call his own to live upon, things would not have come to this pass."

Yin was by nature a generous man and a loyal friend. When he heard what Miss Ren had said, he immediately let her go and apologized for his mad behavior. Presently Zheng Liu returned and the two friends grinned at each other for joy, one for his own good fortune and the other for the happiness of his friend.

Henceforward Yin supplied all her wants and never stinted anything that struck her fancy. He visited her every day. They took great pleasure in each other's company, but their intimacy never exceeded the bounds of propriety. Realizing how much he loved her, Miss Ren said to him one day, "I am grateful to you for your love and kindness and I wish I could repay you, however unworthy I am. I cannot give myself to you because I am pledged to Zheng Liu, but perhaps there are things that I can do to show my gratitude. As I am a native of Chang'an and come from a family of professional entertainers, I have many cousins much favored by men, besides many acquaintances in the profession. If there is any one among these that you have desired in vain, I shall undertake to bring her to you."

"That would be wonderful," Yin said, and asked her if she knew of a certain milliner by the name of Zhang whom he had seen and liked. "She is one of my cousins," Miss Ren said. "It will be easy to get her." And indeed in about ten days she brought her to him. When after a few months he grew tired of her and sent her away, Miss Ren said to him, "It is so little trouble to secure women of the marketplace. I should like to have an opportunity to exercise my abilities in a more difficult task. If there is any one that you fancy but have put out of your mind because she is inaccessible, name her, and I shall try my best." Yin said, "While visiting Thousand Blessings Temple with some friends during the Clear Bright Festival, I observed, at a musicale that General Diao Mian was giving, a flageolet player of striking beauty. She was about sixteen and had not yet done up her hair. Do you know her?" Miss Ren answered, "She is the general's favorite and her mother is one of my cousins. I can get her for you." Yin bowed to her in gratitude.

Thereafter she began to visit the General's mansion frequently and when about a month later Yin asked her how she was progressing in her scheme, she asked him for two bolts of silk for a bribe. These he gave to her, and two days later as Miss Ren and Yin were at dinner, an old servant from the General's house came with a black horse to fetch her. When she was told of the presence of the messenger, she said to Yin, smiling, "Success is at hand." For she had caused the General's favorite to be afflicted with an illness that neither the needle nor simples could dispel, and when she heard that the girl's mother and master were distraught with anxiety and were about to consult a fortune teller, she bribed the latter to suggest that the patient must be moved to her own house before she could get well. So at the examination of the patient, the exorcist said that she was subject to a certain malign influence in her own house and that she must be moved to a certain distance southeast of where she lived. When the girl's mother and the General located the spot indicated by the exorcist, it turned out to be the site of Miss Ren's house. The General asked Miss Ren to let his favorite stay a while in her house. Miss Ren pretended to refuse, pleading that her place was small and unsuitable, and affected reluctance when she finally yielded at his importunities. The girl and her mother were escorted to Miss Ren's house and there she almost immediately recovered. After a few days Miss Ren secretly took Yin to her and brought about their union. A month later the girl showed signs of pregnancy, and her mother, becoming frightened, took her back to the General's house, and there the affair ended.

Some time later Miss Ren said to Zheng Liu, "Could you raise five or six thousand cash? If so, I can make it possible for you to reap a large profit." "I can," Zheng Liu said, and when he managed to borrow the money, Miss Ren said to him, "Go to the market and look for a horse with a mole on its left haunch. When you find it, buy it and hold it until you can sell it at a profit." Zheng went to the market and sure enough there he encountered a man with a horse for sale that had a black mole on its left haunch. He bought it and returned with it much to the amusement of his wife's brothers, who laughed at him and said, "It is a worthless horse. What are you going to do with it?"

Soon afterwards, Miss Ren said to Zheng, "Now the time has come to sell the horse. You should get thirty thousand for it." At the market a man offered him twenty thousand for the horse but Zheng would not sell it, much to the astonishment of people around. "What merits does the horse have," they exclaimed, "that one should offer so much for it and the other refuse to sell?" As Zheng rode back to his house, the prospective buyer followed him and raised his offer again and again until it reached twenty-five thousand, but Zheng refused and said that he would not sell for a copper cash less than thirty thousand. In the meantime his wife's brothers called him a fool to refuse, but Zheng stuck to his position and finally got his thirty thousand. Being curious to know why the buyer should have paid such a high price, Zheng trailed him and asked him about it. He discovered that the buyer was an officer in charge of the imperial stables at Zhaoying and that he was about to vacate his post. A horse with a mole in the identical place as the one he had just bought had died three years previously. As the horse was valued at sixty thousand cash he would not only stand to gain thirty thousand if he could substitute a horse of that description in the official register, but could also pocket the money he had saved on feed over those three years. The horse was therefore cheap at the price he paid for it and it was for that reason he had bought it.

Once, her clothes having become worn, Miss Ren asked Yin to get her some new dresses. Yin offered her some silks, but Miss Ren refused them, saying that she preferred to have garments ready-made. Yin called in a merchant by the name of Zhang Da so that he could ascertain from Miss Ren just what she wanted. When Zhang Da saw her he was so struck with her beauty that he said to Yin, "A lady of such beauty could not be found outside the Emperor's palace or the mansion of some great nobleman. If you have indeed kidnapped her, you should return her at once so as to avoid the terrible consequences of detection." From this one can imagine how striking her beauty must have been. She never sewed but always bought ready-made clothes, a circumstance that neither Zheng nor Yin could understand.

A year or so later Zheng received an order to go to Jincheng on a military mission. Now Zheng had been able to spend only the day with Miss Ren since he was married and had to return to his wife at night, and he had been regretting the fact that he could not always be with Miss Ren. So he asked Miss Ren to accompany him on the mission. This she showed a reluctance to do, saying, "The mission will only take about a month. I would rather that you make provision for my needs and let me wait for your return."

Zheng repeated his request several times but Miss Ren was adamant. Finally Zheng asked Yin to use his influence, which the latter did, at the same time asking her why she was so stubborn in her refusal. After a long while Miss Ren said, "It is because a fortune teller once told me that it is unlucky for me to journey westward that I do not wish to go." Because of the urgency of his desire, Zheng thought nothing of her fears, but laughed as did Yin and said, "How could one as intelligent as you are

permit yourself to give in to such superstitious fears!" "But should the
fortune teller's predictions be true," Miss Ren said, "I shall die without
any benefit to anyone." "But how could that be?" the two men said and
continued to importune her. Finally, she yielded. Yin lent them horses
and went to see them off as far as Lingao, where they drank some farewell
cups and parted.

They reached Mawei the next day. Miss Ren rode ahead on a palfrey,
followed by Zheng on his own donkey and a maid servant still farther
behind on her mount. It happened that for the past days some dog
trainers from around the West Gate of Mawei had been running their
hounds on the bank of the River Luo and as Zheng's party rode by, the
hounds suddenly rushed out on the road from the grass. At the sight of
the dogs, Miss Ren fell to the ground, resumed her original shape and
ran off in a southerly direction, pursued closely by the hounds. Zheng
followed them and called to the dogs but he could not stop them. After
about a *li* the fox was captured by the dogs. With tears in his eyes, Zheng
took out some money, redeemed the animal and buried it, marking the
spot with a wooden tablet. When he returned to where she had left her
horse, it was grazing by the roadside. On the saddle he found the clothes
that Miss Ren had last worn and on the stirrups were her shoes, cast off
by her in the transformation as a cicada might have cast its larva shell. On
the ground he found her jewels, but otherwise there was no trace of her.
The maid, too, had vanished.

At the conclusion of his mission he returned to Chang'an. Yin was
delighted to see him and asked him if all was well with Miss Ren. "She has
passed away," Zheng answered, his eyes wet with tears. Yin also grieved
when he heard the sad news and asked him what had brought about her
death. "She was killed by some dogs," he answered. "But how could dogs,
however fierce they may be, kill a human being?" Yin asked. "But she was
not human," came the answer. "Then what was she?" Yin asked in
astonishment. Then Zheng told him the story from beginning to end,
much to the wonder and amazement of his friend. The next day they
rode together to Mawei, where they disinterred and examined Miss Ren's
remains and wept most grievously over them. Later when they indulged
in reminiscences of Miss Ren the only thing they could recall about her
that marked her from other women was that she never made her own
clothes.

In after years Zheng rose to be a superintendent and became very
wealthy. At one time he kept more than ten horses in his stables. He died
at the age of sixty-five.

During the Da-li period (766–780) I, Shen Jiji, lived at Zhongling and
used to see something of Wei Yin. I learned, therefore, all the details of

that extraordinary story. Later Yin became a censor and concurrently governor of Longzhou, where he died.

The story shows that there is no lack of virtue even in the animal world. In her ability to protect her chastity in the face of violence and to remain faithful to her lord to death, she was superior to many of her sex among mankind today. It is a pity that Zheng, a man with little subtle insight, cared only for her beauty and appreciated nothing of her true character. If he had been a man of learning and profundity, he would have been able, through his life with her, to learn something of the principles that underlie Nature's mysterious transformations, and the line that marks the mundane world from the world of the spirit, and to preserve for us in worthy language her great love; he would not have been satisfied with the enjoyment of the mere beauty of her outside form. What a pity it was, alas!

In the second year of Jian-zhong (781) I was appointed to a post in the southeast and made the journey with General Pei Ji; Sun Cheng, the assistant prefect of the metropolitan district; Cui Xu of the Board of Revenue; and Assistant Counselor Lu Chun, who all happened to be going to that region, and also the Counselor Zhu Fang, who was on a tour of the empire. While we floated down the Ying and crossed the Huai we spent the long evenings in telling one another of the strange things we had heard. When the company heard the story of Miss Ren they all sighed in wonder and amazement and said that I should preserve this remarkable event in writing. It was at their request I wrote this record.

CHEN XUANYOU (fl. 779)

The Departed Spirit

Translated by E. D. Edwards

This story deals with the theme of "spiritual union," whereby lovers, frustrated by some worldly impediment, are united on the spirit plane. The theme subsequently found its supreme expression in the Ming lyric drama "The Peony Pavilion" (see volume 2), which was undoubtedly influenced by this story.

— Editors

Zhang Yi was a native of Qinghe in the province of Hebei. In the third year of the Tian-shou period (A.D. 692), he was made governor of Hengzhou, in the province of Hunan, and moved there with his family. Being an austere and rather solitary individual, he did not make many friends. He had only two children, both daughters. The elder died in childhood, while the younger, who was called Qianniang, grew into a girl of rare beauty with an air of quiet dignity.

Wang Zhou of Taiyuan was the son of Zhang's sister. He was an intelligent youth with an alert mind and a handsome face. Zhang thought highly of him and repeatedly said: "One of these days I must marry Qianniang to him."

When they grew up Wang and Qianniang often dreamed about one another. No one in their families guessed this, however, and when later Zhang's best assistant asked him for Qianniang's hand he readily gave his consent.

The proposal threw Qianniang into a state of great agitation, while Wang was both disappointed and disgusted. He asked his uncle's leave to go away, saying that he ought to report to the capital for service. As he could not be dissuaded from going he was given a handsome allowance by his uncle, and then, hiding his resentment and distress as best he could, he went to his boat with his deepest grief in his heart.

When evening came the boat anchored near a hill-village. About midnight, unable to sleep, Wang heard hurried footsteps approaching along the riverbank. It was Qianniang, who had followed him barefoot. Wang was nearly insane with surprise and delight. He grasped her hands and asked why she was there.

"Your love has moved me even in my dreams," she told him between her sobs, "and I know that your feelings will not change. My father would never have allowed me to marry you, so I have run away from home."

Wang was so excited by his unexpected good fortune that he laughed and capered about in delight. Keeping Qianniang out of sight in the boat, he pushed on day and night without stopping until, after a journey lasting several months, they reached the province of Sichuan. There they lived for five years, and during that time two sons were born to them. They heard nothing of Qianniang's parents, but she thought of them constantly and one day spoke of them to Wang, weeping.

"Because I could not give you up I ignored the duty of a daughter and ran away from home," she said. "That was five years ago. What a disgrace it is to have lived apart from my parents all this time!"

"Don't fret," Wang replied, soothing her, "we will go back soon," and almost at once they set out for Hengzhou.

When they arrived Wang went on ahead to beg his uncle's forgiveness.

"Qianniang is lying sick in the women's apartments," said Zhang. "Why do you tell me such lies?"

"Go and look in my boat," replied Wang.

Zhang was puzzled. He sent a servant hurriedly down to the boat, and there Qianniang sat, charming and gay.

"Are my parents well?" she asked the astonished servant, who ran quickly back and told his master.

Meanwhile, the sick girl in the inner room, hearing the noise of Wang's arrival, rose from her bed and dressed, smiling to herself, but saying nothing. Then she ran out of the room to meet the newcomers. When the two girls met they melted into one body, and their clothes fused together.

To the girl's family the affair appeared rather improper, so they kept it to themselves and only told a few of their near relatives privately.

Forty years afterwards Wang and Qianniang died. Their sons were remarkable for their filial piety and honesty, and when they grew to manhood both achieved good positions.

In my youth I often heard this tale. It has many versions, and some people say that it is pure fantasy. Towards the end of the Da-li reign period (766–780) I happened to meet Zhang Zhonggui, who was Prefect of Laiwu in the province of Shandong. He informed me of the events recounted here. Since he was the great-nephew of Zhang Yi, he knew all the details. I merely wrote down what he told me.

LI CHAOWEI (8th century)

The Dragon King's Daughter

Translated by John Minford

The story of Liu Yi and the beautiful daughter of the Dragon King of Dongting Lake (a large body of water south of the Yangtze River, in Hunan province) has long been a theme for Chinese storytellers and dramatists (including writers for contemporary Peking opera and Cantonese opera). Little is known of the author of this version, which has been slightly abridged in translation.

During the Yi-feng period (676–678), there lived a young scholar by the name of Liu Yi, who, having failed in the examinations, was making his way back from the capital to his home south of the Yangtze River.[2] He had not traveled far when he recalled that an old friend of his lived nearby, and decided to make a slight detour and bid him farewell. A mile or two further on, a bird flew up in front of him and his horse bolted off the road. It galloped on for several miles, and when it finally halted Liu caught sight of a young shepherd girl by the roadside, tending her sheep. He gazed at her in astonishment, for although he could see she was a

---

[2] To be more precise, the area of the River Xiang, in present-day Hunan province.

young lady of striking beauty, there was something strangely listless and forlorn about her expression, and her clothes were worn and drab. She stood there listening expectantly, as though waiting for something. When Liu spoke to her, and asked what her trouble was, at first she seemed too shy to reply, then finally she burst into tears and said:

"What a wretch am I! What a disgrace, to open my heart to a stranger! But my sorrow is so bitter, I cannot do otherwise! This is my tale. I am the youngest daughter of the Dragon King of Dongting Lake. My parents married me to the second son of the god of the River Jing, which flows through these parts.[3] But my husband is a libertine, and let himself be seduced by his maidservants. He treated me more and more cruelly, and finally I complained to his parents. But they have always doted on their son, and would not control him. Instead, they merely punished me by sending me here to mind these sheep."

She gave way to a fit of helpless sobbing, before continuing:

"I do not know how far it is from here to Dongting Lake. It seems such a hopeless distance, far too far to send a message. My heart is broken, and no one knows of my grief. I know you are traveling to the South, sir, and will pass close by Dongting Lake. Might you be willing to carry a letter for me?"

"I am a man who believes in honor above all things," replied Liu. "Your tale has touched me to the quick! Would that I had wings to fly! Of course I will take your letter for you. But Dongting Lake is a watery world, very dark and very deep, and I am a mere creature of dry land. How can I hope to journey down into those deeps? Do you know of some magic art that may help me to fulfil my pledge?"

Still weeping, she replied:

"What you are promising to do for me is so precious, sir, I shall say no more than this: if my letter receives a reply, one day I shall reward you for your great kindness even if it means giving you my very life. If you will truly do this for me, then believe me when I tell you that a journey to the depths of Dongting Lake is in no way different from a journey to the capital."

Liu asked her to say more.

"On the southern shore of the lake," she went on, "there is a large orange tree, which the people living thereabouts worship. You must take off your belt, and wear something else in its place. Then knock three times on the tree, and you will receive a response. Follow whoever it is

---

[3] The river flows eastwards through Gansu and Shaanxi provinces.

that comes for you, no obstacle will stand in your way. I know I can trust in you."

She took a letter from inside her jacket and handed it to him, bowing repeatedly. Then she gazed eastwards, and uncontrollable tears of sorrow welled up again in her eyes. Liu, who was deeply moved on her behalf, put the letter in his bag, saying:

"I do not understand why you are tending these sheep? Surely the gods are not planning to slaughter them, are they?"

"These are not sheep, they are rain-works."

"What do you mean?"

"They are like peals of thunder, or bolts of lightning."

To Liu they seemed nothing more than a healthy, rather frisky flock of sheep.

"When I have acted as your messenger," he said, "if I ever come back one day to Dongting, I hope you will not shun me."

"Certainly not," she said. "On the contrary. I will think of you as part of my family."

With these words they made their farewell, and he set off on his way towards the east. After a few paces he glanced back, and girl and sheep had all vanished.

That night he took leave of his friend and after a month's traveling he arrived back in his hometown. He made his way to Dongting, and there on the southern shores of the lake he found the Orange Tree. He changed his belt as he had been instructed and knocked three times on the tree, whereupon a warrior emerged from the waves, bowed and addressed him:

"From what place do you hail, sir?"

"I come to seek audience with your noble King," replied Liu, not wishing to divulge the true purpose of his mission.

The warrior parted the waves and pointing the way, led Liu forward.

"Close your eyes for a few breaths, and you will be there," he said.

Liu did as he was told, and presently found himself in the grounds of a large palace. Looking around him he saw countless marvels, vista upon vista of terraces and towers, gateways in their thousands, myriads of wondrous herbs and rare trees. His warrior escort brought him to a halt in the corner of a great room, saying:

"Please be so kind as to wait here, sir."

"What manner of place is this?" asked Liu.

"The room in which you now find yourself is called the Hall of the Spirit Void," replied the warrior.

Liu looked about him and beheld a grand hall fashioned with every conceivable kind of material considered precious on earth. The pillars

were of whitest jade, the steps of deepest green jade, the couches
were carved from coral, the blinds were strung with the finest crystal.
The turquoise eaves were inlaid with colored glass, the rainbow rafters
were studded with amber. It was altogether an indescribably strange and
wonderful sight. Liu waited a long while for the King to arrive. Finally he
asked the warrior:

"Where is your master the King?"

"Our Lord is visiting the Pavilion of the Mystic Pearl, consulting with
the Taoist Master of the Supreme Yang on the *Classic of Fire*. He will be
finished in a little while."

"Pray, what is the *Classic of Fire?*" asked Liu.

"My master is a dragon," replied the warrior, "and dragons revere
water. With one drop of it they can submerge the highest mountain, or
drown the greatest valley. The Taoist is a man. Men consider fire to be
sacred. One flame from a single lamp could burn down the First
Emperor's mighty Abang Palace. The spiritual application of these two
elements, and their mystic alchemical properties, are totally different.
The Taoist Master is deeply skilled in the arts of humanity, and my Lord
has invited him here to seek his counsel."

Even as he finished speaking the palace gates were thrown open and
in swept a man, accompanied by a great cloud of attendants. He was clad
all in purple, and in his hands he held a sceptre of green jade. The
warrior leapt up, and crying, "Here comes my Lord!", hurried forward to
announce Liu's presence. The Dragon King looked Liu up and down
and remarked:

"Are you not a human?"

"I am," said Liu, bowing. The King bowed in return, and bade him be
seated down in the Hall of the Spirit Void. Then he continued:

"Who are you, and what has brought you here to the depths of my
watery realm?"

"My name is Liu, and I hail from the same province as yourself, my
Lord. I grew up in the southern realm of Chu, but later travelled west to
study. Recently I was unsuccessful in my examination, and went wandering in the region of the River Jing, where I happened upon your
daughter tending sheep in the wilds. I could not bear to see the wretched
state she was in. When I questioned her, she told me that she had been
mistreated by her husband, and her husband's parents had thrown her
out of house and home. She shed many bitter tears, it was a distressing
sight to behold. She asked me to deliver a letter, and so here I am."

He took out the letter and presented it. The King read it, and as he did
held his sleeve before his face to conceal his tears.

"This was all my fault!" he sobbed. "I should have listened to her.

Instead I was blind to her needs, deaf to her entreaties. I sent a delicate maid from the inner chambers to suffer a cruel fate in a distant land. You sir, a complete stranger, took pity on her distress. As long as I live I shall be endebted to you."

He sighed heavily, and on both sides his courtiers wept. The King gave one of the eunuchs a message to carry into the inner palace, and presently the whole palace filled with the noise of lamentation. The King turned in some alarm to his courtiers and gave orders that the noise must be stilled, for fear of disturbing Lord Qiantang.

"And who is Lord Qiantang?" asked Liu.

"He is my beloved younger brother," replied the King. "He used to be in charge of the Qiantang River, but has retired."

"And why must this news not reach his ears?"

"Because he is a man of supernatural courage. And prone to excess. In ancient times, when the Great Emperor Yao suffered nine years of flooding, that was all the work of one moment of my brother Lord Qiantang's anger. Recently he had a falling out with the Heavenly Generals, and caused water to rise around the Five Sacred Mountains. The Supreme Lord of Heaven was lenient with him, on account of some small merit I have accumulated. But he is still confined here, and the people of Qiantang await his return."

Before he had finished speaking, a great earth-rending, sky-shattering roar was heard from within, the walls trembled to their foundations and a confused halo of cloud and mist seethed about the palace. Then all of a sudden a huge red dragon over a thousand feet in length appeared before them, with blazing eyes and gory tongue, crimson scales and fiery whiskers, a great golden chain trailing from its neck, and a pillar of jade dangling from the end of the chain. The dragon was heralded by a myriad flashes of lightning and a myriad peals of thunder, and as it approached the heavens disgorged huge quantities of driving sleet and snow, of pelting rain and hail. The red dragon now soared up into the air, and went cleaving its way through the azure vault of the sky. Liu fell to the ground in abject terror, and the Dragon King lifted him up.

"Do not be afraid, he will cause you no harm."

Liu gradually regained his composure, and begged to take his leave.

"I should like to reach home alive. I really do not want to be here when he returns."

"Have no fear. He will not return in the same manner. In the meantime, we must entertain you as best we can."

And he ordered wine to be served, and they toasted each other.

Presently a balmy breeze blew through the palace, wafting with it clouds of a joyful hue, which enveloped the assembled company in a warm aura of contentment. Banners were born aloft, cunningly crafted, the heavenly music of flutes could be heard drifting on the breeze, and a bevy of fair maidens clad in fine gowns, smiling and chattering brightly amongst themselves, paraded into the hall. They were followed by a young lady of the greatest beauty, her brows fair as the fairest gossamer, her ears bedecked with pendant jewels, her shimmering silken gown trailing around her. When Liu looked more closely he recognized her as the young lady for whom he had delivered the letter. Through her tears, which flowed down her cheeks in silken rivulets, could be detected both joy and sorrow. A crimson mist swirled on one side of her, a purple haze floated on the other, and a wondrous aroma pervaded the air, as she made her way into the hall. The King said to Liu:

"The prisoner from the River Jing has returned!"

And with these words he took his leave, and returned to his own palace.

Presently, the sound of long-drawn lamentation could be heard. When it had died away, the King returned, and entertained Liu. While they were feasting, another man entered, dressed in a purple robe, holding a sceptre of green jade in his hand. He stood proudly to the King's right.

"This is Lord Qiantang," said the King to Liu.

Liu rose and promptly bowed to him. Lord Qiantang responded most graciously, saying:

"My niece suffered cruelly at the hands of that worthless husband of hers. It was thanks to your chivalry and devotion to the cause of honor that news of her fate reached us. Else she would have been buried by the River Jing. We owe you more than we can hope to express in words."

Liu modestly demurred, bowing and murmuring politely. Lord Qiantang turned to his brother the King:

"Just now, when I set out from the Hall of the Spirit Void, it was early morning: I reached Jingyang by mid-morning, fought there at noon, and was back here by mid-afternoon. Between times I sped up to the Ninth Heaven and informed the Supreme One of what I had done. He knew of the injustice suffered by your daughter, and forgave me my misdemeanours. I have even been pardoned my former crime. But I must apologize to our guest for any offence I may have caused earlier by my somewhat violent departure."

He drew back and bowed several times.

"How many did you kill?" asked the King.

"Six hundred thousand."

"How many crops were destroyed?"

"Over a distance of three hundred miles."

"And the man — the heartless husband — is he still alive?"

"I ate him."

"However unforgivable his cruelty may have been," said the King in a tone of disapproval, "that was too hasty of you, you went too far. You are lucky that the Supreme One has shown you mercy. You must not behave like that again."

Lord Qiantang bowed once more.

That night Liu lodged in the Hall of Frozen Light.

The next day another feast was held for him, in the Hall of Green Light. Friends and relatives were invited, there were performances of music and dancing, and the choicest food and wines were served. In the first ballet, which was danced to the sound of reed pipe and drum, a vast corps de ballet of male dancers leapt onto the righthand side of the stage, brandishing swords and halberds, and waving flags and banners. One of them stepped forward and announced:

"We present 'Lord Qiantang Demolishes the Enemy Ranks.'"

The ballet consisted of a series of hair-raising military acrobatic displays. When it was finished, the music changed: now it was all delicate bells and chimes, soft strings and flutes, and massed ranks of female dancers came onto the lefthand side of the stage, their silken gowns resplendent with pearls and precious stones. One of them came forward and announced:

"We present 'The Return of the Princess.'"

The music had such a deeply haunting sound, it seemed to express the keenest longings and yearnings of the captive princess, and there was hardly a dry eye in the audience.

When the two performances were over, the Dragon King seemed greatly pleased and presented gifts of costly silk to the dancers. Then the banqueters set to in earnest, drawing their seats closer together and engaging in enthusiastic drinking. Soon the company were well in their cups, and the Dragon King beat a rhythm on the mat he was sitting on and began to sing:

Boundless the Heaven above
Vast the Earth below;
To each and every Man a goal
Unfathomable.
Fox Sprite and
Rat Sprite
Nest by altar,
Cling to wall;
But when thunder strikes
Which of them stands firm?

This brave man and true
This chevalier
Brought our daughter home.
To him we owe
A debt
We will never forget.

When the Dragon King had finished, his brother Lord Qiantang
bowed again and began his song:

High Heaven made the match,
Life and death go each their way.
Hers was not to be his wife;
Nor his to be her mate.
The dear heart
Suffered such cruelty
By the River Jing.
Frost and wind bleached her raven locks,
Rain and snow spoiled her silken gown.
This noble gentleman carried her letter,
Brought our daughter safely home.
His kindness we'll remember
For ever and a day.

When Lord Qiantang had finished his song, the Dragon King rose
with him and poured Liu a cup of wine. This Liu accepted graciously, and
when he had drunk he offered them each a goblet, and sang:

The pale clouds drifted by,
The River Jing flowed east.
A fair maiden stood in such distress
Tears streaked her flowerlike face.
The letter travelled far
To dispel my lord's grief.
A wrong has been righted,
She returns to take her ease.
I thank you for this banquet. And now
My mountain hut is deserted
And I must return;
Even as I make my farewell
Sorrow tangles my heart.

When he had finished singing they all applauded. The Dragon King
presented Liu with a blue jade casket containing a rhinoceros horn for

parting the waters; Lord Qiantang presented him with a tray of red amber on which lay a large Night-shining Pearl. Liu accepted them, after first politely declining them. Then the ladies of the palace cast all manner of gifts in heaps beside him: silks, pearls, jades. The glistening pile grew so tall that presently he disappeared behind it. Liu looked around him, smiling, scarcely able to bow his thanks for such an abundance of gifts. When they had all drunk their fill he rose to take his leave, and lodged once more that night in the Hall of Frozen Light.

The next day they feasted him again, this time in the Hall of Pure Light. Lord Qiantang, when he had become somewhat the worse for drink, squatted down unceremoniously and said to Liu:

"You have surely heard the saying, 'a strong rock may be shattered but it can never be bent; a man of honor may be killed but never corrupted.' I have a proposal in my mind that I should like to put to you. Agree, and we will all of us be in heaven; reject it, and we will be at the bottom of a dung-pile. What do you say?"

Liu asked him to explain his meaning a little more clearly.

"It is like this. The wife newly returned from the River Jing is our King's beloved daughter. She has a pure nature, and a fine character, and is prized by all her kin. She suffered at that man's hands, but that is all over now and in the past. We wish to entrust her to a man of honor, a man fit to be her husband and our kin. There is a way to find such a man. If we choose that way, then she who received the kindness will know the man to whom she is to be united; and we who love her will know whither she is destined to go. What say you? Is this not the perfect conclusion for a man of honor such as yourself?"

Liu rose solemnly to his feet, and gave a grim laugh.

"Indeed I never thought that you, my Lord Qiantang, could stoop so low as this! From your exploits, when in your mighty rage you bestrode the Nine Provinces and enfolded the Five Sacred Peaks, when you snapped your golden chain and dragged the jade pillar behind you, fiercely rushing to the maiden's rescue, I thought you a hero without equal. I knew you as fearless in the face of danger and death. And look at you now! In the middle of this happy family gathering, where the music of joyous flutes resounds, you have the baseness to try and intimidate me! This is not the behavior I would have expected of you! If I had encountered you amid waves and torrents, or on some dark mountain top, bristling with whiskers and scales and robed in your panoply of clouds and rain, and if then you had pressed me to the point of death, I would have looked upon you as a mere beast and would have had no grounds for complaint. But here you are in your lordly robes, sitting and talking about what is proper and honorable, talking of duty and the subtleties of right and wrong, better than many a human, let alone some dragon, some River Spirit! And you dare to tower over me with your great frame and your foul temper, you dare to make wine an excuse for your bullying! Is that any way to carry on? I am an insignificant mortal, so insignificant I should easily disappear between two of your scales; but I have the courage to resist, to defy your outrageous proposal. Consider well what I have said."

Lord Qiantang was greatly dismayed by this.

"I grew up in the palace," he said falteringly. "I never received instruction in the matters of which you speak. Please forgive my clumsiness, and do not let it come between us."

That evening another banquet was held, and they made merry as before. Liu and Lord Qiantang were the very best of friends despite everything. The following day Liu took his leave, and the Dragon Queen held a parting banquet for him in the Hall of Submerged Splendor. Everyone came, men and women, servants and concubines. With tears in her eyes the Queen addressed Liu:

"My daughter desires to repay your great kindness to her; but alas now you are departing, and that cannot be."

She called her daughter forward and bade her bow in gratitude to Liu in front of the banqueters.

"Since you are leaving us, I suppose we will never see you again!"

Although Liu had rejected Lord Qiantang's proposal of marriage, as a matter of honor, now that it it came to leaving, he felt a keen sense of sorrow. Once the banquet was over, he took his leave, and the whole palace was filled with grief at his departure. They loaded him with precious gifts beyond counting. And so he returned and emerged from the water at a riverbank, with a dozen men still escorting him, bearing his many gifts. They followed him home, and then went their way.

Liu went to the jeweller's shop in Guangling[4] to sell the gifts he had been given, and found that a hundredth part of it was enough to make him a very wealthy man, the envy of the neighborhood. Some time later he married a young lady of the Zhang family, who died. He married again, this time to a Miss Han, who also died within a few months. He moved house to the city of Jinling,[5] and finding himself excessively lonely there, began to consider finding a third wife. A matchmaker mentioned a young lady of the Lu family from Fanyang. Her father, a certain Lu Hao, had once been the magistrate of Qingliu. In his old age he had

---

[4] Present-day Yangzhou, in Jiangsu province.
[5] Present-day Nanjing, or Nanking.

taken to the Tao, and spent his time wandering alone in the remotest depths of the countryside. At present no one knew of his whereabouts. The girl's mother, Lady Zheng, had remarried the previous year a Mr Zhang of Qinghe, but to her sorrow he had died shortly afterwards. She was now looking for a husband for her young daughter, hoping to find a man worthy of the girl's great beauty and intelligence. Liu consulted the almanac for a propitious day, and the ceremony was performed. Theirs were two of the most eminent families of Jinling, and the marriage was a very grand one.

One evening, a month or so later, Liu came home and when he looked at his wife he was struck by her resemblance to the Dragon King's daughter. If anything she was even more ethereal and beautiful. He spoke to her of that whole adventure of his, and she replied:

"How could such things happen in this human world? But I have some real news for you. You and I are going to have a child."

Liu loved her all the more for this. When the child was born, and when the first month was over, she dressed herself up in all her finery and summoned Liu into her chamber. She smiled at him and said:

"Do you not remember me from the past?"

"We were never friends before, so how could I remember you?"

"I am the Dragon King's daughter," she replied. "You saved me from my miserable plight. I promised I would reward you one day. But then you refused my uncle Lord Qiantang's proposal, and we went our separate ways, and I had no news of you. My parents wanted to marry me to another young man but I locked my door and cut my hair, to show them I would never agree to do so. Even though you had rejected me, and I saw no chance of meeting you again, I could never put aside my resolve. Then I heard that you had married, not once but twice, and that both your wives had died. My parents saw this as a chance for me to reward you for your past kindness to me. Now that I can serve you, and we can spend our days happily together, I shall die without regret."

She broke down and began sobbing. Presently she looked him in the face and continued:

"I did not tell you this before, because I thought you were not susceptible to a woman's charms. But now I see that you have some feeling towards me, and love your son, and so I have told you everything. Tell me how you feel. I am so afraid. That day you agreed to deliver my letter, I remember you saying to me that you hoped I would not shun you when you returned to Dongting. I wonder if you were already thinking then of marrying me one day? Was your refusal of my uncle's offer just a passing fit of anger? Please tell me!"

"This does all seem to have been ordained by fate," Liu replied. "That day long ago when I saw you with your sheep by the roadside, looking so sad and forlorn, I felt sorry for you, and agreed to be your messenger, to help you right a wrong. I had no other thought in mind. My words had no special meaning. Then later, when your uncle Lord Qiantang tried to bully me into marrying you, I felt angry and insulted. He was almost suggesting I had planned your husband's death so that I could have you for myself! Nothing could have been further from the truth. I have always believed in championing the cause of justice and honor in whatever way I can. I was not going to let myself be pushed around in that way. We had both had quite a lot to drink, and I know I was very outspoken myself. But then when I came to leave and saw the sadness on your face, I felt a pang of regret. Somehow at the time I was unable to respond to your feelings. But now we are married, and can love each other truly for the rest of our days."

His wife was moved to tears by these words. She explained to Liu that though she was a daughter of the dragon race, he must not think her incapable of feeling. She was determined to repay him for all his kindness. Now that he had married an immortal denizen of the deep, he too would be granted long life, and the ability to travel anywhere on water or land.

Liu seemed delighted by this.

"I never thought that marrying a beautiful lady would also bring me immortality!"

They went together to pay their respects to her parents in Dongting Lake, and were welcomed with a lavish display of hospitality.

Afterwards they moved to live in Nanhai.[6] In a matter of forty years Liu's wealth came to rival that of princes and dukes of the realm. His whole clan shared in it. What astounded the people of Nanhai even more was that as he grew older, he preserved his youthful appearance unchanged. During the Kai-yuan period (713–742), the Emperor Xuanzong, in his quest for the secret of immortality, scoured his kingdom for adepts of the Taoist arts, and Liu and his wife thought it safer to leave. So they went together to Dongting, and there was no sight or sound of them for more than ten years. Then towards the end of the Kai-yuan period, Liu's cousin Xue Gu, having served as a magistrate in the Metropolitan area, was demoted and sent to serve in the south-east. His journey took him across Dongting Lake. It was a sunny day and he was gazing across the water when suddenly he saw in the distance a blue hill emerging from the waves. The sailors gathered to the side of the boat, crying in astonishment:

---

[6] Present-day Guangzhou, or Canton.

"There was never a hill here before. It must be some sort of water monster!"

Presently the hill came closer to the boat and a brightly colored skiff set out from the foot of the hill and came as if to greet Xue Gu. A man on board the skiff called out:

"My master Lord Liu wishes to wait upon you!"

Suddenly Gu recalled the story of his cousin, and he bade them row the boat close to the hill, where he hitched up his gown and stepped ashore. On the hillside stood a palace like those in the world of men, and there in the middle of it stood Liu. String and wind instruments played in front of him, and gorgeously arrayed ladies paraded behind him. The richness of ornamentation far surpassed anything ever seen by human eyes. Liu's speech was dark and mysterious, and his complexion was more youthful than ever. He welcomed Gu at the palace steps, taking him by the hand and saying:

"It is only a moment since we last met, and your hair is quite turning grey!"

Gu laughed.

"You are an immortal, cousin. I am dry bones. Such is fate."

Liu gave Gu fifty large pills, saying:

"Each one of these pills will grant you one extra year of life. When the years are gone, come back. Do not linger too long in the world of men; you will only bring suffering on yourself."

He feasted Gu, and then the time came for Gu to leave. After this, there was no further trace of Liu and his wife. Gu would often tell the story of their encounter. And then, some fifty years later, he too vanished.

Li Chaowei of Longxi wrote this account, adding with a sigh of wonder:

"Of the five Highest Creatures,[7] each has a unique spiritual endowment that sets it apart. Man the Naked Creature can feel compassion towards the Scaly Creatures. The Dragon Lord of Dongting had a measured sense of righteousness; Lord Qiantang was impulsive and forthright; these Scaly Creatures had their virtues too.

"Xue Gu's tale was never written down; he was the only one to visit that realm.

"I saw in this a tale of honor, so I wrote it down."

---

[7] The highest of each category of creature.

YUAN ZHEN (779–831)

The Story of Yingying

Translated by J. R. Hightower

This classical tale, which is supposedly autobiographical, is without doubt the single best-known love story in Chinese literature. The author is widely held to have been Yuan Zhen, the prominent Tang poet, and close friend of Bo Juyi (see chapter 23). Sometimes known as "The Encounter with an Immortal," the story was later expanded many times into ballad and drama (under the name "The Western Chamber," see volume 2), with substantial modification of the plot. Discussion of the original story has tended to dwell on the behavior of Zhang, his seemingly casual abandonment of the beautiful Yingying, and subsequent attempt at self-justification. The young scholar's ethical shortcomings have not however detracted from the story's ability to capture and sustain the reader's interest. Its powerful narration of the course of human passion, conveyed in understated, but emotionally charged, classical prose, has won this short work an important place in the development of Chinese romantic literature.

— Editors

During the Zhen-yuan period (785–804) there lived a young man named Zhang. He was agreeable and refined, and good looking, but firm and self-contained, and capable of no improper act. When his companions included him in one of their parties, the others could all be brawling as though they would never get enough, but Zhang would just watch tolerantly without ever taking part. In this way he had gotten to be twenty-three years old without ever having had relations with a woman. When asked by his friends, he explained. "Master Dengtu[8] was no lover, but a lecher. I am the true lover — I just never happened to meet the right girl. How do I know that? It's because things of outstanding beauty never fail to make a permanent impression on me. That shows I am not without feelings." His friends took note of what he said.

Not long afterward Zhang was traveling in Pu.[9] where he lodged some ten *li* east of the city in a monastery called the Temple of Universal Salvation. It happened that a widowed Mrs. Cui had also stopped there on her way back to Chang'an. She had been born a Zheng; Zhang's mother had been a Zheng, and when they worked out their common

---

[8] Master Dengtu is the archetypal lecher. This allusion originates from the character in Song Yu's rhapsody. "The Lechery of Master Dengtu."
[9] Puzhou, also known as Hezhong in Tang times, was under the jurisdiction of Jiangzhou. It is modern Yongji County in Shanxi Province, located east-northeast of Chang'an.

ancestry, this Mrs. Cui turned out to be a rather distant cousin once removed on his mother's side.

This year Hun Zhen[10] died in Pu, and the eunuch Ding Wenya proved unpopular with the troops, who took advantage of the mourning period to mutiny. They plundered the citizens of Pu, and Mrs. Cui, in a strange place with all her wealth and servants, was terrified, having no one to turn to. Before the mutiny Zhang had made friends with some of the officers in Pu, and now he requested a detachment of soldiers to protect the Cui family. As a result all escaped harm. In about ten days the imperial commissioner of inquiry, Du Que,[11] came with full power from the throne and restored order among the troops.

Out of gratitude to Zhang for the favor he had done them, Mrs Cui invited him to a banquet in the central hall. She addressed him: "Your widowed aunt with her helpless children would never have been able to escape alive from these rioting soldiers. It is no ordinary favor you have done us: it is rather as though you had given my son and daughter their lives, and I want to introduce them to you as their elder brother so that they can express their thanks." She summoned her son Huanlang, a very attractive child of ten or so. Then she called her daughter: "Come out and pay your respects to your brother, who saved your life." There was a delay; then word was brought that she was indisposed and asked to be excused. Her mother exclaimed in anger, "Your brother Zhang saved your life. You would have been abducted if it were not for him — how can you give yourself airs?"

After a while the girl appeared, wearing an everyday dress and no makeup on her smooth face, except for a remaining spot of rouge. Her hair coils straggled down to touch her eyebrows. Her beauty was extraordinary, so radiant it took the breath away. Startled, Zhang made her a deep bow as she sat down beside her mother. Because she had been forced to come out against her will, she looked angrily straight ahead, as though unable to endure the company. Zhang asked her age. Mrs Cui said, "From the seventh month of the fifth year of the reigning emperor to the present twenty-first year, it is just seventeen years."

Zhang tried to make conversation with her, but she would not respond, and he had to leave after the meal was over. From this time on Zhang was infatuated but had no way to make his feelings known to her.

---

[10] Hun Zhen, the regional commander of Jiangzhou, died in Puzhou in 799.

[11] Du Que, originally prefect of Tongzhou (in modern Shaanxi), was appointed, after the death of Hun Zhen, the prefect of Hezhong as well as the imperial commissioner of inquiry of Jiangzhou.

She had a maid named Crimson with whom Zhang had managed to exchange greetings several times, and finally he took the occasion to tell her how he felt. Not surprisingly, the maid was alarmed and fled in embarrassment. Zhang was sorry he had said anything, and when she returned the next day he made shame-faced apologies without repeating his request. The maid said, "Sir, what you said is something I would not dare repeat to my mistress or let anyone else know about. But you know very well who Miss Cui's relatives are; why don't you ask for her hand in marriage, as you are entitled to do because of the favor you did them?"

"From my earliest years I have never been one to make any improper connections," Zhang said. "Whenever I have found myself in the company of young women, I would not even look at them, and it never occurred to me that I would be trapped in any such way. But the other day at the dinner I was hardly able to control myself, and in the days since, I walk without knowing where I am going and eat without hunger — I am afraid I cannot last another day. If I were to go through a regular matchmaker, taking three months and more for the exchange of betrothal presents and names and birthdates[12] — you might just as well look for me among the dried fish in the shop.[13] Can't you tell me what to do?"

"Miss Cui is so very strict that not even her elders could suggest anything improper to her," the maid replied. "It would be hard for someone in my position to say such a thing. But I have noticed she writes a lot. She is always reciting poetry to herself and is moved by it for a long time after. You might see if you can seduce her with a love poem. That is the only way I can think of."

Zhang was delighted and on the spot composed two stanzas of "spring verses" which he handed over to her. That evening Crimson came back with a note on colored paper for him, saying, "By Miss Cui's instructions." The title of her poem was "Bright Moon on the Night of the Fifteenth":

I await the moon in the western chamber,
Where the breeze comes through the half-opened door.
Sweeping the wall the flower shadows move;
I imagine it is my lover who comes.

Zhang understood the message: that day was the fourteenth of the second month, and an apricot tree was next to the wall east of the Cuis' courtyard. It would be possible to climb it.

---

[12] To determine an astrologically suitable date for a wedding.
[13] An allusion to the parable of help that comes too late in chapter 9 of the pre-Qin philosophical work *Zhuangzi*.

On the night of the fifteenth Zhang used the tree as a ladder to get over the wall. When he came to the western chamber, the door was ajar. Inside, Crimson was asleep on a bed. He awakened her, and she asked, frightened, "How did you get here?"

"Miss Cui's letter told me to come," he said, not quite accurately. "You go tell her I am here."

In a minute Crimson was back. "She's coming! She's coming!"

Zhang was both happy and nervous, convinced that success was his. Then Miss Cui appeared in formal dress, with a serious face, and began to upbraid him: "You did us a great kindness when you saved our lives, and that is why my mother entrusted my young brother and myself to you. Why then did you get my silly maid to bring me that filthy poem? You began by doing a good deed in preserving me from the hands of ravishers, and you end by seeking to ravish me yourself. You have substituted seduction for rape — is there any great difference? My first impulse was to keep quiet about it, but that would have been to condone your wrongdoing, and not right. If I told my mother, it would amount to ingratitude, and the consequences would be unfortunate. I thought of having a servant convey my disapproval, but feared she would not get it right. Then I thought of writing a short message to state my case, but was afraid it would only put you on your guard. So finally I composed those vulgar lines to make sure you would come here. It was an improper thing to do, and of course I feel ashamed. But I hope that you will keep within the bounds of decency and commit no outrage."

As she finished speaking, she turned on her heel and left him. For some time Zhang stood, dumbfounded. Then he went back over the wall to his quarters, all hope gone.

A few nights later Zhang was sleeping alone by the veranda when someone shook him awake. Startled, he rose up, to see Crimson standing there, a coverlet and pillow in her arms. She patted him and said, "She's coming! She's coming! Why are you sleeping?" And she spread the quilt and put the pillow beside his. As she left, Zhang sat up straight and rubbed his eyes. For some time it seemed as though he were still dreaming, but nonetheless he waited dutifully. Then there was Crimson again, with Miss Cui leaning on her arm. She was shy and yielding, and appeared almost not to have the strength to move her limbs. The contrast with her stiff formality at their last encounter was complete.

This evening was the night of the eighteenth, and the slanting rays of the moon cast a soft light over half the bed. Zhang felt a kind of floating lightness and wondered whether this was an immortal who had visited him, not someone from the world of men. After a while the temple bell sounded. Daybreak was near. As Crimson urged her to leave, she wept softly and clung to him. Crimson helped her up, and they left. The whole time she had not spoken a single word. With the first light of dawn Zhang got up, wondering, was it a dream? But the perfume still lingered, and as the day grew lighter he could see on his arm traces of her makeup and the teardrops sparkling still on the mat.

For some ten days afterward there was no word from her. Zhang composed a poem of sixty lines on "An Encounter with an Immortal" which he had not yet completed when Crimson happened by, and he gave it to her for her mistress. After that Yingying [for that was Miss Cui's name, meaning Golden Oriole] let him see her again, and for nearly a month he would join her in what her poem called the "western chamber," slipping out at dawn and returning stealthily at night. Zhang once asked what her mother thought about the situation. Yingying said, "She knows there is nothing she can do about it, and so she hopes you will regularize things."

Before long Zhang was about to go to Chang'an, and he let her know his intentions in a poem. Yingying made no objections at all, but the look of pain on her face was very touching. On the eve of his departure he was unable to see her again. Then Zhang went off to the west. A few months later he again made a trip to Pu and stayed several months with Yingying.

She was a very good calligrapher and wrote poetry, but for all that he kept begging to see her work, she would never show it. Zhang wrote poems for her, challenging her to match them, but she paid them little attention. The thing that made her unusual was that, while she excelled in the arts, she always acted as though she were ignorant, and although she was quick and clever in speaking, she would seldom indulge in repartee. She loved Zhang very much, but would never say so in words. At the time she was subject to moods of profound melancholy, but she never let on. She seldom showed on her face the emotions she felt. On one occasion she was playing her zither alone at night. She did not know Zhang was listening, and the music was full of sadness. As soon as he spoke, she stopped and would play no more. This made him all the more infatuated with her.

Some time later Zhang had to go west again for the scheduled examinations. It was the eve of his departure and though he had said nothing about what it involved, he sat sighing unhappily at her side. Yingying had guessed that he was going to leave for good. Her manner was respectful, but she spoke deliberately and in a low voice: "To seduce someone and then abandon her is perfectly natural, and it would be presumptuous of me to resent it. It would be an act of charity on your part if, having first seduced me, you were to go through with it and fulfill your oath of lifelong devotion. But in either case, what is there to be so upset about in this trip? However, I see you are not happy and I have no way to cheer you up. You have praised my zither playing, and in the past I have been embarrassed to play for you. Now that you are going away, I shall do what you so often requested."

She had them prepare her zither and started to play the prelude to the "Rainbow Robe and Feather Skirt."[14] After a few notes, her playing grew wild with grief until the piece was no longer recognizable. Everyone was reduced to tears, and Yingying abruptly stopped playing, put down the zither, and ran back to her mother's room with tears streaming down her face. She did not come back.

The next morning Zhang went away. The following year he stayed on in the capital, having failed the examinations. He wrote a letter to Ying ying to reassure her, and her reply read roughly as follows:

I have read your letter with its message of consolation, and it filled my childish heart with mingled grief and joy. In addition you sent me a box of ornaments to adorn my hair and a stick of pomade to make my lips smooth. It was most kind of you: but for whom am I to make myself attractive? As I look at these presents my breast is filled with sorrow.

Your letter said that you will stay on in the capital to pursue your studies, and of course you need quiet and the facilities there to make progress. Still it is hard on the person left alone in this far-off place. But such is my fate, and I should not complain. Since last fall I have been listless and without hope. In company I can force myself to talk and smile, but come evening I always shed tears in the solitude of my own room. Even in my sleep I often sob, yearning for the absent one. Or I am in your arms for a moment as it used to be, but before the secret meeting is done I am awake and heartbroken. The bed seems still warm beside me, but the one I love is far away.

Since you said good-bye the new year has come. Chang'an is a city of pleasure with chances for love everywhere. I am truly fortunate that you have not forgotten me and that your affection is not worn out. Loving you as I do, I have no way of repaying you, except to be true to our vow of lifelong fidelity.

Our first meeting was at the banquet, as cousins. Then you persuaded my maid to inform me of your love; and I was unable to keep my childish heart firm. You made advances, like that other poet, Sima

---

[14] After this Brahman music was introduced into China, it was dignified by the elegant name given to it by Emperor Xuanzong of the Tang Dynasty and by the performance of his favorite consort Guifei.

Xiangru.[15] I failed to repulse them as the girl did who threw her shuttle.[16] When I offered myself in your bed, you treated me with the greatest kindness, and I supposed, in my innocence, that I could always depend on you. How could I have foreseen that our encounter could not possibly lead to something definite, that having disgraced myself by coming to you, there was no further chance of serving you openly as a wife? To the end of my days this will be a lasting regret — I must hide my sighs and be silent. If you, out of kindness, would condescend to fulfill my selfish wish, though it came on my dying day it would seem to be a new lease on life. But if, as a man of the world, you curtail your feelings, sacrificing the lesser to the more important, and look on this connection as shameful, so that your solemn vow can be dispensed with, still my true love will not vanish though my bones decay and my frame dissolve: in wind and dew it will seek out the ground you walk on. My love in life and death is told in this. I weep as I write, for feelings I cannot express. Take care of yourself: a thousand times over, take care of your dear self.

This bracelet of jade is something I wore as a child; I send it to serve as a gentleman's belt pendant. Like jade may you be invariably firm and tender: like a bracelet may there be no break between what came before and what is to follow. Here are also a skein of multicolored thread and a tea roller of mottled bamboo. These things have no intrinsic value, but they are to signify that I want you to be true as jade, and your love to endure unbroken as a bracelet. The spots on the bamboo are like the marks of my tears,[17] and my unhappy thoughts are as tangled as the thread: these objects are symbols of my feelings, and tokens for all time of my love. Our hearts are close, though our bodies are far apart and there is no time I can expect to see you. But where the hidden desires are strong enough, there will be a meeting of spirits. Take care of yourself a thousand times over. The springtime wind is often chill: eat well for your health's sake. Be circumspect and careful, and do not think too often of my unworthy person.

Zhang showed her letter to his friends, and in this way word of the

---

[15] An allusion to the story of the Han poet Sima Xiangru (179–117 B.C.), who enticed the young widow Zhuo Wenjun to elope by his zither playing.

[16] A neighboring girl, named Gao, repulsed Xie Kun's (280–322) advances by throwing her shuttle in his face. He lost two teeth.

[17] Alluding to the legend of the two wives of the sage ruler Shun, who stained the bamboo with their tears.

affair got around. One of them, Yang Juyuan,[18] a skillful poet, wrote a
quatrain on "Young Miss Cui":

For clear purity jade cannot equal his complexion;
On the iris in the inner court snow begins to melt.
A romantic young man filled with thoughts of love.
A letter from the Xiao girl,[19] brokenhearted.

Yuan Zhen of Henan[20] wrote a continuation of Zhang's poem "Encounter with an Immortal," also in thirty couplets:

Faint moonbeams pierce the curtained window;
Fireflies glimmer across the blue sky.
The far horizon begins now to pale;
Dwarf trees gradually turn darker green.
A dragon song crosses the court bamboo;
A phoenix air brushes the wellside tree.
The silken robe trails through the thin mist;
The pendant circles tinkle in the light breeze.
The accredited envoy accompanies the Queen Mother of the West:[21]
From the cloud's center comes Jade Boy.[22]
Late at night everyone is quiet;
At daybreak the rain drizzles.
Pearl radiance shines on her decorated sandals;
Flower glow shows off the embroidered skirt.
Jasper hairpin: a walking colored phoenix;
Gauze shawl: embracing vermilion rainbow.
She says she comes from Jasper Flower Bank
And is going to pay court at Green Jade Palace.

---

[18] The poet Yang Juyuan (fl. 800) was a contemporary of Yuan Zhen.
[19] In Tang times the term "Xiaoniang" referred to young women in general. Here it means Yingying.
[20] The Henan Circuit in Tang times covered the area to the south of the Yellow River in both of the present provinces of Shandong and Henan, up to the north of the Huai River in modern Jiangsu and Anhui.
[21] The Queen Mother of the West is a mythological figure supposedly dwelling in the Kunlun Mountains in China's far west. In early accounts she is sometimes described as part human and part beast, but since early post-Han times she has usually been described as a beautiful immortal. Her huge palace is inhabited by other immortals. Within its precincts grow the magic peach trees which bear the fruits of immortality once every three thousand years. This might be an allusion to Yingying's mother.
[22] The Jade Boy might allude to Yingying's brother.

On an outing north of Luoyang's wall,[23]
By chance he came to the house east of Song Yu's.[24]
His dalliance she rejects a bit at first,
But her yielding love already is disclosed.
Lowered locks put in motion cicada shadows;[25]
Returning steps raise jade dust.
Her face turns to let flow flower snow;
As she climbs into bed, silk covers in her arms.
Love birds in a neck-entwining dance;
Kingfishers in a conjugal cage.
Eyebrows, out of shyness, contracted;
Lip rouge, from the warmth, melted.
Her breath is pure: fragrance of orchid buds;
Her skin is smooth: richness of jade flesh.
No strength, too limp to lift a wrist;
Many charms, she likes to draw herself together.
Sweat runs: pearls drop by drop;
Hair in disorder: black luxuriance.
Just as they rejoice in the meeting of a lifetime
They suddenly hear the night is over.
There is no time for lingering;
It is hard to give up the wish to embrace.
Her comely face shows the sorrow she feels;
With fragrant words they swear eternal love.
She gives him a bracelet to plight their troth;
He ties a lovers' knot as sign their hearts are one.
Tear-borne powder runs before the clear mirror;
Around the flickering lamp are nighttime insects.
Moonlight is still softly shining
As the rising sun gradually dawns.
Riding on a wild goose she returns to the Luo River.[26]
Blowing a flute he ascends Mount Song.[27]
His clothes are fragrant still with musk perfume;

---

[23] Possibly a reference to the goddess of the Luo River. This river, in modern Henan, is made famous by the rhapsody of Cao Zhi, "The Goddess of the Luo." [See chapter 6.]

[24] In "The Lechery of Master Dengtu," Song Yu tells about the beautiful girl next door to the east who climbed up on the wall to flirt with him.

[25] Referring to her hairdo in the cicada style.

[26] Again the goddess of the Luo River theme.

[27] This is also known as the Central Mountain; it is located to the north of Dengfeng County in Henan Province. Here the one ascending the mountain may refer to Zhang.

The pillow is slippery yet with red traces.
Thick, thick, the grass grows on the dyke;
Floating, floating, the tumbleweed yearns for the isle.
Her plain zither plays the "Resentful Crane Song";
In the clear Milky Way she looks for the returning wild goose.[28]
The sea is broad and truly hard to cross;
The sky is high and not easy to traverse.
The moving cloud is nowhere to be found —
Xiao Shi stays in his chamber.[29]

All of Zhang's friends who heard of the affair marveled at it, but Zhang had determined on his own course of action. Yuan Zhen was especially close to him and so was in a position to ask him for an explanation. Zhang said, "It is a general rule that those women endowed by Heaven with great beauty invariably either destroy themselves or destroy someone else. If this Cui woman were to meet someone with wealth and position, she would use the favor her charms gain her to be cloud and rain or dragon or monster — I can't imagine what she might turn into. Of old, King Xin of the Shang and King Yu of the Zhou[30] were brought low by women, in spite of the size of their kingdoms and the extent of their power; their armies were scattered, their persons butchered, and down to the present day their names are objects of ridicule. I have no inner strength to withstand this evil influence. That is why I have resolutely suppressed my love."

At this statement everyone present sighed deeply.

Over a year later Cui Yingying was married, and Zhang for his part had taken a wife. Happening to pass through the town where she was living, he asked permission of her husband to see her, as a cousin. The husband spoke to her, but Yingying refused to appear. Zhang's feelings of hurt showed on his face, and she was told about it. She secretly sent him a poem:

Emaciated, I have lost my looks,
Tossing and turning, too weary to leave my bed.
It's not because of others I am ashamed to rise;
For you I am haggard and before you ashamed.

---

[28] Which might be carrying a message.

[29] Xiao Shi was a well-known flute-playing immortal of the Spring and Autumn period.

[30] Xin (Zhou) was the familiar last ruler of the Shang Dynasty, whose misrule and fall are attributed to the influence of his favorite Daji. King Yu (r. 781–771 B.C.), last ruler of the Western Zhou, was misled by his consort Baosi. The behavior of both rulers is traditionally attributed to their infatuation with the wicked women they loved.

She never did appear. Some days later when Zhang was about to leave, she sent another poem of farewell:

Cast off and abandoned, what can I say now,
Whom you loved so briefly long ago?
Any love you had then for me
Will do for the one you have now.

After this he never heard any more about her. His contemporaries for the most part conceded that Zhang had done well to rectify his mistake. I have often mentioned this among friends so that, forewarned, they might avoid doing such a thing, or if they did, that they might not be led astray by it. In the ninth month of a year in the Zhen-yuan period, when an official, Li Gongchui,[31] was passing the night in my house at the Pacification Quarter, the conversation touched on the subject. He found it most extraordinary and composed a "Song of Yingying" to commemorate the affair. Cui's child-name was Yingying, and Gongchui used it for his poem.

ANON

The Curly-Bearded Hero

Translated by Cyril Birch

Attributed by some to the Late Tang Taoist writer Du Guangting (850–933), this story deals with the period at the end of the Sui dynasty (581–618), and the emergence of the man who was to become the founder of the Tang dynasty, Li Shimin. Its idealized picture of the One Man, Li Shimin (who in fact won the throne by killing his older brother), seems to reflect Late Tang nostalgia for a golden age. Despite its concluding moral ("The subject who harbors foolish thoughts of rebellion is like the mantis which would stop a chariot with its feelers"), the story has always been popular for its colorful characterization (Curly-Beard and Red Whisk) and for vivid episodes such as the slicing and eating of the human heart and liver. Like other Tang tales, this one was later adapted many times for the stage.

— Editors

When the Emperor Yang of the Sui dynasty visited Yangzhou he left his western capital, Chang'an, in the charge of Councilor Yang Su. This was a man whom high birth had made arrogant, and in the troubled state of the times he had begun to regard his own power and prestige as

---

[31] Gongchui was the style of the Tang poet Li Shen (?–846).

unrivaled in the land. He maintained a lavish court and departed from the mode of conduct appropriate to a subject. Whether it was a high officer requesting interview or a private guest paying his respects, Yang would receive his visitor seated on a couch; when he rose to leave his hall it would be to walk, supported on either side by a beautiful girl, down between rows of attendant maidens. In these and other ways he arrogated to himself the imperial prerogatives. With age his behavior grew more extreme, until he no longer seemed aware of the responsibility he owed to sustain the realm against peril.

One day Li Jing, later to be ennobled as Duke of Wei but at that time still a commoner, requested an interview with Yang Su in order to present certain policies to which he had given much thought. As with everyone else, Yang Su remained seated to receive him. But Li Jing came forward, bowed and said, "The whole empire is now in turmoil, as would-be leaders strive for mastery. Your Highness is supreme in the service of our imperial house. Your first concern should be to win the respect of men of heroic mettle, and this you are hindering by remaining seated to receive those who seek audience."

Yang Su composed his features to an expression of more fitting gravity, rose to his feet and apologized. He derived great pleasure from the discussion which followed, and Li Jing, when the time came for him to withdraw, was assured of the acceptance of his proposals.

Throughout his spirited conversation with the Councilor, Li Jing had been subjected to the gaze of a girl who stood before them, a girl of remarkable beauty who held in her hand a red whisk. When Li had taken his leave this girl followed him into the anteroom and pointed him out to an attendant, whom she asked to ascertain Li's position, family situation and address. Li answered the attendant, and the girl nodded her head and withdrew.

Li Jing returned to his lodging. But that night, toward dawn, suddenly there came a knocking at his door and a call in a low voice. Li Jing rose to find a being dressed in a purple robe and with covered head, who carried a staff and a single traveling-bag.

"Who are you?" asked Li.

"I am the maid-servant from Councilor Yang's residence, the girl with the red whisk," came the reply.

Li at once invited her to enter. The removal of outer robe and headwear revealed a girl of superb beauty, perhaps seventeen or eighteen years old. Her face was free of cosmetics though her clothes were of the gayest style. She bowed to Li Jing, who though startled, returned her greeting.

"I have been for a long time in the service of the Councilor Yang," she said, "and I have seen many of the leading figures of the empire; but none have I seen to equal you. I have come to seek your favor as the creeper, helpless alone, seeks the support of the sturdiest tree."

"But what can I do," Li Jing asked, "when Councilor Yang has such power now in the capital?"

"There is little to fear from him. He is the corpse in which a little breath remains. We his women know him to be a failure and though many have run away they have not been pursued very far. I have carefully considered all this, and pray that you will not reject me."

Li Jing asked her surname and her position in her family, and she replied that she was the eldest child of the Zhang family. Her form and face, her speech and her bearing were all beyond the mortal range, and Li Jing could not find it in him to reject her. But his joy was no greater than the fears her action raised in him. Each new moment a thousand causes for anxiety would present themselves, and outside the door there was always someone new trying to spy on them. Then, after a few days, they heard news of a search. Convinced of the danger of their situation, they put on riding dress, left their lodging in the capital and rode out on the Taiyuan road to seek refuge there.

They broke their journey at an inn at Lingshi. A bed had been made ready for them and meat boiling in a pot on the stove was almost cooked. Miss Zhang had to stand up by the bed to comb her hair, which was so long that it reached to the floor. Li Jing was brushing down the horses just outside the door. At this moment there rode up to them a stranger mounted on a lame donkey. The man was of middle height and had a ruddy, curling beard. Dismounting he threw a leather bag down by the stove, took a pillow and lay down on his side, his gaze fixed on Miss Zhang as she combed her hair.

Li Jing was infuriated by this behavior but went on with his grooming while he tried to decide what to do about it. Miss Zhang studied the stranger's face. Then, one hand holding out her hair as a screen, with the other she signed to Li not to show anger. She hastily finished her toilet, then approached the stranger, bringing together her sleeves before her in token of greeting and asking to know his name.

"My name is Zhang," said the stranger without shifting his position.

"I also have the name Zhang," said the girl, "so you should regard me as your younger sister." She swiftly performed the prescribed obeisance, then asked further what position he had in his family.

"I am the third," he replied, and asked what was her position.

"The eldest."

"Then I am most fortunate today in encountering First Sister," said the stranger with a smile.

Now Miss Zhang called out to Li Jing, "Come now and greet my Third Brother." Li hastened to salute him, then the three seated themselves round the stove.

"What sort of meat is cooking there?" asked the stranger.

"Mutton. It must be ready by now."

"Good," said the stranger, "for I am hungry."

While Li went out to buy wheaten cakes the stranger drew a dagger from his belt and sliced the meat for them to share. When they had eaten their fill he chopped up what remained and fed it to his donkey. He was extremely swift in all his movements.

"From your appearance I should judge you to be an impoverished gentleman," said the stranger to Li Jing. "How do you come to be accompanied by such an outstanding beauty as this?"

"It is true that I am poor," Li replied, "yet there is good reason for this. If it were anyone else who asked I should not care to say, but from you I shall hide nothing." And he told him all that had taken place.

"Then where do you plan to go?" asked the stranger.

"We shall take refuge in Taiyuan," answered Li Jing.

"In that case I shall not be able to accompany you," said the stranger. Then, "Do you have wine?" he asked.

"There is a wineshop just to the west of the inn," said Li Jing, and he brought a gallon of wine.

"I have something here just to go with the wine. I hope you will join me, Li," said the stranger when the wine had been passed round. Courteously Li thanked the stranger, who opened his leather bag and drew from it first a human head, then a human heart and liver. The head he dropped back into the bag; the heart and liver he sliced with his dagger and shared with Li Jing.

"This man was unrivaled throughout the empire for mean ingratitude," he said. "For ten years I have nursed my feud with him, but now at last I have taken him and found some vent for my wrath." And he continued: "Li, your bearing is that of a true man of valor. Have you heard, as I have, that there is in Taiyuan a man marked out from his fellows?"

"I have known for some time of a youth whom I consider to be the One Man," replied Li. "Other than this I know only of men destined to be generals or ministers."

"What is his name?" asked the stranger.

"Li, as mine is," said Li Jing.

"How old is he?"

"Nineteen only."

"And what is his position at present?"

"He is the son of a garrison commander," said Li Jing.

"This sounds very like the man I heard of," said the stranger. "I must see him. Li, can you arrange for me to meet him?"

"I have a friend named Liu Wenjing, who knows him well," answered Li Jing. "I can arrange an introduction through him. But what is it you want of him?"

"A soothsayer spoke of an aura of portent over Taiyuan, and advised me to seek out this man. When do you expect to reach Taiyuan?"

Li Jing told him, and he continued, "Let us agree to meet on the day following your arrival. Wait for me at daybreak at the Fenyang Bridge."

With these words he mounted his donkey and rode off, so fast that when they looked he was already lost to sight. For some time Li Jing and the girl discussed him with both pleasure and amazement. Then they said, "There is no distrust among true heroes. We have nothing to fear from him." And they hastened on their journey.

They reached Taiyuan by the appointed day, entered the city and awaited Zhang's arrival. He was as good as his word and they met with great pleasure. Together they proceeded to the house of Liu Wenjing. Li Jing disguised their purpose: "This gentleman is a gifted physiognomist who is anxious to meet the youth Li. Would you be so kind as to invite him here?"

Now Liu Wenjing had long been convinced of the boy's high destiny. On learning that his visitor practised the science of the physiognomist he dispatched a messenger to summon him with all speed, and in the shortest possible time he was with them. The youth wore neither outer robe nor shoes, but had on a simple fur-lined jacket. There was about him an air of elation, and his whole appearance was of great distinction.

The bearded Zhang remained silent in his seat in the corner of the room: at sight of the youth his will had died within him. They drank a few cups of wine, then Zhang summoned Li Jing to him: "This is the true Son of Heaven," he said. Li Jing told this to Liu Wenjing, who was delighted to be confirmed in his own conviction.

When they had left, the bearded man said to Li Jing, "Now that I have seen him I am almost completely certain, but I need confirmation from a friend of mine, a Taoist. You must take First Sister back to the capital. At noon on such-and-such a day, come to me at the wine-shop to the east of the horse market. Outside you will find this donkey of mine with another one, a very lean beast: this will indicate that my Taoist friend and myself are upstairs together. You must come up to us straight away."

Again he left them, and again Li Jing and the girl Zhang followed his instructions and sought him out on the chosen day. They saw the two donkeys as he had described them. Lifting up the skirts of their robes, they climbed the stairs to find the bearded man and the Taoist drinking together. Their arrival gave fresh pleasure to the bearded Zhang. He summoned them to be seated, passed wine to them, and after a dozen cups gave them further instructions: "In a cupboard downstairs here, you will find one hundred thousand cash. Find a quiet, safe place to settle First Sister, then on such-and-such a day meet me again at the Fenyang Bridge."

Li Jing kept the appointment and found the Taoist and the bearded man already there. Together the three of them went to visit Liu Wenjing. The latter was playing chess when they arrived. He rose, bowed and talked to them, then shortly afterward sent a messenger in haste to summon the youth Li Shimin to watch their game. The protagonists were the Taoist and Liu Wenjing; the bearded man stood with Li Jing at one side, looking on. Very soon Li Shimin came in, bowed and took a seat. So bright, so distinct was the charm of his manner that the whole room seemed filled with a freshness of spirit; and his eyes, as he looked about him, seemed to glow with an inner light.

At sight of him the face of the Taoist saddened, and he cleared away the chessmen and said, "The game is over! My position had become impossible. Who could have told? — but there was no way out."

The chess at an end, they took their leave, and as soon as they were outside the Taoist addressed the bearded man: "This realm is not to be your realm. But strive hard, and there will be a place for you elsewhere — do not let this bring you to despair."

After this they all returned to the capital together. On the journey the bearded man spoke to Li Jing: "You will not be in the capital before such-and-such a day," he said. "The day after you arrive, I want you to bring First Sister to my home in such-and-such a ward of the city. I am afraid you have been put to a great deal of journeying, and First Sister must fear that you will be destitute. I should like my wife to meet you, and we can talk things over then. Please do not decline this request."

With a sigh he left them at this point, while Li Jing and the girl Zhang whipped up their horses and hastened on. Before long they arrived in the capital. Together they made their way to the address given them. They found themselves before an unimposing wooden doorway. Their knock was answered by servants who made obeisance and said, "We have long been awaiting you, sir, and First Sister, on our master's orders." And they were led through a series of gates, each more magnificent than the last. Over thirty maidens now stood ranged before them, and twenty servants led them into the eastern wing of the mansion.

Here everything they saw was of the rarest excellence, and there was an abundance of wardrobes and toilet-cases, of headgear, of mirrors and hair ornaments, all of a quality seldom seen on earth. When they had washed and combed their hair they were invited to change their robes, and the most exquisite garments were brought for them. No sooner were they ready than word came of the master's approach, and the bearded Zhang entered. In headdress of gauze and robe of purple, his bearing truly regal, he strode toward them and greeted them with gladness. His wife, fittingly a being of rare beauty, he commanded to come forward and make obeisance to them. Then he brought them to the central hall where a banquet had been prepared whose lavishness neither king nor noble could have matched. The two couples seated themselves to face each other, and delicacies were passed. And now there filed into the courtyard twenty girl musicians who entertained them with music of a sweetness heard perhaps in heaven, but seldom here below.

The banquet ended, wine was brought, and while they drank, a procession of household retainers carried in twenty couches from the western hall, each covered with a sheet of brocade. The covers were then removed to reveal sets of keys and account-books, which the bearded Zhang explained to Li Jing in the following words: "Here you will find complete lists of my treasure in jewels and silks. All that I possess I now give over to you. I must tell you my reason for this. My design was to carve a place for myself in this realm, perhaps to establish what power I could after two years or three years of campaigning for the throne. But now that I recognize my overlord there is no cause for me to linger on here. Li of Taiyuan is the true lord of us all: within half-a-dozen years he will have brought the empire to order. You, Li Jing, a man of heroic stature in the service of a prince unrivalled, you must bend your every effort to the supreme tasks of a minister. First Sister, rare beauty matched by great gifts, will support you in your advancement and share in your high nobility. None but First Sister could have foreseen your greatness; none but yourself could have secured her service. As men of wisdom and virtue join with each other in succession, their coming together is as though prearranged: 'storm rises when the tiger roars, clouds gather when the dragon soars'; there is nothing here of mere chance. Put my treasure at the service of our true lord, and strive with all your power to secure his mastery. If in a dozen years from now you hear of stirring happenings in the southeast, a thousand miles away, then you will know that I have found my season of success. You, First Sister, and you, Li Jing, make then together a libation in my honor."

Zhang now ordered the servants of his household to assemble and make obeisance, and said, "Li Jing and First Sister are now your master and mistress. Serve them with diligence." And it remained only for Zhang and his wife both to put on warrior's clothes and ride off, attended by a single servant; and a few paces took them out of sight.

After taking over the mansion Li Jing became a wealthy man and was able to make his contribution to Li Shimin's conquest of the empire. By the time of the reign-period Zhen-guan (627–650) he had risen to be Chief Minister of the Left. It was now that reports came from the Man tribes of the southeast: "A force of a thousand ships carrying hundreds of thousands of armed men has invaded the country of Fuyu. They have killed the king and set up their own leader in his place, and settled down in occupation of the land."

Li Jing realized that the bearded man had found his success. On his return from court he told Madam Zhang of the news, and together they made a libation with obeisances toward the southeast in his honor.

From this history we may know that not even a hero, far less a common being, may expect to come forward as the One Man. The subject who harbors foolish thoughts of rebellion is like the mantis which would stop a chariot with its feelers. True it is that our dynastic house shall flourish from age to age, time without end.

LI FUYAN (c. 775–833)

Betrothal Inn

Translated by Robert Joe Cutter

A powerful treatment of the theme of predestination.

Wei Gu of Duling, some fifty *li* south of the capital Chang'an, was orphaned when young, and wished to marry as early as possible. He sought matrimony in many places, but was totally unsuccessful and gave up. In the second year of the Yuan-he period (807), he was traveling to Qinghe and stopped at an inn south of Songcheng. Among the guests was one who proposed the daughter of Pan Fang, the former commandery assistant of Qinghe. They made an appointment for daybreak the next morning at the gate of Longxing Monastery west of the inn. Gu was anxious to wed, and he set off at the crack of dawn, while the setting moon was still bright.

On his way he saw an old man who sat leaning against a cloth sack upon the steps and was examining some writing by moonlight. Gu walked over and stole a glance at it, but did not recognize the script. It was neither in the insect seal, "eight-part," or tadpole styles, nor was it Sanskrit. "What's that you're reading?" he asked the old man. "When I was young, I studied quite hard for a while and thought I knew every script in the world. I can even read Sanskrit. How come I've never seen this writing before?"

The old man laughed and said, "It's not of this world, so how could you have seen it?"

Gu queried, "If it's not of this world, then what is it?"

"The writing of the underworld," came the reply.

"What brings someone from the underworld to this place?" Gu asked.

"It's not that I shouldn't be here," the old man said. "It's just that you're out too early. Every agent of darkness controls some human affair, so we have to walk among men, don't we? At this moment humans and ghosts each make up half of the traffic on the roads. It's just that you can't tell the difference."

"Then what do you control?" Gu inquired.

"Oh, just the world's marriage register," the old man replied.

Gu said happily, "I was orphaned young and have always wanted to marry as early as possible, and continue the family line. These past ten years I've tried every way to find a wife, but have never had any luck. Now I have an appointment here to discuss the possibility of a match with the daughter of Commandery Assistant Pan. Will I succeed?"

"Not yet," the old man replied. "If the thing is not in your destiny, you will never succeed, even by lowering your sights and seeking matrimony among butchers and gamblers, much less commandery assistants. *Your* future wife is just three years old now. When she is seventeen, she will enter your home."

Gu then asked, "What's in your sack?"

"Just red cord," the old man answered. "I use it to tie the feet of future husbands and wives. Even if they are from feuding families or different classes, even if they are sent to serve at the ends of the world, or are from places as different as Wu and Chu, they are secretly joined from birth. This cord once tied can never be loosened. Your foot is already tied to another. What point is there in seeking elsewhere?"

"Where is my wife?" Gu asked. "What does her family do?"

"She is none other than the daughter of the woman Chen who sells vegetables north of this inn," the old man replied.

"May I see her?" Gu asked.

"Chen often carries her along when she comes to the market to sell vegetables. You can go with me, and I'll show you right now."

It was getting light, and the person he had made an appointment with had not arrived. The old man rolled up his documents, hoisted his sack, and walked off. Gu followed him and they went to the vegetable market. An old woman, blind in one eye, arrived carrying a three-year-old girl. She was very tattered and ugly.

The old man pointed to her and said, "This is your wife."

"What if I kill her?" Gu exploded.

The old man answered, "By destiny it is meet that she enjoy Heaven's blessings. Because of her son, she shall have a fief. How could she be slain?" And with these words he disappeared.

Gu swore, "You cursed old goat! How absurd! Mine is a family of officials and the woman I marry must be of equal rank. If I couldn't marry such a woman, then I might just keep an attractive geisha. But I would never marry the ugly daughter of an old woman blind in one eye!"

Whetting a small knife, he gave it to his servant and said, "You've always been very resourceful. Kill that girl for me, and I'll give you ten thousand cash."

"Done," said the servant.

The next day, concealing the knife in his sleeve, the servant went among the vegetable sellers. He stabbed the girl in the crowd and fled. The whole market was thrown into chaos. Gu and his servant fled and were able to escape.

Gu asked his servant, "Did you hit the mark?"

"I tried to stab her in the heart," he replied, "but unfortunately struck her between the eyebrows."

Afterwards, Gu repeatedly sought marriage without success. Fourteen years later he was serving on the administrative staff of Xiangzhou, a hereditary privilege handed down to him by his father. The Prefect, Wang Tai, employed him as acting administrator in charge of revenue, where he specialized in investigating litigation. Because the Prefect considered him able, he gave his daughter to him in marriage. She was about seventeen and a great beauty. Gu proclaimed his utmost satisfaction. However, she always affixed a beauty spot between her eyebrows, which she never removed for a moment, even in the bath. Gu wondered about this for over a year. Then suddenly he remembered that day in the past and how his servant had struck between the girl's eyebrows. He pressed his wife for an explanation.

"I am the prefect's niece," she said tearfully, "not his daughter. Formerly, my father was in charge of Songcheng and died in office. At the time I was still in swaddling clothes. Then my mother and elder brother died. I went to live in a village south of Songcheng with my wet-nurse, Mrs. Chen. She sold vegetables near an inn to supply our daily needs. Mrs. Chen loved me very much and couldn't bear to put me aside for a moment. When I was three, she carried me into the market, where I was stabbed by some crazed thug. The knife scar is still there, so I always cover it with a beauty spot. Seven or eight years ago, uncle was posted to Lulong, so I came to live with him. It was kind of him to give me to you in marriage as his daughter."

"Was Mrs. Chen blind in one eye?" Gu asked.

"Yes!" she exclaimed. "How did you know?"
"I was the one who had you stabbed," Gu answered.
"Amazing!" she cried. "This is fate!"
Then they talked all about it and their mutual affection gradually grew deeper and deeper. Later she gave birth to a boy, Gun. He became Prefect of Yanmen, and she was enfeoffed as Grand Mistress of Taiyuan Commandery. Thus, we know that what is determined by secret predestination may not be altered. When the magistrate of Songcheng learned of it, he named the inn Betrothal Inn.

The Alchemist

Translated by J. R. Hightower

Again, this story presents the Taoist theme of the illusory nature of human existence. Unlike the dream allegory of "The World in a Pillow," "The Alchemist" presents a powerful picture of the harrowing quest for the reality that lies beyond the illusion of the emotions. The Taoist alchemist possesses the means to transcend this illusion, but Du Zichun is unable to persevere to the end of the lengthy ordeal prescribed for him, and is conquered by the force of love.

— Editors

Du Zichun lived, apparently, around the time of the Zhou[32] and Sui dynasties. As a young man he was extravagant and unmindful of his patrimony. Being a man of free and easy spirit, he gave himself over to drinking and dissipation until he had squandered all his wealth. When he appealed to his relatives, they disowned him, one and all, as irresponsible.

Winter was coming on, his clothing was in rags, and his belly was empty. As he walked about Chang'an, the sun set and he still had had nothing to eat. He found himself at the west gate of the East Market, uncertain where to turn. His hunger and chill were obvious, and he looked up to heaven and sighed.

An old man there leaning on a staff asked him, "What are you sighing about, sir?"

Zichun said what was on his mind. As he grew eloquent over the shabby treatment he had received from his relatives, his indignation showed on his face.

"How many strings of cash would you need to feel well off?" the old man asked.

---

[32] This is the Northern Zhou Dynasty (557–581), the last of the non-Chinese regimes that occupied North China during the Northern and Southern Dynasties period.

"With thirty or fifty thousand I could get along."

"That's not enough."

"A hundred thousand."

"Still not enough."

"A million."

"Still not enough."

"Three million."

"That should do," the old man said at last, and drew from his sleeve a single string of cash, saying, "This is for tonight. Tomorrow at noon be waiting for me at the Persian Hostel in the West Market. Don't be late!"

Zichun went at the appointed time, and the old man actually delivered the three million, leaving without telling his name.

Now that he was rich, Zichun's profligate nature flared up again; he was convinced that he would never again be a pauper. He rode sleek horses and dressed in light furs: he assembled drinking companions, hired musicians, singers, and dancers in the gay quarter with never a thought for the future. Within a year or two he had gradually exhausted his resources. Fine clothes and carriage were replaced by cheap ones, he surrendered his horse for a donkey, and then gave up the donkey and walked. In no time he was as destitute as before.

At his wits' end, he stood at the gate to the market, bemoaning his lot. As if in response to his sighs, the old man appeared. Seizing Zichun's hand he exclaimed, "Amazing, that this should happen again! I will help you again — how much do you need?"

Zichun was too embarrassed to reply and, to the old man's urgings, he could only shake his head in shame.

"Come again at noon tomorrow, the same place," the old man said.

Swallowing his shame, Zichun went, and was given ten million strings of cash. Before receiving them, he was filled with determination to invest his money wisely in the future, putting Shi Chong and Yi Dun[33] quite in the shade. But once the money came into his hands, his resolve grew unstable and his irresponsible character reasserted itself. Within a couple of years he was poorer than ever.

Again he ran into the old man in the same old place. Humiliated past endurance, he covered his face and fled. The old man seized the skirt of his robe and stopped him. "Too bad!" he said. "You have had bad luck." And he offered him thirty million, with the warning, "If this does not cure you, poverty is in your blood."

---

[33] Shi Chong was a legendary rich man of the Jin Dynasty. Yi Dun was an exceptionally rich salt merchant of the Spring and Autumn period.

Zichun thought, "When I lost all I had through extravagance and dissipation, my relatives and high connections spared me not a glance. Yet this old man has come to my aid three times — how can I repay him?" And to the old man he said, "With what you have given me I can put my affairs in order. It enables me to provide for widows and orphans and restore my name as a man of honor. I am deeply touched by your great generosity, and when I have accomplished this task, I will be at your disposal."

"It is what I had hoped. When you have taken care of your affairs, meet me next year on the fifteenth of the seventh month by the twin junipers at the Temple of Laozi."

Reckoning that most widows and orphans of his clan were to be found in the area to the south of River Huai, he transferred his capital to Yangzhou, where he bought some fifteen hundred acres of good land. Within the city he built a large house, and on the main roads he erected over a hundred hostels, in which he lodged the widows and orphans of the whole region. He married off his nieces and nephews and had the unburied remains of his relatives moved to the clan cemetery. He requited those who had been kind to him and avenged his wrongs. When this was all done, the date was approaching, and he went to the appointed place, where he found the old man whistling in the shade of the twin junipers.

Together they climbed the Cloud Terrace Peak in the Hua Mountains. When they had gone forty *li* or so, they came upon an imposing edifice, not the dwelling of any ordinary person. High above them were colored clouds, and wary cranes were soaring overhead. The main hall stood out against the sky; inside was an alchemist's furnace over nine feet high emitting purple flames that lit up the door and windows.

Nine jade damsels[34] stood around the furnace, which rested on a green dragon in front and a white tiger behind. Just before sunset the old man appeared, no longer in ordinary dress, but now wearing the yellow cap and red robe of a Taoist priest. In his hands he held three pills of hornblende and a cup of wine, which he gave to Zichun, instructing him to swallow them. Then he spread a tiger skin against the inner wall on the west side and seated him on it, facing east.

"Be careful not to speak," he warned. "Though you see imposing spirits or fearful demons, or yakshas, or fierce wild beasts or hell itself — even though your dearest relatives are bound and tortured, none of it will be real. Through it all you must neither move nor speak; quiet your heart and fear not, and in the end you will suffer no harm. Just put your mind on what I have said." And he went out.

---

[34] The Taoist fairies.

Zichun looked around in the hall. There was only a large earthen jar filled to the brim with water, and nothing else. No sooner had the Taoist departed than the slopes of the hillside were covered with armed men carrying flags and banners, a thousand chariots and ten thousand horsemen. The roar of their shouts shook heaven and earth. One of them they addressed as "Great General"; he was over ten feet tall, clad, as was his horse, all in golden armor of a dazzling radiance. His bodyguard of several hundred men, all holding swords or drawn bows, dashed into the hall shouting, "Who are you that dare face the Great General?"

On both sides they raised their swords and advanced, demanding to know Zichun's name and what sort of person he was, to which he made no response. Enraged, they made a great uproar as if they were about to slash him, and shoot arrows into him, but he paid them no attention. The general left in a fury.

All at once there were all sorts of creatures — fierce tigers and poisonous dragons, griffins and lions, cobras and scorpions — roaring and snatching as they rushed forward to seize and bite, even leaping into the air over his head. Zichun remained unperturbed, and in a little while they were all gone.

Then a great rain fell in torrents, with thunder and lightning in the murky air, and fire wheels racing by to the left and the right, the lightning striking in front and behind, until he could not open his eyes. In a moment the water in the hall was over ten feet deep, lightning came in an unbroken stream, and the thunder roared, as though the very hills and rivers were split open. In no time the waves had reached the place where Zichun sat, but he did not budge at all and paid no attention to anything around him.

Before long, the general appeared again, leading a troop of ox-headed jailers and demons of extraordinary appearance. They carried a huge cauldron which they placed in front of Zichun. They surrounded him on all sides with long, forked spears. He was given an ultimatum: if willing to tell his name, he would be set free. If not, he would be impaled through the heart and thrust into the boiling cauldron. He made no response.

Next they brought in his wife and dragged her to the foot of the steps. Pointing to her the general said, "Tell your name and we will let her go."

When he did not respond, she was whipped until the blood flowed. They shot her with arrows, cut her with knives, poured boiling water on her, and seared her flesh with irons until she could not endure it and screamed and wept, "I am of no account, a disgrace to a gentleman like you. But I have after all had the good fortune to serve you more than ten years as your wife. Now I am tormented past endurance by these demons.

I would never expect you to get down on your knees and beg favors of them, but all it would take to save my life is just one single word!" Her tears rained down as she alternately prayed and cursed.

When Zichun persisted in paying no attention, the general shouted, "You think we can't hurt your wife?" And he ordered them to bring the knife and block and slice her, inch by inch, beginning with her feet. She screamed and wept even more desperately, but to the end Zichun never once paid her the slightest attention.

The general then announced, "This villain has perfected his black magic and cannot be allowed on earth any longer." He ordered the attendants to behead him, and when it was done, they led his ghost before the Yama King, who said, "Is this the sorcerer of the Cloud Terrace Peak? Deliver him to the tortures of hell."

There he experienced in complete form all the tortures — swallowing molten bronze, being beaten with an iron cudgel, pounded in a mortar, ground in a mill, buried in a fiery pit, boiled in a cauldron: he climbed the mountain of knives and the tree of swords. Through it all he remembered the Taoist master's injunction, and it all seemed bearable, so never a sigh escaped him. The torturers reported that he had suffered all the punishments, and the Yama King said, "This man is a secret villain. It is not fitting that he should be reborn a man: we will have him born a daughter in the family of Wang Quan, the deputy magistrate of Shanfu County in Songzhou."[35]

From birth the little girl was sickly, and hardly a day passed without acupuncture or moxa burning or some nasty medicine. And she was always falling out of bed or into the fire, but whatever the pain she never made a sound. Soon she was grown into an extraordinarily beautiful girl, but because she never spoke, she was thought by her family to be dumb. Her relatives would take liberties with her and offer her all sorts of insults, but she would not respond.

In the same town was a *jinshi* scholar named Lu Gui who, hearing of her beauty, sought her through an intermediary for his wife. The family declined on the grounds that she was dumb, but Lu said, "If my wife is worthy, what need has she for speech? She will serve as a reproach to sharp-tongued women." They agreed to the match, and Lu married her as his wife, with all the six rites.

For several years their love was very deep. She bore him a son, who at two years was unusually bright and clever. His father held the child in his arms and talked to her, but she did not respond. He tried all sorts of ways

---

[35] In modern Jiangsu Province.

to get her to talk, but never a word would she say. In a fury he exclaimed, "Minister Jia's wife [of the Spring and Autumn period] despised her husband and would never smile, until he shot a pheasant, which made her feel better about him. I cannot do as well as he did, though I should think my accomplishments as a man of education were better than any mere archery. If you are not ever going to speak, what use to a man of honor is the child of a wife who despises him?"

And he took the child by its two feet and dashed its head against a stone, spattering blood for several paces around. In Zichun's heart love welled up, and for an instant he forgot his vow, inadvertently letting slip a sound of distress: "No —"

The sound was still in the air as he found himself sitting in his old place, the Taoist standing in front of him. It was just the beginning of the fifth watch. He saw the purple flames shoot up through the roof and all at once they were surrounded by a fire. Roof and walls were all in flames.

"You have failed me!" the Taoist said with a sigh.

He seized Zichun's hair and threw him in the water jar, and the flames subsided.

"My son, your heart was purged of joy and anger, grief and fear, loathing and desire," the Taoist said to him. "It is only love that binds you still. If you had not uttered that cry, my elixir would have been ready, and you, too, could have become an immortal with me. It is hard, alas, to find someone with the capacity for immortality. I can smelt my elixir again, but your body must remain earthbound. Take heed!"

Pointing out the distant road back, he sent Zichun on his way. Zichun climbed up on the platform to look. The furnace had split apart and inside was an iron rod thick as a man's forearm and several feet long. The Taoist had put off his robe and was cutting at the rod with a knife.

When Zichun returned home, he was filled with shame that he had forgotten his vow, and resolved to go back and try to make amends. He went to the Cloud Terrace Peak, but there was no sign of anyone, and he returned home again, sighing and chagrined.

LIU ZONGYUAN (773–819)

Mid-River

Translated by William H. Nienhauser

For poetry and prose by Liu Zongyuan, see chapters 22 and 27. This strangely modern story reveals an unexpected side of this many-faceted Tang man of letters.

— Editors

Mid-River was a lewd woman. I do not wish to disclose her identity and have therefore named her after the district in which she lived. In the beginning, she lived in Relatives' Village[36] and was known for her virtue. Even before she married, she abhorred the disorderly behavior of her relatives and deemed it a disgrace to be associated with them. She remained discreetly in her quarters and attended to her dress designs, to her spinning, weaving, and knitting.

When she married, her father-in-law was already dead, and she waited upon her mother-in-law most respectfully. She was not given to gossip and was properly reverential to her husband. They treated one another with great courtesy and seemed to share each other's very thoughts.

Certain of her more disreputable relatives got together and plotted against her, asking, "What can we do about Mid-River?" The worst amongst them said, "We must try to corrupt her." They took a carriage and called on her as a group. They invited her to go out and enjoy herself with them, while at the same time flattering her: "Since you came here, the people of Relatives' Village have all been encouraged to cultivate and restrain themselves day and night. If they commit even the slightest of misdemeanors, they are afraid of people hearing of it. Now we wish to improve their behavior still further, by affording them an opportunity to emulate your propriety. We want them to observe your proper bearing so that morning and night they may be watchful of their own."

Mid-River firmly declined the offer, but her mother-in-law said angrily, "They have come with compliments; they regard you as their teacher. Why did you reject them so strongly?" "I have heard," Mid-River replied, "that a woman should be chaste, obedient, quiet, and loyal. To show off fancy carriages, to flaunt costumes and jewelry, to go out carousing in a group, to eat, drink, and be merry — these are not proper ways for a woman." But her mother-in-law remained adamant, so she finally consented and went with the company.

As they passed the market, someone said: "A little south of here, we shall enter a Buddhist temple. There Old Wu, a painter known throughout the nation, has just finished some frescoes on the southeastern wall. These paintings are quite uncanny.[37] We can have the groom clear the way so we can go in to look at them." After they had

---

[36] Relatives' Village was the residence of imperial relations during the Han; it is possible that Liu Zongyuan thereby intends to indicate that Mid-river was a member of the Tang aristocracy.
[37] "Old Wu" refers to Wu Daozi, well known for his depictions of hell, in scenes which involved considerable nudity or semi-nudity.

finished viewing, she was invited to take the honored seat, where food
was spread out beside a curtained bed. Suddenly, she heard a man's
cough and was so frightened that she ran out without her shoes, ordering
an attendant to take her home post-haste in a carriage. She wept for
several days and thereafter confined herself even more closely to her own
house, having nothing to do with her relatives.

Then they came to offer their apologies, saying, "Why were you so
rash? Are you blaming us, because of what happened? The man who
coughed that day was only a kitchen hand."

"But why did several people laugh near the door?" she asked. Upon
hearing this, the relatives withdrew.

It was not until a whole year later that the relatives dared call on
Mid-River's mother-in-law again to invite Mid-River out. They were
sure she would make her go with them. And she did. They went to a
place between two ponds in a temple at Feng River. They knocked at the
animal pen, and fish and turtles were brought out to feed.[38] Mid-River
smiled, and her companions were pleased. She was soon led to a dining-
room without any curtains where the corridors were open and spacious.
Mid-River consented to enter this room. Earlier, a number of wicked
youths had been hidden behind a partition under the northern window.[39] Then the curtain was let down, and some girls were ordered to
play Qin music.[40] Mid-River and the others squatted down to watch them.

Shortly afterward, from among those hidden behind the partition,
one selected for his good looks and large organ emerged to take care
of Mid-River. He embraced her, and she screamed and cried. Female
servants held her between them, taking turns to urge her on and to scold
or mock her. Mid-River stole a glance at the man who had her in his
arms and found him very handsome. Those around her were meanwhile indulging themselves more and more freely, breathing more and
more heavily, and she could not avoid being aroused herself. As she
relaxed her resistance a little, her adversary had his way with her. He
carried her off to a separate room, and Mid-River soon stopped crying
and began to enjoy herself exceedingly. She congratulated herself on this
newly discovered pleasure.

Toward evening, when dinner was being served and she was called to

---

[38] These animals were presumably held to be "released from captivity," as is the Buddhist
custom.
[39] The northern window indicates in a number of classical texts a place for sleeping — thus
there must have been beds nearby.
[40] One of the traditional types of music considered licentious.

partake of it, she said, "I do not wish to eat." Later, the carriage was harnessed and they warned her they were going back, but Mid-River said, "I am not going back. I will not be parted from this man until I die." Her relatives were at a great loss and they had no alternative but to stay there overnight.

Mid-River's husband came to fetch her home, but he was not able to see her. She consented to go home the next day only when prevailed upon by those about her. As she was about to leave, she embraced her lover and cried bitterly, swearing eternal loyalty and biting his arm. On her arrival home, she could not bear to look at her husband, but closed her eyes and pleaded illness. He gave her all kinds of food, but she refused to eat. He fed her good medicine, but she waved it away. She was as tense as a lute string about to snap. Whenever her husband came near her, she berated him severely. She never opened her eyes, and became more and more resentful of him. The distress was more than the husband could bear. "I am so sick that I shall soon die!" she said several days later. "I shall never be cured by medicine. Summon a spirit to release me; but it must be done by night."

Since Mid-River had become sick and had started her ravings, her husband had been prepared to go to any lengths to please her. The ruling emperor abhorred the practice of praying to spirits at night, but the husband was not deterred. The utensils for the ceremony were all arranged. Then Mid-River ordered the local officials to accuse her husband of sorcery. Officials of various ranks looked into the matter, and the husband was beaten with the bamboo until he died. Even on the point of death, he cried, "I have failed my wife! I have failed my wife!"

Mid-River was greatly pleased and did not mourn for her husband. She opened her door and sent for her paramour. Chasing about the house naked, they lost themselves in an orgy of carnal pleasure. But after a year of this, the man showed signs of flagging. She was tired of him and drove him out.

Then she called together a group of good-for-nothings from Chang'an, and they engaged in orgies day and night in her home. Still not satisfied, she set up a wineshop at the southwestern corner of the house and positioned herself upstairs to spy on her customers. She had a small door cut and sought to attract passers-by, using young servant girls as bait. Of the men who went in to drink, she chose only those with big noses, the robust, the young, and the handsome, the ones who showed the most talent during wine games, to be taken upstairs to give her satisfaction. As they coupled, she would keep an eye to the door, lest she miss even one man. And yet daily she continued to sigh dreamily, showing that her thirst was still not slaked.

After more than a decade of dissipation, she was exhausted, her bones began to dry up, and soon she died. Thereafter, even the reprobates of Relatives' Village would wince at the name of Mid-River. No one cared to talk about her.

Mr. Liu Zongyuan comments: "Of the scholars of the world, who can compare in virtue and purity with Mid-River when she first became a wife? Of friends who are said to have admired one another, have any been as close as Mid-River was to her husband? And yet she succumbed to force, she tasted pleasure and returned home even to oppose her husband. She treated him like a robber and an enemy. She could not bear to see his face and finally plotted his death, not grieving for him for a moment. Can those, then, who are joined together by affection and love be free from the evil influence of self-interest? Indeed, it is enough for us to know that mutual affection is something difficult to rely upon. Since this is certainly true of friends, is it not even more terrifying in the relationships between a ruler and his subjects? I have therefore taken the liberty to enumerate these events."

ꍈ *Further Reading* ꍈ

Bauer, Wolfgang, & Herbert Franke, trans. (trans. from the German by Christopher Levenson). *The Golden Casket: Chinese Novellas of Two Millenia.* New York: Harcourt, Brace & World, 1964.

Birch, Cyril, trans. "The Curly-Bearded Hero." In Birch, ed., *Anthology of Chinese Literature*, vol. 1.

Chang, H. C., ed. and trans. *Chinese Literature, Vol. 3: Tales of the Supernatural.* Edinburgh: University of Edinburgh Press, 1984.

Dudbridge, Glen. *The Tale of Li Wa. Study and Critical Edition of a Chinese Story from the Ninth Century.* London: Ithaca Press, 1983.

Edwards, E. D., ed. and trans. *Chinese Prose Literature of the T'ang Period.* 2 vols. London: Arthur Probsthain, 1937–38.

Hightower, J. R., trans. "The Story of Yingying" and "The Alchemist (Tu Tzu-ch'un)." In Y. W. Ma & Joseph S. M. Lau, eds. *Traditional Chinese Stories: Themes and Variations.* New York: Columbia University Press, 1978.

Kao, Karl S. Y., ed. *Classical Chinese Tales of the Supernatural and the Fantastic: Selections from the Third to the Tenth Century.* Bloomington: Indiana University Press, 1985.

Lu, Xun (trans. Yang Xianyi & Gladys Yang). *A Brief History of Chinese Fiction.* Beijing: Foreign Languages Press, 1959.

Ma, Y. W., & Joseph S. M. Lau, eds. *Traditional Chinese Stories: Themes and Variations.* New York: Columbia University Press, 1978.

Wang, Chi-chen, trans. *Traditional Chinese Tales.* New York: Columbia University Press, 1944.

Yang, Xianyi, & Gladys Yang, trans. *The Dragon King's Daughter: Ten Tang Dynasty Stories.* Beijing: Foreign Languages Press, 1954.

Chapter 29

Turning the Scrolls

Ballads and Stories from Dunhuang

Popular recitation of Buddhist stories by the monk preachers developed very early in the Tang period, at the latest by the end of the seventh century. Poems written in the seven-word form were introduced for singing by the reciter, perhaps with accompaniment by some instrument. Illustrative pictures may have been shown at the recitation to arouse greater audience interest. In Chang'an, a number of Buddhist monks attracted a large following with their popular lectures. When the Japanese monk Ennin visited the city, he went to some of these recitations and recorded in his diary for the year 841 the names of several Buddhist reciters, among whom the most famous was Wenxu. He was noted for his melodious and deeply moving voice in chanting the sutras as well as in reciting noncanonical Buddhist tales. Once he was accused by a contemporary writer of telling vulgar and lewd stories: "Ignorant men and dissolute women were fond of hearing his tales. The listeners packed the monastery compounds."

— Liu Wu-chi, from *An Introduction to Chinese Literature*, 1966

Introduction

Arthur Waley

The Dunhuang manuscripts come from a hidden library found by the Taoist Wang Yuanlu in 1900. Wang was a discharged soldier who, finding himself at a loose end, settled in one of the famous "Caves of the Thousand Buddhas" at Dunhuang in the extreme northwest of China and made a living by selling Taoist spells. These were in demand because the spell-trade was in the hands of the Mongolian lamas who catered for Buddhists, and the considerable Chinese population had, at the time of Wang's arrival, nowhere to go for native Chinese spells.

The exact circumstances of the find are unknown. One version of the story is that Wang was removing sand from a cave when he discovered the walled-up library. Nor is it known when the library-cave was walled up nor for what reason. The dated documents found in it are said to range from A.D. 406 to A.D. 996. At least three-quarters of the texts are copies of well-known Buddhist scriptures in Chinese, almost word for word as we have them in the printed Canon today.... But to me the most interesting part of the collection are the eighty or so specimens of popular literature — ballads, stories and legendary expansions and expositions of Buddhist scriptures.

But to return to the history of the finds. In 1907 Sir Aurel Stein, acting on behalf of the British Museum and the Government of India, induced the Taoist Wang Yuanlu in return for small sums of money to hand over large numbers of manuscripts and paintings on silk. All the manuscripts in Chinese and half of the paintings on silk are now at the British Museum. In 1908 Professor Pelliot made a similar haul, not so large as Stein's but more discriminating, since he could read Chinese and Stein could not.

— from *Ballads and Stories from Dunhuang,* 1960

Victor Mair and Maxime Weinstein

Although the bulk of the Chinese materials found at Dunhuang are copies of canonical Buddhist texts written for members of the religious establishment, there are also a significant number of writings intended for laymen. These are particularly important for students of popular literature, for among them are the earliest examples of extended prosimetrical narrative (chantefable) and the forerunners of lyric verse (ci), all of which are unprecedentedly written in a colloquial language.

Perhaps the single most noteworthy genre to emerge from the study of the Dunhuang manuscripts has been the *bianwen*. This designation may be rendered in English as "transformation text" and is intimately related to pictures that were known as *bianxiang* ("transformation tableaux"). Indeed, it may be demonstrated that the "transformation text" was a type of story-telling with pictures and that its origins can be traced through Central Asia to India.

The subjects of the "transformation texts" may be either secular or religious.... Among the most celebrated religious stories is "The Great Maudgalyāyana Rescues His Mother from Hell." There is also among the Dunhuang manuscripts a uniquely precious illustrated scroll which closely matches the "transformation text" version of another story.

One of the most intriguing problems about the "transformation texts" is how they came to be written down and by whom. Clearly they have an intimate connection to an eighth- and ninth-century story-telling tradition known as *zhuanbian* ("turning transformation scrolls"). The best information now available indicates that the performers of these "transformations" were professional entertainers and that individuals who became enamored of their performances transcribed them as "transformation texts" so that they might have a more permanent record. The copyists of the extant manuscripts were mostly lay students studying a largely secular curriculum in schools attached to Buddhist monasteries.

Other types of popular narrative were also discovered at Dunhuang. Some, like the story of Meng Jiangnü, resemble "transformation texts" in certain respects, but seem less likely to have been the immediate products of an oral tradition.

— Indiana Companion, 1986

Meng Jiangnü at the Long Wall

Translated by Arthur Waley

This is one of the best-known Chinese legends. It has existed in various forms for over two thousand years and has been the subject of innumerable ballads and plays. In the present version the story is placed in the time (third century B.C.) of the First Emperor, who built the Long Wall ("Great Wall"). Meng Jiangnü's husband, who was employed in the building of the wall, succumbs to the hardships of the task, and is buried in the wall. His wife comes to bring him winter clothes, and is told that he has been buried in the wall. She prays that the wall may crumble, and the intensity of her love is such that it falls down, she finds her husband's bones and brings them back for burial.... The text is incomplete at the beginning.

"... weary and destitute (?) Farewell! If you were to send me winter clothes, I do not know what return I could make."

At the time of his taking leave from his wife he did not speak for
    long,
For he hoped as it were between morning and evening
    to come back to his home.
Who could think that he would suddenly meet disaster by pestle and
    hammer,
His soul be dissolved, his life finished — that he should perish
    at the frontier wall?
After he had taken leave and reached the Long Wall
The officials in charge of the work there treated him with bitter
    harshness.
When he died his body was at once built into the wall,
His wandering soul strayed afar amid the thorns and brambles:
"Weary and destitute on this long journey you came on purpose
    to see me
Bravely meeting wind and frost, wasting your energy.
A thousand times farewell! Go quickly home;

A poor soldier[1] under the earth will not ever forget you."
When his wife heard this, she burst into great sobbing;
"Little did I know that you my lord had perished at the Long Wall!
You tell me now that the bones of your body are built in
    to the Long Wall,
But how am I to know in what part of this Long Wall to look?"
Jiangnü smote herself and wailed to mighty Heaven,
Making plaint that so good a husband had perished all too soon.
A wedded wife's intense devotion can move rivers and hills;
Her great wailing had such power that the Long Wall fell.

An old poem says:

Over the ridges sad clouds rise,
In the empty wastes sorrowful is the voice of wailing.
If you say that men have not the power to move,[2]
How was it that the Long Wall toppled?
Those stone ramparts, ranging over a thousand cubits,
At one stroke melted into the streams and hills.
Could it be that the Wall had crashed and fallen
Only because a wedded wife had come?
This frontier land — strange beyond reason —
With cold heart could not endure to hear.

When she had finished wailing, her heart and soul were still lost in
sorrow, grieving that her husband had suddenly been destroyed. She
sighed out her faithful heart, anguish ever added to anguish. There were
skulls without number; many dead men lay there. Among all the bones
that were strewn this way and that, how was she to tell which were his?
    She bit her finger till it bled, and dripped the blood on to the Long
Wall to show her singleness of heart, that she might be able to pick out
her husband's bones.

Jiangnü said sobbing, "I am at my wit's end;
His lovely substance is scattered about among the yellow sands.
I say to all these ridges and hummocks 'Vouchsafe me a clear sign;
Among all these piles of skulls, tell me which is his.'
Alas, alas, it is very hard to choose;
To see them causes sad thoughts to rise."
One by one she takes them in her hand and looks hard at them;
Then she bites her finger and draws blood and puts them to the test:

---

[1] These four lines are spoken by the ghost of the husband.
[2] That is, to affect Nature.

"If it is my husband, the blood will sink deep into the bones;
But if it is not Ji Liang, the blood will remain apart.
If only I can recognize them, I will take them home with me;
Let them not on my account leave me still in doubt."
Stifled by her great sobbing, her voice then ceased,
From her two eyes there still flowed tears that were hard to stop.
"If Mighty Heaven does not consent to give me what I ask
Then certainly I too will die at the Long Wall."

(The text here becomes fragmentary; but it is clear that the test works. Meng Jiangnü recovers all her husband's bones.)

But there were as well many skulls that had no one to carry them away. Jiangnü was sorry for them and asked them: "All you skulls, in what prefecture is your home? When taking my husband's bones back, I could bring a message for you. If you have souls, I could guide them on their way."

The skulls having thus been questioned by Meng Jiangnü
Knew now that they could send a message to their homes.
The souls of the dead then replied to Ji Liang's wife:
"All of us were sons born into good families;
But the ruler of Qin sent us to work on the building of the Long
　　Wall;
The hardship were endured were more than we could bear and
　　we all died at our tasks:
Our corpses were scattered over the wastelands, no one knew
　　what had become of us,
Spring and winter for ever we lie amid the yellow sands.
Bring word to our wives that pine desolate in their bowers
Telling them to chant the Summons to the Soul and keep up
　　the sacrifices.
Make sure to record in your heart what we tell you now,
And if you see our fathers and mothers do us the kindness
　　to tell them."

(Here the manuscript again becomes fragmentary. It ends with the sacrificial address, *qi wen*, which accompanies Meng Jiangnü's offerings to the souls of the dead; but this, too, is fragmentary.)

The Emperor Taizong in Hell

Translated by Arthur Waley

Popular Chinese ideas about what happens to the dead were in Dunhuang times a mixture of Buddhism and Taoism. The Buddhist World of the Dead was reigned over by King Yama, who enquires or gets his subordinates to enquire into the record of the dead person and gives judgment accordingly. The number of people who had behaved sufficiently well to be sent to the Halls of Heaven was very small. There was a proverb that said, "In the Halls of Heaven things are very quiet." The great majority of the dead were "sinners" who were sent to one section or another of Hell to be tortured.

The Taoist Hell was under or on Mount Tai in Shandong, near the eastern coast, and its authorities are often conceived of as working in with King Yama and his judicial Court. Finally the ancient Chinese ideas of Heaven (*Tian*) as arbiter of human destinies comes into play, and both Yama and Mount Tai are shown as subject to the higher dictates of Heaven.

Most of what the living know about the dead comes, naturally, from people who have, for one reason or another, returned to life after spending some time in the World of the Dead. They may have been sent for by mistake, they may have influence with the authorities of the underworld or they may be employed by King Yama or Mount Tai on secret missions in the World of the Living. Or they may have been sent for to do some special job for King Yama, such as painting his portrait or curing his ague, after which they were returned to their families on earth....

It might be assumed that proceedings at the Court of the Dead are naively modeled on those of the living world, without any intention of parody or "take off." I am inclined to think that this is seldom so and that a "dig" at mundane institutions is usually intended.

"Taizong in Hell" is not likely to be earlier than the ninth century. The manuscript is fragmentary, and I have only translated the more intelligible parts of it.

"I (i.e., the Emperor Taizong) remember that from the third of the fifth year of Wu-de (A.D. 620–622) I went on several military expeditions, took part in every engagement and killed a large number of people. I have not yet paid the penalty for those sins of former days, and how can I now return on the road to life?" Very despondent, the Emperor staggered on like a drunk man. However, led by his escort, he managed to follow on till they came to the gates of the Court, and going in halted at the screen-wall. Here his escort announced, "We wish to leave in your hands the living wraith of a certain person called Li, known in the world as His Majesty Taizong, Emperor of Tang." The Court servants said, "By all means," and brought the Emperor into the Audience Hall to make his obeisances. His Majesty, however, did not perform the rite of prostration. A certain high-ranking official up in the hall shouted out, "Why does not the Emperor of Tang perform the dance of homage?" If he had not been shouted at like this, the Emperor might not have been altogether unwilling to make the obeisance. But nettled by being shouted at he retorted in a loud voice, "Who was it that ordered me to perform the dance of homage? When I was in Chang'an, people did homage to me; I am quite unused to doing homage to others. Is the person up in the hall who ordered me to do homage by any chance a subject of mine? I am the Emperor of Great Tang. King Yama is only sector-leader of a parcel of demons; how can I be expected to dance homage to him?"

King Yama, hearing himself spoken of in this insulting way, hung his head, ashamed to look Hell in the face, humiliated in the presence of all his officials. Scowling angrily he ordered those about him....

(There are now gaps in the text; but it appears that King Yama orders the case to be enquired into by the Assessor Cui Ziyu, so famous in Chinese legend.)

When the Emperor reached the gate of the courtyard, the escort said to him, "I must trouble your Majesty to wait here for a little, while I go in and announce to the Assessor that you are here. I'll be back in a minute." The escort went to the Assessor's office and, bowing low, announced that in accordance with the Great King's orders he had brought the living wraith of the Emperor Taizong to be put on trial by the Assessor. "He is outside the door," said the escort. "I did not venture to bring him in." When Cui Ziyu heard this, he hurriedly rose to his feet and muttering, "This is most unfortunate!" he added, "I am a subject of the Emperor's and as such I ought to have gone a long way to welcome him; instead of which I have kept a lord of men waiting outside the gate! This is an act of gross impoliteness on the part of a minor official like myself. Moreover, in the living world I am clerk in the town of Fuyang. My household consists of more than five hundred persons and all of us have a horse to ride and meat to eat, a state of affairs we owe entirely to his Majesty's bounty. But now owing to my having this post in the Underworld I am neglecting my governmental duties at Fuyang. If on looking into his Majesty's record I find that his span of life is at an end, there is no more to say. But if it turns out that he still has some years to live, and goes back to reign at Chang'an, those five hundred and more members of my household will have to change over to a fish diet, and that will all be the result of my rudeness on this occasion to his Majesty in my capacity of Assessor in the World Below." Cui Ziyu continued to be very worried about this.

Meanwhile the Emperor, seeing that his escort was a long time before coming out to fetch him, thought to himself, "Perhaps he is telling the Assessor about various wicked deeds of mine." So the Emperor, too, could not help being very worried. Now however Cui Ziyu hastened to ask for his official dress and tablet and, going to his office, tried to compose himself. After a while he came running out to where the Emperor was waiting, himself announcing his name and rank. When he reached the Emperor he did the dance of homage before him, crying, "May your Majesty live ten thousand years!" and, crawling toward him with his face on the ground, awaited the Emperor's commands. "It seems then that you who are doing homage to me are Cui Ziyu, the clerk of

Fuyang. Is that so? — I give you leave to interview me without standing on ceremony, in an ordinary posture."

The Emperor now remembered the letter that he was carrying in his bosom, and he said to Cui Ziyu, "I believe that you knew Li Qianfeng at Court. Is not that so?" "Yes," said Cui Ziyu, "from the time we began to be at Court together we were like Guan and Bao."[3] "That is to say, very close friends indeed," observed the Emperor. "He gave me a letter for you. I've got it here." When Cui Ziyu heard there was a letter for him, he did not seem best pleased. The Emperor then took the letter and gave it to Cui Ziyu, who knelt to receive it and did a dance of homage to thank the Emperor. But instead of reading it, he put it in the folds of his dress. "Why don't you read the letter?" the Emperor asked. "I am low in rank," replied Cui Ziyu. "It would be a breach of Court etiquette if I were to read it in your Majesty's presence." "But I gave you leave not to stand on ceremony," said the Emperor. "I have no objection to your reading it." Having received this command and bowed, Cui Ziyu in the Emperor's presence opened the letter and read it. What he read so much agitated him that he abandoned all the etiquette belonging to a subject in the presence of his ruler, and looking afar towards Chang'an he said, "Li Qianfeng! It is true that we served together at Court. But does that give you the right to demand things of this sort from me?"

When the Emperor heard him say this, he felt as though the ground had been withdrawn from under his feet, and very humbly, with soft words, he asked Cui Ziyu, "Is there any chance of your being able to do what the letter suggests? Please, tell me at once, so as to put my mind at rest." "There's nothing impossible about it," said Cui Ziyu, "but under the circumstances it might be rather difficult." When the Emperor heard that it might be "rather difficult," his spirits fell. "You have had me brought here under arrest," he said, "and I am entirely at your disposition. But the Crown Prince is very young and important points of policy have to be settled. I don't expect to be allowed to return to life for very long. But if you could allow me three or even five days at Chang'an, it would give me time to leave instructions about State affairs and about the Crown Prince, and it would still not be too late for me to come and report here." When he spoke of the Crown Prince the Emperor wept floods of tears. When Cui Ziyu saw how upset he was, he said, "Your Majesty may put your mind at rest. Come with me, and we will discuss terms."

---

[3] Guan Yiwu and Bao Shuya were statesmen of the 7th century B.C., whose deep friendship was famous.

The Emperor, as desired by Cui Ziyu, then followed him, and once inside the screen-wall he saw that on the east side there were more than twenty offices. In No. 6 office there were two men wailing. "What are they so unhappy about?" asked the Emperor. "Who else should they be," replied Cui Ziyu, "but the two princes Jiancheng and Yuanji?"[4] "If you had not brought me here," said the Emperor, "I should never have had a chance to see my brothers!" "Since they've been here," replied Cui Ziyu, "the two princes have been constantly sending in statements about you, demanding that you should be brought here for trial. They feel they have been deeply wronged and their complaints are worded in the most bitter terms. It was to meet these charges that you were sent for. If you keep away from the princes, I may be able to find some way of arranging matters for you fairly well; but if you insist on going into that office and meeting them, you will be face to face with your accusers, and even I will not be able to save you. In that case you will certainly not be able to get back to Chang'an. Your Majesty had better not even go and look at them; it would be far safer not to." When the Emperor heard this, he did not dare insist, but hurried on to the Assessor's office and took a seat there. Cui Ziyu did not go in, but stood on the steps, calling for the heads of the six offices to come and pay their respects. After they had bowed and enquired after the Emperor's health, they bowed again and retired. "Who were those people?" asked the Emperor. "Why did they bow to me in front of your office?" "They are the heads of the six offices," said Cui Ziyu. "In the World of the Living," said Cui Ziyu, "there are people called 'the heads of the six offices' and in the World of the Dead they have the same name." "Why don't you come up into your office," said the Emperor, "and keep me company?" "I am too low in rank," said Cui Ziyu. "It would not be fitting for me to sit with you in the same office." "When you were in Chang'an," said the Emperor, "you held a low rank. But here in the Court of the Dead it is quite otherwise, and there is no reason you should not come up." Cui Ziyu bowed and, coming up into the office, took a seat.

(The text here becomes fragmentary, but it is evident that the Two Boys, who record good and evil deeds, are sent for.)

Cui Ziyu asked the boy who records good deeds, "What good deeds did his Majesty do when he was in Chang'an?" The boy pressed together the palms of his hands and said, "It does not appear that at Chang'an he did any good deeds. He certainly did not have any *sutras* copied or any images painted...."

---

[4] Murdered by Taizong in 626 in order to clear his path to the throne.

(Two incomplete lines follow, and the text then breaks off. The second portion, after an incomplete line, goes on with words spoken by Cui to the Emperor.)

"The three rolls of writing here on my desk contain the facts about your Majesty's life-span and fortunes. If you want me to go through them for you and make changes, I must have your authority for doing so." "Do as you propose," said the Emperor. "Make any changes for me that you think desirable." Cui Ziyu returned to his seat and began to examine the documents.

He ... and then added the minute "Ten years as Emperor; to go back again to the World of the Living." But when he had given the Emperor this extra span, he thought to himself, "My rank in the Living World is so low that if the Emperor had not been brought for trial here, I should never have set eyes on him. I ought to avail myself of this opportunity to get from him a post in the Government." So he ... his tablet and said, "I have made the necessary changes in your Majesty's papers." "To what effect?" said the Emperor. "Do tell me at once." But Cui Ziyu again thought to himself, "I had better not tell him at once that I have put in 'To be Emperor for ten years,' for if he doesn't in return give me what I've set my heart on, I shall have no remedy. I had better pitch it lower than that, and tell him 'three years' or 'five years'." So he said to the Emperor, "Your humble servant is deeply indebted to your Majesty for coming here in person, and as a small return he has altered the record of your destiny to five further years and a return to the World of Life." "If I do succeed in reaching the city of Chang'an," said the Emperor, "all the things sent as tribute to my Palace shall be yours." Cui Ziyu again thought to himself, "I've allowed him five years, and this has only led to his giving me money and precious things. If I were to allow him another five years, I should surely get a government post out of him." "I have already marked you as returning to the Living World for five years," he said. "Li Qianfeng is, as you know, a great friend of mine and he gave you a letter to bring to me, urgently requesting me to do what I could for you. For his sake I will give you another five years, making ten in all, which you will be able to spend in Chang'an city." The Emperor, hearing this, said to Cui Ziyu, "I really feel ashamed that you should have the trouble of keeping on making these alterations. If I get to Chang'an city, I assure you I'll give you all the things that are sent to me as tribute."

Cui Ziyu again thought to himself, "That's the second time he has only offered me money and precious things. Not a word about any official post! He's evidently very mean about official posts." For a long time he remained silent. Presently the Emperor said, "When you were talking to me just now, you spoke of my returning to the Living World. If I return to

Chang'an I shall take you with me, and you must come and pay your respects to me at Court." "Certainly I will do so," said Cui Ziyu. "When are you going to let me start?" asked the Emperor. "Your Majesty will first have to draw up a document to be kept in the files," said Cui Ziyu. "When I was alive," said the Emperor, "I never learnt how to draw up documents. How does one do it?" Cui Ziyu thought to himself, "If I don't bully him a bit, I shall never be able to get an official post out of him." "If your Majesty does not know how to draw up official documents, I've got a written question here. If you can answer it, there is no reason you shouldn't start for Chang'an at once; but if you can't answer it, it won't be possible to send you back to the World of the Living." When the Emperor heard this he was very frightened, and he entreated Cui Ziyu to give him an easy question. "I won't forget you kindness, if you do," he said.

Cui Ziyu, his heart set on getting a job, asked for paper and when he had dutifully bowed to the Emperor he set to work to write out the following question: "His Majesty Taizong, Emperor of Tang, is asked why, in the seventh year of Wu-de, he slew his brothers in front of the Palace and imprisoned his loving father in the women's apartments? An answer is requested!" He handed the paper to the Emperor who took it and read it. He was very much upset and his heart pounded as though hammered with a pestle. He threw the question-paper to the ground saying, "This question that you have set me is one I can't possibly answer!" Seeing how upset he was Cui Ziyu took the question-paper back and said, "If your Majesty can't answer it, would you perhaps allow me to answer it for you?" On hearing this the Emperor was much relieved. Great joy spread over the dragon-countenance. "Pray do as you suggest," he said. "If I answer this for you," said Cui Ziyu, "I shall certainly expect your Majesty to open your mouth wide." "You promise to answer for me and also tell me to open my mouth wide," said the Emperor. "What are you going to put into it?" "Not *that* kind of opening the mouth wide," said Cui. "What I mean is that in the Living World my rank is low; I am only Clerk at Fuyang. What I hoped was that your Majesty would bestow on me 'enough land for one foot to tread upon,' and I shall be eternally grateful." "What government post is it that you want?" asked the Emperor. "I do wish you had mentioned this before! Where does your family come from?" he continued. "I am a Puzhou man," said Cui Ziyu. "Very well then," said the Emperor. "I appoint you Governor of Puzhou and concurrently Investigating Commissioner of the twenty-four districts of Hebei, with the rank of Senior Censor and the right to wear the purple and gold fish-bag. In addition to this I bestow upon you twenty thousand strings of cash, to be paid by the treasury at Fuyang to provide for your household." Having at last been promised official rank Cui Ziyu did the dance of homage below the dais of the office in order to express his thanks to the Emperor, and then coming up on to the dais, took a seat there. While he was conversing with the Emperor, it was announced that an envoy from the office of the Heavenly Tally had arrived from Chang'an. "What have you come for?" asked Cui Ziyu. "I have come to inform you," said the envoy, "that you are appointed Governor of Puzhou and concurrently Investigating Commissioner of the twenty-four districts of Hebei, with the rank of Senior Censor and the right to wear the purple and gold fish-bag. In addition to this you are to receive twenty thousand strings of cash, to be paid by the treasury at Fuyang, to provide for your household. Issued today by the office of the Heavenly Tally, for the attention of Cui Ziyu." "Well, they didn't take long hearing about it at the office of the Heavenly Tally," said the Emperor. "I have always heard that 'appointments made in the Realm of the Dead take effect in the Land of the Living.' It seems it really is so."

The answer that Cui Ziyu framed for the Emperor consisted only of these words: "A great Sage will exterminate a family in order to save a kingdom." When Cui Ziyu had written this out the Emperor was uncommonly pleased. Having shown his answer to the Emperor, Cui Ziyu took it back, and then said, "When you get to Chang'an you must do good works; for example send out envoys galloping to every quarter of the Empire announcing an amnesty, and also order the director of the monasteries in the quarter to the west of the high road leading to the Red Sparrow Gate to have the *Great Cloud Sutra* expounded in public. And your Majesty should at your own expense have copies of this *sutra* made."

Cui Ziyu then, at the Emperor's request, fetched paper and wrote out a list of the good works the Emperor was to perform. When it was ready, the Emperor took the list and put it into the folds of his dress. Then he said to Cui Ziyu, "I feel absolutely famished. How could I get something to eat?" "If your Majesty is hungry," said Cui Ziyu, "I will get you some food."

Cui Ziyu then gave orders to those about him....

(Here the manuscript breaks off.)

The Quest of Mulian or
The Great Maudgalyāyana Rescues His Mother from Hell

Translated by Eugene Eoyang

Among the Dunhuang *bianwen* ("transformation texts"), an important position is occupied by the various versions (at least eight) of the tale of Maudgalyāyana (Mulian

Figure 64. Tortures of the Buddhist Hell. Traditional illustration. (Source: C.A.S. Williams, *Encyclopedia of Chinese Symbolism and Art Motives* [Shanghai: Kelly & Walsh, 1932])

in Chinese), the disciple of the Buddha who searches through all the hells to find his sinful mother and save her from her tortures. This translation is made from the version known as P2319, kept in the Bibliothèque Nationale in Paris. (It is so numbered because it was among the many manuscripts taken to Paris by Paul Pelliot in 1908.)

During his wanderings through the hells, Mulian, filial to the point of naïveté, refuses to believe that his mother has committed any sins. His journey takes him through numerous chambers and compounds, before the storyteller presents the final confrontation between the pious son and impious mother. Mulian's purpose is to redeem his mother, but as he descends into hell he is moved by the sorrowful sight of the condemned, and his quest is thus instrumental in bringing about the eventual salvation of many a pitiful soul on the River of Futility.

Now on the fifteenth day of the seventh month, the heavens open up, the gates of hell swing wide, the karma of the Three Paths of Pain[5] is dissolved, and the Ten Commandments[6] overflow. The assembly of monks, the *sangha*, has set down this date as a holy day of thanksgiving,

---

[5] They are the Hell of Fires, the Hell of Blood, and the Hell of Swords.

[6] Against killing, stealing, adultery, lying, speaking with a double tongue, slandering, filthy language, covetousness, anger, and perverted views.

and so the eight classes of supernatural beings[7] all come to observe this occasion. The assembly makes offerings of its worldly goods so that those who have passed away may change their fate and improve their lot. For this reason, on the Avalamba Festival[8] we offer up a hundred tasty sacrifices to the Honorable Triad[9] in supplication for divine mercy on the entire congregation, and first to rescue those who hang upside down from their distress.[10]

Long ago, when Buddha lived in this world, he had a disciple, Mulian,[11] whose secular name, before he joined the order, was Luobu, or Turnip. Mulian was deeply committed to the Three Treasures,[12] and revered the Greater Vehicle, the Mahāyāna.[13] Once he wanted to go to another country for new adventures, so he divided up his worldly possessions. He instructed his mother to initiate offerings, and to supply provisions to wandering Buddhist monks as well as any other mendicants who came by. But after Turnip left, his mother became stingy and selfish, and the wealth which had been entrusted to her was secretly hidden away. Her son, in the course of time, completed his travels and returned home. The mother told the son, "I have, as you instructed, given alms and built up our blessings." And so, because she had deceived both the

---

[7] They are the eight classes of supernatural beings mentioned in the *Lotus Sutra: deva* (celestial spirits), *nāga* (dragons), *yaksha* (demons in earth, air, and hell), *gandharva* (musicians of the Shakra heaven — one of the eight heavens), *asura* (war demons), *garuda* (mythical birds), *kinnara* (musicians with men's bodies and horses' heads), and *mahoraga* (demons shaped like the boa).

[8] This is the festival of All Souls (*Yulan pen* in Chinese), when prayer services are said by Buddhist monks and Taoist priests and elaborate offerings are made to the Buddhist triad for the purpose of releasing from the purgatory the souls of those who have died on land and sea.

[9] The Buddha, the Law, and the Ecclesia [*sangha*].

[10] Hanging upside down refers to the condition of certain condemned souls, especially those for whom the Festival of Avalamba is held.

[11] Maudgalyāyana (or Mahā-Maudgalyāyana, or Maudgalaputra), noted for his miraculous powers, was one of the ten disciples of Shākyamuni, the principal Buddha. Formerly an ascetic, Maudgalyāyana agreed with Shāriputra, another major disciple of the Buddha known for his wisdom and learning, that whoever first found the truth would reveal it to the other. In Buddhist iconography, Shāriputra appears on Buddha's right, Maudgalyāyana on his left.

[12] Same as the Buddhist triad.

[13] The Mahāyāna school is one of the main traditions of Buddhism. It is now made up of various syncretistic sects found chiefly in Tibet, Nepal, China, and Japan. Emphasis is placed on compassion, universal salvation, enlightenment, and wisdom.

secular and the holy community, when she died she dropped straight away down to the Avīchi Hell[14] to suffer innumerable tortures.

Turnip, after three years of mourning, offered himself to the service of Buddha, was admitted into the holy order, and devoted himself to religious practices. By obeying the Law, he attained the blessed state of an arhat in the end.[15] Then, with his transcendent eyes, he looked all over for his dear mother, but in all the six realms of life and death,[16] there was no trace of her. Mulian consulted the World-Honored One, the Buddha: "Where is my good mother enjoying eternal bliss?"

To this, the World-Honored One answered Mulian, "Your mother has already descended down to the Avichi Hell, where she is suffering innumerable tortures. Although you've attained the heights of arhatship, what can you do? Only the efforts of the assembled monks from all directions[17] on the day of the summer sacrifices, with their cumulative strength, can save her. This is why the Buddha, in his compassion, instituted this means, and established the Festival of the Avalamba especially for this purpose."

Turnip from the time his parents died
Mourned three years until the obligation was over.
To hear music and not rejoice spoils one's appearance;
To eat delicacies and not find them tasty is bad for flesh and bone.
It is said that the Tathāgata, the Buddha, when he was
    in the Deer Park,[18]
Took pity at once on all the people of the world.
Today, I search for the Way in order to find the Tathāgata,
And go to the Twin Grove[19] to ask the Buddha. *Yun, yun* ...[20]

---

[14] The Avīchi Hell, the last and deepest of the eight hot hells (vs. the eight cold hells), is the place where the condemned go through endless cycles of suffering, death, and rebirth without intermission.

[15] An arhat is one who has acquired transcendent powers over nature, matter, time, and space. Arhatship is to be succeeded either by buddhahood or by immediate entrance into nirvāna (the state of perfect freedom and the absorption of the individual into the supreme spirit).

[16] These represent the six directions of reincarnation, i.e., three upper forms (the spirits of heaven, men, and awesome demons), and three lower forms (animals, hungry ghosts, and denizens of hell).

[17] The text reads "the ten directions," which include the four cardinal and the four intercardinal directions as well as "up" and "down."

[18] The Deer Park, the site of the Buddha's famous first sermon, was a retreat of the wise.

[19] The sāl trees under which the Buddha entered nirvāna.

[20] *Yun, yun* in Chinese is a formula used in the text to indicate either an opportunity for further elaboration or an omission.

On the day when Mulian went to the trees in the Twin Grove, he had already become an arhat. How did this come about? Truly the *Lotus Sūtra* says, "The prodigal son first accepts the value, then is cleansed of impurity." This is it. First one attains arhatship, then one follows the Way. Look at Mulian, sitting deep in the mountains in attitudes of meditation! His father was living in Devapura.[21]

> Mulian cut off his hair, shaved his beard,
> And thereupon went deep into the mountains.
> Dark and deep, where it was quiet, with no one around.
> There he sat down, facing the void, in meditation, etc., etc....
> From the moment Mulian emerged from meditation,
> He quickly achieved supernatural power.
> He came as suddenly as a clap of thunder,
> And went away like the whirlwind....
> With the supernatural status, he achieved spontaneity;
> Throwing his magical begging bowl in the sky, he leaped into
> heaven.
> In almost no time, he went
> All the way up to the realm of Brahmā.[22] *Yun, yun* ...

Mulian went to Devapura to look for his father. At one gate, he met an old man, to whom he said, "I, a poor monk, was named Turnip when I was young. After my parents passed away, I left home and entered the order of Buddha, cutting off my hair and shaving my beard. I'm now known as Mulian, and I'm well known for my supernatural power."

When the old man was told Mulian's childhood name, he knew that he was his son. "It's been so long since we last saw each other. How have you been?"

Turnip, or Mulian, recognized his good father and, after inquiring as to his welfare, asked, "And my good mother, where is she now receiving the rewards of happiness?"

"Your mother's karma," the old man answered, "while she lived, was different from mine. I observed the Ten Commandments, and obeyed the Five Prohibitions,[23] and so when I died my spirit lived on in heaven. But your mother, all the days of her life, committed numerous sins; so

---

[21] Devapura (or Devaloka) is the palace of the devas (the heavenly beings) and the abode of the gods.
[22] Brahmā is the Supreme Being, the father of all living beings.
[23] The first five of the Ten Commandments.

when she died, she dropped down to hell. Ask around for your mother in the dark alleys of Jambudvīpa."[24]

After hearing this, Mulian said farewell to his father and descended from heaven. But he was unable to find his mother. Instead, he saw eight or nine men and women who were wandering around with nothing to do. Mulian stepped forward and asked their business and where they came from:

"No, no! Don't bow toward me.
Good souls, who are you?
Why are you all milling around here,
Wandering about with nothing to do?"

They replied, telling the monk:

"It's only because we have the same surnames and given names,
That our names were confused, and we were summoned here.
We wandered around for a few days.
Proven innocent, we were released, and then went home,
But we had been buried prematurely by our families....
To moan and bewail our fate does no good in the end....
Please go to tell the men and women in our families,
Tell them to perform good works to save the dead
        from misfortune." *Yun, yun ...*

Mulian remained silent for a while, and then he said, "Do you know a certain Lady Qingti?"

"No one among us knows her," they replied.

"Where does Yama, the King of the Dead, live?" Mulian then asked.

"Your Reverence," they answered, "go north several steps further, and you'll see in the distance a triple-layered gate, guarded by thousands of strong men, all wielding swords and staffs. This is the gate of the Yama King."

Mulian, upon hearing this, went north several paces and then saw the triple-layered gate, where the strong men were herding and prodding numberless sinners and driving them in. Mulian went forward looking for his mother and, not being able to find her, he stood by the side of the road and cried loudly. Afterward he dried his tears and proceeded forward. After explaining why he was there, he was permitted an

---

[24] Jambudvīpa is the southern one of the four continents which, according to Indian mythology, comprise the world.

audience with the King. The gatekeeper let him in to see the King, who asked him to state his business.

> When the King saw Mulian come in,
> He clasped his hands, shrank back, and was about to stand.
> "Your Reverence, how can you have any business here?"
> Then, hastily behind the desks, the two bowed
>   to each other. *Yun, yun* ...

When Mulian had finished, the King called him up the dais to meet the Bodhisattva Kshitigarbha,[25] and Mulian paid his respects.

"You've come to look for your mother?"

"Yes, I've come to look for my mother."

"Your mother committed many sins when she was alive; she was completely and utterly evil, and must have dropped down to hell. You just go on, I'll be there right away."

The King then summoned the Keeper of Karma, the Commissioner of Fate, and the Custodian of Records, who all responded immediately and came before him.

"This monk's mother is Lady Qingti. How long ago did she die?"

"Your Majesty," the Keeper of Karma said, "Lady Qingti has already been dead now for three years. The record of her penance is filed with the Recorder of the Heavenly Court as well as the Commandant of the Tai Mountains."[26] The King summoned the two boys who respectively record good and evil deeds and sent them to the Tai Mountains to check out which hell Lady Qingti was in. The King added, "Your Reverence, you'd better go along with these two boys, and ask the General of the Five Ways.[27] He should know where she's gone."

When Mulian heard this, he took his leave of the King and went on. Before he had gone but a few steps, he came upon the River of Futility.[28] There he saw countless sinners who had doffed their clothes and hung them up on the trees, crying over and over again in loud lament, wanting

---

[25] Kshitigarbha, one of a group of eight Dhyāni or Meditation Bodhisattvas, is the savior of lost souls and the deliverer from hell.

[26] Since the Han period, the worship of the Tai Mountains was combined with the Buddhist concept of hell, and the god of the Tai Mountains was the counterpart of the Yama King on earth; hence it is his line of duty to administer matters concerning life, death, reincarnation, the government of men and spirits.

[27] He is a general in the retinue of the ten kings of the underworld responsible for keeping the book of life. After the Song period, this term is used to designate five individual spirits who were bandits in their former existence.

[28] This is the river in purgatory, to be crossed by all souls.

to cross the river but unable to, pacing back and forth, at sixes and
sevens, holding their heads and sobbing. Mulian asked them what had
happened:

"The waters of Futility rush toward the west;
Shattered rock, jagged cliffs — the way is rough.
Clothes taken off and hung on three branches;
We have not been transferred, and must stay here.
By the riverbank we ask that our names be called;
Without our knowing it, our chests are soaked through.
Only today we've come to realize what death means.
Two by two, under the trees, our tears of grief stream down....
Oxhead demons, staffs in hand, on the southern bank;
Hell's guardians, wielding tridents, on the northern shore.
The eyes of those in the water bulge out;
The tears of those on the riverbank gush forth.
Had we known how bitter death would be,
How would we not have cultivated good deeds in life!"

Mulian then asked those who stood under the trees by the River of
Futility:

"So heaven and hell are no fairy tale!
For those who sin and do not care, comes the punishment of
    heaven....
I had a mother without much merit.
Her departed soul, therefore, dropped down here to the Three
    Paths;
After hearing this, I've ventured to come down to hell.
Tell me if you have any news of her."

The sinners all looked at Master Mulian, all weeping and sobbing till
their eyes were sore:

"We have been dead only a very short time;
Your mother, good monk, we really don't know.
In life we all committed many sins;
Only in suffering today do we begin to repent.
You may have wives and concubines by the droves,
But who would be willing to die in your stead?
When you have departed from these depths,
Please report this to our sons and grandsons:
'Never mind the white jade for our coffins;
In vain, the yellow gold buried in our tombs.

Persistent mourning, signs of sorrow are of no use,
And tabor music, stringed dirges, we can't hear.
If you want to end our torment and suffering,
Nothing is better than works of charity to save lost souls.'"

"Your Reverence, please pass on the message for us, asking them to do more works of charity in order to save the deceased. Aside from the Buddha himself, no one is able to save us. Good monk, may the boat of your perfect wisdom and the boat of perfect freedom constantly appear to deliver all living beings. May the sword of wisdom be constantly sharpened, and the grove of worries be cut down, that majesty may spread to all the hearts of the world. Thus will the ideal of all the Buddhas be fulfilled. If we are to be delivered from the mire and the mud, this is indeed due to your great benevolence."

Mulian, after making inquiries, again went on. In a short while, he arrived at the place of the General of the Five Ways. There he asked for news of his mother:

The General of the Five Ways had a hateful mien;
His gold armor glimmered and his sword dazzled,
Intimidating millions of souls around him —
All took flight on their hands and feet.
His roar sounded like thundering earthquake;
His angry eyes flashed like blinding light.
Some had their chests cut open, their hearts exposed;
Others had the skins of their faces peeled.
Although Mulian was a sage,
He was scared to death....
The General clasped his hands and said to the monk:
"Don't let tears spoil your appearance;
Those who come this way are as many as the sands in the Ganges.
If I ask them about Lady Qingti, who may know
        the answer?" *Yun, yun* ...

"Have any of you seen Lady Qingti?" the General asked those around him.

From the left, a chief officer answered, "General, three years ago, there was a certain Lady Qingti whose name was inscribed on the tablets of the Avīchi Hell. Now she is suffering there."

Mulian, upon hearing this, said to the General, "Would you please tell me, although all sinners receive judgment from the Yama King before they are sent down here, why my mother has never been brought before the King?"

"Good monk," the General replied, "there are two kinds of people in the world who are not allowed an audience with the King. One includes those who have observed the Ten Commandments and the Five Prohibitions — these don't have to meet the King after their death, for their spirits will live on in heaven. The second category includes those who in their lives did not practice good deeds, but gave themselves to evil karma, so that when they die, they are sent forthwith into hell. They also do not see the King. Only those who are half good and half evil get to see the King to have their fate judged. They will first go through reincarnation, and then they will be rewarded or punished according to what they deserve."

After Mulian had heard this, he started to search through the various hells for his mother.

Mulian's tears flowed as he thought of the past;
The fate of all creatures seemed tossed on the wind.
His good mother came to death's vale of suffering;
Her spirit had long been wasted away. *Yun, yun …*

When Mulian had finished, he moved on, and in a wink, he reached one of the hells. Mulian inquired of the guardian, "Does this prison have a Lady Qingti or not? She is my mother, and I have come looking for her."

"Your Reverence," the guardian replied, "this prison is full of men; there are no women here. A little further ahead, there is the Asipattra Hell of Swords. If you ask there, you will, no doubt, be able to see her."

Mulian went on, and came upon another hell; the left side was called the Mountain of Knives, and the right, the Forest of Swords. In this hell, the tips of swords were locked in confrontation, with blood dripping down from them. There Mulian saw the guardian pushing countless sinners into this hell.

"What is this hell?" Mulian asked.

"This is the Asipattra Hell of Swords," a raksha demon replied.

"What sins have been committed by the sinners here that they should be in this hell?" Mulian then asked.

"These sinners," the guardian said, "when they were alive, violated the temples, defiled the monasteries, and were fond of picking the fruits of the temples and stealing firewood and kindling from the temples. Now let them attempt to pull the sword trees with their hands; see if their limbs and joints can stay together."

The Mountain of Knives, bleached bones strewn in profusion;
The Forest of Swords, human heads by the millions.

> If you want to put an end to the sinners' climbing
>   the Mountain of Knives,
> The best way is to cultivate the temple grounds.
> Plant fruit trees within the monastery walls,
> Liberally sow seedlings to grace the temple.
> Of course, you can't give pleasure to these sinners,
> Who will forever suffer torments numberless as the sands
>   of Ganges....
> Bronze-tipped arrows whizz straight into the eye —
> Mountain of Knives, Forest of Swords, cut them down.
> They cannot return to life in a thousand years,
> But they still must suffer incessantly in the jungle
>   of iron knives and swords.

Mulian, when he heard this, broke down in tears and went forward to ask the guardian, "In this hell, is there a Lady Qingti?"

"Good monk, is she related to you?"

"She's my mother."

"Your Reverence," the guardian then replied, "in this hell there's no Lady Qingti, but if you go a little further, there is a hell which is only for women. You should get to see her there."

Mulian, on hearing this, went on ahead until he reached a hell that was a *yōjana* high from top to bottom, with black smoke gushing up from it,[29] and a stench that fouled the sky. He came upon a horse-headed raksha demon with an iron staff in his hand, standing there looking haughtily.

"What's the name of this hell?" Mulian asked.

"This is the Hell of Bronze Pillars and Iron Beds," the raksha replied.

"What sins did these poor souls commit in life that they should have dropped down to this hell?"

"In life," the guardian replied, "girls who seduced boys, boys who seduced girls, as well as parents and children who had incestuous relations, teachers and students who had affairs, and masters and servants who had liaisons — they have all dropped down into this hell, where the east is separated from the west, and men and women each occupy one division."

---

[29] *Yōjana* was a rather ambiguous unit of measurement. It has been described as the distance covered by a day's march of an army, and as forty, thirty, or sixteen *li*, and as eight *kroshas* (four *kroshas* being equivalent to nearly thirty *li*). [Compare chapter 14, note 21.]

The women lie on the iron beds, their bodies nailed down:
The men are wrapped around the bronze pillars to rot....
The knives cut bone and flesh, pierce right through;
The swords cut liver and gall into little pieces....
Their parents, if still alive, are building up blessings for them,
But only one out of seven may be saved.
Even should the Eastern Sea turn into a mulberry field:
The sinners will have yet to be released. *Yun, yun ...*

When Mulian finished his inquiries, he went on ahead. In a twinkling of an eye, he was at another hell. There, he asked the guardian, "Does this place have a Lady Qingti in it?"

"Good monk," the guardian said, "is Lady Qingti your mother?"

"Yes, she's my mother."

"Three years ago, there was a Lady Qingti who was among those who dropped down here, but she was put on the roster for the Avīchi Hell. So now she is over there."

Mulian fainted for a moment. He resumed his normal breath after a long while, and then slowly went on ahead. Then he ran into a raksha demon, who guarded the way. Mulian questioned him and the raksha replied:

"It appears we have a Lady Qingti here,
Though I can't completely confirm that report....
Bodies of new arrivals are strewn about.
Please take my advice and go back home.
To look for someone here is to look in vain.
You'd better go quickly to see the Tathāgata;
What use is there in beating your breast in despair?"

After Mulian learned of all these obstacles in the various hells, he immediately turned back. Then, sailing up with his magic begging bowl, in a wink, he was in the Grove of Brahma, where he circled the Buddha three times before sitting down in front of him. He looked up in reverence at the honored visage, his eyes not wavering. He spoke to the World-Honored One:

It has been so long since I received instructions from the Tathāgata;[30]
Throughout heaven and earth, I have constantly searched.
Only my father has been able to live in heaven,

---

[30] This term means literally "One who has come to Truth," or "One who has discovered Truth." It refers to the Buddha. *Eds.*

But my mother I have been unable to meet face-to-face.
When I heard she was suffering torments in the Avīchi Hell,
The mere thought tore at my entrails.
Raging fires, dragon serpents obstructed my progress:
In my consternation, I could think of no other way.
The Tathāgata's holy power moves mountains and oceans.
All living creatures benefit from his benevolence.
So I have hurried here to have you explain
How mother and son can meet once again."

The World-Honored One comforted the Mulian:

"Now, please, stop your tears of grief.
The sins of the world are drawn out like string:
They are not stuck on from the outside.
Someone hurry to bring him my abbot's staff;
It can ward off the Eight Obstacles,[31] the Three Calamities.[32]
As often as possible, chant my name;
All the hells should be accessible to you."

Mulian assumed the Buddha's power, soared away, and went down as fast as a windborne arrow. In a wink, he reached the Avīchi Hell. Even as he was passing through in the sky, he saw fifty ox-headed, horse-brained rakshas and yakshas, with teeth like jagged stumps, mouths like bowls of blood, voices like thunderclaps, eyes like flashes of lightning, on their way to heaven to report for duty. When they encountered Mulian, they yelled at him from afar: "Good monk! Don't come to these regions. This is not a good place to come to. This is the road to hell. In the west, there is black smoke full of hell's poisonous vapors; if you inhale it, Your Reverence, here and now you will turn to ashes and dust."

"Good monk, have you not heard about the Avīchi Hell?
Even iron and rock, in passing through it, will not be spared.
Where is the hell one speaks of?
Toward the west, black fumes spurt forth over there."

---

[31] This term refers to the eight conditions in which it is difficult for someone to see the Buddha or to hear his Dharma (Law) — in the hells: as hungry ghosts; as animals; in Utarakuru (the northern continent where all is pleasant); in the long-life heavens; as deaf, blind, and dumb: as a philosopher on earth; in the intermediate period between a Buddha and his successor.

[32] There are two kinds of calamities. The minor three calamities, appearing during a decadent period in the world, are war, pestilence, and famine; the major ones, for the destruction of the world, are fire, water, and wind.

Mulian chanted Buddha's name countless times:

"Hell was once my domain."
Then he wiped his tears and shook the staff in the air,
And all the demons fell like puffballs on the spot.
Sweat poured out like moisture from rainfall;
Bewildered, hardly conscious, they could not help but sigh.
Three-pronged halberds dropped from their hands;
Six-pointed pitchforks flew out of their arms.
"Buddha has sent me to see my mother,
To save her from the calamities of the Avīchi Hell."
Mulian did not stay still, but soared right over;
The lictors of hell looked, but dared not block his way.

Mulian went on ahead until he reached another part of the Avīchi hell. When he was about one hundred steps away, he was so overcome by fire and smoke that he almost fainted away. This Avīchi Hell had iron walls that were high and steep, so tall that they almost touched the sky. The horrors within were beyond description. All of the lictors were oxheads and horsefaces. Even hearts of iron and stone would quake with fear and lose their souls.

Mulian, holding his staff, moved forward to listen,
To learn something about the Avīchi Hell.
In most hells there would normally be some rest,
But in this Avīchi Hell, there was no such respite....
Suddenly, they spied the monk standing there;
Moreover, they had never made his acquaintance.
Certainly no one person could be held to account,
Only the merciful power of the Three Treasures.

"Good monk," the guardian of this hell asked, "what business do you have here that you should open the gates of hell?"

"The World-Honored One gave me the means to open them."

"What did he give you to open them with?"

"He gave me his twelve-ringed abbot's staff to open the gates."

"Good monk," the lictors, too, asked, "what is your reason for coming here?"

"My mother is named Lady Qingti," Mulian replied, "and I have come to look for her."

When the guardian heard this, he went up to a high tower in the compound of hell, raised a white flag, and beat on an iron drum. "Is there a Lady Qingti in the first cell?"

No answer from the first.

He went to the second cell, then to the third, the fourth, the fifth, and the sixth — and each time the answer was no. The lictors went to the seventh cell and saw Lady Qingti nailed down on a platform with forty-nine spikes, and called out, "Are you Lady Qingti?"

"Yes," she said.

Then the guardian told her, "There's a monk outside who claims to be your son."

Qingti, when she heard this, replied, "Guardian, I have no son who is a monk. He must be mistaken."

When the guardian heard this, he returned to the high tower to report: "Your Reverence, how could you have made such an error, thinking that sinner in the hell to be your mother? What's the reason for this nonsense?"

Mulian, when he heard this, broke down in tears. He told the guardian, "I was called Turnip when I was small. After my parents passed away, I entered the order of Buddha and became a monk, assuming the name of Mulian. I beg you, do not be angry. Go back once more and make the inquiry."

When the guardian heard this, he went back to the sinner: "The monk outside claims his name was Turnip when he was small."

"If he was called Turnip as a child," Qingti said, "then he is my son, my precious offspring, this sinner's own flesh and blood!"

Hearing this, the guardian helped lift Qingti up, drawing out the forty-nine spikes, tied iron chains around her waist, put shackles on her, and drove her to outside the gate. This was how the mother and the son met.

> The shackles around her, bristled with pricks like fish scales.
> A thousand years of punishment that cannot be imagined.
> From the seven apertures in her head, blood spurted forth;
> Fire flared out from the woman's mouth....
> Oxheads held the cangue on both sides;
> Stepping and stumbling, she came forward.
> Mulian embraced his mother, bursting into tears,
> And crying: "This comes from my not being a devoted son!"
>   *Yun, yun ...*

His mother was then driven back into the cell. When Mulian saw his mother go back in, his bones snapped, his heart broke, and he choked on his sobs. Then he stood up and beat his breast. It was as if the Five Mountains trembled. And the seven apertures in his head all gushed blood. In the end, he seemed to die, but in time revived, and he pushed himself up from the ground with his arms and put his clothes in order. Then he leaped into the sky and to the place of the World-Honored One.

Mulian's feelings were all in a turmoil.
What others said seemed blurred: he heard not at all.
After a long while, he woke with a revelation;
Throwing his begging bowl and leaping to the sky, he went
    to ask the Buddha.
Mulian told the Buddha all about his sorrow and suffering,
And spoke of the Mountain of Knives and the Forest of Swords.
"By the grace of Buddha's overwhelming power,
I have managed to see my mother in the Avīchi Hell." ...
"Your mother committed many sins in the life before,
So her soul went straight down to the Avīchi Hell.
She cannot absolve herself from sin, after all this time;
And no one but the Buddha, no ordinary mortal can
    understand all this."
Then he called Ananda[33] and the other disciples:
"I must go down to save her myself."

The Tathāgata, leading the eight groups of supernatural beings, surrounded in front and back, shining forth radiance, shaking the ground, went to release the souls from suffering in hell:

The exalted wisdom of the Tathāgata is equitable,
And in his compassion, he saves the multitude in hell.
Innumerable worthies, a congregation from all eight sectors,
Followed in procession and moved as one.
Deep and hidden was the procession,
Heaven above, heaven below — nothing quite so extraordinary!
On the left, it was overwhelming; on the right, devastating:
Like mountain peaks peeking out from above the clouds.
High and lofty,
The vaults of heaven and of hell opened together;
Moving like rain, shaking like thunder,
Just like the moon rising round over the sea.
In the clouds, heaven's music wafts on the willows:
On the air, a flurry of plum-blossoms floats down.
The Buddha-king steps forth, the jade tablet in hand;
The Brahma-lord from the rear holds the golden tablet.
What cannot be fathomed cannot be fathomed:
The transcendent power of the Tathāgata liberates hell.
Left and right, the supernatural beings of all classes;

---

[33] Ananda was the most learned disciple of the Buddha.

Here and there, imperial guards of all directions.
In the Buddha's eyebrows flashed a thousand hues;
Behind his head, a halo-cloud in dazzling colors.
When the radiance permeates hell, it disintegrates —
The Forest of Swords, the Grove of Knives, crushed to dust.
The lictors of the hells, accepting grace, bow down on their knees
And clasp their hands in supplication to the Buddha....
The sinners all gain rebirth in heaven;
Only Mulian's mother still goes hungry.
Hell then is totally transformed;
In the end, the majesty of Shākyamuni prevails.

Mulian, beneficiary of Buddha's power, once again saw his beloved mother. But her sin was too deeply rooted, and her karma was difficult to cast off; although she was able to avoid the stench of hell, she nevertheless fell into the realm of the "hungry ghosts."[34] Although the misery is greatly reduced, there is no comparison between the conditions of the realms of bitterness and happiness. Her throat felt like the tiny aperture of a needle, so small that water could not drip through it; while her head was like the Tai Mountains, which the waters of three rivers are not enough to cover. She heard not so much as a hint of water and drink, but the months went by, the years passed, and the miseries of starvation had to be endured. From a distance, pure, cool, refreshing waters could be seen, but up close, they turned into a stream of pus. Delicious food, delectable meals, turned into blazing fire.

Lady Qingti told her son, "Your mother is suffering from hunger-pangs, and her life is hanging by a thread. If you don't take pity on me, how can you be called a devoted son? The paths of life and death are

---

[34] Hungry Ghosts are the unhappy spirits who no longer have human descendants to care for them. Such spirits suffer from hunger and thirst, and must so suffer uninterruptedly, unless someone attends to their needs. Otherwise, they meddle maliciously with human affairs. During the popular Buddhist festival of the *Yulanpen*, for one whole month the souls of these ghosts are released from hell and permitted to enjoy the feasts prepared for them. On the last day of the sixth moon, the "mouth of the pit" opens, to close again on the last night of the seventh. At the festival Buddhist priests everywhere hold masses for the dead. Weird words, talismanic words, summon from the Ten Directions of Space the Hungry Ghosts freed by the Breaking of the Gates of Hell. "Let the merit of this action be extended to all suffering souls, and let the power of this merit spread the truth through the Dark World, and assist all beings there towards the Supreme Enlightenment. It is our desire that you may quickly become Buddhas, and thus be fully and finally delivered out of the Hell of the Hungry Ghosts." Based on Juliet Bredon and Igor Mitrophanow, *The Moon Year: A Record of Chinese Customs and Festivals* (Shanghai: Kelly & Walsh, 1927), pp. 376–380. *Eds.*

separate, and any future meeting is beyond prediction. If you wish to rescue me from these perils, the matter should not be delayed. The life of a monk is to rely on faith and devotion. Please, son, leave me, go to Rājagriha,[35] and see that I get something to eat."

Mulian took leave of his mother, tossed up his begging bowl, and ascended into the heavens. In a wink, he arrived in the city of Rājagriha. At one house after another, he begged for food, and came to the residence of an elder. Seeing that it was not the hour for begging, the elder stopped him and asked him the reason: "Good monk, breakfast is over and the time for eating has passed. What are you going to do with this food you're begging for?"

Mulian responded to him, "Worthy elder,
After she passed away, this monk's mother's
Soul was sent directly down to the Avīchi Hell.
Of late the Tathāgata saved her,
Her body all withered bones, her breath a wisp.
This poor monk's heart broke, bit by bit;
How could a bystander know the pain?
I know I have come at the wrong time to beg;
I only intend to bring my mother some food to eat."
When the elder heard this, he was startled,
His thoughts unsettled, his feelings uneasy.
The elder's subordinates said:
"Golden saddles cannot touch the pearl-bright heart.
No reason to add makeup to a pretty face.
So, let us sing, let us be happy;
A man's life is as uncertain as a flickering candle.
No one sees those enjoying bliss in heaven;
We only hear of crowds of sinners in hell.
There's time to eat and time to clothe oneself.
Don't learn to hoard things like a fool:
Better build up karma for the time to come.
For who can guarantee life from day to day?
When two people meet, no one thinks of death;
Wealth and riches must not be spared for the body.
One day, we pass away and are placed in coffins.

---

[35] This ancient Indian city, a little to the southwest of the present city of Bihar, was important in early Buddhism. It was the site of the council that is said to have been held right after the death of the Buddha for the purpose of verifying the sayings of the Buddha and for establishing the basic disciplinary code.

What use is it to water the graves in vain?
Those who are wise use wealth to do charity,
Whereas fools use money to buy land and property.
All through life, one struggles in search of riches;
But after death, in the end, others will portion them out."

The elder, hearing these words, was started by doubt:

"The blessed land, the Three Treasures, are difficult to meet."
Hurriedly, he urged his subordinates not to waste any more time;
From the house, they took out food for the monk.
In a twinkling, hell disintegrated and dissolved,
And the ineffable power of Buddha was manifested.
The elder held offerings of food in his hands,
Went over to the monk, and wished him well:
"This is not just for Your Reverence to give to your mother,
But so that all the sinners can eat their fill."
After Mulian had received the delicious food,
He put the food in the begging bowl to tend to his mother.
Then he went to the wilderness to meet his waiting mother,
And with a golden spoon, he fed her himself.

Although Lady Qingti had suffered the ordeals of hell, her stinginess
and greed had still not been rooted out. When she saw her son coming
with food, she succumbed to her miserliness and avarice: "The monk
who comes is my son, and he is bringing for me the food he has collected
from the world of humans. Now all of you have to be patient. I will tend
to myself. There is little I can do for the rest of you."

Mulian took the food and offered it to her in his begging bowl. But his
mother was afraid that someone might snatch it from her; so, glaring at
the companions all around her, she used her left hand to cover up the
bowl, and scooped up the food with the right hand. Before the food
reached her mouth, it turned into raging flame. The devotion of the
elder who had donated the food had been profound, but it was not
enough to expiate a selfishness that was deeply ingrained.

When Mulian saw his mother like this, his insides were unstrung: "I
have but the puny strength of a lowly monk; my ability is limited, and I
am but an insignificant man. Only by consulting the World-Honored
One can one know the road to salvation." Now, let us see how his mother
ate:

When she saw the food, she went forward to take it.
Even before she ate it, out of greed, she was already defending it.
"My son brought food from the world of humans,

With which he intended to cure my hunger pangs.
The food does not seem to be enough for myself;
All of you, be patient and wait."
Qingti's karma of greed and selfishness was deep.
So when the food entered her throat, it caught fire.
And when Mulian saw his mother touched by flames,
He beat his breast and fell to the ground like a mountain collapsing.
From his ears and nose, blood came streaming out,
And he cried out, "Oh, my poor mother!" ... She replied:
"Now, the food cannot be put in my mouth,
And the fire hurts me.
Those who are covetous should remember this;
They will encounter a hundred or more misfortunes.
Good monk, you are my most devoted son;
Get me some cold water to salve my empty stomach."

Mulian, when he heard his mother asking for water, her breath scorched, her voice hoarse, remembered in a flash that south of Rājagriha there was a great river, with vast expanses of water without end, named the Ganges, where he could find relief for his fire-singed, suffering mother. When people in the southern continent Jambūdvīpa saw this water, it was a pure, clear, refreshingly cool river; when the mortals of heaven saw this water, it was a crystal pond; when the fish and the tortoises saw it, it was a babbling brook; but when Qingti saw this water, it became a stream of blazing pus. She went to the water's edge and, without waiting for her son's blessings, out of greed supported herself on the shore with her left hand, and out of avarice dipped her right hand into the water, because her greed and avarice knew no bounds. The water had not reached her lips when it turned into fire.

When Mulian saw the food his mother ate turn into fire, and the water she drank also turn into fire, he pounded his head and beat his breast in loud lamentation and tears. He came before the Buddha, paid homage three times, and addressed him: "World-Honored One, in your grace and mercy, please rescue my mother from her misery. Now when she eats food, it turns into fire, and when she drinks water, it also turns into fire. How may she be spared this ordeal of fire?"

"Mulian," the World-Honored One replied, "your mother cannot eat anything, and there is no way to overcome this without first celebrating, one year from now, on the fifteenth day of the seventh month, the Festival of the Avalamba. Only then can she begin to eat."

Mulian, seeing his mother starve, said, "World-Honored One, can this be achieved on the thirteen or fourteenth day of each month? Must she wait for the fifteenth day of the seventh month each year before she can eat?"

"It is not just for your mother that the Festival of Avalamba has been established on this day; it is also for meditative exercises, the day for the arhats to attain the Way, the day of absolution for Devadatta,[36] the day of rejoicing for the Yama King, the day when all the hungry ghosts eat their fill."

When Mulian heard the Buddha's instructions, he went to a temple tower on the outskirts of the city of Rājagriha and recited the sutras of the Mahāyāna school and established the blessings of the Avalamba, so that his mother might have a meal to eat from that offering.

Once she was fed, mother and son again lost sight of each other. Mulian looked for his mother everywhere, but could not find her; so mournfully, with tears streaming down both cheeks, he came before the Buddha. Paying homage to him three times, he stood in front of him, his hands clasped together, and, on his knees, said, "World-Honored One, when my mother took food and it turned to fire, when she drank water which also turned into fire, it was possible for me to save her from her ordeal of fire only through the compassion of the World-Honored One. So, on the fifteenth day of the seventh month, she was able to eat a meal. But since then, my mother and I have not seen each other. Is it because she has dropped down to hell and is again on the way to becoming a hungry ghost?"

"Your mother has not fallen into hell nor into the realm of hungry ghosts," the World-Honored One replied. "Because you attained merit from reciting the sutras and establishing the blessings of the Avalamba Festival, your mother has been transformed from the form of a hungry ghost into that of a black dog in Rājagriha. If you wish to see her, you must go, without any discrimination, begging at each house, whether rich or poor, until you arrive at the gate of a very wealthy elder, where a black dog will come out and nip at your cassock, mouthing words as if it were human. This, then, is your mother."

Mulian received these intructions and took his begging bowl and plate to look for his mother. Without any regard to the wealth or humbleness of the dwelling, he went through every lane and alley, all around, but could find no trace of her. Then he came upon the residence of an elder and saw a black dog running out of the house, which began nipping at

---

[36] Devadatta was a cousin of Shākyamuni and his enemy. For his plots against the Buddha, he is said to have been swallowed up alive in hell.

Mulian's cassock, at the same time making sounds very much like human speech: "Oh, my own devoted son, if you could save your mother from the realm of the underworld in no time at all, why can't you release me from this miserable state of being a dog?"

"Dear mother," Mulian said, "because your son was not devoted, calamity has befallen you, and you have descended down to the Three Paths. Now, surely you prefer life in this form as a dog, or would you rather go on in the world of the hungry ghosts?"

"Obedient son," his mother answered, "in this dog's life, I can yap, move about, stay in one spot, sit or sleep. If I am hungry, I can always go to the sewage pit and eat human offal; if I am parched, I can always drink from the gutters to quench my thirst. In the morning, I hear the elders chanting praises of the Three Treasures; in the evening, I hear the women reciting scripture. Of course I prefer this life as a dog, even if I have to pick up filth from all around, just so long as I don't have to hear the word 'hell' in my ears again."

Mulian then took his mother to the front of a Buddhist stupa in Rājagriha, and for seven days and seven nights he chanted the Mahāyāna sutras, made his confessions, and recited the abstinences. His mother, having benefited from these devotions, was able to shed her dog skin and hang it up on a tree, once again assuming the body of a woman.

"Mother," Mulian said, "it is not easy to achieve human form; it is not easy to be born in the Central Kingdom;[37] it is not easy to hear the law of Buddha; and it is not easy to develop a good heart. I ask you, mother, now that you have attained human form, to perform good works."

Mulian then took his mother beneath the sāl trees in the Twin Grove, where he performed his homage to Buddha three times and, standing in front of him, said, "World-Honored One, would you look at the course of my mother's karma, examine it from the beginning, and see if there is any sin left still?"

The World-Honored One did not refuse to do what Mulian asked. He looked over the three realms of karma, examining her for the slightest bit of sin.

Mulian saw that his mother's sins were expiated and was overjoyed. He said, "Mother, you should go to where you belong. The world of Jambūdvīpa is no place for you. Birth and death, there is no end to it. But in the west, the Land of the Buddha is most perfect."

---

[37] India, not China.

Then, she felt herself spirited away by the *devas* and dragons and escorted by the Heavenly Maidens, and taken to the Trayastrinshā Heaven,[38] there to enjoy everlasting bliss.

The first time the first sutra was chanted, there were eighty thousand bodhisattvas, eighty thousand monks, eighty thousand male deacons, and eighty thousand female deacons, performing the ritual around and around, in joy and in the faith that this teaching would prevail.

The Great Maudgalyāyana transformation text, one scroll.

▣ *Further Reading* ▣

Eoyang, Eugene, trans. "The Great Maudgalyayana Rescues His Mother from Hell." In Ma and Lau, eds., *Traditional Chinese Stories.*

Ma, Y. W., & Joseph S. M. Lau, eds. *Traditional Chinese Stories: Themes and Variations.* New York: Columbia University Press, 1978.

Mair, Victor H. *Painting and Performance: Chinese Picture Recitation and Its Indian Genesis.* Honolulu: University of Hawaii Press, 1988.

———. *T'ang Transformation Texts: A Study of the Buddhist Contribution to the Rise of Vernacular Fiction and Drama in China.* Cambridge, Mass.: Harvard University Press, 1989.

Waley, Arthur. *Ballads and Stories from Tun-huang: An Anthology.* London: Allen & Unwin, 1960.

"Calm the spirit within; be rid of desire without."
Seal carved by Gao Fenghan (1683–1743)

---

[38] Trayastrinshā is the heaven of Indra, one of the twelve spirits associated with the cult of the Master of Healing. The capital of this heaven is situated on Mount Sumeru, the central mountain of the nine mountain ranges of the universe.

Chapter 30

Among the Flowers

Lyrics of the Tang and Five Dynasties

Zhang Huiyan (1761–1802), in the preface to his *Lyric Anthology*, gives a most succinct account of the origins of the lyric: "It originated with the poets of the Tang dynasty, who made metres out of popular songs, adding their own words, or 'lyrics'."

Chen Zilong (1608–1647) wrote: "The lyric is a fragile form. Pearls and kingfisher feathers are too heavy for it, let alone dragon and phoenix." That is not to say that the lyric is trivial. In a lyric, a very serious idea would still be expressed in a light and ethereal fashion.

Although poetry in general deals with the subtler aspects of human experience, there is a still more elusive and refined level of subtlety, a still greater delicacy of nuance, that cannot find expression in the regular poetic forms, even if these are stretched to their utmost limits. A new form is needed, a form at once lighter and more supple than regular verse. This is where the lyric comes in. Poets came to discover that the lyric was perfectly suited to the expression of those very experiences, those subtle feelings and fugitive melancholy moods, that were beyond the reach of the old regular forms.

Regular verse seems explicit when compared with the even more suggestive and veiled mode of expresson found in the lyric; it seems plainspoken and exhaustive, when compared with the more symbolic and restrained style of the lyric. To quote Wang Guowei (1877–1927), writing in his *Poetic Remarks in the Human World*:

> The lyric form is one of exquisite refinement and sophisticated beauty. While this enables it to deal with subjects that are beyond the scope of regular verse, it also limits its range. Regular verse is broader in scope, the lyric deeper in expression.

When describing the sky, the lyric poet will prefer a faint rain, a solitary cloud, scattered stars and a pale moon. His landscape will tend to be one of distant peaks, meandering banks, misty isles and fishermen's shoals. His preferred emotions will be groundless grief, sweet musings, quiet enjoyment, and feelings of seclusion.

The lyric poet's perceptions and impressions arise from the depth of his personal joy and sorrow, and although they may appear far-fetched or confused, they have an aesthetic unity and intricate balance of their own — rounded like a pearl, smooth as jade, and with the translucent clarity of a carved miniature. The world of the lyric is like a mountain viewed through the mist, or a flower seen in the moonlight. Its beauty resides in its elusive ambiguity.

— Miao Yue (1904–), "The Chinese Lyric" (*translated by John Minford*)

Introduction

Kang-i Sun Chang

The lyric (*ci* or "song-words"), one of the major poetic genres in China, was originally a song text set to existing musical tunes. It emerged in the Tang dynasty in response to the popularity of foreign musical tunes newly imported from Central Asia. At first, the lyric replaced the old *yuefu* ballad [see chapter 8] and thus came to be regarded as a continuation of the ballad. The ancient musical notations have been lost, and it is no longer possible to know how the lyric melodies differed from those of ballad music. It is certain, however, that the lyric finally formed its own special tradition of composition: titles of ballad poems do not refer to fixed metric patterns, whereas lyric titles always point to particular tune patterns for which the poems are composed. These patterns, totaling about 825 if the numerous variant forms are excluded, came to be viewed as definite verse patterns. Even today, poets still write to these tune patterns without knowing the original melodies. This unique practice of composition is called "filling in words."

Lyric poetry is characterized often by lines of unequal length, in sharp contrast to Regulated Verse with its strictly five-character or seven-character lines. Long before the Tang poets began to view the lyric as a serious poetic genre, it already flourished as a "popular" song-form. The Dunhuang songs [lyrics found among the manuscripts in the caves at Dunhuang], which have given so many clues to Tang and Five Dynasties popular culture, attest to this fact. The early "popular" songs were vital to the development of lyric poetry; many devices formerly restricted to the "popular" song style later became important ingredients in the "literati" lyric. The evolution of the genre was a history of the intermingling of the "literati" style and the "popular" style. Wen Tingyun was the first prolific lyric poet in China, but before him such poets as Bo Juyi and Liu Yuxi had already experimented with occasional lyrics. These early writers composed lyrics primarily to meet the needs of the singing-girls in the entertainment quarters. Yangzhou, Suzhou, and Hangzhou were among the cities known for this newly emerging Tang song culture. When Ouyang Jiong, the compiler of the first lyric anthology, *Among the Flowers* (940), said that the literati lyrics were written for the "Southern singing-girls," he was no doubt referring to the growing demand for lyrics in the entertainment quarters of the Lower Yangtze Region.

As with other literary genres, the cumulative efforts of the numerous poets throughout the centuries contributed to the evolution of the lyric. Some focused more on stylistic changes and some on the innovations of formal structure. Some were revolutionary and introduced new blood into the lyric. Others were conservative and stayed within the orthodox tradition.

The Late Tang poet Wen Tingyun has been traditionally regarded as the pioneer poet of the form. His poetic style of refined subtlety became typical of the early lyric. The only poet of the *Among the Flowers* circle to break away from the overwhelming influence of Wen Tingyun was Wei Zhuang. Wei's style was deliberately more direct, and thus represented a style contrary to Wen's. A few decades later the last monarch of the Southern Tang, Li Yu, went a step further and synthesized these two stylistic modes.

— *Indiana Companion*, 1986

Eight Popular Lyrics from the Dunhuang Manuscripts

Translated by Marsha Wagner

The audience was not necessarily the same for every lyric found in the Dunhuang manuscripts. Some of these songs were local products; others were probably carried to Dunhuang from Chang'an and perhaps even Suzhou or Hangzhou. Just as the composers of the poems ranged from emperors and literati to artisans and semi-literate courtesans, those for whom the songs were performed also represented a broad social spectrum. The thematic content of particular lyrics — such as traveling merchants' songs, students' songs, and patriotic songs — suggests somewhat special-ized audiences and occasions. Perhaps performances were held in the marketplace, or particular meeting halls. Similarly, many of the love songs were performed in erotic settings or urban entertainment quarters, usually by courtesans. It was there that the ninth-century literati in the audience learned the tunes and themes that they even-tually adopted and modified to create the style of the anthology *Among the Flowers*. Thus, the popular lyric audience became the creators of the literary lyric, indicating a complex interaction among social and literary levels.

The Girl and Her Companion

(to the tune "Western Yangtze Moon")

The girl and her companion together search for the misty water;
Tonight the moon on the river is clear.
The tip of the rudder moves effortlessly, the boat floats sideways;
On the surface of the waves a light breeze imperceptibly arises.
Rowing the oars and riding the boat, with no fixed destination;
The sound of fishermen's songs is heard here and there.
The river's waves stretch to the sky, soaking the autumn stars;
By mistake the pair enters the water smartweed thicket.

Reed Flowers Turn White

(tune unknown)

Reed flowers turn white,
Autumn nights grow longer.
In front of my courtyard, the leaves of trees turn yellow,
Before the door it is cold.
Soon the grass will be covered with frost:
It will be time for winter clothing to come.
Husband and wife are in different places:
Tears fall in a thousand streams.

Over the Pillow

(to the tune "Strangers in Saint's Coif")

Over the pillow I made a thousand kinds of vows:
If you want me to stop loving you, then you must wait until the green
    mountains crumble,
Until iron floats on top of water,
Even until the Yellow River becomes dry.

Until Orion appears in broad daylight,
Until the Big Dipper points south;
If you want me to stop, I cannot stop yet,
You must wait until the sun is seen at the third watch of the night.

Yesterday Morning

(to the same tune)

Yesterday morning I went early to bid farewell to the traveling man,
The fifth watch was not yet over; the golden cock crowed.
We parted, and he passed beyond the river bridge.
The sound of water: hearing it broke my heart.
I recall only the grief of separation,
And how hard it was for him to set off on the long road.
He stopped his horse, then again plied the whip,
To send me one hundred thousand words.

Behind the Mountain

(to the tune "Washing Silk in the Creek")

Behind the mountain I cultivated a garden and planted herbs
    and sunflowers;
In front of the cave I dug a pond for fish and stocked it.
On a single frame of purple vines, flowers cluster;
The rain is light and fine.
Sitting I hear the gibbons cry, I sing an old rhapsody;
Walking I see the swallows chattering, I recite a new poem.
Since I have no affairs, I return to my library,
And close the wicker gate.

The Red Stove Warms the Room

(to the tune "Strangers in Saint's Coif")

The red stove warms the room where a beautiful woman sleeps,
Beyond the curtains flying snow increases the coldness.
In the small garden, they are playing mouth organs and singing,
The fragrant breeze gathers robes of silk and gauze.
Wine is poured, the golden cups are full;
Amidst orchid musk, the feast is offered again.
The young gentleman is as drunk as mud,
On the Avenue of Heaven his horse is heard neighing.

Drop by Drop

(to the same tune)

Drop by drop and drip by drip, rain on the winding banks,
Pair by pair and one by one, mandarin ducks chatter.
Lush, lush, the fragrance of wild flowers,
Soft, soft, the yellow of the golden willow-threads.
Lovely, lovely, the girls on the river,
Two by two, dancers beside the stream.
Bright, bright, the gleam of silk and gauze robes,
Dainty, dainty, the adornments of cloud hair and cosmetics.

Do Not Pluck Me

(to the tune "Gazing to the South")

Do not pluck me,
Plucking me is too unfair.
I'm a willow near the pond by the Qu River.
This man broke me, that man plucked me:
Each one's love lasted only a moment.

WEI YINGWU (737–c. 792)
Two Lyrics

(to the tune "Tiaoxiao")

Translated by Marsha Wagner

For Wei Yingwu, see chapter 21. — Editors

Tartar Horse

Tartar horse
Tartar horse,
Let free far off below Yanzhi Mountain,
Runs on the sand, runs on the snow, neighing alone;
Looking east, looking west, lost his way.
Lost his way
Lost his way,
The frontier grasses extend without end, the sun sets.

Milky Way

Milky Way
Milky Way,
At daybreak hanging over the autumn city, ever so dim.
The grieving one rises and gazes with longing;
South of the river, north of the border: separation.
Separation
Separation,
Milky Way: although the stars are the same, the road is cut off.

WANG JIAN (c. 768–833)
Two Lyrics

(to the tune "Tiaoxiao within the Palace")

Translated by Marsha Wagner

Wang Jian was a Mid Tang poet best known for his "palace-style" poems and *yuefu* ballads in the new style. He was an official, courtier, and recluse during his long career.

Round Fan

Round fan
Round fan,
When illness comes to the beautiful woman you cover his face.
Her jade face has been haggard and sad for three years:
Who will again tune up her pipes and strings?
Pipes and strings
Pipes and strings,
Amidst spring grass the road to Zhaoyang is cut off.

Willow

Willow
Willow,
At dusk standing by the White Sand Ford.
Ahead of the boat, the river waters are so vast:
The merchant and young woman are heartbroken.
Heartbroken
Heartbroken,
Partridges flying at night miss their mates.

LIU YUXI (772–842)

Red Blossoms

(to the tune "Bamboo Branch Song")

Translated by Burton Watson

[For Liu Yuxi, see chapters 22 and 27.] The "Bamboo Branch Song" was patterned
after a folk song of the region of Shu, present-day Sichuan.

Red blossoms of mountain peach crowd the uplands,
spring waters of Shu rivers buffet the mountains as they flow.
Crimson blossoms so quickly fading, like my lover's ardor;
flowing waters so endless, like the sorrow I feel.

Parrot Island

(to the tune "Wave-Washed Sand")

Translated by Marsha Wagner

On the shores of Parrot Island, waves beat on the sand.
From the blue mansion, I gaze out at spring in the setting sun.
Carrying mud in their beaks the swallows hurry to return to nest
    for the night;
Only my crazy lover does not long for home.

BO JUYI (772–846)
Three Lyrics

(to the tune "Remembering the South")

Translated by Marsha Wagner

For Bo Juyi, see chapter 23. — Editors

Jiangnan

Jiangnan, "South of the Yangtze River," was a region famous for its rivers and lakes, for its mountains and historic cities, for its lush landscape and beautiful women.

— Editors

Jiangnan is wonderful!
Once I knew its scenery so well.
The sun rises, river flowers redder than fire;
Spring comes, river waters blue as indigo.
How could I not long for Jiangnan?

Hangzhou

When I remember Jiangnan,
What I remember most is Hangzhou.
From mountain temples I would search for the cassia tree in the
     moon,
From the pavilion, I would watch the crests of waves from my pillow.
When can I go there again?

Wu

The southern region of Wu (named after the ancient southern state of Wu) includes much of Zhejiang and Jiangsu Provinces, and the great cities of Nanjing, Suzhou, and Hangzhou.

— Editors

When I remember Jiangnan,
What I remember next are the palaces of Wu.
A cup of Wu wine, leaves of spring bamboo,
A pair of dancing Wu beauties, wine-flushed hibiscus faces.
When can I meet them again?

WEN TINGYUN (c. 813–870)
Five Lyrics

(to the tune "Strangers in Saint's Coif")

Translated by Glen Baxter

For Wen Tingyun, see chapter 24. — Editors

Gold Glimmers and Fades

On the bedscreen's folding panels, gold glimmers and fades.
Clouds of hair verge upon the fragrant snow of cheeks.
Languorous she rises, pencils the moth-eyebrows,
Dawdles over her toilet, slowly washing, combing.
Mirrors front and back reflect her flowers;
Face and blossoms illumine one the other.
Upon her new embroidered silken jacket
Pairs and pairs of partridges in gold.

News So Seldom Comes

Blue tail-feathers and markings of gold on a pair of mandarin ducks,
And tiny ripples of water stirring the blue of a pond in spring;
Beside the pond there stands a crabapple tree,
Its branches filled with pink after the rain.
Her figured sleeve covers a dimpled smile
As a flying butterfly lights on the mistlike grass.
Her window gives on all this loveliness —
And news so seldom comes from the Jade Pass![1]

In Her Moonlit Chamber

There in her moonlit chamber she is dreaming of him still:
How delicate the willows, how languorous the spring!
In the grasses growing thick outside the gate
She hears his horse neigh as she waves goodbye....
By her colored quilt with kingfishers worked in gold
The scented candle has melted into tears.
Among the falling blossoms a nightjar cries —
And behind her green-gauze window the dream dissolves.

In the South Courtyard

In the south courtyard everywhere willow floss covers the ground.
Sadly she listens to the sound of a sudden spring's-end shower;
After the rain, the slanting rays of sunset
And scent of almond blossoms fallen and scattered.

---

[1] Frontier garrison west of Dunhuang.

She silently makes up her sleepy face
And sets the folding screen about her pillow.
The time of day is nearing yellow twilight
As languorous and alone she leans by the gate.

A Brilliant Moon

A brilliant moon has just now reached the zenith of the night.
Behind the lowered blind all's still, no one to say a word.
Secluded there amid perpetual incense
She goes to bed in her same old careless makeup.
Sufficient are her sorrows of this year —
How could she bear to think about the past?
Flowers lie fallen as the moonlight pales,
And under her quilt she knows the chill of dawn.

Embers of Incense

(to the tune "The Water Clock")

Translated by John Minford

Embers of incense
In the jade brazier
With candle's crimson tears
Conspire
To glow on gilded walls,
Autumnal mood,
Faded makeup, hair awry,
Coverlet and pillow cold,
A long night
Ahead.

At midnight the rain
On the *wutong* tree
Not knowing the pain
Of loneliness
Falls leaf to leaf
Dripping
On the bare steps
Till dawn.

WEI ZHUANG (c. 836–910)
Four Lyrics

Translated by Lois Fusek

For Wei Zhuang, see chapter 24. — Editors

A Candle Dies

(to the tune "Speaking of Love")

A candle dies, and incense fades by the closed curtains.
She awakes with a sudden start.
The flowers are soon to wither.
In deep night, the moon rises bright and splendid.
From somewhere comes the faintest murmur of music.
So low, so soft the song.
Her dancing robes lie dark and dusty with neglect.
He turned his back on her love.

A Green Pond

(to the same tune)

A green pond and red flowers lie in the soft misty rain.
She rests on the magnolia boat.
Drops of jade hang at her side.
Her sash winds around her slim and delicate waist.
Love's dream is kept apart by the Bridge of Stars.
So far, so very far away.
The sweet scent from her silken gown slowly fades.
A coronet of feathers dips low.

Hidden Tears

(to the tune "The Water Clock")

The bells and drums lie cold.
The towers stand in darkness.
The moon shines on the *wutong* trees by a golden well.
The inner gardens are closed.
The small courtyard is empty.
The falling flowers redden the fragrant dew.

The smoky willows grow heavy.
The spring fog rolls lightly.
A lamp still shines in a high window facing the waters.
Idly I lean against the door.
Hidden tears fall on my robe.
I wait for a gentleman never more to return.

The Moon Dips Low

(to the tune "Song of the Wine Spring")

The moon dips low and the stars grow dim.
In the tower, a lovely girl sleeps in sweet abandon.
Her radiant hair falls tousled.
Her pillow glistens with tears.
It is quiet within the screens.

The sudden cry of the cuckoo shatters love's tender dream.
A pale shimmer lights the east as she first awakens.
A thin mist covers the willows.
The flowers are heavy with dew.
Her thoughts become unbearable.

I Remember

(to the tune "The Lotus Leaf Cup")

Translated by John Minford

I remember
That year among the flowers
Deep in the night
Meeting my love
For the first time:
West of the Water Pavilion
Behind painted curtains,
Holding hands,
A secret tryst.

Heartache
At the morning oriole's cry,
As the tattered moon went down,
And we said goodbye!
Since then,

Not a word.
We are both far from home.
Why should we ever meet again?

LI CUNXU (885–926)

Deep Peach Glades

(to the tune "Memories of Fairy Grace")

Translated by C. H. Kwock and Vincent McHugh

Feasted once
            in deep peach glades
one song
      phoenix to phoenix
      danced and sang
I recall
      — how long!
            saying goodbye to her
Tears mingled together
            hand on arm to the door
   like a dream
   like a dream
faded moon
fallen blossoms
            thick mist
            over all

NIU XIJI (fl. 925)

Spring Mountains

(to the tune "The Unripe Hawthorn Berries")

Translated by C. H. Kwock and Vincent McHugh

Spring mountains
            Fog
            about to disperse
Sky clear
      stars few

A fading moon
        shines on your cheek
We cry at parting
        as the day comes up

So many words!
        but the feeling
        strong as ever
Turning your head
to look back
        you call
        over and over
"Remember the Green-Skirt Girl
        and everywhere on earth
        be tender with the grass"

FENG YANSI (c. 903–960)

The Cloud That Drifted

(to the tune "The Butterfly Loves the Flowers")

Translated by John Minford

The cloud that drifted days ago
Forgot to come home
Doesn't know
Spring's on the wane.
Down in the holiday street
Flowers and pretty faces,
And that fancy carriage
Parked at someone else's door.

Up at the window, tears
and faltering soliloquy:
"Swallows, swallows,
On your way,
By the footpath,
Did you see … ?"
Tangled spring-sorrow
Like catkins
Won't let go:
But dreaming
Never finds.

LI JING (916–961)

Two Lyrics

(to the tune "Washing Silk in the Creek")

Translated by Alan Ayling and Duncan Mackintosh

Li Jing was the second emperor of the Southern Tang dynasty and father of Li Yu.

Sorrow for Spring

Now, as my hand rolls up the blind to reach its hook of jade,
Sorrow for spring again assails me in my cloistered shade.
Who is the master once the wind-blown blossom's fallen free?
       I wonder anxiously.

The orioles bring no messages from cloudland's distant groves.
My troubles grow entwined as rain-drenched blossom on the
       cloves.
Green billows in the three ravines I watch as day goes by
       Press on to reach the sky.

The West Wind Ferries Grief

Dead now the water-lily's scent, kingfisher gloss of leaf.
Across green waves to the lake-side the west wind ferries grief.
I who shared spring's glory share in autumn life's decay.
       Appalled, I turn away.

The distant Cock Fort fills my dream; I wake to a fine rain.
Sheng notes sound from the small pavilion, cold yet sweet their
       strain.
Tears, so many tears; what end to grief? I wonder, leaning
       Disconsolate on the railing.

ZHANG BI (tenth century)

Butterfly

(to the tune "The Butterfly")

Translated by John Scott

Butterfly
       time of late spring

girl slender in a light yellow dress
leans in the window trying to paint him
As if she's with him in the flowers
    coupled, together and flying
She can't help it if her tears wet the paint
Making his wings heavy to lift

MAO WENXI (tenth century)

I Mustn't Ask

(to the tune "Drunk Among the Flowers")

Translated by Burton Watson

I mustn't ask about him —
I'm afraid to ask —
asking would only add to my heartache —
Spring waters swell and flood the pond,
the crested ducks follow each other around.

Last night the rain came pouring down,
toward dawn a cold spell set in,
and all I do is think of that man in his lookout tower —
how long since I've had news from the border!

LI YU (937–978)

Five Lyrics

Translated by Sam Houston Brock

The sixth son of Li Jing, and the last emperor of the Southern Tang, Li Yu was taken prisoner in 975 when the House of Song conquered his kingdom. Li is considered by many to be the first true master of the lyric.

The critic Wang Guowei (1877–1927) wrote: "The lyrics of Li Yu can truly be said to have been written in blood." Wang compares Li Yu with earlier lyric poets: "Wen Tingyun's artistry lies in the lines; Wei Zhuang's in the bone; Li Yu's in the spirit. By Li Yu's time the lyric's range of vision had begun to widen. The emotions grew more profound and the lyric moved out of the world of the singsong-girls and actors into that of the literati."

— Editors

Nightlong I Wander

(to the tune "The Butterfly Loves the Flowers")

Nightlong I wander aimlessly about the palace lawn.
The Qing Ming Festival is gone
And suddenly I feel with sadness spring's approaching end.
Now and then a splashing raindrop comes along the wind
And passing clouds obscure the paling moon.

Plum and peach trees, lingering, scent the evening air.
But someone is whispering in the swing,
Laughing and whispering in the swing!
The heart is a single skein, but with a thousand straggling threads
     that tear.
In all the world is no safe place to spread it out and leave it there.

My Idlest Dreams

(to the tune "Viewing the River Plum-Blossom")

1

My idlest dreams go farthest,
South to a land of brilliant days in fall,
A thousand miles of hills and rivers, cold-colored sunsets,
Flowering reeds that hid the boats of solitary men,
And flutes played overhead in moonlit rooms.

2

My idlest dreams go farthest,
South to a land of fragrant springs
And rivers green beneath our boat-borne flutes and strings,
Back to a town of floating catkins mixed with golden dust
And crowds that fought to see the flowers.

The Flowered Woods

(to the tune "Night Crow Calling")

The flowered woods have dropped their springtime rose festoon,
So soon, so soon.
But night-blowing winds and the cold dawn rain were bound
     to be.

Your tear-stained rouge will keep me
Drinking here beside you.
Then — who knows when again?
Out lives are sad like rivers turning always toward the sea.

The Past

(to the tune "Wave-Washed Sand")

The past is only fit to be regretted.
It stares unbanished in my face
Now autumn winds have claimed the court and moss usurped
    the stairs.
The shades hang down in rows, idle and unraised,
Throughout the day, for no one calls.

My golden sword is laid away.
My valor lies in weeds.
When nights are cold, the weather still, and a haloed moon is out,
I think of all that marble palace
Mirrored empty in the Huai.

One Dream

(to the tune "Washing Silk in the Creek")

One dream that scarce outlasts the burning of a candle or a petal's
    fall
And then we go.
I should like to visit ruins and weep for men no longer there,
But heaven makes our circumstances contradict our hearts.

In the river-house I watch the heedless, flowing waters, waiting for
    the moon,
And when it comes, slanting vaguely on the darkened flowers and
    the house,
I climb up to look, not minding if my sleeves be wetter still.

Immeasurable Pain!

(to the tune "Gazing to the South")

Translated by Arthur Waley

Immeasurable pain!
My dreaming soul last night was king again.

As in past days
I wandered through the Palace of Delight,
And in my dream
Down grassy garden-ways
Glided my chariot, smoother than a summer stream;
There was moonlight,
The trees were blossoming,
And a faint wind softened the air of night,
For it was spring.

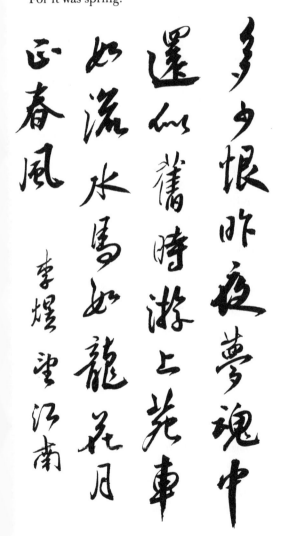

Figure 65. "Immeasurable
Pain!" Calligraphy by T. C.
Lai.

The River Rolling Eastward

(to the tune "The Beautiful Lady Yu")

Translated by Cyril Birch

When will the last flower fall, the last moon fade?
So many sorrows lie behind.
Again last night the east wind filled my room —
O gaze not on the lost kingdom under this bright moon.

Still in her light my palace gleams as jade
(Only from bright cheeks beauty dies).
To know the sum of human suffering
Look at this river rolling eastward in the spring

Shaken, They Cling Again

(to the tune "Light Flowing Music")

Translated by John Turner

To one who lonely sees the springtime close,
Each thing that strikes the eye bids the heart break,
Plum-blossoms tumbling as dishevelled snows
    Down over steps of stone, 'tis vain
    From off one's dress to shake:
    Shaken, they cling again.

See, the wild geese are come,
But voice, but word, is dumb.
So long a road no wistful dream may take.
    Farewell's sorrowing
    Is like grass in spring:
    How far soe'er you go,
    Yet faster will it grow.

Silent and Alone

(to the tune "Happiness of Meeting")

Translated by Amy Lowell and Florence Ayscough

Silent and alone, I ascended the West Cupola.
The moon was like a golden hook.
In the quiet, empty, inner courtyard, the coolness of early
    Autumn enveloped the *wutong* tree.

Scissors cannot cut this thing;
Unraveled, it joins again and clings.
It is the sorrow of separation,
And none tastes to the heart like this.

🔲 Further Reading 🔲

Ayling, Alan, & Duncan Mackintosh, trans. *A Collection of Chinese Lyrics.* London: Routledge & Kegan Paul, 1965.

———. (in collaboration with Ch'eng Hsi & T'ung Ping-cheng). *A Further Collection of Chinese Lyrics and Other Poems.* London: Routledge & Kegan Paul, 1969.

———. (in collaboration with T'ung Ping-cheng). *A Folding Screen: Selected Chinese Lyrics from T'ang to Mao Tse-tung.* London: Whittington Press, 1974.

Baxter, Glen W. "Hua-chien chi: Songs of Tenth Century China: A Study of the First Tz'u Anthology." Ph.D. dissertation, Harvard University, 1952. Translations also included in Birch, ed., *Anthology of Chinese Literature.*

Brock, Sam Houston Brock, trans. "Lyrics of Li Yü." In Birch, ed., *Anthology of Chinese Literature* Vol. 1. New York: Grove Press, 1965.

Bryant, Daniel. *Lyric Poets of the Southern T'ang: Li Yü and Feng Yen-ssu.* Vancouver: University of British Columbia Press, 1983.

Chang, Kang-i Sun. *The Evolution of Chinese Tz'u Poetry.* Princeton: Princeton University Press, 1980.

Fusek, Lois. *Among the Flowers: The Hua-chien chi.* New York: Columbia University Press, 1982.

Kwock, C. H., & Vincent McHugh, trans. *Old Friend from Far Away: 150 Chinese Poems from the Great Dynasties.* San Francisco: North Point, 1980.

Minford, John, trans. "Miao Yüeh: The Chinese Lyric." In Soong, ed. *Song Without Music: Chinese Tz'u Poetry.* Hong Kong: The Chinese University Press, 1985.

Rickett, Adele, trans. *Wang Kuo-wei's Jen-chien Tz'u-hua: A Study in Chinese Literary Criticism.* Hong Kong: Hong Kong University Press, 1977.

Scott, John (with Graham Martin), ed. and trans. *Love and Protest: Chinese Poems from the Sixth Century B.C. to the Seventeenth Century A.D.* London: Rapp & Whiting, 1972.

Soong, Stephen C., ed. *Song Without Music: Chinese Tz'u Poetry.* Hong Kong: The Chinese University Press, 1980.

Wagner, Marsha. *The Lotus Boat: The Origins of Chinese Tz'u Poetry in T'ang Popular Culture.* New York: Columbia University Press, 1984.

Wixted, John Timothy. *The Song-Poetry of Wei Chuang.* Tempe, Ariz.: Center for Asian Studies, 1979.

Yu, Pauline, ed. *Voices of the Song Lyric in China.* Berkeley and Los Angeles: University of California Press, 1994.

"In my dream I forgot that I was in a strange land."
Li Yu, "To the tune Wave-Washed Sand"
Seal carved by Wu Xizai (1799–1870)

Note on Pronunciation

In this anthology, Chinese words, names and place-names are in general spelt according to the Chinese system of romanisation known as *Hanyu Pinyin*, which is now internationally accepted. Occasional exceptions to this rule include well-established geographical names (such as the Yangtze River, Peking, Canton, Hong Kong), the widely used philosophical term the Tao, and a few translations where older systems have been preserved in the interests of historical authenticity (e.g. Du Halde, Ezra Pound).

Hanyu Pinyin is for the most part quite straightforward. The following short list of approximations may help readers with some of the more awkward sound values of the system.

Letter	Pronunciation
C	*ts*
Q	*ch*
X	*sh*
Z	*dz*
ZH	*j*

A handy guide to the system as a whole can be found at the front of any one of the five volumes of the Penguin Classics translation of the 18th-century novel *The Story of the Stone* by Cao Xueqin and Gao E (Penguin, Harmondsworth: 1973–1986).

Conversion Tables

Hanyu Pinyin to Wade-Giles

Hanyu Pinyin	Wade-Giles	Hanyu Pinyin	Wade-Giles
a	a	chai	ch'ai
ai	ai	chan	ch'an
an	an	chang	ch'ang
ang	ang	chao	ch'ao
ao	ao	che	ch'e
		chen	ch'en
ba	pa	cheng	ch'eng
bai	pai	chi	ch'ih
ban	pan	chong	ch'ung
bang	pang	chou	ch'ou
bao	pao	chu	ch'u
bei	pei	chua	ch'ua
ben	pen	chuai	ch'uai
beng	peng	chuan	ch'uan
bi	pi	chuang	ch'uang
bian	pien	chui	ch'ui
biao	piao	chun	ch'un
bie	pieh	chuo	ch'o
bin	pin	ci	tz'u
bing	ping	cong	ts'ung
bo	po	cou	ts'ou
bu	pu	cu	ts'u
		cuan	ts'uan
ca	ts'a	cui	ts'ui
cai	ts'ai	cun	ts'un
can	ts'an	cuo	ts'o
cang	ts'ang		
cao	ts'ao	da	ta
ce	ts'e	dai	tai
cei	(ts'ei)	dan	tan
cen	ts'en	dang	tang
ceng	ts'eng	dao	tao
cha	ch'a	de	te

Hanyu Pinyin	Wade-Giles	Hanyu Pinyin	Wade-Giles
dei	tei	gong	kung
den	(ten)	gou	kou
deng	teng	gu	ku
di	ti	gua	kua
dian	tien	guai	kuai
diao	tiao	guan	kuan
die	tieh	guang	kuang
ding	ting	gui	kuei
diu	tiu	gun	kun
dong	tung	guo	kuo
dou	tou		
du	tu	ha	ha
duan	tuan	hai	hai
dui	tui	han	han
dun	tun	hang	hang
duo	to	hao	hao
		he	he/ho
e	e/o	hei	hei
en	en	hen	hen
er/r	erh	heng	heng
		hong	hung
fa	fa	hou	hou
fan	fan	hu	hu
fang	fang	hua	hua
fei	fei	huai	huai
fen	fen	huan	huan
feng	feng	huang	huang
fo	fo	hui	hui
fou	fou	hun	hun
fu	fu	huo	huo
ga	ka	ji	chi
gai	kai	jia	chia
gan	kan	jian	chien
gang	kang	jiang	chiang
gao	kao	jiao	chiao
ge	ke/ko	jie	chieh
gei	kei	jin	chin
gen	ken	jing	ching
geng	keng	jiong	chiung

Hanyu Pinyin	Wade-Giles	Hanyu Pinyin	Wade-Giles
jiu	chiu	lin	lin
ju	chü	ling	ling
juan	chüan	liu	liu
jue	chüeh	long	lung
jun	chün	lou	lou
		lu	lu
ka	k'a	luan	luan
kai	k'ai	lun	lun
kan	k'an	luo	lo
kang	k'ang	lü	lü
kao	k'ao	lüan	lüan
ke	k'e/k'o	lüe	lüeh
kei	k'ei	lün	lün
ken	k'en		
keng	k'eng	ma	ma
kong	k'ung	mai	mai
kou	k'ou	man	man
ku	k'u	mang	mang
kua	k'ua	mao	mao
kuai	k'uai	mei	mei
kuan	k'uan	men	men
kuang	k'uang	meng	meng
kui	k'uei	mi	mi
kun	k'un	mian	mien
kuo	k'uo	miao	miao
		mie	mieh
la	la	min	min
lai	lai	ming	ming
lan	lan	miu	miu
lang	lang	mo	mo
lao	lao	mou	mou
le	le	mu	mu
lei	lei		
leng	leng	na	na
li	li	nai	nai
lia	lia	nan	nan
lian	lien	nang	nang
liang	liang	nao	nao
liao	liao	nei	nei
lie	lieh	nen	nen

Hanyu Pinyin	*Wade-Giles*	*Hanyu Pinyin*	*Wade-Giles*
neng	neng	qian	ch'ien
ni	ni	qiang	ch'iang
nian	nien	qiao	ch'iao
niang	niang	qie	ch'ieh
niao	niao	qin	ch'in
nie	nieh	qing	ch'ing
nin	nin	qiong	ch'iung
ning	ning	qiu	ch'iu
niu	niu	qu	ch'ü
nong	nung	quan	ch'üan
nou	nou	que	ch'üeh
nu	nu	qun	ch'ün
nuan	nuan		
nun	nun	ran	jan
nuo	no	rang	jang
nü	nü	rao	jao
nüe	nüeh	re	je
		ren	jen
ou	ou	reng	jeng
		ri	jih
pa	p'a	rong	jung
pai	p'ai	rou	jou
pan	p'an	ru	ju
pang	p'ang	rua	(jua)
pao	p'ao	ruan	juan
pei	p'ei	rui	jui
pen	p'en	run	jun
peng	p'eng	ruo	jo
pi	p'i		
pian	p'ien	sa	sa
piao	p'iao	sai	sai
pie	p'ieh	san	san
pin	p'in	sang	sang
ping	p'ing	sao	sao
po	p'o	se	se
pou	p'ou	sei	(sei)
pu	p'u	sen	sen
		seng	seng
qi	ch'i	sha	sha
qia	ch'ia	shai	shai

Hanyu Pinyin	Wade-Giles	Hanyu Pinyin	Wade-Giles
shan	shan	tou	t'ou
shang	shang	tu	t'u
shao	shao	tuan	t'uan
she	she	tui	t'ui
shei	shei	tun	t'un
shen	shen	tuo	t'o
sheng	sheng		
shi	shih	wa	wa
shou	shou	wai	wai
shu	shu	wan	wan
shua	shua	wang	wang
shuai	shuai	wei	wei
shuan	shuan	wen	wen
shuang	shuang	weng	weng
shui	shui	wo	wo
shun	shun	wu	wu
shuo	shuo		
si	ssu	xi	hsi
song	sung	xia	hsia
sou	sou	xian	hsien
su	su	xiang	hsiang
suan	suan	xiao	hsiao
sui	sui	xie	hsieh
sun	sun	xin	hsin
suo	so	xing	hsing
		xiong	hsiung
ta	t'a	xiu	hsiu
tai	t'ai	xu	hsü
tan	t'an	xuan	hsüan
tang	t'ang	xue	hsüeh
tao	t'ao	xun	hsün
te	t'e		
tei	(t'ei)	ya	ya
teng	t'eng	yan	yen
ti	t'i	yang	yang
tian	t'ien	yao	yao
tiao	t'iao	ye	yeh
tie	t'ieh	yi	i/yi
ting	t'ing	yin	yin
tong	t'ung	ying	ying

Hanyu Pinyin	Wade-Giles	Hanyu Pinyin	Wade-Giles
yong	yung	zhen	chen
you	yu	zheng	cheng
yu	yü	zhi	chih
yuan	yüan	zhong	chung
yue	yüeh	zhou	chou
yun	yün	zhu	chu
		zhua	chua
za	tsa	zhuai	chuai
zai	tsai	zhuan	chuan
zan	tsan	zhuang	chuang
zang	tsang	zhui	chui
zao	tsao	zhun	chun
ze	tse	zhuo	cho
zei	tsei	zi	tzu
zen	tsen	zong	tsung
zeng	tseng	zou	tsou
zha	cha	zu	tsu
zhai	chai	zuan	tsuan
zhan	chan	zui	tsui
zhang	chang	zun	tsun
zhao	chao	zuo	tso
zhe	che		

Wade-Giles to Hanyu Pinyin

Wade-Giles	Hanyu Pinyin	Wade-Giles	Hanyu Pinyin
a	a	chang	zhang
ai	ai	ch'ang	chang
an	an	chao	zhao
ang	ang	ch'ao	chao
ao	ao	che	zhe
		ch'e	che
cha	zha	chei	zhei
ch'a	cha	chen	zhen
chai	zhai	ch'en	chen
ch'ai	chai	cheng	zheng
chan	zhan	ch'eng	cheng
ch'an	chan	chi	ji

Wade-Giles	Hanyu Pinyin	Wade-Giles	Hanyu Pinyin
ch'i	qi	chü	ju
chia	jia	ch'ü	qu
ch'ia	qia	chüan	juan
chiang	jiang	ch'üan	quan
ch'iang	qiang	chüeh	jue
chiao	jiao	ch'üeh	que
ch'iao	qiao	chün	jun
chieh	jie	ch'ün	qun
ch'ieh	qie		
chien	jian	e,o	e
ch'ien	qian	ei	ei
chih	zhi	en	en
ch'ih	chi	eng	eng
chin	jin	erh	er
ch'in	qin		
ching	jing	fa	fa
ch'ing	qing	fan	fan
chiu	jiu	fang	fang
ch'iu	qiu	fei	fei
chiung	jiong	fen	fen
ch'iung	qiong	feng	feng
cho	zhuo	fo	fo
ch'o	chuo	fou	fou
chou	zhou	fu	fu
ch'ou	chou		
chu	zhu	ha	ha
ch'u	chu	hai	hai
chua	zhua	han	han
chuai	zhuai	hang	hang
ch'uai	chuai	hao	hao
chuan	zhuan	hei	hei
ch'uan	chuan	hen	hen
chuang	zhuang	heng	heng
ch'uang	chuang	ho	he
chui	zhui	hou	hou
ch'ui	chui	hsi	xi
chun	zhun	hsia	xia
ch'un	chun	hsiang	xiang
chung	zhong	hsiao	xiao
ch'ung	chong	hsieh	xie

Wade-Giles	Hanyu Pinyin	Wade-Giles	Hanyu Pinyin
hsien	xian	kan	gan
hsin	xin	k'an	kan
hsing	xing	kang	gang
hsiu	xiu	k'ang	kang
hsiung	xiong	kao	gao
hsü	xu	k'ao	kao
hsüan	xuan	ke, ko	ge
hsüeh	xue	k'e, k'o	ke
hsün	xun	kei	gei
hu	hu	ken	gen
hua	hua	k'en	ken
huai	huai	keng	geng
huan	huan	k'eng	keng
huang	huang	ko, ke	ge
hui	hui	k'o, k'e	ke
hun	hun	kou	gou
hung	hong	k'ou	kou
huo	huo	ku	gu
		k'u	ku
i, yi	yi	kua	gua
		k'ua	kua
jan	ran	kuai	guai
jang	rang	k'uai	kuai
jao	rao	kuan	guan
je	re	k'uan	kuan
jen	ren	kuang	guang
jeng	reng	k'uang	kuang
jih	ri	kuei	gui
jo	ruo	k'uei	kui
jou	rou	kun	gun
ju	ru	k'un	kun
juan	ruan	kung	gong
jui	rui	k'ung	kong
jun	run	kuo	guo
jung	rong	k'uo	kuo
ka	ga	la	la
k'a	ka	lai	lai
kai	gai	lan	lan
k'ai	kai	lang	lang

Wade-Giles	Hanyu Pinyin	Wade-Giles	Hanyu Pinyin
lao	lao	mu	mu
le	le		
lei	lei	na	na
leng	leng	nai	nai
li	li	nan	nan
lia	lia	nang	nang
liang	liang	nao	nao
liao	liao	ne	ne
lieh	lie	nei	nei
lien	lian	nen	nen
lin	lin	neng	neng
ling	ling	ni	ni
liu	liu	niang	niang
lo	luo	niao	niao
lou	lou	nieh	nie
lu	lu	nien	nian
luan	luan	nin	nin
lun	lun	ning	ning
lung	long	niu	niu
lü	lü	no	nuo
lüan	lüan	nou	nou
lüeh	lüe	nu	nu
		nuan	nuan
ma	ma	nun	nun
mai	mai	nung	nong
man	man	nü	nü
mang	mang	nüeh	nüe
mao	mao		
mei	mei	o, e	e
men	men	ou	ou
meng	meng		
mi	mi	pa	ba
miao	miao	p'a	pa
mieh	mie	pai	bai
mien	mian	p'ai	pai
min	min	pan	ban
ming	ming	p'an	pan
miu	miu	pang	bang
mo	mo	p'ang	pang
mou	mou	pao	bao

Wade-Giles	Hanyu Pinyin	Wade-Giles	Hanyu Pinyin
p'ao	pao	shei	shei
pei	bei	shen	shen
p'ei	pei	sheng	sheng
pen	ben	shih	shi
p'en	pen	shou	shou
peng	beng	shu	shu
p'eng	peng	shua	shua
pi	bi	shuai	shuai
p'i	pi	shuan	shuan
piao	biao	shuang	shuang
p'iao	piao	shui	shui
pieh	bie	shun	shun
p'ieh	pie	shuo	shuo
pien	bian	so	suo
p'ien	pian	sou	sou
pin	bin	ssu	si
p'in	pin	su	su
ping	bing	suan	suan
p'ing	ping	sui	sui
po	bo	sun	sun
p'o	po	sung	song
pou	(bou)		
p'ou	pou	ta	da
pu	bu	t'a	ta
p'u	pu	tai	dai
		t'ai	tai
sa	sa	tan	dan
sai	sai	t'an	tan
san	san	tang	dang
sang	sang	t'ang	tang
sao	sao	tao	dao
se	se	t'ao	tao
sen	sen	te	de
seng	seng	t'e	te
sha	sha	tei	dei
shai	shai	teng	deng
shan	shan	t'eng	teng
shang	shang	ti	di
shao	shao	t'i	ti
she	she	tiao	diao

Wade-Giles	Hanyu Pinyin	Wade-Giles	Hanyu Pinyin
t'iao	tiao	ts'un	cun
tieh	die	tsung	zong
t'ieh	tie	ts'ung	cong
tien	dian	tu	du
t'ien	tian	t'u	tu
ting	ding	tuan	duan
t'ing	ting	t'uan	tuan
tiu	diu	tui	dui
to	duo	t'ui	tui
t'o	tuo	tun	dun
tou	dou	t'un	tun
t'ou	tou	tung	dong
tsa	za	t'ung	tong
ts'a	ca	tzu	zi
tsai	zai	tz'u	ci
ts'ai	cai		
tsan	zan	wa	wa
ts'an	can	wai	wai
tsang	zang	wan	wan
ts'ang	cang	wang	wang
tsao	zao	wei	wei
ts'ao	cao	wen	wen
tse	ze	weng	weng
ts'e	ce	wo	wo
tsei	zei	wu	wu
tsen	zen		
ts'en	cen	ya	ya
tseng	zeng	yai	(yai)
ts'eng	ceng	yang	yang
tso	zuo	yao	yao
ts'o	cuo	yeh	ye
tsou	zou	yen	yan
ts'ou	cou	yin	yin
tsu	zu	ying	ying
ts'u	cu	yu	you
tsuan	zuan	yung	yong
ts'uan	cuan	yü	yu
tsui	zui	yüan	yuan
ts'ui	cui	yüeh	yue
tsun	zun	yün	yun

Further Reading

General Reference: Bibliographies, Companions, Guides, China and the West, Translation

Bailey, Roger B., rev. Richard J. Lynn. *Guide to Chinese Poetry and Drama*. Boston: G. K. Hall, 1984.

Barrett, T. H. *Singular Listlessness: A Short History of Chinese Books and British Scholars*. London: Wellsweep, 1989.

Cameron, Nigel. *Barbarians and Mandarins: Thirteen Centuries of Western Travellers in China*. Hong Kong: Oxford University Press, 1989.

Chan, Sin-wai. *A Topical Bibliography of Translation and Interpretation: Chinese-English, English-Chinese*. Hong Kong: The Chinese University Press, 1995.

———, & David E. Pollard, eds. *An Encyclopedia of Translation: Chinese-English, English-Chinese*. Hong Kong: The Chinese University Press, 1995.

Ch'ien Chung-shu. "China in the English Literature of the Seventeenth Century." In *Quarterly Bulletin of Chinese Bibliography*, New Series, Vol. I:4, 1940.

———. "China in the English Literature of the Eighteenth Century." In *Quarterly Bulletin of Chinese Bibliography*, New Series, Vol. II:1–2, 1941.

Cordier, Henri. *Bibliotheca Sinica: Dictionnaire bibliographique des ouvrages relatifs à l'Empire Chinois*. 2nd ed., 5 vols. Paris: Guilmoto and Geuthner, 1904–24.

Couling, Samuel. *The Encyclopedia Sinica*. Shanghai: Kelly & Walsh, 1917.

Davidson, Martha. *A List of Published Translations from Chinese into English, French and German*. Vol. 1 (Literature Exclusive of Poetry), Ann Arbor: J. W. Edwards, 1952; Vol. 2 (Poetry), New Haven: Yale University Far Eastern Publications, 1957.

Dawson, Raymond. *The Chinese Chameleon*. Oxford: Oxford University Press, 1967.

De Bary, William T., W. T. Chan & Burton Watson, eds. *Sources of Chinese Tradition*. New York: Columbia University Press, 1960.

Eberhard, Wolfram. *A Dictionary of Chinese Symbols*. London: Routledge, 1986.

Eliot, T. S. *Introduction to Selected Poems of Ezra Pound*. London: Faber and Faber, 1928.

Eoyang, Eugene. *The Transparent Eye: Reflections on Translation, Chinese Literature, and Comparative Poetics*. Honolulu: University of Hawaii Press, 1993.

———, & Lin Yao-fu, eds. *Translating Chinese Literature*. Bloomington: Indiana University Press, 1995.

Franke, Wolfgang. *China and the West: The Cultural Encounter, 13th to 20th Centuries*. New York: Harper, 1967.

Fung, Sydney S. K. and Lai, S. T. *Twenty-five T'ang Poets: Index to English Translations*. Hong Kong: The Chinese University Press, 1984.

Giles, Herbert A. *A Chinese Biographical Dictionary*. Shanghai: Kelly & Walsh, 1898.

Hightower, J. R. *Topics in Chinese Literature*. Rev. ed., Cambridge, Mass.: Harvard University Press, 1953.

Honour, Hugh. *Chinoiserie: The Vision of Cathay*. New York: Harper and Row, 1961.

Hsia, Adrian. *Chinesia: The European Construction of China in the Literature of the Seventeenth and Eighteenth Centuries*. Tübingen: Max Niemeyer, 1998.

———, ed. *The Vision of China in the English Literature of the Seventeenth and Eighteenth Centuries*. Hong Kong: The Chinese University Press, 1998.

Hsiao, Ch'ien. *A Harp with a Thousand Strings: A Chinese Anthology in Six Parts*. London:

Pilot Press, 1944.

Hudson, G. F. *Europe and China: A Survey of Their Relations from the Earliest Times to 1800.* London: Arnold, 1931.

Johns, Francis A. *A Bibliography of Arthur Waley.* New Brunswick: Rutgers University Press, 1968.

Kircher, Athanasius, S. J. *China Monumentis qua Sacris qua Profanis Illustrata.* Amsterdam: 1667. English translation by Charles D. Van Tuyl, Muskogee, Oklahoma, 1986.

Koss, Nicholas. "Western Images of China from the first century B.C. to the seventh century A.D." In *Fu Jen Studies: Literature & Linguistics,* 27 (1994).

————. "China in the medieval accounts of John of Plano Carpini and William of Rubruck." In *Fu Jen Studies: Literature & Linguistics,* 28 (1995).

————. "China in *The Description of the World,* usually attributed to Marco Polo." In *Fu Jen Studies: Literature & Linguistics,* 29 (1996).

Lach, Donald, et al. *Asia in the Making of Europe.* Several vols. Chicago: Chicago University Press, 1965–

Lee, Thomas H. C., ed. *China and Europe: Images and Influences in the Sixteenth to Eighteenth Centuries.* Hong Kong: The Chinese University Press, 1991.

Leslie, Donald D., Colin Mackerras and Wang Gungwu, eds. *Essays on the Sources for Chinese History.* Canberra: Australian National University Press, 1973.

Li, T'ien-yi. *Chinese Fiction: A Bibliography of Books and Articles in Chinese and English.* New Haven: Yale University Far Eastern Publications, 1968.

————. *The History of Chinese Literature: A Selected Bibliography.* New Haven: Yale University Far Eastern Publications, 1970.

Lust, John. *Index Sinicus: A Catalogue of Articles Relating to China in Periodicals and Other Collective Publications, 1920–1955.* Cambridge: Heffer, 1964.

————. *Western Books on China Published up to 1850 in the Library of the School of Oriental and African Studies.* London: Bamboo Press, 1987.

Lynn, Richard J. *Chinese Literature: A Draft Bibliography in Western European Languages.* Canberra: Australian National University Press, 1979.

Mayers, William F. *The Chinese Reader's Manual.* Shanghai: American Presbyterian Press, 1874.

Morris, Ivan, ed. *Madly Singing in the Mountains: An Appreciation and Anthology of Arthur Waley.* London: Allen & Unwin, 1970.

Mungello, David. *Curious Land: Jesuit Accommodation and the Origins of Sinology.* Honolulu: University of Hawaii Press, 1985.

Needham, Joseph, et al. *Science and Civilisation in China.* Several vols. Cambridge: Cambridge University Press, 1954–

Nienhauser, William H., ed. *Indiana Companion to Traditional Chinese Literature.* Bloomington: Indiana University Press, 1986.

————. *Bibliography of Selected Western Works on T'ang Dynasty Literature.* Taipei: Center for Chinese Studies, 1988.

Paper, Jordan P. *Guide to Chinese Prose.* Boston: G. K. Hall, 1973.

Pfister, Louis. *Notices biographiques et bibliographiques sur les Jésuites de l'ancienne mission de la Chine.* 2 vols. Shanghai: Mission Press, 1932–1934.

Reichwein, A., trans. J. C. Powell. *China and Europe: Intellectual and Artistic Contacts in the Eighteenth Century.* London: Kegan Paul, 1925.

Rule, Paul A. *K'ung-tzu or Confucius? The Jesuit Interpretation of Confucianism.* Sydney: Allen & Unwin, 1986.

Teele, Roy Earl. *Through a Glass Darkly: A Study of English Translations of Chinese Poetry.*

Ann Arbor: University of Michigan Press, 1949.

Tsien, Tsuen-hsuin & James K. M. Cheng. *China: An Annotated Bibliography of Bibliographies.* Boston: G. K. Hall, 1978.

Werner, E. T. C. *A Dictionary of Chinese Mythology.* Shanghai: Kelly & Walsh, 1932.

Williams, C. A. S. *Encyclopedia of Chinese Symbolism and Art Motives.* Shanghai: Kelly & Walsh, 1932.

Wood, Frances. *Did Marco Polo Go to China?* London: Secker & Warburg, 1995.

Wylie, Alexander. *Memorials of Protestant Missionaries to the Chinese.* Shanghai: American Presbyterian Mission Press, 1867.

———. *Notes on Chinese Literature.* Shanghai: American Presbyterian Mission Press, 1867.

Yip, Wai-lim. *Ezra Pound's Cathay.* Princeton: Princeton University Press, 1969.

Yuan, Tung-li. *China in Western Literature: A Continuation of Cordier's Bibliotheca Sinica.* New Haven: Yale University Far Eastern Publications, 1958.

Yule, Henry. *Cathay and the Way Thither: Being a Collection of Medieval Notices of China.* New ed., rev. Henri Cordier. London: Hakluyt Society, 1915.

———. *The Travels of Marco Polo: The Complete Yule-Cordier Edition.* London: Constable, 1903.

General Reference: Histories and Critical Studies of Chinese Literature

Bush, Susan and Christian Murck, eds. *Theories of the Arts in China.* Princeton: Princeton University Press, 1983.

Chang, Kang-i Sun. *Six Dynasties Poetry.* Princeton: Princeton University Press, 1986.

Ch'en, Shou-yi. *Chinese Literature, a Historical Introduction.* New York: Ronald Press, 1961.

Cheng, François. *L'écriture poétique chinoise.* Paris: Editions du Seuil, 1977. *Chinese Poetic Writing: With an Anthology of T'ang Poetry* (English trans. by Donald A. Riggs & Jerome P. Seaton). Bloomington: Indiana University Press, 1982.

Davis, Sir John Francis. *The Poetry of the Chinese : Poeseos Sinicae Commentarii.* London: J. L. Cox, 1829; rev. ed., London: Asher, 1870.

Dawson, Raymond, ed. *The Legacy of China.* Oxford: Oxford University Press, 1964.

Du Halde, Jean-Baptiste. *Description géographique, historique, chronologique, politique de l'Empire de la Chine.* 4 vols. Paris: Lemercier, 1735 (trans. by Brookes as *A Description of the Empire of China.* 2 vols. London: Edward Cave, 1738; trans. by Green and Guthrie as *The General History of China.* 4 vols. London: J. Watts, 1741).

Feifel, Eugen. *Geschichte der Chinesischen Literatur* (after Nagasawa, *Shina gakujutsu bungeishi.* Tokyo: Sanseido, 1957). Rev. ed. Hildesheim: Olms, 1982.

Giles, Herbert A. *A History of Chinese Literature.* London: Heinemann, 1901.

Hawkes, David. *Classical, Modern and Humane: Essays in Chinese Literature.* Hong Kong: Chinese University Press, 1989.

Lai, Ming. *A History of Chinese Literature.* New York: John Day, 1964.

Lin, Shuen-fu and Stephen Owen, eds. *The Vitality of the Lyric Voice: Shih Poetry from the Late Han to T'ang.* Princeton: Princeton University Press, 1986.

Liu, James J. Y. *The Art of Chinese Poetry.* Chicago: Chicago University Press, 1962.

———. *Chinese Theories of Literature.* Chicago: Chicago University Press, 1975.

Liu, Wu-chi. *An Introduction to Chinese Literature.* Bloomington: Indiana University Press, 1966.

Lu, Xun (trans. by Gladys Yang & Yang Xianyi). *A Brief History of Chinese Fiction*. Peking: Foreign Languages Press, 1959.

Owen, Stephen. *The Poetry of the Early T'ang*. New Haven: Yale University Press, 1977.

——. *The Great Age of Chinese Poetry: The High T'ang*. New Haven: Yale University Press, 1981.

——. *Remembrances: The Experience of the Past in Classical Chinese*. Cambridge, Mass.: Harvard University Press, 1985

——. *Traditional Chinese Poetry and Poetics: Omen of the World*. Madison: University of Wisconsin Press, 1985.

Rickett, Adele, ed. *Chinese Approaches to Literature from Confucius to Liang Ch'i-ch'ao*. Princeton: Princeton University Press, 1978.

Soong, Stephen C., ed. *A Brotherhood in Song: Chinese Poetry and Poetics*. Hong Kong: The Chinese University Press, 1985.

Strachey, Lytton. "An Anthology." In *Characters and Commentaries*. London: Chatto & Windus, 1933.

Watson, Burton. *Early Chinese Literature*. New York: Columbia University Press, 1962.

——. *Chinese Lyricism: Shih Poetry from the Second to the Twelfth Century*. New York: Columbia University Press, 1971.

Whincup, Greg. *The Heart of Chinese Poetry*. New York: Anchor Books, 1987.

Wu, John C. H. *The Four Seasons of T'ang Poetry*. Rutland, Vermont: Tuttle, 1972.

Yu, Pauline. *The Reading of Imagery in the Chinese Tradition*. Princeton: Princeton University Press, 1987.

General Reference: Anthologies of Translations

(These anthologies cover several authors, genres and periods. For more specific anthologies, see under the relevant chapter.)

Ayling, Alan & Duncan Mackintosh, trans. *A Collection of Chinese Lyrics*. London: Routledge and Kegan Paul, 1965.

—— (in collaboration with Ch'eng Hsi and T'ung Ping-cheng). *A Further Collection of Chinese Lyrics and Other Poems*. London: Routledge and Kegan Paul, 1969.

—— (in collaboration with T'ung Ping-cheng). *A Folding Screen: Selected Chinese Lyrics from T'ang to Mao Tse-tung*. London: Whittington Press, 1974.

Barnstone, Tony & Chou Ping. *The Art of Writing: Teachings of the Chinese Masters*. Boston: Shambhala, 1996.

Bauer, Wolfgang & Herbert Franke, trans. (trans. from the German by Christopher Levenson). *The Golden Casket: Chinese Novellas of Two Millenia*. New York: Harcourt, Brace and World, 1964.

Birch, Cyril, ed. *Anthology of Chinese Literature*. Vol. 1. New York: Grove Press, 1965.

Birrell, Anne, trans. *New Songs from a Jade Terrace: An Anthology of Early Chinese Love Poetry*. London: Allen and Unwin, 1982.

Budd, Charles, trans. *Chinese Poems*. Oxford: Oxford University Press, 1912.

Bynner, Witter, trans. (from the texts of Kiang Kang-hu). *The Jade Mountain, a Chinese Anthology: Being Three Hundred Poems of the T'ang Dynasty*. New York: Knopf, 1929.

Chang, H. C., ed. and trans. *Chinese Literature. Vol. 2: Nature Poetry*. Edinburgh: Edinburgh University Press, 1977.

——. *Chinese Literature. Vol. 3: Tales of the Supernatural*. Edinburgh: Edinburgh University Press, 1984.

Ch'en, Jerome & Michael Bullock, trans. *Poems of Solitude*. London: Abelard-Schuman, 1960.

Chinese Literature. Journal of translations from Chinese literature, classical and modern, published by the Foreign Languages Press, Peking.

Davis, A. R. ed., Kotewall, Robert & Norman L. Smith, trans. *The Penguin Book of Chinese Verse.* Harmondsworth, 1962.

De Bary, William T., W. T. Chan & Burton Watson, eds. *Sources of Chinese Tradition.* New York: Columbia University Press, 1960.

Demiéville, Paul. ed. *Anthologie de la poésie chinoise classique.* Paris: Gallimard, 1962.

Edwards, E. D., ed. *The Dragon Book.* London: William Hodge, 1938.

————. and trans. *Chinese Prose Literature of the T'ang Period.* 2 vols. London: Probsthain, 1937–8.

Fletcher, W. J. B., trans. *Gems of Chinese Verse, Translated into English Verse.* Shanghai: Commercial Press, 1918.

————. *More Gems of Chinese Poetry.* Shanghai: Commercial Press, 1919.

French, Joseph Lewis, ed. *Lotus and Chrysanthemum: An Anthology of Chinese and Japanese Poetry.* New York: Liveright, 1927.

Frodsham, John D., ed. and trans. (with the collaboration of Ch'eng Hsi). *An Anthology of Chinese Verse: Han, Wei, Chin and the Northern and Southern Dynasties.* Oxford: Oxford University Press, 1967.

Gautier, Judith, trans. *Le Livre de Jade.* Paris: Alphonse Lemerre, 1867.

Giles, Herbert A., ed. and trans. *Gems of Chinese Literature.* 2 vols. 2nd rev. ed. London: Quaritch, 1926.

Graham, A. C., trans. *Poems of the Late T'ang.* Harmondsworth: Penguin Books, 1965.

Hart, Henry H., trans. *A Chinese Market.* Peking: French Bookstore, 1931.

————. *A Garden of Peonies.* Stanford: Stanford University Press, 1938.

————. *Poems of the Hundred Names.* Stanford: Stanford University Press, 1954.

Hawkes, David, trans. *The Songs of the South: An Ancient Chinese Anthology of Poems by Qu Yuan and Other Poets.* Harmondsworth: Penguin Books, 1985.

Herdan, Innes, trans. *The Three Hundred T'ang Poems.* Taipei: Far East Book Co., 1973.

Hervey de Saint-Denys, trans. *Poésies de l'époque des Thang.* Paris: Amyot, 1862.

Holbrook, David, ed. *Plucking the Rushes: An Anthology of Chinese Poetry in Translations.* London: Heinemann, 1968.

Jenyns, Soame, trans. *Selections from the 300 Poems of the T'ang Dynasty.* London: John Murray, 1940.

————. *Further Selections from the 300 Poems of the T'ang Dynasty.* London: John Murray, 1944.

Kao, Karl S. Y., ed. *Classical Chinese Tales of the Supernatural and the Fantastic: Selections from the Third to the Tenth Century.* Bloomington: Indiana University Press, 1985.

Knechtges, David, trans. *Wen Xuan or Selections of Refined Literature.* Several vols. Princeton: Princeton University Press, 1982–.

Kwock, C. H. & Vincent McHugh, trans. *Why I Live on the Mountain.* San Francisco: Golden Mountain Press, 1958.

————. *The Lady and the Hermit.* San Francisco: Golden Mountain Press, 1962.

————. *Old Friend from Far Away: 150 Chinese Poems from the Great Dynasties.* San Francisco: North Point, 1980.

Lattimore, David, trans. *The Harmony of the World.* Providence: Copper Beech Press, 1980.

Lin, Yutang, ed. and trans. *The Importance of Living.* London: Heinemann, 1938.

————. *The Wisdom of China.* London: Michael Joseph, 1944.

————. *The Importance of Understanding: Translations from the Chinese.* London: Heinemann, 1961.

Liu, Wu-chi & Irving Yucheng Lo, eds. *Sunflower Splendor: Three Thousand Years of Chinese Poetry.* Bloomington: Indiana University Press, 1975.

Lowell, Amy (with Florence Ayscough), trans. *Fir-Flower Tablets: Poems Translated from the Chinese.* Boston: Houghton Mifflin, 1922.

Lü, Shuxiang & Xu Yuanzhong, eds. *Gems of Classical Chinese Poetry in Various English Translations.* Hong Kong: Joint Publishing, 1988.

Ma, Y. W. & Joseph S. M. Lau, eds. *Traditional Chinese Stories: Themes and Variations.* New York: Columbia University Press 1978.

Mair, Victor, ed. *The Columbia Anthology of Traditional Chinese Literature.* New York: Columbia University Press, 1994.

McNaughton, William, ed. *Chinese Literature: An Anthology from the Earliest Times to the Present Day.* Rutland, Vermont: Tuttle, 1974.

Owen, Stephen. *Readings in Chinese Literary Thought.* Cambridge, Mass.: Harvard University Press, 1992.

———, ed. and trans. *An Anthology of Chinese Literature: Beginnings to 1911.* New York: W. W. Norton, 1996.

Payne, Robert, ed. *The White Pony: An Anthology of Chinese Poetry from the Earliest Times to the Present Day.* New York: John Day, 1947.

Percy, Thomas, ed. *Fragments of Chinese Poetry* (appendix to vol. 4 of *Hau Kiou Choaan or The Pleasing History*). London: Dodsley, 1761.

Pound, Ezra, trans. (from the notes of the late Ernest Fenollosa, and the decipherings of the Professors More & Ariga.) *Cathay* (for the most part from the Chinese of "Rihaku"). London: Elkin Mathews, 1915.

Renditions. Journal of translations from Chinese literature published by the Chinese University of Hong Kong.

Rexroth, Kenneth, trans. *One Hundred Poems from the Chinese.* New York: New Directions, 1956.

———. *One Hundred More Poems from the Chinese: Love and the Turning Year.* New York: New Directions, 1970.

———, & Ling Chung, trans. and eds. *Women Poets of China.* New York: New Directions, 1982. (First published as *The Orchid Boat: Women Poets of China.* New York: Seabury Press, 1972.)

Roberts, Moss, trans. *Chinese Fairy Tales and Fantasies.* New York: Pantheon, 1979.

Scott, John (with Graham Martin), ed. and trans. *Love and Protest: Chinese Poems from the Sixth Century B.C. to the Seventeenth Century A.D.* London: Rapp and Whiting, 1972.

Trevelyan, R. C., ed. *From the Chinese.* Oxford: Oxford University Press, 1945.

Turner, John A., trans. *A Golden Treasury of Chinese Poetry: 121 Classical Poems in New Translations.* Hong Kong: The Chinese University Press, 1976.

Waddell, Helen, trans. *Lyrics from the Chinese.* London: Constable, 1934.

Waley, Arthur, trans. *One Hundred and Seventy Chinese Poems.* London: Constable, 1918.

———. *More Translations from the Chinese.* London: Allen and Unwin, 1919.

———. *The Temple and Other Poems.* London: Allen and Unwin, 1923.

———. *Chinese Poems.* London: Allen and Unwin, 1946.

Wang, Chi-chen, trans. *Traditional Chinese Tales.* New York: Columbia University Press, 1944.

Watson, Burton, trans. *Chinese Rhyme-Prose: Poems in the Fu Form from the Han and Six Dynasties Periods.* New York: Columbia University Press, 1971.

———, ed. and trans. *The Columbia Book of Chinese Poetry: From Early Times to the*

Thirteenth Century. New York: Columbia University Press, 1984.
Wong, Man, trans. *Poems from China.* Hong Kong: Creation Books, 1950.
Wong, Siu-kit, ed. and trans. *Early Chinese Literary Criticism.* Hong Kong: Joint Publishing, 1983.
Yang, Gladys & Xianyi Yang, trans. *The Dragon King's Daughter: Ten Tang Dynasty Stories.* Peking: Foreign Language Press, 1954.
———. *The Man Who Sold a Ghost: Chinese Tales of the 3rd–6th Centuries.* Hong Kong: Commercial Press, 1958.
———. *Stories about Not Being Afraid of Ghosts.* Peking: Foreign Languages Press, 1961.
———. *Poetry and Prose of the Han, Wei and Six Dynasties.* Peking: Foreign Languages Press, 1986.
———. *Poetry and Prose of the Tang and Song.* Peking: Foreign Languages Press, 1984.
Yip, Wai-lim, ed. and trans. *Chinese Poetry: Major Modes and Genres.* Berkeley: University of California Press, 1976.
Young, David, trans. *Wang Wei, Li Po, Tu Fu, Li Ho: Four T'ang Poets.* Ohio: Field Translation Series, 1980.

"The Han Stone Classics."
Seal carved by Zhao Zhiqian (1829–1884)

Major Chinese Dynasties and Periods

Xia	c. 2100–c. 1600 B.C.
Shang	c. 1600–c. 1028 B.C.
Zhou	c. 1027–256 B.C.
Western Zhou	c. 1027–771 B.C.
Eastern Zhou	c. 770–256 B.C.
Spring & Autumn	722–481 B.C.
Warring States	403–221 B.C.
Qin	221–207 B.C.
Han	206 B.C.–A.D.220
Former Han	206 B.C.–A.D. 8
Xin	A.D. 9–25
Later Han	A.D. 25–A.D. 220
Three Kingdoms	220–265
Wei	220–265
Shu	221–263
Wu	222–280
Six Dynasties (Wu, Eastern Jin, Liu Song, Southern Qi, Southern Liang, Southern Chen)	222–589
Jin	265–420
Western Jin	265–317
Eastern Jin	317–420
Southern Dynasties	420–589
Former (Liu) Song	420–479
Southern Qi	479–502
Southern Liang	502–557
Southern Chen	557–589
Northern Dynasties	386–581
Northern Wei (Toba)	386–534
Eastern Wei	534–550
Western Wei	535–577
Northern Qi	550–577
Northern Zhou	557–581
Sui	581–618
Tang	618–907
Five Dynasties	907–960

Liao (Khitan)	916–1125
Song	960–1279
Northern Song	960–1126
Southern Song	1127–1279
Jin (Jurchen)	1115–1234
Yuan (Mongol)	1260–1368
Ming	1368–1644
Qing (Manchu)	1644–1911

List of Permissions

Permissions to use materials from the following copyrighted works in this *Anthology* have been granted by their respective publishers or otherwise specified, to whom we wish to make our acknowledgements. Every effort has been made to trace copyright holders, but if any have been inadvertently overlooked, we will be pleased to make the necessary arrangement at the first opportunity.

Among the Flowers: The Hua-chien Chi, by Lois Fusek, pp. 71–73. Copyright © 1982, Columbia University Press. Reprinted with permission of the publisher.

Anthology of Chinese Literature: From Early Times to the Fourteenth Century, by Cyril Birch, pp. 162–63, 314–22, 336–37, 349–52. New York: Grove Press, 1965.

An Anthology of Chinese Verse: Han, Wei, Chin and the Northern and Southern Dynasties, ed. and trans. by John D. Frodsham, pp. 9–13, 16–17, 26–29, 32–35, 44–50, 72, 89, 91–94, 99–101, 104–8, 111, 123, 131–36, 142–46, 151, 159, 163–66, 168, 184–92, 198. Oxford: Oxford University Press, 1967.

Ballads and Stories from Tun-huang: An Anthology of Early Chinese Love Poetry, Translated with Annotations and an Introduction, trans. by Arthur Waley. London: George Allen & Unwin, 1960. Reprinted with permission of the Arthur Waley Estate.

Basic Writings of Mo Tzu, Hsun Tzu, and Han Fei Tzu, by Burton Watson, pp. 80–81. Copyright © 1967, Columbia University Press. Reprinted with permission of the publisher.

The Book of Odes, trans. by Bernhard Karlgren, p. 2. Stockholm: Museum of Far Eastern Antiquities, 1950.

The Book of Songs, trans. by Arthur Waley. London: George Allen and Unwin, 1937. Reprinted with permission of Grove/Atlantic Inc. and the Arthur Waley Estate.

A Brief History of Chinese Fiction, by Lu Xun, trans. by Xianyi and Gladys Yang. Beijing: Foreign Languages Press, 1931.

Larsen, Jeanne; BROCADE RIVER POEMS: SELECTED WORKS OF THE TANG DYNASTY COURTESAN XUE TAO, pp. 4, 5, 51, 54, 75.

Copyright © 1987 by Princeton University Press. Reprinted by permission of Princeton University Press.

Chan-kuo T'se, by J. I. Crump, pp. 164–65, 179, 226–27, 279–81. Oxford: Oxford University Press, 1996.

Chinese Love Poetry: A Medieval Anthology, New Songs from a Jade Terrace, trans. by Anne Birrell. New York: Penguin, 1995. Reprinted with permission of the author.

Chinese Lyricism: Shih Poetry from the Second to the Twelfth Century, by Burton Watson, pp. 59, 174–76. Copyright © 1971, Columbia University Press. Reprinted with permission of the publisher.

Chinese Poems, trans. by Arthur Waley. London: George Allen & Unwin, 1962. Reprinted with permission of the Aruthur Waley Estate.

Chinese Poetic Writing: With an Anthology of T'ang Poetry, trans. by Donald A. Riggs and Jerome P. Seaton, Bloomington: Indiana University Press, 1982, from *L'Ecriture poetique chinoise. Suivi d'une anthologie des poemes des T'ang (608–907)*, by Francois Cheng. Copyright © 1977, 1996 by Editions du Seuil. Reprinted by permission of the copyright holder and Georges Borchardt, Inc. (commentaries) and Jerome P. Searon (poems).

Chinese Prose Literature of the T'ang Period, Vol. 2, ed. and trans. by E. D. Edwards, pp. 314–16. London: Arthur Probstain, 1938.

Chinese Theories of Literature, by James J. Y. Liu, pp. 108–9. Chicago: University of Chicago Press, 1975.

Chinese, by Jerry Norman, pp. 58–61. New York: Cambridge University Press, 1988.

Chuang Tzu: Taoist Philosopher and Chinese Mystic, by Herbert Giles, pp. 32–33, 44–46, 48–49, 159–60. London: George Allen & Unwin, 1961. Reprinted with permission of HarperCollins Publishers.

The Classical Anthology Defined by Confucius, by Ezra Pound, pp. 2–3, 7–8, 10, 12–13, 34, 36–38, 43–44, 53–54, 82–83, 89–90. London: Faber and Faber, 1955. Reprinted with permission of the publisher.

A Collection of Chinese Lyrics, trans. by Alan Ayling and Duncan Mackintosh, pp. 7–8. London: Routledge, 1965.

The Columbia Book of Chinese Poetry: From Early Times to the Thirteenth Century, by Burton Watson, pp. 12–13, 18, 23, 33, 35–38, 68, 80, 82–95, 104, 107–9, 123–24, 171, 193–94, 205–6, 218–24, 226–34, 238–39. Copyright © 1984, Columbia University Press. Reprinted with permission of the publisher.

Courtier and Commoner in Ancient China: Selections from the History of the Former Han, by Burton Watson, pp. 1, 2, 4, 79–83, 247–49, 251. Copyright © 1974, Columbia University Press. Reprinted with permission of the publisher.

Doctors, Diviners, and Magicians of Ancient China: Biographies of Fang-shih, ed., and trans. by Kenneth DeWoskin. New York: Columbia University Press, 1983. Reprinted with permission of the author.

Du Mu: Plantains in the Rain, trans. by Richard F. Burton, pp. 47, 49, 53, 60, 63, 69. London: Wellsweep Press, 1990. Reprinted with permission of the author and the publisher.

Early Chinese Literature, by Burton Watson, pp. 21, 25, 40–42, 74–75, 125–126, 130, 157, 158, 160–61, 163–65, 175, 207–8, 210–11, 259. Copyright © 1962, Columbia University Press. Reprinted with permission of the publisher.

Early Chinese Literature Criticism, by Wong Siu-kit, pp. 19–22. Hong Kong: Joint Publishing, 1983.

Family Instructions for the Yen Clan, trans. by Teng Ssu-yu, pp. 209–11. Leiden: E. J. Brill, 1968.

Festivals and Songs of Ancient China, by Marcel Granet, trans. by E. D. Edwards. London: Routledge, 1932.

A Gallery of Chinese Immortals, by Lionel Giles, pp. 17–18, 22–23, 35–36, 53. London: John Murray, 1948.

The Great Age of Chinese Poetry: The High T'ang, by Stephen Owen, pp. xi–xii, 25–26, 62–63, 91–92, 99–100, 107–8, 150, 153–56, 179–80, 235, 247. Copyright © 1981 Yale University Press. Reprinted by permission of the publisher.

Reprinted by permission of the publisher from HAN SHIH WAI CHUAN by James Robert Hightower. Copyright © 1952 by the Harvard-Yenching Institute.

Harmony of the World, by David Lattimore, pp. 16–20, 23, 26. Providence: Copper Beech Press, 1980.

Hiding the Universe: Poems by Wang Wei, trans. by Wai-lim Yip. New York: Munshinsha, 1972. Reprinted with permission of the author and the publisher.

A History of Chinese Civilization, by Jacques Garnet, pp. 202, 206–7. Cambridge: Cambridge University Press, 1982.

Wilhelm, R., trans. by Cary F. Baynes; *THE I CHING, OR BOOK OF CHANGES*, pp. xxvii–xxix, 200–4. Copyright © 1950 by Princeton University Press. Reprinted by permission of Princeton University Press.

In the Voice of Others: Chinese Music Bureau Poetry, by Joseph R. Allen. © 1992 by Center for Chinese Studies, The University of Michigan. Reprinted with Permission.

The Jade Mountain, a Chinese Anthology: Being Three hundred Poems of the T'ang Dynasty, trans. by Witter Bynner, pp. 4, 7, 18–19, 87, 89–91, 97–99, 108, 112, 114–15, 161, 183, 206, 209–11, 213–14. New

York: Alfred A. Knopf, 1957. Reprinted by permission of the publisher.

Li Po and Tu Fu, trans. by Arthur Cooper, pp. 105, 111, 136, 149, 167, 231–32. New York: Penguin, 1973. Copyright © Arthur Cooper 1973. Reproduced by permission of Penguin Books Ltd.

The Lotus Boat: The Origins of Chinese Tz'u Poetry in T'ang Popular Culture, by Marsha Wagner, pp. X, 11, 37, 44–45, 86, 107–8, 111, 113–15. Copyright © 1984, Columbia University Press. Reprinted with permission of the publisher.

Reprinted from *Memories of Loyang: Yang Hsuan-chih and the Lost Capital* translated by W. J. E. Jenner (1981) by permission of Oxford University Press.

The Murmuring Stream: The Life and Works of the Chinese Nature Poet Hsieh Ling-yun, by John Frodsham, pp. 94, 101–2, 125, 146, 148. Kuala Lumper: University of Malaya Press, 1967.

A New Account of Tales of the World, trans. by Richard B. Mather, pp. 185, 213, 282, 319, 323, 331, 372–74, 377, 389–90, 457, 459, 462, 465, 487. Minneapolis: University of Minnesota Press, 1976.

Old Friend from Far Away: 150 Chinese Poems from the Great Dynasties, trans. by C. H. Kwock and Vincent McHugh, pp. 20, 80. New York: North Point Press, 1980. Reprinted by permission of C. H. Kwock and Mrs. McHugh.

By Kenneth Rexroth, from ONE HUNDRED POEMS FROM THE CHINESE. Copyright © 1971 by Kenneth Rexroth. Reprinted by permission of New Directions Publishing Corp.

By Kenneth Rexroth, from ONE HUNDRED MORE POEMS FROM THE CHINESE. Copyright © 1970 by Kenneth Rexroth. Reprinted by permission of New Directions Publishing Corp.

Perspectives on the T'ang, by Arthur F. Wright and Dennis Twitchett, pp. 372–74. Copyright © 1973 Yale University Press. Reprinted by permission of the publisher.

Poems of the Late T'ang, trans. by A. C. Graham, pp. 41, 45, 49, 69, 74, 123, 126, 137, 145–49, 167–68, 171. New York: Penguin, 1965. Copyright © A. C. Graham 1965. Reproduced by permission of Penguin Books Ltd.

Poetry and Politics: The Life and Work of Juan Chi (A.D. 210–263), by Donald Holzman, pp. 85–87. Cambridge: Cambridge University Press, 1976.

The Poetry of Li Shang-yin: Ninth-Century Baroque Chinese Poet, by James J. Y. Liu, pp. 78–81, 158–59, 254. Chicago: University of Chicago Press, 1969.

The Poetry of Meng Chiao and Han Yu, by Stephen Owen, pp. 83–86. Copyright © 1975 Yale University Press. Reprinted by permission of the publisher.

The Poetry of T'ao Ch'ien, trans. by James R. Hightower, pp. 4, 254–56, 268–70. Oxford: Oxford University Press, 1970.

The Poetry of the Early T'ang, by Stephen Owen, pp. xi, 66, 68, 70–71, 105–11, 127, 134, 141, 148–49, 158, 160, 170–71, 175, 189–90, 196–97, 205–6, 284–85, 291–92, 334–36, 356–57, 401, 406. Copyright © 1977 Yale University Press. Reprinted by permission of the publisher.

The Poetry of Wang Wei: New Translations and Commentary, trans. by Pauline Yu, pp. 134, 152. Bloomington: Indiana University Press, 1980.

Popular Songs and Ballads of Han China, trans. by Anne Birrell, pp. 37, 58, 91–92, 96, 98, 119–20, 125, 129–30, 146–47, 169–70. Honolulu: University of Hawaii Press, 1989.

Yu, Pauline; THE READING OF IMAGERY IN THE CHINESE POETIC TRADITION, pp. 49–52. Copyright © 1986 by Princeton University Press. Reprinted by permission of Princeton University Press.

From READINGS IN CHINESE LITERARY THOUGHT. Copyright © 1992 by the President and Fellows of Harvard College. Reprinted by permission of Harvard University Press.

The Secret of the Golden Flower: A Chinese Book of Life, by Richard Wilhelm, trans. by Cary F. Baynes, pp. 159–60. Arkana, 1984. Reproduced by permission of Penguin Books Ltd.

Selections from the "Book of Songs," trans. by Xianyi and Gladys Yang. Beijing: Foreign Languages Press, 1983.

Selling Wilted Peonies: Biography and Songs of Yu Hsuan-chi, T'ang Poetess, by Genevieve Wimsatt, ch. 25. Copyright © 1936, Columbia University Press. Reprinted with permission of the publisher.

Shan Hai Ching: Legendary Geography and Wonders of Ancient China, trans. by H. C. Cheng, H. C. Pai Cheng, and K. L. Thern. Taipei: National Institute for Compilation and Translation, 1985.

Reprinted by permission of the publisher from SHIH-CHING: THE CLASSIC ANTHOLOGY DEFINED BY CONFUCIUS by Ezra Pound (tr.), pp. 2–3, 7–8, 10–13, 34, 36–38, 43–44, 53–54, 82–83, 89–90, Cambridge, Mass.: Harvard University Press, Copyright © 1954, 1982 by the President and Fellows of Harvard College.

Six Dynasties Poetry, by Kang-I Sun Chang, pp. 88–89, 91. New Jersey: Princeton University Press, 1986. Reprinted by permission of the author.

The Songs of the South: An Anthology of Ancient Chinese Poems by Qu Yuan and Other Poets, introduced and trans. by David Hawkes, 15–19, 67–68, 95–117, 122–23, 127–34. New York: Penguin, 1985. Copyright © David Hawkes 1985. Reproduced by permission of Penguin Books Ltd.

Sources of Shang History: The Oracle-Bone Inscriptions of Bronze Age China, by David Knightley. California: University of California Press, 1978.

T'ao the Hermit: Sixty Poems by T'ao Ch'ien, trans. by William Acker, pp. 45–48, 52–57, 62–63, 65–67, 72, 77, 82–84, 87–89, 94–95, 97–98, 121–22. London: Thames & Hudson, 1952.

The Temple and Other Poems, trans. by Arthur Waley. New York: K. K. Knopf, 1923. Reprinted with permission from the Arthur Waley Estate.

The Three Hundred Tang Poems, trans. by Innes Herden, pp. 138–43. Taipei: Far East Book Company, 1973.

TOPICS IN CHINESE LITERATURE by James Robert Hightower. Copyright © 1952, 1953 by the Harvard-Yenching Institute. Reprinted by permission of Harvard University Press.

Traditional Chinese Stories: Themes and Variations, edited by W. Ma and Joseph S. M. Lau, ch. 25. Copyright © 1978, Columbia University Press. Reprinted with permission of the publisher.

Traditional Chinese Tales, by Wang Chi-chen, pp. 20–34, 139–45, 416–19, 443–55. Copyright © 1944, Columbia University Press. Reprinted with permission of the publisher.

The Travels of Fa-hsien, by Herbert Giles. Cambridge: Cambridge University Press, 1923.

The Tso Chuan: Selections from China's Oldest Narrative History, by Burton Watson, pp. 11–12, 40–44, 120–21, 178–79, 207–13. Copyright © 1989, Columbia University Press. Reprinted with permission of the publisher.

Tu Fu, the Autobiography of a Chinese Poet, A.D. 712–770, Vol. 2: *Travels of a Chinese Poet: Tu Fu, Guest of Rivers and Lakes, A.D. 759–770*, by Florence Ayscough. London: Jonathan Cape, 1929–34.

Wang Wei, Li Po, Tu Fu, Li Ho, Li Shang-yin: Five T'ang Poets, trans. by David Young, pp. 56, 65, 69, 74. Ohio: Oberlin College Press, 1990.

The Way and Its Power: A Study of the Tao Te Ching and Its Place in Chinese Thought, trans. by Arthur Waley. New York: Grove Press, 1958. Reprinted with permission from the publisher and the Arthur Waley Estate.

Knechtges, David R.; WEN XUAN OR SELECTIONS OF REFINED LITERATURE, VOLUME TWO: RHAPSODIES ON SACRIFICES, HUNTING, SIGHTSEEING, PALACES AND HALLS, RIVERS AND SEAS, pp. 17–39, 305–19. Copyright © 1982 by Princeton University Press. Reprinted by permission of Princeton University Press.

Western Chou Civilization, by Cho-yun Hsu and Katheryn M. Linduff, p. 115. Copyright © 1988 Yale University Press. Reprinted by permission of the publisher.

By Kenneth Rexroth and Ling Chung, from WOMEN POETS OF CHINA. Copyright © 1973 by Kenneth Rexroth and Ling Chung. Reprinted by permission of New Directions Publishing Corp.

"Cold Mountain Poems," trans. by Gary Snyder, in *Evergreen Review* (autumn 1958) and *Riprap & Cold Mountain Poems*. San Francisco: Four Seasons Foundation, 1965.

"For the Danger of the King of Wu When She Is Half Drunk," "The Mallards," trans. by Robert Payne, in *The White Pony: An Anthology of Chinese Poetry from the Earliest Times to the Present Day*. New York: John Day, 1947. Reprinted by permission of David Higham Associates.

"The Fortunate Banishment: Liu Tsung-yuan in Yung-chou," by A. R. Davis, in *Journal of the Oriental Society of Australia*, 4:2 (1996). School of Asian Studies, The University of Sydney.

"In Passing an Old Friend's Farm," from *Selections from the 300 Poems of the T'ang Dynasty*, trans. by Soames Jenyns. London: John Murray, 1940.

"In Search of the Supernatural — Selections from the Sou-shen Chi," trans. by Kenneth DeWoskin, from *Renditions*, 7 (Spring 1997), pp. 103–14. Reprinted by permission of Research Centre for Translation, The Chinese University of Hong Kong.

"Kuan Kuan, The Ospreys," in *Chinese Poetry: An Anthology of Major Modes and Genres*, ed. and trans. by Yip Wai-lim, p. 35. Copyright 1997, Duke University Press. Reprinted with permission.

"The Lament of the Lady of Ch'in," trans. by Lionel Giles, in *Toung Pao*, 24 (1926). Reprinted by permission of E. J. Brill.

"Mineral Imagery in the Paradise Poems of Kuan-hsiu," by Edward Schafer, in *Asia Major*, New Series, 10 (1963), p. 77. Reprinted by permission of Asia Major.

"Mortals," in *Records of the Grand Historian of China*, Vol. 2, translated by Burton Watson. Copyright © 1961, Columbia University Press. Reprinted with permission of the publisher.

"Rhymeprose on Literature: The Wen-fu of Lu Chi," trans. by Achilles Fang, first appeared in *Harvard Journal of Asiatic Studies*, 14 (1951), pp. 527–29. Reprinted by permission of the editors.

"Risks," trans. by Graeme Wilson, from *Renditions*, 2 (Spring 1974), p. 116. Reprinted by permission of Research Centre for Translation, The Chinese University of Hong Kong.

"Shih Ch'ung and His Chin-ku-Yuan," by Helmut Wilhelm, in *Monumenta Serica*, 18 (1959), pp. 324–25. Reprinted by permission of Monumenta Serica.

"Some Characteristics of Parallel Prose," by J. R. Hightower, in Soren Egerod and Else Glahn, eds., *Studia Serica Bernhard Karlgren Dedicata*, pp. 70–74 (Copenhagen: Ejnar Munksgaard, 1959). Reprinted by permission of the author.

"Some Mid-T'ang Quatrains," trans. by Stephen Owen, from *Renditions*, 21&22 (Spring & Autumn 1984), pp. 145–46, 148, 157, 161, 178.

Reprinted by permission of Research Centre for Translation, The Chinese University of Hong Kong.
"Tao: Buddha: Zen," by Graeme Wilson, *Denver Quarterly*, 12:2 (1977).

Index of Authors

Where no author is known, the title of the book is given in English, followed by the romanization. For entries taken from footnotes, the page numbers are printed in italics. A list of authors' names in the Wade-Giles system of romanization, with their Hanyu Pinyin equivalents, is added for the convenience of readers accustomed to the old style. No entry is given where the spelling is identical (e.g. Yang Fang), or identical apart from a minor difference such as a hyphen (e.g. Yuan Haowen) or a superscript.

Wade-Giles Finding List

Index of Translators & Commentators